Shooter's Bible

105TH EDITION

Shooter's Bible

105TH EDITION

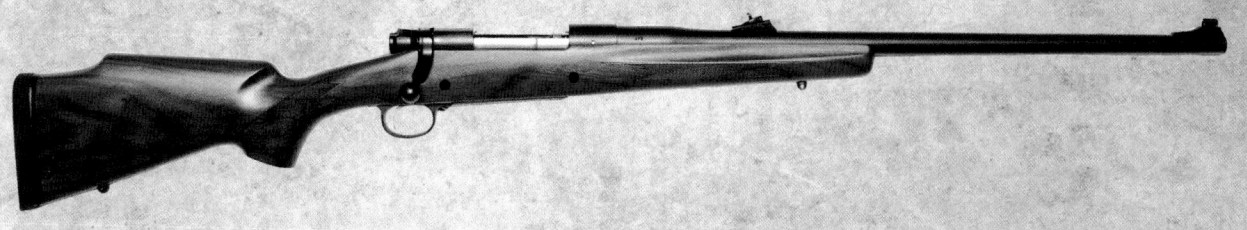

SKYHORSE PUBLISHING

Skyhorse Publishing books may be purchased in bulk at special discounts for sales promotion, corporate gifts, fund-raising, or educational purposes. Special editions can also be created to specifications. For details, contact the Special Sales Department, Skyhorse Publishing, 307 West 36th Street, 11th Floor, New York, NY 10018 or info@skyhorsepublishing.com

Skyhorse® and Skyhorse Publishing® are registered trademarks of Skyhorse Publishing, Inc.®, a Delaware corporation.

Visit our website at www.skyhorsepublishing.com.

10 9 8 7 6 5 4 3 2 1

ISBN: 978-1-62636-066-2
ISSN: 0080-9365

Printed in Canada

Note: Every effort has been made to record specifications and descriptions of guns, ammunition, and accessories accurately, but the Publisher can take no responsibility for errors or omissions. The prices shown for guns, ammunition, and accessories are manufacturers' suggested retail prices (unless otherwise noted) and are furnished for information only. These were in effect at press time and are subject to change without notice. Purchasers of the book have complete freedom of choice in pricing for resale.

CONTENTS

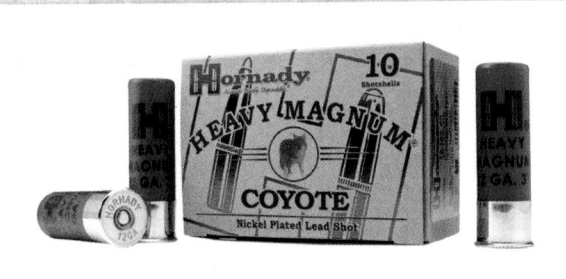

INTRODUCTION

It's hard to believe that another year has gone by and here we are, publishing the 105th edition of the *Shooter's Bible*. It goes without saying that it has been a tumultuous year for gun owners. Despite this, the gun industry itself saw unprecedented sales in 2012, with a 40 percent increase in sales of firearms and ammunition in 2012 over 2011 (based on excise tax data). This, in turn, has lead to increased industry contributions to the Federal Aid in Wildlife Restoration Fund (aka the Pittman-Robertson Act).

By all accounts, the coming year should be just as prosperous, and arms manufacturers everywhere are ramping up their production to meet the insatiable demands of the gun-buying public. Many companies have come out with new and exciting firearms this year. Doubletap's titanium two-barrel derringer,

Chiappa Firearms' triple-barrel shotgun, and the ZiP gun from U.S. Fire Arms are just a few examples of the high-tech manufacturing techniques that are changing firearms design throughout the industry.

As you pore over the more than one hundred pages in the New Products section, you'll be amazed at the wide array of new firearms that is now available. You'll also be pleased to see Remington coming out with the fiftieth anniversary edition of the revered Model 1100, while Winchester Repeating Arms is relaunching the Winchester 1873, one hundred forty years after the Gun That Won The West was introduced.

As you move on to the meat of the *Shooter's Bible*, the existing products section, starting on page 107, you'll find practically every gun in production on the planet, with totally up-to-date prices and specs. I'm

EDITORIAL DIRECTOR JAY CASSELL TRACKS AN INCOMING CANADA GOOSE FROM A LAYOUT BLIND IN NORTHERN MANITOBA. HE WAS USING A 12-GAUGE BROWNING MAXUS ON THIS HUNT. BROWNING HAS ADDED A SPORTING GOLDEN CLAYS MODEL TO THE MAXUS LINE OF GAS-OPERATED SEMIAUTO SHOTGUNS THIS YEAR.

Return of "The Gun That Won the West"

The Model 1873 lever-action rifle (MSRP: $1,300)—the real thing, the genuine article—is again being produced by Winchester Repeating Arms. The '73 rifle is the stuff of legends with some 720,610 rifles, carbines, and muskets produced from 1873 up until 1919 by the original Winchester factory located in New Haven, Connecticut. Along with the rifle, Winchester also debuted a new cartridge named the .44 Winchester or .44 WCF (Winchester Center Fire), but the cartridge is more commonly known as the .44-40; a .44 caliber bullet atop 40 grains of black powder. Later it was chambered in .38-40 and .32-20. Lawmen, settlers, outlaws, hunters, and renegades used the 1873 with efficiency. It was the first truly strong repeating rifle that offered rapid rifle when muzzleloaders and single shots were common. Many paired the rifle with a pistol in the same caliber. Since then the company has gone through numerous reorganizations and Italian-manufactured 1873 clones have been imported to the U.S. The new Winchester 1873 has an oil-finished walnut stock with a classic blued-steel crescent buttplate and a 20-inch round barrel. It is chambered in .357 Mag./.38 Spl.

—Robert A. Sadowski

WINCHESTER MODEL 1873 SHORT RIFLE

guessing that everyone reading this book owns some firearms that are in this section. (If you own a gun that isn't in this section, it is probably out of production, in which case you need to pick up a copy of another Skyhorse Publication, the 35th edition of the *Gun Trader's Guide*.) Optics, ammunition, and accessories are also covered in this year's edition of the *Shooter's Bible*, as they are every year.

If this is first time you have picked up a copy of the *Shooter's Bible*, you should know that it has a long and storied past. The first numbered edition of the *Shooter's Bible* was published in 1925; it has been published annually, and in some cases bi-annually, ever since. More than seven million copies have been sold in that time, and it continues to be the ultimate reference book for millions of people who want information on new guns, ammunition, optics, and accessories, as well as up-to-date prices and specs for thousands of in-production firearms.

The Skyhorse staff—including head researcher Lindsey Breuer (below) as well as intern Ryan Gerhardt—is proud of this newest edition of the *Shooter's Bible*, a book that has been continually updated and fact-checked for the past twelve months. Not content to rest on our laurels, however, we have also continued to produce more and more

RESEARCHER LINDSEY BREUER HOLDING HER NEW BENELLI ULTRA LIGHT 28-GAUGE.

A Classic Shotgun 50 Years in the Making and Still Going Strong

The Remington Model 1100 is America's favorite semiauto shotgun. Back in 1963 it debuted to compete against recoil-operated shotgun designs. The 1100 uses a gas system to cycle the semiautomatic action. This system not only quickly and reliably cycled the action; it also greatly reduced recoil. It's also lightweight and points naturally. Hunters have used the 1100 for duck, pheasant, turkey, grouse, rabbit, and deer—to name just a few. Over the years more than four million 1100s have been manufactured in a variety of finishes, barrel lengths, and types. It has been chambered in the tiny .410 and 28-gauge to 20-, 16- and 12-gauge. Visit a trap, skeet, or sporting clays field and you will no doubt see an 1100 in action. The military and LE have also specified certain features on the 1100 for tactical use. A special 12-gauge Model 1100 50th Anniversary collectors' edition (MSRP: $1,999) features a machine-cut engraved receiver with gold fill, B-grade walnut stock with a white-diamond grip cap and white line spacer, and 28-inch vent rib barrel with Rem. chokes. —Robert A. Sadowski

REMINGTON 1100 50TH ANNIVERSARY EDITION

Shooter's Bible guidebooks. In the past year, we have added a number of new volumes to our growing lineup, including the *Shooter's Bible Guide to Gun Assembly, Disassembly, and Cleaning*, by Robert A. Sadowski; the *Shooter's Bible Guide to Planting Food Plots*, by Peter Fiduccia; the *Shooter's Bible Guide to Bowhunting*, by Todd A. Kuhn; the *Shooter's Bible Guide to Concealed Carry*, by Brad Fitzpatrick, and the *Shooter's Bible Guide to the Hunting Rifle and Its Ammunition*, by Thomas C. Tabor.

Other guidebooks include the *Shooter's Bible Guide to Cartridges*, the *Shooter's Bible Guide to Rifle Ballistics*, the *Shooter's Bible Guide to Optics*, the *Shooter's Bible Guide to AR-15s*, the *Shooter's Bible Guide to Combat Handguns*, the *Shooter's Bible Guide to Knives*, and the *Shooter's Bible Guide to Whitetail Strategies*. All of these must-have books include useful, up-to-date information on topics that shooters and outdoorsmen value.

What does the future hold? How about the *Shooter's Bible Guide to Extreme Iron*, the *Shooter's Bible Guide to Long-Range Tactical Rifles*, and the *Shooter's Bible Guide to Home Defense*?

As you can see, we're trying to cover all of your specialized needs, needs that merit guidebooks of their own. And in the meantime, we hope you enjoy this, the 105th edition of the *Shooter's Bible*. It's got something for everyone.

Jay Cassell
Editorial Director
Skyhorse Publishing

ADVANCED ARMAMENT CORP. MULTI PURPOSE WEAPON (MPW)

ANSCHÜTZ 1416 D HB WALNUT THUMBHOLE

ANSCHUTZ 1727F IMAGE

ARMALITE AR-30A1 STANDARD RIFLE

ADVANCED ARMAMENT CORP. MULTI PURPOSE WEAPON (MPW)

Action: Bolt
Stock: Magpul CTR
Barrel: 9 in., 12.5 in., 16 in.
Sights: None
Weight: N/A
Caliber: 7.62x35mm (300 AAC Blackout)
Magazine: 30 rounds
Features: Bolt carrier features a proprietary design with a modified cam path and nickel-boron finish to enhance reliability and ease of cleaning; bolt machined from Carpenter 158 steel; freefloating forearm; lower receiver features a Geissele two-stage trigger; six-position Mil-Spec collapsing stock
MSRP **$1599.95**

ANSCHÜTZ 1416 D HB WALNUT THUMBHOLE

Action: Bolt
Stock: Walnut
Barrel: 23 in.
Sights: None
Weight: 6 lb. 8 oz.
Caliber: .22 LR
Magazine: 5 rounds
Features: Luxus repeating rifle; single-stage trigger; black buttplate; carved German checkering on the pistol grip; sling swivel studs; wave-style V-block dovetail rail for telescopic sight
MSRP **$1517**

ANSCHÜTZ 1727F

Action: Lever
Stock: Walnut German stock
Barrel: 22 in.
Sights: None
Weight: 7 lb. 10 oz.
Caliber: .17 HMR

Magazine: None
Features: Two-stage trigger; precision barrel; rubber buttplate
MSRP **$3409**

ARMALITE AR-30A1 STANDARD RIFLE

Action: Bolt
Stock: Aluminum
Barrel: 24 in., 26 in.
Sights: None
Weight: 12 lb. 13 oz.–13 lb. 6 oz.
Caliber: .300 Win. Mag., .338 Lapua
Magazine: 5 rounds
Features: Cheekpiece is at the optimum height for viewing through a telescopic sight; buttstock is ergonomically correct; steel magazine; ambidestrous magazine catch; fixed stock; detachable sight rail, hard case, and sling included
MSRP . . . . **$3264–$3404**

ARMALITE AR-30A1 TARGET RIFLE

Action: Bolt
Stock: Aluminum
Barrel: 24 in., 26 in.
Sights: None
Weight: 14 lb. 8 oz.–15 lb. 5 oz.
Caliber: .300 Win. Mag., .338 Lapua
Magazine: 5 rounds
Features: MOA Picatinny rail over receiver and barrel; cheekpiece vertically adjustable; adjustable buttstock; 1913 accessory rail at the bottom of the buttstock; buttpad is adjustable for height
MSRP . . . . $3460–$3599

ARSENAL, INC. SAM7R

Action: Semiautomatic
Stock: Polymer
Barrel: 16.25 in.
Sights: Scope rail
Weight: 8 lb.
Caliber: 7.62x39mm
Magazine: 10 rounds
Features: Milled receiver; chrome-lined, hammer-forged barrel; muzzle brake; cleaning rod; intermediate length US-made 10 in. trapdoor buttstock
MSRP $1299

ARSENAL, INC. SLR-106F

Action: Semiautomatic
Stock: Synthetic
Barrel: 16.25 in.
Sights: Scope rail
Weight: 7 lb. 5 oz.
Caliber: 5.56 NATO
Magazine: 5 rounds
Features: Stamped receiver; chrome-lined, hammer-forged barrel; bayonet lug; stainless steel heat shield handguards; left-side folding buttstock; also available in desert sand color
MSRP $1080

BERETTA USA ARX100

Action: Semiautomatic
Stock: Telescopic folding
Barrel: 12 in., 16 in.
Sights: Removable back-up sights
Weight: 6 lb. 13 oz.
Caliber: 5.56 NATO (other barrels available)
Magazine: 30 rounds
Features: Cold hammer forged barrel can be replaced with barrels in different lengths and calibers; case injections switch from right to left at a button push; completely ambidextrous; technopolymer receiver; contains no pins and can be disassembled without the use of tools; optional .300 Black Out kit available
MSRP $1950

ARMALITE AR-30A1 TARGET RIFLE

ARSENAL, INC. SAM7R

ARSENAL, INC. SLR-106F

BERETTA USA ARX100

BLASER USA R8 PROFESSIONAL SUCCESS

BROWNING AB3 (A-BOLT III) COMPOSITE STALKER

BROWNING BAR SHORTRAC HOG STALKER REALTREE MAX-1

BROWNING BLR LIGHTWEIGHT '81 HOG STALKER TAKEDOWN GREEN

BLASER USA R8 PROFESSIONAL SUCCESS

Action: Bolt
Stock: Synthetic
Barrel: 22.8 in., 25.6 in.
Sights: Open
Weight: 7 lb.
Caliber: .222 Rem., .204 Ruger, .223 Rem., .22-250, .243 Win., 6XC, 6.5x55 SE, 6.5x57, 6.5x65 RWS, .270 Win., 7x64, .308 Win., .30-06, 8x57 IS, 8.5x63, 9.3x57, 9.3x62, 6.5x68, 7.5x55 Suisse, 8x68 S, .257 Wby. Mag., .270 Wby. Mag., .270 WSM, 7mm Blaser Mag., 7mm Rem. Mag., .300 Blaser Mag., .300 Win. Mag., .300 Wby. Mag., .300 WSM, .338 Blaser Mag., .338 Win. Mag., .375 Blaser Mag., .375 H&H
Magazine: 3+1, 4+1, 5+1 rounds
Features: Blaser precision trigger; radial locking system; ergonomically optimized stock in dark green or dark brown and elastomer grips; double loading option; leather model available
MSRP....................**$4148**
Leather:.................**$5198**

BROWNING AB3 (A-BOLT III) COMPOSITE STALKER

Action: Bolt
Stock: Composite
Barrel: 22 in., 26 in.
Sights: None
Weight: 6 lb. 10 oz.–7 lb. 3 oz.
Caliber: .270 Win., .30-06 Spfd., 7mm Rem. Mag., .300 Win. Mag.
Magazine: 3 rounds (magnum), 4 rounds (standard)
Features: Matte blued barreled action; matte black synthetic stock; barrel is individulally finished with a hand-reamed chamber; free-floating barrel; receiver drilled and tapped for scope mounts; generous trigger guard; top-tang safety; sling swivel studs
MSRP................. **$599.99**

BROWNING BAR SHORTRAC HOG STALKER REALTREE MAX-1

Action: Gas-operated autoloader
Stock: Composite Realtree Max-1
Barrel: 20 in.
Sights: None
Weight: 9 lb. 5 oz.
Caliber: .308 Win.

Magazine: 10 rounds
Features: Aircraft-grade alloy receiver; drilled and tapped for scope mount; three interchangeable cheekpieces and recoil pads for different fit options; ambidextrous magazine release
MSRP................ **$1669.99**

BROWNING BLR LIGHTWEIGHT '81 HOG STALKER TAKEDOWN GREEN

Action: Lever
Stock: Green laminate wood
Barrel: 18 in.
Sights: TruGlo/Marble fiber optic fron
Weight: 6 lb. 11 oz.
Caliber: .223 Rem., .308 Win.
Magazine: Detachable box
Features: Satin nickel finish on receiver; matte finish on barrel; receiver drilled and tapped for scope mounts; checkered straight grip on stock; separates for storage or transportation; sling swivel studs; Picatinny rail scope base; Hog Stalker soft case included
MSRP................. **$1339.99**

BUSHMASTER 300 AAC BLACKOUT

Action: Semiautomatic
Stock: Magpul ACS stock
Barrel: 16 in.
Sights: None
Weight: 6 lb. 9 oz.
Caliber: .300 AAC Blackout
Magazine: Accepts all AR-types
Features: A compact 30-caliber solution for the AR platform; sound and flash suppression; use existing AR magazines; low-profile milled gas block; Magpul MOW grip; quad rail; Magpul enhanced trigger guard
MSRP $1471.39

CENTURY INTERNATIONAL ARMS CENTURION 39 SPORTER

Action: Semiautomatic
Stock: Synthetic
Barrel: 16.5 in.
Sights: Front post, adjustable rear
Weight: 8 lb. 3 oz.
Caliber: 7.62x39mm
Magazine: 30 rounds
Features: Milled receiver machined from an 11-pound block of 4140 ordnance quality steel; rear sight adjustable for windage and elevation; high visibiliy from sight postl buttstock 1 in. longer than military-style stocks; upper and lower handguard have four Picatinny rails; two 30 round magazines included; 100 percent American made
MSRP $999.95

CHIAPPA FIREARMS LITTLE BADGER

Action: Single shot
Stock: Metal foldable
Barrel: 16.5 in.
Sights: Adjustable rear
Weight: 3 lb. 8 oz.
Caliber: .22LR
Magazine: None
Features: Single barrel; foldable rifle; extremely light for comfortable carry; folds to 16.5 in. total length; nylon carry bad and special cartridge holder available
MSRP . . . .$179.95–$189.95

CHIAPPA FIREARMS M1-22

Action: Semiautomatic
Stock: Wood or black synthetic
Barrel: 18 in.
Sights: Adjustable rear
Weight: 5 lb. 8 oz.
Caliber: .22LR
Magazine: 10 rounds
Features: The M1 carbine is a lightweight, easy-to-use semiautomatic carbine that became a standard firearm for the U.S. military during World War II, the Korean War, and the Vietnam War, and was produced in several variants.
Synthetic: $349
Wood: $399

BUSHMASTER 300 AAC BLACKOUT

CENTURY INTERNATIONAL ARMS CENTURION 39 SPORTER

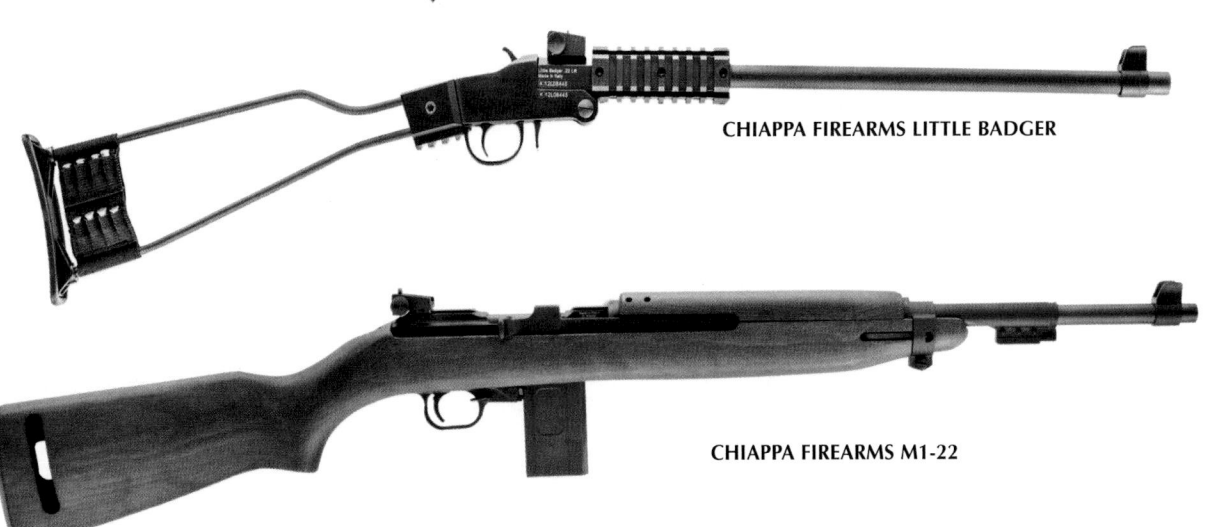

CHIAPPA FIREARMS LITTLE BADGER

CHIAPPA FIREARMS M1-22

NEW Products: **Rifles**

CIMARRON 1886 BOAR BUSTER

CIMARRON 1886 CLASSIC

CIMARRON 1886 BOAR BUSTER

Action: Lever
Stock: Walnut
Barrel: 19 in.
Sights: Fiber optic
Weight: N/A
Caliber: .45-70
Magazine: Fixed tube
Features: Carbine model; scout rail; pistol grip stock
MSRP **$1792.70**

CIMARRON 1886 CLASSIC

Action: Lever
Stock: Walnut
Barrel: 26 in.
Sights: Open
Weight: N/A

Caliber: .45-70
Magazine: Fixed tube
Features: Blued receiver; pistol grip stock
MSRP **$1792.70**

CIMARRON 1886 PREMIUM

Action: Lever
Stock: Premium Walnut
Barrel: 26 in.
Sights: Open
Weight: N/A
Caliber: .45-70
Magazine: Fixed tube
Features: Case colored receiver
MSRP **$1883.70**

CIMARRON SADDLE SHORTY

Action: Lever
Stock: Wood
Barrel: 18 in.
Sights: Open
Weight: N/A
Caliber: .357 Mag./.38 Spl., .45 Colt, .44 WCF
Magazine: Fixed tube
Features: Full octagon barrel; straight stock with checkered forearm and stock
MSRP **$1059**

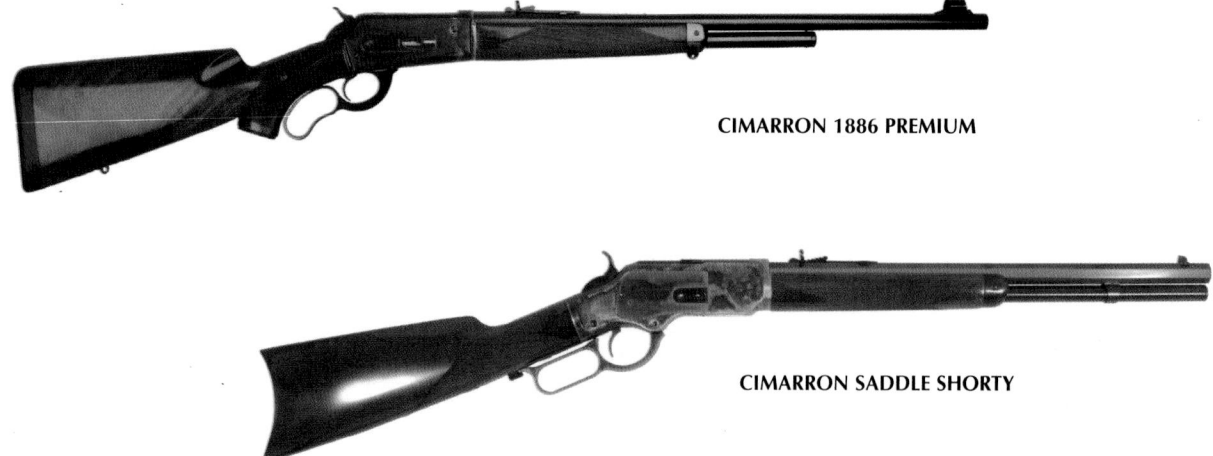

CIMARRON 1886 PREMIUM

CIMARRON SADDLE SHORTY

COLT COMPETITION MARKSMAN CRX-16

Action: Semiautomatic
Stock: M4 carbine-style
Barrel: 16 in.
Sights: None
Weight: 6 lb. 7 oz.
Caliber: .223 Rem.
Magazine: 30 rounds
Features: Match-grade chrome-moly steel barrel; twin-port muzzle brake; vented modular float-tube handguard; low profile gas block; charging handle with extended tactical latch; match-target trigger coated with nickel-Teflon
MSRP....................**$1399**

COLT COMPETITION CRX-16

COLT COMPETITION PRO CRP-18

Action: Semiautomatic
Stock: Magpul CTR adjustable
Barrel: 18 in.
Sights: None
Weight: 7 lb. 3 oz.
Caliber: .223 Rem.
Magazine: 30 rounds
Features: Match-grade, polished 416 stainless steel barrel; gas-operated, original direct-impingement system; triple port muzzle brake; Picatinny top handguard rail and accessory rail; Magpul MOE grip with extended backstrap; low profile adjustable gas block
MSRP....................**$2019**

COLT COMPETITION CRP-18

COOPER FIREARMS MODEL 51

COOPER FIREARMS MODEL 51

Action: Bolt
Stock: Classic, Custom Classic, Western Classic, Schnabel, Mannlicher, Jackson Game, Jackson Hunter, Excaliber, Varminter, Montana Varminter, Varmint Extreme, Varmint Laminate, Phoenix
Barrel: 22 in., 24 in.
Sights: None
Weight: 6 lb. 4 oz.–7 lb. 4 oz.
Caliber: .17 Rem., .19-223, Tactical .20, .204 Ruger, .222 Rem., .222 Rem. Mag., .223 Rem., .223 Rem. AI, 6x45, 6x47, .300 Blackout
Magazine: None
Features: Longer barrel standard on all varmint models; fully adjustable single-stage trigger; Sako style extraction machined from solid bar stock
MSRP.............. **$2225–$5095**

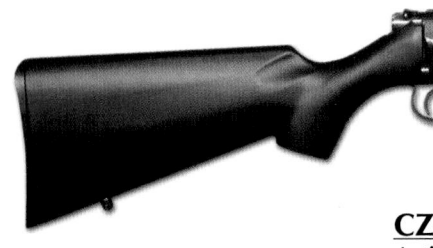

CZ-USA 455 AMERICAN

CZ-USA 455 AMERICAN

Action: Bolt
Stock: Black polymer
Barrel: 20.5 in.
Sights: None
Weight: 5 lb. 13 oz.

Caliber: .22LR
Magazine: Detachable box, 5 rounds
Features: New black synthetic stock; cold hammer-forged barrel; interchangeable barrel system; adjustable trigger
MSRP................... **$374**

CZ-USA 455 VARMINT TACTICOOL

CZ-USA 455 VARMINT TACTICOOL

Action: Bolt
Stock: Black laminate
Barrel: 20.5 in.
Sights: None
Weight: 7 lb. 6 oz.
Caliber: .22LR
Magazine: Detachable box, 5 rounds
Features: Built as a tactical trainer with

a number of ergonomic features; stock has ambidextrous palm swells on its pistol grip and an especially high Monte Carlo to accommodate larger scopes; beavertail forend is great for riding bags or affixing bipod; cold hammer-forged barrel; interchangeable barrel system; adjustable trigger
MSRP................... **$522**

CZ-USA 455 VARMINT THUMBHOLE SST FLUTED

CZ-USA 455 VARMINT THUMBHOLE SST FLUTED

Action: Bolt
Stock: Forest camo laminate
Barrel: 20.5 in.
Sights: Integrated 11mm dovetail
Weight: 7 lb.
Caliber: .17 HMR
Magazine: Detachable box, 5 rounds

Features: Fitted into a vented thumbhole stock in forest camo laminate; barrel is fluted to cut down on weight and speed cooling; CZ's new SST for the 455 platform
MSRP................... **$615**

DAKOTA ARMS MODEL 76 PH

DEL-TON DTI EVOLUTION

DEL-TON DT SPORT OR

DEL-TON ECHO 316H OR

DAKOTA ARMS MODEL 76 PH

Action: Bolt
Stock: Fiberglass
Barrel: 23 in.
Sights: Fixed blade banded front, fiber optic bead
Weight: 9 lb.
Caliber: .375 H&H, .404 Jeffrey, .416 Rem., .416 Rigby, .458 Lott, .450 Dakota, .450 Rigby
Magazine: None
Features: Custom fiberglass stock; Douglas premium stainless steel barrel; barrel band; CeraKote matte black, black decelrator pad; right- and left-hand models available
MSRP **$7995**

DEL-TON DTI EVOLUTION

Action: Semiautomatic
Stock: Magpul CTR Mil-Spec
Barrel: 16 in.
Sights: Folding front, flip rear
Weight: 7 lb. 3 oz.
Caliber: 5.56x45mm
Magazine: 30 rounds
Features: Chrome-lined barrel; Samson Evolution free-float rail; Quick Flip Dual Aperture rear sight; Magpul MOE+ grip
MSRP **$1300**

DEL-TON DT SPORT OR

Action: Semiautomatic
Stock: M4 six-position
Barrel: 16 in.
Sights: None
Weight: 5 lb. 13 oz.
Caliber: 5.56x45mm
Magazine: 30 rounds

Features: Low profile gas block; six-position M4 stock; CAR handguards with single heat shields; A2 flash hider; anodized receiver; gun lock included
MSRP **$699**

DEL-TON ECHO 316H OR

Action: Semiautomatic
Stock: M4 five-position
Barrel: 16 in.
Sights: None
Weight: 6 lb. 10 oz.
Caliber: 5.56x45mm
Magazine: 30 rounds
Features: Single rail gas block; CAR handguards with single heat shields; A2 flash hider; forged 7075 T6 aluminum upper and lower receivers
MSRP **$864**

DPMS PANTHER ARMS DPMS 3G2

Action: Semiautomatic
Stock: Synthetic
Barrel: 16 in.
Sights: Magpu Gen 2 BUS
Weight: 7 lb. 1.6 oz.
Caliber: 5.56x45mm
Magazine: Detachable box, 30 rounds
Features: Stainless lightweight barrel with Miculek compensator; full length M111 handguard allows for the placement of back-up sights either on the top rail or on a 45-degree angle for rapid close-range target acquisition; Ergo grip and Magpul STR stock round out this range-ready carbine; pistol grip stock
MSRP..................**$1239**

DPMS 3G2

DPMS PANTHER ARMS 300 PERSONAL DEFENSE

Action: Semiautomatic
Stock: AP4 com. tube
Barrel: 23.75 in.
Sights: Magpul vertical
Weight: 5 lb. 8 oz.
Caliber: 5.56 NATO
Magazine: 30 rounds
Features: The DPMS Personal Defense Weapon, or PDW, is designed to bring maximum firepower into a small package. Features forged 7075 T6 A3 flattop upper receiver; chromoly barrel standard AR-15 fire control; PDW free float handguard with vertical grip
MSRP..................**$1289**

DPMS PDW

DPMS PANTHER ARMS DPMS 6.8 HUNTER

Action: Semiautomatic
Stock: A2-style
Barrel: 20 in.
Sights: N/A, optics ready
Weight: 7 lb. 2 oz.
Caliber: 6.8 SPC
Magazine: 25 rounds
Features: Carbon-fiber free-float tube handguard; flattop upper; fluted teflon coated barrel; two-stage match fire control
MSRP..................**$1269**

DPMS 6.8 HUNTER

DPMS PANTHER ARMS DPSM .22 BULL BARREL

Action: Semiautomatic
Stock: Fixed A2 synthetic
Barrel: 16 in.

DPMS .22 BULL BARREL

Sights: None
Weight: 7 lb. 5 oz.
Caliber: .22LR
Magazine: 10 rounds

Features: Capable of accepting aftermarket stocks, grips, fire control components; integral feed ramp; fixed ejector
MSRP....................**$1029**

FNH FN/UNIQUE ALPINE BALLISTA

Action: Bolt
Stock: Collapsible
Barrel: 26 in.
Sights: N/A, scope compatible
Weight: 15 lb.
Caliber: .308 Win., .300 Win. Mag., .338 Lapua Mag.
Magazine: 8 or 15 rounds (.308 Win.), 6 or 10 rounds (.300 Win. Mag.), 5 or 8 rounds (.338 Lapua)
Features: Modular, multi-caliber designed for long-range precision work; aluminum alloy receiver; adjustable trigger; ambidextrous stock; vibration-isolated aluminum alloy receiver; Mil-Std 1913 rail
MSRP.....................**$9995**

FNH FN-UNIQUE ALPINE BALLISTA

FNH FN SPR A5 XP

FNH FN SPR A5 XP

Action: Bolt
Stock: McMillan fiberglass
Barrel: 20 in., 24 in.
Sights: None
Weight: 11 lb. 5 oz.-11 lb. 13 oz.
Caliber: .300 WSM, .308 Win.
Magazine: 4 or 5 rounds
Features: Threaded tactical bolt knob; barrel threaded muzzle; Mil-Std 1913 rail; external claw extractor with controlled round feeding; integral recoil lug; three-position safety; knurled bolt handle
MSRP.....................**$2899**

HECKLER & KOCH MR762A1 (LRP)

HECKLER & KOCH MR762A1 (LRP)

Action: Semiautomatic
Stock: Synthetic
Barrel: 16.5 in.
Sights: 3-9x40mm scope
Weight: 9 lb. 15 oz.
Caliber: 7.62x51mm
Magazine: 10, 20 rounds
Features: Rifle; Leupold 3-9 VX-R Patrol scope and mount; HK G28 buttstock; LaRue Tactical BRM-S bipod; ERGO Pistol Grip; Blue Force Gear sling; Manta rail covers; OTIS cleaning kit; a 10- and 20-round magazine; Model 1720 Pelican case
MSRP.....................**$6895**

HENRY REPEATING ARMS THE ORIGINAL HENRY RIFLE

Action: Lever
Stock: Walnut
Barrel: 24.5
Sights: Folding ladder rear
Weight: 9 lb.
Caliber: .44-40
Magazine: 13+1 rounds
Features: True to original specifications; first time the Original Henry has been offered in the U.S. by an American manufacturer in 150 years
MSRP.....................**$2300**

HENRY REPEATING ARMS THE ORIGINAL HENRY RIFLE

NEW Products: Rifles

HOWA BY LEGACY SPORTS WHITETAIL PACKAGE

Action: Bolt
Stock: Synthetic
Barrel: 20 in.
Sights: 2.5-10x42mm scope
Weight: 9 lb.
Caliber: .204, .223, .22-250, .243, .308, 7mm-08
Magazine: 5 round detachable
Features: Contour barrel; shaved receiver and hollowed bolt handle; two-stage trigger; three-position safety; forged bolt with two locking lugs; three MoonShine Camo patterns: Muddy Girl, Harvest Moon, and Outshine; Nikko Stirling Nighteater 2.5-10x42 scope with #4 duplex reticle; Buffalo River bipod also included
MSRP $762

HOWA WHITETAIL OUTSHINE

J. P. SAUER & SOHN SAUER 101

Action: Bolt
Stock: Walnut
Barrel: 22 in., 24 in.
Sights: Adjustable open sights optional
Weight: 6 lb. 12 oz.
Caliber: .22-250 Rem., .243 Win., .270 Win., .308 Win., .30-06, 6.5x55, 7x64, 8x57IS, 9.3x62, 7mm Rem. Mag., .300 Win. Mag., .338 Win. Mag.
Magazine: 5+1 rounds (standard), 4+1 rounds (magnum)
Features: 60-degree bolt lift; six locking lugs; available in standard and magnum calibers; matte black finish; DURA SAFE firing pin safety; EVER REST action bedding; ambidextrous stock
MSRP . . . . $1499–$1699

J. P. SAUER & SOHN SAUER 101

KRISS VECTOR SBR

Action: Semiautomatic
Stock: Polymer
Barrel: 5.5 in.
Sights: Custom flip-up iron
Weight: 5 lb. 10 oz.
Caliber: .45 ACP
Magazine: 13 rounds
Features: Also available in Carbine and Special Duty Pistol configurations; adjustable folding stock; picatinny rails; ambidextrous F/S controls; foregrip; cable lock
MSRP $1995

KRISS VECTOR SBR

K-VAR SGL 31-95

K-VAR SGL 31-95

Action: Semiautomatic
Stock: Mil-Spec black polymer
Barrel: 16.3 in.
Sights: Rear leaf
Weight: 7 lb. 5 oz.
Caliber: 5.45x39.5mm
Magazine: 30, 45 rounds
Features: Manufactured at the Izhmash Factry in Russia; authentic Russian polymer side-folding buttstock; chrome-lined, hammer-forged barrel; scope rail; accessory lug
MSRP....................$1299

MAGNUM RESEARCH MAGNUM LITE MLR22 WIN MAG

Action: Semiautomatic
Stock: Hogue Overmolded; Barracuda
Barrel: 18 in.
Sights: Rail for Weaver style rings
Weight: 7 lb. 5 oz.
Caliber: .22 Win. Mag
Magazine: 9 rounds
Features: Barrel features an 11 degree crown; patented gas system and block under barrel; available in nutmeg, pepper, forest camo, stainless steel, or matte
MSRP............... $727–$819

MASTERPIECE ARMS MPAR 556 RIFLE

Action: Semiautomatic
Stock: Synthetic
Barrel: 16 in.
Sights: None
Weight: 7 lb. 13 oz.
Caliber: 5.56mm NATO (.223 Rem.)
Magazine: N/A
Features: Short stroke piston design; lightweight, free-floating, two-piece aluminum handguard; user located Picatinny rails; side-folding collapsible stock; full length top rail
MSRP.................... $999

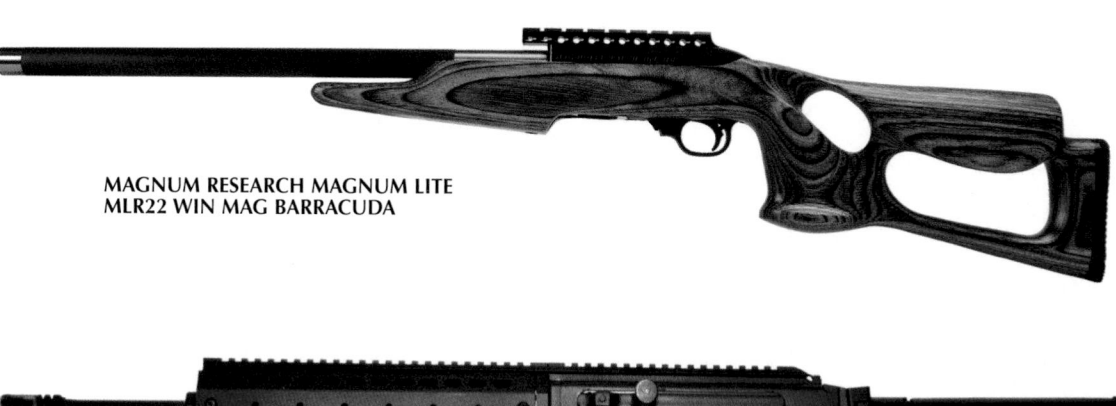

MAGNUM RESEARCH MAGNUM LITE
MLR22 WIN MAG BARRACUDA

MASTERPIECE ARMS
MPAR 556 RIFLE

NEW Products: Rifles

MAUSER M12 HUNTING RIFLE

Action: Bolt
Stock: Wood, Synthetic
Barrel: 22 in., 24.5 in.
Sights: None
Weight: 7 lb.
Caliber: .22-250 Rem., .243 Win., 6.5x55 SE, .270 Win., 7x64, .308 Win., .30-06 Spfd., 8x57 IS, 9.3x62, 7mm Rem., .300 Win. Mag., .338 Win. Mag.
Magazine: 5+1 rounds
Features: 60-degree bolt lift; detachable magazine; open sights available; drilled and tapped for scopes; stock extension available
MSRP $1799
Extreme:. $1499

MCMILLAN FIREARMS EOL MOUNTAIN EXTREME ALPINE

Action: Bolt, McMillan G30 Long Action
Stock: Composite, khaki and gray
Barrel: 26 in.
Sights: 20 MOA Picatinny style scope bases
Weight: 7 lb. 4 oz.
Caliber: 6.5x284 Norma
Magazine: N/A
Features: Jewell trigger; metal black finish; NP3 muzzle brake; EDGE graphite technology
MSRP $6775

MCMILLAN FIREARMS EOL MOUNTAIN EXTREME DENALI

Action: Bolt, McMillan G30 Long Action
Stock: EDGE A3-5 composite, khaki and gray
Barrel: 28 in.
Sights: 40 MOA Picatinny style scope bases
Weight: 9 lb. 8 oz.
Caliber: 7mm EOL Mag./7mm Rem. Ultra Mag., .300 EOL Mag./.300 Rem. Ultra Mag., .338 Lapua
Magazine: N/A
Features: Jewell trigger; metal black finish; NP3 muzzle brake; EDGE graphite technology; hand-lapped match grade barrel
MSRP $6895

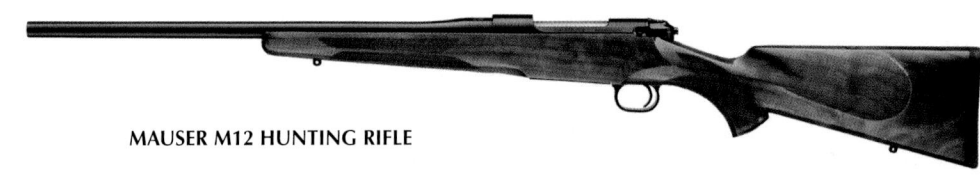

MAUSER M12 HUNTING RIFLE

MCMILLAN EOL MOUNTAIN EXTREME ALPINE

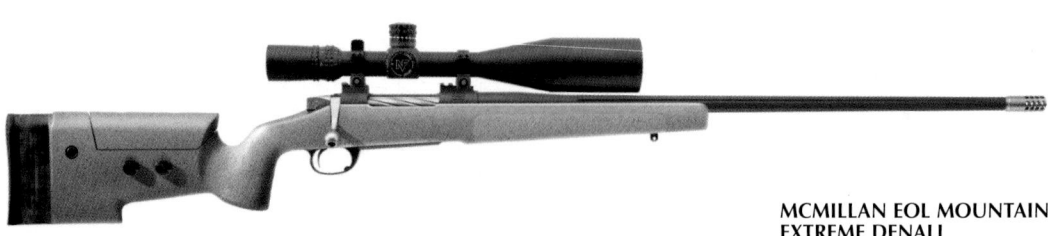

MCMILLAN EOL MOUNTAIN EXTREME DENALI

MCMILLAN FIREARMS EOL MOUNTAIN EXTREME YUKON

MCMILLAN FIREARMS EOL MOUNTAIN EXTREME YUKON

Action: Bolt, McMillan G30 Long Action
Stock: EDGE Outdoorsman composite, khaki and gray
Barrel: 27 in.
Sights: 20 MOA Picatinny style scope bases

Weight: 8 lb. 4 oz.
Caliber: 7mm EOL Mag./7mm Rem. Ultra Mag., .300 EOL Mag./.300 Rem. Ultra Mag., .338 EOL Mag./.338 Lapua
Magazine: N/A
Features: Jewell trigger; metal black finish; NP3 muzzle brake; EDGE graphite technology; hand-lapped match grade barrel
MSRP **$6775**

MONTANA RIFLES AMERICAN VANTAGE RIFLE (AVR)

MONTANA RIFLES AMERICAN VANTAGE RIFLE (AVR)

Action: Bolt
Stock: Walnut, Synthetic
Barrel: 24 in.
Sights: Marble replaceable front and rear
Weight: 9 lb.

Caliber: .35 Whelen, .375 H&H, .375 Ruger, .416 Rem. Mag., .416 Ruger, .458 Lott, .458 Win. Mag.
Magazine: N/A
Features: Matte blued chrome moly steel or stainless steel barreled actions; available in right or left hand configurations
MSRP **$1279**

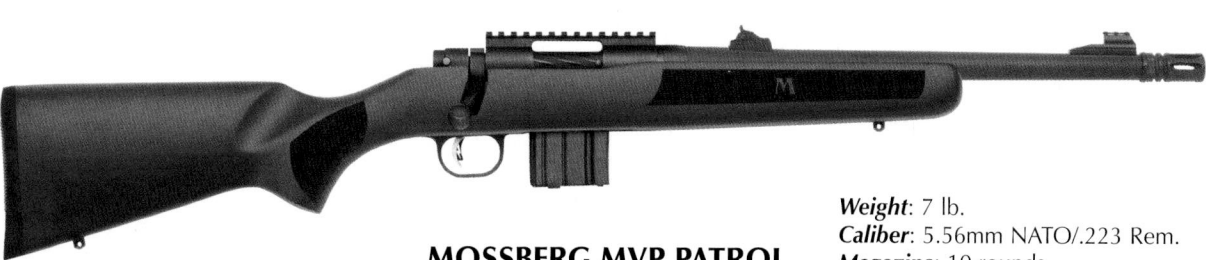

MOSSBERG MVP PATROL RIFLE

MOSSBERG MVP PATROL RIFLE

Action: Bolt
Stock: Birch, black textured
Barrel: 16.25 in.
Sights: Front fiber optic, adjustable rear; optional 3-9x32mm scope

Weight: 7 lb.
Caliber: 5.56mm NATO/.223 Rem.
Magazine: 10 rounds
Features: MVP Drop-Push bolt design; A2 flash suppressor; Lightning Bolt Action Trigger System; matte blue finish; picatinny rails; spiral fluted bolts; front and rear swivel studs; available threaded barrel
MSRP . . . . $681–$829

REMINGTON MODEL 700 SPS WOOD TECH

Action: Bolt
Stock: Synthetic walnut finish
Barrel: 22 in., 24 in.
Sights: None
Weight: 7 lb. 6 oz.–7 lb. 10 oz.
Caliber: .270 Win., 30-06 Spfd., .300 Win., 7mm Rem. Mag.
Magazine: 4 rounds
Features: Hammer-forged barrel; X-Mark Pro externally adjustable trigger ensures peak shot control; over-molded grip panels on stock; SuperCell recoil pad
MSRP **$800**

REMINGTON MODEL 783

Action: Bolt
Stock: Black synthetic
Barrel: 22 in., 24 in.
Sights: None
Weight: 7 lb.–7 lb. 4 oz.
Caliber: .270 Win., 30-06 Spfd., .308 Win., 7mm Rem. Mag.
Magazine: 4 rounds
Features: CrossFire trigger system; carbon steel magnum contour button rifled barrel; pillar-bedded stock and free-floated barrel; SuperCell recoil pad
MSRP **$451**

REMINGTON MODEL 700 SPS WOOD TECH

REMINGTON MODEL 783

ROCK RIVER ARMS LAR-15 DELTA CAR/DELTA MID-LENGTH

Action: Semiautomatic
Stock: Synthetic
Barrel: 16 in.
Sights: None
Weight: 7 lb.-7 lb. 4.8 oz.
Caliber: 5.56mm NATO, .223

Magazine: 30 rounds
Features: Delta Quad Rail two piece drop-in and gas system, available in CAR or Mid-length; low profile gas block; Ergo SureGrip; two stage trigger
MSRP.....................$1085

ROCK RIVER ARMS LAR-15 DELTA CAR/ DELTA MID-LENGTH

ROCK RIVER ARMS LAR-15LH LEF-T COYOTE RIFLE & CARBINE

Action: Semiautomatic
Stock: Synthetic A2
Barrel: 16 in., 20 in.
Sights: None
Weight: 7 lb.-8 lb. 6.4 oz.
Caliber: 5.56mm NATO, .223

Magazine: 20 rounds
Features: Smith Vortex Flash Hider; Hogue free float tube; Hogue grip; two stage trigger
Carbine: $1400
Rifle: $1450

ROCK RIVER ARMS LAR-15LH LEF-T COYOTE RIFLE & CARBINE

ROCK RIVER ARMS LAR-15 R3 COMPETITION RIFLE

Action: Semiautomatic
Stock: Synthetic A2 or CAR
Barrel: 18 in.
Sights: None
Weight: 7 lb. 9.6 oz.
Caliber: 5.56mm NATO, .223
Magazine: 30 rounds
Features: RRA tuned and ported

muzzle brake; low profile gas block; two stage trigger; Hogue Rubber grip
MSRP.....................$1310

ROCK RIVER ARMS LAR-15 R3 COMPETITION RIFLE

ROSSI CIRCUIT JUDGE .44 MAG.

Action: SA/DA
Stock: Hardwood
Barrel: 18.5 in.
Sights: Red fiber optic front
Weight: 5 lb. 3 oz.
Caliber: .44 Mag.
Magazine: 6 rounds
Features: Yoke detent; transfer bar; Taurus Security System
MSRP **$684**

ROSSI CIRCUIT JUDGE CONVERTIBLE

Action: SA/DA
Stock: Synthetic
Barrel: 18.5 in.
Sights: Red fiber optic front
Weight: N/A
Caliber: .22LR, .22 Mag.
Magazine: 6 rounds
Features: Removable cylinder to change easily from .22LR to .22 Mag.; blued finish
MSRP **$732**

RUGER 10/22 TAKEDOWN

Action: Autoloading
Stock: Black synthetic
Barrel: 16.6 in.
Sights: Gold bead front, adjustable rear
Weight: 4 lb. 10.7 oz.
Caliber: .22LR
Magazine: 10 rounds
Features: Built of alloy steel with satin black finish; threaded barrel with flash suppressor; easy takedown and reassembly; detachable rotary magazine; extended magazine release; combination scope base adapter; push-button manual safety
MSRP **$419**

ROSSI CIRCUIT JUDGE .44 MAG.

ROSSI CIRCUIT JUDGE CONVERTIBLE

RUGER 10/22 TAKEDOWN

RUGER GUIDE GUN

RUGER GUNSITE SCOUT RIFLE STAINLESS

RUGER M77 HAWKEYE MAGNUM HUNTER

RUGER SR-556VT

RUGER GUIDE GUN WITH MUZZLE BRAKE SYSTEM

Action: Bolt
Stock: Green Mountain laminate
Barrel: 20 in.
Sights: Bead front, adjustable rear
Weight: 8 lb.-8 lb. 2 oz.
Caliber: .300 RCM, .300 Win. Mag., .30-06 Spfd., .338 RCM, .338 Win. Mag., .375 Ruger
Magazine: 3 rounds (4 rounds in .30-06 Spfd.)
Features: LC6 Trigger; Mauser-type extractor; muzzle brake system; three-position safety; manner-forged barrel; integral scope mounts; stainless steel bolt; swivel studs;
MSRP $1199

RUGER GUNSITE SCOUT RIFLE STAINLESS

Action: Bolt
Stock: Black laminate
Barrel: 18 in.

Sights: Post front, adjustable rear
Weight: 7 lb. 2 oz.
Caliber: .308 Win.
Magazine: 10 rounds
Features: Flash suppressor; picatinny rail; detachable box magazine; recoil pad; integral scope mounts; Mauser-type extractor; "Gunsite Approved"; stainless steel bolt; muzzle thread protector; available in both left and right hand
MSRP $1099

RUGER M77 HAWKEYE MAGNUM HUNTER WITH MUZZLE BRAKE SYSTEM

Action: Bolt
Stock: Green Hogue
Barrel: 24 in.
Sights: None
Weight: 8 lb.
Caliber: .300 Win. Mag.
Magazine: 3 rounds

Features: Hawkeye matte stainless finish; LC6 trigger; Mauser-type controlled extractor; steel floorplate; muzzle brake system; integral scope mounts; three-position safety; stainless steel bolt
MSRP $1099

RUGER SR-556VT

Action: Autoloading
Stock: Black synthetic
Barrel: 20 in.
Sights: None
Weight: 8 lb. 8 oz.
Caliber: 5.56mm NATO
Magazine: 5 rounds
Features: Two-stage piston with adjustable regulator; handguard; target-style trigger; hammer-forged barrel; pistol grip; charging handle; chrome-plated bolt
MSRP $1995

NEW Products: **Rifles**

SAVAGE ARMS AXIS XP YOUTH CAMO

Action: Bolt
Stock: Synthetic
Barrel: 20 in.
Sights: Scope included
Weight: 6 lb. 13 oz.
Caliber: .223 Rem., .243 Win., 7mm-08 Rem.
Magazine: 4 rounds, detachable box
Features: Made with cooperation from the Youth Shooting Sports Alliance; carbon steel barrel with matte black finish; stock comes in camo or muddy girl
MSRP **$475**

SAVAGE ARMS LAW ENFORCEMENT SERIES 110 BA LEFT HAND MODEL

Action: Bolt
Stock: Aluminum
Barrel: 26 in.
Sights: Drilled and tapped for scope
Weight: 15 lb. 12 oz.
Caliber: .300 Win. Mag., .338 Lapua Mag.
Magazine: 5 rounds, detachable box
Features: Also available in right hand model; AccuTrigger; matte black carbon steel barrel; 20 MOA scope rail
MSRP **$2465**

SAVAGE ARMS SPECIALTY SERIES MODEL 42

Action: Break-action
Stock: Synthetic
Barrel: 20 in.
Sights: Adjustable
Weight: 6 lb. 2 oz.
Caliber: .22LR, .22 WMR
Magazine: None
Features: Rifle-shotgun combo; break-open combination gun over 410 bore; carbon steel matte black barrel; matte black synthetic stock;
MSRP **$480**

SAVAGE ARMS AXIS XP YOUTH CAMO

SAVAGE ARMS LAW ENFORCEMENT
SERIES 110 BA LEFT HAND MODEL

SAVAGE ARMS SPECIALTY SERIES
MODEL 42

SIG SAUER SIG716 PRECISION

SIG SAUER SIG716 PRECISION

Action: Semiautomatic
Stock: Magpul UBR
Barrel: 18 in.
Sights: None
Weight: 11 lb.
Caliber: 7.62x51mm NATO
Magazine: 20 rounds
Features: Short-stroke push rod operating system; 1913 Mil-Std rail; free-floating barrel; telescoping stock; Magpul PMAG; Match grade trigger group
MSRP....................**$2666**

STAG ARMS MODEL 8T

Action: Gas-operated piston
Stock: 6 position collapsible
Barrel: 16 in.
Sights: Diamondhead premium flip up sight set
Weight: N/A
Caliber: 5.56 NATO
Magazine: 30 rounds
Features: Short-stroke piston system; left or right-handed versions; ergonomic modular free-floating VRS-T handguard; chrome-lined barrel; Mil-spec trigger; lifetime warranty
MSRP....................**$1275**

STAG ARMS MODEL 8T

NEW Products: **Rifles**

TURNBULL MFG. CO TAR-15

Action: Semiautomatic
Stock: Black Walnut
Barrel: 16 in.
Sights: None
Weight: 8 lb. 8 oz.
Caliber: .223
Magazine: 5 and 10 rounds
Features: AR-15 gas impingement system; 8620 carbon steel receivers; color case hardened steel; oversized integral trigger guard; picatinny rail; screw on muzzle brake; also available in 7.62x39 and .300 AAC Blackout
MSRP. $2750

WEATHERBY MARK V ACCUMARK RC RIFLE

Action: Bolt
Stock: Monte Carlo composite
Barrel: 24 in., 26 in., 28 in.
Sights: None
Weight: 7 lb. 4 oz.–9lb.
Caliber: .240 Wby. Mag., .270 Win., .308 Win., .30-06 Spfd., .257 Wby. Mag., .270 Wby. Mag., 7mm Rem. Mag., 7mm Wby. Mag., .300 Win. Mag., .300 Wby. Mag., .30-378 Wby. Mag., .338-378 Wby. Mag., .340 Wby. Mag., .338 Lapua
Magazine: 5+1, 3+1, or 2+1 rounds
Features: "Range Certified" model comes with a SUB-MOA guarantee; button-rifled stainless steel barrel; free floated barrel with a recessed target crown; Pachmayr Decelerator pad
MSRP. . . . . $2400–$2700

WEATHERBY VANGUARD 2 BACK COUNTRY

Action: Bolt
Stock: Monte Carlo composite
Barrel: 24 in.
Sights: None
Weight: 6 lb. 12 oz.
Caliber: .240 Wby. Mag., .270 Win., .257 Wby. Mag., .30-06 Spfd., .300 Win. Mag., .300 Wby. Mag.
Magazine: 5+1 or 3+1 rounds
Features: SUB-MOA guarantee; chrome moly metalwork with Cerakote Tactical Grey finish; pillar-bedded stock; two-stage trigger; 3-position safety; auxiliary trigger sear; Pachmayr Decelerator pad
MSRP. $1399

TURNBULL MFG. CO TAR-15

WEATHERBY MARK V ACCUMARK RC RIFLE

WEATHERBY VANGUARD 2 BACK COUNTRY

NEW PRODUCTS

WEATHERBY VANGUARD 2 SYNTHETIC PACKAGE

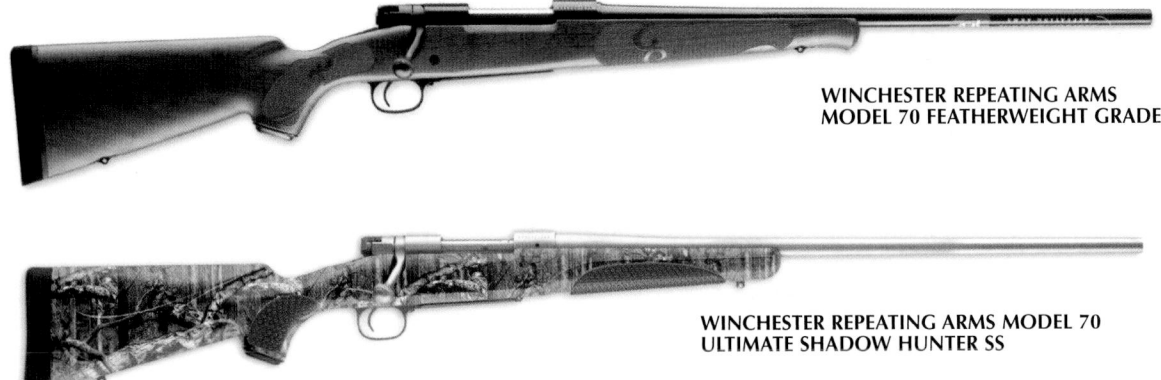

WINCHESTER REPEATING ARMS
MODEL 70 FEATHERWEIGHT GRADE III

WINCHESTER REPEATING ARMS MODEL 70
ULTIMATE SHADOW HUNTER SS

WEATHERBY VANGUARD 2 SYNTHETIC PACKAGE

Action: Bolt
Stock: Synthetic
Barrel: 24 in.
Sights: 3-9x42mm Redfield Revenge scope
Weight: 8 lb. 4 oz.–8 lb. 8 oz.
Caliber: .223 Rem., .22-250 Rem., .243 Win., .25-06 Rem., .270 Win., 7mm-08 Rem., .308 Win., .30-06 Spfd., .257 Wby. Mag., 7mm Rem. Mag., .300 Win. Mag., .300 Wby. Mag., .338 Win. Mag.
Magazine: 5+1 or 3+1 rounds
Features: SUB-MOA guarantee; mounted and boresighted Redfield scope with matte finish and 4-plex reticle; Talley-designed mounts; adjustable nylon sling; injection-molded scoped rifle case
MSRP $999

WINCHESTER REPEATING ARMS MODEL 70 FEATHERWEIGHT GRADE III

Action: Bolt
Stock: Walnut
Barrel: 22 in.
Sights: None
Weight: 7 lb.
Caliber: .270 Win.
Magazine: 5 rounds
Features: Polished blued steel; free-floating barrel with target crown; adjustable M.O.A. Trigger System; three-position safety; controlled round feed and ejection; hinged floorplate; jeweled bolt body; Pachmayr Decelerator pad
MSRP $1019.99

WINCHESTER REPEATING ARMS MODEL 70 ULTIMATE SHADOW HUNTER SS

Action: Bolt
Stock: Synthetic MO Break-Up Infinity Camo
Barrel: 22 in., 24 in., 26 in.
Sights: None
Weight: 6 lb. 12 oz.–7 lb. 4 oz.
Caliber: .243 Win., 7mm-08 Rem., .308 Win., .270 Win., 30-06 Spfd., .300 Win. Mag., .338 Win. Mag., .300 WSM, .270 WSM, .325 WSM
Magazine: 3 rounds
Features: Gray overmolded rubberized gripping surfaces; matte metal; alloy one-piece bottom metal; pre-'64 style controlled round feed with claw extractor; three-position safety; free-floating stainless steel barrel; recessed target crown; blade-type ejector; M.O.A. Trigger System; available in blued and stainless steel
Blued: . . . . $829.99–$869.99
SS: . . . .$1039.99–$1079.99

WINCHESTER REPEATING ARMS MODEL 94 CARBINE

Action: Lever
Stock: Walnut
Barrel: 20 in.
Sights: Adjustable semi-buckhorn rear, Marble Arms front
Weight: 6 lb. 8 oz.
Caliber: 30-30 Win., 38-55 Win.
Magazine: N/A
Features: Triple-checked button rifled barrel; round locking bolt trunnions; top-tang safety; rebounding hammer; bolt relief cut; steel loading gate; articulated cartridge stop; available knurled hammer spur extension
MSRP. $1199.99

WINCHESTER REPEATING ARMS MODEL 1873 SHORT RIFLE

Action: Lever
Stock: Walnut
Barrel: 20 in.
Sights: Semi-buckhorn rear, Marble Arms gold bead front
Weight: 7 lb. 4 oz.
Caliber: 357 Mag.
Magazine: 10 rounds (357 Mag.) or 11 rounds (38 Spl.)
Features: Blued steel crescent buttplate; steel loading gate; receiver rear tang; round barrel; based off the original Model 73
MSRP. $1299.99

WINCHESTER REPEATING ARMS MODEL 1885 LOW WALL HUNTER RIMFIRE OCTAGON

Action: Lever
Stock: Walnut
Barrel: 24 in.
Sights: Semi-buckhorn rear, gold bead front
Weight: 7 lb. 8 oz.
Caliber: .22LR, .22 WMR, .17 HMR, .17 WSM
Magazine: Single shot
Features: Gloss blued steel receiver; octagon barrel; pistol grip buttstock; Pachmayr rubber butt pad; sling swivel studs
MSRP. $1469.99

WINCHESTER REPEATING ARMS MODEL 94 CARBINE

WINCHESTER REPEATING ARMS MODEL 1873 SHORT RIFLE

WINCHESTER REPEATING ARMS MODEL 1885 LOW WALL HUNTER RIMFIRE OCTAGON

NEW PRODUCTS

AIRFORCE AIRGUNS CONDOR SS

BEEMAN PRECISION AIRGUNS RAM DELUXE

BEEMAN PRECISION AIRGUNS
SILVER KODIAK X2 DC

AIRFORCE AIRGUNS CONDOR SS

Power: Compressed air
Stock: Composite
Overall Length: 38.125 in.
Sights: Open or optical may be installed
Weight: 6 lb. 2 oz.
Caliber: .177, .20, .22, .25
Features: CondorSS combines the major attributes of the TalonSS's quiet operation and the Condor's high power levels; new sound reduction technology; 18-inch barrel blue, red, or original black; 600-1300 fps; two-stage trigger; single shot
Quick-Detach: **$717**
Spin-Loc: **$737**

BEEMAN PRECISION AIRGUNS RAM DELUXE

Power: Break action, spring piston
Stock: Hardwood
Overall Length: 47.5 in.
Sights: 4x32 scope
Weight: 9 lb.
Caliber: .177, .22
Features: Checkered European hardwood stock; ported muzzle brake; 1000 fps max velocity
MSRP **$239**

BEEMAN PRECISION AIRGUNS SILVER KODIAK X2 DC

Power: Break action, spring piston
Stock: All-weather synthetic
Overall Length: 47.5 in.
Sights: 3-9x32 scope
Weight: 8 lb. 12 oz.
Caliber: .177, .22
Features: Two airguns in one; satin nickel plated barrel and receiver; ported muzzle brake; 1000 fps max velocity
MSRP . . . . **$245–$249**

NEW Products: Air Rifles

BEEMAN PRECISION AIRGUNS SILVER PANTHER

Power: Break action, spring piston
Stock: All-weather synthetic
Overall Length: 47.5 in.
Sights: 4x32 scope
Weight: 8 lb. 12 oz.
Caliber: .177, .22
Features: Satin nickel plated barrel and receiver; ported muzzle brake; 1000 fps max velocity
MSRP **$189**

CROSMAN BENJAMIN LEGACY JIM SHOCKEY SIGNATURE SERIES

Power: Break action Nitro Piston
Stock: Synthetic
Overall Length: 43 in.
Sights: 3-9x40mm scope
Weight: 6 lb. 11 oz.
Caliber: .22
Features: Nitro Piston technology delivers smooth cocking, reduced vibration and shoots with 70% less noise; over-molded barrel with soft-touch inserts; adjustable comb; 800-950 fps max velocity
MSRP **$349.99**

CROSMAN FURY NP

Power: Break action Nitro Piston
Stock: Synthetic all-weather
Overall Length: 45 in.
Sights: 4x32mm scope
Weight: 6 lb. 6 oz.
Caliber: .177
Features: Velocities up to 1200 fps; rifled steel barrel; adjustable two-stage trigger; Nitro Piston technology delivers smooth cocking, reduced vibration and shoots with 70% less noise
MSRP **$139.99**

BEEMAN PRECISION AIRGUNS SILVER PANTHER

CROSMAN BENJAMIN LEGACY JIM SHOCKEY SIGNATURE SERIES

CROSMAN FURY NP

CROSMAN MTR77NP

CROSMAN MTR77NP

Power: Break action Nitro Piston
Stock: Synthetic all-weather
Overall Length: 40 in.
Sights: 4x32mm scope
Weight: 6 lb. 2 oz.
Caliber: .177
Features: Nitro Piston technology delivers smooth cocking, reduced vibration and shoots with 70% less noise; sling mounts; storage in false magazine; up to 1200 fps; carry handle available
MSRP................... **$300**

CROSMAN TORRENT SX

CROSMAN TORRENT SX

Power: Variable pump
Stock: Synthetic
Overall Length: 36.75 in.
Sights: Fiber optic front, adjustable rear
Weight: 2 lb. 15 oz.
Caliber: .177
Features: Lightweight, variable pump BB/pellet rifle; adjustable stock; customized length of pull; up to 695 fps; five-shot clip; olive-drab stock and forearm
MSRP.................**$49.95**

NEW Products: Air Rifles

DAISY WINCHESTER MODEL 1100SS

DAISY WINCHESTER MODEL 1250WS

GAMO USA BIG CAT 1400

DAISY WINCHESTER MODEL 1100SS

Power: Break action/spring piston
Stock: Composite
Overall Length: 46.25 in.
Sights: Blade front, micro-adjustable rear
Weight: 6 lb. 10 oz.
Caliber: .177
Features: Rifled steel barrel; 1100 fps with alloy pellets; single shot; thumb safety engages when rifle is cocked
MSRP $129.99

DAISY WINCHESTER MODEL 1250WS

Power: Break action/spring piston
Stock: Hardwood
Overall Length: 46.25 in.
Sights: Fiber optic front, 3–9x32mm scope
Weight: 6 lb. 10 oz.
Caliber: .177
Features: Rifled steel barrel; 1250 fps with alloy pellets; folding bipod; single shot; thumb safety engages when rifle is cocked
MSRP $149.99

GAMO USA BIG CAT 1400

Power: Break action/spring piston
Stock: Synthetic
Overall Length: 43.3 in.
Sights: 4x32 scope
Weight: 6 lb. 2 oz.
Caliber: .177
Features: 33mm power plant enabling it to shoot at up to 1,400 fps with PBA Platinum Ammo; Smooth Action Trigger to maximize pinpoint accuracy; all-weather synthetic stock with rubberized grips; Shock Wave Absorber recoil pad
MSRP $229.95

GAMO USA LITTLE CAT

GAMO USA WHISPER FUSION PRO

STOEGER AIRGUNS ATAC SUPPRESSOR

GAMO USA LITTLE CAT

Power: Break action/spring piston
Stock: Beechwood
Overall Length: 36 in.
Sights: Front, rear fiber optics
Weight: 5 lb. 10 oz.
Caliber: .177
Features: Newest addition to the Youth Precision Airguns family from Gamo; 525 fps with Match Lead Pellets and up to 750 fps with PBA Platinum; metal barrel; grooved cylinder for optional scope mounting
MSRP...................**$139.95**

GAMO USA WHISPER FUSION PRO

Power: Break action/spring piston
Stock: Synthetic
Overall Length: 43 in.
Sights: 3–9x40 adjustable objective scope
Weight: 8 lb.
Caliber: .177
Features: Includes the latest noise dampening technology developed exclusively by Gamo that is integrated in the barrel; noise is reduced by up to 89.5%; Smooth Action Trigger; new recoil pad Shock Wave Absorber that is able to absorb the recoil up to 74%; rubberized grips; all-weather black stock with adjustable cheekpiece; max velocity 1400 fps
MSRP...................**$329.95**

STOEGER AIRGUNS ATAC SUPPRESSOR

Power: Break action/gas-operated
Stock: Synthetic
Overall Length: 42.5 in.
Sights: 4–16x40 scope
Weight: 8 lb. 14 oz.
Caliber: .177, .22
Features: Airflow control technology and dual-stage noise reduction system; automatic ambidextrous safety; black tactical stock; up to 1200 fps with alloy pellets (.177); adjustable length of pull; integral Picatinny rails
MSRP.....................**$299**

AYA ADARRA

BENELLI M2 FIELD COMPACT

BENELLI MONTEFELTRO BLACK SYNTHETIC

BENELLI VINCI SPEEDBOLT

AYA (AGUIRRE Y ARANZABAL) ADARRA

Action: Side-by-side hammerless boxlock ejector shotgun
Stock: Walnut
Barrel: 28 in., with other lengths to order
Chokes: Screw-in tubes
Weight: 6 lb. 10 oz.
Bore/ Gauge: 12, 16, 20, 28, .410
Magazine: None
Features: Double locking mechanism with replaceable hinge pin; disc set firing pins; double trigger;
MSRP **$4800**

BENELLI M2 FIELD COMPACT

Action: Inertia operated semiautomatic
Stock: Black synthetic
Barrel: 24 in., 26 in.

Chokes: C, IC, M, IM, F
Weight: 5 lb. 10 oz.–7 lb.
Bore/ Gauge: 12, 20
Magazine: 3+1 rounds
Features: M2 Field now in compact model; ComforTech gel recoil pad and comb insert; ComforTech shim kit; red bar front sight
MSRP . . . . **$1359–$1409**

BENELLI MONTEFELTRO BLACK SYNTHETIC

Action: Semiautomatic
Stock: Black synthetic
Barrel: 26 in.
Chokes: IC, M, F
Weight: 6 lb. 14 oz.
Bore/ Gauge: 12
Magazine: 4 +1 rounds
Features: Now with a black synthetic stock; red bar front sight; black rubber

ventilated recoil pad; hard case included
MSRP **$1139**

BENELLI VINCI SPEEDBOLT

Action: Inertia operated semiautomatic
Stock: Black synthetic
Barrel: 24 in.
Chokes: C, IC, M, IM, F
6 lb. 13 oz.
Bore/ Gauge: 12
Magazine: 3+1 rounds
Features: Practical Speed Performance with new Speed-Bolt, a bolt inset with tungsten that is designed for faster cycling and loads as weighing one ounce or greater; QuadraFit buttstock; vent rib; drilled and tapped for scope mounting; red bar front sight and metal bead mid-sight
MSRP **$1599**

BERETTA 692 SPORTING

Action: Over/under
Stock: Walnut
Barrel: 30 in., 32 in.
Chokes: 5 OCHP
Weight: 7 lb. 11 oz.
Bore/ Gauge: 12
Magazine: None
Features: Steelium Plus barrels; longer forcing cone; Beretta Fast Adjustment System Technology; Adjustable Balance System; adjustable trigger
MSRP $4755

BERETTA DT11 SPORTING

Action: Over/under
Stock: Walnut
Barrel: 30 in., 32 in.
Chokes: OCHPe
Weight: 9 lb.
Bore/ Gauge: 12
Magazine: None
Features: Steelium Pro barrel; top rib with hollowed bridges; ergonomic top lever; safety selector switch; increased receiver side wall thickness; select high-quality walnut wood finished in oil; stock and forend can be fitted to customer's measurement; pistol grip and forend are hand-checkered; B-Fast adjustable stock available
MSRP $8999

BERNARDELLI MEGA

Action: Semiautomatic
Stock: Walnut, synthetic
Barrel: 24 in., 26 in., 28 in., 30 in.
Chokes: 5 tubes
Weight: 5 lb. 14 oz.
Bore/ Gauge: 12, 20
Magazine: 5+1 rounds
Features: Gas-operated system with partial autocompensator for a more uniform action bar speed; plasma technology to increase corrosion resistance; Made in Italy and steel proof tested; four shims to adjust drop; also available in silver, sporting, and synthetic
MSRP . . . . . Available upon request

BERETTA 692 SPORTING

BERETTA DT11 SPORTING

BERNARDELLI MEGA

NEW Products: Shotguns

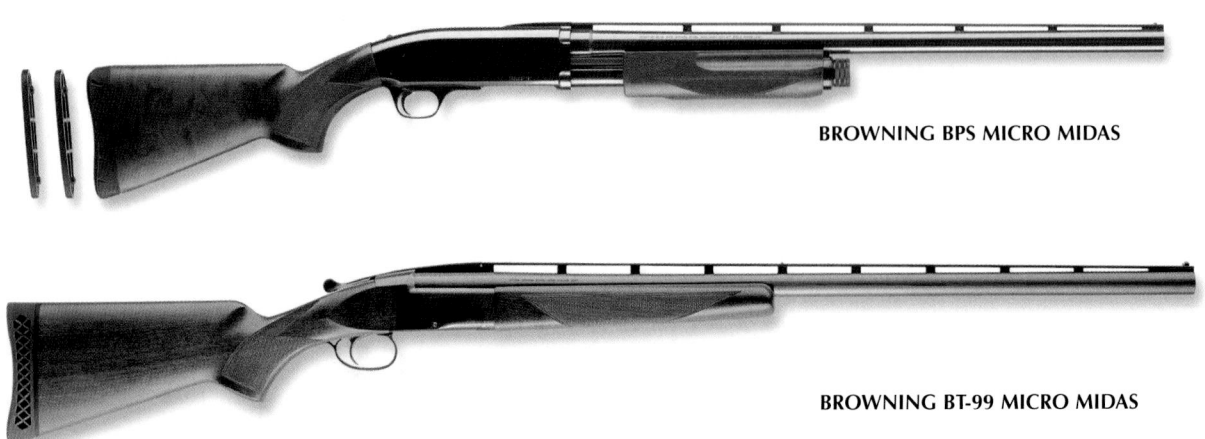

BROWNING BPS MICRO MIDAS

BROWNING BT-99 MICRO MIDAS

BROWNING BPS MICRO MIDAS
Action: Bottom ejection pump
Stock: Walnut
Barrel: 24 in., 26 in.
Chokes: 3 Invector-Plus (12, 20 Ga.), 3 Standard Invector (28, .410 Ga.)
Weight: 6 lb. 15 oz.-7 lb. 10 oz.
Bore/ Gauge: 12, 20, 28, .410
Magazine: None
Features: Ventilated rib barrel; dual steel action bars; top-tang safety; scaled down for smaller shooters; Inflex Technology recoil; silver colored front bead sight; stock spacers
MSRP . . . . $649.99–$689.99

BROWNING BT-99 MICRO MIDAS
Action: Pump, extractor only
Stock: Walnut
Barrel: 28 in., 30 in.
Chokes: 1 Invector-Plus
Weight: 7 lb. 11 oz

Bore/ Gauge: 12
Magazine: None
Features: Blued finish; high-post ventilated rib barrel; beavertail forearm; scaled down for smaller shooters; Vector-Pro lengthed forcing cone; recoil pad; ivory front and mid-bead sights
MSRP $1429.99

BROWNING CITORI 725 FEATHER
Action: Over/under
Stock: Walnut
Barrel: 26 in., 28 in.
Chokes: 3 Invector-DS
Weight: 6 lb. 7 oz.
Bore/ Gauge: 12
Magazine: None
Features: Lightweight alloy receiver; low-profile; silver nitride finish; ventilated top rib barrel; Fire Lite Mechanical Trigger system; hammer

ejectors; ivory front and mid-bead sights
MSRP $2649.99

BROWNING MAXUS SPORTING GOLDEN CLAYS
Action: Autoloader, gas operated
Stock: Walnut
Barrel: 28 in., 30 in.
Chokes: 5 Invector-Plus
Weight: 7 lb. 3 oz.
Bore/ Gauge: 12
Magazine: None
Features: Gold-enhanced engraving; lightweight aluminum alloy; flat, ventilated rib; 3 in. chamber; Power Drive Gas System; Speed Lock Forearm; Vector Pro lengthened forcing cone; HiViz Pro-Comp fiber optic front sight
MSRP $1999.99

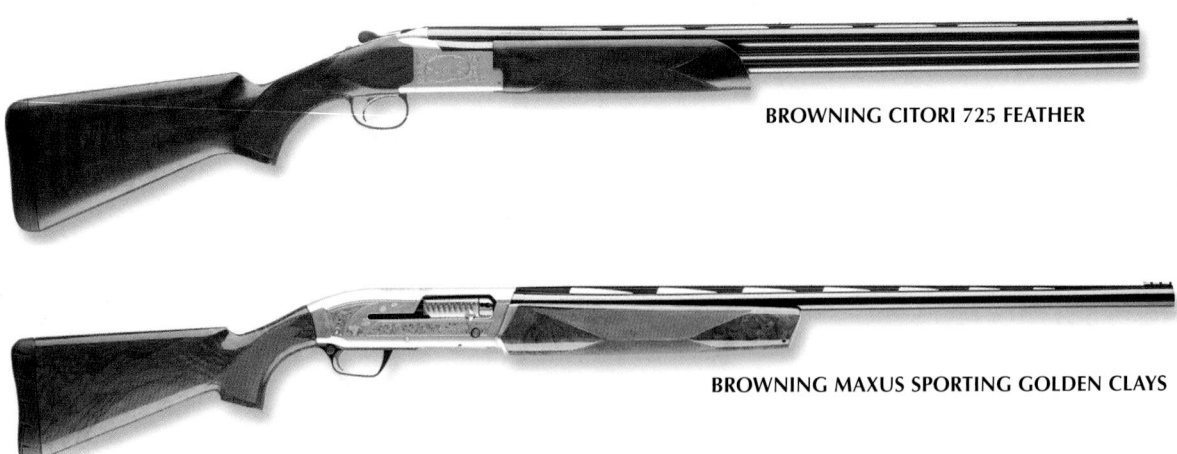

BROWNING CITORI 725 FEATHER

BROWNING MAXUS SPORTING GOLDEN CLAYS

CAESAR GUERINI CHALLENGER ASCENT

Action: Over/under
Stock: Hand rubbed oil
Barrel: 30 in., 32 in.
Chokes: 6 MAXIS competition chokes
Weight: 8 lb. 6 oz.–8 lb. 8 oz.
Bore/ Gauge: 12
Magazine: None
Features: 10mm high tapered top rib is designed to shoot at 50/50% point-of-impact; White Bradley style front sight, with brass center bead; DTS trigger system; manual safety
MSRP. **$5995**

CAESAR GUERINI ELLIPSE

Action: Round body
Stock: Hand rubbed oil on walnut
Barrel: 28 in., 30 in.
Chokes: 5 nickel plated, flush fitting
Weight: 6 lb. 1 oz.–7 lb. 4 oz.
Bore/ Gauge: 12, 20, 28
Magazine: None
Features: Engraving pattern coated with Invisalloy; brass front bead sight; single (selective optional) trigger; manual safety; tapered, solid top rib
MSRP. . . . . **$4195–$5995**

CAESAR GUERINI MAGNUS SPORTING

Action: Over/under
Stock: Hand rubbed oil on walnut
Barrel: 30 in., 32 in., 34 in.
Chokes: 6 CCP competition chokes (6 MAXIS for 12 Ga. models)
Weight: 7 lb. 2 oz.–8 lb. 2 oz.
Bore/ Gauge: 12, 20, 28, .410
Magazine: None
Features: Single selective trigger; manual safety; ventilated center rib; available 20/28 gauge combo and 20/28/.410 gauge combo
MSRP. **$4995**
Combo gauges:. . . . . . **$6795–$8770**

CAESAR GUERINI CHALLENGER ASCENT

CAESAR GUERINI ELLIPSE

CAESAR GUERINI MAGNUS SPORTING

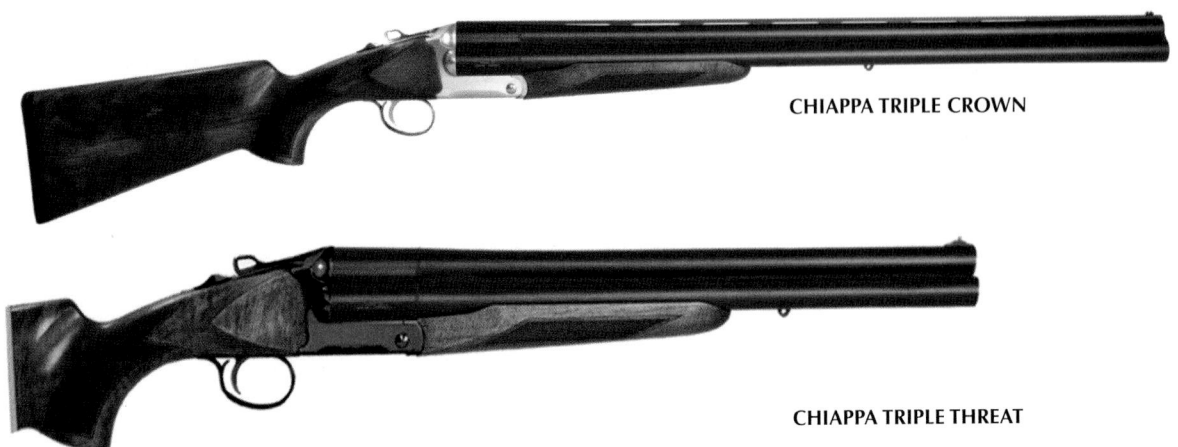

CHIAPPA TRIPLE CROWN

CHIAPPA TRIPLE THREAT

CHIAPPA TRIPLE CROWN

Action: Break-action
Stock: Wood
Barrel: 28 in.
Chokes: Rem-choke in all barrels
Weight: 8 lb. 11 oz.
Bore/ Gauge: 12
Magazine: None
Features: Side-by-side and middle arrangement sporting model with three shotgun barrels; chokes in all three barrels; sling swivel studs
MSRP **$1629**

CHIAPPA TRIPLE THREAT

Action: Break-action
Stock: Wood
Barrel: 18.5 in.
Chokes: Rem Choke in all barrels

Weight: 8 lb.
Bore/ Gauge: 12
Magazine: None
Features: Side-by-side and middle arrangement defense model with three shotgun barrels; chokes in all three barrels; sling swivel studs; wooden stock can be partly disassembled
MSRP **$1629**

CIMARRON 1878 COACH GUN

Action: Side-by-Side
Stock: Wood
Barrel: 20 in., 26 in.
Chokes: Open
Weight: 8 lb.–8 lb. 15 oz.
Bore/ Gauge: 12
Magazine: None

Features: 3 in. blue steel real working hammers; available in standard blue, original finish, or USA finish
MSRP . . . . **$574.60–$851.10**

CIMARRON WYATT EARP SHOTGUN

Action: Side-by-Side
Stock: Walnut
Barrel: 20 in.
Chokes: Open
Weight: N/A
Bore/ Gauge: 12
Magazine: None
Features: Built on the Doc Holliday model with "Wyatt Earp" engraved on the receiver; case hardened steel frame with standard blue finish
MSRP **$1558.70**

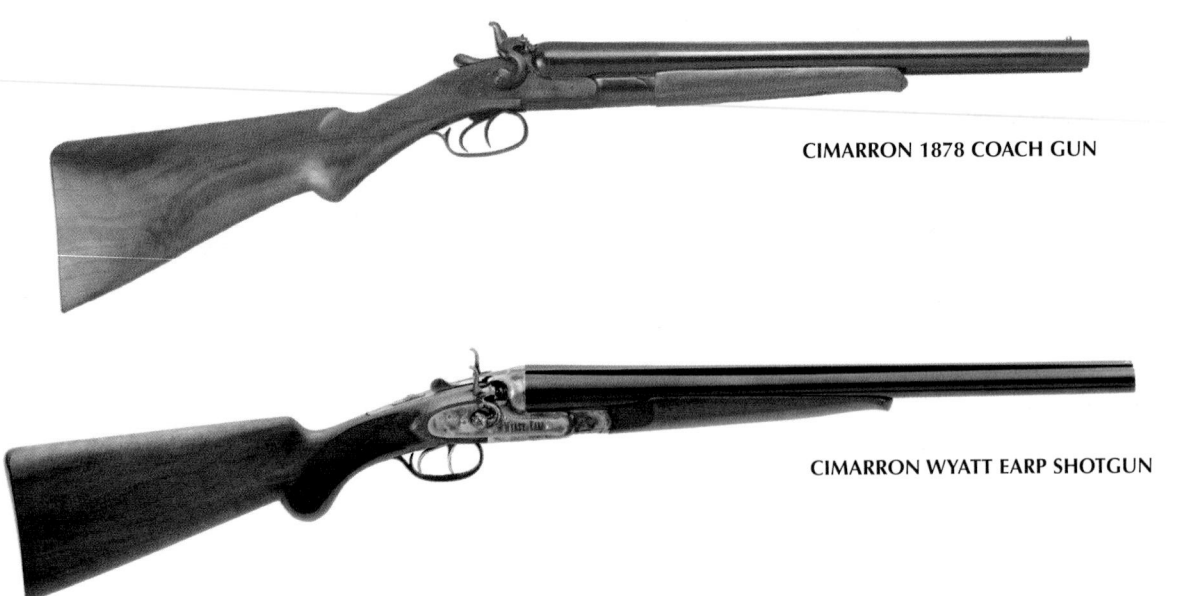

CIMARRON 1878 COACH GUN

CIMARRON WYATT EARP SHOTGUN

NEW Products: **Shotguns**

CZ-USA 612 HC-P
Action: Pump
Stock: Black polymer
Barrel: 20 in.
Chokes: Removable cylinder
Weight: 6 lb. 8 oz.
Bore/ Gauge: 12
Magazine: None
Features: Full-length pistol grip stock; ghost ring sights with glow fiber dots for fast zombie target acquisition; full-length pump forend; barrel accepts CZ choke tubes and ships with one cylinder choke
MSRP **$349**

CZ-USA 612 HOME DEFENSE
Action: Semiautomatic
Stock: Polymer
Barrel: 18.5 in.
Chokes: Fixed cylinder
Weight: 6 lb.
Bore/ Gauge: 12
Magazine: 5+1
Features: Cylinder-bore barrel; a 26-inch vent-rib barrel is available for purchase that easily converts the 612 Home Defense into a field gun
MSRP **$290**

CZ-USA SPORTER STANDARD GRADE
Action: Over/under
Stock: Grade 2 Turkish walnut
Barrel: 30 in.
Chokes: 6 Kicks extended SS
Weight: 8 lb. 8 oz.
Bore/ Gauge: 12
Magazine: None
Features: Designed specifically with the sporting clay enthusiast in mind; single selectable trigger system; Grade 2 Monte Carlo sporting stock with adjustable comb and right-hand palm swell; ships with a set of 6 Kicks stainless steel extended choke tubes
MSRP **$1799**

CZ-USA SUPER SCROLL COMBO SET
Action: Over/under
Stock: Grade 5 Turkish walnut
Barrel: 30 in.
Chokes: 5 per gauge
Weight: 6 lb. 11 oz.
Bore/ Gauge: 20, 28
Magazine: None

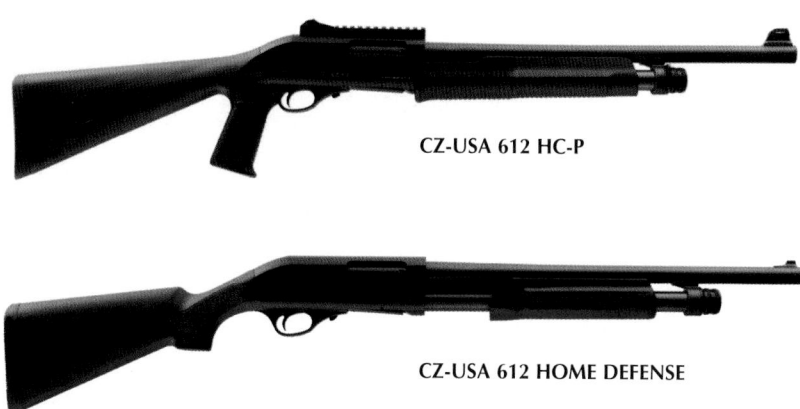
CZ-USA 612 HC-P

CZ-USA 612 HOME DEFENSE

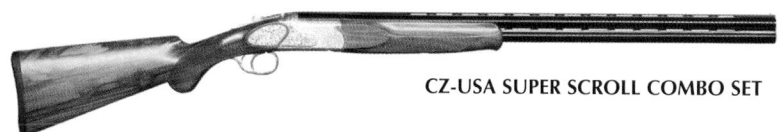
CZ-USA SPORTER STANDARD GRADE

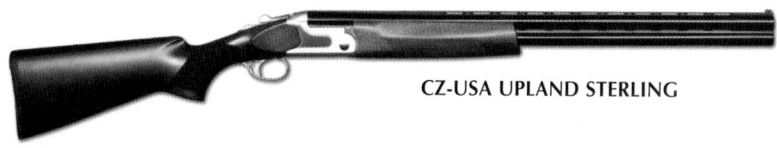
CZ-USA SUPER SCROLL COMBO SET

CZ-USA UPLAND STERLING

Features: Intended for the hunter or sporting clays shooter who wants to carry an absolutely gorgeous shotgun; ornate hand-engraved scrollwork on receiver, faux sideplates, trigger guard and mono-block; both barrel sets are equipped with ejectors; five chokes per gauge and a full grip, making it an excellent crossover gun between clay and feather
MSRP **$3899**

CZ-USA UPLAND STERLING
Action: Over/under
Stock: Turkish walnut

Barrel: 28 in.
Chokes: 5 screw-in
Weight: 7 lb. 8 oz.
Bore/ Gauge: 12
Magazine: None
Features: Built on a new platform featuring a CNC-milled steel receiver, resulting in mechanical components that operate with clockwork precision and consistency; Turkish walnut stock features a stippled grip area on the wrist and forend rather than the traditional checkering
MSRP **$979**

NEW Products: **Shotguns**

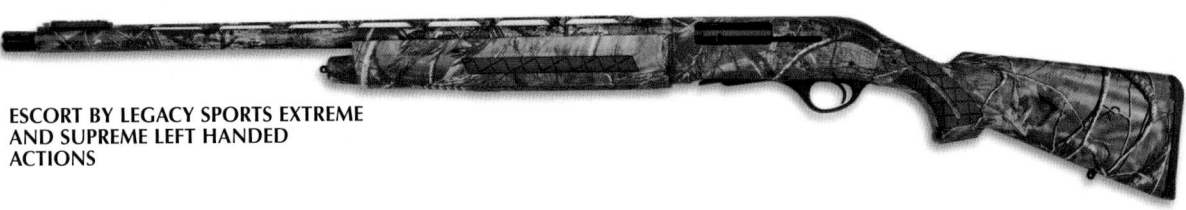

ESCORT BY LEGACY SPORTS EXTREME AND SUPREME LEFT HANDED ACTIONS

ESCORT BY LEGACY SPORTS EXTREME AND SUPREME LEFT HANDED ACTIONS

Action: Semiautomatic
Stock: Black synthetic, Realtree camo (Supreme model only), or Wood
Barrel: 26 in., 28 in.
Chokes: F, M, IM, IC, Skeet (Extreme Camo models also come with MR Waterfowl)
Weight: 6 lb. 8 oz.–7 lb. 10 oz.
Bore/ Gauge: 12, 20
Magazine: Tubular, 5+1 rounds
Features: Available in Magnum and Supreme Magnum models; cycle rate of 3 shots/second with 7/8oz. loads; true left-handed action and receiver; SMART valve cycling for blowback; nickel chrome moly lined barrel; ventilated rib and fiber optic front sight; magazine cut-off for quick load changes
MSRP . . . . **$549–$799**

ESCORT BY LEGACY SPORTS YOUTH 20 GAUGE

Action: Semiautomatic
Stock: Wood, Black Synthetic, Realtree Max4 and AP camo, and Moon Shine Muddy Girl camo
Barrel: 22 in., 26 in. (Ladies Muddy Girl)
Chokes: Multi-3
Weight: 6 lb. 6 oz.
Bore/ Gauge: 20
Magazine: Cut-off for single round loading
Features: TRIO recoil pad; top of receiver milled with 3/8 in. dovetail for sights; raised, ventilated sight rib with fiber optic sight; nickel chrome moly lined barrel
Synthetic **$499**
Wood **$525**
Camo **$549**

FABARM ELOS DELUXE

Action: Over/under
Stock: European walnut
Barrel: 28 in.
Chokes: 5 Inner HP
Weight: 5 lb. 14 oz.–7 lb. 1 oz.
Bore/ Gauge: 20
Magazine: None
Features: Round action and trim stock provide speed in keeping up with wild birds; Fabarm Tribore HP tapered bore; steel or aluminum frame
MSRP . . . . **$2895–$2995**

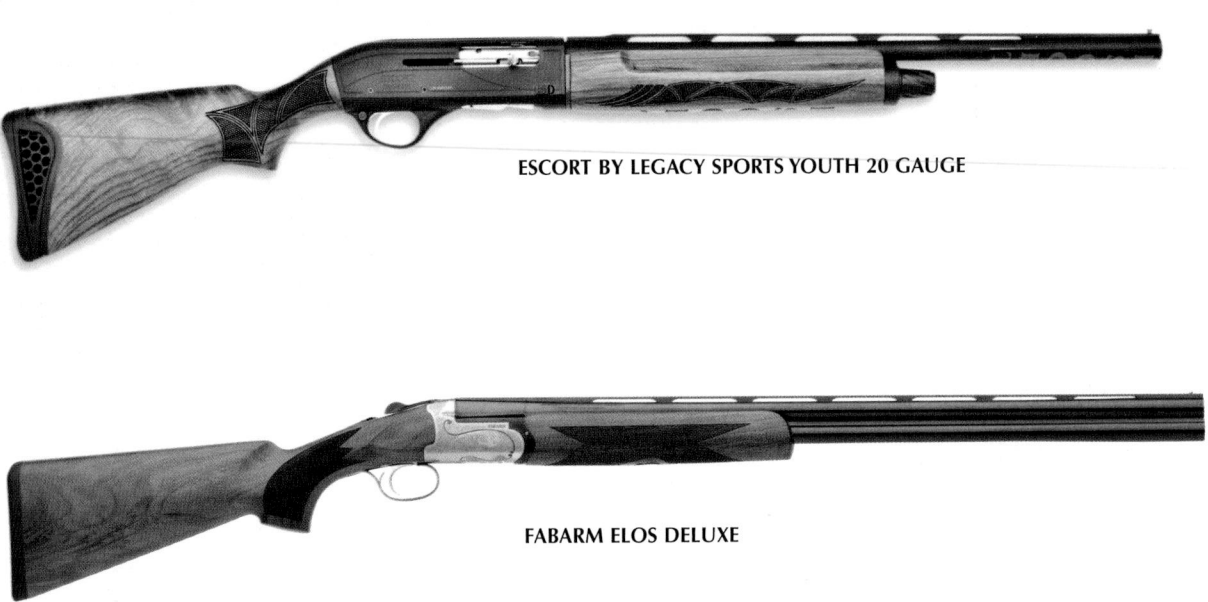

ESCORT BY LEGACY SPORTS YOUTH 20 GAUGE

FABARM ELOS DELUXE

FRANCHI ASPIRE

FRANCHI INTENSITY

FRANCHI ASPIRE

Action: Over/under
Stock: Walnut
Barrel: 28 in.
Chokes: IC, M, F
Weight: 5 lb. 13 oz.
Bore/ Gauge: 28, .410
Magazine: None
Features: Slim, round-action receiver; color-case hardened receiver; automatic safety with built-in barrel selector;
MSRP **$2299**

FRANCHI INTENSITY

Action: Semiautomatic, inertia driven
Stock: Black synthetic, Realtree Max4, Realtree APG, Bottomlands
Barrel: 26 in., 28 in., 30 in.
Chokes: IC, M, F
Weight: 6 lb. 11 oz.
Bore/ Gauge: 12
Magazine: 4+1 rounds
Features: Inertia Driven system; recoil spring encircles the magazine tube forward the receiver; stepped, ventilated-rib, red fiber optic front sight; three extended choke tubes
MSRP . . . . **$1099–$1199**

ITHACA GUN COMPANY MODEL 37 WATERFOWL

Action: Bottom ejection
Stock: Camo, synthetic black
Barrel: 28 in., 30 in.
Chokes: Briley choke tubes
Weight: 7 lb. 3 oz.-7 lb. 6 oz.
Bore/ Gauge: 12, 20
Magazine: 4+1 rounds
Features: 3 in. chamber; gold plated trigger; gamescene engraving; perma-guard protection
MSRP **$759**

ITHACA GUN COMPANY MODEL 37 WATERFOWL

NEW Products: **Shotguns**

KRIEGHOFF MODEL KX-6

Action: Single-shot trap
Stock: Walnut
Barrel: 34 in.
Chokes: IM, LIM, F
Weight: 8 lb. 12 oz.
Bore/ Gauge: 12
Magazine: None
Features: White pearl front sight and metal center bead; case hardened, long lasting black nitro carbonized finish; semi-automatic ejector; adjustable tapered rib; available choke tubes: CY, SK, IC, M, SF
MSRP **$5490**

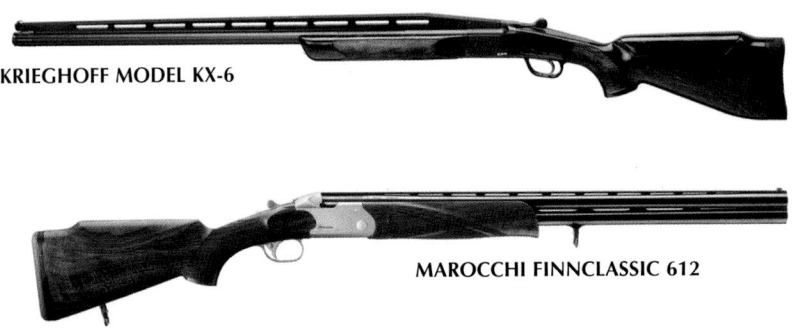

KRIEGHOFF MODEL KX-6

MAROCCHI FINNCLASSIC 612

MAROCCHI FINNCLASSIC 612

Action: Over/under
Stock: Wood
Barrel: 24 in., 28 in., 30 in.
Chokes: 5 choke tube Maxi 70 plus key
Weight: 6 lb. 8 oz.
Bore/ Gauge: 12
Magazine: None
Features: 3 in. chamber; available Maxi 90 choke tubes; special steel, proof tested by the Italian National Proof House; scroll work
MSRP **$1375**

MOSSBERG 835 ULTI-MAG-RECOIL REDUCTION SYSTEM

Action: Pump
Stock: Recoil Reduction System/ Mathews
Barrel: 24 in., 28 in.
Chokes: Accu-Mag set, Modified tube, or Ulti-full tube
Weight: 8 lb. 8 oz.
Bore/ Gauge: 12
Magazine: 6 rounds
Features: Exclusive stock incorporating Mathews Harmonic Damper Technology; two interchangeable low and high profile combs; 3.5 in. chamber; ported barrels; free gun lock and 10-year limited warranty
MSRP **$630**

MOSSBERG SILVER RESERVE II FIELD

Action: Over/under
Stock: Walnut, satin
Barrel: 26 in., 28 in.
Chokes: 5, Field set
Weight: 7 lb. 8 oz.
Bore/ Gauge: 12, 20, 28, .410
Magazine: 2 rounds
Features: Bead front sight; 3 in. chamber; blued barrels with silver receiver and scroll engraving; 12 Ga. model features shell ejectors
MSRP **$799**

MOSSBERG 835 ULTI-MAG-RECOIL REDUCTION SYSTEM

MOSSBERG SILVER RESERVE II FIELD

REMINGTON MODEL 1100 50TH ANNIVERSARY LIMITED EDITION

REMINGTON VERSA MAX SPORTSMAN

REMINGTON VERSA MAX ZOMBIE

REMINGTON MODEL 1100 50TH ANNIVERSARY LIMITED EDITION

Action: Autoloading
Stock: Walnut
Barrel: 28 in.
Chokes: N/A
Weight: 8 lb. 4 oz.
Bore/ Gauge: 12
Magazine: 4+1 rounds
Features: After 50 years the Model 1100 has cemented its name as the most famous autoloading shotgun of all time. Featuring a machine-cut engraved receiver with a commemorative 1963 serial number prefix; B-Grade walnut stock with white diamond grip cap; vent rib barrel with Rem Choke tube; shipped in green Remington hard case
MSRP **$1999**

REMINGTON VERSA MAX SPORTSMAN

Action: Autoloading
Stock: Synthetic
Barrel: 22 in., 26 in., 28 in.
Chokes: Modified Pro Bore Flush Mount; Pro Bore Wingmaster Turkey TXF Extended
Weight: 7 lb. 8 oz.
Bore/ Gauge: 12
Magazine: 3+1, 2+1 rounds
Features: VersaPort Gas System; 4140 Hammer-Forged barrel; available in Mossy Oak Camo, Realtree AP Camo, and black oxide; SuperCell Recoil Pad; ivory front bead sights, steel mid bead
MSRP . . . . **$1025–$1175**

REMINGTON VERSA MAX ZOMBIE

Action: Autoloading
Stock: Synthetic
Barrel: 22 in.
Chokes: IC and Tactical Extended Choke Tubes
Weight: 7 lb. 12 oz.
Bore/ Gauge: 12
Magazine: 8+1 rounds
Features: Oversized bolt release button and bolt release; oversized trigger guard; Picatinny rail on receiver; HiViz front sight; vent rib barrel; synthetic stock available in gargoyle green or pink explosion
MSRP **$1599**

STOEGER MODEL 3000

STOEGER MODEL 3000
Action: Semiautomatic
Stock: Black synthetic, Realtree APG,
Realtree APG SteadyGrip
Barrel: 24 in.
Chokes: IC, M, XFT, wrench
Weight: 7 lb. 5 oz.
Bore/ Gauge: 12
Magazine: 4+1 rounds
Features: Intertia Driven; red-bar front
sight; drilled and tapped; shim kit; 3
in. loads
MSRP. . . . .**$529–$629**

TAYLOR'S & CO. WYATT EARP SHOTGUN
Action: Side-by-side
Stock: Walnut checkered pistol grip
Barrel: 20.06 in.
Chokes: N/A
Weight: 7 lb. 1 oz.
Bore/ Gauge: 12
Magazine: 2 rounds
Features: Easily opened with one hand
for fast shell loading; case-hardened
frame stamped with 'Wyatt Earp';
chromed barrel bores with blued finish
MSRP. **$1738**

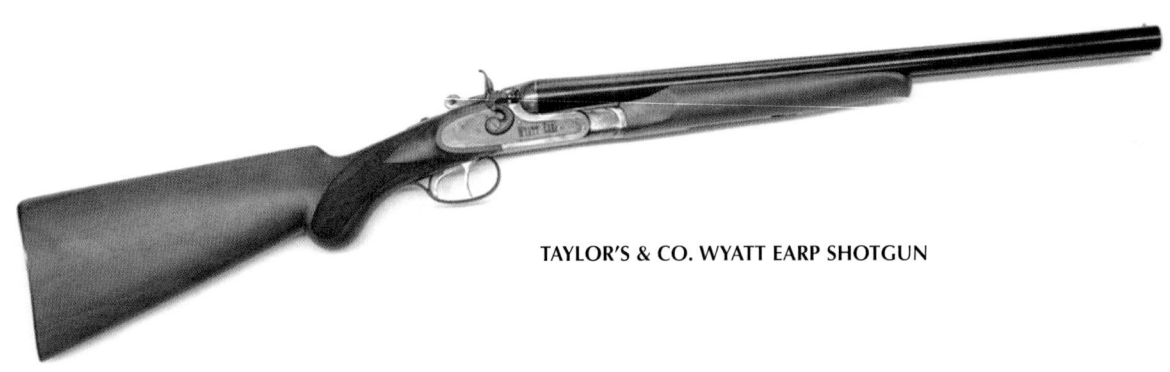

TAYLOR'S & CO. WYATT EARP SHOTGUN

TRISTAR SPORTING ARMS
HUNTER EX LT

TRISTAR SPORTING ARMS
RAPTOR A-TAC

TRISTAR SPORTING ARMS HUNTER EX LT

Action: Over/under
Stock: Wood
Barrel: 26 in.
Chokes: SK, IC, M, IM, F
Weight: 5 lb. 6.4 oz.
Bore/ Gauge: 20
Magazine: N/A
Features: Aluminum alloy receiver; steel hinge and firing pins; chambered for 3 in.; fiber optic sight
MSRP $659

TRISTAR SPORTING ARMS RAPTOR A-TAC

Action: Semiautomatic
Stock: Synthetic, fixed pistol grip
Barrel: 20 in.
Chokes: Extended Tactical Beretta/Benelli/Style choke
Weight: 6 lb. 8 oz.
Bore/ Gauge: 12
Magazine: N/A
Features: 3 in. chamber; bridge-front sight with fiber optic bead; picatinni rail; ghost ring sight; swivel studs; 5-year warranty
MSRP $449

TRISTAR SPORTING ARMS TEC 12

Action: Pump/Auto
Stock: Black synthetic
Barrel: 20 in.
Chokes: External Ported Cylinder choke
Weight: 7 lb. 6.4 oz.
Bore/ Gauge: 12
Magazine: N/A
Features: Capable of operating in Pump or Semi-Auto mode; 3 in. chamber; picatinny rail; ghost ring sight; raised front bridge sight with fiber optic bead; fixed rubber pistol grip; military sling swivels and swivel studs
MSRP $689

TRISTAR SPORTING ARMS TEC 12

NEW Products: **Shotguns**

TRISTAR SPORTING ARMS VIPER G2 LH

UTAS UTS-15 NAVY

WEATHERBY PA-459 TR 20 GAUGE

TRISTAR SPORTING ARMS VIPER G2 LH
Action: Semiautomatic
Stock: Synthetic
Barrel: 28 in.
Chokes: IC, M, F
Weight: 6 lb. 14.4 oz.
Bore/ Gauge: 12
Magazine: N/A
Features: Chrome lined chambers; barrels threaded for Beretta/Benelli style choke tubes; 3 in. chambers
MSRP . . . . **$549–$629**

UTAS UTS-15 NAVY
Action: Pump
Stock: Polymer
Barrel: 18.5 in.
Chokes: N/A
Weight: 6 lb. 15 oz.
Bore/ Gauge: 12
Magazine: 15 rounds
Features: Corrosion-resistant, satin-nickel plating that is black-chromed
MSRP **$1200**

WEATHERBY PA-459 TR 20 GAUGE
Action: Pump
Stock: Synthetic
Barrel: 18.5 in.
Chokes: Extended Ported Cylinder
Weight: 5 lb. 12 oz.
Bore/ Gauge: 20
Magazine: 5+1 or 4+1 rounds
Features: Short length of pull (13.5 in.) and ergonomic buttstock; chrome-lined barrel; adjustable rear LPA-style ghost ring sight; matte black metalwork; swivel studs; also available in 12 gauge
MSRP **$499**

WINCHESTER REPEATING ARMS SUPER X PUMP MARINE DEFENDER

Action: Pump
Stock: Synthetic
Barrel: 18 in.
Chokes: Invector-Plus cylinder
Weight: 7 lb. 5 oz.
Bore/ Gauge: 12
Magazine: 6 rounds
Features: Matte hard chrome plating; alloy receiver; tactical ribbed forearm; brass bead front sight; rotary bolt; crossbolt safety; Inflex technology recoil pad
MSRP $399.99

WINCHESTER REPEATING ARMS SUPER X3 WATERFOWL HUNTER

Action: Autoloader
Stock: Synthetic
Barrel: 26 in., 28 in.
Chokes: Invector-Plus tube
Weight: 6 lb. 10 oz.–7 lb. 2 oz.
Bore/Gauge: 12, 20
Magazine: None
Features: Mossy Oak Shadow Grass Blades; .742 Back-Bored technology; hard chrome chamber and bore; vent rib; TruGlo Long Bead fiber optic front sight; Active Valve Gas System; Quadra-Vent Ports; ambidextrous crossbolt safety
MSRP . . . .$1139.99–$1199

WINCHESTER REPEATING ARMS SXP COMPACT FIELD

Action: Pump
Stock: Satin finish
Barrel: 26 in., 28 in.
Chokes: Three Invector-Plus chokes
Weight: 6 lb. 8 oz.–6 lb. 10 oz.
Bore/ Gauge: 12
Magazine: None
Features: Aluminum alloy receiver; matte black finish; hard chrome chamber and bore; Speed plug system; brass bead front sight; Inflex technology recoil pad
MSRP $399.99

WINCHESTER REPEATING ARMS SUPER X PUMP MARINE DEFENDER

WINCHESTER REPEATING ARMS SUPER X3 WATERFOWL HUNTER

WINCHESTER REPEATING ARMS SXP COMPACT FIELD

NEW Products: **Handguns**

ACCU-TEK FIREARMS
LT-380

Action: SA semiautomatic
Grips: Composite
Barrel: 2.8 in.
Sights: Adjustable rear sight
Weight: 15 oz.
Caliber: .380 ACP
Capacity: 6 rounds
Features: Aluminum frame; stainless steel slide; exposed hammer; manual safety; European type magazine release
MSRP **$308**

ACCU-TEK
FIREARMS
LT-380

AMERICAN DERRINGER LM4
SIMMERLING

AMERICAN DERRINGER
LM4 SIMMERLING

Action: Hinged breech
Grips: Mesquite, Rosewood, custom
Barrel: 3.85 in.
Sights: Open, fixed
Weight: 24 oz.
Caliber: .45 ACP
Capacity: 5 rounds
Features: Vest pocket pistol; first round carried in the chamber; only 1in. thick; stainless steel
MSRP **$4250**

AMERICAN DERRINGER
LM5

Action: Hinged breech
Grips: Rosewood
Barrel: 2 in.
Sights: Open, fixed
Weight: 15 oz.
Caliber: .25 Auto, .32 Mag.
Capacity: 4 (.32) or 5 (.25) rounds
Features: Stainless steel; cam lock safety
MSRP **$715**

AMERICAN DERRINGER LM5

AMERICAN TACTICAL
IMPORTS FX45 FATBOY
LIGHTWEIGHT

ARSENAL INC. SAM7K

AMERICAN TACTICAL
IMPORTS FX45 TITAN
LIGHTWEIGHT

AUTO-ORDNANCE
1911TC THOMPSON
CUSTOM 1911 STAINLESS

AMERICAN TACTICAL IMPORTS FX45 FATBOY LIGHTWEIGHT

Action: Semiautomatic
Grips: Alloy, no panels
Barrel: 3.2 in.
Sights: Black post, white dot front, Novak-style rear
Weight: 27 oz.
Caliber: .45 ACP
Capacity: 12+1 rounds
Features: Alloy frame; 1911-style slide and controsl; wide-body, high-capacity frame; cone barrel with no bushing; blued finish
MSRP **$699.95**

AMERICAN TACTICAL IMPORTS FX45 TITAN LIGHTWEIGHT

Action: Semiautomatic
Grips: Wood
Barrel: 3.13 in.
Sights: Black post, white dot front, Novak-style rear
Weight: 27.9 oz.
Caliber: .45 ACP
Capacity: 7 rounds
Features: Alloy frame; 1911-style slide and controsl; ambidextrous safety; target trigger; blued finish
MSRP **$597.95**

ARSENAL INC. SAM7K

Action: Semiautomatic
Grips: Black Polymer
Barrel: 10.5 in.
Sights: Peep rear
Weight: 129.5 oz.
Caliber: 7.62x39mm
Capacity: 5 rounds
Features: Milled receiver; short gas system; front sight block; gas block system; chrome-lined hammer-forged barrel; ambidextrous safety lever; scope rail; sling included
MSRP **$1235**

AUTO-ORDNANCE 1911TC THOMPSON CUSTOM 1911 STAINLESS

Action: Semiautomatic
Grips: Checkered laminate
Barrel: 5 in.
Sights: Low-profile iron sights
Weight: 39 oz.
Caliber: .45 ACP
Capacity: 7+1 rounds
Features: Frames machined on high precision computerized machinery from a 420 stainless steel casting; slide is machined from a solid stainless steel billet utilizing specialized tooling to reduce set-up and refixturing; matte finish on slide and frame; front and rear sights are black with serrations; extended beavertail grip safety; extended magazine release
MSRP **$813**

NEW Products: **Handguns**

BERETTA PICO .380

Action: Semiautomatic
Grips: Technopolymer
Barrel: 2.7 in.
Sights: Front and rear adjustable
Weight: 11.5 oz.
Caliber: .380 ACP
Capacity: 6+1 rounds
Features: Stainless steel sub-chassis engraved with serial number; snag-free slide and frame; barrel can be replaced with a .32 ACP barrel; dovetail quick-change sights; frames available in flat dark earth, white, or purple
MSRP **$399**

BERETTA PICO .380

BROWNING BUCK MARK CAMPER UFX

Action: Blowback
Grips: Overmolded Ultragrip FX
Barrel: 5.5 in.
Sights: Pro-Target adjustable
Weight: 34 oz.
Caliber: .22LR
Capacity: 10+1 rounds
Features: Built from aircraft-grade aluminum alloy; single-action trigger; target-crowned; large manual thumb safety; ambidextrous grip and slide release; available in blued or stainless finish
MSRP . . . . **$379.99–$419.99**

BROWNING BUCK MARK CAMPER UFX

CABOT GUN COMPANY AMERICAN JOE 1911

Action: Semiautomatic
Grips: Aluminum
Barrel: 5 in.
Sights: Adjustable 2-dot rear
Weight: 40 oz.
Caliber: .45 ACP
Capacity: 8+1 rounds
Features: For this art gun crossing the rubicon between firearms and art, Cabot commissioned rock star designer Joe Faris to design art that represents Detroit and Americana, and the result is a limited edition run of a new iconic 1911, the American Joe. Features top slide serrations; 420 stainless steel frame and slide; 20 LPI front strap checkering; tristar trigger
MSRP **$7450**

CABOT GUN COMPANY AMERICAN JOE 1911

CENTURY INTERNATIONAL ARMS, INC. TP-9

CENTURY INTERNATIONAL ARMS, INC. TP-9
Action: DA semiautomatic
Grips: Polymer, interchangeable backstraps
Barrel: 4 in.
Sights: Adjustable 3-dot
Weight: 26.4 oz.
Caliber: 9mm
Capacity: 17+1 rounds
Features: Double-action striker-fired mechanism with de-cocking button; polymer frame and steel slide; modeled after S&W 99; available titanium, OD green, and desert finish
MSRP $425.95

CHIAPPA FIREARMS M9-22

CHIAPPA FIREARMS M9-22
Action: Semiautomatic
Grips: Wood or plastic
Barrel: 5 in.
Sights: Fixed front, adjustable rear; Novak-style fiber optic (tactical)
Weight: 37 oz.
Caliber: .22LR
Capacity: 10 rounds
Features: A replica of the U.S. Military sidearm chambered in .22 rimfire and is available in two versions, the Standard model featuring fixed front sight and windage adjustable rear sight, and the Tactical model with Novak style fiber optic sights.
MSRP . . . . $329–$369

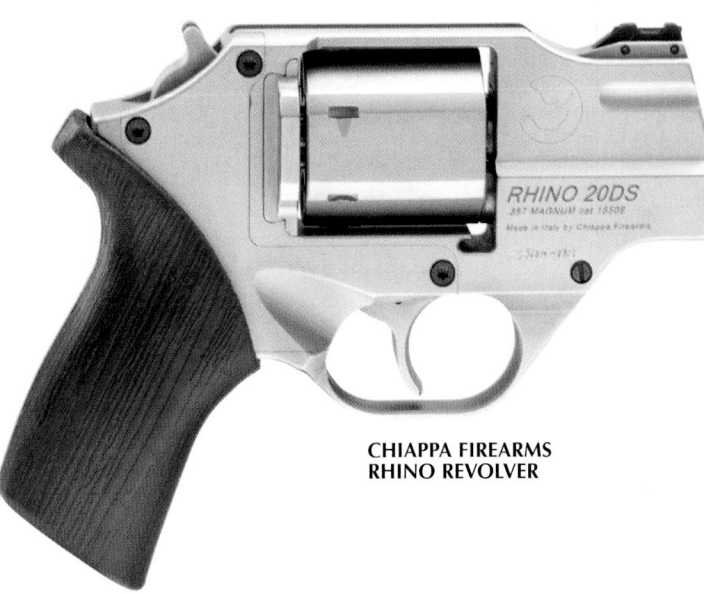

CHIAPPA FIREARMS RHINO REVOLVER

CHIAPPA FIREARMS RHINO REVOLVER
Action: Revolver
Grips: Wood
Barrel: 6 in.
Sights: Front blade; adjustable rear
Weight: 37 oz.
Caliber: .357, .40 S&W, 9x19, 9x21
Capacity: 6 rounds
Features: Rhino barrel is aligned with the bottom most chamber, which lowers the center of gravity and yields a centerline of the bore more in line with the shooter's arm allowing for the most natural "point ability" while engaging a target; reduces both recoil and muzzle flip which insures subsequent shots are on target faster; frame available in chrome, black, or gold finish
MSRP . . . . $849–$1079

NEW Products: **Handguns**

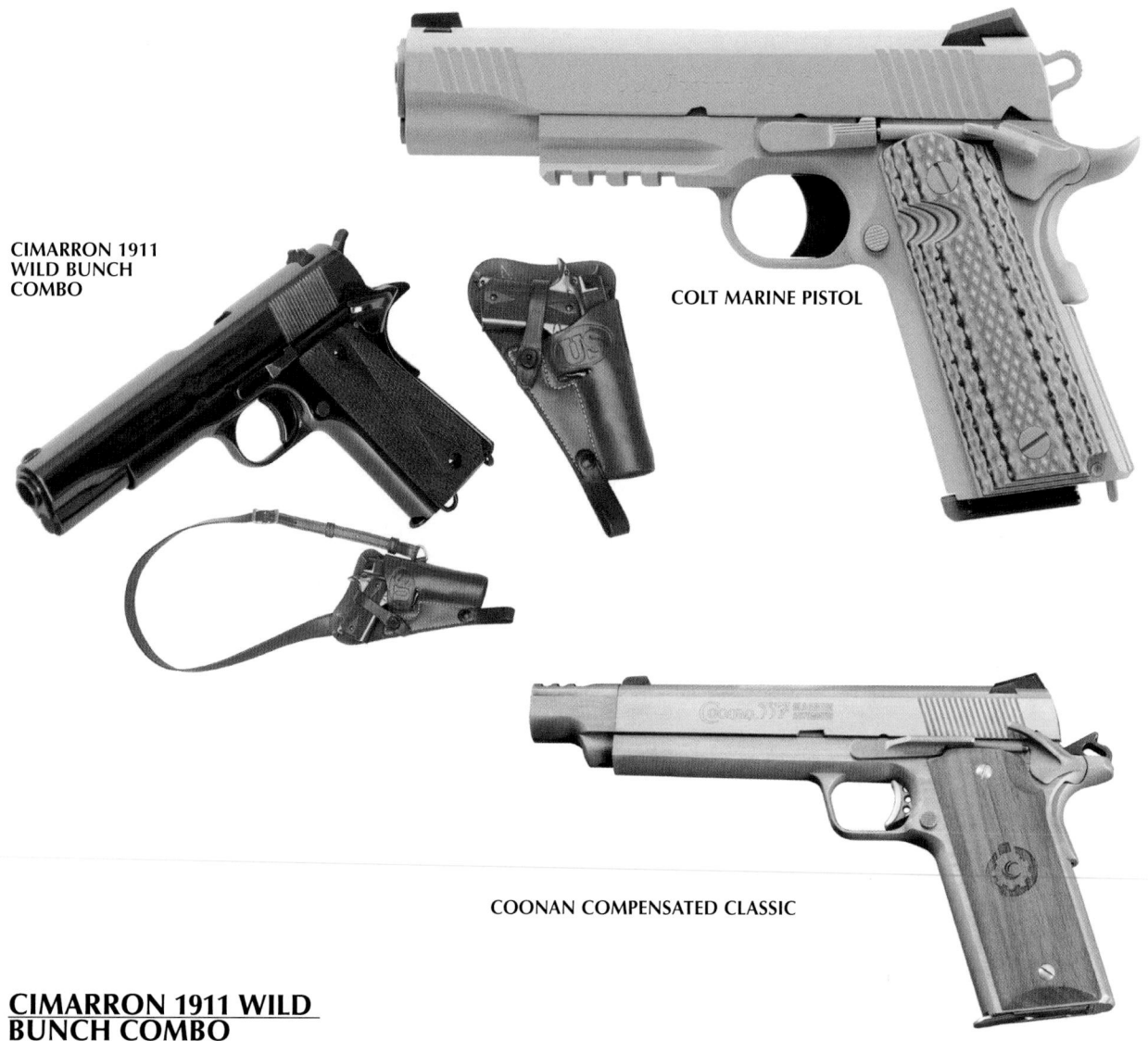

CIMARRON 1911 WILD BUNCH COMBO

COLT MARINE PISTOL

COONAN COMPENSATED CLASSIC

CIMARRON 1911 WILD BUNCH COMBO

Action: Semiautomatic
Grips: Diamond checkered walnut
Barrel: 5 in.
Sights: Fixed
Weight: 39.52 oz.
Caliber: .45 ACP
Capacity: 8+1 rounds
Features: Correct historical markings; the original 1911 frame with a Type 1 smooth mainspring housing; combo includes the 1911 in polished blue finish and the Tanker shoulder holster, a reproduction of the rig used by William Holden in the movie The Wild Bunch
MSRP **$817.70**

COLT MARINE PISTOL

Action: Semiautomatic
Grips: Composite
Barrel: 5 in.
Sights: Novak 3-dot night sights
Weight: 40 oz.
Caliber: .45 ACP
Capacity: 7 rounds
Features: Desert Tan Cerakoted stainless steel receiver and slide; serrated mainspring housing with lanyard loop; enhanced hammer; Colt tactical ambidextrous safety lock; National Match barrel; 1913 accessory rail
MSRP **$1995**

COONAN COMPENSATED CLASSIC

Action: Semiautomatic
Grips: Smooth black walnut
Barrel: 5 in.
Sights: Dovetail front and rear
Weight: 42 oz.
Caliber: .357 Mag.
Capacity: 7+1 rounds
Features: Coonan Classic with compensator barrel; recoil operated; extended slide catch and thumb lock; custom carry case
MSRP **$1375**
Compensator: **$1625**

CZ-USA 75 SHADOW SAO

CZ-USA 75 SP-01 ACCU-SHADOW

CZ-USA P-09 DUTY

CZ-USA 75 SHADOW SAO

Action: SAO semiautomatic
Grips: Plastic
Barrel: 4.6 in.
Sights: Fiber optic front
Weight: 35.2 oz.
Caliber: 9mm
Capacity: 16+1
Features: Fitted with a redesigned unit originally used in the CZ 75 Champion, the hammer of the SAO is slightly wider with modified sear engagement, resulting in smoother release and more positive ignition. The CZ single action aluminum trigger has an overtravel adjustment screw; to further smooth the trigger pull and improve trigger reset distance, the CZ 85 Combat-style slide without a firing pin block is used; ships with three 16-round magazines
MSRP $979

CZ-USA 75 SP-01 ACCU-SHADOW

Action: SA/DA semiautomatic
Grips: Thin aluminum
Barrel: 4.6 in.
Sights: Fiber optic front, HAJO rear
Weight: 38.4 oz.
Caliber: 9mm
Capacity: 18+1
Features: The Accu-Bushing system holds the barrel with much more precision; pistols returned test groups substantially less than 3″ at 50 yards (using Fiocci 124 JHP); competition hammer; lighter springs; stainless steel guide rod and polished internals; short-reset disconnector is used to greatly reduce trigger reset between shots; fiber optic front and HAJO serrated target rear (adjustable for height, also drift adjustable for windage)
MSRP $1665

CZ-USA P-09 DUTY

Action: DA/SA semiautomatic
Grips: Three interchangeable backstraps
Barrel: 4.39 in.
Sights: Dovetailed, low profile front post, drift-adjustable, dovetailed rear notch
Weight: 30.39 oz.
Caliber: .40 S&W, 9mm
Capacity: 19+1
Features: This full-size version of the P-07 boasts an impressive 19+1 capacity in its flush-fitting magazine that is unsurpassed by any other 9mm service pistol; Omega trigger system; shipped with decockers installed but can easily be converted to a manual safety with the supplied parts and instructions; three interchangeable backstraps; integrated 1913 Picatinny rail
9mm: $514
.40 S&W: $528

NEW Products: **Handguns**

DOUBLETAP DEFENSE LLC DOUBLETAP

Action: DAO semiautomatic
Grips: Synthetic
Barrel: 3 in.
Sights: Front blade
Weight: 12 oz.–14 oz.
Caliber: .45 ACP, 9mm
Capacity: 2+2 rounds
Features: Titanium frame with a MIL-STD finish that resists corrosion; integral grips house additional two spare rounds; ported barrel reduces muzzle flip and recoil; ambidextrous thumb latch to eject spent rounds; quick-change interchangable barrels; comes with one barrel and you can purchase extra conversion kits

Aluminum: . . . . **$499–$569**
Titanium: . . . . **$729–$799**
Conversion kits: . . . . **$199–$269**

DOUBLETAP DEFENSE LLC DOUBLETAP

EAGLE IMPORTS MAC 1911 BOBCUT

Action: SA semiautomatic
Grips: Hardwood
Barrel: 4.25 in.
Sights: Adjustable rear, dovetail front
Weight: 34.58 oz.
Caliber: .45 ACP
Capacity: 8+1 rounds
Features: 4140 steel frame and hammer forged slide; fully adjustable Novak-type rear sight; dovetail front sight with fiber optic; flared and lowered ejection port; enhanced beavertail grip safety; skeletal hammer; combat trigger; stippled front strap serration; throated forged steel barrel

Deep Blue: **$902**
Hard Chrome: **$978**

EAGLE IMPORTS MAC 1911 BOBCUT

EAGLE IMPORTS MAC 1911 BULLSEYE

EAGLE IMPORTS MAC 1911 BULLSEYE

Action: SA semiautomatic
Grips: Hardwood
Barrel: 6 in.
Sights: Adjustable rear, dovetail front
Weight: 46.91 oz.
Caliber: .45 ACP
Capacity: 8+1 rounds
Features: The largest of the MAC 1911 pistol line; 4140 steel frame and hammer forged slide; fully adjustable Bomar-type rear sight; dovetail front sight; flared and lowered ejection port; enhanced beavertail grip safety; skeletal hammer; combat trigger; checkered front strap serration; ramped match grade bull barrel

Deep Blue: **$1204**
Hard Chrome: **$1279**

EAGLE IMPORTS MAC 1911 CLASSIC

Action: SA semiautomatic
Grips: Hardwood
Barrel: 5 in.
Sights: Adjustable rear, dovetail front
Weight: 40.56 oz.
Caliber: .45 ACP
Capacity: 8+1 rounds
Features: 4140 steel frame and hammer forged slide; fully adjustable bomar-type rear sight; dovetail front sight with fiber optic; flared and lowered ejection port; enhanced beavertail grip safety; skeletal hammer; combat trigger; checkered front strap serrations; ramped match grade bull barrel
Deep Blue: **$1038**
Hard Chrome: **$1112**

EAGLE IMPORTS MAC
1911 CLASSIC

EAGLE IMPORTS SPS
PANTERA

EAGLE IMPORTS SPS PANTERA

Action: SA semiautomatic
Grips: Glass-filled nylon polymer
Barrel: 5 in.
Sights: Adjustable rear, dovetail front
Weight: 36.68 oz.
Caliber: .45 ACP
Capacity: 12+1 rounds
Features: IPSC Standard or Open Competition ready; fully adjustable Bomar-type rear sight, dovetail front sight with fiber optic; light weight polymer trigger; wide front and rear slide serrations; ambidextrous thumb safety; black chrome finish
MSRP **$1895**

EAGLE IMPORTS SPS VISTA LONG AND SHORT

Action: SA semiautomatic
Grips: Glass-filled nylon polymer
Barrel: 5 in., 5.5 in.
Sights: Sight mount included
Weight: 41.62 oz.–43.38 oz.
Caliber: 9mm (Short), .38 Super (Long)
Capacity: 21 rounds
Features: Hammer forged steel slide; scope mount for C-MORE optical sight included; checkered front strap serration; ramped match grade threaded barrel; wide magwell; black chrome finish
MSRP **$2450**

EAGLE IMPORTS SPS VISTA
LONG AND SHORT

NEW Products: **Handguns**

ED BROWN SPECIAL
FORCES CARRY

ED BROWN SPECIAL FORCES CARRY

Action: Autoloader
Grips: Double diamond checkered Cocobolo wood
Barrel: 4.25 in.
Sights: Fixed dovetail 3-dot night sights
Weight: 35 oz.
Caliber: .45 ACP
Capacity: 7 rounds
Features: Commander model slide, single stack Bobtail frame; chainlink treatment on forestrap; Bobtail housing; slide coated with Gen III low glare protection; high visibility white outlines for sights; available stainless finish
MSRP $2795

E.M.F. COMPANY, INC. GREAT WESTERN II ALL BLUE "PALADIN"

Action: Revolver
Grips: Ultra Ivory
Barrel: 3.5 in., 5.5 in., 7.5 in.
Sights: Fixed
Weight: N/A
Caliber: 45 LC
Capacity: 6 rounds
Features: Single action; all blued barrel, cylinder, and frames as seen in Hollywood westerns
MSRP $560

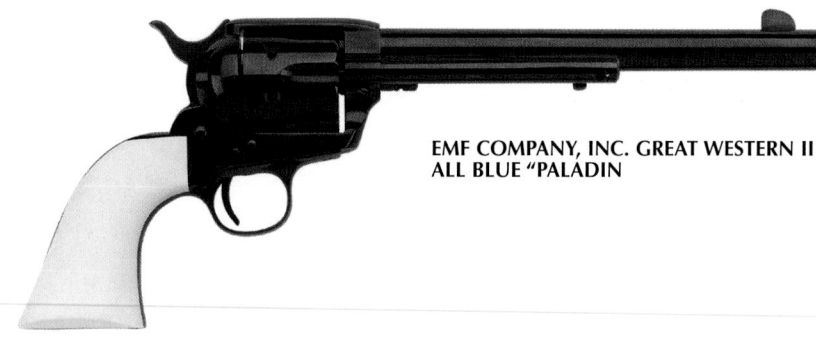

EMF COMPANY, INC. GREAT WESTERN II
ALL BLUE "PALADIN

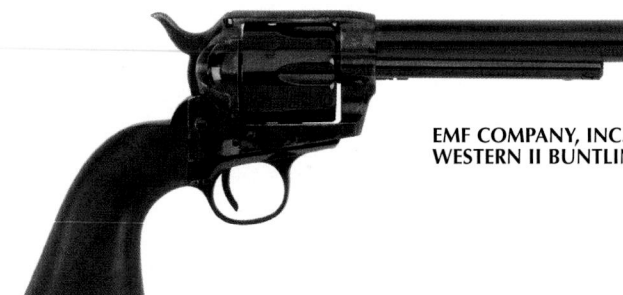

EMF COMPANY, INC. GREAT
WESTERN II BUNTLINE

E.M.F. COMPANY, INC. GREAT WESTERN II BUNTLINE

Action: Revolver
Grips: Walnut or Ultra Stag
Barrel: 12 in.
Sights: Fixed
Weight: N/A
Caliber: 45 LC
Capacity: 6 rounds
Features: Deep color case hardened finish; first version was designed by Colt for Ned Buntline
MSRP $580

E.M.F. COMPANY, INC. GREAT WESTERN II DELUXE SHERIFF

Action: Revolver
Grips: Ultra Ivory
Barrel: 3 in.
Sights: Fixed
Weight: N/A
Caliber: .357 Mag., 45 LC
Capacity: 6 rounds
Features: Manufactured in Italy; stainless steel with factory laser engraving
MSRP **$800**

E.M.F. COMPANY, INC. GREAT WESTERN II "LIBERTY"

Action: Revolver
Grips: Ultra Ivory
Barrel: 4.75 in., 5.5 in.
Sights: Fixed
Weight: N/A
Caliber: .357 Mag., 45 LC
Capacity: 6 rounds
Features: Manufactured in Italy; all blued barrel, cylinder, and frame; factory laser engraved
MSRP **$630**

EUROPEAN AMERICAN ARMORY SARSILMAZ ST10

Action: Autoloader
Grips: Polymer
Barrel: 4.4 in.
Sights: 3-dot, low-profile
Weight: 34 oz.
Caliber: 9mm
Capacity: 16 rounds
Features: Steel frame and slide; adjustable sight; accessory rail; manual safety; low barrel axis; slide serrations; upper and lower barrel lockup; external hammer; available in blue steel or two-tone
MSRP . . . . **$712–$776**

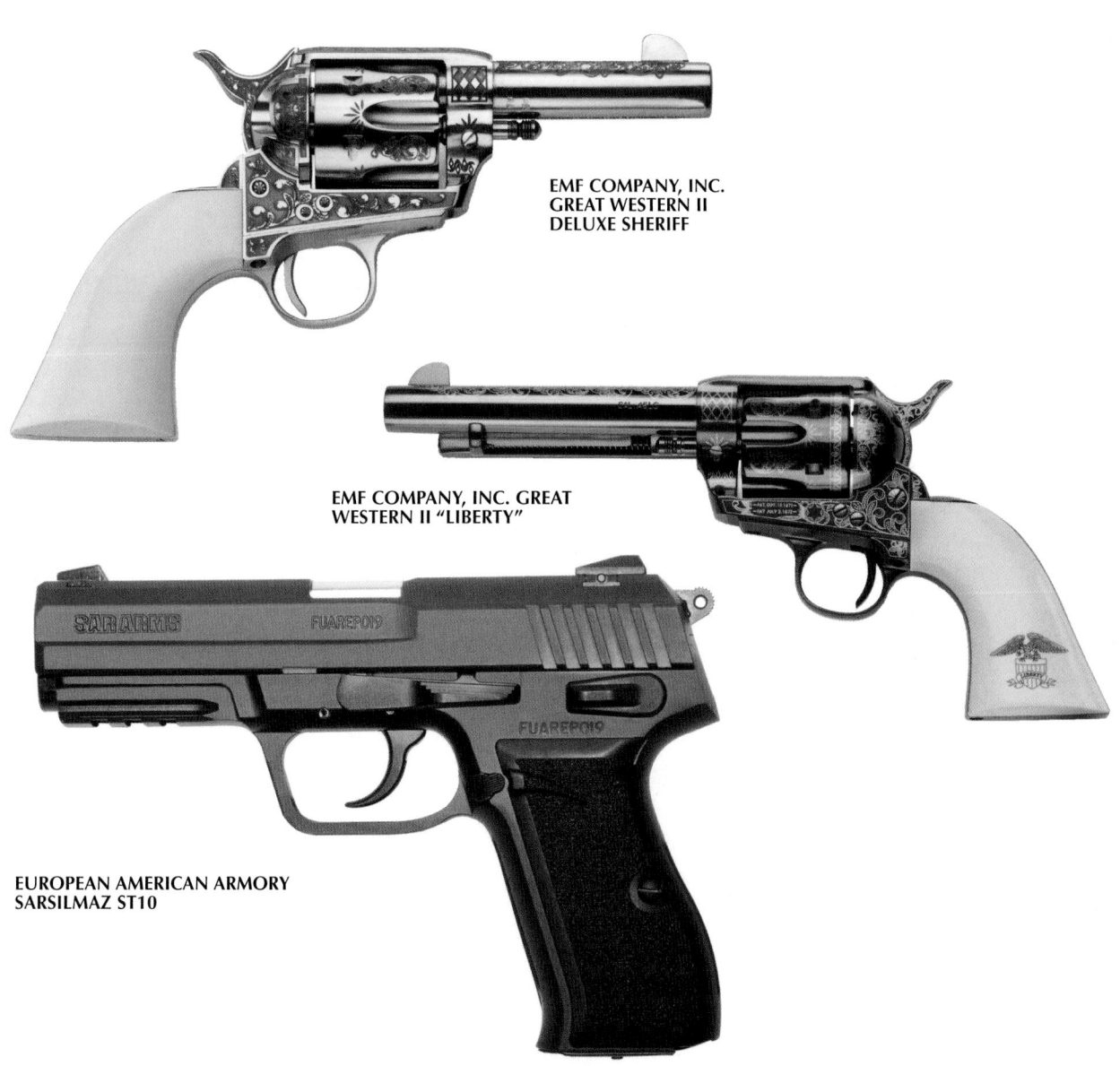

EMF COMPANY, INC.
GREAT WESTERN II
DELUXE SHERIFF

EMF COMPANY, INC. GREAT
WESTERN II "LIBERTY"

EUROPEAN AMERICAN ARMORY
SARSILMAZ ST10

FNH FNX-45

FNH FNX-45

Action: DA/SA Autoloader
Grips: Interchangeable backstraps with lanyard eyelets
Barrel: 4.5 in.
Sights: Fixed 3-dot
Weight: 33.2 oz.
Caliber: .45 ACP
Capacity: 15 rounds
Features: Polymer frame with stainless steel barrel; external extractor with loaded chamber indicator; front and rear cocking serrations; 1913 accessory rail; manual, ambidextrous safety; available in black or flat dark earth
MSRP $824

GLOCK G20 GEN4

Action: Autoloader
Grips: Textured polymer
Barrel: 4.61 in.
Sights: 3-dot fixed sights
Weight: 27.51 oz.
Caliber: 10mm
Capacity: 15 rounds
Features: Full-size polymer frame; multiple backstrap frame with reduced short-frame trigger mechanism housing; three grip options; Rough Textured Frame; reversible magazine release catch; dual recoil spring
MSRP $637

GLOCK G20 GEN4

GLOCK G29 GEN4

GLOCK G29 GEN4

Action: Autoloader
Grips: Textured polymer
Barrel: 3.78 in.
Sights: 3-dot fixed sights
Weight: 24.34 oz.
Caliber: 10mm
Capacity: 10 rounds
Features: Subcompact polymer frame; trigger safety; multiple backstrap frame with reduced short-frame trigger mechanism housing; three grip options; Rough Textured Frame; reversible magazine release catch; dual recoil spring
MSRP $637

GLOCK G33 GEN4

GLOCK G33 GEN4
Action: Autoloader
Grips: Textured polymer
Barrel: 3.43 in.
Sights: 3-dot fixed sights
Weight: 19.75 oz.
Caliber: .357 SIG
Capacity: 9 rounds
Features: Subcompact polymer frame; trigger safety; multiple backstrap frame with reduced short-frame trigger mechanism housing; three grip options; Rough Textured Frame; reversible magazine release catch; dual recoil spring
MSRP $599

GLOCK G30S
Action: Autoloader
Grips: Textured polymer
Barrel: 3.78 in.
Sights: White-dot front, white-outlines rear
Weight: 20.28 oz.
Caliber: .45 Auto
Capacity: 10 rounds
Features: "Slim"model built with the "Short Frame" Glock 30SF; polymer frame; dual recoil spring assembly; accessory rail; cold-hammer-forged barrel with octagonal rifling
MSRP $637

GLOCK G30S

HECKLER & KOCH HK45 TACTICAL

HECKLER & KOCH HK45 TACTICAL
Action: Autoloader
Grips: Polymer with finger grooves
Barrel: 5.16 in.
Sights: 3-dot tritium night sights
Weight: 31.7 oz.
Caliber: .45 ACP
Capacity: 10 rounds
Features: Polymer frame; recoil-operated with modified Browning locking system; threaded barrel; 1913 Picatinny rail; key-based HK Lock-Out system; nine different trigger firing modes; available in black, tan, and green
MSRP . . . . $1392–$1461

NEW Products: **Handguns**

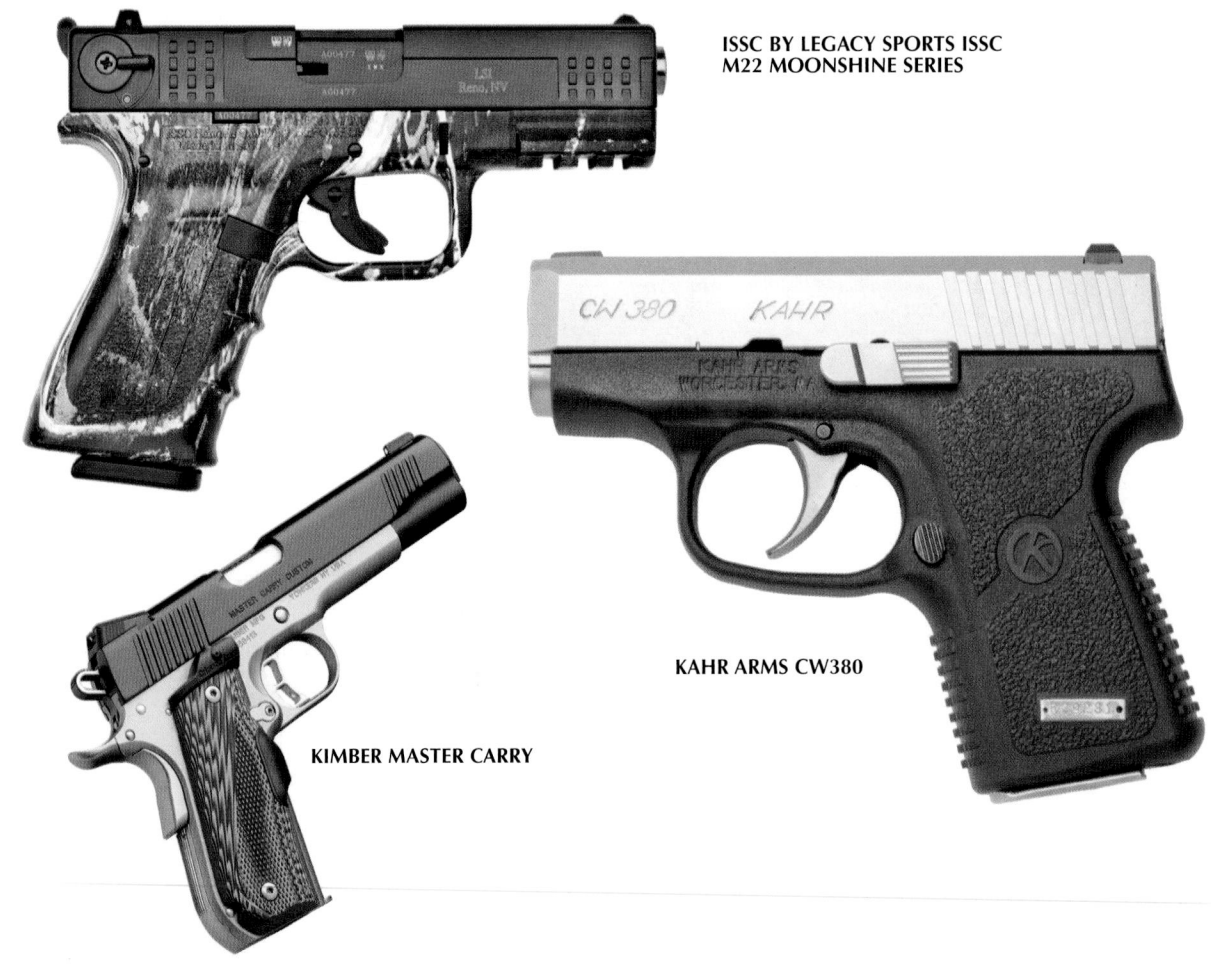

ISSC BY LEGACY SPORTS ISSC M22 MOONSHINE SERIES

KAHR ARMS CW380

KIMBER MASTER CARRY

ISSC BY LEGACY SPORTS ISSC M22 MOONSHINE SERIES

Action: Semiautomatic
Grips: Polymer
Barrel: 4 in.
Sights: White dot front, adjustable rear
Weight: 21.4 oz.
Caliber: .22LR
Capacity: 10 rounds
Features: Five safety features: hammer drop-down, loaded chamber indicator, external key lock, trigger safety tab, and magazine disconnect; windage-adjustable rear sight; white dot front sight; polymer frame; MoonShine Attitude Attire series features new camo patterns Harvest Moon, Outshine, and Muddy Girl
MSRP **$469**

KAHR ARMS CW380

Action: DAO
Grips: Black polymer
Barrel: 2.58 in.
Sights: Adjustable white bar-dot combat rear, pinned in polymer front
Weight: 10.2 oz.
Caliber: .380 ACP
Capacity: 6+1 rounds
Features: Lock breech; modified Browning type recoil lug; "safe cam" action; conventional rifled barrel; metal-injection-molded slide stop lever; slide lock after last round; black and stainless matte finish
MSRP **$419**

KIMBER MASTER CARRY

Action: Autoloader
Grips: Crimson Trace Lasergrips
Barrel: 3in. (Ultra), 5 in.
Sights: Fixed low profile
Weight: 25 oz.–31 oz.
Caliber: .45 ACP
Capacity: 7 or 8 rounds
Features: Aluminum, round-heel frame; satin silver finish; dovetailed night sights; recessed slide-stop pin; serrated mainspring housing; stainless steel slide; available in a Custom model, Pro, or Ultra
MSRP **$1568**

KIMBER MICRO CARRY
Action: Autoloader
Grips: Black synthetic or Rosewood, double diamond
Barrel: 2.75 in.
Sights: Fixed low profile
Weight: 13.4 oz.
Caliber: .380 ACP
Capacity: 6 rounds
Features: Aluminum frame; stainless steel barrel; dovetailed sights; single-side thumb safety; available in black, stainless, CDP, and CDP with Crimson Trace Lasergrips
MSRP. **$651**
Stainless:. **$679**
CDP: **$1121**
CDP Lasergrips:. **$1406**

KIMBER WARRIOR SOC
Action: Autoloader
Grips: Kimber G10
Barrel: 5 in.
Sights: Fixed tactical wedge tritium night sights, desert tan Crimson Trace Rail Master laser sight
Weight: 39 oz.
Caliber: .45 ACP
Capacity: 7 rounds
Features: Steel frame; front and rear slide serrations; 1913 Picatinny rail; ambidextrous thumb safety; checkered front strap; stainless steel barrel and bushing; beavertail grip; KimPro II dark green finish
MSRP. **$1665**

MG ARMS WRAITHE
Action: Semiautomatic
Grips: Custom G10
Barrel: 4.5 in.
Sights: Night or fixed
Weight: 18 oz.–20 oz.
Caliber: .45, 9mm
Capacity: 8+1, 9+1 rounds
Features: Aluminum alloy bobtail frame, custom grip panels, high ride beavertail safety, two Wilson magazines included, available in olive drab, black, desert tan, or limited edition 2011 Ti titanium frame
MSRP. **$2595**
Titanium:. **$2995**

MG ARMS WRAITHE

KIMBER MICRO CARRY

KIMBER WARRIOR SOC

NIGHTHAWK CUSTOM T4

NIGHTHAWK CUSTOM T4
Action: Autoloader
Grips: Slim
Barrel: 3.8 in.
Sights: Fixed
Weight: 34.3 oz.
Caliber: 9mm
Capacity: 9 or 10 rounds
Features: Thinned aluminum frame and mainspring housing
MSRP. **$3350**

NEW Products: **Handguns**

NORTH AMERICAN ARMS SIDEWINDER

Action: Revolver
Grips: Laminated rosewood
Barrel: 1 in.
Sights: Stainless steel post
Weight: 6.7 oz.
Caliber: .22 Mag.
Capacity: 5 rounds
Features: Features NAA's safety cylinder; stainless steel frame; available .22LR conversion
MSRP **$349**

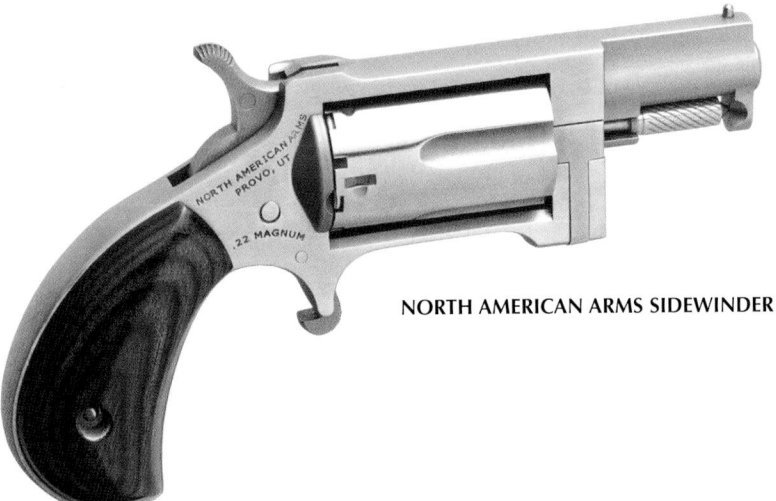

NORTH AMERICAN ARMS SIDEWINDER

OLYMPIC ARMS WHITNEY WOLVERINE

Action: Autoloader
Grips: Black checkered
Barrel: 4.625 in.
Sights: Blade type front sight, dovetail rear sight
Weight: 19.2 oz.
Caliber: .22LR
Capacity: 10+1 rounds
Features: Revival of ray-gun style semiauto pistol; polymer frame; ventilated rib; thumb safety; available in black, pink, coyote brown, and desert tan
MSRP **$294**

OLYMPIC ARMS WHITNEY WOLVERINE

PARA BLACK OPS 14.45

Action: Autoloader
Grips: Beavertail
Barrel: 5 in.
Sights: Trijicon 3-dot night sights
Weight: 41 oz.
Caliber: .45 ACP
Capacity: 14+1 rounds
Features: Stainless steel frame; oversized flared ejection port; ramped barrel; adjustable skeletonized trigger; black IonBond finish
MSRP **$1299**

PARA BLACK OPS 14.45

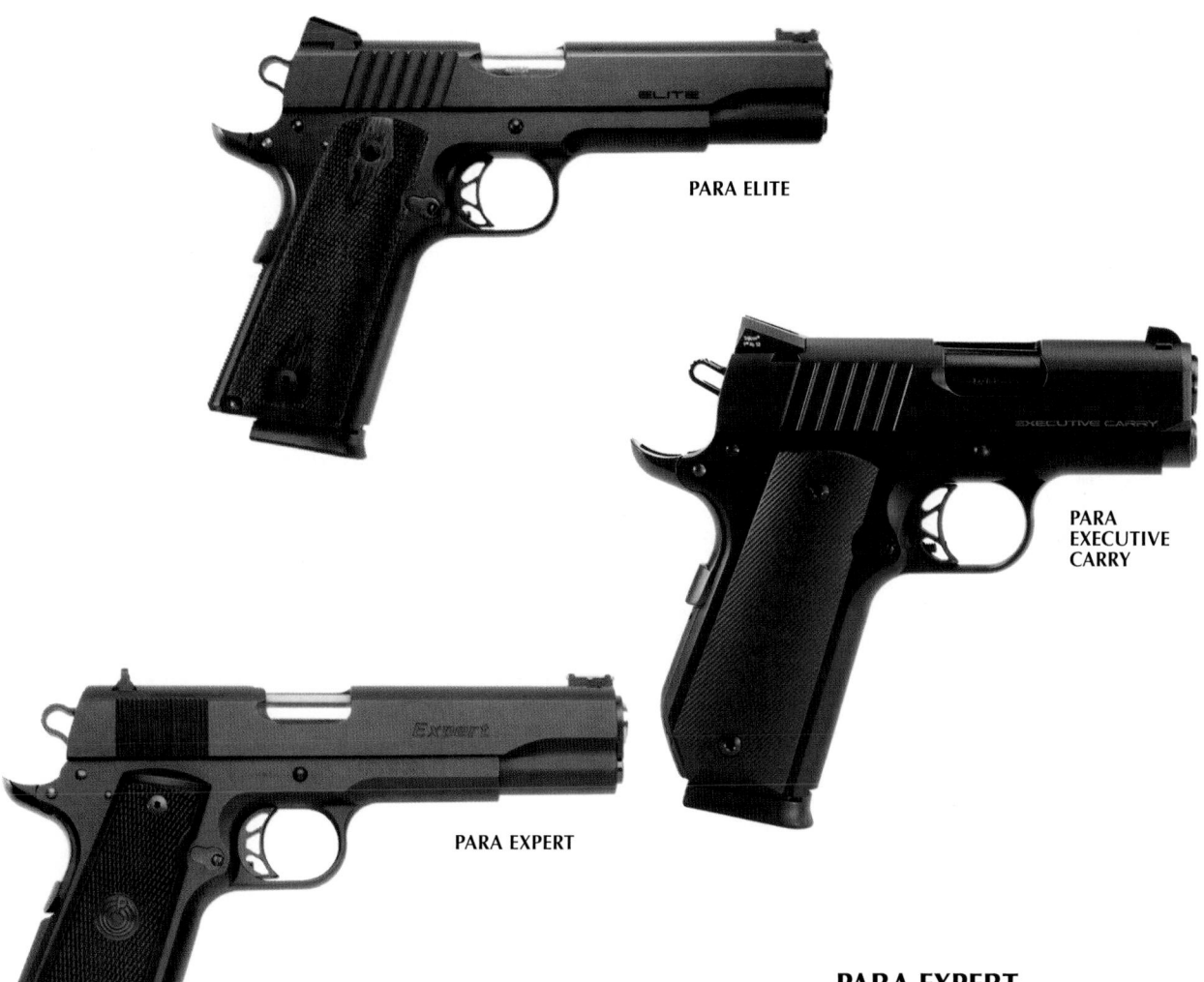

PARA ELITE

PARA EXECUTIVE CARRY

PARA EXPERT

PARA ELITE

Action: Autoloader
Grips: Beavertail
Barrel: 5 in.
Sights: 2-dot dovetail rear, green fiber optic front
Weight: 39 oz.
Caliber: .45 ACP
Capacity: 8+1 rounds
Features: Stainless steel frame; oversized flared ejection port; ramped barrel; adjustable skeletonized trigger; black IonBond PVD slide and frame
MSRP **$949**

PARA EXECUTIVE CARRY

Action: Autoloader
Grips: VZ G10
Barrel: 3 in.
Sights: Trijicon night sights
Weight: 26 oz.
Caliber: .45 ACP
Capacity: 8+1 rounds
Features: Ed Brown Bobtail mainspring housing; lightweight aluminum frame; adjustable skeletonized trigger; two magazines included
MSRP **$1449**

PARA EXPERT

Action: Autoloader
Grips: Polymer
Barrel: 5 in.
Sights: Green fiber optic front; 2-dot combat rear
Weight: 39 oz.
Caliber: .45 ACP
Capacity: 8+1 rounds
Features: Double-stack stainless steel frame; stainless match-grade barrel; adjustable skeletonized trigger; two magazines included
MSRP **$949**

NEW Products: **Handguns**

PARA LDA CARRY
Action: Autoloader
Grips: Polymer
Barrel: 3 in.
Sights: 2-dot combat rear, green fiber optic front
Weight: 30 oz.
Caliber: .45 ACP, 9mm
Capacity: 6+1, 8+1 rounds
Features: Oversized, flared ejection port; steel frame and slide; beavertail grip safety; adjustable skeletonized trigger; black nitride finish available
MSRP **$1025**

REMINGTON MODEL 1911 R1 CARRY
Action: Autoloader
Grips: Cocobolo wood
Barrel: 5 in.
Sights: Novak sights with tritium front night sight
Weight: 38.5 oz.
Caliber: .45 Auto
Capacity: 7 or 8 rounds
Features: De-horned forged carbon steel frame and de-horned carbon steel slide; beavertail grip safety with checkered memory bump; checkered front strap and mainspring housing; ambidextrous safety; satin black oxide finish
MSRP **$1299**

PARA LDA CARRY

**REMINGTON MODEL
1911 R1 CARRY**

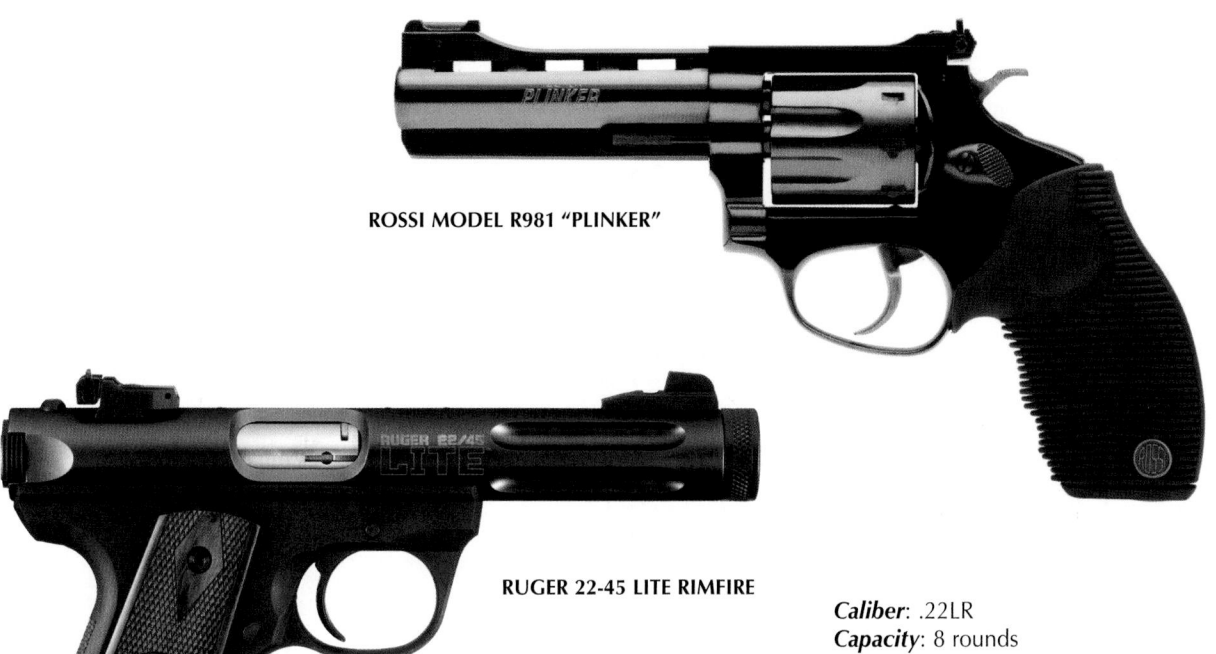

ROSSI MODEL R981 "PLINKER"

RUGER 22-45 LITE RIMFIRE

Caliber: .22LR
Capacity: 8 rounds
Features: Alloy steel frame; key-based Taurus security system; transfer bar/ hammer block safety; yoke detent system; blued finish
MSRP **$431**

RUGER 22/45 LITE RIMFIRE PISTOL

Action: SA autoloader
Grips: Black laminate
Barrel: 4.4 in.
Sights: Fixed front, adjustable rear
Weight: 23 oz.
Caliber: .22LR
Capacity: 10 rounds
Features: Aluminum upper, black anodized finish; stainless barrel sleeve; polymer grip frame; manual safety; loaded chamber indicator; magazine disconnect
MSRP **$499**

RUGER LC380

RUGER LC380

Action: Autoloader
Grips: Black, glass-filled nylon
Barrel: 3.12 in.
Sights: Adjustable 3-dot
Weight: 17.2 oz.
Caliber: .380 Auto
Capacity: 7+1 rounds
Features: Hardened alloy steel slide; checkered grip frame; finger grip extension floorplate; three safeties and loaded chamber indicator; blued finish
MSRP **$449**

ROSSI MODEL R981 "PLINKER"

Action: DA/SA revolver
Grips: Ribber
Barrel: 4 in.
Sights: Fixed red fiber optic front, adjustable rear
Weight: 29 oz.

RUGER SR45

Action: Autoloader
Grips: Black, glass-filled nylon
Barrel: 4.5 in.
Sights: Adjustable 3-dot
Weight: 30.15 oz.
Caliber: .45 ACP
Capacity: 10+1 rounds
Features: Reversible backstrap; ambidextrous safety and magazine release; mouting rail; loaded chamber indicator; black nitride or brushed stainless finish
MSRP **$529**

RUGER SR45

RUGER SR1911

Action: Autoloader
Grips: Hardwood
Barrel: 4.25in., 5 in.
Sights: Windage adjustable Novak 3-dot
Weight: 36.4 oz.–39 oz.
Caliber: .45 ACP
Capacity: 7+1, 8+1 rounds
Features: Checkered backstrap; stainless steel barrel and bushing; positive barrel lock-up; lightweight, aluminum, skeletonized trigger and hammer; beavertail grip safety; low-glare stainless finish
MSRP **$829**

RUGER SR1911

SIG SAUER 1911 .22LR CAMO

Action: SAO
Grips: Polymer Camo
Barrel: 5 in.
Sights: Contrast sights
Weight: 34 oz.
Caliber: .22LR
Capacity: 10 rounds
Features: Lightweight metal frame and slide; low-profile sights; ambidextrous thumb safety; camo coating
MSRP **$518**

SIG SAUER 1911 .22LR CAMO

SIG SAUER 1911 SPARTAN

Action: SAO
Grips: Hogue Spartan
Barrel: 5 in.
Sights: Low profile night sights
Weight: 41.6 oz.
Caliber: .45 ACP
Capacity: 8 rounds
Features: Oil-rubbed bronze Nitron finish; gold inlay engraving; 1911 design and ergonomic feel; ancient Greek inscription on slide and grip supposedly spoken by Spartan King Leonidas: "Molon labe," or "Come and take it"
MSRP **$1356**

SIG SAUER 1911 SPARTAN

SIG SAUER M11-A1

SIG SAUER M11-A1

Action: DA/SA
Grips: Polymer
Barrel: 3.9 in.
Sights: Siglite night sights
Weight: 32 oz.
Caliber: 9mm
Capacity: 15 rounds
Features: Stainless steel slide; Short Reset Trigger; flush fit magazines; phosphate coated internals; Nitron slide finish; black hard anodized
MSRP **$1125**

SIG SAUER P227

Action: DA/SA
Grips: One-piece polymer
Barrel: 4.4 in.
Sights: Contrast or Siglite night sights
Weight: 32 oz.
Caliber: .45 ACP
Capacity: 10 rounds
Features: Full-size and carry lengths; double stack magazines; integral accessory rail; black hard anodized; Nitron slide finish
MSRP **$993**
w/Night Sights: **$1085**

SIG SAUER P227

NEW Products: **Handguns**

SMITH & WESSON M&P PRO SERIES C.O.R.E. PISTOL

Action: Striker Fire Double Action
Grips: Polymer
Barrel: 4.25 in., 5 in.
Sights: White dot dovetail front, fixed 2-dot rear
Weight: 24 oz.–26 oz.
Caliber: 9mm, .40 S&W
Capacity: 17+1 and 15+1 rounds
Features: Competition Optics Ready Equipment; mounting platform on slide; engineered as a competition platform; polymer frame; ambidextrous operating controls; interchangeable back strap; Performance Center sear; Melonite finish
MSRP **$729**

SMITH & WESSON M&P SHIELD PISTOL

Action: Striker Fired
Grips: Polymer
Barrel: 3.1 in.
Sights: White dot front, white 2-dot rear
Weight: 19 oz.
Caliber: 9mm, .40 S&W
Capacity: 6, 7, and 8 round
Features: Slim, concealable, and lightweight defense firearm; high-strength polymer frame; Melonite coated; consistent 6.5 lb. trigger pull; loaded chamber indicator
MSRP **$449**

SMITH & WESSON SD9 VE AND SD40 VE

Action: Striker Fired
Grips: Textured polymer
Barrel: 4 in.
Sights: White dot front, fixed 2-dot rear
Weight: 22.7 oz.
Caliber: 9mm, .40 S&W
Capacity: 10+1, 14+1, and 16+1 rounds
Features: Lightweight polymer frame; front and rear slide serrations; Self Defense Trigger; ergonomic grip; Picatinny rail; two-tone finish
MSRP **$379**

SMITH & WESSON M&P PRO SERIES C.O.R.E. PISTOL

SMITH & WESSON M&P SHIELD PISTOL

SMITH & WESSON SD9 VE

NEW PRODUCTS

**SPRINGFIELD
ARMORY XD-S**

STI INTERNATIONAL
DUTY ONE SERIES

STEYR L-A1

STI INTERNATIONAL
TACTICAL SS FAMILY

SPRINGFIELD ARMORY XD-S

Action: DAO autoloader
Grips: Polymer
Barrel: 3.3 in.
Sights: Steel dovetail rear, fiber optic front
Weight: 21.5 oz.
Caliber: .45 ACP
Capacity: 5+1 rounds
Features: Slim contour, single stack frame; Ultra Safety Assurance Trigger System; loaded chamber indicator; fail-safe disassembly; Picatinny rail system; Mould-Tru backstraps; Melonite finish
MSRP . . . . $599–$669

STEYR L-A1

Action: Autoloader
Grips: Synthetic
Barrel: 4.5 in.
Sights: Fixed triangular/trapezoid

Weight: 28.6 oz.
Caliber: 9mm, .40 S&W
Capacity: 12 or 15 rounds
Features: Rectangular sights with or without Trilux, match sights; full size service pistol; matte finish
From $549.99

STI INTERNATIONAL DUTY ONE SERIES

Action: Autoloader
Grips: STI patented modular polymer
Barrel: 3 in., 4.37 in., 5.11 in.
Sights: STI Ramped front, Tactical Adjustable Rear Sight
Weight: 31.6 oz.–37.2 oz.
Caliber: 9mm, .40 S&W, .45 ACP
Capacity: 8, 9 rounds
Features: STI government frame; integral tactical rail; ambidextrous thumb safeties and beavertail grip safety; lowered and flared ejection port; STI RecoilMaster guide rod

system; front and rear serrations; blued matte finish
MSRP $1330

STI INTERNATIONAL TACTICAL SS FAMILY

Action: Autoloader
Grips: STI patented modular polymer
Barrel: 3.76 in., 4.26 in., 5 in.
Sights: STI Ramped front, STI Fixed Ledge Style Rear
Weight: 34.4 oz.–41.1 oz.
Caliber: 9mm, .40 S&W, .45 ACP
Capacity: 8+1 rounds
Features: Tactical line features in a traditional 1911 package; fully forged frames with Picatinny rail system; flat top slide with front and rear serrations; ambidextrous thumb safety and beavertail grip safety; blued matte finish
MSRP $2030

**TRADITIONS FIREARMS
FRONTIER**

TRADITIONS FIREARMS FRONTIER SERIES

Action: SA revolver
Grips: Simulated ivory or walnut
Barrel: 4.75 in., 5.5 in., 7.5 in.
Sights: Front blade
Weight: N/A
Caliber: .357, .44 Mag., .45 LC, .44/40
Capacity: 6 rounds
Features: 1873 single action revolvers; deep bluing and nickel frames and barrel or color case hardened frame, all polished to perfection; transfer bar safety system provides the highest lever of safety offered in an 1873 single action firearm
MSRP . . . . $515–$609

**TRADITIONS FIREARMS
RAWHIDE**

TRADITIONS FIREARMS RAWHIDE SERIES

Action: SA revolver
Grips: Walnut
Barrel: 4.75 in., 5.5 in., 7.5 in.
Sights: Front blade
Weight: N/A
Caliber: .45 LC, .357, .22LR, and .22LR/.22 Mag.
Capacity: 6 rounds
Features: Quality single action shooter features at an affordable price; matte black finish that provides excellent corrosion resistance; transfer bar system provides the highest level of safety offered in an 1873 single action
MSRP . . . . $440–$485

TRISTAR ARMS C-100

Action: DA/SA semiautomatic
Grips: Polymer
Barrel: 3.9 in.
Sights: Rear dovetail, fixed front
Weight: 24.48 oz.–26.08 oz.
Caliber: 9mm, .40 S&W
Capacity: 11, 15 rounds
Features: Produced to NATO specs; rear snag-free dovetail sights; fixed blade front sight; black polycoat finish; black polymer checkered grips; includes two magazines and a hard plastic case
MSRP . . . . $429–$439

TRISTAR ARMS C-100
CHROME

TRISTAR ARMS P-120

TRISTAR ARMS P-120

Action: DA/SA semiautomatic
Grips: Polymer
Barrel: 4.7 in.
Sights: Rear dovetail, fixed front
Weight: 29.9 oz.
Caliber: 9mm
Capacity: 17 rounds
Features: Originally created for military use; constructed from steel alloy; blued or chrome finish; rear snag-free dovetail sights; fixed blade front sight; includes two magazines, cleaning kit, gun lock, and a black carrying case
MSRP . . . . $429–$439

TRISTAR ARMS T-100

Action: DA/SA semiautomatic
Grips: Polymer
Barrel: 3.7 in.
Sights: Rear dovetail, fixed front
Weight: 26.24 oz.
Caliber: 9mm
Capacity: 15 rounds
Features: Compact pistol perfect for concealed carry; constructed from steel alloy; blued or chrome finish; rear snag-free dovetail sights; fixed blade front sight; includes two magazines, cleaning kit, gun lock, and a black carrying case
MSRP . . . . $429–$439

TRISTAR ARMS
T-100 BLUED

UBERTI 1873 CATTLEMAN .22LR

UBERTI 1873 CATTLEMAN .22LR
Action: SA revolver
Grips: Walnut
Barrel: 4.75 in., 5.5 in., 7.5in.
Sights: Fixed, open
Weight: 36.8 oz.
Caliber: .22LR
Capacity: 6 and 12 round models
Features: Ideal for cowboy-action shooting practice; light recoil; six-shot comes with brass or steel backstrap and trigger guard; available in six- or twelve-shot; case-hardened frame; blued finish
MSRP . . . .$509–$559

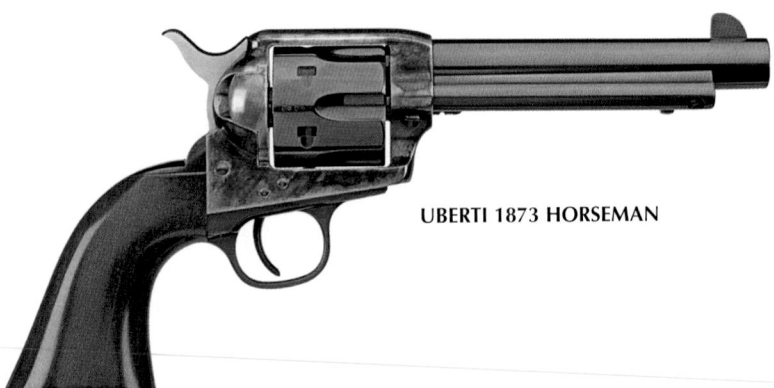

UBERTI 1873 HORSEMAN

UBERTI 1873 HORSEMAN
Action: SA revolver
Grips: Walnut
Barrel: 4.75 in., 5.5 in., 7.5in.
Sights: Fixed, open
Weight: 36.8 oz.
Caliber: .45 Colt, .357 Mag.
Capacity: 6 rounds
Features: Transfer-bar safety system; coil main spring; wider trigger; case-hardened frame; blued finish
MSRP $559

U.S. FIREARMS ZIP

U.S. FIREARMS ZIP
Action: SA striker fired
Grips: Polymer, checkered
Barrel: 5.25 in.
Sights: Fixed, open
Weight: 15.2 oz.
Caliber: .22LR
Capacity: N/A
Features: Modular firearm system built on a polymer frame; configurations include striker-fired gun as a pistol or short barreled rifle; features an accessory rail; accepts Ruger 10/22-style magazines; available in black, gray, coyote tan, and blue
MSRP . . . . $199.99–$219.99

WALTHER PPK/S .22

Action: DA/SA autoloader
Grips: Polymer
Barrel: 3.3 in.
Sights: Fixed, open
Weight: 24 oz.
Caliber: .22LR
Capacity: 10 rounds
Features: Manual safety; top strap waved to reduce glare; internal slide stop; iconic PPK/S frame; beaver tail extension; nickel plated or black finish
MSRP . . . . $399–$429

WALTHER PPK/S .22

WALTHER PPQ M2

Action: Striker fire action autoloader
Grips: Polymer
Barrel: 4 in., 4.1 in., 4.6 in., 5 in.
Sights: 3-dot adjustable low-profile
Weight: 24 oz. (9mm), 25.6 oz. (.40 S&W)
Caliber: 9mm, 9mm (Navy SD), .40 S&W
Capacity: 15 rounds (9mm), 15/17 rounds (9mm Navy SD), 11 rounds (.40 S&W)
Features: Quick defense trigger; three safeties; ergonomic grip with checkered trigger guard; ambidextrous slide stop and magazine release button; Tenifer coated slide and barrel with matte finish
MSRP . . . . $599–$699

WALTHER PPQ M2

WALTHER PPX

WALTHER PPX

Action: Hammer fire action autoloader
Grips: Polymer
Barrel: 4 in., 4.6 in. (9MM SD)
Sights: 3-dot adjustable low-profile
Weight: 27.2 oz.
Caliber: 9mm, 9mm (SD), .40 S&W
Capacity: 16 rounds (9mm), 14 rounds (.40 S&W)
Features: Constant 6.5 lb. trigger pull; three safeties; ergonomic grip; ambidextrous slide stop and reversible push button magazine release; loaded chamber viewport; Mil-Std-1913 Picatinny accessory mounting rail; Tenifer coated slide and barrel; available in black and stainless
MSRP . . . . $449–$499

CONNECTICUT VALLEY ARMS (CVA) OPTIMA V2

LYMAN PRODUCTS MODEL OF 1878
SIDE-HAMMER SHARPS BY PEDERSOLI

CONNECTICUT VALLEY ARMS (CVA) OPTIMA V2

Lock: Break-action muzzleloading
Stock: Realtree Xtra Green or black
Barrel: 26 in.
Sights: Fiber optic sights or mount
Weight: 6 lb. 10 oz.
Bore/Caliber: .50
Features: Modeled on the Accura V2; stainless steel barrel; quick release breech plug; 100% ambidextrous stock; includes DuraSight Dead-On scope mount and ramrod
Realtree: .... **$391.95–$425.95**
SS/Black: .... **$338.95–$348.95**
Blued/Black:...... **$307.95–$317.95**

LYMAN PRODUCTS MODEL OF 1878 SIDE-HAMMER SHARPS BY PEDERSOLI

Lock: Centerfire
Stock: Walnut
Barrel: 30 in.
Sights: Lyman's tang and globe sights
Weight: 9 lb.
Bore/Caliber: .45-70
Features: Reproduced for today's single shot enthusiast, Sharps' final iconic side-hammer design and Lyman's sights combine to create Lyman's "Model of 1878" .45/70 barrel; double-set triggers; shotgun-style butt; forend finished with premium ebony tip; laser engraved; black powder cartridge optional
MSRP **$1995**

PEDERSOLI BOUTET 1ER EMPIRE

Lock: Flintlock
Stock: Hardwood
Barrel: 10 in.
Sights: Fixed
Weight: 2 lb. 14 oz.
Bore/Caliber: .45
Features: Napoleon often wrote with flattering appreciation about the style and prestige of the Boutet guns, which Pedersoli now proudly introduces with fine checkering on the sides; metal buttplate; ramrod has a horn tip; single set trigger; on the lock two lines are engraved with MANUF RE/a Versailles.
MSRP **$2200**

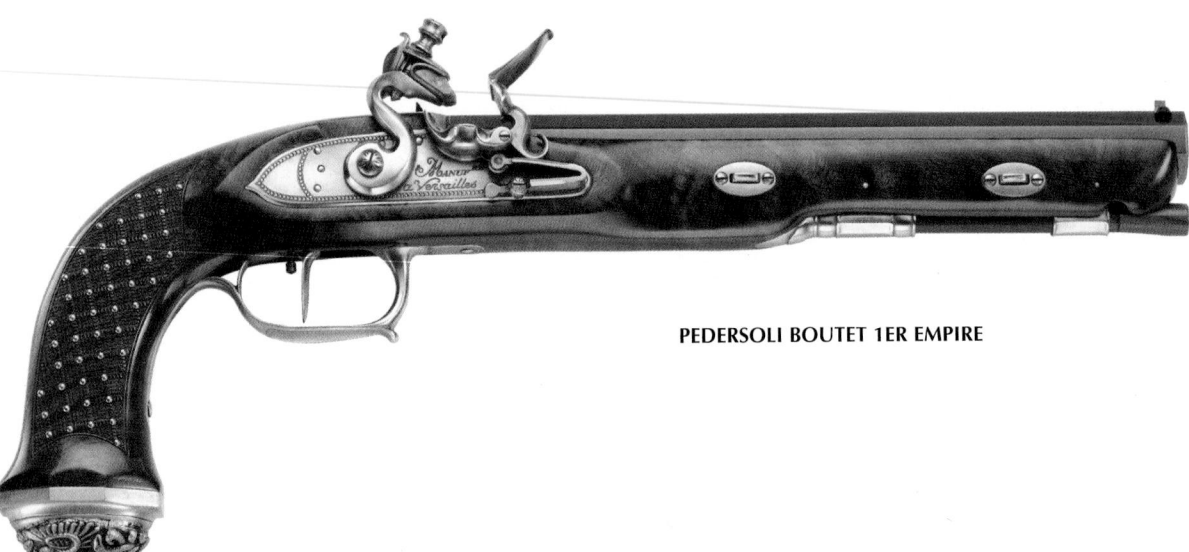

PEDERSOLI BOUTET 1ER EMPIRE

PEDERSOLI KODIAK EXPRESS MK VI

Lock: Breechloading
Stock: Hardwood
Barrel: 24.25 in.
Sights: Creedmore
Weight: 10 lb. 2 oz.
Bore/Caliber: .50, .54, .58
Features: A very manageable gun, perfectly balanced; particularly suitable for wild boar hunting; practical rubber buttplate; half pistol grip stock; equipped with ghost sights
MSRP **$1388**

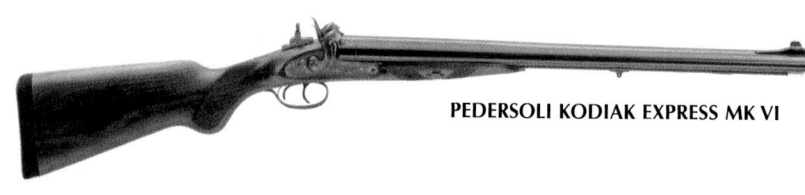
PEDERSOLI KODIAK EXPRESS MK VI

PEDERSOLI MAMELOUK

Lock: Flintlock
Stock: Hardwood
Barrel: 7.6 in.
Sights: Fixed
Weight: 1 lb. 10 oz.
Bore/Caliber: 14.5mm
Features: Like all the firearms equipping Napoleon's Imperial Guards, the Mameluke pistols were made at the Manufacture of Versailles under the technical management of Nicolas-Noël Boutet; the trigger guard, buttcap, screw washers of the lock, and ramrod tip are brass
MSRP **$978**

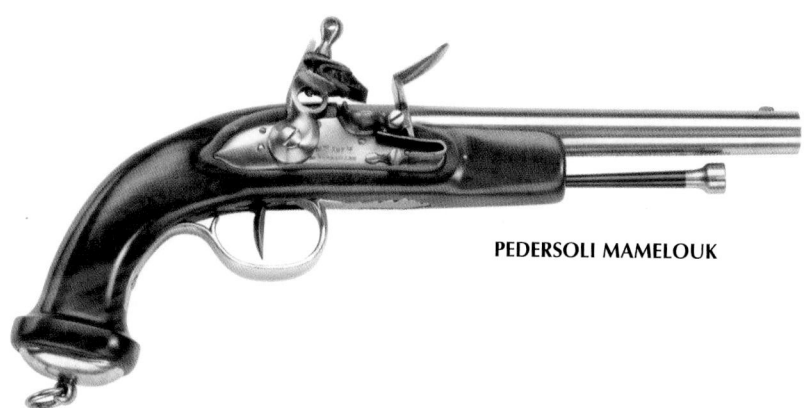
PEDERSOLI MAMELOUK

PEDERSOLI ZOUAVE U.S. MODEL 1863

Lock: Caplock
Stock: Hardwood
Barrel: 33 in.
Sights: Front, rear
Weight: 9 lb. 4 oz.
Bore/Caliber: .58
Features: Intended for the U.S. Artillery Department and never distributed to any Civil War army division; features brass furnitures; ramrod with a tulip tip; three-leaf rear sight; two sling swivels; the lock shows the Eagle stamp and the U.S. letters in front of the hammer
MSRP **$1241**

PEDERSOLI ZOUAVE U.S. MODEL 1863

TRADITIONS FIREARMS VORTEK STRIKERFIRE

Lock: Break-action muzzleloading
Stock: Soft Touch synthetic
Barrel: 28 in.
Sights: Fiber optic
Weight: N/A
Bore/Caliber: .50

TRADITIONS FIREARMS VORTEK STRIKERFIRE

Features: This patent-pending rifle takes in-line muzzleloaders to the next level by taking away the external hammer and using an internal StrikerFire™ System. To cock the gun, simply slide the striker button forward until it locks and fire. The recessed de-cocking buttons allows for quick and quiet de-cocking of the firearm and the gun is also equipped with an automatic de-cocking mechanism - when the gun is opened, it is automatically de-cocked. Also includes: two-stage trigger; CeraKote finish; Realtree Xtra or black stock
MSRP: . . . . **$489–$649**

SCOPES

ALPEN APEX XP 6-24X50MM RIFLESCOPE MODEL 4058

Weight: 24 oz.
Length: 15.5 in.
Power: 6-24x
Obj. Dia.: 50mm
Main Dia.: 30mm
Exit Pupil: 8-2mm
Field of View: 16-4ft @ 100yds
Twilight Factor: 17.3-34.6
Eye Relief: 3.5 in.
Features: WBDC-TACT reticle; shock tested to 1,000 g's magnum load; fully multi-coated lenses; waterproof; fogproof; shockproof; zero-set low profile windage and elevation adjustments; black matte finish; Alpen's No-Fault, No Problem Lifetime Warranty
MSRP **$653**

ALPEN APEX XP 6-24X50MM RIFLESCOPE MODEL 4058

BRUNTON ECHO 3.5-10X50MM RIFLESCOPE

Weight: 17.6 oz.
Length: 13 in.
Power: 3.5-10x
Obj. Dia.: 50mm
Main Dia.: 1 in.
Exit Pupil: N/A
Field of View: 28.3ft @ 3.5x @ 100yds
Twilight Factor: 13.2-22.4
Eye Relief: 3.34–2.95 in.
Features: Fast focus eyepiece; fully multi-coated optics; waterproof; fogproof; shockproof; glass etched reticle; precision finger turrets; also available in 1.5-5x20 Duplex Reticle, 1.5-6x40 Duplex Reticle, 1.5-6x40 Crossbow Reticle, 3-9x40 BDC Reticle, 3.5-10x50 BDC Reticle, and 6-24x50 Mil-Dot Reticle; matte finish
MSRP **$265**

BRUNTON ECHO 3.5-10X50MM RIFLESCOPE

BURRIS 2X-7X SCOUT SCOPE

Weight: 13 oz.
Length: 9.7 in.
Power: 2-7x
Obj. Dia.: 32mm
Main Dia.: 1 in.
Exit Pupil: 16-4.6mm
Field of View: 21-7ft @ 100yds
Twilight Factor: 8-15
Eye Relief: 11–21 in.
Features: Ballistic Plex reticle; fully multi-coated; variable power; low mounting capabilities; black matte finish
MSRP **$399**

BURRIS 2X-7X SCOUT SCOPE

BURRIS C4 RIFLESCOPE
4.5X-14X42MM

BURRIS ELIMINATOR 3.5X-10X40MM

BURRIS ELIMINATOR II 4X-12X42MM

BURRIS C4 RIFLESCOPE 4.5X-14X42MM

Weight: 18 oz.
Length: 12.2 in.
Power: 4.5-14x
Obj. Dia.: 42mm
Main Dia.: 1 in.
Exit Pupil: 9-3mm
Field of View: 23-8ft @ 100yds
Twilight Factor: 13.7-24.2
Eye Relief: 3.2–3.9 in.
Features: Custom knob to match elevation adjustment and a specified catridge and bullet; index matched Hi-Lume multi-coatings; ergonomic power rings; black matte finish; available in 3x-9x-40mm and 4.5x-14x-42mm in both 1 in. and 30 mm tubes
MSRP $449–749

BURRIS ELIMINATOR 3.5X-10X40MM

Weight: 26 oz.
Length: 13 in.
Power: 3.5-10x
Obj. Dia.: 40mm
Main Dia.: 39mm
Exit Pupil: 11.4-4.0mm
Field of View: 25.4-9.6ft @ 100yds
Twilight Factor: 11.8-20
Eye Relief: 3.5–4 in.
Features: Laser rangefinder; range of 800 yards; aiming dot with storable programming; black matte finish
MSRP $1235

BURRIS ELIMINATOR II 4X-12X42MM

Weight: 26 oz.
Length: 13 in.
Power: 4-12x
Obj. Dia.: 42mm
Main Dia.: 39mm
Exit Pupil: 10.5-3.5mm
Field of View: 25-9ft @ 100yds
Twilight Factor: 13-22.4
Eye Relief: 3–3.5 in.
Features: Laser rangefinder; range of 999 yards; accurate at any magnification; ergonomic activation buttons; enhanced extreme range ballistic programming; black matte finish
MSRP $1584

BURRIS ELIMINATOR III 4X-16X50MM

Weight: 26 oz.
Length: 15.75 in.
Power: 4-16x
Obj. Dia.: 50mm
Main Dia.: 39mm
Exit Pupil: 12.5-3.1mm
Field of View: 25-7ft @ 100yds
Twilight Factor: 14.1-28.3
Eye Relief: 3.5–4 in.
Features: Laser rangefinder with wind compensation; range of 1,200+ yards; accurate at any magnification; ergonomic activation buttons; parallax adjustment 50 yards-infinity; black matte finish; fully multi-coated
MSRP **$2413**

BURRIS ELIMINATOR III 4X-16X50MM

BUSHNELL AR OPTICS 1-4X24MM THROW DOWN PCL

Weight: 17.3 oz.
Length: 3.6 in.
Power: 1-4x
Obj. Dia.: 24mm
Main Dia.: 30mm
Exit Pupil: 13-6mm
Field of View: 110-36ft @ 100yds
Twilight Factor: 4.9-9.8
Eye Relief: 3.6 in.
Features: Illuminated BTR-1 reticle; first focal plane; Throw Down PCL lever for power changes; fully multi-coated optics; holdovers out to 500 yds; target turrets; matte finish
MSRP $280.95

BUSHNELL AR OPTICS 1-4X24MM THROW DOWN PCL

BUSHNELL AR OPTICS 2-7X32MM RIMFIRE

Weight: 19.6 oz.
Length: 11.3 in.
Power: 2-7x
Obj. Dia.: 32mm
Main Dia.: 1 in.
Exit Pupil: 13.5-4.6mm
Field of View: 50-17ft @ 100yds
Twilight Factor: 8-15
Eye Relief: 3.7 in.
Features: Target turrets; Drop Zone 22 LR BDC reticle; fully multi-coated optics; matte finish
MSRP $209.95

BUSHNELL AR OPTICS 2-7X32MM RIMFIRE

BUSHNELL AR OPTICS 3-12X40MM
Weight: 21.3 oz.
Length: 12 in.
Power: 3-12x
Obj. Dia.: 40mm
Main Dia.: 1 in.
Exit Pupil: 13.7-3.7mm
Field of View: 33-11ft @ 100yds
Twilight Factor: 11-21.9
Eye Relief: 3.7 in.
Features: Target turrets; side parallax adjustment; Drop Zone 223 BDC reticle; second focal plane; fully multi-coated optics; 600 yard range; matte finish
MSRP. $280.95

BUSHNELL AR OPTICS 4.5-18X40MM
Weight: 21.5 oz.
Length: 12.4 in.
Power: 4.5-18x
Obj. Dia.: 40mm
Main Dia.: 1 in.
Exit Pupil: 8.6-2.3mm
Field of View: 22-7.3ft @ 100yds
Twilight Factor: 13.4-26.8
Eye Relief: 3.7 in.
Features: Target turrets; side parallax adjustment; Drop Zone 223 BDC reticle; second focal plane; fully multi-coated optics; 600 yard range; matte finish
MSRP. $349.95

BUSHNELL ELITE TACTICAL 1-8.5X24MM
Weight: 23 oz.
Length: 10.2 in.
Power: 1-8.5x
Obj. Dia.: 24mm
Main Dia.: 34mm
Exit Pupil: 13.2-3.2mm
Field of View: 105-14ft @ 100yds
Twilight Factor: 4.9-14.3
Eye Relief: 3.5 in.
Features: Illuminated BTR-2 reticle; first focal plane; .1 Mil click value; eleven brightness settings; T-Lok turrets; black matte finish
MSRP. $2149.95

BUSHNELL AR OPTICS
3-12X40MM

BUSHNELL AR OPTICS 4.5-18X40MM

BUSHNELL ELITE
TACTICAL 1-8.5X24MM

NEW PRODUCTS

BUSHNELL ELITE TACTICAL 4.5-30X50MM XRS

Weight: 37 oz.
Length: 10.2 in.
Power: 4.5-30x
Obj. Dia.: 50mm
Main Dia.: 34mm
Exit Pupil: 9-1.7mm
Field of View: 24-3.6ft @ 100yds
Twilight Factor: 15-38.7
Eye Relief: 3.7 in.
Features: T-Lok locking target turrets; Z-Lok zero stop; G2 reticle; first focal plane; side parallax adjustment; 1. Mil Clicks, 10 Mils/rev; blacked-out finish
MSRP $3252.95

BUSHNELL ELITE TACTICAL
4.5-30X50MM XRS

BUSHNELL ELITE TACTICAL ERS 3.5-21X50MM

Weight: 35 oz.
Length: 13 in.
Power: 3.5-21x
Obj. Dia.: 50mm
Main Dia.: 34mm
Exit Pupil: 10-2.4mm
Field of View: 26-5ft @ 100yds
Twilight Factor: 13.2-32.4
Eye Relief: 3.7 in.
Features: T-Lok locking turrets; Z-Lok zero stop; G2 reticle; first focal plane; side parallax adjustment; 1. Mil Clicks, 10 rev; available in matte black or flat dark earth finishes
MSRP $2975.95

BUSHNELL ELITE TACTICAL ERS
3.5-21X50MM

CARL ZEISS SPORTS OPTICS CONQUEST HD5 2-10X42MM

Weight: 17.5 oz.
Length: 13.19 in.
Power: 2-10x
Obj. Dia.: 50mm
Main Dia.: 25.4mm
Exit Pupil: 10.6-4.2mm
Field of View: 52-10ft @ 100yds
Twilight Factor: 6.5-20.5
Eye Relief: 3.5 in.
Features: Versatile in close encounters from cover to mid-range; parallax free to 100yds; available in z-Plex reticle, Rapid-Z 600, or standard hunting turrets; matte finish
MSRP . . . . $889–$972

CARL ZEISS SPORTS OPTICS
CONQUEST HD5 2-10X42MM

CARL ZEISS SPORTS OPTICS
CONQUEST HD5 5-25X50MM

CARL ZEISS SPORTS OPTICS CONQUEST HD5 3-15X42MM

Weight: 18.4 oz.
Length: 13.8 in.
Power: 3-15x
Obj. Dia.: 50mm
Main Dia.: 25.4mm
Exit Pupil: 10-2.8mm
Field of View: 35-7ft @ 100yds
Twilight Factor: 9.5-25.1
Eye Relief: 3.5 in.
Features: Mid- to long-range; low profile; parallax adjustment; Z-Plex reticle; hunting turret or lockable target turret; available Rapid-Z 600 or 800 reticle for hunting turret; most versatile of HD5 line; matte finish
MSRP . . . . $999–$1111

CARL ZEISS SPORTS OPTICS CONQUEST HD5 5-25X50MM

Weight: 26.6 oz.
Length: 14 in.
Power: 5-25x
Obj. Dia.: 60mm
Main Dia.: 25.4mm
Exit Pupil: 8.5-2mm
Field of View: 21-4.2ft @ 100yds
Twilight Factor: 14.5-35.4
Eye Relief: 3.5 in.
Features: Mid- to extra-long range; wide magnification range provide flexibility; side parallax adjustment; Z-Plex reticle with lockable target turret, Rapid-Z 800 with hunting turret, Rapid-Z 1000 with lockable target turret, or Rapid-Z Varmint reticle and hunting turret; matte finish
MSRP . . . . $1111–$1194

CARL ZEISS SPORTS OPTICS
CONQUEST HD5 3-15X42MM

CARL ZEISS SPORTS
OPTICS TERRA 3X
3-9X42MM

CARL ZEISS SPORTS OPTICS TERRA 3X 3-9X42MM

Weight: 14.8 oz.
Length: 12.4 in.
Power: 3-9x
Obj. Dia.: 42mm
Main Dia.: 25.4mm
Exit Pupil: 13.8-4.6mm
Field of View: 35.9-12.3ft @ 100yds
Twilight Factor: 11.2-19.4
Eye Relief: 3.5 in.
Features: MC anti-reflective coatings; standard Z-Plex or RZ 600 and 800 ballistic reticles available; all-purpose scope; larger objective for better low light situations; waterproof; matte finish
MSRP . . . . $444–$499

NEW Products: **Optics**

LEICA ERI 3-12X50MM RIFLESCOPE

Weight: 21.9 oz.
Length: 13.4 in.
Power: 3-12x
Obj. Dia.: 50mm
Main Dia.: 30mm
Exit Pupil: 14.9-4.1mm
Field of View: 35-10ft @ 100yds
Twilight Factor: 12.2-24.5
Eye Relief: 4 in.
Features: Illuminated reticle; four reticle options; optional rapid reticle adjustment; matte finish
MSRP **$1979**

LEICA ERI 3-12X50MM RIFLESCOPE

LEUPOLD MARK 6 1-6X20MM

LEUPOLD MARK 6 1-6X20MM

Weight: 17 oz.
Length: 10.3 in.
Power: 1-6x
Obj. Dia.: 20mm
Main Dia.: 1.34 in.
Exit Pupil: 10.2-3.3mm
Field of View: 103.2-17.4ft @ 100yds
Twilight Factor: 4.5-11
Eye Relief: 3.7 in.
Features: Xtended Twilight Lens System with Diamond Coat 2; illuminated front focal plane reticles; zerolock adjustments with available BDC; waterproof; fogproof; matte finish
MSRP **$2439.99**

LEUPOLD MARK 6 3-18X44MM

Weight: 23.6 oz.
Length: 11.9 in.
Power: 3-18x
Obj. Dia.: 44mm
Main Dia.: 1.34 in.
Exit Pupil: 10.3-2.4mm
Field of View: 36.8-6.3ft @ 100yds
Twilight Factor: 11.5-28.1
Eye Relief: 3.8–3.9 in.
Features: Xtended Twilight Lens System with Diamond Coat 2; M5B2 Autolocking Pinch & Turn; Elevation Zero Stop with Revolution Indicator; factory or custom quick change BDC rings available; waterproof; matte finish
MSRP **$2749.99**

LEUPOLD MARK 6 3-18X44MM

LEUPOLD VX6 2-12X42MM IR

LEUPOLD VX6 2-12X42MM IR
Weight: 17.8 oz.
Length: 12.5 in.
Power: 2-12x
Obj. Dia.: 42mm
Main Dia.: 1.18 in.
Exit Pupil: 10-3.5mm
Field of View: 57.5-10.2ft @ 100yds
Twilight Factor: 9.2-22.4
Eye Relief: 3.8 in.
Features: Xtended Twilight lens;

Diamond Coat 2 and Edge Blackened Lenses; lead-free optical design; FIREDOT illumination; waterproof; fogproof; matte finish
MSRP **$1249.99**

LEUPOLD VX6 3-18X50MM
Weight: 20.7 oz.
Length: 13.5 in.
Power: 3-18x
Obj. Dia.: 50mm

Main Dia.: 1.18 in.
Exit Pupil: 10-2.4mm
Field of View: 75.9-13.7ft @ 100yds
Twilight Factor: 12.2-30
Eye Relief: 3.7 in.
Features: Xtended Twilight lens; Diamond Coat 2 and Edge Blackened Lenses; lead-free optical design; Motion Sensor Technology (MST); FIREDOT illumination; waterproof; fogproof; matte finish
From: **$1374.99**

LEUPOLD VX6 3-18X50MM

MINOX ZE 5I 1-5X24MM
Weight: 16.9 oz.
Length: 11.2 in.
Power: 1-5x
Obj. Dia.: 24mm
Main Dia.: 30mm
Exit Pupil: 11.4-4.8mm
Field of View: 110.6-23.1ft @ 100yds
Twilight Factor: 4.9-11
Eye Relief: 3.94 in.
Features: Illuminated central red-dot with eleven brightness settings; automatic shut down to conserve battery; German A4, BDC, and Dot reticles available; finished with Minox's M* coating; waterproof; shockproof; Z-rail mount
MSRP **$1649**

MINOX ZE 5I 1-5X24MM

MINOX ZE 5I 2-10X50MM

Weight: 22.9 oz.
Length: 13.2 in.
Power: 2-10x
Obj. Dia.: 50mm
Main Dia.: 30mm
Exit Pupil: 11.4-5.1mm
Field of View: 55.2-11.5ft @ 100yds
Twilight Factor: 10-22.4
Eye Relief: 3.94 in.
Features: Illuminated central red-dot with eleven brightness settings; automatic shut down to conserve battery; German A4, BDC, and Dot reticles available; finished with Minox's M* coating; waterproof; shockproof; Z-rail mount
MSRP **$1849**

MINOX ZE 5I 2-10X50MM

MINOX ZE 5I 3-15X56MM

MINOX ZE 5I 5-25X56MM

MINOX ZE 5I 3-15X56MM

Weight: 26.1 oz.
Length: 14.6 in.
Power: 3-15x
Obj. Dia.: 56mm
Main Dia.: 30mm
Exit Pupil: 11.4-3.8mm
Field of View: 36.3-7.6ft @ 100yds
Twilight Factor: 13-29
Eye Relief: 3.94 in.
Features: Illuminated central red-dot with eleven brightness settings; automatic shut down to conserve battery; German A4, BDC, and Dot reticles available; finished with Minox's M* coating; waterproof; shockproof; Z-rail mount
MSRP **$1949**

MINOX ZE 5I 5-25X56MM

Weight: 27.9 oz.
Length: 16.9 in.
Power: 5-25x
Obj. Dia.: 56mm
Main Dia.: 30mm
Exit Pupil: 10.9-2.5mm
Field of View: 21.6-4.5ft @100yds
Twilight Factor: 16.7-37.4
Eye Relief: 3.94 in.
Features: Illuminated central red-dot with eleven brightness settings; automatic shut down to conserve battery; German A4, BDC, and Dot reticles available; finished with Minox's M* coating; waterproof; shockproof; Z-rail mount
MSRP **$2049**

NIGHTFORCE OPTICS, INC. 5-25X56MM ADVANCED TACTICAL RIFLESCOPE (ATACR)

Weight: 38 oz.
Length: 14.3 in.
Power: 5-25x
Obj. Dia.: 56mm
Main Dia.: 34mm
Exit Pupil: 10.52-2.28mm
Field of View: 17.96-4.92ft @ 100yds
Twilight Factor: 16.7-37.4
Eye Relief: 3.54 in.
Features: Fully multi-coated ED glass; ZeroStop comes standard; available in MOAR and MIL-R reticles; 120 MOA/34.9Mils elevation adjustment; matte finish
From: **$2328**

NIGHTFORCE OPTICS, INC. 5-25X56MM
ADVANCED TACTICAL RIFLESCOPE (ATACR)

NIGHTFORCE OPTICS, INC. 5-25X56MM B.E.A.S.T.

Weight: 39 oz.
Length: 15.37 in.
Power: 5-25x
Obj. Dia.: 56mm
Main Dia.: 34mm
Exit Pupil: 8.3-2.3mm
Field of View: 18.7-4.92ft @ 100yds
Twilight Factor: 16.7-37.4
Eye Relief: 3.35–3.54 in.
Features: First focal plane precision; Nightforce Digillum illumination; 90%+ light transmission; i4F intelligent four-function elevation control, ZeroStop system; XtremeSpeed adjustments; available with MIL-R, MOAR, MD2.0, TReMoR, and H59 reticles; matte finish
From: . . . . **$3298–$3783**

NIGHTFORCE OPTICS, INC.
5-25X56MM B.E.A.S.T.

NIGHTFORCE OPTICS, INC. 15-55X52MM COMPETITION

Weight: 27.87 oz.
Length: 16.2 in.
Power: 15-55x
Obj. Dia.: 52mm
Main Dia.: 30mm
Exit Pupil: 3.54-.93mm
Field of View: 6.91-1.83ft @ 100yds
Twilight Factor: 27.9-53.5
Eye Relief: 3.15 in.
Features: ED glass; 92% light transmission; fast-focus European-style eyepiece; side parallax adjustment; available with CTR-1 or DDR reticles; available in matte and silver
From: **$2231**

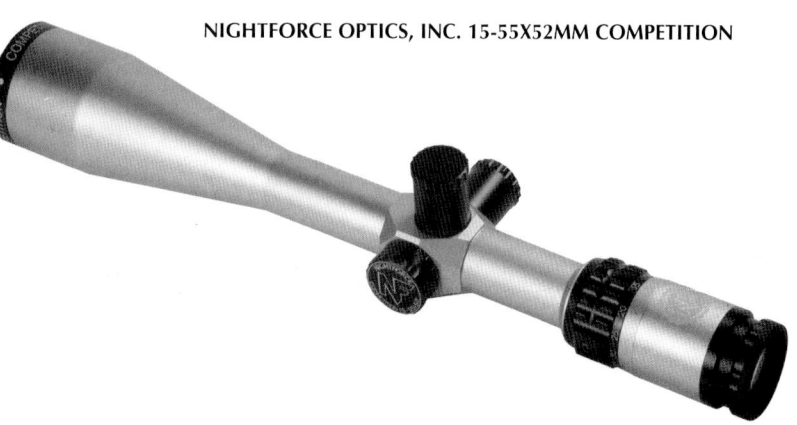

NIGHTFORCE OPTICS, INC. 15-55X52MM COMPETITION

NIKON INLINE XR 3-9X40MM BDC 300

Weight: 13.8 oz.
Length: 11.3 in.
Power: 3-9x
Obj. Dia.: 40mm
Main Dia.: 1 in.
Exit Pupil: 4.4-13.3mm
Field of View: 8.4-25.2ft @ 100yds
Twilight Factor: 11-19
Eye Relief: 5 in.
Features: Long range muzzleloader; BDC 300 reticle; ¼-MOA adjustments; Spring-Loaded Zero-Reset Turrets; silver finish; waterproof; fogproof; shockproof
From:.................$199.95

NIKON MONARCH 3 1-4X20MM BDC

Weight: 12.2 oz.
Length: 10.35 in.
Power: 1-4x
Obj. Dia.: 20mm
Main Dia.: 1 in.
Exit Pupil: 5-20mm
Field of View: 23.1-92.9ft @ 100yds
Twilight Factor: 4.5-8.9
Eye Relief: 4 in.
Features: BDC reticle; designed for big game hunting; Spot On Ballistic Match technology; Spring Loaded Instant Zero-Reset Turrets; quick-focus eyepiece; enhanced mount ring spacing; waterproof; fogproof
MSRP.................$279.95

NIKON MONARCH 3 4-16X42MM SIDE FOCUS MILDOT

Weight: 19 oz.
Length: 13.5 in.
Power: 4-16x
Obj. Dia.: 42mm
Main Dia.: 1 in.
Exit Pupil: 2.6-10.5mm
Field of View: 6.3-25.2ft @ 100yds
Twilight Factor: 13-25.9
Eye Relief: 4 in.
Features: Mildot reticle; Max Adj. 40 MOA; waterproof; fogproof; Spring Loaded Instant Zero-Reset Turrets; Spot On Ballistic Match technology; Monarch 3 Eyebox technology; matte finish
MSRP.................$469.95

NIKON INLINE XR 3-9X40MM BDC 300

NIKON MONARCH 3 1-4X20MM BDC

NIKON MONARCH 3 4-16X42MM SIDE FOCUS MILDOT

NIKON P-300 BLK
2-7X32MM BDC SUPERSUB

NIKON PROSTAFF 5 2.5-
10X50MM MATTE BDC

NIKON PROSTAFF 5 3.5-
14X50MM ILLUMINATED
NIKOPLEX

NIKON P-300 BLK 2-7X32MM BDC SUPERSUB

Weight: 16.1 oz.
Length: 11.5 in.
Power: 2-7x
Obj. Dia.: 32mm
Main Dia.: 1 in.
Exit Pupil: 4.6-16mm
Field of View: 12.7-44.5ft @ 100yds
Twilight Factor: 8-15
Eye Relief: 3.8 in.
Features: BDC SuperSub reticle; optimized for use with supersonic and subsonic ammo; Max Adj. 80 MOA; waterproof; fogproof; matte black
MSRP..................**$199.95**

NIKON PROSTAFF 5 2.5-10X50MM MATTE BDC

Weight: 18 oz.
Length: 13.7 in.
Power: 2.5-10x
Obj. Dia.: 50mm
Main Dia.: 1 in.
Exit Pupil: 5-20mm
Field of View: 9.9-40.4ft @ 100yds
Twilight Factor: 11.2-22.4
Eye Relief: 4 in.
Features: Hand-turn reticle adjustments with Spring-Loaded Zero-Reset turrets; BDC reticle; multi-coated optics; Max Adj. 70 MOA; waterproof; fogproof; parallax setting
MSRP..................**$379.95**

NIKON PROSTAFF 5 3.5-14X50MM ILLUMINATED NIKOPLEX

Weight: 19.9 oz.
Length: 14.3 in.
Power: 3.5-14x
Obj. Dia.: 50mm
Main Dia.: 1 in.
Exit Pupil: 2.9-14.3mm
Field of View: 7.2-28.6ft @ 100yds
Twilight Factor: 13.2-26.5
Eye Relief: 4 in.
Features: Illuminated reticle; hand-turn reticle adjustments with Spring-Loaded Zero-Reset turrets; waterproof; fogproof; parallax adjustment; matte finish
MSRP..................**$569.95**

REDFIELD (LEUPOLD) BATTLEZONE 3-9X42MM

Weight: 14.8 oz.
Length: 12.4 in.
Power: 3-8.6x
Obj. Dia.: 42mm
Main Dia.: 1 in.
Exit Pupil: 14.2-14.9mm
Field of View: 32.9-11.4ft @ 100yds
Twilight Factor: 11.2-19
Eye Relief: 3.5 in.
Features: Pop-up resettable ¼ MOA finger-click adjustments; BDC dials; TAC-MOA Reticle Matches Adjustments; waterproof; fogproof; shockproof; Redfield Lifetime Warranty; matte finish
From:................**$199.99**

REDFIELD (LEUPOLD) BATTLEZONE 3-9X42MM

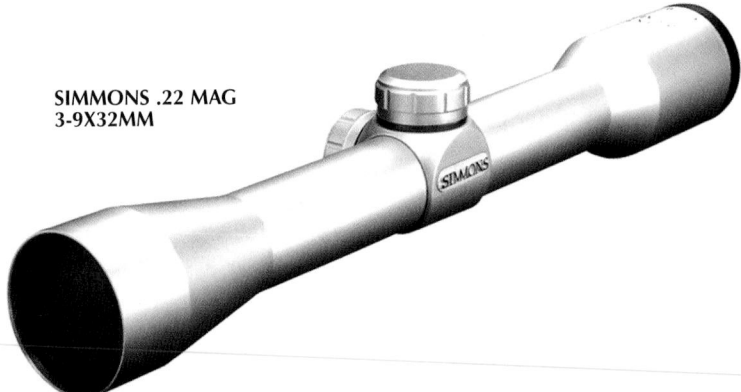

SIMMONS .22 MAG
3-9X32MM

SIMMONS .22 MAG 3-9X32MM

Weight: 10 oz.
Length: 12 in.
Power: 3-9x
Obj. Dia.: 32mm
Main Dia.: 1 in.
Exit Pupil: 10.7-3.6mm
Field of View: 31.4-10.5ft @ 100yds
Twilight Factor: 9.8-17
Eye Relief: 3.75 in.
Features: One piece tube construction; fully coated optics; waterproof; fogproof; shockproof; Truplex reticle; RF Rings with available Adjustable Objective; also available in 4x32; matte or silver finish
From:...........**$70.95–$106.95**

SIMMONS 8-POINT 3-9X40MM

Weight: 10 oz.
Length: 13.125 in.
Power: 3-9x
Obj. Dia.: 40mm
Main Dia.: 1 in.
Exit Pupil: 10.7-3.6mm
Field of View: 31.4-10.5ft @ 100yds
Twilight Factor: 11-19
Eye Relief: 3.75 in.
Features: TrueZero fingertip adjustments; Quick Target Acquisition; fully coated optics; waterproof; fogproof; recoilproof; Truplex reticle; also available in 4x32, 3-9x32, and 3-9x50; matte finish
From:................**$70.95**

SIMMONS 8-POINT 3-9X40MM

SIMMONS PROSPORT 4-12X50MM

Weight: 14 oz.
Length: 13 in.
Power: 4-12x
Obj. Dia.: 50mm
Main Dia.: 1 in.
Exit Pupil: 12.5-4.2mm
Field of View: 23.8-8.2ft @ 100yds
Twilight Factor: 14.1-24.5
Eye Relief: 3.75 in.
Features: Adjustable Objective (AO); fully coated optics; TrueZero fingertip adjustments; Quick Target Acquisition eyepiece with Fast Focus; waterproof; fogproof; recoilproof; Truplex reticle; also available in 3-9x40, 3-9x50, 4-12x40 (AO), and 6-18x50 (AO); matte finish with silver or Realtree available for the 3-9x40 model
From:.................$158.95

SIMMONS PROSPORT 4-12X50MM

TRIJICON 3X30MM ACOG WITH 300 AAC BLACKOUT RETICLE

TRIJICON 3X30MM ACOG WITH 300 AAC BLACKOUT RETICLE

Weight: 11.64 oz.
Length: 6.1 in.
Power: 3x
Obj. Dia.: 30mm
Main Dia.: N/A
Exit Pupil: 10mm
Field of View: 19.3ft @ 100yds
Twilight Factor: 9.5
Eye Relief: 1.9 in.
Features: TA60 Mount; designed for law enforcement and military applications; 300 AAC Blackout Ballistic Reticle for subsonic and supersonic rounds; bullet drop compensator; Bindon Aiming Concept (BAC), fiber optics & tritium illuminated; available with amber, green, or red crosshair reticle
MSRP...................$1257

TRIJICON 3.5X35MM ACOG NICKEL BORON DUAL ILLUMINATED .223 BALLISTIC RETICLE

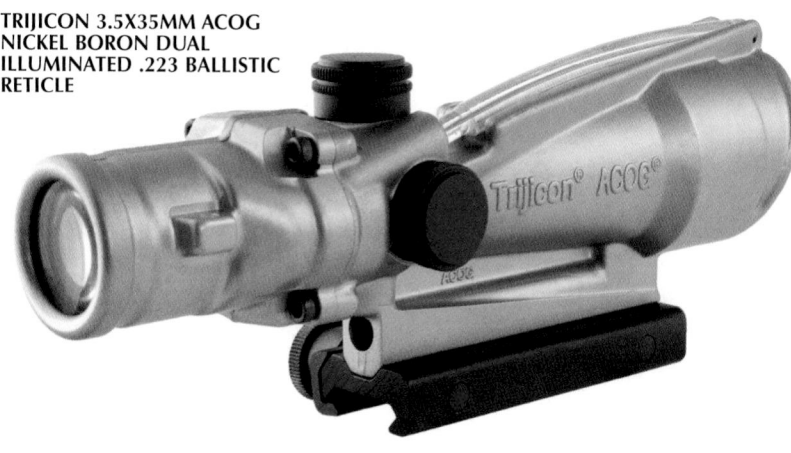

TRIJICON 3.5X35MM ACOG NICKEL BORON DUAL ILLUMINATED .223 BALLISTIC RETICLE

Weight: 14 oz.
Length: 8 in.
Power: 3.5x
Obj. Dia.: 35mm
Main Dia.: N/A
Exit Pupil: 10mm
Field of View: 28.9ft @ 100yds
Twilight Factor: 11.1
Eye Relief: 2.39 in.
Features: Nickel Boron plating; red or green Chevron BAC reticle; Flat Top Adapter; range up to 800 meters; 5.53 MOA; fiber optics & tritium illumination; bullet drop compensator; available in 4x32, and with Horseshoe or Crosshair reticle
MSRP...................$1476

NEW Products: **Optics**

TRIJICON VCOG 1-6X24MM RIFLESCOPE

Weight: 23.2 oz.
Length: 10.05 in.
Power: 1-6x
Obj. Dia.: 24mm
Main Dia.: N/A
Exit Pupil: 10.4-3.8mm
Field of View: 95-15.9ft @ 100yds
Twilight Factor: 12
Eye Relief: 4 in.
Features: Designed and built in the U.S.; Mil Spec, hard-coat finish; 90 MOA of windage and elevation adjustment; fully multi-coated lenses; waterproof; seven different reticle choices, between centered crosshair and horseshoe/dot reticle; red illuminated reticle; six brightness settings; matte finish
MSRP **$2270**

TRIJICON VCOG 1-6X24MM RIFLESCOPE

WEAVER GRAND SLAM 3-12X50MM

Weight: 16.6 oz.
Length: 12.6 in.
Power: 3-12x
Obj. Dia.: 50mm
Main Dia.: 1 in.
Exit Pupil: 13.6-4.2mm
Field of View: 32.7-8.4ft @ 100yds
Twilight Factor: 12.2-24.5
Eye Relief: 3.19–3.46 in.
Features: 4x magnification ranges; ground, fully multi-coated lenses; fogproof; side focus parallax adjustments on select models; multiple reticle options; available in 2-8x36, 3-12x42, and 4-16x44; matte finish
MSRP . . . . **$518.95–$530.95**

WEAVER GRAND SLAM 3-12X50MM

WEAVER KASPA TACTICAL 1-4X24MM

Weight: N/A
Length: 10.5 in.
Power: 1-4x
Obj. Dia.: 24mm
Main Dia.: 30mm
Exit Pupil: 6-13mm
Field of View: 27-109ft @ 100yds
Twilight Factor: 4.9-9.8
Eye Relief: 3.54–4 in.
Features: Illuminated Dual-X reticle; tactical 30 mm tube; ¼" MOA adjustments; fully multi-coated lenses; fogproof; matte finish
MSRP **$329.99**

WEAVER KASPA TACTICAL 1-4X24MM

SIGHTS

AIMPOINT 9000SC
Weight: 7.4 oz.
Length: 6.3 in.
Obj. Dia.: 38mm
Features: Ideal for short length action rifles, semi-automatic firearms, and magnum handguns; ACET technology for longer battery life; available in 2 or 4 MOA dot sizes; two-ring configuration for mounting; waterproof; matte finish
From: **$419**

AIMPOINT 9000SC

BROWNING 2-1 HUNTING SIGHTS
Features: Magnetic base attaches to shotgun rib; features both red and green LitePipes; comes with both round and triangular LitePipe systems; designed for guns with narrow ribs
MSRP **$39**

BROWNING 2-1 HUNTING SIGHTS

BURRIS AR-132
Weight: 11.5 oz.
Length: 5.25 in.
Power: 1x
Obj. Dia.: 32mm
Field of View: 50ft @ 100yds
Eye Relief: 2.5 in.
Features: 4 MOA red dot sight; integrated lens covers; three Picatinny rail mounting brackets; tethered windage and elevation caps; black matte finish; Max Adj. 60 MOA; one-year warranty
MSRP **$422**

BURRIS AR-132

BURRIS AR-536
Weight: 18.75 oz.
Length: 5.75 in.
Power: 5x
Obj. Dia.: 36mm
Field of View: 20ft @ 100yds
Eye Relief: 2.5–3.5 in.
Features: Ballistic/CQTM lighted reticle; 600 yard range; multi-coated lenses; adjutable diopter; three Picatinny rail mounting points; black matte finish; Max Adj. 60 MOA; one-year warranty
MSRP **$602**

BURRIS AR-536

BUSHNELL FIRST STRIKE RED DOT

BUSHNELL 1X MP ZOMBIE ASSAULT SIGHT
Power: 1x
Features: Illuminated T-Dot reticle; five brightness settings; red or green reticle display; multi-coated optics for transition and glare; waterproof; fogproof; shockproof
MSRP **$199.99**

BUSHNELL 1X MP ZOMBIE ASSAULT SIGHT

BUSHNELL FIRST STRIKE RED DOT
Weight: 2.1 oz.
Length: 2.4 in.
Field of View: unlimited
Eye Relief: unlimited
Features: 5 MOA red dot reticle; multi-coated optics; self-regulating brightness; integrated mount; waterproof; fogproof; shockproof; matte finish
MSRP **$149.99**

BUSHNELL AR OPTICS 1X28MM RED DOT
Weight: 6 oz.
Length: 5.5 in.
Power: 1x
Obj. Dia.: 28mm
Exit Pupil: 28mm
Field of View: 68ft @ 100yds
Eye Relief: unlimited
Features: 6 MOA red dot sight; eleven brightness settings; tactical rings for variably mounts and heights; matte finish
MSRP   **$116.95**

BUSHNELL AR OPTICS 1X28MM RED DOT

NEW Products: **Optics**

BUSHNELL SCOUT DX 1000

Weight: 6.6 oz.
Power: 6x
Features: Built-in inclinometer; ARC Bow and Rifle Modes; Variable Sight-in; range up to 1,000yds; diopter adjustment; waterproof; compatible with magnetic attachment system; available in black or RealTree AP
MSRP **$476.95**

BUSHNELL TRS-25 HIRISE

Weight: 6.3 oz.
Length: 2.4 in.
Power: 1x
Obj. Dia.: 25mm
Exit Pupil: 22mm
Field of View: unlimited
Eye Relief: unlimited
Features: 3 MOA red dot reticle; eleven brightness settings; multi-coated; waterproof; fogproof; shockproof; riser block; matte finish
MSRP **$129.99**

CABELA'S TACTICAL RED DOT SIGHT

Features: Bullet-drop-compensating reticle; reticle features three selectable colors; five adjustable brightness settings; multi-coated optics for low-light shooting; waterproof; shockproof; runs up to 300 hours on one battery
MSRP **$299.99**

BUSHNELL SCOUT DX 1000

BUSHNELL TRS-25 HIRISE

CABELA'S TACTICAL REFLEX SIGHT

Features: Automatically turns on when cap is lifted; automatic reticle-brightness control; multi-coated optics with 5-MOA center-dot reticle; waterproof; shockproof; mounts to any MIL-STD-1913 rail; runs for up to 300 hours on one battery
MSRP **$149.99**

EOTECH XPS2-300 BLACKOUT

Weight: 8 oz.
Length: 3.5 in.
Power: 1x
Field of View: 90ft @100yds
Eye Relief: unlimited
Features: 2-dot ballistic drop reticle for either subsonic or supersonic rounds; mounts to 1 in. Weaver on MIL-

STD-1913 rail; repeatable to within 1 MOA when remounting; runs 600 continuous hours; 65 MOA Ring with (2) 1 MOA aiming dots; waterproof to 10ft; fogproof; 20 brightness settings; anti-glare coating
MSRP **$549**

EOTECH XPS2-300 BLACKOUT

CABELA'S TACTICAL RED DOT SIGHT

CABELA'S TACTICAL REFLEX SIGHT

LEICA RANGEMASTER CRF 1000-R

Weight: 7.8 oz.
Length: 4.4 in.
Power: 7x
Obj. Dia.: 24mm
Field of View: 345ft @ 100yds
Features: Starter model; basic ballistic funtionality; measures linear and horizontal distance; integrated diopter compensation; automatic brightness control; LED display; angle-of-inclination display
MSRP $599

LEICA RANGEMASTER CRF 1600-B

Weight: 8.1 oz.
Length: 4.4 in.
Power: 7x
Obj. Dia.: 24mm
Field of View: 345ft @ 100yds
Features: Point-of-aim correction, angle, temperature, and barometric pressure readings; ABC intelligent ballistics program; LED display; range up to 1600 yds; waterproof
MSRP $799

LUCID M7 MICRO RED DOT

Weight: 4.6 oz.
Obj. Dia.: 21mm
Field of View: 48ft @ 100yds
Eye Relief: unlimited
Features: 2MOA dot 25MOA circle reticle; auto brightness sensor; auto shut off; seven brightness levels; capped and leashed turrets; ½ MOA adjustments; parallax free; waterproof; fogproof; shockproof; cast aluminum; Limited Lifetime Warranty
MSRP $229

LEICA RANGEMASTER
CRF 1000-R

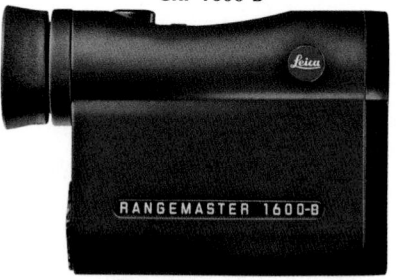

LEICA RANGEMASTER
CRF 1600-B

LUCID M7 MICRO RED DOT

NIKON PROSTAFF 7 LASER RANGEFINDER

Weight: 5.8 oz.
Length: 4.4 in.
Power: 6x
Obj. Dia.: 21mm
Exit Pupil: 3.5mm
Field of View: 11-600yds
Eye Relief: 0.7 in.
Features: Multi-coated optics; waterproof; fogproof; Tru Target Technology; switchable display; Nikon's ID Technology; angle compensation
MSRP $299.95

MILLETT OPTICS SCOPES (BUSHNELL) SP SERIES RED DOT

Features: Precision-click adjustments; dot intensity control with eleven settings; waterproof; shockproof; available with 1 in. or 30mm tube; available 3Min Dot, 5Min Dot, and 3, 5, 8, 10 Min Multi Dot; available in matte or silver
MSRP . . . . $86.95–$118.95

PENTAX RD MINI WATERPROOF DOT SIGHT

Weight: 4.4 oz.
Field of View: 41.8ft @ 100yds
Features: 5 MOA dot size; waterproof and nitrogen filled; seven brightness settings; parallax-free; black matte finish
From: $98.49

MILLETT
OPTICS SCOPES
(BUSHNELL) SP
SERIES RED DOT

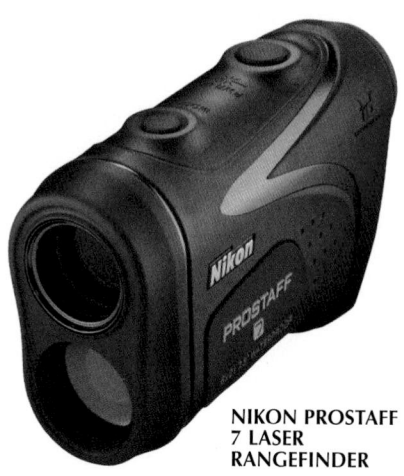

NIKON PROSTAFF
7 LASER
RANGEFINDER

PENTAX RD MINI
WATERPROOF
DOT SIGHT

NEW Products: Optics

PEDERSOLI FOLDING FRONT SIGHT

Features: Globe sight for long-range when raised, or fold down for built-in blade for close range; ball/detent locking mechanism; 3/8 in. dovetail base; 1/2 in. high
From: **$69.35**

PEDERSOLI FOLDING FRONT SIGHT

REDFIELD BY LEUPOLD COUNTERSTRIKE 1X30MM TACTICAL RED DOT

Weight: 14.8 oz.
Length: 5.9 in.
Power: 1x
Obj. Dia.: 30mm
Exit Pupil: 30mm
Eye Relief: unlimited
Features: Coin-click ½ MOA adjustments; tethered adjustment covers; 4 MOA red/green dot; auto shut off; up to 5,000 hour battery life; waterproof; fogproof; shockproof; Redfield "No Excuses" Warranty
From: **$179.99**

REDFIELD BY LEUPOLD COUNTERSTRIKE 1X30MM TACTICAL RED DOT

TRIJICON GLOCK SUPPRESSOR BRIGHT & TOUGH NIGHT SIGHTS

Features: Three-dot iron sights; shock-resistant design; increase night-fire accuracy by as much as 5x; fits the 17, 17L, 19, 22, 23, 24, 26, 27, 33, 34, 35, 38, and 39 Glock Models; available in black or white outline, with a green, orange, or yellow tritium lamp
MSRP **$145**

TRIJICON GLOCK SUPPRESSOR BRIGHT & TOUGH NIGHT SIGHTS

TRIJICON RMR 3.25MOA NICKEL BORON SIGHT

Weight: 1.2 oz.
Length: 45mm
Power: 1x
Features: LED illuminated; up to 2 years of typical battery use; aluminum housing; nickel boron plating; easy-to-use adjusters with audible clicks; also available in 7MOA Dual-Illuminated Amber Dot, 9MOA Dual-Illuminated Green Dot, and 12.9MOA Dual-Illuminated Green Triangle
MSRP **$644**

TRIJICON RMR 3.25MOA NICKEL BORON SIGHT

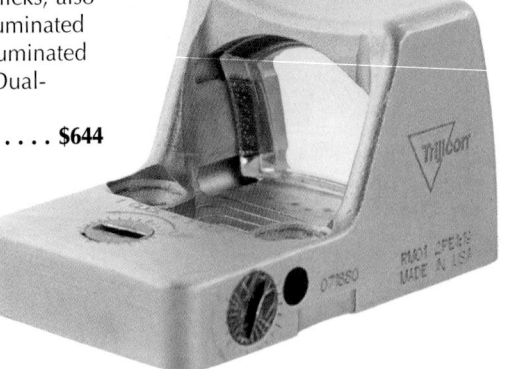

WEAVER MICRO DOT SIGHT

Weight: 2.8 oz.
Length: 1.9 in.
Power: 1x
Eye Relief: unlimited
Features: 4 MOA red dot reticle; matte finish; mounts to most firearms; adjustable brightness
MSRP **$108.45**

WEAVER MICRO DOT SIGHT

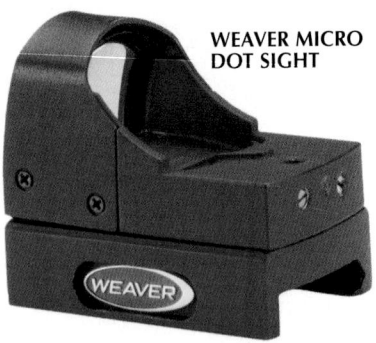

BARNES BULLETS TAC-XPD AMMUNITION

Features: Loaded with Barnes TAC-XP bullets, the all-copper construction and very large, deep hollow-point cavity expand, penetrate, and perform consistently and optimally for personal and home defense.

Available in: .380 Auto; 9mm Luger +P; .40 S&W; .45 Auto +P

Box 20: . . . . **$24.99–$29.99**

BARNES BULLETS TAC-XPD AMMUNITION

BRENNEKE USA MAGNUM CRUSH

Features: Delivers a force of more than 3.800ft/lbs, weighs a full 1 ½ ounce / 666 grains, and the flat trajectory is ideal for bigger game. Special coating to reduce lead fouling and broad ribs for optimum groove engagement.

Available in: 12 Ga. (3 in.)

Box 5: **$12.37**

BRENNEKE USA MAGNUM CRUSH

CCI AMMUNITION TROY LANDRY SIGNATURE SERIES

Features: Gator-tested performance endorsed by Troy Landry, clean-burning propellants, reliable cycling, and sure-fire CCI priming. The Mini-Mag is 36-grain, copper-plated hollow point; 1,260 fps. The Maxi-Mag is 40-grain, jacketed hollow point; 1,875 fps.

Available in: .22 LR Mini-Mag; .22 WMR Maxi-Mag

.22 LR Box 375: **$23.99–29.99**
.22 WMR Box 250: . . . **$46.99–$52.99**

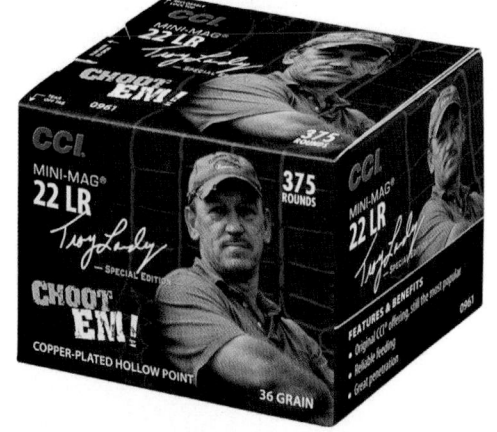

CCI AMMUNITION TROY LANDRY SIGNATURE SERIES

COR-BON AMMUNITION DPX THUNDER RANCH AMMUNITION

Features: Teamed up with Thunder Ranch Training Center for exclusive ammunition package. Solid Copper X Bullet, deep penetrating, barrier blind, impressive expansion, and environmentally friendly.

Available in: .38 Special +P 110GR; 9mm Luger 1115GR; .357 Mag. 125 GR; .40 S&W 140 GR; .45 Auto +P 185 GR

Box 20: . . . . **$33.53–$41.09**

COR-BON AMMUNITION DPX THUNDER RANCH AMMUNITION

NEW Products: **Ammunition**

ENVIRON-METAL HEVI DUTY HOME DEFENSE

Features: Frangible, non-toxic, low recoil home defense load. 00 buckshot loads coming soon.
Available in: 12 Ga. (2 ¾ in.) Shot sizes: 4
Box 5:.....................$8.99

FEDERAL PREMIUM HST (HANDGUN AMMUNITION)

Features: Provides near 100% weight retention through most barriers. Consistent expansion, optimum penetration, and superior terminal performance, it's specially designed hollow point won't plug while passing through a variety of barriers.
Available in: 9mm Luger, .40 S&W, .45 Auto
Box 20:............ $23.99–$25.99

FEDERAL PREMIUM WOODLEIGH HYDRO SOLID (RIFLE AMMUNITION)

Features: Provides safari hunters superb accuracy, consistent performance, and tremendous impact. Special heavy jackets provide excellent weight retention, up to 100% for solids.
Available in: 9.3x62 Mauser, 9.3x74 R, .370 Sako Mag. (Cape-Shok), .375 H&H Mag., .416 Rigby, .416 Rem. Mag., .458 Win. Mag., 458 Lott, .470 Nitro Express, .500 Nitro Express 3
Box 20:.......... $114.99–$212.99

ENVIRON-METAL HEVI DUTY HOME DEFENSE

FEDERAL PREMIUM HST (HANDGUN AMMUNITION)

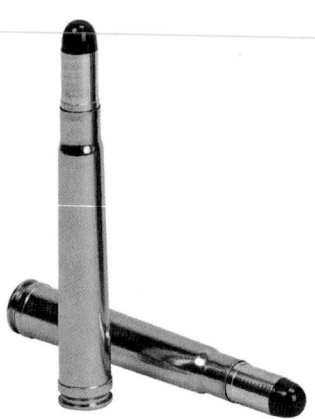

FEDERAL PREMIUM WOODLEIGH HYDRO SOLID (RIFLE AMMUNITION)

FEDERAL FUSION FUSION MSR

Features: Modern sporting rifles (MSRs) represent a very versatile class of firearms, handling a wide range of ammo and game. Shooters often build these rifles from the ground up and trick them out with accessories to match their specific needs. All-new Fusion® MSR loads provide that same degree of customization in ammunition.
Available in: .223 Rem., .308 Win., .338 Fed., 6.8 SPC
Box 20: . . . . **$20.99-$28.99**

FEDERAL FUSION
FUSION MSR

FEDERAL FUSION FUSION SP

Features: Real-world recoil can translate to inaccurate shooting and missed trophies. For this reason, bullet weights and velocities have been developed to be lethal on whitetails, without pounding the shooter.
Available in: .357 Mag., .41 Rem. Mag., .44 Rem. Mag., .454 Casull, .460 S&W, .500 S&W, 50 Action Express
Box 20: . . . . **$16.99–$38.49**

FEDERAL FUSION
FUSION SP

HORNADY AMERICAN WHITETAIL

Features: Loaded with Hornady InterLock Bullets, optimized loads specifically for deer hunting, and select propellants for greater consistency.
Available in: .243 Win.; 25-06 Rem.; .270 Win.; 7mm-08 Rem.; 7mm Rem. Mag; 30-30 Win.; .308 Win.; 30-06 Spfd.; .300 Win. Mag
Box 20: . . . . **$26.65–$38.33**

HORNADY AMERICAN
WHITETAIL

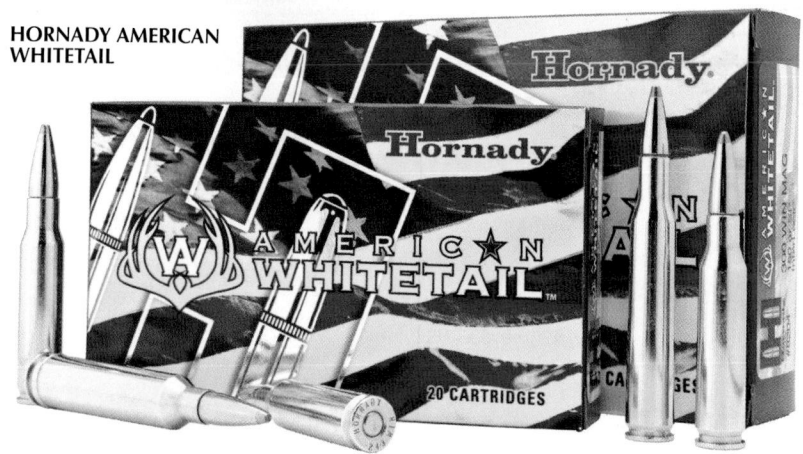

HORNADY HEAVY MAGNUM COYOTE

Features: Loaded with 1 ½ oz. of nickel plated lead shot in either a BB or 00 buckshot for close range predators. Features Hornady Versatite wad for more impact on target; 1,300 fps.
Available in: 12 Ga. (3 in., 00 buckshot or BB)
Box 10: **$17.08**

HORNADY HEAVY
MAGNUM COYOTE

NORMA AMERICAN PH

Features: In the "American" style, this line of ammunition features lighter bullets, higher muzzle velocity, and longer average ranges.

Available in: .222 Rem.; .223 Rem.; .243 Win.; .257 Roberts; 6.5 Jap; 6.5 Carcano; 6.5x55; 6.5-284; .270 Win.; .270 WSM; 7mm-08; .280 Rem.; 7mm Rem. Mag; .308 Win.; .30-06; .308 Norma Magnum; .300 Win. Mag; .300 WSM; .300 RUM; 7.65 Arg; 7.7 Jap; .338 Win. Mag; 9.3*62; 9.3*74R; .375 H&H Mag; .338 Lapua Mag; .257 Wby.; .270 Wby.; 7mm Wby.; .300 Wby.; .30-378 Wby.; .340 Wby.

From:............ **$38.34–$129.60**

NORMA AMERICAN PH

NOSLER DEFENSE HANDGUN AMMUNITION

Features: Bonded 'Performance' bullets for higher weight retention and maximum barrier penetration; either jacketed hollow point or polymer tipped configuration.

Available in: 9mm Luger +P; .40 S&W; 45 ACP +P

MSRP.....................**N/A**

NOSLER DEFENSE HANDGUN AMMUNITION

PMC AMMUNITION X-TAC MATCH

Features: X-TAC ammo performance comined with Sierra Bullets' ballistics, with a match grade .50 caliber bullet.

Available in: .223 Rem., .308 Win.

Box 20:........... **$27.99–$39.99**

PMC AMMUNITION X-TAC MATCH

REMINGTON AMMUNITION 300 AAC BLACKOUT

Features: A great 30-cal solution for the R-15 platform. It matches the ballistic power of the 7.62x39mm AK, but at 300 meters has 16.7% more energy. Optimal for sound and flash-suppressed fire, all in a low-recoiling package. Featuring waterproofed primers, crimped and cannelured open-tip match bullets, and a low-drag design.

Available in: .300 AAC Blackout

Box 20:........... **$15.29–$29.49**

REMINGTON AMMUNITION 300 AAC BLACKOUT

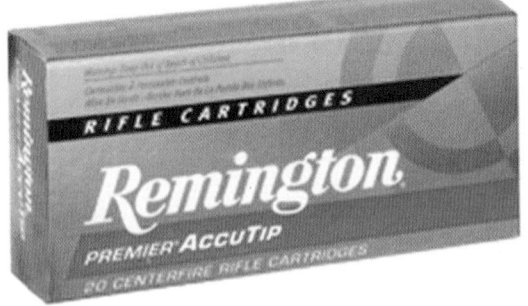

REMINGTON AMMUNITION HD ULTIMATE HOME DEFENSE

Features: Loaded with high-performance Brass Jacket Hollow Point (BJHP), these new rounds deliver massive expansion and deep penetration for ultimate stopping power. Premium nickel-plated cases resist corrosion and cycle dependably through extended storage.
Available in: .380 Auto, 9mm Luger, .38 Spl. +P, .40 S&W, .45 Auto
Box 20: **$21.99**

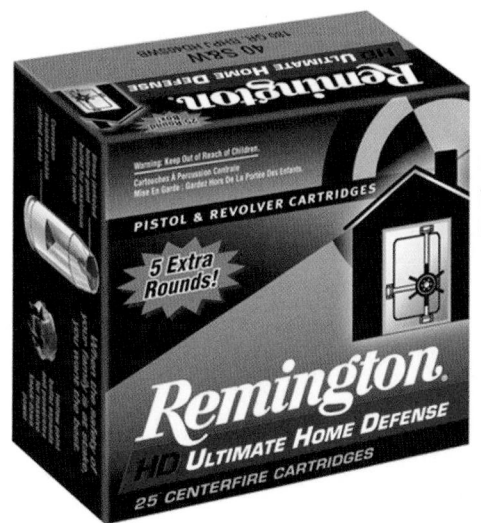

REMINGTON AMMUNITION HD ULTIMATE HOME DEFENSE

REMINGTON AMMUNITION HOG HAMMER

Features: Penetrating even the thickest-skinned pigs with a Barnes TSX® Bullet at its heart, the all copper construction provides for 28% deeper penetration than standard lead-core bullets. One of the toughest expanding bullets on the market, it offers near 100% weight-retention on-hog, while expanding rapidly to deliver devastating wound channels. Hog Hammer utilizes a flash-suppressed propellant for nighttime or low light hunts, and uses nickel-plated cases for reliable feeding in today's hog rifles.
Available in: .300 AAC Blackout, .223 Rem., .30 Rem. AR, .30-30 Win., .30-06 Spfd., .308 Win., .450 Bushmaster
Box 20: . . . . **$28.99–$43.99**

REMINGTON AMMUNITION HOG HAMMER

RWS EVOLUTION GREEN

Features: New lead-free Evolution Green bullets made of food-safe metal. Features a specially pre-fragmented front core and RWS Speed Tip bullet points for shock effect. Maximum knock-down power with a flat trajectory, for humane and successful hunting.
Available in: .30 R Blaser; .300 Win. Mag; .30-06; .308 Win.; 7mm Rem. Mag; 7x57 R; 7x64; 7x65 R; 8x57 JRS; 8x57 JS; 9,3x62; 9,3x74 R
MSRP . . . .**N/A**

RWS EVOLUTION GREEN

WINCHESTER AMMUNITION VARMINT X

Features: Polymer tip, alloy jacket, lead core, and rapid fragmentation.
Available in: .204 Ruger; .22-250 Rem.; .223 Rem.; .243 Win.
From: . . . .**$18.99–$25.99**

WINCHESTER AMMUNITION VARMINT X

NEW Products: MZ Ammunition

MUZZLELOADING BULLETS

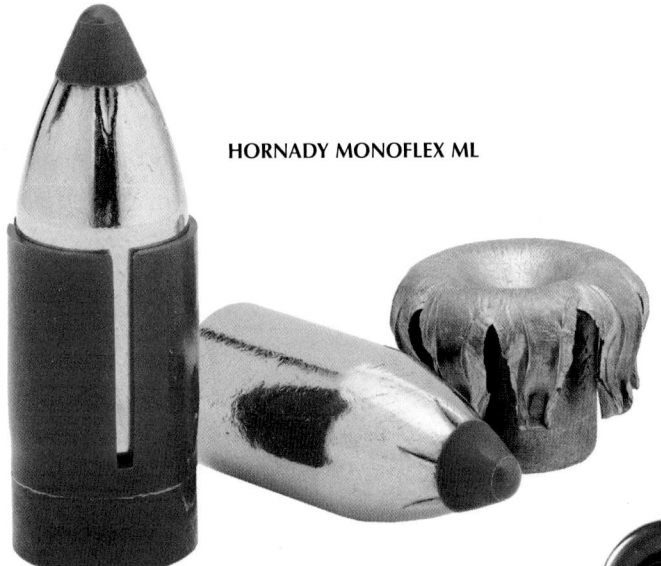

HORNADY MONOFLEX ML

HORNADY MONOFLEX ML

Features: Constructed with the Hornady Flex Tip and retaining 95% of its original weight, it's available in both a High Speed/Low Drag sabot and Lock-N-Load Speed Sabot.
Available in: .50 cal. sabot with .45 cal. (250 gr.) bullet
Box 20:. . . . . $24.84–$26.71

KNIGHT RIFLES BLOODLINE BULLETS

Features: Individually machined, double knurled bullets for increased visual blood trails.
Available in: .45 (185, 200 gr.); .50 (220, 250, 275, 300 gr.); .52 (220, 275, 300 gr.); .54 (325 gr.)
Box 20:. . . . . $25.99–$31.49

KNIGHT RIFLES BLOODLINE BULLETS

THOMPSON/CENTER SUPER 45 XR SABOTS

THOMPSON/CENTER SUPER 45 XR SABOTS

Features: Centerfire weight performance without the recoil, Super 45 XR sabots have a flatter trajectory, provide deep penetration, and nearly 2 times the expansion of its original diameter.
Available in: .45 (155, 180 gr.)
Box 30:. . . . . $25.36–$27.39

NEW Products: **Handloading Equipment**

POWDERS

ALLIANT POWDER RELODER 33

Features: Specifically designed for the .338 Lapua, this powder is also suited to a variety of large magnum rifle cartridges. Double base formulation provides consistency, and it meters well.

1lb:.....................$19.15
8lb:.....................$137.50

ALLIANT POWDER POWER PRO 1200-R

Features: Specifically formulated for high-volume .223 progressive loadings. Double base formulation provides consistency, it meters well, and is made in the U.S.

1lb:.....................$18.10
8lb:.....................$129.25

ALLIANT POWDER
POWER PRO 1200-R

ALLIANT POWDER
RELODER 33

HORNADY HOT TUB SONIC CLEANER

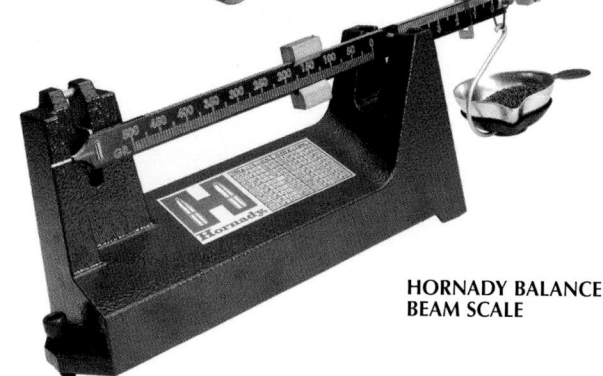

HORNADY BALANCE
BEAM SCALE

RELOADING TOOLS

HORNADY HOT TUB SONIC CLEANER

Features: Featuring a 9 liter capacity, the Hot Tub is long enough to clean a 16 inch AR-15 upper. It has 4 transducers as well as a heating element for cleaning action. The microjet action removes carbon residue and other debris, and can clean internal and external surfaces. Available inner tanks for separating batches and solutions. 110V.

MSRP.................$658.33

HORNADY BALANCE BEAM SCALE

Features: A traditional analog scale for powder measurement, this high tolerance scale is consistent to .1 of a grain. East to read laser etched beam.

MSRP...................$82.17

NEW Products: **Handloading Equipment**

LYMAN E-ZEE PRIME HAND PRIMING TOOL

Features: Provides an ergonomic shape to minimize hand fatigue, accepts popular brands of standard shell holders like Hornady, RCBS, and Redding, and plenty of leverage. Features integral primer tray and primer punch assembly with built-in shut-off gate.

MSRP $47.50

LYMAN E-ZEE PRIME HAND PRIMING TOOL

LYMAN GEN5 TOUCH SCREEN POWDER SYSTEM

Features: New touch-screen controls with extra large, easy-to-read LCD display. An auto repeat function, quick-drain, and fast operation all make the Gen5 efficient and easy to use. Accurate to .1 grain, anti-static/anti-drift technologies and electronic interferences shields all improve performance. 115V and 230V.

MSRP $349.95

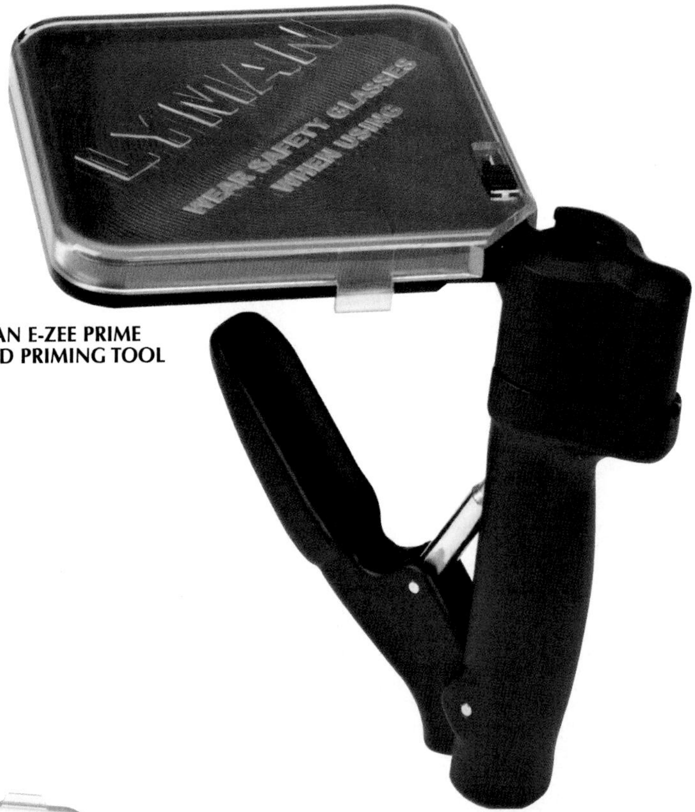

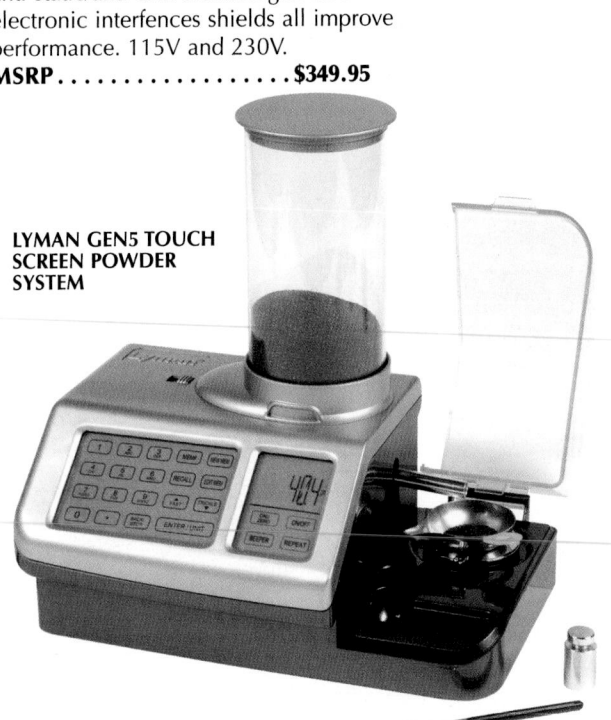

LYMAN GEN5 TOUCH SCREEN POWDER SYSTEM

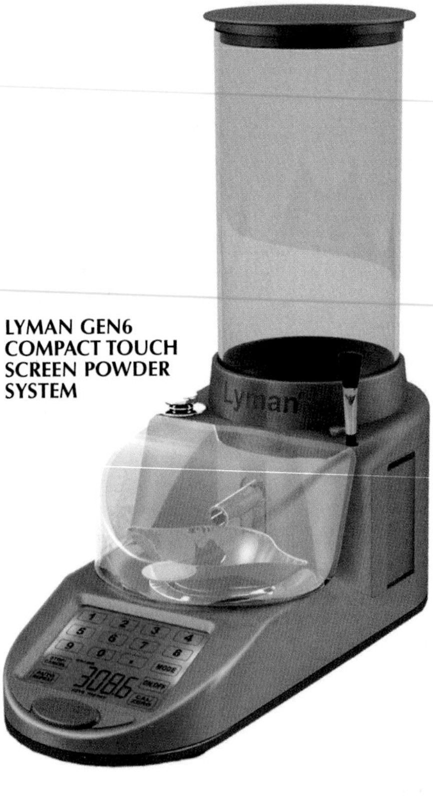

LYMAN GEN6 COMPACT TOUCH SCREEN POWDER SYSTEM

LYMAN GEN6 COMPACT TOUCH SCREEN POWDER SYSTEM

Features: New touch-screen controls and compact size maximize efficiency and space use. Auto repeat, quick-drain, fast operation, and easy access for right and left hand users make the Gen6 effective and user friendly. Anti-static/anti-drift technologies and electronic interferences shields all improve performance. 115V and 230V.

MSRP $289.95

LYMAN POWER PRO ULTRASONIC CLEANER

Features: Designed for high volume cleaning, the 34 ¾ inch heated stainless steel tank can handle most barreled actions and upper receivers. Ten powerful industrial transducers clean the parts inside and out, and also accomodates quick changing from cleaning to lubrication. Has both a timer and adjustable heat control. 115V.

LYMAN POWER PRO ULTRASONIC CLEANER

MEC RELOADERS 600 SLUGGER

MSRP **$1395**

MEC RELOADERS 600 SLUGGER

Features: Self-inclusive device; folds plastic into shell like a roll crimp; available in 12 and 20 gauges; available primer feed upgrade.
MSRP. **$275**

MEC RELOADERS SIZEMASTER ZOMBIE RELOADER

Features: "Power Ring" collet resizer returns every base back to factory specification. Resizing station handles brass or steel heads. E-Z Prime auto primer is standard. 12 and 20 Ga., adjustable for 3 in. shells.
MSRP **$283.50**

MEC RELOADERS SIZEMASTER ZOMBIE RELOADER

RCBS EXPLORER AND EXPLORER PLUS RELOADING KITS

RCBS SUMMIT SINGLE STAGE RELOADING PRESS

RCBS EXPLORER AND EXPLORER PLUS RELOADING KITS

Features: Explorer includes: Reloader Special-5 press, Uniflow Powder Measure, 1,500-grain Digital Pocket Scale, Nosler 7th Edition Reloading Manual, Hand Priming Tool, Universal Case Loading Block, Debur Tool, Powder Funnel, Case Slick Spray Lube, and Powder Trickler-2. Explorer Plus includes all Explorer items plus: Advanced Powder Measure Stand, Pow'r Pull Kit, Stainless Steel Dial Caliper, Measure Cylinder, six die lock rings, and No. 2, 3, 4, 10, and 43 shell holders.

Explorer From:. $279.99
Explorer Plus From:. $369.99

RCBS SUMMIT SINGLE STAGE RELOADING PRESS

Features: The ambidextrous Summit Single Stage Reloading Press provides for bench-top operation and full frontal access. With a 2-inch diameter ram, press adapter bushing, and quick die change, convenience and efficiency are maximized.

From:. $209.99

RCBS ULTRASONIC CASE CLEANER

RCBS ULTRASONIC CASE CLEANER

Features: 3.2 quart stainless steel tank, powerful 60W transducer and 100W ceramic heater, and 36kHz ultrasonic frequency. User-friendly keypad and display, sensor to indicate when to change out solution, de-gas function, and convenient drain valve.

From:. $139.99

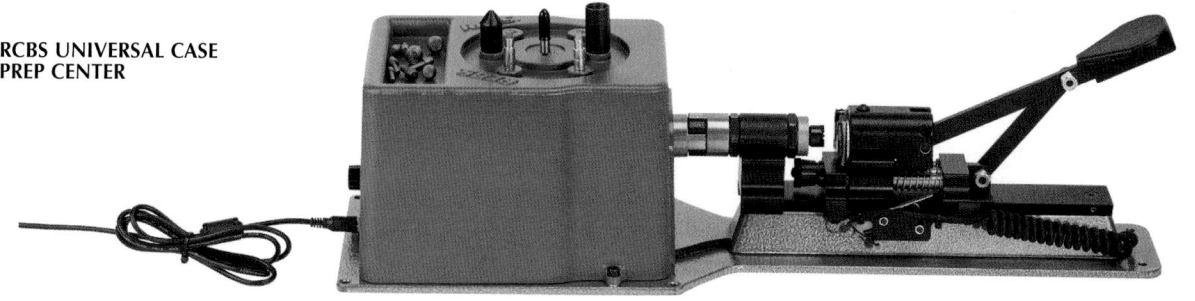

RCBS UNIVERSAL CASE PREP CENTER

RCBS UNIVERSAL CASE PREP CENTER

Features: With an ambidextrous design, powerful 24-VDC motor, and ability to accommodate case head diameters from .25–.625 inches and lengths from .72-3.375 inches, the Universal Case Prep Center provides for a quick trim and prep for high volumes of cases. Carries a two-year limited warranty.

From:. $399.99

REDDING RELOADING .17 HORNET DIE SETS

Features: The 17 Hornet provides an exciting low noise, low recoil cartridge for varmint hunting. Available in Standard Die Sets, Type-S Die Sets, and as a Competition Seating Die.

MSRP .N/A

REDDING RELOADING MICRO ADJUSTABLE TAPER CRIMP DIES

REDDING
DIE SET
TYPE S - MATCH
38279
DESCRIPTION
17 HORNET
☒ NECK DIE SET
☐ FULL DIE SET

REDDING RELOADING .17 HORNET DIE SETS

REDDING RELOADING MICRO ADJUSTABLE TAPER CRIMP DIES

Features: Being top adjusting, these dies avoid the need to remove the die and reposition the lock ring like traditional taper crimp dies. Uses a knurled, micrometer type head for quicker and more precise adjustments. Available in .17 Hornet, 9mm/38 Super, 45 Acp/45Cap, and 40 S&W/10mm.

From:. $59.99

NEW PRODUCTS

Advanced Armament Corp.

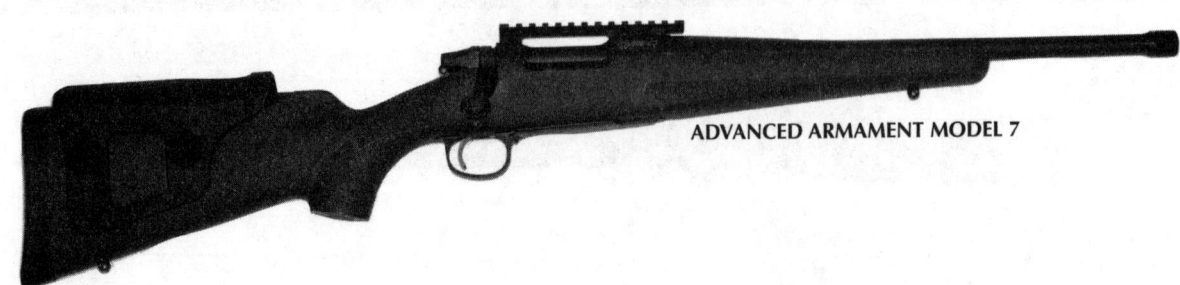

ADVANCED ARMAMENT MODEL 7

MODEL 7
Action: Bolt
Stock: Synthetic
Barrel: 16 in.
Sights: None
Weight: 6 lb. 8 oz.

Caliber: 7.62x35mm
Magazine: None
Features: Factory-threaded barrel; receiver mounted Picatinny rail; externally adjustable X-Mark Pro trigger; sling swivels; weatherproof synthetic stock with AAC adjustable cheekpiece
MSRP **$899**

J. G. Anschütz

ANSCHÜTZ 1416 D HB NUSS CLASSIC

ANSCHÜTZ 1416 D KL

ANSCHÜTZ 1517 D HB NUSS CLASSIC

1416 D HB
Action: Bolt
Stock: Walnut
Barrel: 23 in.
Sights: None
Weight: 6 lb. 6 oz.
Caliber: .22LR, .17 Mach 2, .17 HMR
Magazine: Detachable box, 5 rounds
Features: Heavy barrel; lacquered walnut wood stock (optional beavertail); pistol grip; black buttplate; studs for sling swivel; lateral sliding safety
MSRP $1099

1416 D KL
Action: Bolt
Stock: Walnut
Barrel: 22 in.
Sights: Open
Weight: 5 lb. 15 oz.
Caliber: .22LR
Magazine: Detachable box, 5 rounds
Features: Folding leaf adjustable sights; lacquered walnut wood stock; pistol grip; black buttplate; studs for sling swivel; lateral sliding safety
MSRP **$1099**

1517
Action: Bolt
Stock: Walnut, hardwood
Barrel: 22 in.
Sights: None
Weight: 6 lb. 2 oz.–8 lb. 9 oz.
Caliber: .17 HMR
Magazine: 4 rounds
Features: Single- or two-stage adjustable trigger; optional beavertail stock
MSRP . . . . **$1079–$1429**

J. G. Anschütz

ANSCHÜTZ 1710 D HB NUSS CLASSIC

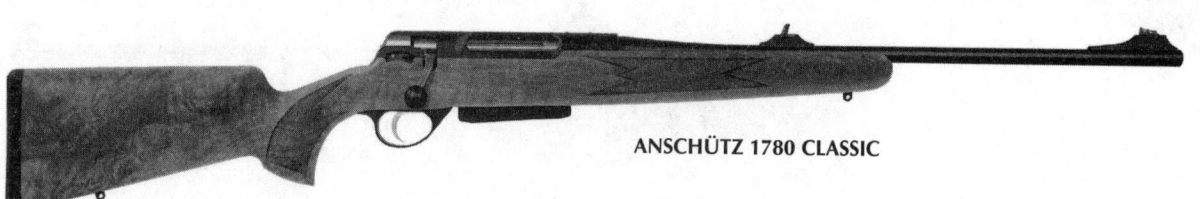

ANSCHÜTZ 1780 CLASSIC

1710
Action: Bolt
Stock: Walnut
Barrel: 22 in.
Sights: Open
Weight: 7 lb. 8 oz.
Caliber: .22LR
Magazine: 5 rounds
Features: Drilled and tapped for scope mounts; sliding safety catch; two-stage or single-stage trigger; adjustable folding leaf sights and pear front adjustable ramp; Meistergrade has engraved forestock and trigger guard; black plastic buttplate
Classic: . . . . **$1899–$2159**
Monte Carlo: . . . . **$2039–$2269**

1770
Action: Bolt
Stock: Walnut
Barrel: 22 in.
Sights: Drilled and tapped for scopes
Weight: 7 lb. 11 oz.
Caliber: .223 Rem.
Magazine: Detachable, 3-shot, in-line
Features: Six locking lug action for strength and reliability; adjustable, single-stage match trigger; hand checkered stock with oval cheekpiece and rubber buttpad; detachable sling swivel studs
MSRP **$2499**

1780
Action: Bolt
Stock: Walnut
Barrel: 22 in.
Sights: Drilled and tapped for scopes
Weight: 7 lb.
Caliber: .308 Win., .30-06, 8x57 IS, 9.3x62
Magazine: 5 rounds
Features: Single-stage trigger; fast acquisition sight; sliding safety catch; stock made of walnut heartwood, thumbhole optional
Classic: **$2757**
German: **$3077**
Thumbhole: **$3398**
Monte Carlo: **$3495**

ANSCHÜTZ 1827 FORTNER SPRINT

1827 FORTNER SPRINT
Action: Bolt
Stock: Biathlon, walnut
Barrel: 22 in.
Sights: None
Weight: 8 lb. 2 oz.

Caliber: .22LR
Magazine: Detachable box, 5 rounds
Features: Combination of an extra light 1827 Fortner barreled action with the stock of the 1827 model; lacquered walnut stock with stippled checkering; heavy, cylindrical match barrel; match stage two or single trigger
MSRP **$3398**

J. G. Anschütz

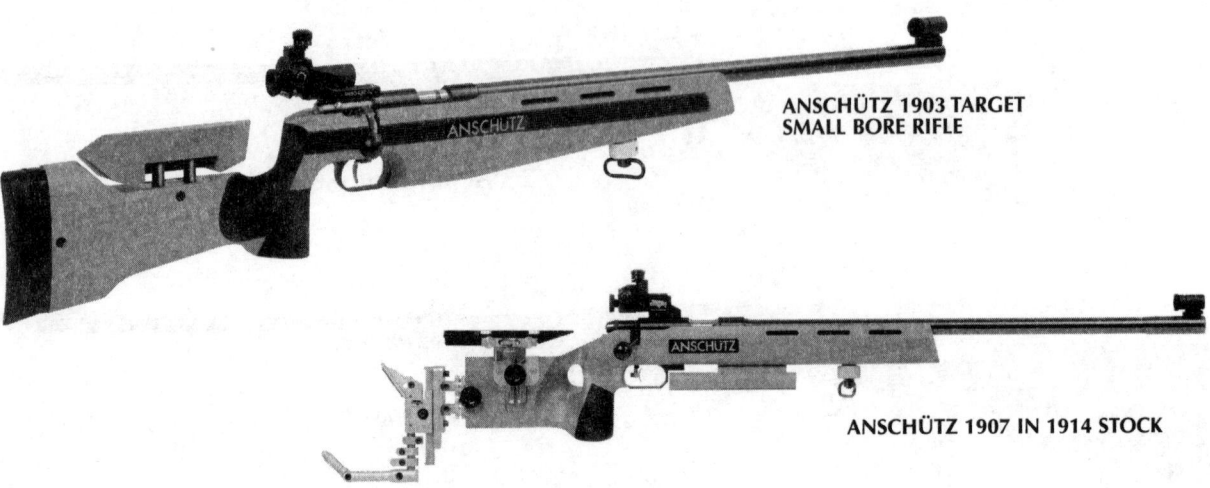

ANSCHÜTZ 1903 TARGET
SMALL BORE RIFLE

ANSCHÜTZ 1907 IN 1914 STOCK

1903 TARGET SMALL BORE RIFLE

Action: Bolt
Stock: Hardwood
Barrel: 26 in., heavy
Sights: None
Weight: 9 lb. 11 oz.
Caliber: .22LR
Magazine: None
Features: A match rifle for small bore shooters; anatomically perfect walnut stock with vertically adjustable cheek piece; optional aluminum, hook, or rubber buttplate; aluminum accessories rail
MSRP $1282

1907 IN 1914 STOCK

Action: Bolt
Stock: Walnut
Barrel: 32.28 in.
Sights: None
Weight: 10 lb. 12 oz.
Caliber: .22LR
Magazine: None
Features: Match 54 action; heavy, cylindrical barrel; match two-stage or single-stage trigger; safety signal pin
MSRP $3013

2007/660, 2013/690 WITH 2018 PRECISE STOCK

Action: Bolt
Stock: Aluminum
Barrel: 32 in., 33 in.
Sights: None
Weight: 13 lb., 13 lb. 10 oz.
Caliber: .22LR
Magazine: None
Features: Single loader; two-stage trigger; optional buttplate; new backend

offers large range of adjustment for small shooters
MSRP $4296

MSR RX 22

Action: Semiautomatic
Stock: Laminated wood, plastic
Barrel: 16.5 in.
Sights: None
Weight: 7 lb.
Caliber: .22LR
Magazine: 10 rounds
Features: Folding stock; aluminum grooved Picatinny rail for accessories; 6 possible positions for cocking lever; optional buttplate and sight set; black, desert, aluminum colors available
Precision, Precision Black: . . . $995
Black Hawk, Desert: $895

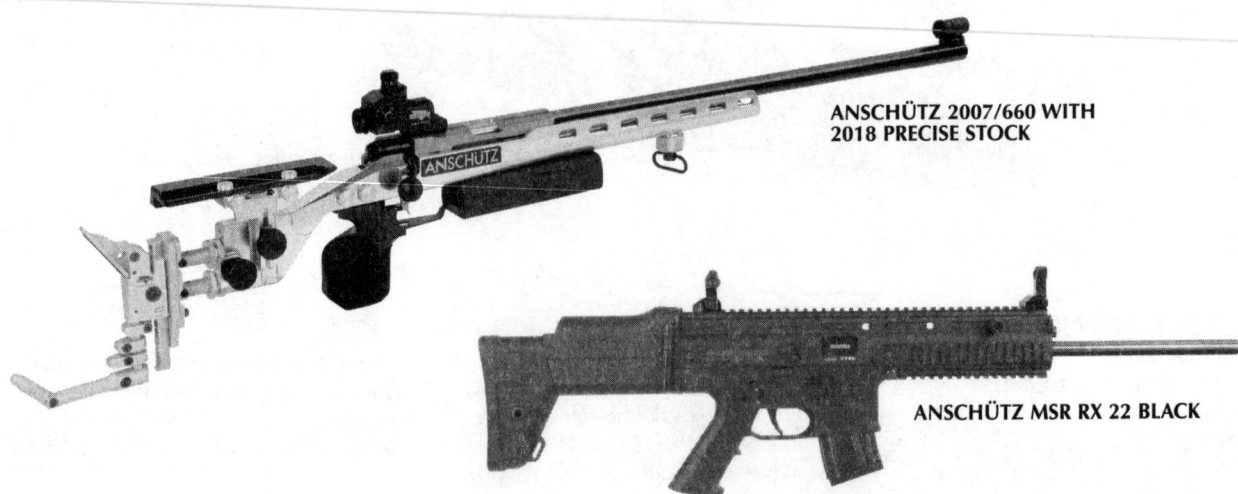

ANSCHÜTZ 2007/660 WITH
2018 PRECISE STOCK

ANSCHÜTZ MSR RX 22 BLACK

ArmaLite

ARMALITE AR-10 A4 CARBINE

ARMALITE AR-10A2CF CARBINE

AR-10 A4 CARBINE

Action: Semiautomatic
Stock: Synthetic
Barrel: 16 in.
Sights: Front
Weight: 7 lb. 14 oz.
Caliber: 7.62/.308
Magazine: Detachable box, 20 rounds
Features: Functionally identical to the AR-10B family, the AR-10A family is designed to accept early ArmaLite AR-10 "Waffle" magazines and good quality magazines copied from them, including Magpul PMAG 20LR, Knight's Armament, and DPMS. Gas block with Picatinny rail; black synthetic stock; sling, hard case, and sling swivel mounts included
MSRP **$1571**

AR-10A2CF CARBINE

Action: Semiautomatic
Stock: Synthetic
Barrel: 16 in.
Sights: Open
Weight: 9 lb.
Caliber: .308
Magazine: Detachable box, 10, 20 rounds
Features: Chrome-lined barrel; forged A2 receiver; sling; black case; flash suppressor; tactical two-stage trigger; black or green stock; stage trigger
MSRP **$1583**

AR-10 SUPER SASS

Action: Semiautomatic
Stock: Synthetic
Barrel: 20 in.
Sights: Adjustable front
Weight: 11 lb. 13 oz.
Caliber: 7.62/.308
Magazine: Detachable box, 20 rounds
Features: Functionally identical to the AR-10B family, the AR-10A family is designed to accept early ArmaLite AR-10 "Waffle" magazines and good quality magazines copied from them, including Magpul PMAG 20LR, Knight's Armament, and DPMS. Adjustable gas block front sight; black synthetic stock; sling, hard case, and sling swivel mounts included
MSRP **$3100**

AR-10 TBNF

Action: Semiautomatic
Stock: Synthetic
Barrel: 20 in.
Sights: None
Weight: 10 lb. 2 oz.
Caliber: .308
Magazine: Detachable box, 10-round
Features: Free-float handguard in black; two-stage NM trigger; black case; triple-lapped barrel; black or green stock
MSRP **$1914**

AR-10T CARBINE

Action: Semiautomatic
Stock: Synthetic
Barrel: 16 in.
Sights: Open
Weight: 8 lb. 10 oz.
Caliber: .308
Magazine: Detachable box, 10, 20 round
Features: Free-float handguard in black; two-stage NM trigger; flash suppressor; black case; black stock
MSRP **$1914**

ARMALITE AR-10 SUPER SASS

ARMALITE AR-10T CARBINE

ARMALITE AR-10 TBNF

ArmaLite

ARMALITE M-15 A2

ARMALITE M-15 A2
CARBINE

AR-50A1 NM

Action: Bolt
Stock: Synthetic
Barrel: 33 in.
Sights: None
Weight: 33 lb. 3 oz.
Caliber: .50 BMG
Magazine: None
Features: Chromoly barrel; muzzle-brake; 15minute rail; single-stage trigger
MSRP **$4230**

M-15 A2

Action: Semiautomatic
Stock: Synthetic
Barrel: 20 in.
Sights: Open
Weight: 8 lb. 1 oz.
Caliber: .223
Magazine: Detachable box, 30 rounds
Features: Double-lapped, chrome-lined barrel; flash suppressor; forged A2 Receiver; tactical two-stage trigger;

sling; black case; black or green synthetic stock
MSRP **$1174**

M-15 A2 CARBINE

Action: Semiautomatic
Stock: Synthetic
Barrel: 16 in.
Sights: Open
Weight: 6 lb. 13 oz.
Caliber: .223
Magazine: Detachable box, 30 rounds
Features: Forged A2 receiver; double-lapped, chrome-lined barrel; sling; handguards; black or green synthetic stock; black case; tactical two-stage trigger; flash suppressor
MSRP **$1174**

M-15 A2 NATIONAL MATCH RIFLE

Action: Semiautomatic
Stock: Synthetic
Barrel: 20 in.

Sights: Open
Weight: 9 lb. 3 oz.
Caliber: .223
Magazine: Detachable box, 30 rounds
Features: Forged A2 receiver with NM hooded rear sight; triple-lapped, stainless steel barrel with NM sleeve; A2 front sight assembly; two-stage NM trigger; black or green stock
MSRP **$1422**

M-15 A4 CARBINE

Action: Semiautomatic
Stock: Synthetic
Barrel: 16 in.
Sights: None
Weight: 6 lb. 7 oz.
Caliber: 7.62x39mm
Magazine: Detachable box, 10 rounds
Features: Forged flattop with Picatinny rail; forged aluminum receiver; tactical two-stage trigger; A2 flash suppressor; sling; black case; black or green stock
MSRP **$1115**

ARMALITE AR-50A1 NM

ARMALITE M-15 A2
NM RIFLE

ARMALITE M-15 A4
CARBINE

M-15 A4 CBK WITHOUT CARRY HANDLE

Action: Semiautomatic
Stock: Synthetic
Barrel: 16 in.
Sights: None
Weight: 6 lb. 3 oz.
Caliber: .223
Magazine: Detachable box, 30 rounds
Features: Chrome-lined barrel; muzzle flash suppressor; forged flattop; Picatinny rail; tactical two-stage trigger; no carry handle; black stock; sling; black case
MSRP **$989**

SPR MOD 1 LE CARBINE

Action: Semiautomatic, short gas system
Stock: Synthetic
Barrel: 16 in.
Sights: 3 detachable rails
Weight: 6 lb. 8 oz.

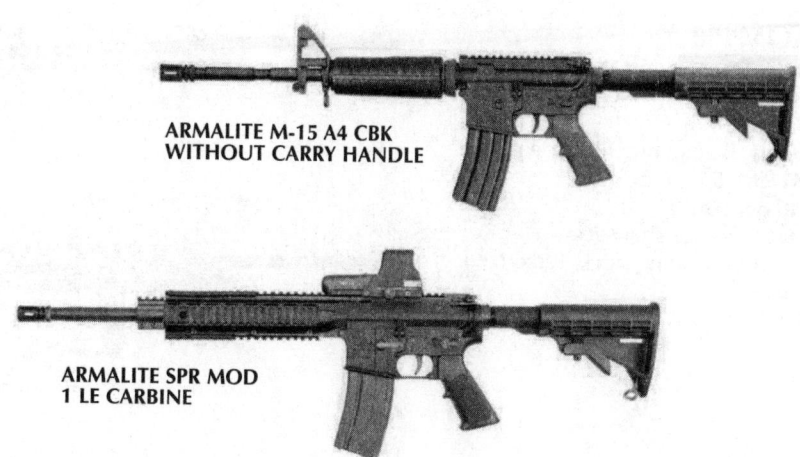

ARMALITE M-15 A4 CBK
WITHOUT CARRY HANDLE

ARMALITE SPR MOD
1 LE CARBINE

Caliber: .223, 6.8mm SPC, 7.62x39mm
Magazine: Detachable box, 30 rounds
Features: Muzzle flash suppressor; black synthetic tactical stock; aluminum handguard; tactical two-stage trigger, sling; black case
MSRP **$1554**

Arsenal, Inc.

ARSENAL SA RPK-3R

ARSENAL SAM7R-61C (CALIFORNIA
COMPLIANT)

SAM7R-61C (CALIFORNIA COMPLIANT)

Action: Gas-operated autoloader
Stock: Black polymer
Barrel: 16.3 in.
Sights: Open
Weight: 8 lb. 2 oz.
Caliber: 7.62x39mm
Magazine: 10-round U.S.-made

Features: Milled receiver; non-detachable magazine; includes muzzle nut, cleaning rod, and bayonet lug
MSRP **$1349**

SA RPK-3R

Action: Gas-operated autoloader
Stock: Black polymer or blond wood
Barrel: 23.2 in.
Sights: Open

Weight: 10 lb. 8 oz.
Caliber: 5.45x39.5mm
Magazine: 45-round
Features: RPK heavy barrel; milled receiver; U.S.-made; paddle style buttstock and scope rail; includes sling, oil bottle, and cleaning kit
MSRP . . . . **$2500–$2750**

Auto-Ordnance

AOM150

Action: Semiautomatic
Stock: Walnut; handguard
Barrel: 18 in.
Sights: Blade front; flip style rear
Weight: 5 lb. 6 oz.
Caliber: .30
Magazine: 15-shot stick
Features: Folding stock; Parkerized finish
MSRP **$903**

AUTO-ORDNANCE AOM150

M1SB THOMPSON M1 SBR

Action: Semiautomatic
Stock: Walnut, vertical foregrip
Barrel: 10.5 in.
Sights: Blade front, fixed battle rear
Weight: 10 lb. 8 oz.
Caliber: .45 ACP
Magazine: 30-shot stick
Features: Will not accept drum magazines; frame and receiver made from solid steel
MSRP **$1970**

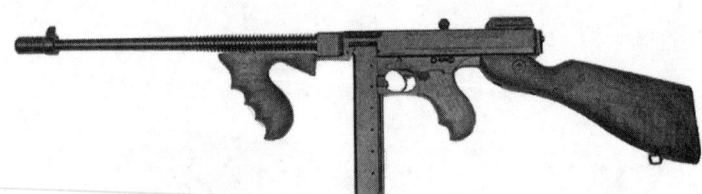

AUTO-ORDNANCE T1
THOMPSON 1927 A-1

AUTO-ORDNANCE
M1SB THOMPSON
M1 SBR

T1 THOMPSON 1927 A-1

Action: Semiautomatic
Stock: Walnut, vertical foregrip
Barrel: 16.5 in.
Sights: Blade front, open rear adjustable
Weight: 13 lb.
Caliber: .45 ACP
Magazine: 30-shot stick
Features: Frame and receiver made from solid steel; compensator; optional 50-round drum magazine
MSRP **$1420**
With 50rd drum: **$1668**

Auto-Ordnance

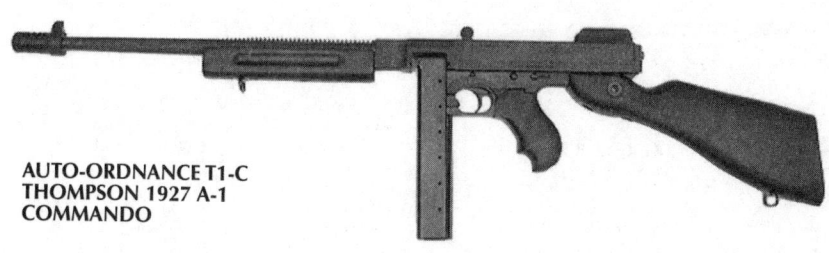

AUTO-ORDNANCE T1-C
THOMPSON 1927 A-1
COMMANDO

T1-C THOMPSON 1927 A-1 COMMANDO

Action: Semiautomatic
Stock: Black finish stock and forend
Barrel: 16.5 in.
Sights: Blade front, open rear adjustable
Weight: 13 lb.
Caliber: .45 ACP
Magazine: 30-shot stick
Features: Frame and receiver made from solid steel; compensator; black nylon sling
MSRP $1393

T1SB THOMPSON 1927 A-1 SBR SHORT BARREL RIFLE

Action: Semiautomatic
Stock: Walnut, vertical foregrip
Barrel: 10.5 in.
Sights: Blade front, open rear adjustable
Weight: 12 lb.
Caliber: .45 ACP
Magazine: 30-shot stick
Features: Frame and receiver made from solid steel; blued steel finish
MSRP $2053
Detachable butt stock: $2554

AUTO-ORDNANCE T1SB THOMPSON
1927 A-1 SBR SHORT BARREL RIFLE

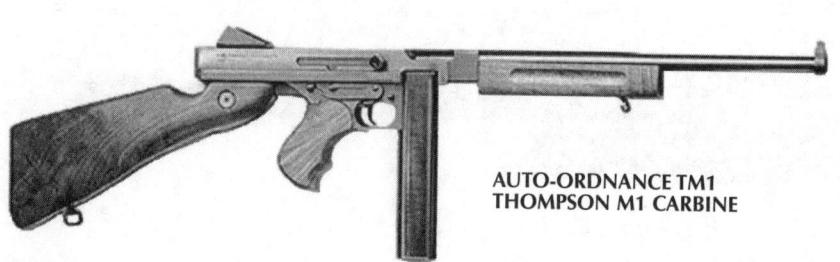

AUTO-ORDNANCE TM1
THOMPSON M1 CARBINE

TM1 THOMPSON M1

Action: Semiautomatic
Stock: Walnut, vertical foregrip
Barrel: 16.5 in.
Sights: Blade front, fixed battle rear
Weight: 8 lb., 11 lb. 8 oz.
Caliber: .45 ACP
Magazine: 30-shot stick
Features: Side bolt action; frame and receiver made from solid steel; lightweight model features a frame and receiver made from solid aluminum
MSRP $1334

Barrett

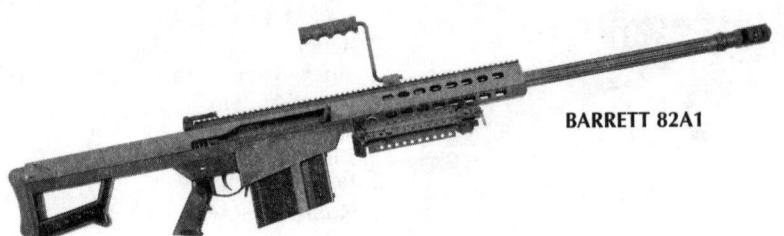

BARRETT 82A1

BARRETT 98B

MODEL 82A1

Action: Semiautomatic
Stock: Synthetic
Barrel: 20 in., 29 in.
Sights: Flip-up iron sights or Leupold scope
Weight: 30 lb. 14 oz.
Caliber: .416, .50 BMG
Magazine: Detachable box, 10 rounds
Features: Pelican case; detachable adjustable bipod legs; cleaning kit; carry handle; muzzlebrake; M1913 optics rail; chrome-lined barrel
MSRP. . . . . $8900–$9100

MODEL 95

Action: Semiautomatic
Stock: Synthetic
Barrel: 29 in.
Sights: Flip-up iron sights
Weight: 25 lb.
Caliber: .50 BMG
Magazine: Detachable box, 5 rounds
Features: Pelican case; detachable adjustable bipod legs; cleaning kit; M1913 optics rail
MSRP. $6500

MODEL 98B

Action: Bolt
Stock: Synthetic
Barrel: 20 in., 26 in.
Sights: None
Weight: 13 lb. 8 oz.
Caliber: .338 Lapua Mag.
Magazine: Detachable box, 10 rounds
Features: Ergonomic pistol grip; muzzlebrake; heavy or fluted barrel; Harris bipod; monopod; cleaning kit; side accessory rail; Air/watertight hard case; black stock
MSRP. . . . . $4699–$4849

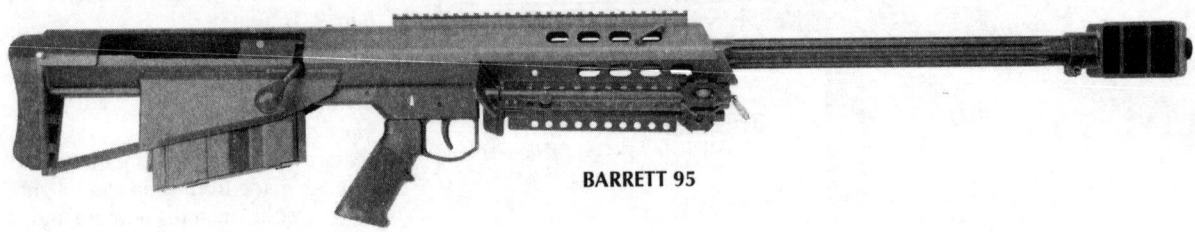

BARRETT 95

Barrett

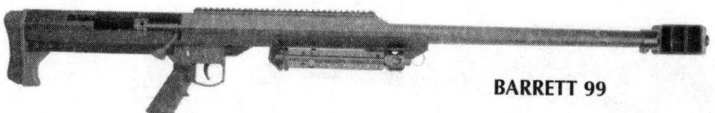
BARRETT 99

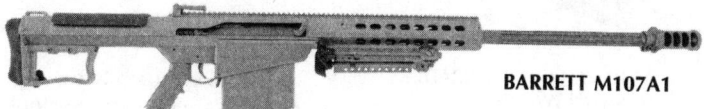
BARRETT M107A1

BARRETT MRAD

MODEL 99
Action: Bolt
Stock: Synthetic
Barrel: 29 in., 32 in.
Sights: None
Weight: 25 lb.
Caliber: .416, .50 BMG
Magazine: None
Features: M1913 optics rail; pelican case; detachable adjustable bipod; cleaning kit
MSRP . . . . **$3849–$4099**

M107A1
Action: Semiautomatic
Stock: Synthetic
Barrel: 20 in., 29 in.
Sights: Flip-up iron sights
Weight: 30 lb. 14 oz.
Caliber: .50 BMG
Magazine: Detachable box, 10 rounds
Features: Chrome-lined barrel, Flat Dark Earth stock finish; suppressor-ready muzzlebrake; pelican case; M1913 optics rail; detachable adjustable lightweight bipod legs; lightweight monopod
MSRP **$12000**

MRAD
Action: Bolt action repeater
Stock: Synthetic
Barrel: 20 in., 24.5 in., 27 in.
Sights: None
Weight: 14 lb. 13 oz.
Caliber: .338 Lapua Mag.
Magazine: Detachable box, 10 rounds
Features: Fluted barrel; multi-role brown finish stock; folding stock; adjustable cheekpiece and buttplate; includes two 10-round magazines, two sling loops, and three adjustable accessory rails
MSRP . . . . **$5850–$6000**

Benelli USA

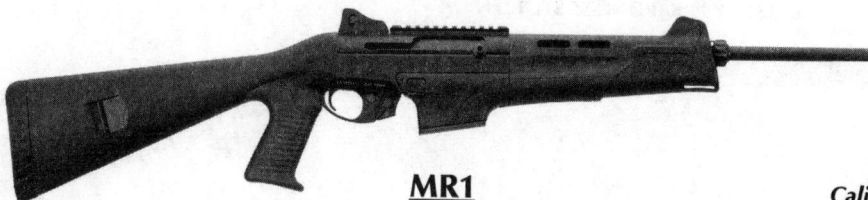
BENELLI MR1

MR1
Action: A.R.G.O (Auto-Regulating-Gas-Operated)
Stock: Synthetic tactical pistol grip (ComforTech optional)
Barrel: 16 in.
Sights: Military-style aperture sights with Picatinny rail
Weight: 7 lb. 14 oz.

Caliber: .223 Rem.
Magazine: Detachable box, 5 shot
Features: Self-cleaning stainless piston system with gas port forward of chamber; accepts high-capacity M-16 magazines; hard chrome-lined barrel
Pistol Grip: **$1339**
ComforTech: **$1461**

RIFLES

Benelli USA

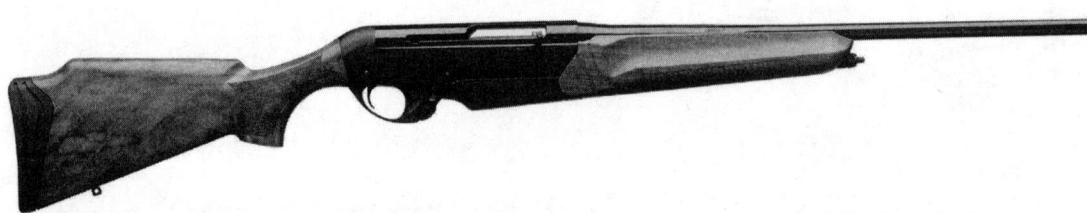

**BENELLI R1 AA-GRADE
SATIN WALNUT**

R1
Action: Semiautomatic
Stock: AA-grade satin walnut,
synthetic or Realtree APG
Barrel: 22 in., 24 in.
Sights: None
Weight: 7 lb. 2 oz.–7 lb. 5 oz.
Caliber: .30-06 Spfd., .300 Win. Mag.,
.338 Win. Mag.

Magazine: Detachable box, 3+1, 4+1
rounds
Features: Picatinny rail; synthetic and
APG finish come with GripTight coat-
ing; raised comb; auto-regulating gas-
operated system
Walnut: **$1019**
ComforTech: .... **$1039–$1249**

Beretta USA

BERETTA CX4 STORM

CX4 STORM
Action: Single-action
Stock: Synthetic
Barrel: 16.6 in.
Sights: Front sight post
Weight: 5 lb. 12 oz.
Caliber: 9mm, .40 S&W, .45 ACP
Magazine: Detachable box,
10,15,17,20 (9mm); 10, 11, 12, 14, 17
(40 S&W); 8 (.45 ACP) rounds

Features: Picatinny rail; allows for
reverse ejection and extraction; ideal
for left-handed shooters; adjustable
length-of-pull; easy to accessorize
MSRP **$915**

Blaser USA

BLASER K95 BARONESSE STUTZEN

K95 BARONESSE STUTZEN
Action: Single shot
Stock: Walnut
Barrel: 19.75 in.
Sights: None
Weight: 5 lb. 11 oz.
Caliber: .222 Rem., 5.6xR Mag.,
5.6xR, .243 Win., 6.5x57R, 7x57 R,
.308 Win., .30-06, 8x57 IRS

Magazine: None
Features: Octagonal barrel standard,
barrels are interchangeable; available
from grade Lexus; split forearm for
continuous precision even in extreme
weather; black forearm tip; range of
ornamentation and game engravings
MSRP **$16931**

RIFLES

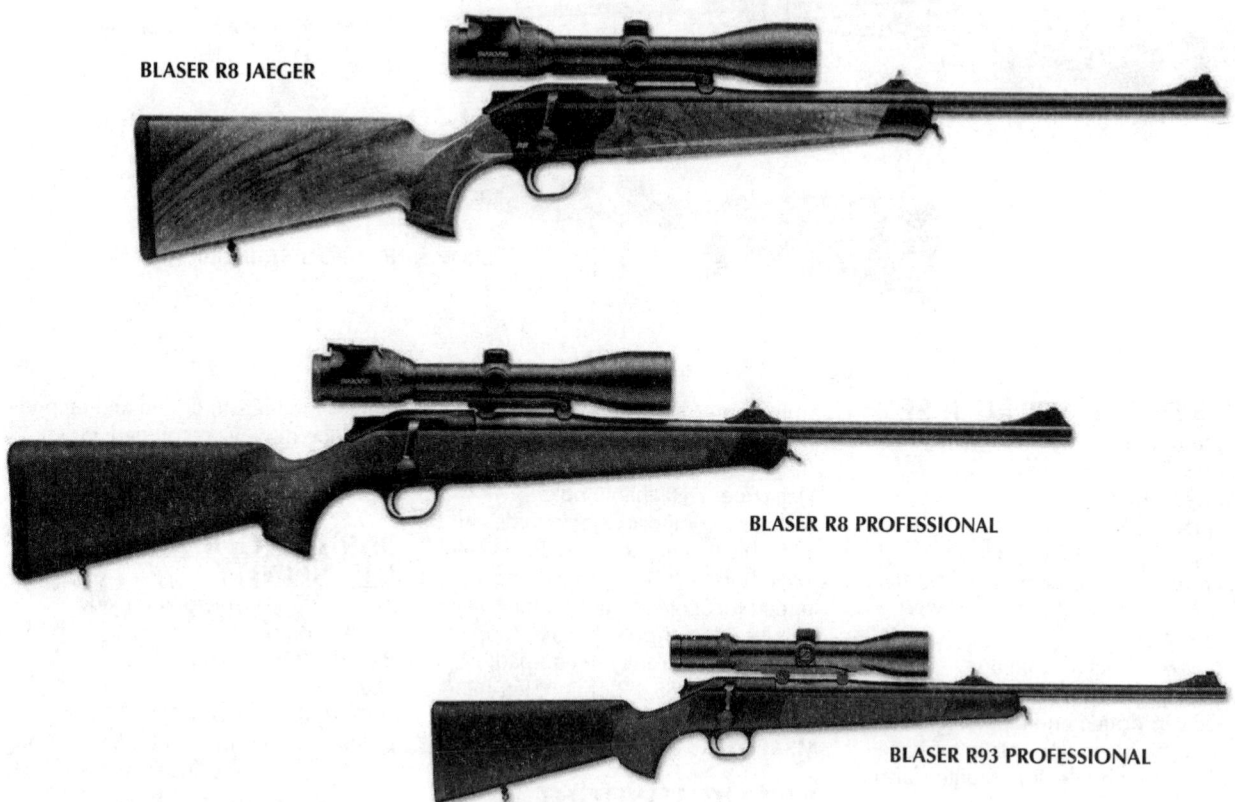

BLASER R8 JAEGER

BLASER R8 PROFESSIONAL

BLASER R93 PROFESSIONAL

R8 JAEGER

Action: Straight-pull bolt-action
Stock: Walnut, pistol grip
Barrel: 20.5 in., 23 in., 25.75 in.
Sights: None
Weight: 6 lb. 6 oz.
Caliber: .222 Rem. to .338 Win. Mag.
Magazine: Detachable box, 3 rounds with lock
Features: Cold-hammer-forged barrels and chambers; black forearm tip; synthetic stock in dark green or walnut, straight comb; manual cocking system; integrated trigger/magazine unit; original Blaser saddle mount
MSRP **$4195**

R8 PROFESSIONAL

Action: Straight-pull bolt-action
Stock: Matte dark green synthetic stock, pistol grip
Barrel: 20.5 in., 23 in., 25.75 in.
Sights: None
Weight: 6 lb. 6 oz.
Caliber: .222 Rem. to .338 Win. Mag.
Magazine: Detachable box, 3 rounds with lock

Features: Shatter-proof, synthetic dark green stock; detachable magazine/trigger unit; single-stage trigger; quick-release scope mount; ergonomically optimized pistol grip; kickstop optional; precision trigger; black forearm tip; integrated receiver
MSRP **$3623**

R93 PROFESSIONAL

Action: Straight-pull bolt-action
Stock: Synthetic
Barrel: 25.50 in. (Magnum), 25.59 (Ultra Magnum); 27.56 in. (Swiss Kaliber)
Sights: None
Weight: 6 lb. 6 oz.–6 lb. 13 oz.
Caliber: .222 Rem., .223 Rem., .22-250, .243 Win., 6x62 Freres, .25-06, 6.5x5.5, 6.5x57, 6.5-284 Norma, 6.5x65 RWS, .270 Win., .280 Rem., 7x57, 7mm-08, 7x64, .308 Win., .30-06, 8x57IS, 8x64 S, 8.5x63, 9.3x62, 6.5x68, 7.5x55, 8x68 S, .257 Wby. Mag., .270 Wby. Mag., 7mm Rem. Mag., .300 Win. Mag., .300 Wby.

Mag., .338 Win. Mag., .375 H&H Mag., 7mm STW, .300 Rem. Ultra Mag., 1.3x60 R
Magazine: In-line box, 2, 3, 4 rounds
Features: Anodized barrel; quick-release scope mount; shatter-proof stock comes in natural stone, slate gray, dark green, Mossy Oak camo; left-handed version optional
MSRP **$3145**
Left-hand versions add **$459**

S2 SAFARI DOUBLE RIFLE

Action: Tilting block, double-barrel
Stock: Grained walnut
Barrel: 24.4 in.
Sights: None
Weight: 11 lb. 11 oz.
Caliber: .375 H&H Mag., .470 NE, .500/.416 NE, .500 NE
Magazine: None
Features: Straight Safari stock with Monte Carlo cheekpiece; kickstop; rubber recoil pad; half-beavertail forend
MSRP **$11060**

Browning

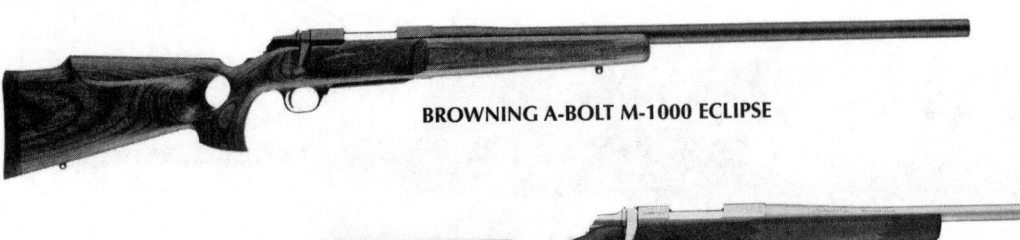

BROWNING A-BOLT M-1000 ECLIPSE

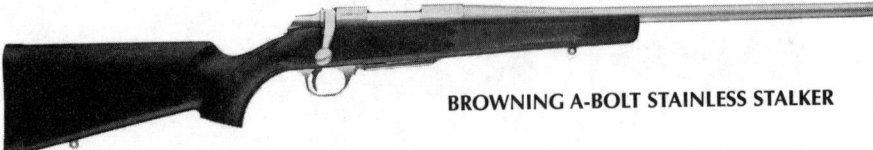

BROWNING A-BOLT STAINLESS STALKER

A-BOLT M-1000 ECLIPSE

Action: Bolt
Stock: Gray Laminated
Barrel: 26 in.
Sights: None
Weight: 9 lb. 14 oz.–10 lb.
Caliber: .22-250 Rem., 7mm-08 Rem., .308 Win., .300 WSM, .270 WSM, 7mm WSM
Magazine: Detachable box
Features: Steel, matte blued finish receiver; drilled and tapped for scope mounts; hinged floor plate; top-tang safety; thumbhole grip; Monte Carlo cheekpiece
MSRP. . . . .$1339.99–$1469.99

A-BOLT STAINLESS STALKER

Action: Bolt
Stock: Composite
Barrel: 22 in., 23 in., 24 in., 26 in.
Sights: None
Weight: 6 lb. 4 oz.–6 lb. 11 oz.
Caliber: .243 Win., 7mm-08 Rem., .308 Win., .270 Win., .30-06 Spfd., 7mm Rem. Mag., .388 Win. Mag., .300 WSM, .270 WSM, 7mm WSM, .325 WSM
Magazine: Detachable box
Features: Composite stock comes in matte black, checkered; stainless steel, matte finish receiver; drilled and tapped for scope mounts; adjustable stainless steel trigger; hinged floor plate; top-tang safety; recoil pad; BOSS and BOSS-CR option; left-hand version available
MSRP. . . . .$1239.99–$1269.99

BAR LIGHTWEIGHT STALKER

Action: Gas-operated autoloader
Stock: Composite
Barrel: 23 in.
Sights: None
Weight: 7 lb. 4 oz.
Caliber: 7mm WSM
Magazine: Detachable box
Features: Composite stock in matte black; aircraft-grade alloy receiver in matte blued finish; drilled and tapped for scope mounts; recoil pad; cross-bolt safety
MSRP. $1339.99

BAR LONGTRAC, BREAK-UP INFINITY

Action: Gas-operated autoloader
Stock: Composite
Barrel: 22 in., 24 in.
Sights: None
Weight: 6 lb. 15 oz.–7 lb. 8 oz.
Caliber: .270 Win., .30-06 Spfd., 7mm Rem. Mag., .300 Win. Mag.
Magazine: Detachable box
Features: Aircraft-grade alloy receiver; drilled and tapped for scope mounts; hammer-forged barrel; multi-lug rotary bolt; composite trigger guard and floor plate; cross-bolt safety; Dura-Touch Armor coating; composite stock comes in Mossy Oak camo finishes; interchangeable recoil pad
MSRP. . . . .$1359.99–$1459.99

BROWNING BAR LIGHTWEIGHT STALKER

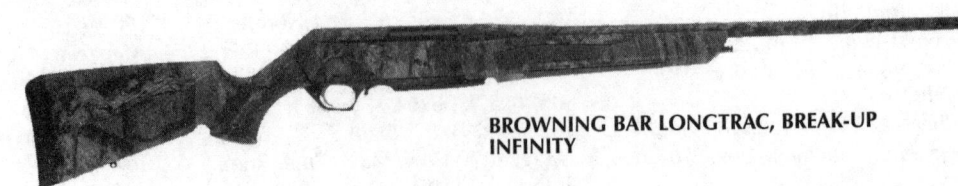

BROWNING BAR LONGTRAC, BREAK-UP INFINITY

BROWNING BAR LONGTRAC STALKER

BROWNING BAR SAFARI

BROWNING BAR SHORTTRAC

BROWNING BAR
SHORTTRAC, LEFT-HAND

BAR LONGTRAC STALKER

Action: Gas-operated autoloader
Stock: Composite
Barrel: 22 in., 24 in.
Sights: None
Weight: 6 lb. 15 oz.–7 lb. 8 oz.
Caliber: .270 Win., .30-06 Spfd., 7mm Rem. Mag., .300 Win. Mag.
Magazine: Detachable box
Features: Aircraft-grade alloy receiver with matte blued finish; drilled and tapped for scope mounts; hammer-forged; multi-lug rotary bolt; composite stock in matte black finish; gripping panels; recoil pad; composite trigger guard and floor plate
MSRP . . . .$1259.99–$1339.99

BAR SAFARI

Action: Gas-operated autoloader
Stock: Walnut
Barrel: 22 in., 23 in., 24 in.
Sights: None
Weight: 7 lb. 6 oz.–8 lb. 6 oz.
Caliber: .243 Win., .308 Win., .25-06 Rem., .270 Win., .30-06 Spfd., 7mm

Rem. Mag., .300 Win. Mag., .338 Win. Mag., .270 Win. (BOSS), 7mm Rem. Mag. (BOSS), .300 Win. Mag. (BOSS), .338 Win. Mag. (BOSS), .300 WSM (BOSS), .270 WSM (BOSS), 7mm WSM (BOSS)
Magazine: Detachable box
Features: Checkered, select gloss finish walnut stock; steel receiver with blued finish and scroll engraving; drilled and tapped for scope mounts; multi-lug rotary bolt; recoil pad BOSS and BOSS-CR option; sling swivel studs installed
MSRP . . . .$1229.99–$1499.99

BAR SHORTTRAC

Action: Gas-operated autoloader
Stock: Walnut
Barrel: 23 in.
Sights: None
Weight: 6 lb. 10 oz.–7 lb. 4 oz.
Caliber: .243 Win., 7mm-08 Rem., .308 Win., .300 WSM, .270 WSM, 7mm WSM, .325 WSM
Magazine: Detachable box

Features: Oil finish walnut stock with stylized forearm; aircraft-grade alloy receiver with blued finish; drilled and tapped for scope mounts; interchangeable recoil pad
MSRP . . . .$1229.99–$1339.99

BAR SHORTTRAC, LEFT-HAND

Action: Gas-operated autoloader
Stock: Walnut
Barrel: 22 in., 23 in.
Sights: None
Weight: 6 lb. 10 oz.–7 lb. 4 oz.
Caliber: .243 Win., 7mm-08 Rem., .308 Win., .300 WSM, .270 WSM, 7mm WSM, .325 WSM
Magazine: Detachable box
Features: Aircraft-grade alloy receiver; drilled and tapped for scope mounts; hammer-forged barrel; grade II walnut stock with oil finish; stylized, checkered forearm; sling swivel studs installed; interchangeable recoil pad
MSRP . . . .$1269.99–$1359.99

RIFLES

Browning

BROWNING BLR LIGHTWEIGHT '81

BROWNING BLR LIGHTWEIGHT STAINLESS

BROWNING BLR LIGHTWEIGHT '81 STAINLESS TAKEDOWN

BROWNING BLR WHITE GOLD MEDALLION

BLR WHITE GOLD MEDALLION

Action: Lever-action
Stock: Walnut, pistol grip
Barrel: 20 in., 22 in.
Sights: Open
Weight: 6 lb. 8 oz.–6 lb. 12 oz.
Caliber: .243 Win., 7mm-08 Rem., .308 Win., .300 WSM, .270 WSM
Magazine: Detachable box
Features: Aircraft-grade aluminum receiver with nickel finish; high-relief engraving on receiver; drilled and tapped for scope mounts; crowned muzzle; stainless steel barrel; stock comes in grade IV/ V walnut with a checkered pistol grip and forearm; rosewood forend cap; silver pistol grip cap; adjustable sights; recoil pad; sling swivel studs installed
MSRP . . . .$1469.99–$1549.99

BLR LIGHTWEIGHT '81

Action: Lever-action
Stock: Walnut, straight grip
Barrel: 20 in., 22 in., 24 in.
Sights: None
Weight: 6 lb. 8 oz.–7 lb. 12 oz.

Caliber: .223 Rem., .22-250 Rem., .243 Win., 7mm-08 Rem., .308 Win., .358 Win., .270 Win., .30-06 Spfd., 7mm Rem. Mag., .300 Win. Mag., .300 WSM, .270 WSM, 7mm WSM, .450 Marlin, .325 WSM
Magazine: Detachable box
Features: Aircraft-grade alloy receiver; drilled and tapped for scope mounts; crowned muzzle; adjustable sights; gloss finish walnut stock; recoil pad
MSRP . . . . $959.99–$1039.99

BLR LIGHTWEIGHT '81 STAINLESS TAKEDOWN

Action: Lever-action
Stock: Laminate, straight grip
Barrel: 20 in., 22 in., 24 in.
Sights: Open
Weight: 6 lb. 8 oz.–7 lb. 12 oz.
Caliber: .223 Rem., .22-250 Rem., .243 Win., 7mm-08 Rem., .308 Win., .358 Win., .270 Win., .30-06 Spfd., 7mm Rem. Mag., .300 Win. Mag., .300 WSM, .270 WSM, 7mm WSM, .450 Marlin, .325 WSM
Magazine: Detachable box
Features: Aircraft-grade alloy receiver; drilled and tapped for scope mounts;

stainless steel barrel with matte finish; gray laminate wood stock in satin finish; recoil pad; separates for storage or transportation; optional Scout-style scope mount; TRUGLO/Marble's fiber optic front sight
MSRP . . . .$1229.99–$1299.99

BLR LIGHTWEIGHT STAINLESS

Action: Lever-action
Stock: Walnut, pistol grip
Barrel: 20 in., 22 in., 24 in.
Sights: None
Weight: 6 lb. 8 oz.–7 lb. 12 oz.
Caliber: .223 Rem., .22-250 Rem., .243 Win., 7mm-08 Rem., .308 Win., .358 Win., .270 Win., .30-06 Spfd., .300 Win. Mag., .300 WSM, .270 WSM, 7mm WSM, .450 Marlin, .325 WSM
Magazine: Detachable box
Features: Aircraft-grade alloy receiver; drilled and tapped for scope mounts; steel barrel with matte finish; crowned muzzle; adjustable sights; gloss finish walnut stock with pistol grip; sling swivel studs installed; recoil pad
MSRP . . . .$1019.99–$1099.99

Browning

BROWNING RMEF X-BOLT WHITE GOLD

BROWNING X-BOLT HUNTER

RMEF X-BOLT WHITE GOLD

Action: Bolt
Stock: Walnut
Barrel: 23 in.
Sights: None
Weight: 7 lb. 3 oz.
Caliber: .325 WSM
Magazine: Detachable rotary box
Features: Monte Carlo stock; stainless steel barrel and receiver, receiver etched in gold; raised cheekpiece; Inflex technology recoil pad; adjustable feather trigger; top-tang safety with bolt unlock button
MSRP $1499.99

X-BOLT HUNTER

Action: Bolt
Stock: Satin finish walnut stock
Barrel: 22 in., 23 in., 24 in., 26 in.
Sights: None
Weight: 6 lb. 13 oz.–7 lb.
Caliber: .243 Win., 7mm-08 Rem., .308 Win., .25-06 Rem., .270 Win., .280 Rem., .30-06 Spfd., 7mm Rem. Mag., .388 Win. Mag., .300 WSM,
.270 WSM, 7mm WSM, .325 WSM, .223 Rem., .22-250 Rem.
Magazine: Detachable rotary box
Features: Adjustable feather trigger; top-tang safety with bolt unlock button; sling swivel studs installed; Inflex technology recoil pad
MSRP . . . . $899.99–$939.99

X-BOLT MEDALLION

Action: Bolt
Stock: Walnut
Barrel: 22 in., 23 in., 24 in., 26 in.
Sights: Open
Weight: 6 lb. 6 oz.–7 lb.
Caliber: .223 Rem., .22-250 Rem., .243 Win., .308 Win., .25-06 Rem., .270 Win., .280 Rem., .30-06 Spfd., 7mm Rem. Mag., .300 Win. Mag., .338 Win. Mag., .300 WSM, .270 WSM, 7mm WSM, .325 WSM
Magazine: Detachable rotary box
Features: Gloss finish walnut stock, rosewood forend grip and pistol cap; Inflex technology recoil pad; adjustable feather trigger; drilled and tapped for scope mounts; left-hand option
MSRP . . . . $1029.99–$1069.99
Left-hand: . . . . . . $1069.99–$1099.99

X-BOLT MICRO MIDAS

Action: Bolt
Stock: Walnut
Barrel: 20 in.
Sights: None
Weight: 6 lb. 1 oz.
Caliber: .243 Win., 7mm-08 Rem., .308 Win., .22-250 Rem.
Magazine: Detachable rotary magazine
Features: Drilled and tapped for scope mounts, low-luster blued finish, free-floating barrel; adjustable feather trigger; top-tang safety; left-hand option
MSRP $839.99

X-BOLT STAINLESS STALKER

Action: Bolt
Stock: Composite
Barrel: 22 in., 23 in., 24 in., 26 in.
Sights: None
Weight: 6 lb. 3 oz.–6 lb. 13 oz.
Caliber: .243 Win., 7mm-08 Rem., .308 Win., .25-06 Rem., .270 Win., .280 Rem., .30-06 Spfd., 7mm Rem. Mag., .300 Win. Mag., .388 Win. Mag., .300 WSM, .270 WSM, 7mm WSM, .325 WSM, .223 Rem., .22-250 Rem.
Magazine: Detachable rotary box
Features: Composite stock in matte black with textured gripping surfaces; Dura-Touch armor coating; adjustable feather trigger; top-tang safety; bolt unlock button; palm swell
MSRP . . . . $1119.99–$1159.99

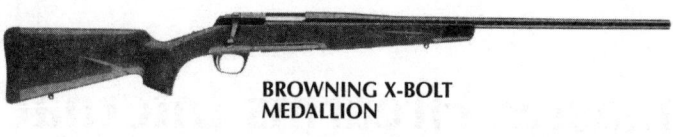

BROWNING X-BOLT MEDALLION

BROWNING X-BOLT MICRO MIDAS

BROWNING X-BOLT STAINLESS STALKER

Browning

BROWNING X-BOLT STALKER CARBON FIBER FLUTED

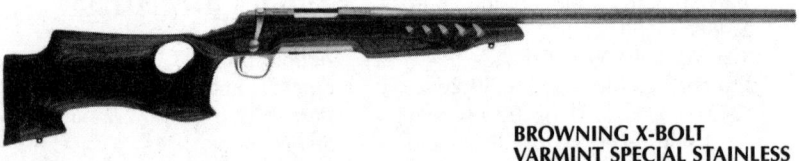

BROWNING X-BOLT VARMINT SPECIAL STAINLESS

RIFLES

X-BOLT STALKER CARBON FIBER FLUTED

Action: Bolt
Stock: Composite
Barrel: 22 in., 23 in., 26 in.
Sights: None
Weight: 6 lb. 3 oz.–6 lb. 11 oz.
Caliber: .308 Win., .270 Win., .30-06 Spfd., .300 Win. Mag., .300 WSM, .270 WSM
Magazine: Detachable rotary
Features: Matte blued receiver glass bedded; drilled and tapped for scope mounts; matte blued barrel; hand chambered; target crown; eight flutes to reduce weight and increase cooling; adjustable feather trigger; top-tang safety; bolt unlock button; Dura-Touch® armor coating; Inflex technology recoil pad; sling swivel studs installed
MSRP . . . .$1269.99–$1329.99

X-BOLT VARMINT SPECIAL STAINLESS

Action: Bolt
Stock: Altamont Paladin, black laminated
Barrel: 24 in., 26 in.
Sights: None
Weight: 8 lb. 8 oz.–8 lb. 11 oz.
Caliber: .223 Rem., .22-250 Rem., .308 Win., .300 WSM
Magazine: Detachable rotary box
Features: Stainless steel, free-floating barrel; adjustable feather trigger; top-tang safety; bolt unlock button; Inflex technology recoil pads; sling swivel studs installed
MSRP $1069.99

Bushmaster Firearms Internat'l

.308 HUNTER

Action: Semiautomatic
Stock: Synthetic
Barrel: 20 in.
Sights: None
Weight: 8 lb. 6 oz.
Caliber: .308 Win., 7.62 NATO
Magazine: Detachable box, 5 rounds
Features: Two riser blocks, A2 grip on Vista; free-floating, vented aluminum forend; MOE trigger guard for gloved finger
Hunter: $1685.32

BUSHMASTER .308 HUNTER

Bushmaster Firearms Internat'l

BUSHMASTER .308 ORC

BUSHMASTER .450 RIFLE & CARBINE

.308 ORC

Action: Semiautomatic
Stock: Synthetic
Barrel: 16 in. (carbine), 20 in. (rifle)
Sights: None
Weight: 7 lb. 12 oz.
Caliber: .308 Win. 7.62 NATO
Magazine: Detachable box, 20 rounds
Features: Milled gas block; heavy, chrome-lined barrel; A2 Birdcage flash hider; receiver-length Picatinny optics rail with two .5-in. optic raisers; heavy oval hand guards; six-position tele-scoping stock; shipped in lockable hard case with yellow safety block; black web sling included
MSRP **$1476.99**

.450 RIFLE & CARBINE

Action: Semiautomatic
Stock: Synthetic, A2 pistol grip
Barrel: 16 in. (carbine), 20 in. (rifle)
Sights: None
Weight: 8 lb. 2 oz. (carbine), 8 lb. 8 oz. (rifle)
Caliber: .450 Bushmaster
Magazine: Detachable box, 5 rounds
Features: Chromoly steel barrels; free-floating aluminum forends; forged aluminum receivers; solid A2 buttstock with trapdoor storage compartment; Pictatinny rail; black web sling included; shipped in lockable hard plastic case with orange safety block
Rifle: **$1484.76**
Carbine: **$1500.31**

BUSHMASTER ACR BASIC FOLDER COMBINATION

ACR BASIC FOLDER COMBINATION

Action: Semiautomatic
Stock: Synthetic
Barrel: 10.5 in., 14.5 in., 16.5 in.
Sights: None
Weight: N/A
Caliber: .223/5.56mm NATO to 6.8mm Rem. SPC
Magazine: 30-round PMAG
Features: Cold-hammer-forged barrel with melonite coating; A2 birdcage-type hider; toolless quick-change bar-rel system; quick and easy multi-cali-ber bolt carrier assembly; free-floating MIL-STD 1913 monolithic top rail for optic mounting; high-impact compos-ite hand guard with heat shield; ambi-dextrous controls; composite stock comes in black or coyote
MSRP **$2490**

Bushmaster Firearms Internat'l

BUSHMASTER A-TACS PREDATOR

BUSHMASTER A-TACS VARMINTER

A-TACS PREDATOR
Action: Semiautomatic
Stock: Synthetic
Barrel: 20 in.
Sights: None
Weight: 8 lb.
Caliber: 5.56mm or .223 Rem.
Magazine: Detachable box, 5 rounds
Features: Coated in A-Tacs digital camouflage; fluted extra-heavy barrel with competition muzzle crown; two-stage competition trigger
MSRP. **$1518.97**

A-TACS VARMINTER
Action: Semiautomatic
Stock: Synthetic
Barrel: 24 in.
Sights: None
Weight: 8 lb. 6 oz.
Caliber: 5.56mm or .223 Rem.
Magazine: Detachable box, 5 rounds
Features: Coated in A-Tacs digital camouflage; free-floated barrel with a vented aluminum forend; two-stage competition trigger
MSRP. **$1534.51**

BA50 RIFLES
Action: Bolt
Stock: Synthetic
Barrel: 30 in.
Sights: None
Weight: 30 lb.
Caliber: .50 BMG
Magazine: Detachable box, 10 rounds
Features: MIL-STD1913 rail; steel bipod with folding legs; ErgoGrip deluxe tactical pistol grip; LimbSaver Butt Pad; Magpul PRS adjustable buttstock; aluminum receiver; recoil reducing brake
MSRP. **$5519.27**

CARBON 15 9MM CARBINE
Action: Semiautomatic
Stock: Composite

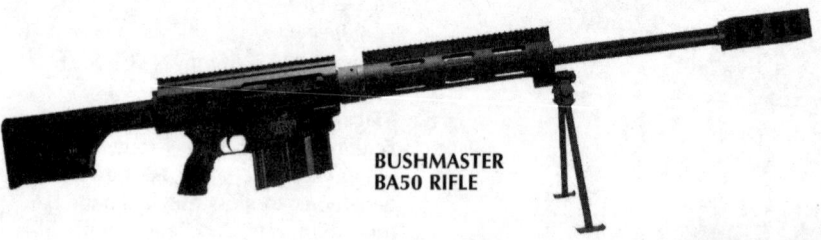

BUSHMASTER BA50 RIFLE

Barrel: 16 in.
Sights: None
Weight: 5 lb. 11 oz.
Caliber: 9mm NATO
Magazine: Detachable box, 30 rounds
Features: Carbon fiber composite receivers; birdcage flash hider; chromoly steel barrel; manganese phosphate bolt carrier; Picatinny rail mounted on upper receiver; six-position telescoping buttstock; shipped in lockable Bushmaster carrying case
MSRP. **$932.99**

DCM-XR
Action: Semiautomatic
Stock: Synthetic
Barrel: 20 in.
Sights: Open, adjustable
Weight: 13 lb. 1 oz.
Caliber: 5.56mm, .223 Rem.
Magazine: Detachable box, 10 rounds (accepts all M16/AR15 type)
Features: M16A2 Dual aperture rear sight with interchangeable apertures; competition front sight; extra heavy competition barrel; barrel is lead lapped and hardened to Rockwell C26 to 32; two-stage competition trigger; competition free-floater tube handguard; shipped in lockable hard case
MSRP. **$1360.39**

BUSHMASTER DCM-XR

Bushmaster Firearms Internat'l

BUSHMASTER M4 TYPE CARBINE

BUSHMASTER MOE 308 MID-LENGTH

M4 TYPE CARBINES

Action: Semiautomatic
Stock: Synthetic
Barrel: 16 in.
Sights: Open
Weight: 6 lb. 3 oz.
Caliber: 5.56mm, .223 Rem.
Magazine: Detachable box, 30 rounds (accepts all M16/ AR15 type)
Features: Six-position telestock; "Izzy" flash suppressor; hard chrome-lined barrels are designed to accept M203 grenade launcher; upper receivers available in A2 or A3 configurations; A2 receiver has 300-800 meter rear sight system; A3 receiver is mounted with Pictatinny rail, 300-600 meter rear sight system and removable carry handle; shipped in lockable hard case with orange safety block
A2:. . . . . **$1197.14–$1274.88**
A3:. **$1391.48**

MOE 308 MID-LENGTH

Action: Semiautomatic
Stock: Synthetic
Barrel: 16 in.
Sights: Magpul MSBUS rear flip sight
Weight: 6 lb. 2 oz.
Caliber: .308 Win., 7.62 NATO
Magazine: Detachable box, 20 rounds
Features: Receiver length Picatinny optics rail; Magpul MOE polymer mid-length handguard; Magpul MOE adjustable buttstock with strong A-frame design; rubber buttplate; Magpul MOE vertical grip; MOE enhanced trigger guards; shipped in lockable hard case with yellow safety block; stock comes in black, Flat Dark Earth, or OD green
MSRP. **$1508.08**

O.R.C. (OPTICS READY CARBINE)

Action: Semiautomatic
Stock: Synthetic
Barrel: 16 in.
Sights: None
Weight: 6 lb.
Caliber: 5.56mm, .223 Rem.
Magazine: Detachable box, 30 rounds (accepts any AR type mag)
Features: Flat-top upper receiver made for easy optic attachment; chrome-lined barrel; A2 birdcage suppressor; receiver length Picatinny optics rail with .5-inch optics risers; milled gas block; heavy oval M4 type handguards; telestock
MSRP. **$1391.48**

PREDATOR

Action: Semiautomatic
Stock: Synthetic, ambidextrous pistol grip
Barrel: 20 in.
Sights: None
Weight: 8 lb.
Caliber: 5.56mm, .223 Rem.
Magazine: Detachable box, 5 rounds (accepts all M16/AR 15 type)
Features: Steel lined fluted barrel; two-stage competition trigger; vented tubular aluminum free-floater forend with bipod stud; shipped with safety block in lockable, foam-padded hard case
MSRP. **$1414.80**

BUSHMASTER O.R.C.

BUSHMASTER PREDATOR

Bushmaster Firearms Internat'l

QUAD RAIL A3

Action: Semiautomatic
Stock: Synthetic
Barrel: 16 in.
Sights: None
Weight: 8 lb. 5 oz.
Caliber: 5.56mm, .223 Rem.
Magazine: Detachable box, 30 rounds
Features: Chrome-lined barrel; A2 birdcage-type suppressor; free-float quad rail forend; six-position telestock for light weight and quick handling; ships with lockable hard case and yellow safety block
A3:................... **$1391.48**

BUSHMASTER QUAD RAIL A3

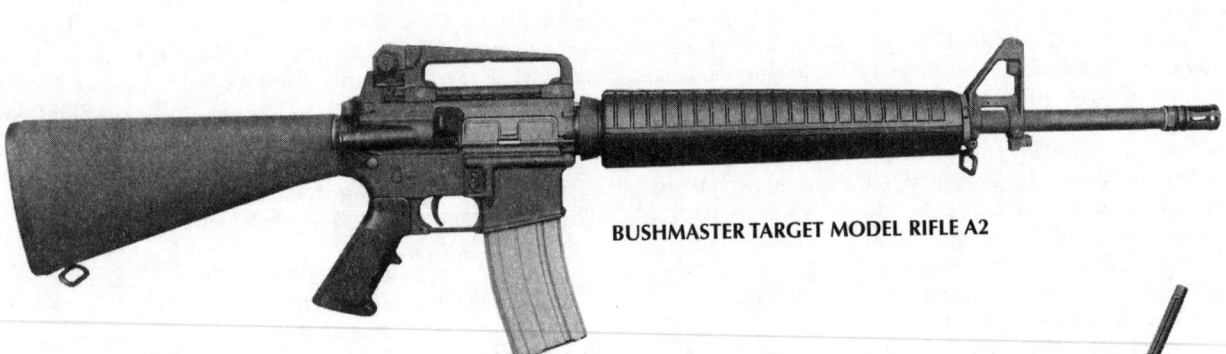

BUSHMASTER TARGET MODEL RIFLE A2

TARGET MODEL RIFLES

Action: Semiautomatic
Stock: Synthetic
Barrel: 20 in, 24 in.
Sights: None
Weight: 8 lb. 7 oz. (A2), 8 lb. 12 oz. (A3)
Caliber: 5.56mm, .223 Rem.
Magazine: Detachable box, 30 rounds (accepts all M16 / AR15 type)
Features: A3 upper receiver incorporates Pictatinny rail; A2 upper receiver 300-800 meter rear sight system; A3 receiver has 300-600 meter rear sight system; chromoly steel or polished stainless steel barrels; shipped in a lockable hard case with orange safety block
A2:..................... **$1105**
A3:..................... **$1187**
SSA2:................... **$1112**
SSA3:................... **$1187**

VARMINTER

Action: Semiautomatic
Stock: Synthetic, ambidextrous pistol grip
Barrel: 24 in.
Sights: None
Weight: 8 lb. 6 oz.
Caliber: 5.56mm, .223 Rem.
Magazine: Detachable box, 5 rounds (accepts all M16/AR 15 type)
Features: Competition crowned muzzle; chromoly vanadium steel barrel with full-length fluting; two-stage competition trigger; twelve cooling vents in forend; bipod stud installed on forend; black stock with rubberized, non-slip surface; shipped in hard plastic, lockable storage case complete with orange safety block
MSRP................ **$1430.34**

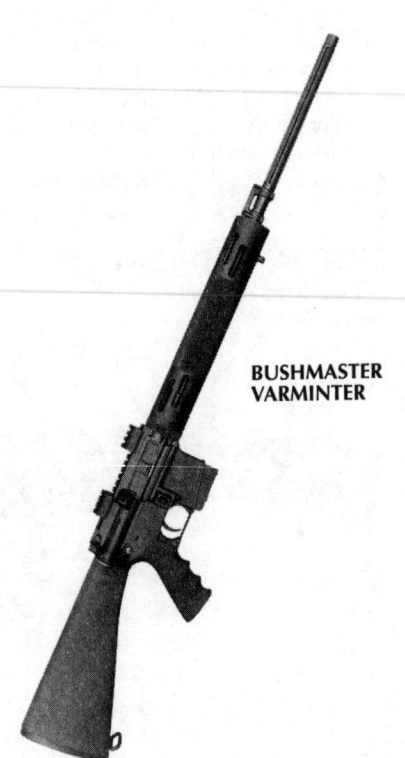

BUSHMASTER VARMINTER

Century International Arms

CENTURY INTERNATIONAL ARMS M70

CENTURY INTERNATIONAL ARMS M85 MINI MAUSER

M70 STANDARD/MAGNUM

Action: Bolt
Stock: Walnut
Barrel: 23.6 in.
Sights: Adjustable
Weight: 7 lb. 11 oz.
Caliber: .30-06, .270 Win., .308 Win., .243 Win., 7mm Rem. Mag., .300 Win. Mag.
Magazine: 5 rounds
Features: New rifle from the famous Zastava factory in Serbia; oiled European walnut stock; adjustable sights; modernized thumb actuated safety; cold forged chrome-vanadium steel
MSRP . . . . $530.95–$697.95

M85 MINI MAUSER

Action: Bolt
Stock: Walnut
Barrel: 20.07 in., 22.04 in.
Sights: Adjustable
Weight: 6 lb. 2 oz.–6 lb. 6 oz.
Caliber: .223 Rem., 7.62x39mm, .22 Hornet
Magazine: 5 rounds
Features: New rifle from the famous Zastava factory in Serbia; oiled European walnut stock; adjustable sights; modernized thumb actuated safety; cold forged chrome-vanadium steel
MSRP . . . . $530.95–$697.95

Chipmunk Rifles

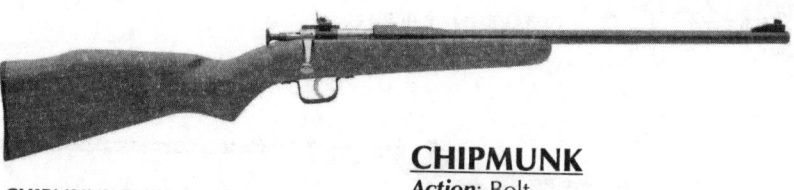

CHIPMUNK RIFLES CHIPMUNK

CHIPMUNK

Action: Bolt
Stock: Walnut, laminated
Barrel: 16.125 in.
Sights: Target
Weight: 2 lb. 8 oz.
Caliber: .22LR
Magazine: None
Features: Designed with younger shooters in mind; single-shot; manual-cocking action; receiver-mounted rear sights; metal with blued finish or stainless steel; post sight on ramp front, fully adjustable peep rear; adjustable trigger; extendable buttplate and front rail; available in black, walnut, deluxe walnut, camo laminate, and brown laminate
MSRP . . . . $163.99–$230.99

Cimarron Firearms Co.

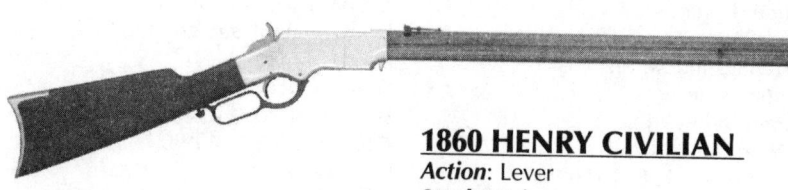

CIMARRON 1860 HENRY CIVILIAN

1860 HENRY CIVILIAN

Action: Lever
Stock: Walnut
Barrel: 24 in.
Sights: Open
Weight: 9 lb. 1 oz.–9 lb. 2 oz.
Caliber: .45 LC, .44 WCF
Magazine: Under barrel tube, 12 rounds
Features: Reproduction of 1860 Civil War Henry rifle; includes military sling swivels; frame comes in charcoal blue or original finish
Standard blue: $1350.70
Charcoal blue: $1420.70
Original finish: $1450.70

Cimarron Firearms Co.

RIFLES

1876 CENTENNIAL

Action: Lever
Stock: Walnut
Barrel: 28 in.
Sights: Open
Weight: 9 lb. 15 oz.–10 lb. 2 oz.
Caliber: .45-60, .45-75, .40-60, .50-95
Magazine: Under barrel tube, 12 rounds
Features: The favorite rifle of Teddy Roosevelt. Reproduction of 1876 Civil War Henry rifle; includes military sling swivels; frame comes in charcoal blue or original finish
MSRP $1558.70

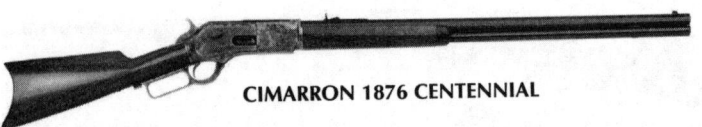

CIMARRON 1876 CENTENNIAL

1876 CROSSFIRE CARBINE

Action: Lever
Stock: Walnut
Barrel: 22 in.
Sights: None
Weight: 8 lb. 15 oz.
Caliber: .45-60, .45-75
Magazine: Under barrel tube, 8 rounds
Features: Gun was glorified in the movie *Crossfire Trail;* case-hardened stock with standard blued finish
MSRP $1706.90

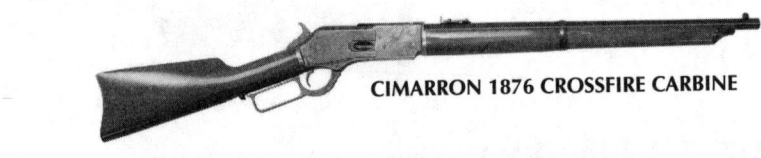

CIMARRON 1876 CROSSFIRE CARBINE

1876 N.W.M.P. (NORTH WEST MOUNTED POLICE) CARBINE

Action: Lever
Stock: Walnut
Barrel: 22 in.
Sights: None
Weight: 8 lb. 15 oz.
Caliber: .45-60, .45-75
Magazine: Under barrel tube, 8 rounds
Features: Available in walnut stock and all blued metal; reproduction of popular firearm used by mounted police in 1870s
MSRP $1748.50

CIMARRON 1876 N.W.M.P. CARBINE

1885 HIGH WALL SPORTING RIFLE

Action: Dropping block
Stock: Walnut, pistol grip
Barrel: 30 in.
Sights: Open
Weight: 9 lb. 4 oz.–10 lb. 6 oz.
Caliber: .45-70, .40-65, .38-55, .45-90, .30-40 KRAG, .405 Win.
Magazine: None
Features: Reproduction of the Winchester single-shot hunting rifle popular in 1880s; standard blued

CIMARRON 1885 HIGH WALL SPORTING RIFLE

CIMARRON 1886 RIFLE

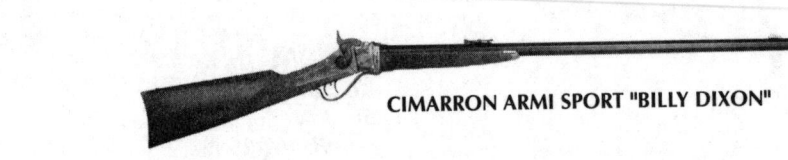

CIMARRON ARMI SPORT "BILLY DIXON"

finish on octagonal barrel; single- or double- set triggers
MSRP . . . . $1033.50–$1363.70

1886 RIFLE

Action: Lever
Stock: Walnut
Barrel: 22 in., 26 in.
Sights: None
Weight: 8 lb.–9 lb.
Caliber: .45/70 Govt.
Magazine: 7+1, 8+1 rounds
Features: Made by Armi Sport in Italy; color case-hardened receiver and butt-plate; octagonal barrel; standard blued finish; carbine version available

MSRP $1558.70
Carbine $1258.60

ARMI SPORT "BILLY DIXON" SHARPS

Action: Dropping block
Stock: Walnut, straight grip
Barrel: 32 in.
Sights: Open
Weight: 10 lb. 4 oz.–10 lb. 10 oz.
Caliber: .45-70, .45-90, .45-110, .50-90, .38-55
Magazine: None
Features: Single-shot reproduction; patent markings as on original sharps
MSRP $1324.70

Cimarron Firearms Co.

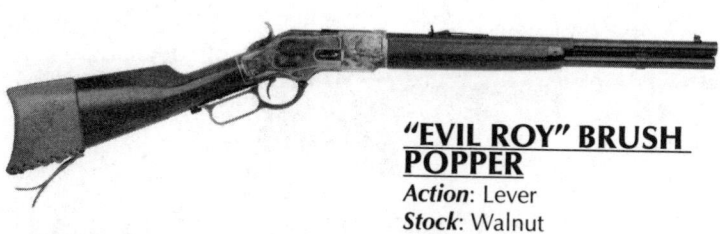

CIMARRON "EVIL ROY" BRUSH POPPER

"EVIL ROY" BRUSH POPPER

Action: Lever
Stock: Walnut
Barrel: 18.5 in.
Sights: Open
Weight: 7 lb. 2 oz.–7 lb. 5 oz.

Caliber: .45 Colt, .44 WCF, .357/.38 Spl.
Magazine: Under barrel tube, 10 rounds
Features: Custom marble sights; Evil Roy signature barrel; leather butt sheath; short stroke kit; walnut straight stock with standard blued finish on metal; case-hardened frame; pistol grip optional
MSRP $1277.70
Pistol grip: $1350.70

Citadel by Legacy Sports

M-1 .22

Action: Bolt
Stock: Wood, synthetic
Barrel: 18 in.
Sights: Adjustable rear, fixed front
Weight: 4 lb. 13 oz.
Caliber: .22LR
Magazine: 10 rounds, 2 rounds
Features: Recreation of the M-1 carbine carried by the U.S. Military in

WWII and Korea; traditional wood stock and synthetic stock models; blow-back action

Wood: $399
Synthetic: $319

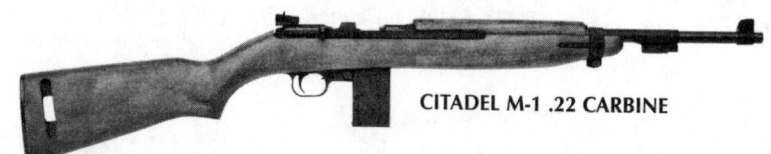

CITADEL M-1 .22 CARBINE

Colt's Manufacturing Company

ACCURIZED RIFLE

Action: Semiautomatic
Stock: Combat-style, synthetic
Barrel: 20 in., 24 in.
Sights: None
Weight: 9 lb.–9 lb. 4 oz.
Caliber: 5.56 NATO, .223
Magazine: Detachable box, 9 rounds
Features: Black stock with matte finish; heavy barrel; target crown muzzle; A2 rifle buttstock; free-floating tubular handguard; match trigger
MSRP . . . . $1374–$1653

LE901-16S

Action: Semiautomatic
Stock: Combat-style, synthetic
Barrel: 16.1 in.
Sights: Flip-up front, adjustable post, flip-up rear

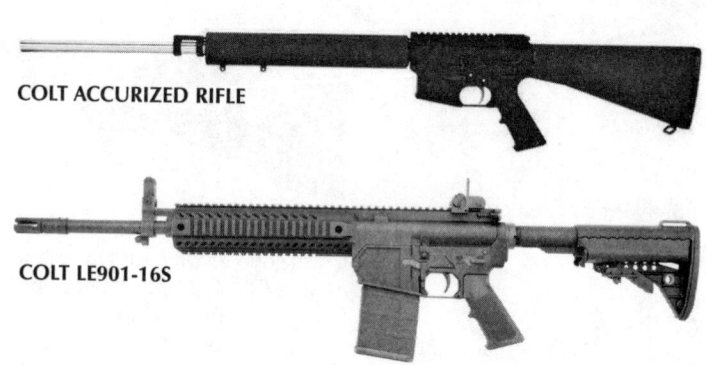

COLT ACCURIZED RIFLE

COLT LE901-16S

Weight: 9 lb. 6 oz.
Caliber: .308 Win.
Magazine: Detachable box, 20 rounds
Features: Matte black, monolithic upper receiver; .308 Winchester upper receiver group can be swapped out for

Mil-Spec Colt upper in 5.56x45 NATO; ambidextrous controls on magazine release, bolt catch and safety selector; back up iron sights; full floated barrel; bayonet lug and flash hider
MSRP $2423

Colt's Manufacturing Company

LE6940, LE6920 CARBINES

Action: Semiautomatic
Stock: Combat-style, synthetic
Barrel: 16.1 in.
Sights: Flip-up front, adjustable post, flip-up rear
Weight: 6 lb. 13 oz.–7 lb.
Caliber: 5.56x45 NATO
Magazine: Detachable box 20, 30 rounds
Features: Chrome-lined barrel; direct gas or articulating link piston system with locking bolt; Magpul MOE handguards, MOE carbine stock, MOE pistol grip, MOE vertical grip, and a Magpul back-up sight; flip-up front sight with adjustable post for elevation; flip-up rear sight adjustable for both windage and elevation; matte black finish; additional models available: LE6920MP-FDE, LE6920MP-B, LE6920SOCOM, LE6940P, LE6920CA, LE6940CA, LE6920CMP-B
MSRP . . . . **$1155–$2105**

COLT LE6940

COLT MATCH TARGET RIFLE

MATCH TARGET RIFLE

Action: Semiautomatic
Stock: Combat-style, synthetic
Barrel: 16.1 in., 20 in.
Sights: None
Weight: 7 lb. 5 oz.–9 lb. 4 oz.
Caliber: 5.56 NATO, .223
Magazine: Detachable box, 9 rounds

Features: Flat top with optional carry handle and scope mount; two-position safety; available with free-floating monolithic handguard; available with flip-up sights; available with match trigger; black stock with matte finish
MSRP . . . . **$1230–$1825**

Connecticut Valley Arms (CVA)

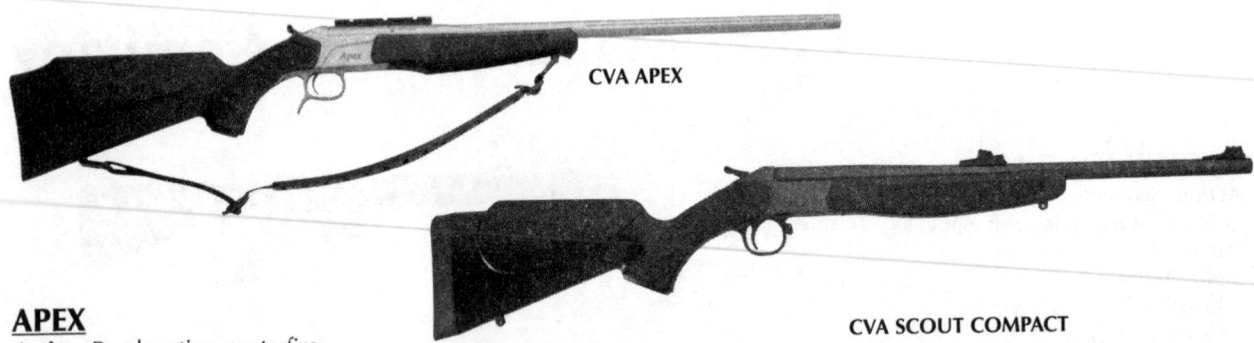

CVA APEX

CVA SCOUT COMPACT

APEX

Action: Break-action centerfire
Stock: Synthetic
Barrel: 25 in.
Sights: None
Weight: 7 lb. 8 oz.
Caliber: .45-70, 7mm-08, .308, .30-06, .300 Win. Mag., .35 Whelen, .270, .243, .223, .222, .22-250
Magazine: None
Features: Ambidextrous synthetic stock with rubber grip panels; comes in black or Realtree APG camo; stainless steel, fluted Bergara barrel; adjustable trigger; interchangeable barrels;

CrushZone recoil pad; DuraSight rail mount; QRBP (Quick Release Breech Plug); reversible hammer spur; Quake Claw Sling; also available in muzzleloading models
MSRP . . . . **$652.95–$737.95**

SCOUT

Action: Centerfire, single shot
Stock: Synthetic
Barrel: 20 in. (compact), 22 in. (standard fluted barrels)

Sights: None
Weight: 5 lb. 13 oz.
Caliber: 7mm-08, .270, .30-06, .35 Whelen, .243 (compact only)
Magazine: None
Features: Stainless steel or blued barrel; ambidextrous black synthetic stock; DuraSight Dead-On integral scope rail; CrushZone recoil pad; reversible hammer spur; compact and alternate length stocks available
MSRP . . . . **$319.95–$369.95**

Cooper Firearms

MODEL 21

Action: Bolt
Stock: 1, 2, 3, 4, 10, 11, 13, 14, 15, 17 (see key on page 135)
Barrel: 22 in., 24 in.
Sights: None
Weight: 6 lb. 8 oz.–7 lb. 8 oz.
Caliber: .17 Rem., .19-.223, Tactical .20, .204 Ruger, .222 Rem., .222 Rem. Mag., .223 Rem., .223 Rem. Al., 6x45, 6x47, 6.8 SPC, .17 Fireball, .20 VarTarg, .221 Fireball
Magazine: None
Features: Three-front locking lug bolt action single shot; Sako style extraction machined from solid bar stock; plunger style ejector machined from solid bar; fully adjustable single-stage trigger
MSRP . . . . $1825–$4395

COOPER FIREARMS MODEL 21 VARMINT EXTREME

MODEL 22

Action: Bolt
Stock: 1, 2, 3, 4, 10, 11, 13, 14, 15
Barrel: 24 in., 26 in.
Sights: None
Weight: 7 lb. 8 oz.–8 lb. 4 oz.
Caliber: .22-250 Rem., .22-250 Rem. Al., .220 Swift, .25-06 Rem., .25-06 Rem. Al., .243 Win., .243 Rem. Al., .250 Savage, .250 Savage Al., .22BR, 6BR, .257 Roberts, .257 Roberts Al., .284 Win., 7mm-08, 6mm Rem., .260 Rem., 6x284, 6.5x284, 6.5x55 Swede, 6.5 Creedmoor, 7x57 Mauser, .308 Win.
Magazine: None
Features: Three-front locking lug bolt action single-shot; Sako style extraction machined from solid bar stock; plunger style ejector machined form solid bar; fully adjustable single-stage trigger
MSRP . . . . $1825–$4495

COOPER FIREARMS MODEL 21 VARMINT LAMINATE

MODEL 38

Action: Bolt
Stock: 1, 2, 3, 4, 10, 11, 13, 14, 15, 17
Barrel: 22 in., 24 in.
Sights: None
Weight: 6 lb. 8 oz.–7 lb. 8 oz.
Caliber: .17 Squirrel, .17 Ackley Hornet, .17 He Bee, .19 Hornet, .22 Hornet, .22 K-Hornet, .22 Squirrel, .218 Bee, .218 Mashburn Bee
Magazine: None
Features: Three-front locking lug bolt action single-shot; Sako style extraction machined from solid bar stock;

COOPER FIREARMS MODEL 38 JACKSON VARMINTER

retractable tab ejector; fully adjustable single-stage trigger
MSRP . . . . $1825–$4395

MODEL 52

Action: Bolt
Stock: 1, 2, 3, 4, 5, 6, 8, 9
Barrel: 22 in., 23 in., 24 in.
Sights: None
Weight: 7 lb. 8 oz.–8 lb.
Caliber: .30-06, .25-06, .25-06 Al.,

COOPER FIREARMS MODEL 52 WESTERN CLASSIC

6.5x284, 6.5-06, .270, .284, .280, .280 Al., .338-06, .35 Whelen
Magazine: 3 rounds
Features: Three-rear locking lug bolt action magazine fed repeater; center-fire action, also available in stainless steel; Sako style extraction machined from solid bar stock; retractable tab ejector machined from solid bar; fully adjustable single-stage trigger
MSRP . . . . $1975–$4995

Cooper Firearms

**COOPER FIREARMS MODEL 57M
CLASSIC**

**COOPER FIREARMS MODEL 57 LIGHT
VARMINT TARGET - LVT**

MODEL 54
Action: Bolt
Stock: 1, 2, 3, 4, 5, 6, 8, 9, 10, 11, 13, 14, 15
Barrel: 22 in., 23 in., 24 in.
Sights: None
Weight: 6 lb. 8 oz.–8 lb.
Caliber: .22-250 Rem., .22-250 Rem. Al., .220 Swift, .243 Win., .243 Rem. Al., 6mm Rem., .250 Savage, .250 Savage Al., .257 Roberts, .257 Roberts Al., 7mm-08, .260 Rem., 6.5 Creedmoor, 6.5x47 Lapua, .308 Win.
Magazine: 3 rounds
Features: Three-rear locking lug bolt action magazine fed repeater; center-fire action, also available in stainless steel; Sako style extraction machined from solid bar stock; plunger style ejector machined form solid bar; fully adjustable single-stage trigger
MSRP . . . . $1975–$4995

MODEL 56
Action: Bolt
Stock: 1, 2, 3, 4, 5, 6, 8, 9
Barrel: 22 in., 23 in., 24 in.
Sights: None
Weight: 8 lb. 4 oz.–8 lb. 8 oz.
Caliber: .257 Wby. Mag., .264 Win. Mag., .270 Wby. Mag., 7mm Rem. Mag., 7 mm Wby. Mag., 7mm STW, .300 H&H, .300 Win. Mag., .300 Wby. Mag., .308 Norma Mag., 8mm Rem. Mag., .338 Win. Mag., .340 Wby. Mag., .375 H&H
Magazine: 3 rounds
Features: Three-rear locking lug bolt action magazine fed repeater; center-fire action, also available in stainless steel; Sako style extraction machined from solid bar stock; retractable tab ejector machined from solid bar; fully adjustable single-stage trigger
MSRP . . . . $2795–$5995

MODEL 57M
Action: Bolt
Stock: 1, 2, 3, 4, 5, 7, 9, 12, 15, 16
Barrel: 22 in., 24 in.
Sights: None
Weight: 6 lb.–8 lb.
Caliber: .17 Mach 2, .22LR, .22 WMR, .17 HMR
Magazine: 4, 5 rounds
Features: Three-rear locking lug bolt action magazine fed repeater; twin extractor claw; fixed ejector; feed block; fully adjustable single-stage trigger
MSRP . . . . $1855–$4395

Cooper Stocks

COOPER FIREARMS EXCALIBUR

1. CLASSIC
AA Claro Walnut; steel grip; four-panel hand checkering; oil finish; matte metal finish; no options

2. CUSTOM CLASSIC
AAA Claro walnut; steel grip and stock metal; ebony tip; western-fleur wrap-around hand checkering; oil finish; 4140 blued steel match barrel; gloss metal finish; all options

3. WESTERN CLASSIC
AAA Claro walnut; steel grip and stock metal; Doug Turnbull case color metal; octagon barrel; matte metal finish; wrap-around western-fleur hand checkering; oil finish; ebony tip; 4140 blued steel match barrel; all options

4. MANNLICHER
AAA Claro walnut; shadowline beaded cheek piece; African ebony tip; multi-point wrap around hand checkering; oil finish; Pachmayr pad; standard sling swivel studs; steel grip cap; chromoly premium match grade barrel; high gloss finish on metalwork; all options available

5. SCHNABEL
Available in models 52, 54, 56, and 57; AA+ Claro walnut; raised comb; slim taper forearm; multi-point two panel hand checkering; oil finish; standard grade sling swivel studs; Pachmayr pad; steel grip cap; chromoly premium match grade barrel; metal work is matte finished; all options available

6. EXCALIBUR
Synthetic copy of the Classic; M52 only

7. JACKSON SQUIRREL
AA Select walnut; roll-over cheekpiece; fluted forearm; hand checkering; oil finish; steel grip cap

8. JACKSON GAME
Characteristics of Jackson Squirrel stock with a North American Hunting rifle (M52); some options

9. JACKSON HUNTER
Synthetic version of Jackson Squirrel in M57; in M52, this is a version of the Jackson Game

10. VARMINTER
AA Claro walnut; stainless match barrel; hand checkering; hand oil finish; matte metal finish; no options

11. MONTANA VARMINTER
AA Select Claro walnut; steel grip cap; cooling vents; stainless match barrel; hand checkering and hand oil finish; matte metal finish; all options

12. LIGHT VARMINT TARGET
AA Select Claro walnut; steel grip cap; cooling vents; stainless match barrel; hand checkering and hand oil finish; matte metal finish; all options

13. VARMINT EXTREME
AAA Claro walnut; steel grip and stock metal; stainless match barrel; hand checkering with cross-over grip pattern; hand oil finish; egg shell matte metal finish; all options

14. PHOENIX
Synthetic in flat black and brown spider-web finish; stainless match barrel; aluminum bedding block; cooling vents; matte metal finish; no options

15. VARMINT LAMINATE
Laminated hardwood stock; oil finish; Pachmayr pad; steel grip cap; ventilated forearm; stainless steel, striaght taper, premium grade match barrel; sling swivel studs available upon request

16. TRP-3
Benchrest style; synthetic BR stock; straight stainless match barrel; matte metal finish; some options

17. JACKSON VARMINTER
AA Select walnut; roll-over cheekpiece; fluted forearm; hand checkering; oil finish; steel grip cap; stainless match barrel; matte metal finish; some options

CZ-USA (Ceska Zbrojovka)

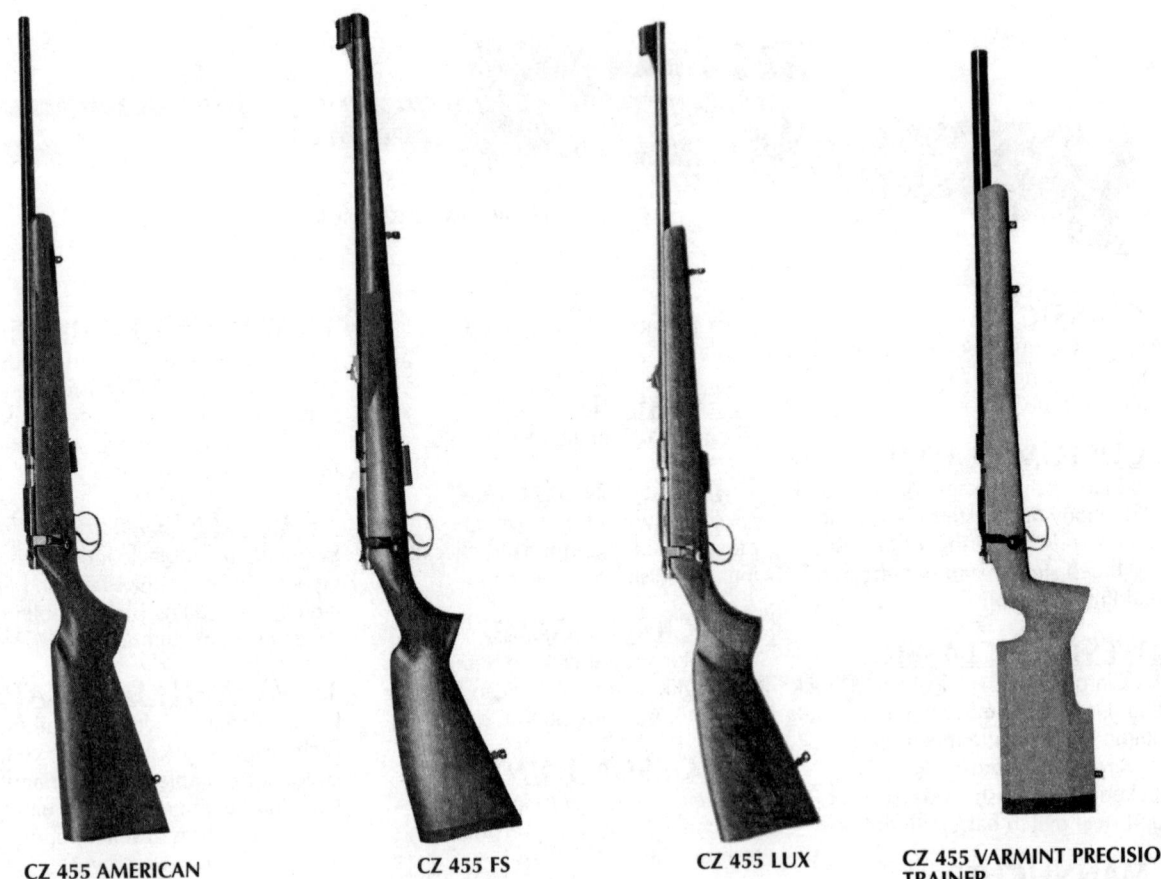

CZ 455 AMERICAN   CZ 455 FS   CZ 455 LUX   CZ 455 VARMINT PRECISION TRAINER

455 AMERICAN

Action: Bolt
Stock: Walnut
Barrel: 20.5 in.
Sights: None
Weight: 6 lb. 2 oz.
Caliber: .17 HMR, .22LR, .22 WMR, Combo .22LR with .17 HMR replacement barrel
Magazine: Detachable box, 5 rounds
Features: Cold hammer-forged barrel; blued receiver and barrel finish; integrated dovetail scope base; interchangeable barrel system; adjustable trigger
MSRP . . . .$374–$541

455 FS

Action: Bolt
Stock: Walnut
Barrel: 20.6 in.
Sights: Adjustable iron sights

Weight: 6 lb. 6 oz.
Caliber: .22LR, .17 HMR
Magazine: Detachable box, 5 rounds
Features: Action machined from bar stock; adjustable trigger; detachable feed magazine; cold-hammer-forged barrels; standard 11mm optic-mounting dovetail; full length Mannlicher walnut stock; adjustable iron sights
MSRP . . . .$499–$524

455 LUX

Action: Bolt
Stock: Walnut
Barrel: 20.6 in.
Sights: Open
Weight: 6 lb. 2 oz.
Caliber: .22LR, .22 WMR
Magazine: Detachable box, 5 rounds
Features: Interchangeable barrel system; adjustable trigger; hammer-forged barrel and billet machined receiver;

adjustable iron sights; lux pattern walnut stock
MSRP . . . .$427–$456

455 VARMINT PRECISION TRAINER

Action: Bolt
Stock: Composite
Barrel: 20.5 in.
Sights: Optic mounting dovetail
Weight: 8 lb. 2 oz.
Caliber: .22LR
Magazine: Detachable box, 5 rounds
Features: Action machined from bar stock; adjustable trigger; detachable feed magazine; cold-hammer-forged barrels; standard 11mm optic-mounting dovetail; MCS-T4 Manners composite stock; heavy .886-inch diameter barrel; available in coyote tan; stocks can be ordered with custom weighting/filling
MSRP $899

RIFLES

CZ-USA (Ceska Zbrojovka)

CZ 455 VARMINT

CZ 455 VARMINT
EVOLUTION

CZ 512 RIMFIRE

CZ 527 VARMINT

455 VARMINT
Action: Bolt
Stock: Walnut
Barrel: 20.5 in.
Sights: Optic mounting dovetail
Weight: 7 lb. 1 oz.
Caliber: .22LR, .22 WMR, .17 HMR
Magazine: Detachable box, 5 rounds
Features: Action machined from bar stock; adjustable trigger; detachable feed magazine; cold-hammer-forged barrels; standard 11mm optic-mounting dovetail; heavier and stiffer barrel for enhanced accuracy; accepts all accessory barrels for the 455 models
MSRP. . . . .$456–$483

455 VARMINT WITH SS EVOLUTION STOCK
Action: Bolt
Stock: Laminate
Barrel: 20.5 in.
Sights: Optic mounting dovetail
Weight: 7 lb. 2 oz.
Caliber: .17 HMR, .22LR

Magazine: Detachable box, 5 rounds
Features: Action machined from bar stock; adjustable trigger; detachable feed magazine; cold-hammer-forged barrels; standard 11mm optic-mounting dovetail; sky blue/gray laminated stock; ambidextrous; free floated barrel; accepts all accessory barrels for the 455 models
MSRP. . . . .$522–$549

512 RIMFIRE RIFLE
Action: Semiautomatic
Stock: Lacquered beech wood
Barrel: 20.7 in.
Sights: Adjustable
Weight: 5 lb. 14 oz.
Caliber: .22LR, .22 WMR
Magazine: Detachable box, 5 rounds
Features: Aluminum alloy upper receiver and fiberglass reinforced polymer lower half; dual guide rods; hammer-forged CZ barrel; integral 11mm dovetail for mounting optics
MSRP. . . . .$465–$496

527
Action: Bolt
Stock: Walnut
Barrel: 18.5 in.-24 in.
Sights: Open
Weight: 5 lb. 14 oz.–7 lb. 13 oz.
Caliber: .222 Rem., .223 Rem., .22 Hornet; American: .17 Hornet .204 Ruger, .221 Fireball; Carbine: 7.62x39; Varmint Target: .204 Ruger
Magazine: Detachable box, 5 rounds
Features: Hammer-forged barrel; controlled round feed; single-set trigger; each model comes in a variety of calibers and a different stock; Turkish walnut stock in Bavarian pattern on Lux model; Varmint model comes in walnut, Kevlar, or laminated; left-hand version available in American model
American: . . . .$711–$764
Carbine: $711
FS: $762
Lux: . . . .$711–$755
Varmint: . . . .$704–$752
Varmint Target $885

CZ-USA (Ceska Zbrojovka)

CZ 550 CARBINE

CZ 550 MEDIUM, KEVLAR

550
Action: Bolt
Stock: Walnut, Kevlar
Barrel: 20.5 in., 23.6 in.
Sights: Open
Weight: 7 lb.–7 lb. 10 oz.
Caliber: .22-250, .243 Win., .270 Win., .30-06, .308 Win.; 6.5x55, 9.3x62; (Medium Lux): 6.5x55 Swede
Magazine: Detachable box, 4, 5 rounds
Features: Adjustable single-set trigger; detachable magazine optional; full stocked model (FS) available; American model includes Pachmayr recoil pad; carbine has Kevlar stock
American: . . . .$815–$998
Carbine: . . . . $1049–$1096
FS: . . . .$864–$911

550 MEDIUM
Action: Bolt
Stock: Walnut, Kevlar
Barrel: 20.5 in., 23.6 in.

Sights: Open
Weight: 7 lb. 5 oz.–7 lb. 11 oz.
Caliber: .300 Win. Mag., 7mm Rem. Mag.
Magazine: Detachable box, 3 rounds
Features: Adjustable single-set trigger; detachable magazine optional; Battue model has hog-back cob and red fiber optic front sight; Kevlar model has adjustable back iron sights
Kevlar: $1096
Lux: $919

550 SAFARI MAGNUM
Action: Bolt
Stock: Walnut
Barrel: 25 in.
Sights: Express sights
Weight: 9 lb. 6 oz.
Caliber: .375 H&H Mag., .416 Rigby, .458 Win. Mag.
Magazine: Fixed, 3 (.416 Rigby), 5 rounds

Features: Known worldwide as the 602 BRNO; hammer-forged barrel; single-set trigger; controlled round feed and fixed ejector make the rifle reliable enough for heavy and dangerous game; express sights (1 standing, 2 folding); select Trukish walnut stock with classic safari shape
MSRP . . . . $1180–$1280

550 ULTIMATE HUNTING RIFLE
Action: Bolt
Stock: Walnut, Kevlar
Barrel: 23.6 in.
Sights: Open
Weight: 7 lb. 11 oz.
Caliber: .300 Win. Mag.
Magazine: Fixed, 3 rounds
Features: Hammer-forged, blued barrel; single-stage trigger
MSRP $1321
Kevlar: $1453

CZ 550 SAFARI MAGNUM

CZ 550 ULTIMATE HUNTING RIFLE

CZ-USA (Ceska Zbrojovka)

CZ 550 VARMINT

CZ 550 URBAN COUNTER-SNIPER

CZ 750 SNIPER

550 URBAN COUNTER-SNIPER

Action: Bolt
Stock: Synthetic
Barrel: 16 in.
Sights: None
Weight: 8 lb. 5 oz.
Caliber: .308 Win.
Magazine: Detachable box, 10 rounds
Features: Floated bull barrel with target crown; Surefire muzzlebrake; Teflon coating; single-stage trigger; Bell & Carlson fiberglass stock; aluminum bedding block
MSRP. **$2530**

550 VARMINT

Action: Bolt
Stock: Walnut, laminate, Kevlar
Barrel: 25.6 in.
Sights: Open
Weight: 9 lb. 11 oz.
Caliber: .22-250, .308
Magazine: Detachable box, 4 rounds

Features: Heavy barreled, two position manual safety; firing-pin-block and bolt lock
MSRP. . . . . **$840–$979**

750 SNIPER

Action: Bolt
Stock: Synthetic thumbhole
Barrel: 26 in.
Sights: Open

Weight: 11 lb. 14 oz.
Caliber: .308 Win.
Magazine: Detachable box, 10 rounds
Features: Adjustable comb; underside of forend is fitted with a 220mm-long rail for bipod attachment; muzzlebrake; thread protector; mirage shield; blued barrel; single-stage trigger
MSRP. **$1999**

Dakota Arms

MODEL 10

Action: Falling block
Stock: Walnut
Barrel: 23 in.
Sights: None

Weight: 6 lb.–7 lb.
Caliber: .22LR to .300 Win., .338 to .375 H&H Mag.
Magazine: None
Features: Point wrap checkering; scope

ring bases installed; custom length of pull; barrel break in
MSRP. . . . . from **$5260**
Deluxe: . . . . from **$6690**

DAKOTA MODEL 10

Dakota Arms

DAKOTA MODEL 76 CLASSIC

DAKOTA MODEL 97 HUNTER

MODEL 76 CLASSIC

Action: Bolt
Stock: Walnut
Barrel: 23 in.
Sights: None
Weight: 6 lb. 8 oz.–9 lb. 8 oz.
Caliber: Classic: .257 Roberts, .260 Rem., .270 Win., .280 Rem., .30-06 Spfd., .300 Dakota, .300 Win. Mag., .300 WSM, .308 Win., .330 Dakota, .416 Rem., 7mm Rem. Mag., 7mm-08 Rem.; Safari: .300 H&H, .375 Dakota, .416 Rem., 7mm Dakota; African: .338 Win. Mag., .375 H&H, .416 Rem., .404 Jeffery, .416 Rigby, .450 Dakota, .458 Lott
Magazine: Box, 4 rounds
Features: Barrel break in; custom length of pull; optional engraving; point panel checkering; Dakota swivel studs; 1-inch recoil pad; straddle floor plate; right- or left-hand configurations; Safari model has front island sight with flip-up night sight; African model has quarter rib sights with banded front sights and flip-up night sights

Classic: . . . . from $6030
Safari: . . . . from $8010
African: . . . . from $8890

MODEL 97 HUNTER

Action: Bolt
Stock: Fiberglass, composite, walnut
Barrel: 22 in. (short action), 25 in. (long action)
Sights: None
Weight: 7 lb.
Caliber: All-Weather: .30-06, .338 Win. Mag., .375 H&H, 7mm Rem. Mag., 7mm-08; Long Range: .280

Rem., .338 Win. Mag., 7mm Rem. Mag., 7mm-08
Magazine: Blind box
Features: Stainless Douglas barrel; black composite stock with two inletted Ken Howell swivel studs; stainless trigger bow

All-weather: . . . . from $4050
Deluxe: . . . . from $4820
Long Range: . . . . from $3720

SHARPS

Action: Falling block
Stock: Walnut
Barrel: 26 in.
Sights: Open
Weight: 8 lb.
Caliber: .17 HMR, .22 Hornet, .30-30, .30-40 Krag., .375 H&H
Magazine: None
Features: Octagon barrel; steel butt-plate; single blade rear sight with front bead; matte blued metal finish

Sharps: . . . . from $4490
Miller: . . . . from $5590

VARMINTER

Action: Bolt
Stock: Walnut
Barrel: 22 in.
Sights: None
Weight: 8 lb. 4 oz.
Caliber: .17 VarTag, .17 Rem., .17 Tactical, .20 PPC, .204 Ruger, .221 Rem. Fireball, .22 PPC, .223 Rem., 6mm PPC, 6.5 Grendel
Magazine: None
Features: Available in walnut sporter-style stock or XXX walnut varmint style stock with semi-beavertail forend; checkered grip; recessed target crown; vapor hone matte bead blast finish on stainless; stainless steel barrel

MSRP . . . . from $2840
All-weather: . . . . from $3390
Deluxe: . . . . from $3390
Heavy: . . . . from $2840

DAKOTA SHARPS

DAKOTA VARMINTER

Dixie Gun Works

1873 TRAPDOOR OFFICER'S MODEL BY PEDERSOLI

Action: Breechloading
Stock: Walnut
Barrel: 26 in.
Sights: Adjustable
Weight: 8 lb.
Caliber: .45-70
Magazine: None
Features: Single-shot rifle; front sight is blued steel with brass bead; rear sight is adjustable tang sight; color case-hardened steel furniture, pewter nose cap; single set trigger; chambered for black powder cartridges or factory-loaded smokeless ammo
MSRP. **$1900**

1874 SHILOH SHARPS MODEL

Action: Breechloading
Stock: Walnut, pistol grip
Barrel: 34 in. long range; 30 in. Sporting rifle No. 1; 26 in. Sporting Rifle
Sights: Adjustable
Weight: 10 lb.
Caliber: .45-70,.30-40 Krag. Sporting rifle
Magazine: None
Features: Sporting model has a spirit level dovetail; part round, part octagonal barrel; frame, lock plate, hammer, and lever have all the original color case-hardening; buttstock is mounted with checkered hard rubber plate; double-set triggers; chambered for black powder cartridges or factory-loaded smokeless ammo
MSRP. **$2850**

KODIAK DOUBLE RIFLE BY PEDERSOLI

Action: Lever
Stock: Walnut, pistol grip
Barrel: 24 in.
Sights: Flip up sights
Weight: 10 lb.–10 lb. 12 oz.
Caliber: .50, .54, .58 Kodiak, .45-70 Mark IV, .72 Express
Magazine: None
Features: Express has dovetail, steel ramp with brass bead as front sight; blued barrels; external hammers are rebounding style; double triggers; sling is included; English walnut buttstock and forearm are checkered; rubber recoil pad; chambered for black powder cartridges or factory-loaded smokeless ammo
MSRP. . . . . **$1395–$1450**

DIXIE GUN WORKS 1873 TRAPDOOR OFFICER'S MODEL

DIXIE GUN WORKS 1874 SHILOH SHARPS MODEL

DIXIE GUN WORKS KODIAK DOUBLE RIFLE

DPMS Panther Arms

24 SPECIAL
Action: Semiautomatic
Stock: Synthetic; pistol grip
Barrel: 24 in.
Sights: None
Weight: 10 lb. 4 oz.
Caliber: .233 Rem
Magazine: Detachable box, 30 rounds
Features: Aircraft aluminum alloy, A3 style flattop receiver coated in black Teflon; aluminum trigger guard; black standard A2 Zytel Mil-Spec stock with Panther Tactical grip; aluminum ribbed free-float tube; nylon web sling included; adjustable buttplate
MSRP $1229

A2 CLASSIC
Action: Semiautomatic
Stock: Synthetic
Barrel: 20 in.
Sights: Open
Weight: 9 lb.
Caliber: 5.56x45mm
Magazine: Detachable box, 30 rounds
Features: Chromoly steel barrel with A2 flash hider; forged aircraft aluminum alloy receiver with A2 fixed carry handle; black standardized A2 black style Mil-Spec stock; standard A2 round handguards; dual aperture adjustable rear sights, Mil-Spec front sight post
MSRP $869

AP4 CARBINE
Action: Semiautomatic
Stock: Synthetic
Barrel: 16 in.
Sights: Open
Weight: 7 lb. 2 oz.
Caliber: 5.56x45mm
Magazine: Detachable box, 30 rounds
Features: Chromoly steel barrel with A2 Flash hider; A3 aircraft aluminum alloy receiver with detachable carrying handle; adjustable rear sight and A2 front sight assembly; black AP4-6 position, telescoping fiber reinforced polymer stock; oval, carbine length GlacierGuards
MSRP $959

ARCTIC PANTHER
Action: Semiautomatic
Stock: Synthetic
Barrel: 20 in.
Sights: None
Weight: 9 lb.
Caliber: .223 Rem.
Magazine: Detachable box, 30 rounds
Features: Fluted and black Teflon coated barrel; aircraft aluminum alloy, A3 style flattop receiver coated in white; standard A2 black Zytel Mil-Spec stock; aluminum ribbed free-float handguard tube (coated white)
MSRP $1129

DPMS 24 SPECIAL

DPMS A2 CLASSIC

DPMS AP4 CARBINE

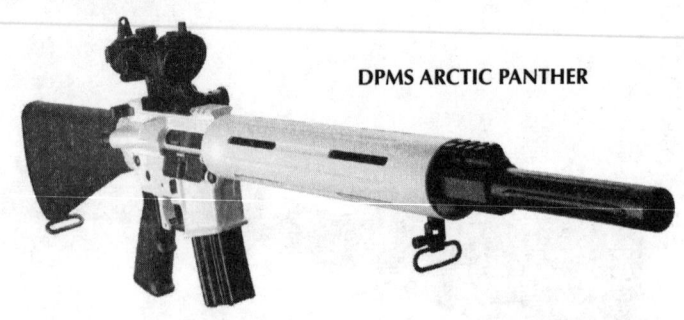

DPMS ARCTIC PANTHER

RIFLES

DPMS CARBINE A2

DPMS DCM

DPMS COMPACT HUNTER

DPMS LO-PRO CLASSIC

DPMS LITE LR-308

CARBINE A2

Action: Semiautomatic
Stock: Synthetic
Barrel: 16 in.
Sights: Open
Weight: 6 lb. 14 oz.
Caliber: 5.56x45mm
Magazine: Detachable box, 30 rounds
Features: Chromoly steel barrel with flash hider; A3 aircraft aluminum alloy receiver with detachable carrying handle; adjustable rear sight and A2 front sight assembly; DPMS Pardus black stock; oval, carbine length GlacierGuards
MSRP **$859**

COMPACT HUNTER

Action: Semiautomatic
Stock: Synthetic
Barrel: 16 in.
Sights: None
Weight: 7 lb. 12 oz.
Caliber: .308 Win.
Magazine: 4, 10, 20 rounds
Features: Designed for smaller statures and suitable for youth, female, and hunters who prefer a compact firearm; Teflon-coated stainless steel barrel; carbon fiber free-float tube; Hogue pistol grip; B5 Systems-Special Operations Peculiar Modification (SOPMOD) stock
MSRP **$1499**

DCM

Action: Semiautomatic
Stock: Synthetic
Barrel: 20 in.
Sights: Adjustable NM
Weight: 9 lb. 6 oz.
Caliber: .233 Rem.
Magazine: Detachable box, 30 rounds
Features: National Match dual aperture rear sight, NM front sight post; A2 fixed carry handle; forged aircraft aluminum alloy receiver; receiver coated in Teflon; aluminum trigger guard; standard black A2 style Mil-Spec stock with trap door assembly; DCM free-float handguard system
MSRP **$1129**

LITE LR-308

Action: Semiautomatic
Stock: Synthetic
Barrel: 24 in.
Sights: None
Weight: 10 lb. 4 oz.
Caliber: .308 Win.
Magazine: 4, 10, 20 rounds
Features: 416 stainless steel light-weight fluted barrel; improved 2012 carbon fiber free-float tube; A3 receiver
MSRP **$1499**

LO-PRO CLASSIC

Action: Semiautomatic
Stock: Synthetic
Barrel: 16 in.
Sights: None
Weight: 7 lb. 12 oz.
Caliber: 5.56x45mm
Magazine: Detachable box, 30 rounds
Features: Chromoly steel barrel; flattop Lo-Pro, extruded receiver made of aircraft aluminum alloy; semiauto trigger group; standard A2 black Zytel Mil stock with trap door assembly; GlacierGuards
MSRP **$769**

DPMS Panther Arms

DPMS LR-204

DPMS LR-243H

DPMS LR-308

DPMS LR-260

DPMS PRAIRIE PANTHER KING'S DESERT SHADOW

LR-204

Action: Semiautomatic
Stock: Synthetic
Barrel: 24 in.
Sights: None
Weight: 10 lb. 4 oz.
Caliber: .204 Ruger
Magazine: Detachable box, 30 rounds
Features: Fluted barrel; standard A2 black stock; aluminum ribbed free-float tube; aircraft aluminum alloy, Teflon coated, forged A3 style receiver; nylon web sling included
MSRP. **$1059**

LR-243H, LR-243L

Action: Semiautomatic
Stock: Synthetic
Barrel: 20 in. (LR-243), 18 in. (LR-243L)
Sights: None
Weight: 8 lb.–10 lb. 10 oz.
Caliber: .243 Win.
Magazine: Detachable box, 19 rounds
Features: Custom Miculek compensator, lightweight gas block (LR-243L); black Teflon-covered stainless steel barrel with 308 Panther Flash hider (LR-243H); A3 flattop lightweight receiver, extruded from T-5 Aluminum (LR-243L); A3 flattop thick walled aluminum receiver (LR-243H); two-stage trigger (LR-243L); standard AR-15 trig-

ger group (LR-243H); Carbon Fiber Free-Float tube with bipod stud (LR-243L); standard length ribbed free-float handguard tube (LR-243H)
LR-243H: **$1239**
LR-243L: **$1499**

LR-260

Action: Semiautomatic
Stock: Synthetic
Barrel: 24 in.
Sights: None
Weight: 11 lb. 4 oz.
Caliber: .260 Rem.
Magazine: Detachable box, 19 rounds
Features: 416 Stainless steel bull barrel; A3 style flattop receiver made of thick walled aluminum; standard AR-15 trigger group; standard A2 black style Mil-Spec stock with trap door assembly; standard length ribbed free-float handguard tube
MSRP. **$1239**

LR-308

Action: Semiautomatic
Stock: Synthetic
Barrel: 24 in.
Sights: None

Weight: 11 lb. 3 oz.
Caliber: .308 Win.
Magazine: Detachable box, 19 rounds
Features: 416 Stainless steel bull barrel; thick walled aluminum receiver coated with Teflon; internal trigger guard; raised Picatinny rail for easy scope mounting; standard A2 Black Zytel Mil-Spec stock
MSRP. **$1199**

PRAIRIE PANTHER CAMO

Action: Semiautomatic
Stock: Synthetic
Barrel: 20 in.
Sights: None
Weight: 7 lb. 2 oz.
Caliber: .223 Rem.
Magazine: Detachable box, 20 rounds
Features: Target crowned, stainless steel heavy barrel; A3 flattop aircraft aluminum alloy receiver; Magpul winter trigger guard; King's Desert Shadow camo, King's Snow Shadow camo, or Mossy Oak Brush camo stock; receiver features durable ceramic over coat in either type of camo; nylon web sling included
MSRP. **$1289**

DPMS Panther Arms

RECON

Action: Semiautomatic
Stock: Synthetic
Barrel: 16 in.
Sights: Magpul BUIS
Weight: 9 lb.
Caliber: 5.56mm
Magazine: Detachable box, 30 rounds
Features: Bead-blasted stainless, mid length gas system; semi-auto trigger group; Magpul MOE stock in Teflon black
MSRP $1129

DPMS RECON

REPR

Action: Semiautomatic
Stock: Synthetic
Barrel: 20 in.
Sights: None
Weight: 9 lb. 12 oz.
Caliber: 7.62 NATO
Magazine: Detachable box, 19 rounds
Features: Two-stage match grade trigger; dark earth Magpul PRS stock; Hogue rubber grip with finger grooves; A3 style flattop; ambi-selector installed; milled from solid billet of aluminum; AAC flash hider/suppressor adapter
MSRP $2589

DPMS REPR

SWEET 16, BULL 20, BULL 24

Action: Semiautomatic
Stock: Synthetic
Barrel: 16 in., 20 in., 24 in.
Sights: None
Weight: 7 lb. 14 oz.–9 lb. 13 oz.
Caliber: .223 Rem.
Magazine: Detachable box, 30 rounds
Features: Aircraft aluminum alloy, A3 style flattop receiver coated in black Teflon; aluminum trigger guard; black standard A2 Zytel Mil-Spec stock; aluminum ribbed free-float tube; Nylon web sling included
Bull Sweet 16: $939
Bull 20: $969
Bull 24: $999

DPMS SWEET 16

TACTICAL 16

Action: Semiautomatic
Stock: Synthetic
Barrel: 16 in.
Sights: Open
Weight: 8 lb. 3 oz.
Caliber: 5.56x45mm
Magazine: Detachable box, 30 rounds

DPMS TACTICAL 16

Features: Chromoly steel barrel with A3 Flash hider; A2 front and rear sight assembly; forged aircraft aluminum alloy receiver coated in Teflon; black standard A2 style mil stock; nylon web sling included
MSRP $859

E.M.F. Company

1866 "YELLOWBOY" SHORT RIFLE

Action: Lever
Stock: Walnut
Barrel: 20 in.
Sights: Open
Weight: 8 lb. 3 oz.
Caliber: .38 Spl., .45LC
Magazine: 10+1 rounds
Features: First true cowboy lever-action rifle; loading gate passes cartridges through side of the receiver; SASS badge engraved on both sides
MSRP **$1175**

ROSSI 1892 TRAPPER CARBINE

Action: Lever
Stock: Hardwood

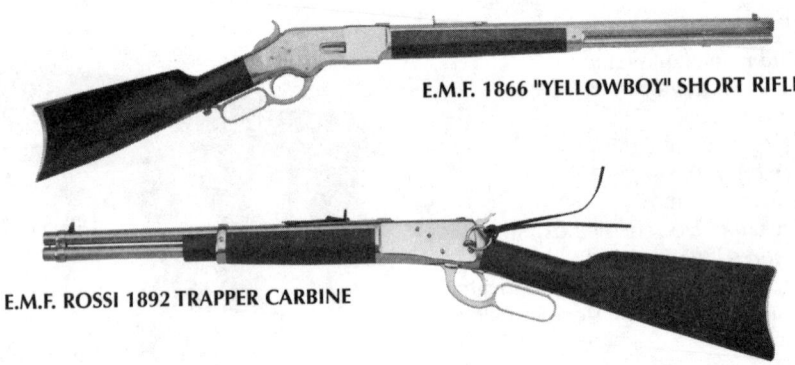

E.M.F. 1866 "YELLOWBOY" SHORT RIFLE

E.M.F. ROSSI 1892 TRAPPER CARBINE

Barrel: 16 in.
Sights: Fixed
Weight: 4 lb. 13 oz.
Caliber: .44 Mag.
Magazine: 8+1 rounds

Features: Stainless steel frame; round stainless steel barrel; hardwood forend and buttstock; fast western-style lever; crescent buttplates
MSRP **$585**

E.R. Shaw

E.R. SHAW MARK VII CUSTOM

Action: Bolt
Stock: Walnut, laminate wood, or synthetic
Barrel: 16.25 in.–26 in.
Sights: None
Weight: Depending on specifications
Caliber: 75 caliber choices from .17 Rem. to .458 Lott
Magazine: Internal magazine

Features: Right- or left-hand actions; stainless receivers; contour barrels; polished or matte blued finish; recoil pads and swivel studs; choice of two

barrel contours, stainless steel or blued chromoly steel
Base price: **$775**

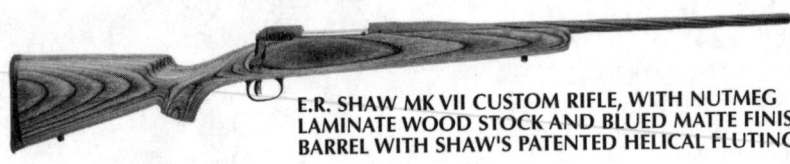

E.R. SHAW MK VII CUSTOM RIFLE, WITH NUTMEG LAMINATE WOOD STOCK AND BLUED MATTE FINISH BARREL WITH SHAW'S PATENTED HELICAL FLUTING

Excel Arms

EXCEL ARMS ACCELERATOR RIFLE

ACCELERATOR RIFLE

Action: Semiautomatic
Stock: Polymer composite, pistol grip
Barrel: 18 in.

Sights: Standard includes Red/Green dot optic
Weight: 8 lb.
Caliber: .22 WMR, .17 HMR
Magazine: Detachable box, 9 rounds
Features: Weaver rail for scope, sights, and optics; pin-block safety; stainless steel barrel; polymer composite stock available in black or silver shroud
MR-22: . . . . **$512–$549**
MR-5.7: . . . . **$640–$795**

RIFLES

Excel Arms

EXCEL ARMS X-5.7R

EXCEL ARMS X-22R

X-5.7R

Action: Semiautomatic
Stock: Synthetic
Barrel: 18 in.
Sights: None
Weight: 6 lb. 4 oz.
Caliber: 5.7x28mm
Magazine: 25, 10 rounds
Features: CNC-machined aluminum; Picatinny rail; tactical AR styling; collapsible stock; tapped holes in the hand guard for mounting accessory rails
MSRP. $795
Iron sights: $916

X-22R RIFLE

Action: Semiautomatic
Stock: Synthetic
Barrel: 18 in.
Sights: None
Weight: 4 lb. 12 oz.
Caliber: .22LR HV
Magazine: Detachable box, 25 rounds, (10 rounds optional)
Features: CNC-machined aluminum frame; optional 3-9x40 scope; tapped holes in hand guard for mounting accessory rails; integral weaver base to mount scopes, sights, and optics
Basic: $461
Scoped: $548
10 RD: $461

FNH USA

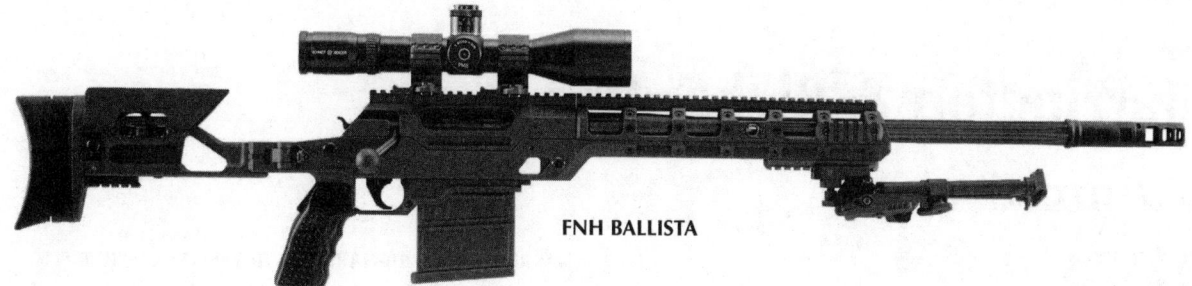

FNH BALLISTA

BALLISTA

Action: Semiautomatic
Stock: Synthetic
Barrel: 26 in.
Sights: None
Weight: 15 lb. 13 oz.
Caliber: .338 Lapua Mag., .300 Win. Mag., .308 Win.
Magazine: Detachable box, 6/9, 8/12, 9/13 rounds
Features: High strength vibration-isolated aluminum alloy receiver with a top mounted Mil-Spec 1913 rail; ambidextrous folding stock; integrated folding rear monopod; optional scopes and bipod
MSRP. $6999

FNH USA

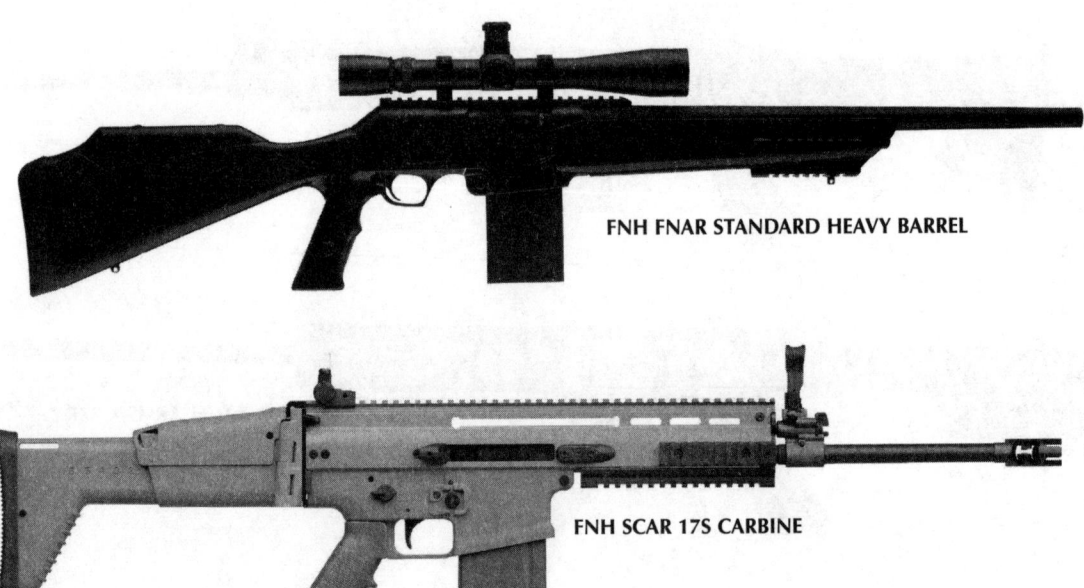

FNH FNAR STANDARD HEAVY BARREL

FNH SCAR 17S CARBINE

FNAR STANDARD

Action: Gas-operated autoloader
Stock: Synthetic
Barrel: 16 in., 20 in. standard fluted, 20 in. heavy fluted
Sights: Receiver mounted rail
Weight: 8 lb. 13 oz.–10 lb.
Caliber: .308 Win. (7.62x51mm NATO)
Magazine: 10, 20 rounds
Features: Extended bolt handle, hammer-forged barrel with crown; comes with one magazine, three interchange-able recoil pads, three comb inserts and shims for adjusting for cast-on, cast-off, and drop at comb; stock is matte black synthetic with pistol grip and adjustable comb
MSRP **$1699**

SCAR 17S CARBINE

Action: Gas-operated autoloader
Stock: Polymer
Barrel: 16.25 in.
Sights: Adjustable, folding, removable
Weight: 8 lb.
Caliber: .308 Win. (7.62x51mm NATO)
Magazine: 10, 20 rounds
Features: Fully adjustable stock; MIL-STD 1913 optical rail plus three accessory rails for attaching a variety of sights and lasers; free-floating, cold-hammer-forged barrel; available in black or Flat Dark Earth tactical, tele-scoping, side-folding polymer stock
MSRP **$3349**

Harrington & Richardson

BUFFALO CLASSIC RIFLE

Action: Lever
Stock: Walnut
Barrel: 32 in.
Sights: Open
Weight: 8 lb.
Caliber: .45-70
Magazine: None
Features: Antique color case-hardened frame; cut-checkered American black walnut with case colored crescent steel buttplate
MSRP $479

HARRINGTON & RICHARDSON BUFFALO CLASSIC RIFLE

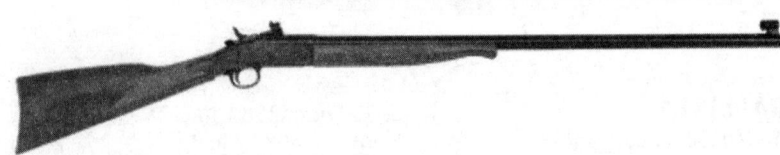

Harrington & Richardson

HARRINGTON & RICHARDSON HANDI-GRIP HANDI RIFLE

HARRINGTON & RICHARDSON HANDI-RIFLE

HARRINGTON & RICHARDSON STAINLESS ULTRA HUNTER

HARRINGTON & RICHARDSON SUPERLIGHT
HANDI-RIFLE COMPACT WITH SCOPE

RIFLES

HANDI-GRIP HANDI RIFLE
Action: Hinged breech
Stock: Ambidextrous thumbhole black polymer
Barrel: 22 in., 24 in., 26 in.
Sights: Scope mount rail and hammer extension
Weight: 7 lb.
Caliber: .204 Ruger, .223 Rem., .22-250 Rem., .308 Win., .45-70 Govt., .243 Win., .35-06 Rem.
Magazine: None
Features: Molded checkering at grip and forend for sure handling; transfer bar system
MSRP. **$341**

HANDI-RIFLE
Action: Lever
Stock: Walnut finish hardwood stock
Barrel: 22 in.
Sights: None
Weight: 7 lb.
Caliber: .35 Whelen
Magazine: None
Features: Blued finish; scope mount included; hammer spur
MSRP. **$313**

STAINLESS ULTRA HUNTER WITH THUMBHOLE STOCK
Action: Lever
Stock: Laminate
Barrel: 24 in.
Sights: None
Weight: 8 lb.
Caliber: .45-70
Magazine: None
Features: Cinnamon laminate stock with thumbhole pistol grip, swivel studs, and rubber rifle buttpad
MSRP. **$516**

SUPERLIGHT HANDI-RIFLE COMPACT WITH SCOPE
Action: Lever
Stock: High-density polymer, matte black
Barrel: 20 in.
Sights: Open
Weight: 5 lb. 5 oz.
Caliber: .243 Win.
Magazine: None
Features: Sling swivel studs; recoil pad; ramp front sight, adjustable rear; drilled and tapped for scope rail; includes 3-9x32 scope, factory mounted and bore sighted
MSRP. **$359**

Harrington & Richardson

SURVIVOR
Action: Lever
Stock: Polymer
Barrel: 22 in., 24 in.
Sights: None
Weight: 6 lb. 8 oz.
Caliber: .223 Rem, .308 Win.
Magazine: None
Features: Bull barrel with blued finish; high-density polymer stock with black matte finish, thumbhole design; butt-stock storage compartment; sling swivel studs and sling
MSRP **$326**

HARRINGTON & RICHARDSON SURVIVOR

ULTRA VARMINT RIFLE
Action: Lever
Stock: Cinnamon laminated American hardwood
Barrel: 24 in. bull barrel
Sights: None
Weight: 7 lb.–8 lb.
Caliber: .223 Rem., .243 Win.
Magazine: None
Features: Monte Carlo pistol grip with checkering; sling swivel studs; ventilated recoil pad; scope mount and hammer extension, no iron sights; thumbhole optional
MSRP **$381**

**HARRINGTON & RICHARDSON
ULTRA VARMINT THUMBHOLE**

Heckler & Koch

G28
Action: Semiautomatic gas operated
Stock: Synthetic
Barrel: 16.5 in.
Sights: Mounted 3-20x50 scope
Weight: 16 lb. 8 oz.
Caliber: 7.62mm
Magazine: 10, 20 rounds
Features: Steel upper receiver; STANAG 4694 NATO accessory rails; new two-stage gas regulator designed for suppressed and unsuppressed use; free-floating chrome-lined cold-hammer-forged steel barrel; retractable buttstocks; green/brown finish with special low IR observable color
MSRP . . . .**N/A**
(Special order only)

**HECKLER & KOCH
G28 STANDARD**

Heckler & Koch

HECKLER & KOCH
MR556A1

HECKLER & KOCH MR762A1

HECKLER & KOCH USC

MR556A1

Action: Autoloading
Stock: Synthetic
Barrel: 16.50 in.
Sights: Open
Weight: 8 lb. 15 oz.
Caliber: 5.56x44mm
Magazine: Detachable box, 10 rounds
Features: Free-floating four-quadrant rail system; four Mil-Spec 1913 Picatinny rails; two-stage trigger; retractable buttstock
MSRP **$3295**

MR762A1

Action: Semiautomatic gas operated
Stock: Synthetic
Barrel: 16.5 in.
Sights: None
Weight: 9 lb. 15 oz.
Caliber: 7.62mm
Magazine: 10, 20 rounds
Features: Match rifle features; direct descendant of HK416/417 series, but made for civilians; uses a piston and a solid operating "pusher" rod in place of the common gas tube normally used in AR-style rifles; cold-hammer-forged barrel; adjustable stock
MSRP **$3995**

USC

Action: Autoloading
Stock: Synthetic
Barrel: 16.13 in.
Sights: None
Weight: 6 lb.
Caliber: .45 ACP
Magazine: Detachable box, 10 rounds
Features: Black reinforced polymer stock; steel barrel; skeletonized butt-stock is topped with rubber cheek rest and recoil pad; Picatinny rails; ambidextrous safety
MSRP **$1788**

Henry Repeating Arms

HENRY .30-30

.30-30

Action: Lever
Stock: Walnut
Barrel: 20 in.
Sights: Open
Weight: 7 lb.
Caliber: .30-30
Magazine: 5 rounds
Features: Steel round barrel: deluxe checkered American walnut with rubber buttpad; XS Ghost Rings sights; blued steel receiver, drilled and tapped for easy scope mounting. Brass octagon barrel: straight-grip American walnut with buttplate; marble fully adjustable semi-buckhorn rear sight, with diamond insert, beaded front sight; brass receiver, drilled and tapped for easy scope mounting

Steel: $749.95
Brass: $950

HENRY .45-70 LEVER ACTION

.45-70 LEVER ACTION

Action: Lever
Stock: Walnut
Barrel: 18.43 in.
Sights: Closed rear, blade front
Weight: 7 lb. 1 oz.
Caliber: .45-70
Magazine: 4 rounds
Features: Pistol-grip American walnut with buttplate; blued steel drilled and tapped for easy scope mounting; XS Ghost Rings rear sight with blade front
MSRP $799.95

HENRY ACU-BOLT

ACU-BOLT

Action: Bolt
Stock: Synthetic
Barrel: 20 in.
Sights: Open
Weight: 4 lb. 4 oz.
Caliber: .22LR, .22 Mag., .17 HMR
Magazine: None
Features: Single-shot; one-piece fiberglass synthetic stock; Williams fire sights; stainless steel receiver and barrel
MSRP $399.95

HENRY BIG BOY

BIG BOY

Action: Lever
Stock: Walnut
Barrel: 20 in.
Sights: Open
Weight: 8.68 lb.
Caliber: .44 Mag., .45 Colt, .357 Mag.
Magazine: Under-barrel tube, 10 rounds
Features: Adjustable marble semi-buckhorn rear with white diamond insert and brass beaded front sight; solid top brass receiver, brass buttplate and brass barrel band; straight-grip American walnut stock; octagonal barrel
MSRP $899.95

RIFLES

HENRY GOLDEN BOY DELUXE

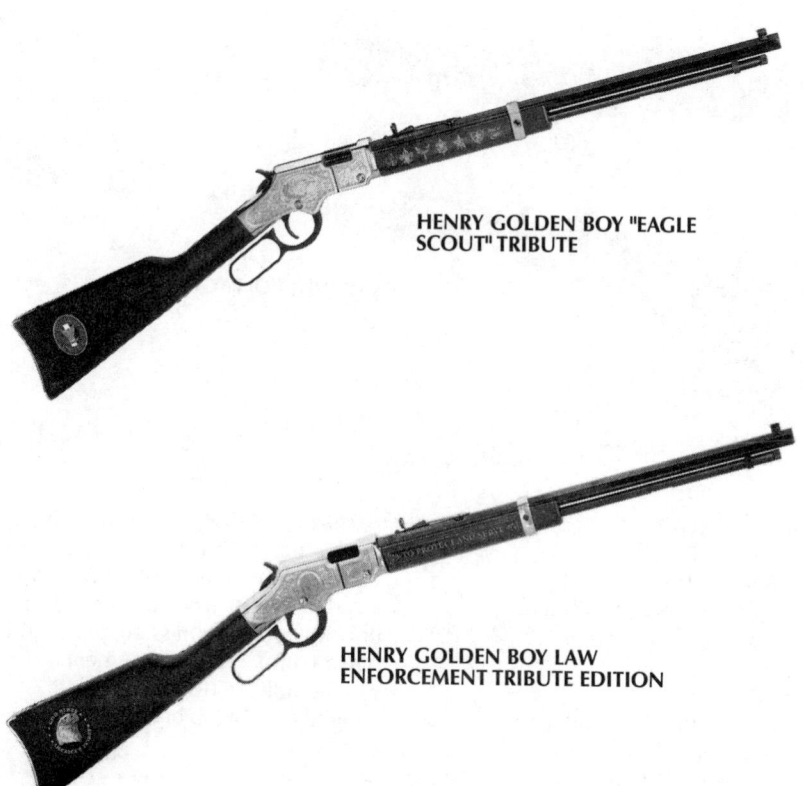

HENRY GOLDEN BOY "EAGLE SCOUT" TRIBUTE

HENRY GOLDEN BOY LAW ENFORCEMENT TRIBUTE EDITION

GOLDEN BOY DELUXE ENGRAVED II

Action: Lever
Stock: Walnut
Barrel: 20 in.
Sights: Open
Weight: 6 lb. 12 oz.
Caliber: .22
Magazine: Under-barrel tube, 16 rounds (LR), 21 rounds (S)
Features: American walnut stock; adjustable buckhorn rear sight, beaded front sight; brasslite receiver, brass buttplate, and blued barrel
MSRP................... **$1585**

GOLDEN BOY "EAGLE SCOUT" TRIBUTE

Action: Lever
Stock: American Walnut with Boy Scout Medallion on side
Barrel: 20 in.
Sights: Adjustable semi-buckhorn rear and brass bead front
Weight: 6 lb. 12 oz.
Caliber: .22LR, .22 Short
Magazine: 16 round (LR) and 21 round (short)
Features: Nickel-plated receiver with hand engraved eagle and Boy Scout motto in 24-karat gold; brass buttplate, barrel band, and receiver; blued barrel and lever
MSRP................ **$1049.95**

GOLDEN BOY LAW ENFORCEMENT TRIBUTE

Action: Lever
Stock: Walnut
Barrel: 20 in.
Sights: Open
Weight: 6 lb. 12 oz.
Caliber: .22 S/L/LR
Magazine: Under-barrel tube, 16 rounds (LR), 21 rounds (S)
Features: 24-kt. gold-plated engravings in American-style scrollwork; right side features law enforcement badge and banner, left side features Michael the Archangel with sword, scales, and banner; American walnut stock
MSRP................... **$899.95**

Henry Repeating Arms

HENRY LEVER ACTION .22

HENRY LEVER OCTAGON FRONTIER

HENRY MARE'S LEG

HENRY MINI BOLT YOUTH

LEVER ACTION .22

Action: Lever
Stock: Walnut
Barrel: 16.13 in. (carbine, youth), 18.25 in.
Sights: Open
Weight: 4 lb. 8 oz. (carbine, youth), 5 lb. 4 oz., 5 lb. 8 oz. (Mag.)
Caliber: .22, .22L, .22LR
Magazine: Under-barrel tube, 11 rounds (.22 Mag.), 15 rounds (.22LR), 17 rounds (.22L), 18 rounds (.22S), 21 rounds (.22)
Features: Straight-grip American walnut stock; deluxe checkered American walnut stock (.22 Magnum); adjustable rear, hooded front sight; blued round barrel and lever
Rifle, Youth, Carbine: . . . $340–$355
Magnum: $475

LEVER OCTAGON FRONTIER

Action: Lever
Stock: Walnut
Barrel: 20 in.

Sights: Open
Weight: 6 lb. 4 oz.
Caliber: .22LR, .22S, .17 HMR
Magazine: Under-barrel tube, 21 rounds (.22S), 16 rounds (.22LR); 12 rounds (.22 Mag.); 11 rounds (.17 HMR)
Features: American walnut; marble fully adjustable semi-buckhorn rear with reversible white diamond insert and brass beaded front sight; blued barrel and lever
.22LR, .22S: $430
.22 Mag.: $545
.17 HMR: $540

MARE'S LEG

Action: Lever
Stock: Walnut
Barrel: 12.9 in.
Sights: Open
Weight: 4 lb. 7 oz. (.22S/L/LR), 5 lb. 7 oz. (.45 Colt)
Caliber: .22S/L/LR, .45 Colt
Magazine: Under-barrel tube, 10 rounds (.22 S/L/LR); 5 rounds (.45 Colt)

Features: .45 Colt: American walnut; marble fully adjustable semi-buckhorn rear with reversible white diamond insert and brass beaded front sights; brasslite receiver, brass buttplate, and blued barrel. .22 S/L/LR: American walnut; fully adjustable rear, with hooded front sight; blued metal barrel and lever
.22 S/L/LR: $415
.45 Colt, .44 Mag., .357 Mag.: . . . $975

MINI BOLT YOUTH

Action: Bolt
Stock: Synthetic
Barrel: 16.25 in.
Sights: Open
Weight: 3 lb. 4 oz.
Caliber: .22LR, .22S
Magazine: None
Features: Single-shot; one-piece fiberglass synthetic stock in orange or black; Williams fire sights; stainless steel receiver and barrel
MSRP. $260

Henry Repeating Arms

PUMP ACTION OCTAGON
Action: Pump
Stock: Walnut
Barrel: 19.75 in.
Sights: Open
Weight: 6 lb.
Caliber: .22LR, .22S, .22Mag

Magazine: Under-barrel tube, 15 rounds (.22LR, .22S), 12 rounds (.22 Mag.)
Features: American walnut stock; adjustable rear, beaded front sight; blued octagonal barrel
MSRP. **$510**
Magnum:. **$585**

HENRY PUMP ACTION OCTAGON

HENRY U.S. SURVIVAL AR-7

HENRY VARMINT EXPRESS

U.S. SURVIVAL AR-7
Action: Semiautomatic
Stock: ABS Plastic
Barrel: 16 in.
Sights: Open
Weight: 2 lb. 4 oz.
Caliber: .22LR
Magazine: Detachable box, 8 rounds
Features: ABS plastic in black; adjustable rear sight, blade front sight; Teflon coated receiver and coated steel barrel
Black:. **$280**
Camo: **$345**

VARMINT EXPRESS
Action: Lever
Stock: Walnut
Barrel: 20 in.
Sights: Open
Weight: 5 lb. 12 oz.
Caliber: .17 HMR
Magazine: Under-barrel tube, 11 rounds
Features: Checkered American walnut stock; Williams fire sights; blued round barrel and lever
MSRP. **$540**

RIFLES

High Standard

AR-15 ENFORCER

Action: Semiautomatic
Stock: Synthetic
Barrel: 16 in.
Sights: Flip-up
Weight: 7 lb. 6 oz.
Caliber: 5.56mm NATO
Magazine: 20, 30 rounds
Features: SOCOM style six position synthetic stock; A2 flash hider; YHM quad rail with smooth side; YHM same plane flip-up sights; ergonomical grip; two-stage match trigger
MSRP $2275

HIGH STANDARD AR-15 MIL-SPEC SERIES

HIGH STANDARD AR-15 ENFORCER WITH EOTECH AND SIGHTS RS VIEW

AR-15 MIL-SPEC SERIES

Action: Gas-operated autoloader
Stock: 6-position
Barrel: 20 in. (16 in. carbine)
Sights: Adjustable
Weight: 8 lb. (7 lb. 5 oz. carbine)

Caliber: 5.56 NATO
Magazine: Detachable box, 30 rounds
Features: Matte black collapsible

stock, G.I. style; hard chrome bore; A2 flash holder
MSRP . . . . $925–$1200

Hi-Point Firearms

HI-POINT FIREARMS MODEL 995TS

MODEL 995TS

Action: Blow-back autoloader
Stock: Black, skeleton-style, all-weather molded polymer
Barrel: 16.5 in.
Sights: Adjustable
Weight: 7 lb.
Caliber: 9mm
Magazine: Detachable box, 10 rounds
Features: Sling, swivels, and base mount included; last round lock-open latch; multiple Picatinny rails; internal recoil buffer
MSRP $285

Howa by Legacy Sports

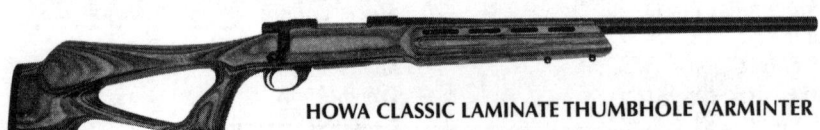

HOWA CLASSIC LAMINATE THUMBHOLE VARMINTER

CLASSIC LAMINATE VARMINTER

Action: Bolt
Stock: Laminate
Barrel: 24 in.

Sights: None
Weight: 9 lb. 14 oz.
Caliber: .223, .204 Ruger, .22-250 Rem., .243 Win., .308 Win.
Magazine: Internal box, 5 rounds
Features: Nutmeg or Pepper stock color; optional thumbhole stock; heavy blued or stainless barrel; black recoil pad; sling swivel studs
Blued barrel $813
Stainless barrel. $918

RIFLES

Howa by Legacy Sports

HOWA/HOGUE RANCHLAND COMPACT

HOWA/HOGUE RANCHLAND COMPACT

Action: Bolt
Stock: Synthetic
Barrel: 20 in.
Sights: None
Weight: 7 lb. 2 oz.–8 lb. 12 oz.
Caliber: .223, .204 Ruger, .22-250 Rem., .243 Win., .308 Win., 7mm-08
Magazine: Internal box
Features: Black, green, or sand over-molded stock; includes one-piece scope rail; color match combo option includes Nikko Stirling 3-10x42 Nighteater scope; rings and one-piece base; full camo packages include Desert Camo Stock
MSRP . . . . **$585–$782**

HOWA/HOGUE RIFLES

Action: Bolt
Stock: Synthetic
Barrel: 20 in., 22 in., 24 in.
Sights: None
Weight: 7 lb. 12 oz.
Caliber: Standard Blue, Stainless: .223, .204 Ruger, .22-250 Rem., .243 Win., .308 Win., 7mm-08, 6.5x 55SW, .25-06, .270 Win., .30-06; Magnum Blue, Stainless: .300 Win. Mag., .375 Ruger, .338 Win. Mag, 7mm Rem. Mag.
Magazine: Internal box
Features: Stainless or blued barrel; synthetic stock comes in black, sand, or green with matching Hogue Soft Grip; recoil pad; hinged floor plate; sling; swivel studs
Standard: . . . . **$570–$680**
Magnum: . . . . **$599–$704**
Varmint: . . . . **$631–$717**

HOWA/HOGUE OR TALON SNOWKING

Action: Bolt
Stock: Synthetic
Barrel: 22 in.
Sights: Mounted 4-16x44 scope
Weight: 9 lb. 6 oz.
Caliber: .223, .243, .22-250, .308
Magazine: 4+1 rounds
Features: HACT 2-stage trigger system; 3 position safety; Blackhawk Talon or Hogue overmolded stock in Kings Snow Shadow Camo; Nikko Stirling Gameking 4-16x44 scope with LRK Range-finding Reticle; color matched scope, rings, and one-piece base; limited edition and limited availability only through Bill Hicks & Co.
Hogue: **$799**
Talon: **$1136**

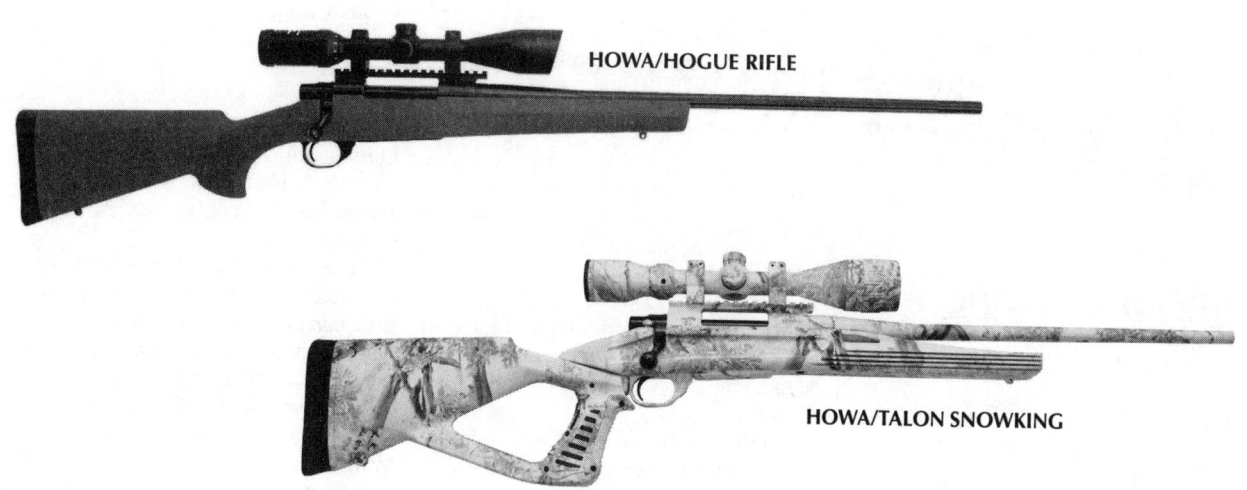

HOWA/HOGUE RIFLE

HOWA/TALON SNOWKING

Howa by Legacy Sports

HOWA/HOGUE/TARGETMASTER COMBO

Action: Bolt
Stock: Synthetic
Barrel: 20 in.
Sights: Mounted 4-16x44 scope
Weight: 9 lb. 6 oz.
Caliber: .223 Win., .22-250 Rem., .308 Win.
Magazine: 4+1 rounds
Features: Fluted barrels and heavy standard barrels available; black or OD green Hogue overmolded stocks; Nikko-Stirling Targetmaster 4-16x44 scopes; HACT two-stage trigger system; three-position safety; forged flat-bottomed receiver
MSRP . . . .$787–$837

HOWA HUNTER

Action: Bolt
Stock: Walnut
Barrel: 20 in., 22 in., 24 in.
Sights: Optional mounted scope

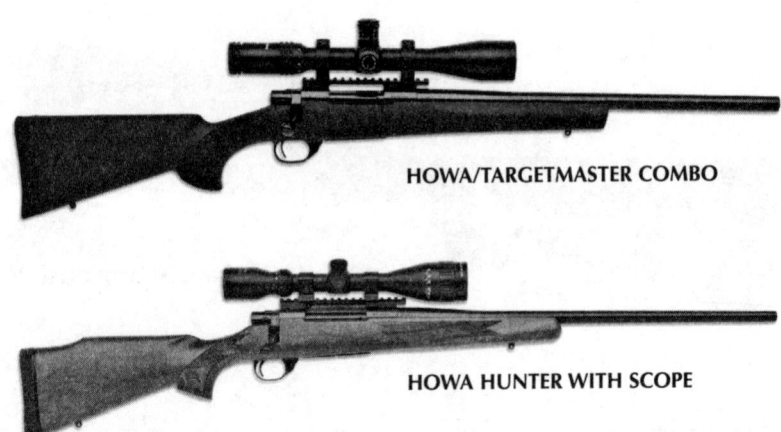

HOWA/TARGETMASTER COMBO

HOWA HUNTER WITH SCOPE

Weight: 7 lb. 7 oz.
Caliber: .223 Rem., .204 Ruger, .22-250 Rem., .243 Win., 6.5x55SW, .25-06, .270 Win., .308 Win., .30-06, .300 Win. Mag., .338 Win. Mag., 7mm Rem. Mag., .375 Ruger
Magazine: 4+1 rounds

Features: Blued or stainless steel barrels; one-piece high grade walnut stock; checkering at forend and pistol grip; Monte Carlo cheekpiece; rubber recoil pad; sling swivel studs; scopes optional on blued models
MSRP . . . .$709–$880

H-S Precision

H-S PRECISION HTR

H-S PRECISION PHR

HTR (HEAVY TACTICAL RIFLE)

Action: Bolt
Stock: Synthetic
Barrel: 20 in., 22 in., 24 in., 26 in., 28 in.
Sights: None
Weight: 10 lb. 12 oz.–11 lb. 4 oz.
Caliber: Any standard SAAMI, LR calibers
Magazine: Detachable box, 3, 10 rounds
Features: Pro-Series 2000; fully adjustable synthetic stock comes in a wide range of colors combinations including sand, black, olive, gray, and spruce green; heavy fluted barrel
MSRP $3600

PHR (PROFESSIONAL HUNTER RIFLE)

Action: Bolt
Stock: Synthetic
Barrel: 20 in., 22 in., 24 in., 26 in., 28 in.
Sights: None
Weight: 7 lb. 12 oz.–8 lb. 4 oz.
Caliber: All popular magnum calibers up to .375 H&H and .338 Lapua
Magazine: Detachable box, 3, 4 rounds
Features: Pro-Series 2000; cheekpiece and built-in recoil reduction system; steel barrel; optional muzzlebrake; synthetic stock comes in a wide range of color combinations including sand, black, olive, gray, and spruce green; left-hand available for additional cost
MSRP $3555

RIFLES

H-S Precision

H-S PRECISION TTD

TTD (TACTICAL TAKE-DOWN RIFLE)
Action: Bolt
Stock: Composite
Barrel: 22 in., 24 in.
Sights: None
Weight: 11 lb. 4 oz.–11 lb. 12 oz.
Caliber: Available in all standard SA SAAMI and LR calibers

Magazine: Detachable box, 3, 4 rounds
Features: Stainless steel barrel and floor plate; synthetic stock with full length bedding block chassis system; metal parts are finished in matte black Teflon; wide variety of stock colors including sand, black, olive, gray, and spruce green
MSRP **$5500**

Jarrett Rifles

JARRETT BEANFIELD

JARRETT PROFESSIONAL HUNTER

JARRETT WIND WALKER

BEANFIELD
Action: Bolt
Stock: Synthetic
Barrel: Various lengths available
Sights: None
Weight: Varies depending on options
Caliber: Any popular standard or magnum chambering
Magazine: Comes with 20 rounds
Features: Can build rifle on any receiver provided; optional caliber, stock style, color, muzzlebrake, barrel size, and taper; includes load data and 20 rounds of custom ammo
MSRP . . . . **starting at $5380**

PROFESSIONAL HUNTER
Action: Bolt
Stock: Synthetic or walnut
Barrel: Various lengths available
Sights: None
Weight: Varies depending on options
Caliber: .375 H&H, .416 Rem., .416 Rigby, .450 Rigby
Magazine: Comes with 40 rounds
Features: Includes 40 rounds of soft pointed bullets and solids created custom for each gun; ballistics printout and last three targets the gun shot also provided; optional scopes; .416 Rem. comes with Jarrett Tri-Lock receiver
MSRP . . . . **starting at $10400**

WIND WALKER
Action: Bolt
Stock: Synthetic
Barrel: Up to 24 in.
Sights: None
Weight: 7 lb. 8 oz.
Caliber: Any popular short-action
Magazine: Comes with 20 rounds
Features: Jarrett Tri-Lock action; muzzlebrake; Tally scope mounting system; phenolic resin metal finish with choice of stock colors; ballistic print out included
MSRP . . . . **starting at $7380**

J.P. Sauer & Sohn

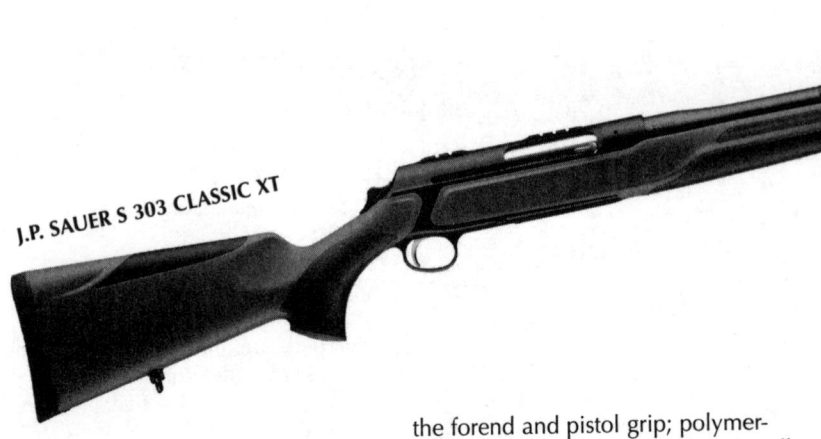

J.P. SAUER S 303 CLASSIC XT

S 202 CLASSIC BOLT ACTION RIFLE
Action: Bolt
Stock: Walnut
Barrel: 24 in.
Sights: None
Weight: 7 lb. 11 oz.
Caliber: .22, .22 Mag.
Magazine: Detachable box, 5 rounds
Features: Features stable, dark tan walnut heartwood; Monte Carlo stock with cheek-piece; luxury wood tip on the forend and pistol grip; polymer-coated steel surface; round bolt handle
MSRP **$3509**
Left-hand: **$4192**

S 303 CLASSIC XT
Action: Semiautomatic
Stock: Synthetic with anti-slip elasto-mer inlays
Barrel: 20 in., 22 in.
Sights: Yellow triangle rear sight; red-dot front sight
Weight: 7 lb. 5 oz.
Caliber: .30-06, .300 Win. Mag.
Magazine: Detachable box, 2, 5 rounds

Features: Light-metal receiver; manual cocking safety; straight comb stock for either left- or right-handed shooters; rust protection with Nitrobond-X finish
MSRP **$3352**

S 303 ELEGANCE
Action: Semiautomatic
Stock: Walnut
Barrel: 20 in., 22 in.
Sights: High contrast
Weight: 7 lb. 3 oz.–7 lb. 6 oz.
Caliber: .30-06, .300 Win. Mag.
Magazine: Detachable box, 2, 5 rounds
Features: Manual cocking at the upper wrist; crisp single-stage trigger; four bolt lugs engage directly into the bar-rel; free-floating barrel
MSRP **$4752**

Kel-Tec

KEL-TEC SUB-2000

SUB-2000
Action: Autoloader
Stock: Polymer
Barrel: 16.1 in.
Sights: Target
Weight: 4 lb.
Caliber: 9mm, .40 S&W
Magazine: 10+1 rounds
Features: Self-loading carbine for pis-tol cartridges; by rotating the barrel upwards and back, it can be reduced to a size of 16"x7" to facilitate secure storage
MSRP **$409**

RIFLES

KIMBER CAPRIVI

KIMBER MODEL 84L CLASSIC SELECT GRADE

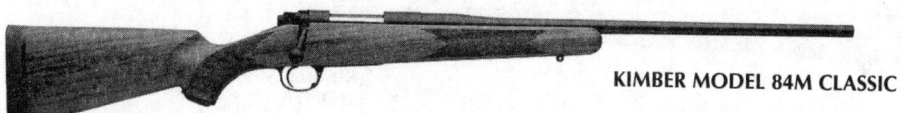

KIMBER MODEL 84M CLASSIC

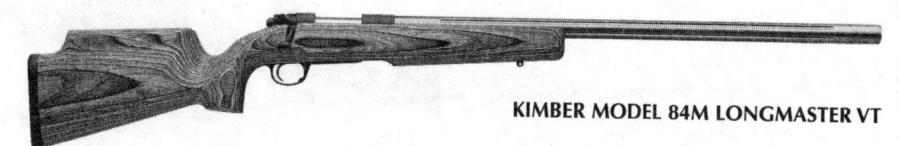

KIMBER MODEL 84M LONGMASTER VT

CAPRIVI

Action: Bolt
Stock: Walnut
Barrel: 24 in.
Sights: None
Weight: 8 lb. 8 oz.–8 lb. 10 oz.
Caliber: .375 H&H Mag., .416 Rem. Mag., .458 Lott
Magazine: Internal box, 4 rounds
Features: AA-grad walnut stock with wrap checkering; ebony forend tip; cheekpiece; double cross-bolts; sling swivel studs; front barrel band swivel stud; recoil pad; steel barrel with matte blued finish; front locking repeater; Mauser claw extractor; adjustable trigger
MSRP **$3263**

MODEL 84L SERIES

Action: Bolt
Stock: Walnut, synthetic
Barrel: 24 in.
Sights: None
Weight: 5 lb. 5 oz.–6 lb. 3 oz.
Caliber: .270 Win., .30-06 Spfd.,
.25-06 Rem., .280 Ackley Improved
Magazine: Internal box, 5 rounds
Features: Full-length Mauser claw exactor; 1-in. Pachmayr recoil pad; full-length match-grade barrel with pillar and glass bedding; match-grade trigger and three-postion wing safety; Classic Select has French walnut stock with ebony forend tip; Montana has Kevlar/carbon fiber stocks
Classic: **$1223**
Classic Select Grade: **$1427**
Classic SS Select Grade **$1495**
Montana: **$1359**

MODEL 84M CLASSIC

Action: Bolt
Stock: Walnut
Barrel: 18 in., 22 in., 24 in.
Sights: None
Weight: 5 lb. 9 oz.–5 lb. 13 oz.
Caliber: .243 Win., .7mm-08 Rem., .308 Win.
Magazine: Internal box, 5, 6 rounds
Features: A-grade walnut stock with checkering panel, or AA walnut with ebony forend on Select Grade; recoil pad; sling swivel studs; steel matte blued or satin stainless steel finish; front locking repeater
Classic: **$1223**
Classic Select Grade: **$1427**
Classic SS Select Grade: **$1495**

MODEL 84M LONGMASTER

Action: Bolt
Stock: Laminate
Barrel: 26 in.
Sights: None
Weight: 7 lb. 5 oz.–10 lb.
Caliber: Classic: .223 Rem., .308 Win.; VT: .22-250 Rem.
Magazine: Internal box, 5 rounds
Features: A-grade walnut with oil finish on Classic or gray laminated stock on VT model; sling swivel stud or front swivel stud for bipod; recoil pad; stainless steel barrel with satin finish; steel action with matte blued finish
Classic: **$1291**
VT: **$1427**

RIFLES

Kimber

MODEL 84M SERIES

Action: Bolt
Stock: Walnut, laminate, Kevlar/carbon fiber
Barrel: 22 in.
Sights: None
Weight: 4 lb. 13 oz.–8 lb. 5 oz.
Caliber: 7mm-08 Rem., .308 Win., .204 Ruger, .22-250 Rem., .204 Ruger, .223 Rem., .243 Win., .257 Roberts, .338 Federal (among the various models)

Magazine: Internal box, 4, 5, 6 rounds
Features: A-grade walnut on Varmint; AAA-grade walnut stock with checkering panel on SuperAmerica; gray laminate on ProVarmint and SVT; Kevlar/carbon fiber on Montana; recoil pad; stainless steel barrel and action; front locking repeater; adjustable trigger

Montana: **$1359**
ProVarmint: **$1427**
SuperAmerica: **$2240**
SVT: **$1427**
Varmint: **$1291**

KIMBER MODEL 84M MONTANA

KIMBER MODEL 8400 POLICE TACTICAL

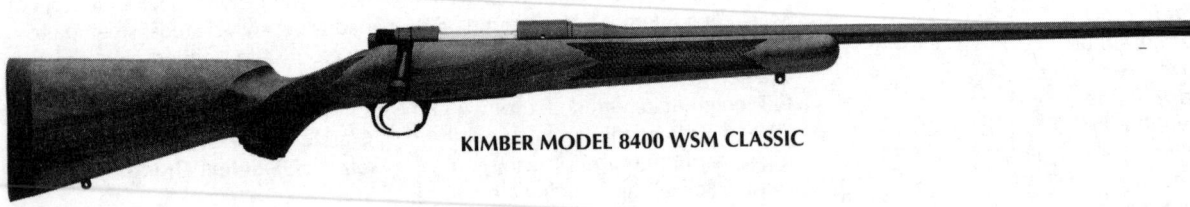

KIMBER MODEL 8400 WSM CLASSIC

MODEL 8400 POLICE TACTICAL

Action: Bolt
Stock: Laminate
Barrel: 24 in.
Sights: None
Weight: 8 lb. 12 oz.
Caliber: .308 Win., .300 Win. Mag.
Magazine: Internal box, 5 rounds
Features: Laminated wood stock with black epoxy finish; sling swivel studs; front swivel stud for bipod; recoil pad; steel barrel with matte blued finish; fluted bolt front locking repeater; adjustable trigger
MSRP **$1495**

MODEL 8400 WSM

Action: Bolt
Stock: Walnut, synthetic
Barrel: 24 in.
Sights: None
Weight: 6 lb. 3 oz.–6 lb. 10 oz.
Caliber: .270 WSM, .300 Swam, .325 Swam; SuperAmerica: .270 WSM, .300 WSM
Magazine: Internal box, 3 rounds

Features: Stock options: A-grade walnut with checkered panels, A-grade French walnut with checkered panels, gray synthetic Kevlar/carbon fiber stock; sling swivel studs; recoil pad; steel barrel with matte blued finish or stainless steel satin finish; front locking repeater; Mauser claw extractor

Classic: **$1223**
Classic Select Grade: **$1427**
Classic SS Select Grade: **$1495**
SuperAmerica: **$2240**
Montana: **$1359**

RIFLES

KRIEGHOFF CLASSIC BIG FIVE

KRIEGHOFF CLASSIC STANDARD

KRIEGHOFF SEMPRIO

KRIEGHOFF SEMPRIO
THUMBHOLE

CLASSIC BIG FIVE

Action: Hinged breech
Stock: Walnut
Barrel: 23.5 in.
Sights: Open
Weight: 9 lb. 8 oz.–10 lb. 8 oz.
Caliber: .375 H&H Mag., .375
Flanged Magnum N.E., .450/.400 NE,
.500/.416 N.E., .470 N.E., .500 N.E.
Magazine: None
Features: Double triggers; V-shaped
rear sight with a white, vertical middle
line and a pearl front sight; optional
Super-Express sight; Monte Carlo style
cheekpiece; European walnut stock
with small game scene engraving; steel
trigger and floor plate; straight comb
and large recoil pad
MSRP. **$13995**

CLASSIC STANDARD

Action: Hinged breech
Stock: Walnut
Barrel: 23.5 in.
Sights: Open
Weight: 7 lb. 4 oz.–8 lb. 4 oz.
Caliber: 7x57R, 7x65R, .308 Win.,
.30-06, 8X57JRS, 8x75RS, 8.5x75RS,
9.3x74R
Magazine: None
Features: European walnut stock with
conventional rounded cheekpiece and
Kaiser Grip; adjustable, removable
muzzle wedge integrated in the front
sight ramp; Universal-Trigger-System;
Combi-cocking device; ergonomically
shaped "Kickspanner" manual cocking
device
MSRP. **$10995**

SEMPRIO

Action: Hinged breech
Stock: Walnut
Barrel: 21.5 in., 25 in.
Sights: Open
Weight: 7 lb. 8 oz.

Caliber: .223 Rem., .243 Win.,
6.5x55SE, 6.5x57, .270 Win., 7x64,
.308 Win., .30-06 Spfd., .338 Win.
Mag., 8x57JS, 9.3x62; Magnum calibers: 7mm Rem. Mag., .300 Win.
Mag., .375 Ruger
Magazine: Detachable box
Features: Barrels are plasma nitrated
and blued to resist corrosion; open
sights feature fluorescent front bead
and rear sight, designed for target
acquisition in low light conditions;
accepts various types of scope-mounts;
Turkish walnut stock available with or
without the Semprio cheekpiece; rubber recoil pad; sling swivels; optional
BreaKO recoil reducer; includes fitted
case. New stock options include
thumbhole stock and Next G-1 Vista
Forest Green or Blaze Orange camouflage finishes
Standard Caliber: **$4690**
Magnum Caliber: **$4990**

L.A.R. Grizzly Firearms

GRIZZLY BIG BOAR
Action: Bolt
Stock: Steel
Barrel: 36 in.
Sights: None
Weight: 30 lb. 6 oz.
Caliber: .50 BMG
Magazine: None
Features: Bullpup single-shot; match grade steel barrel; steel receiver; very low recoil; thumb safety and bolt top safety; Harris bipod; Weaver scope mount; leather cheekpad; hard carry case

Standard Blued:	**$2350**
Parkerized:	**$2450**
Blued with Nickel Trigger Housing Finish:	**$2600**
Full Nickel Finish:	**$2700**
Stainless Steel Barrel:	**$2600**

GRIZZLY T-50
Action: Bolt
Stock: Steel
Barrel: 32 in.–36 in.
Sights: None
Weight: 30 lb. 6 oz.
Caliber: .50 BMG
Magazine: None

Features: Bullpup single-shot; steel stock; aircraft grade aluminum scope mount, bipod and monopod rails; steel receiver; very low recoil; thumb safety and bolt stop safety; 20 MOA scope mount Picatinny rail; integrated cheekpad; hard carry case
MSRP **$3200**

L.A.R. GRIZZLY T-50

Lazzeroni Rifles

L2012LLT LONG MAGNUM LITE
Action: Bolt
Stock: Graphite/composite
Barrel: 26 in.
Sights: None
Weight: 7 lb. 5 oz.
Caliber: 6.53 (.257) Scramjet, 7.82 (.308) Warbird, 7.21 (.284) Firebird, 8.59 (.338) Titan
Magazine: 4 rounds
Features: All new precision CNC-machined chromoly receiver; one-piece diamond-fluted bolt shaft; stainless steel match-grade button-barrel; custom molded hand-bedded graphite/composite stock designs; precision-machined aluminum alloy floor plate/trigger guard assembly; jewel competition trigger; Vais muzzlebrake; Limbsaver recoil pad
MSRP **$5999.99**

LAZZERONI L2012LLT LONG MAGNUM LITE

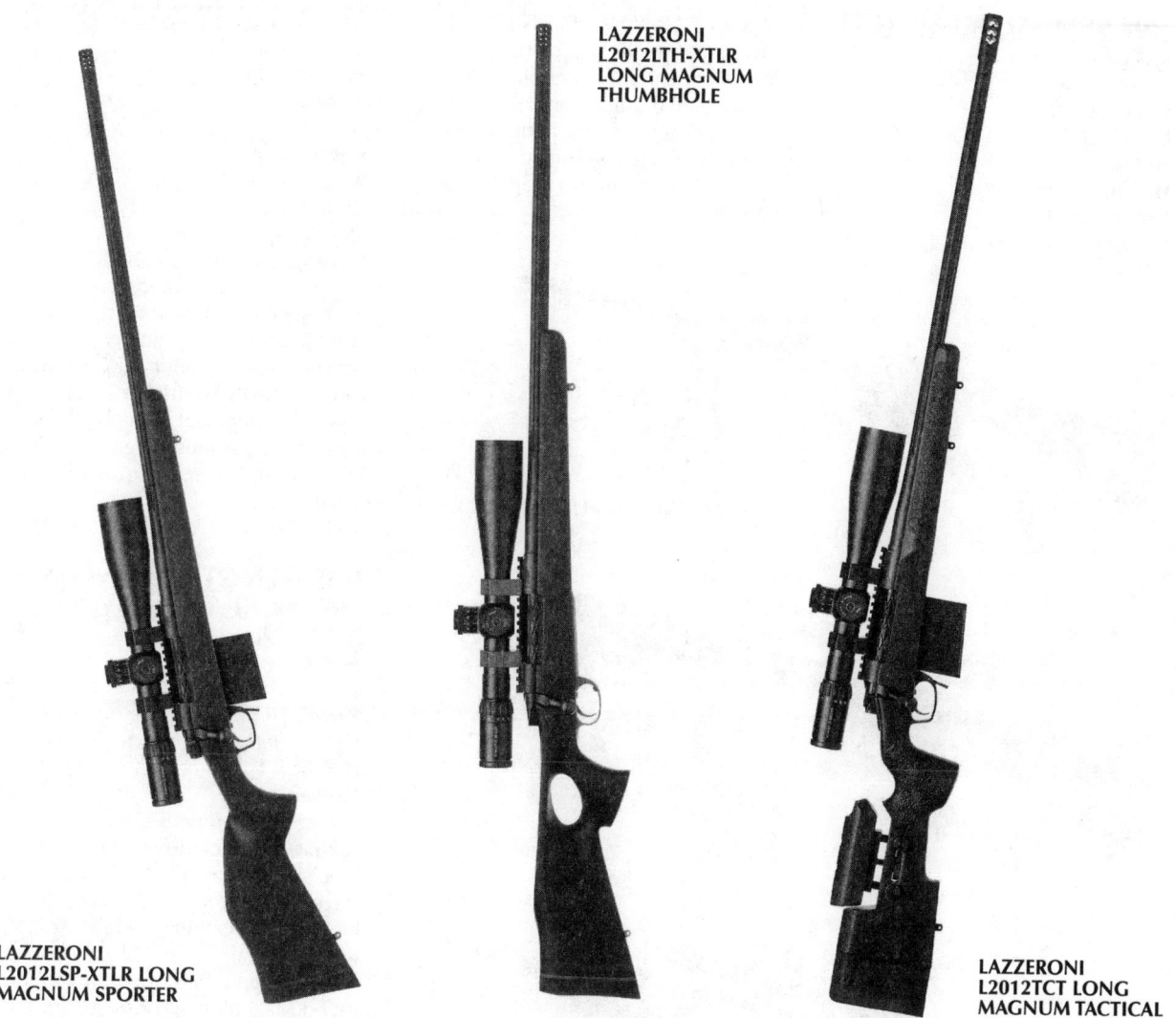

LAZZERONI
L2012LTH-XTLR
LONG MAGNUM
THUMBHOLE

LAZZERONI
L2012LSP-XTLR LONG
MAGNUM SPORTER

LAZZERONI
L2012TCT LONG
MAGNUM TACTICAL

L2012LSP-XTLR LONG MAGNUM SPORTER

Action: Bolt
Stock: Graphite/composite
Barrel: 28 in.
Sights: None
Weight: 8 lb. 13 oz.
Caliber: 6.53 (.257) Scramjet, 7.82 (.308) Warbird, 7.21 (.284) Firebird, 8.59 (.338) Titan
Magazine: 6 rounds
Features: Heavy barrel contour; recoil reducing roll-over cheekpiece incorporated into stock design; 20 MOA Picatinny rail; 34mm or 30mm rings
MSRP **$6999.99**

L2012LTH LONG MAGNUM THUMBHOLE

Action: Bolt
Stock: Graphite/composite
Barrel: 25 in.
Sights: None
Weight: 7 lb. 11 oz.
Caliber: 6.53 (.257) Scramjet, 7.82 (.284) Warbird, 7.21 (.284) Firebird, 8.59 (.338) Titan
Magazine: 4 rounds
Features: 20 MOA Picatinny style rail; 34mm or 30mm ring sets; right hand only
MSRP **$6699.99**

L2012TCT LONG MAGNUM TACTICAL

Action: Bolt
Stock: Graphite/composite
Barrel: 26 in.
Sights: None
Weight: 10 lb. 14 oz.
Caliber: 7.82 (.308) Warbird, 8.59 (.338) Titan
Magazine: 6 rounds
Features: Tactical black rifle; right hand only
MSRP **$7999.99**

Les Baer Custom

.308 SEMI-AUTO MATCH RIFLE

Action: Bolt
Stock: Synthetic
Barrel: 18 in. or 20 in.
Sights: None
Weight: 11 lb. 3 oz.
Caliber: .308
Magazine: 20-round Magpul

Features: No forward assist; Picatinny style flat top rail; LBC carrier, chromed; chromed precision bolt; Geissele two-stage trigger group; steel gas block; LBC Custom grip; Harris bipod; DuPont S coating on barrel; enforcer muzzlebrake; Magpul stock
MSRP $3190

LES BAER .308 SEMI-AUTO MATCH RIFLE

LES BAER AR .223 SUPER VARMINT

LES BAER MID-LENGTH MONOLITH .308 SEMI-AUTO SWAT MODEL

LES BAER MONOLITH .308 SEMI-AUTO SWAT

AR .223 SUPER VARMINT

Action: Bolt
Stock: Synthetic
Barrel: 20 in. (optional 18 in., 22 in., 24 in.)
Sights: None
Weight: 9 lb.
Caliber: .223
Magazine: 20 rounds
Features: Includes targets; LBC forged and precision machined upper and lower receivers; Picatinny style flat top rail; LBC National Match chromed carrier; LBC chromed bolt; LBC extractor; Geissele two-stage trigger group; adjustable free-float handguard with locking ring; aluminum gas block; stainless steel barrel; Versa Pod installed
MSRP $2290

MID-LENGTH MONOLITH .308 SEMI-AUTO SWAT MODEL

Action: Semiautomatic
Stock: Synthetic
Barrel: 16 in.
Sights: Optional scope and rings
Weight: 11 lb. 5 oz.
Caliber: .308
Magazine: 20 rounds
Features: LBC carrier, chromed; LBC precision chromed bolt; Geissele two-stage trigger group; LBC steel gas block with Picatinny rail; LBC bench rest 416R stainless steel barrel with rifling; Magpul PRS stock; two twenty-round Magpul magazines
MSRP $3940

MONOLITH .308 SEMI-AUTO SWAT

Action: Bolt
Stock: Synthetic
Barrel: 20 in. (optional 18 in., 24 in.)
Sights: None
Weight: 9.04 lb.
Caliber: .308
Magazine: 20-round Magpul
Features: Geissele two-stage trigger group; LBC Steel gas block with Picatinny rail on top; LBC bench rest, stainless steel barrel; Magpul PRS stock in black; special Versa Pod and adapter; DuPont S coating in barrel
MSRP $3940

RIFLES

LWRC International

M6A2

Action: Short-stroke gas piston
Stock: Vltor Emod
Barrel: 10.5 in., 12.7 in., 14.7 in., 16.1 in.
Sights: LWRC Skirmish BUIS
Weight: 7 lb. 6 oz. (16.1 in. barrel)
Caliber: 5.56mm, 6.8mm
Magazine: 30 rounds
Features: Ideal for optical sights with low-profile gas block and no A-frame front sight to obscure field of view; longer mid-length free-float rail system with a removable return-to-zero top; lightweight, self-regulating, self-scraping operating system; match grade cold rotary hammer-forged barrel with target crown; barrel treated with NiCorr surface conversion technology; available in black, OD green, patriot brown, and Flat Dark Earth Cerakote
5.56mm: $2216
6.8mm: $2327

M6A2 SPR

Action: Short-stroke gas piston
Stock: Magpul ACS
Barrel: 16.1 in.
Sights: LWRC Skirmish BUIS
Weight: 7 lb. 6 oz.
Caliber: 5.56mm
Magazine: 30 rounds
Features: Rifles uses a lightweight sculpted rail derived from the LWRC REPR platform; SPR-MOD rail is lighter and longer than Mark-II-B rail; cold-hammer-forged barrel; spiral fluting; enhanced fire control group; Magpul MIAD pistol grip; Magpul ACS stock; available in black, Flat Dark Earth, OD green, and patriot brown
MSRP. $2425

M6 IC (INDIVIDUAL CARBINE)

Action: Short-stroke gas piston operation
Stock: Magpul MOE
Barrel: 14.7 in.
Sights: LWRCI folding BUIS
Weight: 6 lb. 14 oz.
Caliber: 5.56mm NATO, 6.8mm SPC
Magazine: 30 rounds
Features: New fully ambidextrous lower receiver with dual controls for bolt catch/release, magazine release, and fire control; 2-position gas block; user configurable rail system; features

LWRCI M6A2

LWRCI M6A2 SPR

LWRCI M6 IC

LWRCI M6-SL

RIFLES

non-IR reflective Cerakote Stealth that makes the rifle "disappear" to image intensifying night vision (U.S. Military applications only); initial production run will be flat dark earth only
MSRP. .N/A

M6-SL (STRETCH LIGHTWEIGHT)

Action: Short-stroke gas piston operation
Stock: Magpul MOE
Barrel: 16.1 in.

Sights: Fixed front, Daniel Defense rear
Weight: 6 lb. 7 oz.
Caliber: 5.56mm
Magazine: 30 rounds
Features: Magpul MOE furniture; MOE mid-length handguard; MOE stock; MOE pistol grip; light contour barrel; EXO (nickel-boron) plated advanced combat bolt; one-piece EXO coated carrier; EXO-coated enhanced fire control group
MSRP. $1675

LWRC International

PSD (PERSONAL SECURITY DETAIL)

Action: Short-stroke gas piston operation
Stock: Magpul CTR
Barrel: 8 in.
Sights: LWRC Skirmish BUIS
Weight: 6 lb. 2 oz.
Caliber: 5.56mm, 6.8mm
Magazine: 30 rounds
Features: Patent-pending ARM-R rail system; removable top platform; return-to-zero reinstallation with no tools required; carbine-length rail over low profile gas block; available in black, OD green, patriot brown, and Flat Dark Earth Cerakote

5.56mm:................. $2216
6.8mm: $2327

LWRCI PSD

LWRCI R.E.P.R., 20 INCH

R.E.P.R. (RAPID ENGAGEMENT PRECISION RIFLE)

Action: Short-stroke gas piston operation
Stock: Vltor Emod, Magpul UBR, Magpul PRS
Barrel: 12.7 in., 16 in., 18 in., 20 in.
Sights: LWRC Skirmish BUIS
Weight: 9 lb. 8 oz. (16 in. barrel)
Caliber: 7.62mm
Magazine: 20 rounds
Features: Patented self-regulating, short-stroke, gas-piston operating system; side-mounted charging handle, ARM-R top rail available in three models: Standard, Designated Marksman, Sniper; available in black, OD green, Flat Dark Earth, and patriot brown
MSRP.............. $3600–$3800

UCIW (ULTRA COMPACT INDIVIDUAL WEAPON)

Action: Short-stroke gas piston operation
Stock: 4-position collapsible stock
Barrel: 7 in.
Sights: LWRC Skirmish BUIS
Weight: 6 lb. 4 oz.
Caliber: 5.56mm
Magazine: 30 rounds
Features: Custom-made buffer tube; overall length of only 22 inches with stock collapsed; available in black, FDE, and OD green
MSRP................. $2216

LWRCI UCIW

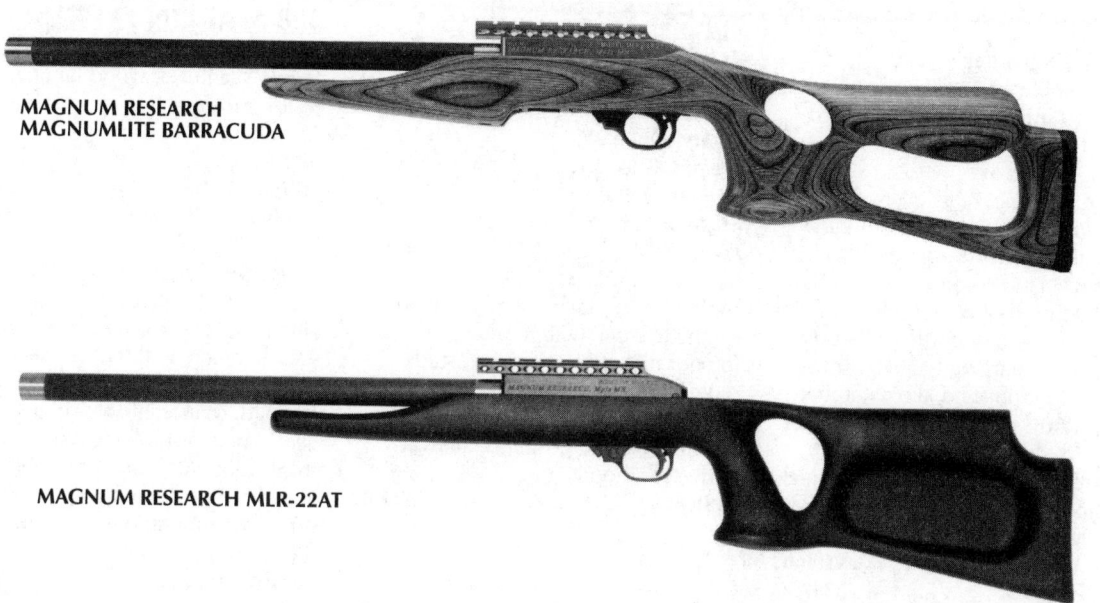

MAGNUM RESEARCH
MAGNUMLITE BARRACUDA

MAGNUM RESEARCH MLR-22AT

MAGNUMLITE BARRACUDA

Action: Semiautomatic
Stock: Composite or laminate
Barrel: 17 in.
Sights: None
Weight: 4 lb. 7 oz.–7 lb. 5 oz.
Caliber: .22LR, .22 Win. Mag.
Magazine: Box, 9, 10 rounds
Features: 17 in., 19 in. models have graphite barrels; 18 in. barrels come in stainless steel; .22 Win. Mag. version has patented gas-assisted blowback operation; CNC receivers machined from aircraft aluminum; include integral Weaver type rail for optics; heat treated steel with tight bolt face depth tolerances
MSRP **$819**

MLR-22AT

Action: Semiatuomatic rimfire
Stock: Synthetic
Barrel: 17 in.
Sights: None
Weight: 4 lb. 4 oz.
Caliber: .22LR
Magazine: 10+1
Features: Ambidextrous lightweight thumbhole stock made of polypropylene with fiber additives; semi palm swell on both sides of the pistol grip; molded-to-fit hard rubber buttplate attached with screws; graphite bull barrel with uni-directional graphite fibers parallel to the bore axis; full floating barrel; French gray anodized finish
MSRP **$599**

MOUNTAIN EAGLE MAGNUM LITE GRAPHITE

Action: Bolt
Stock: Composite
Barrel: 24 in., 26 in.
Sights: None
Weight: 7 lb. 4 oz.–9 lb. 2 oz.
Caliber: .30-06, .223, .308, .280, 7mm Rem. Mag., .300 Win. Mag., .22/250, .300 WSM, 7mm WSM
Magazine: Box, 4, 5 rounds
Features: Adjustable trigger; Kevlar-graphite stock in H-S Precision or Hogue Overmolded; open grip; free-floating match-grade barrel; hinged floor plate of solid steel; recoil pad; sling swivel studs; left-hand available for most calibers; action has been drilled and tapped for scope
MSRP . . . . **$2173–$2475**

MAGNUM RESEARCH MOUNTAIN
EAGLE MAGNUM LITE GRAPHITE

Marlin

60

Action: Autoloading
Stock: Laminated hardwood
Barrel: 19 in.
Sights: Open
Weight: 5 lb. 8 oz.
Caliber: .22LR
Magazine: Tubular mag, 14 rounds with patented closure system
Features: Manual and automatic "last-shot" bolt hold-opens; receiver top has serrated, non-glare finish; cross-bolt safety; steel charging handle; Monte Carlo walnut-finished laminated hardwood; M60C comes with camouflage patterned Monte Carlo hardwood stock; full pistol grip; tough Mar-Shield finish; adjustable open rear sight, front ramp sight

60: $196.83
60C: $232.06
60SB: $249.60

70PSS

Action: Autoloading
Stock: Synthetic
Barrel: 16.25 in.
Sights: Open
Weight: 3 lb. 4 oz.
Caliber: .22LR
Magazine: Clip, 7 rounds
Features: Automatic "last-shot" bolt hold-open; manual bolt hold-open; Monte Carlo black fiberglass-filled synthetic stock with abbreviated forend; nickel plated swivel studs; molded-in checkering; adjustable open rear sight; front ramp sight with high visibility orange post and cutaway wide-scan hood
MSRP $328.82

308 MARLIN EXPRESS

Action: Lever
Stock: Walnut or wood laminate with pistol grip
Barrel: 22 in., 24 in.
Sights: None
Weight: 7 lb.
Caliber: .308 Marlin Express, .338 Marlin Express
Magazine: Tubular mag, 5 rounds
Features: Hammer block safety; American black walnut stock or black/gray laminate with cut checkering; stainless steel receiver; rubber rifle buttpad; Mar-Shield finish; adjustable semi-buckhorn folding rear and ramp front sight with brass bead and wide-scan hood; solid top receiver tapped for scope mount; offset hammer spur for scope use

Laminate: $904.57
Walnut: $685.52

MARLIN 60

MARLIN 70PSS

MARLIN 308 MARLIN EXPRESS

336C

Action: Lever
Stock: Walnut
Barrel: 20 in.
Sights: Open
Weight: 7 lb.
Caliber: .30-30 Win., .35 Rem.
Magazine: Tubular mag, 6 rounds
Features: Deeply blued surfaces; hammer block safety; American black walnut stock with pistol grip and checkering
MSRP. $592.42

336SS

Action: Lever
Stock: Walnut
Barrel: 20 in.
Sights: Open
Weight: 7 lb.
Caliber: .30-30 Win., .35 Rem.
Magazine: Tubular mag, 6 rounds
Features: Stainless steel receiver, barrel, lever, and trigger guard; hammer block safety; American black walnut pistol grip stock with fluted comb and cut checkering; rubber rifle buttpad; adjustable semi-buckhorn folding rear, ramp front sight with brass bead and wide-scan hood; solid top receiver tapped for scope mount; offset hammer spur for scope use
MSRP. $727.03

336XLR

Action: Lever
Stock: Laminated hardwood
Barrel: 24 in.
Sights: Open
Weight: 7 lb.
Caliber: .30-30
Magazine: Tubular mag, 5 rounds
Features: Stainless steel receiver, barrel, lever, and trigger guard plate; black/gray laminated hardwood stock with pistol grip and checkering; deluxe recoil pad; nickel plates swivel studs; adjustable semi-buckhorn folding rear sight and brass bead front sight with wide-scan hood; receiver tapped for scope mount
MSRP. $904.57

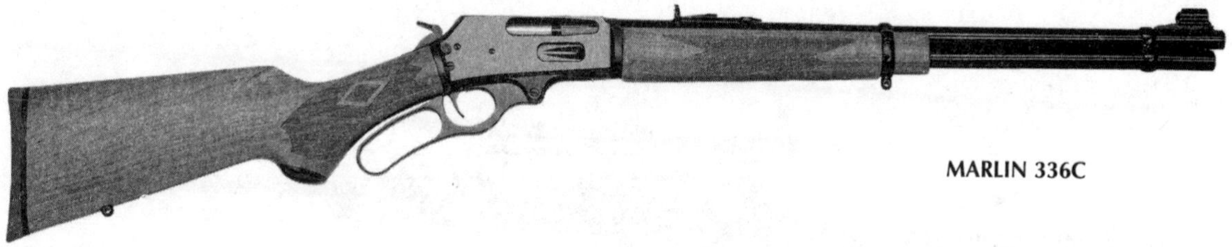

MARLIN 336C

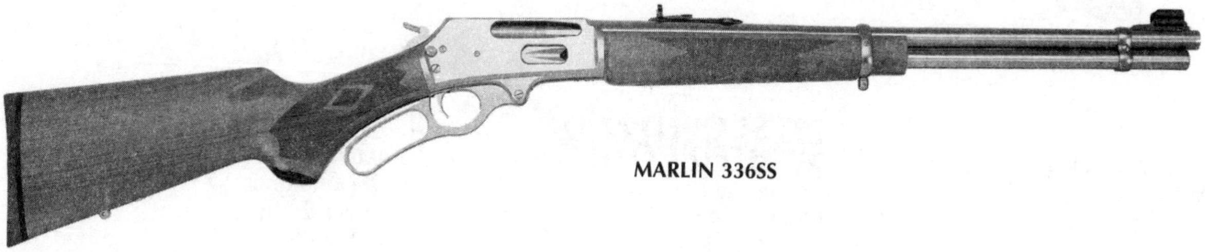

MARLIN 336SS

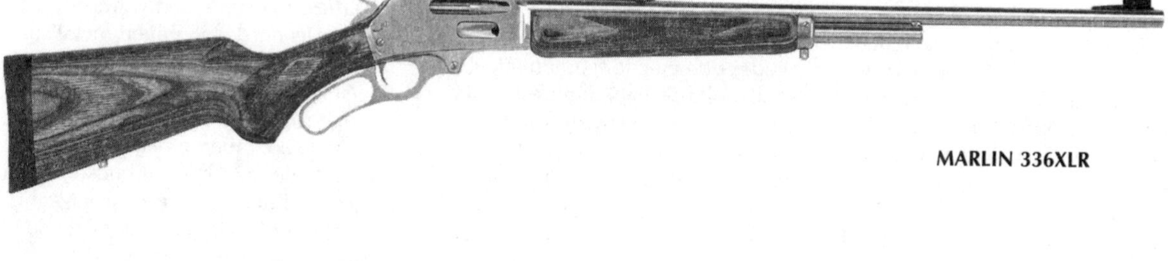

MARLIN 336XLR

Marlin

MARLIN 795SS

MARLIN 1894 COWBOY

MARLIN 795 SCOPED AND SIGHTED COMBO

RIFLES

795

Action: Autoloading
Stock: Synthetic
Barrel: 18 in.
Sights: Open
Weight: 4 lb. 8 oz.
Caliber: .22LR
Magazine: Clip, 10 rounds
Features: Automatic "last-shot" bolt hold-open, manual bolt hold-open; cross-bolt safety; Monte Carlo black fiberglass-filled synthetic stock with swivel studs and molded in checkering; adjustable open rear sight and front ramp sight; receiver grooved for scope mount
795: $181.21
795SS: $259.13

795 SCOPED AND SIGHTED COMBO

Action: Autoloading
Stock: Synthetic
Barrel: 18 in.
Sights: Mounted 4x20 scope
Weight: 4 lb. 8 oz.
Caliber: .22LR
Magazine: 10 rounds
Features: Autoloading rimfire rifle; factory-mounted and bore-sighted 4x20 scope; side ejection; automatic "last-shot" bolt hold-open; nickel-plated clip magazine; Monte Carlo black fiberglass-reinforced synthetic stock with molded-in checkering; swivel studs
MSRP $219.25

1894 COWBOY

Action: Lever
Stock: Walnut
Barrel: 20 in.
Sights: Open
Weight: 6 lb. 8 oz.
Caliber: .45 Colt, .357 Mag./.38 Spl., .44 Mag./.44 Spl.
Magazine: Tubular mag, 10 rounds
Features: Lever action with squared finger lever; deeply blued metal surfaces; straight-grip American black walnut stock; hard rubber buttplate; tough Mar-Shield finish; blued steel forend cap; tapered octagon barrel; adjustable marble semi-buckhorn rear sight and marble carbine front sight; solid top receiver tapped for scope mount
MSRP $1010.19

Marlin

1895GBL

Action: Lever
Stock: Laminate
Barrel: 18.5 in.
Sights: Open
Weight: 7 lb.
Caliber: .45-70 Govt.
Magazine: Full length tubular magazine, 6 rounds
Features: Lever action with big loop finger lever; deeply blued metal surfaces; hammer block safety; American pistol grip two-tone brown laminate stock with cut checkering; ventilated recoil pad; tough Mar-Shield finish; swivel studs; adjustable semi-buckhorn folding rear sight and ramp front sight with brass bead; receiver tapped for scope mount; offset hammer spur for scope use
MSRP $712.62

1895SBL

Action: Lever
Stock: Laminated hardwood
Barrel: 18.5 in.
Sights: Open
Weight: 8 lb.
Caliber: .45-70 Govt.
Magazine: Full length tubular magazine, 6 rounds
Features: Lever action with big loop finger lever; deeply blued metal surfaces; stainless steel barrel and receiver; black/gray laminated hardwood with pistol-grip stock and cut checkering; fluted comb; deluxe recoil pad; compact version available
MSRP $1038.76

CLASSIC 1895

Action: Lever
Stock: Walnut
Barrel: 22 in.
Sights: Open
Weight: 7 lb. 8 oz.
Caliber: .45-70 Govt.
Magazine: Tubular mag, 4 rounds
Features: Deeply blued metal surfaces; hammer block safety; American black walnut pistol grip with fluted comb and cut checkering; rubber rifle buttpad; tough Mar-Shield finish; swivel studs; adjustable semi-buckhorn folding rear sight and front ramp sight with brass bead and wide-scan hood; model 1985 G has 18.5-in. barrel and straight grip; model 1985 Cowboy has a 26-in. octagonal barrel and straight grip
Classic 1895: $675.41
1895G: $680.17
1895GS: $812.59

MARLIN 1895GBL

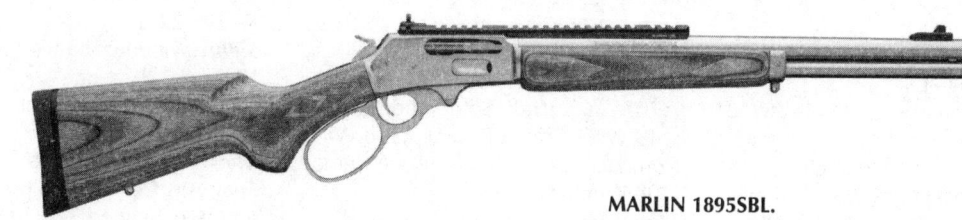

MARLIN 1895SBL.

MARLIN CLASSIC 1895

Marlin

MARLIN GOLDEN 39A

MARLIN X7

MARLIN X7 SCOPED AND
SIGHTED COMBO

GOLDEN 39A
Action: Lever
Stock: Walnut
Barrel: 24 in.
Sights: Open
Weight: 6 lb. 8 oz.
Caliber: .22S, L, LR
Magazine: Tubular mag, holds 26S, 21 LR or 19 LR rounds
Features: Rebounding hammer; hammer safety block; one-step takedown; deeply blued metal surfaces; gold plated steel trigger; genuine American black walnut with full pistol grip and forend; blued steel forend cap; swivel studs; rubber rifle buttpad; tough Mar-Shield finish; adjustable semi-buckhorn folding rear sight and front ramp sight with brass bead and wide-scan hood
MSRP **$702.22**

X7
Action: Centerfire Bolt
Stock: Synthetic
Barrel: 22 in.
Sights: None
Weight: 6 lb. 8 oz.
Caliber: Long action: .25-06 Rem., .270 Win., .30-06 Spfd.; Short-action: .243 Win., 7mm-08 Rem., .308 Win.; Compact: .243 Win., 7mm-08 Rem., .308 Win., .223 Rem.
Magazine: 4+1 rounds
Features: Pro-Fire adjustable trigger; button-fired barrel with a target-style muzzle crown; soft-tech recoil pad; stainless steel barrel and receiver; pillar-bedded black synthetic stock with raised cheekpiece; Realtree APG HD stock for X7C long action version; two-position safety; red cocking indicator; fluted bolt design
MSRP **$391.03**

X7 SCOPED AND SIGHTED COMBO
Action: Bolt
Stock: Synthetic
Barrel: 22 in.
Sights: Mounted 3-9x40mm riflescope
Weight: 7 lb. 4 oz.
Caliber: .243 Win., 7mm-08 Rem., .308 Win.
Magazine: 4+1 rounds
Features: Comes with pre-mounted and bore-sighted 3-9x40 riflescope; Pro-Fire adjustable trigger; Soft-Tech recoil pad; black synthetic stock; precision button rifled barrel; fluted bolt; compact version available in .243 Win., .270 Win., 30-06 Spfd.
MSRP **$443.27**

Marlin

X7 VARMINT HEAVY BARREL

Action: Bolt
Stock: Walnut
Barrel: 26 in.
Sights: None
Weight: 7 lb. 12 oz.
Caliber: .22-250 Rem., .308 Win.
Magazine: 4+1 rounds
Features: Pro-Fire adjustable trigger; fluted bolt; two-position safety; red cocking indicator; pillar-bedded satin-finished walnut with raised cheek piece; soft-tech recoil pad
MSRP $396.95

XT-22

Action: Bolt
Stock: Hardwood
Barrel: 22 in.
Sights: Open
Weight: 6 lb.
Caliber: .22LR
Magazine: Clip, 7 rounds
Features: Pro-Fire adjustable trigger; Micro-Groove rifling; blued bolt action; thumb safety; red cocking indicator; Monte Carlo walnut-finished hardwood with swivel studs; full pistol grip; tough Mar-Shield finish; adjustable rear sight and front ramp sights; receiver grooved for scope mount, drilled and tapped for scope bases
MSRP . . . . $219.89–$265.31

MARLIN X7 VARMINT HEAVY BARREL

MARLIN XT-22

McMillan

50 LBR

Action: Bolt
Stock: Synthetic
Barrel: 32 in.
Sights: None
Weight: 28 lb.
Caliber: .50
Magazine: Internal box
Features: McMillan 50 light benchrest stock in orange and gray marbling; fluted match barrel with McMillan BR muzzlebrake and precision target crown; pillar-bedded action; adjustable Jewell trigger
MSRP $9450

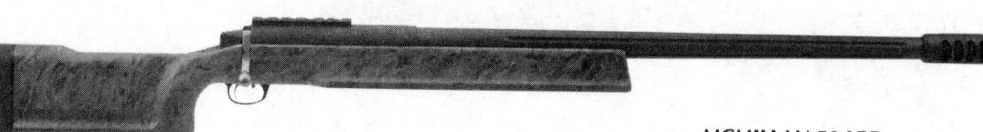

MCMILLAN 50 LBR

McMillan

MCMILLAN CS5

CS5

Action: Semiautomatic
Stock: Synthetic
Barrel: 12.5 in., 18.5 in.
Sights: None
Weight: 10 lb. 10 oz., 11 lb. 10 oz.
Caliber: .308 Win.
Magazine: 10/20 rounds
Features: Concealable Subsonic/Supersonic Suppressed Sniper System; available in "Stubby" suppressed configuration for military and law enforcement use; with buttstock and suppressor detached, will fit in backpack; adjustable buttstock; tactile safety button can be operated without moving your trigger finger

MSRP	**$6500**
Standard:	**$5500**

CUSTOM HUNTING RIFLES - LEGACY

Action: Bolt
Stock: Synthetic
Barrel: 22 in., 24 in.
Sights: None
Weight: 6 lb. 10 oz.–7 lb.
Caliber: .270 Win., .308 Win., .30-06, .300 Win. Mag.
Magazine: Internal box
Features: McMillan classic sporter fiberglass stock with shadow line cheekpiece; McMillan G30 custom action in long or short; match-grade stainless steel barrel, with a matte finish and target crown; custom machined one-piece aluminum hinged floor plate; custom Jewell trigger; includes scope base and travel case with rollers

MSRP	**$6235**

LONG RANGE HUNTING RIFLE

Action: Bolt
Stock: Synthetic
Barrel: 24 in., 26 in., 27 in.
Sights: None
Weight: 9 lb. 8 oz.–10 lb.
Caliber: .243 Win., 7mm Rem. Mag., 7mm Rem. Ultra Mag., .308 Win., .300 Win. Mag., .338 Lapua Mag.
Magazine: Internal box
Features: McMillan A-3 Fiberglass stock with fixed cheekpiece and recoil pad; McMillan G30 Custom long or short action; match grade, stainless steel barrels with matte finish and target crown; hinged steel floor plate; Remington-style trigger; optional box magazine; comes with travel case with rollers

LRH .243, .308:	**$6575**
LRH 7mm, .300:	**$6575**
LRH .338:	**$6575**

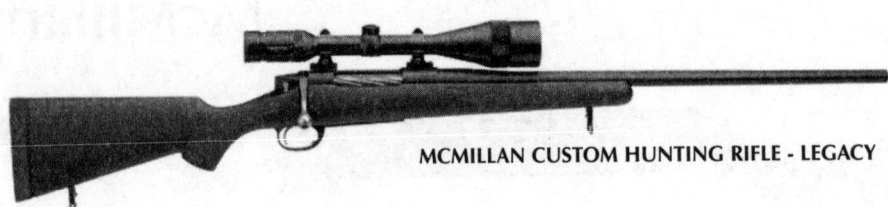

MCMILLAN CUSTOM HUNTING RIFLE - LEGACY

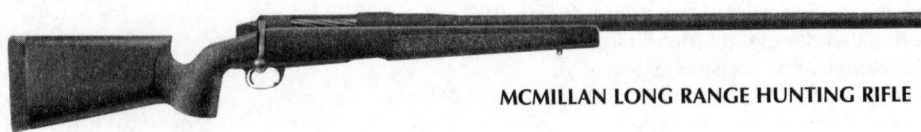

MCMILLAN LONG RANGE HUNTING RIFLE

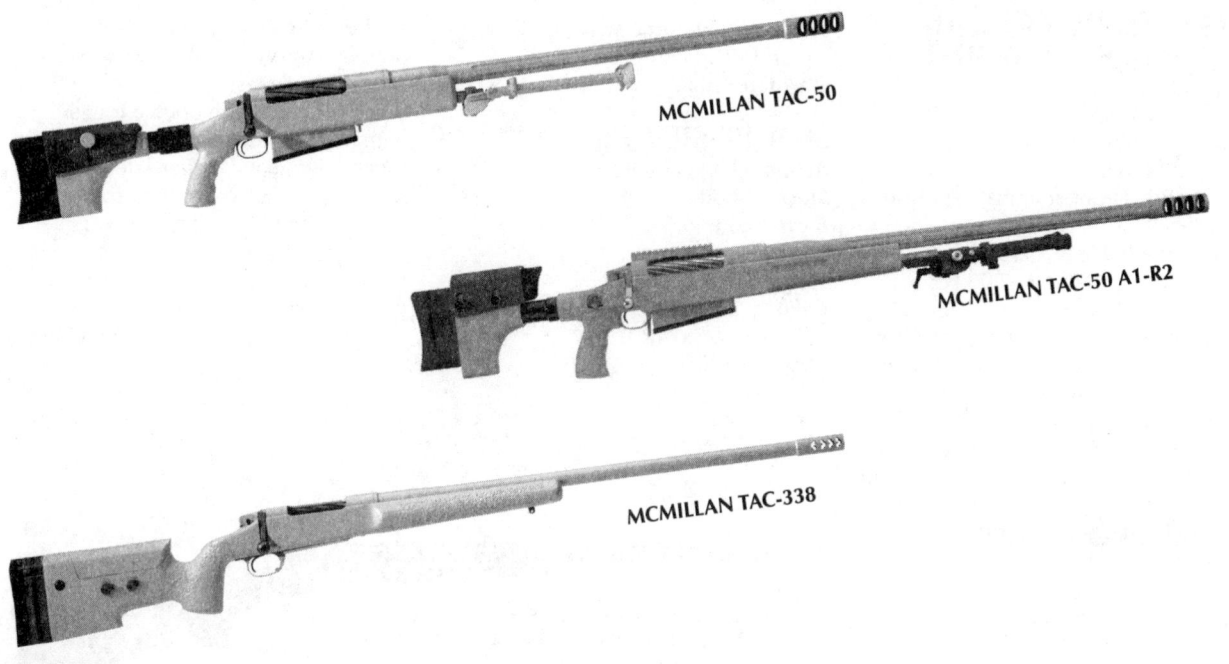

MCMILLAN TAC-50

MCMILLAN TAC-50 A1-R2

MCMILLAN TAC-338

TAC-50

Action: Bolt
Stock: Composite
Barrel: 29 in.
Sights: None
Weight: 26 lb.
Caliber: .50 BMG
Magazine: Detachable box
Features: Bipod; match grade, stainless steel barrel; muzzlebrake; anti-glare Dura Coating; square-surfaced recoil lug; extra long bolt handle; tight benchrest tolerances; saddle cheekpiece; metal finish comes in black, olive, gray, tan, or dark earth to match composite stock
MSRP. **$9990**

TAC-50 A1

Action: Semiautomatic
Stock: Synthetic
Barrel: 29 in.
Sights: Drilled and tapped for scopes
Weight: 26 lb.
Caliber: .50
Magazine: Detachable box, 5 rounds
Features: Take-down fiberglass stock with a longer forend that moves the balance point for the bipod forward; integral cheekpiece; monopod on the buttstock; smaller pistol grip; lighter,

sturdier bipod; positive, self-locking magazine latch; magazine release lever repositioned ahead of trigger bow; match grade free floating barrel
MSRP. **$9990**

TAC-50 A1-R2

Action: Semiautomatic
Stock: Synthetic
Barrel: 29 in.
Sights: Drilled and tapped for scopes
Weight: 26 lb.
Caliber: .50
Magazine: Detachable box, 5 rounds
Features: New hydraulic recoil mitigation system reducing peak recoil by 90 percent; take-down fiberglass stock with a longer forend that moves the balance point for the bipod forward; integral cheekpiece; monopod on the buttstock; smaller pistol grip; lighter, sturdier bipod; positive, self-locking magazine latch; magazine release lever repositioned ahead of trigger bow; match grade free floating barrel
MSRP. **$11990**

TAC-338

Action: Bolt
Stock: Composite
Barrel: 26.5 in.

Sights: None
Weight: 11 lb.
Caliber: .338 Alpha Mag., .338 Norma Mag.
Magazine: Detachable box, 1 to 5 rounds
Features: G30 McMillan Long Action; hinged floor plate system; metal finish (to match stock)—black, olive, gray, tan, or dark earth; Vanguard Case; adjustable cheekpiece; tight benchrest tolerances; square-surfaced recoil lugs; threaded cap provided; match grade, stainless steel barrel with matte finish
MSRP. **$6895**

TAC-416

Action: Single shot
Stock: Synthetic
Barrel: 29 in., 30 in.
Sights: Drilled and tapped for scopes
Weight: 26 lb.
Caliber: .416 Barrett
Magazine: None
Features: Stock with integral cheekpiece; action finished to match stock in variety of colors: black, olive, gray, tan, and dark earth; Lilja match grade barrel; configured as a single shot; Picatinny sight base
MSRP. **$9990**

Merkel

AFRICAN SAFARI SERIES DOUBLE RIFLE MODEL 140AE

Action: Boxlock
Stock: Walnut
Barrel: 23.6 in.
Sights: Bead front, four-leaf express rear
Weight: 10 lb. 8 oz.
Caliber: .375 H&H, .416 Rigby, .450/400 NE, .470 NE, .500 NE
Magazine: None
Features: Classic styling with cheekpiece, half luxus Turkish walnut; hand-engraved, English-style arabesque, gold relief Cape buffalo; tapered, octagonal barrel with rust blued finish
MSRP................. **$12595**

B3 OVER-AND-UNDER RIFLE

Action: Over/under
Stock: Checkered walnut
Barrel: 21.6 in.
Sights: Driven-hunt sight with integrated light elements
Weight: 6 lb. 6 oz.
Caliber: .30-06 and 9.3x74R
Magazine: None
Features: Short, light, and responsive; manual cocking mechanism; tilting breech block can be removed without tools; adjustable single trigger; pistol grip; cheekpiece and hogback comb; rubber buttpad
Hunting: **$5495**

RX HELIX HUNTING COMBINATION RIFLE/SHOTGUN

Action: Break-action
Stock: Walnut
Barrel: 23.6 in.
Sights: Open sights, 11mm prismatic scope mount rail
Weight: 6 lb. 6 oz.
Caliber: Rifle: .222 Rem., .243 Win., .308 Win., 7x65R, .30-06 Spfd., .30R Blaser, 8x57 IRS, 9.3x74R; Shotgun: 12 Ga./3-inch
Magazine: None
Features: Rotary bolt head with seven locking lugs; fully enclosed action with integral rail; interchangeable barrels and mags for tool-free caliber change in 60 seconds; tang-mounted safety, 8 models available; aluminum action; European walnut stock; manual cocking system; Elastomer recoil pad;

European style sling swivels; checkering on forend and pistol grip
Standard:................ **$3795**

SIDE-BY-SIDE RIFLE 140

Action: Hinged breech
Stock: Wood
Barrel: 23.6 in.
Sights: None
Weight: 7 lb. 8 oz.
Caliber: 7x65R, .30-06, .30R Blaser, 8x57IRS, 9, 3x74R
Magazine: None
Features: Interchangeable barrel options; Anson & Deeley locks; steel action; Greener-style cross-bolt and double bottom bite; double trigger with front set trigger, optional single trigger; automatic trigger safety; optional with ejectors; hard soldered barrels with muzzle adjustment; engraving English arabesque or game scene "JAGD"; rubber buttplate; pistol grip; cheekpiece and hogback comb
MSRP................. **$11995**

MERKEL AFRICAN SAFARI SERIES DOUBLE RIFLE MODEL 140AE

MERKEL B3 OVER-AND-UNDER RIFLE

MERKEL RX HELIX HUNTING COMBINATION RIFLE/SHOTGUN

MERKEL SIDE-BY-SIDE RIFLE 140

RIFLES

Mossberg

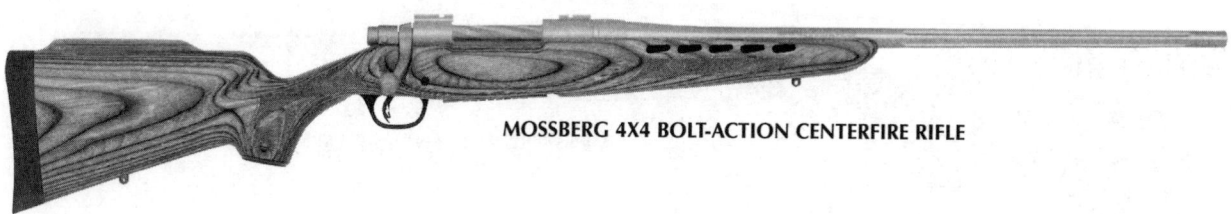

MOSSBERG 4X4 BOLT-ACTION CENTERFIRE RIFLE

4X4 BOLT-ACTION CENTERFIRE RIFLE

Action: Bolt
Stock: Synthetic, walnut, laminate
Barrel: 24 in.
Sights: None
Weight: 6 lb. 12 oz.–7 lb. 8 oz.
Caliber: .25-06 Rem., .270 Win., .30-06 Spfd., 7mm Rem., .300 Win. Mag., .338 Win. Mag., .22-250 Rem., .243 Win., 7mm-08 Rem., .308 Win.
Magazine: Detachable box, Standard: 5 rounds; Magnum: 4 rounds
Features: Classic style, gray laminate stock in Marinecote finish; free-floating, fluted, button rifled barrel with muzzlebrake; scoped combos available
MSRP . . . . **$643–$742**

464 LEVER-ACTION RIFLE

Action: Lever
Stock: Walnut
Barrel: 18 in., 20 in.
Sights: Adjustable rifle sights
Weight: 5 lb. 8 oz.–6 lb. 12 oz.
Caliber: .330
Magazine: 18 in.: 14 rounds, 20 in.: 7 rounds
Features: Adjustable rifle sights; 18 in. model has dovetail receiver; drilled and tapped for scope; walnut stock with optional pistol grip
18 in.: **$468**
20 in.: . . . . **$497–$535**

464 SPX

Action: Lever
Stock: Synthetic
Barrel: 16.25 in., 18 in.
Sights: Open
Weight: 6 lb.–6 lb. 8 oz.
Caliber: .22LR, .30-03 Win.
Magazine: 14, 6 rounds
Features: 6-position adjustable stocks; tri-rail forends with rail covers; adjustable fiber optic sights; optional flash suppressor and muzzlebrake; top-tang safety; dovetail receiver rifle sights or fiber optic 3-dot sights
MSRP . . . . **$497–$504**

MOSSBERG 464 LEVER-ACTION RIFLE

MOSSBERG 464 SPX

Mossberg

MOSSBERG 702 BANTAM PLINKSTER

MOSSBERG 715T TACTICAL FLAT TOP

MOSSBERG 802 PLINKSTER BOLT-ACTION

MOSSBERG 817 BOLT-ACTION

702 BANTAM PLINKSTER
Action: Autoloading
Stock: Synthetic
Barrel: 18 in.
Sights: Rear sight
Weight: 4 lb. 2 oz.
Caliber: .22LR
Magazine: Detachable box, 10 rounds
Features: Fold down rear sight; synthetic stock comes in black or pink; blued finish on barrel and metal
MSRP $176

715T TACTICAL FLAT TOP
Action: Autoloading
Stock: Synthetic
Barrel: 16.25 in.
Sights: Adjustable
Weight: 5 lb. 4 oz.
Caliber: .22LR, .30-03 Win.
Magazine: 11, 26 rounds
Features: Fixed stock or six-position adjustable stock versions available;

stock finish is black matte or Mossy Oak Brush camo; Red-Dot Combo package; optional 10 round or 25 round magazine; flat top receiver with full-length Picatinny top rail; free-floating barrels with matte blued finish; removable rear and front adjustable sights; pistol grip
MSRP . . . . $364–$421

802 PLINKSTER BOLT-ACTION
Action: Bolt
Stock: Synthetic or wood
Barrel: 18 in., 21 in.
Sights: Adjustable rifle sights
Weight: 4 lb. 2 oz.–4 lb. 10 oz.
Caliber: .22LR
Magazine: Detachable box, 11 rounds
Features: Stock comes in black, pink, or marble pink finish; receiver grooved to accept .375-inch scope mounts; cross-bolt safety and magazine release

buttons; free-float barrel with blued or brushed chrome finish; includes free gun lock
MSRP . . . . $162–$199

817 BOLT-ACTION
Action: Bolt
Stock: Synthetic or wood
Barrel: 21 in.
Sights: None
Weight: 4 lb. 8 oz.–5 lb.
Caliber: .17 HMR
Magazine: Detachable box, 5 rounds
Features: Factory-mounted Weaver-style scope bases; cross-bolt safety and magazine release buttons; free gun lock included; stock available in black synthetic or wood; metal finishes include blued or brushed chrome; optional scope; optional muzzlebrake
MSRP . . . . $205–$301

Mossberg

ATR SHORT ACTION
Action: Bolt
Stock: Synthetic, walnut
Barrel: 22 in.
Sights: None
Weight: 6 lb. 12 oz.–7 lb.
Caliber: .270 Win., .30-06, .243 Win., .308 Win.
Magazine: Top loading mag, 4+1 rounds
Features: Integral synthetic trigger guard; Weaver-style scope bases; integral swivel studs; free-floating, button-rifled barrels; recessed muzzle crown; barrel finishes include matte blued or Marinecote; rugged synthetic stocks include black, camo, and synthetic walnut finishes; rubber recoil pad; free gunlock; available in long-action and short-action
MSRP **$416**

MMR HUNTER
Action: Semiautomatic
Stock: Synthetic
Barrel: 20 in.
Sights: None
Weight: 7 lb. 8 oz.
Caliber: 5.56mm NATO
Magazine: 5+1 rounds
Features: Carbon steel barrel with black phosphate finish; black synthetic, Mossy Oak Treestand, or Mossy Oak Brush stocks; single-stage trigger; oversized trigger guard for use with gloves; integral Picatinny rail
Black: **$978**
Mossy Oak: **$1072**

MVP SERIES PREDATOR
Action: Bolt
Stock: Laminate
Barrel: 18.5 in., 20 in.
Sights: Weaver-style bases
Weight: 7 lb. 8 oz.
Caliber: 5.56mm NATO
Magazine: 11 rounds
Features: Mossberg Varmint Predator series; gray laminate sporter-style stock; optional compact barrel lengths; scoped combo package available; Weaver-style bases for adding optics; carbon steel barrels; varmint style muzzle crown; helically-fluted bolt and barrel fluting; metalwork has dura-ble, non-reflective matte blued finish; front and rear sling swivel studs
MSRP **$729**

MVP SERIES VARMINT
Action: Bolt
Stock: Laminate
Barrel: 24 in.
Sights: Weaver-style bases
Weight: 7 lb. 8 oz.
Caliber: 5.56mm NATO
Magazine: 10+1 rounds
Features: Mossberg Varmint Predator series; Weaver-style bases for optics customization; button-rifled medium bull barrel; varmint style crown; fluting on the barrel; helically-fluted bolt; metalwork has matte blued finish; gray laminate benchrest stock with pistol grip
MSRP **$861**

MOSSBERG ATR SHORT ACTION

MOSSBERG MMR HUNTER - MOSSY OAK TREESTAND

MOSSBERG MVP SERIES PREDATOR

MOSSBERG MVP SERIES VARMINT

New Ultra Light Arms

MODEL 20 ULTIMATE MOUNTAIN RIFLE

Action: Bolt
Stock: Kevlar/graphite composite
Barrel: 22 in.
Sights: None
Weight: 5 lb.
Caliber: .308, .243 Win., 6mm Rem., .257 Roberts, 7mm-08, .284
Magazine: Detachable box
Features: Available in left-hand; choice of stock colors; 20-oz. action; two-position safety
MSRP $3600
Left-handed: $3700

MODEL 20 RIMFIRE

Action: Bolt
Stock: Kevlar/graphite composite
Barrel: 22 in.
Sights: None
Weight: 5 lb. 4 oz.
Caliber: .22LR
Magazine: None or detachable box, 5 rounds
Features: Single-shot or repeater; drilled and tapped for scope; recoil pad; sling swivels; color stock options; left-hand models available for no extra charge
Single shot: $1900
Repeater: $1958

MODEL 209 MUZZLELOADER

Action: Bolt
Stock: Kevlar/graphite composite
Barrel: 24 in.
Sights: None
Weight: 4 lb. 14 oz.
Caliber: .45, .50
Magazine: None
Features: Adjustable Timney trigger; positive primer extraction; button-rifled barrel; Kevlar/graphite stock comes in various colors; recoil pad; sling swivels; ULA scope mounts; hard case; optional black powder
MSRP $1800

NEW ULTRA LIGHT ARMS MODEL 20 ULTIMATE MOUNTAIN RIFLE

NEW ULTRA LIGHT ARMS MODEL 20 RIMFIRE

NEW ULTRA LIGHT ARMS MODEL 209

Nosler

NOSLER M48 CUSTOM SPORTER

M48 CUSTOM SPORTER

Action: Bolt
Stock: Kevlar and carbon fiber
Barrel: 24 in.
Sights: None
Weight: 6 lb. 8 oz.–7 lb. 8 oz.
Caliber: .22-250 Rem., .257 Roberts +P, 6.5-284 Norma, .270 Win., .280 Ack. Imp., .30-06, .300 Win. Mag., .228 Win. Mag., .35 Whelen
Magazine: Internal box, 3, 4 rounds
Features: Onyx black stock with slate metal finish; rifle Basix trigger; glass pillar-bedded Kevlar and carbon fiber stock with Teflon overcoat; Cerakote and Micro Slick finishes prevent corrosion and weather damage; match-grade stainless Pac-Nor, fully free-floated hand lapped barrel
MSRP $3195

M48 CUSTOM VARMINT
Action: Bolt
Stock: Composite
Barrel: 24 in.
Sights: None
Weight: 7 lb. 4 oz.
Caliber: .204 Ruger, .223 Rem., .22-250 Rem.
Magazine: Internal box, 4 rounds
Features: Coyote tan stock with graphite metal finish or onyx black with slate metal finish; rifle Basix trigger; glass pillar-bedded Kevlar and carbon fiber stock with Teflon overcoat; match-grade stainless Pac-Nor, full free-floated hand-lapped barrel
MSRP.................. **$3195**

M48 LEGACY
Action: Bolt
Stock: Walnut
Barrel: 24 in.
Sights: None
Weight: 7 lb. 8 oz.–8 lb.
Caliber: Short: .257 Roberts+P, .308 Win., .300 Win. Mag.; Long: .270 Win., .280 Ack. Imp., .30-06 Spfd., .388 Win. Mag., .35 Whelen
Magazine: Internal box, 3, 4 rounds
Features: Model 48 action; hand lapped PAC-NOR match-grade chromoly, fully free-floated barrel; hinged floor plate; custom rifle Basix trigger; hand oiled black walnut with 20 LPI checkering; classic American styled stock with shadow-line cheekpiece; glass-pillar bedded; sling swivel studs; Pachmayr decelerator recoil pad
MSRP.................. **$2695**

M48 TROPHY GRADE RIFLE
Action: Bolt
Stock: Composite
Barrel: 24 in., 24.75 in.
Sights: None
Weight: 6 lb. 8 oz.–7 lb. 8 oz.
Caliber: Short: .243 Win., .257 Roberts+P, .270 WSM, 7mm-08 Rem., .308 Win., .300 WSM, .325 WSM; Long: .270 Win., .280 Ack. Imp., 7mm Rem. Mag., .30-06 Spld., .300 Win. Mag., .338 Win. Mag., .35 Whelen
Magazine: Internal box, 3, 4 rounds
Features: Custom aluminum-bedded Bell and Carson composite stock in black with gray; Pachmayr Decelerator; recoil pad; sling swivel studs; Nosler Custom Action with standard scope mount; match-grade Pac-Nor chromoly barrel; two-position safety; Basix trigger; Cerakote and Micro Slick finishes
MSRP.................. **$1995**

NOSLER CUSTOM RIFLE
Action: Bolt
Stock: Walnut
Barrel: 24 in., 24.75 in.
Sights: Open
Weight: 8 lb. 4 oz.–8 lb. 12 oz.
Caliber: .300 WSM, .280 Ack. Imp., .338 Win. Mag.
Magazine: Internal box, 3, 4 rounds
Features: Leupold Custom Shop; match-grade stainless, fully free-floated hand lapped barrel; three-stage safety; glass pillar-bedded fancy walnut stock; custom case cruzer by Pelican; custom leather sling
MSRP.................. **$4195**

NOSLER M48 CUSTOM VARMINT

NOSLER M48 LEGACY

NOSLER M48 TROPHY GRADE RIFLE

NOSLER CUSTOM RIFLE

RIFLES

Olympic Arms

GAMESTALKER

Action: Gas-operated autoloader
Stock: ACE Skeleton stock in camo
Barrel: 22 in. stainless fluted
Sights: None
Weight: 7 lb. 8 oz.
Caliber: .243 WSSM, .25 WSSM, .300 OSSM
Magazine: Detachable box, 5 rounds
Features: Flat-top upper receiver; free-floating aluminum handguard; ERGO grip; Picatinny rail
MSRP **$1363.70**

ULTIMATE MAGNUM AR (UMAR)

Action: Semiautomatic, gas-operated
Stock: Synthetic
Barrel: 24 in.
Sights: None
Weight: 9 lb. 6 oz.
Caliber: .22-250 Rem., .223 WSSM, .243 WSSM, .25 WSSM, .300 OSSM
Magazine: 5 rounds
Features: Aluminum forged receiver machined by Olympic Arms; black matte anodized receiver, Parkerized steel parts; flat top with Picatinny rails; heavy match grade bull barrel; side-sling mount or bi-pod mount
MSRP **$1588.70**

OLYMPIC ARMS GAMESTALKER

OLYMPIC ARMS UMAR

RIFLES

Pedersoli

1763 LEGER (1766) CHARLEVILLE

Action: Dropping block
Stock: Walnut
Barrel: 44.7 in.
Sights: Open
Weight: 10 lb. 2 oz.
Caliber: .69
Magazine: None
Features: Creedmoor sight; tunnel front sight; replica of French infantry musket
MSRP **$1506**

1874 SHARPS OLD WEST MAPLE

Action: Dropping block
Stock: Maple
Barrel: 30 in.
Sights: None
Weight: 11 lb. 7 oz.
Caliber: .45-70
Magazine: None
Features: Optional Creedmoor and tunnel sights; brass plate on right side of butt stock can be personalized; forend has wedge plates; pistol grip cap is made of hardened steel
MSRP **$2279**

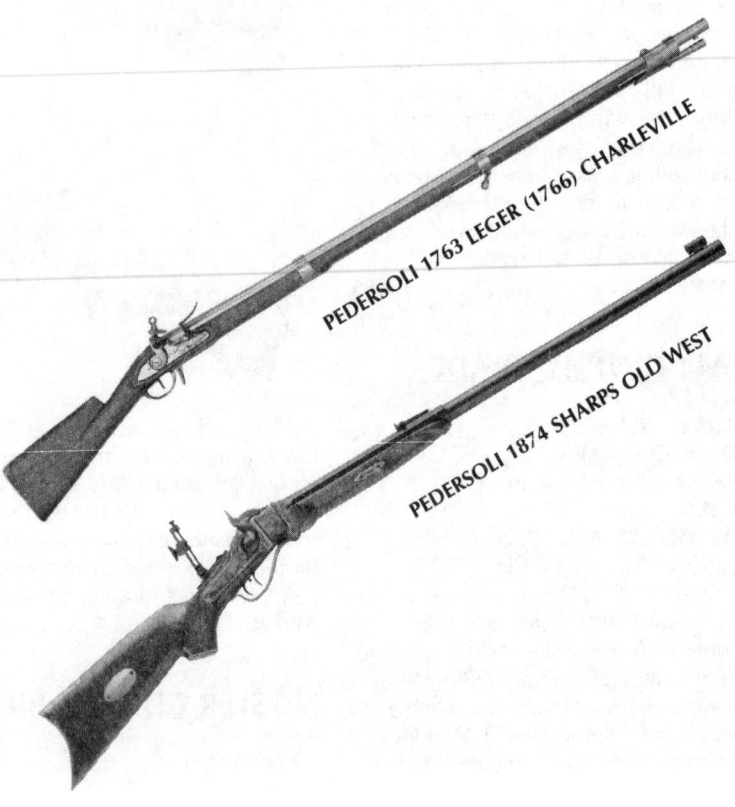

PEDERSOLI 1763 LEGER (1766) CHARLEVILLE

PEDERSOLI 1874 SHARPS OLD WEST

Pedersoli

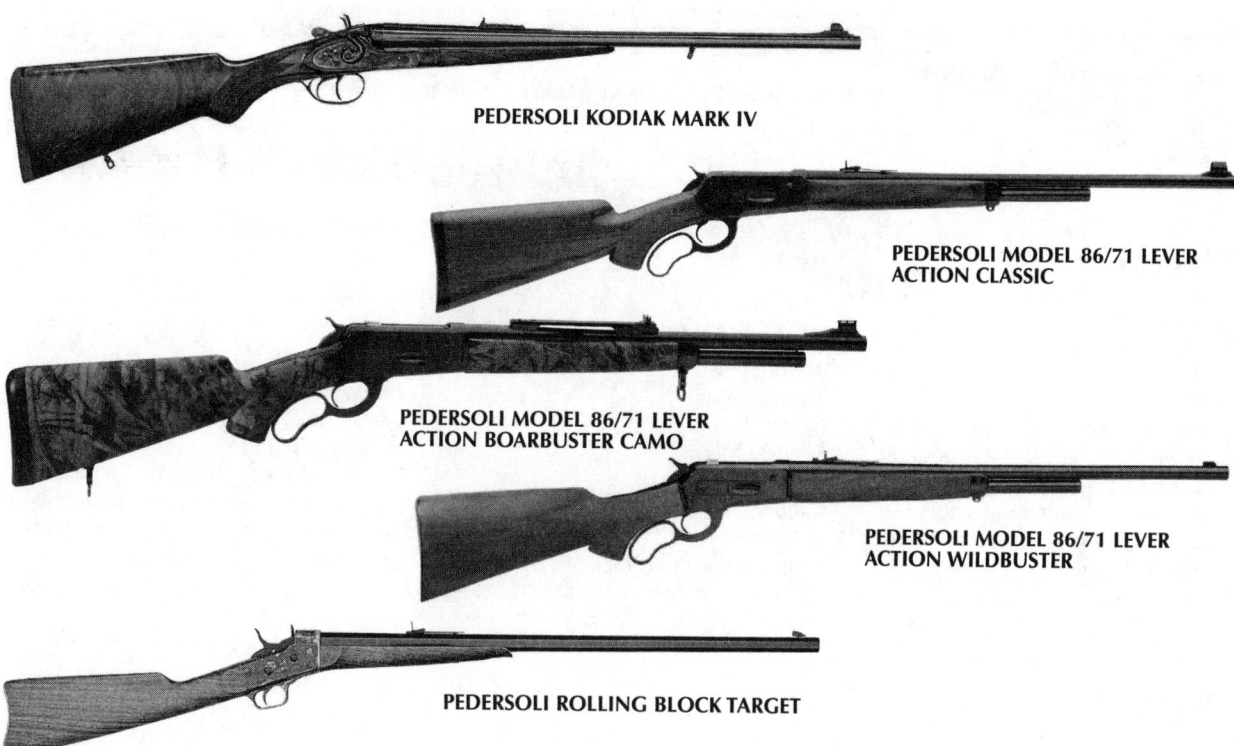

PEDERSOLI KODIAK MARK IV

PEDERSOLI MODEL 86/71 LEVER
ACTION CLASSIC

PEDERSOLI MODEL 86/71 LEVER
ACTION BOARBUSTER CAMO

PEDERSOLI MODEL 86/71 LEVER
ACTION WILDBUSTER

PEDERSOLI ROLLING BLOCK TARGET

KODIAK MARK IV
Action: Breech loading
Stock: Walnut
Barrel: 22 in., 24 in.
Sights: Open
Weight: 9 lb. 11 oz.–10 lb. 5 oz.
Caliber: .45-70; 8x57JRS; 9.3x74R
Magazine: None
Features: Double-leave rear sight in a dovetail; tapered round barrels made of blued steel; select walnut stock with checkering and oil finish
MSRP **$6009**

MODEL 86/71 LEVER ACTION BOARBUSTER
Action: Lever
Stock: Walnut
Barrel: 19 in.
Sights: Drilled and tapped for scopes
Weight: 7 lb. 4 oz.
Caliber: .444 Marlin, .45-70
Magazine: 5 rounds
Features: Barrel equipped with European Picatinny style base with integral rear sight; half cock safety on hammer; safety slide catch at the rear of the frame; checkered pistol grip stock and forend are made from walnut; also available in soft touch orange

camo color; metal parts are blued; drilled and tapped for sights
MSRP **$1771**

MODEL 86/71 LEVER ACTION CLASSIC
Action: Lever
Stock: Walnut
Barrel: 24 in.
Sights: Drilled and tapped for scopes
Weight: 8 lb. 3 oz.
Caliber: .45-70
Magazine: 5 rounds
Features: Last "big frame" rifle for Winchester; drilled and tapped for scopes; broach rifled barrel and magazine are blued finished; checkered walnut pistol grip; frame is forged and CNC-machined, with a blued finish on the standard version and case-hardened frame and buttcap on the Premium model with select walnut stock and forend
MSRP **$1771**

MODEL 86/71 LEVER ACTION WILDBUSTER
Action: Lever
Stock: Walnut
Barrel: 24 in.

Sights: Drilled and tapped for scopes
Weight: 8 lb. 3 oz.
Caliber: .45-70
Magazine: 5 rounds
Features: Ramp rear sight; walnut forend and pistol grip stock with checkered buttplate; blued finish on metal parts; drilled and tapped for scopes
MSRP **$1709**

ROLLING BLOCK TARGET
Action: Dropping block
Stock: Walnut
Barrel: 30 in.
Sights: Open
Weight: 10 lb. 9 oz.
Caliber: .357 Mag., .45-70
Magazine: None
Features: Octagonal, conical blued barrel; case-hardened color frame is equipped with ramp rear sight adjustable in elevation; steel buttplate and trigger guard; straight stock and forend made of walnut with oil finish
MSRP **$1151**

Puma By Legacy Sports

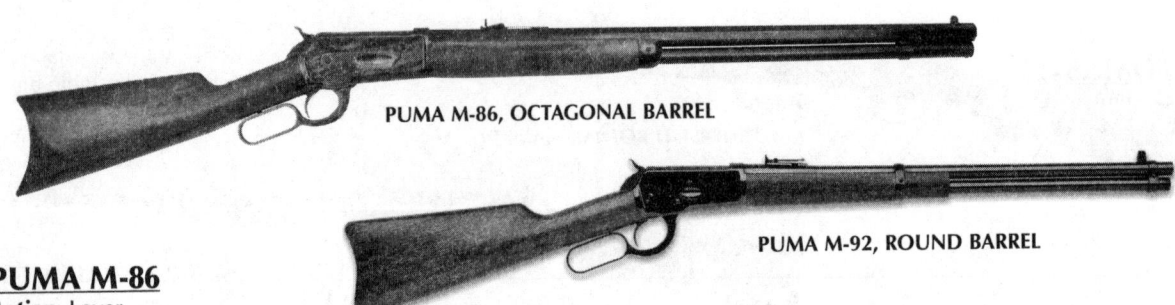

PUMA M-86, OCTAGONAL BARREL

PUMA M-92, ROUND BARREL

PUMA M-86

Action: Lever
Stock: Walnut
Barrel: 22 in., 26 in.
Sights: Open
Weight: 9 lb.
Caliber: .45-70
Magazine: Tubular mag, 7, 8 rounds
Features: Octagonal steel barrel; graduated rear and blade front sights; double locking lugs; high grade Italian walnut stock; standard loop lever
MSRP $1390

PUMA M-92

Action: Lever
Stock: Walnut
Barrel: 16 in., 20 in., 24 in.
Sights: Open
Weight: 6 lb. 10 oz.
Caliber: .45 Colt, .357 Mag., .44/40, .44 Mag.
Magazine: Tubular mag, 16-in. holds 9 rounds, 20-in. holds 10 rounds, octagonal barrels hold 10 rounds
Features: Octagonal or round steel barrel available; walnut stock with straight grip; crescent buttplate; blued barrel; color case receiver; factory magazine tube plug is included limiting it to 5 rounds until removed; high grade Italian walnut stock
MSRP $1053

Purdey

PURDEY BOLT ACTION RIFLE

PURDEY DOUBLE RIFLE

DOUBLE RIFLES

Action: Self-Opening
Stock: Walnut
Barrel: 23 in.–26 in.
Sights: Open
Weight: 12 lb. 4 oz.
Caliber: .375, .416, .470, .475, .500, .577, .600
Magazine: None
Features: Hinged front trigger; bolted non-automatic safety catch; sling swivels optional; full pistol grip; cheekpiece and leather covered recoil pad; chopper lump barrel construction; express rear sights with bead foresight with flip-up moon sight; optional beavertail forend and telescopic sights
.375 or smaller: $166091
.416, .470, .475, .500: $175493
.557, .600: $175493
(All prices excluding UK taxes)

BOLT ACTION RIFLES

Action: Bolt
Stock: Walnut
Barrel: 25 in.
Sights: Open
Weight: 10 lb. 8 oz.
Caliber: .375 H&H, 7mm Mag.
Magazine: None
Features: Original Mauser '98 or modern Mauser type magnum square bridge; model 70 type safety catch for use with telescopic sights; quick detachable claw or Purdey rail mounts depending on the type of action and telescopic sight chosen; Purdey's rail mount system with integral recoil bar; Turkish walnut stock with pistol grip; cheekpiece and rubber recoil pad; single trigger
Original Mauser Action: . . . $43873
Magnum Square Bridge Action (.375 caliber & above): $43873
(All prices excluding UK taxes)

Remington Arms

MODEL 552 BDL SPEEDMASTER

Action: Semiautomatic
Stock: Walnut
Barrel: 22 in.
Sights: Open
Weight: 5 lb. 12 oz.
Caliber: .22S, L, LR
Magazine: Tubular mag
Features: Adjustable iron sights for open sight plinking; grooved receiver for scope mounts; high-gloss American walnut stock and forend checkering; richly blued carbon-steel barrel; positive cross-bolt safety
MSRP. **$650**

MODEL 572 BDL FIELDMASTER

Action: Pump
Stock: Walnut
Barrel: 21 in.
Sights: Open
Weight: 5 lb. 12 oz.
Caliber: .22S, L, LR
Magazine: Tubular mag
Features: Smooth classic side action; high-gloss American walnut stock and forend with cut checkering; richly blued carbon-steel barrel; adjustable iron sights for open slight plinking; receiver grooved for scope mounts; positive cross-bolt safety
MSRP. **$665**

MODEL 597

Action: Semiautomatic
Stock: Synthetic
Barrel: 22 in.
Sights: Open
Weight: 5 lb. 8 oz.
Caliber: .22LR, .22 WMR
Magazine: Detachable box, 10 rounds
Features: Bolt-guidance system features twin, tool-steel guide rails; sear and hammer are Teflon/nickel-plated; non-glare matte finish; adjustable big game iron sights; last-shot "hold open" bolt for added safety
MSRP. **$204**

MODEL 597 HEAVY BARREL

Action: Semiautomatic
Stock: Synthetic
Barrel: 22 in.
Sights: None
Weight: 5 lb. 12 oz.
Caliber: .22 LR
Magazine: Detachable box, 10 rounds
Features: Heavy barrel with rugged green synthetic stock; bolt-guidance system features twin tool-steel guide rails; Teflon nickel plated sear and hammer; patented drop-out staggered stack, detachable metal magazine; last-shot "hold open" bolt; scope rail
MSRP. **$249**

RIFLES

REMINGTON MODEL 552 BDL SPEEDMASTER

REMINGTON MODEL 572 BDL FIELDMASTER

REMINGTON MODEL 597 WITH SCOPE

REMINGTON MODEL 597 HB

Remington Arms

REMINGTON MODEL 597
HEAVY BARREL A-TACS CAMO

REMINGTON MODEL 700 BDL

REMINGTON MODEL 700 BDL
50TH ANNIVERSARY EDITION

MODEL 597 HEAVY BARREL A-TACS CAMO

Action: Semiautomatic
Stock: Synthetic
Barrel: 22 in.
Sights: None
Weight: 5 lb. 12 oz.
Caliber: .22 LR
Magazine: Detachable box, 10 rounds
Features: Heavy barrel with A-TACS camo synthetic stock; bolt-guidance system features twin tool-steel guide rails; Teflon nickel plated sear and hammer; patented drop-out staggered stack, detachable metal magazine; last-shot "hold open" bolt; scope rail
MSRP **$349**

MODEL 700 BDL

Action: Bolt
Stock: Walnut
Barrel: 22 in., 24 in., 26 in.
Sights: Open
Weight: 7 lb. 4 oz.–7 lb. 10 oz.
Caliber: .243 Win., .270 Win., .30-06 Spfd., 7mm Rem. Mag., .300 Rem. Ultra Mag.
Magazine: Internal box
Features: Adjustable X-Mark Pro Trigger system; walnut stock with black forend cap; Monte Carlo comb with raised cheekpiece and skipline cut checkering; hinged magazine floor plate; sling swivel studs; hooded ramp front sight and adjustable rear sight; cylindrical receiver machined from solid-steel bar
MSRP **$985**

MODEL 700 BDL 50TH ANNIVERSARY EDITION

Action: Bolt
Stock: Walnut
Barrel: 24 in.
Sights: Open
Weight: 7 lb. 10 oz.
Caliber: 7mm Rem. Mag.
Magazine: Internal box
Features: 50th anniversary edition in the first chambering released in 1962, 7mm Remington Magnum; laser-engraved commemorative floorplate; B grade walnut stock with fleur-de-lis checkering and white line spacers at the recoil pad, grip cap, and forend; sling swivel studs; black vented recoil pad; satin bluing on the receiver; X-Mark Pro externally adjustable trigger
MSRP **$1399**

Remington Arms

REMINGTON MODEL 700 CDL

REMINGTON MODEL 700 CDL 375 H&H 100TH ANNIVERSARY EDITION

REMINGTON MODEL 700 CDL DM

REMINGTON MODEL 700 CDL SF LIMITED EDITION

RIFLES

MODEL 700 CDL

Action: Bolt
Stock: Walnut
Barrel: 24 in., 26 in.
Sights: None
Weight: 7 lb. 5 oz.–7 lb. 10 oz.
Caliber: .243 Win., .270 Win., 7mm-08 Rem., .300 Win. Mag., .300 Rem. Ultra Mag.
Magazine: Internal box
Features: Adjustable X-Mark Pro Trigger system; cylindrical receiver machined from solid-steel bar stock; walnut stock with oil finish
MSRP. **$1019**

MODEL 700 CDL 375 H&H 100TH ANNIVERSARY EDITION

Action: Bolt
Stock: Walnut
Barrel: 22 in.

Sights: Front and rear
Weight: 7 lb. 10 oz.
Caliber: .375 H&H
Magazine: Internal box
Features: Walnut stock with satin finish; matte-finished rifle sighted barrel; externally adjusted X-Mark Pro trigger system; rear sling swivel stud; front barrel band; New England custom gun rear adjustable sight and hooded front sight; steel hinged floorplate
MSRP. **$1450**

MODEL 700 CDL DM

Action: Bolt
Stock: Walnut, synthetic
Barrel: 24 in., 26 in.
Sights: None
Weight: 7 lb. 5 oz.–7 lb. 10 oz.
Caliber: .243 Win., 7mm-08 Rem., .270 Win., .30-06 Spfd., 7mm Rem. Mag., .300 Win. Mag.

Magazine: Detachable box
Features: Receiver machined from solid-steel bar stock; X-Mark Pro externally adjustable trigger system; walnut stock with satin finish
MSRP. **$1041**

MODEL 700 CDL SF LIMITED EDITION

Action: Bolt
Stock: Walnut
Barrel: 24 in.
Sights: None
Weight: 7 lb. 6 oz.
Caliber: 7mm Rem. Mag.
Magazine: Internal box
Features: 50th anniversary edition; satin-finished American walnut stock; sling swivel studs; satin finished stainless steel drilled and tapped barrel; X-Mark Pro trigger
MSRP. **$1250**

Remington Arms

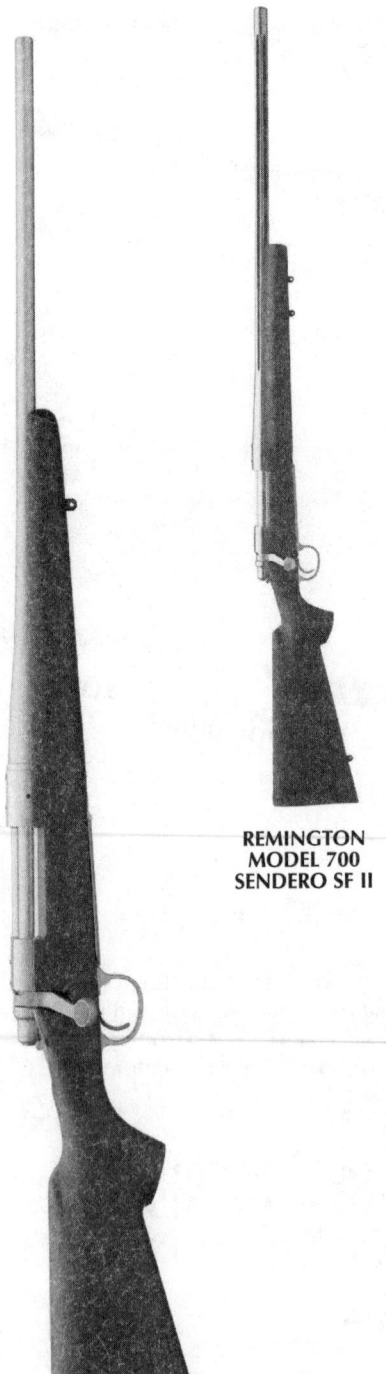

REMINGTON MODEL 700 SENDERO SF II

REMINGTON MODEL 700 MOUNTAIN SS

MODEL 700 MOUNTAIN SS

Action: Bolt
Stock: Synthetic
Barrel: 22 in.
Sights: Drilled and tapped for scopes
Weight: 6 lb. 8 oz.
Caliber: .25-06 Rem., .270 Win., .280 Rem., .30-06 Spfd., 7mm-08 Rem., .308 Win.
Magazine: Internal box
Features: Bell & Carson aramid fiber reinforced stock; X-Mark Pro trigger system; cylindrical receiver design; sling swivel studs; stainless steel barrel and action; hinged magazine floor plate
MSRP **$1123**

MODEL 700 SENDERO SF II

Action: Bolt
Stock: Composite
Barrel: 26 in.
Sights: None
Weight: 8 lb. 8 oz.
Caliber: 7mm Rem. Mag., .300 Win. Mag., .300 Rem. Ultra Mag.
Magazine: Internal box
Features: Composite stock in black with gray webbing, reinforced with aramid fibers; features contoured beavertail forend with ambidextrous finger grooves and palm swells; heavy contour barrels are fluted for rapid cooling; full-length aluminum bedding stocks; twin front swivel studs for sling and bipod; concave target-style barrel crown
MSRP **$1451**

MODEL 700 SPS

Action: Bolt
Stock: Synthetic
Barrel: 24 in., 26 in.
Sights: None
Weight: 7 lb.–7 lb. 10 oz.
Caliber: .270 WSM, .300 WSM, .223 Rem., .243 Win., 7mm-08 Rem., .308 Win., .270 Win., .20-06 Spfd., .300 Win. Mag., .300 Rem. Ultra Mag., 7mm Rem. Mag.
Magazine: Internal box
Features: Black ergonomic synthetic stock; carbon steel sight drilled and tapped for scope mounts; exterior metal-work features matte blued finish; hinged floor plate; swivel studs
MSRP **$702**

MODEL 700 SPS CAMO

Action: Bolt
Stock: Synthetic
Barrel: 20 in., 22 in., 24 in.
Sights: None
Weight: 7 lb.–7 lb. 6 oz.
Caliber: .270 Win., .30-06 Spfd., 7mm Rem. Mag., .300 Win. Mag., .243 Win., 7mm-08 Rem.
Magazine: None
Features: Hammer-forged barrel; X-Mark Pro externally adjustable trigger system; SuperCell recoil pad; synthetic stock in Mossy Oak Break-Up Infinity pattern; Hogue over-molded grips; receivers tapped and drilled
MSRP **$777**

REMINGTON MODEL 700 SPS LEFT-HAND

REMINGTON MODEL 700 SPS CAMO

MODEL 700 SPS TACTICAL

Action: Bolt
Stock: Synthetic
Barrel: 20 in.
Sights: None
Weight: 7 lb. 4 oz.–7 lb. 11 oz.
Caliber: .223 Rem., .308 Win.
Magazine: Detachable box
Features: Ergonomic tactical stock in black; sling swivel studs; carbon steel barrel is drilled and tapped for sights; metal features blued finish; X-Mark Pro adjustable trigger; SuperCell recoil pad; semi-beavertail forend; hinged floor plate
MSRP $757

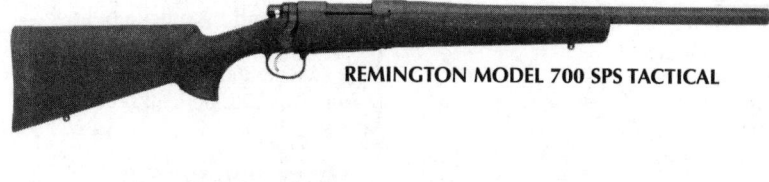

REMINGTON MODEL 700 SPS TACTICAL

MODEL 700 SPS TACTICAL AAC-SD

Action: Bolt
Stock: Synthetic
Barrel: 20 in.
Sights: None
Weight: 7 lb. 5 oz.
Caliber: .308 Win.
Magazine: Internal box
Features: Heavy barrel with threaded muzzle; accepts AAC and other threaded flash hiders, muzzlebrakes and suppressors; Hogue overmolded hillier green pillar bedded stock; X-Mark Pro adjustable trigger; optional Leupold Mark IV scope
MSRP $833

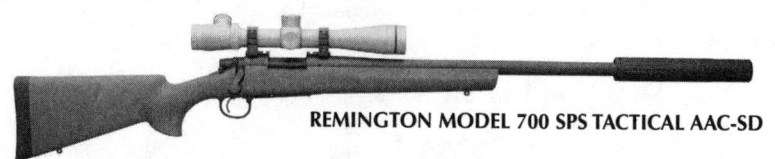

REMINGTON MODEL 700 SPS TACTICAL AAC-SD

MODEL 700 SPS VARMINT

Action: Bolt
Stock: Synthetic
Barrel: 26 in.
Sights: None
Weight: 8 lb. 8 oz.
Caliber: .204 Ruger, .223 Rem., .22-250 Rem., .243 Win., .308 Win.
Magazine: Internal box
Features: Ergonomic black synthetic stock has a vented beavertail forend; non-reflective matte blued finish on barrel and receiver; hinged floor plate; sling swivel studs; drilled and tapped for scope mounts
MSRP $732

REMINGTON MODEL 700 SPS VARMINT

MODEL 700 TARGET TACTICAL

Action: Bolt
Stock: Synthetic

REMINGTON MODEL 700 TARGET TACTICAL WITH SCOPE

Barrel: 26 in.
Sights: Target
Weight: 11 lb. 12 oz.
Caliber: .308 Win.
Magazine: Internal box
Features: Triangular VTR barrel configuration; Bell & Carson Medalist varmint/tactical stock in black; 5-R hammer-forged tactical target rifling; adjustable length of comb and pull; tactical style bolt knob; X-Mark Pro adjustable trigger
MSRP $2117

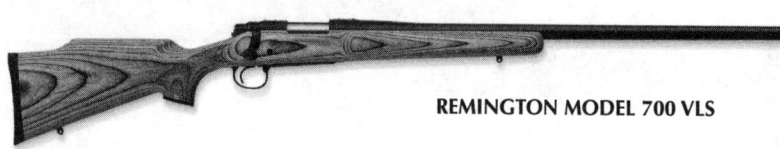

REMINGTON MODEL 700 VLS

MODEL 700 VLS

Action: Bolt
Stock: Laminate
Barrel: 26 in.
Sights: Target
Weight: 9 lb. 6 oz.
Caliber: .204 Ruger, .22-250 Rem., .223 Rem., .243 Win., .308 Win.
Magazine: Internal box
Features: Varmint laminated stock; Monte Carlo cheekpiece; beavertail shape forend; blued, satin finish metal; concave target-style barrel crown
MSRP $1045

Remington Arms

MODEL 700 VTR

Action: Bolt
Stock: Synthetic
Barrel: 22 in.
Sights: None
Weight: 7 lb. 8 oz.
Caliber: .223 Rem., .308 Win., .243 Win., .204 Ruger, .223 Rem., .22-250 Rem.
Magazine: Internal box
Features: Triangular barrel contour; integral muzzlebrake; green stock with black overmolded grips
MSRP **$825**

MODEL 700 VTR A-TACS

Action: Bolt
Stock: Synthetic, laminate
Barrel: 22 in.
Sights: None
Weight: 7 lb. 1 oz.
Caliber: .308 Win.
Magazine: 4 rounds
Features: Triangular barrel design; A-TACS camo pattern on synthetic or laminate stock; integral muzzlebrake; vents in forend for quick cooling; X-Mark Pro adjustable trigger; dual front swivel studs; concave target-style barrel crown; SuperCell recoil pad
MSRP **$930**

MODEL 700 XCR II

Action: Bolt
Stock: Synthetic
Barrel: 24 in., 26 in.
Sights: Iron sights on .375 chamberings
Weight: 7 lb. 6 oz.–7 lb. 10 oz.
Caliber: .270 Win., .30-06 Spfd., 7mm Rem. Mag., .300 WSM, .300 Win. Mag., .338 Win. Mag., .300 Rem. Ultra Mag., .338 Rem. Ultra Mag., .375 H&H
Magazine: Internal box
Features: Engraved floor plate; synthetic stock in; drilled and tapped for scope mounting; rubber overmolding on grip and forestock; SuperCell recoil pad; TriNyte corrosion-control system; X-Mark Pro trigger system
MSRP **$1005**

MODEL 750 WOODSMASTER

Action: Semiautomatic, gas action
Stock: Walnut, synthetic
Barrel: 22 in.
Sights: Open
Weight: 7 lb. 8 oz.
Caliber: .270 Win., .30-06 Spfd., .308 Win., .243 Win.
Magazine: None
Features: American walnut or black synthetic stock and forend; iron sights; receiver drilled and tapped for model 7400 scope mounts; rotary-bolt lock-up; sling swivel studs
MSRP **$1004**

REMINGTON MODEL 700 VTR

REMINGTON MODEL 700 VTR A-TACS

REMINGTON MODEL 700 XCR II

REMINGTON MODEL 750 WOODSMASTER

RIFLES

Remington Arms

MODEL 770
Action: Bolt
Stock: Synthetic
Barrel: 22 in.
Sights: Boresighted 3-9x40mm scope
Weight: 8 lb. 8 oz.–8 lb. 10 oz.
Caliber: .243 Win., 7mm-08 Rem., .270 Win., .30-06 Spfd., 7mm Rem. Mag., .300 Win. Mag., .308 Win.
Magazine: Detachable box, standard 4 rounds, magnum 3 rounds
Features: Button rifling; ergonomically contoured stock with a raised cheekpiece; textured grips; black synthetic stock; blued or stainless barrel with nickel-plated action and bolt; easy-camming 60 degree bolt; stainless steel barrel
MSRP. $373

MODEL 770 STAINLESS CAMO
Action: Bolt
Stock: Synthetic
Barrel: 22 in., 24 in.
Sights: Boresighted 3-9x40mm scope
Weight: 8 lb. 8 oz.
Caliber: .270 Win., .30-06 Spfd., 7mm Rem. Mag., .300 Win. Mag.
Magazine: Detachable box, standard 4 rounds, magnum 3 rounds
Features: Realtree AP HD camo synthetic stock design; molded swing swivel studs; stainless barrel with nickel-plated action and bolt; easy-camming 60 degree bolt
MSRP. $455

MODEL 7600
Action: Pump
Stock: Wood
Barrel: 22 in.
Sights: Open
Weight: 7 lb. 8 oz.
Caliber: .243 Win., .270 Win., .30-06 Spfd., .308 Win.
Magazine: Detachable box, 4 rounds
Features: Free-floated barrel; Monte Carlo walnut stock with satin finish as standard; metal work has black non-reflective finish; iron sights and drilled and tapped receiver for scope mounts; rotary-bolt lock-up
MSRP. $900

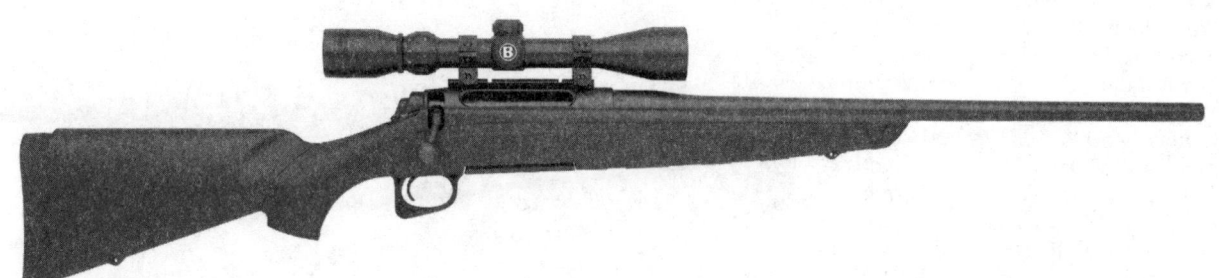

REMINGTON MODEL 770

REMINGTON MODEL 770 STAINLESS CAMO

REMINGTON MODEL 7600

Remington Arms

MODEL 7600 SYNTHETIC

Action: Pump
Stock: Synthetic
Barrel: 22 in.
Sights: Open
Weight: 7 lb. 8 oz.
Caliber: .243 Win., .270 Win., .30-06 Spfd., .308 Win.
Magazine: Detachable box, 4 rounds
Features: Fiberglass-reinforced synthetic stock and forend; free-floated barrel; metal work has black non-reflective finish; iron sights and drilled and tapped receiver for scope mounts; rotary-bolt lock-up
MSRP **$756**

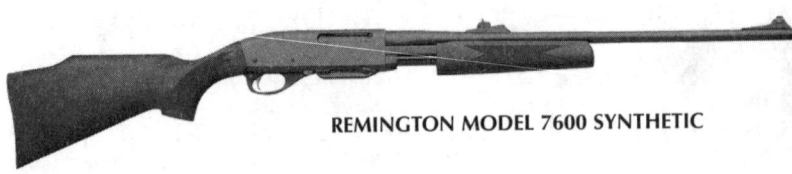

REMINGTON MODEL 7600 SYNTHETIC

MODEL R-15 450 BUSHMASTER

Action: Semiautomatic, gas action
Stock: Synthetic
Barrel: 18 in., 22 in.
Sights: None
Weight: 7 lb. 8 oz.–7 lb. 12 oz.
Caliber: .450 Bushmaster, .30 Rem. AR
Magazine: Detachable box, 4 rounds
Features: Free-floated, fluted barrel; clean-breaking single-state trigger; receiver-length Picatinny rail; aluminum receiver; synthetic full Mossy Oak camo stock with ergonomic pistol grip; lockable hard case included
MSRP **$1276**

REMINGTON MODEL R-15 450 BUSHMASTER WITH SCOPE

REMINGTON MODEL R-25

MODEL R-25

Action: Semiautomatic, gas action
Stock: Synthetic
Barrel: 20 in.
Sights: None
Weight: 8 lb. 12 oz.
Caliber: .243 Win, 7mm-08 Rem., .308 Win.
Magazine: Detachable box, 4 rounds
Features: Free-floated, fluted barrel; clean-breaking single state trigger; receiver length Picatinny rail; aluminum receiver; synthetic full Mossy Oak camo stock with ergonomic pistol grip; lockable hard case included
MSRP **$1631**

REMINGTON MODEL SEVEN CDL

MODEL SEVEN CDL

Action: Bolt
Stock: Walnut
Barrel: 20 in.
Sights: Open
Weight: 6 lb. 8 oz.
Caliber: .243 Win., .260 Rem., 7mm-08 Rem., .308 Win.
Magazine: Internal box
Features: SuperCell recoil pad; American walnut CDL stock with satin-finished barrel; compact design for fast handling; cylindrical receiver; available in Rem. short-action magnum and Winchester short magnum
MSRP **$1029**

Remington Arms

REMINGTON MODEL SEVEN PREDATOR

REMINGTON MODEL SEVEN SYNTHETIC

MODEL SEVEN PREDATOR
Action: Bolt
Stock: Synthetic
Barrel: 22 in.
Sights: None
Weight: 7 lb.
Caliber: .223 Rem., .22-250 Rem., .243 Win.
Magazine: Internal box
Features: Mossy Oak Brush camo stock; fluted magnum-contour barrel; X-Mark Pro trigger system
MSRP **$886**

MODEL SEVEN SYNTHETIC
Action: Bolt
Stock: Synthetic
Barrel: 18 in., 20 in.
Sights: None
Weight: 6 lb. 2 oz.–6 lb. 8 oz.

Caliber: .223 Rem., .243 Win., .260 Rem., 7mm-08 Rem., .308 Win.
Magazine: Internal box
Features: Synthetic black stock; compact design for fast handling; cylindrical receiver design
MSRP **$702**

Rifles Inc.

RIFLES

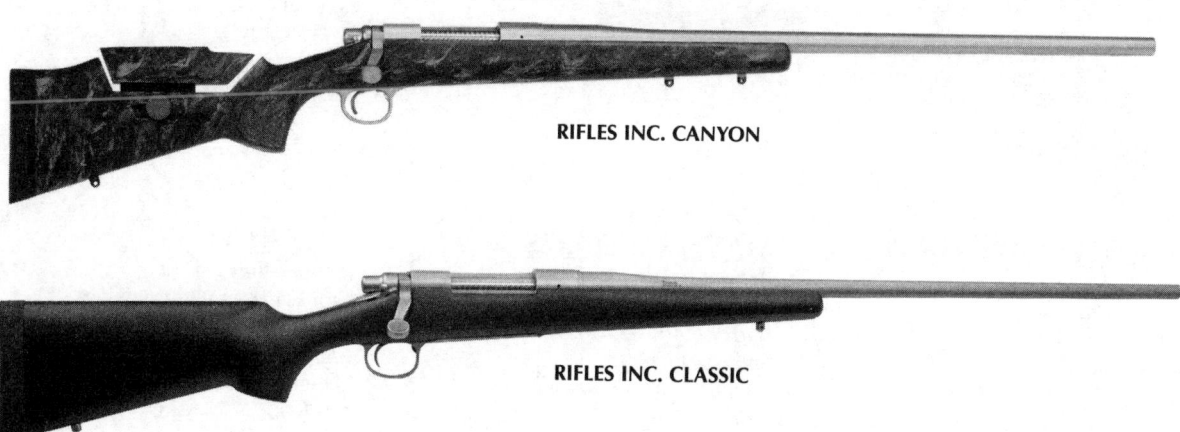

RIFLES INC. CANYON

RIFLES INC. CLASSIC

CANYON
Action: Bolt
Stock: McMillan HTG
Barrel: 24 in.
Sights: None
Weight: 10 lb.
Caliber: Most popular calibers
Magazine: Internal box
Features: Blind or hinged floor plate; customer-supplied Rem. 700 action; match grade stainless steel Lilja number 6 barrel; optional muzzlebrake; matte stainless metal finish,

optional black Teflon; adjustable cheekpiece; custom buttpad
MSRP **$3500**

CLASSIC
Action: Bolt
Stock: Laminated fiberglass
Barrel: 24 in.-26 in.
Sights: None
Weight: 6 lb. 8 oz.

Caliber: All popular chamberings up to .375 H&H
Magazine: Internal box
Features: Customer-supplied Rem. 700 action; match grade stainless steel Lilja barrel; blind or hinged floor plate; matte stainless metal finish, optional Black Teflon finish; black laminated fiberglass, pillar glass bedded stock
MSRP **$2600**

Rifles Inc.

RIFLES INC. LIGHTWEIGHT STRATA

RIFLES INC. MASTER'S SERIES

RIFLES INC. SAFARI

LIGHTWEIGHT STRATA

Action: Bolt
Stock: Laminate
Barrel: 22 in.-26 in.
Sights: None
Weight: 4 lb. 8 oz.–5 lb. 12 oz.
Caliber: All popular chamberings up to .375 H&H
Magazine: Internal box
Features: Customer-supplied Rem. 700 action; match grade stainless steel Lilja barrel; fluted bolt and hollowed-handle; blind or hinged floor plate; matte stainless metal finish, optional black Teflon finish; hand-laminated blend of Kevlar/graphite and boron, pillar glass bedded stock; Titanium Strata has hand-laminated graphite stock with pillar glass bedded; custom buttpad; Quiet Slimbrake II muzzlebrake

Lightweight Strata: **$2900**
Lightweight 70: **$2800**
Titanium Strata: **$3500**

MASTER'S SERIES

Action: Bolt
Stock: Laminated fiberglass
Barrel: 24 in.-27 in.
Sights: None
Weight: 7 lb. 12 oz.
Caliber: All popular chamberings up to .375 H&H
Magazine: Internal box
Features: Customer-supplied Rem. 700 action; match grade stainless steel Lilja number 5 barrel; hinged floor plate; matte stainless metal finish, optional black Teflon finish; black laminated fiberglass, pillar glass bedded stock; optional muzzlebrake

MSRP **$2900**

SAFARI

Action: Bolt
Stock: Laminated fiberglass
Barrel: 23 in.-25 in.
Sights: Optional Express Sights
Weight: 8 lb. 8 oz.
Caliber: .375 H&H, .416 Rem. Mag., and other large game cartridges
Magazine: Drop box, 4 rounds
Features: Customer-supplied Winchester Model 70 Classic action; lapped and face trued bolt; match grade stainless steel Lilja barrel; Quiet Slimbrake II muzzlebrake; hinged floor plate or optional drop box; matte stainless finish, optional black Teflon; double laminated fiberglass, pillar glass bedded stock; Pachmayr decelerator; optional barrel band

MSRP **$3200**

RIFLES

Rock River Arms

ROCK RIVER ARMS LAR-6.8 COYOTE CARBINE

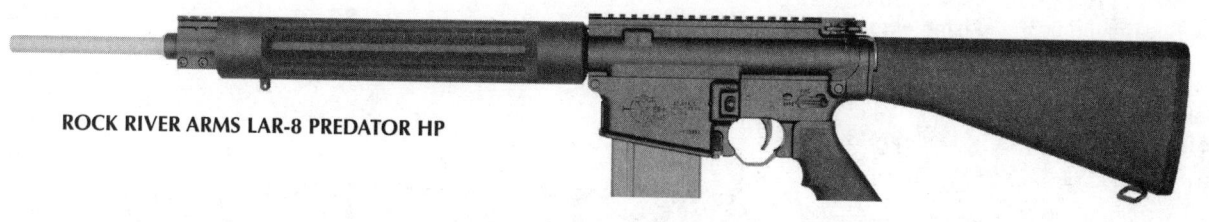

ROCK RIVER ARMS LAR-8 PREDATOR HP

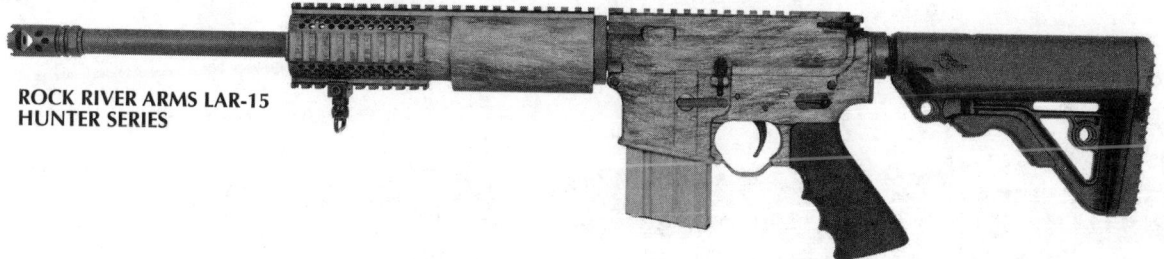

ROCK RIVER ARMS LAR-15 HUNTER SERIES

LAR-6.8 COYOTE CARBINE

Action: Semiautomatic
Stock: Synthetic
Barrel: 16 in.
Sights: None
Weight: 7 lb.
Caliber: 6.8mm SPC II
Magazine: 1 round
Features: Smith Vortex flash hider; chromoly barrel; RRA two-stage match trigger
MSRP $1270

LAR-8 PREDATOR HP

Action: Semiautomatic
Stock: Synthetic
Barrel: 20 in.
Sights: None
Weight: 8 lb. 10 oz.
Caliber: .308 Win., 7mm-08 Rem., .243 Win.
Magazine: Detachable box
Features: Forged A4 receiver with forward assist and port door; stainless steel barrel; gas block sight Base; two-stage trigger; Hogue rubber grip; RRA aluminum free-float tube; A2 buttstock or operator stock
MSRP . . . . $1605–$1655

LAR-15 HUNTER SERIES

Action: Semiautomatic
Stock: Synthetic
Barrel: 16 in.
Sights: None
Weight: 7 lb. 10 oz.
Caliber: 5.56mm NATO, .223
Magazine: 20 rounds
Features: Finish in choice of WYL-Ehide or PRK-Ehide, digitalized imagery of real coyote or wild hog; finish is in the hardcoat anodizing, not a film dip or applique; camo anodized to the lower receiver, upper receiver, charging handle, trigger guard, and RRA half quad rail handguard; Hogue rubber pistol grip; low profile gas block; RRA operator CAR stock
MSRP $1550

Rock River Arms

LAR-15LH LEFT-HANDED SERIES

Action: Semiautomatic
Stock: Synthetic
Barrel: 16 in.
Sights: None
Weight: 8 lb.
Caliber: 5.56mm NATO, .223
Magazine: 30 rounds
Features: Re-engineered and outfitted specifically for the left-handed shooter; left side ejection port; right side safety selector and bolt catch; ambidextrous mag release and charging handle; mid-length gas system; RRA tactical muzzle break; RRA two-stage triggerr; RRA operator CAR stock
MSRP . . . . **$1360–$1415**

LAR-40 MID-LENGTH A4

Action: Semiautomatic
Stock: Synthetic
Barrel: 16 in.
Sights: None
Weight: 7 lb. 2 oz.
Caliber: .40 S&W
Magazine: 1 round
Features: Flash hider; single-stage trigger; RRA tactical CAR stock with Hogue grip
A4: **$1260**

LAR-47 CAR A4

Action: Semiautomatic
Stock: Synthetic
Barrel: 16 in.
Sights: None
Weight: 6 lb. 6 oz.
Caliber: 7.62x39mm
Magazine: 30 rounds, standard AK-47 mag
Features: RRA 6-postion tactical CAR stock; A2 pistol grip; CAR handguards; RRA two-stage trigger; A2 flash hider; ambidextrous mag release
MSRP **$1270**

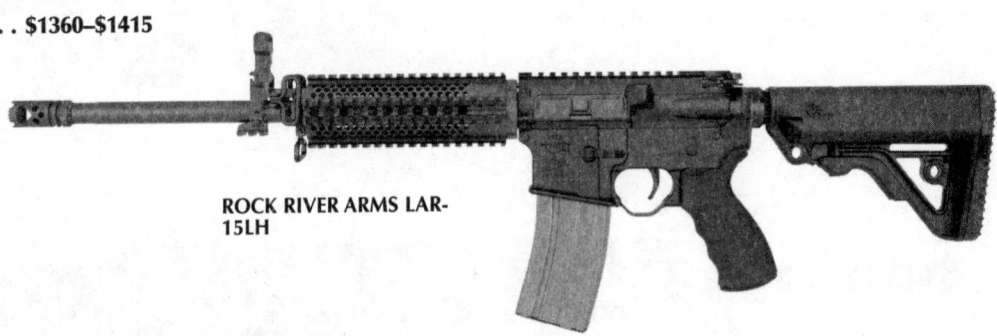

ROCK RIVER ARMS LAR-15LH

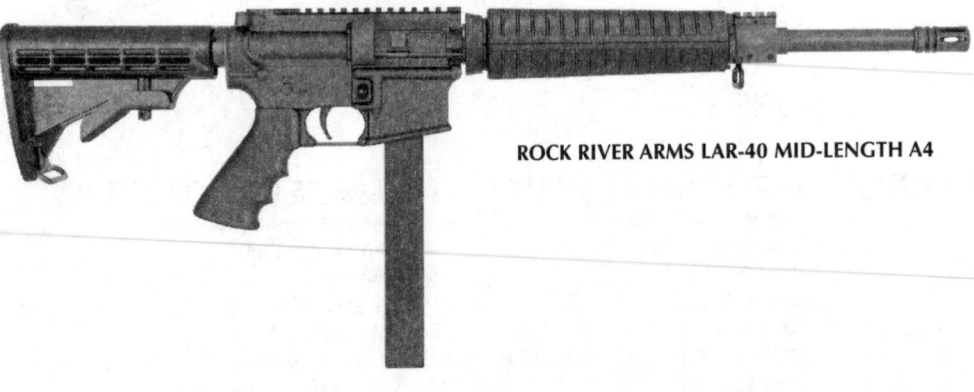

ROCK RIVER ARMS LAR-40 MID-LENGTH A4

ROCK RIVER ARMS LAR-47 CAR A4

RIFLES

Rock River Arms

ROCK RIVER ARMS LAR-47 DELTA
CARBINE

ROCK RIVER ARMS LAR-458 CAR A4

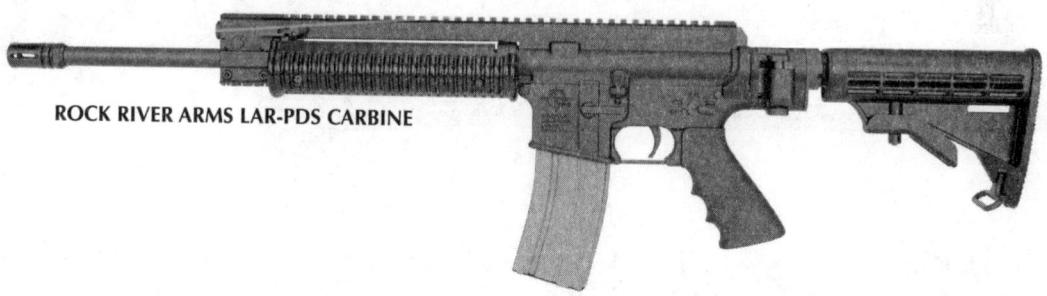

ROCK RIVER ARMS LAR-PDS CARBINE

LAR-47 DELTA CARBINE
Action: Semiautomatic
Stock: Synthetic
Barrel: 16 in.
Sights: None
Weight: 7 lb. 12 oz.
Caliber: 7.62x39mm
Magazine: 30 rounds, standard AK-47 mag
Features: RRA 6-position delta CAR stock; RRA delta pistol grip; RRA 2-piece quad rail; RRA delta muzzle-brake; RRA two-stage trigger; ambidextrous mag release
MSRP **$1545**

LAR-458 CAR A4
Action: Semiautomatic
Stock: Synthetic
Barrel: 16 in.
Sights: None
Weight: 7 lb. 10 oz.
Caliber: .458 SOCOM
Magazine: Detachable box
Features: Forged A4 receiver; A2 flash hider; chromoly bull barrel; varmint gas block with sight rail; RRA two-stage trigger; RRA aluminum free-float tube; A2 pistol grip; A2 buttstock
MSRP **$1220**

LAR-PDS CARBINE
Action: Semiautomatic
Stock: Synthetic
Barrel: 16 in.
Sights: None
Weight: 7 lb. 6 oz.
Caliber: .223 Rem.
Magazine: Detachable box
Features: Ambidextrous non-reciprocating charging handle; A2 flash hider; RRA two-stage trigger; Hogue rubber grip; tri-rail handguard available
MSRP . . . . **$1595–$1750**

Rossi

ROSSI CIRCUIT JUDGE

ROSSI CIRCUIT JUDGE TACTICAL SYNTHETIC

ROSSI FULL SIZE CENTERFIRE MATCHED PAIR

CIRCUIT JUDGE

Action: DA Revolver
Stock: Hardwood
Barrel: 18.5 in.
Sights: Fiber optic front sight
Weight: 5 lb. 5 oz.
Caliber: .410 Ga./.45LC
Magazine: 5 rounds
Features: Shotgun/rifle crossover allows you to fire .410 3-inch magnum shotshells, .410 2.5-inch shotshells, and .45 Colt ammunition in any order without switching barrels; available in smooth-bore shotgun or rifled barrel shotgun; yoke detent; transfer bar; Taurus Security System
MSRP **$732**

CIRCUIT JUDGE TACTICAL SYNTHETIC

Action: Revolver
Stock: Synthetic
Barrel: 18.5 in.
Sights: Red fiber optic front sight
Weight: 4 lb. 11 oz.
Caliber: .45 LC, .410 Ga.
Magazine: 5 rounds
Features: This gun utilizes the revolver and extends its range for hunting and shooting. One can fire .410 Ga 3-inch magnum shotshells, .410 Ga. 2.5-inch shotshells, and .45 Colt ammunition in any order, without switching barrels. It includes modern features like yoke detent, transfer bar, and the Taurus Security System.
MSRP **$684**

FULL SIZE CENTERFIRE MATCHED PAIR

Action: Break Open, single-shot
Stock: Synthetic
Barrel: 23 in., 28 in.
Sights: Adjustable sights
Weight: 5 lb. 4 oz.–6 lb. 4 oz.
Caliber: 20 Ga./.243 Win., 12 Ga., .243 Win., 20 Ga./.223 Rem., 12 Ga./.223 Rem.
Magazine: None
Features: Quick-interchangeable rifle and shotgun barrels; single shot; recoil pad; sling swivels; black synthetic stock; steel barrel with matte blued finish; button rifled barrel
MSRP **$352**

Rossi

R92 .44-40

Action: Lever
Stock: Wood
Barrel: 20 in., 24 in.
Sights: None
Weight: 7 lb.
Caliber: Most popular calibers: .38/.357 Mag., .44 Mag., .45 Colt, .44-40 Win.
Magazine: 12+1 rounds
Features: Octagonal barrel with a variety of metal finishes: blued, blued/case-hardened, blued/brass, and stainless; curved buttplate
MSRP. **$577**

R92 CARBINE .45 COLT STAINLESS

Action: Lever
Stock: Wood
Barrel: 20 in.
Sights: Open
Weight: 5 lb.
Caliber: .45 Colt
Magazine: Tubular mag, 10+1 rounds
Features: Stainless steel or blued round barrel; crescent buttplates and extended front sight; for brush hunting and wilderness packing; recoil absorbing buttpad
MSRP. **$599**

RIO GRANDE

Action: Lever
Stock: Hardwood
Barrel: 20 in.
Sights: Open
Weight: 5 lb. 13 oz.–7 lb.
Caliber: .30-30 Win., .45-70, .410,
Magazine: 6+1 rounds
Features: Blued or stainless steel barrel; authentic buckhorn sights; Taurus Safety System
MSRP. . . . . **$541–$644**

ROSSI R92 .44-40

ROSSI R92 CARBINE .45 STAINLESS COLT

ROSSI RIO GRANDE

Rossi

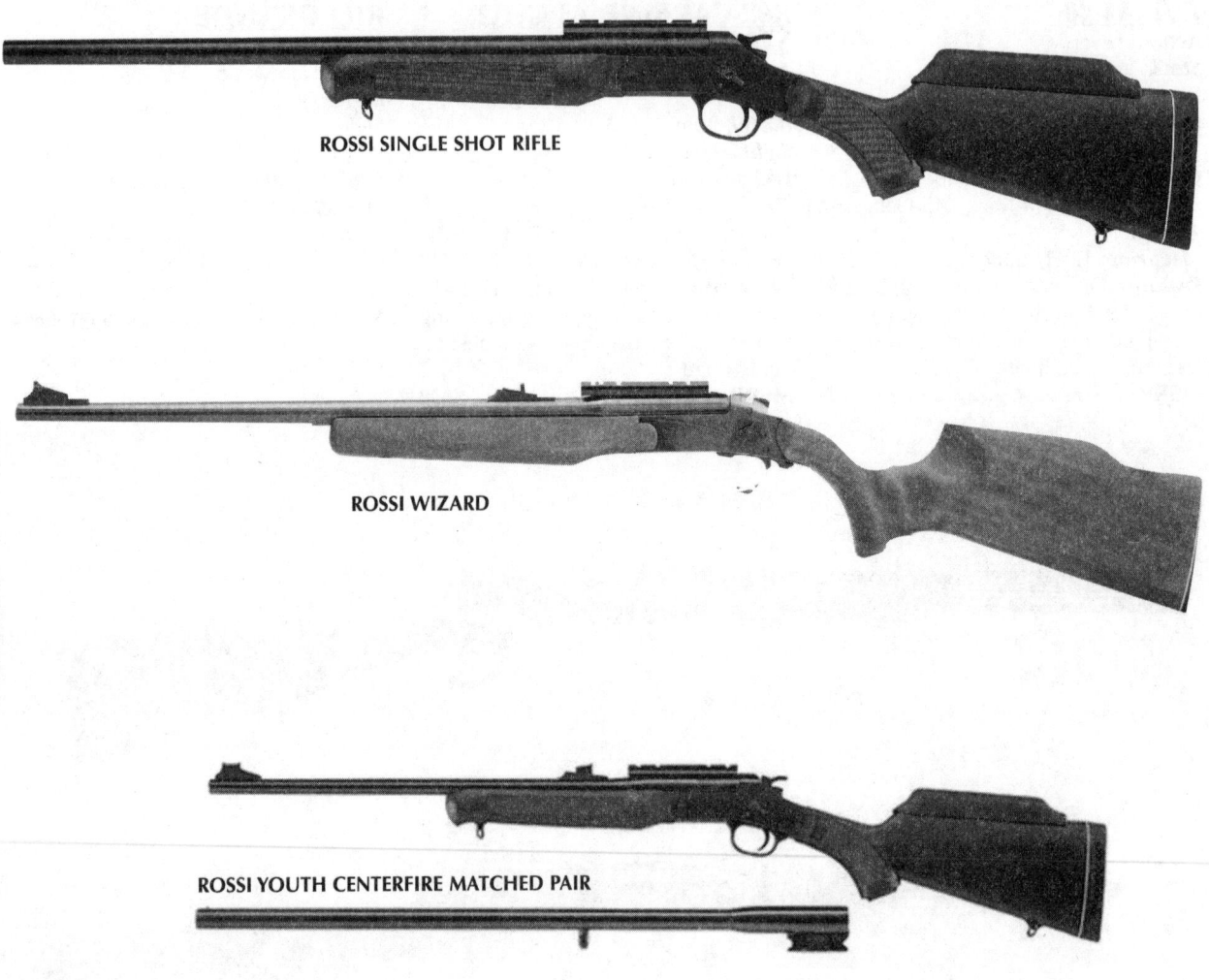

ROSSI SINGLE SHOT RIFLE

ROSSI WIZARD

ROSSI YOUTH CENTERFIRE MATCHED PAIR

SINGLE SHOT RIFLE

Action: Break-open, single-shot
Stock: Synthetic
Barrel: 23 in.
Sights: Adjustable fiber optic front
Weight: 6 lb. 4 oz.–7 lb.
Caliber: .243 Win., .44 Mag.
Magazine: None
Features: Steel barrel in matte blued finish; equipped with scope rail and hammer extension that accommodates all popular optics; black synthetic stock with removable cheekpiece; soft recoil pad; white line spacer; button rifled barrels; sling swivels
MSRP . . . . $314–$320

WIZARD

Action: Single-shot
Stock: Wood or Hi-Def Green camo
Barrel: 23 in.
Sights: Fiber optic front sight
Weight: 7 lb.
Caliber: .243 Win., .308 Win., .22-250 Win., .223 Win., .30-06 Win., .270 Win.
Magazine: None
Features: Interchangeable rifle and barrel system allows barrels to be changed quickly without tools; blued finish, cushioned recoil pad; Monte Carlo stock
MSRP $378

YOUTH SIZE CENTERFIRE MATCHED PAIR

Action: Break-open, single-shot
Stock: Synthetic
Barrel: 22 in.
Sights: Adjustable fiber optic front (rifle barrels), brass bead front (shotgun)
Weight: 5 lb., 6 lb. 4 oz.
Caliber: 20 Ga./.44 Mag., 20 Ga./.243 Win., 20 Ga./.223 Rem.
Magazine: None
Features: Quick-interchangeable rifle and shotgun barrels in youth size; matte blued finish
MSRP $352

Ruger

RUGER 10/22 CARBINE

RUGER 10/22 TACTICAL

RUGER 10/22 TARGET

10/22 CARBINE

Action: Autoloading
Stock: Synthetic or hardwood
Barrel: 18.5 in.
Sights: Gold bead front sight, adjustable rear
Weight: 5 lb.
Caliber: .22LR
Magazine: Rotary, 10 rounds
Features: Stock comes in black synthetic and hardwood; extended magazine release; push-button manual safety; combination scope base adapter; hammer-forged barrel; polymer trigger housing; aluminum receiver; contoured buttpad; barrel band; available LaserMax laser
MSRP. . . . . $279–$399

10/22 TACTICAL

Action: Autoloading
Stock: Synthetic
Barrel: 16.1 in.
Sights: None
Weight: 4 lb. 5 oz.
Caliber: .22LR
Magazine: Rotary box, 10 rounds
Features: Precision-rifled cold-hammer-forged alloy-steel barrel in black matte finish; black synthetic stock or black Hogue overmolded
Synthetic: $329
Hogue: $579

10/22 TARGET

Action: Autoloading
Stock: Laminate
Barrel: 20 in.
Sights: None
Weight: 7 lb. 8 oz.

Caliber: .22LR
Magazine: Rotary, 10 rounds
Features: Stock comes in black or brown laminate; extended magazine release; push-button manual safety; combination scope base adapter; hammer-forged barrel; polymer trigger housing; aluminum receiver; target trigger; flat buttplate
MSRP. . . . . $529–$569

77/17

Action: Bolt
Stock: Walnut or laminate
Barrel: 22 in., 24 in.
Sights: None
Weight: 6 lb. 8 oz.–7 lb. 8 oz.
Caliber: .17 HMR
Magazine: Detachable rotary, 9 rounds
Features: Stock options include American walnut with blued finish or black laminate with target gray finish;

alloy steel or stainless steel barrel; integral scope mounts; three-position safety; sling swivel stud mounts
Walnut: $899
Laminate:. $969

77/22

Action: Bolt
Stock: Laminate, walnut, synthetic
Barrel: 20 in., 24 in.
Sights: None
Weight: 6 lb.–7 lb. 8 oz.
Caliber: .22LR, .22 Mag., .22 Hornet
Magazine: Detachable rotary, 6, 9, 10 rounds
Features: Stock options include black synthetic, American walnut, or brown laminate; alloy steel or stainless steel barrel in target gray, blued, or brushed stainless finish; integral scope mounts; three-position safety; sling swivel studs
Walnut, Synthetic: $899
Laminate:. $969

77/44

Action: Bolt
Stock: Vista Camo, synthetic
Barrel: 18.5 in.
Sights: Front bead sight, adjustable rear
Weight: 5 lb. 4 oz.
Caliber: .44 Mag.
Magazine: Detachable rotary, 4 rounds
Features: Stock options include Next G1 Vista Camo or black synthetic; stainless steel barrel with brushed steel finish; integral scope mounts; three-position safety; sling swivel studs
Vista Camo: $999
Synthetic: $969

RUGER 77/17

RUGER 77/22

RUGER 77/44

Ruger

RUGER AMERICAN RIFLE

RUGER GUNSITE SCOUT RIFLE

RUGER M77 HAWKEYE

RUGER M77 HAWKEYE AFRICAN

AMERICAN RIFLE

Action: Bolt
Stock: Synthetic
Barrel: 22 in.
Sights: Drilled and tapped for scopes
Weight: 6 lb. 2 oz.–6 lb. 4 oz.
Caliber: .22-250 Rem., 7mm-08 Rem., .243 Win., .270 Win., .30-06 Spfd., .308 Win.
Magazine: Rotary, 4 rounds
Features: Ruger Marksman adjustable trigger; ergonomic, lightweight stock; soft rubber recoil pad; three-lug 70 degree bolt; Power Bedding positively locates the receiver and free-floats the barrel; hammer-forged barrel; tang safety; round rotary magazine
MSRP **$449**

GUNSITE SCOUT RIFLE

Action: Bolt
Stock: Laminate
Barrel: 16.50 in.
Sights: Post front sight, adjustable rear
Weight: 7 lb.
Caliber: .308 Win.
Magazine: Detachable box, 10 rounds
Features: Flash suppressor, Picatinny rail; recoil pad; accurate sighting system; integral scope mounts; Mauser-type extractor; developed with Gunsite and features their logo
MSRP **$1039**

M77 HAWKEYE

Action: Bolt
Stock: Walnut
Barrel: 22 in., 24 in.
Sights: None
Weight: 7 lb.–8 lb. 4 oz.
Caliber: .204 Ruger, .22-250 Rem., .223 Rem., .243 Win., 6.5 Creedmoor, .257 Roberts, .270 Win., 7mm Rem. Mag., 7mm-08 Rem., .300 RCM, .30-06 Spfd., .300 Win. Mag., .308 Win., .338 RCM, .338 Win. Mag.
Magazine: 5 rounds
Features: American walnut stock; alloy steel, satin blued barrel; LCG Trigger; positive floor plate latch; integral scope mounts; three-position safety
MSRP **$899**

M77 HAWKEYE AFRICAN

Action: Bolt
Stock: Walnut
Barrel: 23 in.
Sights: Bead front sight, adjustable rear V notch sight
Weight: 7 lb. 12 oz.
Caliber: .223 Rem., .300 Win. Mag., .338 Win. Mag., 9.3x 62, .375 Ruger
Magazine: 3, 4, 5 rounds
Features: Walnut stock with pistol grip; LC6 Trigger; non-rotating, Mauser-type controlled round feed extractor; steel floor plate; three-position safety; integral scope mounts; muzzle brake
MSRP **$1199**

M77 HAWKEYE PREDATOR

Action: Bolt
Stock: Green Mountain Laminate
Barrel: 22 in., 24 in.
Sights: None
Weight: 7 lb. 12 oz.–8 lb.
Caliber: .204 Ruger, .22-250 Rem., .223 Rem., 6.5 Creedmoore, .308 Win.

Magazine: 4, 5 rounds
Features: Hawkeye matte stainless steel finish on barrel; two-stage adjustable target trigger; non-rotating, Mauser-type controlled round feed extractor; hinged solid-steel floor plate; three-position safety; integral scope mounts; sling swivel studs
MSRP **$1029**

M77 MARK II TARGET

Action: Bolt
Stock: Laminate
Barrel: 26 in., 28 in.
Sights: None
Weight: 9 lb. 4 oz.–9 lb. 12 oz.
Caliber: .204 Ruger, .22-250 Rem., .223 Rem., .243 Win., .25-06 Rem., 6.5 Creedmoor, .308 Win.
Magazine: 4, 5 rounds
Features: Black laminate stock; stainless steel barrel; two-stage target trigger; non-rotating, Mauser-type controlled round feed extractor, hinged solid-steel floor plate, three-position safety; integral scope mounts; sling swivel studs
MSRP **$1029**

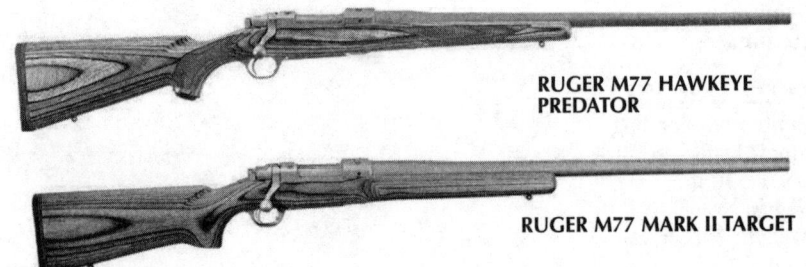

RUGER M77 HAWKEYE PREDATOR

RUGER M77 MARK II TARGET

RIFLES

Ruger

RUGER MINI-14 RANCH RIFLE

RUGER MINI-14 TACTICAL

RUGER MINI-14 TARGET RIFLE

RUGER MINI THIRTY RIFLE

MINI-14 RANCH RIFLE

Action: Autoloading
Stock: Hardwood, synthetic
Barrel: 18.5 in.
Sights: Blade front sight, adjustable rear
Weight: 6 lb. 12 oz.–7 lb.
Caliber: .56mm NATO/ .223 Rem., 6.8 SPC
Magazine: 5 rounds, or detachable box, 20 rounds
Features: Stock comes in hardwood or black synthetic; Garand style action; hammer-forged barrel; sighting system; integral scope mounts; flat buttpad; integral sling swivels on hardwood or black synthetic stocks
MSRP . . . . $909–$1039

MINI-14 TACTICAL

Action: Autoloading
Stock: Synthetic
Barrel: 16.1 in.
Sights: Adjustable
Weight: 6 lb. 12 oz.–7 lb. 4 oz.
Caliber: 7.62x39mm
Magazine: 5, 20 rounds
Features: Black synthetic stock; blued barrel with a flash suppressor; adjustable ghost ring rear sight, non-glare protected-post front sight
MSRP . . . . $989–$1069

MINI-14 TARGET RIFLE

Action: Autoloading
Stock: Laminate or Hogue overmolded
Barrel: 22 in.
Sights: None
Weight: 8 lb. 8 oz.–9 lb. 8 oz.
Caliber: .223 Rem.
Magazine: 5 rounds
Features: Black laminate with thumb hole stock or Black Hogue overmolded stock; matte stainless finish on stainless steel barrel; Garand style action; hammer-forged barrel; integral scope mounts; harmonic dampener; sling swivel studs
MSRP $1149

MINI THIRTY RIFLE

Action: Autoloading
Stock: Synthetic
Barrel: 16.12 in., 18.5 in.
Sights: Blade front sight, adjustable rear
Weight: 6 lb. 12 oz.
Caliber: 7.62x39mm
Magazine: 5 rounds, or detachable box, 20 rounds
Features: Garand style action, hammer-forged barrel; sighting system; integral scope mounts; black synthetic stock; sling swivels; stainless steel or alloy steel barrel in matte or blued finish
MSRP . . . . $979–$1039

Ruger

NO. 1 LIGHT SPORTER

Action: Falling block, single-shot
Stock: Walnut
Barrel: 22 in.
Sights: Front bead sight, adjustable rear
Weight: 7 lb. 4 oz.
Caliber: .222 Rem.
Magazine: None
Features: Falling block breech mechanism, sliding tang safety; sculptured receiver; Ruger scope mounting system; Alexander Henry-style forend; sporting style buttpad; grip cap and sling swivel studs; American walnut stock
MSRP $1349

NO. 1 VARMINTER

Action: Falling block, single-shot
Stock: Walnut
Barrel: 26 in.
Sights: None
Weight: 8 lb. 8 oz.
Caliber: 6.5 Creedmoor, .22-250 Rem., .223 Rem., .25-06 Rem.
Magazine: None
Features: Falling block breech mechanism, sliding tang safety; sculptured receiver; Ruger scope mounting system; Alexander Henry-style forend; sporting style buttpad; grip cap and sling swivel studs; American walnut stock
MSRP $1349

SR-22

Action: Autoloading
Stock: Synthetic
Barrel: 16.12 in.
Sights: None
Weight: 6 lb. 8 oz.–6 lb. 14 oz.
Caliber: .22LR
Magazine: Detachable rotary, 10 rounds
Features: Black laminate stock in standard or collapsible; AR-style ergonomic Hogue Monogrip and six-position telescoping buttstock; hammer-forged barrel; round handguard; barrel support block
MSRP $649

SR-556

Action: Autoloading
Stock: Synthetic
Barrel: 16.12 in.

Sights: Folding BattleSights
Weight: 7 lb. 15 oz.
Caliber: 5.56mm NATO/.223 Rem., 6.8 SPC
Magazine: Detachable box, 10, 30 rounds
Features: Stock options include black synthetic standard or collapsible; two-stage piston with adjustable regulator; chrome-lined gas block; quad rail handguard; Troy Industries Sights; telescoping buttstock; hammer-forged barrel; pistol grip stock; rail covers and soft case
MSRP $1995

SR-556E

Action: Autoloading
Stock: Synthetic
Barrel: 16.12 in.
Sights: Folding battle sights
Weight: 7 lb. 6 oz.
Caliber: 5.56mm NATO/.223 Rem.
Magazine: 10, 30 rounds
Features: Stock is black synthetic standard; two-stage piston with adjustable regulator; chrome-lined gas block; quad rail handguard; Troy Industries sights; telescoping buttstock; hammer-forged barrel; pistol grip stock; rail covers and soft case
MSRP $1375

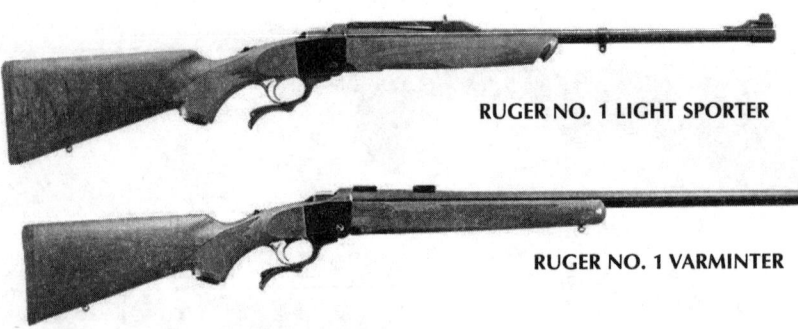

RUGER NO. 1 LIGHT SPORTER

RUGER NO. 1 VARMINTER

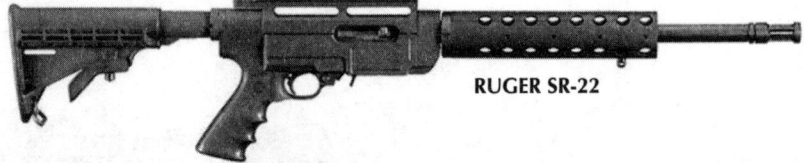

RUGER SR-22

RUGER SR-556

RUGER SR-556E

85 BAVARIAN

Action: Bolt
Stock: Walnut
Barrel: 22 in., 24 in.
Sights: None
Weight: 7 lb.–7 lb. 8 oz.
Caliber: .308 Win., .270 Win., .30-06 Spfd., .300 Win. Mag., .270 WSM, .300 WSM, 6.5x55 Swede, 7mm-08 Rem., 7mm Rem. Mag.
Magazine: 4, 5 rounds
Features: High grade walnut stock in traditional European style; single-set trigger
MSRP . . . . $2200–$2250

85 BLACK BEAR

Action: Bolt
Stock: Black composite
Barrel: 21.25 in.
Sights: Adjustable Express "V" rear, white bead front and integral dovetail for scope mounts
Weight: 6 lb. 13 oz.–7 lb.
Caliber: .308 Win., .338 Fed., .30-06 Spfd., 8x57IS, 9.3x62, 9.3x66 Sako
Magazine: Detachable box, 5 rounds
Features: Purpose built weapon for bear and wild boar hunters; adjustable single-stage trigger; adjustable shallow "V" Express style rear sight with white bead front sight for fast target acquisition and a barrel band for front swivel; patented Total Control Magazine Latch (TCL) prevents accidental release of the stainless steel magazine under the heaviest recoil or harshest hunting conditions
MSRP $1850

85 BROWN BEAR

Action: Bolt
Stock: Brown laminate
Barrel: 21.25 in.
Sights: Adjustable open rear, blade style front and integral dovetail for

SAKO 85 BAVARIAN

SAKO 85 BLACK BEAR

SAKO 85 BROWN BEAR

scope mounts
Weight: 7 lb. 15 oz.
Caliber: .338 Win. Mag., .375 H&H Mag.
Magazine: Detachable box, 4 rounds
Features: Open adjustable rear sight and blade style front sight; short free-floated bull barrel has a band type front swivel; forged one-piece bolt with three locking lugs offers fast, smooth cycling with controlled round feed and mechanical case ejection; patented Total Control Magazine Latch (TCL) prevents accidental release of the stainless steel magazine
MSRP $2500

85 CLASSIC

Action: Bolt
Stock: Walnut
Barrel: 22.4 in., 24.4 in.
Sights: Open
Weight: 7 lb.–7 lb. 12 oz.
Caliber: (Short): .243 Win., .260 Rem., 7mm-08 Rem., .308 Win., .338 Federal; (SM) .270 Win. S Mag., .300 Win. S Mag.; (Medium) .25-06 Rem., 6.5x55 SE, .270 Win., .30-06 Spfd., 9.3x66 Sako; (Long): 7mm Rem. Mag.,

.300 Win. Mag., .338 Win. Mag., .375 H&H Mag.
Magazine: Detachable box, S/M 6 rounds, SM/L 5 rounds
Features: Comes in short actions Extra Short (XS), Short (S) and Short Magnum (SM), medium action (M), and long action (L); straight, classic walnut stock with rosewood forend tip and pistol grip cap; integral rails for scope mounts; free-floating barrel is cold-hammer-forged; adjustable single-stage trigger
MSRP . . . . $2200–$2250

85 FINNLIGHT ST

Action: Bolt
Stock: Synthetic
Barrel: 20.25 in., 22.4 in.
Sights: None
Weight: 6 lb. 3 oz.–6 lb. 13 oz.
Caliber: (Short): .22-250 Rem., .243 Win., .260 Rem., .7mm-08 Rem., .308 Win.; (SM) .270 Win. Short Mag., .300 Win. Short Mag.; (Medium): .25-06 Rem., 6.5x55 SE, .270 Win., .30-06 Spfd.; (Long) 7mm Rem. Mag., .300 Win. Mag.
Magazine: Detachable box, S/M 6 rounds, SM/L 5 rounds
Features: Comes in short actions Short (S) and Short magnum (SM), Medium action (M), and Long action (L); single-stage trigger; two-way Sako safety locks both trigger and bolt handle; black synthetic stock with soft gray grip areas; pistol grip stock; integral rails for scope mounts; free-floating barrel is cold-hammer-forged of stainless steel
MSRP . . . . $1650–$1700

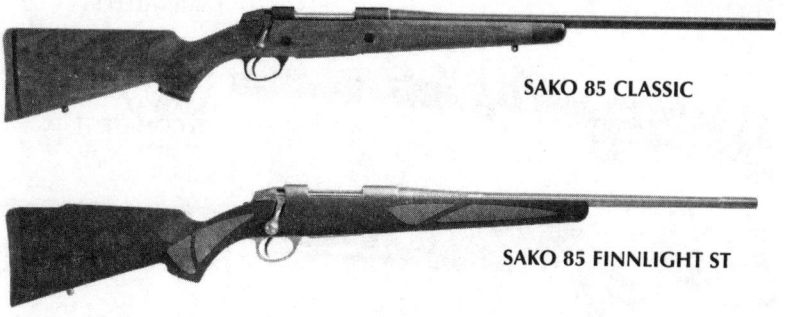

SAKO 85 CLASSIC

SAKO 85 FINNLIGHT ST

Sako

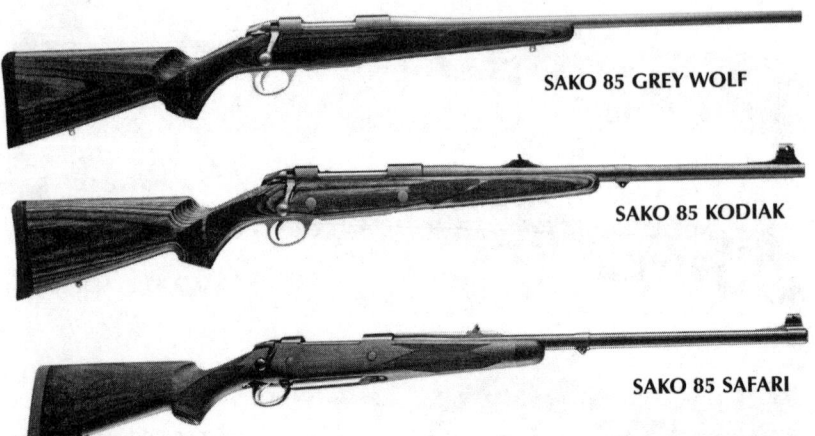

SAKO 85 GREY WOLF

SAKO 85 KODIAK

SAKO 85 SAFARI

85 GREY WOLF

Action: Bolt
Stock: Gray laminate
Barrel: 22 in., 24 in.
Sights: None
Weight: 7 lb. 4 oz.
Caliber: .270 Win., .30-06 Spfd., .300 Win. Mag., .270 WSM, .300 WSM, 7mm Rem. Mag.
Magazine: 4 or 5 rounds
Features: Stainless steel barrel and action; Warp-free stock makes the rifle suitable for hunting in extreme conditions
MSRP. . . . . $1600–$1650

85 KODIAK

Action: Bolt
Stock: Laminated hardwood
Barrel: 12.25 in.
Sights: Open
Weight: 7 lb. 15 oz.
Caliber: .338 Win. Mag., .375 H&H Mag.
Magazine: Detachable box, 5 rounds
Features: Adjustable single-stage trigger; barrel band for front swivel; integral dovetail rails for secure scope mounting; straight stock made of gray matte-lacquered laminated hardwood and reinforced with two cross-bolts; free-floating "bull" barrel
MSRP. $1925

85 SAFARI

Action: Bolt
Stock: Walnut
Barrel: 24.2 in.
Sights: Front bead, adjustable iron sights rear
Weight: 9 lb.
Caliber: .375 H&H Mag.

Magazine: Detachable box, 6 rounds
Features: Free-floating barrel; ergonomic walnut stock with checkering; staggered, two-row magazine with total control latch; single-set adjustable trigger; steel trigger guard; two-way Sako safety locks both trigger and bolt handle; Pachmayr recoil pad; limited models imported to U.S.
MSRP. . . . . $10000–$10500

85 VARMINT LAMINATED STAINLESS

Action: Bolt
Stock: Laminated hardwood
Barrel: 20 in., 23.6 in.
Sights: None
Weight: 8 lb. 10 oz.–9 lb.
Caliber: (XS) .204 Ruger, .222 Rem., .223 Rem.; (Short) .22-250 Rem., .243 Win., .260 Rem., 7mm-08 Rem., .308 Win., .338 Federal
Magazine: Detachable box, XS 7 rounds, S 6 rounds
Features: Comes in short actions Extra Short (XS) and Short (S); single-set trigger; two-way Sako safety locks both

trigger and bolt handle; straight stock with wide forend is made of brown matte laquered laminated hardwood; integral rail for scope mounts
MSRP. $2000

A7 TECOMATE ST

Action: Bolt
Stock: Synthetic
Barrel: 22 in., 24 in.
Sights: None
Weight: 6 lb. 8 oz.–7 lb.
Caliber: .22-250 Rem., .243 Win., .308 Win., .25-06 Rem., .270 Win., .30-06 Spfd., .300 Win. Mag., .270 WSM, .300 WSM, 7mm-08 Rem., 7mm Rem. Mag.
Magazine: 4 rounds
Features: Stainless or blued finish
MSRP. $1375

TRG 22

Action: Bolt
Stock: Synthetic
Barrel: 20 in., 26 in., 27.1 in.
Sights: None
Weight: 10 lb. 4 oz.–10 lb. 12 oz.
Caliber: .308 Win, .300 Win. Mag., .338 Lapua Mag.
Magazine: Detachable box, 5, 7, 10 rounds
Features: Double-stage trigger; two-way Sako safety locks both trigger and bolt handle; base of stock is made of polyurethane with aluminum skeleton; adjustable cheekpiece and buttplate; Ambidextrous stock in green or desert tan color; includes integral dovetail on receiver and is drilled and tapped for Picatinny rail mounting
Green:. $3450
Tan: . . . . $5825–$6800

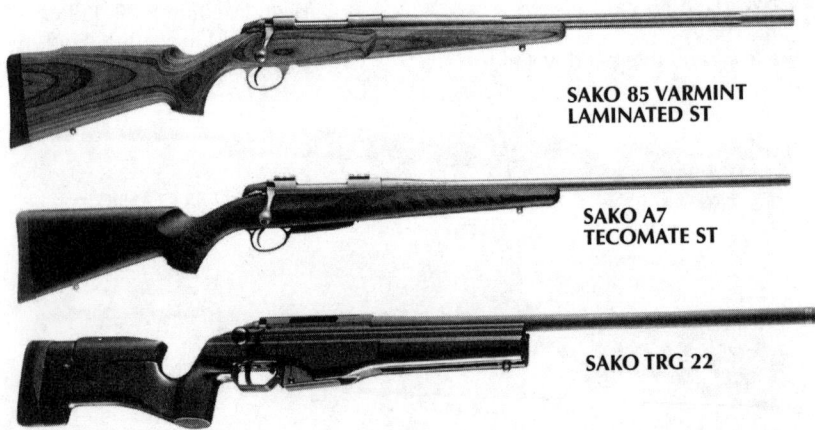

SAKO 85 VARMINT LAMINATED ST

SAKO A7 TECOMATE ST

SAKO TRG 22

Savage Arms

10 XP PREDATOR HUNTER PACKAGE BRUSH
Action: Bolt
Stock: Synthetic
Barrel: 22 in.
Sights: 4-12x40mm Scope
Weight: 8 lb. 8 oz.
Caliber: .223 Rem., .204 Ruger, .22-250 Rem., .243 Win.
Magazine: 4 rounds
Features: Mounted and bore-sighted scope; AccuTrigger; carbon steel barrel; synthetic camo stock
MSRP **$945**

12 VARMINT SERIES BTCSS
Action: Bolt
Stock: Laminate
Barrel: 26 in.
Sights: None
Weight: 10 lb.
Caliber: .204 Ruger, .223 Rem., .22-250 Rem.
Magazine: Detachable box, 4 rounds
Features: Drilled and tapped for scope mounts; stainless steel barrel with high luster finish; AccuTrigger; wood laminate with thumbhole and satin finish
MSRP **$1175**

14/114 AMERICAN CLASSIC
Action: Bolt
Stock: Wood
Barrel: 22 in., 24 in.
Sights: None
Weight: 7 lb. 4 oz.–7 lb. 12 oz.
Caliber: .243 Win., .250 Sav., .270 Win., .300 WSM, .30-06 Spfd., .300 Win. Mag., .308 Win., 7mm Rem. Mag., 7mm-08 Rem.
Magazine: Hinged floor plate, 2, 4 rounds
Features: Drilled and tapped for scope mounts; carbon steel barrel with matte blued finish; short action; AccuTrigger; satin finish wood stock
MSRP **$885**

SAVAGE ARMS 10 XP PREDATOR HUNTER PACKAGE BRUSH

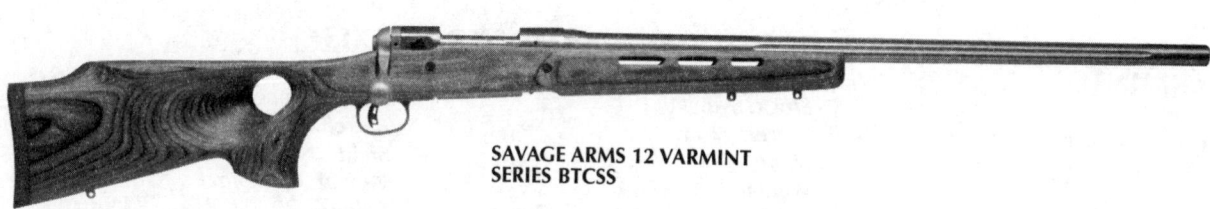

SAVAGE ARMS 12 VARMINT SERIES BTCSS

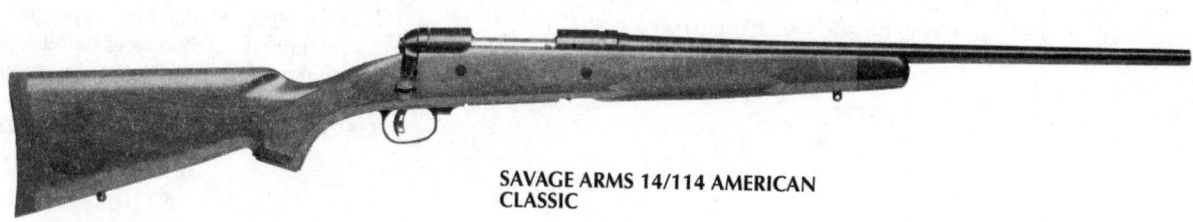

SAVAGE ARMS 14/114 AMERICAN CLASSIC

Savage Arms

SAVAGE ARMS 25 LIGHTWEIGHT VARMINTER

SAVAGE ARMS 25 WALKING VARMINTER

SAVAGE ARMS AXIS

25 LIGHTWEIGHT VARMINTER

Action: Bolt
Stock: Wood laminate
Barrel: 24 in.
Sights: None
Weight: 8 lb. 4 oz.
Caliber: .17 Hornet, .204 Ruger, .22 Hornet, .223 Rem.
Magazine: Detachable box, 4 rounds
Features: Drilled and tapped for scope mounts; carbon steel barrel with blued satin finish; wood laminate stock with satin finish
MSRP $730

25 WALKING VARMINTER

Action: Bolt
Stock: Synthetic
Barrel: 22 in.
Sights: None
Weight: 6 lb. 14 oz.
Caliber: .17 Hornet, .204 Ruger, .22 Hornet, .222 Rem., .223 Rem.
Magazine: Detachable box, 4 rounds
Features: Matte black synthetic stock; matte black carbon steel barrel; AccuTrigger
MSRP $585

AXIS

Action: Bolt
Stock: Synthetic
Barrel: 22 in.
Sights: None
Weight: 6 lb. 8 oz.
Caliber: .22-250 Rem., .223 Rem., .243 Win., .25-06 Rem., .270 Win., .30-06 Spfd., .308 Win., 7mm-08 Rem.
Magazine: Detachable box, 4 rounds
Features: New modern design, smooth bolt operation; drilled and tapped for scope mounts; carbon steel barrel with black matte finish; synthetic stock with matte black finish
MSRP $375

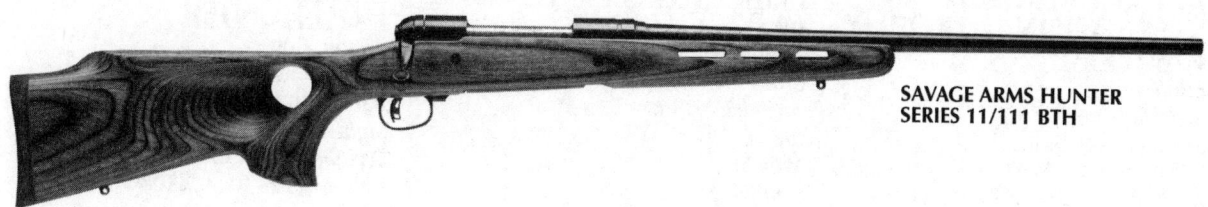

SAVAGE ARMS HUNTER
SERIES 11/111 BTH

HUNTER SERIES 11/111 BTH

Action: Bolt
Stock: Wood laminate
Barrel: 22 in.
Sights: None
Weight: 6 lb. 12 oz.–7 lb.
Caliber: .22-250 Rem., .243 Win.,
.223 Rem., .25-06 Rem., .270 Win.,
.30-06 Spfd., .308 Win.
Magazine: Hinged floor plate, 4
rounds
Features: Drilled and tapped for scope
mounts; carbon steel barrel with blued
satin finish; AccuTrigger; wood lami-
nate stock with thumbhole in satin fin-
ish
MSRP **$890**

MAGNUM SERIES 93 BRJ

Action: Bolt
Stock: Wood laminate
Barrel: 21 in.
Sights: None
Weight: 7 lb.
Caliber: .22 WMR
Magazine: 5 rounds
Features: Carbon steel barrel in blued
satin finish; wood laminate stock;
AccuTrigger
MSRP **$510**

MARK II SERIES BTV

Action: Bolt
Stock: Wood laminate
Barrel: 21 in.
Sights: None
Weight: 6 lb. 8 oz.
Caliber: .22LR
Magazine: Detachable box, 5 rounds
Features: Carbon steel barrel with
blued satin finish; wood laminate
stock with thumbhole; AccuTrigger
MSRP **$445**

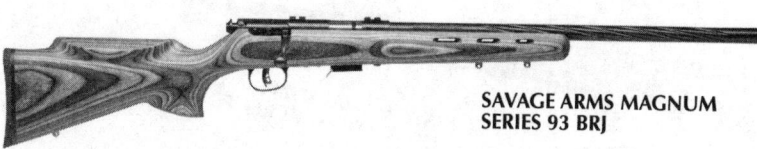

SAVAGE ARMS MAGNUM
SERIES 93 BRJ

SAVAGE ARMS MARK II
SERIES BTV

Savage Arms

RIFLES

PACKAGE SERIES 16-116 INTERNATIONAL TROPHY HUNTER XP

Action: Bolt
Stock: Synthetic
Barrel: 22 in., 24 in.
Sights: Mounted Weaver 3-9x40 scope
Weight: 7 lb. 4 oz.–7 lb. 8 oz.
Caliber: .204 Ruger, .243 Win., .260 Rem., .270 WSM, .300 WSM, .308 Win., .375 Ruger, 6.5 Creedmoor, 7mm-08 Rem.
Magazine: Detachable box, 2, 4 rounds
Features: Matte black synthetic stock; stainless steel barrel with satin finish
MSRP . . . . $795–$825

RASCAL SINGLE SHOT

Action: Bolt
Stock: Synthetic, hardwood
Barrel: 16.125 in.
Sights: Adjustable
Weight: 2 lb. 10 oz.–2 lb. 15 oz.
Caliber: .22LR
Magazine: None
Features: Matte synthetic stock available in seven colors; adjustable peep sights; drilled and tapped for scope mounts; AccuTrigger; carbon steel barrel with satin blued finish
Synthetic: $180
Hardwood: $225

SEMI-AUTOMATIC SERIES 64 F

Action: Semiautomatic
Stock: Synthetic
Barrel: 20.5 in.
Sights: Open
Weight: 5 lb.
Caliber: .22LR
Magazine: Detachable box, 10 rounds
Features: Drilled and tapped for scope mounts; carbon steel barrel with satin blued finish; synthetic matte black stock
MSRP $175

SPECIALTY SERIES 11-111 HOG HUNTER

Action: Bolt
Stock: Synthetic
Barrel: 20 in.
Sights: Adjustable
Weight: 7 lb. 4 oz.–8 lb.
Caliber: .223 Rem., .308 Win., .338 Win.
Magazine: Internal box, 4 rounds
Features: Green composite synthetic stock; matte black carbon steel barrel; LPA adjustable sights; threaded barrel; AccuTrigger
MSRP $535

SAVAGE ARMS PACKAGE SERIES 16-116 INTERNATIONAL TROPHY HUNTER XP

SAVAGE ARMS RASCAL SINGLE SHOT

SAVAGE ARMS SEMI-AUTOMATIC SERIES 64 F

SAVAGE ARMS SPECIALTY SERIES 11-111 HOG HUNTER

SAVAGE ARMS SPECIALTY SERIES 11-111 LADY HUNTER

SAVAGE ARMS SPECIALTY SERIES 11/111 LONG RANGE HUNTER

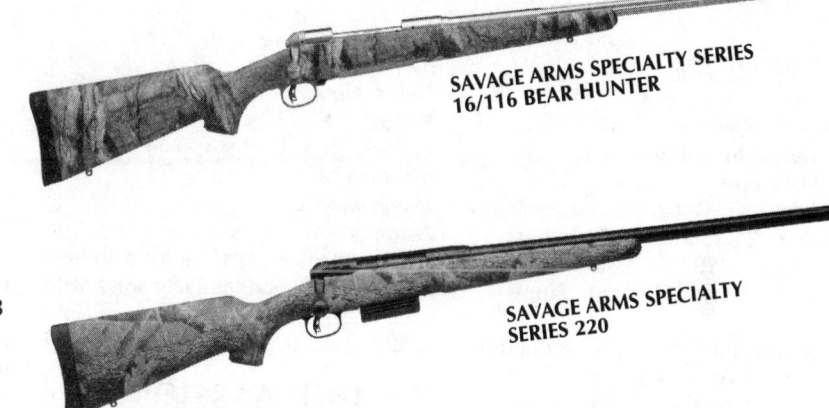

SAVAGE ARMS SPECIALTY SERIES 16/116 BEAR HUNTER

SAVAGE ARMS SPECIALTY SERIES 220

SPECIALTY SERIES 11-111 LADY HUNTER

Action: Bolt
Stock: Wood
Barrel: 20 in.
Sights: None
Weight: 6 lb.–6 lb. 8 oz.
Caliber: .22-250 Rem., .223 Rem., .243 Win., .270 Win., .30-06 Spfd., .308 Win., 6.5 Creedmoor, 7mm-08 Rem.
Magazine: Detachable box, 4 rounds
Features: Oil-finish American walnut stock with ladies-specific geometry; carbon steel barrel in matter black
MSRP $840

SPECIALTY SERIES 11/111 LONG RANGE HUNTER

Action: Bolt
Stock: Synthetic
Barrel: 26 in.
Sights: None
Weight: 8 lb. 6 oz.
Caliber: .25-06 Rem., .260 Rem., .300 Win. Mag., .300 WSM, .308 Win., .338 Lapua Mag., 6.5 Creedmoor, 6.5x284 Norma, 7mm Rem. Mag.
Magazine: Hinged floor plate, 2, 4 rounds
Features: Drilled and tapped for scope mounts; carbon steel barrel with black matte finish; synthetic stock with black matte finish; AccuTrigger
MSRP . . . . $1020–$1290

SPECIALTY SERIES 16/116 BEAR HUNTER

Action: Bolt
Stock: Synthetic
Barrel: 23 in.
Sights: None
Weight: 7 lb. 8 oz.
Caliber: .300 Win. Mag., .300 WSM, .325 WSM, .338 Win. Mag., .375 Ruger
Magazine: Hinged floor plate, 2 rounds
Features: Drilled and tapped for scope mounts; adjustable muzzlebrake; stainless steel barrel; synthetic stock with matte camo finish; AccuTrigger; AccuStock
MSRP . . . . $995–$1030

SPECIALTY SERIES 220 STANDARD, YOUTH, CAMO

Action: Bolt
Stock: Synthetic
Barrel: 22 in.
Sights: None
Weight: 7 lb. 8 oz.
Caliber: 20 Ga.
Magazine: 2 rounds
Features: Drilled and tapped for scope mounts; carbon steel barrel with matte blued finish; AccuTrigger; synthetic stock in matte black finish or camo
Standard: $565
Camo: $630
Youth: $565

Savage Arms

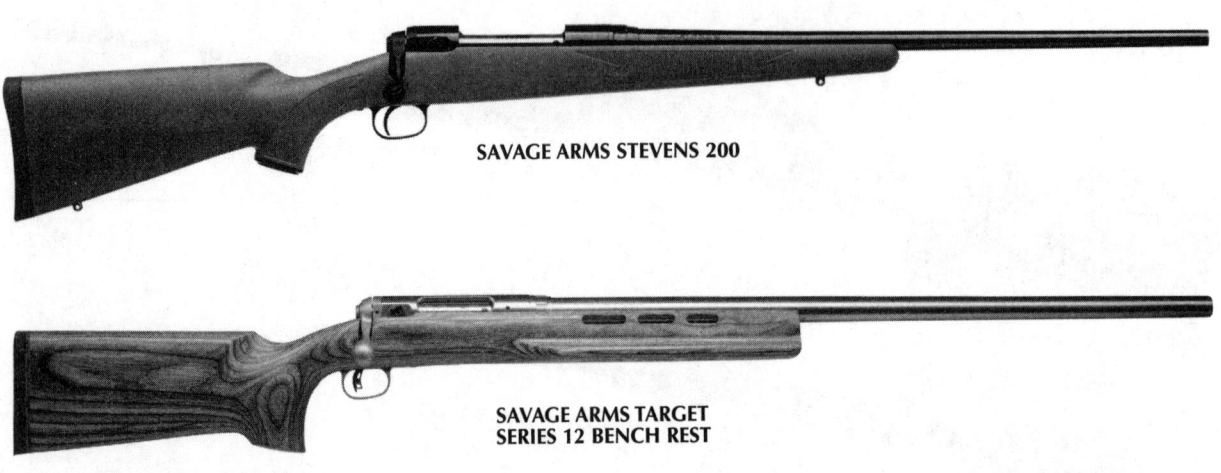

SAVAGE ARMS STEVENS 200

SAVAGE ARMS TARGET SERIES 12 BENCH REST

STEVENS 200
Action: Bolt
Stock: Synthetic
Barrel: 22 in., 24 in.
Sights: None
Weight: 6 lb. 12 oz.
Caliber: .22-250 Rem., .223 Rem., .243 Win., .270 Win., .30-06 Spfd., .300 Win. Mag., .308 Win., 7mm Rem. Mag.
Magazine: Internal box, 3, 4 rounds
Features: Drilled and tapped for scope mounts; carbon steel barrel with satin blued barrel; synthetic stock with matte gray finish stock
MSRP. **$420**

TARGET SERIES 12 BENCH REST
Action: Bolt, single shot
Stock: Wood laminate

Barrel: 29 in.
Sights: None
Weight: 12 lb. 12 oz.
Caliber: .308 Win., 6.5 x284 Norma, 6 Norma BR
Magazine: None
Features: Drilled and tapped for scope mounts; stainless steel barrel with high luster finish; wood laminate stock with satin finish; AccuTrigger
MSRP. **$1550**

WEATHER WARRIOR SERIES 16/116 FCSS
Action: Bolt
Stock: Synthetic
Barrel: 22 in., 24 in.
Sights: None
Weight: 6 lb. 14 oz.–7.15 lb.
Caliber: .204 Ruger, .22-250 Rem., .223 Rem., .243 Win., .25-06 Rem.,

.260 Rem., .270 WSM, .270 Win., .30-06 Spfd., .300 WSM, .300 Win. Mag., .308 Win., .308 Win. Mag., .375 Ruger, 6.5 Creedmoor, 6.5x284 Norma, 7mm Rem. Mag., .7mm-08 Rem.
Magazine: Detachable box, 2, 4 rounds
Features: Drilled and tapped for scope mounts; stainless steel barrel with high luster finish; synthetic stock with black matte finish; AccuTrigger
MSRP. . . . . **$850–$885**

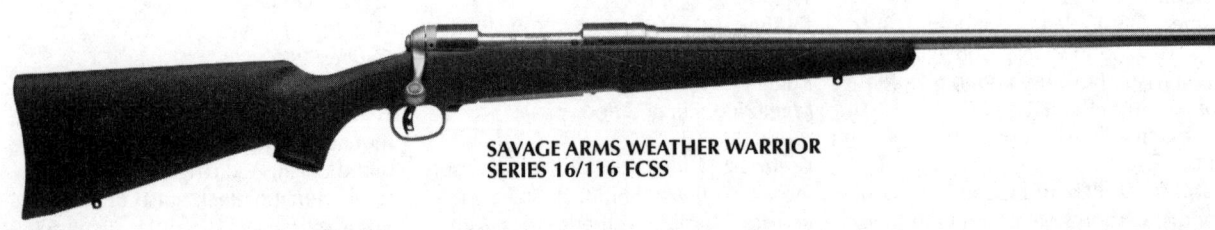

SAVAGE ARMS WEATHER WARRIOR SERIES 16/116 FCSS

SIG SAUER SIG516 PATROL

SIG SAUER 522 COMMANDO

SIG522 COMMANDO

Action: Semiautomatic
Stock: Tactical synthetic
Barrel: 16 in.
Sights: Mini red-dot
Weight: 6 lb. 2 oz.
Caliber: .22LR
Magazine: Detachable box, 10, 25 rounds
Features: Removable inert training suppressor; anodized alloy upper receiver and M1913 mounted rail; folding telescopic stock
MSRP **$600**

SIG SAUER 551-A1

551-A1

Action: Semiautomatic
Stock: Swiss type
Barrel: 16 in.
Sights: Rotary diopter rear and hooded front
Weight: 7 lb.
Caliber: 5.56x45 NATO
Magazine: 20, 30 rounds
Features: Ambidextrous controls; 2-position gas piston operating system; 1:7 chrome-lined barrel; gray finish in honor of the Swiss 550 series barrel; SWAT variant features 1913 quad rail
MSRP **$1599**

SIG516 PATROL

Action: Semiautomatic
Stock: Tactical synthetic
Barrel: 16 in.
Sights: None
Weight: 7 lb. 5 oz.
Caliber: 5.56mm NATO
Magazine: Detachable box, 30 rounds

Features: Gas piston operating system; three-position gas regulator; free-floating military grade chrome-lined barrel; M1913 Picatinny flat top upper; aircraft grade aluminum upper and lower receiver with hard coat anodize finish
MSRP **$1666**

Sig Sauer

SIG556 CLASSIC SWAT

Action: Semiautomatic
Stock: Tactical synthetic
Barrel: 16 in.
Sights: Rear rotary diopter sight
Weight: 8 lb. 3 oz.
Caliber: 5.56 x.45mm NATO
Magazine: Detachable box, 30 rounds
Features: Features full length gas piston operating system; quad rail and rotary diopter sight; black Swiss-type folding stock that adjusts to length; cold-hammer-forged barrel; alloy trigger housing; AR style magazine and flash suppressor
MSRP.................. **$1399**

SIG SAUER SIG556 CLASSIC SWAT

SIG556 PATROL RIFLE

Action: Semiautomatic
Stock: Tactical synthetic
Barrel: 14.4 in.
Sights: Rear rotary diopter sight
Weight: 7 lb. 8 oz.
Caliber: 5.56x45mm NATO, .223
Magazine: Detachable box, 30 rounds
Features: A2 Type flash suppressor; reduced length gas piston with two-position gas valve; improved design trigger casing; Swiss-type folding stock, adjustable for length; Swiss-type reduced lengthy polymer handguards; alloy quad rail reduced length tactical forend; RDSS rotary diopter sight system
MSRP.................. **$1266**

SIG SAUER SIG556 PATROL RIFLE

SIG716

Action: Semiautomatic
Stock: Synthetic
Barrel: 12 in., 14.5 in., 16 in.
Sights: SIG flip-up front & rear
Weight: 9 lb.–9 lb. 11 oz.
Caliber: 7.62x51 NATO
Magazine: 20 rounds
Features: 4-position gas piston system; 1:10 16" chrome-lined chamber and bore; Magpul ACS stock & MIAD grip; M1913 quad rail; ambi selector; ambi mag release; integral QD sling points; machined into lower receiver & quad; offered in black, OD, and FDE; also offered in a 14.5" SBR variant
MSRP.............. **$2066–$2172**

SIG SAUER SIG716

SIG716 PATROL RIFLE

Action: Semiautomatic
Stock: Tactical synthetic
Barrel: 16 in.
Sights: None
Weight: 9 lb. 5 oz.
Caliber: 7.62x51mm NATO
Magazine: Detachable box, 20 rounds
Features: Short stroke pushrod operating system; M1913 MIL-STD rail; free-floating barrel; aluminum quad rail forend; telescoping stock
MSRP.................. **$2132**

SIG SAUER SIG716 PATROL RIFLE

Sig Sauer

SIG M400

Action: Semiautomatic
Stock: Synthetic
Barrel: 16 in.
Sights: Adjustable front post, dual aperture
Weight: 5.59 lb.
Caliber: 5.56x45mm NATO
Magazine: Detachable box, 30 rounds
Features: Military grade, chrome-lined barrel, flat top upper with M1913 accessory rail
MSRP. **$1200**

SIG SAUER SIG M400

SIG M400 ENHANCED

Action: Semiautomatic
Stock: Magpul MOE
Barrel: 16 in.
Sights: None
Weight: 6 lb. 11 oz.
Caliber: 5.56x45 NATO
Magazine: 30 rounds
Features: SIG's first direct gas impingement system; taking the enhancements of the 516 platform into a traditional Stoner design; 1:7 chrome lined barrel; ambi selector & mag release; integral QD sling swivel mounts machined into lower; upper/lower tension adjustment device; offered in traditional configuration with removable carry handle with poly or 1913 quad rail; offered as 'enhanced' variants with Magpul MOE furniture in black, FDE, and OD; new variants also include a Sight Ready Platform (SRP), a lightweight with contoured barrel
MSRP. **$1234**

SIG SAUER M400
ENHANCED CARBINE

Smith & Wesson

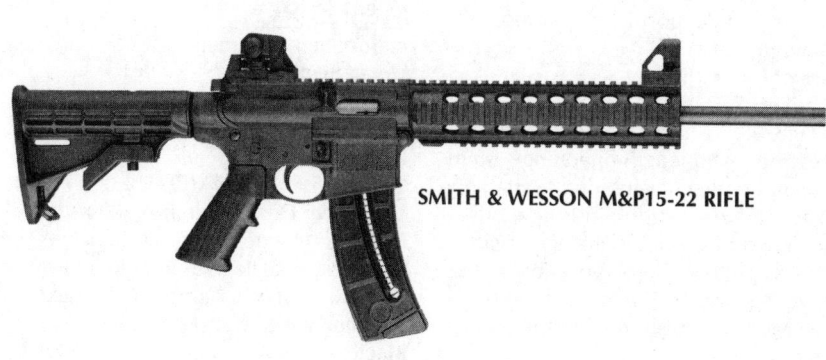

SMITH & WESSON M&P15-22 RIFLE

M&P15-22 RIFLE

Action: Semiautomatic
Stock: Synthetic
Barrel: 18 in.
Sights: Adjustable A2 front post, adjustable dual aperture
Weight: 5 lb. 6 oz.
Caliber: .22LR
Magazine: Detachable box, 25 rounds
Features: Six-position collapsible stock; functioning charging handle; two-position receiver mounted safety selector; cartridge case deflector; bolt catch; recessed magazine release button; match grade precision, threaded barrel
MSRP. **$499**

Smith & Wesson

SMITH & WESSON
M&P15 300 WHISPER

SMITH & WESSON
M&P15 MOE MID

SMITH & WESSON M&P15

SMITH & WESSON M&P15 PC

M&P15 300 WHISPER

Action: Semiautomatic
Stock: Synthetic
Barrel: 16 in.
Sights: None
Weight: 6 lb. 6 oz.
Caliber: .300 Whisper, .300 AAC Blackout
Magazine: Detachable box, 10 rounds
Features: Sub-sonic and super-sonic capabilities; 4140 chromoly steel barrel; forged 7075 aluminum receivers coated with Realtree APG finish; gas-operated rifle; single-stage trigger; integral one-piece trigger guard; six-position collapsible CAR stock; optics ready
MSRP $1119

M&P15

Action: Semiautomatic
Stock: Synthetic
Barrel: 16 in.
Sights: Troy adjustable front post, folding rear battle sight
Weight: 6 lb. 12 oz.
Caliber: 5.56 mm NATO, .223
Magazine: Detachable box, 30 rounds
Features: Six-position telescopic black stock; chrome-lined gas key and bolt carrier; flash suppressor compensator; two-position safety lever
MSRP $1249

M&P15 MOE MID

Action: Semiautomatic
Stock: Synthetic
Barrel: 16 in.
Sights: M4-A2 post front, folding Magpul rear
Weight: 6 lb. 8 oz.
Caliber: 5.56mm NATO
Magazine: Detachable box, 30 rounds
Features: Mid-length operating system, patent-pending flash hider; available in black and dark earth finish; Magpul designed forged lower receiver with flared magazine; one-piece integrated trigger guard; Melonite finish on barrel; MOE six-position collapsible buttstock
MSRP $1259

M&P15 PC

Action: Semiautomatic
Stock: Synthetic
Barrel: 20 in.
Sights: None
Weight: 8 lb. 2 oz.
Caliber: 5.56mm NATO, .223
Magazine: Detachable box, 10 rounds
Features: Hogue Green pistol grip; A2 buttstock; two-stage trigger; Realtree Advantage Max-1 Camo finish stock; chromed gas key and bolt carrier
Black: $1509
Camo: $1539

Smith & Wesson

M&P15 SPORT

Action: Semiautomatic
Stock: Synthetic
Barrel: 16 in.
Sights: Adjustable A2 front post, adjustable dual aperture
Weight: 6 lb. 8 oz.
Caliber: 5.56mm NATO
Magazine: Detachable box, 10, 30 rounds
Features: Six-position telescopic black stock or fixed stock; chrome-lined gas key and bolt carrier; flash suppressor compensator; two-position safety lever
MSRP $839

M&P15T

Action: Semiautomatic
Stock: Synthetic
Barrel: 16 in.
Sights: Folding Magpul
Weight: 6.85 lb.
Caliber: 5.56mm NATO
Magazine: Detachable box, 30 rounds
Features: 10-in. patent-pending, anti-twist, free-floating quad rail; melonite barrel; chromed bolt carrier and gas key; gas operated; single-stage trigger
MSRP $1159

M&P15 VTAC II

Action: Semiautomatic
Stock: Synthetic
Barrel: 16 in.
Sights: None
Weight: 6 lb. 4 oz.
Caliber: 5.56mm NATO
Magazine: Detachable box, 30 rounds
Features: Mid-length operating system, patent-pending flash hider; 4150 CMV steel barrel with Melonite finish; VTAC/Troy Extreme TRX handguard that reduces heat transfer; packaged with 2-inch adjustable Picatinny-style rails; Geissele Super V trigger
MSRP $1949

RIFLES

SMITH & WESSON M&P15 SPORT

SMITH & WESSON M&P15T

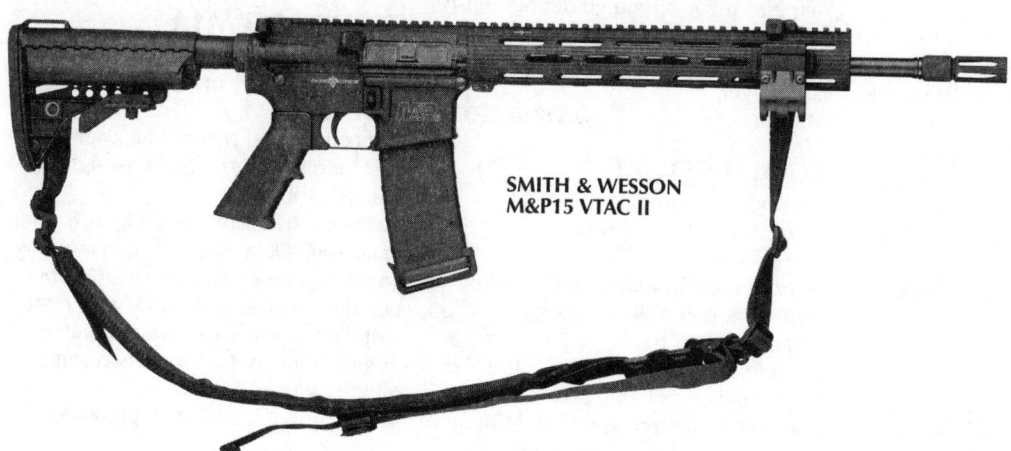

SMITH & WESSON
M&P15 VTAC II

Springfield Armory

SPRINGFIELD ARMORY M1A SOCOM 16

SPRINGFIELD ARMORY NATIONAL MATCH M1A

SPRINGFIELD ARMORY SCOUT SQUAD

SPRINGFIELD ARMORY STANDARD M1A

RIFLES

M1A SOCOM 16
Action: Autoloading
Stock: Composite
Barrel: 16.25 in.
Sights: Tritium front sight
Weight: 8 lb. 13 oz.
Caliber: 7.62x51mm NATO, .308 Win
Magazine: Detachable box, 10 rounds
Features: Muzzlebrake; forward mounted scope base; two-stage military trigger; composite black or green stock
MSRP $1893

NATIONAL MATCH M1A
Action: Autoloading
Stock: Walnut
Barrel: 22 in.
Sights: National Match front military post sight; rear National Match hooded aperture

Weight: 9 lb. 13 oz.
Caliber: 7.62x51mm NATO, .308 Win.
Magazine: Detachable box, 10 rounds
Features: Glass bedded; NM gas cylinder; NM recoil spring guide; NM flash suppressor; walnut stock; stainless steel or carbon barrel; two-stage military trigger
MSRP . . . . $2318–$2373

SCOUT SQUAD
Action: Autoloading
Stock: Walnut, composite
Barrel: 18 in.
Sights: National Match front military post sight; rear military aperture
Weight: 9 lb. 5 oz.
Caliber: 7.62x51mm NATO, .308 Win.
Magazine: Detachable box, 10 rounds
Features: Mounted optical sight base; muzzle stabilizers; black or green

fiberglass composite, American walnut stock or Mossy Oak camo stock; two-stage military trigger
MSRP . . . . $1761–$1893

STANDARD M1A
Action: Autoloading
Stock: Composite or walnut
Barrel: 22 in.
Sights: National Match military front post, adjustable rear aperture sight
Weight: 9 lb. 5 oz.
Caliber: 7.62x51mm NATO, .308 Win.
Magazine: Detachable box, 10 rounds
Features: Black fiberglass with rubber buttplate, Mossy Oak stock with metal buttplate or American walnut with original military buttplate; two-stage military trigger
MSRP . . . . $1640–$1739

MODEL 3G

Action: Semiautomatic
Stock: Synthetic
Barrel: 18 in.
Sights: Optional iron sights
Weight: 7 lb. 13 oz.
Caliber: 5.56 NATO
Magazine: 30 rounds
Features: Stainless steel fluted heavy barrel with rifle length gas system; Stag Arms 3G compensator; Samson Evolution handguard; Geissele Super 3-Gun trigger; Magpul collapsible ACS buttstock and MOE pistol grip; optional Dueck Defense Rapid Transition sights
MSRP.................... **$1459**
Left-hand: **$1479**

MODEL 8

Action: Gas-operated piston autoloader
Stock: Synthetic
Barrel: 20 in.
Sights: Midwest Industries front and rear flip-up
Weight: 6 lb. 14 oz.

Caliber: 5.56 NATO
Magazine: Detachable box, 30 rounds
Features: Right-and left-hand available; six-position collapsible stock; chrome-lined barrel
MSRP.................. **$1145**

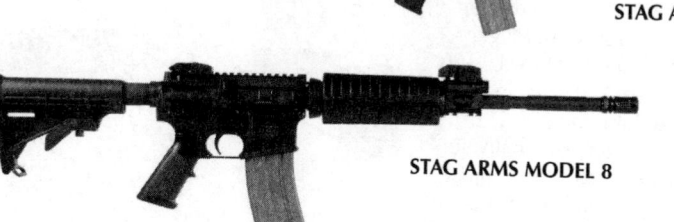

STAG ARMS 3G

STAG ARMS MODEL 8

Steyr Arms

AUG/A3 SA USA

Action: Semiautomatic
Stock: Synthetic
Barrel: 16 in.
Sights: None
Weight: 8 lb. 2 oz.
Caliber: .223 Rem.
Magazine: Detachable transparent box, 30 rounds
Features: Synthetic black stock; lateral push-through type, locks trigger; 1913 Picatinny rail; changeable barrel; includes factory AUG sling and cleaning kit that fits inside butt stock
MSRP.................. **$2099**

DUETT HUNTING COMBINATION RIFLE/ SHOTGUN

Action: Break-action
Stock: Walnut
Barrel: 23.6 in.
Sights: Open sights, 11mm prismatic scope mount rail

STEYR ARMS AUG/A3 SA USA

Weight: 6 lb. 6 oz.
Caliber: Rifle: .222 Rem., .243 Win., .308 Win., 7x65R, .30-06 Spfd., .30R Blaser, 8x57 IRS, 9.3x74R; Shotgun: 12 Ga./3-inch
Magazine: None
Features: Break-action over-under combination rifle/shotgun; dual gold-plated single-stage triggers; free-floated cold-hammer-forged barrels, Mannox finish; tang-mounted manual cocking lever; 5 models available; manual cocking system; European walnut stock; checkered forend and pistol grip
Standard:................ **$2850**

CLASSIC

Action: Bolt
Stock: European Walnut
Barrel: 20 in., 23.6 in., 25.6 in.
Sights: Open
Weight: 7 lb. 5 oz.
Caliber: .222 Rem., .223 Rem., .243 Win., 6.5x55 SE, .270 Win., 7x64, .25-06 Rem., .308 Win., .30-06 Spfd., 8x57 JS, 9.3x62, 6.5x57
Magazine: Detachable box, 3, 4 rounds
Features: Set or direct trigger; sights included for full stock only; Bavarian-styled cheekpiece; safe bolt system; case hardening surface finish on European walnut stock
Half stock: **$2795**
Full stock: **$2995**

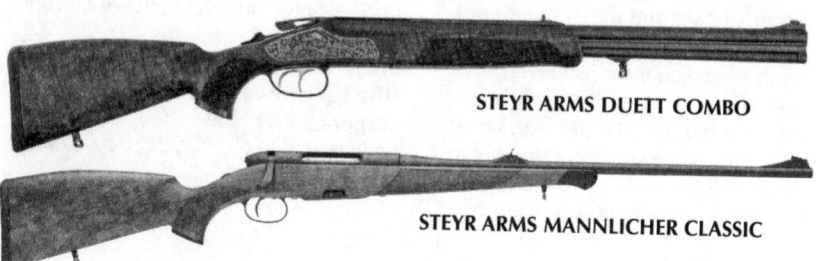

STEYR ARMS DUETT COMBO

STEYR ARMS MANNLICHER CLASSIC

Steyr Arms

PRO HUNTER

Action: Bolt
Stock: Synthetic
Barrel: 20 in., 23.6 in., 25.6 in.
Sights: None
Weight: 7 lb. 5 oz.–8 lb. 3 oz.
Caliber: .222 Rem., .223 Rem., .243 Win., 6.5x55SE, .25-06 Rem., .270 Win., 7x64, 7mm-08 Rem., .308 Win., .30-06 Spfd., 9.3x62, .338 Fed. Mag. Magnum Caliber: .300 Win. Mag., 9.3x62, 7mm Swam, .270 WSM, .300 WSM
Magazine: Detachable box
Features: Direct trigger, optionally set trigger; durable synthetic stock adjusted by spacers; Mannotm metal surface finish protects against corrosion; three-position safety
MSRP $1150
Stainless: $1250

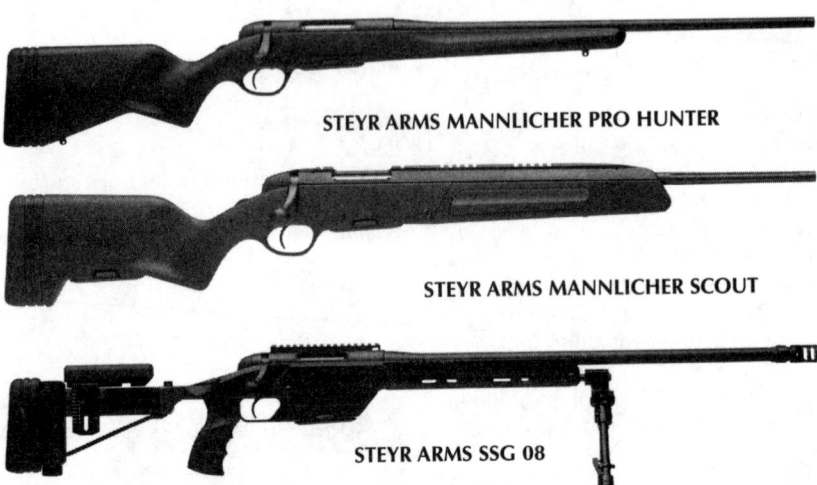

STEYR ARMS MANNLICHER PRO HUNTER

STEYR ARMS MANNLICHER SCOUT

STEYR ARMS SSG 08

SCOUT

Action: Bolt
Stock: Synthetic
Barrel: 19 in.
Sights: None
Weight: 6 lb. 10 oz.
Caliber: .243 Rem., 7mm-08 Rem., .308 Win.
Magazine: Box, 5 rounds (optional 10 round magazine)

Features: Weaver scope mounting rail; set trigger or direct trigger; synthetic stock in black or gray wood imitation; optional bipod integrated into forearm; matte black or stainless steel finish on barrel
MSRP $2099

SSG 08

Action: Bolt
Stock: Synthetic
Barrel: 20 in., 23.6 in.
Sights: None

Weight: 5 lb. 8 oz.–5 lb. 11 oz.
Caliber: .308 Win.
Magazine: Box, 10 rounds
Features: Direct trigger; Mannox TM system; high grade aluminum folding stock; adjustable cheekpiece and buttplate with height marking; ergonomic exchangeable pistol grip; UIT rail and Picatinny rail; muzzlebrake; Versa-Pod
MSRP . . . . $5895–$6795

Szecsei & Fuchs

SZECSEI & FUCHS DOUBLE BOLT REPEATER

DOUBLE BOLT REPEATER

Action: Bolt
Stock: Turkish walnut
Weight: 11 lb. 6 oz. round barrel, 13 lb.–15 lb. 3 oz. octagonal barrel
Caliber: Available in many popular calibers. The larger caliber rifles are available in .17 to .700. Their most affordable options are the .17 and .22 rifles.
Magazine: Detachable box, 4+2 rounds

Features: Hungarian inventor Joseph Szecsei developed his innovative design after being charged simultaneously by three elephants in 1989. Built with great care and much handiwork from the finest materials, it follows a design remarkable for its cleverness. While the rifle is not light-weight, it can be aimed quickly and offers more large-caliber firepower than any competitor. The six-shot magazine feeds two rounds simultaneously, both of

which can then be fired by two quick pulls of the trigger. Optical sight is secured with titanium mounting; triggers have integrated, noiseless double-firing safety catch; titanium and steel barrels in octagon or round; one-piece bolt reloads two rounds. *As these rifles are custom order only and with the fluctuation of the U.S. dollar, it is best to contact the sales representative listed in back to obtain a firm quotation. Average product delivery currently 14 months.
Small caliber (.17 and .22) rifle base price: $30000
Larger caliber rifle base price: $75000

CLASSIC SPORTER

Action: Chimera bolt
Stock: Walnut
Barrel: 22 in.
Sights: None
Weight: 8 lb. 14 oz.
Caliber: .308 Win., .260 Rem., 6.5 Creedmoor and Lapua, .243 Win., 7mm-08 Rem. (short action); .30-06 Spfd., .270 Win., .300 Win. Mag., 7mm Rem. Mag. (long action)
Magazine: 4+1 rounds
Features: Chimera action is constructed from stainless steel with a hand-fitted spiral-groove bolt and "Magnum" extractor; Picatinny rail; XXX grade English walnut stock with 22 lpi checkering at grip and forearm; extreme environment matte black finish
MSRP. **$5895**

SPECIAL PURPOSE GRENDEL (SPG)

Action: Semiautomatic
Stock: Magpul PRS
Barrel: 20 in.
Sights: None
Weight: 10 lb. 8 oz.
Caliber: 6.5 Grendel, .264 Les Baer Custom
Magazine: 17+1 rounds
Features: Stainless steel match grade barrel; SureFire muzzlebrake; enhanced upper and lower receivers; Magpul MOE pistol grip; Picatinny rail
MSRP. **$3595**

TACTICAL L.R.

Action: Bolt, 700 Rem.
Stock: Synthetic
Barrel: 18 in.-26 in.
Sights: None
Weight: 12 lb.–13 lb. 6 oz.
Caliber: 7.62 NATO, .308 Win.
Magazine: Detachable box, 5, 10 rounds
Features: Ergonomic thumbhole stock comes in black or green; raised cheekpiece; free-floating chromoly match grade barrel; ambidextrous sling swivel studs; soft rubber recoil pad; 1913 MIL-STD Picatinny rail; aluminum block chassis stock system; optional bipod
MSRP. **$2950**

RIFLES

TACTICAL RIFLES CLASSIC SPORTER

TACTICAL RIFLES SPG

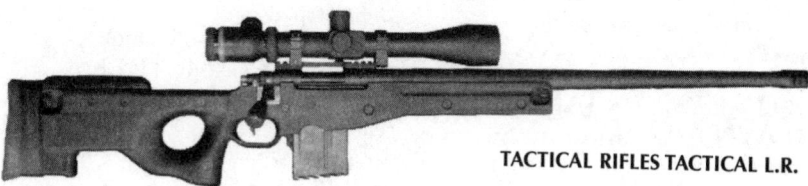

TACTICAL RIFLES TACTICAL L.R.

Taylor's & Co. Firearms

1860 HENRY LEVER ACTION RIFLE

Action: Lever
Stock: Walnut
Barrel: 24.25 in.
Sights: Open
Weight: 9 lb. 3 oz.
Caliber: .44-40
Magazine: Under-barrel tube, 9-13 rounds
Features: Brass frame; octagonal barrel with blued finish; includes sling swivels
MSRP . . . . **$1533–$1663**

1860 HENRY RIFLE WITH STANDARD ENGRAVING

Action: Lever
Stock: Walnut
Barrel: 24.25 in.
Sights: Open
Weight: 9 lb. 3 oz.
Caliber: .45LC
Magazine: Under-barrel tube, 9-13 rounds
Features: Standard engraved brass; octagonal barrel with blued finish
MSRP **$1782**

TAYLOR'S & CO. 1860 HENRY RIFLE WITH STANDARD ENGRAVING

TAYLOR'S & CO. LIGHTNING SLIDE ACTION RIFLE

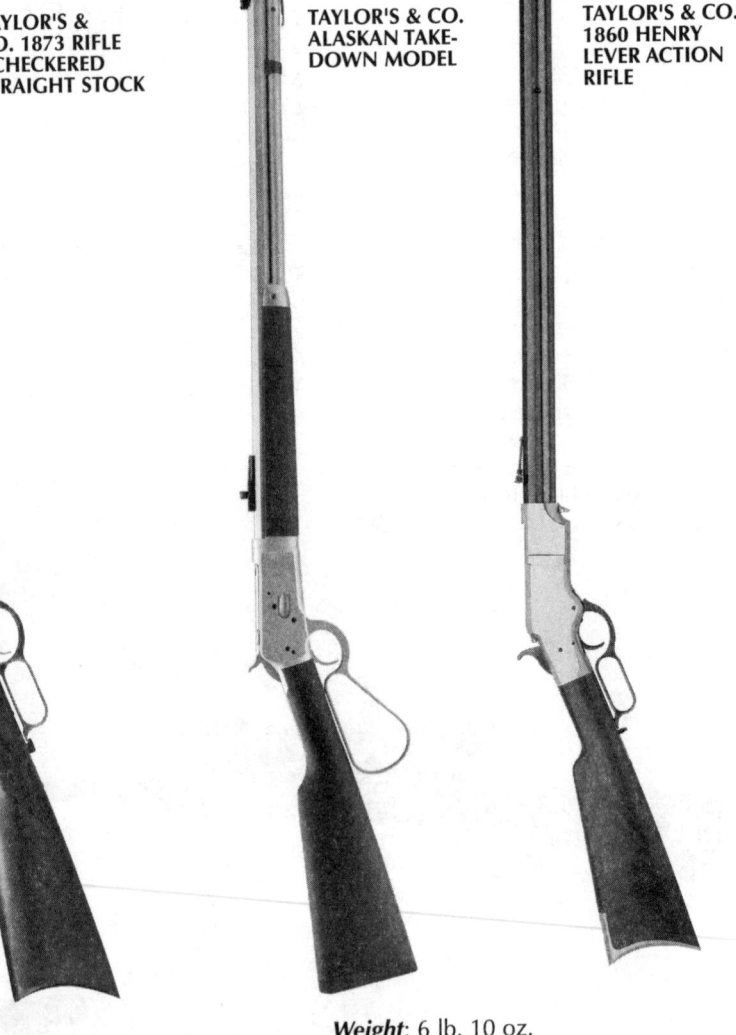

TAYLOR'S & CO. 1873 RIFLE - CHECKERED STRAIGHT STOCK

TAYLOR'S & CO. ALASKAN TAKE-DOWN MODEL

TAYLOR'S & CO. 1860 HENRY LEVER ACTION RIFLE

1873 RIFLE - CHECKERED STRAIGHT STOCK

Action: Lever
Stock: Walnut
Barrel: 20 in.
Sights: Open
Weight: 8 lb. 8 oz.
Caliber: .357 Mag., .45 LC
Magazine: 10+1 rounds
Features: Case-hardened frame; straight stock with checkering; available with full octagon barrel
MSRP **$1341**

1892 ALASKAN TAKE-DOWN MODEL

Action: Lever
Stock: Synthetic
Barrel: 16 in., 20 in.
Sights: Skinner rear

Weight: 6 lb. 10 oz.
Caliber: .44RM, .45 LC
Magazine: 10 rounds
Features: Matte chrome finish; soft touch stock
MSRP **$1324**

LIGHTNING SLIDE ACTION RIFLE

Action: Slide
Stock: Walnut
Barrel: 24.25 in., 26 in.
Sights: Open
Weight: 6 lb. 3 oz.–6 lb. 8 oz.
Caliber: .45LC, .44-40, .357 Mag.
Magazine: Under-barrel tube
Features: Case-hardened frame; walnut stock with checkered forend; octagonal barrel
MSRP . . . . **$1236–$1264**

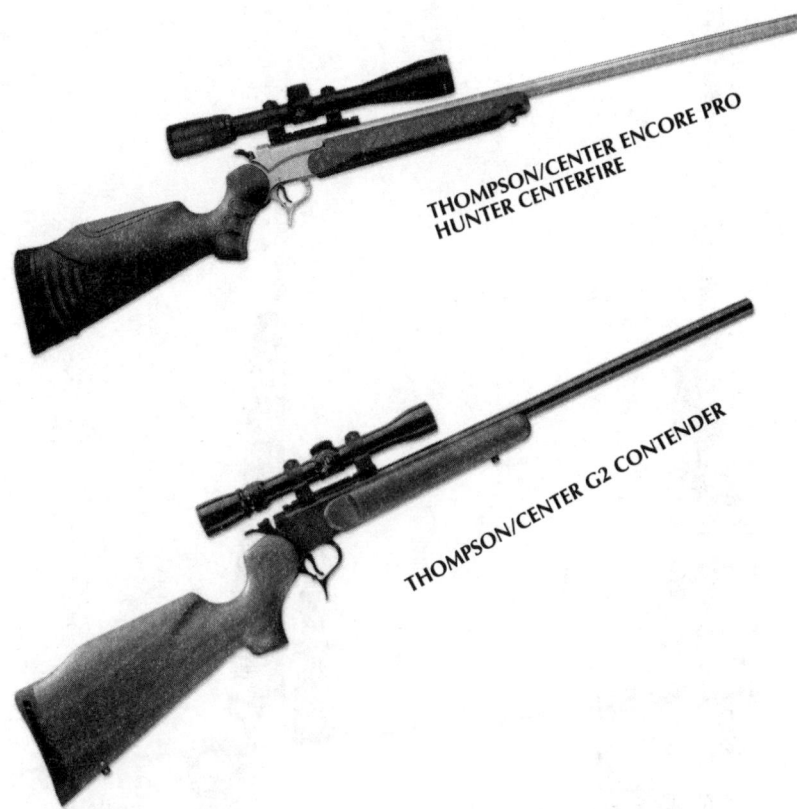

THOMPSON/CENTER ENCORE PRO HUNTER CENTERFIRE

THOMPSON/CENTER G2 CONTENDER

THOMPSON/
CENTER
DIMENSION

DIMENSION

Action: Bolt
Stock: Composite
Barrel: 22 in., 24 in.
Sights: None
Weight: 7 lb.
Caliber: .204 Ruger, .223 Rem., .22-250 Rem., .243 Win., 7mm-08 Rem., .308 Win., .270 Win., .30-06 Spfd., 7mm Rem. Mag., .300 Win. Mag.
Magazine: 3 rounds
Features: A bolt action platform you can build on season after season; switch out barrels, bolts, magazines, and and other components such as scopes and mounts
MSRP **$689**

ENCORE PRO HUNTER CENTERFIRE

Action: Single-shot, break-open
Stock: Composite, hardwood
Barrel: 20 in., 28 in.
Sights: Optional fiber optic sights and peep sights
Weight: 6 lb. 4 oz.–7 lb. 12 oz.
Caliber: .204 Ruger, .223 Ruger, .22-250 Rem., .243 Win., .25-06 Rem., .270 Win., .280 Rem., .7mm Rem. Mag., 7mm-08 Rem., .300 Win. Mag., .308 Win., .30-06 Spfd., .45-70 Govt., .460 S&W, .500 S&W
Magazine: None
Features: Swing hammer; Flextech stock in black or Realtree Hardwoods camo; fluted barrel; thumbhole stock optional; SIMS recoil pad; engraved stainless steel frame; readily interchangeable barrels
MSRP **$1015**

G2 CONTENDER

Action: Single-shot, break-open
Stock: Walnut, composite
Barrel: 18 in., 23 in.
Sights: None
Weight: 5 lb. 6 oz.
Caliber: .17 HMR, .22LR Match, 5mm Rem. Mag., .204 Ruger, .223 Rem., 6.8 Rem., 7-30 Waters, .30-30 Win., .45-70 Govt.
Magazine: None
Features: Blued or stainless steel barrel; automatic hammer block with bolt interlock; drilled and tapped for scope mounts; button rifled
MSRP **$906**

Thompson/Center

**THOMPSON/
CENTER PROHUNTER
PREDATOR**

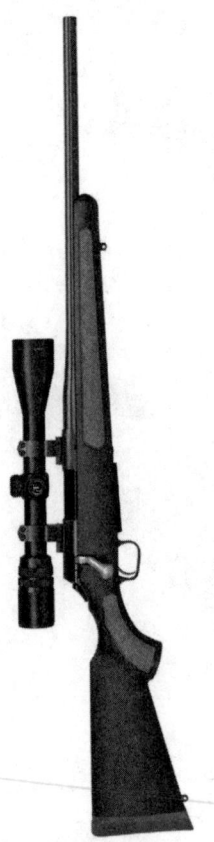

**THOMPSON/
CENTER VENTURE
COMPACT**

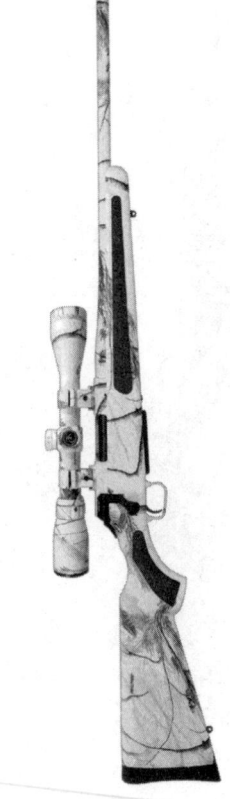

**THOMPSON/
CENTER VENTURE
PREDATOR SNOW**

PROHUNTER PREDATOR

Action: Single-shot, break-open
Stock: Composite
Barrel: 28 in.
Sights: None
Weight: 7 lb. 12 oz.
Caliber: .204 Ruger, .223 Rem., .22-250 Rem., .308 Win.
Magazine: None
Features: Realtree MAX-1 camo composite stock and barrel; FlexTech; mounted and drilled for scopes
MSRP **$882**

VENTURE COMPACT

Action: Bolt
Stock: Composite
Barrel: 20 in.
Sights: None
Weight: 6 lb. 12 oz.
Caliber: .22-250 Rem., .243 Win., .308 Win., 7mm-08
Magazine: Detachable box, 3+1 rounds
Features: Adjustable trigger; included spacer and buttpad; Hogue traction inlays; Melanite coated bolt; two position safety
MSRP **$537**

VENTURE PREDATOR SNOW

Action: Bolt
Stock: Composite
Barrel: 22 in., 24 in.
Sights: Bases for mounting scopes
Weight: 6 lb. 12 oz.
Caliber: 7mm-08, .243 Rem., .22-250 Rem., .308 Win.
Magazine: 3+1 rounds
Features: Adjustable trigger; Hogue rubber inlays; sling swivel studs; Weather Shield bolt handle
MSRP **$638**

TIKKA T3 HUNTER

T3 HUNTER
Action: Bolt
Stock: Walnut
Barrel: 20 in., 22.4 in., 24.4 in.
Sights: None
Weight: 6 lb. 10 oz.–7 lb.
Caliber: .204 Ruger, .222 Rem., .223 Rem., .22-250 Rem., .243 Win., .260 Rem., 7mm-08 Rem., .308 Win., .338 Federal, .25-06 Rem., 6.5x55 SE, .270 Win., 7x64, .30-06 Spfd., 8x57IS, 9.3x62, 7mm Rem. Mag., .300 Win. Mag., .338 Win. Mag., .270 Win. Short Mag., .300 Win. Short Mag.
Magazine: Detachable box, 4, 5 rounds
Features: Sling swivels; free-floating cold-hammer-forged barrel; two locking Lug T3 action; two-stage safety; single-set trigger; walnut stock in oil finish and optional matte lacquered stock; integral scope mounts
MSRP **$745**

T3 LITE
Action: Bolt
Stock: Synthetic
Barrel: 20 in., 22.4 in., 24.4 in.
Sights: None
Weight: 6 lb.–6 lb. 6 oz.
Caliber: .204 Ruger, .222 Rem., .223 Rem., .22-250 Rem., .243 Win., .260 Rem., 7mm-08 Rem., .308 Win., .338 Federal, .25-06 Rem., 6.5x55 SE, .270 Win., 7x64, .30-06 Spfd., 8x57IS, 9.3x62, 7mm Rem. Mag., .300 Win. Mag., .338 Win. Mag., .270 Win. Short Mag., .300 Win. Short Mag.
Magazine: Detachable box, 4, 5 rounds
Features: Stainless steel bolt; two-stage safety; single-set trigger; fiberglass synthetic stock in black; Weaver scope mount bases; free-floating, cold-hammer-forged barrel
MSRP . . . . **$625–$660**
Stainless: . . . . **$750–$800**
Stainless, LH: . . . . **$825–$850**

T3 SPORTER
Action: Bolt
Stock: Laminated wood, oiled
Barrel: 20 in., 24 in.
Sights: Scope rail and threads for Weaver-type scope rail
Weight: 9 lb.–9 lb. 11 oz.
Caliber: .222 Rem., .223 Rem., 6.5x55 SE, .260 Rem., .308 Win.
Magazine: 5, 6 rounds
Features: Adjustable cheekpiece; adjustable recoil pad in length and height; various rail placements that allow rifle to be carried in biathlon style; metal parts are matte blued; limited number of left-handed models imported to U.S.
MSRP **$1850**
Left-handed: **$1925**

RIFLES

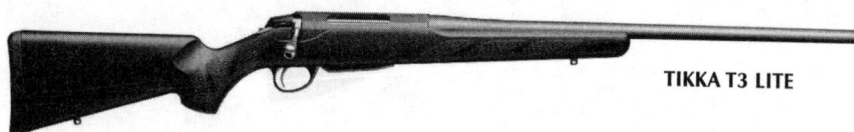

TIKKA T3 LITE

TIKKA T3 SPORTER LEFT-HANDED

Uberti

1860 HENRY RIFLE
Action: Lever
Stock: Walnut
Barrel: 18.5 in., 24.5 in.
Sights: Adjustable
Weight: 9 lb.
Caliber: .45 Colt, .44-40
Magazine: Under-barrel tube, 8+1, 13+1 rounds
Features: Blued or standard buttplate; case-hardened lever and frame; A-grade walnut stock; octagonal barrel
MSRP . . . . **$1399–$1429**

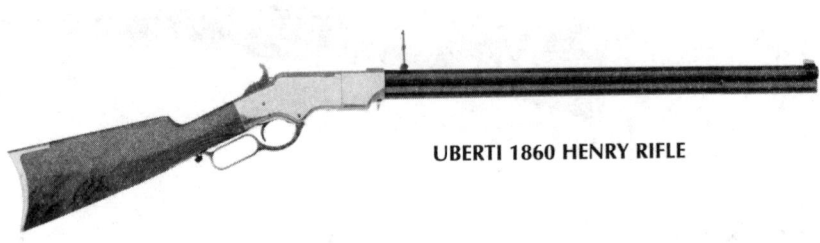

UBERTI 1860 HENRY RIFLE

1866 YELLOWBOY
Action: Lever
Stock: Walnut
Barrel: 19 in., 20 in., 24.25 in.
Sights: Adjustable
Weight: 8 lb. 3 oz.
Caliber: .45 Colt, .44-40, .38 Spl.
Magazine: Under barrel tube, 10+1, 13+1 rounds
Features: Brass forend nose cap; solid brass crescent buttplate; case-hardened lever; brass frame and buttplate
MSRP . . . . **$1099–$1149**

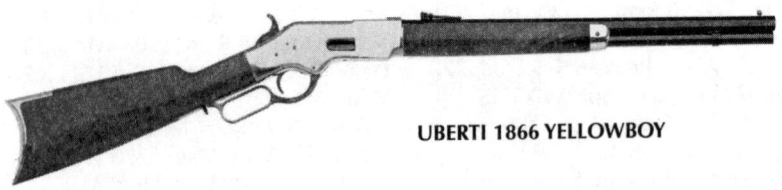

UBERTI 1866 YELLOWBOY

1871 ROLLING BLOCK HUNTER CARBINE
Action: Rolling block
Stock: Walnut
Barrel: 22 in.
Sights: Fixed
Weight: 4 lb. 8 oz.
Caliber: .38-55, .30-30, .45-70
Magazine: None
Features: Rubber buttpad; case-colored receiver
MSRP **$799**

UBERTI 1871 ROLLING BLOCK HUNTER CARBINE

1871 ROLLING BLOCK HUNTER RIMFIRE
Action: Rolling block
Stock: Walnut
Barrel: 22 in.
Sights: Adjustable
Weight: 4 lb. 8 oz.
Caliber: .22LR, .22 Mag., .17 HMR
Magazine: None
Features: Round blued barrel; brass trigger guard; case-hardened frame; A-grade walnut stock with rubber buttpad
MSRP **$709**

UBERTI 1871 ROLLING BLOCK HUNTER RIMFIRE

UBERTI 1873 CARBINE

UBERTI 1874 CAVALRY CARBINE SHARPS

UBERTI 1874 SHARPS RIFLE

UBERTI 1876 CENTENNIAL

UBERTI 1883 BURGESS RIFLE

1873 RIFLE & CARBINE

Action: Lever
Stock: Walnut
Barrel: 16.1 in., 18 in., 19 in., 20 in., 24.5 in.
Sights: Adjustable
Weight: 7 lb. 3 oz.–8 lb. 3 oz.
Caliber: .45 Colt, .357 Mag., .44-44
Magazine: Under-barrel tube, 9+1, 10+1, 13+1 rounds
Features: Octagonal barrel on rifle; round barrel on carbine and trapper; A-grade walnut with checkered pistol grip and forend
Trapper: **$1259**
Rifle: . . . . **$1259–$1309**
Carbine: . . . . **$1219–$1309**
Sporting: . . . . **$1259–$1399**

1874 CAVALRY CARBINE SHARPS

Action: Falling block
Stock: Walnut
Barrel: 22 in.
Sights: Creedmoor Sight
Weight: 8 lb.
Caliber: .45-70
Magazine: None
Features: Round blued barrel; case-hardened levers and blued buttplate
MSRP **$1739**

1874 SHARPS RIFLE

Action: Falling block
Stock: Walnut
Barrel: 32 in., 34 in.
Sights: Creedmoor Sight
Weight: 10 lb. 4 oz.–11 lb.
Caliber: .45-70
Magazine: None
Features: Blued octagonal barrel; checkered walnut stock; case-hardened, except Extra Deluxe model; double-set trigger; pewter forend cap
Special: **$1949**
Deluxe: **$3059**
Down Under: **$2509**
Buffalo Hunter: **$2469**
Extra Deluxe: **$4869**

1876 CENTENNIAL

Action: Lever
Stock: Walnut
Barrel: 28 in.
Sights: Adjustable
Weight: 10 lb.
Caliber: .45-60, .45-75, .50-95
Magazine: 11+1 rounds
Features: Case-hardened frame and lever; blued buttplate; octagonal barrel; straight stock
MSRP **$1609**

1883 BURGESS RIFLE & CARBINE

Action: Lever
Stock: Walnut
Barrel: 20 in. (carbine), 25.5 in. (rifle)
Sights: Fixed
Weight: 7 lb. 10 oz.–8 lb. 2 oz.
Caliber: .45 Colt

Magazine: Under-barrel tube, 10, 13 rounds
Features: Case-hardened, round barrel; straight grip
MSRP **$1499**

Uberti

1885 HIGH-WALL SINGLE-SHOT

Action: Falling block
Stock: Walnut
Barrel: 28 in., 30 in., 32 in.
Sights: Adjustable
Weight: 9 lb. 5 oz. (carbine), 10 lb.
Caliber: .45-70, .45-90, .45-120
Magazine: None
Features: Case-hardened frame and lever; blued buttplate; octagonal barrel; carbine model has round barrel; carbine and sporting rifle have straight stock
Carbine: **$1009**
Sporting Rifle: . . . . **$1079–$1139**
Special Sporting Rifle: . **$1199–$1279**

LIGHTNING

Action: Pump
Stock: Walnut
Barrel: 20 in., 24.25 in.
Sights: Adjustable
Weight: 6 lb. 3 oz.–6 lb. 8 oz.
Caliber: .45 Colt, .357 Mag.
Magazine: Under-barrel tube, 10+1 round (short rifle), 13+1 rounds (standard)
Features: Case-hardened frame and trigger guard; octagonal barrel
MSRP. **$1279**

SILVERBOY LEVER ACTION

Action: Lever
Stock: Walnut
Barrel: 19 in.
Sights: Fixed
Weight: 5 lb. 13 oz.
Caliber: .22LR, .22 Mag.
Magazine: 15+1 rounds
Features: Chrome-plated alloy reciever; walnut straight stock; cartridge-control mechanism allows controlled-round-feed; blued barrel
MSRP. . . . . **$589–$599**

SPRINGFIELD TRAPDOOR CARBINE

Action: Hinged breech
Stock: Walnut
Barrel: 22 in.
Sights: Adjustable
Weight: 7 lb. 5 oz.
Caliber: .45-70
Magazine: None
Features: Blued steel, case-hardened breechblock and buttplate; fitted with sliding ring and bar for cavalryman to

UBERTI 1885 HIGH-WALL SINGLE-SHOT SPECIAL SPORTING MODEL

UBERTI LIGHTNING

UBERTI SILVERBOY LEVER ACTION

UBERTI SPRINGFIELD TRAPDOOR CARBINE

UBERTI SPRINGFIELD TRAPDOOR RIFLE

carry it clipped to carbine sling
MSRP. **$1599**

SPRINGFIELD TRAPDOOR RIFLE

Action: Hinged breech
Stock: Walnut
Barrel: 32.5 in.

Sights: Adjustable
Weight: 8 lb. 13 oz.
Caliber: .45-70
Magazine: None
Features: Blued steel, case-hardened breechblock and buttplate
MSRP. **$1879**

Volquartsen Custom

TF-17 & TF-22
Action: Autoloader
Stock: Ambidextrous birch
Barrel: 18.5 in.
Sights: Picatinny Mil-Spec rail
Weight: 8 lb. 8 oz.
Caliber: .17 HMR, .22 WMR
Magazine: Rotary mag, 9 rounds
Features: Blowback design, TG2000 trigger unit with 2.25-lb. pull; black stainless barrel
MSRP $1086

VOLQUARTSEN CUSTOM TF-17

Walther

Sights: Adjustable on handle and front strut
Weight: 6 lb.
Caliber: .22LR
Magazine: Detachable box, 10 rounds
Features: Single-action trigger; employs an innovative "Bullpup" design; Weaver-style universal rails for sight mounts, bipods, and other accessories; includes Walther safety package with cocking indicator, slide safety and integral lock; available in left-hand models; synthetic stock comes in black or green
MSRP . . . . $420–$530

WALTHER G22 CARBINE

G22 CARBINE
Action: Autoloading
Stock: Synthetic
Barrel: 20 in.

Weatherby

MARK V ACCUMARK
Action: Bolt
Stock: Composite
Barrel: 24 in., 26 in., 28 in.
Sights: None
Weight: 7 lb. 4 oz.–9 lb.
Caliber: .270 Win., .208 Win., .257 Wby. Mag., .270 Wby. Mag., 7mm Rem. Mag., 7mm Wby. Mag., .300 Win. Mag., .300 Wby. Mag., .30-378 Wby. Mag., .340 Wby. Mag., .247 Wby. Mag., .300 Wby. Mag., .30-378

Wby. Mag.
Magazine: Box, 2+1, 3+1, 5+1 rounds
Features: Adjustable trigger; hand-laminated raised comb; Monte Carlo composite stock with matte gel coat finish and spider web accents; Pachmayr

decelerator pad; button rifled; CNC-machined 6061 T-6 aluminum bedding plate; cocking indicator; fluted bolt body
MSRP $2100

WEATHERBY MARK V ACCUMARK

Weatherby

WEATHERBY MARK V
ACCUMARK .338 LAPUA

WEATHERBY MARK V DELUXE

WEATHERBY MARK V FIBERMARK

WEATHERBY MARK V LAZERMARK

MARK V ACCUMARK .338 LAPUA

Action: Bolt
Stock: Composite
Barrel: 26 in.
Sights: None
Weight: 9 lb.
Caliber: .338 Lapua Mag.
Magazine: 2+1 rounds
Features: Button-rifled; chromoly free-floated barrel with recessed target crown; features fluted barrel with matching Accubrake; matte bead blasted blued finish
MSRP $2300

MARK V DELUXE

Action: Bolt
Stock: Walnut
Barrel: 24 in., 26 in., 28 in.
Sights: None
Weight: 6 lb. 12 oz.–10 lb.
Caliber: .270 Win., .308 Win., .30-06 Spfd., .257 Wby. Mag., .270 Wby. Mag., 7mm Wby. Mag., .300 Wby. Mag., .340 Wby. Mag., .378 Wby. Mag., .416 Wby. Mag., .460 Wby. Mag.
Magazine: Box, 2+1, 3+1, 5+1 rounds
Features: Adjustable trigger; walnut Monte Carlo stock with rosewood forend and pistol grip cap and maple-wood spacers; blued metalwork in high luster finish; Pachmayr decelerator pad
MSRP $2400

MARK V FIBERMARK

Action: Bolt
Stock: Composite
Barrel: 24 in., 26 in., 28 in.
Sights: None
Weight: 6 lb.–8 lb. 8 oz.
Caliber: .240 Wby. Mag., .270 Win., .30-06 Spfd., .257 Wby. Mag., .270 Wby. Mag., 7mm Rem. Mag., 7mm Wby. Mag., .300 Win. Mag., .300 Wby. Mag., .30-378 Wby. Mag., .340 Wby. Mag., .375 H&H Mag.
Magazine: Box, 2+1, 3+1 rounds

Features: Adjustable trigger; pillar-bedded, hand-laminated raised comb Monte Carlo composite stock with strategically placed bedding points assures consistent, repeatable accuracy
MSRP $1500

MARK V LAZERMARK

Action: Bolt
Stock: Walnut
Barrel: 26 in.
Sights: None
Weight: 8 lb. 8 oz.
Caliber: .257 Wby. Mag., .270 Wby. Mag., 7mm Rem. Mag., 7mm Wby. Mag., .300 Win. Mag., .300 Wby. Mag.
Magazine: Box, 3+1 rounds
Features: Adjustable trigger; hand-selected, raised comb Monte Carlo stock with laser-carved oak leaf pattern; blued metalwork in high luster finish; Pachmayr decelerator pad
MSRP $2600

Weatherby

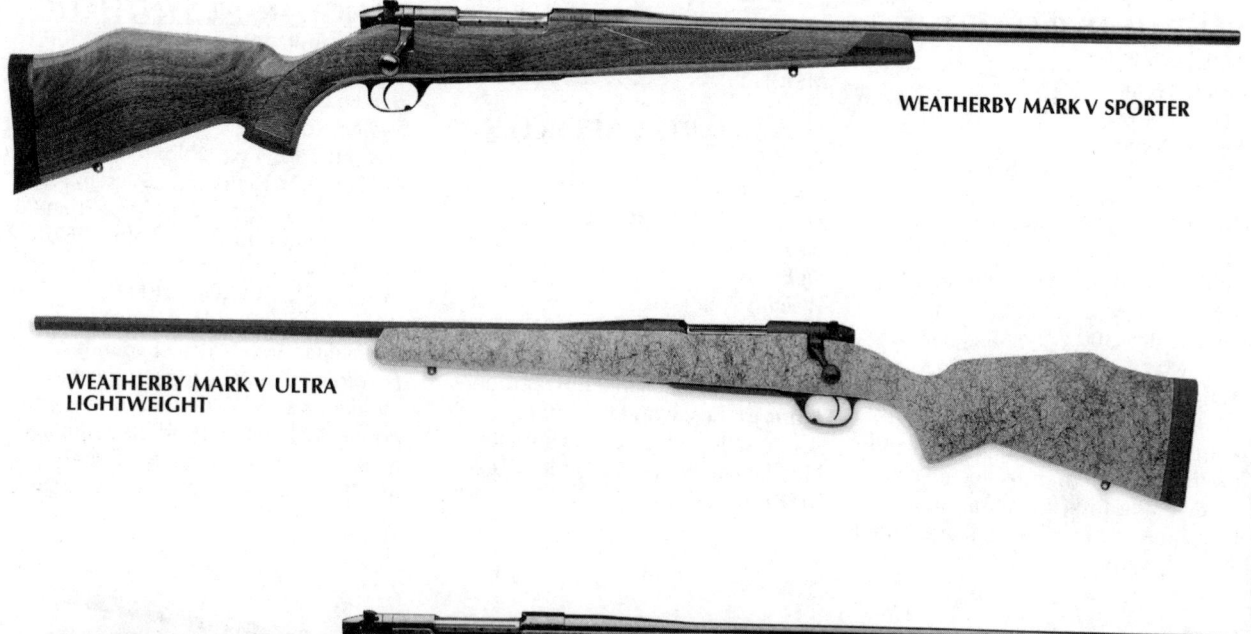

WEATHERBY MARK V SPORTER

WEATHERBY MARK V ULTRA LIGHTWEIGHT

WEATHERBY MARK V ULTRAMARK

MARK V SPORTER

Action: Bolt
Stock: Walnut
Barrel: 24 in., 26 in.
Sights: None
Weight: 8 lb.
Caliber: .257 Wby. Mag., .270 Wby. Mag., 7mm Rem. Mag., 7mm Wby. Mag., .300 Win. Mag., .300 Wby. Mag., .340 Wby. Mag.
Magazine: Box, 3+1 rounds
Features: Adjustable trigger; raised comb Monte Carlo walnut stock with satin finish; features fine line diamond point checkering and rosewood forend and grip cap; bead blasted, blued metalwork with low luster finish; Pachmayr decelerator pad
MSRP **$1600**

MARK V ULTRA LIGHTWEIGHT

Action: Bolt
Stock: Composite
Barrel: 24 in., 26 in.
Sights: None
Weight: 5.75 lb.–6.75 lb.
Caliber: .243 Win., .240 Wby. Mag., .25-06 Rem., .270 Win., 7mm-08 Rem., .308 Win., .30-06 Spfd., .257 Wby. Mag., 7mm Rem. Mag., 7mm Wby. Mag., .300 Win. Mag., .257 Wby. Mag., .300 Wby. Mag.
Magazine: Box, 3+1, 5+1 rounds
Features: Adjustable trigger; contoured fluted stainless steel barrel, blackened to reduce glare; Bell & Carlson composite stock with spider web accents; CNC-machined 6061 T-6 aluminum bedding plate; one-piece forged bolt; Pachmayr decelerator pad
MSRP **$2100**

MARK V ULTRAMARK

Action: Bolt
Stock: Walnut
Barrel: 26 in.
Sights: None
Weight: 8 lb. 8 oz.
Caliber: .257 Wby. Mag., .300 Wby. Mag.
Magazine: Box, 3+1 rounds
Features: Adjustable trigger; hand-selected, AAA fancy exhibition grade walnut stock; features 20 lpi checkering, maplewood/ebony spacers and rosewood forend and grip caps; blued metalwork in high luster finish; Pachmayr decelerator pad
MSRP **$3200**

Weatherby

VANGUARD 2 SPORTER

Action: Bolt
Stock: Walnut
Barrel: 24 in.
Sights: None
Weight: 7 lb. 4 oz.–7 lb. 8 oz.
Caliber: .223 Rem., .22-250 Rem., .243 Win., .25-06 Rem., .270 Win., 7mm-08 Rem., .308 Win., .30-06 Spfd., .257 Wby. Mag., .270 WSM, 7mm Rem. Mag., .300 Win. Mag., .300 WSM, .300 Wby. Mag., .338 Win. Mag.
Magazine: Box 3+1, 5+1 rounds
Features: Two-stage trigger; raised comb, Monte Carlo stock with satin urethane finish; hand-selected A fancy grade Turkish walnut; rosewood forend; low luster, matte blued metalwork; fine line diamond point checkering; low density recoil pad
MSRP.....................$849

VANGUARD 2 SPORTER DBM

Action: Bolt
Stock: Walnut Monte Carlo
Barrel: 24 in.
Sights: None
Weight: 7 lb. 4 oz.
Caliber: .25-06 Rem., .270 Win., .30-06 Spfd.
Magazine: Detachable box, 3 rounds
Features: Rosewood forend; raised comb; satin urethane finish; matte blued metalwork; adjustable trigger
MSRP.....................$899

VANGUARD 2 SYNTHETIC

Action: Bolt
Stock: Synthetic
Barrel: 24 in.
Sights: None
Weight: 7 lb. 4 oz.–7 lb. 8 oz.
Caliber: .223 Rem., .22-250 Rem., .243 Win., .25-06 Rem., .270 Win., 7mm-08 Rem., .308 Win., .30-06 Spfd., .257 Wby. Mag., .270 WSM, 7mm Rem. Mag., .300 Win. Mag., .300 WSM, .300 Wby. Mag., .338 Win. Mag.
Magazine: Box 3+1, 5+1 rounds
Features: Two-stage trigger; injection-molded, Monte Carlo Griptonite composite stock; matte bead blasted blued metalwork; hammer-forged barrel
MSRP.....................$649

WEATHERBY VANGUARD 2 SPORTER

WEATHERBY VANGUARD 2 SPORTER DBM

WEATHERBY VANGUARD 2 SYNTHETIC

RIFLES

Weatherby

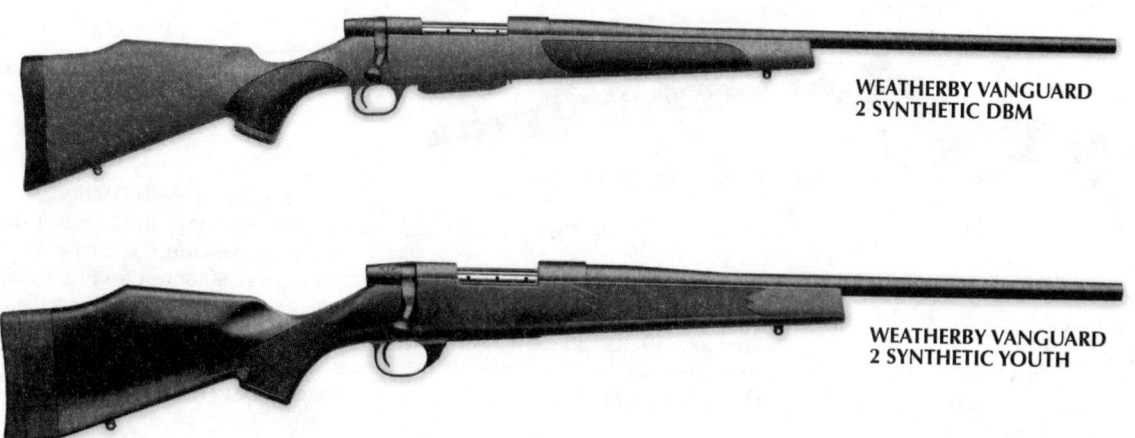

WEATHERBY VANGUARD 2 SYNTHETIC DBM

WEATHERBY VANGUARD 2 SYNTHETIC YOUTH

VANGUARD 2 SYNTHETIC DBM

Action: Bolt
Stock: Injection-molded Monte Carlo
Barrel: 24 in.
Sights: None
Weight: 7 lb. 4 oz.
Caliber: .25-06 Rem., .270 Win., .30-06 Spfd.
Magazine: Detachable box, 3 rounds
Features: Matte bead blasted blued metalwork; low density recoil pad; two-stage trigger
MSRP $749

VANGUARD 2 SYNTHETIC YOUTH

Action: Bolt
Stock: Injection-molded Monte Carlo
Barrel: 20 in.
Sights: None
Weight: 6 lb. 8 oz.
Caliber: .223 Rem., .22-250 Rem., .243 Win., 7mm-08 Rem., .308 Win.
Magazine: Internal box, 5 rounds
Features: Removable spacer to allow stock to be lengthened as shooter grows; low-density recoil pad; two-stage trigger
MSRP $599

VANGUARD 2 TRR RC (RANGE CERTIFIED)

Action: Bolt
Stock: Composite
Barrel: 22 in.
Sights: None
Weight: 8 lb. 12 oz.
Caliber: .223 Rem., .308 Win.
Magazine: 5+1 rounds
Features: Match quality, two-stage trigger; includes factory-shot target certified and signed by Ed Weatherby and special RC engraved floorplate; hand-laminated Monte Carlo composite stock with aluminum bedding plate, beavertail forearm, and Pachmayr decelerator pad
MSRP $1199

VANGUARD 2 VARMINT SPECIAL

Action: Bolt
Stock: Composite
Barrel: 22 in.
Sights: None
Weight: 8 lb. 12 oz.
Caliber: .223 Rem., .22-250 Rem., .308 Win.
Magazine: Box, 5+1 rounds
Features: Adjustable trigger; Monte Carlo composite stock in Griptonite; matte bead blasted blued metalwork; features recessed target crown to enhance accuracy and protect rifling
MSRP $849

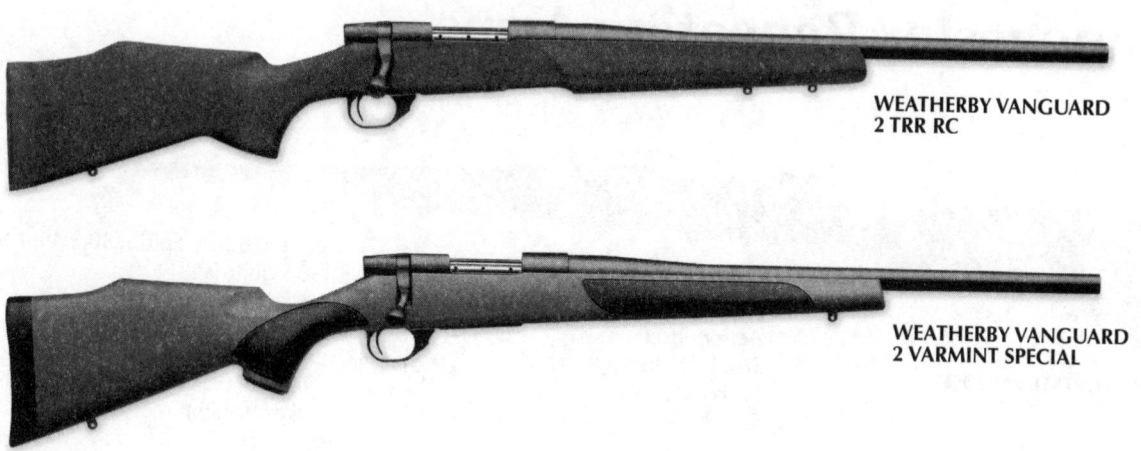

WEATHERBY VANGUARD 2 TRR RC

WEATHERBY VANGUARD 2 VARMINT SPECIAL

Wild West Guns

WILD WEST GUNS ALASKAN CO-PILOT

ALASKAN CO-PILOT
Action: Lever
Stock: Walnut
Barrel: 16 in., 18.5 in., 20 in.
Sights: Fiber optic front bead, ghost ring sight

Weight: 6 lb. 8 oz.
Caliber: .457 Mag., .45-70, .50 Alaskan, .30-30, .35 Rem., .44 Mag., .357, .45 Colt
Magazine: Under-barrel tube

Features: 1859 Marlin Action; features the trigger happy kit; Pachmayr decelerator pad; includes soft carry case; WWG recoil control porting system; WWG bear proof ejector installed; Mil-Spec Parkerized, stainless, or matte blue finish
Base price:. **$2400**

Wilson Combat

RECON TACTICAL
Action: Semiautomatic
Stock: Synthetic tactical
Barrel: 16 in.
Sights: Optional rail
Weight: 7 lb.
Caliber: 5.56mm, 6.8 SPC, .300 Blackout, 7.62x40WT, .458 SOCOM
Magazine: Detachable box, 30 rounds
Features: Match grade medium weight stainnless steel barrel; forged 7075 upper (flat top) and lower receiver; mid-length gas system with low-profile gas block; Wilson Combat T.R.I.M. rail; ergo pistol grip
MSRP. . . . . **$2250–$2600**

WILSON COMBAT RECON TACTICAL

Winchester Repeating Arms

WINCHESTER MODEL 70 ALASKAN

MODEL 70 ALASKAN
Action: Bolt
Stock: Walnut
Barrel: 25 in.
Sights: Open
Weight: 8 lb. 8 oz.

Caliber: .30-06 Spfd., .300 Win. Mag. .338 Win. Mag.
Magazine: None
Features: Satin finish Monte Carlo walnut stock with cut checkering; folding adjustable rear sight with hooded gold bead front sight; recessed target crown
MSRP. **$1269.99**

Winchester Repeating Arms

WINCHESTER MODEL 70 COYOTE LIGHT

MODEL 70 COYOTE LIGHT

Action: Bolt
Stock: Composite
Barrel: 24 in.
Sights: None
Weight: 7 lb. 8 oz.
Caliber: .22-250 Rem., .243 Win., .308 Win., .300 WSM, .270 WSM, 7mm WSM, .325 WSM
Magazine: 3 rounds
Features: Bipod mounting studs; matte-blued receiver and medium-heavy fluted stainless barrel mount; Pachmayr Decelerator
MSRP . . . . $1099.99–$1149.99

WINCHESTER MODEL 70 FEATHERWEIGHT COMPACT

MODEL 70 FEATHERWEIGHT COMPACT

Action: Bolt
Stock: Walnut
Barrel: 20 in.
Sights: None
Weight: 6 lb. 8 oz.
Caliber: .22-250 Rem., .243 Win., 7mm-08 Rem., .308 Win.
Magazine: 5 rounds
Features: Pachmayr decelerator recoil pad; action is drilled and tapped for optics
MSRP $879.99

WINCHESTER MODEL 70 SAFARI EXPRESS

WINCHESTER MODEL 70 ULTIMATE SHADOW

MODEL 70 SAFARI EXPRESS

Action: Bolt
Stock: Satin-finished checkered walnut with deluxe cheekpiece
Barrel: 24 in.
Sights: Hooded-blade front and express-style rear
Weight: 9 lb.
Caliber: .375 H&H Mag., .416 Rem. Mag., .458 Win. Mag.
Magazine: 3 rounds
Features: Pre-'64 type claw extractor; Pachmayr decelerator recoil pad; barrel band front swivel base; dual recoil lugs and three-position safety; MOA trigger system; matte blued finish; two steel cross-bolts and one-piece steel trigger guard and hinged floor plate
MSRP $1419.99

MODEL 70 ULTIMATE SHADOW

Action: Bolt
Stock: Composite
Barrel: 22 in., 24 in., 26 in.
Sights: None
Weight: 6 lb. 12 oz.–7 lb. 4 oz.
Caliber: .300 WSM, .270 WSM, .243 Win., 7mm-08 Rem., .308 Win., .25-06 Rem., .270 Win., .30-06 Spfd., .264 Win. Mag., 7mm Rem. Mag., .300 Win. Mag., .338 Win. Mag., .325 WSM
Magazine: 3 rounds
Features: Features integrated, rubberized oval-dot gripping surfaces; pistol grip; controlled round feed action
MSRP . . . . $759.99–$799.99

Winchester Repeating Arms

MODEL 94 SHORT RIFLE

Action: Lever
Stock: Walnut
Barrel: 20 in.
Sights: Front, adjustable rear
Weight: 6 lb. 12 oz.
Caliber: .30-30 Win., .38-50 Win.
Magazine: Under-barrel tube, 7 rounds
Features: Straight grip; rifle-style fore-arm and black grip cap; semi-buck-horn rear sights, Marble Arms gold-bead front sight; drilled and tapped for optics
MSRP **$1229.99**

WINCHESTER MODEL 94 SHORT RIFLE

MODEL 94 SPORTER

Action: Lever
Stock: Walnut
Barrel: 24 in.
Sights: Marble Arms front, adjustable rear
Weight: 7 lb. 8 oz.
Caliber: .30-30 Win., .38-55 Win.
Magazine: 8 rounds
Features: Half-round, half-octagon blued barrel; straight grip stock with a crescent butt and finely checkered blued-steel buttplate with double-line bordering; drilled and tapped for optics
MSRP **$1399.99**

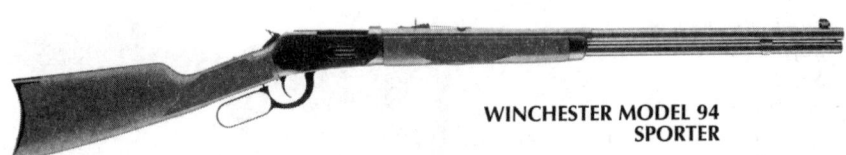

WINCHESTER MODEL 94 SPORTER

MODEL 94 TRAILS END TAKEDOWN

Action: Lever
Stock: Walnut
Barrel: 20 in.
Sights: Adjustable
Weight: 6 lb. 12 oz.

WINCHESTER MODEL 94 TRAILS END TAKEDOWN

Caliber: .30-30 Win., .450 Marlin
Magazine: 2 rounds
Features: Walnut stock and forearm with satin finish and straight-grip styling; blued steel receiver and barrel; Marble Arms front sight with semi-buckhorn rear sight; Pachmayr Decelerator recoil pad (450 model)
MSRP **$1459.99**

MODEL 1886 SHORT RIFLE

Action: Lever
Stock: Walnut
Barrel: 20 in., 24 in.
Sights: Front with brass bead, adjustable rear
Weight: 8 lb. 6 oz.
Caliber: .45-70 Govt.
Magazine: Tubular mag., 6 rounds
Features: Deeply blued receiver and lever; end cap and steel crescent butt-plate; straight grip
MSRP **$1339.99**

MODEL 1892 CARBINE

Action: Lever
Stock: Walnut
Barrel: 20 in.
Sights: Front, adjustable rear
Weight: 6 lb.
Caliber: .45 Long Colt, .44-40 Win., .44 Mag., .357 Mag.
Magazine: 10 rounds
Features: Round, deeply blued finish on receiver and lever; straight grip and satin walnut finish
MSRP **$1159.99**

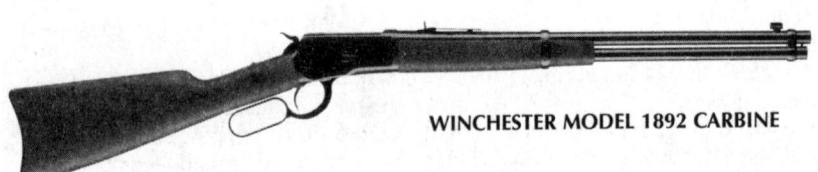

WINCHESTER MODEL 1886 SHORT RIFLE

WINCHESTER MODEL 1892 CARBINE

AirForce Airguns

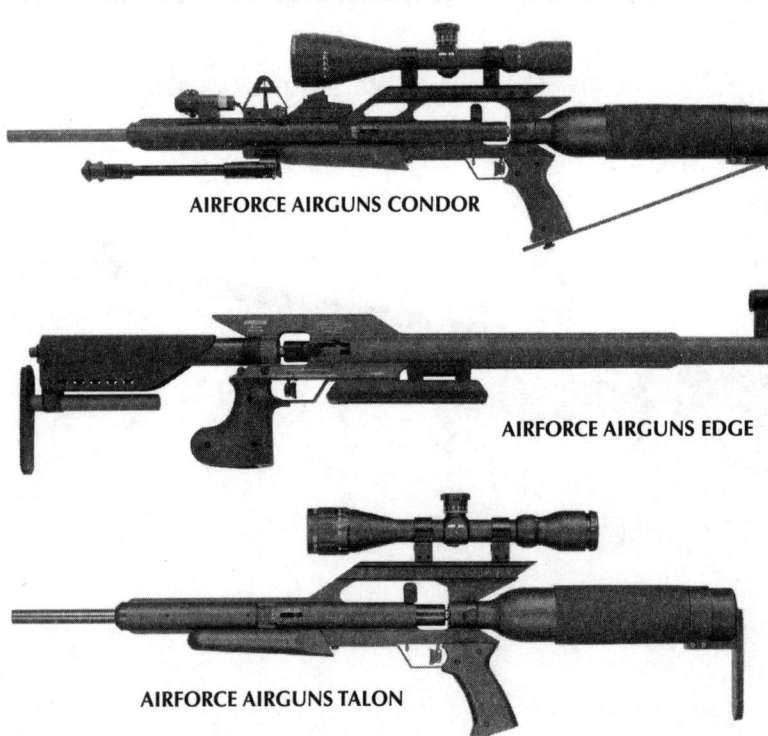

AIRFORCE AIRGUNS CONDOR

AIRFORCE AIRGUNS EDGE

AIRFORCE AIRGUNS TALON

CONDOR
Power: Pre-charged pneumatic, user adjustable
Stock: Composite
Overall Length: 38.7 in.
Sights: None
Weight: 6 lb. 8 oz.
Caliber: .25, .22, .20, .177
Features: Black, red, or blue composite stock; integral extended scope rail; detachable air tank; Lothar Walther barrel; pressure relief device; adjustable power; scopes optional
Quick-Detach:. **$689.50**
Spin-Loc: **$709.50**

TALON
Power: Compressed air
Stock: Composite
Overall Length: 32.6 in.
Sights: None
Weight: 5 lb. 8 oz.
Caliber: .25, .22, .20, .177
Features: Lothar Walther barrel; pressure relief device; adjustable power; detachable air tank; black composite stock; scopes optional
Quick-Detach:. **$562**
Spin-Loc: **$582**

EDGE
Power: Pre-charged pneumatic
Stock: Composite
Overall Length: 35–40 in.
Sights: TS1 peep sight system
Weight: 6 lb. 2 oz.
Caliber: .177
Features: Ambidextrous cocking knob; regulated air system; adjustable length of pull; adjustable forend; hooded front sight only or front and rear sight available; two-stage adjustable trigger; composite stock in red or blue finish; scopes optional
Front sight: **$545.95**
Rear & front sights: **$679.95**

TALON P
Power: Compressed air
Stock: Composite
Overall Length: 24 in.
Sights: None
Weight: 3 lb. 8 oz.
Caliber: .25
Features: Designed to deliver over 50 ft.-lbs. of energy with a .25-caliber hunting pellet; integral extended scope rail; Lothar Walther barrels; scopes optional
Quick-Detach:. **$433.50**
Spin-Loc: **$453.50**

TALON SS
Power: Compressed air
Stock: Composite
Overall Length: 32.7 in.
Sights: None
Weight: 5 lb. 4 oz.
Caliber: .25, .22, .20, .177
Features: Improved sound reduction; Lothar Walther barrel; pressure relief device; adjustable power; detachable air tank; black, red, or blue composite stock; multiple mounting rails; two-stage trigger; innovative muzzle cap that strips away air turbulence and reduces discharge sound levels; scopes optional
Quick-Detach:. **$585**
Spin-Loc: **$605**

AIRFORCE AIRGUNS
TALON P

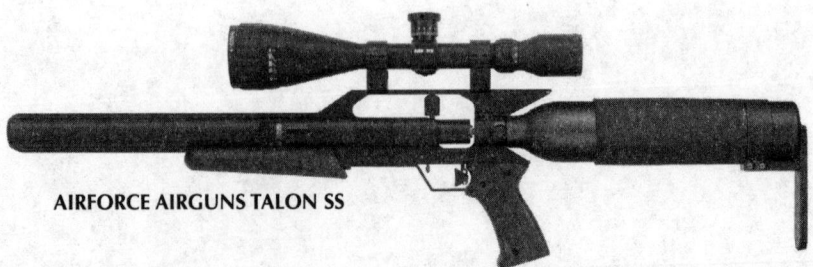

AIRFORCE AIRGUNS TALON SS

J. G. Anschütz

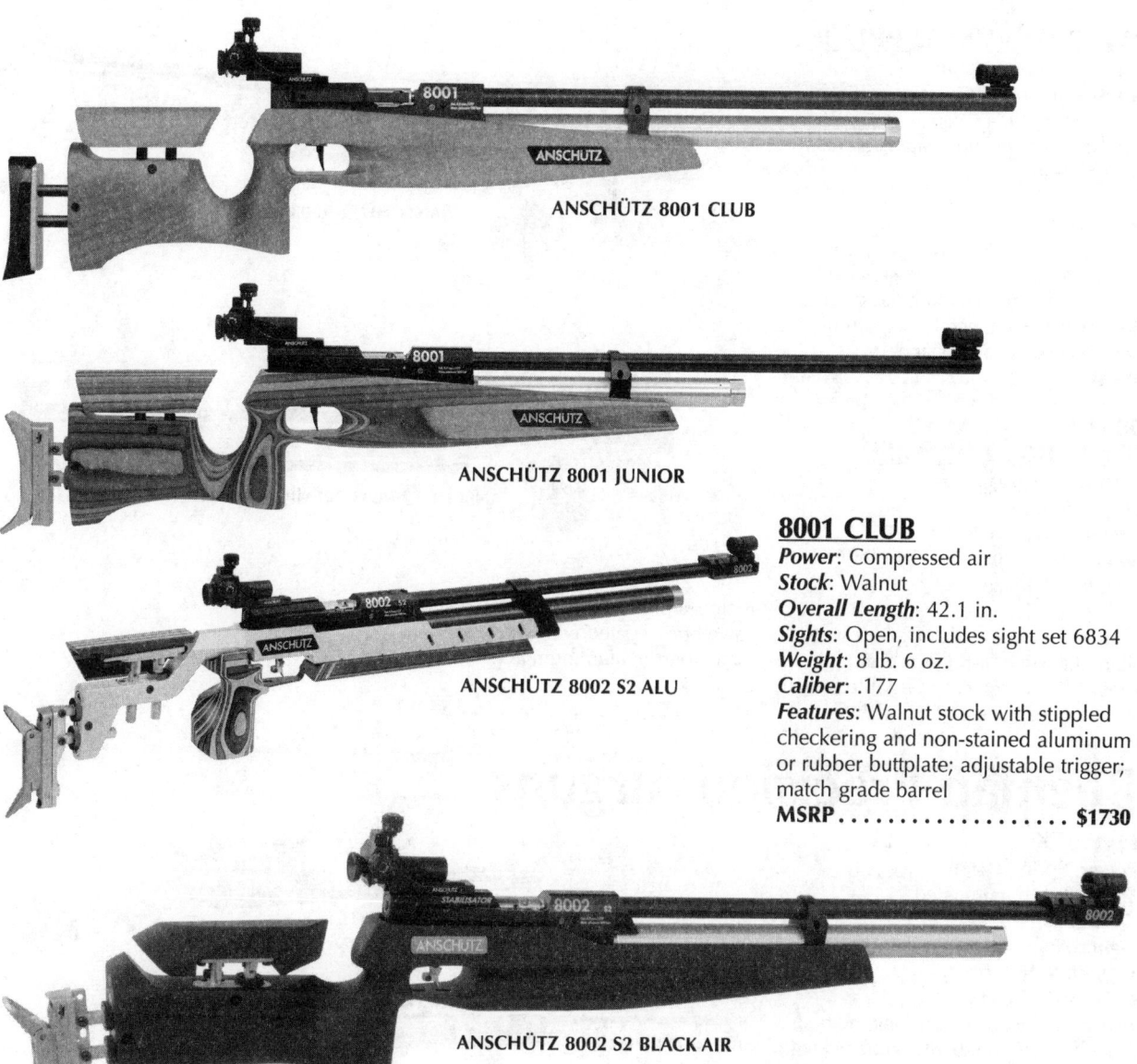

ANSCHÜTZ 8001 CLUB

ANSCHÜTZ 8001 JUNIOR

ANSCHÜTZ 8002 S2 ALU

ANSCHÜTZ 8002 S2 BLACK AIR

8001 CLUB
Power: Compressed air
Stock: Walnut
Overall Length: 42.1 in.
Sights: Open, includes sight set 6834
Weight: 8 lb. 6 oz.
Caliber: .177
Features: Walnut stock with stippled checkering and non-stained aluminum or rubber buttplate; adjustable trigger; match grade barrel
MSRP................... **$1730**

8001 JUNIOR
Power: Compressed air
Stock: Laminate
Overall Length: 37.4 in.
Sights: Open, includes sight set 6834
Weight: 8 lb. 2 oz.
Caliber: .177
Features: Laminated wood in blue and orange with aluminum buttplate stock; cylindrical match grade barrel; comes with accessory box
MSRP................... **$1859**

8002 S2 ALU
Power: Compressed air
Stock: Aluminum and synthetic pistol grip or laminated wood pistol grip
Overall Length: 42.1 in.
Sights: Open, includes sight set 6834
Weight: 10 lb. 2 oz.
Caliber: .177
Features: Aluminum stock in silver and blue with laminated wood or synthetic pistol grip; blue air cylinder; ProGrip cheekpiece and forend; includes accessory box; aluminum accessory rail
Aluminum: **$2564**
Wood: **$2244**

8002 S2 BLACK AIR
Power: Compressed air
Stock: Plastic
Length: 43.3 in.
Sights: Rear, turnable front
Weight: 9 lb. 8 oz.
Caliber: .177
Features: IWA special edition equipped with new Anschütz SOFT-Grip stock, combining the vibration damping and recoil absorbing characteristics of a naturally grown wooden stock with the characteristics of an easy-care and weather-proof plastic stock; match barrel; aluminum buttplate; cheekpiece; two-stage trigger
MSRP................... **$2308**

J. G. Anschütz

9003 PREMIUM S2 PRECISE

Power: Compressed air
Stock: Aluminum
Overall Length: 43.7 in.
Sights: Open, includes sight set 6834
Weight: 9 lb. 15 oz.
Caliber: .177
Features: Silver/black aluminum stock pistol grip; Soft Link shock absorber pads; adjustable forend stock, cheekpiece, and buttplate; includes plastic rifle case; steel match barrel; aluminum accessory rail on stock
MSRP **$4040**

9003 PREMIUM S2 BENCHREST PRECISE

Power: Compressed air
Stock: Aluminum
Length: 39.96 in.
Sights: Open, includes sight set 6834
Weight: 11 lb. 11 oz.
Caliber: .177
Features: Aluminum stock with wedge-shaped design; pistol grip; Soft Link shock absorber pads; adjustable forend stock, cheekpiece and buttplate;

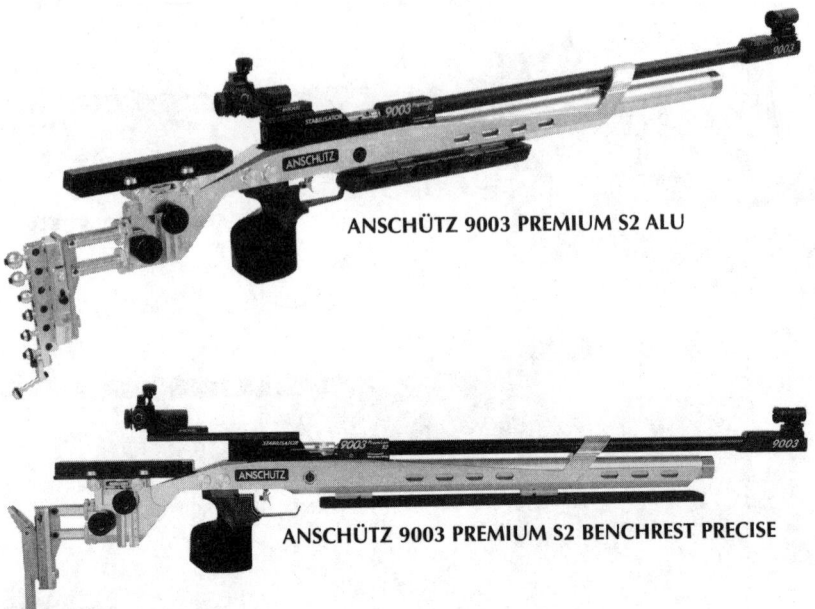

ANSCHÜTZ 9003 PREMIUM S2 ALU

ANSCHÜTZ 9003 PREMIUM S2 BENCHREST PRECISE

includes plastic rifle case; valve and valve body coated with gold; steel match barrel; aluminum accessory rail on stock
MSRP **$4040**

Beeman Precision Airguns

HW 97K

Power: Spring piston
Stock: Beech, laminated
Overall Length: 44.1 in.
Sights: Adjustable
Weight: 9 lb. 6 oz.
Caliber: .177, .20, .22
Features: Underlever cocking method; blued steel action, barrel, and cocking lever; stippling on the pistol grip and forearm; soft rubber recoil pad; grooved receiver for optical sights; adjustable two-stage trigger; automatic safety
Blue: **$839.95**
Elite: **$889.95**
Thumbhole: **$890**

MODEL R1 SUPERMAGNUM, R1 SUPERMAGNUM CARBINE

Power: Spring piston
Stock: Hardwood
Overall Length: 45.2 in., 42 in.
Sights: Adjustable
Weight: 8 lb. 5 oz.–8 lb. 13 oz.
Caliber: .22, .20, .177; Carbine: .177, .20

BEEMAN HW 97K ELITE

BEEMAN R1 ELITE

BEEMAN R9 ELITE

Features: Beech-stained hardwood stock; adjustable two-stage trigger; automatic safety
Carbine: **$734.95**
MSRP **$749.95**

MODEL R9, R9 ELITE

Power: Spring piston
Stock: Hardwood
Overall Length: 43 in.
Sights: Adjustable
Weight: 7 lb. 5 oz.–7 lb. 8 oz.

Caliber: .20, .177
Features: Beech-stained hardwood stock with Monte Carlo cheekpiece; ambidextrous rifle; soft rubber buttplate; adjustable two-stage trigger; automatic safety; R9 Elite has hand checkered panels, pistol cap, carved Monte Carlo cheekpiece, and interchangeable globe front sight
MSRP **$549.95**
Elite: **$669.95**

  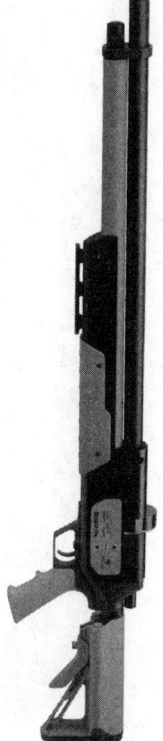 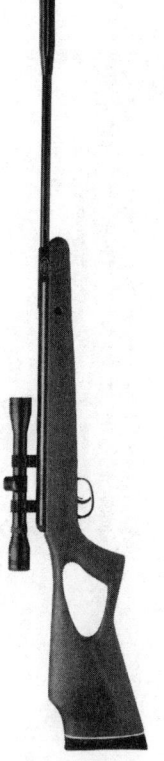 

CROSMAN BENJAMIN DISCOVERY

CROSMAN BENJAMIN MAV 77 UNDERLEVER AIR RIFLE

CROSMAN BENJAMIN ROGUE .357

CROSMAN BENJAMIN TITAN NP

CROSMAN CHALLENGER PCP

BENJAMIN DISCOVERY

Power: Dual fuel compressed air
Stock: Walnut
Overall Length: 39 in.
Sights: Fiber optic front, adjustable rear
Weight: 5 lb. 2 oz.–5 lb. 3 oz.
Caliber: .22, .177
Features: Rifled steel barrel; velocity up to 900 fps; cross-bolt safety; built-in pressure gauge; high pressure pump included
MSRP $409

BENJAMIN MAV 77 UNDERLEVER AIR RIFLE

Power: Spring piston
Stock: Hardwood
Length: 42 in.
Sights: 3-9x32mm scope included
Weight: 8 lb. 14 oz.
Caliber: .177
Features: Fixed barrel design; rifled barrel; two-stage trigger; ambidextrous hardwood stock; includes 3-9x32mm CenterPoint precision scope with a

Mil-Dot reticle; delivers velocities up to 1100 fps with alloy pellets
MSRP $530

BENJAMIN ROGUE .357

Power: Electro pre-charged pneumatic
Stock: Synthetic
Overall Length: 48 in.
Sights: None
Weight: 9 lb. 8 oz.
Caliber: .357
Features: Uses electronic valve technology to provide precise regulation of pressure and provide more shots per fill through the control of pressure; rifled steel barrel; velocity up to 700–1000 fps; built in LCD screen to control eValve and trigger; sling studs; fill adaptor; degassing tool; magazine holds six shots
MSRP $1349

BENJAMIN TITAN NP

Power: Nitro piston
Stock: Hardwood
Length: 43 in., 44.5 in.

Sights: 4x32mm scope included
Weight: 6 lb. 10 oz.–6 lb. 14 oz.
Caliber: .177, .22
Features: Powered by Nitro Piston technology; delivers velocities up to 1200 fps (.177) with alloy pellets; included 4x32mm scope; ambidextrous hardwood stock with thumbhole; two-stage adjustable trigger; ventilated rubber recoil pad
MSRP $159.99

CHALLENGER PCP

Power: Pneumatic pump and CO2
Stock: Synthetic
Overall Length: 41.5 in.
Sights: Open
Weight: 7 lb. 2 oz.
Caliber: .177
Features: Two-stage match grade adjustable trigger; Lothar Walther barrel; adjustable cheekpiece and butt-piece; black synthetic stock; 11mm scope mount rails; ambidextrous
MSRP $529.99

Crosman

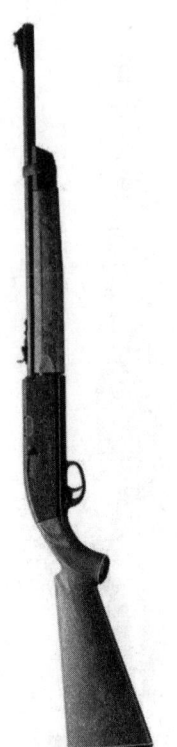

CROSMAN CLASSIC 2100

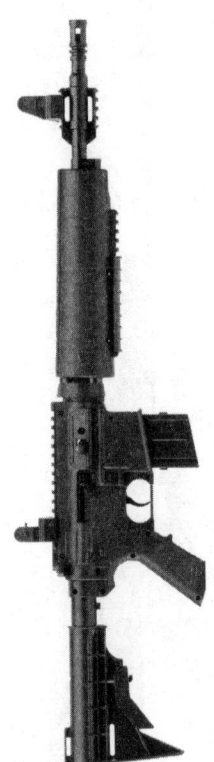

CROSMAN M4-177

CROSMAN MARAUDER

CROSMAN OPTIMUS

CROSMAN PHANTOM 1000

CLASSIC 2100
Power: Pneumatic pump
Stock: Synthetic
Overall Length: 39.75 in.
Sights: Visible impact front, adjustable rear
Weight: 4 lb. 13 oz.
Caliber: .177
Features: Cross-bolt safety; BB up to 755 fps, pellet up to 725 fps
MSRP $69.99

M4-177 RIFLE
Power: Multi-pump pneumatic
Stock: Synthetic
Length: 34 in.
Sights: Adjustable front and rear
Weight: 3 lb. 9 oz.
Caliber: .177
Features: Rifled steel barrel; shoots both pellets and BBs; variable pump action easy to use for right- or left-handed shooters; Picatinny rails; front and rear sights and stock are removable for upgrades; adjustable stock; velocities up to 660 fps with BBs

and 625 fps with 7.9gr, .177 caliber pellets
MSRP $75

MARAUDER
Power: Pre-charged pneumatic
Stock: Hardwood
Overall Length: 42.5 in.
Sights: None
Weight: 7 lb. 2 oz.
Caliber: .177, .22, .25
Features: Crosman custom choked barrel and internal shroud for unsurpassed accuracy and ultra quiet operation; two-stage adjustable match grade trigger; rifle can be filled with Benjamin hand pump or a high pressure tank; velocity up to 1100 fps; ambidextrous hardwood stock
MSRP . . . . $509.99–$529.99

OPTIMUS
Power: Break action
Stock: Hardwood
Overall Length: 43 in.
Sights: 4x32mm CenterPoint scope

Weight: 6 lb. 8 oz.
Caliber: .177, .22
Features: Ambidextrous hardwood stock; relatively light cocking force and a two-stage adjustable trigger; velocities of up to 1200 fps with alloy pellets; barrel incorporates a micro-adjustable rear sight and fiber optic front sight
MSRP $139

PHANTOM 1000
Power: Spring piston
Stock: Synthetic
Overall Length: 44.5 in.
Sights: Fiber optic front, adjustable rear
Weight: 6 lb.
Caliber: .177
Features: All-weather, synthetic black stock and forearm; checkered grip and forearm; velocity up to 1000 fps; rifled steel barrel; two-stage adjustable trigger
MSRP $99.99

AIR RIFLES

Crosman

CROSMAN PUMPMASTER 760

CROSMAN RECRUIT

CROSMAN REPEATAIR 1077

CROSMAN TR77

CROSMAN VANTAGE NP

PUMPMASTER 760

Power: Pneumatic pump
Stock: Synthetic
Overall Length: 33.5 in.
Sights: Fiber optic front, adjustable rear
Weight: 2 lb. 12 oz.
Caliber: .177
Features: Cross-bolt safety; BB up to 625 fps; pellet up to 600 fps
MSRP. $43.99

RECRUIT

Power: Pneumatic pump
Stock: Synthetic
Overall Length: 38.25 in.
Sights: Fiber optic front, adjustable rear
Weight: 2 lb. 15 oz.

Caliber: .177
Features: Adjustable buttstock; adjustable synthetic stock; 11mm dovetail scope rail; cross-bolt safety
MSRP. $69.99

REPEATAIR 1077

Power: CO2
Stock: All-weather, synthetic
Overall Length: 36.88 in.
Sight: Fiber optic front, adjustable rear
Weight: 3 lb. 11 oz.
Caliber: .177
Features: Exclusive 12-shot rotary pellet clip lets you shoot longer; maximum velocity 625 fps; cross-bolt safety
MSRP. $89.99

TR77

Power: Nitro piston
Stock: Synthetic
Length: 41.5 in.

Sights: Fiber optic front, adjustable rear
Weight: 6 lb.
Caliber: .177
Features: Tactical break air rifle with military styling and all-weather tactical, synthetic stock; two-stage adjustable trigger; pistol grip; includes CenterPoint 4x32mm scope; velocities up to 1000 fps
MSRP. $149.95

VANTAGE NP

Power: Break action
Stock: Hardwood
Length: 45 in.
Sights: Fiber optic front, adjustable rear 4x32mm scope included
Weight: 7 lb. 2 oz.
Caliber: .177
Features: Crosman's own version of the Bantage NP; hardwood stock; fiber optic front sight and fully adjustable rear sight
MSRP. $160

Daisy

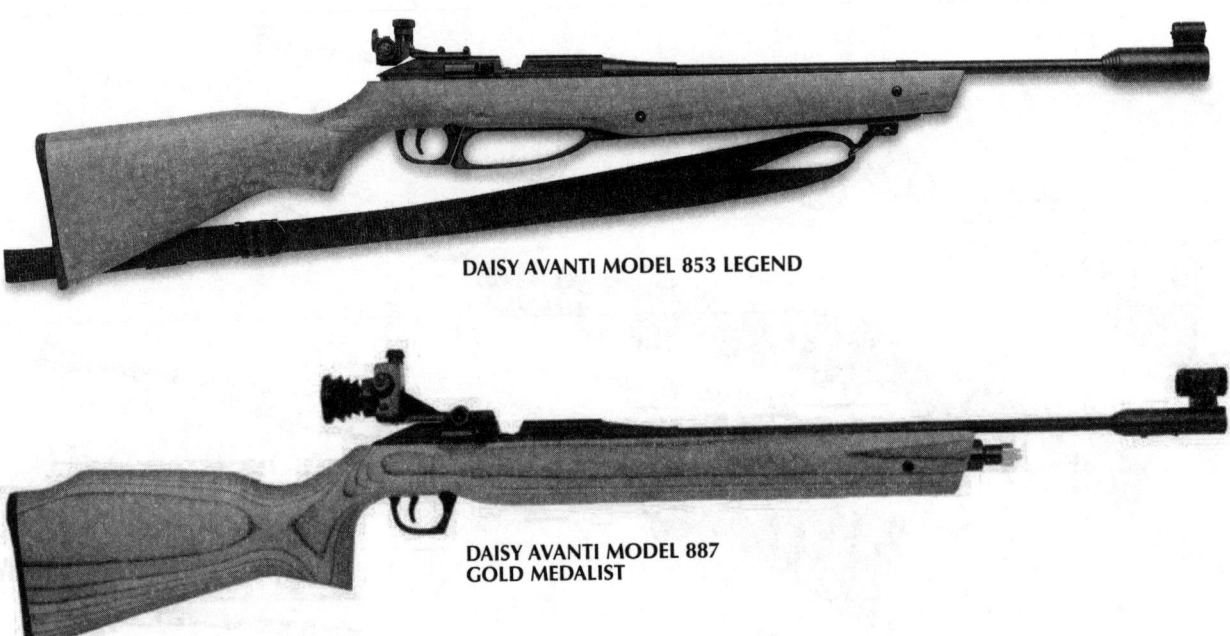

DAISY AVANTI MODEL 853 LEGEND

DAISY AVANTI MODEL 887
GOLD MEDALIST

AVANTI MODEL 853 LEGEND

Power: Single-pump pneumatic
Stock: Hardwood
Overall Length: 38.5 in.
Sights: Hooded front with interchangeable aperture inserts, micrometer adjustable rear
Weight: 5 lb. 8 oz.
Caliber: .177

Features: Diecast receiver with dovetail scope mount; Lothar Walther rifled high-grade steel barrel; full-length, sporter-style hardwood with adjustable length
MSRP **$399.99**

AVANTI MODEL 887 GOLD MEDALIST

Power: CO2 single shot bolt
Stock: Laminated hardwood

Overall Length: 39.5 in.
Sights: Front globe with changeable aperture inserts, rear diopter with micrometer
Weight: 7 lb. 5 oz.
Caliber: .177
Features: Laminated hardwood stock; Lothar Walther rifled high-grade steel barrel; manual, cross-bolt trigger block; includes scope rail adapter
MSRP **$499.99**

DAISY POWERLINE MODEL 880

POWERLINE MODEL 880

Power: Multi-pump pneumatic
Stock: Molded wood grain
Overall Length: 37.6 in.
Sights: TruGlo fiber optic front, adjustable rear
Weight: 3 lb. 11 oz.

Caliber: .177
Features: Wood-grained, Monte Carlo stock and forearm; rifled steel barrel; cross-bolt trigger block; velocity up to 750 fps; engineering resin with dovetail mount for scope
MSRP **$49.99**

AIR RIFLES

Daisy

DAISY POWERLINE MODEL 901

DAISY POWERLINE TARGETPRO 953

DAISY WINCHESTER M-14

DAISY WINCHESTER MODEL 77XS

POWERLINE MODEL 901

Power: Multi-pump pneumatic
Stock: Composite
Overall Length: 37.5 in.
Sights: Fiber optic front, adjustable rear
Weight: 3 lb. 11 oz.
Caliber: .177
Features: Rifled steel barrel; black advanced composite stock; dovetail mounts for optics
MSRP **$69.99**

POWERLINE TARGETPRO 953

Power: Pneumatic single-pump cocking lever
Stock: Composite
Overall Length: 37.75 in.

Sights: Front and rear fiber optic
Weight: 6 lb. 6 oz.
Caliber: .177
Features: Full-length, match-style black composite stock; rifled high-grade steel barrel; diecast metal receiver; manual cross-bolt trigger block with red indicator
MSRP **$119.99**

WINCHESTER M-14

Power: CO2 semiautomatic
Stock: Composite
Length: 44.5 in.
Sights: Blade front, adjustable rear
Weight: 4 lb. 6 oz.
Caliber: .177
Features: Dual ammo BB or pellet rifle; rifled steel barrel; adjustable rear

sight, fixed front sight; brown composite stock; 700 fps maximum velocity
MSRP **$219.99**

WINCHESTER MODEL 77XS

Power: Multi-pump pneumatic
Stock: Composite
Length: 37.6 in.
Sights: TruGlo fiber optic front, adjustable rear
Weight: 3 lb. 2 oz.
Caliber: .177
Features: Rifled steel barrel; TruGlo fiber optic front, adjustable rear sight; 4x32mm air rifle scope included; black composite stock; 800 fps maximum velocity
MSRP **$129.99**

Gamo USA

BIG CAT 1250

Power: Break action/spring piston
Stock: Synthetic
Overall Length: 43.3 in.
Sights: 4x32mm scope
Weight: 6 lb. 2 oz.
Caliber: .177
Features: Tough all-weather molded synthetic stock; ventilated rubber pad for recoil; twin cheekpads; non-slip texture design on grip and forearm; manual trigger system; fluted barrel; two-stage adjustable trigger
MSRP **$199.95**

GAMO BIG CAT 1250

GAMO RECON WHISPER

RECON WHISPER

Power: Break action/spring piston
Stock: Synthetic
Overall Length: 37.2 in.
Sights: 4x20mm scope
Weight: 4 lb. 10 oz.
Caliber: .177
Features: All-weather black molded synthetic stock; ventilated rubber butt-pad; twin cheekpads; automatic cocking safety system; 525 fps maximum velocity
MSRP **$119.95**

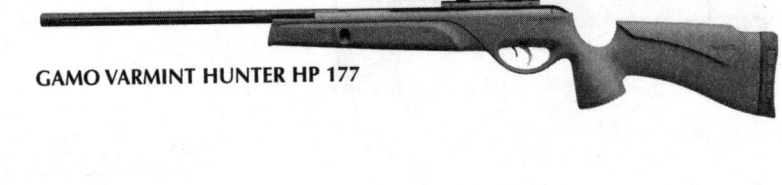

GAMO VARMINT HUNTER HP 177

VARMINT HUNTER HP 177

Power: Break action/spring piston
Stock: Synthetic
Length: 43.78 in.
Sights: Mounted 4x32mm scope
Weight: 6 lb. 10 oz.
Caliber: .177
Features: Lightweight synthetic stock; match grade fluted barrel; 1400 fps maximum velocity; 4x32mm air rifle scope with laser sight and flashlight; break barrel single cocking system
MSRP **$299.95**

GAMO WHISPER

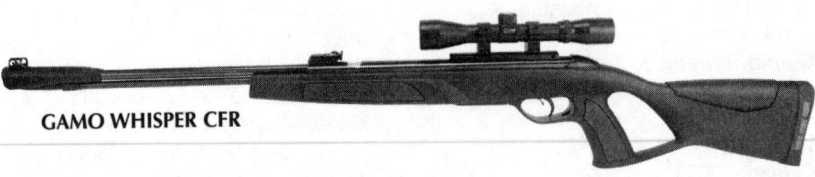

GAMO WHISPER CFR

WHISPER

Power: Break action/spring piston
Stock: Synthetic
Overall Length: 37.2 in.
Sights: Mounted scope with rings
Weight: 4 lb. 10 oz.
Caliber: .177
Features: Raised rail scope mount with 39x40mm scope; two-stage adjustable trigger; manual safety; non-removable noise dampener; black synthetic all-weather stock; ventilated rubber butt-plate; non-slip checkering on grip and forearm
MSRP **$269.95**

WHISPER CFR

Power: Single shot/spring piston
Stock: Synthetic
Length: 46.85 in.
Sights: Fiber optic sights, mounted 4x32 standard reticle scope
Weight: 8 lb.
Caliber: .177
Features: First Whisper Air Rifle with a fixed barrel; integrated ND52 noise dampener system; fixed rifled steel barrel; capable of 1100 fps; newly designed recoil pad with 74 percent more recoil absorbing pressure; all-weather synthetic molded stock with thumbhole
MSRP **$329.95**

AIR RIFLES

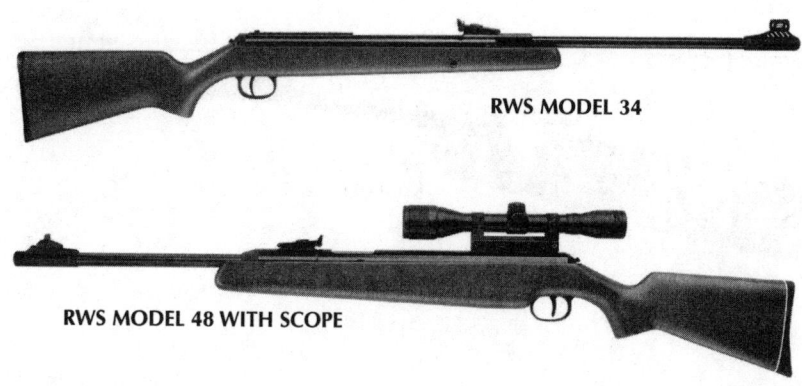

RWS MODEL 34

RWS MODEL 48 WITH SCOPE

MODEL 34

Power: Break action/spring piston
Stock: Hardwood, synthetic
Overall Length: 45 in.
Sights: 4x32mm scope
Weight: 7 lb. 8 oz.–8 lb.
Caliber: .177, .22
Features: Polished with blued metal-work; full-sized hardwood stock; two-stage adjustable trigger; automatic safety; finely rifled barrel; 34 Pro large muzzlebrake
MSRP **$362.90**
With scope: **$419.35**

MODEL 48

Power: Side lever/spring piston
Stock: Hardwood
Overall Length: 42.5 in.
Sights: Adjustable rear
Weight: 8 lb. 8 oz.
Caliber: .177
Features: Extended breech stock to reduce recoil; fixed barrel system; adjustable trigger; automatic safety; optional RWS 4x32mm scope and mounts
MSRP **$564.52**
With scope: **$625.81**

RWS MODEL 54 AIR KING

RWS MODEL 350 MAGNUM

MODEL 54 AIR KING

Power: Side lever/spring piston
Stock: Hardwood
Overall Length: 43.75 in.
Sights: Adjustable rear
Weight: 9 lb.
Caliber: .177, .22, .25
Features: Adjustable trigger; scope rail; Monte Carlo hardwood stock with cheekpiece and checkering; automatic safety; 1100 fps maximum velocity
MSRP **$846.53**
With scope: **$896.77**

MODEL 350 MAGNUM

Power: Break action/spring piston
Stock: Hardwood
Overall Length: 48.3 in.
Sights: 4x32mm scope
Weight: 8 lb. 3 oz.
Caliber: .177, .22
Features: Two-stage trigger; mounted scope rail
MSRP **$564.52**
With scope: **$625.81**

SCHÜTZE

Power: Break action/spring piston
Stock: Hardwood
Overall Length: 41 in.
Sights: TruGlo fiber optic
Weight: 5 lb. 11 oz.
Caliber: .177
Features: Classic straight hardwood stock; ambidextrous safety
MSRP **$222.56**

RWS SCHÜTZE

AIR RIFLES

Stoeger Airguns

STOEGER X-5 SYNTHETIC

STOEGER X-20 SUPPRESSOR

STOEGER X-50 AIR RIFLE COMBO

AIR RIFLES

X-5
Power: Break action/spring piston
Stock: Hardwood, black synthetic
Overall Length: 41 in.
Sights: Hooded front with red, fiber optic insert; rear fiber optic
Weight: 5 lb. 11 oz.
Caliber: .177
Features: Automatic, ambidextrous safety mounted on back of receiver; Monte Carlo-style stock; integral dovetail scope rail on receiver
MSRP **$149**

X-20 SUPPRESSOR
Power: Break action/spring piston
Stock: Black synthetic
Overall Length: 43 in.
Sights: 4x32mm illuminated red green scope
Weight: 7 lb.
Caliber: .177
Features: Air Flow Control system; adjustable two-stage trigger; integral dovetail scope rail on receiver; non-slip, deluxe rubber recoil pad; Monte Carlo-style, black synthetic stock with checkering; rifled, blued steel barrel
MSRP **$249**

X-50
Power: Break action/spring piston
Stock: Black synthetic
Overall Length: 50 in.
Sights: 3-9x40mm parallax adjustable scope with rings
Weight: 9 lb. 14 oz.
Caliber: .177
Features: Ergonomic cocking grip; rifled blued steel barrel; synthetic Monte Carlo-style stock; ambidextrous automatic safety
MSRP **$359**

AYA (Aguirre y Aranzabal)

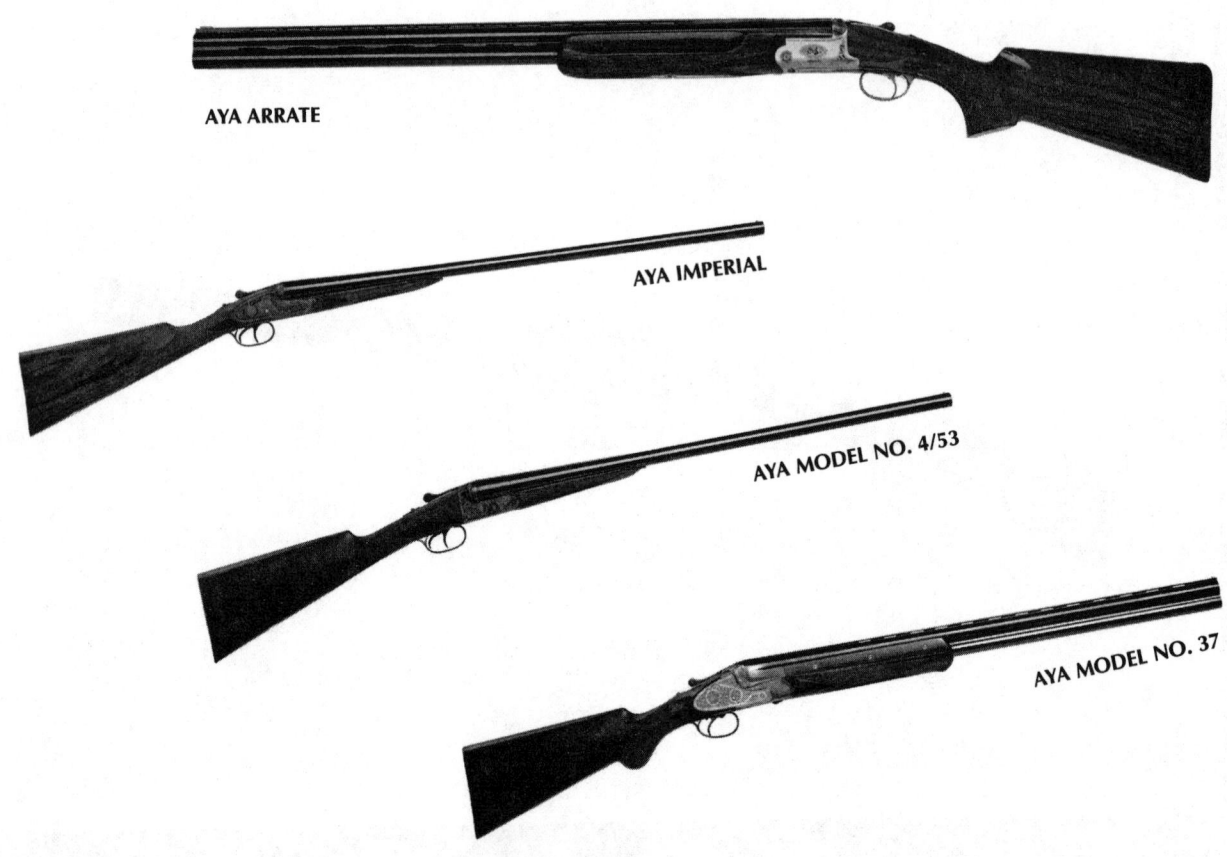

AYA ARRATE

AYA IMPERIAL

AYA MODEL NO. 4/53

AYA MODEL NO. 37

ARRATE

Action: Over/under
Stock: Walnut
Barrel: 28 in.–32 in.
Chokes: Fixed or multichokes
Weight: 6 lb. 10 oz.
Bore/Gauge: 12
Magazine: None
Features: F125 steel receiver; chrome steel barrels; detachable trigger mechanism; walnut stock AYA grade 2
From $6500

IMPERIAL

Action: Side-by-side hammerless sidelock
Stock: Walnut
Barrel: 28 in., with other lengths to order
Chokes: Screw-in tubes
Weight: 6 lb. 12 oz.
Bore/Gauge: 12, 16, 20, 28, .410
Magazine: None
Features: Forged steel action with double locking mechanism and gas vents; gold washed internal lock parts; gold lined cocking indicators; optional selective or non-selective single trigger; concave rib; straight hand, finely checkered walnut stock; gold initial oval
From $20995

MODEL NO. 4/53

Action: Side-by-side hammerless boxlock ejector
Stock: Walnut
Barrel: 28 in., with other lengths to order
Chokes: Screw-in tubes
Weight: 6 lb. 10 oz.
Bore/Gauge: 12, 16, 20, 28, .410
Magazine: None
Features: Double locking mechanism with replaceable hinge pin; disk set firing pins; double trigger; chopper lump barrels with concave rib; light scroll engraving; metal finish available in hardened, old silver, or white finish; automatic safety
From $3895

MODEL NO. 37

Action: Over/under sidelock
Stock: Walnut
Barrel: 28 in.
Chokes: Screw-in tubes
Weight: 7 lb. 8 oz.
Bore/Gauge: 12
Magazine: None
Features: Double underlocking lugs and double crossbolt; chopper lump chrome nickel steel barrels; hardened steel intercepting safety sears; gold line cocking indicators; gold washed internal lock parts; double trigger with hinged front trigger; fine rose and scroll, game scene, or bold relief engraving on action plates; full pistol grip walnut stock
From $14999

Benelli USA

CORDOBA COMFORTECH
Action: Inertia operated semiautomatic
Stock: Synthetic
Barrel: 28 in., 30 in.
Chokes: Extended Crio Chokes
Weight: 7 lb.
Bore/Gauge: 12, 20
Magazine: 4+1 rounds
Features: Black synthetic stock with GripTight; Crio ported barrels; ComforTech gel recoil pad and comb insert; heavy duty magazine cap
MSRP. . . . . **$2069–$2099**

BENELLI CORDOBA COMFORTECH

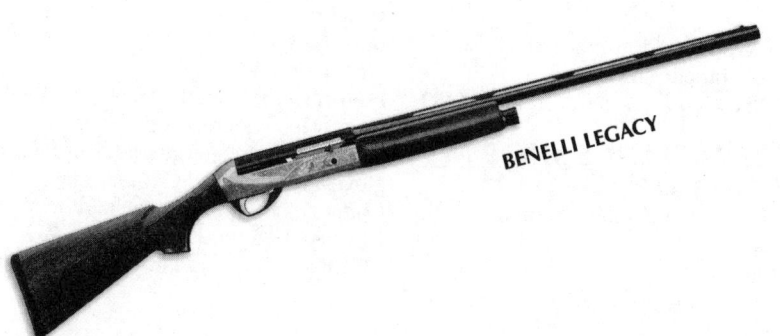

BENELLI LEGACY

LEGACY
Action: Inertia operated semiautomatic
Stock: Walnut
Barrel: 24 in., 26 in., 28 in.
Chokes: Crio Choke (C, IC, M, IM, F); 28 gauge: (C & M)
Weight: 4 lb. 14 oz.–7 lb. 6 oz.
Bore/Gauge: 12, 20, 28
Magazine: 4+1, 28 Ga.: 2+1 rounds
Features: Satin walnut with Weathercoat or AA-grade stock; classic game scene etchings on receiver; red front sight and metal bead mid sight
MSRP. . . . . **$1799–$2039**

LEGACY SPORT
Action: Inertia operated semiautomatic
Stock: Walnut
Barrel: 28 in., 30 in.
Chokes: Extended Crio Chokes (C, CI, M, IM, F)
Weight: 7 lb. 6 oz.–7 lb. 8 oz.
Bore/Gauge: 12
Magazine: 4+1 rounds
Features: Acid-etched game scenes on receiver plates; AA-grade walnut stock; red front sight and metal bead mid sight
MSRP. **$2439**

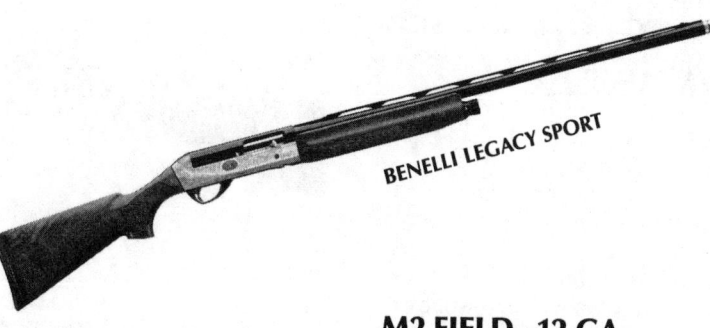

BENELLI LEGACY SPORT

M2 FIELD –12 GA.
Action: Inertia operated semiautomatic
Stock: Synthetic, Realtree APG
Barrel: 21 in., 24 in., 26 in., 28 in.
Chokes: Crio Chokes (IC, M, F)
Weight: 6 lb. 14 oz.–7 lb. 3 oz.
Bore/Gauge: 12
Magazine: 3+1rounds
Features: ComforTech gel recoil pad and comb insert; ComforTech shim kit; red bar front sight; stock comes in black synthetic, Realtree APG, and Realtree MAX-4 Camo
Synthetic: **$1359**
Realtree APG: **$1469**

BENELLI M2 FIELD –12 GA.

SHOTGUNS

Shotguns • 253

Benelli USA

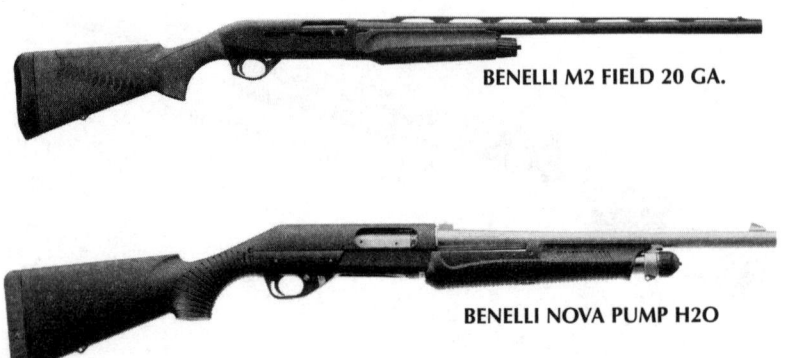

BENELLI M2 FIELD 20 GA.

BENELLI NOVA PUMP H2O

M2 FIELD 20 GA.

Action: Inertia operated semiautomatic
Stock: Synthetic
Barrel: 24 in., 26 in.
Chokes: Crio Chokes (IC, M, F)
Weight: 7 lb. 2 oz.–7 lb. 3 oz.
Bore/Gauge: 20
Magazine: 3+1 rounds
Features: ComforTech gel recoil pad and comb insert; ComforTech shim kit; red bar front sight; synthetic stock in Realtree Max-4 Camo or matte black finish
Synthetic **$1409**
Realtree APG **$1519**

NOVA PUMP H2O

Action: Pump
Stock: Synthetic
Barrel: 18.5 in.
Chokes: Fixed cylinder choke
Weight: 7 lb. 3 oz.
Bore/Gauge: 12
Magazine: 4+1 round
Features: Available with ghost-ring or open rifle sights; push-button shell stop; grooved grip surface black synthetic stock
MSRP **$669**

NOVA PUMP TACTICAL

Action: Pump
Stock: Synthetic
Barrel: 18.5 in.
Chokes: Fixed cylinder choke
Weight: 7 lb. 3 oz.
Bore/Gauge: 12
Magazine: 4+1 rounds
Features: Available with ghost-ring or open rifle sights; push-button shell stop; grooved grip surface stocks in black synthetic stock
MSRP . . . . **$419–$459**

PERFORMANCE SHOP M2 3-GUN COMFORTECH

Action: Inertia operated semiautomatic
Stock: Synthetic
Barrel: 21 in.
Chokes: Crio chokes (C, IC, M, IM, F)

Weight: 7 lb. 5 oz.
Bore/Gauge: 12
Magazine: 8+1 rounds
Features: ComforTech gel recoil pad and comb insert; ComforTech shim kit; extended magazine; ergonomic bolt release
MSRP **$2699**

PERFORMANCE SHOP SUPER BLACK EAGLE II TURKEY EDITION

Action: Inertia operated semiautomatic
Stock: Synthetic
Barrel: 24 in.
Chokes: Custom XTF extended choke
Weight: 7 lb. 2 oz.
Bore/Gauge: 12
Magazine: 3+1 rounds
Features: Burris FastFire sight; ComforTech gel recoil pad and comb insert; larger trigger guard for use with gloves; EDM ported Crio barrel; ComforTech synthetic stock with Realtree APG finish
MSRP **$2949**

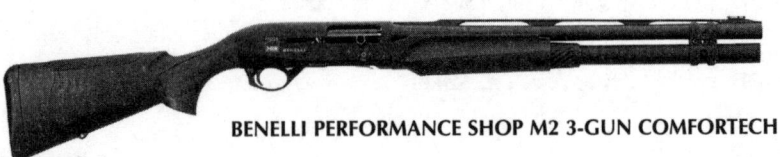

BENELLI NOVA PUMP TACTICAL

BENELLI PERFORMANCE SHOP M2 3-GUN COMFORTECH

BENELLI PERFORMANCE SHOP SUPER BLACK EAGLE II TURKEY EDITION

SHOTGUNS

Benelli USA

BENELLI SPORT II

BENELLI SUPER BLACK EAGLE II

BENELLI SUPERNOVA FIELD

BENELLI SUPERSPORT

SPORT II
Action: Inertia operated semiautomatic
Stock: Walnut
Barrel: 28 in., 30 in.
Chokes: Extended Crio Chokes (C, CI, M, IM, F)
Weight: 6 lb. 5 oz.–7 lb. 5 oz.
Bore/Gauge: 12, 20
Magazine: 4+1 rounds
Features: Red bar front sight and metal bead mid sight; Crio ported barrels; ComforTech gel recoil pad and comb insert; heavy duty magazine cap
MSRP $1899

SUPER BLACK EAGLE II
Action: Inertia operated semiautomatic
Stock: Walnut, synthetic, Realtree APG, Mossy Oak
Barrel: 24 in., 26 in., 28 in.
Chokes: Crio Choke (C, IC, M, IM, F)
Weight: 7 lb. 2 oz.–7 lb. 5 oz.
Bore/Gauge: 12
Magazine: 3+1 rounds

Features: Red bar front sight and metal bead mid sight; ComforTech gel recoil pad and comb insert; larger trigger guard for use with gloves; stock in black synthetic, Realtree Max-4 camo, Realtree APG camo, or walnut
MSRP . . . . $1569–$1999

SUPERNOVA FIELD
Action: Pump
Stock: Synthetic
Barrel: 24 in., 26 in., 28 in.
Chokes: Standard choke (IC, M, F)
Weight: 7 lb. 13 oz.–8 lb.
Bore/Gauge: 12
Magazine: 4+1 rounds
Features: Stock comes in black synthetic, Realtree APG camo, or Realtree Max-4 camo; receiver drilled and tapped for scope mounting; standard chokes; vented recoil pad
ComforTech Stock: . . . . . $549–$669
SteadyGrip Stock: $669

SUPERSPORT
Action: Inertia operated semiautomatic
Stock: Synthetic
Barrel: 28 in., 30 in.
Chokes: Extended Crio Chokes(C, IC, M, IM, F)
Weight: 6 lb. 5 oz.–7 lb. 5 oz.
Bore/Gauge: 12, 20
Magazine: 4+1 rounds
Features: Stock comes in black SuperSport carbon fiber finish; red bar front sight and metal bead mid sight; Crio ported barrels; ComforTech gel recoil pad and comb insert
MSRP $2199

Benelli USA

SUPER VINCI

Action: Inertia operated semiautomatic
Stock: Synthetic, Realtree APG
Barrel: 26 in., 28 in.
Chokes: Crio Chokes (C, IC, M, IM, F)
Weight: 6 lb. 14 oz.–7 lb.
Bore/Gauge: 12
Magazine: 3+1 rounds
Features: In-line inertia driven system; enlarged trigger and trigger guard for use with gloves; ComforTech Plus recoil pad; QuadraFit shim kit; drilled and tapped for scopes; synthetic stock in black, Realtree APG camo, or Realtree MAX-4 camo
MSRP . . . . **$1799–$1899**

ULTRA LIGHT

Action: Inertia operated semiautomatic
Stock: Walnut
Barrel: 24 in., 26 in.
Chokes: Crio Chokes (IC, M, F)
Weight: 5 lb. 3 oz.–6 lb. 2 oz.
Bore/Gauge: 12, 20, 28
Magazine: 2+1
Features: Weather coated walnut stock; red bar front sight and metal bead mid sight; gel recoil pad; option of checkered Montefeltro forend or ultra light forend
MSRP . . . . **$1669–$1799**

VINCI

Action: Inertia operated semiautomatic
Stock: Synthetic
Barrel: 24 in., 26 in., 28 in.
Chokes: Crio Chokes (C, IC, M, IM, F)
Weight: 6 lb. 13 oz.–6 lb. 14 oz.
Bore/Gauge: 12
Magazine: 3+1 rounds
Features: Stock in black, Realtree APG, Realtree APG HD SteadyGrip, or Realtree MAX-4 camo; red bar front sight and metal bead mid sight; drilled and tapped for scope mounting; ComforTech Plus recoil pads
MSRP . . . . **$1359–$1629**

VINCI CORDOBA

Action: Inertia operated semiautomatic
Stock: Synthetic with GripTight coating
Barrel: 28 in., 30 in.
Chokes: Extended Crio Chokes
Weight: 7 lb.–7 lb. 2 oz.
Bore/Gauge: 12
Magazine: 4+1 rounds
Features: Crio ported barrels; ComforTech gel recoil pad and comb insert; heavy duty magazine cap; black synthetic stock; red bar front sight and metal bead mid sight
MSRP **$2069**

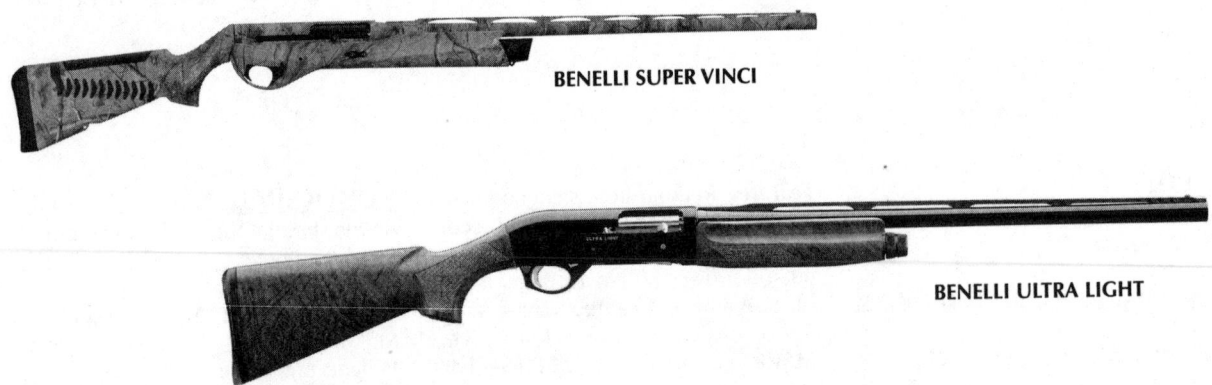

BENELLI SUPER VINCI

BENELLI ULTRA LIGHT

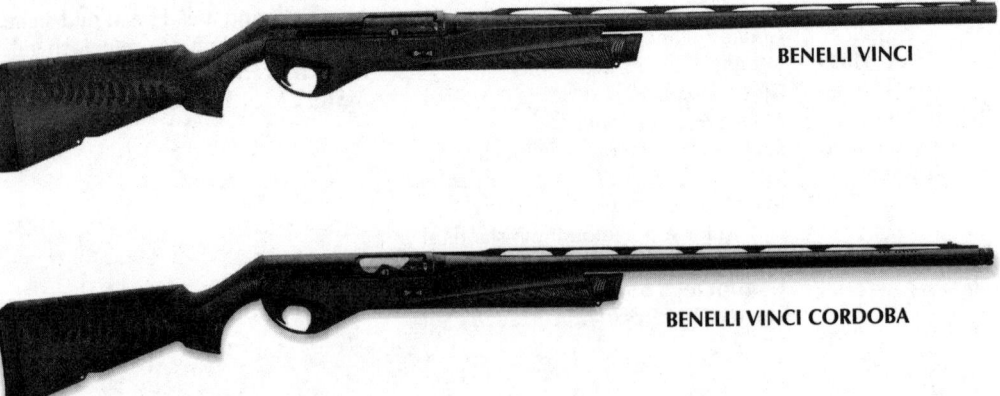

BENELLI VINCI

BENELLI VINCI CORDOBA

Beretta USA

686 SILVER PIGEON I

Action: Over/under
Stock: Walnut
Barrel: 26 in., 28 in., 30 in.
Chokes: MC
Weight: 6 lb. 13 oz.
Bore/Gauge: 12, 20, 28, .410
Magazine: None
Features: Extensive but refined floral and scroll decoration on the frame; dual-conical locking mechanism; automatic safety; oil finish on checkered walnut stock and forend; metal bead sight
MSRP **$2240**

687 SILVER PIGEON V

Action: Over/under
Stock: Walnut
Barrel: 28 in.
Chokes: Screw-in tubes
Weight: 6 lb. 13 oz.
Bore/Gauge: 12, 20, 28, .410
Magazine: None
Features: Oil-finished walnut stock detailed with gold game bird inlays and a gold Beretta medallion underneath; color-case finish; single selective trigger; 3-inch chambers; available with English stock or standard stock with pistol grip
MSRP **$4075**

A300 OUTLANDER

Action: Semiautomatic gas operated
Stock: Synthetic, camo, walnut
Barrel: 28 in.
Chokes: MC3
Weight: 7 lb. 10 oz.
Bore/Gauge: 12
Magazine: 3+1 rounds
Features: Gas operation with compensating exhaust valve and self-cleaning piston; adjustable shim system on stock; aluminum alloy receiver; cross-bolt safety with ergonomics; front metal bead sight; black synthetic, camo, or oiled wood stock finish
Synthetic: **$725**
Wood: **$825**
Camo: **$825**

A400 XCEL PARALLEL TARGET

Action: Semiautomatic gas operated
Stock: Walnut
Barrel: 28 in., 30 in., 32 in.

Chokes: Optima Bore HP Extended
Weight: 7 lb. 11 oz.
Bore/Gauge: 12
Magazine: 3+1, 2+1 rounds
Features: Gun Pod digital display provides digital readout of the ambient air temperature, cartridge pressure, and overall number of rounds fired; interchangeable balance caps; select walnut checkered stock/forend; blued toned aluminum-alloyed receiver; Blink operating system; recoil-dissipating Kick-Off, Micro-core pad; cold-hammer-forged barrel; white front, steel mid-bead
MSRP **$1900**

A400 XPLOR ACTION

Action: Semiautomatic
Stock: Walnut
Barrel: 26 in., 28 in., 30 in.
Chokes: Optima-Choke HP
Weight: 6 lb. 13 oz.
Bore/Gauge: 12
Magazine: 3+1, 2+1 rounds
Features: Blink gas operating system for fast cycling; bronze anodized receiver resistant to corrosion; Kick-Off recoil system; Micro-Core recoil pad; electronic Gun Pod that counts shells, measures temperature, and other functions comes standard
MSRP . . . . **$1620–$1825**

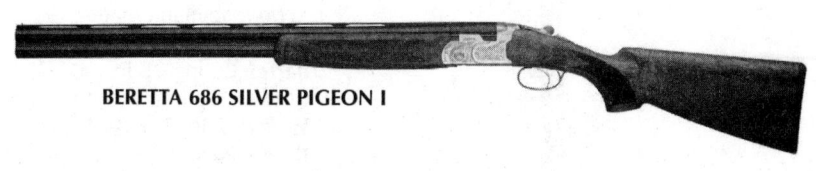
BERETTA 686 SILVER PIGEON I

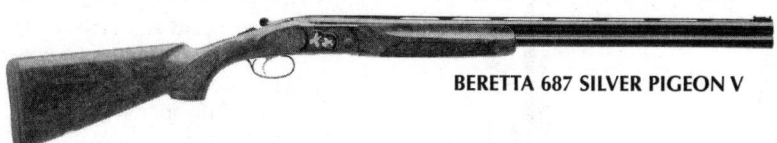
BERETTA 687 SILVER PIGEON V

BERETTA A300 OUTLANDER

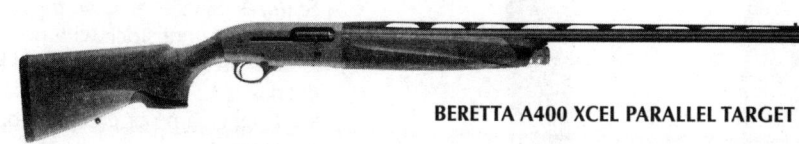
BERETTA A400 XCEL PARALLEL TARGET

BERETTA A400 XPLOR ACTION

SHOTGUNS

Beretta USA

A400 XPLOR LIGHT 12 GA.
Action: Semiautomatic
Stock: Walnut and polymer
Barrel: 26 in., 28 in.
Chokes: OptimaChoke screw-in tube
Weight: 6 lb. 3 oz.–6 lb. 10 oz.
Bore/Gauge: 12
Magazine: 3+1, 2+1 rounds
Features: Steelium barrel design, walnut stock with polymer forend insert, trigger guard and kick-off interface; 3-in. chamber; blink operating system; Micro-Core recoil pad; available with kick-off damper system
MSRP . . . . **$1515–$1620**

A400 XPLOR UNICO
Action: Semiautomatic
Stock: Walnut and polymer
Barrel: 26 in., 28 in.
Chokes: OptimaChoke screw-in tube
Weight: 6 lb. 10 oz.–7 lb.
Bore/Gauge: 12
Magazine: 3+1, 2+1 rounds
Features: Single-selective trigger; green receiver; walnut stock with polymer forend insert, trigger guard and kick-off interface; 3.5-in. chamber; metal bead front sight; camo or green anodized available
MSRP . . . . **$1730–$1865**

A400 XTREME
Action: Semiautomatic
Stock: Synthetic, camo
Barrel: 26 in., 28 in.
Chokes: Optima Bore HP (C, Mod, Full)
Weight: 7 lb. 10 oz.
Bore/Gauge: 12
Magazine: 4+1, 3+1 rounds
Features: Advanced Kick-Off Mega recoil system; Micro-Core recoil pad; overmolded grip panels; Aqua Technology's corrosion proof barrier; synthetic black or MAX4 camo.
Synthetic: **$1730**
MAX4: **$1840**

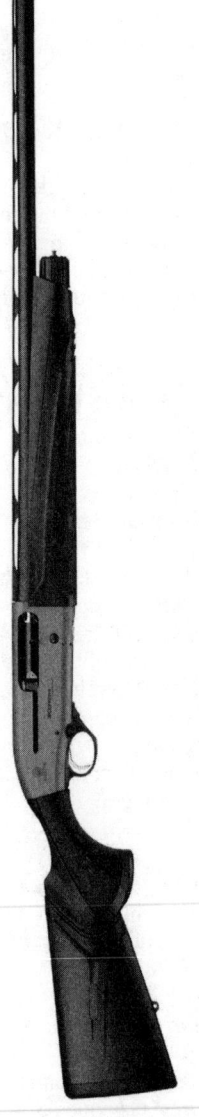

BERETTA A400 XTREME

**BERETTA A400
XPLOR UNICO**

**BERETTA A400
XPLOR LIGHT**

Beretta USA

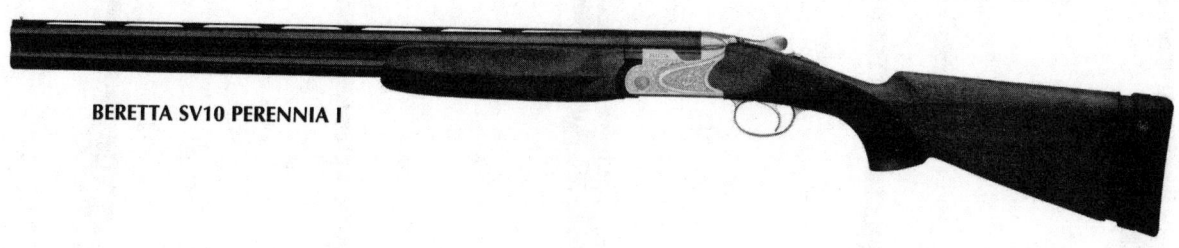

BERETTA SV10 PERENNIA I

SV10 PERENNIA I
Action: Over/under
Stock: Walnut, synthetic
Barrel: 26 in., 28 in., 30 in.
Chokes: Optima-Choke HP
Weight: 7 lb.
Bore/Gauge: 12, 20
Magazine: None
Features: Nano-Ceramic forend iron reduces wear and corrosion; choice between automatic ejection and mechanical extraction; floral engraving; Kick-Off recoil system available; Micro-Core recoil pad.
Standard: **$2890**
KO: **$3295**

SV10 PERENNIA III 20 GA
Action: Over/under
Stock: Walnut
Barrel: 26 in., 28 in.
Chokes: OptimaChoke HP Extended
Weight: 7 lb. 5 oz.
Bore/Gauge: 12
Magazine: None
Features: Optional Kick-Off hydraulic dampening reduction system; sling swivels; plastic pad; Optima-bore high-performance cold, hammer-forged barrels; automatic safety; chrome-lined bore and chamber
MSRP . . . . **$3620–$3945**

SV10 PREVAIL I
Action: Over/under
Stock: Walnut
Barrel: 30 in., 32 in.
Chokes: Optima Bore HP Extended
Weight: 7 lb. 13 oz.
Bore/Gauge: 12
Magazine: None
Features: Kick-Off, extraction/ejection selection system; easy-removable trigger group; Xtra-Grain walnut checkered stock with oil finish; manual safety; white front bead with steel mid-bead sights; available in sporting and trap versions
MSRP . . . . **$2900–$3450**

BERETTA SV10 PERENNIA III 20 GA.

BERETTA SV10 PREVAIL I, SPORTING

SHOTGUNS

Bernardelli

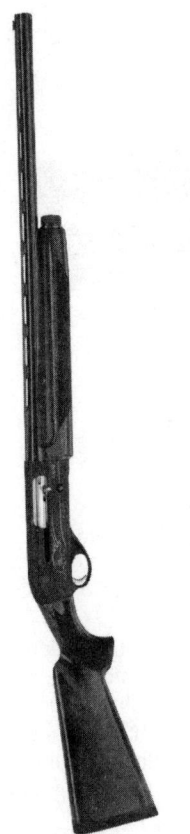
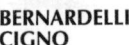

BERNARDELLI CIGNO

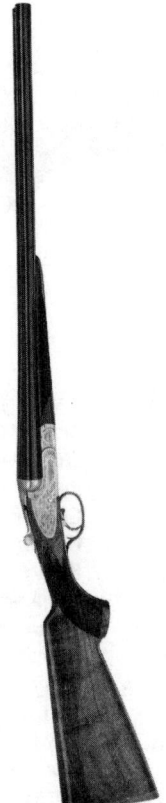

BERNARDELLI HEMINGWAY DELUXE

BERNARDELLI PA 12

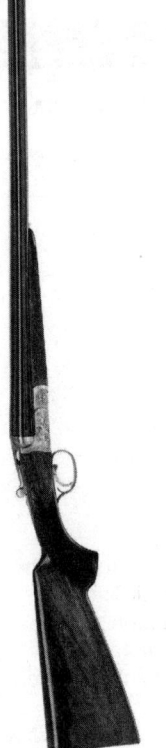

BERNARDELLI RISERVA

BERNARDELLI SIRBONE

CIGNO

Action: Semiautomatic
Stock: Walnut
Barrel: 24 in., 26 in., 28 in., 30 in.
Chokes: Steel chokes (M, F, IM, IC, CYL, F)
Weight: 6 lb. 13 oz.
Bore/Gauge: 12
Magazine: 2+1, 4+1 rounds
Features: Select walnut stock with pistol grip; rubber recoil pad; includes carrying case; receiver is black anodized and finely sand blasted
MSRP **$1269**

HEMINGWAY DELUXE

Action: Side-by-side
Stock: Walnut
Barrel: 24 in., 26 in., 27 in., 28 in., 29 in.
Chokes: Fixed cylinder chokes
Weight: 6 lb. 2 oz.–6 lb. 3 oz.
Bore/Gauge: 12, 20
Magazine: None
Features: Simple or automatic extractors; double trigger or single trigger with selector; beavertail buttstock; forged steel frame; English walnut stock with pistol grip
MSRP **$5887**

PA 12

Action: Pump
Stock: Synthetic
Barrel: 20 in.
Chokes: Steel cylinder chokes
Weight: 6 lb.
Bore/Gauge: 12
Magazine: 6+1 rounds
Features: Synthetic black matte stock; shipped in carton box; steel barrel
MSRP **$596**

RISERVA

Action: Side-by-side
Stock: Walnut
Barrel: 24 in., 26 in., 27 in., 28 in., 29 in.
Chokes: Fixed cylinder chokes
Weight: 6 lb. 13 oz.
Bore/Gauge: 12
Magazine: None
Features: Forged steel frame; double trigger or single trigger with selector; simple or automatic extractor; English walnut stock with pistol grip; beavertail buttstock
Standard: **$5069**
De Luxe: **$5646**

SIRBONE

Action: Semiautomatic
Stock: Walnut
Barrel: 24 in., 26 in., 28 in., 30 in.
Chokes: Steel chokes (M, F, IM, IC, CYL, F)
Weight: 6 lb. 13 oz.
Bore/Gauge: 12
Magazine: 2+1, 4+1 rounds
Features: Optical fiber front sight with rear sight dovetail optical fiber; select walnut stock with pistol grip; rubber recoil pad
MSRP **$1744**

SHOTGUNS

Blaser USA, Inc.

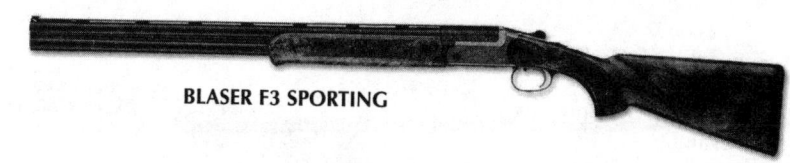

F3 SPORTING

Action: Over/under
Stock: Walnut
Barrel: 28 in., 30 in., 32 in., 34 in.
Chokes: Briley Spectrum chokes (SK, IC, M., IM, F)
Weight: 7 lb. 5 oz.
Bore/Gauge: 12, 20, 28, .410
Magazine: None
Features: Sporting stock, forearm with Schnabel; internal block system; ergonomically optimized, adjustable trigger

BLASER F3 SPORTING

blade; Triplex Bore design; ejection-ball-system; balancer

Standard:................ $7613
Luxus: $9340
Grand Luxus:............ $12233

Super Luxus: $13913
Baronesse:.............. $15010
Exclusive:........Price on request
Super Exclusive:...Price on request
Imperial: ....Price on request

Browning

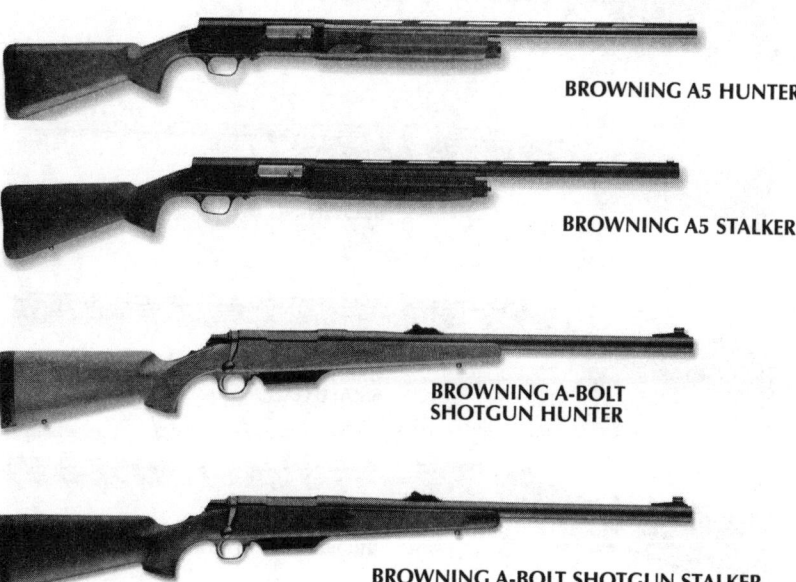

BROWNING A5 HUNTER

BROWNING A5 STALKER

BROWNING A-BOLT SHOTGUN HUNTER

BROWNING A-BOLT SHOTGUN STALKER

Dura-Touch armor coating; Vector Pro lengthened forcing cone; Inflex II technology recoil pad; fiber-optic front sight; included ABS case
MSRP . . . .$1399.99–$1559.99

A-BOLT SHOTGUN HUNTER

Action: Bolt
Stock: Walnut
Barrel: 22 in.
Chokes: None
Weight: 7 lb. 2 oz.
Bore/Gauge: 12
Magazine: Detachable, 2+1 rounds
Features: Sling swivel studs; satin finish walnut stock with checkered forearm; low-luster blued finish, steel receiver; drilled and tapped for scope mounts
MSRP $1279.99

A5 HUNTER

Action: Autoloader
Stock: Walnut
Barrel: 26 in., 28 in., 30 in.
Chokes: Invector-DS
Weight: 6 lb. 15 oz.
Bore/Gauge: 12
Magazine: None
Features: Strong, lightweight aluminum alloy; black anodized bi-tone finish; flat, ventilated rib; recoil operated Kinematic Drive is ultra-reliable and cycles a wide range of loads; gloss finish walnut with close radius pistol grip; 22 lines-per-inch checkering; shim adjustable for length of pull, cast and drop; Vector Pro lengthened forcing cone; three invector-DS™ choke tubes; Inflex II technology recoil pad; brass

front bead sight; ivory mid-bead sight; included ABS case
MSRP . . . .$1559.99–$1699.99

A5 STALKER

Action: Autoloader
Stock: Composite
Barrel: 26 in., 28 in., 30 in.
Chokes: Invector-DS
Weight: 7 lb. 3 oz.–7 lb. 7 oz.
Bore/Gauge: 12
Magazine: None
Features: Strong, lightweight aluminum alloy; flat, ventilated rib; recoil operated Kinematic Drive is ultra-reliable and cycles a wide range of loads; composite with close radius pistol grip; textured gripping surfaces; shim adjustable for cast and drop; matte black finish;

A-BOLT SHOTGUN STALKER & INFINITY CAMO

Action: Bolt
Stock: Composite
Barrel: 22 in.
Chokes: None
Weight: 7 lb.
Bore/Gauge: 12
Magazine: Detachable, 2+1 rounds
Features: Black composite (Stalker model); Mossy Oak Break-Up Infinity composite (Infinity Camo Model); textured gripping surfaces; Dura-touch armor coating; sling swivel studs installed; recoil pad; Truglo/Marble's fiber optic front sight, adjustable rear sight
Stalker: $1149.99
Infinity Camo: $1299.99

Browning

BPS HUNTER

Action: Bottom ejection pump
Stock: Walnut
Barrel: 26 in., 28 in.
Chokes: Three Invector-Plus choke tubes with 12 and 20 gauges; Standard Invectors with 16, 28, and .410
Weight: 6 lb. 15 oz.–7 lb. 11 oz.
Bore/Gauge: 12, 16, 20, 28, .410
Magazine: None
Features: Satin finish walnut stock; forged and machined steel receiver; ventilated rib barrel; top-tang safety
MSRP . . . . **$649.99–$699.99**

BPS RIFLED DEER HUNTER

Action: Bottom ejection pump
Stock: Walnut
Barrel: 22 in.
Chokes: Screw-in tubes
Weight: 7 lb. 4 oz.–7 lb. 10 oz.
Bore/Gauge: 12, 20
Magazine: None
Features: Satin finish walnut stock; forged and machined steel receiver; thick-walled barrel for slug ammunition only; dual steel action bars
MSRP . . . . **$779.99–$799.99**

BPS TRAP

Action: Bottom ejection pump
Stock: Walnut
Barrel: 30 in.
Chokes: Three Invector-Plus choke tubes
Weight: 8 lb. 2 oz.
Bore/Gauge: 12
Magazine: None
Features: Satin finish walnut stock with raised comb; forged and machined steel receiver with engraving; dual steel action bars; top-tang safety; magazine cut-off; HiViz ProComp fiber optic sight with mid-bead
MSRP **$799.99**

BT-99

Action: Bottom ejection pump
Stock: Walnut
Barrel: 32 in., 34 in.
Chokes: Screw-in tubes
Weight: 8 lb. 3 oz.–8 lb. 5 oz.
Bore/Gauge: 12
Magazine: None
Features: Satin finish walnut stock with beavertail forearm; steel receiver with blued finish; high-post ventilated rib
MSRP **$1429.99**

BROWNING BPS HUNTER

BROWNING BPS RIFLED DEER HUNTER

BROWNING BPS TRAP

BROWNING BT-99

BROWNING CITORI 625 SPORTING SMALL GA.

BROWNING CITORI 725 FIELD

CITORI 625 SPORTING SMALL GA.

Action: Over/under
Stock: Walnut
Barrel: 28 in., 30 in., 32 in.
Chokes: Five Diamond Grade Extended Invector-Plus choke tubes on 12 and 2 Standard Invector on 28 and .410
Weight: 6 lb. 15 oz.–7 lb. 7 oz.
Bore/Gauge: 20, 28, .410
Magazine: None
Features: Steel receiver with high-relief engraving with gold embellishment; single selective trigger; hammer ejectors; top-tang barrel selector/safety; sporting recoil pad; triple trigger system; HiViz Pro-Comp fiber optic sight
MSRP . . . . **$3549.99–$3579.99**

CITORI 725 FIELD

Action: Over/under
Stock: Walnut
Barrel: 26 in., 28 in.
Chokes: Invector-DS
Weight: 7 lb. 4 oz.–7 lb. 6 oz.
Bore/Gauge: 12
Magazine: None
Features: Steel receiver with silver nitride finish; accented, high-relief engraving; ventilated top rib action; mechanical trigger system; hammer ejectors; top-tang barrel selector/safety; gloss oil finish Grade II/III walnut with close radius pistol grip; Vector Pro lengthened forcing cones; ivory front and mid-bead sights
MSRP **$2469.99**

SHOTGUNS

Browning

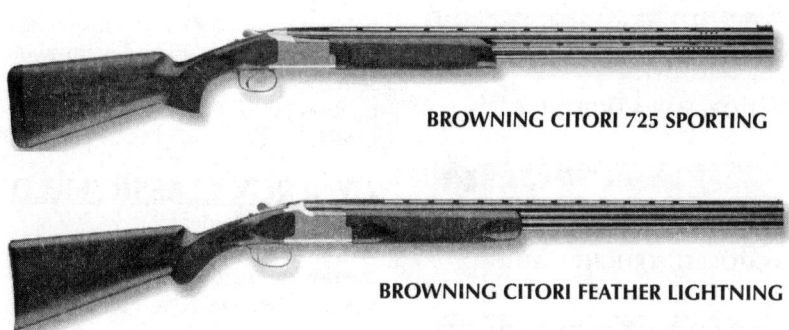

BROWNING CITORI 725 SPORTING

BROWNING CITORI FEATHER LIGHTNING

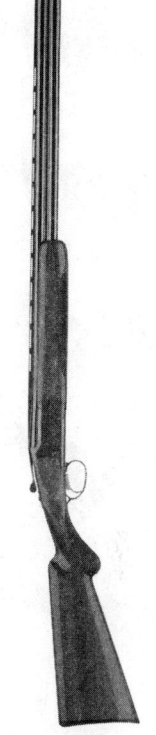

BROWNING CITORI LIGHTNING

CITORI 725 SPORTING

Action: Over/under
Stock: Walnut
Barrel: 28 in., 30 in., 32 in.
Chokes: Invector-DS
Weight: 7 lb. 6 oz.–7 lb. 10 oz.
Bore/Gauge: 12
Magazine: None
Features: Steel receiver with silver nitride finish; gold accented engraving; ventilated top and side rib action; mechanical trigger system; hammer ejectors; top-tang barrel selector/safety; gloss oil finish Grade III/IV walnut with close radius pistol grip; Vector Pro lengthened forcing cones; five Invector-DS choke tubes; HiViz Pro-Comp sight and ivory mid-bead
MSRP $3139.99

CITORI FEATHER LIGHTNING

Action: Over/under
Stock: Walnut
Barrel: 26 in., 28 in.

Chokes: Invector-Plus (F, M, IC)
Weight: 5 lb. 14 oz.–6 lb. 9 oz.
Bore/Gauge: 12, 20
Magazine: None
Features: With a lightweight alloy receiver and lightning style stock and forearm, the popular Browning Citori is now available in the new Citori Feather Lightning model. This lightweight Citori makes it easy to carry for long days on the range or out hunting.
MSRP $2179.99

CITORI GRADE IV LIGHTNING

Action: Over/under
Stock: Walnut
Barrel: 26 in.
Chokes: Three Invector-Plus choke tubes
Weight: 6 lb. 8 oz.–8 lb. 1 oz.
Bore/Gauge: 12, .410
Magazine: None
Features: Steel grayed finish receiver with full coverage engraving; ventilat-

ed rib barrel; single selective trigger; hammer ejectors; lightning style walnut stock and forearm
MSRP . . . . $3499.99–$3589.99

CITORI LIGHTNING

Action: Over/under
Stock: Walnut
Barrel: 26 in., 28 in.
Chokes: Three Invector-Plus choke tubes on 12 and 20, three standard Invector tubes on 28 and .410
Weight: 6 lb. 7 oz.–8 lb. 2 oz.
Bore/Gauge: 12, 20, 28, .410
Magazine: None
Features: Walnut stock with pistol grip; ventilated rib; single selective trigger; hammer ejectors; top-tang barrel selector/safety; ivory front bead sight
MSRP . . . . $1989.99–$2069.99

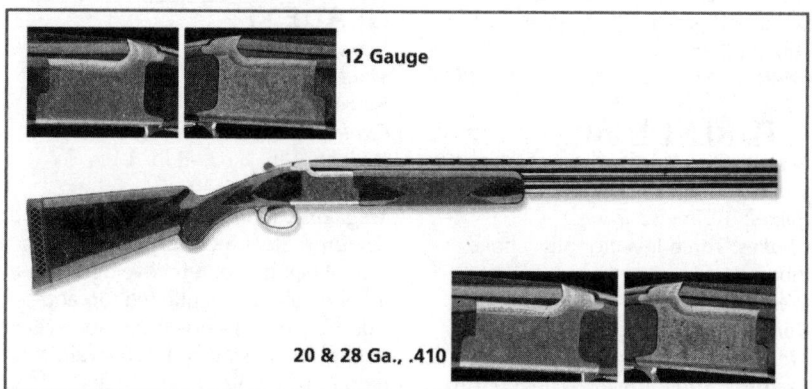

12 Gauge

20 & 28 Ga., .410

BROWNING CITORI GRADE IV LIGHTNING AND VII LIGHTNING

Browning

BROWNING CITORI MAPLE LIGHTNING

BROWNING CITORI SUPERLIGHT FEATHER

BROWNING CITORI XT TRAP

BROWNING CYNERGY CLASSIC FIELD

BROWNING CYNERGY CLASSIC FIELD GRADE III

BROWNING CYNERGY CLASSIC FIELD GRADE VI

CITORI MAPLE LIGHTNING

Action: Over/under
Stock: Maple
Barrel: 26 in., 28 in., 30 in.
Chokes: Invector-Plus (F, M, IC)
Weight: 6 lb. 9 oz.–8 lb.
Bore/Gauge: 12, 20
Magazine: None
Features: Steel receiver with blued finish; high-relief standard Lightning engraving; high gloss blued finish; ventilated rib; single selector trigger; hammer ejectors; top-tang barrel; selector/safety; gloss finish maple; recoil pad on 12 gauge model; ivory front bead sight
MSRP $2069.99

CITORI SUPERLIGHT FEATHER

Action: Over/under
Stock: Walnut
Barrel: 26 in.
Chokes: Invector-Plus
Weight: 5 lb. 11 oz.–6 lb. 4 oz.
Bore/Gauge: 12, 20, 28, .410
Magazine: None
Features: Lightweight alloy receiver with steel breech face and hinge pin; high-relief engraving; single selective trigger; hammer ejectors; top-tang barrel selector/safety; gloss finish walnut, English-style straight grip stock, Schnabel forearm; three Invector-Plus choke tubes
MSRP $2389.99

CITORI XT TRAP

Action: Over/under
Stock: Walnut
Barrel: 30 in., 32 in.
Chokes: Three Invector-plus choke tubes
Weight: 8 lb. 6 oz.–8 lb. 8 oz.
Bore/Gauge: 12
Magazine: None
Features: Triple-trigger system; HiViz Pro-Comp sight; steel receiver with gold accented engravings; ventilated

barrel; walnut stock with close radius pistol grip and right-hand palm swell; semi-beavertail forearm with finger grooves
MSRP $2949.99

CYNERGY CLASSIC FIELD

Action: Over/under
Stock: Walnut
Barrel: 26 in., 28 in.
Chokes: Three Invector-Plus choke tubes on 12 and 20; three standard Invector chokes on 28 and .410
Weight: 6 lb. 4 oz.–7 lb. 13 oz.
Bore/Gauge: 12, 20, 28, .410
Magazine: None
Features: Reverse striker ignition system; impact ejectors; top-tang barrel selector/safety; gloss oil finish on grade III/IV walnut; steel receiver; ivory front and mid-bead sights
MSRP . . . . $2529.99–$2589.99

CYNERGY CLASSIC FIELD GRADE III

Action: Over/under
Stock: Walnut
Barrel: 26 in., 28 in.
Chokes: Three Invector-Plus choke tubes
Weight: 6 lb. 8 oz.–8 lb. 1 oz.
Bore/Gauge: 12, 20
Magazine: None
Features: Steel receiver with MonoLock hinge; full coverage high-relief engraving; ventilated top and side ribs; reverse striker ignition system; gloss finish grade III/IV walnut; recoil pad on 12-gauge model
MSRP . . . . $3999.99–$4049.99

CYNERGY CLASSIC FIELD GRADE VI

Action: Over/under
Stock: Walnut
Barrel: 26 in., 28 in.
Chokes: Three Invector-Plus
Weight: 6 lb. 8 oz.–8 lb. 1 oz.
Bore/Gauge: 12, 20
Magazine: None
Features: Steel receiver with MonoLock hinge; full coverage high-relief engraving; ventilated top and side ribs; reverse striker ignition system; gloss finish grade III/IV walnut; recoil pad on 12-gauge model
MSRP . . . . $6099.99–$6129.99

SHOTGUNS

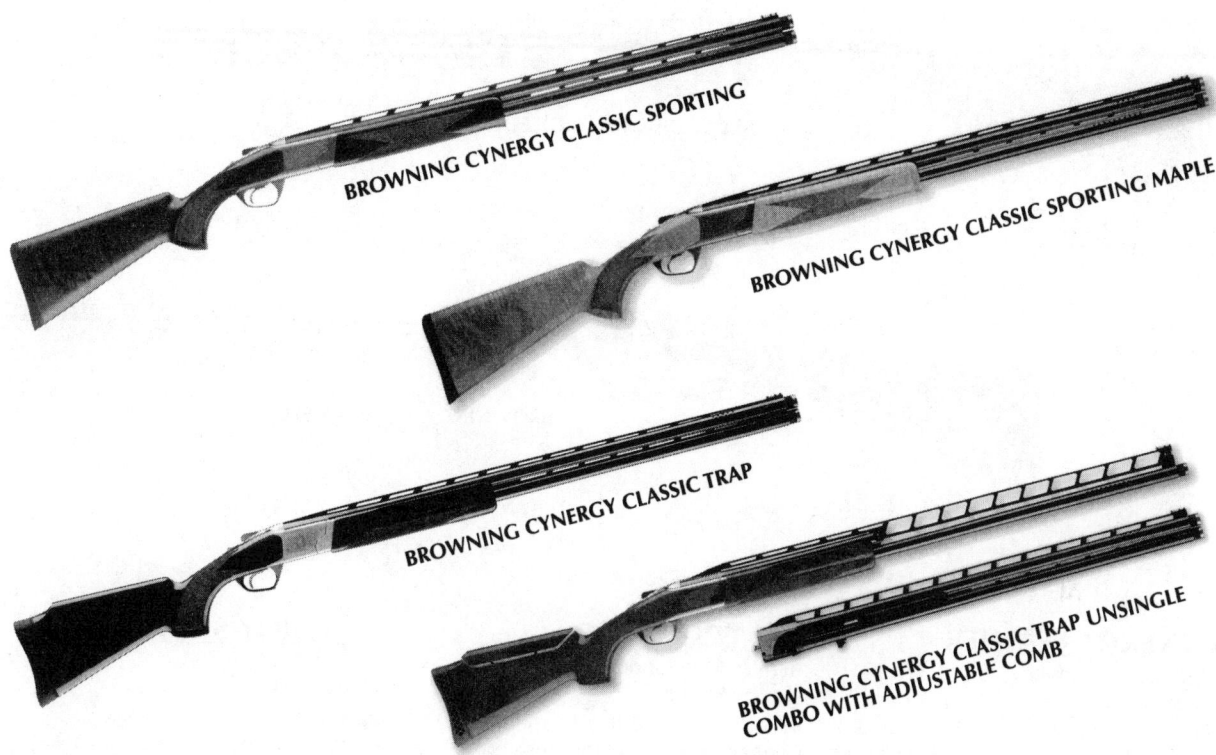

BROWNING CYNERGY CLASSIC SPORTING

BROWNING CYNERGY CLASSIC SPORTING MAPLE

BROWNING CYNERGY CLASSIC TRAP

BROWNING CYNERGY CLASSIC TRAP UNSINGLE COMBO WITH ADJUSTABLE COMB

CYNERGY CLASSIC SPORTING

Action: Over/under
Stock: Walnut
Barrel: 28 in., 30 in., 32 in.
Chokes: Three Invector-Plus Midas Grade choke tubes on 12 and 20; three Standard Invector chokes on 28 and .410
Weight: 6 lb. 4 oz.–7 lb. 15 oz.
Bore/Gauge: 12, 20, 28, .410
Magazine: None
Features: Steel receiver; ventilated top and side ribs; reverse striker ignition system; impact ejectors; top-tang barrel selector/safety; gloss oil finish grade III/IV walnut; HiViz Pro-Comp fiber optic sight
MSRP . . . . $3599.99–$3629.99

CYNERGY CLASSIC SPORTING MAPLE

Action: Over/under
Stock: Maple
Barrel: 28 in., 30 in., 32 in.
Chokes: Midas Grade Invector Plus
Weight: 7 lb. 11 oz.–7 lb. 15 oz.
Bore/Gauge: 12

Magazine: None
Features: Steel receiver with silver nitride finish; jeweled monobloc; MonoLock hinge; high-relief engraving; high gloss blued; ventilated top and side ribs; reverse striker ignition system; impact ejectors; top-tang barrel selector/safety
Stock: Grade III/IV maple, gloss finish
Features: Vector Pro lengthened forcing cones; Three Midas Grade Invector Plus choke tubes (M,IC,SK); Triple Trigger System; HiViz Pro-Comp fiber-optic sight
MSRP $3599.99

CYNERGY CLASSIC TRAP

Action: Over/under
Stock: Walnut
Barrel: 30 in., 32 in.
Chokes: Three Invector-Plus Midas Grade choke tubes
Weight: 8 lb.10 oz.–8 lb. 12 oz.
Bore/Gauge: 12
Magazine: None
Features: Reverse striker ignition system; impact ejectors; top-tang barrel selector/safety; Monte Carlo walnut

stock with right-hand palm swell; HiViz Pro-Comp fiber-optic sight
MSRP $3879.99

CYNERGY CLASSIC TRAP UNSINGLE COMBO WITH ADJUSTABLE COMB

Action: Single shot and over/under
Stock: Walnut
Barrel: 30 in., 32 in.
Chokes: Four Invector-Plus Midas Grade choke tubes
Weight: 8 lb. 13 oz.–8 lb. 15 oz.
Bore/Gauge: 12
Magazine: None
Features: Steel receiver with MonoLock hinge; double- and single-barrel sets included; reverse striker ignition system; impact ejectors; top-tang barrel selector/safety; gloss finish Monte Carlo grade III/IV walnut stock with right-hand palm swell
MSRP $5999.99

Browning

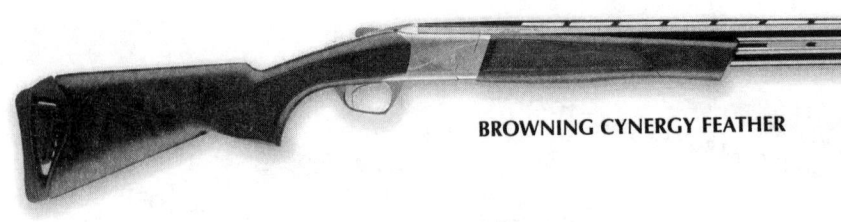

BROWNING CYNERGY FEATHER

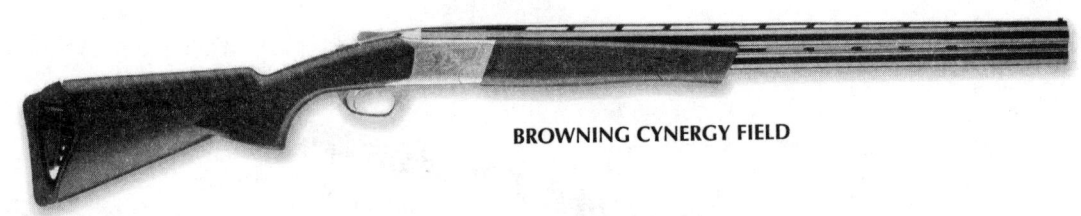

BROWNING CYNERGY FIELD

CYNERGY FEATHER

Action: Over/under
Stock: Walnut
Barrel: 26 in., 28 in.
Chokes: Three Invector-Plus choke tubes on 12 and 20, Standard Invector on 28 and .410
Weight: 5 lb. 8 oz.–6 lb. 13 oz.
Bore/Gauge: 12, 20, 28, .410
Magazine: None
Features: Lightweight alloy receiver; gold enhanced grayed finish; MonoLock hinge; reverse striker ignition system; top-tang barrel selector/safety; Inflex technology recoil pad system; ivory front and mid-bead sights
MSRP . . . . **$2899.99–$2929.99**

CYNERGY FIELD

Action: Over/under
Stock: Walnut
Barrel: 26 in., 28 in.
Chokes: Three Invector-Plus choke tubes on 12 and 20; Standard Invector on 28 and .410
Weight: 6 lb. 1 oz.–7 lb. 11 oz.
Bore/Gauge: 12, 20, 28, .410
Magazine: None
Features: Steel receiver with MonoLock hinge; reverse striker ignition system; impact ejectors; oil finish walnut stock; ivory front and mid-bead sights
MSRP . . . . **$2799.99–$2849.99**

CYNERGY SPORTING

Action: Over/under
Stock: Walnut
Barrel: 28 in., 30 in., 32 in.
Chokes: Three Invector-Plus choke tubes
Weight: 6 lb. 4 oz.–8 lb. 1 oz.
Bore/Gauge: 12, 20
Magazine: None
Features: Reverse striker ignition system; impact ejectors; top-tang barrel selector/safety; gloss oil finish on grade III/IV walnut; steel receiver; Inflex technology recoil pad system; HiViz Pro-Comp fiber optic sight
MSRP . . . . **$3999.99–$4029.99**

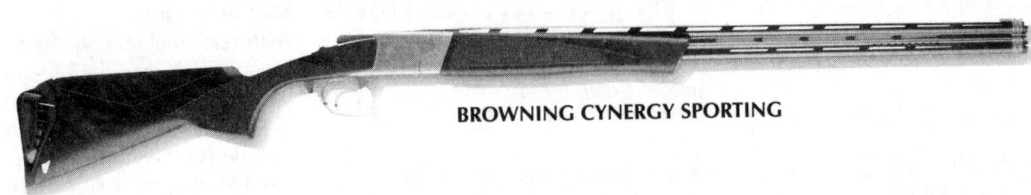

BROWNING CYNERGY SPORTING

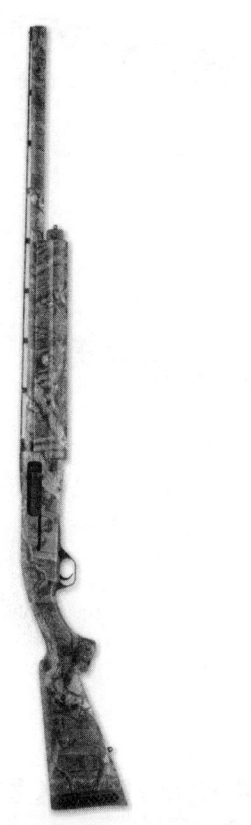

BROWNING GOLD LIGHT 10 GA., MOSSY OAK DUCK BLIND

BROWNING MAXUS HUNTER

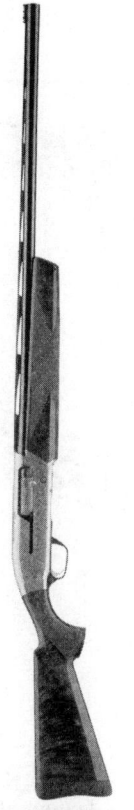

BROWNING MAXUS SPORTING

BROWNING MAXUS STALKER

GOLD LIGHT 10 GA.

Action: Autoloader, gas-operated
Stock: Composite
Barrel: 26 in., 28 in.
Chokes: Three Standard Invector choke tubes
Weight: 9 lb. 9 oz.–9 lb. 10 oz.
Bore/Gauge: 10
Magazine: 4+1 rounds
Features: Aluminum alloy receiver; ventilated rib barrel; composite stock and forearm in MO Break-Up Infinity or MO Shadow Grass Blades; DuraTouch armor coating
MSRP **$1739.99**

MAXUS HUNTER

Action: Autoloader, gas-operated
Stock: Composite
Barrel: 26 in., 28 in., 30 in.
Chokes: Three Invector-Plus

Weight: 6 lb. 15 oz.–7 lb. 1 oz.
Bore/Gauge: 12
Magazine: None
Features: Aluminum alloy receiver with durable satin nickel finish; laser engraving of pheasant and mallard on receiver; Inflex technology recoil pad; ivory front bead sight
MSRP . . . . **$1499.99–$1639.99**

MAXUS SPORTING

Action: Autoloader, gas-operated
Stock: Walnut
Barrel: 28 in., 30 in.
Chokes: Five Invector-Plus choke tubes
Weight: 7 lb. 3 oz.–7 lb. 4 oz.
Bore/Gauge: 12
Magazine: None
Features: Aluminum alloy receiver with durable satin nickel finish; laser engraving of game birds transforming into clay birds; speed lock forearm;

ivory mid bead sight, HiVix Tri-Comp fiber optic front sight
MSRP **$1699.99**

MAXUS STALKER

Action: Autoloader, gas-operated
Stock: Composite
Barrel: 26 in., 28 in.
Chokes: Three Invector Plus choke tubes
Weight: 7 lb.–7 lb. 2 oz.
Bore/Gauge: 12
Magazine: None
Features: Magazine cut-off, matte black composite stock with pistol grip; speed lock forearm; textured gripping surfaces; Dura Touch armor coating; Inflex technology recoil pads; lightning trigger system; ventilated rib
MSRP . . . . **$1339.99–$1499.99**

SHOTGUNS

Browning

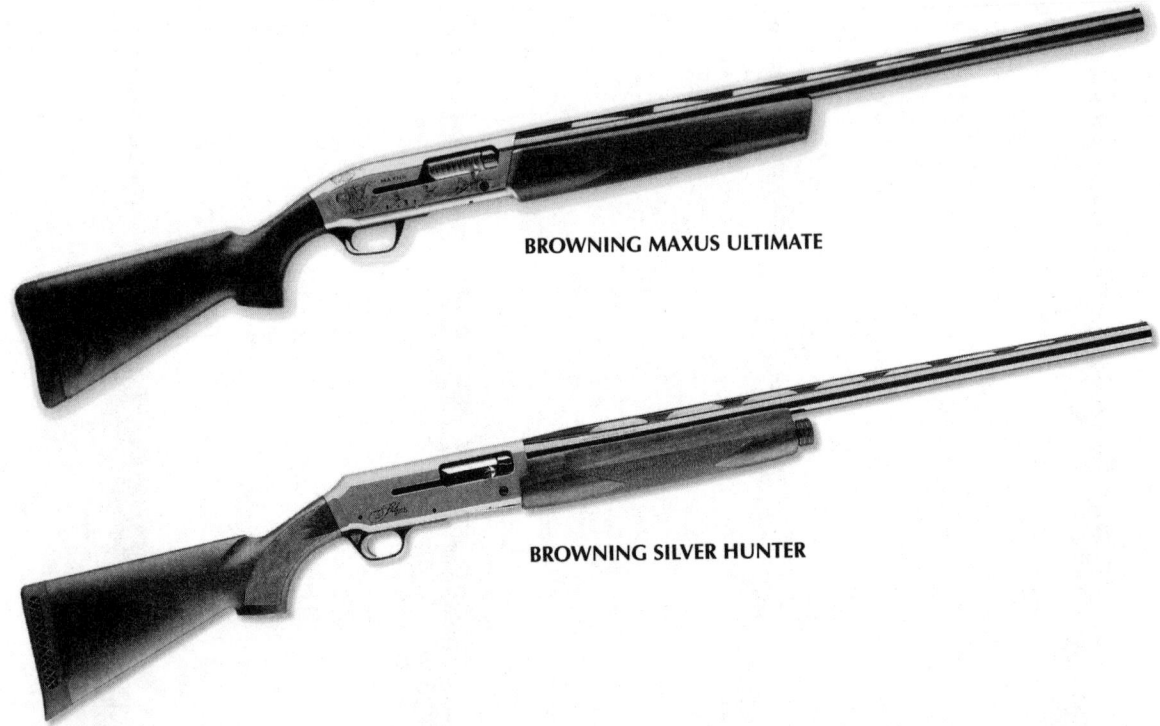

BROWNING MAXUS ULTIMATE

BROWNING SILVER HUNTER

MAXUS ULTIMATE

Action: Autoloader, gas operated
Stock: Walnut
Barrel: 26 in., 28 in., 30 in.
Chokes: Invector Plus (F, M, IC)
Weight: 7 lb. 1 oz.–7 lb. 4 oz.
Bore/Gauge: 12
Magazine: None
Features: Strong, lightweight aluminum alloy receiver; durable satin nickel finish; laser engraved (pintails on the left-hand side and pheasants on the right); gloss blued finish; ventilated rib; gloss oil finished grade III walnut with close radius pistol grip; speed lock forearm; shim adjustable for length of pull, cast, and drop; Inflex technology recoil pad; brass bead front sight; ABS case included
MSRP $1869.99

SILVER HUNTER

Action: Autoloader, gas operated
Stock: Walnut
Barrel: 26 in., 28 in., 30 in.
Chokes: Three Invector-Plus choke tubes
Weight: 6 lb. 5 oz.–7 lb. 9 oz.
Bore/Gauge: 12, 20
Magazine: None
Features: Aluminum alloy receiver; ventilated rib barrel; satin finish walnut stock
MSRP . . . . $1179.99–$1339.99

SILVER HUNTER MICRO MIDAS

Action: Autoloader, gas-operated
Stock: Walnut
Barrel: 24 in., 26 in.
Chokes: Three Invector-Plus choke tubes
Weight: 6 lb.–7 lb. 5 oz.
Bore/Gauge: 12, 20
Magazine: None
Features: Semi-humpback receiver design with silver finish; ivory front bead sight
MSRP $1179.99

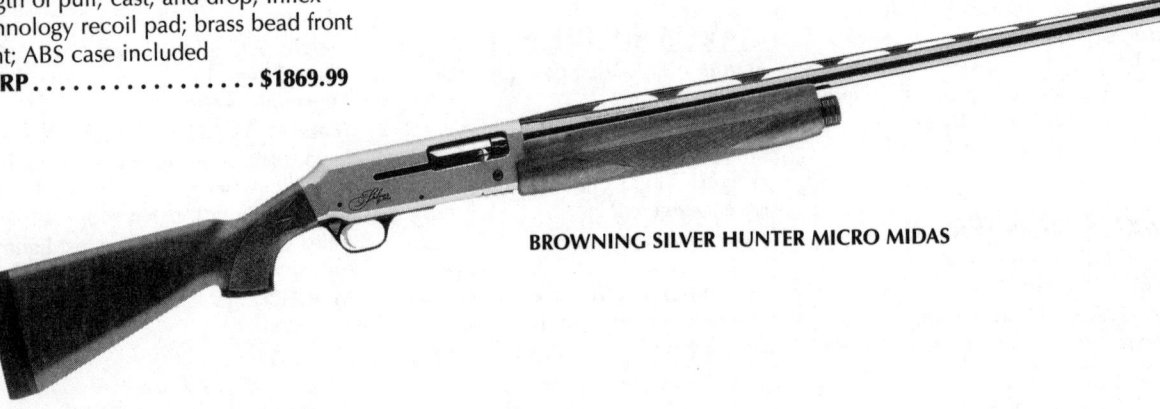

BROWNING SILVER HUNTER MICRO MIDAS

Caesar Guerini

CAESAR GUERINI ELLIPSE EVO

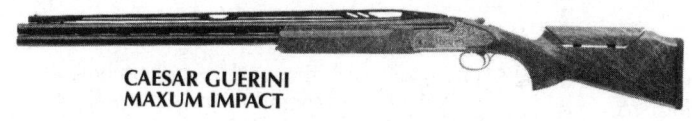

CAESAR GUERINI MAXUM IMPACT

ELLIPSE EVO

Action: Over/under
Stock: Walnut
Barrel: 28 in.
Chokes: 5 choke tube options
Weight: 6 lb.–7 lb. 4 oz.
Bore/Gauge: 12, 20, 28
Magazine: None
Features: Single trigger; rounded forend; chrome-lined barrel; non-ventilated center rib; hand-polished coin finish receiver with Invisalloy protective finish
MSRP . . . . **$5950–$7875**

MAXUM IMPACT

Action: Over/under
Stock: Checkered walnut with adjustable cheekpiece

Barrel: 30 in.–34 in.
Chokes: Maxis choke system
Weight: 7 lb. 11 oz.–8 lb. 7 oz.
Bore/Gauge: 12, 20
Magazine: None
Features: Engraved receiver; 17mm-tall D.T.S. rib for more upright shooting; 5 in. dual conical forcing cones; selective and non-selective triggers available; left-hand available
MSRP . . . . **$8195–$10495**

TEMPIO FIELD GUN

Action: Over/under
Stock: Turkish walnut
Barrel: 26 in., 28 in., 30 in.
Chokes: 5 nickel plated, flush fitting chokes
Weight: 6 lb.–7 lb.

Bore/Gauge: 12, 20, 28, .410
Magazine: None
Features: Designed to be a sleek and fast pointing shotgun in the field; perfect companion for upland game hunters; low-profile receiver matched with a trim stock, classic Prince-of-Wales grip and schnabel forend make the gun a perfect match for fast game birds; contemporary style of "ornato" style scroll with tasteful gold accents; Invisalloy protective coating
MSRP . . . . **$3595–$7070**

WOODLANDER

Action: Over/under
Stock: English walnut
Barrel: 26 in., 28 in., 30 in.
Chokes: Five precision patterned flush chokes (CYL, IC, M, IM, F)
Weight: 6 lb.–7 lb.
Bore/Gauge: 12, 20, 28, .410
Magazine: None
Features: This gun reflects passion for fall coverts, autumn foliage, wet gun dogs, and the smell of wood smoke. With the understated elegance of color case hardening and nicely figured, oil-finished English walnut that speaks of quality from a bygone era, this is a superior-handling upland game gun that's perfect for tight cover and fast-flushing birds.
MSRP . . . . **$3250–$6725**

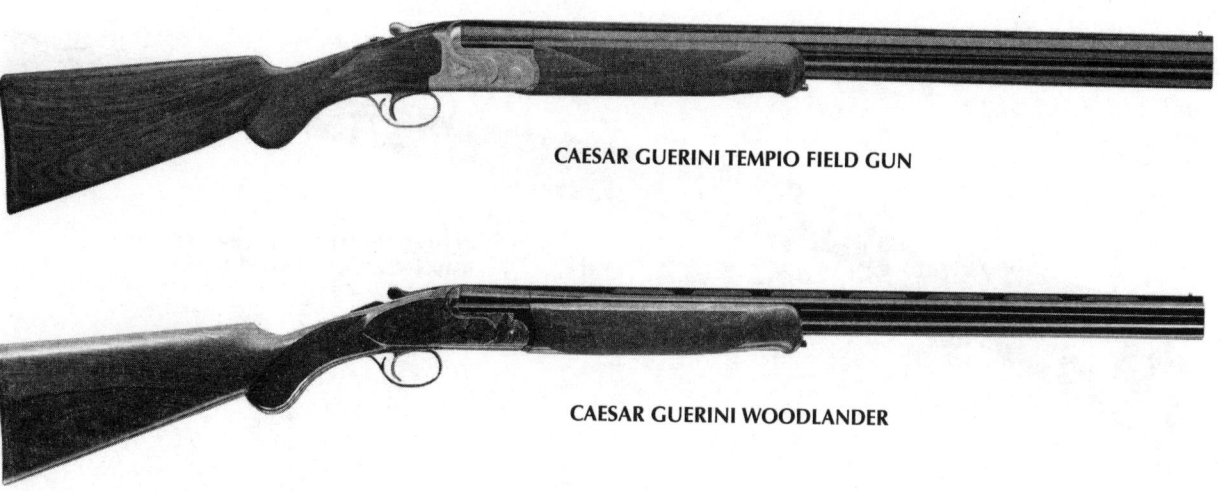

CAESAR GUERINI TEMPIO FIELD GUN

CAESAR GUERINI WOODLANDER

Cimarron Firearms Co.

CIMARRON 1881 HAMMERLESS SHOTGUN

1881 HAMMERLESS SHOTGUN

Action: Side-by-side
Stock: Walnut
Barrel: 20 in., 22 in., 26 in., 28 in., 30 in.

Chokes: Double Barrel STD
Weight: N/A
Bore/Gauge: 12
Magazine: None
Features: Authentic frontier styling; manual ejectors; threaded for inter-

changeable choke tubes; stock and forend is American walnut; deluxe stock available
MSRP . . . . $721.50–$760.50

Connecticut Shotgun Mfg. Co.

A-10 AMERICAN

Action: Sidelock over/under
Stock: Checkered American black walnut
Barrel: 26 in.–32 in.
Chokes: 5 TruLock tubes
Weight: 6 lb. 8 oz.–7 lb. 8 oz.

Bore/Gauge: 12, 20, 28
Magazine: None
Features: Finely engraved, cut checkering; ventilated rib; pistol grip or straight grip; auto ejectors, single selective trigger; Galazan pad

Standard: $7995
Deluxe: $8995
Rose & Scroll: $10000
Platinum: $15000

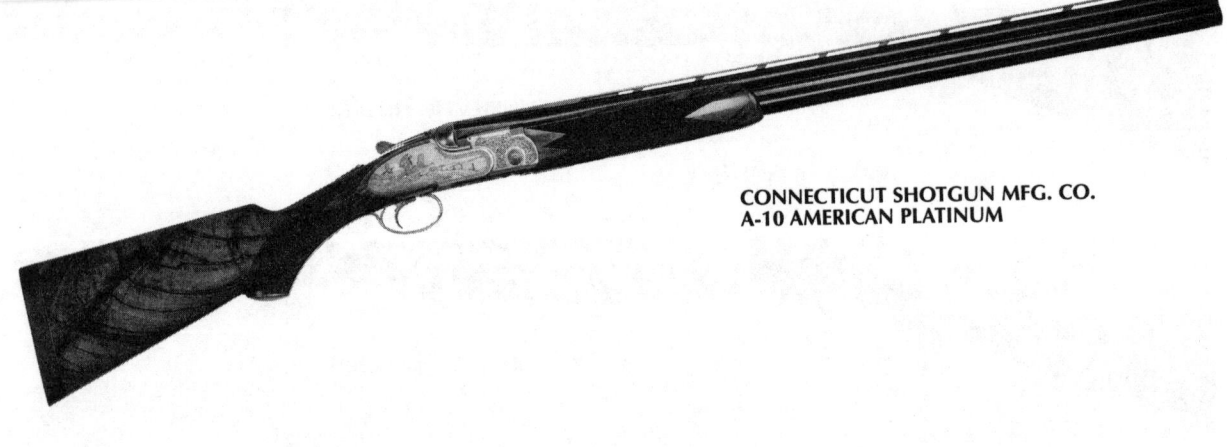

CONNECTICUT SHOTGUN MFG. CO. A-10 AMERICAN PLATINUM

SHOTGUNS

CZ-USA (Ceska Zbrojovka)

712 ADJUSTABLE LENGTH STOCK

Action: Gas-operated semiautomatic
Stock: Polymer
Barrel: 28 in.
Chokes: Interchangeable chokes (F, M, IC)
Weight: 7 lb. 13 oz.
Bore/Gauge: 12
Magazine: 4+1 rounds
Features: Polymer ATI adjsutable stock; fiber optic front sight; adjustable length of pull from 12 to 14 inches
MSRP **$562**

712 SEMIAUTO

Action: Semiautomatic
Stock: Walnut
Barrel: 26 in., 28 in.
Chokes: Screw-in chokes (IC, M, F, C, IM)
Weight: 7 lb. 5 oz.
Bore/Gauge: 12
Magazine: 4+1 rounds
Features: 3-in. chamber; cross bolt safety; matte black chrome barrel finish; matte anodized receiver finish; gas-operated system; chrome-lined barrel
MSRP **$488**

712 TARGET

Action: Gas-operated semiautomatic
Stock: Walnut
Barrel: 30 in.
Chokes: Interchangeable chokes (F, M, IC)
Weight: 7 lb. 10 oz.
Bore/Gauge: 12
Magazine: 4+1 rounds
Features: Gas operated aluminum alloy action with target-grade enhancements; chrome-lined barrel; fiber optic front sight on a 10mm stepped rib; Schnabel forend; smooth rounded heel; Monte Carlo buttstock
MSRP **$660**

712 UTILITY

Action: Semiautomatic
Stock: Synthetic
Barrel: 20 in.
Chokes: Screw-in chokes (F, IM, M, IC, C)
Weight: 6 lb. 10 oz.
Bore/Gauge: 12
Magazine: 4+1 rounds
Features: 3 in.-chamber cross-bolt safety; black synthetic stock; matte

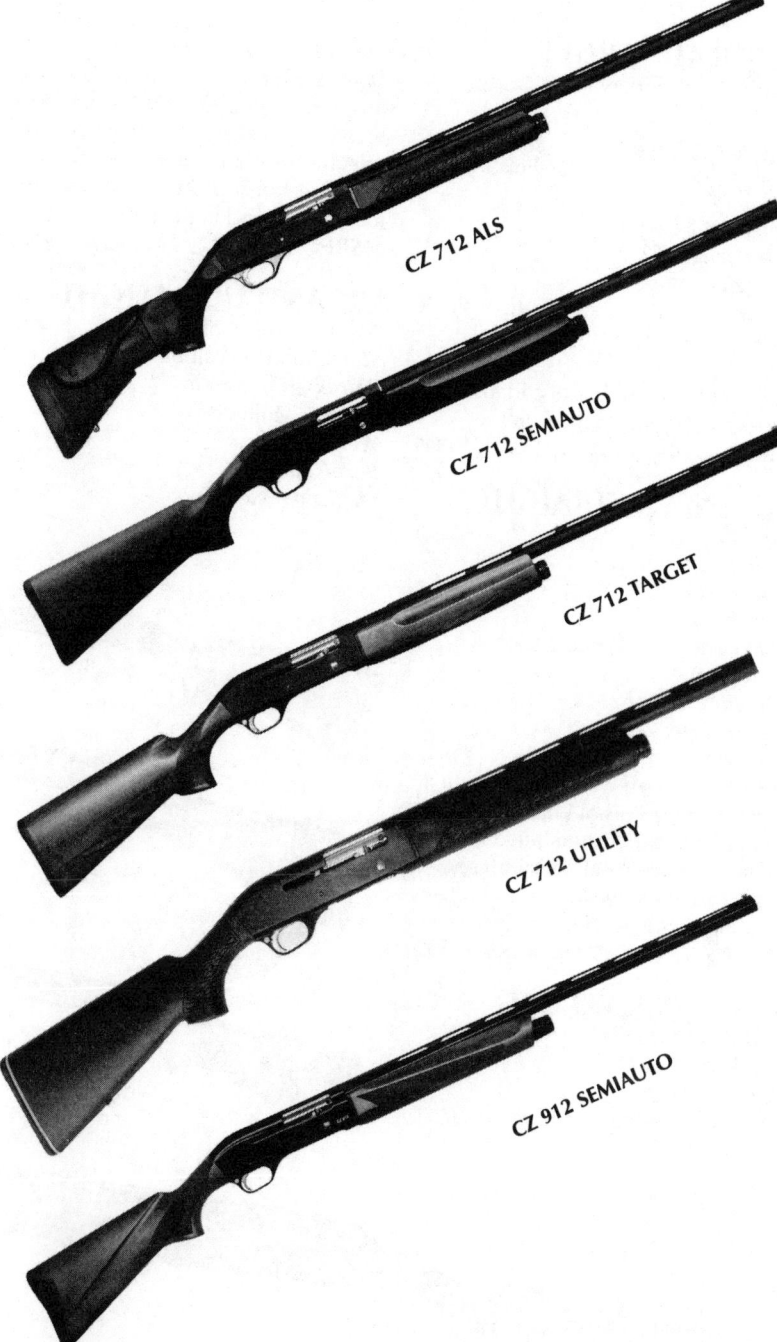

CZ 712 ALS

CZ 712 SEMIAUTO

CZ 712 TARGET

CZ 712 UTILITY

CZ 912 SEMIAUTO

chrome black barrel
MSRP **$488**

912 SEMIAUTO

Action: Recoil-operated semiautomatic
Stock: Walnut
Barrel: 28 in.
Chokes: 5 interchangeable choke tubes
Weight: 7 lb. 5 oz.
Bore/Gauge: 12
Magazine: 4+1 rounds
Features: Fiber optic front bead; features a gloss black finish on metalwork; cross-bolt safety; chrome-lined barrel; aluminum frame
MSRP **$528**

CZ-USA (Ceska Zbrojovka)

REDHEAD TARGET

Action: Over/under
Stock: Walnut
Barrel: 30 in.
Chokes: Interchangeable chokes (C, F, M, IC, IM)
Weight: 8 lb. 4 oz.
Bore/Gauge: 12
Magazine: None
Features: Boxlock frame system; single selective mechanical trigger; coil spring operated hammers; auto ejectors; chrome-lined barrels; Turkish walnut stock; 10mm stepped rib
MSRP $1348

RINGNECK STRAIGHT GRIP

Action: Over/under
Stock: Walnut
Barrel: 26 in.
Chokes: Interchangeable chokes (C, F, M, IC, IM)
Weight: 6 lb. 5 oz.
Bore/Gauge: 20
Magazine: None
Features: Turkish walnut stock with a straight English pistol grip; case hardened receiver; polished blued barrels; single selective mechanical trigger; extractors; Greener Top Cross Bolt system and bottom-locking action
MSRP $993

RINGNECK TARGET

Action: Over/under
Stock: Walnut
Barrel: 30 in.
Chokes: Interchangeable chokes (C, F, M, IC, IM)
Weight: 7 lb. 5 oz.
Bore/Gauge: 12

Magazine: None
Features: Turkish walnut stock with a full size target grip; case-hardened receiver; polished blued barrels; single selective mechanical trigger; extractors; Greener Top Cross Bolt system and bottom-locking action
MSRP $1260

UPLAND ULTRALIGHT

Action: Over/under
Stock: Turkish Walnut
Barrel: 26 in., 28 in.
Chokes: Multi-choke
Weight: 6 lb.
Bore/Gauge: 12
Magazine: None

Features: Lightweight, black alloy receiver; vent rib
MSRP $739

WINGSHOOTER DELUXE

Action: Over/under
Stock: Turkish Walnut
Barrel: 28 in.
Chokes: 5 Interchangeable choke tubes
Weight: 6 lb.–7 lb. 6 oz.
Bore/Gauge: 12, 20
Magazine: None
Features: Single trigger; black chrome barrel finish; box-lock frame; Schnabel forend; manual tang safety
MSRP $999

CZ REDHEAD TARGET

CZ RINGNECK STRAIGHT GRIP

CZ RINGNECK TARGET

CZ UPLAND ULTRALIGHT

CZ WINGSHOOTER DELUXE

SHOTGUNS

Escort by Legacy Sports

AIMGUARD, MARINEGUARD HOME DEFENSE

Action: Pump
Stock: Synthetic
Barrel: 18 in.
Chokes: Cylinder bore
Weight: 6 lb. 4 oz.
Bore/Gauge: 12
Magazine: Tubular, 5 rounds
Features: Rifle-style front sight; black synthetic stock; AimGuard has black metal finish, MarineGuard has water resistant nickel finish; sling swivel studs; dovetail receiver for mounting accessory sights
AimGuard: **$299**
MarineGuard: **$369**

EXTREME MAGNUM SEMI-AUTO

Action: Semiautomatic
Stock: Synthetic
Barrel: 24 in., 26 in., 28 in.
Chokes: 5+1 chokes
Weight: 7 lb.–7 lb. 10.4 oz.
Bore/Gauge: 12, 20
Magazine: Tubular, 5+1 rounds
Features: Non-slip grip pads on the forend and pistol grip; SMART Valve gas pistons; HiVis MagniSight fiber optic, magnetic sight; available in Realtree MAX-4, Realtree AP Camo, Realtree AP Camo Turkey, and black synthetic
Black: . . . . **$549–$649**
Realtree: . . . . **$729–$799**
Realtree Turkey: **$659**

SILVER STANDARD

Action: Over/under
Stock: Walnut, synthetic
Barrel: 28 in.
Chokes: Choke tubes (M, IC, F, IM, Skeet)
Weight: 7 lb. 10 oz.–8 lb. 3 oz.
Bore/Gauge: 12
Magazine: None
Features: 3-in. chamber; Turkish walnut stock; trio recoil pad; blued tang lever; barrel selector switch and trigger guard; auto safety; nickel plated receiver; blued barrel
MSRP **$639**

SILVER SYNTHETIC SHORTY

Action: Over/under
Stock: Synthetic
Barrel: 18 in.
Chokes: Choke tubes (M, IC, F, IM, Skeet)
Weight: 7 lb.
Bore/Gauge: 12
Magazine: None
Features: Nickel plated receiver; adjustable comb; auto safety; blued tang lever, barrel selector switch, and trigger guard; soft rubber grey synthetic stock with cobblestone grip inserts
MSRP **$659**

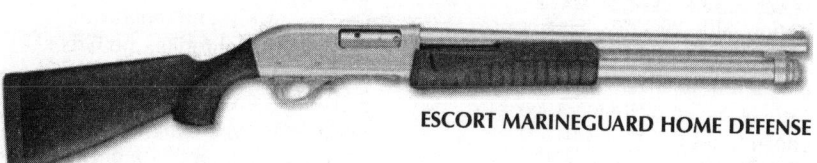

ESCORT MARINEGUARD HOME DEFENSE

ESCORT EXTEME MAGNUM SEMI-AUTO, REALTREE AP CAMO

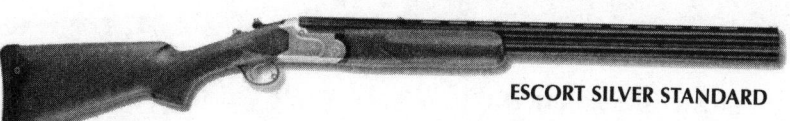

ESCORT SILVER STANDARD

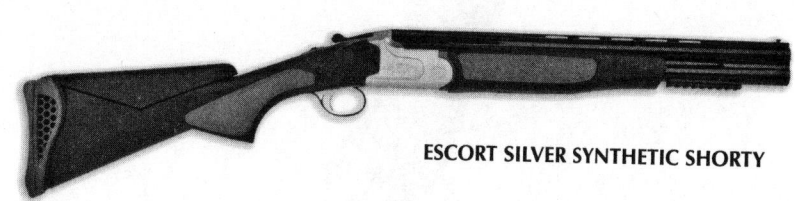

ESCORT SILVER SYNTHETIC SHORTY

SHOTGUNS

Fausti USA

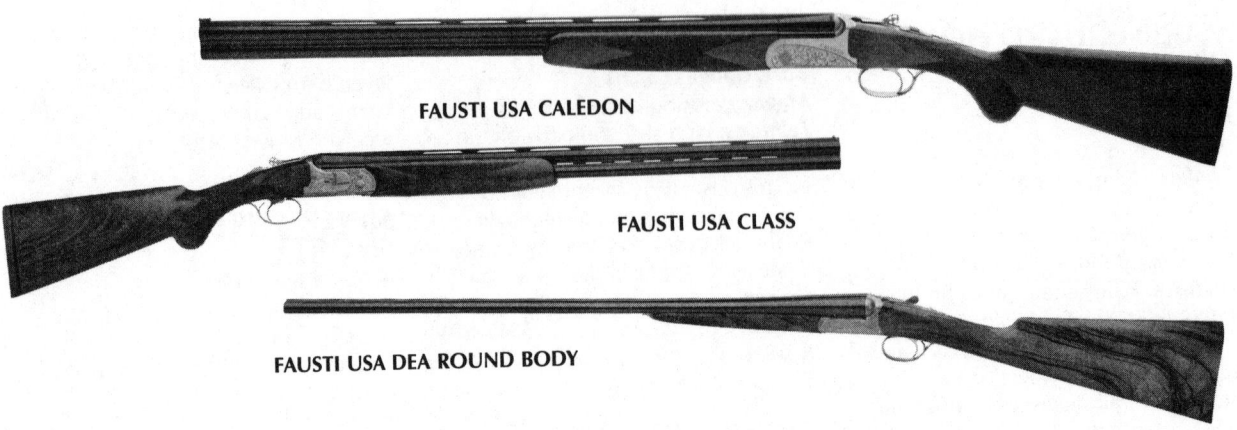

FAUSTI USA CALEDON

FAUSTI USA CLASS

FAUSTI USA DEA ROUND BODY

CALEDON

Action: Over/under
Stock: Walnut
Barrel: 26 in., 28 in., 30 in.
Chokes: Fixed or interchangeable choke tubes
Weight: 5 lb. 12 oz.–7 lb. 4 oz.
Bore/Gauge: 12, 16, 20, 28, .410
Magazine: None
Features: Single selectable trigger; A+ Turkish walnut stock with oil finish; laser-engraved lower receiver; automatic ejectors; metallic bead sight
MSRP . . . . $1999–$2569

CLASS

Action: Over/under
Stock: Walnut
Barrel: 26 in., 28 in., 30 in.
Chokes: Fixed or interchangeable choke tubes
Weight: 5 lb. 12 oz.–7 lb. 5 oz.
Bore/Gauge: 12, 16, 20, 28, .410

Magazine: None
Features: Features automatic ejectors; metallic bead; single-selectable trigger; 14-3/8-in. length of pull; timeless AA walnut oil-polished stock; Prince of Wales style stock; receiver laser-engraved with flushing quail
MSRP . . . . $2449–$2999

DEA ROUND BODY

Action: Side-by-side
Stock: Oil-finished select walnut
Barrel: 28 in.
Chokes: Fixed or interchangeable choke tubes
Weight: 6 lb.
Bore/Gauge: 16, 20
Magazine: None
Features: Scottish-style round-body action and stock; low-profile coin or case-colored receiver; selective ejectors and extractors
MSRP . . . . $5899–$6489

MAGNIFICENT

Action: Over/under
Stock: Walnut
Barrel: 26 in., 28 in., 30 in.
Chokes: Fixed or interchangeable choke tubes
Weight: 5 lb. 12 oz.–7 lb. 6 oz.
Bore/Gauge: 12, 16, 20, 28, .410
Magazine: None
Features: AAA+ walnut stock with oil finish; precision scroll engraving accompanies Aphrodite, the Greek goddess of love and beauty, on the receiver; the Crest of the city of Brescia, Italy, where all Fausti shotguns are produced, is on the underside of the receiver; single selectable trigger; automatic ejectors; metallic bead sight
MSRP . . . . $4999–$5559

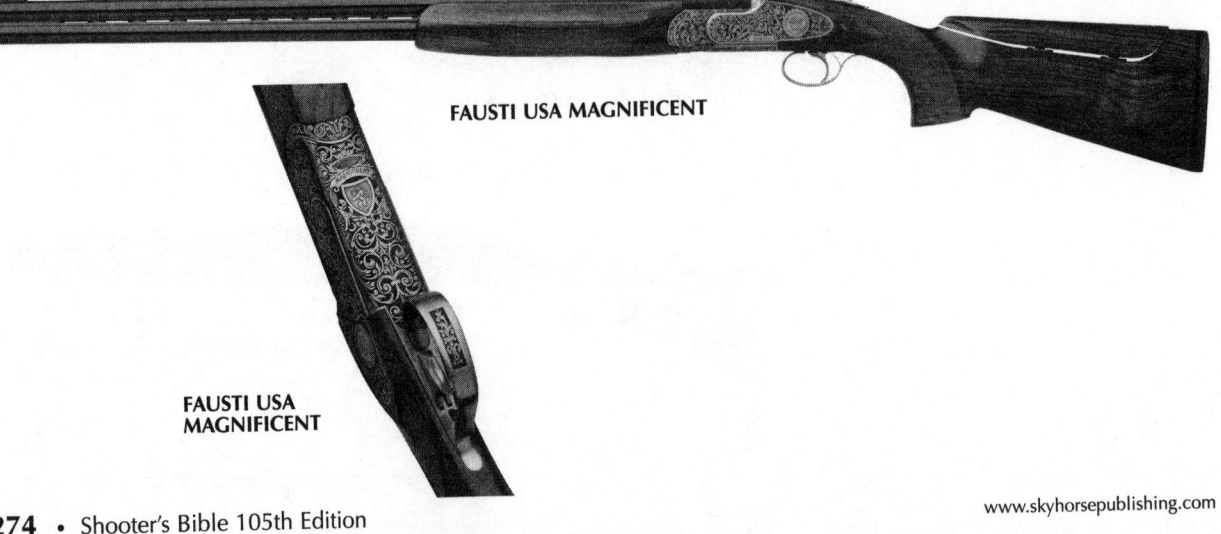

FAUSTI USA MAGNIFICENT

**FAUSTI USA
MAGNIFICENT**

Flodman Guns

FLODMAN SHOTGUN

Action: Over/under
Stock: Walnut
Barrel: 28 in.–34 in.
Chokes: Multichoke
Weight: 6 lb. 3 oz.–8 lb. 6 oz.
Bore/Gauge: 12, 20
Magazine: None
Features: Boxlock offered in any standard gauge or rifle/shotgun combination; walnut stock with pistol grip available; auto or manual safety; Combi stainless steel barrel
From: $23000
Extra double rifle barrels: $18500

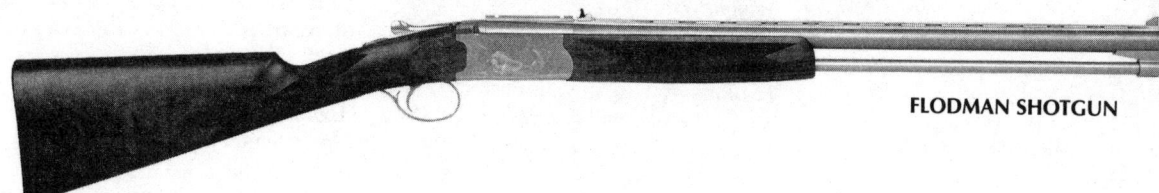

FLODMAN SHOTGUN

Franchi

48 AL

Action: Autoloader
Stock: Walnut
Barrel: 24 in., 26 in., 28 in.
Chokes: Screw-in tubes Standard (IC, M, F, wrench), optional (C, IC, M, IM, F)
Weight: 5 lb. 6 oz.–5 lb. 10 oz.
Bore/Gauge: 20, 28
Magazine: 4+1 rounds
Features: Matte blue steel barrel; polished steel barrel on deluxe model; satin walnut stock on Field model; A-grade satin walnut on Deluxe model; optional custom-fitted hard case
Field: $899
Deluxe: . . . . $999–$1249

FRANCHI AFFINITY

Action: Semiautomatic, inertia driven
Stock: Black synthetic, Realtree Max-4, Realtree APG
Barrel: 24 in., 26 in., 28 in., 30 in.
Chokes: Interchangeable (IC, M, F)
Weight: 5 lb. 8 oz.–6 lb. 12 oz.
Bore/Gauge: 12, 20
Magazine: 4+1 rounds
Features: Red fiber optic bar; durable synthetic stock impervious to all-weather elements as well as gun solvents and lubricants; newly designed recoil pad; aluminum alloy receiver strengthened with steel inserts
Black: $849
Realtree: $949
Compact: . . . . $899–$999
Black, brushed nickel: $1159

FRANCHI INSTINCT L

Action: Over/under
Stock: Walnut

FRANCHI 48 AL FIELD

FRANCHI AFFINITY 20 GA. - REALTREE APG

FRANCHI INSTINCT L 12 GA.

FRANCHI INSTINCT SL 20 GA.

Barrel: 26 in., 28 in.
Chokes: Interchangeable (IC, M, F)
Weight: 6 lb. 2 oz.–6 lb. 6 oz.
Bore/Gauge: 12, 20
Magazine: None
Features: Ventilated raised rib; red fiber optic front sight; blued and color-case-hardened finish on the receiver, with gold inlay; A-grade walnut stock in Prince-of-Wales style with cut checkering on the forend and pistol grip; satin oil finish; single gold-plated trigger; chrome-lined barrels proofed for steel shot; hard-shell custom-fitted gun case included
MSRP. $1149

FRANCHI INSTINCT SL

Action: Over/under
Stock: Walnut
Barrel: 26 in., 28 in.
Chokes: Interchangeable (IC, M, F)
Weight: 5 lb. 6 oz.–5 lb. 11 oz.
Bore/Gauge: 12, 20
Magazine: None
Features: Vent rib; red fiber optic front bead; aluminum alloy receiver; blued barrels; AA-grade satin walnut stock in Prince-of-Wales style with cut checkering and oil finish; tang-mounted automatic safety; custom-fitted, hard-shell gun case included
MSRP. $1349

SHOTGUNS

Harrington & Richardson

HARRINGTON & RICHARDSON PARDNER PUMP

PARDNER PUMP
Action: Pump
Stock: Walnut, synthetic
Barrel: 26 in., 28 in.
Chokes: Screw-in modified choke
Weight: 7 lb. 8 oz.
Bore/Gauge: 12, 20
Magazine: 5 rounds
Features: American walnut stock with grooved and ventilated recoil pad or synthetic with camo; bead front sight; drilled and tapped for scope base; chrome-plated bolt; vent-rib barrel
MSRP **$253**

PARDNER SINGLE-SHOT
Action: Break-open single shot
Stock: Hardwood
Barrel: 22 in., 26 in., 28 in., 32 in.
Chokes: Modified or Full (12 Ga., 20 Ga.), Modified (28 Ga.), Full (12 Ga., .410 bore)
Weight: 5 lb.–6 lb.
Bore/Gauge: 12, 20, 28, .410

Magazine: None
Features: American hardwood, walnut finish with pistol grip; bead front sight; side lever release; automatic ejection; transfer bar safety system
Compact: **$206**
Standard: **$225**

PARDNER TURKEY
Action: Break-open single shot
Stock: Synthetic, hardwood
Barrel: 24 in.
Chokes: Extra-Full Screw-in Chokes, Full in camo 12 Ga.
Weight: 6 lb.–9 lb.
Bore/Gauge: 10, 12
Magazine: None
Features: American hardwood stock in black matte finish or with camo pattern; pistol grip; ventilated rubber recoil pad; sling swivel studs; sling; bead sights; drilled and tapped for scope mount
MSRP **$276**

HARRINGTON & RICHARDSON PARDNER SINGLE-SHOT

HARRINGTON & RICHARDSON PARDNER TURKEY

SHOTGUNS

Harrington & Richardson

HARRINGTON & RICHARDSON TAMER 20 GA.

TAMER 20 GA.
Action: Hinged single-shot
Stock: High density polymer
Barrel: 20 in.
Chokes: Modified choke
Weight: 6 lb.
Bore/Gauge: 20
Magazine: None
Features: High density polymer stock with matte black finish, pistol grip and thumbhole design with storage compartment
MSRP $223

TRACKER II
Action: Single-shot
Stock: Hardwood
Barrel: 24 in.
Chokes: Rifled bore choke
Weight: 5 lb. 4 oz.
Bore/Gauge: 12, 20
Magazine: None
Features: Adjustable rifle sights; American hardwood with walnut finish; full pistol grip; recoil pad; sling swivel studs
MSRP $290

ULTRA LIGHT SLUG HUNTER
Action: Break-open single-shot
Stock: Hardwood
Barrel: 24 in.
Chokes: None
Weight: 5 lb. 4 oz.
Bore/Gauge: 12, 20
Magazine: None
Features: American hardwood with walnut finish, full pistol grip, recoil pad and sling swivel studs; Ultragon rifling; scope base included
MSRP . . . . $290–$293

ULTRA SLUG HUNTER
Action: Hinged single-shot
Stock: Hardwood
Barrel: 24 in.
Chokes: None

Weight: 8 lb.–9 lb.
Bore/Gauge: 12, 20
Magazine: None
Features: Walnut-stained American hardwood Monte Carlo pistol grip

stock; sling swivels; nylon sling; ventilated recoil pad; drilled and tapped for scope mount rail; optional 3-9x32 scope; thumbhole optional
MSRP . . . . $290–$336

HARRINGTON & RICHARDSON TRACKER II

HARRINGTON & RICHARDSON ULTRA SLUG HUNTER

HARRINGTON & RICHARDSON ULTRA LIGHT SLUG HUNTER

SHOTGUNS

Ithaca Gun Company

ITHACA
DEERSLAYER II

ITHACA
LARABEE

ITHACA
DEERSLAYER III

ITHACA MODEL 37
DEFENSE SYNTHETIC

DEERSLAYER II

Action: Pump
Stock: Walnut
Barrel: 24 in.
Chokes: None
Weight: 6.8 lb.–8 lb. 6 oz.
Bore/Gauge: 12, 20
Magazine: 4+1 rounds
Features: Solderless barrel system; thumbhole or standard black walnut Monte Carlo stock; fat deluxe checkered forend; sling swivel studs; Pachmayr 750 Decelerator recoil pad; matte blued finish on barrel; gold-plated trigger; Marble Arms rifle sights; drilled and tapped for Weaver #62 scope rail
MSRP **$899**

DEERSLAYER III

Action: Pump
Stock: Walnut
Barrel: 20 in., 26 in., 28 in.
Chokes: None
Weight: 8.1 lb.–9 lb. 8 oz.
Bore/Gauge: 12, 20
Magazine: 4+1 rounds
Features: Heavy-walled, fluted, fixed barrel in blue matted finish; walnut Monte Carlo stock with optional thumbhole; Pachmayr 750 Decelerator recoil pad; sling swivel studs; gold-plated trigger; Weaver #62 rail pre-installed on receiver
MSRP **$1189**

LARABEE

Action: Single-barrel break-top
Stock: Semi-pistol style
Barrel: 30 in., 32 in., 34 in.
Chokes: 3 interchangeable tubes
Weight: 8 lb. 8 oz.
Bore/Gauge: 12
Magazine: None

Features: Receiver and mono block machined from solid 4140 steel; unique solder-less barrel-attachment system; three possible grades of engraving
MSRP **$1799**

MODEL 37 DEFENSE

Action: Pump
Stock: Synthetic, walnut
Barrel: 18.5 in., 20 in.
Chokes: None
Weight: 6.5 lb.–7 lb. 2 oz.
Bore/Gauge: 12, 20
Magazine: 4+1, 7+1 rounds
Features: Choice of walnut or black synthetic stock; 3 in. chamber; matte blued finish barrel; Pachmayr decelerator recoil pad
Walnut: **$769**
Synthetic: **$685**

Ithaca Gun Company

ITHACA MODEL 37
FEATHERLIGHT

ITHACA MODEL 37 TRAP

ITHACA PHOENIX

MODEL 37 FEATHERLIGHT
Action: Pump
Stock: Walnut
Barrel: 26 in., 28 in., 20 in.
Chokes: 3 Briley Choke tubes (F, M, IC, and wrench)
Weight: 6.1 lb.–7 lb. 10 oz.
Bore/Gauge: 12, 16, 20, 28
Magazine: 4+1 rounds
Features: Solderless barrel system; classic game scene engraving; black walnut stock with semi-pistol butt stock; TruGlo red front sight; Pachmayr 752 Decelerator recoil pad
MSRP . . . . from $859

MODEL 37 TRAP
Action: Pump
Stock: Walnut
Barrel: 30 in.
Chokes: Briley Choke tubes
Weight: 7 lb. 13 oz.
Bore/Gauge: 12
Magazine: 4+1
Features: Bottom ejection; 3 in. chamber; gold plated tubes; walnut Monte Carlo stock; vent rib barrel; classic game scene engraving
MSRP $899

PHOENIX
Action: Over/under
Stock: Semi-pistol style
Barrel: 28 in., 30 in., 32 in., 34 in.
Chokes: 5 interchangeable tubes
Weight: 9 lb.
Bore/Gauge: 12
Magazine: None
Features: Machined from solid steel; barrels attach via front dovetail for a free-floating unit; different engraving grades available
MSRP $2499

SHOTGUNS

Krieghoff

MODEL K-20

Action: Over/under
Stock: Walnut
Barrel: 30 in., 32 in.
Chokes: 5 choke tubes (C, S, IC, LM, M, LIM, IM, F)
Weight: 7 lb. 8 oz.
Bore/Gauge: 20, 28, .410
Magazine: None
Features: Top-tang push safety button; classic scroll engraving; white pearl front bead and metal center bead; single-selective mechanical trigger; hand-checkered select European walnut stock with satin epoxy finish

20 Ga.:	$11395
28 Ga.:	$11495
.410:	$11495
20/28 Ga. Set:	$15890
Set of 3:	$20405

K-20 PRO-SPORTER

Action: Over/under
Stock: Walnut
Barrel: 30 in., 32 in.
Chokes: Titanium choke tubes
Weight: 8 lb.
Bore/Gauge: 20, 28, .410
Magazine: None
Features: Higher rib and stock allows shooter to keep their head more erect, increasing sight range, allowing for quicker target acquisition, reduced neck fatigue, and perceived recoil; high rib easily adjustable

MSRP	$11695–$11795
20/28 Ga. Set:	$16390
3 Ga. Set:	$21105

MODEL K-80

Action: Over/under
Stock: Walnut
Barrel: 30 in., 32 in., 34 in.
Chokes: Steel or Titanium choke tubes (C, S, IC, LM, M, LIM, IM, F, SF)
Weight: 8 lb. 4 oz.
Bore/Gauge: 12
Magazine: None
Features: White pearl front sight and metal center bead; nickel plated steel receiver with satin grey finish; single select trigger; top-tang push button safety; fine-checkered Turkish walnut
Standard Models: . . $10595–$13000

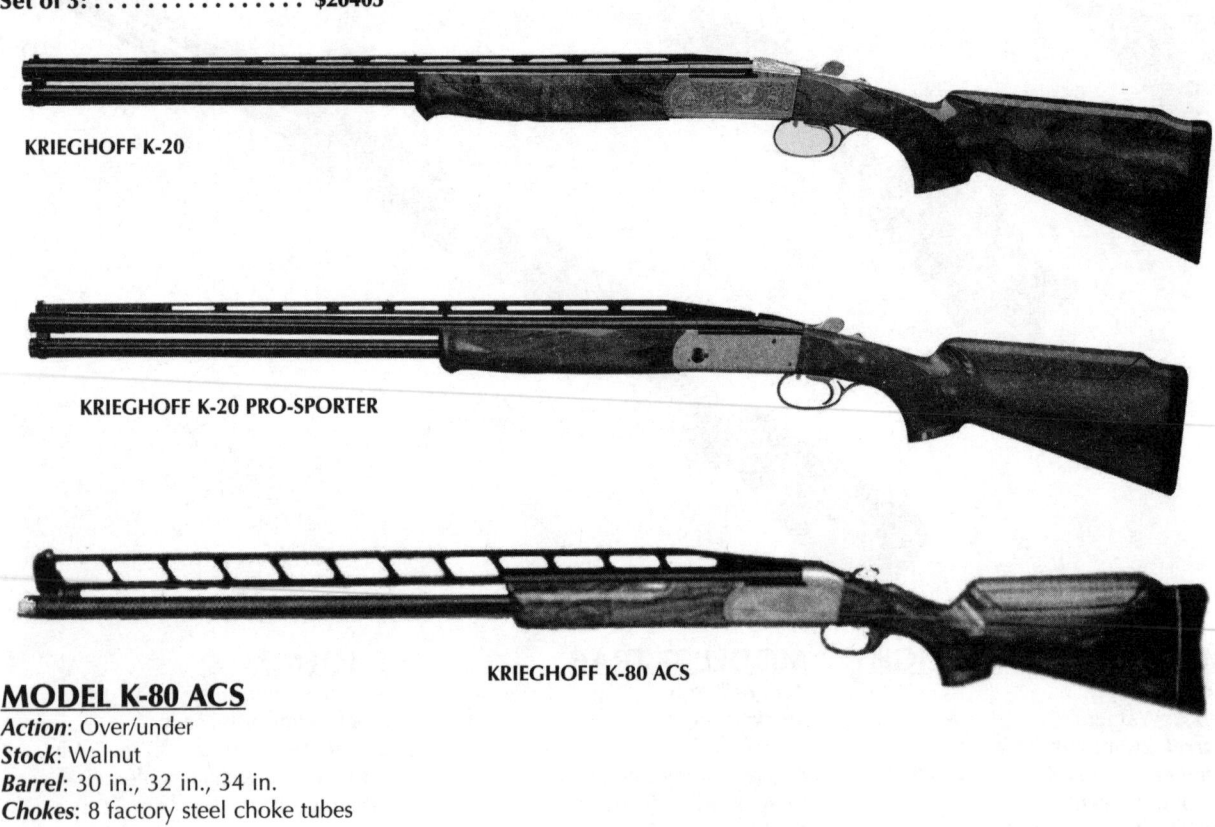

KRIEGHOFF K-20

KRIEGHOFF K-20 PRO-SPORTER

KRIEGHOFF K-80 ACS

MODEL K-80 ACS

Action: Over/under
Stock: Walnut
Barrel: 30 in., 32 in., 34 in.
Chokes: 8 factory steel choke tubes
Weight: 8 lb. 12 oz.
Bore/Gauge: 12
Magazine: None
Features: White pearl front bead and metal center bead sight; case-hardened action, nickel-plated steel receiver with nitride silver finish; single selective trigger

From:	$17370

KRIEGHOFF K-80

Ljutic

ADJUSTABLE RIB MONO GUN

Action: Single barrel
Stock: Walnut
Barrel: 34 in.
Chokes: Fixed or Ljutic SIC
Weight: 10 lb.
Bore/Gauge: .740, 12
Magazine: None
Features: "One Touch" adjustable rib allows you to change your point-of-impact; adjustable comb stock
Adjustable Rib: **$7550**
Stainless Adjustable: **$8495**

MONO GUN

Action: Single barrel
Stock: Walnut
Barrel: 32 in.–34 in.
Chokes: Optional screw in chokes (Fixed, Ljutic SIC, Briley SIC)
Weight: 10 lb.
Bore/Gauge: .740, 12
Magazine: None
Features: Comes with American walnut wood; optional roll over combs and cheek pieces; various upgrades available
Mono: **$7495**
Stainless: **$8495**

PRO 3

Action: Single barrel
Stock: Walnut
Barrel: 34 in.
Chokes: 4 Briley Series 12 chokes
Weight: 9 lb.
Bore/Gauge: .740, 12
Magazine: None
Features: Aluminum baseplate; interchangeable two-pad system; adjustable comb; English or American walnut stock; screw in hinge pin; stainless or blued barrel
Blued barrel: **$8495**
Stainless: **$8995**

LJUTIC ADJUSTABLE RIB MONO GUN

LJUTIC MONO GUN

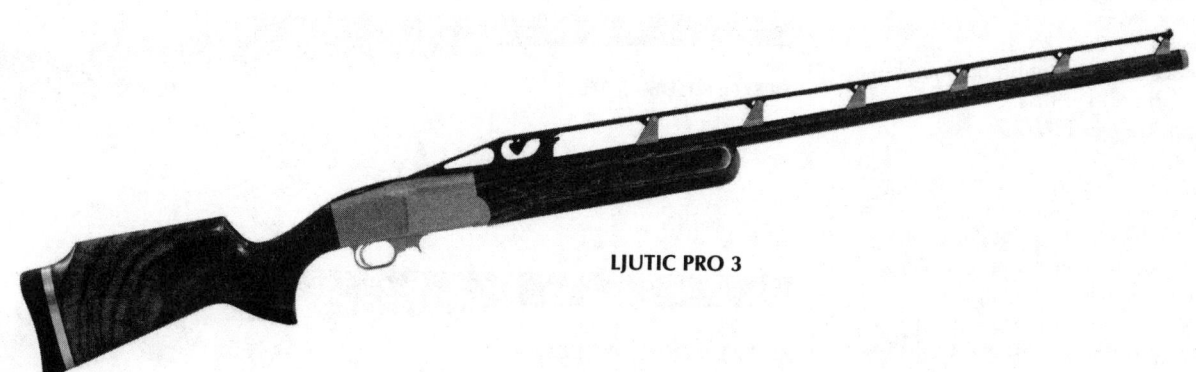

LJUTIC PRO 3

Marocchi

MODEL 100

Action: Over/under
Stock: Walnut
Barrel: 28 in.–32 in.
Chokes: Trap: (IM/F); Sporter (MC), Skeet(SK/SK); Electrocibles (MC);

Double Trap (MC/Full)
Weight: 7 lb. 3 oz.–8 lb. 2 oz.
Bore/Gauge: 12
Magazine: None
Features: Steel action; single adjustable trigger; mechanically assisted

ejector system; steel barrels; boss type locking system; walnut stock available in various grades
Sporting: **$3450**
Trap: **$3400**

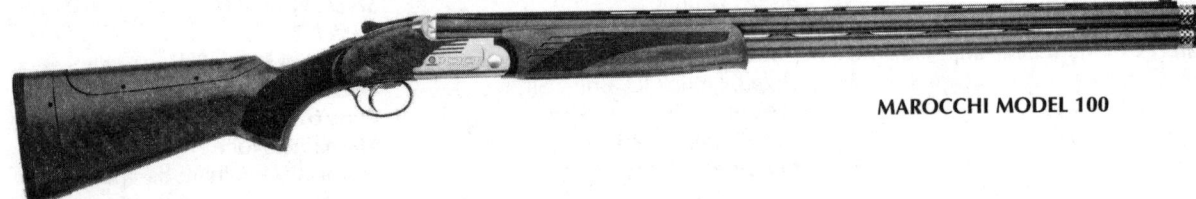

MAROCCHI MODEL 100

Merkel

MODEL 47E, 147E, 147EL

Action: Side-by-side
Stock: Wood
Barrel: 27 in., 28 in.
Chokes: Steel-shot proofed chokes
Weight: 6 lb. 3 oz.
Bore/Gauge: 12, 20
Magazine: None
Features: English stock finished with fine hand-cut checkering at buttplate; silver monogram plate; steel action is gray nitrated; Anson & Deeley locks; Greener-style cross bolt and double bottom bite; double trigger; automatic safety
47E: **$4595**
147E: **$5795**
147EL: **$7195**

MODEL 303EL

Action: Over/under
Stock: Wood
Barrel: 27 in., 28 in.
Chokes: Steel-shot proofed chokes
Weight: 6 lb. 13 oz.
Bore/Gauge: 12/76, 20/76
Magazine: None
Features: Sidelocks with V-springs; Kersten cross-bolt with double conventional bottom bite; double trigger; front trigger articulated; optional selective single trigger; engraving English arabesque; luxury grade walnut stock with pistol grip; optional English-styled stock
MSRP **$24995**

MODEL 2000CL

Action: Over/under
Stock: Wood
Barrel: 27 in., 28 in.
Chokes: 2 interchangeable chokes steel-shot proofed
Weight: 6 lb. 13 oz.
Bore/Gauge: 12/76, 20/76
Magazine: None
Features: Disconnectable ejectors; arabesque engraving; Anson & Deeley locks in steel receiver; Kersten cross-bolt; selective single trigger, adjustable in length; manual safety; wood stock with pistol grip and cheekpiece
MSRP **$8495**

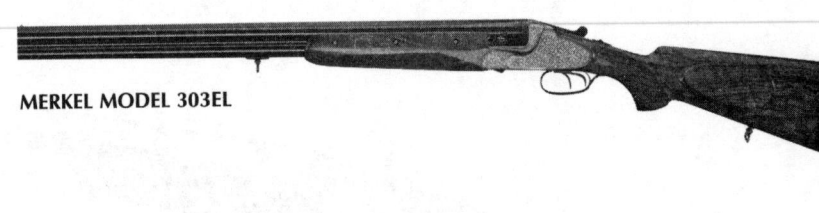

MERKEL MODEL 47E

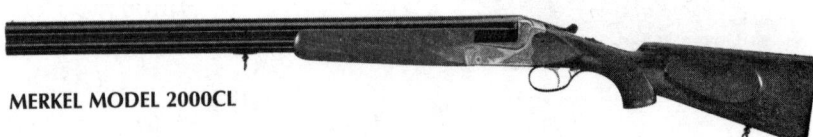

MERKEL MODEL 303EL

MERKEL MODEL 2000CL

SHOTGUNS

MOSSBERG 500 CLASSIC ALL-PURPOSE FIELD

MOSSBERG 500 FLEX ALL-PURPOSE SERIES

500 CLASSIC ALL-PURPOSE FIELD

Action: Pump
Stock: Walnut, synthetic
Barrel: 28 in.
Chokes: Interchangeable Accu-Choke tubes
Weight: 7 lb. 8 oz.

Bore/Gauge: 12
Magazine: 6 rounds
Features: High-gloss walnut stock and forend; fine checkering on the pistol grip and wrapping around the underside of the forend; classic red recoil pad with white Pachmayr line spacer; distinctive jeweled bolt, gold trigger, and high polished blued metal finish; non-binding twin action bars; anodized aluminum receiver; vent rib Accu-Choke barrel; ambidextrous top-mounted safety; available in MO Break-up Infinity
MSRP....................**$401**

500 FLEX ALL-PURPOSE SERIES

Action: Pump
Stock: Synthetic
Barrel: 26 in., 28 in.
Chokes: Accu-Set
Weight: 7 lb. 8 oz.
Bore/Gauge: 12
Magazine: 6 rounds
Features: Matte metal finishes or Marinecote finish; stock with medium recoil pad; stock and forend constructed of synthetic with black matte finish; twin bead sights
MSRP....................**$661**

MOSSBERG 500 FLEX HUNTING SERIES

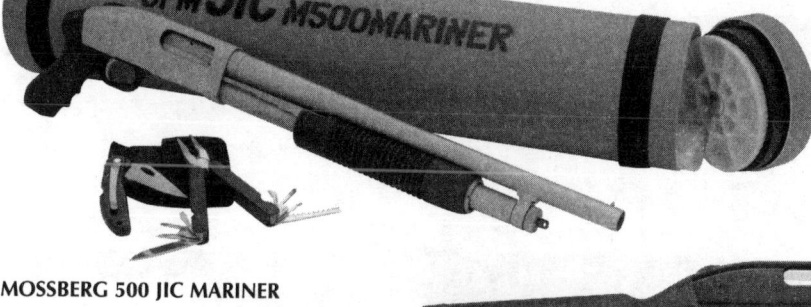

MOSSBERG 500 JIC MARINER

MOSSBERG 500 PERSUADER

500 FLEX HUNTING SERIES

Action: Pump
Stock: Synthetic
Barrel: 24 in.
Chokes: Accu-Set
Weight: 7 lb. 8 oz.
Bore/Gauge: 12
Magazine: 6 rounds
Features: OD green, coyote tan, Mossy Oak Break-Up Infinity, or Realtree Max-4 cam receiver finishes; standard stocks and forends feature Infinity or Realtree Max-4 camo finishes
MSRP....................**$747**

500 JIC MARINER

Action: Pump
Stock: Synthetic
Barrel: 18.5 in.
Chokes: Cylinder bore chokes
Weight: 5 lb. 8 oz.
Bore/Gauge: 12
Magazine: 6 rounds
Features: Bead sight; Marinecote metal finish; comes with multi-tool, survival knife and cordura carrying case; gun lock; swivel studs; black synthetic stock; only pump-action shotguns to pass all U.S. Military Mil-Spec 3443 standards
MSRP....................**$621**

500 PERSUADER, CRUISER

Action: Pump
Stock: Synthetic
Barrel: 20 in.
Chokes: Cylinder bore
Weight: 7 lb.
Bore/Gauge: 12
Magazine: 8 rounds
Features: Ghost ring sights; six-position adjustable stock; matte blued finish; pistol grip standard on some models
MSRP....................**$447**

SHOTGUNS

Mossberg

500 SLUGSTER

Action: Pump
Stock: Synthetic
Barrel: 24 in.
Chokes: None
Weight: 6 lb. 12 oz.–7 lb. 4 oz.
Bore/Gauge: 12
Magazine: 6 rounds
Features: Fully-rifled bore; integral scope base; ported barrel; ambidextrous thumb-operated safety; available in MO Break-up Infinity
MSRP **$434**

500 SUPER BANTAM SLUGSTER

Action: Pump
Stock: Synthetic
Barrel: 24 in.
Chokes: None
Weight: 5 lb. 4 oz.
Bore/Gauge: 20
Magazine: 6 rounds
Features: Fully-rifled bore; adjustable synthetic stock; Blued or Realtree AP finish; drilled and tapped for scopes; ported barrels; adjustable rifle sights
MSRP **$401**

500 SUPER BANTAM TURKEY

Action: Pump
Stock: Synthetic
Barrel: 22 in.
Chokes: Interchangeable Accu-Choke (X-full and wrench)
Weight: 5 lb. 4 oz.
Bore/Gauge: 20
Magazine: 6 rounds
Features: Adjustable synthetic stock in Mossy Oak Break-Up Infinity camo or Hardwoods HD Green camo; adjustable fiber optic sights; drilled and tapped for scopes; gun lock
MSRP **$466**

500 TRI-RAIL TACTICAL

Action: Pump
Stock: Synthetic
Barrel: 18.5 in., 20 in.
Chokes: Cylinder-choked barrel
Weight: 6 lb. 12 oz.
Bore/Gauge: 12
Magazine: 6, 8, 9 rounds
Features: Bead front sight; matte black synthetic, adjustable stock; tri-rail forend
MSRP **$593**

MOSSBERG 500 SLUGSTER

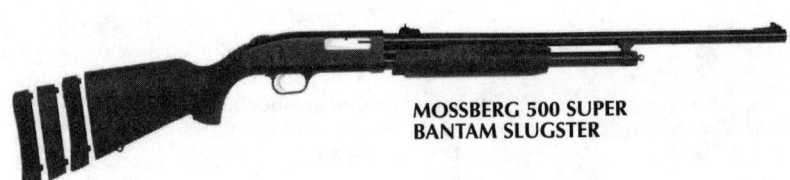

MOSSBERG 500 SUPER BANTAM SLUGSTER

MOSSBERG 500 SUPER BANTAM TURKEY

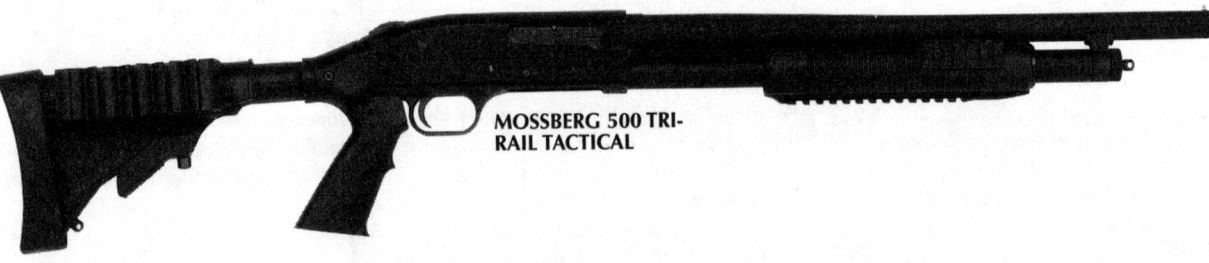

MOSSBERG 500 TRI-RAIL TACTICAL

SHOTGUNS

Mossberg

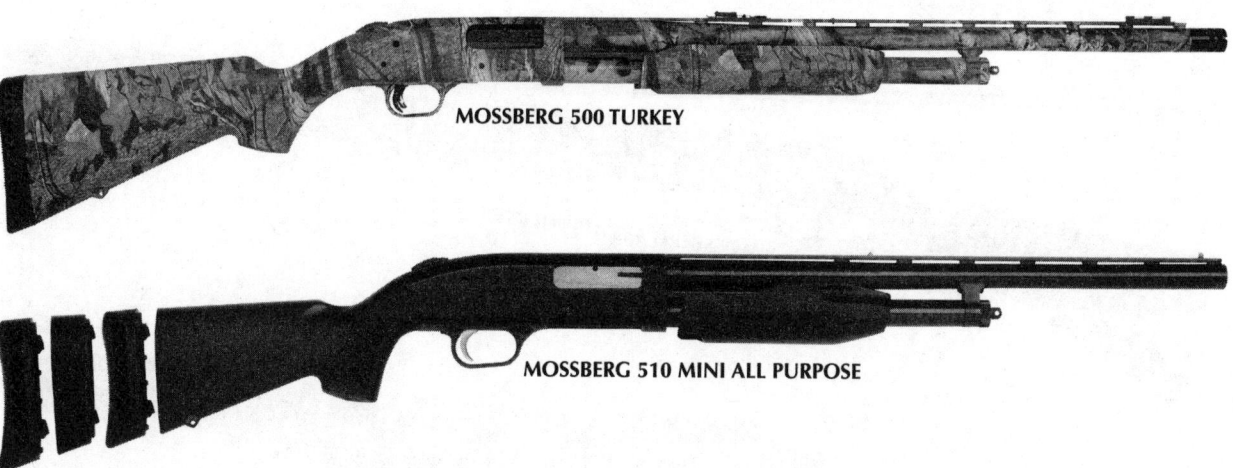

MOSSBERG 500 TURKEY

MOSSBERG 510 MINI ALL PURPOSE

500 TURKEY
Action: Pump
Stock: Synthetic
Barrel: 24 in.
Chokes: Accu-Choke tubes (XX-Full)
Weight: 7 lb. 4 oz.–8 lb. 4 oz.
Bore/Gauge: 12
Magazine: 6, 7 rounds
Features: Adjustable front sight; synthetic finish in Mossy Oak Break-Up Infinity camo; ported barrel; ambidextrous thumb-operated safety; includes gun lock; LPA (Lightning Pump Action) trigger system providing creepfree rifle-like trigger available
MSPR. . . . . **$438–$506**

510 MINI ALL PURPOSE
Action: Pump
Stock: Synthetic
Barrel: 18.5 in.

Chokes: Accu-set in 20 Ga., Fixed-Mod. in .410 bore
Weight: 5 lb.
Bore/Gauge: 20, .410
Magazine: 3 (.410) and 4 (20 Ga.) rounds
Features: Good choice for petite or younger shooter; adjustable synthetic stock in black; blued barrel finish; dual bead sights
MSRP. **$401**

510 MINI CAMO
Action: Pump
Stock: Synthetic
Barrel: 18.5 in.
Chokes: Interchangeable Accu-Choke tubes
Weight: 5 lb.
Bore/Gauge: 20, .410
Magazine: 3, 4 rounds
Features: Dual bead sights; synthetic

stock comes in Mossy Oak Infinity camo
MSRP. **$451**

535 ATS THUMBHOLE TURKEY
Action: Pump
Stock: Synthetic
Barrel: 20 in., 22 in.
Chokes: Interchangeable, X-factor patented choke tube
Weight: 6 lb. 8 oz.
Bore/Gauge: 12
Magazine: 6 rounds
Features: Adjustable front sights; synthetic thumbhole stock comes in black with matte blue metal finish, Mossy Oak break-up infinity or Hardwoods HD green camo; ventilated rib barrel; includes gun lock
MSRP. **$497**

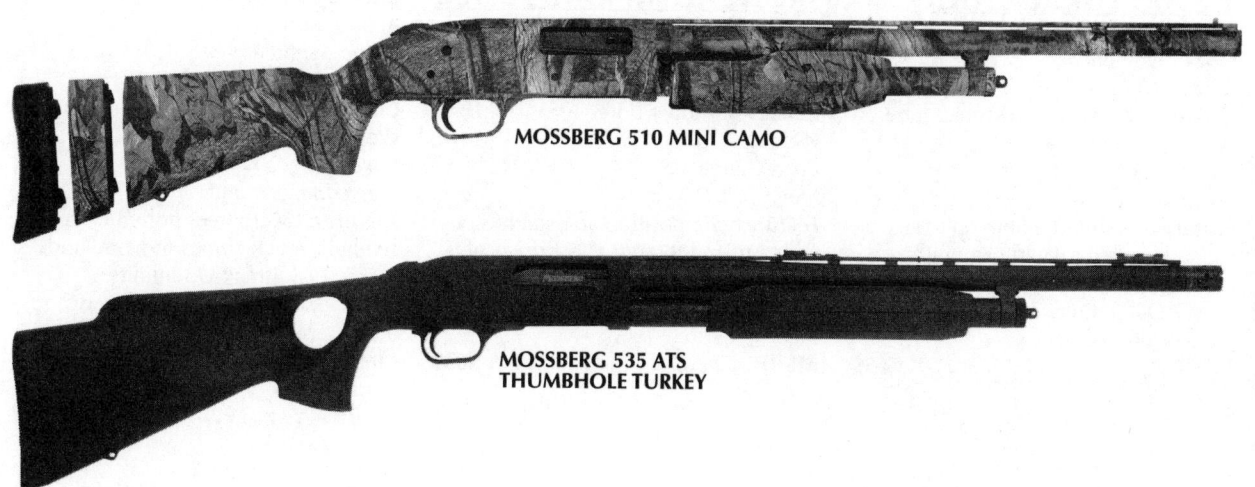

MOSSBERG 510 MINI CAMO

MOSSBERG 535 ATS
THUMBHOLE TURKEY

Mossberg

MOSSBERG 535 ATS TURKEY THUG

MOSSBERG 590A1 ADJUSTABLE TACTICAL TRI-RAIL 9 SHOT

MOSSBERG 835 ULTI-MAG

535 ATS TURKEY THUG

Action: Pump
Stock: Synthetic
Barrel: 20 in.
Chokes: X-factor ported choke tube
Weight: 6 lb. 12 oz.
Bore/Gauge: 12
Magazine: 6 rounds
Features: Adjustable fiber optic sights; user-adjustable trigger; camouflage Picatinny rail; adjustable stock with Mossy Oak Infinity camo finish; TruGlo red-dot sight
MSRP **$656**

590A1 ADJUSTABLE TACTICAL TRI-RAIL 9 SHOT

Action: Pump
Stock: Synthetic
Barrel: 18.5 in., 20 in.
Chokes: Cylinder bore
Weight: 7 lb. 8 oz.
Bore/Gauge: 12
Magazine: 9 rounds
Features: Six-position adjustable stock with a tri-rail forend; ghost ring sights; Parkerized finish; speedfeed, black stock; heavy barrel wall; Blackwater logo
MSRP **$839**

835 ULTI-MAG

Action: Pump
Stock: Synthetic
Barrel: 20 in., 24 in.
Chokes: Ulti-full tube chokes
Weight: 7 lb. 4 oz.
Bore/Gauge: 12
Magazine: 6 rounds
Features: Overbored, ported barrel; synthetic stock comes in woodlands, Mossy Oak Break-Up Infinity, Hardwoods HD Green Camo, or blued; ambidextrous, thumb-operated safety; drilled and tapped for scope mounts
MSRP **$559**

SHOTGUNS

935 MAGNUM TURKEY

Action: Autoloader
Stock: Synthetic
Barrel: 24 in.
Chokes: Ulti-full tube chokes
Weight: 7 lb. 8 oz.
Bore/Gauge: 12
Magazine: 5 rounds
Features: Overbored barrel; synthetic stock in Mossy Oak Break-Up Infinity or Hardwoods HD Green camo; quick-empty magazine button; adjustable fiber optic sights; wide ventilated rib
MSRP **$815**

RHYTHM 930 - PATRICK FLANIGAN SIGNATURE SERIES

Action: Autoloader
Stock: Synthetic
Barrel: 28 in.
Chokes: Accu-Set
Weight: 8 lb. 4 oz.
Bore/Gauge: 12
Magazine: 13 rounds
Features: Dual vent gas-operating autoloading system; Uni-Line stock and receiver alignment; stock drop spacer system; drilled and tapped receiver; versatile Accu-Choke system; synthetic stock and forend with marbled blue and yellow finish; blued metal finishes on metalwork; non-ported vent rib barrel; red fiber optic front bead sight
MSRP **$890**

SA-20 TACTICAL

Action: Autoloader
Stock: Synthetic
Barrel: 20 in.
Chokes: Cylinder bore
Weight: 6 lb.
Bore/Gauge: 20
Magazine: 5 rounds
Features: Quick-load shell elevator; ghost ring sights; Picatinny rail on top of receiver, plus three-sided rail mount below the barrel; standard full-length stock or full-length stock with a pistol grip
MSRP **$518**

**MOSSBERG 935
MAGNUM TURKEY**

**MOSSBERG RHYTHM
930 - PATRICK FLANIGAN
SIGNATURE SERIES**

**MOSSBERG
SA-20 TACTICAL**

SHOTGUNS

Perazzi

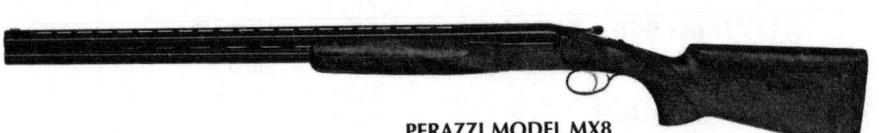

PERAZZI MODEL MX8

MX8 SPORTING CLAYS

Action: Over/under
Stock: Walnut
Barrel: 29 in., 30 in., 31 in.
Chokes: Interchangeable chokes
Weight: 7 lb. 5 oz.
Bore/Gauge: 12, 20
Magazine: None
Features: Custom walnut stock with beavertail forend; half-ventilated side ribs on barrel; removable trigger with flat or coil springs; blue or nickel plating; Sporting, Skeet and Trap models; 28 Ga. and .410 models also available
MSRP $9861

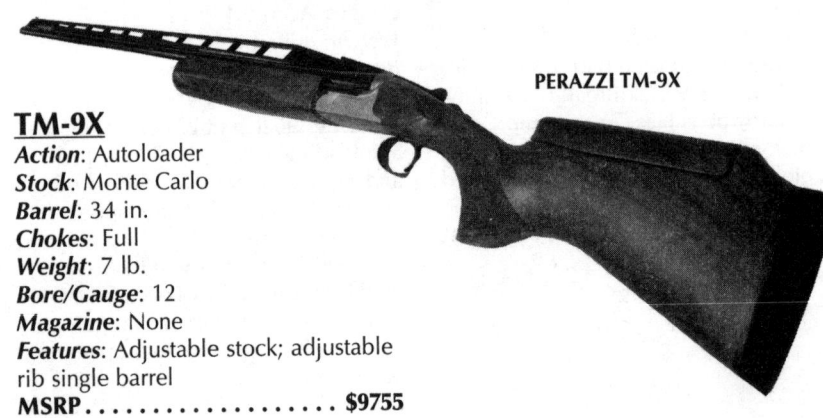

PERAZZI TM-9X

TM-9X

Action: Autoloader
Stock: Monte Carlo
Barrel: 34 in.
Chokes: Full
Weight: 7 lb.
Bore/Gauge: 12
Magazine: None
Features: Adjustable stock; adjustable rib single barrel
MSRP $9755

Purdey

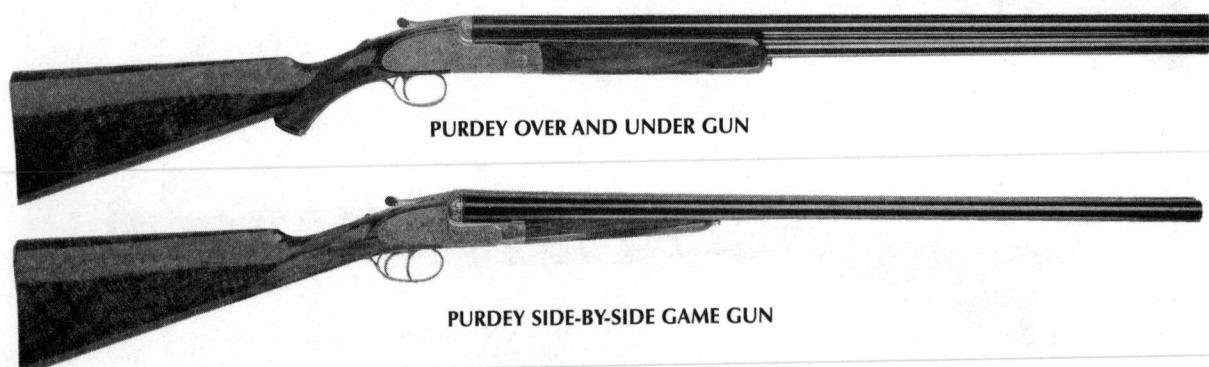

PURDEY OVER AND UNDER GUN

PURDEY SIDE-BY-SIDE GAME GUN

OVER AND UNDER GUN

Action: Over/under
Stock: Walnut
Barrel: 26 in. –30 in.
Chokes: Interchangeable choke tubes
Weight: 4 lb. 14 oz.–7 lb. 8 oz.
Bore/Gauge: 12, 16, 20, 28, .410
Magazine: None
Features: Available in round, square, or ultra-round action shapes; available with double or non-selective single triggers and automatic safety catch; demi-bloc construction; solid game rib with hand matted finish; Turkish walnut with straight, semi, or full pistol grip; gold oval or inlaid gold letters; sporter scroll engraving

Game 12, 16, 20 Ga,: $126144
28 Ga.: $134605
.410: $134605
Sporter: $50144
(All prices excluding UK taxes)

SIDE-BY-SIDE GAME GUN

Action: Side-by-side
Stock: Walnut
Barrel: 26 in. to 30 in.
Chokes: Interchangeable choke tubes
Weight: 4 lb. 10 oz.–6 lb. 12 oz.
Bore/Gauge: 10, 12, 16, 20, 28, .410
Magazine: None
Features: Built on self-opening system; available with double or non-selective single triggers and automatic safety catch; Turkish walnut in straight, semi or full pistol grip; gold oval or inlaid gold letters; sporter scroll engraving; traditional splinter or beavertail forend available

12, 16, 20-bore: $113608
28-bore, .410: $121913
10-bore: $115958
(All prices excluding UK taxes)

SHOTGUNS

REMINGTON MODEL 11-87 SPORTSMAN FIELD

REMINGTON MODEL 870 EXPRESS

REMINGTON MODEL 870 EXPRESS SUPER MAGNUM TURKEY WATERFOWL

MODEL 11-87 SPORTSMAN FIELD

Action: Autoloading
Stock: Walnut
Barrel: 26 in., 28 in.
Chokes: Rem. modified choke
Weight: 7 lb. 4 oz.–8 lb. 4 oz.
Bore/Gauge: 12, 20
Magazine: None
Features: Solid walnut stock and forend with satin finish and fleur-de-lis checkering; nickel-plated bolt and gold-plated trigger; vent rib with dual bead sights
MSRP $845

MODEL 870 EXPRESS

Action: Pump
Stock: Hardwood, synthetic, laminate, or camo
Barrel: 18 in.–28 in.
Chokes: Modified Remington choke, extra full Rem.
Weight: 6 lb.–7 lb. 4 oz.
Bore/Gauge: 12, 20
Magazine: 2–7 rounds depending on model
Features: Single bead sight; standard express finish on barrel and receiver; rubber recoil pad; twin action bars ensure smooth, reliable non-binding action; solid steel receiver; optional thumbhole stock in some models
Express: $411
Syn. 7-round: $428
Syn. Deer: $457
Turkey Camo: $485

MODEL 870 EXPRESS SUPER MAGNUM

Action: Pump
Stock: Hardwood, synthetic, or camo
Barrel: 26 in.
Chokes: Wingmaster HD Waterfowl and Turkey Extra Full Rem chokes
Weight: 7 lb. 4 oz.
Bore/Gauge: 12
Magazine: None
Features: Synthetic stock in full Mossy Oak Bottomland camo; HiVix fiber-optics; SuperCell recoil pad; drilled and tapped receiver
Express Super Mag: $462
Synthetic: $462
Turkey/Waterfowl: $620
Waterfowl Camo: $620

Remington

REMINGTON MODEL 870 EXPRESS TACTICAL A-TACS CAMO

MODEL 870 EXPRESS TACTICAL

Action: Pump
Stock: Synthetic
Barrel: 18.5 in.
Chokes: Screw-in tube
Weight: 7 lb. 8 oz.

Bore/Gauge: 12
Magazine: None
Features: Synthetic stock available in A-tacs digitized camo; Tactical Rem. choke SpeedFeed IV; pistol grip stock; SuperCell recoil pad; adjustable XS Ghost Ring sight rail with removable with bead front sight; Picatinny-style rail
Express Tactical: **$572**
A-Tacs Camo: **$685**

REMINGTON MODEL 870 EXPRESS TACTICAL WITH BLACKHAWK! SPECIAL OPS II

MODEL 870 EXPRESS TACTICAL WITH BLACKHAWK! SPECIAL OPS II

Action: Pump
Stock: Synthetic
Barrel: 18 in.
Chokes: Screw-in tube
Weight: 7 lb.
Bore/Gauge: 12

Magazine: 6+1 rounds
Features: Plain barrel with front bead; 7 position LOP adjustment; recoil reduction system; enhanced pistol grip; sling mount; drilled and tapped receiver; SuperCell recoil pad; Blackhawk Ops II buttstock features built-in recoil reduction system and is adjustable over several increments of length of pull
MSRP **$638**

REMINGTON MODEL 870 SHURSHOT SYNTHETIC SUPER SLUG

MODEL 870 SHURSHOT SYNTHETIC

Action: Pump
Stock: Synthetic
Barrel: 25 in.
Chokes: Screw-in tubes
Weight: 7 lb. 13 oz.
Bore/Gauge: 12

Magazine: None
Features: Ambidextrous Shurshot pistol-grip synthetic stock; rubberized overmolding; SuperCell recoil pad; receiver is drilled and tapped; Weaver rail; sling swivels
Turkey: **$528**
Cantilever: **$571**

REMINGTON MODEL 870 SP MARINE MAGNUM

MODEL 870 SP MARINE MAGNUM

Action: Pump
Stock: Synthetic
Barrel: 18 in.
Chokes: Cylinder chokes

Weight: 7 lb. 8 oz.
Bore/Gauge: 12
Magazine: 6 rounds
Features: Single-bead front sight; padded Cordura; sling swivels; electroless nickel plating covers all metal; twin action bars ensure smooth, reliable non-binding action
MSRP **$829**

REMINGTON MODEL 870 SPS SHURSHOT SYNTHETIC TURKEY

MODEL 870 SPS SHURSHOT SYNTHETIC

Action: Pump
Stock: Synthetic
Barrel: 23 in.
Chokes: Wingmaster HD extended Rem Choke
Weight: 7 lb. 8 oz.

Bore/Gauge: 12
Magazine: None
Features: Synthetic stock covered in Realtree APG HD camo; features ShurShot synthetic pistol grip stock; adjustable TruGlo fiber-optic sights; receiver drilled and tapped for scope mounts
Turkey: **$671**
Super Slug: **$829**

MODEL 870 WINGMASTER

Action: Pump
Stock: Walnut
Barrel: 25 in.
Chokes: Screw-in tubes
Weight: 6 lb.–6 lb. 4 oz.
Bore/Gauge: 12, 20, 28, .410
Magazine: None
Features: Twin action bars for non-binding action; receiver machined from solid billet of steel; highly polished and richly blued receiver; wide array of barrel and choke options
MSRP **$818**

MODEL 870 WINGMASTER CLASSIC TRAP

Action: Pump
Stock: Walnut
Barrel: 30 in.
Chokes: Screw-in tube, Rem. Choke
Weight: 8 lb. 4 oz.
Bore/Gauge: 12
Magazine: None
Features: American walnut, Monte Carlo stock; forend with deep cut checkering and a high-gloss finish; twin bead sights; three specialized trap Rem. choke tubes; twin action bars ensure smooth, reliable non-binding action; choke vent rib barrel
MSRP **$1081**

MODEL 887 NITRO MAG CAMO COMBO

Action: Autoloading
Stock: Synthetic
Barrel: 22 in., 28 in.
Chokes: Screw-in tubes
Weight: 7 lb.–7 lb. 4 oz.
Bore/Gauge: 12
Magazine: None
Features: Synthetic camo stock with ArmorLkt coating; SuperCell recoil pad; HiViz front sight; contoured grip panels; sling swivel
MSRP **$728**

MODEL 1100 CLASSIC TRAP

Action: Autoloading
Stock: Walnut
Barrel: 30 in.
Chokes: Screw-in tubes
Weight: 8 lb. 4 oz.
Bore/Gauge: 12
Magazine: None
Features: American walnut stock with cut-checkering; bead blasted top and bottom radius; blued finish on receiver and barrel; gold triggers and gold embellishments on receiver
MSRP **$1270**

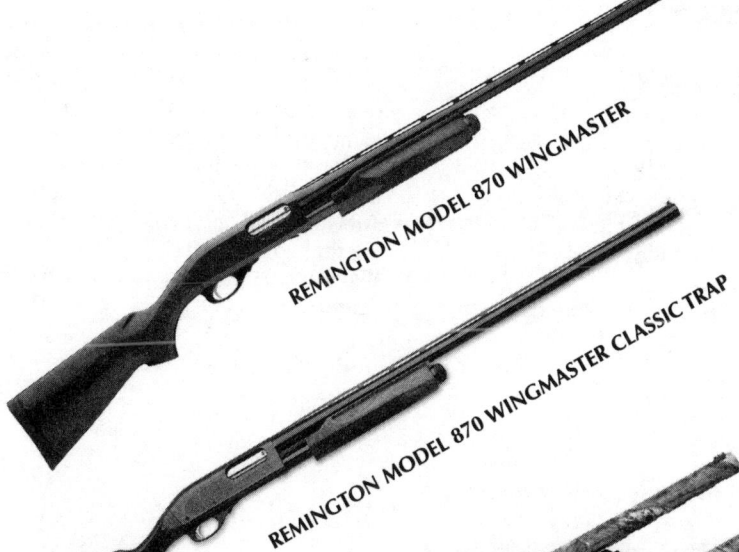

REMINGTON MODEL 870 WINGMASTER

REMINGTON MODEL 870 WINGMASTER CLASSIC TRAP

REMINGTON MODEL 887 NITRO MAG CAMO COMBO

REMINGTON MODEL 1100 CLASSIC TRAP

SHOTGUNS

Remington

**REMINGTON MODEL 1100
COMPETITION SYNTHETIC**

MODEL 1100 COMPETITION SYNTHETIC
Action: Autoloading
Stock: Synthetic
Barrel: 30 in.
Chokes: 5 extended Briley (Target) choke tubes (Skeet, IC, LM, M, Full)
Weight: 8 lb. 2 oz.
Bore/Gauge: 12

Magazine: None
Features: Nickel-Teflon finish on receiver and all internal parts; barrel has 10mm target-style rib; adjustable comb and cast adjustment options; high-gloss blued barrel; fully adjustable target-style stock with recoil reduction; synthetic polymer stock and forend finished with carbon graphite appearance; twin target-style bead sights
MSRP $1242

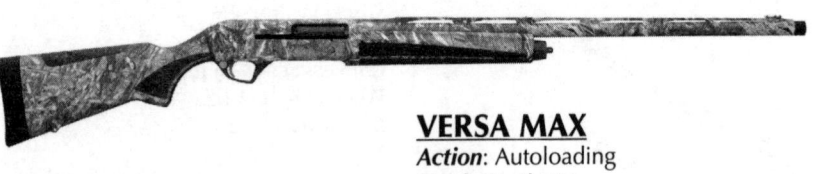

**REMINGTON VERSA MAX
MO DUCK BLIND**

VERSA MAX
Action: Autoloading
Stock: Synthetic
Barrel: 26 in., 28 in.
Chokes: 5 Flush Mount Pro Bore chokes (F, M, IM, LB, IC)
Weight: 7 lb. 8 oz.–7 lb. 11 oz.
Bore/Gauge: 12
Magazine: 3+1, 2+1 rounds

Features: Remington patented gas-piston system; synthetic stock and forend with gray overmolded grips, comes in black or a Mossy Oak Duck blind camo; drilled and tapped receiver; enlarged trigger guard opening and larger safety for easier use with gloves; TriNyte Barrel and nickel Teflon plated internal components
Black: $1399
Camo: $1599

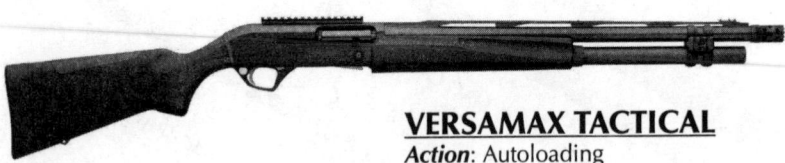

REMINGTON VERSAMAX TACTICAL

VERSAMAX TACTICAL
Action: Autoloading
Stock: Synthetic
Barrel: 22 in.
Chokes: IC and Tactical ProBore tube
Weight: 7 lb. 12 oz.
Bore/Gauge: 12

Magazine: 8+1 rounds
Features: Ventilated rib; fiberoptic HiViz front sight; receiver is drilled and tapped for optics; Picatinny rail; recoil pad; size bolt-release button; oversized trigger guard for easy operation when wearing gloves
MSRP $1399

SHOTGUNS

FIELD GRADE SHOTGUN

Action: Single-shot, break-open
Stock: Synthetic
Barrel: 28 in.
Chokes: Modified screw-in chokes
Weight: 3 lb. 12 oz.–5 lb. 4 oz.
Bore/Gauge: 12, 20, .410
Magazine: None
Features: Steel receiver; black synthetic stock with grips; blue finish metal; transfer bar safety action
Full size: **$175**
Youth 22-in. barrel: **$175**

ROSSI FIELD GRADE SHOTGUN

"TUFFY" .410 SINGLE SHOT

Action: Single-shot, hinged breech
Stock: Synthetic
Barrel: 18.5 in.
Chokes: Screw-in chokes
Weight: 3 lb.
Bore/Gauge: .410
Magazine: None
Features: Black synthetic stock with thumbhole grip; Taurus Security System; matte blued metal finish or matte nickel; steel receiver
MSRP . . . . **$203–$211**

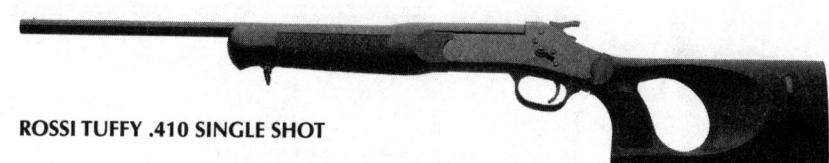

ROSSI TUFFY .410 SINGLE SHOT

YOUTH RIFLED BARREL SLUG GUN

Action: Single shot, break open
Stock: Synthetic
Barrel: 23 in.
Chokes: Screw-in tubes
Weight: 6 lb. 4 oz.
Bore/Gauge: 12
Magazine: None
Features: Steel receiver; black synthetic stock with grips; blued matte finish on metal; removable cheekpiece; Trifecta three-barrel youth gun includes either .243 Win. or 44 Mag. barrel with fiber optic sights or .22 LR barrel with adjustable fiber optics and 20 Ga. shotgun barrel with brass bead front sight
MSRP **$330**

ROSSI YOUTH RIFLED BARREL SLUG GUN

SHOTGUNS

Savage Arms

STEVENS 320 PUMP

Action: Pump
Stock: Synthetic
Barrel: 18.5 in.
Chokes: None
Weight: 7 lb.
Bore/Gauge: 12
Magazine: 5 rounds
Features: Proven rotary bolt design; dual side bars; carbon steel barrel with matte black finish; optional pistol grip, front bead, rifle sights, or ghost ring sights on some models
MSRP . . . . **$245–$295**

SAVAGE ARMS STEVENS 320 PUMP

SAVAGE ARMS STEVENS 350 PUMP FIELD

SAVAGE ARMS STEVENS 350 PUMP SECURITY

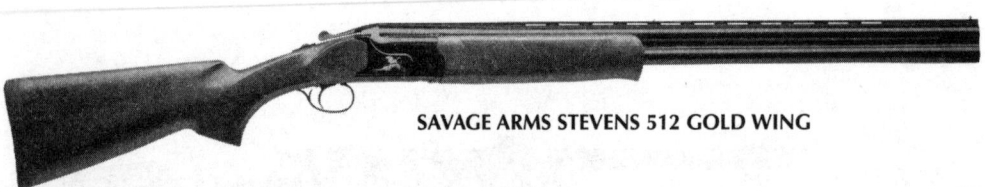

SAVAGE ARMS STEVENS 512 GOLD WING

STEVENS 350 PUMP FIELD

Action: Pump
Stock: Synthetic
Barrel: 28 in.
Chokes: None
Weight: 8 lb. 3 oz.
Bore/Gauge: 12
Magazine: Internal box, 5 rounds
Features: Vent rib, bead sights; carbon steel barrel; blued metal finish; matte black synthetic stock
MSRP **$294**

STEVENS 350 PUMP SECURITY

Action: Pump
Stock: Synthetic
Barrel: 18.25 in.
Chokes: None
Weight: 7 lb. 10 oz.
Bore/Gauge: 12
Magazine: Internal box, 5 rounds
Features: Bead sights; carbon steel barrel with matte blued finish; synthetic stock in matte black finish
MSRP **$285**

STEVENS 512 GOLD WING

Action: Over/under
Stock: Walnut
Barrel: 26 in.
Chokes: None
Weight: 6 lb.–8 lb.
Bore/Gauge: 12, 20, 28, .410
Magazine: None
Features: Vent rib with front sight bead; carbon steel barrel; blued metal finish
Standard: **$690**
Youth: **$690**

SHOTGUNS

Smith & Wesson

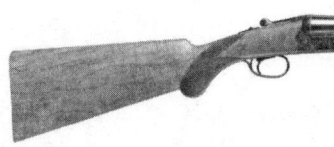

SMITH & WESSON ELITE GOLD GRADE I - PRINCE OF WALES

ELITE GOLD GRADE I
Action: Side-by-side
Stock: Walnut
Barrel: 28 in.
Chokes: Improved cylinder/mod bore
Weight: 6 lb. 11 oz.

Bore/Gauge: 20
Magazine: None
Features: Ivory sight with mid-bead; English or Prince of Wales walnut stock; features the S&W trigger plate; true bone-charcoal case hardening; hand-engraved receiver, English scroll
MSRP $2380

SMITH & WESSON ELITE SILVER GRADE I

ELITE SILVER GRADE I
Action: Over/under
Stock: Walnut
Barrel: 30 in.
Chokes: 5 Thin-wall, English Teague Style Choke Tubes (C, K, M, IM, F)

Weight: 7 lb. 13 oz.
Bore/Gauge: 12
Magazine: None
Features: Ivory sight with mid-bead; English or Prince of Wales walnut stock; features the S&W trigger plate; true bone-charcoal case hardening; hand-engraved receiver, English scroll
MSRP $2380

Stoeger

COACH GUN
Action: Side-by-side
Stock: Walnut, hardwood
Barrel: 20 in.
Chokes: Fixed chokes (IC, M)
Weight: 6 lb. 5 oz.–6 lb. 8 oz.
Bore/Gauge: 12, 20, .410
Magazine: None

Features: A-grade satin or black finished hardwood stock; brass bead sights; nickel or blued metal finish
MSRP . . . . $449–$499

CONDOR
Action: Over/under
Stock: Walnut
Barrel: 22 in., 24 in., 26 in., 28 in.
Chokes: Screw-in and fixed chokes on 12 Ga., 20 Ga., 28 Ga. (IC, M), 16 Ga. (M, F), .410 (F&F)
Weight: 5 lb. 8 oz.–7 lb. 6 oz.
Bore/Gauge: 12, 16, 20, 28, .410
Magazine: None
Features: Walnut stock; brass bead sight; single trigger; auto-ejectors

Condor: $449
Condor Supreme: $599
Condor Youth: $449
Condor Longfowler: $449

CONDOR COMPETITION
Action: Over/under
Stock: Walnut
Barrel: 30 in.
Chokes: Screw-in (IC, M, F)
Weight: 7 lb. 5 oz.–7 lb. 13 oz.
Bore/Gauge: 12, 20
Magazine: None
Features: Walnut stock; brass bead with silver mid-bead sight; single selective trigger; automatic ejector; ported barrel
MSRP $669

STOEGER COACH GUN

STOEGER CONDOR

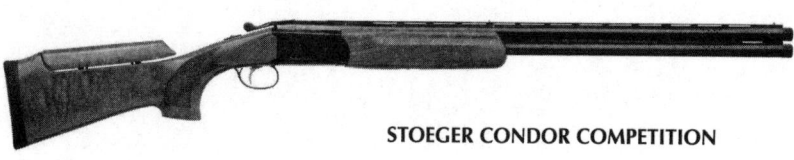

STOEGER CONDOR COMPETITION

Stoeger

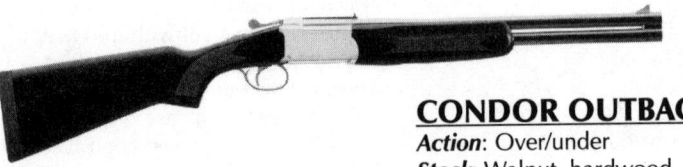

STOEGER CONDOR OUTBACK

CONDOR OUTBACK

Action: Over/under
Stock: Walnut, hardwood
Barrel: 20 in.
Chokes: Screw-in (IC, M)
Weight: 6 lb. 8 oz.–7 lb.

Bore/Gauge: 12, 20
Magazine: None
Features: Notched rear sight and fixed blade front sight; shell extractor; single trigger; A-grade satin walnut or black finished hardwood
MSRP . . . . $449–$499

STOEGER DOUBLE DEFENSE OVER/UNDER

DOUBLE DEFENSE OVER/UNDER

Action: Over/under
Stock: Hardwood
Barrel: 20 in.
Chokes: Screw-in chokes (IC/IC fixed)
Weight: 6 lb. 3 oz.–6 lb. 8 oz.

Bore/Gauge: 12, 20
Magazine: None
Features: Black hardwood stock; green fiber optic front sight; ported barrels; two Picatinny rails; single trigger design; tang-mounted automatic safety
MSRP $479

STOEGER DOUBLE DEFENSE

DOUBLE DEFENSE SIDE-BY-SIDE

Action: Side-by-side
Stock: Hardwood
Barrel: 20 in.
Chokes: Screw-in chokes (IC/IC fixed)
Weight: 6 lb. 8 oz.

Bore/Gauge: 12, 20
Magazine: None
Features: Black hardwood stock; fiber optic front sight; ported barrels; two Picatinny rails; single trigger design; tang-mounted automatic safety
MSRP $499

Stoeger

STOEGER MODEL 3500

STOEGER P350 PUMP

STOEGER UPLANDER

MODEL 3500

Action: Semiautomatic
Stock: Synthetic
Barrel: 24 in., 26 in., 28 in.
Chokes: Screw-in choke tubes (C, IC, M, F, XFT) and wrench
Weight: 7 lb. 7 oz.–7 lb. 10 oz.
Bore/Gauge: 12
Magazine: 4+1 rounds
Features: Synthetic stock comes in black or camo finish in Advantage Max-4, Realtree APG, inertia drive sys- tem; recoil reducer; red-bar front sight; Weaver scope base; includes shim kit

Black synthetic: **$629**
Realtree: **$719**

P350 PUMP

Action: Pump
Stock: Walnut
Barrel: 18.5 in., 24 in., 26 in., 28 in.
Chokes: Screw-in (C, IC, M, F, XFT)
Weight: 6 lb. 6 oz.–6 lb. 14 oz.
Bore/Gauge: 12

Magazine: 4+1 rounds
Features: Red bar front sight and metal bead mid-sight; shipped with limiter plug installed; synthetic stock comes in black, Realtree APG, or Realtree Max-4 HD; ergonomic forend

Synthetic: **$349**
Realtree: **$449**
Realtree APG Steady Grip: **$479**
Synthetic Pistol Grip: **$379**

UPLANDER

Action: Side-by-side
Stock: Walnut
Barrel: 22 in. (youth), 26 in., 28 in., 28 in.
Chokes: Screw-in and fixed tubes
Weight: 6 lb. 8 oz.–7 lb. 8 oz.
Bore/Gauge: 12, 16, 20, 28, .410
Magazine: None
Features: Brass bead sights; A-grade satin walnut stock; tang-mounted safe- ty; single or double triggers; extractors included

Uplander: **$449**
Uplander Supreme: **$539**
Uplander Youth: **$449**
Uplander Longfowler: **$449**

Taylor's & Co.

TAYLOR'S & CO. 1887
T-SERIES PISTOL

1887 T-SERIES PISTOL

Action: Lever
Stock: Synthetic
Barrel: 18.5 in.
Chokes: None
Weight: 7 lb.

Bore/Gauge: 12
Magazine: 5+1 rounds
Features: Black soft touch stock, matte blued finish; available in Zombie Blaster Edition and Bootleg Model
MSRP **$995**

Thompson/Center

THOMPSON/CENTER PRO
HUNTER TURKEY

PRO HUNTER TURKEY

Action: Hinged-breech single-shot
Stock: AP camo with Flextech
Barrel: 24 in. or 26 in.
Chokes: T/C extra full

Weight: 6 lb. 4 oz.–6 lb. 12 oz.
Bore/Gauge: 12, 20
Magazine: None
Features: Fiber optic sights; 14 in. length pull
MSRP **$879**

SHOTGUNS

Tristar Sporting Arms

COBRA FIELD PUMP

Action: Pump
Stock: Synthetic
Barrel: 24 in., 26 in., 28 in.
Chokes: 1 Berretta-style choke (M)
Weight: 6 lb. 8 oz.–6 lb. 14 oz.
Bore/Gauge: 12
Magazine: None
Features: Fiber optic front sight; extended forearm to keep out dirt; sling swivel studs
MSRP . . . . $329–$379
Camo: . . . . $409–$469

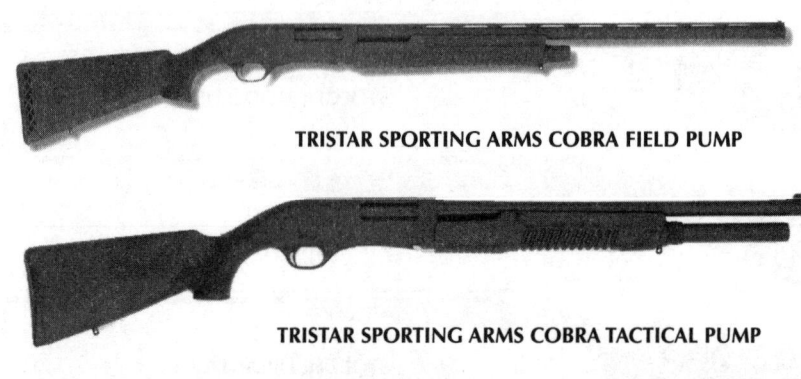

TRISTAR SPORTING ARMS COBRA FIELD PUMP

TRISTAR SPORTING ARMS COBRA TACTICAL PUMP

COBRA TACTICAL PUMP

Action: Pump
Stock: Synthetic
Barrel: 20 in.
Chokes: Screw-in tubes
Weight: 6 lb. 5 oz.
Bore/Gauge: 12
Magazine: 5+1 rounds
Features: Faux extended magazine tube; spring-loaded forearm; synthetic stock in matte black; 3-in. chamber
MSRP $304

HUNTER MAG BLACK 3 1/2 IN.

Action: Over/under
Stock: Black synthetic
Barrel: 26 in., 28 in.
Chokes: Interchangeable tubes (SK, IC, M, IM, F)
Weight: 7 lb. 6 oz.–7 lb. 10 oz.
Bore/Gauge: 12

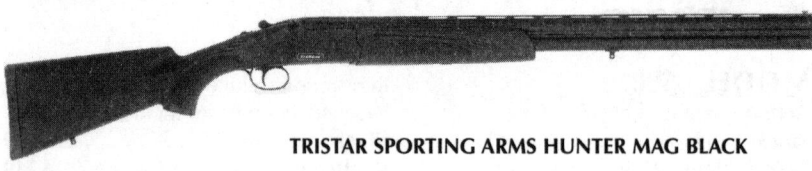

TRISTAR SPORTING ARMS HUNTER MAG BLACK

Magazine: 2 rounds
Features: Fiber optic front sight; synthetic stock and forearm; single selective trigger
MSRP $619
Camo: $719

SETTER S/T

Action: Over/under
Stock: Walnut
Barrel: 26 in., 28 in.
Chokes: 3-Beretta style tubes (IC, M, F)
Weight: 6 lb. 5 oz.–7 lb. 3 oz.
Bore/Gauge: 12, 20
Magazine: None

Features: Fiber optic front sight; high-gloss wood; single selective trigger; extractors; ventilated rib
MSRP $549

TSA 3 1/2" BLACK

Action: Semiautomatic
Stock: Black synthetic
Barrel: 24 in., 26 in., 28 in.
Chokes: Interchangeable tubes (IC, M, F)
Weight: 7 lb. 3 oz.–7 lb. 6 oz.
Bore/Gauge: 12
Magazine: 5+1 rounds
Features: Now in black synthetic stock; also available in camo; two piston system; magnum recoil pad; fiber optic front sight
MSRP $639
Camo: $699

VIPER G2 YOUTH CAMO

Action: Semiautomatic
Stock: Camo synthetic
Barrel: 24 in.
Chokes: Beretta/Benelli style chokes (IC, M, F)
Weight: 5 lb. 11 oz.
Bore/Gauge: 20
Magazine: 5+1 rounds
Features: Now in Realtree Advantage Timber stock; manual E-Z load magazine cut-off; vent rib with matted sight plane; fiber optic front sight; chrome-lined chamber and barrel; soft touch stock
MSRP $589

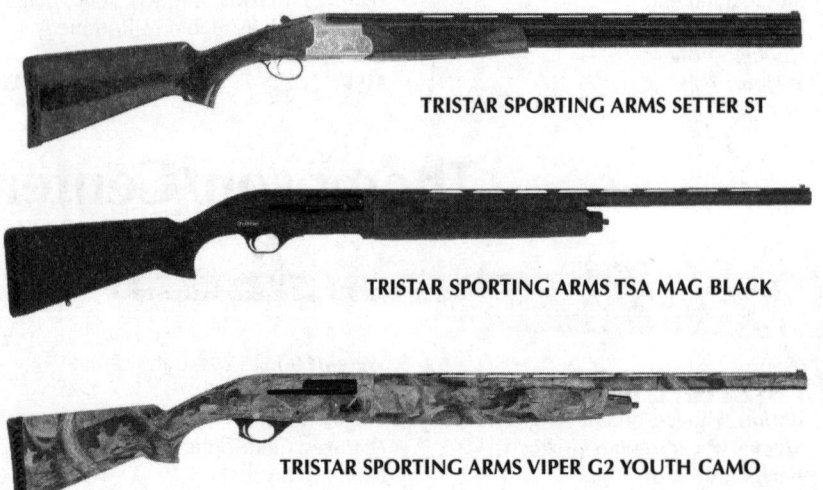

TRISTAR SPORTING ARMS SETTER ST

TRISTAR SPORTING ARMS TSA MAG BLACK

TRISTAR SPORTING ARMS VIPER G2 YOUTH CAMO

SHOTGUNS

Weatherby

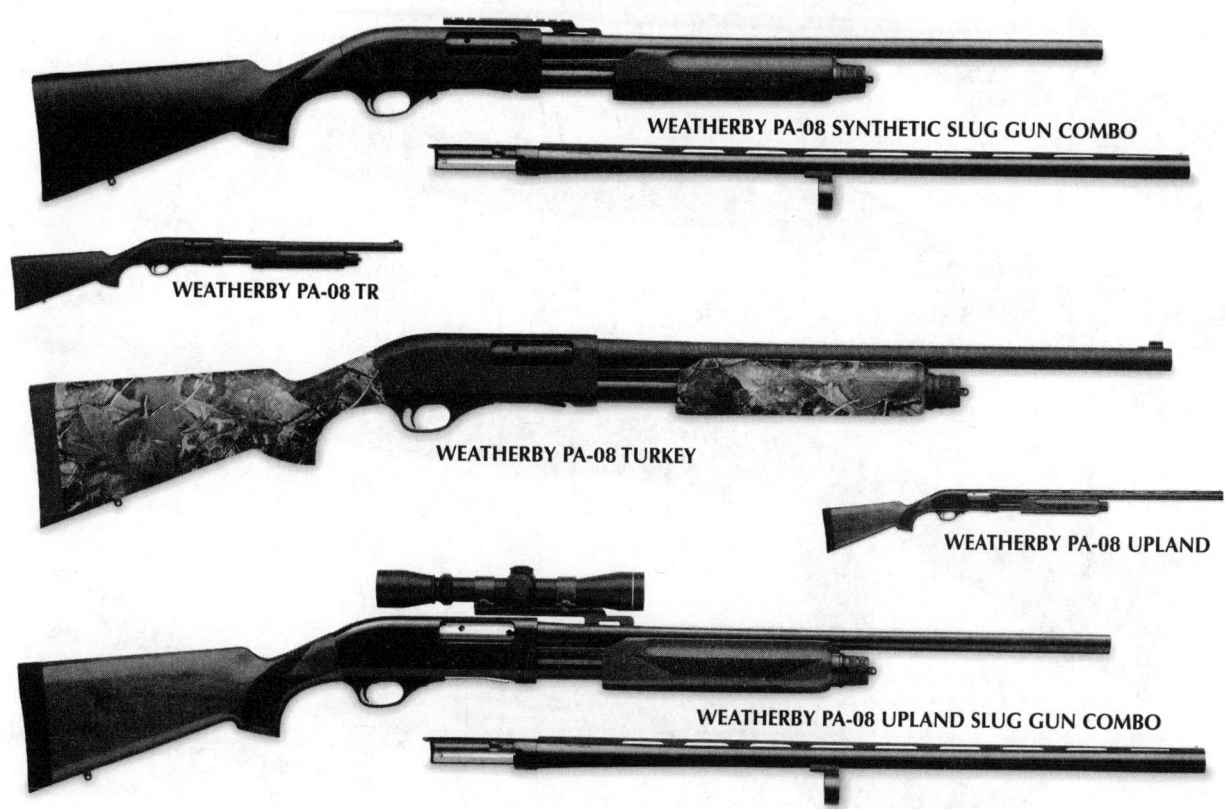

WEATHERBY PA-08 SYNTHETIC SLUG GUN COMBO

WEATHERBY PA-08 TR

WEATHERBY PA-08 TURKEY

WEATHERBY PA-08 UPLAND

WEATHERBY PA-08 UPLAND SLUG GUN COMBO

PA-08 SYNTHETIC SLUG GUN COMBO
Action: Pump
Stock: Synthetic
Barrel: 24 in., 28 in.
Chokes: Interchangeable tubes (IC, M, F)
Weight: 7 lb. 4 oz.
Bore/Gauge: 12
Magazine: 4+1, 5+1 rounds
Features: Lightweight and durable injection-molded synthetic stock; comes with 28 in. field barrel and 24 in. rifled barrel with cantilever scope mount base; swivel studs; aircraft-grade aluminum alloy action; chrome-plated bolt in operating action
MSRP. **$549**

PA-08 TR
Action: Pump
Stock: Synthetic
Barrel: 18.5 in.
Chokes: Cylinder
Weight: 6 lb.–6 lb. 8 oz.
Bore/Gauge: 12, 20
Magazine: None
Features: Dual-action-bar pump; black, injection-molded synthetic

composite stock; black metal finish; white blade front sight
MSRP. **$399**

PA-08 TURKEY
Action: Pump
Stock: Synthetic with Mothwing Spring Mimicry camo
Barrel: 22 in.
Chokes: Removeable choke tube (F)
Weight: 6 lb. 12 oz.
Bore/Gauge: 12
Magazine: 4+1, 5+1 rounds
Features: Dependable dual action bar system; features Mothwing Spring Mimicry camouflage pattern; special "dipping" process adheres camo directly to all stock components; swivel studs included; chrome-lined barrels
MSRP. **$399**

PA-08 UPLAND
Action: Pump
Stock: Walnut
Barrel: 26 in., 28 in.
Chokes: Screw in tubes (IC, M, F)
Weight: 6 lb. 8 oz.–7 lb. 4 oz.
Bore/Gauge: 12, 20

Magazine: None
Features: Walnut stock with gloss finish; gloss black finish on metalwork; vented top dissipates heat and aids in target acquisition; chrome-lined barrels
MSRP. **$449**

PA-08 UPLAND SLUG GUN COMBO
Action: Pump
Stock: Walnut
Barrel: 24 in., 28 in.
Chokes: Interchangeable tubes (IC, M, F)
Weight: 7 lb. 4 oz.
Bore/Gauge: 12
Magazine: 4+1, 5+1 rounds
Features: Walnut stock with gloss finish; receiver with 28 in. field barrel is gloss black for a distinctive look; 24 in. rifled barrel with cantilever scope mount base in matte black; swivel studs; aircraft-grade aluminum alloy action; chrome-plated bolt in operating action
MSRP. **$649**

Weatherby

WEATHERBY SA-08 DELUXE

WEATHERBY SA-08 UPLAND

WEATHERBY SA-459 TR

WEATHERBY SA-459 TURKEY

SA-08 DELUXE

Action: Semiautomatic
Stock: Walnut
Barrel: 26 in., 28 in.
Chokes: Screw in tubes (IC, M, F)
Weight: 6 lb.–6 lb. 12 oz.
Bore/Gauge: 12, 20
Magazine: None
Features: Walnut stock with high–gloss finish and metalwork; vented top rib dissipates heat and aids in target acquisition; dual valve system
MSRP **$799**

SA-08 UPLAND

Action: Semiautomatic
Stock: Walnut
Barrel: 26 in., 28 in.

Chokes: Screw-in tubes (IC, M, F)
Weight: 6 lb.–6 lb. 12 oz.
Bore/Gauge: 12, 20
Magazine: None
Features: Walnut stock with satin finish; matte black finish on metalwork; vented top rib dissipates heat and aids in target acquisition; dual valve system
MSRP **$799**

SA-459 TR

Action: Semiautomatic
Stock: Synthetic
Barrel: 18.5 in.
Chokes: Ported cylinder choke tube
Weight: 6 lb.–6 lb. 8 oz.
Bore/Gauge: 12, 20
Magazine: 5+1 rounds
Features: Pistol grip stock with a rubber textured area; chrome-lined barrel; Picatinny rail for mounting scopes and optics; ghost ring style rear sight, front

bead sight; black synthetic injection-molded stock is matched by black matte metal finishing
MSRP **$699**

SA-459 TURKEY

Action: Semiautomatic, gas-operated
Stock: Synthetic with Mothwing Spring Mimicry camo
Barrel: 21.25 in.
Chokes: Interchangeable tubes (X-F)
Weight: 6 lb. 4 oz.–6 lb. 12 oz.
Bore/Gauge: 12, 20
Magazine: 4+1, 5+1 rounds
Features: Trimmer forend for easier handling; swivel studs; Mil-Spec Picatinny rail for mounting optics; LPA-style ghost ring rear sight that is adjustable for windage and elevation; front blade sight with fiber optic insert; over-size hourglass-shaped bolt handle for quick and positive chambering; pistol grip stock
MSRP **$699**

Winchester Repeating Arms

MODEL 101
Action: Over/under
Stock: Walnut
Barrel: 26 in., 28 in., 30 in., 32 in.
Chokes: Invector-Plus choke system, 3 tubes
Weight: 6 lb. 12oz.–7 lb. 6 oz.
Bore/Gauge: 12
Magazine: None
Features: Solid brass bead front sight on Field; Truglo front sight on Sporting; deep relief receiver engraving; high-gloss grade II/III walnut stock; vented Pachmayr Decelerator pad with classic white line spacer
Field: $1869.99
Sporting: $2320

SUPER X PUMP BLACK SHADOW
Action: Pump
Stock: Synthetic
Barrel: 26 in., 28 in.
Chokes: Invector Plus
Weight: 6 lb. 12 oz.–7 lb.
Bore/Gauge: 12
Magazine: 4 rounds
Features: Hard chrome chamber and bores; drop-out trigger group for easy cleaning; synthetic stock with non-glare black matte finish on barrel and receiver
MSRP . . . . $379.99–$429.99

SUPER X PUMP DEFENDER
Action: Pump
Stock: Composite
Barrel: 18 in.
Chokes: Fixed cylinder choked barrel
Weight: 6 lb. 4 oz.
Bore/Gauge: 12
Magazine: 5+1 rounds
Features: Uses Foster-type slugs; non-glare metal surfaces with a tough black composite stock; deeply grooved fore-arm for control and stability
MSRP $400

SUPER X PUMP TURKEY HUNTER
Action: Pump
Stock: Synthetic
Barrel: 24 in.
Chokes: Invector Plus
Weight: 6 lb. 10 oz.
Bore/Gauge: 12
Magazine: 4 rounds
Features: Hard chrome chamber and bores; drop-out trigger group for easy cleaning; Invector Plus Extra-Full Turkey Choke Tube; crossbolt safety; Inflex technology recoil pad; synthetic stock with textured gripping surfaces in Mossy Oak Break-Up Infinity
MSRP $519.99

SUPER X PUMP WATERFOWL HUNTER
Action: Pump
Stock: Synthetic
Barrel: 26 in.
Chokes: Invector Plus
Weight: 6 lb. 14 oz.
Bore/Gauge: 12
Magazine: 4 rounds
Features: Hard chrome chamber and bores; drop-out trigger group for easy cleaning; synthetic stock with textured gripping surfaces in Mossy Oak Shadow Grass Blades
MSRP $499.99

WINCHESTER MODEL 101 FIELD

WINCHESTER SUPER X PUMP BLACK SHADOW

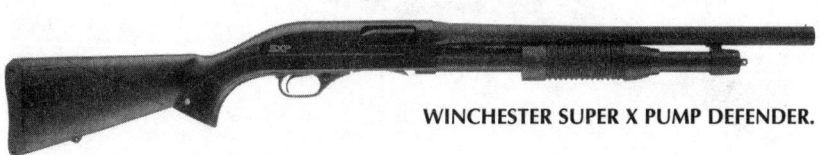

WINCHESTER SUPER X PUMP DEFENDER.

WINCHESTER SUPER X PUMP TURKEY HUNTER

WINCHESTER SUPER X PUMP WATERFOWL HUNTER

SHOTGUNS

Winchester Repeating Arms

SUPER X3 BLACK FIELD
Action: Semiautomatic
Stock: Walnut
Barrel: 26 in., 28 in.
Chokes: Invector Plus
Weight: 6 lb. 8 oz.–6 lb. 14 oz.
Bore/Gauge: 12, 20
Magazine: 4 rounds
Features: Satin oil finish walnut stock with classic cut checkering; matte black receivers in lightweight aluminum alloy; Invector Plus choke system
MSRP **$1069.99**

WINCHESTER SX3 BLACK FIELD

SUPER X3 FIELD COMPACT
Action: Semiautomatic
Stock: Walnut
Barrel: 26 in., 28 in.
Chokes: Invector Plus
Weight: 6 lb. 6 oz.–6 lb. 14 oz.
Bore/Gauge: 12, 20
Magazine: 4 rounds
Features: Stock dimensions trimmed for smaller-frame shooters and hunters with a 13-inch length of pull; satin oil finish walnut stock with classic cut checkering; matte black receivers in lightweight aluminum alloy
MSRP **$1069.99**

WINCHESTER SX3 BLACK FIELD COMPACT

SUPER X3 SPORTING ADJUSTABLE
Action: Autoloader
Stock: Walnut
Barrel: 28 in., 30 in., 32 in.
Chokes: Five extended signature choke tubes
Weight: 7 lb. 6 oz.–7 lb. 10 oz.
Bore/Gauge: 12
Magazine: holds up to 4 rounds depending on shell size
Features: Aluminum-alloy receiver, and barrel; ventilated rib; buttstock features an adjustable comb; chrome-plated chamber and bore; Pachmayr decelerator recoil pad; molded red case included
MSRP **$1699.99**

WINCHESTER SX3 SPORTING ADJUSTABLE

Accu-Tek

ACCU-TEK AT-380 II

AT-380 II
Action: Semi-automatic
Grips: Composite
Barrel: 2.8 in.
Sights: Target
Weight: 23.5 oz.
Caliber: .380 ACP
Capacity: 6+1 rounds
Features: Stainless steel construction;
adjustable rear sight; one hand manual
safety blocks; stainless steel magazine
MSRP $275

HC-380
Action: Semi-automatic
Grips: Composite
Barrel: 2.8 in.
Sights: Target
Weight: 26 oz.
Caliber: .380 ACP
Capacity: 13 rounds
Features: Adjustable rear sight; black
checkered grip; one hand manual
safety block; includes two magazines
and cable lock
MSRP $314

ACCU-TEK HC-380

American Derringer

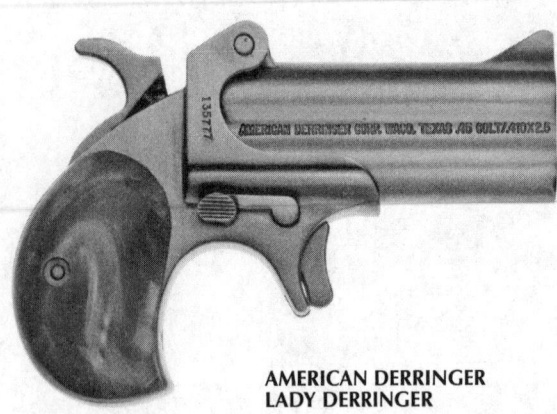

**AMERICAN DERRINGER
LADY DERRINGER**

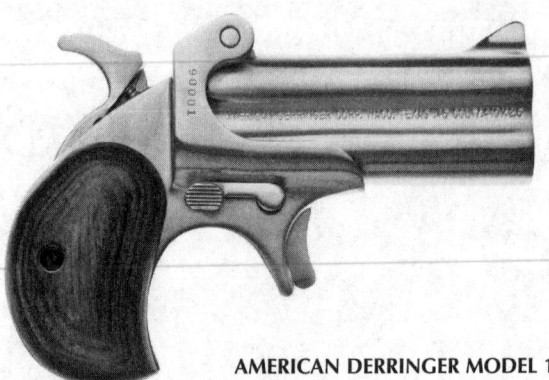

AMERICAN DERRINGER MODEL 1

LADY DERRINGER
Action: Hinged breech
Grips: Camo, Pink, Scrimshaw
Barrel: 3 in.
Sights: Open, fixed
Weight: 15.5 oz.
Caliber: .38 Special, .32 Mag.
Capacity: 2 rounds

Features: Lady Derringer Survivor
Series in memory of breast cancer
survivors; highly-polished brass or
stainless steel frame; each pistol is
handmade, custom serial numbers are
available
Camo/Pink: $835
Engraved Scrimshaw: $2300

MODEL 1
Action: Hinged breech
Grips: Rosewood or stag
Barrel: 3 in.
Sights: Fixed, open
Weight: 15 oz.
Caliber: .45, .410
Capacity: 2 rounds
Features: Single-action; automatic
barrel selection; manually operated
hammer-block safety
MSRP $710

HANDGUNS

American Derringer

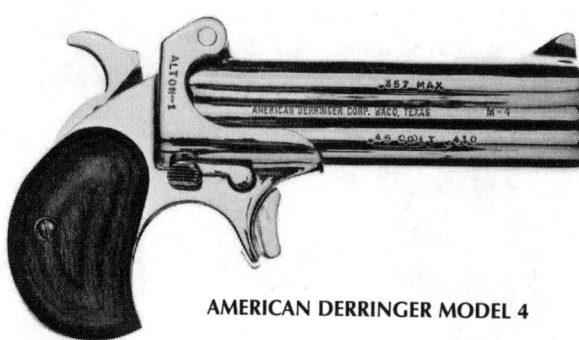

AMERICAN DERRINGER MODEL 4

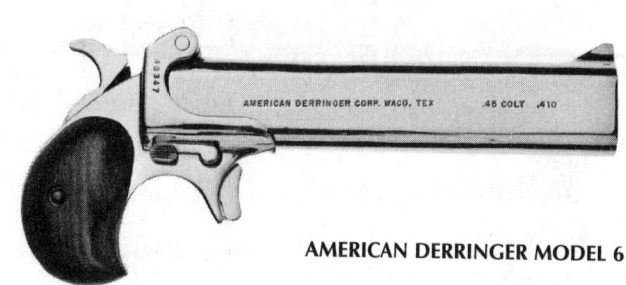

AMERICAN DERRINGER MODEL 6

MODEL 4
Action: Hinged breech
Grips: Rosewood
Barrel: 4.1 in
Sights: Fixed open
Weight: 16.5 oz.
Caliber: .375 Mag., 357 Max., 45-70, .45 Colt/.410, .44 Mag.
Capacity: 2 rounds
Features: Satin or high polish stainless steel finish; single-action; automatic barrel selection; manually operated hammer-block type safety
MSRP . . . . **$760–$870**

MODEL 6
Action: Hinged breech
Grips: Rosewood, walnut, black
Barrel: 6 in.
Sights: Fixed open
Weight: 21 oz.
Caliber: .357 Mag., .45 Auto, .45 Colt/.410
Capacity: 2 rounds
Features: Satin or high polish stainless steel finish; single-action; automatic barrel selection; manually operated hammer-block type safety
MSRP **$895**

MODEL 7 LIGHTWEIGHT & ULTRA LIGHTWEIGHT
Action: Hinged breech
Grips: Blackwood
Barrel: 3 in.
Sights: Fixed open
Weight: 7.5 oz.
Caliber: .44 Special, .380 Auto, .38 Special, .32 Mag./.32 S&W Long, .22LR, .22 Mag.
Capacity: N/A
Features: Grey matte finish; single-action; automatic barrel selection; manually operated hammer-block type safety
MSRP **$700**

AMERICAN DERRINGER MODEL 7

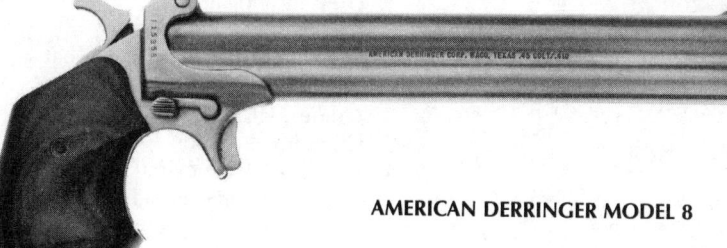

AMERICAN DERRINGER MODEL 8

MODEL 8
Action: Hinged breech
Grips: Rosewood, walnut, black
Barrel: 6 in.
Sights: Optional Adco red dot scope
Weight: 24 oz.
Caliber: .357 Mag., .45 Auto, .45 Colt/.410
Capacity: 2 rounds
Features: Satin or high polish stainless steel finish; single-action; automatic barrel selection; manually operated hammer-block type safety
MSRP **$935**

American Tactical Imports

AMERICAN TACTICAL IMPORTS
FX 45 1911 GI

AMERICAN TACTICAL
IMPORTS FX 45 1911
MILITARY

AMERICAN TACTICAL
IMPORTS FX 1911
THUNDERBOLT

FX 1911 GI

Action: Semi-automatic
Grips: Mahogany
Barrel: 4.25 in.
Sights: Fixed
Weight: 32 oz.
Caliber: .45 ACP
Capacity: 8+1 rounds
Features: Steel parts; black matte military-style fixed front and rear sights; military-style slide stop and thumb safety, solid mahogany grip panels
MSRP $499.95

FX 1911 MILITARY

Action: Semi-automatic
Grips: Mahogany
Barrel: 5 in.
Sights: Fixed
Weight: 37 oz.
Caliber: .45 ACP
Capacity: 8+1 rounds
Features: Steel parts; black matte military-style fixed front and rear sights; military-style slide stop and thumb safety, solid mahogany grip panels
MSRP $499.95

FX 1911 THUNDERBOLT

Action: Semi-automatic
Grips: Mahogany
Barrel: 5 in.
Sights: Fixed
Weight: 39 oz.
Caliber: .45 ACP
Capacity: 8+1 rounds
Features: Picatinny rail; steel parts; Solid mahogany grips
MSRP $857.95

FX 1911 TITAN BLUE & STAINLESS

Action: Semi-automatic
Grips: Mahogany
Barrel: 3.13 in.
Sights: Fixed
Weight: 28 oz.
Caliber: .45 ACP
Capacity: 7+1 rounds
Features: Carbon-steel construction or stainless-steel construction; two-stage recoil spring system; low-profile rear sights with a dovetailed front sight; military-style slide stop and thumb safety; bull barrel
Titan Blue: $584.95
Titan Stainless: $669.95

AMERICAN TACTICAL
IMPORTS FX 1911
TITAN BLUE

FX THUNDERBOLT ENHANCED

Action: Semiautomatic
Grips: Mahogany
Barrel: 5 in.
Sights: Adjustable 3-dot combat sights
Weight: N/A
Caliber: .45 ACP
Capacity: 8 rounds
Features: Picatinny rail; ambidextrous safety; grip checkering; enhanced model has barrel porting for less felt recoil
MSRP $869.95
Blued: $899.00

AMERICAN TACTICAL
IMPORTS FX
THUNDERBOLT
STAINLESS

American Tactical Imports

GSG 922

Action: Semiautomatic
Grips: Plastic
Barrel: 3.2 in.
Sights: Click-adjustable target
Weight: 31 oz.
Caliber: .22 LR
Capacity: 10 rounds
Features: Frame is constructed of Zamak-5 zinc alloy; loaded chamber indicator, grip safety, magazine safety, firing-pin-block, external hammer; optional AD OP's faux suppressor
MSRP................$374.95
With suppressor:........$399.95

AMERICAN TACTICAL
IMPORTS GSG 922

GSG 1911 PISTOL

Action: Semi-automatic
Grips: Classic wood (standard), or black polymer grips
Barrel: 3.2 in., 5 in.

Sights: Fixed
Weight: 39.5 oz.
Caliber: .22LR
Capacity: 10 rounds
Features: Picatinny rail; faux suppressor optional

AMERICAN TACTICAL
IMPORTS GSG 1911
PISTOL

MSRP.................$374.95
Black:.................$367.00
Suppressor:............$391.00

Arsenal Firearms

ARSENAL FIREARMS
AF-1 STRIKE ONE

AF-1 STRIKE ONE

Action: Semiautomatic
Grips: 3D polymer
Barrel: 5 in.
Sights: Fixed or adjustable
Weight: 26.4 oz. (poly), 31.4 oz. (ergal)
Caliber: 9x19 Para, 9x21 IMI, .357 SIG, .40 S&W
Capacity: 17 rounds
Features: Geometric lock, semiautomatic hammerless pistol; short recoil, in line barrel, patented locking block system; automatic

safety; single-action only trigger; ambidextrous magazine release button; reinforced polymer or ergal light alloy frame in ordnance black, desert tan, and olive drab with 360 degree integral mini-skirt; underbarrel integral Picatinny rail; interchangeable back plate/sight, fixed or adjustable, or Micro-Dot ready; available with a Long Range Conversion
MSRP .... **Price on request**

AF2011-A1 DOUBLE BARREL PISTOL

Action: Semiautomatic double barrel
Grips: Steel
Barrel: 4.9 in.
Sights: Fixed or adjustable
Weight: 65.3 oz.
Caliber: .45 ACP, .38 Super Auto
Capacity: 18 rounds
Features: First industrial double barrel semiautomatic pistol; single slide, single frame, single spur double hammer; single grip safety; single body double

mainspring housing and single double cavity magazine floorplate (two single magazines); long and double magazine latch; most internal parts are interchangeable with standard 1911 replacement parts; can be ordered with two independent triggers and one sear group or with two triggers permanently joined and one or two sear groups; deep blued mirror finish or 3400 Vickers surface hardness white ash nitrite coating
MSRP .... **$4400–$4950**

ARSENAL FIREARMS AF2011-A1 DOUBLE BARREL PISTOL

Auto-Ordnance

1911PKZSE

Action: Semi-automatic
Grips: Brown checkered plastic, checkered wood grips
Barrel: 5 in.
Sights: Blade front, rear drift adjustable sight
Weight: 39 oz.
Caliber: .45 ACP
Capacity: 7+1 rounds
Features: Single-action 1911 Colt design; WWII parkerized; stainless steel or blued metal finish
MSRP **$668**

AUTO-ORDNANCE 1911PKZSE

Beretta USA

BERETTA 21 BOBCAT

BERETTA 87 TARGET

21 BOBCAT

Action: Autoloader
Grips: Plastic
Barrel: 2.4 in.
Sights: Fixed, open
Weight: 11.5 oz.
Caliber: .22LR, .25 ACP
Capacity: 7 or 8 rounds
Features: Double-action; tip-up barrel; stainless steel slide and barrel; alloy gray frame; other metal parts come in black or Inox finish
Black Finish: **$310**
Inox Finish: **$350**

BERETTA 90-TWO TYPE F

87 TARGET

Action: Autoloader
Grips: Plastic
Barrel: 5.9 in.
Sights: Fixed open
Weight: 2.1 oz.
Caliber: .22LR
Capacity: 10+1 rounds
Features: Optional wood grips; ambidextrous safety; steel barrel with hard chromed bore; open slide design; firing pin block; reversible magazine release; anodized alloy frame with matte black finish or nickel; combat-style trigger guard; double-action trigger
MSRP **$880**

90-TWO TYPE F

Action: Autoloader
Grips: Technopolymer single-piece wraparound, standard or slim size
Barrel: 4.9 in.
Sights: Super-Lumi Nova
Weight: 32.5 oz.
Caliber: 9mm, .40 S&W
Capacity: 12 or 17 rounds, restricted capacity 10 rounds
Features: Slide serrations; Guigiaro Design grips; removable front sight; internal recoil buffer; Picatinny MIL-STD-1913 rail
MSRP **$700**

92A1

Action: Autoloader
Grips: Plastic
Barrel: 4.9 in.
Sights: 3-Dot System
Weight: 34.4 oz.
Caliber: 9mm, .40 S&W
Capacity: 12 or 17 rounds, restricted capacity 10 rounds
Features: Removable front sight; MIL-STD-1913, internal recoil buffer; captive recoil spring assembly
MSRP **$725**

92FS TYPE M9A1

Action: Autoloader
Grips: Plastic
Barrel: 4.9 in.
Sights: 3-Dot System
Weight: 33.9 oz.
Caliber: 9mm
Capacity: 15+1 rounds, restricted capacity 10+1 rounds
Features: Picatinny MIL STD-1913 rail; magazine well bevel; sand-resistant magazine
MSRP **$725**

3032 TOMCAT

Action: Autoloader
Grips: Plastic
Barrel: 2.5 in.
Sights: Fixed, open
Weight: 14.5 oz.
Caliber: .32 ACP, .380
Capacity: 7+1 round
Features: Double-action; tip-up barrel latch; Inox has stainless steel slide and barrel; titanium alloy frame in black or gray; double- or single-trigger
Standard: **$390**
Inox: **$430**

BU-9 NANO

Action: Autoloader
Grips: Technopolymer
Barrel: 3.07 in.
Sights: 3-dot low profile
Weight: 17.67 oz.
Caliber: 9mm
Capacity: 6+1 rounds
Features: Interchangeable sights; ambidextrous magazine release button; serialized sub-chassis; patent-pending striker deactivator; technopolymer grip frame
MSRP **$475**

BERETTA 92A1

BERETTA BU-9 NANO

BERETTA 92FS TYPE M9A1

BERETTA 3032 TOMCAT

Beretta USA

**BERETTA M9
COMMERCIAL**

M9 COMMERCIAL

Action: Autoloader
Grips: Plastic
Barrel: 4.9 in.
Sights: Dot-and-Post system
Weight: 33.3 oz.
Caliber: 9mm
Capacity: 15 rounds, restricted capacity 10+1 rounds
Features: Has distinctive military style markings; chrome-lined bore; double-action; automatic firing pin block; ambidextrous manual safety; lightweight forged aluminum alloy frame w/ combat-style trigger guard
MSRP $700

BERETTA PX4 STORM COMPACT

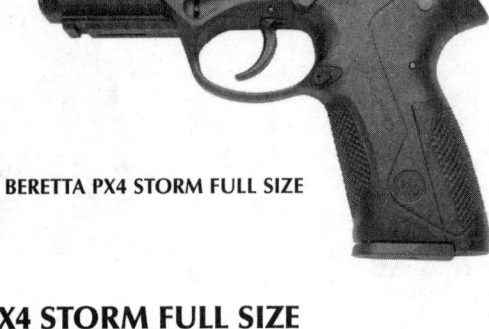

BERETTA PX4 STORM FULL SIZE

PX4 STORM COMPACT

Action: Autoloader
Grips: Plastic
Barrel: 3.2 in.
Sights: 3-Dot System
Weight: 27.3 oz.
Caliber: 9mm, .40 S&W
Capacity: 12 or 15 rounds; full size magazines 9mm: 17 or 20 rounds, .40: 14 or 17 rounds; restricted capacity 10 rounds
Features: Ambidextrous side stop lever; integral Picatinny MIL-STD-1913 rail; bruiton non-reflective black coating; visible automatic firing pin block
MSRP $575

PX4 STORM FULL SIZE

Action: Autoloader
Grips: Plastic
Barrel: 4 in.
Sights: 3-Dot System
Weight: 27.7 oz.
Caliber: 9mm, .40 S&W, .45 ACP
Capacity: 14 or 17 rounds, restricted Capacity: 10 rounds
Features: Picatinny MIL STD-1913 rail; innovative locked-breech with a rotating barrel system; visible automatic firing pin block; ambidextrous safety; reversible magazine release; available in Inox finish
MSRP . . . . $575–$650

U22 NEOS

Action: Autoloader
Grips: Plastic
Barrel: 4.5 in., 6 in.
Sights: Target
Weight: 31.7–36.2 oz.
Caliber: .22LR
Capacity: 10+1 rounds
Features: Single-action; removable colored grip inserts; deluxe model features adjustable trigger, replaceable sights; optional 7.5 in. barrel
Standard: $280
Inox: $375

BERETTA U22 NEOS

BERSA BP CC 9

BERSA THUNDER 40 ULTRA COMPACT PRO

BP CC 9

Action: Short reset DAO
Grips: Integral to frame
Barrel: 3.3 in.
Sights: Interchangeable front and rear
Weight: 21.5 oz.
Caliber: 9mm, .40 SW
Capacity: 6+1, 8+1 rounds
Features: Bersa polymer concealed carry; high impact polymer frame; Picatinny rail, polygonal rifling, and loaded chamber indicator; ambidextrous magazine release; striker fired; micro-polished bore with sharp, deep rifling; 3-dot sight system; integral locking system; automatic firing pin safety; matte black or duotone finish
MSRP . . . .**$427–$440**

THUNDER 9 ULTRA COMPACT

Action: Autoloader
Grips: Black polymer
Barrel: 3.25 in.
Sights: 3-Dot system
Weight: 23 oz.
Caliber: 9mm
Capacity: 10+1, 13+1 rounds
Features: Picatinny rail; precision machined lightweight alloy; ambidextrous safety; lifetime service contract; integral locking system; anatomically designed polymer grips; double-action; available in matte or duotone finish
Matte: **$500**
Duotone: **$510**

THUNDER 40 ULTRA COMPACT

Action: Autoloader
Grips: Black polymer
Barrel: 3.25 in.
Sights: 3-Dot system
Weight: 23 oz.
Caliber: .40 S&W
Capacity: 10+1 rounds
Features: Picatinny rail; precision machined lightweight alloy; ambidextrous safety; lifetime service contract; integral locking system;

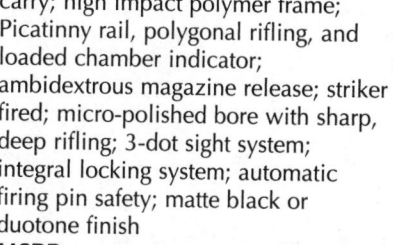

BERSA THUNDER 9 ULTRA COMPACT PRO

BERSA THUNDER 45 ULTRA COMPACT PRO

BERSA THUNDER 380

anatomically designed polymer grips; double-action; available in matte or duotone finish
Matte: **$500**
Duotone: **$510**

THUNDER 45 ULTRA COMPACT

Action: Autoloader
Grips: Black polymer
Barrel: 3.6 in.
Sights: 3-Dot system
Weight: 27 oz.
Caliber: .45 ACP
Capacity: 7+1 rounds
Features: Double-action; Picatinny rail; precision machined lightweight alloy; ambidextrous safety; lifetime service contract; integral locking system; anatomically designed polymer grips; available in matte or duotone finish
Matte: **$500**
Duotone: **$510**

THUNDER 380

Action: Autoloader
Grips: Black polymer
Barrel: 3.5 in.
Sights: 3-Dot system
Weight: 20 oz.
Caliber: .380 ACP
Capacity: 7+1 rounds
Features: Combat style trigger guard; extended slide release; micro-polished bore with sharp, deep rifling; integral locking system; available in matte, satin, nickel, or duotone finish
Matte: **$335**
Duotone: **$335**
Nickel: **$353**
Combat: **$353**

Bersa

THUNDER 380 CONCEALED CARRY

Action: Autoloader
Grips: Black polymer
Barrel: 3.2 in.
Sights: Blade front and notched-bar dovetailed rear
Weight: 16.4 oz.
Caliber: .380 ACP
Capacity: 8+1 rounds
Features: Extra low profile sights; combat style trigger guard; slim slide release; integral locking system
Matte: **$350**
Duotone: **$360**

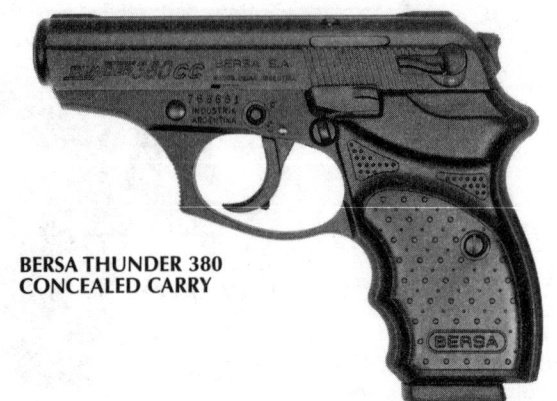

BERSA THUNDER 380 CONCEALED CARRY

Bond Arms

BOND MINI

Action: SA
Grips: Rosewood or pink
Barrel: 2.5 in.
Sights: Blade front, fixed rear
Weight: 18 oz.–19 oz.
Caliber: .357 Mag./.38 Spl., .45 ACP, .45 Colt, .45 Glock Auto, .44 Spl., .44-40 Win., .40 S&W, 10mm, 9mm, .32 H&R Mag., .22 LR, .22 Mag. (3 in. barrel .410/.45 LC with 2.5 in. chambers-rifled)
Capacity: 2 rounds
Features: The Bond Mini was developed as a special edition gun that is even easier to conceal and carry, but still packs the same power Bond Arms guns are known for. This gun comes in two models the Mini .45 and the Girl Mini (.357/.38). The Girl Mini has slightly smaller barrel included and pink grips.
MSRP **$395**

BOND ARMS BOND MINI

BOND RANGER

Action: SA
Grips: Black ash star
Barrel: 4.25 in.
Sights: Blade front and fixed rear
Weight: 23.5 oz.
Caliber: .357 Mag./.38 Spl., .45 ACP, .45 Colt, .45 Glock Auto, .44 Spl., .44-40 Win., .40 S&W, 10mm, 9mm, .32 H&R Mag., .22 LR, .22 Mag.; .410/.45 LC with 3 in. chambers-rifled
Capacity: 2 rounds
Features: Interchangeable barrels; automatic extractor; retracting firing pins; crossbolt safety; spring-loaded cammed locking lever; stainless steel with satin polish finish
MSRP **$634**

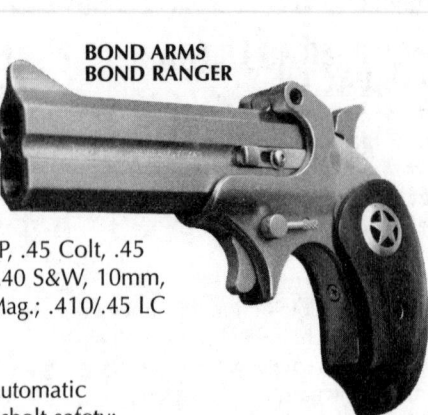

BOND ARMS BOND RANGER

BOND ARMS BOND GIRL MINI

BOND ARMS CENTURY 2000

BOND ARMS SNAKE SLAYER

BOND TEXAS RANGER - SPECIAL EDITION

BOND ARMS SNAKE SLAYER IV

BOND ARMS TEXAS DEFENDER

CENTURY 2000

Action: SA
Grips: Custom laminated black ash or rosewood
Barrel: 3.5 in.
Sights: Blade front and fixed rear
Weight: 21 oz.
Caliber: .357 Mag./.38 Spl., .45 ACP, .45 Colt, .45 Glock Auto, .44 Spl., .44-40 Win., .40 S&W, 10mm, 9mm, .32 H&R Mag., .22 LR, .22 Mag.; .410/.45 LC
Capacity: 2 rounds
Features: Interchangeable barrels; automatic extractor; rebounding hammer; retracting firing pins; crossbolt safety; spring-loaded cammed locking lever; trigger guard; stainless steel with satin polish finish
MSRP.....................**$420**

SNAKE SLAYER

Action: SA
Grips: Extended custom rosewood
Barrel: 4.25 in.
Sights: Blade front and fixed rear
Weight: 22 oz.
Caliber: .357 Mag./.38 Spl., .45 ACP, .45 Colt, .45 Glock Auto, .44 Spl., .44-40 Win., .40 S&W, 10mm, 9mm, .32 H&R Mag., .22 LR, .22 Mag.; .410/.45 LC with 3 in. chambers-rifled
Capacity: 2 rounds

Features: Interchangeable barrels; automatic extractor; rebounding hammer; retracting firing pins; crossbolt safety; spring-loaded cammed locking lever; trigger guard; stainless steel with satin polish finish
MSRP.....................**$489**

SNAKE SLAYER IV

Action: SA
Grips: Extended custom rosewood
Barrel: 4.25 in.
Sights: Blade front and fixed rear
Weight: 23.5 oz.
Caliber: .357 Mag./.38 Spl., .45 ACP, .45 Colt, .45 Glock Auto, .44 Spl., .44-40 Win., .40 S&W, 10mm, 9mm, .32 H&R Mag., .22 LR, .22 Mag.; .410/.45 LC with 3 in. chambers-rifled
Capacity: 2 rounds
Features: Automatic extractor; interchangeable barrels; rebounding hammer; retracting firing pins; crossbolt safety; spring-loaded cammed locking lever; trigger guard; stainless steel with satin polish finish
MSRP.....................**$519**

TEXAS DEFENDER

Action: SA
Grips: Custom laminated black ash or rosewood

Barrel: 3 in.
Sights: Blade front and fixed rear
Weight: 20 oz.
Caliber: 45 Colt/.410 Shot Shell(rifled), .357 Mag/.38 Spl, .357 Max, .45 ACP, .45 Colt, .45 Glock Auto, .44-40 Win., .40 S&W, 10mm, .32 H&R Mag., .22LR
Capacity: 2 rounds
Features: Interchangeable barrels; automatic extractor; rebounding hammer; retracting firing pins; crossbolt safety; spring-loaded cammed locking lever; trigger guard; stainless steel with satin polish finish
MSRP.....................**$415**

TEXAS RANGER - SPECIAL EDITION

Action: SA
Grips: Texas mesquite
Barrel: 4.25 in.
Sights: Blade front, fixed rear
Weight: 23.5 oz.
Caliber: .410/.45LC, .357 Mag., .45 ACP, .45 Colt., .45 Glock Auto, .44 Spl., .44-40 Win., .40 S&W, 10mm, 9mm, .32 H&R Mag., .22 LR, .22 Mag.
Capacity: 2 rounds
Features: Bond Arms has been chosen to represent the prestigious Texas Rangers in their historic 200th Anniversary. The gun and knife grips are made from real Texas mesquite wood, the Texas Ranger Stars are handmade by Texas inmates in the Texas Department of Corrections, and it is gold engraved on the barrel. Custom glass top display case included.
MSRP.....................**$1297**

Browning

BROWNING 1911-22 A1

BROWNING BUCK MARK CAMPER

BROWNING BUCK MARK LITE GREEN 5.5

BROWNING BUCK MARK PLUS UDX

BROWNING BUCK MARK PRACTICAL URX

1911-22 A1
Action: Autoloader
Grips: Brown composite
Barrel: 4.25 in.
Sights: Fixed
Weight: 16 oz.
Caliber: 22 L.R.
Capacity: 10+1 rounds
Features: Alloy frame in matte blued finish; stainless steel barrel block with matte blued finish; blowback action; single-action trigger; detachable magazine; manual thumb safety; grip safety
MSRP **$599.99**

BUCK MARK LITE GREEN 5.5
Action: Autoloader
Grips: Ultragrip RX ambidextrous
Barrel: 5.5 in.
Sights: Pro-Target adjustable rear sight; Truglo/Marble's fiber-optic front
Weight: 28 oz.
Caliber: 22 L.R.
Capacity: 10+1 rounds
Features: Matte green finish; fluted barrel; alloy sleeved barrel; matte black grips and receiver; single action trigger
MSRP **$559.99**

BUCK MARK PLUS UDX
Action: Autoloader
Grips: Rosewood, black laminated, or walnut Ultragrip DX ambidextrous
Barrel: 5.5–7.25 in.
Sights: Adjustable pro-target rear sight, Truglo/Marble fiber-optic front
Weight: 34 oz.
Caliber: 22 L.R.
Capacity: 10+1 rounds
Features: Matte blued, polished barrel flats; blowback action; single-action trigger
Walnut: **$519.99**
Rosewood: **$519.99**
Black laminated: **$559.99**

BUCK MARK PRACTICAL URX
Action: Autoloader
Grips: Ultragrip RX ambidextrous
Barrel: 5.5 in.
Sights: Pro-target adjustable rear; Truglo/Marble's fiber-optic front
Weight: 34 oz.
Caliber: .22LR
Capacity: 10+1 rounds
Features: Tapered bull barrel with matte blued finish; matte gray finish receiver
MSRP **$429.99**

BUCK MARK SERIES
Action: Autoloader
Grips: Composite, black
Barrel: 5.5–7.25 in.
Sights: Adjustable
Weight: 34–39 oz.
Caliber: .22LR
Capacity: 10+1 rounds
Features: Alloy, matte blued finish receiver; tapered barrel; blowback action; single-action trigger; URX ambidextrous grip in contour models; cocobolo, ambidextrous grip on hunter model; lite gray model has matte gray barrel finish and truglo/marble fiber-optic front sight
Camper UFX: **$429.99**
Stainless UFX: **$429.99**
Contour 5.5 URX: **$539.99**
Contour 7.25 URX: **$549.99**
Hunter: **$479.99**
Lite Gray 5.5: **$559.99**

Browning

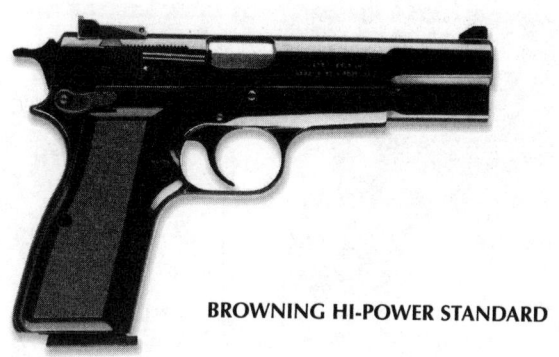

BROWNING HI-POWER STANDARD

HI-POWER STANDARD
Action: Autoloader
Grips: Select walnut, cut checkering
Barrel: 4.6 in.
Sights: Low profile fixed or adjustable with ramped front post
Weight: 32 oz.
Caliber: 9mm
Capacity: 10+1 rounds
Features: Locked breech action; single-action trigger; ambidextrous thumb safety; extra magazine; steel, polished blued finish barrel
MSRP . . . .$1069.99–$1149.99

Charter Arms

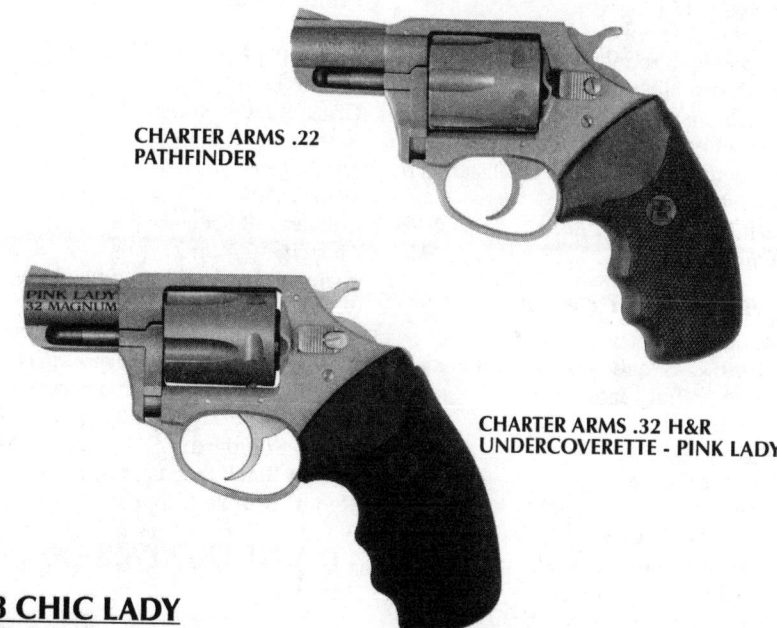

CHARTER ARMS .22 PATHFINDER

CHARTER ARMS .32 H&R UNDERCOVERETTE - PINK LADY

CHARTER ARMS .38 CHIC LADY DAO

.22 PATHFINDER
Action: DA revolver
Grips: Rubber; Crimson Trace lasergrips
Barrel: 2 in., 4 in., 5 in.
Sights: Fixed, adjustable rear on Target model
Weight: 19 oz.–20 oz.
Caliber: .22LR, .22 Mag.
Capacity: 6 rounds
Features: Stainless steel frame
Standard: . . . .**$369–$410**
Target: . . . .**$412–$472**
Target Combo: **$548**

.32 H&R UNDERCOVERETTE
Action: DA revolver
Grips: Rubber; Crimson Trace lasergrips
Barrel: 2 in.
Sights: Fixed
Weight: 12 oz.–16 oz.
Caliber: .32 H&R
Capacity: 5 rounds
Features: Gun with less kick for women; standard or Crimson Trace grip; two-tone pink, stainless, gold & black, or lavender finish; high-grade cast aluminum revolver features
Pink Lady: **$428**
Gold & Black: **$477**
Lavender Lady: **$428**
SS Standard: **$378**

.38 CHIC LADY
Action: DA/SA, DAO revolver
Grips: Rubber
Barrel: 2 in.
Sights: Fixed
Weight: 12 oz.
Caliber: .38 Special
Capacity: 5 rounds
Features: High-polish stainless-steel pink anodized aluminum frame; comes in a faux alligator pink attaché case with high-polish stainless-steel trim; serrated front sight; quick-release cylinder
DA/SA: **$481**
DAO: **$492**

Charter Arms

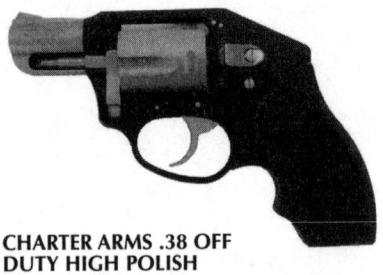

CHARTER ARMS .38 OFF DUTY HIGH POLISH

CHARTER ARMS .38 UNDERCOVER

CHARTER ARMS .38 UNDERCOVER LITE

.38 OFF DUTY HIGH POLISH

Action: DA revolver
Grips: Crimson Trace lasergrip
Barrel: 2 in.
Sights: Serrated front, rear notch
Weight: 12 oz.
Caliber: .38 Special +P
Capacity: 5 rounds
Features: High-polish stainless-steel finish; matte black frame; off duty model has internal DA hammer; Undercover Lite has external standard hammer
Off Duty:. $445
Crimson: $669

.38 UNDERCOVER

Action: DA revolver
Grips: Checkered compact rubber or Crimson Trace lasergrips
Barrel: 2 in.
Sights: Fixed
Weight: 16 oz.
Caliber: .38 Special +P
Capacity: 5 rounds
Features: Stainless steel frame; blued, stainless, tiger & black, OD green & black, grey/SS finishes; DAO available; Crimson Trace grips available; compact and lightweight, this revolver

is ideal for concealed carry situations; 3-point cylinder lock-up
Blue/Black:. . . . . $319–$429
SS:. . . . . $331–$337
Crimson Trace: $576

.38 UNDERCOVER LITE

Action: DA revolver
Grips: Rubber, compact
Barrel: 2 in.
Sights: Fixed
Weight: 12 oz.
Caliber: .38 Special +P
Capacity: 5 rounds
Features: Frame is constructed from aircraft-grade aluminum and steel; traditional spurred hammer; optional DAO (double action trigger); many finishes and special editions available
Black DAO: $428
Alum. Standard: $404
Red or Black & SS:. $422
Red or Bronze & Black: $422

.38 UNDERCOVER ON DUTY

Action: DA revolver
Grips: Rubber; Crimson Trace lasergrips
Barrel: 2 in.
Sights: Fixed
Weight: 12 oz.
Caliber: .38 Special +P
Capacity: 5 rounds
Features: Unique hammer block design; constructed of heat-treated aluminum; allows single-action and double-action operations while minimizing the risk of snagging the hammer on clothing; standard or Crimson Trace grip
Standard:. $410
Crimson Trace: $664

.44 BULLDOG HELLER COMMEMORATIVE

Action: DA revolver
Grips: Walnut
Barrel: 2.5 in.
Sights: Fixed
Weight: 12 oz.
Caliber: .44 Special
Capacity: 5 rounds
Features: This fully engraved .44 Bulldog commemorates the historic win of the U.S. Supreme Court case "Heller vs. D.C." In this case the Supreme Court struck down Washington D.C.'s handgun ban and affirmed the Second Amendment as an individual right. Only 250 models will be made. Each firearm will be packaged with an engraved knife, hardcase with etched glass top, and certificate of authenticity.
MSRP. $1595

CHARTER ARMS .38 UNDERCOVER ON DUTY

CHARTER ARMS .44 BULLDOG HELLER COMMEMORATIVE

.44 SPECIAL BULLDOG

Action: DA revolver
Grips: Rubber; Crimson Trace lasergrips
Barrel: 2.5 in., 4 in. or 5 in. in target model
Sights: Fixed, adjustable rear on Target model
Weight: 21 oz.
Caliber: .44 Special
Capacity: 5 rounds
Features: Stainless steel frame; optional DAO trigger; standard hammer; stainless or blued finish

Blued STD: **$414**
SS STD: **$426**
DAO: . . . . **$431–$465**
Target Bulldog: . . . . **$479–$485**
Crimson: **$696**

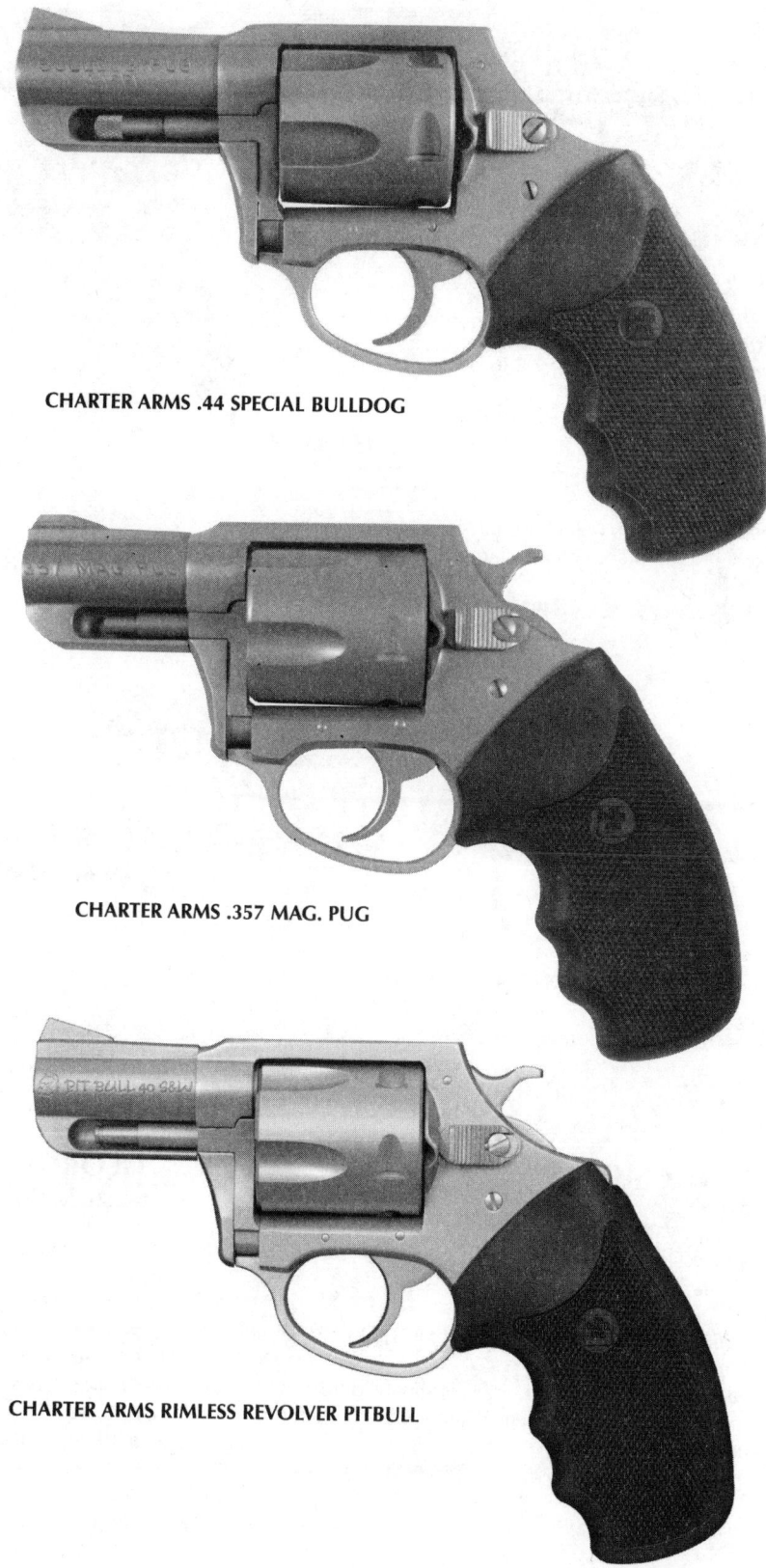

CHARTER ARMS .44 SPECIAL BULLDOG

.357 MAG. PUG

Action: DA revolver
Grips: Rubber; Crimson Trace lasergrips
Barrel: 2.2 in., 4 in., 5 in.
Sights: Fixed, adjustable rear on Target model
Weight: 23 oz.
Caliber: .357 Mag.
Capacity: 5 rounds
Features: Traditional spurred hammer and full-size grips; optional Crimson Trace grip; stainless steel frame; blued and stainless finish

Standard: **$396**
Crimson: **$665**
Stainless: **$400**
SS DAO: **$404**
Target: . . . . **$479–$496**

CHARTER ARMS .357 MAG. PUG

RIMLESS REVOLVER PITBULL

Action: DA/SA revolver
Grips: Rubber, neoprene
Barrel: 2.2 in., 2.3 in.
Sights: Fixed
Weight: 20 oz.–22 oz.
Caliber: 9mm, .40
Capacity: 5, 6 rounds
Features: Dual coil spring assembly; stainless steel frame; 9mm has spurred hammer, .40 has standard hammer

9mm: **$465**
.40: **$465**

CHARTER ARMS RIMLESS REVOLVER PITBULL

Cimarron Firearms Co.

CIMARRON 1872 OPEN TOP NAVY

1872 OPEN TOP NAVY

Action: SA revolver
Grips: Walnut
Barrel: 4.75 in., 5.5 in., 7.5 in.
Sights: Fixed, open
Weight: 40 oz.
Caliber: .44 Special; .44 Colt & Russian, .45 Schofield, .45 Colt, .38 Colt & Special
Capacity: 6 rounds
Features: Forged, color case-hardened frame; Army or Navy grip; charcoal blued, standard blued, or original barrel finish
MSRP . . . . $492.70–$627.91

1911 .45 ACP

Action: Semi-automatic
Grips: Walnut
Barrel: 5 in.
Sights: Open, fixed
Weight: 39.52 oz.
Caliber: .45 ACP
Capacity: 8+1 rounds
Features: Next generation of firearm widely used in the First World War. Correct historical markings; diamond checkered walnt grips; nickel, polished high luster blued, and standard parkerized finish; optional World
War I-style lanyard magazine
MSRP . . . . $540.80–$633.10

CIMARRON BISLEY MODEL

CIMARRON GEORGE ARMSTRONG CUSTER 7TH U.S. CAVALRY MODEL

BISLEY MODEL

Action: SA revolver
Grips: Walnut
Barrel: 4.75 in., 5.5 in., 7.5 in.
Sights: Fixed, open
Weight: 4.3–44 oz.
Caliber: .45 LC, .44 Special, .44 WCF, .357 Mag.
Capacity: 6 rounds
Features: Reproduction of the original Colt Bisley; forged, color case-hardened frame; blued, charcoal blued, or nickel finish
MSRP $596.70

GEORGE ARMSTRONG CUSTER 7TH U.S. CAVALRY MODEL

Action: SA revolver
Grips: Walnut
Barrel: 7.5 in.
Sights: Fixed, open
Weight: 4.4 oz.
Caliber: .45 LC
Capacity: 6 rounds
Features: Old model case-hardened with 7th Cavalry markings; made with 1 piece of walnut with OWA (Ainsworth) Cartouche; blued, charcoal blued or nickel barrel finish
MSRP . . . . $583.70–$770.90

Cimarron Firearms Co.

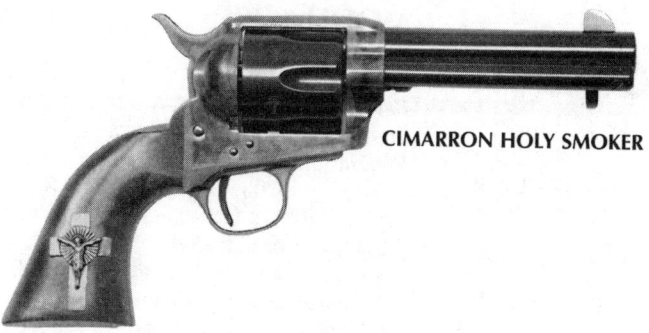

CIMARRON HOLY SMOKER

HOLY SMOKER

Action: SA revolver
Grips: Walnut
Barrel: 4.75 in.
Sights: Open, fixed
Weight: 36 oz.
Caliber: .45 Colt
Capacity: 6 rounds
Features: Revolver made famous in *3:10 to Yuma* film; standard blued finish; case-hardened pre-war frame; gold-plated sterling silver cross inlayed on both sides of one-piece walnut grip
MSRP **$760.50**

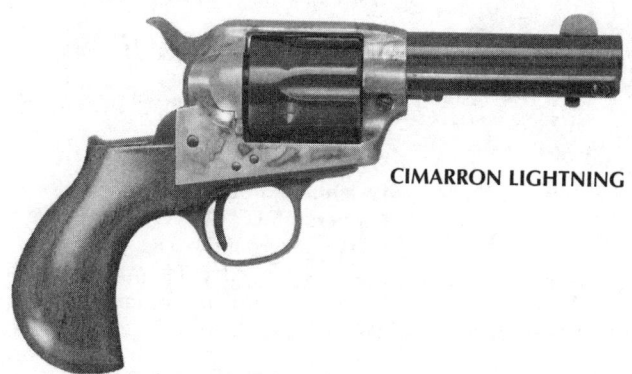

CIMARRON LIGHTNING

LIGHTNING

Action: SA revolver
Grips: Walnut
Barrel: 3.5 in., 4.75 in., 5.5 in., 6.5 in.
Sights: Fixed, open
Weight: 28.5–30.75 oz.
Caliber: .38 Special, .22LR, .41 Colt, 32-20/.32 H&R Dual Cylinder
Capacity: 6 rounds
Features: Forged, pre-war color case-hardened frame; charcoal blued, standard blued, or original barrel finish; walnut stock smooth or checkered
MSRP . . . . **$487.50–$609.70**

CIMARRON MAN WITH NO NAME

MAN WITH NO NAME

Action: SA revolver
Grips: Walnut
Barrel: 4.75 in., 5.5 in.
Sights: Open, fixed
Weight: 42.56 oz.–44.16 oz.
Caliber: .45 Colt
Capacity: 6 rounds
Features: Model P in .45 Colt; sterling silver snake on both sides of walnut grip; conversion version available in .38 Special/.38 Colt
MSRP . . . . **$773.50–$817.70**

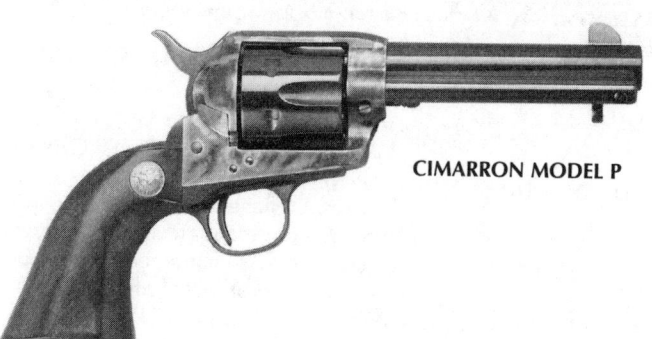

CIMARRON MODEL P

MODEL P

Action: SA revolver
Grips: Walnut
Barrel: 4.75 in., 5.5 in., 7.5 in.
Sights: None
Weight: 44 oz.
Caliber: 32 WCF, 38 WCF, .357 Mag., .44 WCF, .44 Special, .45 LC, .45LC/.45 ACP Dual Cylinder
Capacity: 6 rounds
Features: Fashioned after the 1873 Colt SAA; standard blued, charcoal blued, or original finish; available in old model or pre-war (new) model
MSRP . . . . **$519.87–$630.50**

Cimarron Firearms Co.

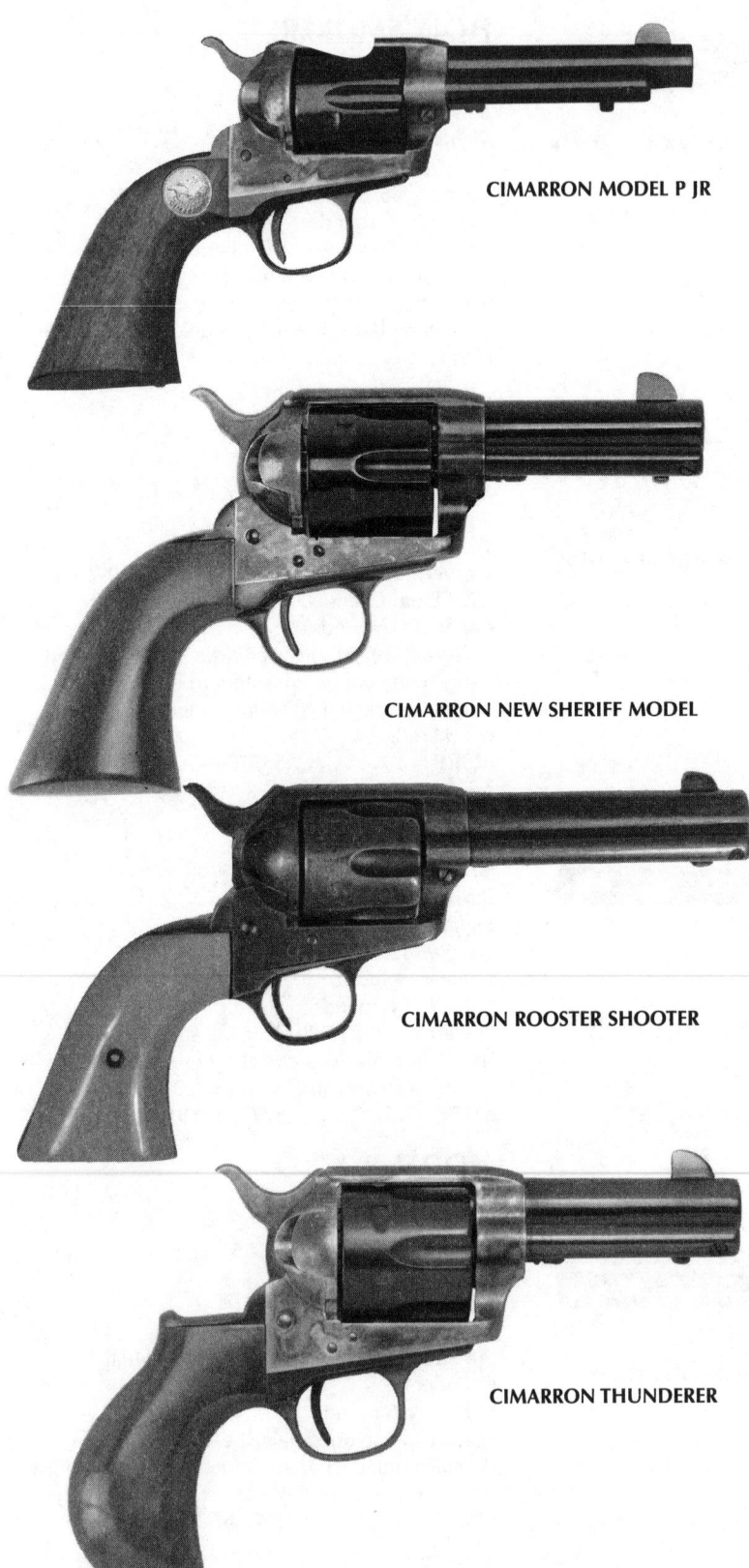

CIMARRON MODEL P JR

CIMARRON NEW SHERIFF MODEL

CIMARRON ROOSTER SHOOTER

CIMARRON THUNDERER

MODEL P JR.
Action: SA revolver
Grips: Walnut
Barrel: 3.5 in., 4.75 in., 5.5 in.
Sights: Fixed, open
Weight: 35.2 oz.
Caliber: .41 Colt, .38 Special, .22LR, .41 Colt, .32-20/.32 H&R Dual Cylinder
Capacity: 6 rounds
Features: Fashioned after the 1873 Colt SAA but on a smaller scale; color case-hardened frame; blue, charcoal blue, or nickel finish
MSRP . . . . $438.10–$583.70

NEW SHERIFF MODEL
Action: SA revolver
Grips: Walnut, black hard rubber
Barrel: 3.5 in.
Sights: Fixed, open
Weight: 33.5 oz.
Caliber: .45 LC, .44 WCF, .357 Mag.
Capacity: 6 rounds
Features: Forged, color case-hardened frame; standard blued barrel finish
MSRP $519.87

ROOSTER SHOOTER
Action: SA revolver
Grips: Orange finger
Barrel: 4.75 in.
Sights: Open, fixed
Weight: 36.68 oz.–40.48 oz.
Caliber: .357/.38 Spl., .45 Colt, .44 W.C.F.
Capacity: 6 rounds
Features: Replica of John Wayne's Colt Single Action
MSRP $882.70

THUNDERER
Action: SA revolver
Grips: Walnut, ivory, mother of pearl or black hard rubber
Barrel: 3.5 in. w/ ejector, 4.75 in., 5.5 in., 7.5 in.
Sights: Fixed, open
Weight: 38–43.60 oz.
Caliber: .45 LC, .44 Special, 44WCF, .357 Mag., .45LC/45 ACP Dual Cylinder
Capacity: 6 rounds
Features: Designed in 1990 by Cimarron founder & president "Texas Jack" Harvey; forged, color case-hardened frame; blued, charcoal blued or nickel finish
MSRP . . . . $544.70–$698.60

Cimarron Firearms Co.

CIMARRON THUNDERSTORM

CIMARRON TITAN DERRINGER, POLISHED STAINLESS STEEL

CIMARRON U.S.V. ARTILLERY MODEL

CIMARRON WYATT EARP BUNTLINE

THUNDERSTORM
Action: SA revolver
Grips: Walnut
Barrel: 3.5 in., 4.75 in.
Sights: Front, rear
Weight: 35.7 oz.–39.68 oz.
Caliber: .45 Colt, .357/.38 Sp.
Capacity: 6 rounds
Features: Checkered grips; stainless steel or standard blued finishes; wide front sights and deep rear notch; smooth action and hand-knurled hammer; available in Model P or Thunderer versions
MSRP . . . . $713.70–$986.70

TITAN DERRINGER
Action: SA revolver
Grips: Rosewood
Barrel: 3.5 in., 4.75 in.
Sights: Open, fixed
Weight: 16.4 oz.
Caliber: .45 LC/.410, 9mm
Capacity: 2 rounds
Features: Largest of Cimarron's pocket pistols; available in polished, brushed, or black stainless steel
MSRP $427.70

U.S.V. ARTILLERY MODEL
Action: SA revolver
Grips: Walnut
Barrel: 5.5 in.
Sights: Fixed, open
Weight: 40 oz.
Caliber: .45 LC
Capacity: 6 rounds
Features: Old model case-hardened with U.S. Artillery markings; stock is a solid piece of walnut with RAC Cartouche; blued, charcoal blued, or original finish
MSRP $583.70

WYATT EARP BUNTLINE
Action: SA revolver
Grips: Walnut
Barrel: 10 in.
Sights: Open, fixed
Weight: 43.04 oz.
Caliber: .45 LC
Capacity: 6 rounds
Features: Revolver made famous in the film *Tombstone*; old model case-hardened; walnut grip hand cast in solid sterling silver and hand inlaid into stock; standard blued or original finish
MSRP . . . . $856.70–$881.40

Citadel by Legacy Sports

M-1911

Action: Semi-automatic
Grips: Full size or compact, wood, or Hogue synthetic grips
Barrel: 3.5 in., 5 in.
Sights: Fixed
Weight: 33.6–37.6 oz.
Caliber: 9mm, .45 ACP, .38 Super
Capacity: 7 or 8 rounds, 2 magazines
Features: Available in compact and full sized models; matte black, brush nickel, or polished nickel finish; optional Hogue wrap around grip in black, green, or sand; comes with lockable, hard plastic case; Wounded Warrior Project model includes laser cut wood grips with WWP insignia and inscription "Never Forget" and engraved commemorative slide
MSRP . . . . **$589–$699**
Wounded Warrior: **$840**

CITADEL M-1911 PISTOLS

M-1911 .22 G.I.

Action: SA autoloader
Grips: Wood
Barrel: 5 in.
Sights: G.I. standard
Weight: 33.6 oz.
Caliber: .22 LR
Capacity: 10 rounds
Features: Alloy and steel parts; standard G.I. sights; two-piece wooden grip panels
MSRP **$310**

CITADEL M-1911 .22 G.I.

CITADEL M-1911 .22 TACTICAL

M-1911 .22 TAC

Action: SA autoloader
Grips: Rubber
Barrel: 5 in.
Sights: Fiber optic
Weight: 33.6 oz.
Caliber: .22 LR
Capacity: 10 rounds
Features: Fixed barrel and blowback action; alloy and steel parts; one-piece wrap around rubber grip from Hogue; fiber optic front and rear sights; two magazines
MSRP **$349**

Colt's Manufacturing Company

.380 MUSTANG POCKETLITE

Action: SA
Grips: Composite
Barrel: 2.75 in.
Sights: High-profile
Weight: 12.5 oz.
Caliber: .380 ACP
Capacity: 6+1 rounds
Features: Aluminum alloy frame
with a CNC-machined stainless steel slide and barrel;
thumb safety and firing-pin-block safety; solid
aluminum trigger; lowered ejection port; electroless
nickeled aluminum receiver
MSRP $649

COLT .380 MUSTANG POCKETLITE

1991 SERIES

Action: Autoloader
Grips: Rosewood or composite
Barrel: 5 in.
Sights: Fixed
Weight: 39 oz.
Caliber: .45 ACP
Capacity: 7+1 rounds
Features: Beveled magazine well; single- and double-
action; carbon steel, aluminum alloy, or stainless steel
frame; standard or beavertail grip safety; blued, black
anodized, brushed stainless steel, bright stainless steel
frame finish
MSRP . . . . $928–$1311

COLT 1991 SERIES

DEFENDER

Action: Autoloader
Grips: Rubber finger-grooved
Barrel: 5 in.
Sights: White dot carry front and rear
Weight: 30 oz.
Caliber: .45 ACP
Capacity: 7+1 rounds
Features: Beveled magazine well; black skeletonized
aluminum trigger; series 80 firing system; beavertail grip
and standard thumb safety; stainless steel slide, Teflon
coated receiver; aluminum alloy frame
MSRP $1066

COLT DEFENDER

Colt's Manufacturing Company

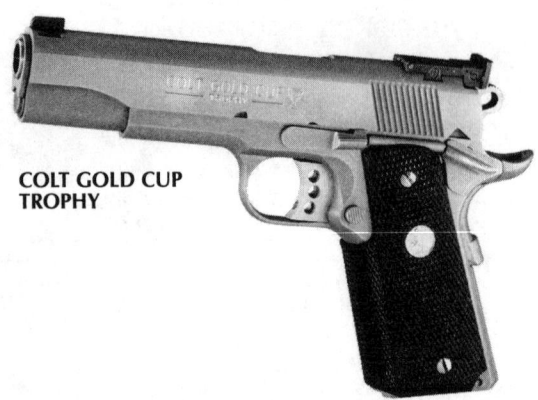

COLT GOLD CUP TROPHY

GOLD CUP SERIES
Action: Autoloader
Grips: Black composite
Barrel: 5 in.
Sights: Dovetail front, adjustable rear
Weight: 39 oz.
Caliber: .45ACP
Capacity: 8+1 rounds
Features: Beveled magazine well; beavertail grip safety; black wrap around grips; wide aluminum 3-Hole trigger adjustable for over travel; stainless steel frame finish and material; enhanced hammer
MSRP . . . . $1158–$1180

COLT NEW AGENT DAO

NEW AGENT
Action: SA or DAO autoloader
Grips: Rosewood, Crimson Trace
Barrel: 3 in.
Sights: Trench style
Weight: 39 oz.
Caliber: .45 ACP, 9mm
Capacity: 7+1, 8+1 rounds
Features: Single-action or .45 ACP double action only; black anodized frame with beveled magazine well; front strap serrations
MSRP . . . . $1041–$1326

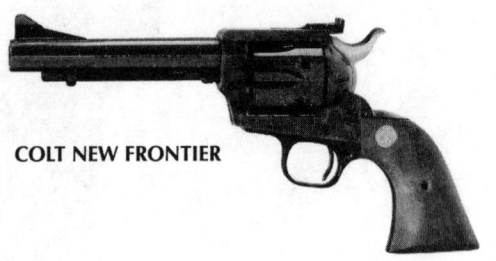

COLT NEW FRONTIER

NEW FRONTIER
Action: SA revolver
Grips: Walnut stock with gold medallions
Barrel: 4.75 in., 5.5 in., 7.5 in.
Sights: Ramp style front; adjustable rear
Weight: 46 oz.
Caliber: .357 Mag., .44 special, .45 Colt
Capacity: 6 rounds
Features: Royal blued barrel and cylinder; flat top case colored frame
MSRP $1455

Colt's Manufacturing Company

COLT RAIL GUN

SERIES 70

Action: Autoloader
Grips: Double diamond rosewood grips
Barrel: 5 in.
Sights: Fixed
Weight: 39 oz.
Caliber: .45 ACP
Capacity: 7+1 rounds
Features: Spur hammer; single-action; blued or brushed steel finish; carbon steel or stainless steel frame; short steel trigger; original series 70 firing system with titanium firing pin
Blued: $1043
Brushed Steel: $1078

SINGLE ACTION ARMY

Action: SA revolver
Grips: Black composite eagle grips
Barrel: 4.75 in., 5.5 in., 7.5 in.
Sights: Fixed
Weight: 46 oz.
Caliber: .32/20, .38 Special, .38/40, .357 Mag., .44/40, .45 Colt
Capacity: 6 rounds
Features: Case-colored frame; transfer bar; 2nd generation style cylinder bushing; features 175th anniversary rollmark; blued or nickel finish
MSRP . . . . $1349–$1551

XSE SERIES

Action: Autoloader
Grips: Checkered, double diamond rosewood
Barrel: 5 in.
Sights: Fixed
Weight: 39 oz.
Caliber: .45 ACP
Capacity: 8+1 rounds
Features: Front and rear slide serrations; extended ambidextrous thumb safeties; enhanced hammer; new roll marking and enhanced tolerances; single-action; white-dot carry sights; beavertail safety grip; blued, brushed stainless steel, Teflon coated, or black anodized finish; carbon steel, stainless steel or aluminum alloy frame
MSRP . . . . $1072–$1223

RAIL GUN

Action: Autoloader
Grips: Double diamond rosewood or blackened rosewood grips
Barrel: 5 in.
Sights: White dot, Novak rear
Weight: 39 oz.
Caliber: .45 ACP
Capacity: 8+1 rounds
Features: Stainless steel, blackened receiver and brushed slide, blackened receiver and slide frame finish options; stainless steel frame material; Colt upswept beavertail with palm swell; enhanced hammer; M1913 Picatinny rail; National Match barrel; single-slide tactical thumb safety
MSRP . . . . $1141–$1223

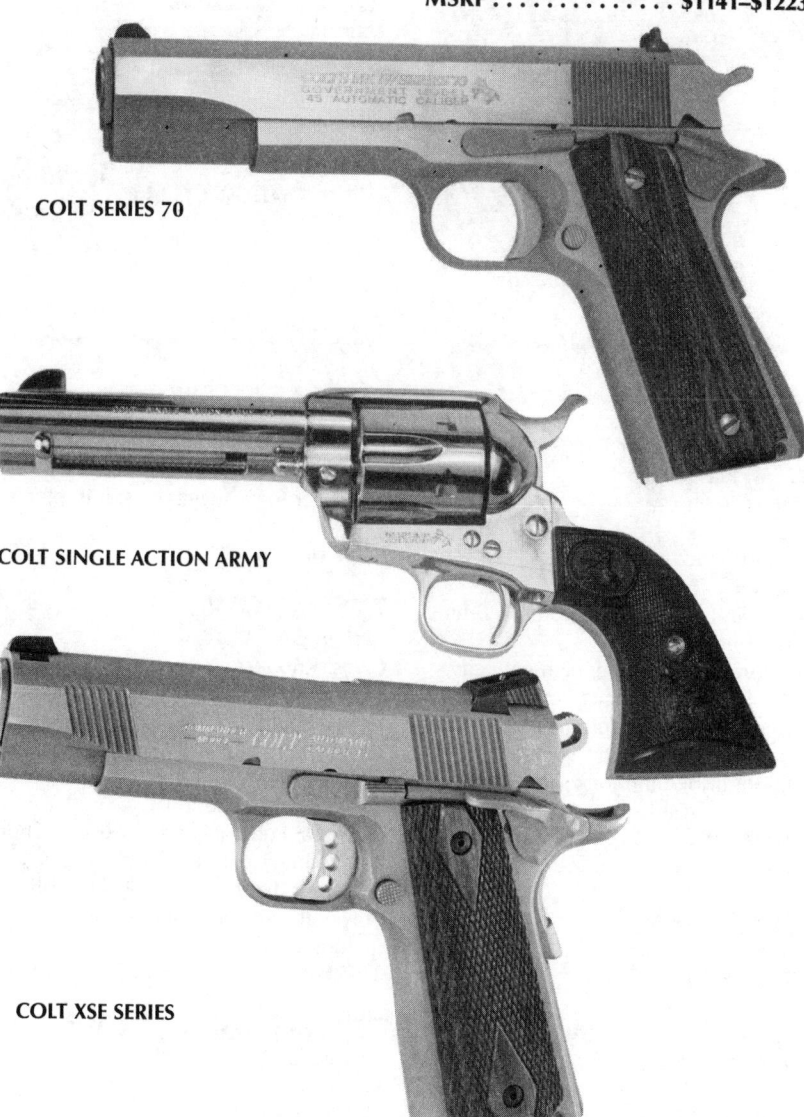

COLT SERIES 70

COLT SINGLE ACTION ARMY

COLT XSE SERIES

CZ-USA (Ceska Zbrojovka)

CZ 75 B

CZ 75 COMPACT

CZ 75 SHADOW

CZ 75 SHADOW CTS LS-P

CZ 75 SHADOW T

75 B

Action: Autoloader
Grips: Plastic
Barrel: 4.6 in.
Sights: Fixed, 3-dot system
Weight: 35.2 oz.
Caliber: .40 S&W, 9mm
Capacity: .40 S&W: 10 rounds, 9mm: 16 rounds
Features: Steel frame; high capacity double column magazines; hammer forged barrels; ergonomic grip and controls; double-action or single-action; firing pin block safety; black polycoat finish
.40 S&W: **$569**
9mm: **$499**

75 COMPACT

Action: Autoloader
Grips: Plastic
Barrel: 3.8 in.
Sights: Fixed, 3-dot system
Weight: 32.48 oz.
Caliber: 9mm Luger
Capacity: 14 rounds

Features: Black polycoat, dual tone, satin nickel frame finishes; manual safety; steel frame; high capacity double column magazines; hammer forged barrels
Black polycoat: **$528**

75 SHADOW

Action: DA/SA
Grips: Rubber
Barrel: 4.61 in.
Sights: Fixed
Weight: 39 oz.
Caliber: 9mm
Capacity: 18+1 rounds
Features: Full package of Custom Shop competition features; Shadow fixed rear sight; fiber optic front sight; black polycoat finish; two magazines included
MSRP **$1053**

75 SHADOW CTS LS-P

Action: DA/SA
Grips: Textured
Barrel: 5.4 in.

Sights: Adjustable rear
Weight: N/A
Caliber: 9mm
Capacity: 18+1 rounds
Features: Long-slide version of the 75 Shadow; fully adjustable Champion rear sight; black frame and blued slide; two magazines included
MSRP **$1450**

75 SHADOW T

Action: DA/SA
Grips: Rubber
Barrel: 4.61 in.
Sights: Adjustable rear, fiber optic front
Weight: 39 oz.
Caliber: 9mm
Capacity: 18+1 rounds
Features: Black rubber grips; adjustable Champion rear sight; fiber optic front sight; black polycoat finish
MSRP **$1180**

CZ-USA (Ceska Zbrojovka)

CZ 75 SP-01

CZ 75 TS CZECHMATE

CZ 75 SP-01
SHADOW TARGET

CZ 97 B

75 SP-01

Action: Autoloader
Grips: Rubber
Barrel: 4.6 in.
Sights: 3-Dot tritium night
Weight: 38.4 oz.
Caliber: 9mm Luger
Capacity: 18 rounds
Features: Based upon the Shadow Target; decocking lever; safety stop on hammer; firing pin safety; steel frame
MSRP **$660**

75 SP-01 SHADOW TARGET

Action: Autoloader
Grips: Cocobolo wood
Barrel: 4.6 in.
Sights: Competition style, fiber optic
Weight: 38.4 oz.

Caliber: 9mm
Capacity: 18 rounds
Features: Single- or double-action; manual safety; steel frame; TRT rear sight; competition springs; CZ custom stainless guide rod
MSRP **$1321**

75 TS CZECHMATE

Action: Autoloader
Grips: Aluminum
Barrel: 5.4 in.
Sights: Fixed, C-more red dot
Weight: 48 oz.
Caliber: 9mm
Capacity: 20 or 26 rounds
Features: Built upon a modified version of the CZ 75 TS frame; interchangeable parts allow the user to quickly configure the gun for both

roles; features a single-action trigger mechanism; red-dot sight; includes spare barrel; includes three 20-round magazines and one 26-round magazine; all-steel pistol is finished in black matte
MSRP **$3220**

97 B

Action: Autoloader
Grips: Plastic
Barrel: 4.8 in.
Sights: Fixed
Weight: 40 oz.
Caliber: .45 ACP
Capacity: 10 rounds
Features: Manual safety; cold hammer-forged barrel; single- or double-action
Black polycoat: **$686**
Glossy blued: **$713**

CZ-USA (Ceska Zbrojovka)

CZ 2075 RAMI

2075 RAMI
Action: Autoloader
Grips: Rubber
Barrel: 3 in.
Sights: Fixed
Weight: 25.6 oz.
Caliber: .40 S&W, 9mm Luger
Capacity: .40 S&W: 7 or 9 rounds,
9mm: 14 rounds
Features: Operates in selective DA and
SA mode depending on shooter's
preferences; firing pin block; manual
safety; double-stack magazine; black
polycoat alloy frame; cold hammer
forged
.40 S&W: $615
9mm Luger: $595

P-01
Action: Autoloader
Grips: Rubber
Barrel: 3.8 in.
Sights: Fixed
Weight: 28.8 oz.
Caliber: 9mm Luger
Capacity: 14 rounds
Features: Decocking lever; safety stop
on hammer; firing pin safety; black
polycoat frame finish; black or pink
grips; single- or double-action
MSRP **$608**

CZ P-01

P-07 DUTY
Action: DA/SA autoloader
Grips: Polymer
Barrel: 3.8 in.
Sights: Fixed
Weight: 27.2 oz.
Caliber: .40 S&W, 9mm Luger
Capacity: .40 S&W: 12 rounds, 9mm: 16 rounds
Features: Omega double- or single-action trigger; cold-hammer-forged
barrel; accessory rail and two magazines included; 9mm available in black
or green poly frame; threaded barrel to accept sound suppressor available;
elevated sights to clear sound suppressor
.40 S&W: $496
9mm: . . . .$483–$528
9mm (OD Green): $489

CZ P-07 DUTY

Dan Wesson Firearms

ECO

Action: SA semiautomatic
Grips: Composite
Barrel: 3.5 in.
Sights: Fixed tritium
Weight: 25 oz.
Caliber: 9mm, .45 ACP
Capacity: 7+1 rounds
Features: Single-stack Officer's size 1991; aluminum alloy frame; undercut trigger guards; 25 lpi checkering; mainspring housing is aluminum with 25 lpi checkering; Ed Brown high rise grip safety; forged steel slide; tritium night sights with tactical ledge rear sight; flush cut ramped bull barrel with target crown
9mm:.................. **$1623**
.45 ACP:................ **$1662**

DAN WESSON ECO

DAN WESSON GUARDIAN

GUARDIAN

Action: SA autoloader
Grips: Stippled shadow
Barrel: 4.25 in.
Sights: Novak low mount style, night
Weight: 28.8 oz.
Caliber: .45 ACP, 9mm
Capacity: 8 rounds
Features: Bobtail alloy frame; aluminum alloy frame; commander length barrel; finished in matte black with tritium sights
.45: **$1619**
9mm:................... **$1558**

DAN WESSON RAZORBACK

DAN WESSON SPECIALIST

RAZORBACK R2-10

Action: SA semiautomatic
Grips: Diamond-checkered cocobolo
Barrel: 5 in.
Sights: Fixed
Weight: 38.4 oz.
Caliber: 10mm
Capacity: 9 rounds
Features: Razorback is back in 2012 in limited quantities; serrated Clark-style target rib; 1911 model; stainless steel frame; manual thumb safety, grip safety
MSRP.................. **$1350**

SPECIALIST

Action: SA semiautomatic
Grips: G10 VZ Operator II grips
Barrel: 5 in.
Sights: Fixed tritium
Weight: 37 oz.
Caliber: .45 ACP
Capacity: 8+1 rounds

Features: Full size single-stack pistol; matte stainless steel or black Duty finishes; forged slide and frame; Clark-style serrated rib with tritium dual-colored night sights stacked in a straight eight-type pattern; tactical ledge rear sight with single rear amber dot and green front with white target ring; 1913 Picatinny rail; undercut trigger guard with 25 lpi front strap checkering; ambidextrous thumb safety; two magazines with bumper pads included
SS:..................... **$1558**
Black:................... **$1870**

DAN WESSON VALOR

VALOR

Action: SA autoloader
Grips: Slim line G10
Barrel: 5 in.
Sights: Heinie Ledge straight eight night
Weight: 35.2 oz.
Caliber: .45 ACP
Capacity: 8 rounds
Features: Matte black duty receiver finish; manual thumb safety; forged stainless steel frame
SS:..................... **$1701**
Black:................... **$2012**

Ed Brown

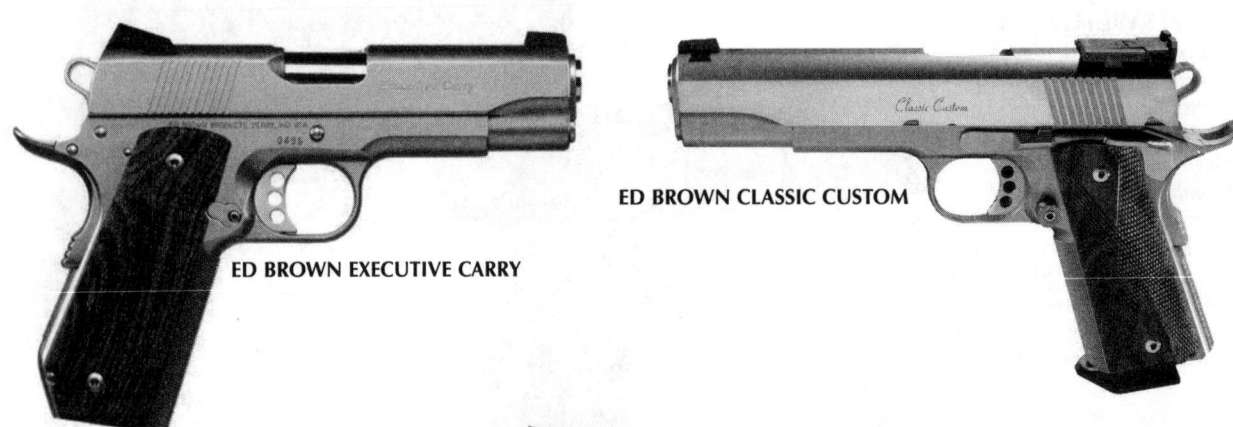

ED BROWN EXECUTIVE CARRY

ED BROWN CLASSIC CUSTOM

ED BROWN KOBRA

ED BROWN EXECUTIVE ELITE

CLASSIC CUSTOM

Action: Autoloader
Grips: Cocobolo wood
Barrel: 5 in.
Sights: Adjustable rear, cross dovetail front
Weight: 40 oz.
Caliber: .45 ACP
Capacity: 7+1 rounds
Features: Single-action; single-stack government model frame; special mirror finished side; two-piece guide rod for smoother cycling and easier disassembly; stainless or blued finish
MSRP **$3495**

EXECUTIVE CARRY

Action: Autoloader
Grips: Checkered cocobolo wood
Barrel: 4.25 in.
Sights: Fixed, night
Weight: 35 oz.
Caliber: .45 ACP
Capacity: 7+1 rounds
Features: Frame modified with an innovative Ed Brown Bobtail; stainless or blued frame finish with stainless, black or blued slide finish; fixed dovetail 3-dot night sights with high visibility white outlines
MSRP **$2945**

EXECUTIVE ELITE

Action: Autoloader
Grips: Checkered cocobolo wood
Barrel: 5 in.
Sights: Fixed, night
Weight: 38 oz.

Caliber: .45 ACP
Capacity: 7+1 rounds
Features: Single-stack government model frame; matte finished slide for low glare, with traditional square cut serrations on rear of slide only; blued or stainless finish
MSRP **$2695**

KOBRA

Action: Autoloader
Grips: Cocobolo wood
Barrel: 5 in.

Sights: Fixed, night
Weight: 38 oz.
Caliber: .45 ACP
Capacity: 7+1 rounds
Features: Single-stack government model frame; John Browning traditional design; exclusive snakeskin treatment on forestrap and mainspring housing; matte finished slide for low glare; 3-dot night sights with high visibility white outlines; blued or stainless finish
MSRP **$2495**

KOBRA CARRY LIGHTWEIGHT

Action: Autoloader
Grips: Cocobolo wood
Barrel: 4.25 in.
Sights: Fixed dovetail front night with high visibility white outlines
Weight: 27 oz.
Caliber: .45 ACP
Capacity: 7+1 rounds
Features: Lightweight aluminum frame and Bobtail housing; all other components are steel; exclusive snakeskin treatment on forestrap and housing; matte finished Gen III coated slide for low glare
MSRP $3120

ED BROWN KOBRA CARRY LIGHTWEIGHT

ED BROWN SIGNATURE EDITION

SIGNATURE EDITION

Action: Autoloader
Grips: Cocobolo wood
Barrel: 5 in.
Sights: Adjustable rear, cross dovetail front
Weight: 40 oz.

Caliber: .45 ACP
Capacity: 7+1 rounds
Features: The Ed Brown Signature Edition is based on our timeless Classic Custom pistol, with hand relief engraving by our master engraver; single stack government model frame; special mirror finished slide; 50 lpi serrations on back of slide to match serrated adjustable sight; hand relief engraved package; adjustable rear sight buried deep into slide; cross dovetail front sight; blued metal parts
MSRP $7195

E.M.F. Company

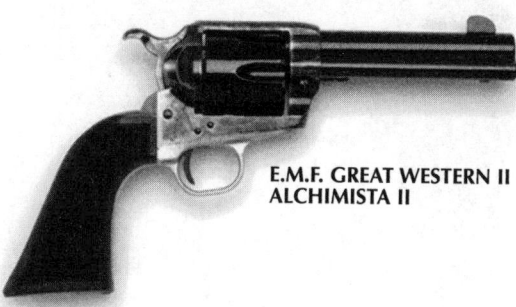

E.M.F. GREAT WESTERN II ALCHIMISTA II

GREAT WESTERN II ALCHIMISTA II

Action: SA revolver
Grips: Walnut
Barrel: 4.75 in., 5.5 in.
Sights: Fixed
Weight: 33.6 oz.
Caliber: .357, .45 LC
Capacity: 6 rounds
Features: Standard case-hardening; stainless steel; checkered walnut grips; express grips available
MSRP $650

E.M.F. Company

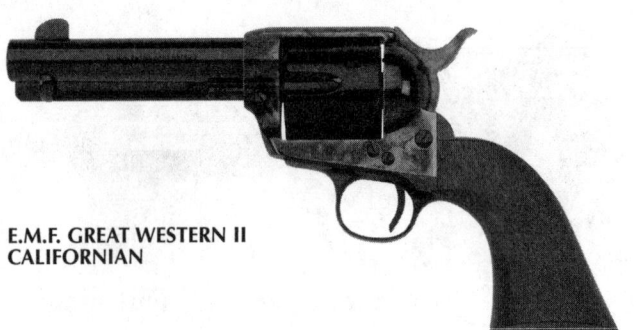

E.M.F. GREAT WESTERN II CALIFORNIAN

E.M.F. GREAT WESTERN II PONY EXPRESS

GREAT WESTERN II CALIFORNIAN

Action: SA revolver
Grips: Walnut
Barrel: 4.75 in., 5.5 in., 7.5 in.
Sights: Fixed
Weight: 48 oz.
Caliber: .22LR, .357, .44 Mag., .44/40, .45 LC
Capacity: 6 rounds
Features: Standard case-hardening; steel frame
MSRP $530

GREAT WESTERN II PONY EXPRESS

Action: SA revolver
Grips: Walnut express grips
Barrel: 3.5 in.
Sights: Fixed
Weight: 32 oz.
Caliber: .357, .45 LC
Capacity: 6 rounds
Features: Case-hardened steel; checkered walnut express grips; turned down hammer
MSRP . . . . $625–$820

Entréprise Arms

ELITE

Action: Autoloader
Grips: Composite
Barrel: 3.25 in., 4.25 in., or 5 in.
Sights: Fixed
Weight: 36–40 oz.
Caliber: .45 ACP
Capacity: 10 or 14 rounds
Features: Three Hi-visible dot sight; black oxide finish; extended thumb lock; match grade disconnector with polished contact points; hardened steel magazine release; adjustable anti-lash match trigger
MSRP $749

ENTRÉPRISE ARMS ELITE

ENTRÉPRISE ARMS MEDALIST

MEDALIST

Action: Autoloader
Grips: Composite
Barrel: 5 in.
Sights: Fixed
Weight: 40 oz.
Caliber: .40 Cal., .45 ACP
Capacity: 10 or 14 rounds
Features: Wide body frame; adjustable

Anti-lash match trigger; High Ride beavertail grip safety; 4140 Chromoly steel firing pin; match extractor
MSRP $999

European American Armory

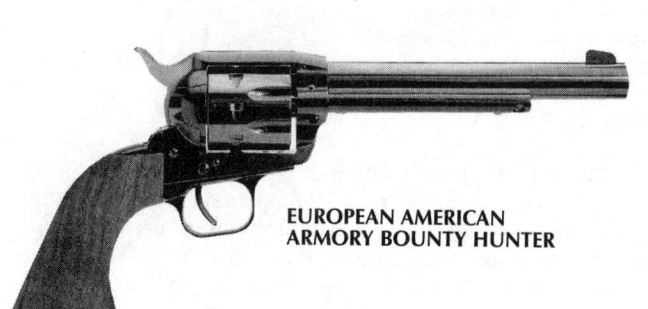

EUROPEAN AMERICAN
ARMORY BOUNTY HUNTER

EUROPEAN AMERICAN ARMORY
WITNESS - POLYMER

EUROPEAN AMERICAN ARMORY
WITNESS COMPACT - STEEL

EUROPEAN AMERICAN ARMORY
WITNESS HUNTER

BOUNTY HUNTER

Action: SA revolver
Grips: Walnut
Barrel: 4.5 in., 6.75 in., 7.5 in.
Sights: Fixed, open
Weight: 39–41 oz.
Caliber: .44 Mag., .22LR/.22WMR, 45LC
Capacity: 6 or 8 rounds
Features: Transfer bar safety; steel or alloy frame; blued, silver, case color, or blued/ivory finish
Nickel: . . . . **$354–$480**
Blued: . . . . **$320–$452**
Case Color: . . . . **$446–$448**

WITNESS

Action: Autoloader
Grips: Rubber
Barrel: 4.5 in.
Sights: 3-Dot
Weight: 33 oz.

Caliber: 9mm, .38 Super, .40 S&W, 10mm, .45ACP, 45/22, 9/22
Capacity: 10+1, 15+1, or 17+1 rounds
Features: Wonder finish, windage adjustable sight; double- or single-action; polymer or steel frame; integral accessory rail
Polymer: **$525**
Steel: **$557**
Combo: **$691**

WITNESS COMPACT

Action: Autoloader
Grips: Rubber
Barrel: 3.6 in.
Sights: Adjustable
Weight: 30 oz.
Caliber: 9mm, .38 Super, .40 S&W, 10mm, .45ACP
Capacity: 8+1, 12+1, or 14+1 rounds
Features: Wonder finish, windage adjustable sight; double- or single-

action; polymer or steel frame; integral accessory rail; blued finish
Polymer: **$525**
Steel: **$557**

WITNESS HUNTER

Action: Autoloader
Grips: Rubber
Barrel: 6 in.
Sights: Dovetail front
Weight: 41 oz.
Caliber: 10mm, .45 ACP
Capacity: 10+1 or 15+1 rounds
Features: Single-action with over travel stop; extended manual safety; super sight; cone barrel, slide lockup; checkered non-slip frame; drilled and tapped for scope mount; auto-firing pin block
MSRP **$1187**

FNH USA

FNH FN FIVE-SEVEN SERIES

FNH FNS-9

FNH FNX-9

FNH FNX-45 TACTICAL

FN FIVE-SEVEN SERIES

Action: SA autoloader
Grips: Plastic
Barrel: 4.8 in.
Sights: Adjustable 3-dot
Weight: 20.8 oz.
Caliber: 5.7x28mm
Capacity: 10 or 20 round magazines
Features: Integrated accessory rail for mounting tactical lights or lasers; reversible magazine button; ambidextrous manual safety levers; hammer-forged, chrome lined barrel; choice of adjustable three-dot target sights or fixed C-More Systems; available with matte black, olive drab green, or flat dark earth
MSRP $1329

FNS-9/FNS-40

Action: DA autoloader
Grips: Polymer
Barrel: 4 in.
Sights: Night sights
Weight: 25.2 oz.
Caliber: 9mm, .40 S&W
Capacity: 17 (FNS-9), 14 (FNS-40) rounds
Features: Striker-fired autoloader; manual safety levers; stainless steel slide in matte black or silver finish; external extractor with loaded chamber indicator; three-dot night sights; hammer-forged stainless steel barrel; black polymer frame; fully ambidextrous
MSRP $699
Night Sights: $749

FNX-9/FNX-40

Action: Autoloader
Grips: Interchangeable backstraps with lanyard eyelets
Barrel: 4 in.
Sights: 3-Dot system
Weight: 21.9 oz. (9mm), 24.4 oz. (.40)
Caliber: 9mm and .40 S&W
Capacity: 17 (9mm), 14 (.40)
Features: Ergonomic polymer black frame with low bore axis; checkered and ribbed grip panels; stainless steel slide and hammer-forged stainless barrel; DA/SA ambidextrous operating controls
MSRP $699

FNX-45 TACTICAL

Action: DA/SA
Grips: Textured polymer
Barrel: 5.3 in.
Sights: High-profile night sights
Weight: 33.6 oz.
Caliber: .45 ACP
Capacity: 15 rounds
Features: Stainless steel slide; external extractor with loaded chamber indicator; high-profile combat night sights; red-dot sight optional; hammer-forged stainless steel barrel; flat dark earth or black polymer frame; Mil-Spec 1913 accessory mounting rail; fully ambidextrous
MSRP $1399

FREEDOM ARMS MODEL 83 PREMIER GRADE

MODEL 83 PREMIER GRADE

Action: SA revolver
Grips: Hardwood
Barrel: 4.75 in., 6 in., 7.5 in., 10 in.
Sights: Fixed or adjustable
Weight: 52.5 oz.
Caliber: .500 Wyoming Express, .475 Linebaugh, .454 Casull, .44 Remington Mag., .41 Remington Mag., .357 Mag.
Capacity: 5 rounds
Features: Adjustable sight models are drilled and tapped for scope mounts; stainless steel, brush finish and impregnated hardwood grips
MSRP . . . . $2365–$2460

MODEL 83 RIMFIRE

Action: SA revolver
Grips: Hardwood
Barrel: 10 in.
Sights: Adjustable
Weight: 55.5 oz.
Caliber: .22LR match grade chambers
Capacity: 5 rounds
Features: Drilled and tapped for scope mounts; stainless steel frame; matte finish
MSRP $2270

FREEDOM ARMS MODEL 83 RIMFIRE

MODEL 97 PREMIER GRADE

Action: SA revolver
Grips: Laminated hardwood
Barrel: 4.5 in., 5.5 in., 7.5 in., or 10 in.
Sights: Adjustable or fixed
Weight: 39 oz.
Caliber: .45 colt, .44 Special, .41 Rem. Mag., .357 Mag, .327 Fed, 224-32 FA, .22LR, .17 HMR,
Capacity: 5 or 6 rounds
Features: Impregnated hardwood grips; stainless steel frame; brush stainless finish
MSRP . . . . $1855–$2020

FREEDOM ARMS MODEL 97 PREMIER GRADE

MODEL 2008 SINGLE SHOT

Action: Hinged breech with top slide latch
Grips: Impregnated hardwood
Barrel: 10–16 in.
Sights: None; drilled and tapped for scope mounts
Weight: 63 oz.
Caliber: .223 Rem. To .375 Win.
Capacity: 1 round
Features: Hammer block safety; stainless matte finish
MSRP $1495

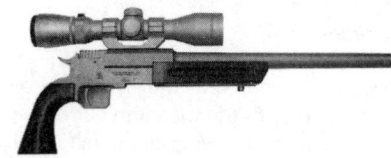

FREEDOM ARMS MODEL 2008 SINGLE SHOT

Glock

COMPACT PISTOLS G19, G23, G25, G32, G38

Action: Autoloader
Grips: Composite
Barrel: 4.02 in.
Sights: Fixed
Weight: 20.11–24.16 oz.
Caliber: 9mm, .40, .45 G.A.P., .380 Auto, .357
Capacity: 8, 10, 13, 15 rounds
Features: Trigger safety; double-action
MSRP . . . . **$599–$696**

GLOCK COMPACT G19

COMPETITION G34, G35

Action: Autoloader
Grips: Synthetic
Barrel: 5.32 in.
Sights: Adjustable
Weight: 22.92–24.5 oz.
Caliber: 9mm, .40
Capacity: 15, 17 rounds
Features: Safe action system; hexagonal barrel; right handed; extended barrel
MSRP . . . . **$679–$729**

GLOCK COMPETITION G34

G21 GEN4

Action: DAO autoloader
Grips: Synthetic
Barrel: 4.61 in.
Sights: Fixed
Weight: 26.28 oz.
Caliber: .45 Auto
Capacity: 13+1 rounds
Features: The GLOCK Pistol that validates the .45 cartridge and its 100 year history by providing all the necessities for superb accuracy and functionality. The dual recoil spring assembly and adjustable backstraps offer increased shooting comfort and control. Sleek, powerful, and affordable are the hallmarks of this remarkable handgun.
MSRP **$687**

GLOCK G21 GEN4

G32 GEN4

Action: DAO autoloader
Grips: Synthetic
Barrel: 4.02 in.
Sights: Fixed
Weight: 21.52 oz.
Caliber: .357
Capacity: 13+1 rounds
Features: The G32 is the size of the old .38 compacts with the magnum performance of the .357 Auto round without the felt recoil and 10/13/14 shots ready to fire when fully loaded. Meet the accurate, powerful, flat-shooting G32, in essence a magnumized GLOCK 19.
MSRP **$649**

GLOCK G32 GEN4

Glock

GLOCK G34 GEN4

GLOCK STANDARD G17

GLOCK SUBCOMPACT G26

GLOCK GEN4 G26

GLOCK SUBCOMPACT SLIMLINE G36

G34 GEN4

Action: DAO autoloader
Grips: Synthetic
Barrel: 5.31 in.
Sights: Fixed
Weight: 22.9 oz.
Caliber: 9mm
Capacity: 10, 17, 19 rounds
Features: This "Tactical/Practical" GLOCK 9x19 is the G17 extended to the overall length of the Government Model 1911 pistols.
MSRP. **$729**

GEN4 G26, G27

Action: Autoloader
Grips: Synthetic
Barrel: 3.46 in.
Sights: Fixed or adjustable
Weight: 19.75 oz.
Caliber: 9x19, .40
Capacity: 15 rounds
Features: Rough textured frame; interchangeable backstrap system; two magazine-release catches for ambidextrous operation; dual-recoil

spring system replaces the original single spring model
Fixed Sights: **$649**
Adjustable: **$667**
Steel: **$671**

STANDARD PISTOL G17, G20, G21, G22, G31, G37

Action: Autoloader
Grips: Composite
Barrel: 4.49 in.
Sights: Fixed
Weight: 22.04–27.68 oz.
Caliber: 9mm, .40, 10mm Auto, .45 G.A.P., .45 Auto, .380 Auto, .357
Capacity: 10, 13, 15, 17 rounds
Features: Double action; safe action trigger system; G20 model has recoil-damping Glock hi-tech polymer
MSRP. . . . . **$599–$734**

SUBCOMPACT PISTOLS G26, G27, G29, G28, G30, G33, G39

Action: Autoloader
Grips: Composite
Barrel: 3.46–3.78 in.

Sights: Fixed
Weight: 18.66–24.69 oz.
Caliber: 9mm, .40, 10mm Auto, .45 G.A.P., .45 Auto, .380 Auto, .357
Capacity: 6, 9, 10 rounds
Features: Trigger safety; double-action
MSRP. . . . . **$599–$734**

SUBCOMPACT SLIMLINE PISTOL G36

Action: Autoloader
Grips: Synthetic
Barrel: 3.78 in.
Sights: Fixed
Weight: 20.11 oz.
Caliber: .45 Auto
Capacity: 6 rounds
Features: Safe action system; single stack magazine for slim grip
MSRP. . . . . **$637–$684**

Hämmerli

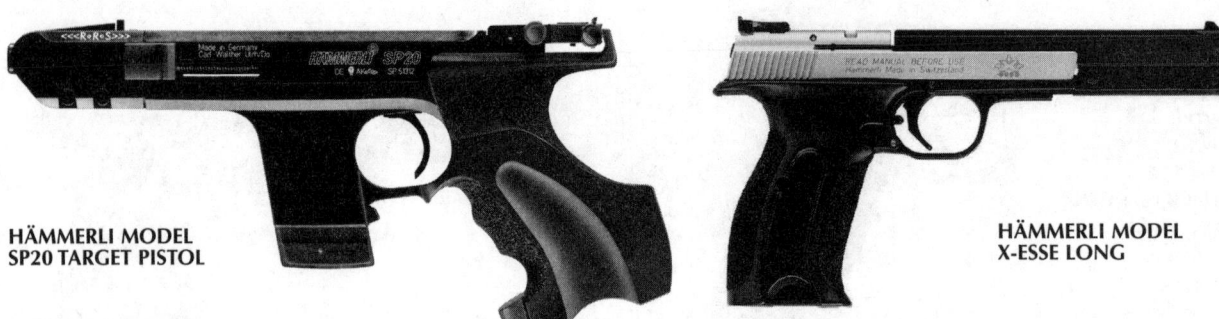

**HÄMMERLI MODEL
SP20 TARGET PISTOL**

**HÄMMERLI MODEL
X-ESSE LONG**

MODEL SP20 TARGET PISTOL

Action: Autoloader
Grips: Synthetic
Barrel: 4.86 in.
Sights: Target
Weight: 41 oz.
Caliber: .22LR, .32 S&W
Capacity: 5 rounds
Features: Front end magazine; counterweight with new recoil reduction system; various grip sizes
MSRP **$1805**

MODEL X-ESSE

Action: Autoloader
Grips: Composite
Barrel: 4.5 in., 5.9 in.
Sights: Adjustable
Weight: 27.9–31 oz.
Caliber: .22LR
Capacity: 10 rounds
Features: Single-action, two-stage trigger; universal hi-grip
MSRP . . . . **$902–$1018**

Heckler & Koch

HK45

Action: Autoloader
Grips: Polymer
Barrel: 4.53 in.
Sights: Fixed
Weight: 31 oz.
Caliber: .45 ACP
Capacity: 10 rounds
Features: DA/SA with control lever; integral Picatinny rail; ambidextrous controls with dual slide releases; modified Browning linkless recoil operating system; polygonal rifling; open square notch rear sight with contrast points; low profile drift adjustable three-dot sights
MSRP **$1187**

**HECKLER &
KOCH HK45**

HECKLER & KOCH MARK 23

HK45 COMPACT TACTICAL

Action: DA/SA
Grips: Textured polymer
Barrel: 4.57 in.
Sights: 3-dot
Weight: 29.12 oz.
Caliber: .45 ACP
Capacity: 10 rounds
Features: Proprietary internal mechanical recoil reduction system; O-ring barrel; cold-hammer-forged barrel
MSRP **$1392**

MARK 23

Action: Autoloader
Grips: Polymer
Barrel: 5.9 in.
Sights: 3-Dot
Weight: 39.4 oz.
Caliber: .45 ACP
Capacity: 12+1 rounds
Features: Threaded O-ring barrel with polygonal bore profile; match grade trigger; one piece machined steel slide; frame mounted decocking lever and separate ambidextrous safety lever; HK recoil reduction system; ambidextrous magazine release lever
MSRP **$2310**

**HECKLER & KOCH HK45
COMPACT TACTICAL**

P30

Action: Autoloader
Grips: Polymer
Barrel: 3.86 in.
Sights: Fixed
Weight: 26.08 oz.
Caliber: 9mm, .40 S&W
Capacity: 15 rounds
Features: Corrosion proof fiber-reinforced polymer frame; multiple trigger firing modes; HK recoil reduction system; blued finish; Picatinny rail; ambidextrous magazine release levers and side release
MSRP **$1054**

P30 L

Action: Autoloader
Grips: Polymer
Barrel: 4.4 in.
Sights: Fixed
Weight: 27.5 oz.
Caliber: 9mm, .40 S&W
Capacity: 10, 13, or 15 rounds
Features: Interchangeable backstraps and side panel grips in small, medium, and large sizes; ambidextrous slide and magazine releases levers; integral Picatinny rail; modular design allows DA trigger or DA/SA system, with a decocking button
MSRP **$1108**

P2000 & P2000 SK

Action: Autoloader
Grips: Polymer
Barrel: 3.26–3.66 in.
Sights: 3-Dot
Weight: 23.8–25.9 oz.
Caliber: 9mm, .40 S&W, .357 SIG
Capacity: 9-13 rounds
Features: LEM trigger system; double-action; pre-cock hammer; ambidextrous magazine release and interchangeable grip straps; mounting rail
P2000: **$941**
P2000 SK: **$1037**

USP

Action: Autoloader
Grips: Polymer
Barrel: 4.25–4.41 in.
Sights: 3-Dot
Weight: 27.2–31.36 oz.
Caliber: 9mm, .40 S&W, .45 Auto
Capacity: 12, 13, 15 rounds
Features: Browning-type action with a

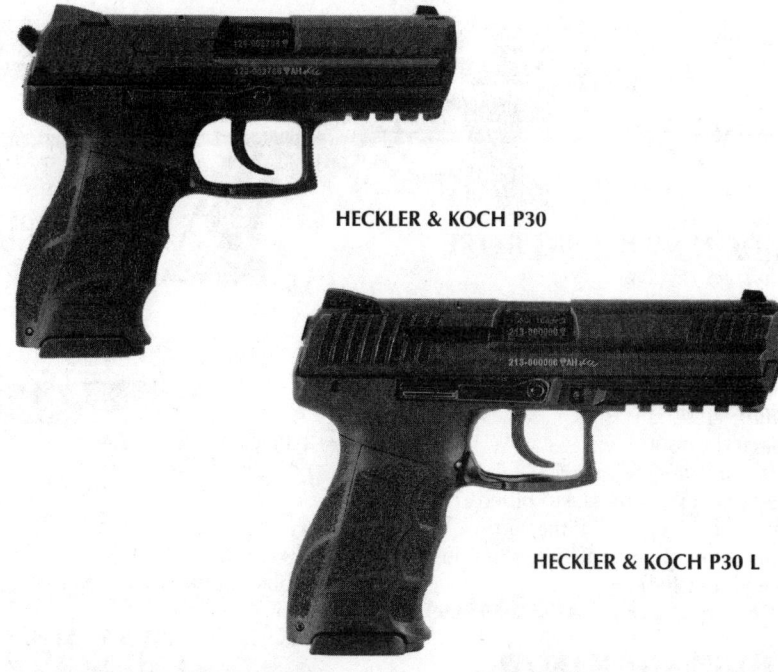

HECKLER & KOCH P30

HECKLER & KOCH P30 L

HECKLER & KOCH USP COMPACT

HECKLER & KOCH P2000

patented recoil reduction system; double and single action modes; available in nine trigger/firing mode configurations; fiber-reinforced polymer frame; blued finish; ambidextrous magazine release trigger
MSRP . . . . **$952–$1056**

USP COMPACT

Action: Autoloader
Grips: Polymer
Barrel: 3.58–3.80 in.
Sights: Fixed
Weight: 25.6–28.2 oz.
Caliber: 9mm, .40 S&W, .45 Auto
Capacity: 8, 12, 13 rounds
Features: Corrosion proof fiber-reinforced polymer frame;

HECKLER & KOCH USP

ambidextrous magazine release lever; grooved target triggers; can be converted to any of nine trigger firing modes
MSRP . . . . **$992–$1108**

Heritage Manufacturing

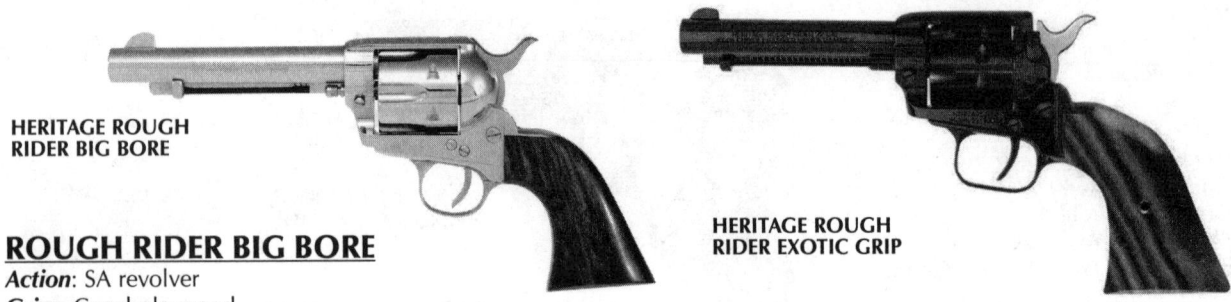

HERITAGE ROUGH RIDER BIG BORE

HERITAGE ROUGH RIDER EXOTIC GRIP

HERITAGE ROUGH RIDER SMALL BORE

ROUGH RIDER BIG BORE

Action: SA revolver
Grips: Cocobolo wood
Barrel: 4.5 in., 5.5 in., 7.5 in.
Sights: Fixed, open
Weight: 38 oz.
Caliber: .357, .45
Capacity: 6 rounds
Features: Patterned after 1873 Colt; blued, nickel, stainless and blued/color-case-hardened finishes are available; frame mounted inertia firing pin and transfer bar
MSRP . . . . $479.99–$549.99

ROUGH RIDER EXOTIC GRIP

Action: SA revolver
Grips: Cocobolo wood
Barrel: 4.75 in.
Sights: Fixed
Weight: 31 oz.
Caliber: .22-9 Shot combo
Capacity: 9 rounds
Features: Machined barrel is micro-threaded; frame finish comes in

ROUGH RIDER SMALL BORE

Action: SA revolver
Grips: Cocobolo wood
Barrel: 3.5 in., 4.75 in., 6.5 in., 9 in.
Sights: Fixed
Weight: 31 oz.
Caliber: .22LR & .22 Mag.
Capacity: 6 rounds
Features: Machined barrel is micro-

smooth silver satin, deep matte black, low gloss black satin or case-hardened finish
MSRP . . . .$279.99–$349.99

threaded; optional cocobolo grips include white mother of pearl, black mother of pearl, or green camo laminate grips; frame finish comes in smooth silver satin, deep matte black, low gloss black satin or case-hardened finish
MSRP . . . . $199.99–$359.99

High Standard

HIGH STANDARD OLYMPIC

HIGH STANDARD SUPERMATIC CITATION

OLYMPIC

Action: Autoloader
Grips: Cocobolo wood
Barrel: 5.5 in.
Sights: Adjustable
Weight: 44 oz.
Caliber: .22 Short
Capacity: 10+1 rounds
Features: Lightweight aluminum alloy slide; precision carbon steel frame; drilled and tapped for scopes; single-action
MSRP $965

SUPERMATIC CITATION

Action: Autoloader
Grips: Walnut

Barrel: 5.5 in.
Sights: Adjustable
Weight: 44 oz.
Caliber: .22LR
Capacity: 10+1 rounds

Features: Durable parkerized finish and black epoxy-finished wood; ambidextrous grips; drilled and tapped for scopes
MSRP . . . . $1095–$1295

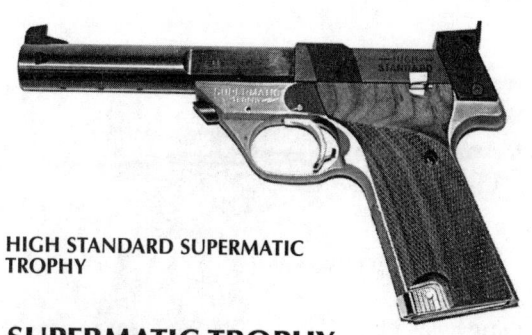

HIGH STANDARD US MODEL 1911 CUSTOM

HIGH STANDARD SUPERMATIC TROPHY

HIGH STANDARD VICTOR

SUPERMATIC TROPHY

Action: Autoloader
Grips: Walnut
Barrel: 5.5 in., 7.25 in.
Sights: Adjustable
Weight: 44 oz.–46 oz.
Caliber: .22LR
Capacity: 10+1 rounds
Features: Features gold plated components: trigger, safety, slide stop and magazine catch; adjustable trigger; checkered deluxe grips; blued finish
MSRP. . . . . **$785–$895**

US MODEL 1911 CUSTOM

Action: Autoloader
Grips: Walnut
Barrel: 5 in.
Sights: Novak style adjustable
Weight: 40 oz.
Caliber: .45 ACP
Capacity: 7+1 rounds
Features: Beveled magazine well; match trigger with overtravel stop; available in stainless steel, blued or parkerized finish
MSRP. **$995**

VICTOR

Action: Autoloader
Grips: Walnut
Barrel: 4.5 in., 5.5 in.
Sights: Adjustable
Weight: 45 oz.
Caliber: .22LR
Capacity: 10+1 rounds
Features: Removable aluminum rib; drilled and tapped for scopes; optional slide conversion kit for .22 short; various customization options
MSRP. . . . . **$785–$845**

Hi-Point Firearms

HI-POINT FIREARMS MODEL CF-380

HI-POINT FIREARMS MODEL C-9 9MM

MODEL C-9 9MM

Action: Autoloader
Grips: Polymer
Barrel: 3.5 in.
Sights: 3-Dots adjustable
Weight: 29 oz.
Caliber: 9mm
Capacity: 8 or 10 rounds
Features: Polymer frame; last round lock open; quick on-off thumb safety; free trigger lock; free extra peep sight; black finish
MSRP. **$179**

MODEL CF-380

Action: Autoloader
Grips: Polymer
Barrel: 3.5 in.
Sights: 3-Dots adjustable
Weight: 29 oz.
Caliber: .380 ACP
Capacity: 8 or 10 rounds
Features: High-impact polymer frame; black powder coat with chrome rail; durable, easy-grip finish; quick on-off

HI-POINT FIREARMS MODEL JHP45 ACP

thumb safety; free extra rear peep sight
MSRP. **$149**

MODEL JHP45 ACP & JCP 40 S&W

Action: Autoloader
Grips: Polymer
Barrel: 4.5 in.
Sights: 3-Dots adjustable
Weight: 35 oz.
Caliber: .40 S&W, .45 ACP
Capacity: 10 rounds
Features: Polymer frame; quick on-off thumb safety; operations safety sheet; +P rated; free extra rear peep sight; free trigger lock; black finish; available with laserlyte laser and green slide
MSRP. **$199**

Kahr Arms

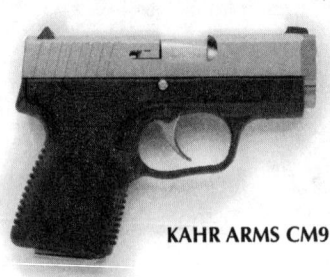

KAHR ARMS CM9

KAHR ARMS CM40

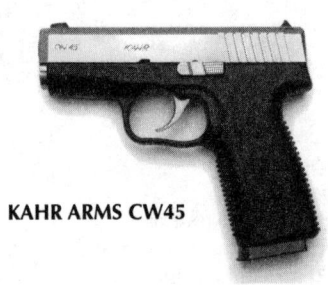

KAHR ARMS CW45

KAHR ARMS P9 SERIES

KAHR ARMS P40 SERIES

CM9
Action: Autoloader
Grips: Textured polymer
Barrel: 3 in.
Sights: Adjustable
Weight: 15.9 oz.
Caliber: 9mm
Capacity: 6+1 rounds
Features: Trigger cocking double-action; lock breech; Browning-type recoil lug; passive striker block; no magazine disconnect; drift adjustable, white bar-dot combat sights; black finish; matte stainless steel slide
MSRP **$517**

CM40
Action: Autoloader
Grips: Textured polymer
Barrel: 3 in.
Sights: Adjustable
Weight: 17.7 oz.
Caliber: .40 S&W
Capacity: 5+1 rounds
Features: Trigger cocking DAO; lock breech; "Browning-type" recoil lug; passive striker block; no magazine disconnect; black polymer frame, matte stainless steel slide
MSRP **$517**

CW45
Action: Autoloader
Grips: Textured polymer
Barrel: 3.64 in.
Sights: Adjustable
Weight: 21.7 oz.
Caliber: .45 ACP
Capacity: 6+1 rounds
Features: Trigger cocking double-action; lock breech; Browning-type recoil lug; passive striker block; no magazine disconnect; drift adjustable, white bar-dot combat rear sight, pinned in polymer front sight; black finish; matte stainless steel slide
MSRP **$485**

P9 SERIES
Action: Autoloader
Grips: Textured polymer
Barrel: 3.6 in.
Sights: Adjustable
Weight: 16.9 oz.
Caliber: 9mm
Capacity: 7+1 rounds
Features: Trigger cocking DAO; lock breech; Browning-type recoil lug; passive striker block; no magazine disconnect; black polymer frame;

model available with external safety and LCI
MSRP . . . . **$739–$996**

P40 SERIES
Action: Autoloader
Grips: Textured polymer
Barrel: 3.6 in.
Sights: Adjustable
Weight: 18.7 oz.
Caliber: .40 S&W
Capacity: 6+1 rounds
Features: Trigger cocking DAO; lock breech; Browning-type recoil lug; passive striker block; no magazine disconnect; black polymer frame
P40: **$739**
P40 w/ Night Sights: **$857**
P40 Black: **$786**
P40 Ext Safety & LCI: **$876**
P40 Ext Safety & LCI w/
Night Sights: **$996**

Kahr Arms

P45 SERIES

Action: Autoloader
Grips: Textured polymer
Barrel: 3.54 in.
Sights: Adjustable
Weight: 18.5 oz.
Caliber: .45 ACP
Capacity: 5+1, 6+1 rounds
Features: Trigger cocking DAO; lock breech; Browning-type recoil lug; passive striker block; no magazine disconnect; black polymer frame
P45: $805
P45 w/ Night Sights: $921
P45 Black: $855
P45 Black w/ Night sights: $973

P380 SERIES

Action: Autoloader
Grips: Textured polymer
Barrel: 2.5 in.
Sights: Adjustable
Weight: 11.27 oz.
Caliber: .380 ACP
Capacity: 6+1 rounds
Features: Trigger cocking DAO; Lock breech; Browning-type recoil lug; passive striker block; no magazine disconnect; black polymer frame, matte stainless steel slide; premium Lothar Walther match grade barrel; available in Black Rose and with night sights or LCI
MSRP . . . . $649–$949

PM9 SERIES

Action: Autoloader
Grips: Textured polymer
Barrel: 3 in.
Sights: Adjustable
Weight: 15.9 oz.
Caliber: 9mm
Capacity: 6+1 or 7+1 rounds
Features: Trigger cocking DAO; lock breech; Browning-type recoil lug; passive striker block; no magazine disconnect; black polymer frame; available in Black Rose, with night sights, LCI, and an external safety
MSRP . . . . $786–$1049

PM40 - EXTERNAL SAFETY & LCI

Action: Autoloader
Grips: Textured polymer
Barrel: 3 in.
Sights: Adjustable
Weight: 17.7 oz.
Caliber: .40 S&W
Capacity: 5+1, 6+1 rounds
Features: Trigger cocking DAO; lock breech; "Browning-type" recoil lug; passive striker block; no magazine disconnect; black polymer frame, matte stainless steel slide; drift adjustable, white bar-dot combat sights (tritium night sights, Crimson Trace laser sight optional)
MSRP $828

PM45 SERIES

Action: Autoloader
Grips: Textured polymer
Barrel: 3.24 in.
Sights: Adjustable
Weight: 19.3 oz.
Caliber: .45 ACP
Capacity: 6+1 rounds
Features: Trigger cocking double action; lock breech; Browning-type recoil lug; passive striker block; no magazine disconnect; drift adjustable, white bar-dot combat sights; black polymer frame, matte blackened stainless steel slide; available with night sights or CT laser sight
MSRP . . . . $855–$1022

KAHR ARMS P380

KAHR ARMS P45 BLACK WITH NIGHT SIGHTS

KAHR ARMS PM9 SERIES

KAHR ARMS PM40 WITH EXTERNAL SAFETY & LCI

KAHR ARMS PM45

Kel-Tec

KEL-TEC P-3AT

KEL-TEC P-11

KEL-TEC P-32

KEL-TEC PF-9

KEL-TEC PMR-30

P-3AT
Action: Autoloader
Grips: Polymer
Barrel: 2.7 in.
Sights: Fixed
Weight: 8.3 oz.
Caliber: .380 Auto
Capacity: 6+1 rounds
Features: Double-action only; steel barrel and slide; aluminum frame; transfer bar
Blued Finish: $318
Parkerized Finish: $361
Hard Chrome Finish: $377

P-11
Action: Autoloader
Grips: Polymer
Barrel: 3.1 in.
Sights: Fixed
Weight: 14 oz.
Caliber: 9mm
Capacity: 10+1 rounds, optional 12 rounds
Features: Double-action only; steel barrel and slide; aluminum frame; locked breech; high-impact polymer DuPont grips
Blued Finish: $333
Parkerized Finish: $377
Hard Chrome Finish: $390

P-32
Action: Autoloader
Grips: Polymer
Barrel: 2.7 in.
Sights: Fixed
Weight: 6.6 oz.
Caliber: 32 Auto
Capacity: 7+1 rounds
Features: Steel barrel and slide; locked breech mechanism
Blued Finish: $318
Parkerized Finish: $361
Hard Chrome Finish: $377

PF-9
Action: Autoloader
Grips: Polymer
Barrel: 3.1 in.
Sights: Adjustable

Weight: 12.7 oz.
Caliber: 9mm
Capacity: 7+1 rounds
Features: Firing mechanism is double-action only with an automatic hammer block safety; grips available in black, grey, and olive drab; rear sight is a new design and is adjustable for windage
Blued Finish: $333
Parkerized Finish: $377
Hard Chrome Finish: $390

PMR-30
Action: SA autoloader
Grips: Nylon
Barrel: 4.3 in.
Sights: Picatinny accessory rail under barrel
Weight: 13.6 oz.
Caliber: .22 WMR
Capacity: 30 rounds
Features: Blowback/locked breech system; lightweight but full sized; urethane recoil buffer; disassembles for cleaning with removal of one pin
MSRP $415

Kimber

KIMBER CLASSIC CARRY PRO

KIMBER COMPACT STAINLESS II

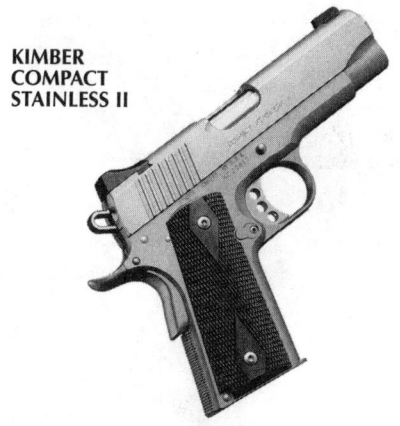

CLASSIC CARRY PRO

Action: SA autoloader
Grips: Bone
Barrel: 4 in.
Sights: Fixed low-profile, 3-dot
Weight: 35 oz.
Caliber: .45 ACP
Capacity: 8 rounds
Features: Deep charcoal blued finish; steel frame and slide; match grade bull barrel; serrated flat top slide; night sights; front strap checkering
MSRP **$2056**

COMPACT STAINLESS II

Action: Autoloader
Grips: Black synthetic double diamond
Barrel: 4 in.
Sights: Fixed, low profile
Weight: 27 oz.
Caliber: .45 ACP
Capacity: 7 rounds
Features: Full-length guide rod; aluminum frame in satin silver finish; steel Match Grade barrel; aluminum match grade trigger
MSRP **$1052**

KIMBER CUSTOM II

KIMBER ECLIPSE ULTRA II

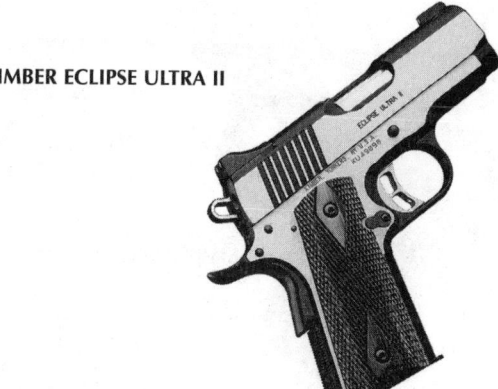

CUSTOM II

Action: Autoloader
Grips: Black synthetic double diamond
Barrel: 5 in.
Sights: Fixed, low profile
Weight: 38 oz.
Caliber: .45 ACP
Capacity: 7 rounds
Features: Full-length guide rod; aluminum frame in matte black finish; steel Match Grade barrel; aluminum match grade trigger
MSRP **$871**

ECLIPSE ULTRA II

Action: Autoloader
Grips: Laminated double diamond
Barrel: 3 in.
Sights: Meprolight Tritium 3-dot night, fixed
Weight: 38 oz.
Caliber: .45 ACP
Capacity: 7 rounds
Features: Full-length guide rod; stainless steel frame with brush polished finish; stainless steel slide; Match Grade steel barrel; aluminum Match Grade trigger
MSRP **$1289**

HANDGUNS

Kimber

KIMBER GOLD MATCH II

KIMBER SAPPHIRE ULTRA II

GOLD MATCH II

Action: Autoloader
Grips: Rosewood double diamond
Barrel: 5 in.
Sights: Kimber adjustable
Weight: 38 oz.
Caliber: .45 ACP
Capacity: 8 rounds
Features: Premium aluminum, Match Grade trigger; full length guide rod; steel frame with highly polished blued finish; stainless steel, Match Grade barrel
MSRP **$1393**

SAPPHIRE ULTRA II

Action: SA autoloader
Grips: G-10 thin grips
Barrel: 3 in.
Sights: Tactical Wedge night sights
Weight: 25 oz.
Caliber: 9mm
Capacity: 8 rounds
Features: Highly-polished stainless steel slide and small parts are finished with bright blue PVD finish accented with fine engraving; blue/black ball-milled G-10 thin grips and short trigger; ambidextrous thumb safety; Tactical Wedge night sights
MSRP **$1652**

KIMBER SOLO CARRY

KIMBER SOLO CDP (LG)

SOLO CARRY

Action: SA autoloader
Grips: Black synthetic checkered/ smooth
Barrel: 2.7 in.
Sights: Fixed low profile
Weight: 17 oz.
Caliber: 9mm
Capacity: 6 rounds
Features: Aluminum finish frame; stainless steel barrel; single-action striker trigger
MSRP **$815**

SOLO CDP (LG)

Action: SA striker-fired
Grips: Synthetic, rosewood finish
Barrel: 2.7 in.
Sights: Fixed 3-dot night sights
Weight: 17 oz.
Caliber: 9mm
Capacity: 6, 8 rounds
Features: Single-action striker-fired trigger system; Crimson Trace Lasergrips; Carry Melt treatment to round endges; black KimPro II frame finish; checkering on front and back straps
MSRP **$1223**

STAINLESS PRO RAPTOR II

Action: SA autoloading, recoil operated
Grips: Zebra wood, scale pattern
Barrel: 4 in.
Sights: Tactical wedge 3-dot
Weight: 35 oz.
Caliber: .45 ACP
Capacity: 8 rounds
Features: Stainless steel slide and frame with satin silver finish; Match Grade barrel; ambidextrous thumb safety; full-length guide rod
MSRP **$1415**

KIMBER STAINLESS
PRO RAPTOR II

STAINLESS PRO TLE II (LG)

Action: Autoloader
Grips: Tactical gray double diamond, Crimson Trace lasergrips
Barrel: 4 in.
Sights: Meprolight tritium 3-dot night, fixed
Weight: 35 oz.
Caliber: .45 ACP
Capacity: 7 rounds
Features: Full-length guide rod; stainless steel frame with satin silver; Match Grade steel barrel; aluminum Match Grade trigger
MSRP **$1518**

KIMBER STAINLESS
PRO TLE II (LG)

STAINLESS ULTRA TLE II

Action: SA autoloader
Grips: Tactical gray double diamond
Barrel: 3 in.
Sights: Meprolight tritium 3-dot night, fixed
Weight: 25 oz.
Caliber: .45 ACP
Capacity: 7 rounds
Features: Full-length guide rod; front strap checkering; aluminum frame with satin silver finish; steel match grade barrel; aluminum match grade trigger
MSRP **$1253**

KIMBER STAINLESS
ULTRA TLE II

SUPER CARRY PRO

Action: SA autoloader
Grips: Micarta/ laminated rosewood
Barrel: 4 in.
Sights: Night, tritium
Weight: 28 oz.
Caliber: .45 ACP
Capacity: 8 rounds
Features: Ambidextrous thumb safety; carry melt; full-length guide rod; aluminum frame in satin silver; super carry serrations; high cut under trigger guard; steel Match Grade barrel; aluminum Match Grade trigger
MSRP **$1596**

KIMBER SUPER
CARRY PRO

Kimber

KIMBER TACTICAL
ENTRY II

KIMBER ULTRA
CARRY II

TACTICAL ENTRY II

Action: SA autoloading, recoil operated
Grips: Laminated double diamond, Kimber logo
Barrel: 5 in.
Sights: Meprolight tritium 3-dot night, fixed
Weight: 40 oz.
Caliber: .45 ACP
Capacity: 7 rounds
Features: Ambidextrous thumb safety; full-length guide rod; stainless steel frame and slide; matte gray Kim Pro II frame finish
MSRP **$1490**

ULTRA CARRY II

Action: SA autoloading, recoil operated
Grips: Black synthetic double diamond
Barrel: 3 in.
Sights: Fixed, low profile
Weight: 25 oz.
Caliber: .45 ACP
Capacity: 7 rounds
Features: Black matte finish; aluminum frame; steel slide; full-length guide rod
MSRP **$919**

KIMBER ULTRA
CDP II

KIMBER ULTRA
CRIMSON CARRY II

ULTRA CDP II

Action: Autoloader
Grips: Rosewood double diamond
Barrel: 3 in.
Sights: Meprolight tritium 3-dot night, fixed
Weight: 25 oz.
Caliber: .45 ACP
Capacity: 7 rounds
Features: Ambidextrous thumb safety; full-length guide rod; matte black Kim Pro frame finish; aluminum frame; stainless steel slide and barrel; Match Grade trigger
MSRP **$1331**

ULTRA CRIMSON CARRY II

Action: SA autoloading, recoil operated
Grips: Rosewood double diamond, Crimson Trace lasergrips
Barrel: 3 in.
Sights: Fixed low profile
Weight: 25 oz.
Caliber: .45 ACP
Capacity: 7 rounds
Features: Full-length guide rod; aluminum frame in satin silver finish; steel Match Grade barrel; aluminum Match Grade trigger
MSRP **$1206**

Kriss USA

SPHINX SDP COMPACT

Action: DA/SA autoloader
Grips: Composite
Barrel: 3.7 in.
Sights: Fiber optic/tritium front, tritium rear
Weight: 27.5 oz.
Caliber: 9mm
Capacity: 15+1 rounds
Features: Upper frame machined from aeronautic-grade hard-anodized aluminum; integral recoil buffer; Mil-Spec 1913 rail; polymer lower frame; interchangeable grip sizes available; Defiance sights feature fiber optic/tritium day-night green front sight with tritium two-dot red rear sight; internal firing pin safety, drop safety, hammer safety, and integrated slide-position safety
MSRP $1295

KRISS USA SPHINX SDP COMPACT

Magnum Research

BABY DESERT EAGLE

Action: Autoloader
Grips: Plastic composite
Barrel: 3.64 in., 3.93 in., 4.52 in.
Sights: 3-Dot combat
Weight: 26.8–38.6 oz.
Caliber: 9mm, .40 S&W, .45 ACP
Capacity: 10, 12, 13, 15 rounds
Features: Black steel or polymer frame; slide safety; decocker; double and single action; polygonal rifling; Picatinny rail; available in full-size, compact, and semi-compact
Polymer: $616
Steel: $630

**MAGNUM RESEARCH
BABY DESERT EAGLE**

BFR (BIG FRAME REVOLVER)

Action: SA revolver
Grips: Rubber, optional wood
Barrel: 5 in., 6.5 in., 7.5 in., 10 in.
Sights: Adjustable rear, fixed front
Weight: 57.6–85 oz.
Caliber: Long Cylinder: .30/30 Win., .444 Marlin, .45 Long Colt/.410, .45/70 Gov't., .450 Marlin, .44 Mag., .460 S&W Mag., .500 S&W Mag.; Short Cylinder: .22 Hornet, .454 Casull, .480 Ruger/ .475 Linebaugh, .50AE

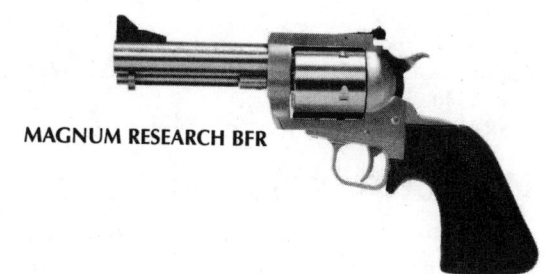

MAGNUM RESEARCH BFR

Capacity: 5 rounds
Features: Both long and short-cylinder models are made of stainless steel; barrels are stress-relieved and cut rifled; current production revolvers are shipped with rubber grips and Weaver style scope mount
MSRP $1050

Magnum Research

HANDGUNS

MAGNUM RESEARCH DESERT EAGLE 1911

MAGNUM RESEARCH MARK XIX DESERT EAGLE

MAGNUM RESEARCH MICRO DESERT EAGLE

MAGNUM RESEARCH MR EAGLE

DESERT EAGLE 1911
Action: SA autoloader
Grips: Checkered wood
Barrel: 5 in., 4.3 in.
Sights: Fixed
Weight: 36 oz. (5 in. barrel), 32 oz. (4.3 in. barrel)
Caliber: .45 ACP
Capacity: 8 rounds
Features: Grip safety; extended thumb safety; blued finish
MSRP $874

MARK XIX DESERT EAGLE
Action: Autoloader
Grips: Plastic composite
Barrel: 6 in., 10 in.
Sights: Fixed combat
Weight: 62.4–71.4 oz.
Caliber: .357 Mag., .44 Mag., .50 A.E.
Capacity: 7, 8, 9 rounds
Features: Gas operated; polygonal rifling; integral scope bases; many finishes available, including: black oxide, brushed/matte/polished chrome, bright/satin nickel, 24K gold, titanium gold, and titanium gold with tiger stripes
MSRP . . . . $1563–$2264

MICRO DESERT EAGLE
Action: Autoloader
Grips: Black polymer
Barrel: 2.22 in.
Sights: Fixed, non-adjustable
Weight: 14 oz.
Caliber: .380 Auto (9mm Browning)
Capacity: 6 rounds
Features: Gas-assisted blowback system; alloy frame; steel slide; oversized trigger guard; nickel finish
Nickel/Nickel-Blued: $479
Blued: $467

MR EAGLE "FAST ACTION"
Action: Autoloader
Grips: Black polymer
Barrel: 4 in. (9mm), 4.15 in. (.40)
Sights: Adjustable rear, fixed front
Weight: 24.8 oz. (9mm), 26.4 oz. (.40 S&W)
Caliber: 9mm or .40 S&W
Capacity: 10, 15 rounds (9mm), 10, 11 rounds (.40 SUW)
Features: 6-groove filing; hammer forged barrel; full Picatinny rail; ergonomic polymer grip frame; four separate safety devices
MSRP $559

MAXIMUM

Action: Hinged breech
Grips: Walnut
Barrel: 8.5 in., 10.5 in., 14 in.
Sights: Adjustable, open
Weight: 56–67 oz.
Caliber: most rifle chamberings from .22 Hornet to .375 H&H
Capacity: single-shot
Features: Falling block action; free

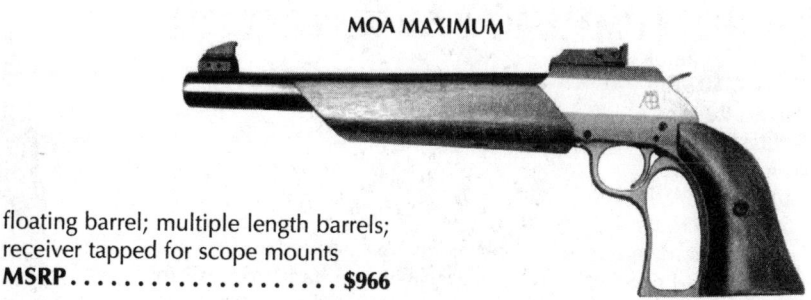

MOA MAXIMUM

floating barrel; multiple length barrels; receiver tapped for scope mounts
MSRP **$966**

Nighthawk Custom

NIGHTHAWK CUSTOM GLOBAL RESPONSE PISTOL

NIGHTHAWK CUSTOM HEINIE SIGNATURE RECON

NIGHTHAWK CUSTOM BOB MARVEL CUSTOM

BOB MARVEL CUSTOM

Action: Autoloader
Grips: Custom Mil Tac
Barrel: 4.25 in.
Sights: Novak tritium night sight front, tritium adjustable rear
Weight: 38 oz.
Caliber: .45
Capacity: 8+1 rounds
Features: Late in 2011 Bob Marvel decided that he would train one of our Master Gunsmiths to build one of his most popular custom models. This model incorporates new Nighthawk/ Marvel Everlast Recoil System, which allows a shooter to go at least 10,000 rounds before a spring change is necessary. Felt recoil and muzzle flip are also dramatically reduced. The proprietary barrel system is unique to any we have ever produced. The groups at 50 yards are beyond the capabilities of the average shooter.
MSRP **$3995**

GLOBAL RESPONSE PISTOL (GRP)

Action: SA autoloader
Grips: Micarta gator grips
Barrel: 5 in.
Sights: Night
Weight: 39 oz.

Caliber: .45 ACP, 10mm, 9mm
Capacity: 8 rounds
Features: 1911 design; Lanyard loop integrated into the mainspring housing; forged slide stop axle is cut flush with the frame; Heinie Slant-Pro Night Sights, Novak Low Mount Night Sights, or Novak Extreme Duty Adjustable Night Sights are standard; Perma Kote finish in black, sniper gray, green, coyote tan, titanium blued, and hard chrome
MSRP **$2895.95**

HEINIE SIGNATURE COMPACT, RECON

Action: Autoloader
Grips: Thin Proprietary G10
Barrel: 4.25 in., 5 in.

Sights: Tritium front night sight, Heinie Slant-Pro Rear
Weight: 38 oz.–40 oz.
Caliber: 9mm, .45
Capacity: 7+1, 8+1 rounds
Features: Features a proprietary thinned frame and mainspring housing that are scalloped to provide a positive grip without the abrasion some people feel from checkering. The grips are a new pattern of G10 that are thinned to make concealed carry even easier, and feature a relieved area on the side to allow easy access to the magazine release.
Compact: **$3450**
PDP: **$3395**
Recon: **$3550**

Nighthawk Custom

T3 - THE ULTIMATE CONCEALED CARRY 1911

Action: SA autoloader
Grips: G10 grips
Barrel: 4.25 in.
Sights: Heinie Straight Eight Slant-Pro, night
Weight: 40 oz.
Caliber: .45 ACP, 9mm
Capacity: 7 rounds
Features: Frame based on Officer model; extended magazine well; Heinie Slant-Pro Straight Eights Night Sights are standard; mainspring housing and rear of slide are horizontally serrated to match; top of slide serrated to reduce glare; Nighthawk Custom lightweight aluminum trigger that has been blacked-out using Perma Kote; available in black, gun metal grey, green coyote tan, titanium blued, and hard chrome Perma Kote or stainless steel model

Standard:. $3250
Stainless: $3400
Thin (35.5 oz.):. $3400

NIGHTHAWK CUSTOM T3

North American Arms

NORTH AMERICAN ARMS .32 ACP GUARDIAN

.32 ACP GUARDIAN

Action: DAO
Grips: Polymer
Barrel: 2.5 in.
Sights: Fixed, open
Weight: 13.5 oz.
Caliber: .32 ACP
Capacity: 6+1 rounds
Features: Stainless steel; double action only; integral locking system safety; also available in .25 caliber
MSRP. $402

.380 ACP GUARDIAN

Action: DAO
Grips: Composite
Barrel: 2.49 in.
Sights: Fixed, open
Weight: 18.72 oz.

Caliber: .380 ACP
Capacity: 6+1 rounds
Features: Stainless steel; double action only; integral locking system safety
MSRP. $449

1860 EARL 4" BARREL

Action: SA revolver
Grips: Rosewood
Barrel: 4 in. heavy octagonal
Sights: Bead front
Weight: 9.1 oz.
Caliber: .22 Mag.
Capacity: 5 rounds
Features: 1860s style mini revolver resembles 150-yr-old percussion revolver; also available with 3 in. barrel
MSRP. $284

NORTH AMERICAN ARMS .380 ACP GUARDIAN

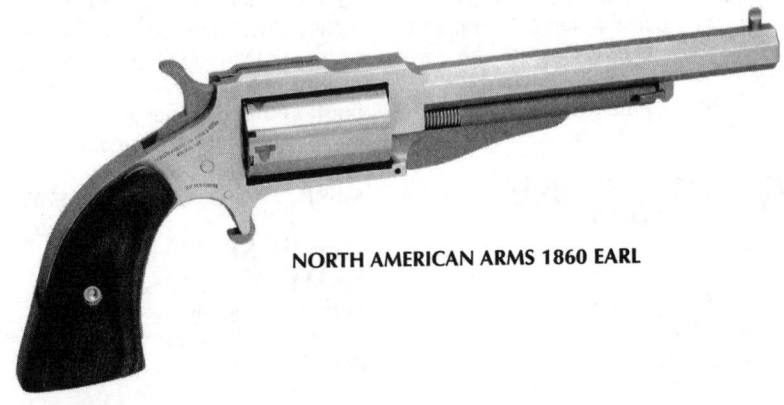

NORTH AMERICAN ARMS 1860 EARL

North American Arms

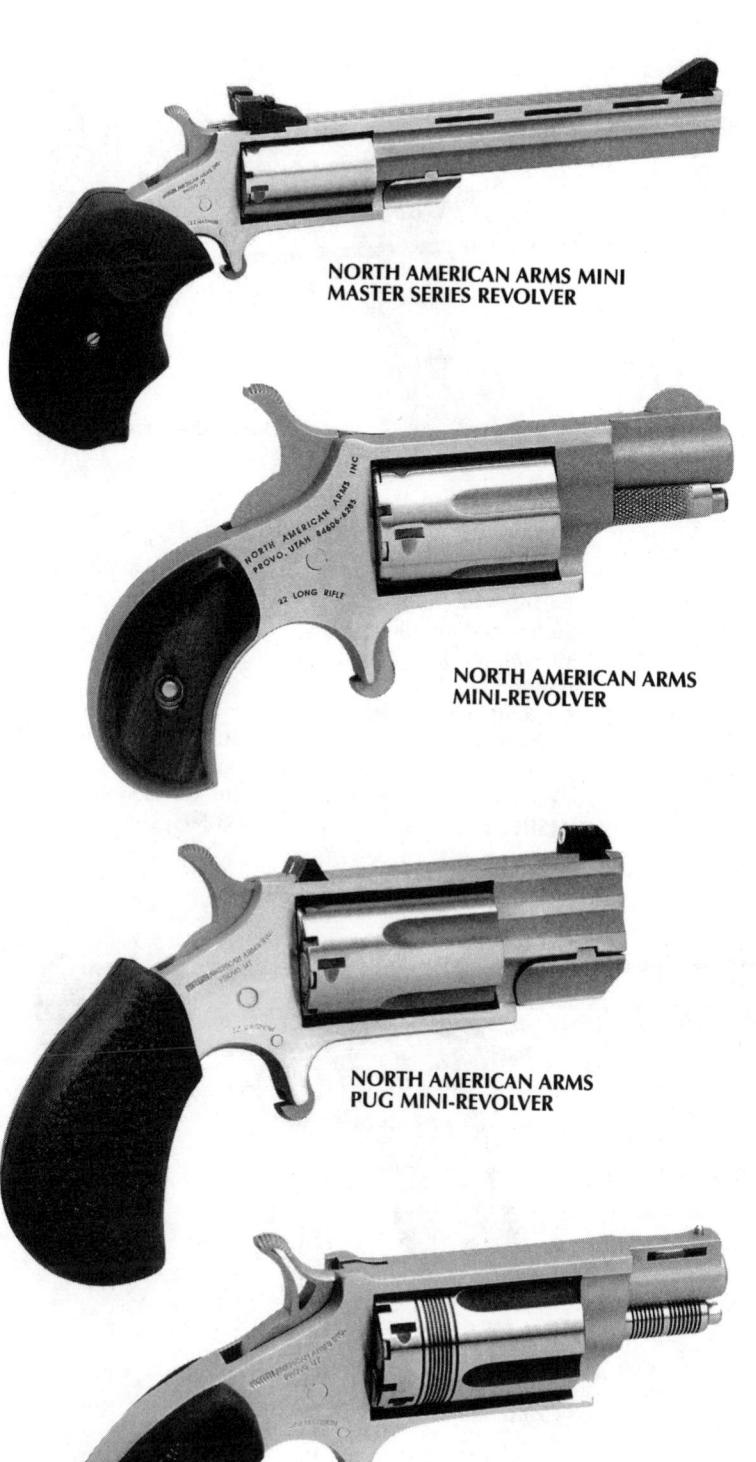

NORTH AMERICAN ARMS MINI MASTER SERIES REVOLVER

NORTH AMERICAN ARMS MINI-REVOLVER

NORTH AMERICAN ARMS PUG MINI-REVOLVER

NORTH AMERICAN ARMS THE WASP

MINI MASTER SERIES REVOLVER

Action: SA revolver
Grips: Rubber
Barrel: 4 in.
Sights: Fixed or adjustable
Weight: 10.7 oz.
Caliber: .22LR, .22 Mag.
Capacity: 5 rounds
Features: Conversion cylinder or adjustable sights available
.22LR, .22 Mag.: . . . . **$284–$314**
Conversion: . . . . **$319–$349**

MINI-REVOLVER

Action: SA revolver
Grips: Laminated rosewood
Barrel: 1.2 in., 1.625 in.
Sights: Fixed, open
Weight: 4 oz.–6.2 oz.
Caliber: .22 Short, .22LR, .22 Mag.
Capacity: 5 rounds
Features: Features NAA's safety cylinder so mini-revolver can be carried fully loaded
.22: **$209**
.22LR: **$209**
.22 Mag: **$219**

PUG MINI-REVOLVER

Action: Revolver
Grips: Rubber
Barrel: 1 in.
Sights: Tritium and white dot
Weight: 6.4 oz.
Caliber: .22 Mag.
Capacity: 5 rounds
Features: Oversized pebble-textured rubber grips enable the handler to keep a firm grip
White dot sight: **$314**
Tritium sight: **$334**

THE WASP

Action: SA revolver
Grips: Rubber pebble finish
Barrel: 1.125 in., 1.625 in.
Sights: Stainless post
Weight: 5.9 oz.–7.2 oz.
Caliber: .22 Mag.
Capacity: 5 rounds
Features: Stainless steel frame; vent rib barrel; skeleton hammer; .22LR conversion cylinders available; brushed sides, matte contours, black inlay
MSRP . . . . **$249–$284**

Olympic Arms

OLYMPIC ARMS COHORT

OLYMPIC ARMS ENFORCER

COHORT

Action: Autoloader
Grips: Walnut, fully checkered
Barrel: 4 in. bull
Sights: Target
Weight: 36 oz.
Caliber: .45 ACP
Capacity: 7+1 rounds
Features: Single-action on 1911 Colt design; short slide on a full size frame; grooved frame front strap; satin bead blast finish
MSRP **$973.70**

ENFORCER

Action: Autoloader
Grips: Smooth, laser etched widow icon, walnut
Barrel: 4 in. bull
Sights: Low-profile
Weight: 35 oz.
Caliber: .45 ACP
Capacity: 6+1 rounds
Features: Single-action on 1911 Colt design; satin bead blast finish; hooked frame trigger guard; Triplex Counterwound self-contained spring recoil system
MSRP **$1033.50**

OLYMPIC ARMS MATCHMASTER

OLYMPIC ARMS WESTERNER

MATCHMASTER

Action: Autoloader
Grips: Smooth, laser etched scorpion icon, walnut
Barrel: 5 in.
Sights: Adjustable rear
Weight: 40 oz.–44 oz.
Caliber: .45 ACP
Capacity: 7+1 rounds
Features: Single-action on 1911 Colt design; satin bead blast or parkerized finish; grooved frame front strap
5 in.: **$1033.50**
6 in.: **$973.70**

WESTERNER

Action: Autoloader
Grips: Smooth, laser etched westerner icon, ivory color
Barrel: 5 in.
Sights: Target
Weight: 39 oz.
Caliber: .45ACP
Capacity: 7+1 rounds
Features: Single-action; color case-hardened frame and slide; stainless steel barrel; round frame trigger guard; straight front frame strap
MSRP **$1163.50**

Puma by Legacy Sports

PUMA M-1873 REVOLVER

M-1873 REVOLVER
Action: SA revolver
Grips: Walnut, synthetic
Barrel: 4.625 in., 5.5 in., 7.5 in.
Sights: Fixed front, rear notch
Weight: 35.2 oz.–38.4 oz.

Caliber: .22LR, .22 Mag
Capacity: 6 rounds
Features: Same frame size and weight of a Single Action Army revolver; antique or matte black finish; checkered grips; key operated, hammer block safety; side loading gate
MSRP . . . .$189–$285

Remington Arms

MODEL 1911 R1
Action: Autoloading
Grips: Double diamond walnut
Barrel: 5 in.
Sights: Fixed
Weight: 38.5 oz.
Caliber: .45 Auto
Capacity: 7 rounds
Features: Short trigger; double diamond walnut grips; modern enhancements include a lowered and flared ejection port; beveled magazine well; loaded chamber indicator; high-profile fixed sights in a three-white-dot pattern; match grade stainless-steel barrel; available in stainless steel
MSRP $729
SS: $789

REMINGTON MODEL 1911 R1

Rock River Arms

ROCK RIVER ARMS 1911 POLY PISTOL

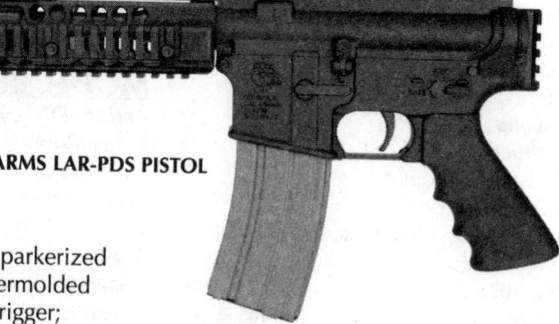

ROCK RIVER ARMS LAR-PDS PISTOL

1911 POLY PISTOL
Action: SA
Grips: Polymer
Barrel: 5 in.
Sights: Dovetail front and rear
Weight: 32.6 oz.
Caliber: .45
Capacity: 7 rounds
Features: Chromoly barrel; polymer frame and mainspring housing; steel frame insert; steel slide; parkerized finish on metal; RRA overmolded grips; aluminum speed trigger; beavertail grip safety; RRA dovetail front and rear sights
MSRP $800

LAR-PDS PISTOL
Action: Gas-operated autoloader with PPS (Performance Piston System)-AR style
Grips: Hogue rubber
Barrel: 8 in. chromoly
Sights: MS 1913 rail
Weight: 80 oz.
Caliber: 5.56mm Nato chamber for 5.56mm & .223
Capacity: 30 rounds
Features: A2 Flash Hider; aluminum tri-rail handguard; ambidextrous non-reciprocating charging handle
MSRP . . . . $1245–$1395

Rossi

ROSSI MODEL R352

ROSSI MODEL R461

ROSSI MODEL R851

ROSSI MODEL R972

ROSSI RANCH HAND

MODEL R351 AND R352

Action: DA revolver
Grips: Rubber
Barrel: 2 in.
Sights: Fixed, open
Weight: 24 oz.
Caliber: .38 Spl., .38 Spl. +P
Capacity: 5 rounds
Features: Blued or stainless steel
finish; checkered grips; forged steel
frame
R35102: . . . . **$401–$414**
R35202: . . . . **$465–$479**

MODEL R462 AND R461

Action: DA revolver
Grips: Rubber
Barrel: 2 in.
Sights: Fixed, open
Weight: 26 oz.
Caliber: .357 Mag.
Capacity: 6 rounds
Features: Blued or stainless steel
finish; checkered grips; forged steel
frame
R46102: . . . . **$401–$414**
R46202: . . . . **$465–$479**

MODEL R851

Action: DA revolver
Grips: Rubber
Barrel: 4 in.
Sights: Adjustable
Weight: 32 oz.
Caliber: .38 Spl., .38 Spl. +P
Capacity: 6 rounds
Features: Adjustable rear sight; blued
finish; forged steel frame
MSRP . . . . **$401–$414**

MODEL R971 AND R972

Action: DA revolver
Grips: Rubber
Barrel: 4 in., 6 in.
Sights: Target
Weight: 35 oz.
Caliber: .357 Mag., .38 Special

Capacity: 6 rounds
Features: Stainless steel or blued
finish; deep contoured finger grooves
in the grip for solid grasp and comfort;
frame forged from steel
Blued: . . . . **$465–$479**
SS: . . . . **$523–$537**

RANCH HAND

Action: Lever-action repeating pistol
Grips: Walnut
Barrel: 12 in.
Sights: Gold-bead front w/adjustable
buckhorn rear
Weight: 64 oz.
Caliber: .38 Special/.357 Mag., .45
Long Colt, .44 Mag., .45 LC
Capacity: 6 rounds
Features: Matte blued finish or blued
case-hardened; Brazilian hardwood
stock; oversize loop lever; investment-
cast receiver
Blued: **$595**
Blued case-hardened: **$676**

RUGER 22/45 TARGET RIMFIRE PISTOL

22/45 TARGET RIMFIRE PISTOL
Action: SA autoloader
Grips: Checkered cocobolo wood
Barrel: 4 in., 5.5 in.
Sights: Adjustable rear
Weight: 31–33 oz.
Caliber: .22LR
Capacity: 10 rounds
Features: Replaceable panels; Zytel polymer frame; blued finish; classic 1911 style pistol
MSRP . . . .**$359–$399**

RUGER BISLEY

BISLEY
Action: SA revolver
Grips: Hardwood
Barrel: 7.5 in.
Sights: Ramp front, adjustable rear
Weight: 48 oz.–50 oz.
Caliber: .44 Mag, .45 Colt
Capacity: 6 rounds
Features: Blued alloy steel frame; patented Ruger transfer bar mechanism and loading gate interlock; traditional western style hand-filling grip featuring rosewood grip panels; ramp front and precision adjustable rear sights
MSRP **$799**

GP100
Action: DA revolver
Grips: Black hogue monogrip
Barrel: 3 in., 4.2 in., 6 in.
Sights: Ramp front, fixed or adjustable rear
Weight: 36 oz.–45 oz.
Caliber: .327 Fed Mag., .357 Mag.
Capacity: 6, 7 rounds
Features: Satin stainless or blued finish; stainless steel or alloy steel frame; cushioned rubber grip; transfer bar; triple-locking cylinder
MSRP . . . .**$699–$759**

RUGER GP100

Ruger

RUGER LC9 9MM

RUGER LCP .380 ACP

RUGER LCP CENTERFIRE PISTOL

RUGER LCR

LC9 9MM

Action: Autoloader
Grips: Glass-filled nylon
Barrel: 3.12 in.
Sights: Adjustable 3-dot
Weight: 17.6 oz.
Caliber: 9mm Luger
Capacity: 7+1 rounds
Features: Alloy steel barrel and slide; blued finish; adjustable 3-dot/LaserMax CenterFire sights; black, high performance, glass-filled nylon grips
MSRP. **$529**

LCP .380 ACP

Action: Autoloader
Grips: Glass-filled nylon
Barrel: 2.75 in.
Sights: Crimson Trace/LaserMax
Weight: 9.9 oz.
Caliber: .380 Auto

Capacity: 6+1 rounds
Features: Alloy steel barrel and slide; blued finish; fixed/LaserMax CenterFire sights; black, high performance, glass-filled nylon grips
MSRP. **$449**

LCP CENTERFIRE PISTOL

Action: DA autoloader
Grips: Black, glass-filled nylon
Barrel: 2.75 in.
Sights: Fixed, optional Crimson Trace laserguard or LaserMax CenterFire
Weight: 9.4–10 oz.
Caliber: .380 Auto
Capacity: 6+1 rounds
Features: Blued, alloy slide and barrel; fixed front and rear sights are integral to the slide; hammer is recessed within the slide; factory-fitted trigger-guard-mounted laser available from

LaserMaz and Crimson Trace
MSRP. . . . . **$379–$449**
Crimson Trace: **$559**

LCR (LIGHTWEIGHT COMPACT REVOLVER)

Action: DA revolver
Grips: Hogue Tamer and Crimson Trace lasergrips
Barrel: 1.8 in.
Sights: U-Notch Integral rear
Weight: 13 oz.–17.1 oz.
Caliber: .22 Mag., .22LR, .38 Spl. +P, .357 Mag.
Capacity: 5, 6, 8 rounds
Features: Advanced target gray cylinder finish; option of replaceable, pinned ramp or XS standard dot tritium front sight
MSRP. . . . . **$529–$879**

Ruger

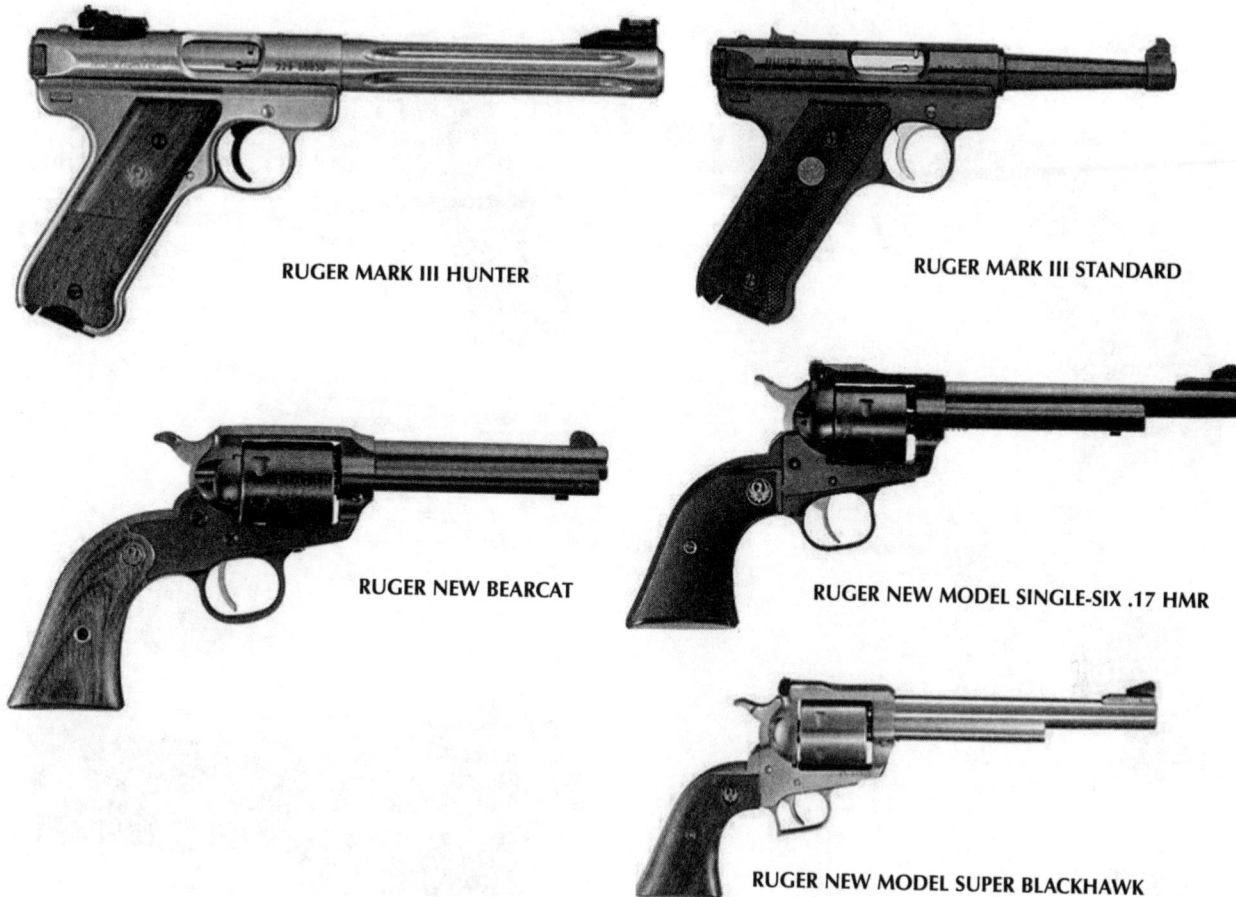

RUGER MARK III HUNTER

RUGER MARK III STANDARD

RUGER NEW BEARCAT

RUGER NEW MODEL SINGLE-SIX .17 HMR

RUGER NEW MODEL SUPER BLACKHAWK

MARK III HUNTER
Action: SA autoloading, recoil operated
Grips: Brown or Target laminate
Barrel: 6.88 in.
Sights: Fiber optic front, adjustable rear
Weight: 41 oz.–43.7 oz.
Caliber: .22LR
Capacity: 10 rounds
Features: Stainless steel frame with satin finish; fluted bull barrel; visible loaded chamber indicator
MSRP. . . . .$679–$729

MARK III STANDARD
Action: Autoloader
Grips: Checkered plastic
Barrel: 4.75 in., 6 in.
Sights: Open, adjustable
Weight: 35–37 oz.
Caliber: .22LR
Capacity: 10 rounds
Features: Steel frame with blued finish;

loaded chamber indicator; manual safety; internal cylindrical bolt
MSRP. $389

NEW BEARCAT
Action: SA revolver
Grips: Hardwood
Barrel: 4.2 in.
Sights: Blade front, integral notch
Weight: 24 oz.
Caliber: .22LR
Capacity: 6 rounds
Features: Alloy steel with blued finish or stainless steel frame with satin stainless finish; decorative cylinder; transfer bar mechanism; features one piece frame reminiscent of old Remington Civil War-era revolvers
Alloy Steel: $569
SS: $619

NEW MODEL SINGLE-SIX .17 HMR
Action: SA revolver
Grips: Black checkered hard rubber

Barrel: 6.5 in.
Sights: Ramp front, adjustable rear
Weight: 35 oz.
Caliber: .17 HMR
Capacity: 6 rounds
Features: Alloy steel frame with blued finish; transfer bar mechanism
MSRP. $569

NEW MODEL SUPER BLACKHAWK
Action: SA revolver
Grips: Hardwood
Barrel: 4.62 in., 5.5 in., 7.5 in., 10.5 in.
Sights: Ramp front, adjustable rear
Weight: 45–55 oz.
Caliber: .44 Mag
Capacity: 6 rounds
Features: Alloy steel or stainless steel frame; blued or satin stainless finish; transfer bar mechanism; western-style grip
MSRP. . . . .$739–$769

Ruger

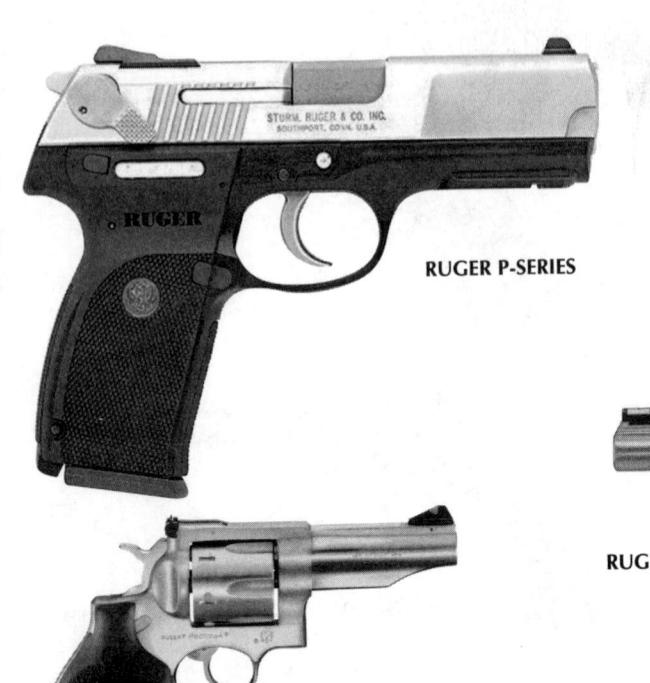

RUGER P-SERIES

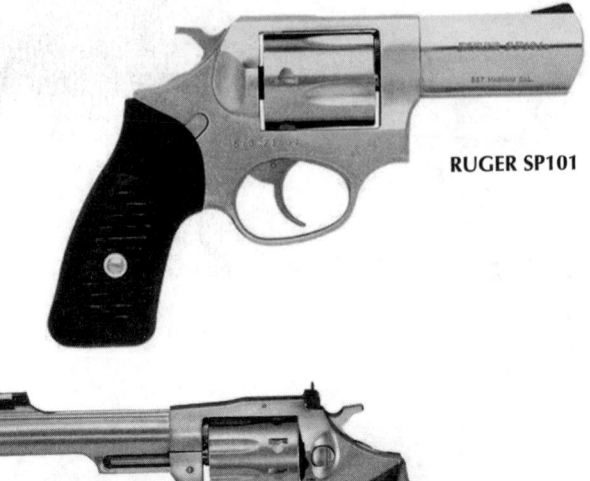

RUGER SP101

RUGER SP101 .22LR

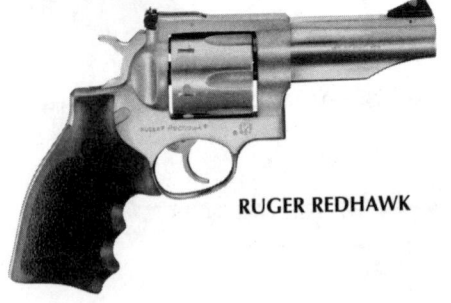

RUGER REDHAWK

RUGER SR9C

P-SERIES
Action: Autoloader
Grips: Black polymer
Barrel: 3.9 in.
Sights: Fixed 3-dot
Weight: 27 oz.
Caliber: .45 Auto, 9mm Luger
Capacity: 10+1, 15+1 rounds
Features: Stainless or blued barrel; ambidextrous manual safety; slide; grip frame; contoured grip
MSRP. . . . .$399–$439

REDHAWK
Action: DA revolver
Grips: Hardwood or black Hogue monogrip
Barrel: 4.2 in., 5.5 in., 7.5 in.
Sights: Ramp front, adjustable rear
Weight: 46–54 oz.
Caliber: .44 Mag., .45 Colt
Capacity: 6 rounds
Features: Satin stainless finish; triple-locking cylinder; single spring mechanism; easy sighting; stainless steel construction; dual chambering; transfer bar
MSRP. . . . .$989–$1049

SP101
Action: DA revolver
Grips: Black rubber
Barrel: 2.25 in., 3.06 in., 4.2 in.
Sights: Fixed, windage adjustable
Weight: 25 oz.–30 oz.
Caliber: .357 Mag., .22LR, .38 Spl.
Capacity: 5 or 6 rounds
Features: Stainless steel frame with satin finish; cushioned rubber grip; grip frame; transfer bar; triple-locking cylinder
MSRP. . . . .$659–$699

SP101 .22LR
Action: DA Revolver
Grips: Rubber, wood
Barrel: 4.20 in.
Sights: Fiber optic
Weight: 29.5 oz.
Caliber: .22LR
Capacity: 8 rounds

Features: Stainless steel frame with satin finish; cushioned rubber grip with engraved wood; grip frame; transfer bar; triple-locking cylinder
MSRP. $699

SR9C
Action: DA autoloader
Grips: Black, glass-filled, nylon
Barrel: 3.4 in.
Sights: Adjustable 3-dot
Weight: 23.4 oz.
Caliber: 9mm Luger
Capacity: 10 or 17 rounds
Features: Compact version of SR9; black alloy or brushed stainless 6-groove rifling; high visibility sights; accessory mounting rail
MSRP. $529

Ruger

RUGER SR22 RIMFIRE PISTOL

RUGER SR40

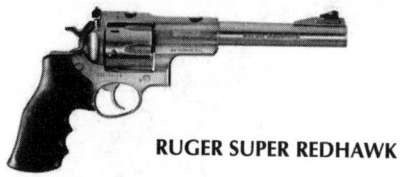

RUGER SUPER REDHAWK

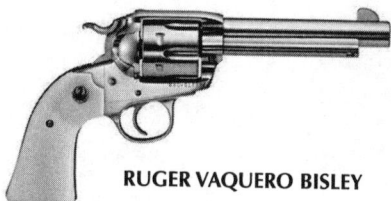

RUGER VAQUERO BISLEY

RUGER VAQUERO BLUED

SR22 RIMFIRE PISTOL

Action: DA autoloader
Grips: Polymer
Barrel: 3.5 in.
Sights: Adjustable 3-dot
Weight: 17.5 oz.
Caliber: .22LR
Capacity: 10 rounds
Features: 3-dot sight system has fixed front sight and adjustable rear sight; polymer frame and two interchangeable rubberized grips; underside Picatinny rail; aluminum slide; ambidextrous manual thumb safety/decocking lever; ambidextrous magazine release
MSRP. $399
Silver: $419
Threaded Barrel: $439

SR40

Action: Autoloader
Grips: Black, high performance, glass-filled nylon
Barrel: 4.1 in.
Sights: Adjustable 3-dot
Weight: 27.25 oz.
Caliber: .40 S&W
Capacity: 10 or 15 rounds

Features: Glass-filled nylon frame; ambidextrous operating controls; trigger system and reversible; fully adjustable three-dot sights; integral accessory rail; backstraps are identical to SR9; Nitridox pro black or brushed stainless finish
MSRP. $529

SUPER REDHAWK

Action: DA revolver
Grips: Black Hogue Tamer monogrip
Barrel: 7.5 in., 9.5 in.
Sights: Ramp front, adjustable rear
Weight: 53 oz.–58 oz.
Caliber: .44 Mag., .454 Casull, .480 Ruger
Capacity: 6 rounds
Features: Satin stainless finish; triple-locking cylinder; integral scope system; corrosion-resistant; extended frame; dual chambering; transfer bar
MSRP. . . . . $1049–$1079

VAQUERO BISLEY

Action: SA revolver
Grips: Simulated ivory
Barrel: 5.5 in.
Sights: Fixed
Weight: 41 oz.–45 oz.
Caliber: .45 Colt, .357 Mag
Capacity: 6 rounds
Features: Stainless steel frame with high-gloss stainless finish
MSRP. $809

VAQUERO BLUED

Action: SA revolver
Grips: Black checkered
Barrel: 4.62 in., 5.5 in.
Sights: Fixed
Weight: 40 oz.–43 oz.
Caliber: .45 Colt, .357 Mag.
Capacity: 6 rounds
Features: Blued finish alloy steel; reverse Indexing Pawl; ejector rod head; transfer bar mechanism; internal lock
MSRP. $739

Sig Sauer

SIG SAUER 1911 TRADITIONAL

SIG SAUER 1911 ULTRA TWO-TONE

SIG SAUER MOSQUITO

SIG SAUER P210

1911 TRADITIONAL

Action: SA autoloader
Grips: Custom shop wood, aluminum, or polymer grips
Barrel: 4.2 in.
Sights: Novak Night, platinum elite model has adjustable combat night sights
Weight: 35.5 oz.
Caliber: .45 ACP
Capacity: 8 rounds
Features: Accessory rail; beavertail frame; checkered grip; match grade barrel, hammer/sear set and trigger; stainless finish on stainless model; duo-tone finish on two-tone model; nitron finish on TACOPS model

Compact stainless:	**$1142**
Match Elite stainless:	**$1128**
Two-Tone Match Elite:	**$1128**
TACOPS:	**$1213**

1911 ULTRA

Action: SA
Grips: Black diamondwood, rosewood
Barrel: 3.3 in.
Sights: Low-pro night sights

Weight: 28 oz.
Caliber: .45 ACP
Capacity: 6+1 rounds
Features: Smallest SIG 1911 yet; stainless slide over alloy frame; unique recoil system; 26 lpi front strap checkering; combine to make a very controllable and comfortable small .45; skeletonized trigger; two variants: Nitron (all black with black diamondwood grips) and Two-Tone (natural stainless slide over black hardcoat anodized aluminum frame; rosewood grips)

Nitron:	**$1142**
Two-Tone:	**$1156**

MOSQUITO

Action: Autoloader
Grips: Black polymer
Barrel: 3.9 in.
Sights: Adjustable rear
Weight: 24.6 oz.
Caliber: .22LR
Capacity: 10 rounds
Features: Integrated accessory rail; rugged blowback system; fixed barrel; superior ergonomic grip; internal locking device; slide mounted ambidextrous safety; blued slide finish; black polymer frame finish; other models available with various color schemes and features

MSRP **$390**

P210

Action: SA autoloader
Grips: Custom wood
Barrel: 4.7 in.
Sights: Post & notch
Weight: 37.4 oz.
Caliber: 9mm
Capacity: 8 rounds
Features: Durable nitron frame and slide finish; chrome-moly barrel; carbon steel slide; frame machined from solid billet steel; slide magazine release

MSRP **$2199**

SIG SAUER P220

SIG SAUER P224
EQUINOX

SIG SAUER P226

SIG SAUER P226 MK25

P220

Action: Autoloader
Grips: Polymer, laminated or custom shop wood
Barrel: 4.4 in.
Sights: Siglite night
Weight: 30.4 oz.–31.2 oz.
Caliber: .45 ACP
Capacity: 8 rounds
Features: Nitron finish, light-weight alloy frame; accessory rail

Standard:................ **$993**
Night Sights: **$1068**
Two-Tone Dak:........... **$1079**

P224

Action: SA/DA or DAO
Grips: Hogue, ergonomic
Barrel: 3.5 in.
Sights: Tritium, fiber optic, or night sights
Weight: 25.4 oz.
Caliber: 9mm, .40, .357
Capacity: 10+1, 11+1 rounds
Features: Classic SIG in a true sub-compact; 4 variants: SIG Anti-Snag (de-horned slide, ergonomic grips, night sights), Equinox (2-tone Nitron SS slide, Tru-Glo Tritium fiber optic front, SIGLITE rear, black diamondwood grips), Nickel (nickel slide and controls, Hogue grips, night sights), Extreme (Hogue black and gray Piranha grips, night sights)

Equinox: **$1218**
Extreme: **$1146**
Nickel:.................. **$1125**
SAS:.................... **$1125**

P226

Action: DA/SA autoloader
Grips: One-piece ergo grip, extreme model features Hogue custom G10 grips, custom wood w/ SIG Medallion
Barrel: 4.4 in.
Sights: Contrast, Siglite night optional
Weight: 34 oz.–34.4 oz.
Caliber: 9mm, .357 Sig, .40 S&W
Capacity: 9mm: 10 or 15 rounds; .357 Sig: 10 or 12 rounds, .40 S&W: 10 or 12 rounds
Features: Black hard anodized frame finish; nitron slide finish; accessory rail; extreme model features SRT trigger and front cocking serrations

Standard:................. **$993**
Night Sights: **$1068**
Extreme: **$1213**
Elite SAO: **$1218**
Engraved:................. **$1289**
Engraved Stainless: **$1402**

P226 MK25

Action: SA/DA
Grips: Polymer
Barrel: 4.4 in.
Sights: SIGLITE night sights
Weight: 34.4 oz.
Caliber: 9mm
Capacity: 10, 15 rounds
Features: New designation of the Navy's P226 9mm variant issued to NSWG; still with phosphated internals; (three) 15 round magazines; classic two-piece polymer grips; anchor engraved on slide; now with M1913 Picatinny rail; actual UID scanable serial number label; packaged with FDE grip band and a certificate of authenticity

MSRP................... **$1142**

Sig Sauer

HANDGUNS

SIG SAUER P229

SIG SAUER P232

SIG SAUER P238

SIG SAUER P239

P229

Action: Autoloader
Grips: Black polymer factor grips
Barrel: 3.9 in.
Sights: Contrast, Siglite night optional
Weight: 32 oz.
Caliber: 9mm, .40 S&W, .357 Sig
Capacity: 9mm: 10, 13 rounds; .357 Sig: 10, 12 rounds, .40 S&W: 10, 12 rounds
Features: Black hard anodized frame finish; nitron slide finish; accessory rail
MSRP **$993**
Night Sights: **$1068**

P232

Action: Autoloader
Grips: Polymer
Barrel: 3.6 in.
Sights: Siglite night
Weight: 18.5 oz.
Caliber: .380 ACP
Capacity: 7 rounds
Features: Black polymer factor grips; blued finish
MSRP **$649**
Night Sights: **$720**

P238

Action: SA autoloader
Grips: Fluted polymer, Rosewood Tribal, Pearl, Tribal Engraved Aluminum, Hogue pink rubber
Barrel: 2.7 in.
Sights: Siglite night
Weight: 15.2 oz.
Caliber: .380 ACP (9mm Short)
Capacity: 6 rounds
Features: Nitron slide finish; beavertail style frame
MSRP . . . . **$679–$779**

P239

Action: DA autoloader
Grips: Polymer, tactical model features black polymer factory grips
Barrel: 3.6 in., 4 in.
Sights: Contrast, Siglite night optional
Weight: 29.5 oz.
Caliber: 9mm, .40 S&W, .357 Sig
Capacity: 8 rounds (9mm), 7 rounds (.40 S&W, .357 Sig)
Features: Black polymer factor grips; black hard anodized frame finish; nitron frame finish
Contrast Sights: **$993**
Night Sights: **$1085**
Tactical: **$1176**
Hogue G-10 Piranha: **$1219**

P250 COMPACT

Action: Locked breech DAO semiauto
Grips: Interchangeable polymer
Barrel: 3.9 in.
Sights: Siglite Night
Weight: 25.1 oz.
Caliber: 9mm, .40 S&W, .45 ACP
Capacity: 9, 13, 15 rounds
Features: Interchangeable polymer grip shell with stainless insert; nitron slide finish; interchangeable grip sizes and calibers
Contrast: **$570**
Night Sights: **$642**

SIG SAUER P250 COMPACT

SIG SAUER P250 2SUM

SIG SAUER P250 2SUM

P250 2SUM

Action: DA autoloader
Grips: Black polymer
Barrel: 4.7 in.
Sights: Siglite Night
Weight: 29.4 oz.
Caliber: 9mm, .40 S&W
Capacity: 17 (full-size 9mm), 14 (full-size .40 S&W) rounds
Features: Full size P250 with all the components to rapidly convert it to the P250 subcompact with 3.6 in. barrel (24.9 oz.)
MSRP. **$813**
Night Sights: **$885**

SIG SAUER P290

SIG SAUER SP2022

P290

Action: Autoloader
Grips: Black polymer
Barrel: 2.9 in.
Sights: Siglite or Contrast
Weight: 20.5 oz.
Caliber: 9mm
Capacity: 6+1 rounds
Features: Polymer frame; slide is machined from solid stainless-steel billet; interchangeable grips; features drift-adjustable Siglite sights or high-contrast black sight; available with Rainbow Titanium-Coated slide finish
MSRP. **$570**

SIG SAUER P938
BLACKWOOD

P938

Action: SA
Grips: Synthetic or wood
Barrel: 3 in.
Sights: SIGLITE night sights, TFO front on Equinox
Weight: 16 oz.
Caliber: 9mm, .40, .357
Capacity: 6+1, 7+1 rounds
Features: Ambi safety; SIG's most compact 9mm; initial offerings in 5 variants: Rosewood (nitron coated stainless slide over hard anodized alloy frame; rosewood grips), Blackwood (natural stainless slide over hard anodized black alloy frame; black diamondwood grips), Extreme (nitron coated stainless slide over hard anodized alloy frame; Hogue G-10 piranha grips in black/gray), SAS (SIG anti-snag dehorned slide and frame; natural stainless slide over hard anodized black alloy frame; walnut stippled grips), Equinox (polished Nitron two-tone slide over hardcoat anodized frame; TFO front with SIGLITE rear; black diamondwood grips)
Black Aluminum: **$823**
Blackwood: **$809**
Equinox: **$823**
Extreme: **$823**
Rosewood: **$795**
SAS: **$838**

SP2022

Action: Autoloader
Grips: Polymer
Barrel: 3.9 in., 4.4 in.
Sights: Contrast, Siglite Night optional
Weight: 29 oz.
Caliber: 9mm, .40 S&W
Capacity: 10 or 15 rounds (9mm), 10 or 12 rounds (.40 S&W)
Features: Accessory rail; wear-resistant polymer frame; black polymer frame finish; nitron slide finish
MSRP. **$570**
Night sights: **$642**
Nitron threaded barrel: **$713**

Smith & Wesson

BODYGUARD 38

Action: DA revolver
Grips: Matte black synthetic
Barrel: 1.9 in.
Sights: Integrated Insight laser system
Weight: 4.3 oz.
Caliber: .38 S&W Special +P
Capacity: 5 rounds
Features: Stainless steel cylinder with PVD coating
MSRP **$509**

SMITH & WESSON BODYGUARD 38

SMITH & WESSON BODYGUARD 380

BODYGUARD 380

Action: DA autoloader
Grips: Polymer
Barrel: 2.75 in.
Sights: Stainless steel drift-adjustable front and rear
Weight: 11.85 oz.
Caliber: .380 Auto
Capacity: 6+1 rounds
Features: Manual thumb safety external takedown lever; external slide stop; barrel and slide stainless with Melonite finish; integrated Insight laser sighting system
MSRP **$419**

SMITH & WESSON CLASSIC M57

SMITH & WESSON CLASSIC M586 REVOLVER

CLASSIC M57

Action: DA N-frame revolver
Grips: Checkered square-butt walnut
Barrel: 6 in.
Sights: Pinned red ramp front, Micro adjustable white outline rear;
Weight: 4.8 oz.
Caliber: .41 Magnum
Capacity: 6 rounds
Features: Bright blued or nickel finish; carbon steel frame; classic style thumbpiece; color case wide spur hammer; color case wide serrated target trigger
M57: **$979**

SMITH & WESSON GOVERNOR

SMITH & WESSON M10

CLASSIC M586 REVOLVER

Action: SA/DA revolver
Grips: Wood
Barrel: 4 in., 6 in.
Sights: Adjustable
Weight: 40.9 oz.–46.3 oz.
Caliber: .357 Mag., .38 S&W Special +P
Capacity: 6 rounds
Features: Carbon steel frame and cylinder with blued finish; adjustable white outline rear sight and red ramp

front sight; square-butt design; checkered wood grips
MSRP **$809**

GOVERNOR

Action: SA/DA revolver
Grips: Synthetic, Crimson Trace
Barrel: 2.75 in.
Sights: Fixed
Weight: 29.6 oz.
Caliber: .45 Colt, .45 ACP, .410 Ga. 2.5 in. shotshells
Capacity: 6 rounds
Features: Patented heat-treated scandium frame; PVD coated cylinder; dovetailed Tritium front night sight; fixed rear sight; matte black finish;

optional factory-installed Crimson Trace Lasergrips
Standard: **$796**
Crimson Trace: **$1019**

M10

Action: SA/DA revolver
Grips: Wood
Barrel: 4 in.
Sights: Black blade, fixed
Weight: 36 oz.
Caliber: .38 S&W Special +P
Capacity: 6 rounds
Features: Carbon steel frame; carbon steel cylinder; blued finish; medium size frame; exposed hammer
MSRP **$719**

SMITH & WESSON
M27 CLASSIC

SMITH & WESSON M29

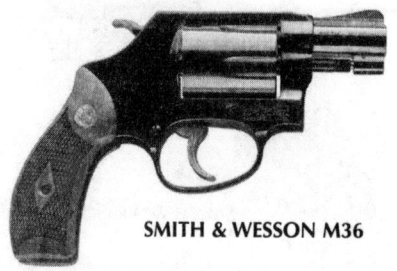

SMITH & WESSON M36

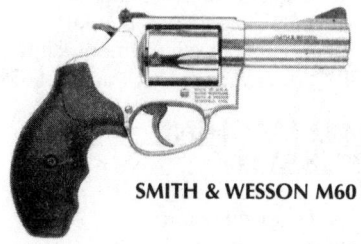

SMITH & WESSON M60

SMITH & WESSON M317

SMITH & WESSON M325
THUNDER RANCH

M27 CLASSIC
Action: SA/DA revolver
Grips: Checkered square butt walnut
Barrel: 4 in.
Sights: Pinned serrated ramp front;
Micro adjustable with cross serrations
Weight: 48.5 oz.
Caliber: .357 Mag., .38 S&W Special +P
Capacity: 6 rounds
Features: Carbon steel frame; bright
blued or blued finish
MSRP $989

M29
Action: Revolver
Grips: Checkered square butt walnut;
6 in. model features Altamont Service
walnut grips
Barrel: 4 in., 6.5 in.
Sights: Red ramp, micro adjustable rear
Weight: 48.5 oz.
Caliber: .44 Mag., .44 S&W Special
Capacity: 6 rounds
Features: Carbon steel frame with
nickel finish, available blued
4 in.: . . . . $969–$1019
6.5 in.: . . . . $1129–$1219

M36
Action: Revolver
Grips: Wood
Barrel: 1.8 in.
Sights: Integral front, fixed rear
Weight: 19.5 oz.
Caliber: .38 S&W Special +P
Capacity: 5 rounds
Features: Small sized frame; exposed
hammer; carbon steel frame and
cylinder; blued or nickel finish; single
or double action
MSRP $729

M60
Action: Revolver
Grips: Synthetic, wood
Barrel: 2.125 in., 3 in.
Sights: Black blade front, adjustable
rear
Weight: 22.6 oz.–23.2 oz.
Caliber: .357 Mag., .38 S&W Special
+P
Capacity: 5 rounds
Features: Satin stainless finish; single-
or double-action; stainless steel fame
and cylinder
MSRP . . . . $729–$779

M317
Action: SA/DA revolver
Grips: Synthetic
Barrel: 1.875 in.
Sights: Integral front, fixed rear
Weight: 10.8 oz.
Caliber: .22LR
Capacity: 8 rounds
Features: Aluminum alloy frame and
cylinder; clear coat finish; small frame
with exposed hammer; double- or
single-action
MSRP $699

M325 THUNDER RANCH
Action: SA/DA revolver
Grips: Synthetic
Barrel: 4 in.
Sights: Interchangeable gold bead
front; adjustable rear
Weight: 31 oz.
Caliber: .45 ACP
Capacity: 6 rounds
Features: Scandium alloy frame;
stainless steel cylinder; matte black
MSRP $1289

Smith & Wesson

SMITH & WESSON M327

SMITH & WESSON M327 TRR8

SMITH & WESSON M386 XL HUNTER

SMITH & WESSON M442

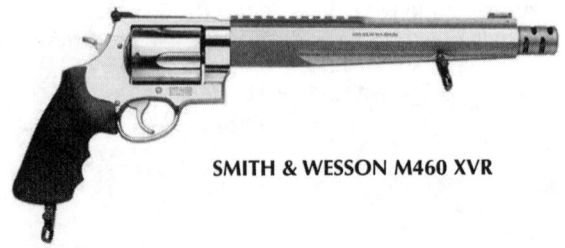

SMITH & WESSON M442 MACHINE ENGRAVED

M327

Action: Revolver
Grips: Wood
Barrel: 2 in.
Sights: Red ramp front, fixed rear
Weight: 21.4 oz.
Caliber: .357 Mag., .38 S&W Special +P
Capacity: 8 rounds
Features: Color case with overtravel stop; color case tear drop with pinned sear; large frame size; exposed hammer; matte black finish; scandium alloy frame and titanium alloy cylinder; Polish button rifling; smooth double action with Wolff Mainspring
MSRP $1269

M327 TRR8

Action: SA/DA revolver
Grips: Synthetic
Barrel: 5 in.
Sights: Interchangeable front; adjustable V-notch rear
Weight: 35.3 oz.
Caliber: .357 Mag., .38 S&W Special +P
Capacity: 8 rounds
Features: Scandium alloy frame; stainless steel cylinder; matte black; large size frame; exposed hammer; equipment rails
MSRP $1289

M386 XL HUNTER

Action: SA/DA revolver
Grips: Synthetic
Barrel: 6 in.
Sights: Hi-Viz fiber optic red front, adjustable rear
Weight: 30 oz.
Caliber: .357 Mag., .38 S&W Special +P
Capacity: 7 rounds
Features: Scandium alloy frame; stainless steel cylinder; matte black; medium size frame; exposed hammer
MSRP $899

M442

Action: DA revolver
Grips: Synthetic
Barrel: 1.87 in.
Sights: Integral front, fixed rear
Weight: 15 oz.
Caliber: .38 S&W Special +P
Capacity: 5 rounds
Features: Aluminum alloy frame; stainless steel cylinder; matte black finish; small size frame; internal hammer; cylinder cut for moon clips
MSRP $459

M442 MACHINE ENGRAVED

Action: DA revolver
Grips: Engraved wood
Barrel: 1.875 in.
Sights: Integral front, fixed rear
Weight: 15 oz.
Caliber: .38 S&W Special +P
Capacity: 5 rounds
Features: Aluminum alloy frame; stainless steel barrel/cylinder; matte black
MSRP $729

M460 XVR

Action: SA/DA revolver
Grips: Synthetic
Barrel: 10.5 in.
Sights: Interchangeable front, adjustable rear
Weight: 82.5 oz.
Caliber: .460 S&W Mag.
Capacity: 5 rounds
Features: Satin stainless finish; stainless steel frame and cylinder; X-Large size frame; exposed tear drop chrome hammer; .312 chrome trigger; multi-caliber capability: .454 Casull, .45 Colt; integral weaver base for optic mounting
MSRP $1519

SMITH & WESSON M460 XVR

Smith & Wesson

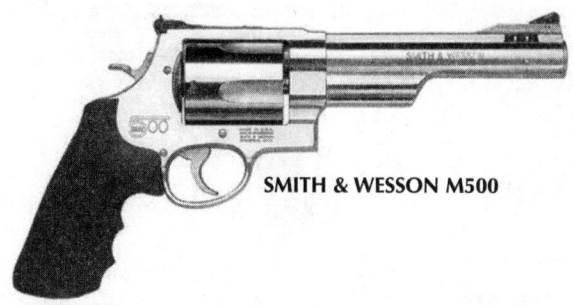

SMITH & WESSON M500

SMITH & WESSON M617

M500
Action: SA/DA revolver
Grips: Synthetic
Barrel: 6.5 in.
Sights: Red ramp front, adjustable white outline rear
Weight: 60.7 oz.
Caliber: .500 S&W mag.
Capacity: 5 rounds
Features: Stainless steel frame and cylinder; satin stainless finish; integral compensator; internal lock; recoil tamed with effective muzzle compensator
MSRP $1249

M617
Action: SA/DA revolver
Grips: Synthetic
Barrel: 4 in.
Sights: Partridge front, adjustable rear
Weight: 38.9 oz.
Caliber: .22LR
Capacity: 10 rounds
Features: Stainless steel frame and cylinder with satin stainless finish; medium size frame with exposed hammer
MSRP $829

M625
Action: SA/DA revolver
Grips: Hogue combat laminate, red, white & blue
Barrel: 4 in.
Sights: Gold bead S&W interchangeable front; Black adjustable rear
Weight: 42 oz.
Caliber: .45 ACP
Capacity: 6 rounds
Features: Stainless steel frame and cylinder with satin stainless finish; deep cut broached rifling; chambered charge holes; PC trigger with stop
MSRP $1049

M625 JM
Action: SA/DA revolver
Grips: Jerry Miculek wood
Barrel: 4 in.
Sights: Gold bead partridge front, adjustable rear
Weight: 40.3 oz.
Caliber: .45 ACP
Capacity: 6 rounds
Features: Stainless steel frame and cylinder; matte stainless; large size frame; exposed hammer; Miculek style .265 wide grooved speed trigger; low reflection bead blast finish
MSRP $979

M627
Action: SA/DA revolver
Grips: Synthetic
Barrel: 5 in.
Sights: Interchangeable front; adjustable rear
Weight: 44 oz.
Caliber: .357 Mag., .38 S&W Special +P
Capacity: 8 rounds
Features: Stainless steel frame and cylinder; matte stainless; large size frame; exposed hammer
MSRP $1249

M629
Action: SA/DA revolver
Grips: Synthetic
Barrel: 5 in.
Sights: Red ramp, adjustable white outline
Weight: 44.3 oz.
Caliber: .44 Mag, .44 S&W Special
Capacity: 6 rounds
Features: Stainless steel frame and cylinder with satin stainless finish; exposed hammer
MSRP $949

SMITH & WESSON M625

SMITH & WESSON M625 JM

SMITH & WESSON M627

SMITH & WESSON M629

Smith & Wesson

SMITH & WESSON M629 V-COMP

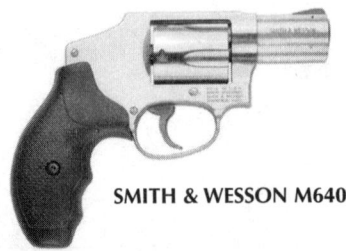

SMITH & WESSON M640

SMITH & WESSON M686

SMITH & WESSON M686 SSR

SMITH & WESSON M&P 9MM

SMITH & WESSON M&P40 COMPACT

SMITH & WESSON M&P45

M629 V-COMP
Action: SA/DA revolver
Grips: Synthetic
Barrel: 4 in.
Sights: Adjustable orange dovetail front, adjustable black rear
Weight: 40.3 oz.
Caliber: .44 Mag., .44 S&W Special
Capacity: 6 rounds
Features: Stainless steel frame and cylinder with matte finish; removable compensator and cap muzzle protector; chambered charge holes; ball detent lock-up; chromed hammer and trigger with overtravel stop
MSRP **$1509**

M640
Action: DA revolver
Grips: Synthetic
Barrel: 2.1 in.
Sights: Black blade front, fixed rear
Weight: 23 oz.
Caliber: .357 Mag., .38 S&W Special +P
Capacity: 5 rounds
Features: Stainless steel frame and cylinder; satin stainless finish; Pro Series
MSRP **$809**

M686
Action: Revolver
Grips: Synthetic
Barrel: 2.5 in.
Sights: Red ramp front, adjustable white outline rear
Weight: 34.7 oz.
Caliber: .357 Mag., .38 S&W Special +P

Capacity: 6 rounds
Features: Stainless steel frame and cylinder; satin stainless finish; exposed hammer; single- and double-action; built on L frame
MSRP **$829**

M686 SSR
Action: Revolver
Grips: Wood
Barrel: 4 in.
Sights: Interchangeable front, adjustable rear
Weight: 38.3 oz.
Caliber: .357 Mag., .38 S&W Special +P
Capacity: 6 rounds
Features: Stainless steel frame and barrel with satin finish; exposed hammer; chambered charge holes; bossed mainspring; ergonomic grip to force high-hand hold; custom barrel with recessed precision crown
MSRP **$969**

M&P 9MM
Action: Autoloader
Grips: Polymer
Barrel: 4.25 in.
Sights: Steel ramp dovetail mount front, steel Novak Lo-Mount Carry
Weight: 24 oz.
Caliber: 9mm
Capacity: 17+1 rounds
Features: Zytel polymer frame, stainless steel barrel/slide and structural components; optional tritium sights; black melonite finish
MSRP **$569**

M&P40 COMPACT
Action: Autoloader
Grips: Polymer
Barrel: 3.5 in.
Sights: White dot dovetail front; steel low profile carry rear
Weight: 21.9 oz.
Caliber: .40 S&W
Capacity: 10 rounds
Features: 3 interchangeable palm swell grip sizes; black melonite; thumb safety
MSRP **$569**

M&P45
Action: Autoloader
Grips: Polymer
Barrel: 4.5 in.
Sights: White dot dovetail front; steel low profile carry rear
Weight: 29.6 oz.
Caliber: .45 ACP
Capacity: 10+1 rounds
Features: Zytel polymer frame, stainless steel barrel/slide and structural components; black melonite finish; CA compliant; 3 interchangeable palm swell grip sizes
MSRP **$599**

SMITH & WESSON M&P357

SMITH & WESSON M&P R8

SMITH & WESSON SW1911 COMPACT ES

M&P357

Action: Autoloader
Grips: Polymer
Barrel: 4.25 in.
Sights: White-dot dovetail front; steel low profile carry rear
Weight: 25.5 oz.
Caliber: .357 Auto
Capacity: 15 rounds
Features: 3 interchangeable palm swell grip sizes; black melonite; thumb safety; polymer frame/stainless steel barrel and slide
MSRP $727

M&P R8

Action: SA/DA revolver
Grips: Polymer
Barrel: 5 in.
Sights: Interchangeable front, adjustable v-notch
Weight: 36.3 oz.

Caliber: .357 Mag., .38 S&W Special +P
Capacity: 8 rounds
Features: Single- or double-action; scandium alloy frame; stainless steel cylinder; integral accessory Picatinny style rail; precision barrel forcing cone
MSRP $1289

SW1911 COMPACT ES

Action: Autoloader
Grips: Wood
Barrel: 4.25 in.
Sights: White-dot dovetail front; steel low profile carry rear
Weight: 29.6 oz.
Caliber: .45 ACP
Capacity: 7+1 rounds
Features: Single-action; scandium alloy frame; stainless steel slide; two-tone finish; compact extended slide
MSRP $1139

Springfield Armory

SPRINGFIELD ARMORY EMP

SPRINGFIELD ARMORY LIGHTWEIGHT CHAMPION OPERATOR

SPRINGFIELD ARMORY LOADED FULL SIZE TROPHY MATCH STAINLESS STEEL

EMP (ENHANCED MICRO PISTOL)

Action: Autoloader
Grips: Thin line cocobolo wood, G10
Barrel: 3 in.
Sights: Fixed low profile combat rear, dovetail
Weight: 26 oz.–33 oz.
Caliber: 9mm, .40 S&W
Capacity: 3–9 rounds (9mm), 3–8 rounds (.40 S&W)
Features: Forged stainless steel, satin finish; dual spring recoil system with full length guide rod
MSRP . . . . $1345–$1424

LIGHTWEIGHT CHAMPION OPERATOR

Action: Autoloader
Grips: Cocobolo wood
Barrel: 4 in.
Sights: Fixed low profile combat rear, dovetail
Weight: 31 oz.
Caliber: .45 ACP
Capacity: 2–7 rounds

Features: Stainless steel match grade, fully supported ramped bull barrel; long aluminum Match Grade trigger; forged aluminum alloy with integral accessory rail; black hard coat anodized; dual spring with full length guide rod
MSRP $1076

LOADED FULL SIZE TROPHY MATCH STAINLESS STEEL

Action: Autoloader
Grips: Cocobolo wood
Barrel: 5 in.
Sights: Low profile adjustable rear, Dovetail front target
Weight: 40 oz.
Caliber: .45 ACP
Capacity: 2–7 rounds
Features: Wide-mouth magazine well; tuned trigger; checkered front strap; forged stainless steel frame; two-piece full length guide rod
MSRP $1605

Springfield Armory

MIL-SPEC FULL SIZE STAINLESS

Action: Autoloader
Grips: Cocobolo wood and black plastic
Barrel: 5 in.
Sights: Fixed combat, 3-dot
Weight: 39 oz.
Caliber: .45 ACP
Capacity: 2–7 rounds
Features: Forged stainless steel, matte rounds with polished flats; GI style recoil system; available Parkerized finish
MSRP.................... **$851**

RANGE OFFICER

Action: Autoloader
Grips: Cocobolo wood
Barrel: 5 in.
Sights: Low profile adjustable target
Weight: 40 oz.
Caliber: .45 ACP
Capacity: 2–7 rounds
Features: Standard guide rod; forged steel frame with blued finish; stainless Match Grade barrel
MSRP.................... **$977**

TRP (TACTICAL RESPONSE PISTOL)

Action: Autoloader
Grips: G10 composite
Barrel: 5 in.
Sights: Front tritium 3-dot, fixed low profile combat rear, dovetail
Weight: 42 oz.
Caliber: .45 ACP
Capacity: 2–7 rounds
Features: Forged steel frame with black armory kote; two piece full length guide rod; wide-mouth magazine well; tuned trigger; available in Armory Kote, Light Rail Armory Kote, and stainless
MSRP.................... **$1777**

XD (M)

Action: DA autoloader
Grips: Polymer
Barrel: 3.8 in., 4.5 in. Match Grade
Sights: 3-dot
Weight: 27.5 oz.–32 oz.
Caliber: 9mm, .40 S&W, .45 ACP
Capacity: 19 (9mm), 16 (.40 S&W), 13 (.45 ACP) rounds
Features: "M" features include carrying case, two magazines, paddle holster, magi loader, double magi pouch and three interchangeable backstraps and two magazines; "all-terrain" texture and deep slide serrations are standard
9mm:................ **$697–$815**
.40 S&W:............ **$697–$876**
.45 ACP:............ **$709–$896**

XD(M) COMPACT

Action: Autoloader
Grips: Synthetic
Barrel: 3.8 in., 5.25 in.
Sights: Fiber optic front, adjustable rear
Weight: 27 oz.–32 oz.
Caliber: 9mm, .45 ACP, .40 S&W
Capacity: 13, 19 rounds
Features: A handgun with improved accuracy, lessened recoil, faster shot recovery and greater sight radius of its newly enhanced performance. The lightening cut in the slide reduces reciprocating mass which allows for faster cycling and allows a larger variety of loads to be used.
MSRP.............. **$705–$797**

SPRINGFIELD ARMORY MIL-SPEC FULL SIZE STAINLESS

SPRINGFIELD ARMORY RANGE OFFICER

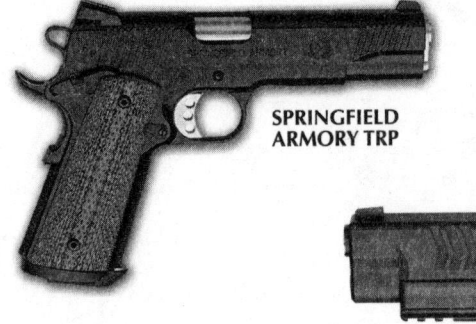

SPRINGFIELD ARMORY TRP

SPRINGFIELD ARMORY XD (M)

SPRINGFIELD ARMORY XD(M) COMPACT

Steyr Arms

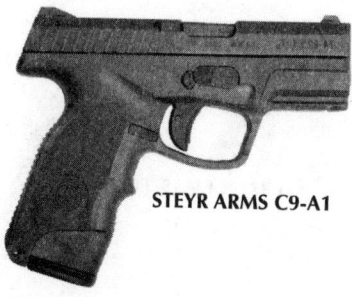

STEYR ARMS C9-A1

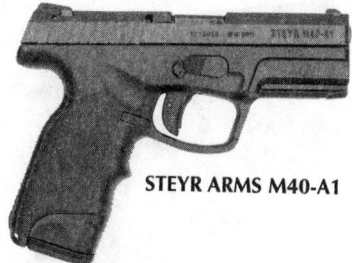

STEYR ARMS M40-A1

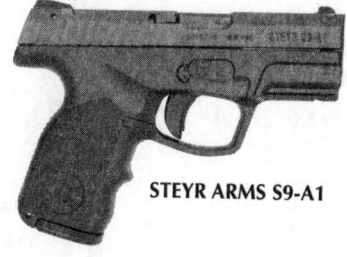

STEYR ARMS S9-A1

C9-A1
Action: Autoloader, striker-fired
Grips: Textured polymer
Barrel: 3.6 in.
Sights: Fixed triangular/trapezoid
Weight: 25.6 oz.
Caliber: 9mm
Capacity: 17+1 rounds
Features: Polymer frame; trigger, internal striker, internal gun-lock safeties; polygonal rifling; black matte Mannox finish; Picatinny rail
MSRP $560

M40-A1
Action: Autoloader
Grips: Synthetic
Barrel: 4 in.
Sights: Fixed triangular/trapezoid
Weight: 27 oz.
Caliber: 9mm, .40 S&W
Capacity: 12 or 15 rounds
Features: Triangular or trapezoid shaped sights; synthetic black grips; Picatinny rail; ergonomic handle
MSRP $560

S9-A1
Action: Autoloader
Grips: Synthetic
Barrel: 3.62 in.
Sights: Fixed triangular/trapezoid
Weight: 23.4–23.9 oz.
Caliber: 9mm, .40 S&W
Capacity: 10 rounds
Features: Ergonomical improved grip with Picatinny rail; low profile; optional sling mount on grip; drop firing safety
MSRP $560

STI International

STI APEIRO

STI EAGLE 5.0

STI EDGE

APEIRO
Action: Autoloader
Grips: STI patented modular polymer
Barrel: 5 in.
Sights: Dawson fiber optic front mounted on barrel, STI adjustable rear
Weight: 39 oz.
Caliber: 9mm, .40 S&W, .45 ACP
Capacity: 11+1, 14+1, 17+1 rounds
Features: Full length stainless steel bar stock slide features STI's unique sabertooth rear cocking serrations; Schuemann barrel; STI recoil master; STI long curved trigger; blued finish with two toned blued/stainless steel slide
MSRP $2805

EAGLE 5.0
Action: Autoloader
Grips: STI patented modular polymer
Barrel: 5 in.
Sights: STI front, STI adjustable rear
Weight: 35.2 oz.
Caliber: 9mm, .357 Sig, .38 Super, .40 S&W, .45 ACP
Capacity: 11+1, 14+1, 17+1 rounds
Features: Stainless STI grip, ambi thumb, ramped bull barrel; STI patented modular steel frame; STI rear serrations; blued finish
MSRP $1985

EDGE
Action: Autoloader
Grips: STI patented modular polymer with aluminum mag well
Barrel: 5 in.
Sights: STI front, STI adjustable rear
Weight: 37.6 oz.
Caliber: 9mm, .38 Super, .40 S&W, .45 ACP
Capacity: 11+1, 14+1, 17+1 rounds
Features: STI fully supported, ramped bull barrel; stainless STI grip and ambi slided thumb; STI recoil master guide rod; blued finish
MSRP $2040

STI International

STI EXECUTIVE

STI LAWMAN 4

STI RANGEMASTER

STI RANGER II

STI TACTICAL

STI TARGETMASTER

EXECUTIVE

Action: Autoloader
Grips: STI patented modular polymer with stainless mag well
Barrel: 5 in.
Sights: Dawson fiber optic front, STI adjustable rear
Weight: 39.2 oz.
Caliber: .40 S&W
Capacity: 14+1 rounds
Features: Stainless STI grip, ambi thumb, ramped bull barrel; STI patented modular steel, long wide frame; STI rear serrations; blued finish
MSRP **$2520**

LAWMAN FAMILY

Action: Autoloader
Grips: G10 Mycarta grip panels
Barrel: 3.24 in., 4.26 in., 5.11 in.
Sights: STI ramped front, tactical adjustable rear
Weight: 23.8 oz.–38.9 oz.
Caliber: 9×19, .45 ACP
Capacity: 6+1 rounds
Features: Forged aluminum frame; carbon steel slide; blue high rise beavertail grip safety and single sided thumb safety; available in traditional polished blue, two tone polymer light brown/coyote tan, and two tone black/olive drab
MSRP **$1455**

RANGEMASTER

Action: Autoloader
Grips: STI logo, checkered, cocobolo wood, standard thickness
Barrel: 5 in.
Sights: STI front, STI adjustable rear
Weight: 41.4 oz.
Caliber: 9mm, .45 ACP
Capacity: 8, 9 rounds
Features: STI long curved trigger; ramped bull barrel; STI polished stainless grip and ambi thumb; STI recoil master guide rod; matte blued finish
MSRP **$1555**

RANGER II

Action: Autoloader
Grips: STI logo, checkered, cocobolo wood, thin
Barrel: 4.26 in.
Sights: STI front, STI fixed low mount snag free rear
Weight: 33.7 oz.
Caliber: 9mm, .40 S&W, .45 ACP
Capacity: 7+1 rounds
Features: STI long curved trigger with stainless bow; STI hi-rise blue grip and single sided thumb safeties; blued finish
MSRP **$1135**

TACTICAL FAMILY

Action: Autoloader
Grips: Polymer
Barrel: 3.75 in., 4.26 in., 5.01 in.
Sights: STI ramped front, Novak style fixed rear
Weight: 30.1 oz.–34.2 oz.
Caliber: 9×19, .40 S&W, .45 ACP
Capacity: 11+1, 14+1, 17+1 rounds
Features: STI International's patented 2011 technology gives the STI Tactical more fire power advantage than 1911 tactical pistols without greatly increasing the size of the grip; less recoil felt; aluminum frame; light tactical rail milled into the dust cover of the frame; STI patented glass filled polymer modular grips; blued slide
MSRP **$2045**

TARGETMASTER

Action: Autoloader
Grips: STI logo, checkered, cocobolo wood, standard thickness
Barrel: 6 in.
Sights: Aristocrat adjustable
Weight: 45.5 oz.
Caliber: 9mm, .45 ACP
Capacity: 8, 9 rounds
Features: STI long curved trigger; STI stainless grip and ambi sided thumb; STI two piece rail guide rod; matte blued finish
MSRP **$1745**

STI TOTAL ECLIPSE

STI VIP

STI TROJAN 5.0

TOTAL ECLIPSE
Action: SA autoloader
Grips: Black polymer
Barrel: 3 in. ramped, bull contour
Sights: 2-dot tritium night
Weight: 23.1 oz.
Caliber: .45 ACP, .40 S&W, 9mm
Capacity: 9+1, 10+1, 12+1 rounds
Features: 2011 double stack pistol; double-column magazine; steel frame; single-sided blued thumb safety and beavertail grip safety
MSRP **$1870**

TROJAN 5.0
Action: Autoloader
Grips: STI logo, checkered, cocobolo

wood, thin
Barrel: 5 in., 6 in.
Sights: STI front, STI adjustable rear
Weight: 36 oz.
Caliber: 9mm, .38 Super, .40 S&W, .45 ACP
Capacity: 8, 9 rounds
Features: STI standard blue grip and single-slided thumb safeties; STI one-piece steel guide rod; flat blued finish
5-inch: **$1135**
6-inch: **$1455**

VIP
Action: Autoloader
Grips: STI patented modular polymer
Barrel: 3.9 in.
Sights: STI front, STI adjustable rear
Weight: 30 oz.
Caliber: 9mm, .40 S&W, .45 ACP
Capacity: 15+1, 12+1, 10+1 rounds
Features: STI rear slide serrations; STI long curved trigger; STI stainless grip and single-sided thumb; matte blued slide with blued steel frame
MSRP **$1690**

Stoeger

STOEGER COUGAR

STOEGER COUGAR COMPACT

COUGAR
Action: DA/SA
Grips: Black plastic
Barrel: 3.6 in.
Sights: White 3-dot
Weight: 32 oz.–32.6 oz.
Caliber: .45 ACP, .40 S&W, 9mm
Capacity: 8+1, 11+1, 15+1 rounds
Features: Ambidextrous safety; rotary-locking principal; available in a non-glare Bruniton silver steel slide with an

anodized alloy matte-silver frame or two-tone style, featuring a matte Bruniton black steel slide combined with an anodized alloy matte-silver frame
MSRP . . . . **$469–$509**

COUGAR COMPACT
Action: DA/SA
Grips: Black plastic
Barrel: 3.6 in.

Sights: Quick read 3-dot
Weight: 32 oz.
Caliber: 9mm
Capacity: 13+1 rounds
Features: Ambidextrous safety; rotary-locking principal; Bruniton matte black finish
MSRP **$469**

Taurus

22BR

Action: Autoloader
Grips: Rosewood
Barrel: 2.75 in.
Sights: Fixed
Weight: 12.3 oz.
Caliber: .22LR
Capacity: 8+1 rounds
Features: Steel/alloy frame with blued finish; manual safety; tip-up barrel; Taurus security system
MSRP **$282**

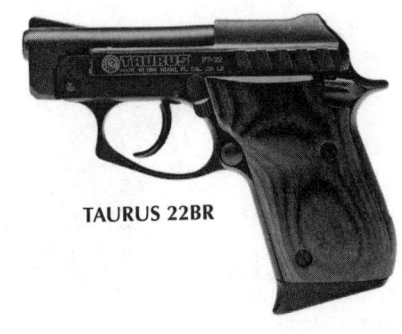

TAURUS 22BR

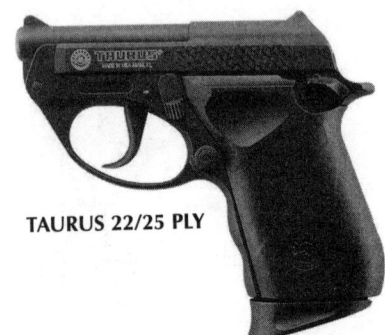

TAURUS 22/25 PLY

22/25 PLY

Action: DA autoloading, recoil operated
Grips: Polymer
Barrel: 2.3 in.
Sights: Fixed
Weight: 11.3 oz.
Caliber: .22LR, .25 ACP
Capacity: 8+1, 9+1 rounds
Features: Polymer/blued steel construction; blued steel finish; tip-up barrel
MSRP **$282**

TAURUS 24/7 G2

TAURUS 44

24/7 G2

Action: DA/SA autoloader
Grips: Checkered polymer with metallic inserts
Barrel: 4.2 in.
Sights: Low-profile, adjustable rear
Weight: 28 oz.
Caliber: 9mm, .40, .45 ACP
Capacity: 17+1 rounds (9mm), 15+1 rounds (.40), 12+1 rounds (.45 ACP)
Features: Blued or stainless steel; DA/SA trigger system; SA or DA only; contoured thumb rests; Picatinny accessory rail; compact model available at same price
Blued: **$539**
Stainless: **$555**

TAURUS 82

44

Action: Autoloader
Grips: Soft rubber
Barrel: 4 in., 6.5 in., 8.4 in.
Sights: Fixed
Weight: 45–57 oz.
Caliber: .44 Mag.
Capacity: 6 rounds
Features: Transfer bar; ported barrel; matte stainless steel finish; double and single-action
4 in.: **$742**
6.5 in.: **$758**
8.4 in.: **$758**

TAURUS 92

82

Action: Autoloader
Grips: Rubber
Barrel: 4 in.
Sights: Fixed
Weight: 36.5 oz.
Caliber: .38 SPL +P
Capacity: 6 rounds
Features: Transfer bar; steel construction with blued finish; single/double-action trigger
Blued: **$481**

92

Action: Autoloader
Grips: Checkered rubber
Barrel: 5 in.
Sights: Fixed-1 dot front, fixed-2 dots rear
Weight: 34 oz.
Caliber: 9mm
Capacity: 10+1 and 17+1 rounds
Features: Blued, stainless steel finish; steel/alloy construction; firing pin block, hammer decocker, manual safety
Blued: **$660**
Stainless: **$668**

94/941

Action: Revolver
Grips: Rubber
Barrel: 2 in., 4 in.
Sights: Fixed front, adjustable rear
Weight: 18.5 oz.–27 oz.
Caliber: .22LR, .22 Mag.
Capacity: 8, 9 rounds
Features: Steel construction; blued or matte stainless steel finish; single- and double-action; transfer bar; 2-inch Ultra-Lite models also available
Blued: $465
Stainless: $513
Ultra-Lite: . . . . $499–$531

.380 MINI REVOLVER

Action: Revolver
Grips: Rubber
Barrel: 1.75 in.
Sights: Adjustable rear
Weight: 15.5 oz.
Caliber: .380 ACP
Capacity: 5 rounds
Features: Double-action trigger; fully enclosed hammer; blued or matte stainless finish; bobbed hammer
Blued: $443
Stainless: $475

605

Action: Revolver
Grips: Rubber
Barrel: 2 in.
Sights: Fixed
Weight: 24 oz.
Caliber: .357 Mag
Capacity: 5 rounds
Features: Transfer bar safety; steel construction with blued or stainless finish; single-double action trigger
Blued: $459
Stainless: $507

608

Action: Revolver
Grips: Rubber
Barrel: 4 in., 6.5 in.
Sights: Fixed front, adjustable rear
Weight: 44 oz.–51 oz.
Caliber: .357 Mag
Capacity: 8 rounds
Features: Matte stainless steel finish; transfer bar; large frame; steel frame; Taurus security system; porting
4 in.: $702
6.5 in.. . . . . $724

709 "SLIM"

Action: Autoloader
Grips: Checkered polymer
Barrel: 3 in.
Sights: Fixed
Weight: 19 oz.
Caliber: 9mm
Capacity: 7+1 rounds
Features: Steel construction; blued or stainless finish; single- and double-action
Blued: $349
Stainless: $513

738 TCP

Action: DA autoloader
Grips: Checkered polymer
Barrel: 2.84 in.
Sights: Fixed
Weight: 10.2 oz.
Caliber: .380 ACP
Capacity: 6+1 rounds
Features: Titanium construction; compact frame; smooth trigger
MSRP. $362

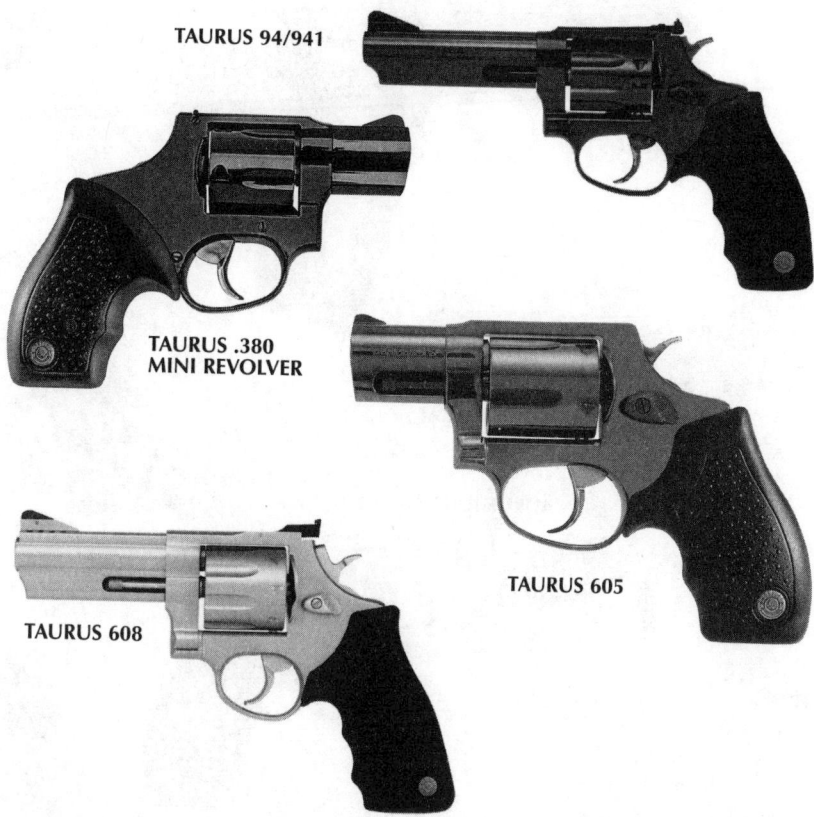

TAURUS 94/941

TAURUS .380 MINI REVOLVER

TAURUS 605

TAURUS 608

TAURUS 709 "SLIM"

TAURUS 738 TCP

Taurus

TAURUS 809

TAURUS 905

TAURUS 1911 AL

TAURUS DT HYBRID

TAURUS JUDGE .45/.410

TAURUS PUBLIC DEFENDER POLYMER

809

Action: Autoloader
Grips: Checkered polymer
Barrel: 3.5 in., 4 in.
Sights: Fixed
Weight: 30.2 oz.
Caliber: 9mm
Capacity: 17+1 rounds
Features: Black Tennifer finish; smooth trigger type; strike-two capability.
MSRP **$497**

905

Action: DA/SA revolver
Grips: Rubber
Barrel: 2 in.
Sights: Fixed
Weight: 22.2 oz.
Caliber: 9mm
Capacity: 5 rounds
Features: Blued finish; transfer bar; steel frame; porting; Taurus security system
Blued: **$491**
Stainless: **$539**

1911 AL

Action: Autoloader
Grips: Checkered black
Barrel: 5 in.
Sights: Heinie
Weight: 38 oz.
Caliber: .45 ACP

Capacity: 8+1 rounds
Features: Steel/alloy construction with blued/gray finish; single-action; forged slide and frame; ventilated trigger type
Blued **$853**
Duotone. **$906**
Stainless. **$927**
Walnut Grip **$975**

DT HYBRID

Action: SA/DA autoloader
Grips: Polymer
Barrel: 3.2 in.
Sights: Adjustable rear
Weight: 24 oz.
Caliber: 9mm, .40
Capacity: 13+1 and 11+1 rounds
Features: Matte stainless steel or blued finish; stainless steel construction; polymer over steel frame
Blued: **$589**
Stainless: **$605**

JUDGE .45/.410

Action: DA/SA revolver
Grips: Taurus rubber grips

Barrel: 3 in.
Sights: Red fiber optic, fixed
Weight: 29–36.8 oz.
Caliber: .45/.410
Capacity: 5 rounds
Features: Firing pin block, transfer bar safety; compact frame; matte stainless steel finish; steel construction
MSRP . . . . **$620–$668**

PUBLIC DEFENDER POLYMER

Action: DA/SA revolver
Grips: Rubber
Barrel: 2 in., 2.5 in.
Sights: Red fiber optic, fixed front
Weight: 27 oz.–28.2 oz.
Caliber: .45/.410
Capacity: 5 rounds
Features: Polymer frame, stainless or blued finish; target hammer and trigger; fires both .410 shotshells and .45 Colt ammunition
Blued: . . . . **$459–$620**
Stainless: **$668**

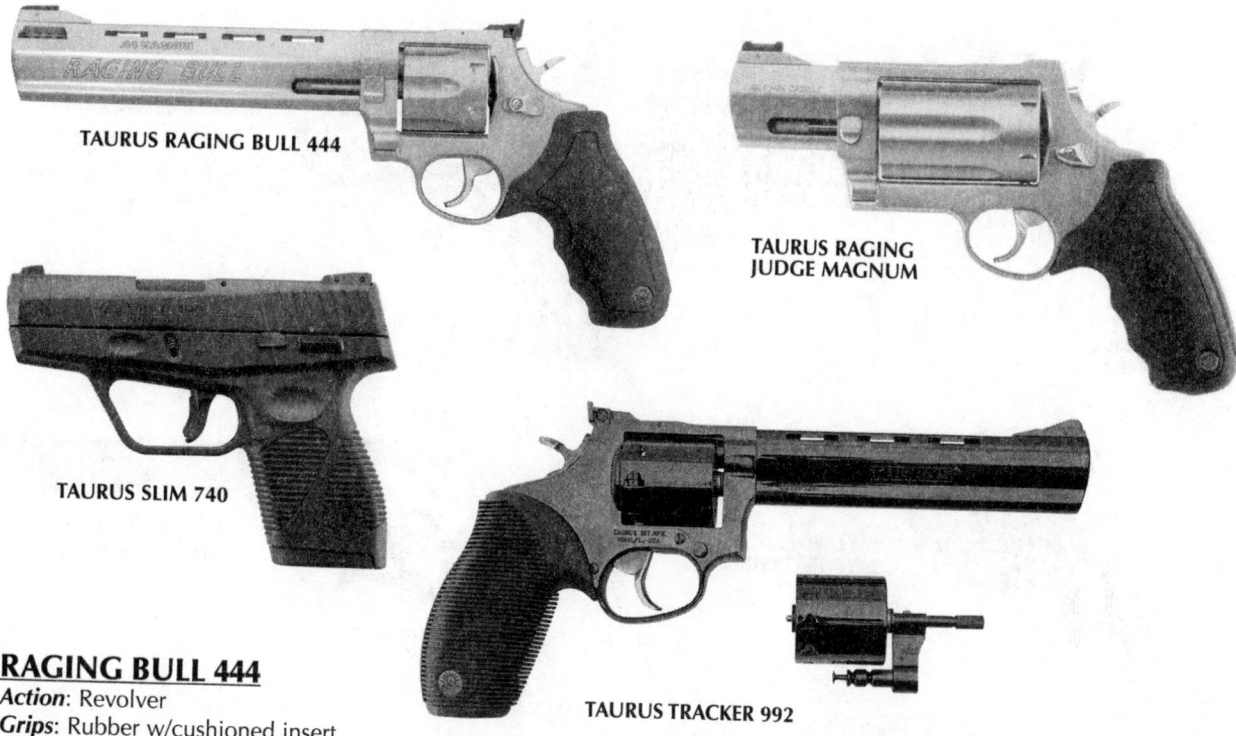

TAURUS RAGING BULL 444

TAURUS RAGING
JUDGE MAGNUM

TAURUS SLIM 740

TAURUS TRACKER 992

TAURUS TRACKER SERIES

RAGING BULL 444

Action: Revolver
Grips: Rubber w/cushioned insert
Barrel: 6.5 in., 8.38 in.
Sights: Partridge front, adjustable rear
Weight: 53 oz.–63 oz.
Caliber: .44 Mag
Capacity: 6 rounds
Features: Steel construction with blued or stainless steel finish; transfer bar; dual lockup cylinder; porting; Taurus security system
Blued: **$769**
Stainless: **$818**

RAGING JUDGE MAGNUM

Action: DA/SA revolver
Grips: Rubber with soft cushion insert
Barrel: 3 in., 6.5 in.
Sights: Fiber optic front, fixed rear
Weight: 60.6 oz.–73 oz.
Caliber: .410/.45 LC, .454 Casull
Capacity: 6 rounds
Features: Stainless steel or blued finish; "Raging Bull" backstrap for added cushioning
Blued: **$1012**
Stainless: **$1061**

SLIM 740

Action: DA/SA autoloader
Grips: Polymer metallic inserts
Barrel: 3.2 in.
Sights: Adjustable rear
Weight: 19 oz.

Caliber: .40
Capacity: 6+1 rounds
Features: Sub-compact pistol in blued, black Tenifer, or stainless steel; loaded chamber indicator; low-profile sights; short, crisp DA/SA trigger pull
Blued: **$349**
Stainless: **$513**

TRACKER 992

Action: SA/DA revolver
Grips: Taurus Ribber
Barrel: 4 in., 6.5 in.
Sights: Adjustable
Weight: 55 oz.
Caliber: .22 LR
Capacity: 9 rounds
Features: The versatile Tracker 992 easily transforms from .22LR to .22

Magnum in seconds with its breakthrough removable cylinder; perfect for plinking, target practice, or varmint hunting
Blued: **$589**
Stainless: **$637**

TRACKER SERIES

Action: Revolver
Grips: Rubber with ribs
Barrel: 4 in., 4.5 in., 6.5 in.
Sights: Fixed front, adjustable rear
Weight: 28.8 oz.–46 oz.
Caliber: .17HMR, .22LR, .22 Mag., .357 Mag., .44 Mag.
Capacity: 5, 7, 9 rounds
Features: Matte stainless steel or blued finish; transfer bar; steel frame; porting
MSRP . . . . **$472–$684**

Taylor's & Co.

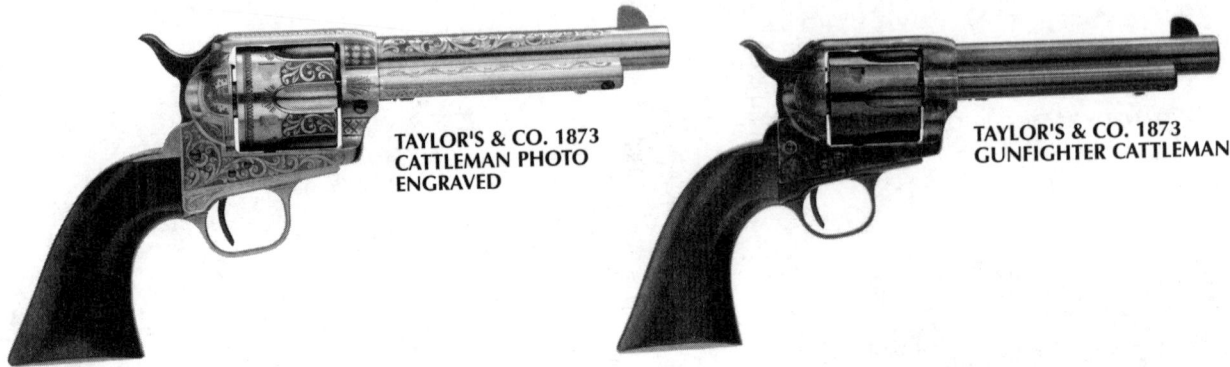

TAYLOR'S & CO. 1873
CATTLEMAN PHOTO
ENGRAVED

TAYLOR'S & CO. 1873
GUNFIGHTER CATTLEMAN

TAYLOR'S & CO. 1873
TAYLOR GAMBLER

TAYLOR'S & CO. 1873
TAYLOR MARSHALL

TAYLOR'S & CO.
RUNNIN' IRON

1873 CATTLEMAN PHOTO ENGRAVED

Action: SA revolver
Grips: Walnut
Barrel: 4.75 in., 5.5 in., 7.5 in.
Sights: Fixed
Weight: 2 lb. 4 oz.–3 lb. 6 oz.
Caliber: .357 Mag., .45 LC
Capacity: 6 rounds
Features: White, heat-treated steel finish with charcoal blued screws; laser-engraved and hand chased; forged frame
MSRP $876

1873 GUNFIGHTER CATTLEMAN

Action: SA revolver
Grips: Walnut
Barrel: 5.5 in.
Sights: Fixed
Weight: 2 lb. 5 oz.

Caliber: .357 Mag., .45 LC
Capacity: 6 rounds
Features: Special Army-sized grip; steel trigger guard and backstrap; blued finish with case-hardened frame; forged frame
MSRP $547

1873 TAYLOR GAMBLER CATTLEMAN

Action: SA revolver
Grips: Walnut
Barrel: 5.5 in.
Sights: Fixed
Weight: 2 lb. 5 oz.
Caliber: .357 Mag., .45 LC
Capacity: 6 rounds
Features: Fancy checkered walnut grip; blued color case-hardened forged frame
MSRP $570

1873 TAYLOR MARSHALL CATTLEMAN

Action: SA revolver
Grips: White PVC
Barrel: 5.5 in.

Sights: Fixed
Weight: 2 lb. 5 oz.
Caliber: .45 LC
Capacity: 6 rounds
Features: Checkered white PVC grip; blued color case-hardened forged frame
MSRP $658

RUNNIN' IRON

Action: SA revolver
Grips: Checkered walnut
Barrel: 3.5 oz.–5.5 in.
Sights: Wider fixed, open
Weight: 39 oz.
Caliber: .45 LC or .357 Mag.
Capacity: 6 rounds
Features: Designed for the sport of mounted shooting; offered in stainless or blued finish with low, wide hammer spur; checkered, one-piece gunfighter style grips in walnut or black polymer; wide trigger and extra clearance at front and rear of cylinder
Stainless: . . . . $705–$852
Blued: . . . . $551–$699

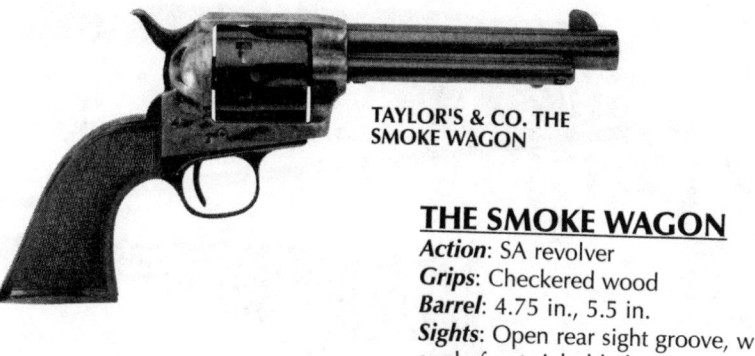

TAYLOR'S & CO. THE SMOKE WAGON

THE SMOKE WAGON

Action: SA revolver
Grips: Checkered wood
Barrel: 4.75 in., 5.5 in.
Sights: Open rear sight groove, wide angle front sight blade

Weight: 40 oz.
Caliber: .38 Sp., .357 Mag., .45 LC, .44-40
Capacity: 6 rounds
Features: Low profile hammer; deluxe edition model includes custom tuning, custom hammer and base pin springs; jig-cut positive angles on trigger and sears; wire bolt and trigger springs
Standard: **$540**
Deluxe: **$650**

Thompson/Center

ENCORE

Action: Single-shot, break open design
Grips: Walnut or rubber
Barrel: 12 in., 15 in.
Sights: Adjustable rear; ramp front blade
Weight: 68–72 oz.
Caliber: .204 Ruger, .223 Rem, .22-250 Rem., .243 Win., .25-06 Rem., .270 Win., 7mm-08 Rem., .308 Win., .30-06 Spfd., .45-70 Gov't., .44 Rem. Mag., .45 Colt/.410, .17HMR, .22LR, .460 S&W, .500 S&W
Capacity: 1 round
Features: Interchangeable barrels; button rifled; drilled and tapped for T/C scope mounts; adjustable trigger for overtravel; ambidextrous pistol grip with finger grooves and butt cap; matching forend; blued or stainless steel finish; patented automatic hammer block with bolt interlock
MSRP. . . . . **$679–$969**
Pro Hunter: **$1199**

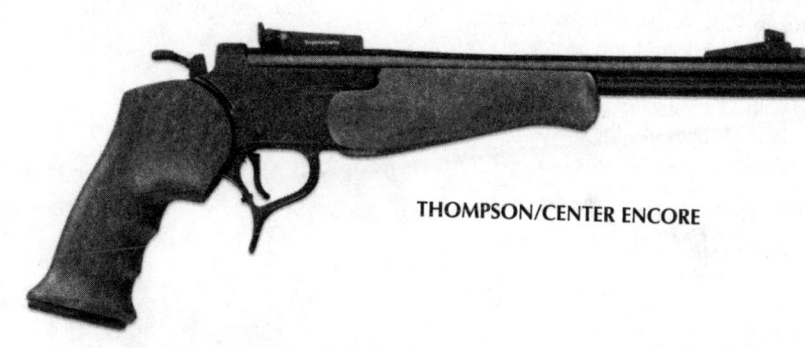

THOMPSON/CENTER ENCORE

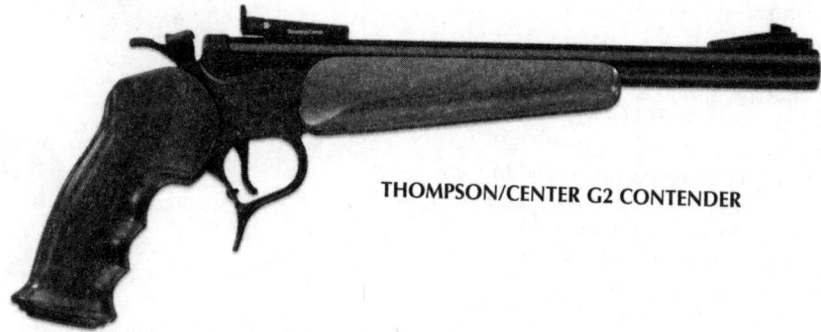

THOMPSON/CENTER G2 CONTENDER

G2 CONTENDER

Action: Single shot, break open design
Grips: Walnut or rubber
Barrel: 12 in., 14 in.
Sights: Adjustable rear; ramp front blade
Weight: 56–60 oz.

Caliber: .22LR Match, .357 Mag., .44 Rem. Mag., .45/410 Vent Rib, .223 Rem., .17 HMR, .204 Ruger, .22 Hornet, 6.8 mm Rem., 7-30 Waters, .45–70 Gov't., .30-30 Win
Capacity: 1 round

Features: .45/410 models include removable choke tube and wrench; stainless steel or walnut frame; manual firing pin selector; button rifled; drilled and tapped for T/C scope mounts
MSRP. **$729**

Uberti

1851 NAVY CONVERSION

Action: SA revolver
Grips: Walnut
Barrel: 4.75 in., 5.5 in., 7.5 in.
Sights: Fixed, open
Weight: 42 oz.
Caliber: .38 Spl.
Capacity: 6 rounds
Features: Case-hardened frame octagonal barrel; brass backstrap and trigger guard; conversion revolver frames are retro-fitted with loading gates to accommodate metallic cartridges like the originals
MSRP **$549**

1860 ARMY CONVERSION

Action: SA revolver
Grips: Walnut
Barrel: 4.75 in., 5.5 in., 8 in.
Sights: Fixed, open
Weight: 42 oz.
Caliber: .38 Spl., .45 Colt
Capacity: 6 rounds
Features: Case-hardened frame; round barrel; steel backstrap and trigger guard; conversion revolver frames are retro-fitted with loading gates to accommodate metallic cartridges like the originals
MSRP **$579**

1871–1872 OPEN-TOP CONVERSION

Action: SA revolver
Grips: Walnut
Barrel: 4.75 in., 5.5 in., 7.5 in.
Sights: Fixed, open
Weight: 42 oz.
Caliber: .38 Spl., .45 Colt
Capacity: 6 rounds
Features: 1872 model has steel backstrap and trigger guard; 1871 model has brass backstrap and trigger guard; case-hardened frame; round barrel; blued finish conversion revolver frames are retro-fitted with loading gates to accommodate metallic cartridges like the originals
1871: **$529**
1872: **$549**

1873 CATTLEMAN BIRD'S HEAD

Action: SA revolver
Grips: Walnut
Barrel: 3.5 in., 4.75 in., 5.5 in.
Sights: Fixed, open
Weight: 35 oz.

UBERTI 1851 NAVY CONVERSION

UBERTI 1860 ARMY CONVERSION

UBERTI 1871–1872 OPEN-TOP CONVERSION

UBERTI 1873 CATTLEMAN BIRD'S HEAD

UBERTI 1873 CATTLEMAN BISLEY

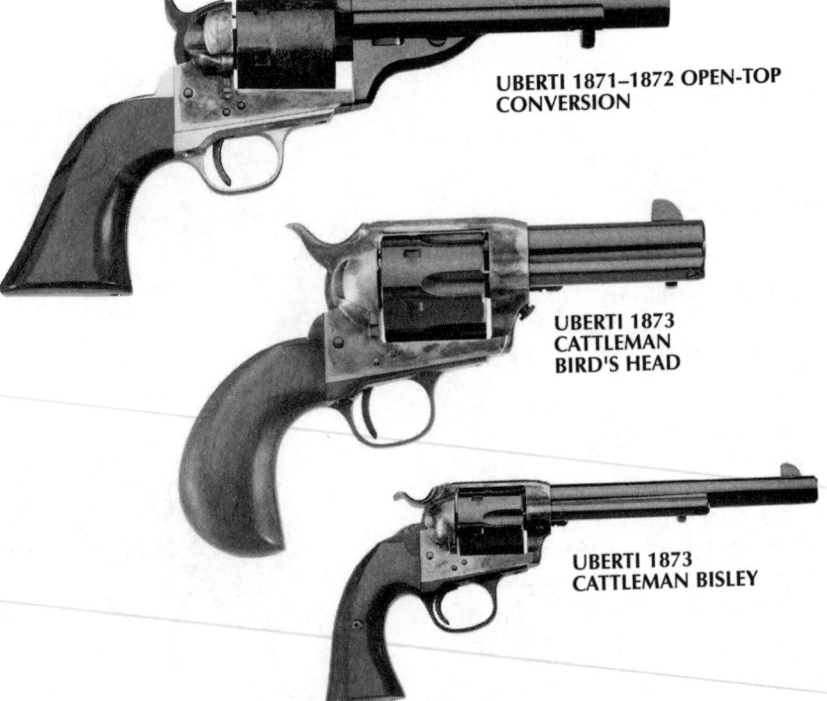

Caliber: .45 Colt, .357 Mag.
Capacity: 6 rounds
Features: Case-hardened frame; steel backstrap and trigger guard; blued finish; bird head shape grip
MSRP **$569**

1873 CATTLEMAN BISLEY

Action: SA revolver
Grips: Bisley target style walnut

Barrel: 4.75 in., 5.5 in., 7.5 in.
Sights: Fixed, open
Weight: 40 oz.
Caliber: .45 Colt, .357 Mag.
Capacity: 6 rounds
Features: Case-hardened frame; steel backstrap and trigger guard; blued finish; fluted barrel
MSRP **$599**

UBERTI 1873 CATTLEMAN CALLAHAN

UBERTI 1873 CATTLEMAN CHISHOLM

1873 CATTLEMAN CALLAHAN

Action: SA revolver
Grips: Walnut, black or mother-of-pearl synthetic
Barrel: 4.75 in., 6 in., 7.5 in.
Sights: Fixed
Weight: 42 oz.
Caliber: .44 Mag.
Capacity: 6 rounds
Features: Blued, stainless, case-hardened or Old West finish; target model has angled front target sight and adjustable notched rear blade sight
MSRP . . . . **$619–$649**

1873 CATTLEMAN CHISHOLM

Action: SA revolver
Grips: Checkered walnut
Barrel: 4.75 in., 5.5 in.
Sights: Fixed, open
Weight: 37 oz.
Caliber: .45 Colt
Capacity: 6 rounds
Features: Complete matte finished steel; fluted barrel
MSRP **$549**

UBERTI 1873 CATTLEMAN DESPERADO

1873 CATTLEMAN DESPERADO

Action: SA revolver
Grips: Bison horn style
Barrel: 4.75 in., 5.5 in.
Sights: Fixed, open
Weight: 37 oz.
Caliber: .45 Colt
Capacity: 6 rounds
Features: Full nickel-plated steel; fluted barrel
MSRP **$819**

1873 CATTLEMAN MATCHING SETS

Action: SA revolver
Grips: Walnut
Barrel: 5.5 in.
Sights: Fixed, open
Weight: 37 oz.
Caliber: .45 Colt and .357 Mag
Capacity: 6 rounds
Features: Fluted barrel; blued case-hardened frame; steel backstrap; trigger guard; the set shares matching serial numbers; also available in nickel and ivory-style grip
Walnut: . . . . **$1079 per set**
Ivory-style: . . . . **$1659 per set**

UBERTI 1873 CATTLEMAN MATCHING SET

Uberti

UBERTI 1873 EL PATRÓN COWBOY MOUNTED SHOOTER (CMS)

1873 EL PATRÓN COWBOY MOUNTED SHOOTER (CMS)

Action: SA revolver
Grips: Checkered walnut
Barrel: 3.5 in., 4 in.
Sights: EasyView
Weight: 37 oz.
Caliber: .45 Colt, .357 Mag.
Capacity: 6 rounds
Features: Blued or stainless steel finish; optional case-hardened frame; fluted barrel; fitted with U.S.-made Wolff springs; numbered cylinders
Blued: **$639**
Stainless steel: **$779**

1873 SINGLE-ACTION CATTLEMAN

Action: SA revolver
Grips: Walnut
Barrel: 4.75 in., 5.5 in., 7.5 in.
Sights: Fixed, open
Weight: 37 oz.
Caliber: .45 Colt, .44/40, .357 Mag.
Capacity: 6 rounds
Features: Case-hardened frame; brass or steel backstrap and trigger guard; blued, nickel or stainless steel finish; fluted barrel
MSRP . . . . **$509–$689**

1873 STALLION/STALLION TARGET

Action: SA revolver
Grips: Walnut
Barrel: 4.75 in., 5.5 in.
Sights: Fixed, open
Weight: 32 oz.
Caliber: .22LR, .22LR/Mag
Capacity: 6 and 10 round models
Features: Case-hardened frame; brass or steel backstrap and trigger guard; blued finish; fluted barrel
MSRP . . . . **$439–$579**

1875 OUTLAW & FRONTIER

Action: SA revolver
Grips: Walnut
Barrel: 5.5 in. (Frontier), 7.5 in.
Sights: Fixed, open
Weight: 40–45 oz.
Caliber: .45 Colt
Capacity: 6 rounds
Features: Case-hardened or full nickel plated steel frame; steel backstrap and

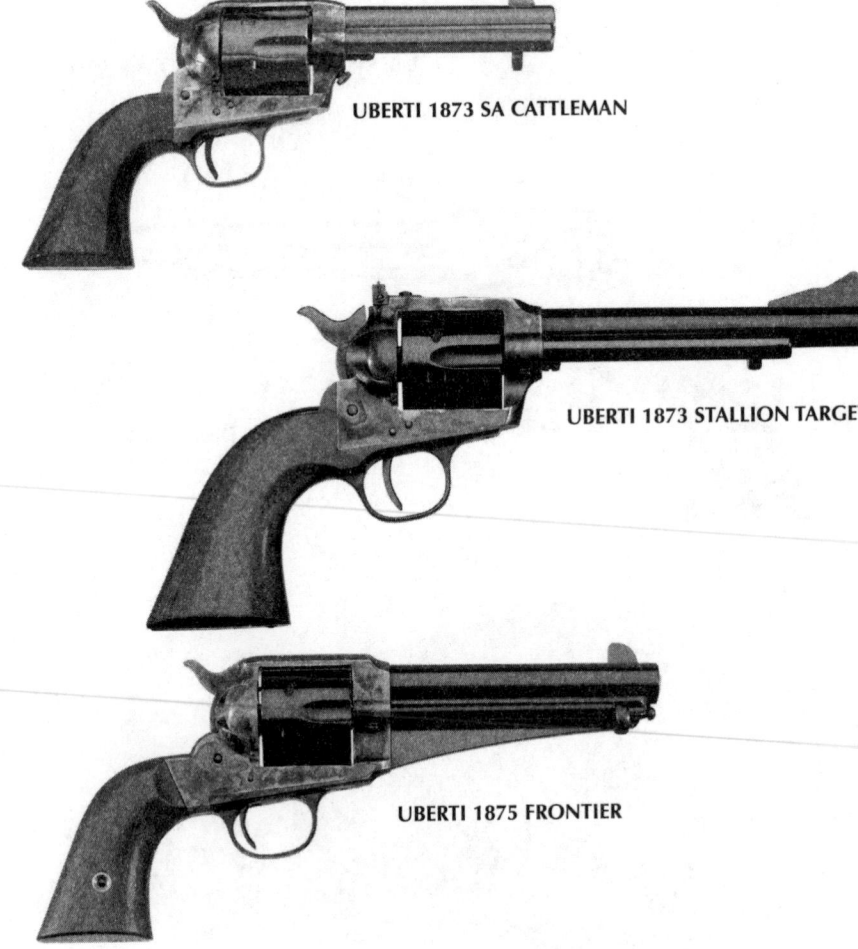

UBERTI 1873 SA CATTLEMAN

UBERTI 1873 STALLION TARGET

UBERTI 1875 FRONTIER

trigger guard; fluted barrel
Outlaw: **$559**
Outlaw Nickel: **$659**
Frontier: **$559**

Uberti

UBERTI 1890 SA POLICE REVOLVER

UBERTI TOP BREAK REVOLVER

1890 SINGLE ACTION POLICE REVOLVER

Action: SA revolver
Grips: Walnut with lanyard ring
Barrel: 5.5 in.
Sights: Fixed, open
Weight: 42 oz.
Caliber: .45, .357 Mag.
Capacity: 6 rounds
Features: Blued steel frame, backstrap and trigger guard; fluted barrel
MSRP $579

TOP BREAK REVOLVERS

Action: SA revolver
Grips: Walnut or pearl-style
Barrel: 3.5 in., 5 in., 7 in.
Sights: Fixed, open
Weight: 40 oz.
Caliber: .45 Colt, .38 Spl., .44/40
Capacity: 6 rounds
Features: Full nickel plated steel or blued steel frame and blackstrap; case-hardened trigger guard; fluted barrel
Pearl-style grip: $1419
Walnut grip: $1069

U.S. Fire Arms

OLD ARMORY ORIGINAL SERIES 1ST GENERATION

Action: SA revolver
Grips: U.S. hard rubber or walnut
Barrel: 4.75 in., 5.5 in., 7.5 in.
Sights: Blade front
Weight: N/A
Caliber: .45 Colt
Capacity: 6 rounds
Features: Historically correct OEM 1st Generation; frame window is smaller; small cylinder profile correct for early Colt production; early flutes and beveled cylinder; choice of B.P. frame, V notch or cross pin frame V notch
MSRP $2095

SHOOTING MASTER .357 MAGNUM

Action: SA revolver
Grips: U.S. hard rubber
Barrel: 7.5 in.
Sights: Front blade, rear golden
Weight: N/A
Caliber: .357 S&W Mag.
Capacity: 6 rounds
Features: Heavy Magnum frame; full dome blued finish
MSRP $1495

SPARROWHAWK .327 MAGNUM

Action: SA revolver
Grips: U.S. hard rubber
Barrel: 7.5 in.
Sights: Fully adjustable rear
Weight: N/A
Caliber: .327 Fed. Mag.

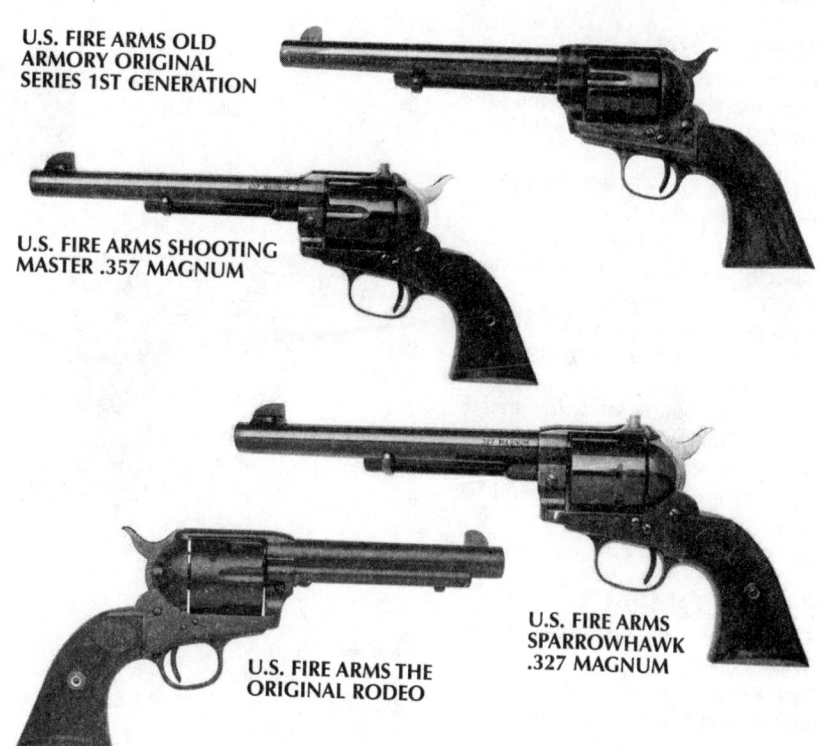

U.S. FIRE ARMS OLD ARMORY ORIGINAL SERIES 1ST GENERATION

U.S. FIRE ARMS SHOOTING MASTER .357 MAGNUM

U.S. FIRE ARMS SPARROWHAWK .327 MAGNUM

U.S. FIRE ARMS THE ORIGINAL RODEO

Capacity: 8 rounds
Features: Full dome blued; new scaled .32 caliber frame; includes removable firing pin
MSRP $1495

THE ORIGINAL RODEO

Action: SA revolver
Grips: U.S. hard rubber
Barrel: 4.75 in., 5.5 in.

Sights: Square notch rear, square front blade
Weight: 37 oz.
Caliber: .45 Colt, .38 Special
Capacity: 6 rounds
Features: Handcrafted with cowboy action in matte blued, glare-reducing finish; standard white sided hammer; cross-pin frame style
MSRP $760

Walther

WALTHER P22

WALTHER P99AS

P22

Action: DA/SA autoloader
Grips: Polymer
Barrel: 3.42 in., 5 in.
Sights: 3-dot adjustable low-profile
Weight: 17.6 oz. (3.42 in. barrel), 21.3 oz. (5 in. barrel)
Caliber: .22LR
Capacity: 10 rounds
Features: Threaded barrel, interchangeable with target barrel; loaded chamber indicator; external slide stop; 3 safeties; two magazine styles; ergonomic grip; ambidextrous magazine release lever; available with integrated laser-set; available in black, nickel, and military finish
MSRP . . . .**$379–$539**

P99AS

Action: DA autoloader
Grips: Black polymer frame and grips
Barrel: 4 in. stainless steel with Tenifer finish
Sights: Front and rear tritium night
Weight: 24 oz.–25.6 oz.
Caliber: 9mm or .40 S&W
Capacity: 15 (9mm), 12 (.40 S&W) rounds
Features: The first pistol with a firing pin block combines advantages of a traditional DA pull with SA trigger and a decocking button safety integrated into slide, allowing users the ability to decock the striker, preventing inadvertent firing in both DA and SA mode
From: **$599**

WALTHER P99AS COMPACT

WALTHER PKK/S

WALTHER PPS

P99AS COMPACT

Action: Striker fire action autoloader
Grips: Polymer
Barrel: 3.5 in.
Sights: 3-dot adjustable low-profile
Weight: 20.8 oz.–22.4 oz.
Caliber: 9mm, .40 S&W
Capacity: 10 rounds (9mm), 8 rounds (.40 S&W)
Features: Flat-bottom magazine buttplate, finger rest magazine buttplate; molded with a Weaver-style rail; interchangeable backstraps; hammerless striker system and integral safety devices come standard
From: **$599**

PPK AND PPK/S

Action: DA/SA autoloader
Grips: Polymer
Barrel: 3.3 in.
Sights: Fixed, open
Weight: 22.4 oz. (PPK), 24 oz. (PPK/S)
Caliber: .380 ACP
Capacity: 6 rounds (PPK), 7 rounds (PPK/S)
Features: Firing pin safety; manual safety with decocking function; double- and single-action trigger; extended beaver tail; nickel plated or blued finish
MSRP **$629**

PPS (POLICE PISTOL SLIM)

Action: Striker fire action autoloader
Grips: Black polymer
Barrel: 3.2 in.
Sights: 3-dot low profile contoured
Weight: 20.8 oz.
Caliber: 9mm, 40 S&W
Capacity: 6 and 8 rounds (9mm), 5 and 7 rounds (.40 S&W)
Features: Ambidextrous magazine release; loaded chamber and cocking indicators; small and large backstrap; trigger safety; Walther QuickSafe safety
MSRP **$599**

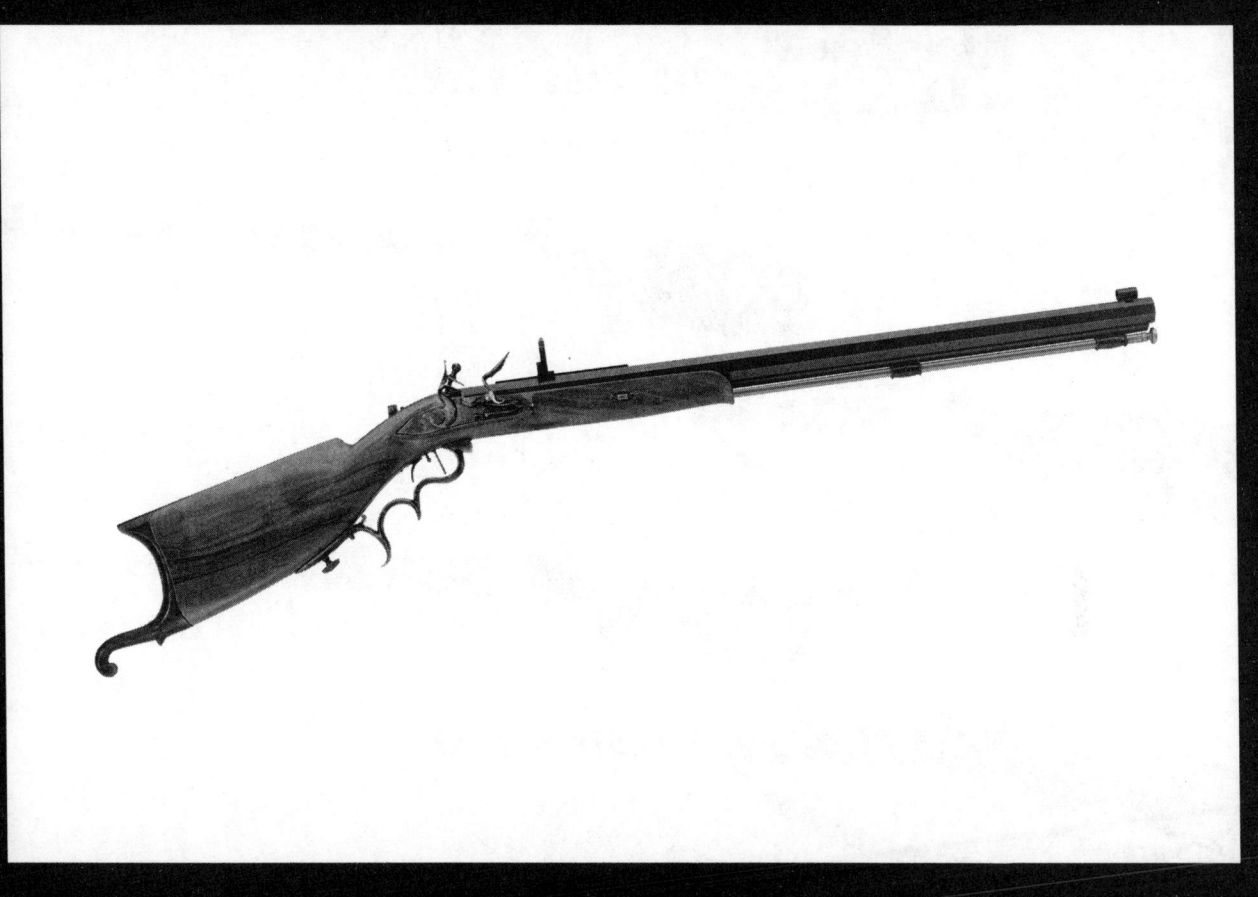

Connecticut Valley Arms (CVA)

CVA ACCURA MR

CVA ACCURA V2

CVA APEX

CVA BUCKHORN

CVA ELKHORN

ACCURA MR

Lock: Break-action in-line
Stock: Synthetic
Barrel: 25 in.
Sights: Scope mount
Weight: 6 lb. 6 oz.
Bore/Caliber: .50
Features: Aluminum frame; quick release breech plug; trigger guard actuated breeching action; Bergara barrel; neutral center of gravity trigger; premium SoftTouch stock with rubber grip panels; WeatherGuard barrel finish on the stainless steel barrel; Realtree Max-1 or black stock finishes; Quake Claw sling included; DuraSight Dead-On scope mount
MSRP . . . . $537.95–$612.95

ACCURA V2

Lock: Break-action muzzle-loading
Stock: Composite stock in standard or thumbhole
Barrel: 27 in.
Sights: DuraSight fiber optic
Weight: 7 lb. 5 oz.
Bore/Caliber: .45 or .50
Features: 416 stainless Bergara barrel; quick-release breech plug; CrushZone recoil pad; drilled and tapped for scope mount; SoftTouch coating and rubber grip panels; Quake Claw sling
MSRP . . . . $493.95–$595.95

APEX

Lock: Hinged breech muzzleloading
Stock: Synthetic
Barrel: 27 in.
Sights: DuraSight rail mount
Weight: 8 lb.
Bore/Caliber: .45 or .50
Features: Multibarrel interchangeable rifle system; ambidextrous buttstock; 416 stainless steel Bergara barrels; quick-release breech plug; Quake Claw sling; CrushZone recoil pad; available in black or Realtree APG camo; also available in centerfire models
MSRP . . . . $652.99–$737.95

BUCKHORN

Lock: In-line
Stock: Solid composite
Barrel: 24 in.
Sights: DuraSight fiber optic
Weight: 6 lb. 5 oz.
Bore/Caliber: .50
Features: 209 ignition; bullet guiding muzzle; DuraSight all-metal fiber optic sights; solid composite stock in black, with molded-in grip panels and sling swivel studs; CrushZone recoil pad; thumb-actuated safety; drilled and tapped for scope mounts
MSRP $176.95

ELKHORN

Lock: Bolt-action muzzleloading
Stock: Synthetic
Barrel: 26 in.
Sights: DuraSight fiber optic
Weight: 7 lb.
Bore/Caliber: .50
Features: Fluted barrel with bullet-guiding muzzle; 3-way ignition with primer ejecting bolt face; DuraBright all metal fiber optic sights; composite stock in Realtree or black; Quake Claw sling; CrushZone recoil pad
MSRP . . . . $289.95–$349.95

Connecticut Valley Arms (CVA)

CVA WOLF

WOLF
Lock: Break-action in-line
Stock: Synthetic
Barrel: 24 in.
Sights: DuraSight fiber optic; includes 3-9x40mm duplex scope
Weight: 6 lb. 4 oz.
Bore/Caliber: .50

Features: Bullet-guiding muzzle; new tool-free QR breech plug system; ambidextrous compact or standard stock in black or camo; CrushZone recoil pad; reversible hammer spur; blued barrel
MSRP . . . . **$238.95–$328.95**

Dixie Gun Works

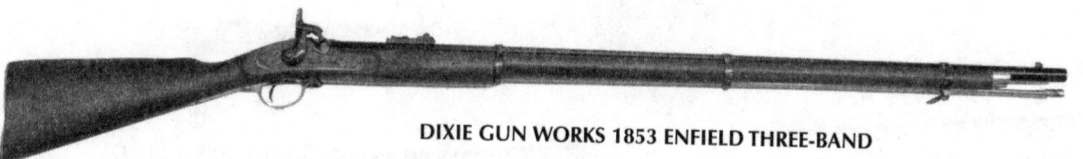

DIXIE GUN WORKS 1853 ENFIELD THREE-BAND

DIXIE GUN WORKS DIXIE SHARPS NEW MODEL 1859 MILITARY CARBINE

1853 ENFIELD THREE-BAND RIFLE MUSKET
Lock: Traditional caplock
Stock: Walnut
Barrel: 39 in.
Sights: Fixed
Weight: 10 lb. 4 oz.
Bore/Caliber: .58
Features: Color case-hardened lock; single trigger; single swivels; steel ramrod
MSRP . . . . **$725–$1695**

DIXIE SHARPS NEW MODEL 1859 MILITARY CARBINE
Lock: Dropping block
Stock: Walnut
Barrel: 22 in.
Sights: Adjustable open
Weight: 8 lb.
Bore/Caliber: .54
Features: Steel furniture; color case-hardened; single trigger; single barrel band; saddle bar with ring
MSRP **$1350**

Dixie Gun Works

FR4055 SPANISH MUSKET

Lock: Flintlock muzzleloading
Stock: Full, European walnut 56 in.
Barrel: 44.75 in.
Sights: Steel stud front
Weight: 10 lb.
Bore/Caliber: .68 round ball
Features: Brass buttplate, trigger guard, and barrel bands; bright steel side-plates; steel ramrod
MSRP **$1400**

DIXIE GUN WORKS FR4055 SPANISH MUSKET

BLACK POWDER

PEDERSOLI SCREW BARREL PISTOL

Lock: Traditional caplock
Stock: European walnut
Barrel: 3 in.
Sights: None
Weight: 12 oz.
Bore/Caliber: .44
Features: Color case-hardened lock; single folding trigger; combination nipple/barrel wrench included
MSRP **$185**

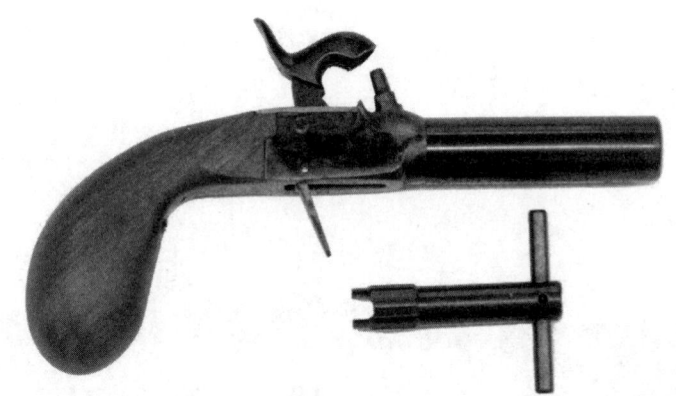

DIXIE GUN WORKS PEDERSOLI SCREW BARREL PISTOL

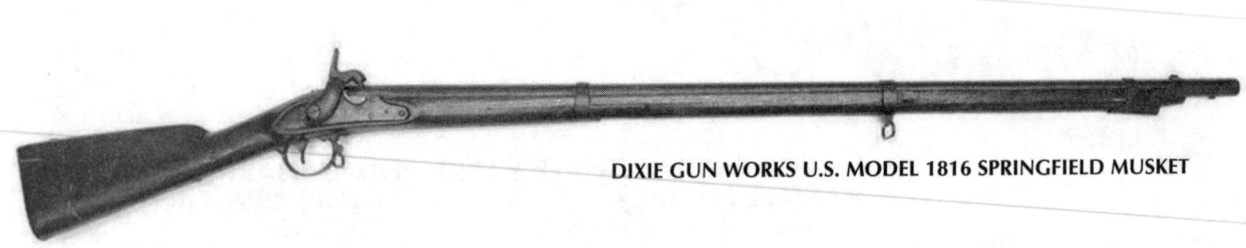

DIXIE GUN WORKS U.S. MODEL 1816 SPRINGFIELD MUSKET

U.S. MODEL 1816 SPRINGFIELD MUSKET

Lock: Traditional flintlock
Stock: Walnut
Barrel: 42 in.
Sights: Fixed

Weight: 9 lb. 13 oz.
Bore/Caliber: .69
Features: Most common military flint-lock from U.S. armories, complete with bayonet lug and swivels
MSRP **$1450**

E.M.F. Company

E.M.F. 1851 NAVY

1851 NAVY
Lock: Caplock revolver
Stock: Walnut
Barrel: 7.5 in.
Sights: Fixed
Weight: 40 oz.
Bore/Caliber: .36, .44
Features: Brass, case-hardened stainless steel frame; blued barrel optional
Brass:.....................$215
Case-hardened:............$240

1851 NAVY SHERIFF
Lock: Caplock revolver
Stock: Walnut
Barrel: 5.5 in.
Sights: None
Weight: 32 oz.
Bore/Caliber: .44
Features: Brass, case-hardened stainless steel frame; blued barrel optional
Brass:.....................$220
Case-hardened:............$250

E.M.F. 1851 NAVY SHERIFF

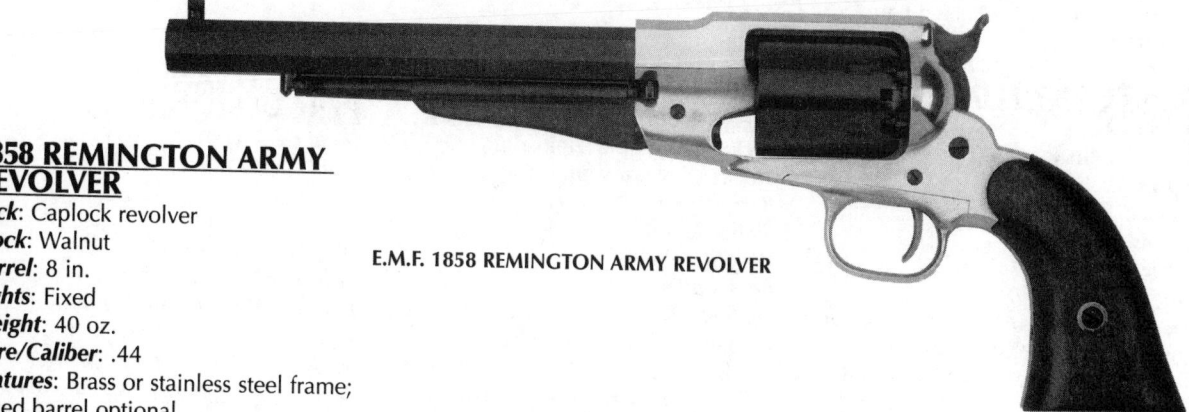

1858 REMINGTON ARMY REVOLVER
Lock: Caplock revolver
Stock: Walnut
Barrel: 8 in.
Sights: Fixed
Weight: 40 oz.
Bore/Caliber: .44
Features: Brass or stainless steel frame; blued barrel optional
Brass:.....................$240
Blued: $290
Stainless: $490

E.M.F. 1858 REMINGTON ARMY REVOLVER

E.M.F. Company

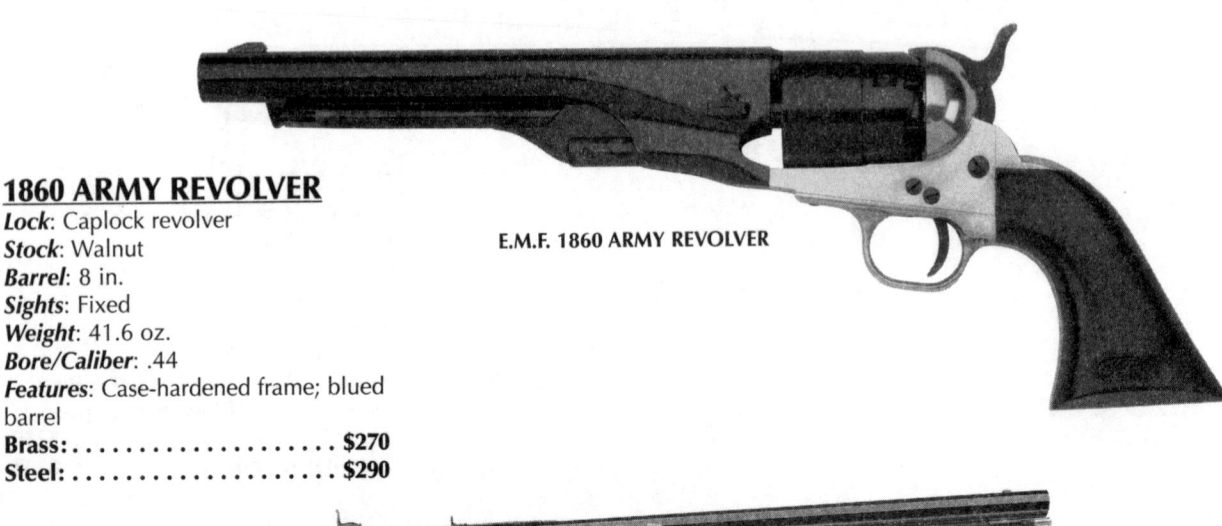

1860 ARMY REVOLVER

Lock: Caplock revolver
Stock: Walnut
Barrel: 8 in.
Sights: Fixed
Weight: 41.6 oz.
Bore/Caliber: .44
Features: Case-hardened frame; blued barrel
Brass: **$270**
Steel: **$290**

E.M.F. 1860 ARMY REVOLVER

E.M.F. MISSOURI RIVER HAWKEN

E.M.F. 1863 POCKET
REMINGTON

1863 POCKET REMINGTON

Lock: Caplock revolver
Stock: Walnut
Barrel: 3.5 in.
Sights: Fixed
Weight: 21 oz.
Bore/Caliber: .36
Features: Steel frame, blued barrel
MSRP **$295**

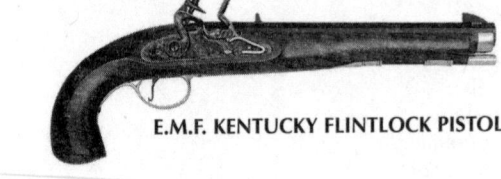

E.M.F. KENTUCKY FLINTLOCK PISTOL

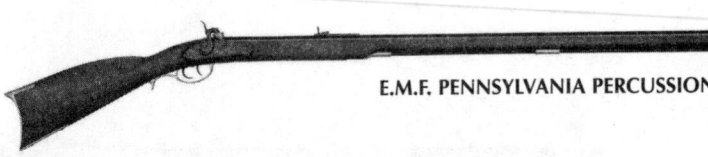

E.M.F. PENNSYLVANIA PERCUSSION RIFLE

KENTUCKY FLINTLOCK PISTOL

Lock: Flintlock
Stock: Walnut
Barrel: 10.375 in.
Sights: Fixed
Weight: 37 oz.
Bore/Caliber: .45, .50
Features: Classic American pistol during the American Revolution and a favorite of pioneers; case-hardened frame; octagonal rifled blued barrel, polished brass fittings
.45: **$525**
.50: **$555**

MISSOURI RIVER HAWKEN BY PEDERSOLI

Lock: Caplock muzzleloading
Stock: Maple or walnut
Barrel: 30 in.
Sights: Open
Weight: 9 lb. 4 oz.
Bore/Caliber: .45, .50
Features: Replica percussion rifle; available in maple or walnut stock in rust brown color finish; barrel features an octagonal cross-section; case-hardened color lock; equipped with a double-set trigger
Maple: **$1360**
Walnut: **$1355**

PENNSYLVANIA PERCUSSION RIFLE

Lock: Caplock
Stock: Walnut
Barrel: 41.625 in.
Sights: Adjustable
Weight: 7 lb. 11 oz.
Bore/Caliber: .45
Features: Reproduction of the American rifles used by Pennsylvania hunters; evolved from the German Jaeger hunting rifle; adjustable rear and front sights; case-hardened frame; double set trigger; rust brown octagonal barrel; polished brass fitting
MSRP **$1035**

BLACK POWDER

Lyman

LYMAN DEERSTALKER FLINTLOCK

LYMAN GREAT PLAINS FLINTLOCK

LYMAN MUSTANG BREAKAWAY 209 MAGNUM

LYMAN PLAINS PISTOL

DEERSTALKER RIFLE

Lock: Traditional cap or flint
Stock: Walnut
Barrel: 24 in.
Sights: Fiber optic front and rear
Weight: 10 lb. 6 oz.
Bore/Caliber: .50 or .54
Features: Quiet single trigger; metal blackened to avoid glare; black rubber recoil pad; left-hand available
Flintlock: . . . . **$559.95–$614.95**
Percussion: . . . . . . **$524.95–$624.95**

GREAT PLAINS RIFLE

Lock: Traditional cap or flint
Stock: Walnut
Barrel: 32 in.
Sights: Adjustable open
Weight: 11 lb. 10 oz.
Bore/Caliber: .50 or .54
Features: Double-set triggers; Hawken style percussion "snail" with clean-out screw; separate ramrod entry thimble and nose cap; reliable coil-spring lock with correct lock plate; left-hand available
Flintlock: . . . . **$769.95–$784.95**
Percussion: . . . . . . **$719.95–$749.95**

MUSTANG BREAKAWAY 209 MAGNUM

Lock: In-line
Stock: Hardwood
Barrel: 26 in.
Sights: Fiber optic front and rear
Weight: 11 lb.
Bore/Caliber: .50
Features: Pachmayr "Decelerator" recoil pad; comes drilled and tapped for Weaver style bases; hammerless; removable, stainless breech plug and easy take-down; "magnetized" primer retention system
MSRP **$525**

PLAINS PISTOL

Lock: Traditional caplock
Stock: Walnut
Barrel: 6 in.
Sights: Fixed
Weight: 3 lb. 2 oz.
Bore/Caliber: .50 or .54
Features: Blackened iron furniture; polished brass trigger guard and ramrod tips; hooked patent breech takes down quickly for easy cleaning; thimble is recessed into the rib; detachable belt hook; spring-loaded trigger
Plains Pistol: **$374.95**
Kit: **$319.95**

TRADE RIFLE

Lock: Traditional cap or flint
Stock: Walnut
Barrel: 28 in.
Sights: Adjustable open
Weight: 10 lb. 13 oz.
Bore/Caliber: .50 or .54
Features: Brass furniture; originally developed for the early Indian fur trade
Flintlock: **$569.95**
Percussion: **$524.95**

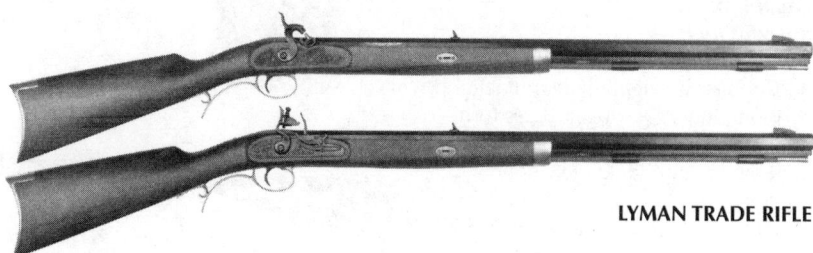

LYMAN TRADE RIFLE

Pedersoli

BAKER STYLE COACH GUN
Lock: Caplock
Stock: Walnut
Barrel: 11.25 in.
Sights: None
Weight: 5 lb. 12 oz.
Bore/Caliber: 12 Ga.
Features: Single trigger back action, side-by-side shotgun; reproduces a gun made by London gunsmith Ezekiel Baker in 1850; case-hardened locks
MSRP **$945**

CAVALRY SHOTGUN WITH SINGLE TRIGGER
Lock: Caplock
Stock: Walnut
Barrel: 20 in.
Sights: None
Weight: 6 lb. 10 oz.
Bore/Caliber: 12 Ga.
Features: Single trigger back action; side-by-side hunting shotgun; shortened barrel for riding a horse; case-hardened locks
MSRP **$913**

COOK & BROTHER ARTILLERY CARBINE
Lock: Caplock
Stock: Walnut
Barrel: 24 in.
Sights: None
Weight: 6 lb. 10 oz.
Bore/Caliber: .58
Features: Inspired by English model guns; originally produced by Cook & Brother beginning in 1861; brass garnitures; blued barrel; case-hardened lock
MSRP **$1055**

DERRINGER PHILADELPHIA
Lock: Flintlock
Stock: Walnut
Barrel: 3.06 in.
Sights: None
Weight: 8.6 oz.
Bore/Caliber: .45
Features: Reproduction of the popular pocket pistols originally manufactured by John Henry Derringer. Brass furniture; case-hardened lock; original markings on the lock: Derringer/Philadelphia
MSRP **$505**

ENFIELD 3 BAND P1853 RIFLE MUSKET
Lock: Caplock
Stock: Walnut
Barrel: 39 in.
Sights: Adjustable rear
Weight: 8 lb. 13 oz.
Bore/Caliber: .577
Features: Ladder rear sight with a slider assembled on a base with steps; steel barrel bands; brass furniture; ramrod tip is shaped with characteristic jag slot; barrel is blued and lock case-hardened
MSRP **$1210**

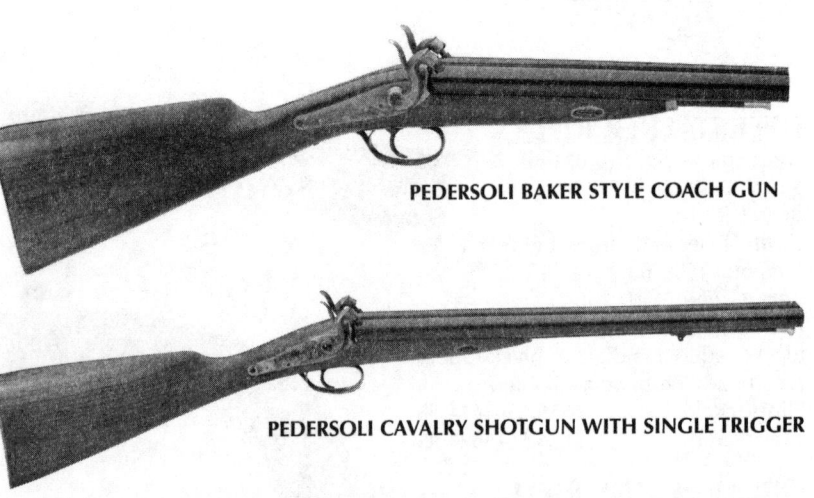

PEDERSOLI BAKER STYLE COACH GUN

PEDERSOLI CAVALRY SHOTGUN WITH SINGLE TRIGGER

PEDERSOLI COOK & BROTHER ARTILLERY CARBINE

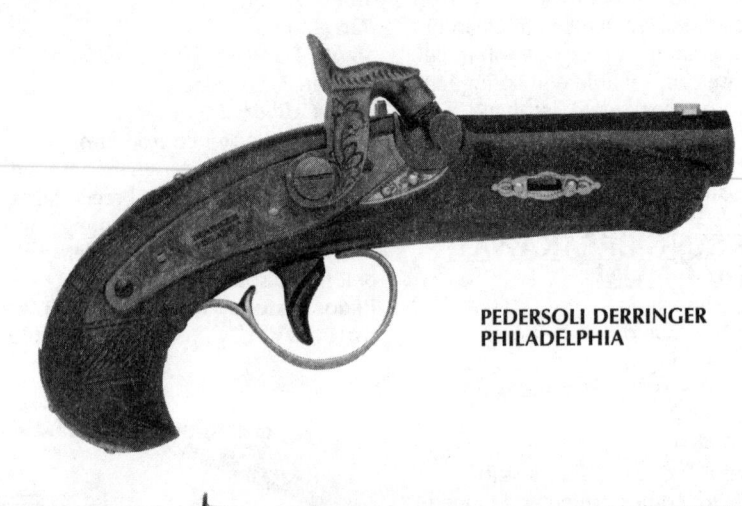

PEDERSOLI DERRINGER PHILADELPHIA

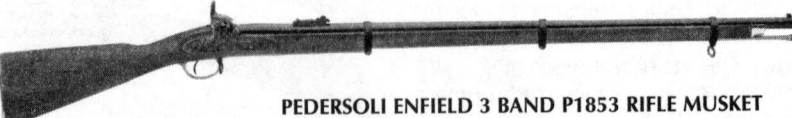

PEDERSOLI ENFIELD 3 BAND P1853 RIFLE MUSKET

Pedersoli

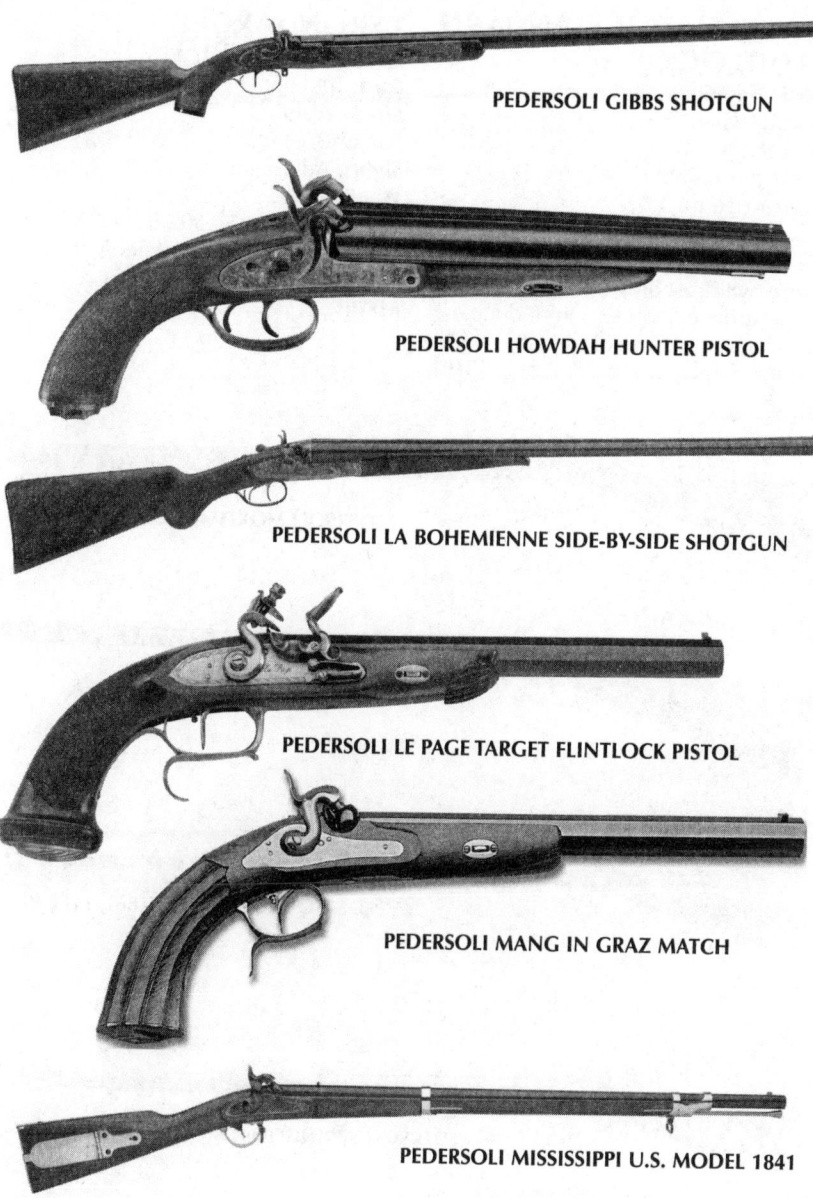

PEDERSOLI GIBBS SHOTGUN

PEDERSOLI HOWDAH HUNTER PISTOL

PEDERSOLI LA BOHEMIENNE SIDE-BY-SIDE SHOTGUN

PEDERSOLI LE PAGE TARGET FLINTLOCK PISTOL

PEDERSOLI MANG IN GRAZ MATCH

PEDERSOLI MISSISSIPPI U.S. MODEL 1841

LA BOHEMIENNE SIDE-BY-SIDE SHOTGUN
Lock: Hinged breech muzzleloading
Stock: Checkered walnut
Barrel: 28 in.
Chokes: cyl/mod choke tubes
Weight: 7 lb.
Bore/Caliber: 12 Ga.
Features: Rust brown finish barrel; interchangeable chokes; color case-hardened frame; hand-engraved locks
MSRP $2050

LE PAGE TARGET FLINTLOCK PISTOL
Lock: Traditional flintlock
Stock: Walnut
Barrel: 10.5 in.
Sights: Adjustable
Weight: 2 lb. 10 oz.
Bore/Caliber: .44 or .45
Features: Smoothbore .45 available; adjustable single-set trigger; brightly polished lock with a roller frizzen spring
MSRP $1230

MANG IN GRAZ MATCH
Lock: Traditional caplock
Stock: Walnut
Barrel: 11.4 in.
Sights: Fixed
Weight: 2 lb. 10 oz.
Bore/Caliber: .38 or .44
Features: Fluted grip; octagonal, rifled barrel in brown rust finish; adjustable single set trigger; breech plug shows a typical mask of the period; barrel and tang enriched with gold inlays
MSRP $1750

MISSISSIPPI U.S. MODEL 1841
Lock: Caplock
Stock: Walnut
Barrel: 33 in.
Sights: Open rear
Weight: 9 lb. 8 oz.
Bore/Caliber: .54, .58
Features: Considered the best-looking ordnance rifle of its period; brass furniture; browned barrel; notched rear sight; case-hardened lock; ramrod with brass tip
MSRP $1261

GIBBS SHOTGUN
Lock: Caplock
Stock: Walnut
Barrel: 32.3 in.
Sights: None
Weight: 8 lb. 9 oz.
Bore/Caliber: 12 Ga.
Features: Octagonal to round barrel; case-hardened color-finished lock; grip and forend caps with ebony inserts; pistol grip stock
MSRP $1514

HOWDAH HUNTER PISTOL
Lock: Caplock
Stock: Walnut
Barrel: 11.25 in.
Sights: None
Weight: 5 lb. 1 oz.
Bore/Caliber: 20 Ga., .50, .58
Features: Engraved locks with wild animal scenes; case-hardened color finish; checkered walnut pistol grip with steel butt cap
MSRP $821

Pedersoli

MORTIMER TARGET RIFLE

Lock: Flintlock
Stock: English-style European walnut
Barrel: 36.4 in.
Sights: Target
Weight: 10 lb. 2 oz.
Bore/Caliber: .54
Features: Case-colored lock; stock has cheekpiece and hand checkering; 7-groove barrel
MSRP **$1758**

PLAINS SHOTGUN "THE FAST BACK ACTION"

Lock: Caplock
Stock: Walnut
Barrel: 27.5 in., 28.5 in.
Sights: None
Weight: 7 lb. 5 oz.–7 lb. 8 oz.
Bore/Caliber: 12, 20 Ga.
Features: Single trigger; side-by-side shotgun; fast second shot, thanks to back action lock reducing minor residues of black powder in lock parts
MSRP **$1191**

RICHMOND 1861, TYPE III

Lock: Caplock
Stock: Walnut
Barrel: 39.75 in.
Sights: None
Weight: 9 lb. 14 oz.
Bore/Caliber: .58
Features: Manufactured based on the U.S. 1855 Model with the Maynard tape ignition system; except for the lock's profile, the brass buttplate, and the stock nose cap, the gun's appearance resembles the U.S. Model 1861
MSRP **$1261**

SPRINGFIELD MODEL 1861 U.S.

Lock: Caplock
Stock: Walnut
Barrel: 40 in.
Sights: None
Weight: 9 lb. 14 oz.
Bore/Caliber: .58
Features: More efficient than earlier smooth bored muskets used by both sides in the American Civil War; satin finish barrel; stock with three bands; coin-colored finish on the steel furniture
MSRP **$1253**

SWISS MATCH STANDARD FLINTLOCK

Lock: Traditional flintlock
Stock: Walnut
Barrel: 30.8 in.
Sights: Adjustable
Weight: 16 lb. 5 oz.
Bore/Caliber: .40
Features: Octagonal conical profile barrel with rust brown finish; lock is case-hardened; steel ramrod; double-set trigger; steel hook buttplate
MSRP **$3191**

TYRON TARGET STANDARD RIFLE

Lock: Traditional caplock
Stock: Walnut
Barrel: 36.4 in.
Sights: Adjustable open
Weight: 9 lb. 11 oz.
Bore/Caliber: .45, .50, .54
Features: Creedmoor version with aperture sight available
MSRP **$1098**

PEDERSOLI MORTIMER TARGET RIFLE

PEDERSOLI PLAINS SHOTGUN

PEDERSOLI RICHMOND 1861, TYPE III

PEDERSOLI SPRINGFIELD MODEL 1861 U.S.

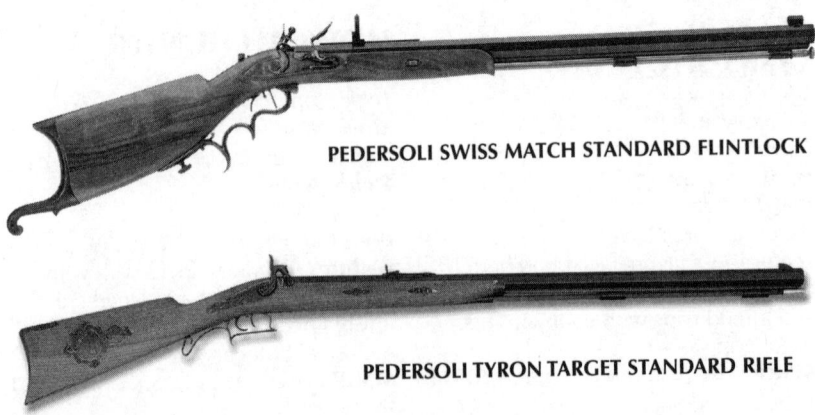

PEDERSOLI SWISS MATCH STANDARD FLINTLOCK

PEDERSOLI TYRON TARGET STANDARD RIFLE

Savage Arms

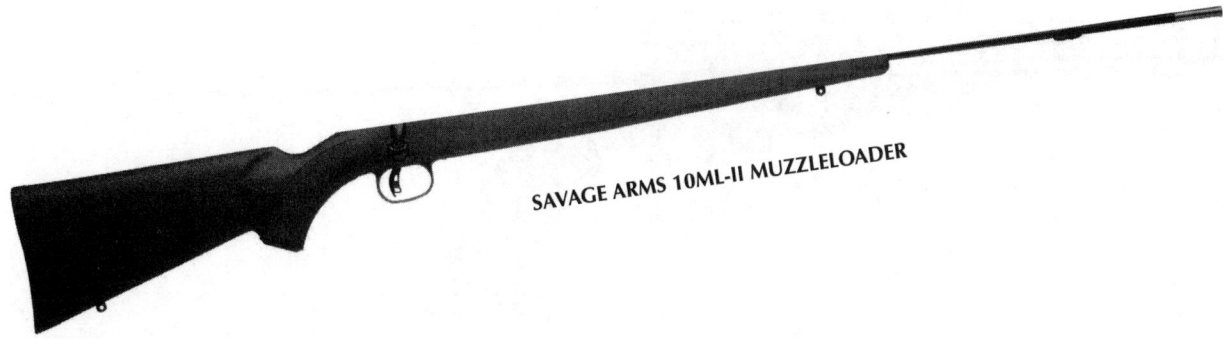

SAVAGE ARMS 10ML-II MUZZLELOADER

10ML-II MUZZLELOADER

Lock: In-line
Stock: Synthetic, camo
Barrel: 24 in.
Sights: Adjustable fiber optics
Weight: 7 lb. 12 oz.
Bore/Caliber: .50

Features: Bolt-action mechanism; drilled and tapped for scope mounts; AccuTrigger; free-floating barreled action; sling swivel studs; stock comes in black synthetic, Realtree Hardwoods HD camouflage synthetic, or brown laminate; blued or stainless steel barrel
Synthetic: **$638**
Camo: **$753**

Shiloh Rifle

SHILOH RIFLE 1874 SHARPS BUFFALO–"QUIGLEY"

SHILOH RIFLE 1874 TARGET CREEDMOOR RIFLE

1863 RIFLES

Lock: Traditional caplock
Stock: Walnut
Barrel: 30 in.
Sights: Adjustable open
Weight: 9 lb. 8 oz.
Bore/Caliber: .50 or .54
Features: Sporting model has half-stock; double set trigger on military model with 3-band full stock; military steel buttstock on all models
Sporting: **$1854**
Carbine: **$1854**
Military: **$2154**

1874 SHARPS BUFFALO– "QUIGLEY"

Lock: Falling block
Stock: Walnut
Barrel: 34 in.
Sights: Semi buckhorn rear, midrange vernier tang, #111 globe aperture front
Weight: 12 lb. 8 oz.
Bore/Caliber: .45-70 or .45-110
Features: Military buttstock; patchbox; heavy octagonal barrel; pewter tip; Hartford collars; double set triggers; antique or standard color finish; gold inlay initials in gold oval
MSRP **$3396**

1874 TARGET CREEDMOOR RIFLE

Lock: Blackpowder cartridge
Stock: Walnut
Barrel: 32 in.
Sights: V aiming rear; blade front
Weight: 9 lb.
Bore/Caliber: All popular black powder cartridges from .38-55 to .50-90
Features: Pistol grip; single trigger; AA finish on American black walnut; polished barrel; octagon barrel; pewter tip
MSRP **$2825**

Taylor's & Co.

TAYLOR'S & CO. 1848 DRAGOONS

TAYLOR'S & CO. LE MAT CAVALRY

TAYLOR'S & CO. 1847 WALKER

TAYLOR'S & CO. 1842 SMOOTHBORE MUSKET

1842 SMOOTHBORE MUSKET

Lock: Caplock
Stock: Walnut
Barrel: 42 in.
Sights: Military style
Weight: 9 lb. 12 oz.
Bore/Caliber: .69
Features: The Springfield replica has all the features of the original, including a one-piece, oil-finished walnut stock; original-style barrel bands; and completely interchangeable parts. The percussion lock has a V-style mainspring. This model features the lock with stamping noting 1842 and Springfield. NSSA approved, with certificate of authenticity and a brass medallion featuring the model and serial number.
MSRP **$750**

1847 WALKER

Lock: Caplock revolver
Stock: Walnut
Barrel: 9 in.
Sights: Fixed
Weight: 4 lb. 12 oz.
Bore/Caliber: .44
Features: Blued finish; round barrel
MSRP **$407**

1848 DRAGOONS

Lock: Caplock revolver
Stock: Walnut
Barrel: 7.5 in.
Sights: Fixed
Weight: 4 lb.–4 lb. 14 oz.
Bore/Caliber: .44
Features: These Dragoon revolvers were first used by the U.S. Army's Mounted Rifles 1st Cavalry in 1833. Soon they went on to see considerable use during the 1850 and during the Civil War. Blued finish; six-round capacity
1st Model: **$381**
2nd Model: **$391**
3rd Model: **$402**

LE MAT CAVALRY

Lock: Caplock revolver
Stock: Walnut
Barrel: 8 in.
Sights: Fixed
Weight: 5 lb.
Bore/Caliber: .44 or 20 Ga.
Features: Blued steel finish; nine-shot .44 caliber revolver with a 20 Ga. single-shot barrel was a favorite among Confederate cavalry troops; case-hardened hammer and trigger; lanyard ring; trigger guard with spur
MSRP **$1169**

THOMPSON/CENTER ENCORE ENDEAVOR PRO HUNTER XT

THOMPSON/CENTER FIRE STORM

THOMPSON/CENTER IMPACT

THOMPSON/CENTER NORTHWEST EXPLORER

THOMPSON/CENTER TRIUMPH BONE COLLECTOR

ENCORE ENDEAVOR PRO HUNTER XT

Lock: Hinged breech muzzleloading
Stock: Camo or black FlexTech with SIMS recoil pad
Barrel: 28 in.
Sights: Fiber optic
Weight: 8 lb. 4 oz.
Bore/Caliber: .50
Features: 209 ignition primer, swing hammer, power rod, QLA muzzle system; speed breech XT; stainless, fluted barrel
MSRP................**$779–$849**

FIRE STORM

Lock: Traditional cap or flint
Stock: Composite
Barrel: 26 in.
Sights: Steel fiber optic

Weight: 7 lb.
Bore/Caliber: .50
Features: Aluminum ramrod; single trigger with large trigger guard bow; Fire Storm positive ignition; magnum capabilities
MSRP.................... **$599**

IMPACT

Lock: Hinged breech muzzleloading
Stock: Black or LongLeaf camo
Barrel: 28 in.
Sights: Fiber optic
Weight: 6 lb. 8 oz.
Bore/Caliber: .50
Features: Triple lead thread breech plug; 1-inch adjustable buttstock
MSRP................**$259–$309**

NORTHWEST EXPLORER

Lock: Dropping block
Stock: Black composite or Realtree Hardwoods camo
Barrel: 28 in.

Sights: Adjustable
Weight: 7 lb.
Bore/Caliber: .50
Features: Design meets legal regulations of western states; exposed breech system; #11 cap ignition and metal sights; QLA (Quick Load Accurizor); weather shield coating available; blued barrel
MSRP...............**$359–$439**

TRIUMPH BONE COLLECTOR

Lock: In-line
Stock: Composite, black or Realtree AP HD camo
Barrel: 28 in.
Sights: Adjustable fiber optic
Weight: 6 lb. 8 oz.
Bore/Caliber: .50
Features: Blued, stainless, and weather shield finish; speed breech XT
MSRP.................... **$669**

Traditions Firearms

**TRADITIONS FIREARMS
1851 NAVY REVOLVER**

**TRADITIONS FIREARMS 1858
ARMY REVOLVER**

**TRADITIONS FIREARMS 1860
ARMY REVOLVER**

TRADITIONS FIREARMS BUCKSTALKER

1851 NAVY REVOLVER

Lock: Caplock revolver
Stock: Walnut
Barrel: 7.5 in.
Sights: Fixed
Weight: 2 lb. 8 oz.
Bore/Caliber: .44
Features: Octagonal barrel and lever-style loader; brass, antiqued, or old silver frame and guard
Brass:..............**$229**
Steel: **$259**

1858 ARMY REVOLVER

Lock: Caplock
Stock: Walnut
Barrel: 8 in.
Sights: Fixed
Weight: 2 lb. 12 oz.
Bore/Caliber: .44
Features: Octagonal barrel and lever style loader; steel, brass, or stainless steel frame and guard; top strap and post sights
Steel: **$335**
Brass: **$269**
SS: **$550**

1860 ARMY REVOLVER

Lock: Caplock
Stock: Simulated ivory, walnut
Barrel: 8 in.
Sights: Fixed
Weight: 2 lb. 12 oz.
Bore/Caliber: .44
Features: Blued barrel; steel frame; brass guard; hammer/blade sights
Walnut/Steel:..............**$305**
Walnut/Brass:..............**$250**
Ivory/Nickel: **$350**

BUCKSTALKER

Lock: Break-action muzzleloading
Stock: Synthetic
Barrel: 24 in.
Sights: Tru-Glo fiber optics
Weight: 7 lb. 8 oz.
Bore/Caliber: .50
Features: Dual safety system; nickel guard coating; synthetic black or G1 Vista camo stock; nickel or blued finish barrel; Monte Carlo stock; drilled and tapped for a scope; sling swivel studs
MSRP...............**$215–$289**

BLACK POWDER

Traditions Firearms

TRADITIONS FIREARMS CROCKETT PISTOL

TRADITIONS FIREARMS DEERHUNTER RIFLE

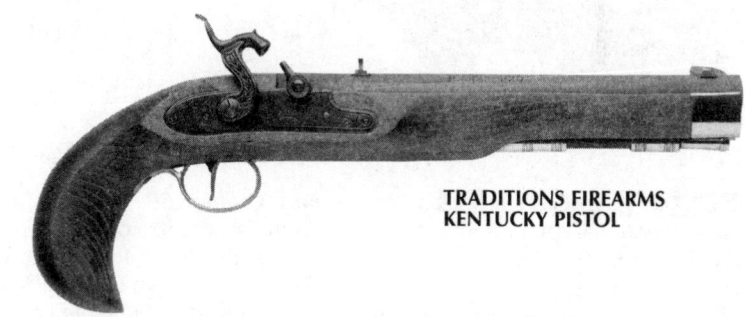

TRADITIONS FIREARMS HAWKEN
WOODSMAN RIFLE

TRADITIONS FIREARMS
KENTUCKY PISTOL

CROCKETT PISTOL

Lock: Traditional caplock
Stock: Hardwood
Barrel: 15 in.
Sights: Fixed
Weight: 2 lb.
Bore/Caliber: .32
Features: Blued, octagonal barrel
MSRP **$248**

DEERHUNTER RIFLE

Lock: Traditional cap or flint
Stock: Synthetic or hardwood
Barrel: 24 in.
Sights: Lite Optic adjustable
Weight: 6 lb.
Bore/Caliber: .32, .50, .54
Features: Octagonal performance barrels; blued or nickel barrel finish; percussion models are drilled and tapped to accept scope mounts; non-slip recoil pad; stock comes in black synthetic, Mossy Oak Tree Stand camo, or hardwood
MSRP . . . . **$249–$389**

HAWKEN WOODSMAN RIFLE

Lock: Traditional cap or flint
Stock: Hardwood
Barrel: 28 in.
Sights: Adjustable rear hunting
Weight: 7 lb. 13 oz.
Bore/Caliber: .50
Features: Hooked breech for easy barrel removal; double-set triggers in an oversized glove-fitting trigger guard; inletted solid brass patch box; left-hand model available; octagonal blued barrel

Flint: **$495**
Percussion: **$454**

KENTUCKY PISTOL

Lock: Traditional caplock
Stock: Hardwood
Barrel: 10 in.
Sights: Fixed
Weight: 2 lb. 8 oz.
Bore/Caliber: .50
Features: Brass furniture; case-colored sidelock and brass ramrod thimble
MSRP **$235**

Traditions Firearms

TRADITIONS FIREARMS PENNSYLVANIA RIFLE

TRADITIONS FIREARMS PURSUIT ULTRALIGHT

TRADITIONS FIREARMS PURSUIT ULTRALIGHT XLT

TRADITIONS FIREARMS TRACKER 209

BLACK POWDER

PENNSYLVANIA RIFLE
Lock: Traditional cap or flint
Stock: Walnut
Barrel: 20 in.
Sights: Adjustable primitive style rear
Weight: 8 lb. 8 oz.
Bore/Caliber: .50
Features: Brass stock inlay ornamentation and toe plate; cheekpiece; solid brass patch box
Percussion: **$754**
Flint: **$799**

PURSUIT ULTRALIGHT
Lock: Hinged breech muzzleloading
Stock: Black synthetic, Reaper Buck camo, or MO Infinity camo
Barrel: 28 in.
Sights: Metal fiber optic
Weight: 5 lb. 2 oz.

Bore/Caliber: .50
Features: Accelerator breech plug; drilled and tapped for scopes; 209 shotgun primer ignition; black synthetic with blued or CeraKote finish; speed load system; fluted barrel; 3-9x40 scope available
MSRP . . . . **$309–$439**

PURSUIT ULTRALIGHT XLT
Lock: Hinged breech muzzleloading
Stock: MO Infinity camo, Monte Carlo style cob
Barrel: 28 in.
Sights: Metal fiber optic
Weight: 5 lb. 14 oz.
Bore/Caliber: .50
Features: Alloy, lightweight frame, aluminum ramrod; QuickRelief recoil pad; SoftTouch rubberized coating on

stock; 209 ignition primer; drilled and tapped for scope mounts; sling swivel; fluted, Premium CeraKote barrel; thumbhole stock available
MSRP . . . . **$339–$429**

TRACKER 209
Lock: In-line
Stock: Synthetic, camo
Barrel: 22 in.
Sights: Light optic adjustable
Weight: 6 lb. 8 oz.
Bore/Caliber: .50
Features: Removable 209 primer ignition; projectile alignment system; in-line bolt with a quiet thumb safety; removable breech plug system; rugged synthetic ramrod
MSRP **$184**

Traditions Firearms

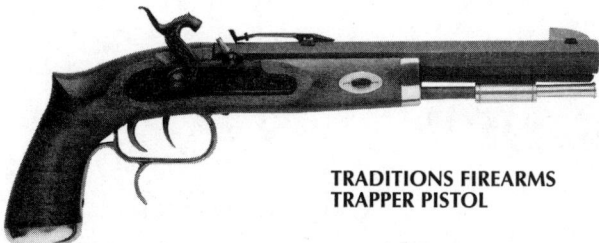

TRADITIONS FIREARMS TRAPPER PISTOL

TRAPPER PISTOL
Lock: Traditional cap or flint
Stock: Hardwood
Barrel: 9.75 in.
Sights: Primitive-style adjustable rear
Weight: 2 lb. 14 oz.
Bore/Caliber: .50
Features: Octagonal blued barrel; double set triggers
MSRP . . . . $316–$355

TRADITIONS FIREARMS VORTEK PISTOL - HARDWOOD

TRADITIONS FIREARMS VORTEK ULTRALIGHT LDR

TRADITIONS FIREARMS VORTEK ULTRALIGHT

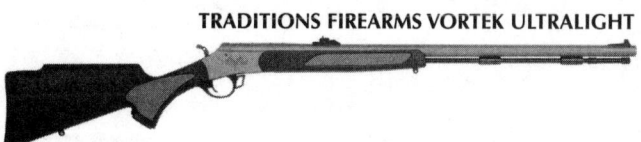

VORTEK PISTOL
Lock: Hinged breech muzzleloading
Stock: Select hardwood, Realtree AP camo, Reaper Buck camo
Barrel: 13 in.
Sights: Fixed open
Weight: 3 lb. 4 oz.
Bore/Caliber: .50
Features: 209 primer ignition, accelerator breech plug; CeraKote finish on frame and barrel
Hardwood: $383
Reaper Buck: $459

VORTEK ULTRALIGHT
Lock: Hinged breech muzzleloading
Stock: Synthetic black Hogue over-mold, Realtree AP camo, or Reaper Buck camo
Barrel: 28 in.
Sights: Fixed, green
Weight: 6 lb. 4 oz.
Bore/Caliber: .50
Features: Drop-out trigger assembly; recoil pad; 3-pound factory trigger; frame and barrel have CeraKote finish
MSRP . . . . $430–$515

VORTEK ULTRALIGHT LDR
Lock: Hinged breech muzzleloading
Stock: Synthetic, Reaper Buck camo
Barrel: 30 in.
Sights: Drilled and tapped for scopes
Weight: 6 lb. 13 oz.
Bore/Caliber: .50
Features: The only break-action muzzle-loader with a 30-inch barrel on the market; accelerator breech plug; LT-1 alloy frame with Premium CeraKote finish; ultralight chromoly tapered, fluted barrel; Hogue comfort grip overmolding; Soft Touch camo stocks
MSRP . . . . $459–$530

Uberti

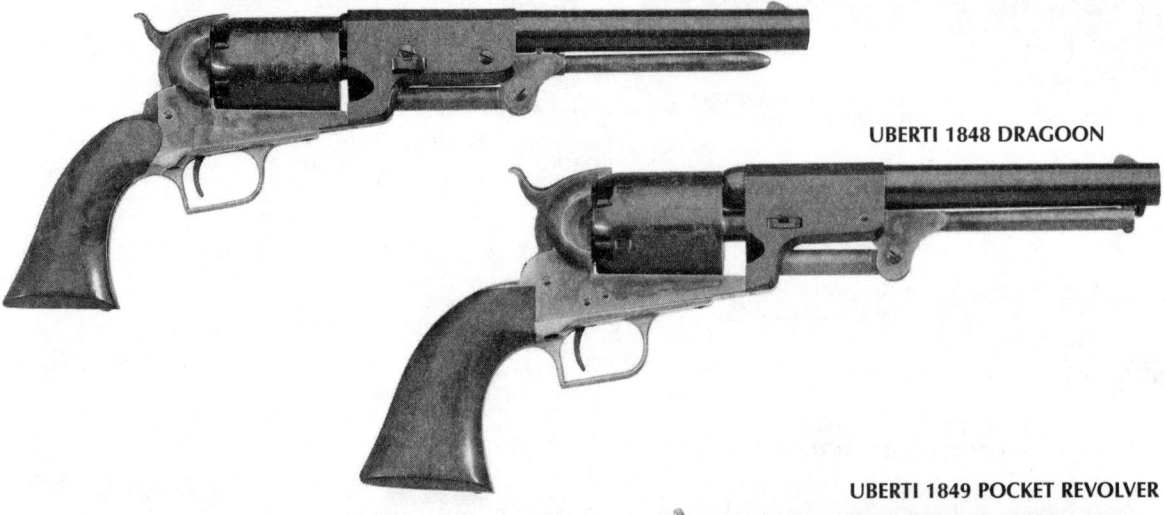

UBERTI 1847 WALKER

UBERTI 1848 DRAGOON

UBERTI 1849 POCKET REVOLVER

UBERTI 1851 NAVY REVOLVER

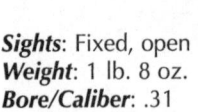

1847 WALKER
Lock: Caplock revolver
Stock: Walnut
Barrel: 9 in.
Sights: Fixed, open
Weight: 4 lb. 8 oz.
Bore/Caliber: .44
Features: Case-hardened frame, steel backstrap, brass trigger guard; blued finish
MSRP **$439**

1848 DRAGOON
Lock: Caplock revolver
Stock: Walnut
Barrel: 7.5 in.
Sights: Fixed, open
Weight: 4 lb. 2 oz.
Bore/Caliber: .44
Features: Case-hardened frame; steel or brass backstrap and trigger guard; engraved
MSRP . . . . **$429–$439**

1848–1849 POCKET REVOLVERS
Lock: Caplock revolver
Stock: Walnut
Barrel: 4 in.

Sights: Fixed, open
Weight: 1 lb. 8 oz.
Bore/Caliber: .31
Features: Case-hardened frame; brass backstrap and trigger guard; blued octagonal barrel; engraved
MSRP **$359**

1851 NAVY REVOLVER
Lock: Caplock revolver
Stock: Walnut

Barrel: 7.5 in.
Sights: Fixed, open
Weight: 2 lb. 10 oz.
Bore/Caliber: .36
Features: Color case-hardened frame; oval or squareback trigger guard; brass or steel backstrap and trigger guard; octagonal barrel (Leech-Rigdon model has round barrel)
MSRP . . . . **$339–$369**

Uberti

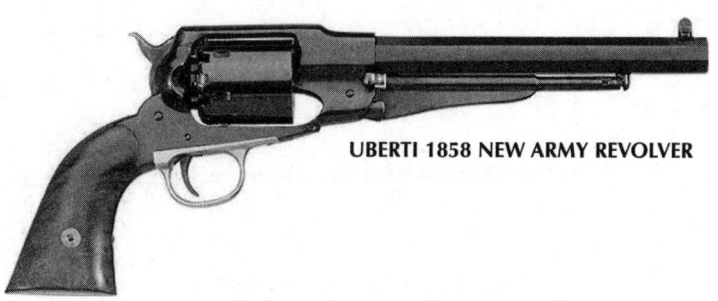

UBERTI 1858 NEW ARMY REVOLVER

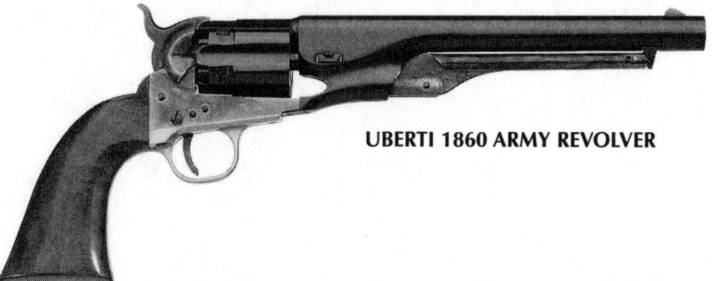

UBERTI 1860 ARMY REVOLVER

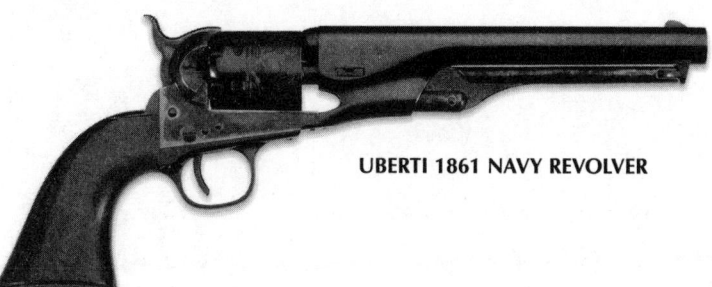

UBERTI 1861 NAVY REVOLVER

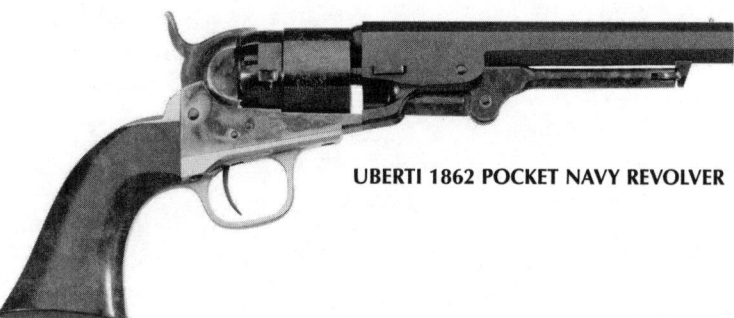

UBERTI 1862 POCKET NAVY REVOLVER

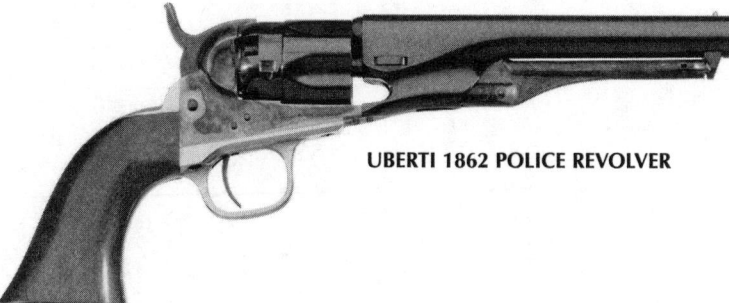

UBERTI 1862 POLICE REVOLVER

1858 NEW ARMY REVOLVER

Lock: Caplock revolver
Stock: Walnut
Barrel: 8 in.
Sights: Fixed, open
Weight: 2 lb. 11 oz.
Bore/Caliber: .44
Features: Blued or stainless steel frame and backstrap; brass trigger guard; octagonal barrel
Blued: **$359**
Stainless Steel:. **$449**

1860 ARMY REVOLVER

Lock: Caplock revolver
Stock: Walnut
Barrel: 7.5 in.
Sights: Fixed, open
Weight: 2 lb. 10 oz.
Bore/Caliber: .44
Features: Case-hardened frame, steel backstrap, brass trigger guard; blued, round barrel
Steel & Brass model: **$349**
Fluted Steel: **$369**

1861 NAVY REVOLVER

Lock: Caplock revolver
Stock: Walnut
Barrel: 7.5 in.
Sights: Fixed, open
Weight: 2 lb. 10 oz.
Bore/Caliber: .36
Features: Case-hardened frame, steel or brass backstrap and trigger guard
Steel: **$359**
Civil Brass:. **$349**

1862 POCKET NAVY REVOLVER

Lock: Caplock revolver
Stock: Walnut
Barrel: 5.5 in., 6.5 in.
Sights: Fixed, open
Weight: 1 lb. 11 oz.
Bore/Caliber: .36
Features: Case-hardened frame; brass backstrap and trigger guard; octagonal, blued barrel
MSRP. **$369**

1862 POLICE REVOLVER

Lock: Caplock revolver
Stock: Walnut
Barrel: 5.5 in., 6.5 in.
Sights: Fixed, open
Weight: 1 lb. 10 oz.
Bore/Caliber: .36
Features: Case-hardened frame; brass backstrap and trigger guard; fluted round barrel
MSRP. **$369**

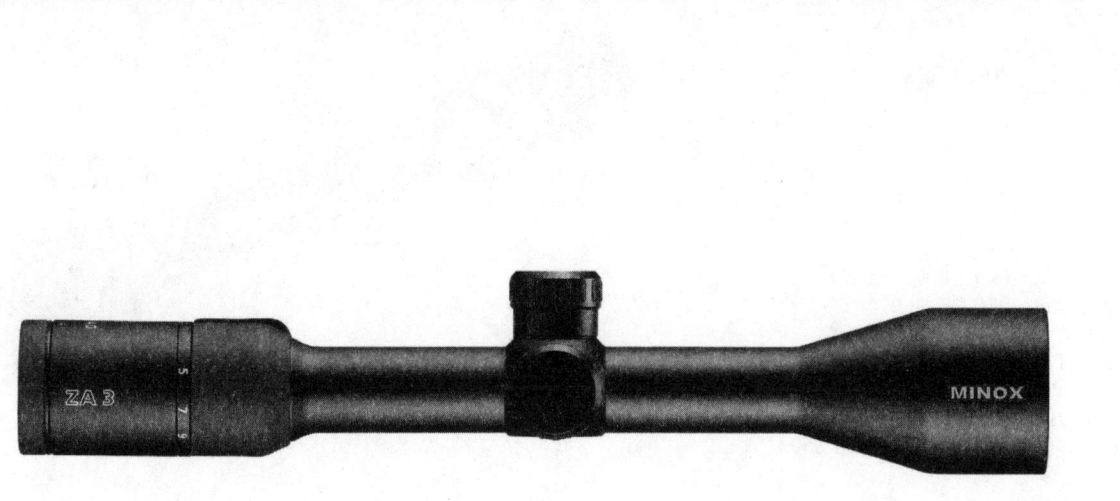

Alpen Optics

APEX XP 3-9X40MM
Weight: 14 oz.
Length: 12.5 in.
Power: 3-9X
Obj. Dia.: 40mm
Main Dia.: 1 in.
Exit Pupil: 13-4.5mm
Field of View: 35-12 ft @ 100 yds
Twilight Factor: 10.95-18.97
Eye Relief: 3.5 in.
Features: Fully multi-coated lens; WBDC-A reticle; matte black finish; fast-focus; side focus adjust; illuminated red-dot reticle
MSRP **$502**

ALPEN APEX
XP 3-9X40MM

APEX XP 6-24X50MM
Weight: 24 oz.
Length: 15.5 in.
Power: 6-24X
Obj. Dia.: 50mm
Main Dia.: 30mm
Exit Pupil: 8-2mm
Field of View: 16-4 ft @ 100 yds
Twilight Factor: 17.3-34.6
Eye Relief: 3.5 in.
Features: Matte black; WBDC-TACT reticle available; also in 1.5-6x42, and in red-dot illuminated-reticle 1.5-6x42, 2.5-10x50, and 4-16x56; 6-24x50 and the 4-16x56 have ⅛ MOA adjustment increments, while the others have ¼ MOA
MSRP **$653**

ALPEN APEX XP
6-24X50MM

KODIAK 3.5-10X50MM
Weight: 21 oz.
Length: 13.2 in.
Power: 3.5-10X
Obj.Dia.: 50mm
Main Dia.: 1 in.
Exit Pupil: 13.5-4.9mm
Field of View: 35-12 ft @ 100 yds
Twilight Factor: 13.2-22.4
Eye Relief: 3 in.
Features: Multi-coated optical design; over-sized zero-reset windage and elevation dials adjustable in ¼ MOA (⅛ MOA in the 6-24x50) clicks; AccuPlex Tapered duplex-style reticle; fast-focus eye piece; matte black; also in 1.5-4x32, 3-9x32, 4x32, 3-9x40, 4-12x40, and 6-24x50
MSRP **$223**

ALPEN KODIAK
3.5-10X50MM

British Small Arms Co. (BSA)

GOLD STAR 2-12X44MM
Weight: 18 oz.
Length: 13.15 in.
Power: 2-12X
Obj.Dia.: 44mm
Main Dia.: 1 in.
Exit Pupil: 22-3.6mm
Field of View: 60-10 ft @ 100 yds
Twilight Factor: 9.38-22.98
Eye Relief: 4 in.
Features: The Gold Star line of rifle-scopes represent the pinnacle of BSA performance optics, exceptional clarity and resolution. 6X zoom system; perfected optical design; EZ Hunter reticle; precision W/E adjustment; side parallax available on some models.
MSRP................$269.95

MAJESTIC DX 4-16X44MM
Weight: 17.6 oz.
Length: 12.66 in.
Power: 4-16X
Obj. Dia.: 44mm
Main Dia.: 1 in.
Exit Pupil: 8-4mm
Field of View: 45-7.3 ft @ 100 yds
Twilight Factor: 13.27-26.53
Eye Relief: 4 in.

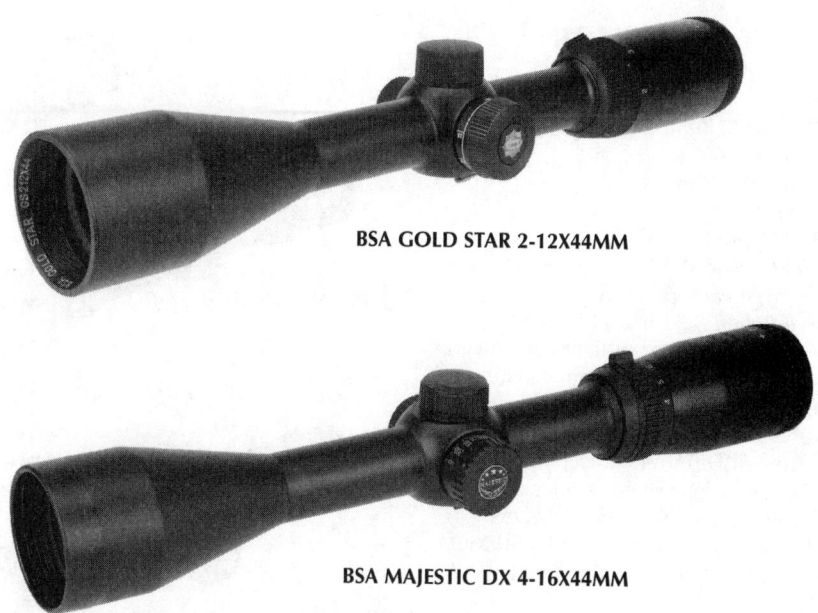

BSA GOLD STAR 2-12X44MM

BSA MAJESTIC DX 4-16X44MM

Features: Newly redesigned one piece tube; fully multi-coated optics; ballistic compensating EZ Hunter reticle; 92 percent light transmission; fast-focus eyepiece
MSRP................$209.95

Burris

FULLFIELD E1 3-9X40MM ILLUMINATED
Weight: 12 oz.
Length: 11.4 in.
Power: 3-9X
Obj. Dia.: 40mm
Main Dia.: 1 in.
Exit Pupil: 17-5mm
Field of View: 45-13 ft @ 100 yds
Twilight Factor: 10.95-18.97
Eye Relief: 3.1-4.1 in.
Features: A series of cascading dots to the left and right of the reticle help compensate for crosswinds. The dots represent a 10 mph crosswind (+/- 1.5" at 400 yds) for most hunting cartridges. For a 5 mph crosswind, halve the distance between dot and reticle. For 20 mph crosswind, simply double the distance. Also available in 2-7x35, 3-9x50, 4.5-14x42, and 6.5-20x50
MSRP................$445

MTAC 4.5-14X42MM
Weight: 17.6 oz.
Length: 13 in.
Power: 4.5-14X
Obj. Dia.: 42mm
Main Dia.: 30mm
Exit Pupil: 24-6mm
Field of View: 22-7.5 ft @ 100 yds
Twilight Factor: 13.75-24.25
Eye Relief: 3.1-3.8 in.
Features: For long-range tactical shooting; adjustable parallax; feature-rich G2B Mil-Dot reticle for precise aiming, distance measurement, holdover, and hold off; new MTAC Mil-Rad knobs with finger-adjustable/resettable dials for windage and elevation; also available in 1-4x-24, 1.5-6x-40, 3.5-10x-42, 6.5-20x-50
MSRP................$828

BURRIS FULLFIELD E1
3-9X40MM

BURRIS MTAC 4.5-14X42MM

Bushnell Performance Optics

BONE COLLECTOR 3-9X40MM DOA 600

Weight: 13 oz.
Length: 12.6 in.
Power: 3-9X
Obj.Dia.: 40mm
Main Dia.: 1 in.
Exit Pupil: 13.3-4.4mm
Field of View: 33.8-11.5 ft @ 100 yds
Twilight Factor: 10.95-18.97
Eye Relief: 3.33 in.
Features: 90-percent light transmission with the "Ultra Wide Band Coating"; RainGuard HD; one-piece aluminum tube with a fast-focus eyepiece; Bushnell DOA reticle technology– DOA 600 for centerfire rifles and DOA 250 for muzzleloaders; ¼ MOA adjustment increments and a 50 MOA range of adjustment for windage and elevation
From: . . . .$349–$434.95

ELITE 3-9X40MM MULTI-X

Weight: 13 oz.
Length: 12.6 in.
Power: 3-9X
Obj.Dia.: 40mm
Main Dia.: 1 in.
Exit Pupil: 13.3-4.44mm
Field of View: 33.8-11.5 ft @ 100 yds
Twilight Factor: 10.95-18.97
Eye Relief: 3.4 in.
Features: Bushnell's "Ultra Wide Band Coating"; lenses treated with moisture shedding RainGuard HD; fingertip windage and elevation adjustments are audible and resettable and in ¼ MOA increments; also in 1.25-4x24, 2.5-10x40, 2.5-10x50, 4-16x40 Multi-X, 4-16x40 DOA 600, 4-16x50, 6-24x40 Mil-Dot, 6-24x40 Multi-X, 8-32x40 Multi-X, 2-7x 32, 3-10x40, 3-9x40 (Gloss/Silver), 3-9x40 FireFly, 3-9x40 DOA 600, 3-9x50 Multi-X, 3-9x50 DOA 600, 3-9x50 FireFly
MSRP $423.95

ELITE 6500 2.5-16X50MM MIL-DOT

Weight: 21 oz.
Length: 13.5 in.
Power: 2.5-16X
Obj.Dia.: 50mm
Main Dia.: 30mm
Exit Pupil: 20-3.12mm
Field of View: 42-7 ft @ 100 yds
Twilight Factor: 11.18-28.28

BUSHNELL BONE COLLECTOR
3-9X40MM DOA 600

BUSHNELL ELITE
3-9X40MM MULTI-X

BUSHNELL
ELITE TACTICAL
3-12X44MM

BUSHNELL
ELITE TACTICAL
6-24X50MM

BUSHNELL ELITE 6500
2.5-16X50MM MIL-DOT

Eye Relief: 3.9 in.
Features: Lenses with 60-layer "Ultra Wide Band Coating"; 91-percent total light transmission through the scope; RainGuard HD; windage and elevation adjustments in ¼ MOA audible increments; also in 1.25x-8x32, 2.5-16x42 Fine Multi-X, 2.5-16x42 Mil-Dot, 2.5-16x50 FMX, 4.5-30x50 DOA 600, 4.5-30x50 Fine Multi-X, 4.5-30x50 Mil-Dot
MSRP $1070.95

ELITE TACTICAL 3-12X44MM

Weight: 24.4 oz.
Length: 13 in.
Power: 3-12X
Obj.Dia.: 44mm
Main Dia.: 30mm
Exit Pupil: 14.66-3.66mm
Field of View: 36-10 ft @ 100 yds
Twilight Factor: 11.48-22.97
Eye Relief: 3.75 in.
Features: Tactical treatment of Elite 6500 riflescope; tactical target-adjustment turrets and non-glare black-matte finish as well as "blacked-out" cosmetics for concealment; Bushnell "Ultra Wide Band Coating" optics; RainGuard HD coating; illuminated and non-illuminated Mil-Dot reticles; also in 10x44, 2.5-16x42, 4.5-30x50, 5-15x40, 6-24x50 Mil-Dot, 6-24x50 Illuminated Mil-Dot
MSRP $1366.95

ELITE TACTICAL 6-24X50MM

Weight: 27 oz.
Length: 13.5 in.
Power: 6-24X
Obj.Dia.: 50mm
Main Dia.: 30mm
Exit Pupil: 7.5-2.1mm
Field of View: 17.5-4.5 ft @ 100 yds
Twilight Factor: 17.32-24
Eye Relief: 4 in.
Features: Exceptional brightness and extended-range magnification with side parallax; RainGuard HD; fully multi-coated optics; ultra-strong, one-piece tube; .1 Mil click value; 3" sunshade; side parallax adjustment; available in Mil-Dot, Illuminated Mil-Dot, G2, and Illuminated BTR-Mil reticles
MSRP $1192.95

Bushnell Performance Optics

ELITE TACTICAL 10X40MM MIL-DOT

Weight: 15.9 oz.
Length: 11.5 in.
Power: 10X
Obj.Dia.: 40mm
Main Dia.: 1 in.
Exit Pupil: 4mm
Field of View: 11-3.7 ft @ 100 yds
Twilight Factor: 20
Eye Relief: 3.5 in.
Features: Fixed-power target scope with Mil-Dot reticle and target turret; RainGuard HD; ultra wide band coating; fully multi-coated optics; blacked-out finish; target turrets
MSRP $379.95

ELITE TACTICAL HDMR AND DMR 3.5-21X50MM

Weight: 32.5 oz.
Length: 13.2 in.
Power: 3.5-21X
Obj. Dia.: 50mm
Main Dia.: 34mm
Exit Pupil: 10.4-2.4mm
Field of View: 25.3 ft @ 100 yds
Twilight Factor: 13.23-21.21
Eye Relief: 3.74 in.
Features: These scopes are part of the Bushnell extended range riflescope (ERS) family designed to give tactical marksmen a powerful optic that works equally well in short or extended range shooting applications. The Bushnell Elite Tactical HDMR is available with the Horus H59 and TreMor 2 reticles, and the Elite Tactical DMR features the G2DMR and Mil-Dot reticles.
MSRP $2119.95

LEGEND ULTRA HD 1.75-5X32MM DOA 200

Weight: 13 oz.
Length: 10.25 in.
Power: 1.75-5X
Obj. Dia.: 32mm
Main Dia.: 30mm
Exit Pupil: 18.2-6.4mm
Field of View: 49-17 ft @ 100 yds
Twilight Factor: 7.48-12.65
Eye Relief: 4.5 in.
Features: The perfect scope for medium range hunting with a shotgun; RainGuard HD; fully multi-coated optics; ultra-strong, one-piece tube; parallax set at 75 yds; waterproof, fog-

BUSHNELL ELITE TACTICAL
10X40MM MIL-DOT

BUSHNELL ELITE TACTICAL HDMR
AND DMR 3.5-21X50MM

BUSHNELL LEGEND
ULTRA HD 1.75-5X32MM

BUSHNELL TROPHY XLT
3-9X40MM MIL-DOT

proof, and shockproof; fast-focus eyepiece; also in 1.75-5x32 Multi-X/DOA Crossbow, 3-9x40 Multi-X/DOA 600, 3-9x50 Multi-X/DOA 600, 4.5-14x44 Multi-X/Mil-Dot
MSRP $378.95

TROPHY XLT 3-9X40MM MIL-DOT

Weight: 14.1 oz.
Length: 11.9 in.
Power: 3-9X
Obj.Dia.: 40mm
Main Dia.: 1 in.
Exit Pupil: 13.3-4.4mm
Field of View: 40-13 ft @ 100 yds
Twilight Factor: 10.95-18.97

Eye Relief: 4 in.
Features: 91-percent total light transmission; one-piece tube with integrated saddle; 1/4 MOA fingertip windage and elevation adjustments with range of adjustment of 80 MOA; Butler Creek flip-up scope covers; some scopes available in gloss, matte, silver, or camo finishes; also in 3-9x40 DOA 250, 3-9x40 DOA 600, 3-9x40 Multi-X, 3-9x40 Circle-X, 3-9x50, 4-12x40 DOA 600, 4-12x40 Multi-X, 1-4x24, 1.5-6x42, 1.5-6x44, 3-12x56, 1.75-4x32, 2-6x32, 2-7x36 DOA Crossbow, 2-7x36 DOA 200, 3-9x40 DOA 200, 6-18x50
MSRP $204.95

Bushnell Performance Optics

TROPHY XLT CROSSBOW SCOPE 2-7X36MM

Weight: 14.3 oz.
Length: 13 in.
Power: 2-7X
Obj.Dia.: 36mm
Main Dia.: 1 in.
Exit Pupil: 13.3-4.4mm
Field of View: 33-11 ft @ 100 yds
Twilight Factor: 8.5-15.9
Eye Relief: 5 in.
Features: One-piece tube with an integrated mounting saddle; Butler Creek flip-up caps; 91-percent light transmission; DOA Crossbow reticle; ¼ MOA fingertip windage and elevation adjustments allow for extended-range shooting out to 60 yards
MSRP **$227.95**

BUSHNELL TROPHY
XLT CROSSBOW SCOPE
2-7X36MM

Cabela's

30MM TACTICAL CLASSIC 6-18X50MM EXT SF

Weight: 17.5 oz.
Length: 13.23 in.
Power: 6-18X
Obj.Dia.: 50mm
Main Dia.: 30mm
Exit Pupil: 8.33-2.77mm
Field of View: 15.88-5.24 ft @ 100 yds
Twilight Factor: 17.32-30
Eye Relief: 4 in.
Features: Tactical-grade 30mm tube; Guidetech broadband lens technology; machined to military-grade tolerances; low-profile turrets with ⅛ MOA click windage and elevation adjustments; hard-blasted anodized finish and moisture- and dust-repelling lenses; also in 2.5-10x50 and 8-32 SFx50 with both EXT and Duplex reticles
MSRP **$439.99**

ALASKAN GUIDE 1-INCH EXT 3-10X40MM

Weight: 13.5 oz.
Length: 12.8 in.
Power: 3-10X
Obj.Dia.: 40mm
Main Dia.: 1 in.
Exit Pupil: 13.33-4mm
Field of View: 33.65-10.48 ft @ 100 yds
Twilight Factor: 10.95-20
Eye Relief: 3.75 in.
Features: EXT— "extended range"; "Guidetech" broadband lens coating technology; one-piece tube; components machined to military-grade tolerances; low-profile turrets with ¼ MOA click windage and elevation adjustments; hard-blasted anodized finish for durability and corrosion resistance; moisture- and dust-repelling lenses; also in 4-12x44SF, 6-18x50SF EXT, and 3-10x40, 4-12x44SF, and 6-18x50SF
MSRP **$269.99**

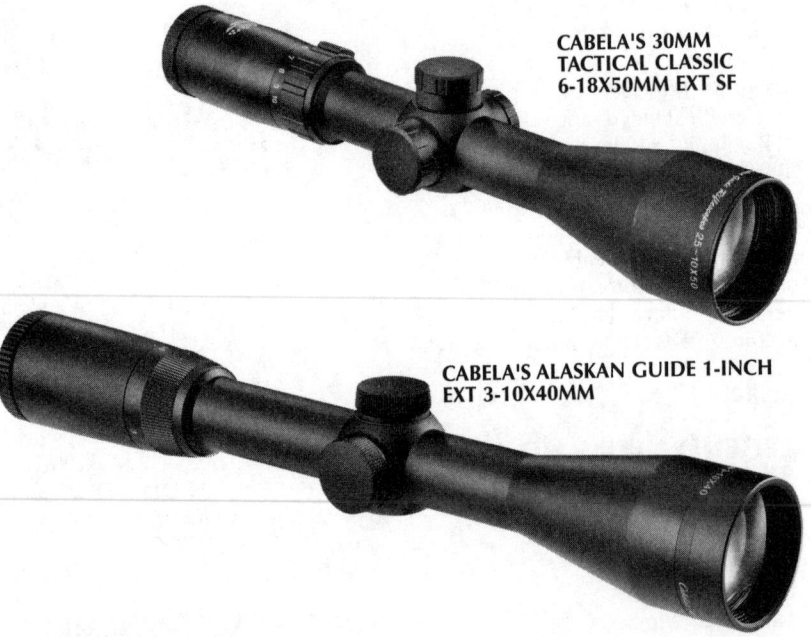

CABELA'S 30MM
TACTICAL CLASSIC
6-18X50MM EXT SF

CABELA'S ALASKAN GUIDE 1-INCH
EXT 3-10X40MM

ALASKAN GUIDE 30MM RANGEFINDING 3-12X52MM SF

Weight: 21.9 oz.
Length: 14 in.
Power: 3-12X
Obj.Dia.: 52mm
Main Dia.: 30mm
Exit Pupil: 17.33-4.33mm
Field of View: 31.5-7.8 ft @ 100 yds
Twilight Factor: 12.48-24.97
Eye Relief: 4 in.
Features: Also in 4-16SFx52, and both with side-focus parallax adjustment and with Duplex and EXT reticles; 30mm tube and 52mm objective for added light gathering an enhanced field of view with less aberration
MSRP $269.99

ALASKAN GUIDE PREMIUM RIFLESCOPES

Weight: 14.7 oz.–15 oz.
Length: 14.3-15.75 in.
Power: 4-12X, 6-20X
Obj.Dia.: 40mm
Main Dia.: 1 in.
Exit Pupil: 13.33-4.44mm
Field of View: 25.5-8.4 ft @ 100 yds, 16.1 ft @ 100 yds
Twilight Factor: 10.95-18.97
Eye Relief: 3.5 in.
Features: One-piece aluminum tube; rubber coated power adjustment; positive-click increments on the fast-focus eyepiece; metal-to-metal contact between the windage and elevation adjustments and the erector tube; and ½ MOA adjustments; knurled AO ring on higher magnification scopes; adjustable objective–AO
MSRP . . . . $399.99–$449.99

CALIBER-SPECIFIC RIFLESCOPES

Weight: 14.6 oz.–15.3 oz.
Length: 12-13.2 in.
Power: 3-9X, 3-12X (.223)
Obj. Dia.: 40mm
Main Dia.: 1 in.
Exit Pupil: 13.33-4.44mm, 13.33-3.33mm (.223)
Field of View: 32.3-11.3 ft @ 100 yds, 28.8-7 ft @ 100 yds (.22 Mag.)
Twilight Factor: 10.95-18.97
Eye Relief: 4.1-3.8 in., 4.3-3.7 in. (.22 Mag.)
Features: Precision scopes specifically built to match your favorite target and varmint calibers; caliber-specific EXT bullet-drop reticles (in .17 HMR, .22 LR, .22 Mag., and .223) take the guesswork out of long-range shooting with crosshairs precisely calibrated to the bullet drop of a specific caliber; ¼-MOA adjustments; matte finish
MSRP . . . . $99.99–$149.99

CABELA'S ALASKAN GUIDE PREMIUM EXT 3-9X40MM

OPTICS

CABELA'S ALASKAN GUIDE 30MM RANGEFINDING 3-12X52MM SF

CABELA'S CALIBER-SPECIFIC RIFLESCOPES

Cabela's

EURO RIFLESCOPE DUPLEX 3-9X42MM

Weight: 16 oz.
Length: 12.4 in.
Power: 3-9X
Obj.Dia.: 42mm
Main Dia.: 1 in.
Exit Pupil: 14-4.66mm
Field of View: 36.3-12.1 ft @ 100 yds
Twilight Factor: 11.22-19.44
Eye Relief: 3.75 in.
Features: CNC machined from a single billet of aircraft-aluminum; ELOX (electrolytic oxidation) anodization for a reduced-glare black matte, abrasion-resistant finish; fully multi-coated lenses; fast-focus eyepieces; elevation and windage turrets are finger adjustable in ¼ MOA clicks; also with EXT reticle, and in 4-12x50 and 6-18x50 with EXT and Duplex reticles
MSRP $449.99

LEVER ACTION 3-9X40MM

Weight: 14.64 oz.
Length: 13 in.
Power: 3-9X
Obj.Dia.: 40mm
Main Dia.: 1 in.
Exit Pupil: 13.33-4.44mm
Field of View: 30.55-9.6 ft @ 100 yds
Twilight Factor: 10.95-18.97
Eye Relief: 5.5 in.
Features: Ballistic Glass Reticles specifically engineered for use with a particular Hornady LEVERevolution round; tube is machined aluminum and lenses are multi-coated; windage and elevation are adjustable in ¼ MOA clicks; .30-30 Winchester Reticle (also in .308 Marlin, .338 Marlin Express, .444 Marlin, .35 Rem., and .45-70 Govt. reticles)
MSRP $119.99

POWDERHORN MUZZLELOADER 3-10X40MM

Weight: 11.6 oz.
Length: 12.2 in.
Power: 3-10X
Obj.Dia.: 40mm
Main Dia.: 1 in.
Exit Pupil: 13.33-4mm
Field of View: 31.5-10.5 ft @ 100 yds
Twilight Factor: 10.95-20

CABELA'S EURO RIFLESCOPE DUPLEX 3-9X42MM

Eye Relief: 3.75 in.
Features: Ballistic reticle regulated to match bullet drop; when the scope is sighted in at 100 yards at 10X, the next bar down is calibrated for a drop at 150 yards and the lowest bar down for 250 yards; loading data is based on the 250-grain saboted bullet and 150 grains of Triple Se7en FFg powder; hand-turn ¼ MOA click adjustments; also in silver and camo
MSRP $99.99

CABELA'S LEVER ACTION 3-9X40MM

CABELA'S POWDERHORN MUZZLELOADER 3-10X40MM

OPTICS

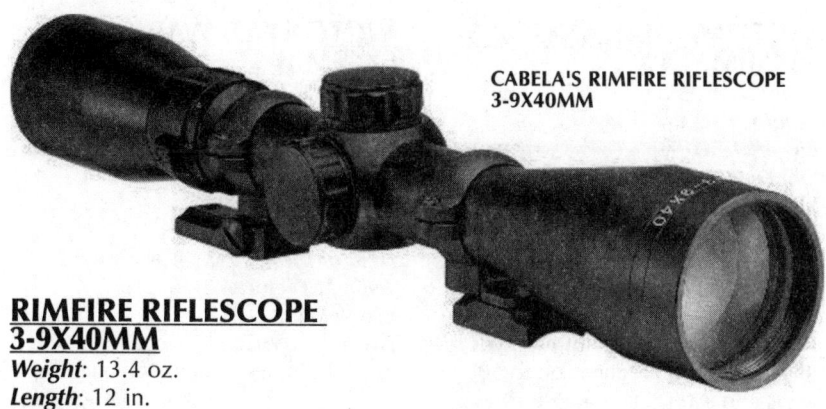

CABELA'S RIMFIRE RIFLESCOPE 3-9X40MM

SHOTGUNS/ BLACKPOWDER 2.5-7X32MM

Weight: 12.2 oz.
Length: 11.8 in.
Power: 2.5-7X
Obj.Dia.: 32mm
Main Dia.: 1 in.
Exit Pupil: 12.8-4.57mm
Field of View: 40.03-14.15 ft @ 100 yds
Twilight Factor: 8.94-14.96
Eye Relief: 4 in.
Features: For use with slug guns and muzzleloading rifles; extended eye relief and expanded exit pupil to promote faster target acquisition; rigid machined-aluminum tube; low-profile turrets for windage and elevation adjustments; also available in Seclusion 3D camouflage; Diamond reticle; also with Duplex reticle and in camo, and in 2.5x32 fixed power with Diamond reticle
MSRP. . . . . **$99.99–$119.99**

RIMFIRE RIFLESCOPE 3-9X40MM

Weight: 13.4 oz.
Length: 12 in.
Power: 3-9X
Obj.Dia.: 40mm
Main Dia.: 1 in.
Exit Pupil: 13.33-4.44mm
Field of View: 37.7-12.4 ft @ 100 yds
Twilight Factor: 10.95-18.97
Eye Relief: 4 in.
Features: For hunting, target shooting, or plinking with a rimfire rifle; parallax-free at 50 yards; multi-coated glass optics; extended eye relief and an expanded exit pupil; low-profile windage and elevation turrets; Duplex reticle; also in 4x32
MSRP. **$79.99**

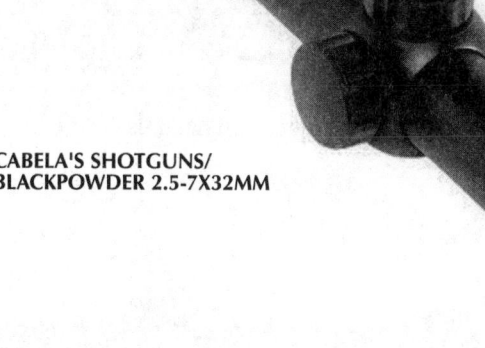

CABELA'S SHOTGUNS/ BLACKPOWDER 2.5-7X32MM

OPTICS

Carl Zeiss Sports Optics

CONQUEST 3-9X40MM

Weight: 15.17 oz.
Length: 12.9 in.
Power: 3-9X
Obj.Dia.: 40mm
Main Dia.: 1 in.
Exit Pupil: 13.3-4.4mm
Field of View: 34-11 ft @ 100 yds
Twilight Factor: 8.5-19.0
Eye Relief: 4 in.
Features: Classic, all-purpose scope with excellent light gathering ability; wide fields of view, brilliant contrast and high resolution images; perfect for shotguns, muzzle loaders and centerfire rifles; variety of reticles including the Rapid-Z Ballistic Reticle; featured with #20 reticle, also in 3-9x40; 3.5-10x44, 4.5-14x44, 3-9x50, 3.5-10x50, 4.5-14x50, 6.5-20x50, 3-12x56
MSRP. **$555.54**

CARL ZEISS CONQUEST 3-9X40MM

Carl Zeiss Sports Optics

CONQUEST 6.5-20X50MM
Weight: 21.83 oz.
Length: 15.6 in.
Power: 6.5-20X
Obj.Dia.: 50mm
Main Dia.: 1 in.
Exit Pupil: 7.7-2.5mm
Field of View: 18-6 ft @ 100 yds
Twilight Factor: 18-31.6
Eye Relief: 3.5 in.
Features: Parallax adjustment for varmints or long-range shooting; available with either target or hunting turret; variety of reticles including the Rapid-Z 800 and Rapid-Z 1000 Ballistic Reticles; featured with #4 or #20 reticles
MSRP $1144.43

VICTORY DIARANGE 2.5-10X50MM T*
Weight: 31.75 oz.
Length: 13.2 in.
Power: 2.5-10X
Obj.Dia.: 56.5mm
Main Dia.: 56.5mm
Exit Pupil: 15-5mm
Field of View: 43.5-12 ft @ 100 yds
Twilight Factor: 7.1-22.4
Eye Relief: 3.5 in.
Features: Laser ranges from 10 yds to 999 yds ± 1 yd at ranges up to 600 yards and ± 0.5% at ranges beyond 600 yards in a measuring time of 0.5 seconds; used in temperatures between -13° to 122°F; illuminated #43 Mil-Dot and illuminated Rapid-Z® 600 & 800 reticles; also in 3-12x56 T*
MSRP $4444.43

VICTORY DIAVARI 1.5-6X42MM T*
Weight: 15.52 oz.
Length: 12.25 in.
Power: 1.5-6X
Obj.Dia.: 42mm
Main Dia.: 30mm
Exit Pupil: 15-7mm
Field of View: 72-23 ft @ 100 yds
Twilight Factor: 4.2-15.9
Eye Relief: 3.5 in.
Features: LotuTec lens coating and ZEISS T* multi-coating; compact, lightweight, low profile scope designed for fast target acquisition; available with rail mount and with illumination on select models; also in 2.5-10x50 T*, 3-12x56 T*, 4-16x50 T* FL, 6-24x56 T* FL, and 6-24x72 T* FL
MSRP $1888.88

CARL ZEISS CONQUEST 6.5-20X50MM

CARL ZEISS VICTORY DIARANGE
2.5-10X50MM T*

CARL ZEISS VICTORY DIAVARI
1.5-6X42MM T*

OPTICS

Carl Zeiss Sports Optics

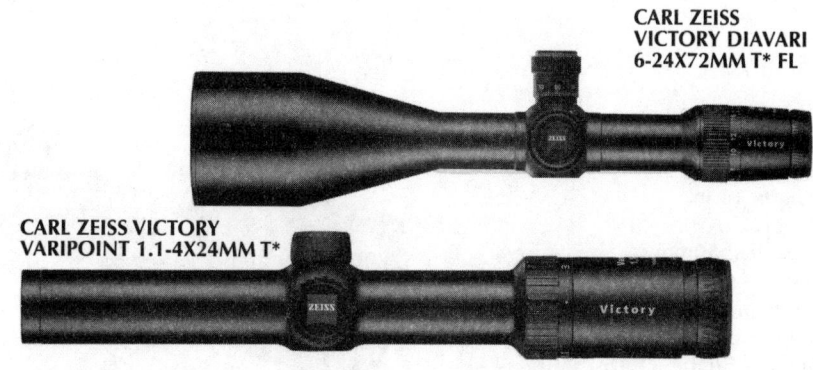

CARL ZEISS
VICTORY DIAVARI
6-24X72MM T* FL

CARL ZEISS VICTORY
VARIPOINT 1.1-4X24MM T*

VICTORY DIAVARI 6-24X72MM T* FL

Weight: 37.39 oz.
Length: 14.9 in.
Power: 6-24X
Obj.Dia.: 72mm
Main Dia.: 34mm
Exit Pupil: 12-3mm
Field of View: 18.3-5.1 ft @ 100 yds
Twilight Factor: 16.9-41.6
Eye Relief: 3.5 in.
Features: FL glass objective and LotuTec coating; two ballistic-compensation options—BDC Ballistic Turret and Rapid Z Ballistic reticle; designed for tactical marksmen, varmint or predator hunters, and long-range hunters and shooters; parallax compensation and ¼ MOA lockable windage and elevation turrets; available with illumination
MSRP **$3999.99**

VICTORY HT 1.1-4X24MM

Weight: 15.5 oz.
Length: 11.37 in.
Power: 1.1-4X
Obj. Dia.: 30mm
Main Dia.: 30mm
Exit Pupil: 14.8mm
Field of View: 114-31.5 ft @ 100 yds
Twilight Factor: 3.1-9.8
Eye Relief: 3.54 in.
Features: With its large exit pupil and wide field of view on low power, this smallest VICTORY HT is perfect for any shooting requiring extremely fast target acquisition; the new reticle #54 with the fine cross on the illuminated dot allows you to shoot with confidence, even when the illuminated red-dot is turned off; also available with reticle #60; LotuTec coating
MSRP **$2555.54**

VICTORY HT 2.5-10X50MM

Weight: 20.2 oz.
Length: 13.66 in.
Power: 3-12X
Obj. Dia.: 63mm
Main Dia.: 30mm
Exit Pupil: 14.9-4.7mm
Field of View: 37.5-25.9 ft @ 100 yds
Twilight Factor: 8.5-25.9
Eye Relief: 3.54 in.
Features: The largest of the VICTORY HT line, this 3-12x56 model makes targets visible in the very last of shooting light; the combination of the advanced HT glass, high-performance 56mm objective lens, the super-fine illuminated dot, and ASV+ turret option makes this scope deadly accurate at any distance, in any light; LotuTec lens coating
MSRP **$2666.66**

VICTORY VARIPOINT 1.1-4X24MM T*

Weight: 15.87 oz.
Length: 11.8 in.
Power: 1.1-4X
Obj.Dia.: 24mm
Main Dia.: 30mm

Exit Pupil: 14.8-6mm
Field of View: 108-31 ft @ 100 yds
Twilight Factor: 3.1-9.9
Eye Relief: 3.5 in.
Features: Illuminated red-dot reticle for fast target acquisition; LotuTec "hydrophobic" lens coating; also in 1.5-6x42 T*, 2.5-10x50 T*, and 3-12x56 T*
MSRP **$2499.99**

VICTORY VARIPOINT 3-12X56MM T*

Weight: 21.34 oz.
Length: 14 in.
Power: 3-12X
Obj.Dia.: 56mm
Main Dia.: 30mm
Exit Pupil: 14.7-4.7mm
Field of View: 37.5-10.5 ft @ 100 yds
Twilight Factor: 8.5-25.9
Eye Relief: 3.5 in.
Features: The large objective lens of the Victory Varipoint 3-12x56 T*, is traditional for European scopes that are often used from shooting towers in low light.
MSRP **$2666.66**

OPTICS

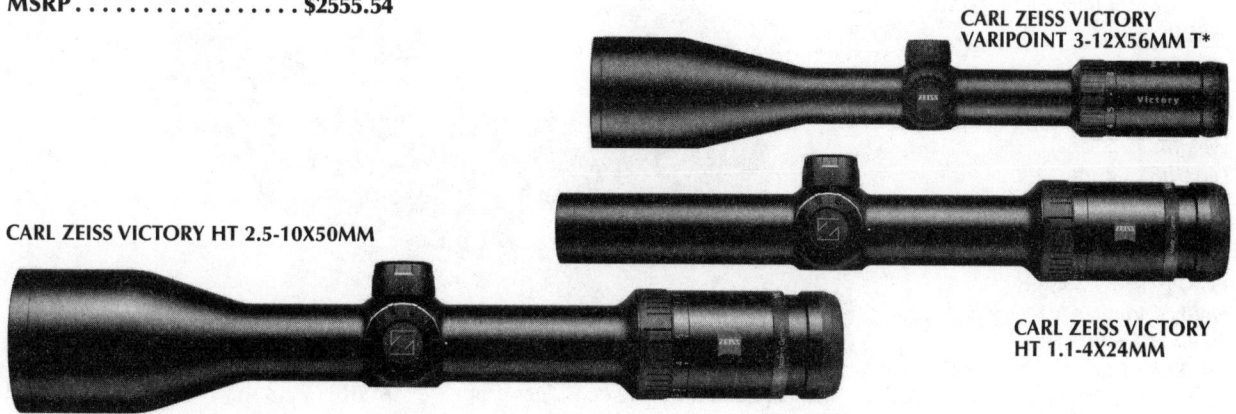

CARL ZEISS VICTORY
VARIPOINT 3-12X56MM T*

CARL ZEISS VICTORY HT 2.5-10X50MM

CARL ZEISS VICTORY
HT 1.1-4X24MM

Kruger Optical

TACDRIVER T4I 2.5-10X50MM

Weight: 24 oz.
Length: 13 in.
Power: 2.5-10X
Obj. Dia.: 50mm
Main Dia.: 30mm
Exit Pupil: 5-12mm
Field of View: 38-10.5 ft @ 100 yds
Twilight Factor: 11.18-23.36
Eye Relief: 3.25 in.
Features: These scopes are equipped with proprietary illuminated glass-etched reticles with multiple brightness levels for low-light target engagement. The easy-to-operate 4x magnification system provides a solid zoom range for target acquisition at various distances. Also available in 1-4x24, 1.5-5x32, 6-24x50, and 10-40x56
MSRP **$399.99**

KRUGER TACDRIVER T4I 2.5-10X50MM

Leatherwood/Hi-Lux

CLOSE MEDIUM RANGE (CMR) 1-4X24MM

Weight: 16.5 oz.
Length: 10.2 in.
Power: 1-4X
Obj.Dia.: 24mm
Main Dia.: 30mm
Exit Pupil: 11.1-6mm
Field of View: 94.8-26.2 ft @ 100 yds
Twilight Factor: 4.89-9.79
Eye Relief: 3 in.
Features: Zero-locking turrets; large external target-style windage and elevation adjustment knobs; power-ring extended lever handle for power change; CMR ranging reticle for determining range and also BDC hold over value good for .223, .308, and other calibers; green or red illuminated reticle; turrets adjustable in ½ MOA clicks
MSRP **$399**

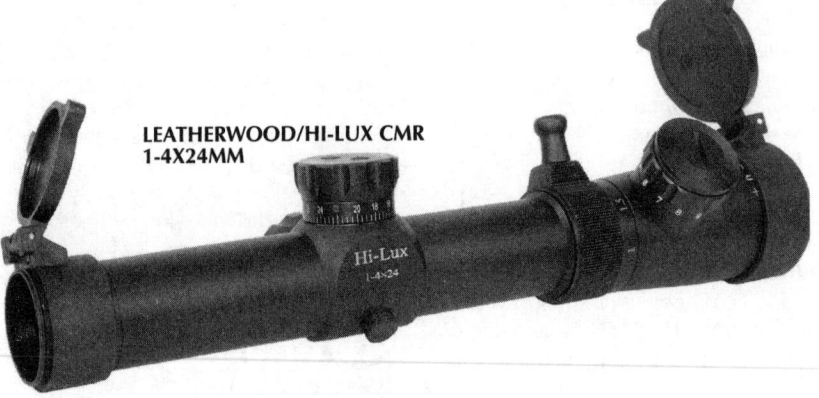

LEATHERWOOD/HI-LUX CMR 1-4X24MM

LEATHERWOOD/HI-LUX M-1000 ART 2.5-10X44MM

M-1000 AUTO RANGING TRAJECTORY 2.5-10X44MM

Weight: 25.2 oz.
Length: 13.2 in.
Power: 2.5-10X
Obj.Dia.: 44mm
Main Dia.: 1 in.
Exit Pupil: 10.2-4mm
Field of View: 47.2-11.9 ft @ 100 yds
Twilight Factor: 10.5-21
Eye Relief: 3.1 in.
Features: Compensates for the bullet

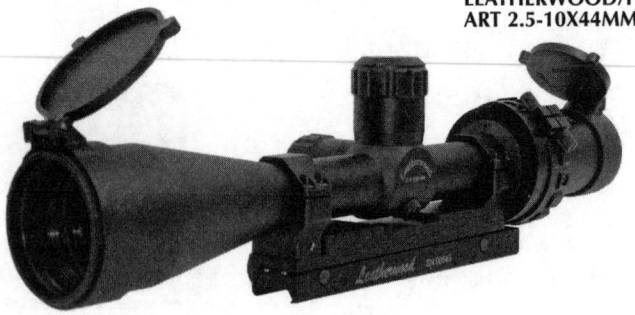

drop automatically by using an external cam system; can be calibrated for most centerfire rifle cartridges–from .223 to .50 BMG; comes with mount and rings; "No-Math Mil-Dot" reticle
MSRP **$459**

OPTICS

MALCOLM 8X USMC SNIPER SCOPE

Weight: 25.4 oz.
Length: 22.1 in.
Power: 8X
Obj. Dia.: 31mm
Main Dia.: .75 in.
Exit Pupil: 4.2mm
Field of View: 11 ft @ 100 yds
Twilight Factor: 15.75
Eye Relief: 3.15 in.
Features: Fully multi-coated lens; fine cross reticle; elevation and wind adjustment ¼ MOA per click at the mounts
MSRP **$521.55**

LEATHERWOOD/HI-LUX MALCOLM 8X USMC SNIPER SCOPE

TOBY BRIDGES SERIES HIGH PERFORMANCE MUZZLELOADING 3-9X40MM MATTE BLACK

Weight: 15.8 oz.
Length: 12.5 in.
Power: 3-9X
Obj.Dia.: 40mm
Main Dia.: 1 in.
Exit Pupil: 13.3-4.4mm
Field of View: 39-13 ft @ 100 yds
Twilight Factor: 10.9-19
Eye Relief: 3.25 in.
Features: The TB/ML scope is designed for in-line ignition muzzleloaders and saboted bullets. It offers multiple reticles for shooting at ranges out to 250 yards.
Blue: **$179**
Silver: **$189**

LEATHERWOOD/HI-LUX TOBY BRIDGES MUZZLELOADING

TOP ANGLE SERIES 30X50MM

Weight: 39.8 oz.
Length: 17.2 in.
Power: 7-30X
Obj.Dia.: 50mm
Main Dia.: 30mm
Exit Pupil: 6.9-2.3mm
Field of View: 10.6-3.5 ft @ 100 yds
Twilight Factor: 18.70-38.72
Eye Relief: 3.33 in.
Features: Larger diameter turret housing offers additional windage-elevation adjustment in ¼ MOA clicks; top-angle objective lens focus rather than adjustment on the objective lens bell; and Mil-Dot reticle for determining range; also in 3-12x50 and 4-16x50
MSRP **$475**

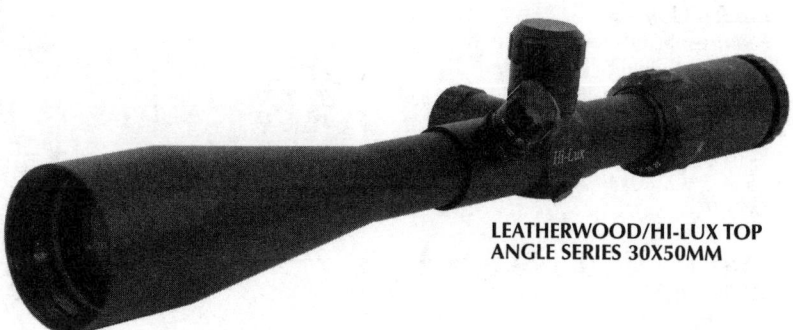

LEATHERWOOD/HI-LUX TOP ANGLE SERIES 30X50MM

OPTICS

Leatherwood/Hi-Lux

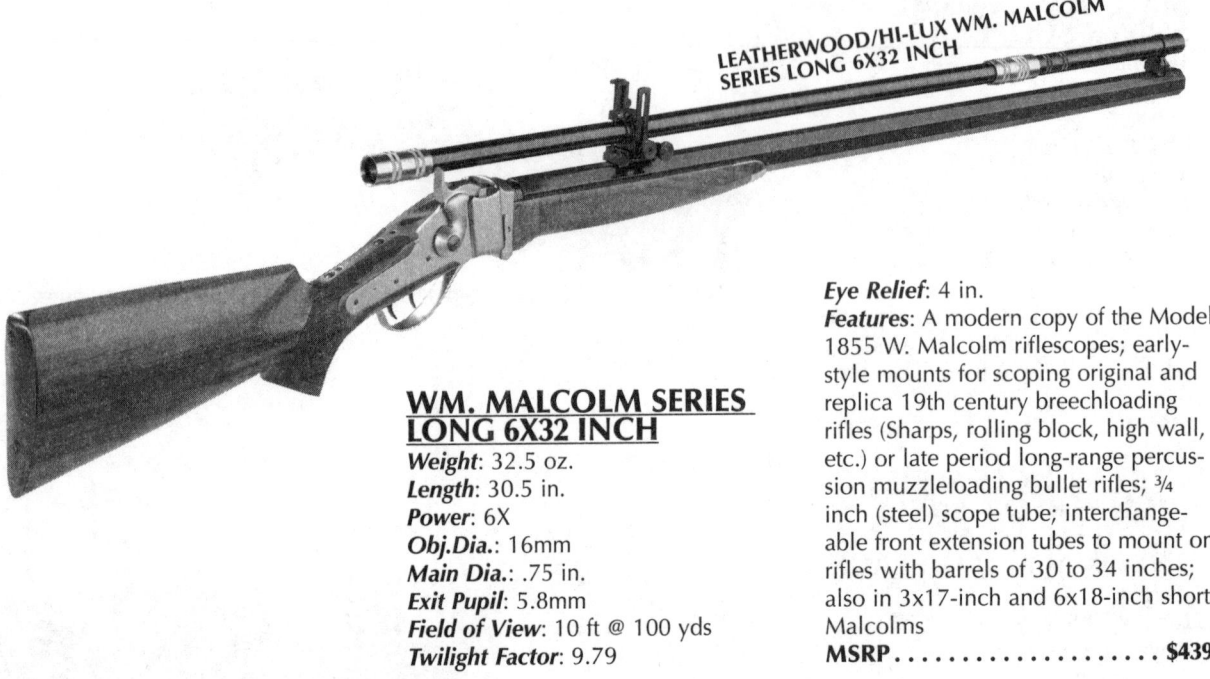

LEATHERWOOD/HI-LUX WM. MALCOLM SERIES LONG 6X32 INCH

WM. MALCOLM SERIES LONG 6X32 INCH
Weight: 32.5 oz.
Length: 30.5 in.
Power: 6X
Obj.Dia.: 16mm
Main Dia.: .75 in.
Exit Pupil: 5.8mm
Field of View: 10 ft @ 100 yds
Twilight Factor: 9.79

Eye Relief: 4 in.
Features: A modern copy of the Model 1855 W. Malcolm riflescopes; early-style mounts for scoping original and replica 19th century breechloading rifles (Sharps, rolling block, high wall, etc.) or late period long-range percussion muzzleloading bullet rifles; ¾ inch (steel) scope tube; interchangeable front extension tubes to mount on rifles with barrels of 30 to 34 inches; also in 3x17-inch and 6x18-inch short Malcolms
MSRP $439

Leupold & Stevens

FX-3 COMPETITION HUNTER 6X42MM
Weight: 15 oz.
Length: 12.2 in.
Power: 6X
Obj.Dia.: 42mm
Main Dia.: 1 in.
Exit Pupil: 7mm
Field of View: 17.3 ft @ 100 yds
Twilight Factor: 15.87
Eye Relief: 4.4 in.
Features: Fixed-power riflescope; Xtended Twilight Lens System; DiamondCoat 2; blackened lens edges; windage and elevation adjustments are ¼ MOA; also available in 12x40 AO, 25x40 AO, 30x40 AO, and 6x42
MSRP $589.99

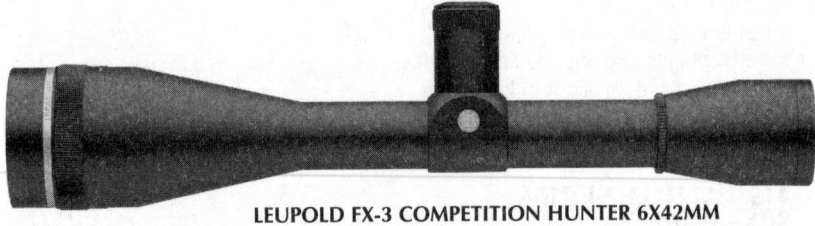

LEUPOLD FX-3 COMPETITION HUNTER 6X42MM

LEUPOLD MARK 4 CQ/T 1-3X14MM

MARK 4 CQ/T 1-3X14MM
Weight: 17.5 oz.
Length: 8.8 in.
Power: 1-3X
Obj.Dia.: 30mm
Main Dia.: 2.9 in.
Exit Pupil: 30-10mm
Field of View: 112-41 ft @ 100 yds
Twilight Factor: 3.74-6.48

Eye Relief: 2.8-2 in.
Features: Close Quarters/Tactical (CQ/T) riflescope combines a red dot at close range with a variable-power optic; Circle Dot reticle is visible with or without illumination or batteries; eleven reticle-illumination settings; slotted ½ MOA click adjustments for windage and elevation
MSRP $1374.99

OPTICS

MARK 4 MR/T 2.5-8X36MM M1

Weight: 16 oz.
Length: 11.33 in.
Power: 2.5-8X
Obj.Dia.: 36mm
Main Dia.: 30mm
Exit Pupil: 14.4-4.5mm
Field of View: 35.5-13.6 ft @ 100 yds
Twilight Factor: 9.48-16.97
Eye Relief: 3.7-3 in.
Features: Xtended Twilight Lens System and DiamondCoat 2; M1 dials are ¼ MOA for windage and elevation; finger-adjustable with audible, tactile clicks; illuminated Mil-Dot, Tactical Milling Reticle (TMR),and non-illuminated TMR versions available; flip-open lens covers; also available in 1.5-5x20, 1.5-5x20 M2, and 2.5-8x36 M2 models
MSRP **$1189.99**
IR: **$1374.99**

MARK AR 3-9X40MM T2

Weight: 12.5 oz.
Length: 12.4 in.
Power: 3-9X
Obj.Dia.: 40mm
Main Dia.: 1 in.
Exit Pupil: 13.33-4.44mm
Field of View: 32.3-14.0 ft @ 100 yds
Twilight Factor: 10.95-18.97
Eye Relief: 4.7-3.7 in.
Features: Multi-coated 4 lens system; ½ MOA T2 elevation adjustment includes a pre-engraved Bullet Drop Compensation (BDC) dial to match the ballistics of most 55-grain loads, including the .223 Rem. and 5.56 NATO; large power selector dial with aggressive knurling; also available in 1.5-4x20, 4-12x40 AO T2, and 6-18x40 AO T1 models
Duplex reticle: **$374.99**
Mil-Dot: **$439.99**

RIFLEMAN 3-9X40MM

Weight: 12.6 oz.
Length: 12.33 in.
Power: 3.3-8.5X (actual)
Obj.Dia.: 40mm
Main Dia.: 1 in.
Exit Pupil: 12-4.7mm
Field of View: 329-131 ft @ 1000 yds
Twilight Factor: 10.95-18.97
Eye Relief: 4.2-3.7 in.
Features: Fully coated lenses for excellent low light brightness; durable waterproof construction; also in 2-7x33, 4-12x40, and 3-9x50
MSRP **$274.99**

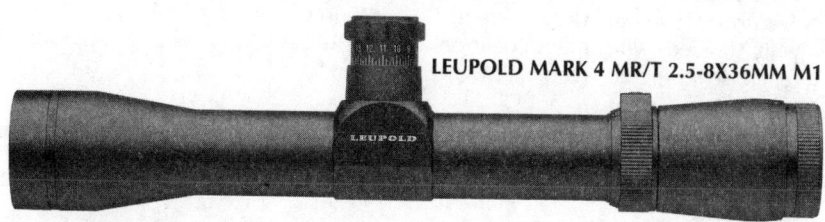

LEUPOLD MARK 4 MR/T 2.5-8X36MM M1

LEUPOLD MARK AR 3-9X40MM T2

LEUPOLD RIFLEMAN 3-9X40MM

OPTICS

Leupold & Stevens

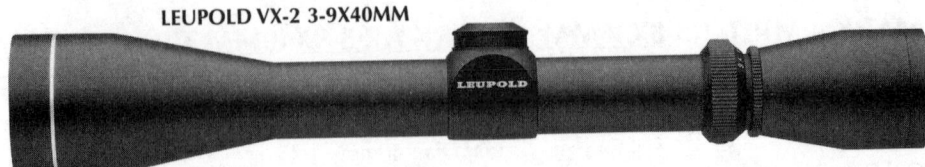

LEUPOLD VX-2 3-9X40MM

VX-2 3-9X40MM

Weight: 12 oz.
Length: 12.4 in.
Power: 3.3-8.6X (actual)
Obj.Dia.: 40mm
Main Dia.: 1 in.
Exit Pupil: 12-4.6mm
Field of View: 323-140 ft @ 1000 yds
Twilight Factor: 10.95-18.97
Eye Relief: 4.7-3.7 in.
Features: Multi-coated 4 Lens System for 92% light transmission; coin click ¼ MOA windage and elevation dials; also in 1-4x20, 4-12x40 AO, 6-18x40 AO and Target, 3-9x50, 4-12x50
MSRP . . . . $374.99–$437.99

VX-3 3.5-10X40MM CDS

Weight: 12.6 oz.
Length: 12.66 in.
Power: 3.3-9.7X (actual)
Obj.Dia.: 40mm
Main Dia.: 1 in.
Exit Pupil: 12.1-4.1mm
Field of View: 298-110 ft @ 1000 yds
Twilight Factor: 11.83-20
Eye Relief: 4.4-3.5 in.
Features: X-Tended Twilight Lens System; ¼ MOA windage and elevation dials; Diamond Coat 2 external lens coatings; dual spring erector assembly; available CDS dial options and illuminated reticles; also in 1.5-5x20, 1.5-5x20 IR, 1.75-6x32, 2.5-

8x36, 4.5-14x40, 4.5-14x40 CDS, 4.5-14x40 SF, 4.5-14x40 AO, 6.5-20x40 AO, 6.5-20x40 SF, 3.5-10x50, 3.5-10x50 IR, 3.5-10x50 IR Metric, 4.5-14x50, 4.5-14x50 SF, 4.5-14x50 SF IR, 6.5-20x50 SF Target, and 8.5-23x50 SF Target
MSRP . . . . $599.99–$664.99

VX-6 ILLUMINATED 2-12X42MM

Weight: 17.8 oz.
Length: 12.5 in.
Power: 2-12X
Obj. Dia.: 42mm
Main Dia.: 30mm
Exit Pupil: 10-3.5mm
Field of View: 112-20.3 ft @ 100 yds
Twilight Factor: 9.17-22.45
Eye Relief: 3.8 in.
Features: Quantum optical system with Xtended Twilight lens coatings; 7 reticle styles include Duplex, Boone & Crockett, Illum. Duplex, Illum. LR Duplex, and Illum. German #4 Dot; also available in 1-6x24, 3-18x44, 3018x50, 4-24x52
MSRP . . . . $1124.99–$1249.99

VX-R 4-12X40MM CDS

Weight: 15.1 oz.
Length: 12.4 in.
Power: 4.4-11.7X (actual)
Obj.Dia.: 1.8 in.
Main Dia.: 30mm
Exit Pupil: 8.6-3.3mm
Field of View: 21.5-10 ft @ 100 yds
Twilight Factor: 14.2-23.1
Eye Relief: 3.7 in.
Features: Fire Dot reticle system with fiber optic technology; DiamondCoat lens coatings; finger click adjustments; index matched lens system; proprietary Motion Sensor Technology
MSRP $789.99

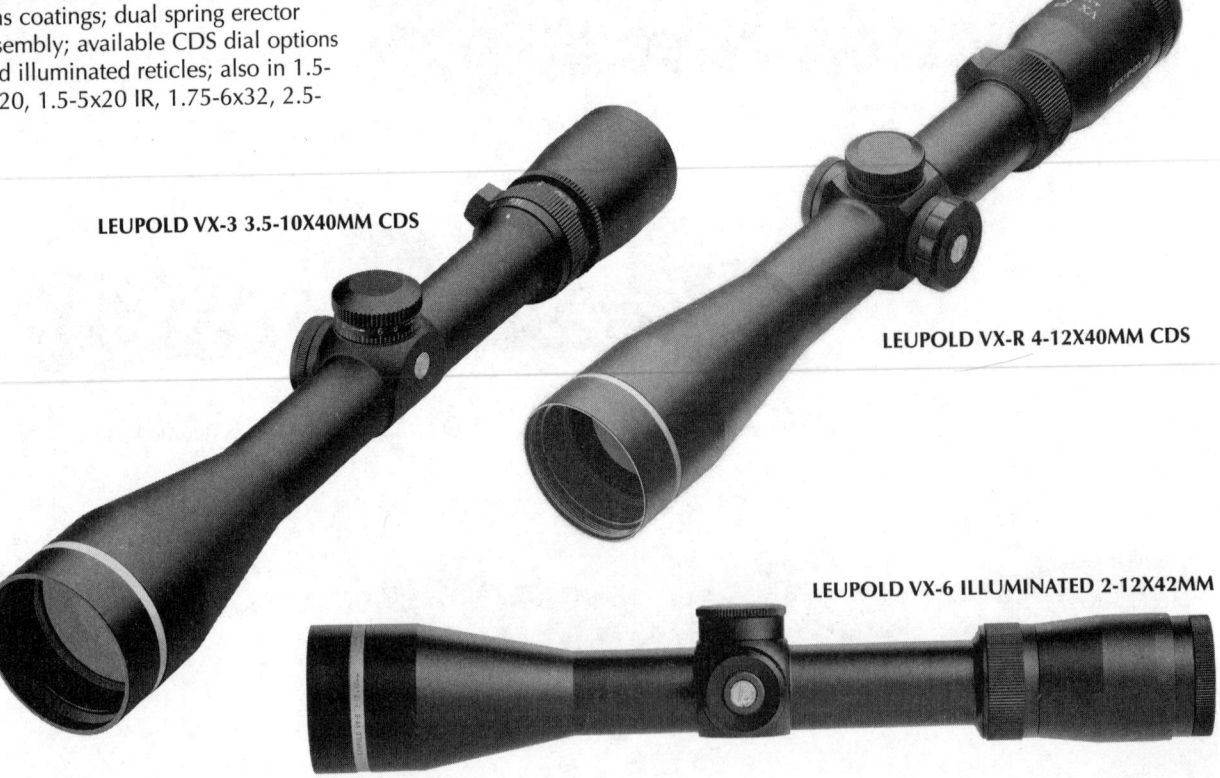

LEUPOLD VX-3 3.5-10X40MM CDS

LEUPOLD VX-R 4-12X40MM CDS

LEUPOLD VX-6 ILLUMINATED 2-12X42MM

6-24X50MM ADVANTAGE RIFLE SCOPE

Weight: 24.5 oz.
Length: 15.5 in.
Power: 6-24X
Obj. Dia.: 50mm
Main Dia.: 30mm
Exit Pupil: 8.3-2mm
Field of View: 16.5-4.3 ft @ 100 yds
Twilight Factor: 17.32-34.64
Eye Relief: 4.25-3.25 in.
Features: Sniper-style rifle scope with the new L5 reticle; multi-coated lenses; ⅛ MOA turret click value; water-, fog-, and shockproof; matte black finish; available in STRELOK
MSRP **$449**

LUCID 6-24X50MM ADVANTAGE RIFLE SCOPE

Millett Optics

DMS 1-4X25MM

Weight: 18 oz.
Length: 11.8 in.
Power: 1-4X
Obj.Dia.: 25mm
Main Dia.: 30mm
Exit Pupil: 24-6mm
Field of View: 90-23 ft @ 100 yds
Twilight Factor: 4.89-9.79
Eye Relief: 3.5 in.
Features: Designated Marksman Riflescope (DMS) features a Donut Dot illuminated reticle; "donut" subtending 18 MOA for ranges as close as three meters; illuminated dot 1 MOA for medium to extended ranges out to 500 yards; available in matte or ATAC finish
Matte: **$385.95**
ATAC: **$429.95**

LRS 6-25X56MM ILLUMINATED .1 MIL

Weight: 35 oz.
Length: 18 in.
Power: 6-25X
Obj.Dia.: 56mm
Main Dia.: 35mm
Exit Pupil: 9.33-2.24mm
Field of View: 45-17 ft @ 100 yds
Twilight Factor: 18.33-37.41
Eye Relief: 3 in.
Features: For extreme-duty and extended-range for calibers such as the .50 BMG and .338 Lapua; one-piece tube; precision controls with 140 MOA range of adjustment; several glass-etched Mil-DotBar reticle and

MILLETT DMS 1-4X24MM

click value configurations; available in a matte or A-TACS finish; also in 6-25x56 Mil-DotBar Reticle .25 or .1 Click Value, 6-25x56 Illuminated Mil-DotBar Reticle A-TACS or Matte Finish
MSRP **$813.95**

TRS 4-16X50MM .1 MIL

Weight: 29.5 oz.
Length: 16.4 in.
Power: 4-16X
Obj.Dia.: 50mm
Main Dia.: 30mm
Exit Pupil: 12.5-3.12mm

Field of View: 29-8 ft @ 100 yds
Twilight Factor: 14.14-28.28
Eye Relief: 3.5 in.
Features: Mil-DotBar reticle system functions as a standard Mil-Dot with the addition of a thin line for easier alignment for rangefinding and holdover; illuminated reticle is green and adjustable; scope has side-focus parallax adjustment knob; also in fixed 10x50 model and several 4-16x50 models finished in either matte or A-TACS
MSRP **$539.95**

MILLETT LRS 6-25X56MM
ILLUMINATED .1 MIL

MILLETT LRS 6-25X56MM
ILLUMINATED .1 MIL

OPTICS

Minox

ZA 3 3-9X40MM
Weight: 13.6 oz.
Length: 12.2 in.
Power: 3-9X
Obj. Dia.: 40mm
Main Dia.: 1 in.
Exit Pupil: 13.5-4.32mm
Field of View: 31.5-10.5 ft @ 100 yds
Twilight Factor: 10.95-18.97
Eye Relief: 4 in.
Features: MINOX M* coating—up to 21 different layers applied to the glass surface to greatly improve light transmission, brightness, contrast, detail, and color rendering; ¼ MOA adjustable windage and elevation; zero-resettable; fast-focus eyepiece; soft-touch rubber variable power ring; Scopecoat protective field cover
MSRP. . . . .$479–$499

MINOX ZA 3 3-9X40MM

ZA 5 4-20X50MM SF
Weight: 19.2 oz.
Length: 13.5 in.
Power: 4-20X
Obj.Dia.: 50mm
Main Dia.: 1 in.
Exit Pupil: 12.45-2.54mm
Field of View: 23.6 ft @ 100 yds
Twilight Factor: 14.14-31.62
Eye Relief: 4 in.
Features: Fully multi-coated Schott-glass lenses with 5-times magnification zoom range; also in 1.5-8x32, 2-10x40, 2-10x50, 3-15x42, 4-20x56, 6-30x56
MSRP. . . . .$839–$869

MINOX ZA 5 4-20X50MM SF

ZA 5 6-30X56MM SF
Weight: 23.6 oz.
Length: 14.8 in.
Power: 6-30X
Obj. Dia.: 55.88mm
Main Dia.: 29.97mm
Exit Pupil: 9.398-1.778mm
Field of View: 15.75-3.16 ft @ 100 yds
Twilight Factor: 18.31-40.94
Eye Relief: 3.9 in.
Features: Side focus parallax adjustment for extreme range shooting; lightweight; waterproof and fogproof; matte-black scope; bullet-drop-compensating reticle available; good in poor light because of 21-layer coating applied
MSRP. . . . .$959–$999

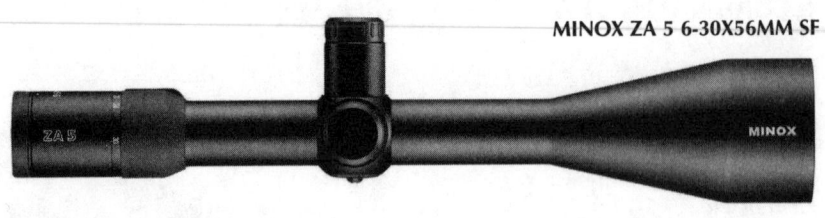

MINOX ZA 5 6-30X56MM SF

Nightforce Optics, Inc.

1-4X24MM NXS COMPACT
Weight: 17 oz.
Length: 8.8 in.
Power: 1-4X
Obj.Dia.: 24mm
Main Dia.: 30mm
Exit Pupil: 1-6mm
Field of View: 100-25 ft @ 100 yds
Twilight Factor: 4.89-9.79
Eye Relief: 3.5 in.
Features: Ideal for the hunter pursuing dangerous or running game at close quarters; low profile complements big bore bolt action and double rifles; as quick as open sights yet vastly more precise; shooter can keep both eyes open for instant target acquisition in high-stress situations
MSRP $1263
ZeroStop: $1450

NIGHTFORCE 1-4X24MM
NXS COMPACT

NIGHTFORCE 2.5-10X32MM
NXS COMPACT

2.5-10X32MM NXS COMPACT
Weight: 19 oz.
Length: 12 in.
Power: 2.5-10X
Obj.Dia.: 32mm
Main Dia.: 30mm
Exit Pupil: 13.3-3.3mm
Field of View: 44-11 ft @ 100 yds
Twilight Factor: 8.94-17.88
Eye Relief: 3.4 in.
Features: Lightweight, low profile; provides low-light performance that exceeds most optics with much larger objective lenses; large exit pupil for fast target acquisition and no parallax or focusing issues; available with the Nightforce Velocity 600 yard reticle, which provides precise shot placement to 600 yards
MSRP $1357
ZeroStop: $1627

3.5-15X50MM F1 NXS
Weight: 30 oz.
Length: 14.8 in.
Power: 3.5-15X
Obj.Dia.: 50mm
Main Dia.: 30mm
Exit Pupil: 11.5-3.2mm
Field of View: 28-8.7 ft @ 100 yds
Twilight Factor: 13.22-27.38
Eye Relief: 3.2 in.
Features: First focal plane reticle design, applicable to a wide range of targets at various distances; five specialized reticles available to maximize first focal plane design; offered with ¼ MOA or .1 Mil-Radian adjustments; ZeroStop standard; Nightforce Ultralight rings
MSRP $2467

3.5-15X50MM NXS
Weight: 30 oz.
Length: 14.8 in.
Power: 3.5-15X
Obj.Dia.: 50mm
Main Dia.: 30mm
Exit Pupil: 14.3-3.6mm
Field of View: 27.6-7.3 ft @ 100 yds
Twilight Factor: 13.22-27.38
Eye Relief: 3.9 in.
Features: Excellent choice for all-around hunting and professional shooters; low mounting profile; full 110 MOA of internal adjustment; available with ¼ MOA and .1 Mil-Radian adjustments; offered with Nightforce's patented ZeroStop, which provides an instant return to the shooter's chosen zero point under any conditions
MSRP $1655
ZeroStop: $1862

NIGHTFORCE 3.5-15X50MM F1 NXS

NIGHTFORCE 3.5-15X50MM NXS

Nightforce Optics

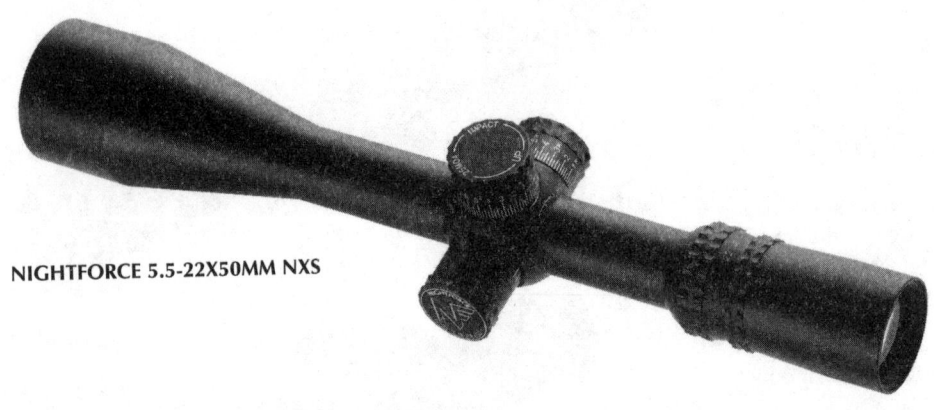

NIGHTFORCE 5.5-22X50MM NXS

NIGHTFORCE 5.5-22X56MM NXS

5.5-22X50MM NXS
Weight: 31 oz.
Length: 15.1 in.
Power: 5.5-22X
Obj.Dia.: 50mm
Main Dia.: 30mm
Exit Pupil: 9.1-2.3mm
Field of View: 17.5-4.7 ft @ 100 yds
Twilight Factor: 16.58-33.16
Eye Relief: 3.8 in.
Features: Originally developed for the U.S. military's extreme long range shooting and hard target interdiction; 100 MOA of elevation travel make it ideal for use on the .50 BMG, allowing accurate shots to 2000 yards and beyond; slim profile, easily adaptable to a wide range of mounting systems
MSRP **$1821**
ZeroStop: **$2025**

5.5-22X56MM NXS
Weight: 32 oz.
Length: 15.2 in.
Power: 5.5-22X
Obj.Dia.: 56mm
Main Dia.: 30mm
Exit Pupil: 10.2-2.5mm
Field of View: 17.5-4.7 ft. @ 100 yds
Twilight Factor: 17.54-35.09
Eye Relief: 3.9 in.
Features: Advanced field tactical riflescope for long-range applications; maximum clarity and resolution across the entire magnification range, exceptional low-light performance; available with ZeroStop technology and $1/8$ and $1/4$ MOA or .1 Mil-Radian adjustments
MSRP **$1766**
ZeroStop: **$2025**

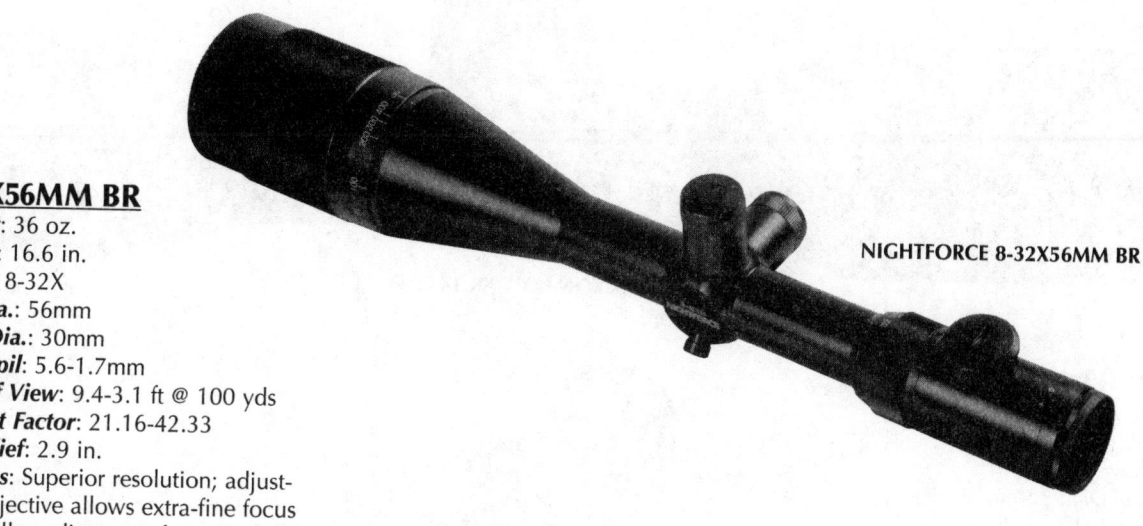

NIGHTFORCE 8-32X56MM BR

8-32X56MM BR
Weight: 36 oz.
Length: 16.6 in.
Power: 8-32X
Obj.Dia.: 56mm
Main Dia.: 30mm
Exit Pupil: 5.6-1.7mm
Field of View: 9.4-3.1 ft @ 100 yds
Twilight Factor: 21.16-42.33
Eye Relief: 2.9 in.
Features: Superior resolution; adjustable objective allows extra-fine focus for parallax adjustment from 25 yards to infinity; target adjustments are calibrated in true ⅛ click) MOA values, and can be re-indexed to zero after sighting in; eyepiece allows for fast reticle focusing and a glass-etched illuminated reticle, with eight different reticles
MSRP $1286

8-32X56MM NXS
Weight: 34 oz.
Length: 15.9 in.
Power: 8-32X
Obj.Dia.: 56mm
Main Dia.: 30mm
Exit Pupil: 7-1.8mm
Field of View: 12.1-3.1 ft @ 100 yds
Twilight Factor: 21.16-42.33
Eye Relief: 3.8 in.

Features: For long-range hunting, competition, and target shooting; choice of five different reticles for the shooter's chosen application; offered with .125 MOA, .250 MOA or .1 Mil-Radian Hi-Speed adjustments; ZeroStop also available
MSRP $1899
ZeroStop: $2092

OPTICS

NIGHTFORCE 8-32X56MM NXS

Nikon

NIKON BOLT XR 3X32MM BDC

BOLT XR 3X32MM BDC
Weight: 11.2 oz.
Length: 8.1 in.
Power: 3-32X
Obj.Dia.: 32mm
Main Dia.: 1 in.
Exit Pupil: 10.7mm
Field of View: 35.6 ft @ 100 yds
Twilight Factor: 9.79
Eye Relief: 3.4 in.
Features: 3x Nikon optics; large ocular; quick focus eye-piece with ±4 diopter adjustment; BDC 60 reticle offers aiming points out to 60 yards based upon velocity of approximately 305 fps; ¼ inch at 20 yards adjustments with a 150 MOA adjustment range (at 100 yards); parallax-free at 20 yards.
MSRP **$218.95**

**NIKON BUCKMASTERS
3-9X40MM NIKOPLEX**

BUCKMASTERS 1X20MM BLACKPOWDER MATTE NIKOPLEX
Weight: 10.6 oz.
Length: 9.1 in.
Power: 1X
Obj.Dia.: 20mm
Main Dia.: 1 in.
Exit Pupil: 20mm
Field of View: 52.5 ft @ 75 yds
Twilight Factor: 4.47
Eye Relief: 4.3-13 in.
Features: For muzzleloading hunting where only 1X power scopes are allowed; uses Nikon's Brightvue multi-coating with a stated 92-percent light transmission; hand-turn ½ MOA positive-click adjustments, plus quick-focus eyepiece
MSRP **$199.95**

BUCKMASTERS 3-9X40MM REALTREE APG HD NIKOPLEX
Weight: 16.1 oz.
Length: 13.1 in.
Power: 3-9X
Obj.Dia.: 40mm
Main Dia.: 1 in.
Exit Pupil: 13.3-4.4mm
Field of View: 35.7-11.9 ft @ 100 yds
Twilight Factor: 10.95-18.97
Eye Relief: 3.6-3.6 in.
Features: Built for centerfire rifle, muzzleloader, or rimfire, the Buckmasters 3-9x40 has Brightvue multi-coating, quick-focus eyepiece, hand-turn ¼ MOA click adjustments, and is adaptable for a sunshade. Also in 4.5-14x40, 6-18x40, 3-9x50, and 4-12x50, and in matte and silver with BDC, Mil-Dot, and fine crosshair with dot.
MSRP **$259.95**

**NIKON BUCKMASTERS
1X20MM BLACKPOWDER
MATTE NIKOPLEX**

OPTICS

Nikon

COYOTE SPECIAL 3-9X40MM MOSSY OAK BRUSH BDC PREDATOR

Weight: 16 oz.
Length: 13.1 in.
Power: 3-9X
Obj.Dia.: 40mm
Main Dia.: 1 in.
Exit Pupil: 13.3-4.4mm
Field of View: 35.7-11.9 ft @ 100 yds
Twilight Factor: 10.95-18.97
Eye Relief: 3.6-3.6 in.
Features: Utilizes the BDC Predator Reticle for ranges out to 450 yards and beyond; open BDC's ballistic circles don't obscure the target; hand-turn ¼ MOA click adjustments; quick-focus eyepiece and lead- and arsenic-free "Eco-Glass"; ARD (Anti Reflective Device) scope cover to eliminate glare but permit shooting; also in 4.5-14x40 and in matte and RealTree Max-1
MSRP **$279.95**

M-223 LASER IRT 3-12X42MM SF RAPID ACTION TURRET NIKOPLEX

Weight: 19.93 oz.
Length: 13.1 in.
Power: 3-12X
Obj.Dia.: 42mm
Main Dia.: 1 in.
Exit Pupil: 14-3.5mm
Field of View: 33.6-8.4 ft @ 100 yds
Twilight Factor: 11.22-22.44
Eye Relief: 4-3.8 in.
Features: Side-focus parallax adjustment from zero out to 600 yards; Nikon's Rapid Action Turret technology based on a .223/5.56mm 55-grain polymer tipped bullet; 4-time zoom range, one-piece main body tube and "Ultra ClearCoat optics; variable-magnification reference numbers are viewable from the shooter's position; also in 1-4x20 and 2-8x32 and with BDC 600 reticle)
MSRP **$459.95**

M-308 4-16X42MM

Weight: 19 oz.
Length: 13.5 in.
Power: 4-16X
Obj. Dia.: 42mm
Main Dia.: 1 in.
Exit Pupil: 10.5-2.6mm
Field of View: 25.2-6.3 ft @ 100 yds
Twilight Factor: 12.96-25.92

NIKON COYOTE SPECIAL 3-9X40MM BDC PREDATOR

NIKON M-223 LASER IRT 3-12X42MM SF RAT NIKOPLEX

NIKON M-308 4-16X42MM

NIKON MONARCH 2.5-10X42MM NIKOPLEX

Eye Relief: 4-3.7 in.
Features: Available with the all-new BDC 800 reticle or Nikoplex reticle with Rapid Action Turrets; developed specifically for the trajectory of the .308 Winchester/7.62x51 NATO round with 168-grain hollow point boat-tail Match bullet; Ultra ClearCoat optical system; Eye Box technology; smooth zoom control
MSRP **$529.95**

MONARCH 2.5-10X42MM NIKOPLEX

Weight: 16.6 oz.
Length: 12.6 in.
Power: 2.5-10X
Obj.Dia.: 42mm

Main Dia.: 1 in.
Exit Pupil: 16.8-4.2mm
Field of View: 40.3-10.1 ft @ 100 yds
Twilight Factor: 10.24-20.49
Eye Relief: 4.0-3.8 in.
Features: Enhanced ring spacing for mounting on rifles including magnum-length actions; see-through "ballistic circle" BDC reticle available; Ultra ClearCoat optical system; customized with accessory target-style windage and elevation adjustment knobs and caps; available in 2-8x30, 3-12x42, 4-16x42, 5-20x44, 2.5-10x50, 4-16x50, 6-24x50, and 8-32x50, in matte and silver with ED glass, SF Mil-Dot, and fine crosshair with dot
MSRP **$419.95**

Nikon

MONARCH GOLD 2.5-10X50MM SF BDC

Weight: 21.2 oz.
Length: 13 in.
Power: 2.5-10X
Obj.Dia.: 50mm
Main Dia.: 30mm
Exit Pupil: 19.2-5.2mm
Field of View: 38.8-10.5 ft @ 100 yds
Twilight Factor: 11.18-22.36
Eye Relief: 4.1-4 in.
Features: Ultra ClearCoat optical system; larger internal lenses for less spherical aberration; locking side focus adjustment dials out parallax; aircraft grade aluminum; hand-turn ¼ MOA windage and elevation adjustments; also in 1.5-6x42 and 2.5x10x56 and with Nikoplex and German #4 reticles
MSRP $709.95

MONARCH X 2.5-10X44MM SF NIKOPLEX

Weight: 23.5 oz.
Length: 13.9 in.
Power: 2.5-10X
Obj.Dia.: 44mm
Main Dia.: 30mm
Exit Pupil: 17.6-4.4mm
Field of View: 42-10.5 ft @ 100 yds
Twilight Factor: 10.24-20.49
Eye Relief: 3.5-3.8 in.
Features: Nikoplex, Mil-Dot, or Dual Illuminated Mil-Dot reticle options; Ultra ClearCoat system; one-piece body tube milled from aircraft grade aluminum; hand-turn ¼ MOA windage and elevation adjustments and side-focus parallax adjustment; also in 4-16x50 with Mil-Dot and dual-illuminated Mil-Dot
MSRP $1299.95

P-22 2-7X32MM

Weight: 13.9 oz.
Length: 11.5 in.
Power: 2-7X
Obj. Dia.: 32mm
Main Dia.: 1 in.
Exit Pupil: 16-4.6mm
Field of View: 33.4-9.5 ft @ 100 yds
Twilight Factor: 8-14.97
Eye Relief: 3.8-3.8 in.
Features: P-22 riflescopes are the rimfire-optimized variant of Nikon's growing line of precision optics for AR rifles; designed for extreme sighting speed and superior accuracy from rimfire AR platform rifles and .22 long rifle cartridges, the P-22 is offered with BDC 150 reticle or 2-7x32 with Nikoplex reticle; Nikon's Rapid Action Turret system
MSRP $179.95

PROSTAFF 3-9X40MM NIKOPLEX

Weight: 15 oz.
Length: 12.4 in.
Power: 3-9X
Obj.Dia.: 40mm
Main Dia.: 1 in.
Exit Pupil: 13.3-4.4mm
Field of View: 33.8-11.3 ft @ 100 yds
Twilight Factor: 10.95-18.97
Eye Relief: 3.6-3.6 in.
Features: ¼ MOA hand-turn reticle adjustments with "Zero-Reset" turrets; quick-focus eyepiece; also in 2-7x32– and in Shotgun Hunter with BDC 200 reticle–4-12x40, and 3-9x50 and in silver, RealTree APG and with BDC reticle
MSRP . . . . $179.99–$199.99

NIKON MONARCH GOLD 2.5-10X50MM SF BDC

NIKON MONARCH X 2.5-10X44MM SF

NIKON P-22 2-7X32MM

NIKON PROSTAFF 3-9X40MM NIKOPLEX

OPTICS

Nikon

NIKON PROSTAFF
TARGET EFR 3-9X40MM

PROSTAFF TARGET EFR 3-9X40MM

Weight: 15.7 oz.
Length: 12.5 in.
Power: 3-9X
Obj. Dia.: 40mm
Main Dia.: 1 in.
Exit Pupil: 13.3-4.4mm
Field of View: 16.9-5.7 ft @ 50 yds
Twilight Factor: 10.95-18.97
Eye Relief: 3.6-3.6 in.
Features: Designed and engineered for .22LR, air rifle, and other applications where the versatility of focusing at extended ranges is desired; new Nikon Precision Reticle featuring a fine crosshair with dot; adjustable objective lens that allows parallax adjustments; large ocular with quick focus eyepiece; zero-reset turrets
MSRP **$189.95**

SLUGHUNTER 1.65-5X36MM MATTE BDC 200

Weight: 13.58 oz.
Length: 11.14 in.
Power: 1.65-5X
Obj.Dia.: 36mm
Main Dia.: 1 in.
Exit Pupil: 7.2mm (at 5X)

NIKON SLUGHUNTER 1.65-
5X36MM MATTE BDC 200

Field of View: 45.3-15.1 ft @ 100 yds
Twilight Factor: 7.7-13.41
Eye Relief: 5 in.
Features: Increased exit pupil for low-light performance and a 75-yard parallax setting; BDC 200 trajectory-compensating reticle, with "ballistic circle" aiming points, calibrated for the lower power range and smaller objective; "Eco-Glass" multi-coated optics; hand-turn ¼ MOA click adjustments; also in 3-9x40 and in RealTree APG
MSRP **$229.95**

Pentax Imaging Co.

PENTAX GAMESEEKER 30 3-10X40MM

GAMESEEKER 30 3-10X40MM

Weight: 15.2 oz.
Length: 13.1 in.
Power: 3-10X
Obj.Dia.: 40mm
Main Dia.: 1 in.
Exit Pupil: 13.3-4.44mm
Field of View: 35.6-10.5 ft @ 100 yds
Twilight Factor: 10.95-20
Eye Relief: 3.3-3 in.
Features: Variable scope; bullet-drop-compensating "Precision Plex" reticle; also in 4-16x50, 6-24x50, and 8.5-32x50
MSRP **$179**

OPTICS

Pentax Imaging Co.

GAMESEEKER II
4-16X50MM
Weight: 16.1 oz.
Length: 13.9 in.
Power: 4-16X
Obj.Dia.: 50mm
Main Dia.: 1 in.
Exit Pupil: 12.5-3.125mm
Field of View: 26.2-6.8 ft @ 100 yds
Twilight Factor: 14.14-28.28
Eye Relief: 3 in.
Features: One-piece tube; finger-adjust-able windage and elevation turrets; also in 2-7x32, 3-9x40, 4-12x40, 3-9x50, and 5-10x56, and P and LPP reticles
MSRP **$149**

PENTAX GAMESEEKER II 4-16X50MM

GAMESEEKER III
4-12X40MM
Weight: 13.4 oz.
Length: 13.2 in.
Power: 4-12X
Obj. Dia.: 40mm
Main Dia.: 1 in.
Exit Pupil: 9.2-3.4mm
Field of View: 27.6-10.6 ft @ 100 yds
Twilight Factor: 12.65-21.91
Eye Relief: 3.7-3.3 in.
Features: New slim line construction and improved optics; fully multi-coat-ed optics; Precision Plex reticle; high quality turrets; one-piece, aluminum construction, waterproof and fogproof; also in 3-9x40, 3-9x50, 4-16x50
MSRP **$149**

LIGHTSEEKER 30
3-10X40MM
Weight: 20 oz.
Length: 13.1 in.
Power: 3-10X
Obj.Dia.: 40mm
Main Dia.: 30mm
Exit Pupil: 13.3-4mm
Field of View: 34-14 ft @ 100 yds
Twilight Factor: 10.95-20
Eye Relief: 3.5-4 in.
Features: Finger-adjustable windage and elevation turrets; side parallax adjustment; also in 4-16x50 and 6-24x50, and with Mil-Dot reticle
MSRP **$519**

LIGHTSEEKER XL
4-16X44MM
Weight: 23 oz.
Length: 14 in.
Power: 4-16X
Obj.Dia.: 44mm
Main Dia.: 1 in.
Exit Pupil: 11-2.8mm
Field of View: 24-8 ft @ 100 yds
Twilight Factor: 9.4-26.5
Eye Relief: 3.5-4 in.
Features: Finger-adjustable windage and elevation turrets; "European-style" eyepieces; also in 3-9x40 and 2.5-10x50, and with P and Twilight Plex reticles
MSRP **$489**

PENTAX GAMESEEKER III 4-12X40MM

PENTAX LIGHTSEEKER 30 3-10X40MM

PENTAX LIGHTSEEKER XL 4-16X44MM

OPTICS

Redfield

REVENGE 3-9X42MM
Weight: 14.8 oz.
Length: 12.4 in.
Power: 3-9X
Obj. Dia.: 42mm
Main Dia.: 1 in.
Exit Pupil: 14.2-4.9mm
Field of View: 32.9-11.4 ft @ 100 yds
Twilight Factor: 11.22-19.44
Eye Relief: 3.5 in.

Features: Built-in optical rangefinder means you never need to take your eye off the target; flexible magnification range; available with 4-Plex, Accu-Ranger Hunter, and Accu-Ranger Sabot reticles; also avavilable in 2-7x34, 3-9x52, 4-12x42, and 6-18x44
MSRP . . . . $199.99–$224.99

REVOLUTION 3-9X40MM
Weight: 12.6 oz.
Length: 12.33 in.
Power: 3-9X
Obj.Dia.: 40mm
Main Dia.: 1 in.
Exit Pupil: 12.1-4.7mm
Field of View: 32.9-13.1 ft @ 100 yards
Twilight Factor: 10.95-18.97
Eye Relief: 3.7-4.2 in.
Features: Black matte finish and either a 4-Plex or Accu-Range reticle; Illuminator Lens System with premium lenses and vapor-deposition multi-coatings; Accu-Trac windage and elevation adjustment system has resettable stainless steel ¼ MOA finger click adjustments; "Rapid Target Acquisition" (RTA) lockable eyepiece; also available in 2-7x33, 3-9x50, and 4-12x40
4-Plex: $249.99
Accu-Range: $264.99

REDFIELD REVENGE 3-9X42MM

REDFIELD REVOLUTION 3-9X40MM

Schmidt & Bender

1.1-4X20MM PM SHORT-DOT LOCKING POLICE MARKSMAN
Weight: 20.11 oz.
Length: 10.6 in.
Power: 1.1-4X
Obj.Dia.: 20mm
Main Dia.: 30mm
Exit Pupil: 14-5mm
Field of View: 96-30 ft @ 100 yds
Twilight Factor: 4.69-8.94
Eye Relief: 3.5 in.
Features: Includes locking turrets and CQB reticle; M855, 75 gr. TAP, and M118LR calibration rings standard; also in 1.5-6x20 and 1-8x24 Short Dots and 1.1-4x24 PM Zenith Short-Dot LE
MSRP $2739

1.5-6X42MM ZENITH FLASH-DOT
Weight: 21.52 oz.
Length: 12.33 in.
Power: 1.5-6X
Obj.Dia.: 42mm
Main Dia.: 30mm
Exit Pupil: 28-7mm
Field of View: 60-19.5 ft @ 100 yds
Twilight Factor: 4.2-15.9
Eye Relief: 3.5 in.
Features: Flash-Dot reticle in the center of the crosshairs performs like front bead sight on shotgun when illuminated; Flash Dot can also be shut off; click values on the windage and elevation adjustments are ½ MOA on the 1.1-4x24 and ⅓ MOA on the rest; also in 1.1-4x24, 1-8x24, 3-12x50, and 2.5-10x56 with Flash Dot and in 1.1-4x24, 1.5-6x42, 1-8x24, 3-12x50, and 2.5-10x56 with non-illuminated reticle
MSRP $2459

SCHMIDT & BENDER 1.1-4X20MM SHORT-DOT LOCKING POLICE MARKSMAN

SCHMIDT & BENDER 1.5-6X42MM ZENITH FLASH-DOT

OPTICS

Schmidt & Bender

SCHMIDT & BENDER 2.5-10X40MM SUMMIT

2.5-10X40MM SUMMIT
Weight: 16.8 oz.
Length: 13.2 in.
Power: 2.5-10X
Obj.Dia.: 40mm
Main Dia.: 1 in.
Exit Pupil: 16-4mm
Field of View: 40.4-12.3 ft @ 100 yds
Twilight Factor: 14-20
Eye Relief: 3.93 in.
Features: Built for the American market with its 1 inch tube; adjustments are ¼ MOA
MSRP................... **$1999**

3-12X42MM PRECISION HUNTER
Weight: 19.9 oz.
Length: 13.66 in.
Power: 3-12X
Obj.Dia.: 42mm
Main Dia.: 30mm
Exit Pupil: 3.5-14mm
Field of View: 31.5-11.4 ft @ 100 yds
Twilight Factor: 8.5-22.4
Eye Relief: 3.5 in.

Features: Enhanced model 3-12x42 Klassik designed for longer ranges; P3 reticle with bullet-drop compensated elevation knob; adjustments are in ⅓ MOA; third-turret parallax adjustment; also in 3-12x50 and 4-16x50
MSRP................... **$2399**

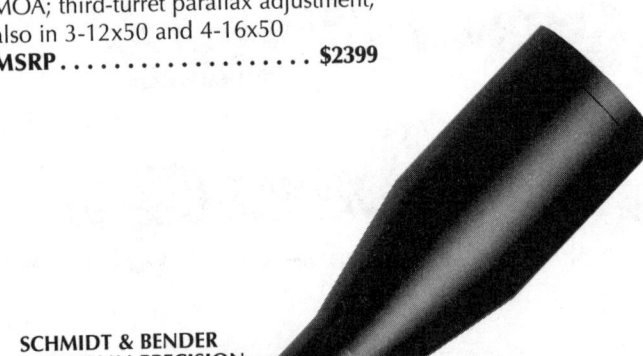

SCHMIDT & BENDER
3-12X42MM PRECISION
HUNTER

3-12X50MM KLASSIK ILLUMINATED
Weight: 21.66 oz.
Length: 13.75 in.
Power: 3-12X
Obj.Dia.: 50mm
Main Dia.: 30mm
Exit Pupil: 4.2-14.4mm
Field of View: 33.3-11.4 ft @ 100 yds
Twilight Factor: 8.5-24.5
Eye Relief: 3.14 in.
Features: All of the Klassik variables have generous objectives for greater light transmission; variety of reticles in illuminated, non-illuminated, and varmint; also in illuminated-reticle 2.5-10x56 and 3-12x42, and in non-illuminated 2.5-10x40, 3-12x42, and 4-16x 50
MSRP................... **$2389**

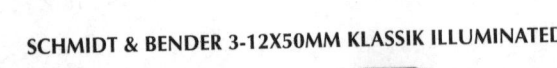

SCHMIDT & BENDER 3-12X50MM KLASSIK ILLUMINATED

OPTICS

Schmidt & Bender

4-16X42MM POLICE MARKSMAN II/LP

Weight: 30.86 oz.
Length: 15.5 in.
Power: 4-16X
Obj.Dia.: 42mm
Main Dia.: 34mm
Exit Pupil: 10.5-2.6mm
Field of View: 22.5-7 ft @ 100 yds
Twilight Factor: 11.3-25.9
Eye Relief: 3.5 in.
Features: Color coded elevation turret; illuminated reticle and parallax adjustment; LP turret system features a color-coded elevation knob for instant reference to the elevation setting; also in 30mm 10x42 and 34mm 3-12x50 with non-IR, 34mm tube 4-16x42, 3-12x50, 3-20x50, 4-16x50, 5-25x56, and 12-50x56
MSRP $3149

6X42MM KLASSIK FIXED

Weight: 16.67 oz.
Length: 13.7 in.
Power: 6X
Obj.Dia.: 42mm
Main Dia.: 1 in.
Exit Pupil: 7mm
Field of View: 21 ft @ 100 yds
Twilight Factor: 15.8
Eye Relief: 3.14 in.
Features: Fixed 6-power magnification applicable to a wide range of hunting situation; windage and elevation adjustments are in 1/3 MOA increments.; classic European 8x56 configuration offers maximum light transmission; also in 10x42, 7x50, and 8x56
MSRP $1239

12.5-50X56MM FIELD TARGET

Weight: 40.56 oz.
Length: 16.4 in.
Power: 12.5-50X
Obj.Dia.: 56mm
Main Dia.: 30mm
Exit Pupil: 4.55-1.18mm
Field of View: 10.5-2.7 ft @ 100 yds

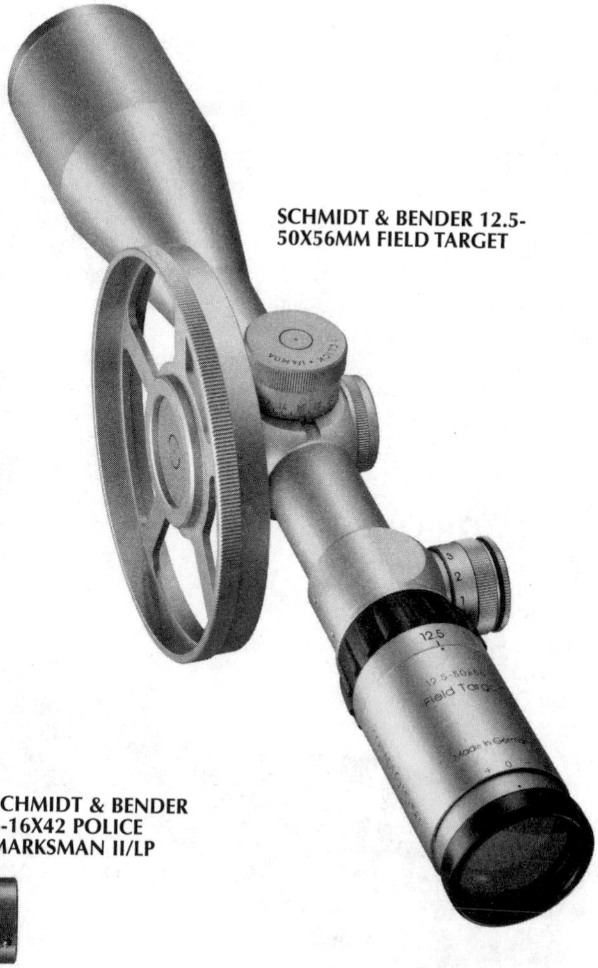

SCHMIDT & BENDER 12.5-50X56MM FIELD TARGET

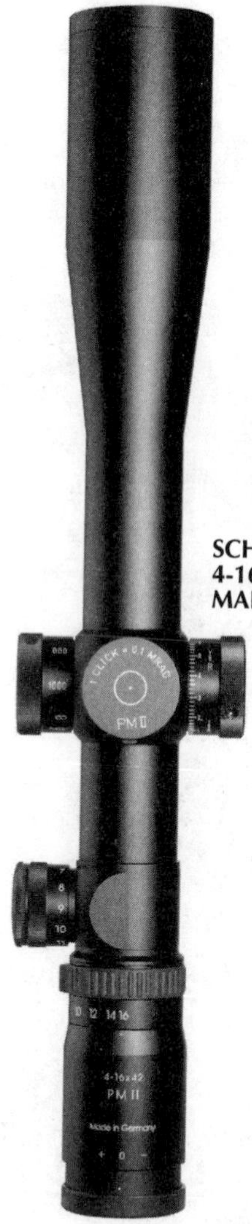

SCHMIDT & BENDER 4-16X42 POLICE MARKSMAN II/LP

Twilight Factor: 26.5-53
Eye Relief: 2.75 in.
Features: High-magnification scope has a shallow depth of field, so the parallax side-focus wheel can be used as a reference for gauging the distance to the target and adjusting the trajectory; extra-large focus wheel to range distances from 7-70m; illuminated reticle with brightness settings adjustable from 1 to 11
MSRP $3439

SCHMIDT & BENDER 6X42MM KLASSIK FIXED

Simmons

.44 MAG. 3-10X44MM
Weight: 11.3 oz.
Length: 12 in.
Power: 3-10X
Obj.Dia.: 44mm
Main Dia.: 1 in.
Exit Pupil: 14.66-4.4mm
Field of View: 33-9.4 ft @ 100 yds
Twilight Factor: 11.48-20.97
Eye Relief: 3.75 in.
Features: Wide field of view with brightness delivered via multi-coated optics; QTA (Quick Target Acquisition) eyepiece; TrueZero windage and elevation adjustment system; also in 4-12x44, 6-21x44, 6-24x44
MSRP **$169.95**

SIMMONS .44 MAG.
3-10X44MM

PREDATOR QUEST 6-24X50MM
Weight: 17 oz.
Length: N/A
Power: 6-24X
Obj.Dia.: 50mm
Main Dia.: 30mm

Exit Pupil: 8.33-2mm
Field of View: 14-4 ft @ 100 yds
Twilight Factor: 17.32-35.35
Eye Relief: 3.9 in.
Features: Inspired by Les Johnson and his popular TV show, the Simmons Predator Quest series; fingertip-adjustable turrets promote quick aim modifications; side focus adjustment for rapid target acquisition; versatile TruPlex reticle; also in 4.5-18x44
MSRP **$372.95**

SIMMONS PREDATOR
QUEST 6-24X50MM

SIMMONS PROHUNTER
3-9X40MM ILLUMINATED
TRUPLEX RETICLE

SIMMONS PROTARGET
3-9X40MM

PROHUNTER 3-9X40MM ILLUMINATED TRUPLEX RETICLE
Weight: 10.8 oz.
Length: 12 in.
Power: 3-9X
Obj.Dia.: 40mm
Main Dia.: 1 in.
Exit Pupil: 13.33-4.44mm
Field of View: 31.4-11 ft @ 100 yds
Twilight Factor: 10.95-18.97
Eye Relief: 3.75 in.
Features: TrueZero windage and elevation adjustment system for a locked-in zero; raised tab on the power change ring for easy grip and surer adjustments; also in 4x32, 1.5-5x32, 3-9x40 TruPlex Reticle, 4x32, 2-6x32 Matte, 2-6x32 Silver
MSRP **$190.95**

PROTARGET 3-9X40MM
Weight: 20.4 oz.
Length: 12 in.
Power: 3-9X
Obj.Dia.: 40mm
Main Dia.: 1 in.
Exit Pupil: 13.33-4.44mm
Field of View: 31-10.5 ft @ 100 yds
Twilight Factor: 10.95-18.97
Eye Relief: 3.9 in.
Features: Calibrated for either .22 LR or .17 HMR; mid- to long-range shooting; TruPlex Reticle makes it easier to pinpoint the smallest targets with a rimfire rifle; fingertip-adjustable turrets with a side focus available on the higher magnification models; also in 3-12x40, 6-18x40
MSRP **$181.95**

OPTICS

MILITARY/TACTICAL 4-16X50MM

Weight: 33.6 oz.
Length: 16.1 in.
Power: 4-16X
Obj.Dia.: 50.8mm
Main Dia.: 34.3mm
Exit Pupil: 11.9-3.3mm
Field of View: 8.7-2.4m @ 100m
Twilight Factor: 14.5-27.2
Eye Relief: 3.0-3.4 in.
Features: Higher magnification range lets you target anything from varmints to big game; side parallax adjustment
MSRP **$2295.99**

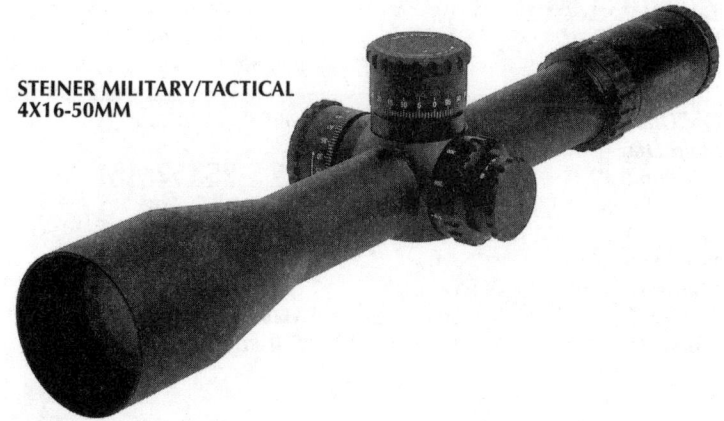

STEINER MILITARY/TACTICAL
4X16-50MM

MILITARY 5-25X56MM

Weight: 36.3 oz.
Length: 16.6 in.
Power: 5-25X
Obj. Dia.: 56mm
Main Dia.: 34mm
Exit Pupil: 9.8-2.24mm
Field of View: 7.23-1.43m @ 100m
Twilight Factor: 16.73-37.42
Eye Relief: 3.54 in.
Features: Extremely high magnification, designed for use on long-range tactical and sniper rifles; high magnification and elevation travel allow to extend the practical shooting range beyond 1,500 meters; broad band anti-reflection coated optic guarantee maximum light transmission; 11 illumination steps; also available in 1-4x24, 3-12x50, 3-12x56, and 4-16x 50
MSRP **$3095**

STEINER MILITARY
5-25X56MM

PREDATOR XTREME 3-12X56MM

Weight: 24 oz.
Length: 14.9 in.
Power: 3-12X
Obj. Dia.: 56mm
Main Dia.: 30mm
Exit Pupil: 13-5mm
Field of View: 36-9 ft @ 100 yds
Twilight Factor: 12.96-25.92
Eye Relief: 3.5-4 in.
Features: Precision-ground lenses with Steiner's unique CAT (Color Adjusted Transmission) technology; engineered lens coating delivers the highest levels of contrast and light transmission; new Steiner Plex S1 Ballistic etched reticle; features ¼-MOA adjustments for windage and elevation; also in 2.5-10x42 and 4-16x50
MSRP **$899.99**

STEINER PREDATOR
XTREME 3-12X56MM

OPTICS

Swarovski Optik

Z3 3-10X42MM
Weight: 12.7 oz.
Length: 12.6 in.
Power: 3-10X
Obj.Dia.: 42mm
Main Dia.: 1 in.
Exit Pupil: 12.6-4.2mm
Field of View: 33-11.7 ft @ 1000 yds
Twilight Factor: 11.22-20.49
Eye Relief: 3.5 in.
Features: Z3 riflescopes have a 3X zoom factor and are the lightest riflescopes in the Swarovski Optik line;

perfect fit for many of today's lightweight rifles; reticles for the Z3 include the 4A, Plex, BRX/BRH (3-10x and 4-12x), and ML in the 3-10x
MSRP **$954**

Z5 5-25X52MM
Weight: 17.5 oz.
Length: 14.6 in.
Power: 5-25X
Obj.Dia.: 52mm
Main Dia.: 1 in.
Exit Pupil: 9.6-2.1mm

SWAROVSKI OPTIK Z3
3-10X42MM

SWAROVSKI OPTIK Z5
5-25X52MM

SWAROVSKI OPTIK Z6
2-12X50MM

SWAROVSKI OPTIK Z6I 5-30X50MM P

Field of View: 21.9-4.5 ft @ 100 yds
Twilight Factor: 16.12-36.05
Eye Relief: 3.75 in.
Features: The Z5 Riflescope line features a 5X zoom factor; a third parallax-adjustment turret; and long eye relief; with reticles available in #4, Plex, Fine in the 5-25x, and BRX/BRH; also available with the ballistic turrets; also in 3.5-18x44
MSRP **$1777**

Z6 2-12X50MM
Weight: 18.3 oz.
Length: 13.4 in.
Power: 2-12X
Obj.Dia.: 50mm
Main Dia.: 30mm
Exit Pupil: 25-4.17mm
Field of View: 63.0-10.5 ft @100 yds
Twilight Factor: 10-24.49
Eye Relief: 3.74 in.
Features: The Z6 line of riflescopes feature a 6X zoom factor, adjustable parallax, and HD glass on select high magnification models; available with illuminated reticles which have a spare battery stored in the turret cap; wide selection of reticles; also in 1-6x24, 1.7-10x42, 2,5-15x44, 2.5-15x56, 3-18x50, and 5-30x50
MSRP **$2477**

Z6I 5-30X50MM P
Weight: 22.6 oz.
Length: 15.67 in.
Power: 5-30X
Obj. Dia.: 48.2-50mm
Main Dia.: 30mm
Exit Pupil: 9.5-1.7mm
Field of View: 23.7-3.9 ft @ 100 yds
Twilight Factor: 14.1-38.7
Eye Relief: 3.74 in.
Features: New 2nd Generation scopes feature slimmer design that enables a clearer view of the controls and of the hunting situation; parallax turret also features a lock-in position at the 100 yds mark; more prominent ribbing on the magnification ring; 4A-1, 4W, Plex, and BRH reticles available; also available in 1-6x24, 1-6x24 BRT, 1-6x24 EE, 1.7-10x42, 2-12x50, 2.5-15x44 P, 2.5-15x56 P, 3-18x50 P
MSRP **$3677**

OPTICS

ACCUPOINT 3-9X40MM

Weight: 13.4 oz.
Length: 12.4 in.
Power: 3-9X
Obj.Dia.: 40mm
Main Dia.: 1 in.
Exit Pupil: 13.3-4.4mm
Field of View: 6.45-2.15 ft @ 100 yds
Twilight Factor: 10.95-18.97
Eye Relief: 3.6 in.
Features: Tritium and fiber battery-free dual-illuminated; manual brightness adjustment override; quick-focus eyepiece; and windage and elevation adjustments; aircraft aluminum with black-matte finish; reticles include BAC Triangle, Standard Cross-Hair with Dot, Mil-Dot Cross-Hair with Dot, and German #4 in red, green, and amber illumination; also in 1-4x24, 1.25-4x24, 5-20x50, and 2.5-10x56
MSRP **$927**

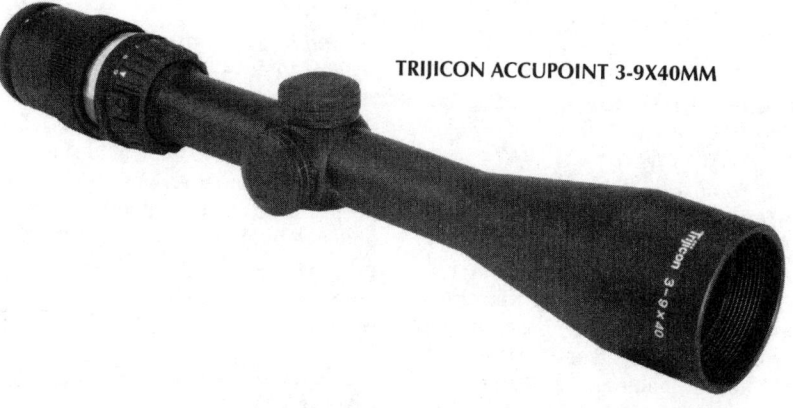

TRIJICON ACCUPOINT 3-9X40MM

ACOG CROSSBOW SCOPE 3X24MM XB

Weight: 5.89 oz.
Length: 5 in.
Power: 3X
Obj. Dia.: 24mm
Exit Pupil: 20-3mm
Field of View: 25.6 ft @ 100 yds
Twilight Factor: 8.49
Eye Relief: 1.4 in.
Features: The first truly high performance optic designed specifically for crossbows; lightest magnified crossbow optic; illuminated reticle accommodates speeds from 300-340 fps; bolt drop stadia lines out to 80 yds; Bad River Outdoors' patented deer/elk ranging capabilities; ability for ranging and hold-over, all in the field of view; fiber optics and tritium illumination
MSRP **$1148**

TRIJICON ACOG CROSSBOW SCOPE 3X24 XB

TARS 3-15X50MM

Weight: 47 oz., 51 oz. with sunshade
Length: 13.9in, 16.9 in. with sunshade
Power: 3-15X
Obj. Dia.: 50mm
Main Dia.: 34mm
Exit Pupil: 16.8-3.3mm
Field of View: 37.5-7.5 ft @ 100 yds
Twilight Factor: 10.1-22.6
Eye Relief: 3.3 in.
Features: Tactical Advanced RifleScope is built for long-range shooting demands; multi-layer coated lenses;

TRIJICON TARS 3-15X50MM

aircraft grade hard anodized aluminum; side-focus parallax compensation, powered by 1 CR2032 battery; constant eye relief; available with MOA, Duplex, JW MIL-Square reticles and MOA or MIL adjusters
MSRP **$3990**

OPTICS

Weaver

40/44 3-10X44MM
Weight: 13.93 oz.
Length: 12.09 in.
Power: 3-10X
Obj.Dia.: 44mm
Main Dia.: 1 in.
Exit Pupil: 14.7-4.4mm
Field of View: 33.5-10.3 ft @ 100 yds
Twilight Factor: 11.49-20.98
Eye Relief: 3 in.
Features: Ballistic-X reticle on some models; one-piece tube construction; aspherical lens system on some models; also available in 2.8-10x44, 3-9x40, 3.8-12x44, 4-12x44, 6.5-20x44; silver finish on some models
MSRP . . . . **$223.49–$233.95**

40/44 SHOTGUN & MUZZLELOADER
Weight: 14-24 oz.
Length: 10.31-13.31 in.
Power: 2-7X
Obj.Dia.: 32mm
Main Dia.: 1 in.
Exit Pupil: 15-5.4mm
Field of View: 44.7-12.7 ft @ 100 yds
Twilight Factor: 8-14.97
Eye Relief: 3.5 in.
Features: Weaver's dedicated shotgun and muzzleloader scopes are engineered specifically for these firearms and give hunters maximum performance out of short to medium-range guns.
MSRP . . . . **$185.49–$195.49**

CLASSIC HANDGUN 2.5-8X28MM
Weight: 9.1 oz.
Length: 9.29 in.
Power: 2.5-8X
Obj.Dia.: 28mm
Main Dia.: 1 in.
Exit Pupil: 11.2-3.5mm
Field of View: 11-4.5 ft @ 100 yds
Twilight Factor: 8.37-14.97
Eye Relief: 24.53 in.
Features: Handguns demand a scope that is built to withstand the brutal pounding from today's most powerful revolvers and single-shot pistols. Designed for the tremendous recoil of 1,000 rounds from a .454 Casull revolver; black or silver; also in 1.5-4x20, 2x28, and 4x28.
MSRP **$348.95**

WEAVER 40/44 3-10X44MM

WEAVER 40/44 SHOTGUN & MUZZLELOADER

WEAVER CLASSIC HANDGUN 2.5-8X28MM

CLASSIC K SERIES 4X28MM
Weight: 14.2 oz.
Length: 9.17 in.
Power: 4X
Obj.Dia.: 38mm
Main Dia.: 1 in.
Exit Pupil: 7mm
Field of View: 8.5 ft @ 100 yds
Twilight Factor: 12.33
Eye Relief: 9.45 in.
Features: Crafted from a one-piece air-craft-grade aluminum tube; built to take heavy recoil punishment and hold zero to 10,000 rounds from a .375 H&H magnum rifle; presents a consistent field of view that's perfect for open field hunting and are among the easiest scopes any instinctive shooter will ever use; also in 4x38, 6x38, 8x56
MSRP **$273.49**

CLASSIC RIMFIRE 3-9X32MM
Weight: 12 oz.
Length: 11.5 in.
Power: 3-9X
Obj.Dia.: 28mm
Main Dia.: 1 in.
Exit Pupil: 10.6mm
Field of View: 33.2-11 ft @ 100 yds
Twilight Factor: 9.17-15.87
Eye Relief: 3.58 in.
Features: Variable and fixed power models; non-glare lenses that produce edge-sharp, low-light brightness; rugged, aircraft-grade, one-piece aluminum construction; parallax is set at 50 yards; also in 2.5-7x28 (matte, silver) and 4x28
MSRP **$372.49**

KASPA TACTICAL SERIES 2.5-10X50MM
Weight: 25.04 oz.
Length: 12.79 in.
Power: 2.5-10X
Obj. Dia.: 50mm
Main Dia.: 30mm
Exit Pupil: 20-5mm
Field of View: 37.3 ft @ 100 yds
Twilight Factor: 11.18-22.36
Eye Relief: 3.74-3.15 in.
Features: Rugged one-piece tube construction; nitrogen purged to eliminate internal fogging; fully multi-coated lenses; crisp ¼-inch MOA adjustments; Dual-X, Ballistic-X, TBX, and Tactical Mil-Dot reticles on various models; also in 1x20, 1.5-6x32, 2.5-10x44, 2-7x32, 309x40, 3-12x44, 3-12x50, 4-16x44
MSRP **$319.99**

WEAVER CLASSIC K SERIES 4X28MM

WEAVER CLASSIC RIMFIRE 3-9X32MM

WEAVER KASPA TACTICAL SERIES 2.5-10X50MM

OPTICS

Weaver

SUPER SLAM 4-20X50MM
Weight: 24 oz.
Length: 13.31 in.
Power: 4-20X
Obj.Dia.: 50mm
Main Dia.: 1 in.
Exit Pupil: 10.5-2.44mm
Field of View: 24.5-4.9 ft @ 100 yds
Twilight Factor: 14.14-31.62
Eye Relief: 3.98 in.
Features: Line of premier riflescopes designed for the serious big game hunter and shooter; side focus parallax adjustment; pull-up turrets; also in 1-5x24, 2-10x42, 2-10x50, 3-15x42, 3-15x50; in silver or matte black; EBX or Dual-x reticle available
MSRP . . . . **$968.49–$1039.49**

WEAVER SUPER SLAM 4-20X50MM

WEAVER TACTICAL 1-5X24MM

TACTICAL 1-5X24MM
Weight: 14.46 oz.
Length: 10.31 in.
Power: 1-5X
Obj.Dia.: 24mm
Main Dia.: 30mm
Exit Pupil: 11.4-4.9mm
Field of View: 100-19.9 ft @ 100 yds
Twilight Factor: 4.9-10.95
Eye Relief: 4.25 in.
Features: Rugged riflescopes designed specifically for tactical applications; extra hard coating on exterior lenses; first focal plane reticles; side focus parallax adjustment; reset-to-zero turrets; one-piece tube construction; also in 3-15x50 and 4-20x50; Mil-Dot, CIRT, and EMDR reticles on some scopes
MSRP **$1069.95**

SIGHTS
Aimpoint

2 MOA MICRO H-1 AND T-1
Weight: 3 oz.
Length: 2.4 in.
Power: 1X
Features: High quality compact red-dot sight; sealed design ensures that no foreign matter will come between the emitter and the lens; can be mounted on nearly any individual weapon platform including: pistols, carbines, personal defense weapons, and sub-machineguns; also available in 4 MOA red-dot
H-1: **$606**
T-1: **$678**

dot for accurate target engagement at all distances; four night vision settings and six daylight settings; modular QRP2 mount includes removable spacer that indexes the sight at optimal height for co-witness with the standard iron sights on AR15/M16/M4 carbine style weapons
MSRP **$405**

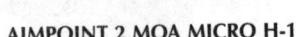

AIMPOINT 2 MOA MICRO H-1

PATROL RIFLE OPTIC (PRO)
Weight: 7.8 oz.
Length: 5.1 in.
Power: 1X
Features: Parallax free optic; 2 MOA

AIMPOINT PATROL RIFLE OPTIC

OPTICS

BROWNING BUCK MARK REFLEX SIGHT

BUCK MARK REFLEX SIGHT

Weight: N/A
Power: 1X
Field of View: 47 ft @ 100 yds
Eye Relief: Unlimited
Features: The Buck Mark has an aluminum housing, four red reticle patterns, a seven-position brightness rheostat powered by a lithium battery, and mounts on a standard Weaver-styled base. Unlimited eye relief.
MSRP.................**$64.99**

Burris

FASTFIRE III RED-DOT REFLEX SIGHT

Weight: 0.9 oz.
Power: 1.07X
Features: Upgraded features such as windage and elevation adjustments that don't require a special tool; 3 or 8 MOA Dot; power button with three levels of brightness; low battery warning indicator and see-through protective cap; ideally suited for use on pistols and AR-15s where fast target acquisition is desired, the FastFire red-dot sight will also match up well with carbines, lever guns, and shotguns; available picatinny mount.
MSRP....................**$372**

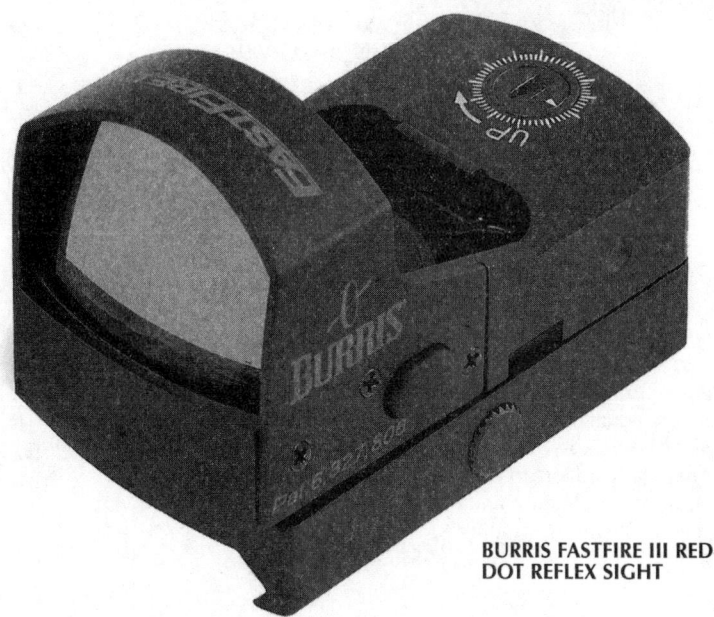

BURRIS FASTFIRE III RED-DOT REFLEX SIGHT

OPTICS

Bushnell

BUSHNELL 2X MP ELECTRONIC SIGHT

2X MP ELECTRONIC SIGHT
Weight: 15.6 oz.
Length: 6.75 in.
Power: 2X
Obj. Dia.: 32mm
Exit Pupil: 32mm
Field of View: 44 ft @ 100 yds
Eye Relief: Unlimited
Features: With the ability to display the T-dot reticle in green during low light and red during bright light, the 2X MP offers the versatility shooters demand from electronic sights. With two power magnification and multi-coated optics, the sight is ideal for acquiring close- to mid-range targets.
MSRP **$340.95**

Carl Zeiss Sports Optics

CARL ZEISS VICTORY COMPACT POINT SIGHT

VICTORY COMPACT POINT SIGHT
Weight: 2.64 oz.
Length: 2.28 in.
Power: 1.05X
Features: LotuTec protective coating; single button on/off and five level brightness; 25 percent wider than conventional reflex sites for natural viewing with both eyes; Blaser integrated mount allows mounting directly on barrel while standard mount allows mounting on Picatinny/Weaver rail
Standard: **$577.77**
Blaser: **$799.99**

CARL ZEISS Z-POINT

Z-POINT (RED DOT REFLEX SIGHT)
Weight: 5.65 oz.
Length: 2.5 in.
Power: 1X
Features: Acquisition sight for shotguns, rifles, and handguns; dual-source illuminated: a solar cell for daylight hours and battery power for dark; red dot automatically adapts to brightness of surroundings and can be regulated manually; available for Weaver or Picatinny mounts
MSRP **$666.66**

OPTICS

EOTech

HOLOGRAPHIC HYBRID SIGHT (HHS)

Power: 3.25X
Eye Relief: 2.2 in.
Features: The HHS kits combine the speed of the EXPS holographic weapon sight and the extended range versatility of the new 3.25X G33 magnifier. The HHS1 includes the night vision compatible EXPS3-4 HWS with the 4-dot reticle calibrated for shooting at 0-300, 400, 500 and 600 meters. The HHS2 includes the EXPS2-2 and non-night vision compatible sight with a 2-dot reticle for fast action targeting.
MSRP . . . . $1002–$1069

EOTECH
HOLOGRAPHIC
HYBRID SIGHT

XPS2-RF

Weight: 7 oz.
Length: 3.5 in.
Power: 1X
Eye Relief: Unlimited
Features: Holographic sight specifically for the rimfire rifle; integrated $3/8$-inch dovetail mount (not compatible with 1-inch Weaver or 1913 rails); lightweight for smaller platforms; single transverse 123 battery to reduce sight length; shortened base; this model is only intended and warranted for calibers .22LR or smaller
MSRP $399

EOTECH XPS2-RF

XPS2-Z ZOMBIE STOPPER

Features: 20 brightness settings; 600 hours of run time on one battery; 65 MOA ring with 1 MOA aiming dot; cool biohazard tails to kill zombies deader
MSRP $588

EOTECH XPS2-Z
ZOMBIE STOPPER

OPTICS

Kruger Optical

DUAL TACTICAL SIGHT (DTS) 1-8X40MM
Weight: 30 oz.
Length: 10 in.
Power: 1X, 2-8X

Obj.Dia.: 40mm
Exit Pupil: 12-4mm
Field of View: 126-13 ft @ 100 yds
Twilight Factor: 8.94-17.89
Eye Relief: Unlimited, 3 in.
Features: Switch instantly with no head movement from a close quarter reflex sight to a 2-8x40 Mil-Dot sight; two independently adjustable windage and elevation systems; rapid target technology eye box; lightweight ultra-strong carbon fiber composite shell
MSRP **$1763.53**

KRUGER DTS 1-8X40MM

Leupold & Stevens

DELTAPOINT REFLEX SIGHT
Weight: 0.6 oz.
Length: 1.66 in.
Features: For use on handguns, shot-guns, and AR-style rifles; includes numerous mounting options; an aspheric lens, motion activation, auto-brightness sensor, locking elevation and windage adjustment system, and a magnesium housing; 7.5 MOA Delta and 3.5 MOA Dot reticles available
Cross-Slot mount: **$499.99**
Other mounts: **$564.99**

PRISMATIC HUNTING 1X14MM
Weight: 12 oz.
Length: 4.5 in.
Power: 1X
Main Dia.: 30mm
Field of View: 83 ft @ 100 yds
Eye Relief: 3 in.
Features: Fast target acquisition of a non-magnifying red-dot sight with a wide field of view; etched-glass reticle that is visible with or without illumination; ½ MOA finger-adjustable wind-age and elevation dials; focusing eye-piece; black matte finish or dark earth anodized finish and with Circle Plex or DCD reticles
MSRP **$599.99**

LEUPOLD PRISMATIC HUNTING 1X14MM

LEUPOLD DELTAPOINT REFLEX SIGHT

OPTICS

Lucid

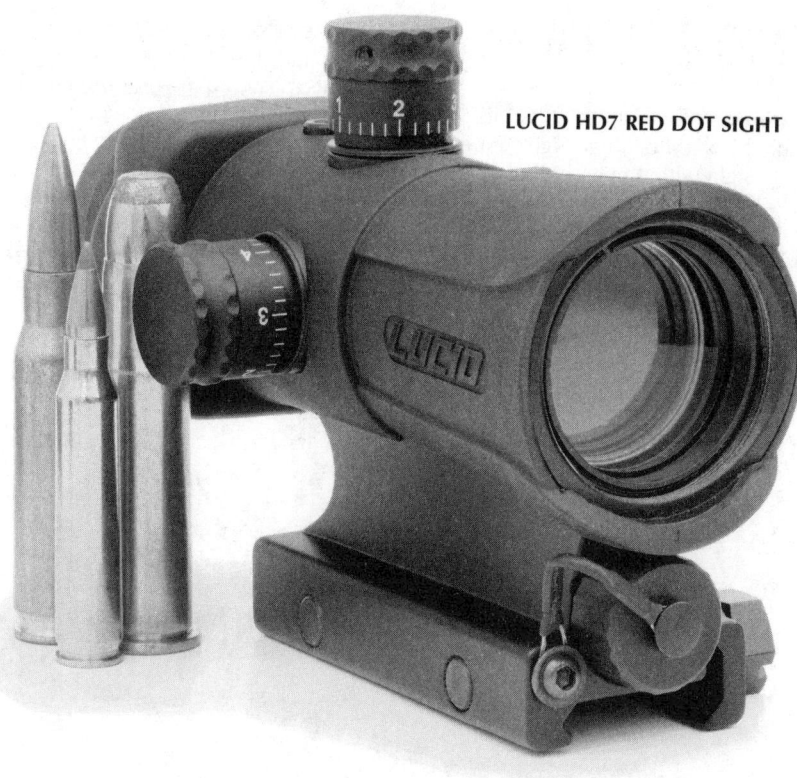

LUCID HD7 RED DOT SIGHT

HD7 RED DOT SIGHT
Weight: 13 oz.
Length: 5.5 in.
Power: 1X
Obj.Dia.: 34mm
Field of View: 44 ft @ 100 yds
Eye Relief: Unlimited
Features: Third Generation Unit. Integral Picatinny rail and reversible mounting pins for bullpup-style firearms. Manual & Auto-Brightness with 12 brightness settings; 4 operator-selectable reticles based on a 2 MOA dot with ½ MOA click adjustments. Parallax free, it is powered by one AAA battery. The frame is cast aluminum armored in chemical rubber and is available with a 2X screw-in eyepiece. Available in tan.
MSRP **$249**

Nikon

NIKON MONARCH DOT SIGHT VSD 1X30MM

MONARCH DOT SIGHT VSD 1X30MM
Weight: 7.8 oz.
Length: 3.8 in.
Power: 1X
Obj.Dia.: 30mm
Exit Pupil: 30mm
Twilight Factor: 5.5
Eye Relief: Unlimited
Features: The Monarch Dot Sight VSD's (Variable Sized Dot) offers selections of 1, 4, 6, 8, or 10 MOA dot size. Includes 11-position rheostat and integral mounting system attachable to any Weaver-style base. Ocular lenses are 30mm. Available in matte, silver, and RealTree APG.
MSRP **$249.95**

OPTICS

Pedersoli

ENGLISH REAR SIGHT, MODEL USA 428

Features: Rear sight with convex base, with two adjustable and folding leaves.

From: **$140**

FIBER OPTIC FRONT AND REAR SIGHT, MODEL USA 409

Features: Front sight and rear sight set for muzzleloading rifles (Model 410 for breechloaders). Front sight with dovetail base; rear sight with base for octagonal barrel.

From: **$125**

"GHOST" TANG SIGHT USA 422

Features: A tang sight inspired by some models in use in the 1800s, economic, functional, and useful for hunting. Adjustable in elevation and windage, it can fit several gun types. The small eye piece ring enables a quick, instinctive aim at the target; when quickly shouldering the rifle, the open ring provides a clear sight picture with low light condition. Distance between the two mounting holes is 1 ¾ inches.

From: **$75**

"SOULE TYPE" MIDDLE RANGE SET, MODEL USA 170

Features: Wooden-box set including Soule XL Middle Range Sight; Tunnel Front Sight with a micrometric screw for windage adjustment, spirit level, and fifteen interchangeable inserts; Professional "Hadley Style" Eyepiece with eight varying diameter viewing holes, depending on available light, on a rotating disk which can be selected without disassembling or loosening the eyepiece, and a rubber ring on the eyepiece; six interchangeable glass bubbles (spirit level) with different colors for varying light conditions. 3 in. elevation adjustment.

From: **$549**

PEDERSOLI ENGLISH REAR SIGHT - 428

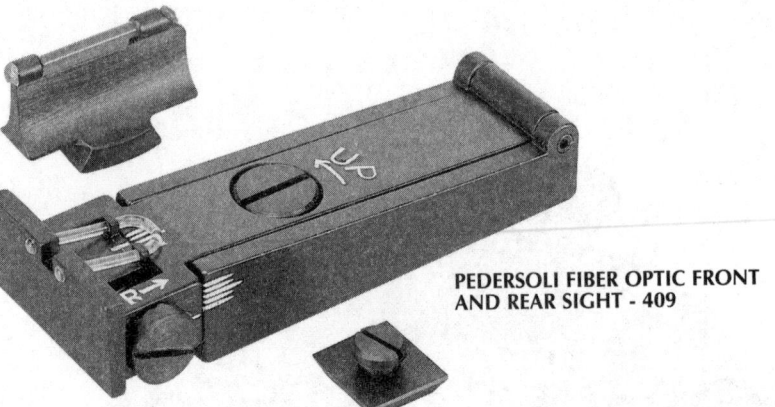

PEDERSOLI FIBER OPTIC FRONT AND REAR SIGHT - 409

PEDERSOLI "SOULE TYPE" MIDDLE RANGE SET - 170

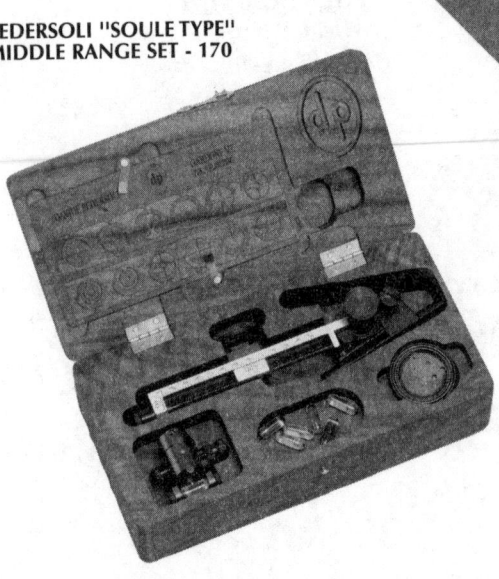

PEDERSOLI "GHOST" TANG SIGHT USA 422

OPTICS

Pedersoli

SPIRIT LEVEL TUNNEL SIGHT ADJUSTABLE WITH 12 INSERTS SET, MODEL USA 425

Features: Spirit level tunnel sight with micrometer adjustment for windage, equipped with twelve interchangeable inserts.

From: . . . . **$29.99–$149.99**

UNIVERSAL CREEDMOOR SIGHT, MIDDLE AND LONG RANGE, MODELS USA 465 AND 430

Features: Tang sight with elevation and windage adjustment in the eye piece. For long-distance target shooting both with muzzle-loading and breech-loading rifles. 2.1875-2.3125 in. between two mounting holes; 2- and 3-inch elevation adjustments

From: . . . . **$162.87–$270.67**

U.S. MODEL 1879 SPRINGFIELD TRAPDOOR REAR SIGHT, MODEL USA 473

Features: Sometimes referred to as "Buckhorn" style. Used on Trapdoor rifles from 1874 until superseded by Buffington style in 1884. Side ramps are graduated to 500 yards and the ladder to 1500 yards. Slide has windage adjustment.

From: **$140**

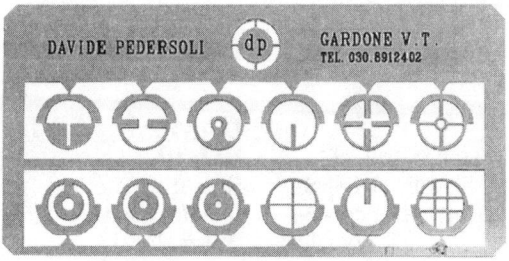

PEDERSOLI SPIRIT LEVEL TUNNEL SIGHT ADJUSTABLE - 425

PEDERSOLI UNIVERSAL CREEDMOOR SIGHT - 430

PEDERSOLI U.S. MODEL 1879 SPRINGFIELD TRAPDOOR REAR SIGHT - 473

Pentax Imaging Co.

GAMESEEKER DOT SIGHT HS-20
Weight: 3.4 oz.
Length: 3.9 in.
Power: 1X
Field of View: 55-50 ft @ 100 yds
Features: 5 MOA dot with 11 brightness settings and 72 hours of continuous battery use; continuous, non-click adjustments; Weaver-style mounting system
MSRP **$59**

GAMESEEKER DOT SIGHT RD-10
Weight: 7.07 oz.
Length: 3.8 in.
Power: 1X
Obj.Dia.: 30mm
Main Dia.: 39mm
Field of View: 54 ft @ 100 yds
Features: Reflex sight with a 4 MOA dot; 11 brightness settings; 72 hours continuous battery life; continuous windage and elevation adjustments; Weaver-style mounting system
MSRP **$69**

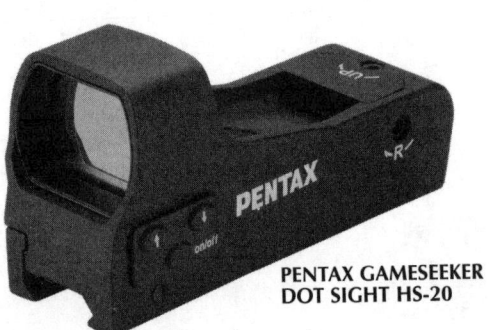

PENTAX GAMESEEKER DOT SIGHT HS-20

PENTAX GAMESEEKER DOT SIGHT RD-10

Trijicon

RMR ADJUSTABLE LED RM06
Weight: 1.2 oz.
Length: 1.77 in.
Power: 1X
Features: LED sight powered by standard CR2032 battery; rugged forged aluminum; adjusters with audible clicks allow for quick windage and elevation adjustments; eight brightness settings; reticle can be manually adjusted; also in Dual-Illuminated RMR with 13.0 MOA dot, 7.0 MOA dot, 9.0 MOA dot, and triangle-reticle RMR LED with 3.25 MOA dot and 6.5 MOA dot
MSRP **$696**

TRIJICON RMR ADJUSTABLE LED RM06

SRS (SEALED REFLEX SIGHT) 1X38
Weight: 13.8 oz.
Length: 3.75 in.
Power: 1X
Obj. Dia.: 38mm
Features: Body length of only 3.75 inches virtually eliminates the "tube-effect" common with other, competitive red-dot sights; field of view provides no obstruction to shooters; LED 1.75 MOA aiming point with 10 brightness settings; SRS powered by solar panel and AA battery; parallax-free objective lens; available in Colt-Style flattop mount or Quick Release flattop mount
MSRP . . . . **$1050–$1125**

TRIJICON SRS 1X38

MUZZLELOADING BULLETS

BULLETS

Barnes Bullets

VOR-TX AMMUNITION

Features: Provides maximum tissue and bone destruction, pass-through penetration, and devastating energy transfer. Multiple grooves in the bullet's shank reduce pressure and improve accuracy. Bullets open instantly on contact causing the nose to peel back into four sharp-edged copper petals destroying tissue, bone, and vital organs for a quick, humane kill. Handgun, Safari, and Rifle lines. **Available in**: .300 AAC Blackout-110 gr., .35 Whelen-180gr.; Rifle Line: .223 Rem., .243 Win., .25-06, .270 Win., .270 WSM, 7mm-08 Rem., 7mm Rem. Mag., 7x64 Brenneke, .30-30 Win., .308 Win., .30-06 Spfd., .300 WSM, .300 Win. Mag., .300 RUM, 8x57 Mauser, .338 Win. Mag., .35 Whelen, 9.3x62 Mauser, .45-70 Govt.; Safari Line: .375 H&H, .416 Rem. Mag., .416 Rigby, .458 Win. Mag., .458 Lott, .470 Nitro, .500 Nitro; Handgun Line: .375 Mag., .41 Rem. Mag., .44 Mag, .45 Colt, .454 Casull
MSRP. . . . . **$22.99–$146.99**

BARNES BULLETS VOR-TX AMMUNITION

Black Hills Ammunition

Rifle Ammunition

BLACK HILLS GOLD

Features: Coupling the finest components in the industry with bullets by Barnes, these lead-free non-toxic rounds set a new standard for high-performance hunting ammunition. 20 rounds per box. **Available in**: .22-250, .243 Win., .25-06 Rem., .260 Rem., .270 Win., 6.5-284 Norma, 7mm Rem. Mag., .300 Win. Mag., .308 Win., .30-06 Spfd., .300 WSM
From:. . . . . **$29.99–$52.99**

FACTORY NEW RIFLE

Features: Coupling the finest components in the industry with bullets by manufacturers such as Hornady, Barnes, and Nosler, these rounds set a new standard for high-performance hunting ammunition. 20 rounds per box. Certain calibers available in Molycoat. **Available in**: .223 Rem., .308 Win. Match, .300 Win. Mag., .338 Lapua, .338 Norma Mag.
From:. . . . . **$38.15–$115.99**

REMANUFACTURED

Features: Ammunition designed with the practice shooter in mind, with incredible accuracy for a great price point. It's the same ammunition used by the U.S. Army Marksmanship Unit in 600-yd. matches. It has the capability to produce 2-in. groups at 300m. 50 rounds per box. **Available in**: .223 Rem. (also in Molycoat) and 9mm Luger, .40 S&W, .45 ACP for handguns
From:. . . . . **$25.99–$39.65**

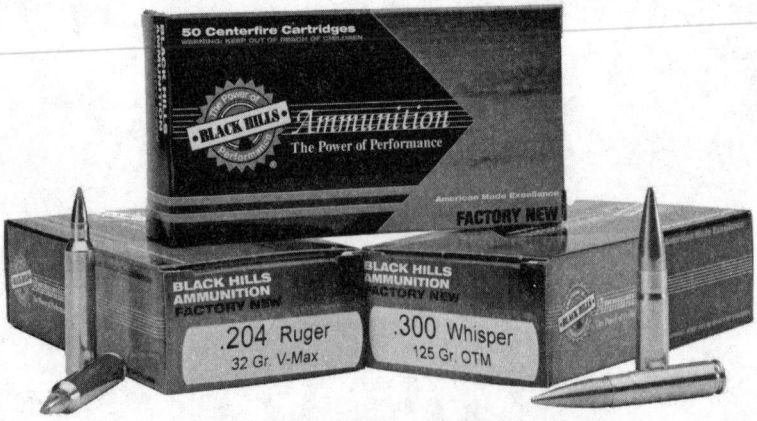

BLACK HILLS FACTORY NEW RIFLE

Black Hills Ammunition

Handgun Ammunition

COWBOY ACTION

Features: Designed to meet the needs of cowboy-action pistol shooters with its new virgin brass and premium-quality hard-cast bullets. Velocities are moderate to provide low recoil and excellent accuracy.
Available in: .32 H&R, .32-20, .38 Long Colt, .38 Spl., .357 Mag., .38-40, .44-40, .44 Russian, .44 Spl., .44 Colt, .45 Schofield, .45 Colt, .38-55, .45-70,
From:.............$30.66–$38.34

FACTORY NEW HANDGUN

Features: Used by the U.S. Military in all four branches for its reliability.
Available in: .300 Whisper, .32 H&R Mag., .380 Auto, 9mm Luger, .38 Spl., .357 Mag., .40 S&W, .44 Mag., .45 Auto Rim, .45 ACP
From:.............$34.99–$50.99

BLACK HILLS COWBOY ACTION

Shotgun Ammunition Slugs

28 GAUGE SLUGS

Features: The moderate recoil makes the 28 Ga. a perfect slug for young hunters who will be introduced to slug shooting. 28 gauge is a multi-talent: small game, home defense, and all around shooting.
Available in: 28 Ga. (2 ¾ in.)
MSRP.............$9.99–$11.99

BLACK MAGIC MAGNUM AND SHORT MAGNUM

Features: The Black Magic Magnum and Black Magic Short Magnum are two of the most powerful cartridges available on the market, offering tremendous knockdown power up to 100/60 yards. The clean speed coating reduces lead fouling inside the barrel by almost 100 percent.
Available in: 12 Ga. (2 ¾ in.), 12 Ga. (3 in.)
From:.............$8.99–$11.99

Brenneke USA

CLASSIC MAGNUM

Features: Invented by Wilhelm Brenneke in 1898, the classic is the ancestor of all modern shotgun slugs. Today this state-of-the-art slug provides long-range stopping power, consistently flat trajectories, and a patented B.E.T. wad column.
Available in: 12 Ga. (2 ¾ in.), 16 Ga. (2 ¾ in.)
Box 5:.............$8.99–$9.99

CLOSE ENCOUNTER

Features: The .410 Close Encounter is the perfect choice if you are a fan of 2 ½-inch .410/.45 revolvers. They are powerful without having bad recoil, and they have an incredible frontal area and the legendary Brenneke penetration.
Available in: .410 (2 ½ in.)
MSRP.............$6.99–$8.99

BRENNEKE CLOSE ENCOUNTER

Brenneke USA

GOLD MAGNUM
Features: Designed for long distance and accuracy. Gold Magnum is designed for rifled barrels only; it is one of the heaviest and most accurate slugs on the market. It has broad ribs for optimum guidance in the rifled barrel and a special coating to reduce lead fouling. Range 100+ yards.
Available in: 12 Ga. (3 in.)
From:.............$8.99–$12.99

HEAVY FIELD SHORT MAGNUM GREEN LIGHTNING
Features: The original "Emerald" slug with patented B.E.T wad and famous stopping power. For all barrel types; range up to 100 yards.
Available in: 12 Ga., 20 Ga. (2 ¾ in.)
From:..............$7.99–$9.99

K.O. SABOT
Features: One of the most affordable sabots on the market, it offers 58 percent more frontal area than standard .50-cal. slugs, resulting in massive energy transfer. Deep penetration, expansion up to .9 in. Range up to 100 yards
Available in: 12 Ga. (2 ¾ in.), 12 Ga. (3 in.)
From:............ $10.99–$13.99

K.O. SLUG
Features: The KO is an improved Foster-type slug with excellent penetration. Range up to 60 yards, for all barrel types.
Available in: 12 Ga. (2 ¾ in.)
From:..............$4.99–$5.99

SUPERSABOT
Features: The SuperSabot has a movable core, lead free construction and an effective range up to more than 100 yards. It mushrooms up to 1 in.
Available in: 12 Ga. (2 ¾ in.), 12 Ga. (3 in.)
From:............ $15.99–$17.99

BRENNEKE HEAVY FIELD SHORT MAGNUM GREEN LIGHTNING SLUGS

BRENNEKE K.O. SABOT

CCI Ammunition

Rifle Ammunition

.22 LONG RANGE AR TACTICAL
Features: This load is designed specifically for AR-style guns being offered in .22 Long Rifle chambering. These rounds get excellent accuracy including 1.5 in. at 100 yards for 10-shot groups. This target bullet has a copper-plated round nose for smooth feeding. CCI case, priming, and bullet lube combined with clean-burning powder. 375 rounds per box
Available in: .22 Long Rifle-40 gr.
From:................. $21.49

GREEN TAG
Features: Our first and still most-popular match rimfire product. Tight manufacturing and accuracy specs mean you get the consistency and accuracy that the unforgiving field of competition demands. The rimfire match ammo leaves the muzzle sub-sonic. That means no buffeting in the transonic zone. Clean-burning propellants keep actions cleaner. Sure-fire CCI priming. Reusable plastic box with dispenser lid
Available in: .22LR-40 grain lead round nose
From:................. $16.49

HMR TNT
Features: CCI extends the usefulness of the exciting .17 Hornady Magnum Rimfire by offering the first hollow point loading. A 17-grain Speer TNT hollow point answers requests from varmint hunters and gives explosive performance over the .17's effective range. Clean-burning propellants keep actions cleaner. Sure-fire CCI priming. Reusable plastic box with dispenser lid.
Available in: .17 HMR-17 grain TNT hollow point
MSRP................... $16.99

CCI Ammunition

LONG HV AND SHORT HV

Features: Designed for rimfire guns that require .22 Long and .22 Short ammunition. Clean-burning propellants keep actions cleaner. Surefire CCI priming. Reusable plastic box with dispenser lid.

Available in: .22 short-29 gr. solid lead bullet; .22 short-27 gr. hollow point bullet; .22 Long-29 gr. solid lead bullet

MSRP **$10.95**

QUIET-22

Features: Ideal for bolt-action and single shot .22LR rifles (and perfectly safe in semiautomatics), this new reduced report cartridge generates ¼ the perceived noise level of standard velocity .22LR round.

Available in: .22 LR

From: . . . .**$2.89–$26.99**

SELECT .22LR

Features: The .22 Long Rifle Select is build for semiautomatic competition. Reliable operation, accuracy, and consistency make Select an ideal choice for competition shooters

Available in: .22LR

MSRP **$16.95**

Handgun and Rifle Ammunition

.22 WIN. MAG. MAXI MAG

Features: A favorite of varmint shooters. 40-gr. TMJ flat nose at 1875 fps, or 40-gr. jacketed HP at 1875 fps. Both loads give over 1400 fps from a 6-in. revolver. Clean-burning propellants keep actions cleaner. Surefire CCI priming. Reusable plastic box with dispenser lid.

Available in: .22 Win. Mag.

MSRP **$13.95**

MINI-MAG. HV

Features: CCI's first rimfire product and still most popular. Mini-Mag. hollow points are high-velocity products and offer excellent all-around performance for small game and varmints. Clean-burning propellants keep actions cleaner. Sure-fire CCI priming. Reusable plastic box with dispenser lid

Available in: .22 Long Rifle-40 gr. gilded round nose or -36 gr. gilded lead hollow point

From: **$6.99**

V-MAX 17 MACH 2

Features: The 17 Mach 2 is a .22LR CCI Stinger case necked down to hold a .17-caliber bullet. CCI loads a super accurate 17-grain polymer-tipped bullet, and drives it 60 percent faster than a .22 Long Rifle 40-gr. hollow point. The loaded cartridge is no longer than a .22LR, greatly expanding the gun actions that can accommodate .17-caliber rimfire cartridges. Reusable 50-count plastic box that protects and dispenses five cartridges at a time

Available in: .17 Mach 2 (V-Max also available in .17 HMR and .22 Mag. RF)

MSRP **$9.95**

PISTOL MATCH

Features: Designed expressly for high-ended semiauto match pistols. Singe-die tooling and great care in assembly lets you wring the last bit of accuracy from your precision pistol. Clean-burning propellants keep actions cleaner. Sure-fire CCI priming. Reusable plastic box with dispenser lid

Available in: .22LR-40 gr. lead round nose bullet

From: **$8.29**

CCI GREEN TAG

CCI QUIET-22

CCI MINI-MAG. HV

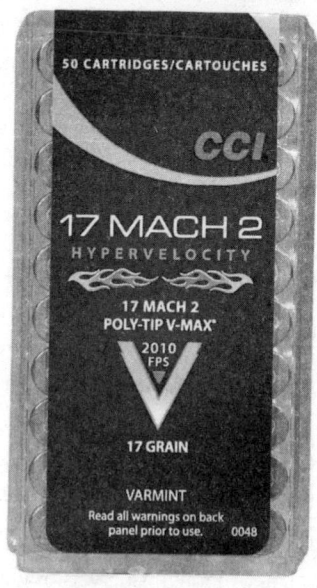

CCI V-MAX 17 MACH 2

Cor-Bon

Rifle Ammunition

.457 WWG

Features: Cor-Bon Ammunition and Wild West Guns teemed up to offer the best in a lever gun big game cartridge.
Available in: .457 WWG-350, 405, 460 gr.
From: **$69.99**

DPX RIFLE

Features: This is an optimum load for Law Enforcement. Lead-free projectile. Reduced recoil due to lighter weight projectile. Deep penetration on soft tissue 12-17 in.
Available in: .223 Rem., .22-250 Rem., .243 Win., .25-06 Rem., .257 Wby. Mag., 6x45mm, 6.5-284 Norma, .260 Rem., 6.8mm Rem. SPC, 7.62x39, .270 Win., .270 Wby. Mag., .270 WSM, 7mm RUM, 7mm WSM, 7mm Rem. Mag., 7mm-08 Rem., .284 Win., .30 Carbon, .308 Win., .30-06 Spfd., .300 Win. Mag., .300 RUM, .300 WSM, .30-30 Win., .338 Win. Mag., .338 Lapua, .338 RUM, .340 Wby. Mag., .375 H&H Mag., .375 RUM, .416 Rigby, .444 Marlin, .45/70 Govt., .458 Win. Mag., .458 Socom, .475 Turnbull
Box 20: . . . . **$33.06–$241.39**

EXPEDITION HUNTER

Features: Available with modern DPX lead free X-panding bullet or the legendary Woodleigh bullet. Both field-tested and engineered specifically to take down thick skinned and dangerous game with deep penetration. All partnered with the outstanding reliability that you have come to trust from Cor-Bon Ammunition.
Available in: 7mm Rem. Mag., .375 Flanged, .375 H&H Mag., .416 Rem. Mag., .416 Rigby, .404 Jeffery, .458 Win. Mag., .458 Lott, .470 Nitro Express, .505 Gibbs, .577 Nitro Express
Box 10: . . . . **$59.49–$187.13**

GLASER SAFETY SLUG

Features: Although slug was originally designed for use by Sky Marshals on airplanes, today the slug is recommended for anyone concerned with over-penetration. The Safety slug uses a copper jacket and is filled with a compressed load of either #12 or #6 lead shot. It is then capped with a round polymer ball that enhances feeding and reloading.
Available in: .25 Auto, .32 Auto, .32 NAA, .380 Auto, 9mm Makarov, 9mm Luger +P, .38 Super Auto, .38 Spl. Std., .38 Special +P, .357 Sig, .357 Mag., .40 S&W, 10mm Auto, .400 Corbon, .44 S&W Spl., .44 Mag., .45 Auto +P, .45 Colt +P, .223 (5.56), 7.62x39, .308 Win., .30-06 Spfd.
Box 6: . . . . **$13.39–$28.93**

HUNTER

Features: Bonded Core Soft Point ammunition retains optimum weight and integrity and provides reliable expansion coupled with deep penetration. The Penetrator features a heavy full-copper jacket enclosed in a hard linotype lead core. Hard Cast bullets are precision cast from hard linotype lead and have the flat, LBT nose design. Both loads cause a through and through hole, penetrating the thickest hides and breaking the heaviest bone.
Available in: .300 Whisper, 7.62x39, .357 Mag., 10mm Auto, .41 Rem. Mag., .44 Auto Mag., .44 Rem. Mag., .440 Corbon, .444 Marlin, .45 Colt +P, .45-70 Govt., .454 Casull, .460 Rowland, .460 S&W Mag., .475 Turnbull, .500 S&W Mag.
Box 12 or 20: . . . . . . **$30.98–$101.12**

Handgun Ammunition

DPX HANDGUN

Features: DPX is a solid copper hollowpoint bullet that combines the best of the lightweight high-speed JHPs and the heavyweight, deep-penetrating JHPs. The copper bullet construction allows it to conquer hard barriers like auto glass and steel while still maintaining its integrity.
Available in: .32 Auto, 9x23 Win., .380 Auto, 9mm Luger, 9mm Luger +P, .38 Super Auto +P, .38 Spl. +P, .357 Sig, .357 Mag., .40 S&W, 10mm Auto, .400 Corbon, .41 Rem. Mag., .44 S&W Special, .44 Rem. Mag., .45 GAP, .45 Auto Rim, .45 Auto, .45 Auto +P, .45 Colt +P, .454 Casull, .480 Ruger, .375 JDJ, .460 S&W Mag., .500 S&W Special, .500 S&W Mag.
Box 20: . . . . **$28.46–$91.17**

GLASER POW'RBALL

Features: Designed for finicky feeding pistols, Pow'Rball is a great choice for your semiauto pistols or revolvers. Reliable feeding and consistent reliable expansion; deeper soft tissue penetration; custom scored jacket; proprietary polymer ball and patented lead core
Available in: .32 Auto, .380 Auto, 9mm Makarov, 9mm Luger +P, 9x23 Win., .38 Super +P, .38 Spl. +P, .357 Sig, .357 Mag, .40 S&W, 10mm Auto, .400 Corbon, .45 GAP, .45 Auto +P
Box 20: . . . . **$21.90–$29.22**

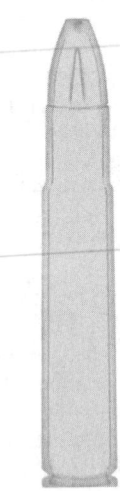

**COR-BON
EXPEDITION
HUNTER**

Shotgun Ammunition

HEVI-METAL TURKEY

Features: HEVI-METAL Turkey is a layered load that combines premium steel shot with HEVI-Shot pellets. Timeless testing of various shot load methods found layering to provide the most pellets on target and the best knockdown performance.
Available in: 12 Ga. (3 in., 3 ½ in.), 20 Ga. (3 in.)
Box 10:. . . . . $8.99–$12.99

HEVI-SHOT CLASSIC DOUBLES

Features: Optimized for your fixed chokes and fine classic doubles; denser than steel but soft like lead which means you get deeper penetration; USFWS-approved non-toxic shot; 45 percent more on target pellets than steel; belted sphere for maximum pellet mass; buffered and nano-treated pellets for tight patterns; weather-resistant crimp
Available in: 12 Ga. (2 ¾ in., 3 in.), 16 Ga. (2 ¾ in.), 20 Ga. (2 ¾ in., 3 in.), .28 Ga. (2 ¾ in.), .410 Ga. (3 in.)
Box 10:. . . . . $30.99–$41.99

HEVI-SHOT DEAD COYOTE!

Features: With these HEVI-Shot T-shot loads, you can be deadly at ranges you never thought possible with a 12 gauge. The 3-in. load pounds out 50 perfectly round pellets at 1,350 fps. 10 percent heavier than lead, 54 percent denser than steel. Every 50 rounds includes a dry-storage box.
Available in: 10 Ga. (3 ½ in.), 12 Ga. (2 ¾ in., 3 in., 3 ½ in.)
Box 10:. . . . . $49.49–$64.99

HEVI-SHOT MAGNUM BLEND

Features: Put more lethal pellets in your pattern with a combination of No. 5, 6, and 7 HEVI-13 shot, and boost your lethal range by 14 to 17 percent. Buffered and moly-coated pellets produce a denser pattern than conventional shot. HEVI-13 delivers 40 percent more knockdown energy and up to 40 percent longer range than lead shells.
Available in: 10 Ga. (3 ½ in.), 12 Ga. (3 in., 3 ½ in.), 20 Ga. (3 in.)
Box 5:. . . . . $26.99–$29.99

SPEED BALL

Features: Speed Ball is an elastomeric ball in the base of the wad that accelerates pellets without boosting chamber pressures. An MV² pellet sits in the base of the shell with a HEVI-Shot layer on top, resulting in higher pellet counts in the 30-inch circle than you get with HEVI-Shot. Nearly matches the lethal energy of HEVI-Shot, out to 60 yards (but far exceeds the energy of anything else).
Available in: 12 Ga. (3 in., 3 ½ in.) 20 Ga. (3 in.); Shot sizes: BB, 1, 3, 5
Box 10: . . . .$8.99–$14.99

ENVIRON-METAL SPEED BALL

ENVIRON-METAL HEVI-METAL TURKEY

ENVIRON-METAL HEVI-SHOT DEAD COYOTE!

AMMUNITION

Federal Fusion Ammunition

FUSION RIFLE AMMO

Features: This specialized deer bullet electrochemically joins pure copper to an extreme pressure-formed core to ensure optimum performance. The result is high terminal energy on impact that radiates lethal shock throughout the target. This energy is optimized through mass weight retention, a top secretive tip-skiving process and superior bullet integrity.
Available in: .223 Rem., .22-250 Rem., .243 Win., .25-06 Rem., 6.5x55 Swedish, .260 Rem., .270 Win., .270 WSM, 7mm-08 Rem., .280 Rem., 7mm Rem. Mag., 7mm WSM, 7.62x39mm Soviet, .30-30 Win., .308 Win., .30-06 Spfd., .300 Win. Mag., .300 WSM, .338 Fed., .338 Win. Mag., .35 Whelen, .375 H&H Mag., .416 Rigby, .416 Rem. Mag., .45-70 Govt., .458 Win. Mag., .458 Lott
Box 20:. . . . . **$18.99–$89.99**

FUSION SAFARI

Features: Fusion's advanced molecular technique of electro-chemically applying the jacket to the core means consistent toughness. With enhanced aerodynamics, internal skiving, and superb accuracy, these bullets provide great performance on a variety of safari animals. Fusion Safari bullets offer high weight retention to ensure deep penetration.
Available in: .375 H&H, .416 Rigby, .416 Rem. Mag., .458 Win. Mag., .458 Lott
Box 20:. . . . . **$59.99–$98.95**

FUSION SHOTGUN SLUGS

Features: Fusion slugs have made shotgunners part of the next generation of deer hunters. Slug hunters can now find the same unequaled energy and deer devastation in their favorite rifled-barrel shotgun.

Available in: 12, 20 Ga. (2 ¾ in., 3 in.)
Box 5:. . . . . **$8.19–$24.99**

FEDERAL FUSION RIFLE AMMO

Federal Premium Ammunition

Rifle Ammunition

FULL METAL JACKET BOAT-TAIL

Features: Accurate, non-expanding bullets. Flat shooting trajectory, leaves small exit holes in game, and put clean holes in paper. Smooth, reliable feeding into semiautomatics too
Available in: .223 Rem., .308 Win., .30-06 Spfd. (American Eagle)
Box 20:. . . . . **$9.09–$23.49**

NOSLER PARTITION

Features: Bullet features a partitioned lead core and shank that allows the front half to mushroom while the rear core remains intact for deep penetration and stopping power.
Available in: .223 Rem., 22-250 Rem., .243 Win., 6mm Rem., 257 Roberts +P, 25-06 Rem., .270 Win., .270 WSM, 7mm Mauser, 7mm-08 Rem., .280 Rem., 7mm Rem. Mag., 30-30 Win., .308 Win., 30-06 Spfd., 300 H&H Mag.
Box 20:. . . . . **$24.99–$57.99**

SIERRA MATCHKING BOAT-TAIL HP

Features: Long ranges are its specialty. Excellent choice for everything from varmints to big game animals. Tapered, boattail design provides extremely flat trajectories. Higher downrange velocity for more energy at the point of impact. Reduced wind drift
Available in: .223 Rem., 6.5x55 Swedish, .260 Rem., .308 Win., 30-06 Spfd., .300 Win. Mag., .338 Lapua Mag.
Box 20:. . . . . **$31.49–$112.99**

SOFT POINT

Features: Proven performer on small game and thin-skinned medium game. Aerodynamic tip for a flat trajectory. Exposed soft point expands rapidly for hard hits, even as velocity slows at longer ranges.
Available in: .22 Hornet (V-Shok), .222 Rem., .223 Rem., .22-250 Rem., .243 Win., 6mm Rem., 6.5x55 Swedish, .270 Win., .270 WSM, .280 Rem., 7mm Rem. Mag., 7mm WSM, 7.62x39 Soviet, .300 Savage, .308 Win., .30-06 Spfd., .300 WSM, .303 British, 8mm Mauser, .338 Fed. (Power-Shok, American Eagle), .375 H&H Mag. (Power-Shok)
Box 20:. . . . . **$18.99–$51.99**

SOFT POINT FLAT NOSE

Features: Great for thick cover, it expands reliably and penetrates deep on light to medium game. The flat nose prevents accidental discharge.
Available in: .30-30 Win., .32 Win. Spl.
Box 20:. . . . . **$15.99–$27.49**

SOFT POINT ROUND NOSE

Features: The choice in heavy cover. Large exposed tip, good weight retention and specially tapered jacket provide controlled expansion.
Available in: .270 Win., 7mm Mauser, .30 Carbine, .30-30 Win., .35 Rem.
Box 20:. . . . . **$15.99–$30.99**

SPEER TNT GREEN

Features: TNT Green brings non-tox technology to the Federal Premium V-Shok varmint hunting line. This is a totally lead-free bullet that couples explosive expansion with match-grade accuracy.
Available in: .22 Hornet, .222 Rem., .223 Rem., .22-250 Rem.
Box 20:. . . . . **$21.99–$25.99**

TROPHY BONDED BEAR CLAW

Features: Ideal for medium to large dangerous game. The jacket and core are 100% fusion-bonded for reliable bullet expansion from 25 yards to extreme ranges. Bullet retains 95 percent of its weight for deep

Federal Premium Ammunition

FEDERAL PREMIUM GUARD DOG HOME DEFENSE

penetration. Hard solid copper base tapering to a soft, copper nose section for controlled expansion
Available in: 7mm Rem. Mag., .30-06 Spfd., .300 Win. Mag., .388 Win. Mag., .35 Whelen (Vital-Shok), .375 H&H Mag., .416 Rigby, .416 Rem. Mag. (Cape-Shok), .45-70 Govt. (Vital-Shok), .458 Win. Mag., .458 Lott, .470 Nitro Express (Cape-Shok)
Box 20:. . . . . $33.99–$199.99

TROPHY BONDED SLEDGEHAMMER
Features: Use it on the largest, most dangerous game in the world. Jack Carter design maximizes stopping power. Bonded bronze solid with a flat nose that minimizes deflection off bone and muscle for a deep straight wound channel.
Available in: .375 H&H Mag., .416 Rigby, .416 Rem. Mag., .458 Win. Mag., .458 Lott, .470 Nitro Express (Cape-Shok)
Box 20:. . . . . $91.99–$213.99

TROPHY BONDED TIP
Features: Built on the Trophy Bonded Bear Claw platform to provide deep penetration and high weight retention. Sleek profile, with tapered heel and translucent polymer tip. Nickel-plated. Available as component and in Federal loaded ammunition
Available in: .270 Win., .270 WSM, .270 Wby. Mag., 7mm-08 Rem., .280 Rem., 7mm Rem. Mag., 7mm WSM, 7mm Wby. Mag., 7mm STW, .308 Win., .30-06 Spfd., .300 H&H Mag., .300 Win. Mag., .300 WSM, .300 Wby. Mag., .300 Rem. Ultra Mag., .338 Federal, .338 Win. Mag.
Box 20:. . . . . $32.99–$59.99

VITAL-SHOK TROPHY COPPER
Features: Tipped bullet cavity for consistent expansion across a broad range of velocities; grooved bullet shank for increased accuracy across a wider range of firearms; a copper-alloy design that achieves up to 99 percent weight retention; nickel-plated case prevents corrosion and aids in easier, faster extraction from the chamber
Available in: .243 Win., .25-06 Rem., .270 Win., .270 WSM, 7mm-08 Rem., .280 Rem., 7mm Rem. Mag., 7mm WSM, .308 Win., .30-06 Spfd., .300 H&H, .300 Win. Mag., .300 WSM, .300 Wby. Mag., .300 Rem. Ultra Mag., .338 Fed., .338 Win. Mag.
Box 20: . . . . $26.99–$56.99

Handgun Ammunition

CASTCORE
Features: Heavyweight, flat-nosed, hard cast-lead bullet that smashes through bone
Available in: .375 Mag., .41 Rem. Mag., .44 Rem. Mag. (Vital-Shok)
Box 20:. . . . . $23.99–$33.99

FULL METAL JACKET
Features: Good choice for range practice and reducing lead fouling in the barrel. Jacket extends from the nose to the base, preventing bullet expansion and barrel leading. Primarily as military ammunition for recreational shooting.
Available in: .25 Auto, .32 Auto, .380 Auto, 9mm Makarov, 9mm Luger, .38 Super +P, .357 Sig, .38 Spl., .40 S&W, 10mm Auto, .45 G.A.P., .45 Auto (American Eagle)
Box 50:. . . . . $13.99–$35.99

FEDERAL PREMIUM TROPHY BONDED TIP

GUARD DOG HOME DEFENSE
Features: Protect your home and loved ones with a cartridge designed exclusively for home defense. Guard Dog packs the terminal performance that stops threats while reducing over-penetration through walls.
Available in: 9mm Luger, .40 S&W, .45 Auto
Box 20:. . . . . $22.99–$26.99

HYDRA-SHOK JHP
Features: Unique center-post design delivers controlled expansion, and the notched jacket provides efficient energy transfer to penetrate barriers while retaining stopping power. Deep penetration satisfies even the FBI's stringent testing requirements.
Available in: .32 Auto, .327 Fed. Mag., .380 Auto, 9mm Luger, .38 Spl., .38 Spl. +P, .357 Mag., .40 S&W, 10mm Auto, .44 Rem. Mag., .45 G.A.P., .45 Auto (Premium Personal Defense)
Box 20:. . . . . $20.49–$32.99

JACKETED HOLLOW POINT
Features: Ideal personal defense round in revolvers and semi-autos. Quick, positive expansion. Jacket ensures smooth feeding into autoloading firearms.
Available in: .32 H&R Mag., 9mm Luger (Personal Defense), .38 Super +P (American Eagle), .357 Sig., .357 Mag. (Premium Personal Defense, Power-Shok), .40 S&W (Personal Defense), .41 Rem. Mag., .44 Rem. Mag. (Power-Shok, American Eagle), .45 Auto (Personal Defense)
Box 20:. $18.49-29.99

LEAD ROUND NOSE
Features: Great training round for practicing at the range. 100 percent lead with no jacket. Excellent accuracy and very economical
Available in: .32 S&W Long (Champion), .38 Special (American Eagle)
MSRP. . . . . $14.99–$20.99

Federal Premium Ammunition

LEAD SEMI-WADCUTTER

Features: Most popular all-around choice for target and personal defense, a versatile design that cuts clean holes in targets and efficiently transfers energy
Available in: .32 H&R Mag. (Champion)
MSRP.................. **$16.49**

NYCLAD HP

Features: Proven NyClad bullets feature a lead core hollow-point with Nylon coating. Offers great stopping power and penetration—ideal qualities for a personal defense round.
Available in: .38 Special-125 gr.
Box 20:........... **$16.99–$21.99**

PREMIUM PERSONAL DEFENSE SHOT SHELLS

Features: The Judge from Taurus has emerged as a very popular handgun for Personal Defense. This specialized gun has been without a specialized load—until now.
Available in: .410 bore (2 ½ in.); Shot sizes: 000 Buck, 4
Box 20:.................**$12.99**

SEMI-WADCUTTER HP

Features: For both small game and personal defense. Hollow point design promotes uniform expansion.
Available in: .44 Special, .45 Colt (Champion)
MSRP........... **$20.99–$24.99**

Shotgun Ammunition

BLACK CLOUD FS STEEL

Available in: 10 Ga. (3 ½ in.), 12 Ga. (2 ¾ in., 3 in., 3 ½ in.) 20 Ga. (3 in.); Shot sizes: 2, 3, 4, BB, BBB
Box 25:........... **$15.99–$27.49**

BLACK CLOUD FS STEEL CLOSE RANGE

Features: Engineered to put more pellets on targets 20 to 30 yards away, Close Range achieves a full pattern within a very short distance; comprised of 100 percent Flitestopper Steel for the most lethal payload imaginable, Close Range produces more open and optimum patterns; crimp and primer sealed
Available in: 12 Ga., 20 Ga. (3 in.)
Box 25: .... **$18.99–$20.49**

BLACK CLOUD HIGH VELOCITY

Features: The Black Cloud High Velocity line pumps up the speed and lethal performance for waterfowl hunters everywhere. Boasting higher velocities, increased energy and shorter lead times, the High velocity offerings bring a renewed sense of excitement to the duck blind.
Available in: 12 Ga. (3 in.); Shot Sizes: 3, 4
Box 25:.................**$20.49**

GAME-SHOK UPLAND GAME

Available in: 12, 16, 20 Ga. (2 ¾ in.); Shot sizes: 6, 8, 7.5
Box 25:............ **$6.69–$11.99**

FEDERAL BLACK CLOUD FS STEEL CLOSE RANGE

GAME-SHOK UPLAND GAME HEAVY FIELD

Available in: 12, 20 Ga. (2 ¾ in.); Shot sizes: 4, 5, 6, 7.5
Box 25:............ **$7.29–$11.49**

GAME-SHOK UPLAND GAME HI-BRASS

Available in: 12, 16, 20 Ga. (2 ¾ in.), .410 bore (2 ½ in., 3 in.); Shot sizes: 4, 5, 6, 7.5
Box 25:............ **$14.49–$16.79**

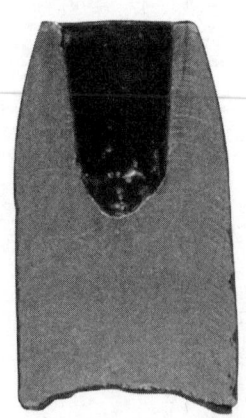

FEDERAL PREMIUM NYCLAD HP

Federal Premium Ammunition

GOLD MEDAL EXTRA-LITE PAPER (LR)
Features: Also available in plastic
Available in: 12 Ga. (2 ¾ in.); Shot sizes: 7.5, 8
Box 25: . . . .**$8.49–$9.99**

GOLD MEDAL-HANDICAP PAPER HV
Features: Also available in plastic
Available in: 12 Ga. (2 ¾ in.); Shot sizes: 7.5, 8
Box 25: . . . .**$8.49–$10.99**

GOLD MEDAL-INTERNATIONAL PAPER
Features: Also available in plastic (with Shot sizes: 7.5, 8)
Available in: 12 Ga. (2 ¾ in.); Shot sizes: 7.5
Box 25: . . . .**$8.99–$10.99**

GOLD MEDAL-PLASTIC
Features: Also available in paper (12 Ga., 2 ¾ in., Shot sizes: 7.5, 8, 9)
Available in: 12, 20, 28 Ga. (2 ¾ in.), .410 bore (2 ½ in.); Shot sizes: 7.5, 8, 8.5, 9
Box 25: . . . .**$7.99–$10.99**

GOLD MEDAL-SPORTING CLAYS PLASTIC
Available in: 12 Ga. (2 ¾ in.); Shot sizes: 7.5, 8, 8.5
Box 25: . . . .**$8.49–$10.99**

MAG-SHOK HEAVYWEIGHT TURKEY
Available in: 10 Ga. (3 ½ in.), 12 Ga. (2 ¾ in., 3 in., 3 ½ in.), 20 Ga. (2 ¾ in., 3 in.); Shot sizes: 5, 6, 7
Box 5: . . . . $14.99–$27.99

MAG-SHOK HIGH VELOCITY LEAD WITH FLITECONTROL
Available in: 10 Ga. (3 ½ in.), 12 Ga. (2 ¾ in., 3 in., 3 ½ in.) 20 Ga. (3 in.); Shot sizes: 4, 5, 6
Box 10: . . . . $11.99–$16.99

MAG-SHOK LEAD WITH FLITECONTROL
Available in: 12 Ga. (3 in., 3 ½ in.); Shot sizes: 4, 5, 6
Box 10: . . . . **$16.99–$19.99**

PRAIRIE STORM - FS STEEL
Available in: 12, 20 Ga. (3 in.); Shot sizes: 3, 4
Box 25: . . . . **$18.29–$20.49**

SPEED-SHOK WATERFOWL
Available in: 10 Ga. (3 ½ in.), 12 Ga. (2 ¾ in., 3 in., 3 ½ in.), 16 Ga. (2 ¾ in.), 20 Ga. (2 ¾ in., 3 in.); Shot sizes: 1, 2, 3, 4, 6, 7, BB, BBB, T
Box 25: . . . .**$7.79–$24.49**

STRUT-SHOK TURKEY
Available in: 12 Ga. (3 in., 3 ½ in.); Shot sizes: 4, 5, 6
Box 10: . . . .**$9.29–$14.49**

TOP GUN TARGET
Available in: 12 Ga., 20 Ga. (2 ¾ in.); Shot sizes: 7.5, 8, 9
Box 25: . . . .**$6.59–$7.69**

TOP GUN TARGET-STEEL
Available in: 12 Ga., 20 Ga. (2 ¾ in.); Shot size: 7
Box 25: . . . .**$7.99–$9.99**

TOP GUN TARGET-SUBSONIC
Available in: 12 Ga. (2 ¾ in.); Shot size: 7.5
Box 25: . . . .**$7.69–$8.99**

V-SHOK HEAVYWEIGHT COYOTE
Available in: 12 Ga. (3 in.); Shot size: BB
Box 5: . . . .**$19.99–$23.99**

WING-SHOK HIGH VELOCITY
Features: Pheasant and Quail Forever versions available
Available in: 12 Ga. (2 ¾ in., 3 in.), 28 Ga. (2 ¾ in.); Shot sizes: 4, 5, 6, 7, 7.5, 8
Box 25: . . . . **$15.29–$24.99**

WING-SHOK MAGNUM
Available in: 10 Ga. (3 ½ in.), 12 Ga. (2 ¾ in., 3 in.), 16 Ga. (2 ¾ in.), 20 Ga. (2 ¾ in., 3 in.); Shot sizes: 2, 4, 5, 6, BB
Box 25: **$24.99-54.99**

Shotgun Ammunition Slugs

POWER-SHOK RIFLED SLUG
Features: Hollow point slug type
Available in: 10 Ga. (3 ½ in.), 12 Ga. (2 ¾ in., 3 in.), 16 Ga. (2 ¾ in.), 20 Ga. (2 ¾ in.), .410 (2 ½ in.)
Box 5: . . . .**$4.39–$6.19**

POWER-SHOK SABOT
Features: Sabot hollow point slug type
Available in: 12 Ga., 20 Ga. (2 ¾ in.)
Box 5: . . . .**$6.69–$8.49**

FEDERAL PREMIUM PRAIRIE STORM - FS STEEL

Federal Premium Ammunition

VITAL-SHOK TROPHY COPPER SABOT SLUG

Features: A copper slug that incorporates some of the most advanced technology in the industry; better accuracy, less drop, manageable recoil (similar to a .30-06) and consistent penetration and expansion; unique two-part sabot design achieves accuracy through a clean launch and improved projectile support

Available in: 12 Ga., 20 Ga. (2 ¾ in., 3 in.)

Box 5: . . . . $10.99–$12.99

VITAL-SHOK TRUBALL RIFLED SLUG

Available in: 12, 20 Ga. (2 ¾ in., 3 in.)

Box 5:. . . . . $4.49–$5.99

FEDERAL PREMIUM VITAL-SHOK TRUBALL RIFLED SLUG

Fiocchi USA

Rifle Ammunition

CANNED HEAT CENTERFIRE RIFLE AMMO

Features: One of the most innovative and effective ways to store ammunition long term. Canned Heat ammo is packed in an oxygen-free nitrogen gas atmosphere to prevent rust and deterioration over time. The cans have an enamel coating inside and out to insulate against electrolysis and prevent corrosion. They stack and store easily, come with resealable plastic lids, and hold up better over time than conventional cardboard packaging.

Available in: .223 Rem., .308 Win., 9x19 Luger, .40 S&W, .45 Auto, .22LR,

From:. . . . . $8.42–$36.13

EXTREMA RIFLE HUNTING LINE

Features: Combining the best bullets in the business with our precision-drawn brass cases gives you the best combination of value and performance. The Fiocchi Extrema Hunting Line uses bullets like the Hornady SST, V Max, and Sierra Game King to provide a combination of accuracy, high ballistic coefficients, and reliable expansion.

Available in: .222 Rem., .204 Ruger, .223 Rem., .22-50 Rem., .243 Win., 6.5x55 Swedish, .270 Win., .308 Win., .30-06 Spfd., .300 Win. Mag.

From:. . . . . $22.49–$34.99

SHOOTING DYNAMICS RIFLE LINE

Features: High-quality reloadable brass cases combined with quality full metal jacket, soft point, or flat soft point (for lever guns) make sure your shooting dollar goes further with Fiocchi. Even our 7.62x39 ammo uses reloadable brass cases, boxer primed (noncorrosive) with copper-jacketed bullets.

Available in: .223 Rem., .22-250 Rem., .243 Win., .270 Win., .30-30 Win., .308 Win., .30-06 Spfd., .300 Win. Mag., 7.62x39

From:. . . . . $10.79–$32.99

Handgun Ammunition

COWBOY ACTION LINE

Features: Loaded with brass reloadable cases, noncorrosive primers, smokeless powders, and lead bullets coated with lube to reduce leading in the barrel. Fiocchi sets the velocity on par with what you would expect from period-correct ammo while keeping the recoil to a minimum for timed Cowboy Action competition and to reduce wear and tear on older guns.

Available in: .32 S&W Long, .38 S&W Short, .38 S&W Special, .357 Mag., .44 Special, .44-40, .45 Long Colt

From:. . . . . $19.99–$34.99

FIOCCHI CANNED HEAT CENTERFIRE RIFLE AMMO

FIOCCHI SHOOTING DYNAMICS PISTOL LINE

AMMUNITION

FIOCCHI GOLDEN PHEASANT SHOT SHELLS

FIOCCHI TUNDRA COMPOSITE

EXTREMA XTP HANDGUN LINE

Features: Combined with nickel-plated cases for positive feeding and extraction when you need it most, qualified primers and clean powders deliver the maximum performance for the ultimate hunting or self-defense application.
Available in: .25 Auto, .32 Auto, .380 Auto, 9mm Luger, .38 Spl., .38 Spl.+P, .357 Mag., .40 S&W, .44 Rem. Mag., .45 Auto,
From: . . . . **$14.99–$24.99**

SHOOTING DYNAMICS PISTOL & REVOLVER LINE

Features: Combining quality brass cases with consistent primers, clean powders, and full metal jacket, jacketed hollow point, and soft point bullets in many calibers, Fiocchi loads bullets of the same weight to velocities that are comparable with high-quality defensive loads so you get realistic training-recoil impulse and point of aim/impact.
Available in: .25 Auto, .32 Auto, .32 S&W Long, .380 Auto, 9mm Luger, 9mm Makarov, 9mm Steyr, 9x21 IMI, .38 Spl., .357 Mag., .38 Super Auto, .40 S&W, .44 Rem. Mag., .44 Spl., .45 Auto
From: . . . . **$12.99–$34.99**

Shotgun Ammunition

CYALUME CHEMICAL TRACER SHOTSHELL

Features: The Fiocchi Chemical Tracer powered by Cyalume, provides a daytime visible trace that travels with the cloud of shot as it hits or misses the clay bird. The Chemical Tracer is non-incendiary, non-toxic, and meets EPA and Consumer Safety compliance. It leaves no residue in the barrel and is non-corrosive.
Available in: 12 Ga. (2 ¾ in.), Shot size: 8
From: . . . . **$16.45–$44.00**

EXACTA TARGET LOADS

Features: Specifically for competitive shooters. The Target Load Line is the offspring of a 50-year tradition of supporting the world of trap, skeet, and now sporting clays, FITASC, and Compaq.
Available in: Steel: 12 Ga., 20 Ga. (2 ¾ in.), Shot size: 7; Helios: 12 Ga. (2 ¾ in.), Shot sizes: 7, 7.5
From: . . . . **$7.99–$8.49**

GOLDEN PHEASANT LINE

Features: Golden Pheasant shot shells utilize a special hard, nickel-plated lead shot, based on Fiocchi's strict ballistic tolerances that ensure proven shot consistency and result in deeper penetration, longer ranges, and much tighter patterns.
Available in: 12 Ga. (2 ¾ in., 3 in.), 16 Ga. (2 ¾ in.), 20, 28 Ga. (2 ¾ in., 3 in.); Shot sizes: 4, 5, 6, 7.5
From: . . . . **$13.99–$18.99**

GOLDEN TURKEY LINE

Features: Copper then nickel-plated shot offers the penetration and patterns you need when you need a turkey for dinner.
Available in: 12 Ga. (3 in., 3 ½ in.); Shot sizes: 4, 5, 6
MSRP . . . .**N/A**

NICKEL PLATED BUCKSHOT

Features: Harder pellets from the nickel plating mean better patterns, better penetration, and no buffer needed.
Available in: 12 Ga. (2 ¾ in.); Shot sizes: 00, 4
From: . . . . **$5.00–$11.99**

OPTIMA SPECIFIC HIGH VELOCITY

Features: High brass hulls, one-piece shot cup and cushioned wads, and round shot pellets make sure you get the bang for your buck you have come to expect from Fiocchi.
Available in: 12 Ga. (2 ¾ in., 3 in.), 16 Ga. (2 ¾ in.), 20 Ga. (2 ¾ in., 3 in.), 28 Ga. (2 ¾ in., 3 in.), .410 (3 in.); Shot sizes: 4, 5, 6, 7.5, 8, 9
From: . . . . **$11.79–$13.46**

TUNDRA COMPOSITE

Features: It's heavier than bismuth for dead-on-delivery performance. Spherical, non-brittle Tundra compound deforms on impact, just like lead. Use with any choke, even full.
Available in: 12 Ga. (2 ¾ in., 3 in.), 20, 28 Ga. (3 in.); Shot size 1, 2, 3, 4, 5, 6, BB
Box 10: . . . . **$21.99–$25.49**

WATERFOWL STEEL HUNTING

Features: Treated steel pellets, the correct wad, and powders that perform in the cold conditions often encountered in waterfowl hunting deliver the kills a waterfowl hunter wants.
Available in: 12 Ga. (2 ¾ in., 3 in.), 20 Ga. (3 in.); Shot sizes: T, BBB, BB, 1, 2, 3, 4, 5, 6
From: . . . . **$8.85–$15.31**

AMMUNITION

Hornady

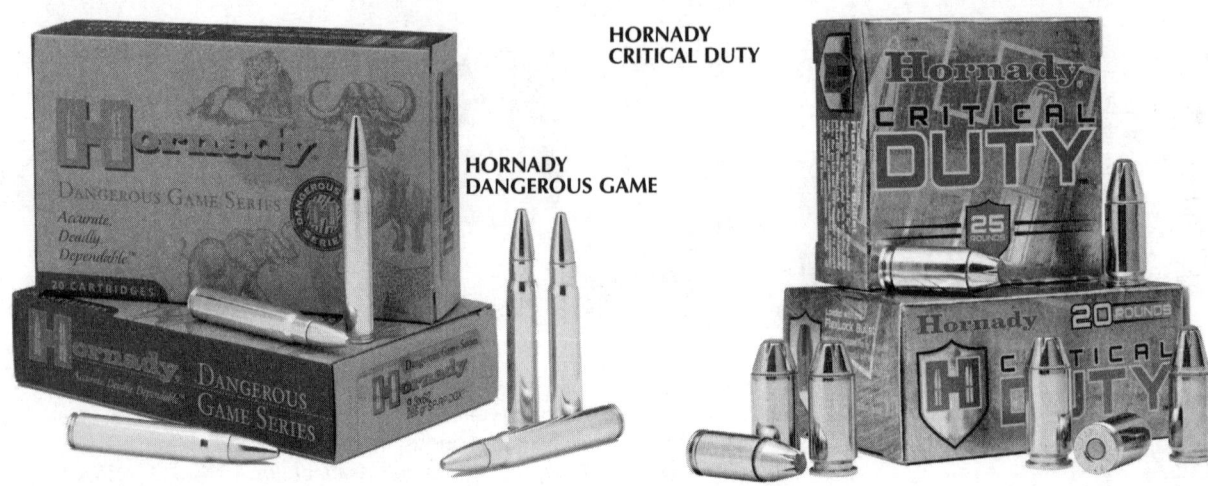

HORNADY
CRITICAL DUTY

HORNADY
DANGEROUS GAME

Rifle Ammunition

CUSTOMLITE
Features: CustomLite ammunition is recommended for children, women, and anyone new to the game. They offer minimum recoil and a reduced muzzle blast. These are often paired with SST and RN bullets.
Available in: .243 Win, .270 Win., 7mm-08 Rem., .30-.30 Win., .308 Win., .30-06 Spfd.
From: . . . . **$25.99–$27.99**

DANGEROUS GAME
Features: These bullets are among the largest offered by Hornady and feature the DGS (Dangerous Game Solid) and the DGX (Dangerous Game eXpanding). They're made with hard lead/antimony alloy cone and surrounded by a copper-clad steel jacket. Straighter penetration comes from a flat meplat that creates more energy than traditional round bullets.
Available in: 9.3X62, 9.3X74R, .376 Steyr., .375 H&H, .375 Ruger, .450-400 Nitro Express, .404 Jeffrey, .416 Rem. Mag., .416 Ruger, .416 Rigby, .458 Win., .450 Nitro Express, .458 Lott, .470 Nitro Express, .500 Nitro Express
From: . . . . **$38.49–$130.99**

LEVEREVOLUTION
Features: LEVERevolution bullets travel at a speed of 250 fps and have a faster muzzle velocity than most other conventional lever gun loads. They are unbelievably accurate and offer incomparable terminal performance. These bullets are available in FTX and MonoFlex.
Available in: .30-.30 Win., .308 Marlin Express, .32 Win. Spl., .338 Marlin Express, .35 Rem., .357 Mag., .44 Mag., .444 Marlin, .45-70 Govt, .450 Marlin
From: . . . . **$24.49–$38.99**

MATCH
Features: Match bullets feature a boattail hollow point design that provides both accuracy and speed. These bullets' jackets feature near-zero wall thickness, which leads to uniformity throughout the jacket. Case weight and internal capacity are also consistent throughout Match ammunition.
Available in: .223 Rem., 6.5 Grendel, 6.5 Creedmoor, .308 Win., .30-06 Springfield, .300 Win. Mag., .338 Lapua, .50 BMG
From: . . . . **$17.99–$84.99**

SUPERFORMANCE
Features: Superformance bullets are 100 to 200 fps faster than any other traditional type of bullet on the market today. In addition to their speed, they also offer minimal recoil, muzzle blast, temperature sensativity, and inaccuracies. These bullets are versatile and can be paired with all types of firearms, including semi-autos, lever guns, and pump actions.
Available in: .223 Rem., .243 Win., .25-06 Rem., .257 Roberts+P, .270 Win., .280 Rem., .30 TC, .30-06 Spfd., .300 RCM., .300 Savage, .300 Win. Mag., .308 Win., .338 RCM, .338 Win. Mag., .35 Whelen, .375 H&H, .375 Ruger, .444 Marlin, .458 Win., 5.56 NATO, 6.5 Creedmoor, 6.5X5.5 Swedish Mauser, 6mm. Rem., 7mm Rem. Mag., 7mm-08 Rem., 7x57 Mauser
MSRP . . . . **$30.27–$118.79**

Handgun Ammunition

COWBOY ACTION SHOOTING
Features: These swaged bullets flatten instead of fragment when they reach their targets. Their diamond knurling ensures that the entire surface of the bullet is well-lubed.
Available in: .44-40, .45 Colt
Box 20: . . . . **$21.93–$24.97**

CRITICAL DEFENSE
Features: Critical Defense bullets are custom-designed for individual loads, and their shiny silver nickel plating prevents bullet corrosion. Heavy clothing such as denim and leather are no match for these bullets. Critical Defense ammunication is cannelured and crimped to avoid bullet setback, and clean burning and stable propellants reduce recoil.
Available in: .410, .22 WMR, 32 NAA, 32 H&R Mag., 9x18mm, .380 Auto, 9mm Luger, .38 Spl., .357 Sig., .357 Mag., 40 S&W, 10mm Auto, .44 Special, .44 Mag., .45 Auto, .45 Colt
From: . . . . **$16.65–$30.35**

AMMUNITION

Hornady

CRITICAL DUTY

Features: Critical Duty ammunition features FlexLock Bullets, crimped and nickel-plated cases, interlocking bands, and a core made of high-antimony lead. These bullets are among the top choices of law enforcement and military professionals and highly reliable.
Available in: 45 Auto +P, 9mm, 9mm Luger+P, .40 S&W
Box 20–25: $28.75

LEVEREVOLUTION

Features: LEVERevolution bullets travel at a speed of 250 fps and are unbelievably accurate. These bullets feature Flex Tip Technology and should not be stored for long periods of time, as the tips may become deformed. They deliver 40 percent more energy than traditional bullets.
Available in: .357 Mag, .44 Mag, .45 Colt
From: . . . . $26.05–$28.51

TAP FPD

Features: Police officers, snipers, and military professionals across the world choose TAP FPD ammunition due to reliability and accuracy of these bullets. Silver-nickel cases prevent corrosion and the minimal muzzle flash protects night vision.

Available in: .380 Auto, 9mm Luger, 40 S&W, .45 Auto+P
Box 20–25 . . . . $23.17–$29.47

Shotgun Ammunition

BUCKSHOT

Features: Buckshot ammunition is specially designed for unmodified semiauto and pump shotguns. Made with Versatite wad technology, these reliable bullets offer a tight, accurate shot.
Available in: 12 Ga. (2 ¾ in.)
Box 10: . . . . $15.52–$17.08

HEAVY MAGNUM TURKEY

Features: Each 3-inch, 12-gauge shotshell contains 1½ ounces of either #4, #5, or #6 nickel-plated lead. Loads don't require modified shotguns or specialized turkey chokes.
Available in: 12 Ga. (3 in.); Shot sizes: 4, 5, 6 nickel
Box 10: $17.81

SST SLUGS

Features: Sharp points at the end of these slugs allow for faster and more accurate shooting. You'll be able to reach your target from an impressive 200 yards away. Each shot delivers more than 1200 ft.-lbs. of energy. Also available in Superperformance (SPF) Slugs.

Available in: 12, 20 Ga. (2 ¾ in)
Box 5: . . . . $15.87–$19.81

Rimfire Ammunition

17 HMR

Features: The 17 HMR is one of the most accurate rimfire bullets ever made. The polymer tip fragments rapidly and dramatically on impact, and its flat trajectory adds to its accuracy and consistency.
Available in: .17 HMR
Box 50: . . . . $17.04–$17.87

17 MACH2

Features: These V-MAX bullets are known for their rapid fragmentation and consistent accuracy. These bullets are made in America and hand inspected. Paired with Varmint Express products, ignition is fast and easy.
Available in: .17 Mach2
Box 50: . . . .$9.91–$11.65

22 WMR

Features: The .22 WMR guarantees accurate shooting from more than 125 feet. It has a muzzle of 2,200 fps and is one of the most requested products Hornady offers. It's available in 25, 30, and 45 gr.
Available in: .22 WMR
Box 50: . . . . $15.77–$17.53

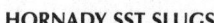

HORNADY SST SLUGS

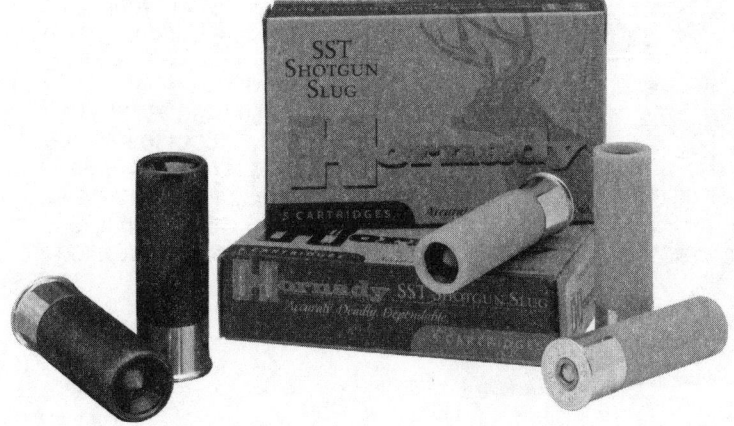

HORNADY 17 HMR

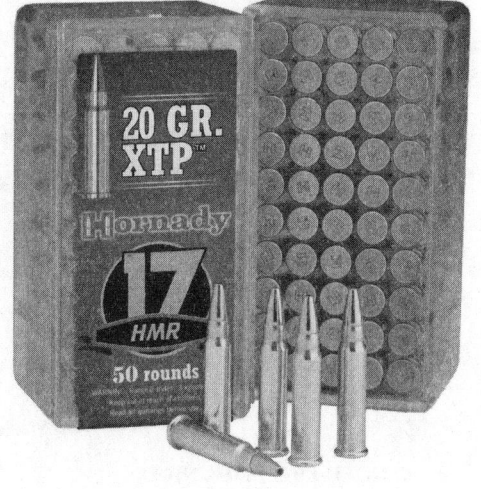

20 GR. XTP
Hornady
17 HMR
50 rounds

AMMUNITION

Jarrett Rifles

TROPHY AMMUNITION

Features: Jarrett's high-performance cartridges are in 10-round boxes. The cases are from Norma with Jarrett's headstamp

Available in: .243 Win., .270 Win., 7mm Rem. Mag., .30-06 Spfd., .300 WM, .300 Jarrett, .375 H&H, .416 Rem. Mag.

MSRP . . . . **$26.68–$76.05**

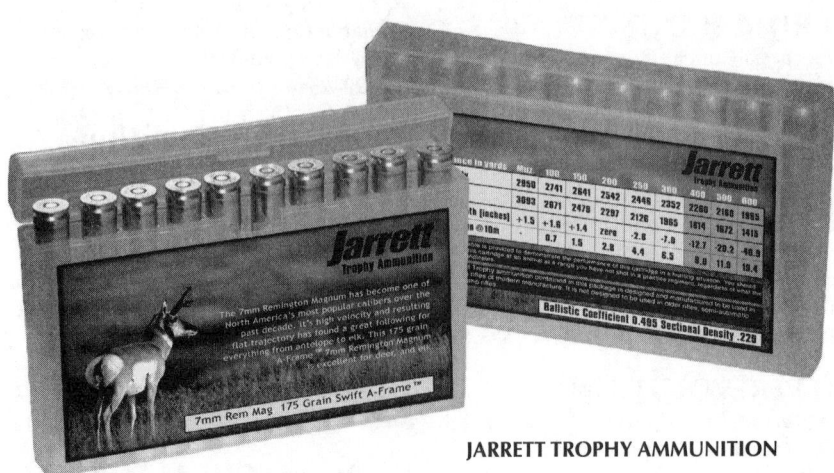

JARRETT TROPHY AMMUNITION

Kynoch Ammunition

KYNOCH RIFLE AMMUNITION

RIFLE AMMUNITION

Features: Kynoch hunting ammunition is now standardized on Woodleigh soft nosed and solid bullets, recognized world wide as the most reliable big game bullets currently manufactured. Kynamco offers virtually the whole range of classic British Nitro Express from its purpose-built factory.

Available in: .300 Flanged, .303 British, .318 Westley Richards, 9.5x57 Mannlicher, .333 Jeffery Flanged, .350 Rigby, .400/.360 Westley Richards, .375 Flanged, .400 Purdey, .405 Win., .450/.400, .416 Rigby, .404 Jeffery, .425 Westley Richards, .450 NE, .450 No. 2 NE, .450 Rigby, .577/.450 Martini Henry, .500/.450 NE, .500/.465 NE, .470 NE, .475 No. 2 Eley, .475 No. 2 Jeffery, .476 Westley Richards, .505 Gibbs, .500 Jeffery, .500 NE, .577 NE, .600 NE, .700 NE

MSRP . . . . **$30–$250**

Lapua

Rifle Ammunition

CENTERFIRE SPORT

Features: Lapua's extremely accurate target shooting cartridges are loaded with the best target bullets—Scenar, FMJBT, D46 and Lock Base. Numerous world championships, Olympic championships, and other top competition gold medals, as well as many official world records in different disciplines, are shot with the Lapua cartridges.
Available in: .222 Rem., .223 Rem., 6mm BR Norma, 6.5x47 Lapua, 6.5x55 SE, 7.62x39, .308 Win., .30-06 Spfd., 7.62x53R/54R, .338 Lapua Mag.
Box 20: . . . . **$37.99–$59.99**

MEGA BULLETS

Features: Soft point bullet designed for big game hunting; lead core and copper jacket that are mechanically bonded together; long jacket protects core and prevents premature bullet expansion or breakage when bullet goes through light brush or grass cover; up to 97 percent weight retention
Available in: 6.5x55 SE, .308 Win., .30-06 Spfd., 7.62x53R/54R, 9.3x62
MSRP . . . . **$43.99–$60.99**

NATURALIS

Features: Bullet mushrooming begins immediately on impact; bullet expands symmetrically and without shattering; gives a maximal shock effect to the hunted game; top premium copper bullet; retains up to 100 percent of its weight after the impact
Available in: .243 Win., 6.5x55 SE, .308 Win., .30-06 Spfd., .338 Lapua Mag., 9.3x62
From: . . . . **$77.99–$127.99**

LAPUA CENTERFIRE SPORT

LAPUA NATURALIS

Magtech Ammunition

Handgun Ammunition

CLEANRANGE

Features: CleanRange ammunition was developed to eliminate airborne lead and the need for lead retrieval at indoor ranges by using a state-of-the-art combination of high-tech, lead-free primers and specially designed Fully Encapsulated Bullets, a unique mix that eliminates lead and heavy metal exposure at the firing point.
Available in: .380 Auto, .38 Spl., .40 S&W, .45 Auto, 9mm Luger
Box 50: . . . . **$20.99–$30.99**

COWBOY ACTION

Features: "Old West" Cowboy Action loads were developed specifically for cowboy action shooting enthusiasts. These flat-nose bullets deliver reliable knockdown power that puts steel targets down on the first shot.
Available in: .357 Mag., .38 Spl., .44-40 Win., .44 Spl., .45 Colt
Box 50: . . . . **$24.99–$36.99**

FIRST DEFENSE

Features: Magtech First Defense rounds are designed with a 100 percent solid copper bullet, unlike traditional hollow points that contain a lead core covered by a copper jacket. First Defense solid copper bullets have no jacket to split or tear away, ensuring every round you fire meets its target with maximum impact and effectiveness.
Available in: 9mm Luger, .38 Spl., .380 Auto, .357 Mag., .40 S&W, .45 Auto
Box 20: . . . . **$17.49–$25.49**

GUARDIAN GOLD

Features: Thanks to its tremendous stopping power, deep penetration, awesome mushrooming, and dead-on accuracy, Guardian Gold is fast-becoming a favorite among those seeking reliable, affordable personal protection.
Available in: 9mm Luger, 9mm Luger+P, .38 Spl.+P, .380 Auto+P, .357 Mag., .40 S&W, .45 Auto+P
Box 20: . . . . **$12.79–$19.49**

MAGTECH AMMUNITION

SPORT SHOOTING

Features: The 100 percent solid copper hollow-point projectile features a six-petal hollow-point specifically designed to deliver tight groups, superior expansion, virtually 100 percent weight retention, and increased penetration over jacketed lead-core bullets.
Available in: .223, .25 Auto, .308, .30 Carbine, .32 Auto, .32 S&W, .357 Mag., .380 Auto, .38 Spl., .38 Super Auto, .38 S&W, .40 S&W, .44-40 Win., .44 Rem. Mag., .454 Casull, .45 Auto, .45 GAP, .500 S&W, .50 BMG, 9mm Luger, 9x21mm
From: . . . . **$12.99–$47.99**

AMMUNITION

Norma Ammunition

Rifle Ammunition

AFRICAN PH

Features: Based on many generations of experience of reputable African Professional Hunters, this range of cartridges has been developed to optimize ballistic criteria such as bullet momentum, sectional density and deep, straight-line, bone-breaking penetration. Loaded cartridges with Woodleigh softnose and solid bullets
Available in: .375 Flanged Mag. NE, .375 H&H Mag., .404 Jeffrey, .416 Rem. Mag., .416 Rigby, .500/.416 NE, .450 Rigby Rimless, .458 Lott, .470 NE, .500 Jeffrey, .500 NE 3, .505 Mag. Gibbs
Box 10: . . . . **$69.99–$192.99**

JAKTMATCH

Features: Target ammunition should have the same quality as your hunting cartridges. Many hunters also use Jaktmatch to hunt birds and small game so there is no reason to distinguish between hunting and target cartridges. The fired cases provide the reloader with a top quality product to reload.
Available in: .222 Rem, .223 Rem, .22-250 Rem., 6mm Norma BR, 6XC, .243 Win., 6.5x55 Swedish Mauser, 6.5-284 Norma, .270 Win., .270 WSM, 7mm Rem. Mag., .308 Win, .30-06 Spfd., .300 WSM, .300 Win. Mag., .338 Win. Mag., .358 Norma Mag., 8x57 JS, 9.3x 57, 9.3x62
Box 10: . . . . **$44.99–$57.99**

KALAHARI

Features: The Kalahari is loaded with selected lots of powder to ensure the highest possible velocity, best possible ballistic coefficient, and lowest wind drift achievable at normal hunting ranges. Bullet expansion is controlled and restricted–only the front third of the bullet will expand into six razor-edged petals, leaving the rear part of the bullet unimpeded, guaranteeing deep penetration.
Available in: .270 Win., .270 WSM, .280 Rem., 7x64, 7mm Rem. Mag., .308 Win., .30-06 Spfd., .300 Win. Mag., .300 WSM
Box 20: . . . . **$48.99–$64.99**

ORYX

Features: The Oryx has a thin forward jacket with internal splitting zones. The bonding and the thicker rear jacket wall ensure a high residual weight after impact (often over 90 percent!) and excellent penetration. Norma is in the process of updating the original Oryx design; the boat tail and a better profile provides a 30-percent increase or more in BC.
Available in: .222 Rem., .223 Rem., .22-250 Rem., .220 Swift, 6mm Norma BR, 6XC, .243 Win., 6.5x55 Swedish Mauser, .270 Win., .270 WSM, .280 Rem., 7x57 R Mauser, 7x57 Mauser, 7x64, 7x65 R, 7mm Rem. Mag., 7mm Blaser Mag., 7.5x55 Swiss, .308 Win., .30-06 Spfd., .300 Win. Mag., .300 WSM, .300 Blaser Mag., .308 Norma Mag., .338 Blaser Mag., .338 Win. Mag., .35 Whelen, .358 Norma Mag., 8x57 JRS, 8x57 JS, 9.3x57, 9.3x62, 9.3x74 R, .375 Blaser Mag., .375 H&H Mag.
Box 20: . . . . **$39.99–$136.99**

NORMA KALAHARI

NORMA ORYX

Nosler

Rifle Ammunition

MATCH GRADE

Features: Match Grade Ammunition consists of Nosler's precisely-designed Custom Competition bullet along with NoslerCustom Brass. Because of Nosler's unsurpassed quality standards, each piece of brass is checked for correct length, neck-sized, chamfered, trued and flash holes are checked for proper alignment. To further ensure our reputation for quality and consistency, powder charges are meticulously weighed and finished rounds are visually inspected and polished.

Available in: .223 Rem.-60, 69, 77 gr., .308 Win.-155, 168, 175 gr.

Box 20:. . . . . $19.99–$26.99

SAFARI

Features: For years, hunters around the globe have relied on the quality and consistency of Nosler bullets. That same quality and consistency is now available in Nosler Safari. Loaded with either the Partition or Nosler Solid and designed for the same point of impact with either bullet, Safari Ammunition provides the ultimate versatility for any dangerous game situation.

Available in: Available in both Partition and Solid Dangerous Game: .375 Flanged, .375 H&H, .416 Rem. Mag., .416 Rigby, .458 Lott, .458 Win. Mag., 9.3x62mm Mauser; SD only: .470 NE, .500 Jeffery, .500 NE, .505 Gibbs; PT only: .500/.416 NE

Box 20:. . . . . $89.99–$229.99

NOSLER TROPHY GRADE VARMINT AMMUNITION

TROPHY GRADE HUNTING

Features: Manufactured to Nosler's strictest quality standards, Trophy Grade Ammunition uses NoslerCustom Brass and Nosler Bullets to attain optimum performance, no matter where your hunting trip takes you. Whether you want your ammunition loaded with AccuBond, Partition Ballistic Tip or, E-Tip, NoslerCustom Trophy Grade Ammunition will have the right load for the right game.

Available in: 243 Win., .25-06 Rem., .257 Roberts +P, .257 Wby., 6.5x55 Mauser, .260 Rem., 6.5x55 Mauser, .260 Rem., 6.5-284 Norma, .264 Win. Mag., .270 Win., .270 WSM, 7mm-08 Rem., .280 Ack. Imp., 7mm SAUM, 7mm Rem. Mag., 7mm STW, 7mm RUM, .308 Win., .30-06 Spfd., .300 H&H Mag., .300 Win. Mag., .300 WSM, .300 SAUM, .300 RUM, .300 Wby., .325 WSM, .338 Lapua Mag., .338 RUM, .338 Win. Mag., .35 Whelen, .375 H&H, .375 H&H Mag.

Box 20:. . . . . $35.99–$79.99

TROPHY GRADE VARMINT

Features: Trophy Grade VARMINT Ammunition consists of the venerable Ballistic Tip VARMINT bullet or the frangible Ballistic Tip Lead Free along with NoslerCustom Brass.

Available in: .204 Ruger-32 gr.; .223 Rem-35, 40 gr.; .22-250 Rem.-35, 40, 55 gr.

Box 20:. . . . . $24.99–$34.99

VARMAGEDDON

Features: Featuring a highly accurate polymer tip or hollow point combined with flat base design, Varmageddon products were created for the high-volume varmint shooter who requires the utmost precision. Loaded with NoslerCustom brass, Varmageddon ammunition provides the highest levels of performance for any varmint hunter. 20 count box.

Available in: .17 Rem., .204 Ruger, .221 Rem. Fireball, .222 Rem., .22-250 Rem., .223 Rem., .243 Win.

Box 20:. . . . . $19.99–$35.49

NOSLER SAFARI AMMUNITION

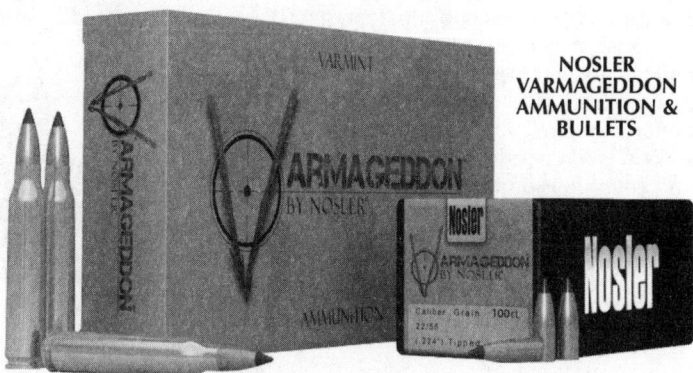

NOSLER VARMAGEDDON AMMUNITION & BULLETS

AMMUNITION

PMC Ammunition

Rifle Ammunition

BRONZE LINE - RIFLE

Features: For shooters and hunters who appreciate affordable quality ammunition, the PMC Bronze Line offers reliable performance for every shooting application. Full Metal Jacket (FMJ) bullet types.
Available in: .223 Rem, .308 Win., 7.62x39, .50
Box 20:. . . . . **$16.99–$39.99**

FRANGIBLE SINTERFIRE

Features: PMC's frangible ammunition combines their incomparable Sinterfire bullet and reduced-hazard primer. Using a lead-free bullet that shatters into non-toxic dust on impact with anything harder than itself, this product virtually eliminates the danger of ricochet from jacket and bullet fragments. Safe for shooting steel plates from any distance or for close-quarters tactical operations.
Available in: 5.56mm, 7.62mm, .50
N/A

PRECISION LINE

Features: PMC's Precision Line incorporates genuine Hornady bullets with precision-drawn cases loaded to stringent manufacturing standards. The result is unparalleled accuracy and consistent performance. It is available in hunting or target versions.
Available in: .223 Rem., .243 Win., .270 Win., 7mm Rem., .300 Win. Mag., .308 Win., .30-06 Spfd., .30-30 Win.
From:. . . . . **$19.30–$24.24**

X-TAC

Features: PMC's exacting adherence to precise specifications of military and law-enforcement organizations assures that X-TAC ammunition will perform perfectly in that fraction of a second when a serious threat arises and your life is on the line. Self-defense depends on reliable, consistent ammunition.
Available in: 5.56mm
Box 20:. **$21.19**

Handgun Ammunition

BRONZE LINE - HANDGUN

Features: The same quality and dependability built into our Starfire ammunition is incorporated throughout our extensive line of PMC training ammunition and standard hollow point or soft point ammunition.
Available in: .25 Auto, .32 Auto, .380 Auto, .38 Spl., .38 Super +P, 9mm Luger, .357 Mag., 10mm Auto, .40 S&W, .44 S&W Spl., .44 Rem. Mag., .45 Auto
From:. . . . . **$12.99–$21.99**

GOLD LINE - STARFIRE

Features: The secret of Starfire's impressive performance lies in a unique, patented rib-and-flute hollow point cavity design. Upon impact, the pre-notched jacket mouth begins to peel back, separating into five uniform copper petals and allowing expansion to begin.
Available in: .380 Auto, .38 Spl. +P, .357 Mag., 9mm Luger, .40 S&W, .44 Rem. Mag., .45 Auto
From:. . . . . **$13.12–$24.78**

SILVER LINE - ERANGE

Features: PMC's eRange environmentally friendly ammunition utilizes a reduced hazard primer that is the first of this type in the industry, an encapsulated metal jacket (EMJ) bullet which completely encloses the surface of the bullet core with precision made copper alloy, and powder with clean-burning characteristics and smooth fire for increased barrel life.
Available in: .380 Auto, .38 Spl., .38 Spl. +P, .357 Mag., 9mm Luger, .40 S&W, .44 Rem., .45 Auto
From:. . . . . **$16.79–$41.15**

Shotgun Ammunition

"ONE SHOT" HIGH VELOCITY PHEASANT LOADS

Features: These maximum velocity loads deliver a knockout punch of copper plating around extra-hard lead shots. Their specially designed plastic wads incorporate an innovative shot cup that ensures dense, uniform patterns needed to buckle late-season game birds and animals made fat by winter and wary by hunting pressure.
Available in: 12, 20 Ga. (2 ¾ in., 3 in.); Shot sizes: 4, 5, 6, 7.5
From:. . . . . **$24.98–$30.48.**

PMC BRONZE LINE - HANDGUN

PMC SILVER LINE - ERANGE

www.skyhorsepublishing.com

Remington Ammunition

Rifle Ammunition

.30 REM. AR
Features: A short, .30-caliber round whose 125-grain bullets match the speed of .308 150s, for hunting deer-size game with the AR-15 modular repeating rifle. Ammo comes with Core-Lokt and AccuTip bullets (125 grains) and, in UMC loads, with full metal case (123 grains) bullets.
Available in: (Exclude Column)
Box 20: . . . . **$21.99–$40.99**

MANAGED RECOIL
Features: Managed-Recoil Ammunition delivers Remington Field proven hunting performance out to 200 yards with half the recoil. Bullets provide 2x expansion with over 75 percent weight retention on shots inside 50 yards and out to 200 yards.
Available in: .260 Rem., .270 Win., .30-06 Spfd., .300 Rem. Ultra Mag., .30-30 Win., .300 Win. Mag., 7mm Rem. Mag., 7mm-08 Rem., .308 Win.
Box 20: . . . . **$17.99–$35.99**

POWER LEVEL
Features: Power Level Ammunition allows you to incrementally tailor the performance of your 7mm or .300 Ultra Mag. rifle to the species and terrain you're hunting, similar to the way shotgunners use 2 ¾ in., 3 in., and 3 ½ in. shells. Plus, point of impact between Power Levels is within 2 in. at 200 yards.
Available in: 7mm Ultra Mag., 7mm Rem. Ultra Mag., .300 Ultra Mag., .300 Rem. Ultra Mag., .375 Rem. Ultra Mag.; three power levels
Box 20: . . . . **$34.99–$67.99**

PREMIER ACCUTIP
Features: Featuring precision-engineered polymer tip bullets designed for match-grade accuracy (sub MOA), Premier AccuTip offers an unprecedented combination of super-flat trajectory and deadly down-range performance.
Available in: .30 Rem. AR, .300 Rem. Ultra Mag., .270 WSM, .300 WSM, .223 Rem., .243 Win., .260 Rem., .270 Win., .280 Rem., 7mm Rem. Mag., .30-06 Spfd., .300 Win. Mag., .308 Win., 7mm-08 Rem.,
Box 20: . . . . **$27.99–$49.99**

PREMIER A-FRAME
Features: A-Frame cartridges use dual-core A-Frame bullets, so that you can expect reliable expansion at long-range decreased velocities, but without over-expansion at short-range high velocities. The combination of A-Frame construction and proprietary bonding process produces extremely uniform, controlled expansion to 2x caliber with nearly 100 percent weight retention.
Available in: .300 Rem. Ultra Mag. (Power Level III), 7mm STW, 8mm Rem. Mag., 7mm Rem. Mag., .270 Win., .338 Win. Mag., 7mm Rem. Ultra Mag. (Power Level III), .375 H&H Mag., .300 Win. Mag., .30-06 Spfd., .416 Rem. Mag., .338 Rem. Ultra Mag., .375 Rem. Ultra Mag.
Box 20: . . . . **$47.99–$149.20**

PREMIER COPPER-SOLID
Features: This polymer-tipped, lead-free, copper bullet is of boattail design and delivers extremely deep penetration with nearly 100 percent weight retention and has a sleek ogive profile.
Available in: .243 Win., .270 Win., 7mm Rem. Mag., .30-30 Win., .30-06 Spfd., .300 Win. Mag., .300 Rem. Ultra Mag., .308 Win.
Box 20: . . . . **$38.99–$66.51**

PREMIER CORE-LOKT ULTRA BONDED
Features: The bonded bullet retains up to 95 percent of its original weight with maximum penetration and energy transfer. Featuring a progressively tapered jacket design, the Core-Lokt Ultra Bonded bullet initiates and controls expansion nearly 2x.
Available in: 7mm Rem. SA Ultra Mag., 7mm Rem. Ultra Mag., .300 Ultra Mag., .300 Rem. SA Ultra Mag., .223 Rem., .243 Win., .25-06 Rem., .260 Rem., .270 Win., 7mm Rem. Mag., .30-06 Spfd., .300 Rem. Ultra Mag., .300 Win. Mag., .338 Win. Mag., .308 Win., 6.8mm Rem. SPC
Box 20: . . . . **$23.99–$59.99**

PREMIER DISINTEGRATOR VARMINT
Features: Frangible bullet design with iron/tin bullet core (no lead), designed to disintegrate upon impact on varmints.

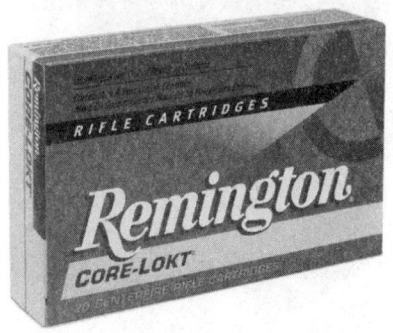

REMINGTON PREMIER CORE-LOKT ULTRA BONDED

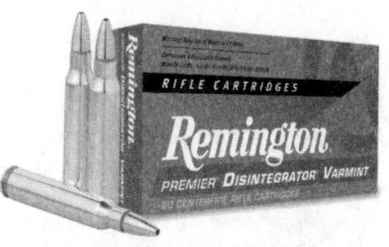

REMINGTON PREMIER DISINTEGRATOR VARMINT

Available in: .223 Rem., .22-250 Rem.
Box 20: **$25.49**

PREMIER MATCH
Features: Loaded with match-grade bullets, this ammunition employs special loading practices to ensure world-class performance and accuracy with every shot.
Available in: .308 Win., .223 Rem., 6.8mm Rem. SPC, .300 Win. Mag., .300 Rem. SA Ultra Mag.
Box 20: . . . . **$29.99–$43.84**

PREMIER SCIROCCO BONDED
Features: The Swift Scirocco Bonded bullet combines polymer tip ballistics with weight retention. The expansion generating polymer tip and the boattail base defy air resistance at the front end, and reduce drag at the back.
Available in: .300 Ultra Mag., .300 Rem. Ultra Mag., 7mm Rem. Mag., .30-06 Spfd., .243 Win., .270 Win., .300 Win. Mag., 7mm Rem. Ultra Mag., .300 WSM
Box 20: . . . . **$43.99–$59.99**

Remington Ammunition

REMINGTON GOLDEN SABER HPJ

Handgun Ammunition

DISINTEGRATOR CTF

Features: Utilizing jacketless, copper tin frangible bullets, the Disintegrator CTF delivers complete breakup at distances as close as 5 feet with no splash back, no jacket fragments, and absolutely no lead residue.
Available in: .38 Spl. (+P), 9mm (+P), .40 S&W, .45 Auto
Box 20: . . . . **$44.49–$49.99**

EXPRESS PISTOL AND REVOLVER

Features: Remington's exceptionally broad line of handgun ammunition covers a comprehensive range of calibers, bullet weights, and bullet styles. Available styles include: Full Metal Case, Lead Round Nose, Jacketed Hollow Point, Lead Hollow Point, Semi-Jacketed Hollow Point, Semi-Wadcutter Lead, Soft Point, and Wadcutter Match
Available in: .45 Auto, .25 Auto, .32 S&W, .32 S&W Long, .32 Auto, .357 Mag., 9mm Luger, .380 Auto, .357 Sig., .38 S&W, .38 Spl., .41 Rem. Mag., .40 S&W, .38 Short Colt, .44 S&W Spl., .45 Colt, .44 Rem. Mag,
From: . . . . **$28.99–$49.99**

GOLDEN SABER HPJ

Features: Designed for law enforcement and personal defense, the Golden Saber High Performance Jacket successfully combines match-type accuracy, deep penetration, maximum expansion, and near 100 percent weight retention. Cases nickel-plated

for reliable feed, function, and extraction.
Available in: .357 Mag., .380 Auto, 9mm Luger (+P), .38 Spl. (+P), .40 S&W, .45 Auto (+P)
Box 25 . . . . **$25.99–$40.49**

Rimfire Ammunition

.22 RIMFIRE TARGET

Features: Whether it's getting young shooters started, practice plinking, small-game hunting, or keeping match shooters scoring high, Remington's rimfire quality stands tall. As in their centerfire ammo, they put the maximum level of quality into their .22s so you can get maximum performance out of them.
Available in: .22LR
From: . . . . **$3.99–$8.99**

MAGNUM RIMFIRE

Features: Premier Gold Box Rimfire ammunition features sleek AccuTip-V bullets. Our standard line of Magnum rimfire ammunition gives shooters the choice of either a Jacketed Hollow Point for quick expansion or a Pointed Soft Point for optimum penetration.
Available in: .22 Mag.
MSRP **$14.22**

PREMIER GOLD BOX RIMFIRE

Features: This ammunition uses the AccuTip-V bullet with precision-engineered polymer tip for match-type accuracy, high on-game energy, and rapid expansion.
Available in: .17 HMR, .22 Win. Mag., .17 Mach 2 Rimfire
From: . . . . **$15.99–$21.99**

REMINGTON-ELEY COMPETITION RIMFIRE MATCH EPS

Features: Remington and Eley offer three grades of their premier .22 Long Rifle ammunition. For the finest performance available Remington/Eley Match EPS offers the ultimate in rimfire accuracy. This match grade load features Eley's innovative Tenex EPS-profile bullet—ideal for aspiring top class shooters and training at the highest level.

Available in: .22LR
Box 50: **$21.99**

Shotgun Ammunition

TARGET-GUN CLUB TARGET

Features: Loaded with Gun Club Grade Shot, Premier STS Primers, and Power Piston One-Piece Wads, these high-quality shells receive the same care in loading as top-of-the-line Premier STS and Nitro .27 shells.
Available in: 12, 20 Ga. (2 ¾ in.); Shot sizes: 7.5, 8, 9
Box 25: **$6.99**

TARGET-MANAGED RECOIL STS TARGET

Features: Managed-Recoil STS target loads offer dramatically reduced recoil (40 percent less in the 12-gauge load) with target-grinding STS consistency and pattern density. Ideal for new shooters and high-volume practice.
Available in: 12, 20 Ga. (2 ¾ in.); Shot size: 8.5
From: . . . . **$8.99–$10.50**

TARGET-PREMIER NITRO 27 TARGET

Features: Designed specifically for back-fence trap and long-range sporting clays. Delivers consistent handicap velocity and pattern uniformity. New, improved powder loading significantly reduces felt recoil while retaining high velocity; both factors allow avid trap shooters to stay fresh for the shoot off.
Available in: 12 Ga. (2 ¾ in.); Shot Sizes: 7.5, 8
From: **$8.99**

REMINGTON TARGET-PREMIER NITRO GOLD SPORTING CLAYS

Remington Ammunition

TARGET-PREMIER NITRO GOLD SPORTING CLAYS

Features: To meet the special demands of avid sporting clays shooters, Remington developed a new Premier Nitro Gold Sporting Clays target load. At 1300 fps, the extra velocity gives you an added advantage for those long crossers—making target leads closer to normal for ultimate target-crushing satisfaction.
Available in: 12, 28 Ga. (2 ¾ in.), .410 (2 ½ in.); Shot sizes: 7.5, 8
From: . . . . **$8.99–$12.99**

TARGET-PREMIER STS TARGET

Features: STS Target Loads have taken shot-to-shot consistency to a new performance level, setting the standard at all major skeet, trap, and sporting clays shooting across the country, while providing handloaders with unmatched reloading ease and hull longevity. Available in most gauges, Premier STS shells are the most reliable, consistent, and reloadable shells you can shoot.
Available in: 12, 20, 28 Ga. (2 ¾ in.), .410 (2 ½ in.); Shot sizes: 7.5, 8, 8.5, 9
From: . . . . **$8.99–$12.99**

TURKEY-NITRO MAG. BUFFERED MAGNUM

Features: The original buffered magnum shotshells from Remington. The shot charge is packed with a generous amount of shock-absorbing polymer buffering and surrounded by our patented Power Piston wad to protect the specially hardened shot all the way down the barrel for dense, even patterns and uniform shot strings.
Available in: 12, 20 Ga. (2 ¾ in., 3 in.); Shot sizes: 2, 4, 6
Box 25: . . . . **$26.08–$34.58**

TURKEY-NITRO TURKEY BUFFERED

Features: These loads contain Nitro Mag. extra-hard lead shot that is as hard and round as copper-plated shot. Nitro Turkey Magnums will pattern as well as other copper-plated, buffered loads without the higher cost.
Available in: 12 Ga. (2 ¾ in., 3 in., 3 ½ in.), 20 Ga. (3 in.); Shot sizes: 4, 5, 6
Box 10: . . . . **$7.50–$16.99**

TURKEY-PREMIER DUPLEX MAGNUM COPPER-PLATED BUFFERED

Features: Shotshell ammunition for the turkey hunter who appreciates dense patterns, deep penetration, and range flexibility. Premier Duplex has No. 4 size shot carefully layered on top of No. 6 shot. When ranges vary, they combine retained energy and penetration from the larger pellets with pattern density from the smaller ones.
Available in: 12 Ga. (2 ¾ in., 3 in.); Shot sizes: 4x6
Box 10: . . . . **$14.79–$16.79**

TURKEY-PREMIER HIGH-VELOCITY MAGNUM COPPER-PLATED BUFFERED

Features: Utilizing a specially-blended powder recipe, Remington's advanced Power Piston one-piece wad, and hardened copper plated shot, these new high-velocity loads result in extremely dense patterns and outstanding knockdown power at effective ranges.
Available in: 12 Ga. (3 in., 3 ½ in.); Shot sizes: 4, 5, 6
From: **$15.99**

TURKEY-PREMIER MAGNUM COPPER-PLATED BUFFERED

Features: Premier Magnum Turkey Loads provide that extra edge to reach out with penetrating power and dense, concentrated patterns. Its magnum-grade, Copper-Lokt shot is protected by our Power Piston wad and cushioned with special polymer buffering.
Available in: 10 Ga. (3 ½ in.), 12 Ga. (2 ¾ in., 3 in., 3 ½ in.), 20 Ga. (3 in.).; Shot sizes: 4, 5, 6
Box 10: . . . . **$11.29–$19.06**

TURKEY-WINGMASTER HD

Features: Comprised of tungsten, bronze, and iron, Wingmaster HD pellets are specifically engineered with a density of 12 grams/cc, 10 percent denser than lead. Wingmaster HD loads also feature a precise balance of payload and velocity that provide turkey hunters with a shotshell that generates nearly 200 ft.-lbs. more energy at 40 yds. than competitive tungsten based shot. This results in deeper penetrating pellets.
Available in: 10 Ga. (3 ½ in.), 12 Ga. (2 ¾ in., 3 in., 3 ½ in.), 20 Ga. (2 ¾ in., 3 in.); Shot sizes: 2, 4, 6, BB, T
From: **$12.99**

UPLAND-EXPRESS EXTRA LONG RANGE

Features: Long considered to be some of the best-balanced, best-patterning upland field loads available, our family of shotshells offer great selections for upland bird hunting. The hunter's choice for a wide variety of game-bird applications, from 12-gauge to .410 bore, with shot-size options ranging from BB's all the way down to 9s; suitable for everything from quail to farm predators.
Available in: 12, 16, 20, 28 Ga. (2 ¾ in.), .410 (2 ½ in., 3 in.); Shot sizes: 2, 4, 5, 6, 7.5, 9
From: . . . . **$13.79–$18.99**

UPLAND-LEAD GAME

Features: For a wide variety of field gaming, these budget-stretching loads include the same quality components as other Remington shotshells, and are available in four different gauges to match up with your favorite upland shotguns.
Available in: 12, 16, 20 Ga. (2 ¾ in.), .410 (2 ½ in.); Shot sizes: 6, 7.5, 8
From: . . . . **$6.99–$13.29**

UPLAND-NITRO PHEASANT

Features: Uses Remington's own Copper-Lokt copper-plated lead shot with high antimony content. Hard shot stays rounder for truer flight, tighter patterns, and greater penetration. Available in both high-velocity and magnum loadings.
Available in: 12, 20 Ga. (2 ¾ in., 3 in.); Shot sizes: 4, 5, 6
From: . . . . **$17.74–$20.49**

AMMUNITION

Remington Ammunition

UPLAND-PHEASANT
Features: For the broadest selection in game-specific Upland shotshells, Remington Upland Loads are the perfect choice. Their high-velocity and long-range performance are just right for any pheasant hunting situation. Standard high-base payloads feature Power Piston one-piece wads.
Available in: 12, 16, 20 Ga. (2 ¾ in.); Shot sizes: 4, 5, 6, 7.5
From: . . . . **$11.99–$15.99**

UPLAND-SHURSHOT HEAVY DOVE
Features: A sure bet for all kinds of upland game, ShurShot loads have earned the reputation as one of the best-balanced, best-pattering upland field loads available. These shells combine an ideal balance of powder charge and shot payload to deliver effective velocities and near-perfect patterns with mild recoil for high-volume upland hunting situations.
Available in: 12, 20 Ga. (2 ¾ in.); Shot sizes: 6, 7.5, 8
From: . . . . **$7.99–$11.36**

UPLAND-SHURSHOT HIGH BASE PHEASANT
Features: The ShurShot High Base Pheasant loads deliver an ideal combination of velocity and payload. Loaded with our reliable Power Piston Wad and hard lead shot
Available in: 12 Ga. (2 ¾ in.); Shot sizes: 4, 5
From: **$12.91**

UPLAND-SPORT
Features: Remington Sport Loads are an economical, multi-purpose utility load for a variety of shotgunning needs. Loaded with Power Piston wads, and plastic unibody hulls, these shells perform effectively for skeet trap and sporting clays, as well as quail, doves, and woodcock.
Available in: 12, 20 Ga. (2 ¾ in.); Shot size: 8
From: **$7.76**

WATERFOWL-HYPERSONIC STEEL
Features: The 1,700 fps HyperSonic Steel from Remington. With unprecedented velocity and the highest downrange pattern energies ever achieved, Remington HyperSonic Steel takes lethality to new heights and lengths.
Available in: 10 Ga. (3 ½ in.), 12 Ga. (3 in., 3 ½ in.), 20 Ga. (3 in.); Shot sizes: BB, BBB, 1, 2, 3, 4
From: . . . . **$21.99–$31.99**

WATERFOWL-NITRO-STEEL HIGH-VELOCITY
Features: Greater hull capacity means heavier charges and larger pellets, which makes these loads ideal for large waterfowl. Nitro-Steel delivers denser patterns for greater lethality and is zinc plated to prevent corrosion.
Available in: 10 Ga. (3 ½ in.), 12 Ga. (2 ¾ in., 3 in., 3 ½ in.), 16 Ga. (2 ¾ in.), 20 Ga. (2 ¾ in., 3 in.); Shot sizes: T, BBB, BB, 1, 2, 3, 4
From: . . . . **$19.05–$28.38**

WATERFOWL-SPORTSMAN HI-SPEED STEEL
Features: Sportsman Hi-Speed Steel's sealed primer, high-quality steel shot,

and consistent muzzle velocities combine to provide reliability in adverse weather, while delivering exceptional pattern density and retained energy. A high-speed steel load that is ideal for short-range high-volume shooting during early duck seasons or over decoys.
Available in: 10 Ga. (3 ½ in.), 12 Ga. (2 ¾ in., 3 in., 3 ½ in.), 20 Ga. (2 ¾ in.); Shot sizes: BB, 1, 2, 3, 4, 6, 7
From: . . . . **$10.49–$26.91**

WATERFOWL-WINGMASTER HD
Features: Wingmaster HD nontoxic shot stretches the kill zone with an ultra-tuned combination of density, shape and energy. At 12 grams/cc, it's 10 percent denser than lead and the scientifically-proven optimum density for pellet count and pattern density. Plus, its smooth, round shape delivers awesome aerodynamics and sustained payload energy.
Available in: 10 Ga. (3 ½ in.), 12 Ga. (2 ¾ in., 3 in., 3 ½ in.), 20 Ga (2 ¾ in., 3 in.); Shot sizes: T, BB 2, 4, 6
From: . . . . **$16.99–$36.99**

Shotgun Ammunition– Buckshot

EXPRESS AND EXPRESS MAGNUM
Features: A combination of heavy cushioning behind the shot column and a granulated polymer buffering helps maintain pellet roundness for tight, even patterns.
Available in: 12 (2 ¾ in., 3 in., 3 ½ in.), 20 Ga. (2 ¾ in.); Shot sizes: 000, 00, 0, 1, 3, 4
From: . . . . **$4.79–$10.79**

REMINGTON EXPRESS BUCKSHOT

REMINGTON WATERFOWL-HYPERSONIC STEEL

AMMUNITION

Remington Ammunition

MANAGED-RECOIL EXPRESS

Features: With less felt recoil than full velocity loads, Express Managed-Recoil Buckshot is an ideal close-range performer. Less recoil means second shot recovery is quicker, allowing the user to get back on target more easily. These loads are buffered for dense patterns, allowing for highly effective performance at up to 40 yards.
Available in: 12 Ga. (2 ¾ in.); Shot size: 00
From:....................$4.99

Shotgun Ammunition– Slugs

BUCKHAMMER LEAD

Features: Specifically designed for rifled barrels and rifled choke tubes, these high-performance slugs are capable of producing 3-inch or better groups at 100 yards with nearly 100 percent weight retention and controlled expansion to nearly one inch in diameter. Unlike traditional sabot slugs, the BuckHammer's unique attached stabilizer allows for a full bore diameter lead slug that delivers devastating terminal performance with unsurpassed accuracy.
Available in: 12, 20 Ga. (2 ¾ in., 3 in.)
From:....................$8.79

MANAGED-RECOIL COPPER SOLID SABOT

Features: With 40 percent less recoil, these slugs are perfect for anyone who wants outstanding on-game results without the rearward punch. Or, use them to sight-in, then step up to full loads. There's no finer slug load for young or recoil-sensitive hunters.
Available in: 12 Ga. (2 ¾ in.)
From:....................$17.26

PREMIER ACCUTIP BONDED SABOT

Features: Guided by our new Power Port Tip, the AccuTip Bonded Sabot Slug delivers a degree of accuracy and terminal performance unmatched by any other we tested. It yields over 95 percent weight retention thanks to its spiral nose cuts, bonded construction, and high-strength cartridge brass jacket.

Designed for fully-rifled barrels only.
Available in: 12, 20 Ga. (2 ¾ in., 3 in.)
From:............$13.79–$15.99

PREMIER CORE-LOKT ULTRA BONDED SABOT

Features: Ultra-high velocities deliver devastating on-game performance and the tightest groups (1.8in) of any shotgun slug with ultra-flat trajectories. Remington patented spiral nose cuts ensure consistent 2x expansion over a wide range of terminal velocities. The 385-grain bonded bullet yields near 100 percent weight retention. Flattest shooting slug in existence—10 percent better than the nearest competition. Designed for use in fully-rifled barrels only.
Available in: 12, 20 Ga. (2 ¾ in.)
From: $20.49

SLUGGER HIGH VELOCITY

Features: This is the first high-velocity Foster-style lead slug. This higher velocity slug exits the barrel at 1800 fps, 13 percent faster than standard 1-oz. slugs. The ⅞ oz. Slugger High Velocity delivers 200 ft.-lbs. more energy at 50 yards with flatter trajectory on deer than standard 1-oz.

slugs. Designed for the avid deer hunter using smooth bore guns.
Available in: 12 Ga. (2 ¾ in., 3 in.), 20 Ga. (2 ¾ in.)
From:...............$4.49–$5.89

SLUGGER MANAGED-RECOIL RIFLED

Features: Slugger Managed-Recoil Rifled Slugs offer remarkably effective performance but with 45 percent less felt recoil than full velocity Sluggers. With effective energy out of 80 Yds., these 1-oz. slugs easily handle the majority of shotgun deer hunting ranges.
Available in: 12 Ga. (2 ¾ in.)
From:....................$4.99

SLUGGER RIFLED

Features: Remington redesigned their 12-gauge Slugger Rifled Slug for a 25 percent improvement in accuracy. Also, at 1760 fps muzzle velocity, the 3-in. 12-ga. Magnum slugs shoot 25 percent flatter than regular 12-Ga. Slugs.
Available in: 12 Ga. (2 ¾ in., 3 in.), 16 Ga. (2 ¾ in.), 20 Ga. (2 ¾ in.), .410 (2 ½ in.)
From:...............$4.39–$5.99

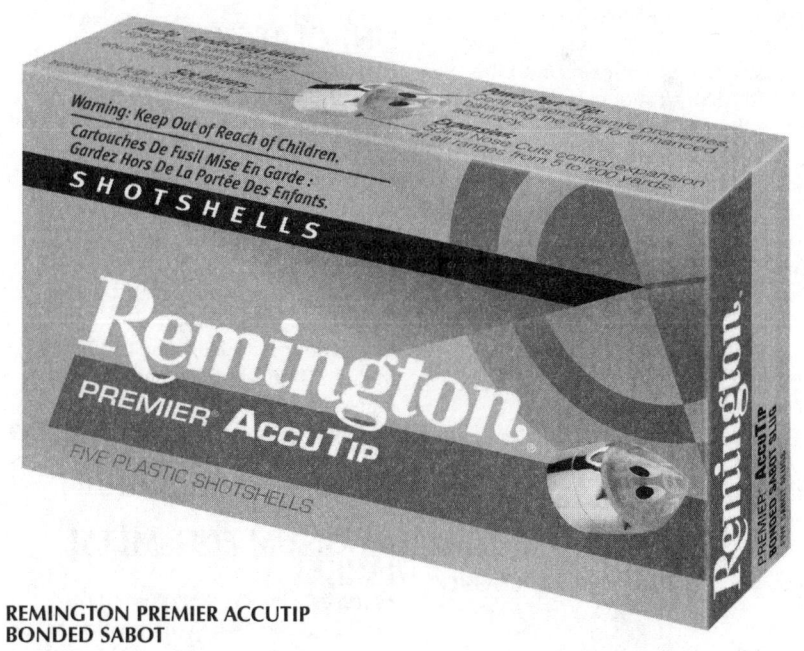

REMINGTON PREMIER ACCUTIP BONDED SABOT

RWS

Centerfire Ammunition

ID-CLASSIC

Features: Penetration and broad effect in the target ideally combine two lead cores of different hardness, which interlock peg-shaped. The soft tip core fragments, the rear core of the ID CLASSIC-bullet strongly mushrooms, the soft steel nickel-plated jacket protects the barrel, and the torpedo-shaped tail of the RWS ID CLASSIC-bullet ensures an especially good flight stability.

Available in: .280 Rem., .30-06, .308 Win., 7mm Rem. Mag., 7x57, 7x57 R, 7x64, 7x65 R, 8x57 JRS, 8x57 JS

Box 20:. . . . . **$21.99–$27.99**

SILVER SELECTION HUNT 36 SHOTSHELLS

Features: Thanks to the nickel-plated shot pellets, the RWS HUNT 36 stands out due to its good patterning at medium range. The shotshell has a selected powder load, which increases the velocity of the shot and the stopping effect of the game.

Available in: 12 Ga.; Shot size: 7

Price:. . . . . **N/A**

SILVER SELECTION WITH UNI PROFESSIONAL

Features: A brand-new twin-core bullet with over 18 percent reduced air resistance in comparison to the UNI CLASSIC-bullet ensures a distinctly extended trajectory and longer hunting ranges. With all of these improvements the responding qualities of the bullet were further optimized.

Available in: .300 Win. Mag., .30-06, .308 Win.

Price:. . . . . **N/A**

RWS ID-CLASSIC

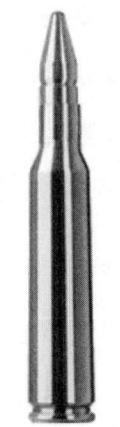

RWS TWIN CORE   **RWS UNI-CLASSIC**

TWIN CORE

Features: The RWS twin-core-bullet (DK-bullet) consists of two lead cores of different hardness. The front core fragments reliably and ensures high instantaneous effectiveness. To regulate this deformation process, a unique Tombac jacket separates the rear bullet core from the softer tip core.

Available in: .30 R Blaser, .300 Win. Mag., .30-06, .308 Win., 6.5x55, 6.5x57, 6.5x57 R, 7x64, 7x65 R, 8x57 JRS, 8x57 JS, 8x68 S, 9.3x62, 9.3x64, 9.3x74 R

Box 20:. . . . . **$21.97–$33.00**

UNI-CLASSIC

Features: The harder and heavier tail core of the bullet has a tendency to mushroom a little bit less, which increases its penetration even more. The front tip core, which fragments reliably, ensures the especially high instantaneous effectiveness. The inceased flight stability of the UNI CLASSIC-bullet is achieved by the torpedo-shaped tail.

Available in: .30 R Blaser, .300 Win. Mag., .30-06, .308 Win., .375 H&H Mag., 9.3x62, 9.3x64, 9.3x74 R

Box 20:. . . . . **$21.99–$27.99**

Rimfire Ammunition

MAGNUM FULL METAL JACKET

Features: The RWS Magnum FMJ reaches an extremely high velocity. This guarantees an extended trajectory of up to 100m for hunting and high energy release in the target. For this reason, this small-caliber ammunition is very good for hunting small game. In addition, it causes very little damage to the games meat because it only minimally perforates the pelt.

Available in: .22 Mag.

Box 50:. . . . . **$9.99–$31.99**

R 50

Features: For competitive shooters demanding the ultimate in precision. This cartridge has been used to establish several world records and is used by Olympic Gold Medalists. Now available in R 50 SC.

Available in: .22LR

From:. **$18.99**

RIFLE MATCH

Features: Perfect for the club-level target competitor. Accurate and affordable.

Available in: .22LR

From:. **$11.29**

SUBSONIC HOLLOW POINT

Features: The RWS Subsonic HP is a special cartridge for low-noise shooting. The bullet velocity stays distinctly below the sound barrier—consequently, there is no sonic boom. For this reason, this rimfire cartridge is very well suited for weapons with silencers.

Available in: .22LR

From:. **$8.69**

TARGET RIFLE

Features: An ideal training and field cartridge, the .22 Long Rifle Target also excels in informal competitions. The target .22 provides the casual shooter with accuracy at an economical price.

Available in: .22LR

From:. **$7.99**

RWS SILVER SELECTION WITH UNI PROFESSIONAL

AMMUNITION

Weatherby

WEATHERBY MAGNUM

WEATHERBY MAGNUM
Features: Weatherby Magnum cartridges are loaded with a variety of popular bullet types for a wide range of shooting purposes.
Available in: .224, .240, .257, .270, 7mm, .300, .340, .30-378, .338-378, .375, .378, .416, .460
MSRP . . . . $43–$193

Winchester Ammunition

Rifle Ammunition

ACCUBOND CT
Features: Fully-bonded lead alloy core, high weight retention, pinpoint accuracy, boattail design, Lubalox coating/red polymer tip.
Available in: .25-06 Rem., .25 WSSM, .270 Win., .270 WSM, .30-06 Spfd., .300 Win. Mag., .300 WSM, .325 WSM, .338 Win. Mag., .338 Lapua Mag., 7mm Rem. Mag., 7mm WSM
From: . . . . $39.99–$87.99

BALLISTIC SILVERTIP
Features: Solid-based boattail design delivers excellent long-range accuracy. In .22 calibers, the ballistic plastic polycarbonate Silvertip bullet initiates rapid fragmentation. In medium to larger calibers, special jacket contours extend range and reduce cross-wind drift. Harder lead core ensures proper bullet expansion.
Available in: .22-250 Rem., .223 Rem., .204 Ruger, .223 WSSM, .243 Win., .243 WSSM, .25-06 Rem., .25 WSSM, .270 Win., .270 WSM, .280 Rem., .300 Win. Mag., .30-06 Spfd., .300 WSM, .30-30 Win., .308 Win., .325 WSM, .338 Win. Mag., 7mm Rem. Mag., 7mm-08 Rem., 7mm WSM
Box 20: . . . . $21.49–$56.99

E-TIP LEAD-FREE
Features: The E-Tip lead-free bullet is developed for big-game hunters and complies with current state non-toxic regulations. Co-developed with Nosler, the bullet features an E2 energy expansion cavity, which promotes consistent upset, and is made of gliding metal instead of pure copper, which helps prevent barrel fouling.
Available in: .270 WSM, .270 Win., .30-06 Spfd., .300 WSM, .300 Win. Mag., .308 Win., 7mm Rem. Mag.
From: . . . . $39.39–$65.99

PDX1 DEFENDER CENTERFIRE RIFLE
Features: Given the recent popularity of modern sporting rifles (MSR) among shooters and hunters, Winchester has designed a product using Split Core Technology (SCT) for personal defense. The SCT technology, using a quick expansion front lead core and a deep driving bonded rear lead core, creates the ultimate .223 Rem. Home Defense load.

Available in: .223 Rem.,.308 Win., 7.62x39mm
Box 20: . . . . $29.99–$39.99

POWER MAX BONDED BULLETS
Features: Key features of the Super-X bullet include: protected hollow point PHP design, lead core bonded to jacket with proprietary process, massive frontal area of mushroom is more than double original diameter, lead remains bonded to jacket after impact.
Available in: .223 Rem., .243 Win., .270 Win., .270 WSM, .30-06 Spfd., .300 WSM, .30-30 Win., .308 Win., .300 Win. Mag., .325 WSM. .338 Win. Mag., 7mm Rem. Mag., .338 Lapua Mag., 7mm WSM
From: . . . . $39.99–$55.99

WINCHESTER
ACCUBOND CT

Winchester Ammunition

RAZORBACK XT

Features: Razorback XT is designed specifically for the rugged demands of boar hunting. It drives through thick hide and bone to deliver lethal force. This lead-free bullet has a beveled profile and is made of solid gilding metal with a hollow point for delayed expansion on extremely tough wild hogs. Flash suppressed powders make Razorback XT perfect for use in low light or after dark with night vision technology.
Available in: .223 Rem., .270 Win., .30-06 Spfd., .308 Win., 7.62x39mm
Box 20: . . . . **$25.99–$37.99**

SUPER-X HOLLOW POINT

Available in: .204 Ruger, .218 Bee, .22 Hornet, .30-30 Win.
From: . . . . **$18.99–$77.99**

SUPER-X HOLLOW SOFT POINT

Available in: .30 Carbine, .44 Rem. Mag.
From: **$22.99**

SUPER-X JACKETED SOFT POINT

Available in: .357 Mag.
Box 50: **$53.93**

SUPER-X JHP

Available in: .45-70 Govt.
Box 20: **$32.99**

SUPER-X LEAD

Available in: .32-20 Win.
Box 20: **$43.49**

SUPER-X POSITIVE EXPANDING POINT

Available in: .25-06 Rem., .25 WSSM
From: . . . . **$30.99–$32.99**

SUPER-X POWER CORE 95/5

Features: Start with a 95/5 copper alloy, integrate a highly engineered contoured cavity—and you have a new benchmark in lead-free big-game cartridges. Featuring a devastating effective bullet with massive initial impact shock plus deep penetration and virtually 100 percent retained weight to assure maximum trauma to bone and vitals.

Available in: .223 Rem., .243 Win., .270 Win., .270 WSM, .30-06 Spfd., .300 Win. Mag., .300 WSM, .30-30 Win., .308 Win., 7mm-08 Rem., 7mm Rem. Mag., 7mm WSM
Box 20: . . . . **$23.99–$46.999**

SUPER-X POWER-POINT

Available in: .22-250 Rem., .223 Rem., .223 WSSM, .243 Win., .243 WSSM, .257 Roberts +P, .264 Win. Mag., .270 Win., .270 WSM, .284 Win., .300 Savage, .30-06 Spfd., .300 WSM, .30-30 Win., .303 British, .30-40 Krag, .307 Win., .308 Win., .300 Win. Mag., .325 WSM, .32 Win. Spl., .338 Win. Mag., .356 Win., 35 Rem., .375 Win., 6mm Rem., 7mm-08 Rem., 7mm Mauser (7 x 57), 7mm Rem. Mag., 7mm WSM, 8mm Mauser (8 x 57)
Box 20: . . . . **$15.99–$52.99**

SUPER-X SILVERTIP HOLLOW POINT

Available in: 44 Rem. Mag.
Box 20: **$26.99**

SUPER-X SOFT POINT

Available in: .22 Hornet, .25-20 Win., .25-35 Win., .38-40 Win., .38-55 Win., .44-40 Win., .458 Win., 6.5x55 Swedish, 7.62x39mm Russian
Box 20: . . . . **$25.99–$71.99**

SUPREME HOLLOW POINT BOATTAIL MATCH

Features: (Exclude Column)
Available in: .308 Win. Match, .338 Lapua Mag.
From: **$36.99**

XP3

Features: The XP3 bullet delivers precision accuracy, awesome knockdown power, and deep penetration all in one package—and it's as effective on thin-skinned game, like deer and antelope, as it is on tough game, like elk, moose, bear, and African animals, at short and long ranges.
Available in: .243 Win., .243 WSSM, .270 WSM, .270 Win., .30-06 Spfd., .300 WSM, .300 Win. Mag., .308 Win., .325 WSM, 7mm Rem. Mag., 7mm WSM
Box 20: . . . . **$39.99–$64.99**

Handgun Ammunition

DUAL BOND

Features: Dual Bond offers a large hollow point cavity, which provides consistent upsets at a variety of ranges and impact velocities. The heavy outer jacket is mechanically bonded to the inner bullet. The inner bullet utilizes a proprietary bonding process for a combination of knockdown power, solid penetration, and significant tissue damage.
Available in: .44 Rem. Mag., .454 Cassull, .460 S&W Mag., .500 S&W Mag.
Box 20: . . . . **$35.99–$60.99**

FULL METAL JACKET

Available in: .45 Auto, .38 Spl., 9mm Luger, .25 Auto, .38 Super Auto +P, .380 Auto, .40 S&W, .32 Auto, .45 G.A.P., 9mm Luger
From: . . . . **$13.99–$48.99**

WINCHESTER RAZORBACK XT

WINCHESTER DUAL BOND

Winchester Ammunition

LEAD FLATNOSE
Available in: .38 Spl., .44-40 Win., .44 S&W Spl., .45 Colt
Box 50: . . . . **$30.99–$39.99**

PDX1 DEFENDER
Features: The new Winchester Supreme Elite Bonded PDX1, which was chosen by the FBI as their primary service round, is engineered to maximize terminal ballistics, as defined by the demanding FBI test protocol, which simulates real-world threats.
Available in: .357 Mag., .357 Sig., .380 Auto, .38 Spl., +P, .40 S&W, .45 Colt, .45 Auto, 9mm Luger +P, 9mm Luger
From: . . . . **$17.79–$25.99**

PLATINUM TIP HOLLOW POINT
Features: Patented notched reserve taper bullet jacket, plated heavy wall jacket, and two-part hollow point cavity for uniform bullet expansion, massive energy depot.
Available in: .41 Rem. Mag., .44 Rem. Mag., .454 Casull, .500 S&W
Box 20: . . . . **$28.49–$59.99**

SUPER-X BLANK-BLACK POWDER
Available in: .32 S&W
Box 50: . . . . **$31.49–$32.99**

SUPER-X BLANK-SMOKELESS
Available in: .38 Special
Box 50: . . . . **$37.49–$39.99**

SUPER-X EXPANDING POINT
Available in: .25 Auto
Box 50: **$38.99**

SUPER-X HOLLOW SOFT POINT
Available in: .30 Carbine, .44 Rem. Mag.
From: **$22.99**

SUPER-X JACKETED SOFT POINT
Available in: .357 Mag., .38 Spl.
From: . . . . **$23.99–$45.49**

SUPER-X JHP
Available in: .357 Mag., .38 Spl. +P, .454 Casull, .45 Win. Mag., .460 S&W

WINCHESTER PLATINUM TIP HOLLOW POINT

WINCHESTER SUPER-X SILVERTIP HOLLOW POINT

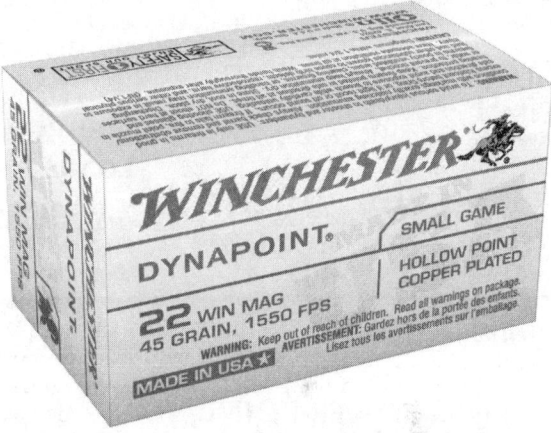

WINCHESTER DYNA POINT - PLATED

Mag.
Box 20: . . . . **$33.99–$50.99**

SUPER-X LEAD ROUND NOSE
Available in: .32 Short Colt, .32 S&W Long, .32 S&W, .38 Spl., .38 S&W, .44 S&W Spl., .45 Colt
From: . . . . **$18.99–$43.99**

SUPER-X LEAD SEMI-WAD CUTTER
Available in: .38 Spl.
Box 50: **$34.99**

SUPER-X LEAD SEMI-WAD CUTTER HP
Available in: .38 Spl. +P
Box 50: **$35.49**

SUPER-X MATCH
Available in: .38 Spl. Super Match
Box 50: **$30.99**

SUPER-X SILVERTIP HOLLOW POINT
Available in: 10mm Auto, .32 Auto, .357 Mag., .380 Auto, .38 Super Auto +P, .38 Spl. +P, .38 Spl., .40 S&W, .41 Rem. Mag., .44 Rem. Mag., .44 S&W Spl., .45 Auto, .45 Colt, .45 G.A.P., 9x23 Win., 9mm Luger
From: . . . . **$20.49–$50.99**

Rimfire Ammunition

DYNA POINT - PLATED
Available in: .22 Win. Mag.
Box 50: **$8.99**

Winchester Ammunition

SUPER-X #12 SHOT
Available in: .22LR
From:.................$8.99

SUPER-X BLANK
Available in: .22 Short
Box 50: $8.49

SUPER-X FULL METAL JACKET
Available in: .22 Win. Mag.
Box 50: $10.99

SUPER-X JHP
Available in: .17 HMR, .17 Win. Super Mag., .22 Win. Mag.
From:............$10.99–$13.99

SUPER-X LEAD HOLLOW POINT
Available in: .22LR
From:............$2.99–$7.89

SUPER-X LEAD ROUND NOSE
Available in: .22LR, .22 Long, .22 Short
From:............$2.99–$3.49

SUPER-X LEAD ROUND NOSE, STANDARD VELOCITY
Available in: .22LR
From:............$3.39–$5.99

SUPER-X POWER-POINT, LEAD HOLLOW POINT
Available in: .22LR
From:............$3.49–$7.89

XPERT LEAD HOLLOW POINT
Available in: .22LR
Box 500: $29.99

VARMINT HIGH ENERGY
Available in: .22LR, .22 Win. Mag., .17 Win. Super Mag.
From:............$6.49–$15.99

VARMINT HIGH VELOCITY
Available in: .22 Win. Mag., .17 HMR, .17 Win. Super Mag.
Box 50: .... $13.99–$14.99

VARMINT LEAD FREE
Available in: .22 Mag., .22LR
From:............$7.59–$13.19

WILDCAT 22 LEAD ROUND NOSE
Available in: .22LR
Box 50: $2.19

Shotgun Ammunition–Loads

AA FEATHERLITE
Features: 20-gauge Featherlite AA shotshells are high-performance, low-recoil training loads for sporting clays, trap, and skeet. This new Featherlite load was designed to address recoil. AA loads use Winchester proprietary one-piece plastic wads, clean burning powder, and hard shot for consistent pattern performance.
Available in: 20 Ga. (2 ¾ in.)
Box 25:.................$8.89

AA TARGET LOADS
Features: The hunter's choice for a wide variety of game bird applications, available in an exceptionally broad selection of loadings, from 12-gauge to .410 bore, with shot size options ranging from BBs all the way down to 9s—suitable for everything from quail to farm predators.
Available in: 12, 20, 28 Ga. (2 ¾ in.), .410 (2½ in.); Shot sizes: 7.5, 8, 8.5, 9
From:............$8.49–$9.99

BLIND SIDE
Features: Blind Side ammunition combines ground-breaking, stacked HEX Shot technology and the Diamond Cut Wad in the most deadly Winchester waterfowl load available. Loaded with 100 percent HEX Shot, you get more pellets on target, a larger kill zone, and more trauma inducing pellets than ever before, meaning quick kill shots.
Available in: 12 Ga. (2 ¾ in., 3 in., 3 ½ in.), 20 Ga. (3 in.); Shot size: BB, 1, 2, 3, 5, 6
From:............$19.99–$26.99

SUPER TARGET LOADS
Available in: 12, 20 Ga. (2 ¾ in.); Shot sizes: 7, 7.5, 8, 9
From:............$5.70–$9.99

SUPER PHEASANT LOADS
Available in: 12 Ga. (2 ¾ in., 3 in.), 20 Ga. (3 in.); Shot sizes: 4, 5, 6
From:............$12.79–$21.49

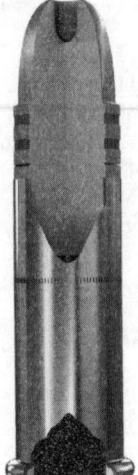

AMMUNITION

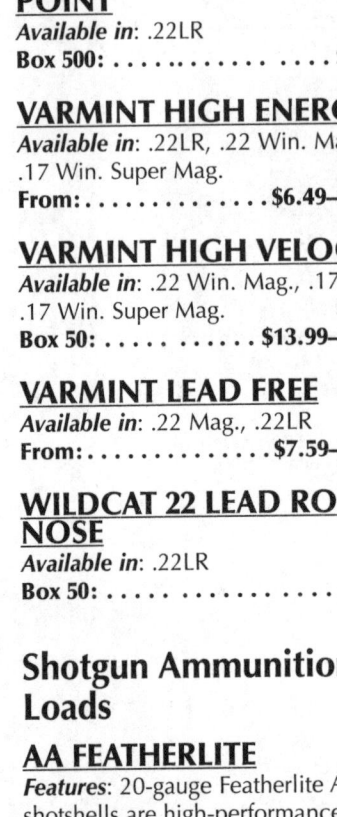

WINCHESTER VARMINT LEAD FREE

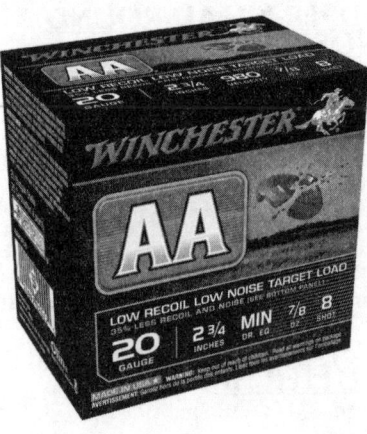

WINCHESTER AA FEATHERLITE

WINCHESTER BLIND SIDE

Winchester Ammunition

SUPER PHEASANT STEEL LOADS
Available in: 12 Ga. (3 in.); Shot size: 4
From: $21.49

SUPER-X TRIALS AND BLANKS
Available in: 10 Ga. (2 $^7/_8$ in.), 12 Ga. (2 ¾ in.)
From: $35.49

SUPER-X TURKEY LOADS
Available in: 12 Ga. (2 ¾ in., 3 in.); Shot sizes: 4, 5, 6
Box 10: ... . $8.79–$10.39

SUPER-X XPERT HI-VELOCITY STEEL LOADS
Available in: 12 Ga. (2 ¾ in., 3 in.), 20 Ga. (3 in.); Shot sizes: BB, 1, 2, 3, 4
From: ....$11.49–$12.99

SUPER-X XPERT STEEL LOADS
Available in: 12, 28 Ga., .410 bore (2 ¾ in.); Shot sizes: 6, 7
From: ....$7.39–$13.59

XTENDED RANGE HD COYOTE
Available in: 12 Ga. (3 in.); Shot size: B
Box 5: $13.99

XTENDED RANGE HD TURKEY
Available in: 12 Ga. (2 ¾ in., 3 in., 3 ½ in.), 20 Ga. (3 in.); Shot sizes: 4, 5, 6
From: ....$22.39–$41.99

XTENDED RANGE HD WATERFOWL
Available in: 12 Ga. (2 ¾ in., 3 in., 3 ½ in.), 20 Ga. (3 in.); Shot sizes: 2, 4, B
From: ....$22.39–$30.59

Shotgun Ammunition–Slugs

SUPER-X BUCKSHOT
Available in: 12 Ga. (2 ¾ in., 3 in., 3½ in.), 20 Ga. (2 ¾ in.), .410 (2½ in., 3 in.); Shot sizes: 4, 3, 1, 00, 000
From: ....$4.79–$16.79

PDX1 12 AND BUCK
Features: The 12-gauge PDX1 Defender ammunition features a distinctive black hull, black oxide high-base head and three pellets of Grex buffered 00 plated buckshot nested on top of a 1 oz. rifled slug. The result is the ideal, tight patterning personal defense load. The slug/buckshot combination provides optimum performance at short and long ranges while compensating for aim error.
Available in: 12 Ga. (2 ¾ in.)
From: $13.99

PDX1 DEFENDER SEGMENTING SLUG
Features: The uniquely designed slug segments into three pieces when fired into FBI protocol barriers such as bare, light cloth, and heavy cloth covered ballistic gelatin. The round is designed to compensate for aim error over traditional slugs.
Available in: 12 Ga. (2 ¾ in.)
Box 10: $14.99

RACKMASTER RIFLED SLUGS
Features: The RackMaster system design consists of a hard-hitting lead nose and the innovative WinGlide rear projectile stabilizer, engineered specifically to improve in-bore alignment and enhance down-range accuracy. RackMaster delivers high accuracy, hard-hitting knockdown performance to hunters shooting shotguns with either smooth bore, rifled choke tube or fully-rifled barrels.
Available in: 12 Ga. (2 ¾ in., 3 in.), 20 Ga. (2 ¾ in.)
From: ....$6.79–$8.99

SUPER-X
Available in: 12, 20 Ga. (2 ¾ in., 3 in.), .410 (2½ in., 3 in.)
From: ....$4.59–$14.17

XP3 SABOT SHOTGUN
Available in: 12 Ga. (2 ¾ in., 3 in.)
Box 5: ....$11.99–$15.49

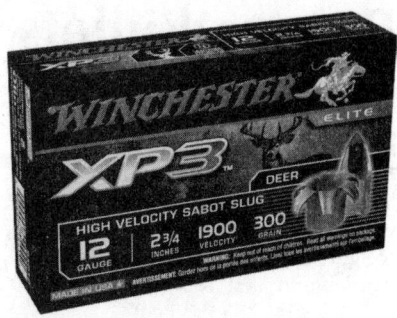

WINCHESTER XP3 SABOT SHOTGUN

WINCHESTER PDX1 DEFENDER SEGMENTING SLUG

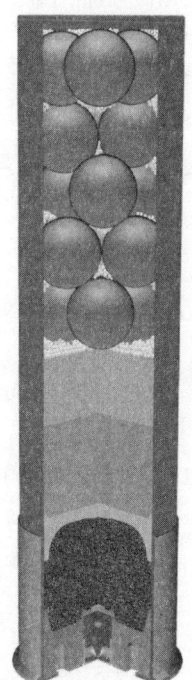

WINCHESTER SUPER-X BUCKSHOT

MUZZLELOADING BULLETS

Barnes Bullets

EXPANDER MZ
Features: 100 percent copper with a large, hollow cavity; six copper petals with double-diameter expansion; full weight retention.
Available in: .45 (195 gr.), .50 (250, 300 gr.), .54 (275, 325 gr.)
Box 24: . . . . $34.15–$77.67

SPIT-FIRE MZ
Features: A streamlined semi-spitzer give, boattail base and tack-driving accuracy; six razor-sharp copper petals create massive shock, deep penetration, and double-diameter expansion; retains virtually 100 percent of its original weight; available in 15-and 24-bullet packs
Available in: .50 (245, 285 gr.)
Box 24: . . . . $36.02–$37.26

SPIT-FIRE TMZ
Features: 100 percent copper boattail design with streamlined polymer tip for faster expansion; expands at 1050 fps.; remains intact at extreme velocities; redesigned sabot loads faster while retaining tight gas seal
Available in: .50 (250, 290 gr.)
Box 24: . . . . $39.75–$42.23

BARNES BULLETS SPIT-FIRE MZ

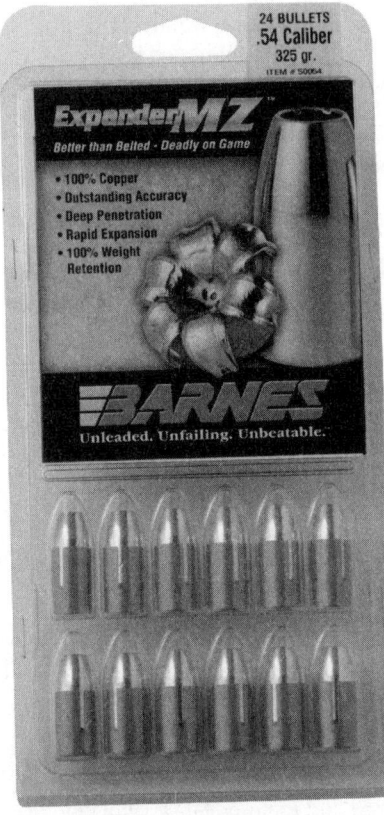

BARNES BULLETS EXPANDER MZ

BARNES BULLETS SPIT-FIRE TMZ

Federal Fusion Ammunition

FUSION MUZZLELOADING SLUGS
Features: Now you can harness the energy of Fusion muzzleloader sabot slugs. Fusion technology gives .50-caliber crush-rib sabots reason to seat themselves at the breech of your T/C.
Available in: .50 (240, 260, 300 gr.)
Box 12: . . . . $12.49–$16.99

FEDERAL FUSION MUZZLELOADING SLUGS

Harvester

SABER TOOTH BELTED
Features: Copper-clad belted bullets in Harvester Crush Rib Sabot.
Available in: .50 (250, 270, 300, 350 gr.)
MSRP $11.99

SCORPION FUNNEL POINT MAG
Features: Electroplated copper plating does not separate from lead core. Loaded in Harvester Crush Rib Sabots.
Available in: .50 (240, 260, 300 gr.); .54 (240, 260, 300 gr.)
MSRP . . . . $8.99–$11.49

SCORPION PT GOLD
Features: Scorpion PT Gold Ballistic Tip Bullets are electroplated with copper plating that does not separate from lead core. The PT Gold offers greater accuracy at longer ranges than

HARVESTER SABER TOOTH BELTED

HARVESTER SCORPION FUNNEL POINT MAG

HARVESTER SCORPION PT GOLD

a hollow point. The 3 percent antimony makes the bullet harder than pure lead.
Available in: .45 (240, 260, 300 gr.); .50 ((240, 260, 300 gr.)
MSRP . . . . $10.99–$21.99

Hornady

GREAT PLAINS - PA CONICAL
Features: Hornady's PA Conical bullets deliver greater accuracy and more knock-down power. PA bullets are prelubed with special knurled grooves on the bearing surface to hold the lubricant on the bullet—no need for a patch or sabot.
Available in: .50 (240, 385 gr.); .54 (425 gr.)
MSRP . . . . $11.41–$14.64

HP/XTP BULLET/SABOT
Features: Hornady XTP bullet/sabot combination with controlled expansion XTP bullet.
Available in: .50 cal. sabot with .44 (240 gr.) or .45 (240, 300 gr.) bullet
MSRP . . . . $12.72–$15.01

HORNADY GREAT PLAINS - PA CONICAL

HORNADY HP/XTP BULLET/SABOT

Knight Rifles

FTX BULLETS
Features: Copper bullet with patented Flex Tip Design and Sabot; 18 pack
Available in: .52 (325 gr.)
MSRP $19.99

JACKETED BULLETS WITH SABOTS
Features: Copper jacketed, hollow point bullet with sabot; 20 pack
Available in: .50 (240, 260, 300 gr.)
MSRP . . . .$14.99–$15.99

LEAD BULLETS WITH SABOTS
Features: Pure lead bullet with sabot; 20 pack
Available in: .50 (260, 310 gr.)
MSRP . . . .$14.99–$15.99

POLYMER-TIP BOAT-TAIL BULLETS
Features: Sabot with all copper polymer tip bullet; expands into six razor-sharp copper petals while retaining 100 percent of original

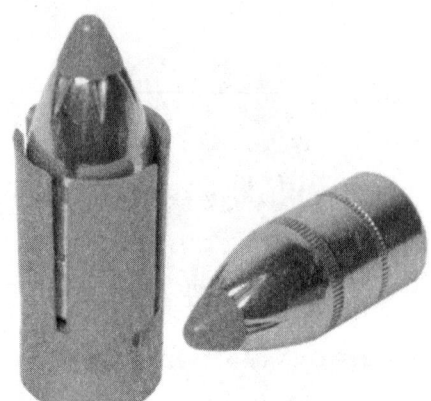

KNIGHT RIFLES FTX BULLETS

weight; 18 pack
Available in: .50 (250, 290 gr.)
MSRP . . . .$25.99–$31.49

RED HOT BULLETS
Features: Saboted Barnes solid copper bullet with superior expansion.

KNIGHT RIFLES JACKETED BULLETS WITH SABOTS
Available in: .45 (175 gr.); .50 (250, 300 gr.); .52 (275, 350, 375 gr.)
MSRP . . . .$22.99–$31.49

SPITZER BOAT-TAIL BULLETS
Features: Sabot loaded with Barnes Spitzer Boat-tail bullet; 18 pack
Available in: .50 (245 gr.)
MSRP $25.99

PowerBelt

AEROLITE
Features: Designed specifically for use with standard 100-grain loads. The AeroLite's shape is noticeably longer and more aerodynamic than other PowerBelts of similar weight. This longer length is made possible by the massive hollow point cavity that is filled by an oversized polycarbonate point.
Available in: .50 (250, 300 gr.)
MSRP . . . .$29.95–$31.95

COPPER
Features: Thin copper plating reduces bore friction while allowing for optimal bullet expansion. Available in four tip designs: Hollow Point, AeroTip, Flat Point, and Steel Tip.
Available in: .45 (175, 195, 225, 275 gr.); .50 (223, 245, 295, 348, 405, 444 gr.); .54 (295, 348, 405, 444 gr.)
MSRP . . . .$21.95–$64.95

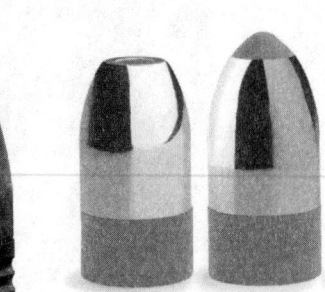
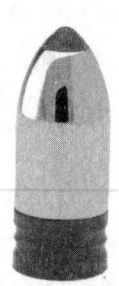

POWERBELT AEROLITE

POWERBELT COPPER

POWERBELT PLATINUM AEROTIP

POWERBELT PURE LEAD HOLLOW POINT

PLATINUM AEROTIP
Features: Proprietary hard plating and aggressive bullet taper design for improved ballistic coefficient. A large-size fluted gas check produces higher and more consistent pressures.
Available in: .45 (223, 300 gr.); .50 (270, 300, 338 gr.)
MSRP . . . .$28.95–$30.95

PURE LEAD
Features: Pure lead, available in four different grain weights in Hollow Point and 444 in Flat Point.
Available in: .50 (295, 348, 405, 444 gr.); .54 (295, 348 , 405, 444 gr.)
MSRP . . . .$21.95–$22.95

Thompson/Center

MAG EXPRESS SABOTS

Features: Mag Express Sabots separate from the projectile quickly. Sabots are preassembled with XTP bullets, but also available separately.
Available in: .50 (240, 300 gr.); .54 (250 gr.)
Box 30: . . . . **$26.38–$28.41**

THOMPSON/CENTER MAXI-BALL SUPERIOR PENETRATION

MAXI-BALL SUPERIOR PENETRATION

Features: An exceptionally accurate bullet and the preferred bullet for penetration needed for large game like elk. Lubricating grooves (maxi wide grooves)
Available in: .50 (320, 370 gr.)
Box 20: . . . . **$27.39–$28.41**

MAXI-HUNTER CONICAL ALL LEAD

Features: Maximum expansion on deer-sized game. Lubricating grooves (maxi hunter multiple grooves)
Available in: .50 (275, 350 gr.)
Box 20: . . . . **$26.38–$29.42**

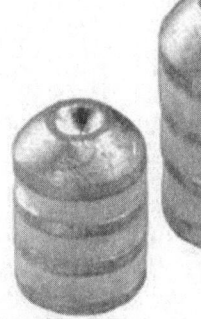

THOMPSON/CENTER MAXI-HUNTER CONICAL ALL LEAD

SHOCK WAVE SABOTS

Features: Polymer tip spire point bullet with sabot. Incorporates harder lead core with walls interlocked with the jacket for maximum weight retention and expansion. Available with spire point or bonded bullets
Available in: .45 (200 gr.); .50 (200, 250, 300 gr.)
Box 15: . . . . **$21.30–$31.45**

THOMPSON/CENTER SHOCK WAVE SABOTS

Winchester Ammunition

SUPREME PLATINUM TIP BULLETS & SABOTS

Features: The Platinum Tip Hollow Point bullet includes Winchester's patented reverse taper jacket and notching technology that delivers expansion and on-target energy delivery.
Available in: .50 (260 gr.); .54 (400 gr.)
Box 30: **$34.49**

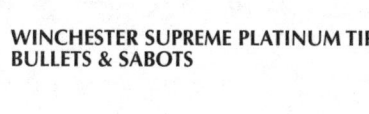

WINCHESTER SUPREME PLATINUM TIP BULLETS & SABOTS

AMMUNITION

BULLETS

Barnes Bullets

Barnes continues to develop leading-edge products with a wide range of workability and functionality using an incredibly broad range of purpose-built components and ammunition. Barnes's most popular hunting bullets, the all-copper TSX line, also comes with a streamlined polymer tip. The Barnes Buster line can be used for both rifles and handguns.

Rifle Bullets

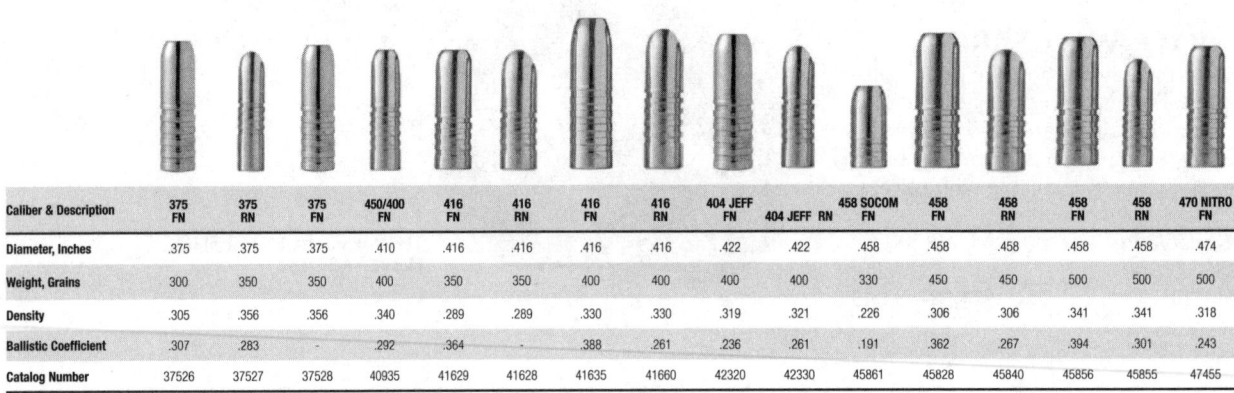

BANDED SOLIDS

Caliber & Description	" 223 S BT"	6MM S BT	25 S BT	6.5MM S BT	270 S BT	7MM S BT	30 S BT	338 FN	338 RN	9.3mm FN	9.3mm RN	9.3MM RN	9.3MM RN	375 RN	375 FN	375 RN
Diameter, Inches	.224	.243	.257	.264	.277	.284	.308	.338	.338	.366	.366	.366	.366	.375	.375	.375
Weight, Grains	45	75	90	110	120	140	165	250	250	250	286	250	286	270	270	300
Density	.128	.181	.195	.225	.223	.248	.248	.313	.313	.267	.305	.267	.305	.274	.274	.305
Ballistic Coefficient	.195	.341	.325	.452	.438	.464	.438	.208	.247	.222	.258	.214	.247	.207	.284	.230
Catalog Number	22425	24375	25793	26422	27763	28464	30816	33824	33825	36602	36604	36611	36612	37512	37513	37525

Caliber & Description	375 FN	375 RN	375 FN	450/400	416 FN	416 RN	416 FN	416 RN	404 JEFF FN	404 JEFF RN	458 SOCOM FN	458 FN	458 RN	458 FN	458 RN	470 NITRO FN
Diameter, Inches	.375	.375	.375	.410	.416	.416	.416	.416	.422	.422	.458	.458	.458	.458	.458	.474
Weight, Grains	300	350	350	400	350	350	400	400	400	400	330	450	450	500	500	500
Density	.305	.356	.356	.340	.289	.289	.330	.330	.319	.321	.226	.306	.306	.341	.341	.318
Ballistic Coefficient	.307	.283	-	.292	.364	-	.388	.261	.236	.261	.191	.362	.267	.394	.301	.243
Catalog Number	37526	37527	37528	40935	41629	41628	41635	41660	42320	42330	45861	45828	45840	45856	45855	47455

Caliber & Description	505 GIBBS RN	505 Gibbs FN	500 NITRO FN	500 JEFF RN	500 JEFF FN	50 BMG BORE RIDER	50 BMG BORE RIDER	577 NITRO FN	600 NITRO FN
Diameter, Inches	.504	.504	.509	.510	.510	.510	.510	.583	.618
Weight, Grains	525	525	570	535	535	750	800	750	900
Density	.295	.294	.314	.294	.294	.412	.439	.315	.337
Ballistic Coefficient	.267	.226	.243	-	.219	1.070	1.095	.257	.380
Catalog Number	50505	50525	50950	51003	51053	510750A	510800A	58525	62025

From: $20.74–$61.91

Barnes Buster

Caliber & Description	"44 MAG. FN FB"	454 CASULL FN FB	45/70 FN FB	500 S&W FN FB
Diameter, Inches	.429	.451	.458	.500
Weight, Grains	300	325	400	400
Density	.233	.228	.272	.229
Ballistic Coefficient	.241	.206	.242	.220
Catalog Number	42982	45135	45884	50040

Box 50: $52.14–$63.31

Barnes Original

Caliber & Description	"348 WIN FN SP"	348 WIN FN SP	375 WIN FN SP	38/55 FN SP	38/55 FN SP	"45/70 SSSP"	45/70 FN SP	45/70 SSSP	45/70 FN SP	50/110 WIN FN SP	50/110 WIN FN SP
Diameter, Inches	.348	.348	.375	.375	.377	.458	.458	.458	.458	.510	.510
Weight, Grains	220	250	255	255	255	300	300	400	400	300	450
Jckt.	.032	.032	.032	.032	.032	.032	.032	.032	.032	.032	.032
Density	.260	.295	.259	.259	.256	.204	.204	.272	.272	.165	.247
Ballistic Coefficient	.301	.327	.290	.290	.290	.291	.227	.389	.302	.183	.274
Catalog Number	34805	34810	375w20	38/5510	38/5520	457010	457020	457030	457040	5011010	5011020

From: $20.85–$58.86

LRX Bullets

Caliber & Description	"6.5MM BT"	270 BT	7MM BT	7MM BT	30 BT	30 BT	338 LAPUA BT	338 LAPUA BT
Diameter, Inches	.264	.277	.284	.284	.308	.308	.338	.338
Weight, Grains	127	129	145	168	175	200	265	280
Density	.257	.240	.257	.257	.264	.301	.331	.350
Ballistic Coefficient	.468	.463	.486	.550	.508	.546	.575	.667
Catalog Number	26403	27740	28404	28407	30807	30880	33882	33881

Box 50: $39.02–$50.83

Match Burner Bullets

Caliber & Description	"22 FB"	22 BT	22 BT	6MM FB	6MM BT	6.5MM BT	7MM BT	"30 PALMA FB"	30 BT
Diameter, Inches	.224	.224	.224	.243	.243	.264	.284	.308	.308
Weight, Grains	52	69	85	68	105	140	171	155	175
Density	.148	.196	.242	.165	.254	.287	.303	.233	.264
Ballistic Coefficient	.224	.339	.410	.267	.511	.586	.645	.467	.521
Catalog Number	22413	22415	22417	24313	24316	26404	28414	30892	30896

Box 100: $20.91–$34.69

AMMUNITION

Barnes Bullets

M/LE Reduced Ricochet, Limited Penetration (RRLP) Bullets

Caliber & Description	"223/5.56 FB"	6.8MM FB	30 FB	7.62X39 FB
Diameter, Inches	.224	.277	.308	.310
Weight, Grains	55	85	150	108
Density	.157	.158	.226	.161
Ballistic Coefficient	.225	.229	.357	.243
Catalog Number	22414	27711	30802	31010

From: $20.74–$31.92

M/LE TAC-TX Bullets

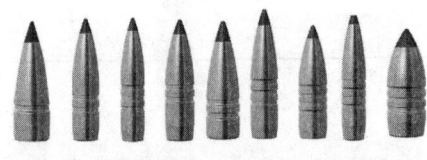

Caliber & Description	300 AAC Blackout	6.5mm BT	6.5mm BT	6.8mm BT	30 FB	30 BT	338 BT	338 BT	458 SOCOM BT
Diameter, Inches	-	.264	.264	.277	.308	.308	.338	.338	.458
Weight, Grains	110	100	120	95	110	168	225	265	300
Density	.166	.205	.246	.177	.166	.253	.281	.331	.204
Ballistic Coefficient	.289	-	.443	.292	.295	.470	.514	.575	.236
Catalog Number	30811	26412	26414	27721	30851	30856	33858	33856	45863

From: $35.01–$54.69

Multi-Purpose Green (MPG) Bullets

Caliber & Description	"223 FB"	6.8MM FB	30 FB	7.62X39 FB
Diameter, Inches	.224	.277	.308	.310
Weight, Grains	55	85	150	108
Density	.157	.158	.226	.161
Ballistic Coefficient	.225	.229	.357	.243
Catalog Number	22476	27701	30817	31008

From: $20.74–$285.00

TSX Bullets

Caliber & Description	"22 FB"	22 FB	22 FB	22 FB	22 BT	22 BT	6MM BT	25 BT	25 FB	6.5MM BT	6.5MM FB	6.8MM FB	6.8MM BT	270 BT	270 BT
Diameter, Inches	.224	.224	.224	.224	.224	.224	.243	.257	.257	.264	.264	.277	.277	.277	.277
Weight, Grains	45	50	53	55	62	70	85	100	115	120	130	85	110	130	140
Density	.128	.142	.151	.157	.177	.199	.206	.216	.249	.246	.266	.158	.205	.242	.261
Ballistic Coefficient	.188	.197	.204	.209	.287	.314	.333	.336	.335	.381	.365	.246	.323	374	.404
Catalog Number	22441	22440	22443	22444	22460	22470	24341	25742	25743	26441	26442	27732	27738	27742	27744

Caliber & Description	270 FB	7MM BT	7MM BT	7MM BT	7MM FB	7MM FB	30 FN FB	30 FB	30 BT	30 BT	30 BT	30 BT	30 BT	30 FB	7.62X39 BT
Diameter, Inches	.277	.284	.284	.284	.284	.284	.308	.308	.308	.308	.308	.308	.308	.308	.310
Weight, Grains	150	120	140	150	160	175	150	110	130	150	165	168	180	200	123
Density	.279	.213	.248	.266	.283	.310	.226	.166	.196	.226	.248	.253	.271	.301	.183
Ballistic Coefficient	.386	.349	.394	.408	.392	.417	.184	.264	.340	.369	.398	.404	.453	.423	.275
Catalog Number	27746	28442	28444	28447	28446	28448	30820	30835	30838	30841	30843	30844	30846	30848	31012

AMMUNITION

Barnes Bullets

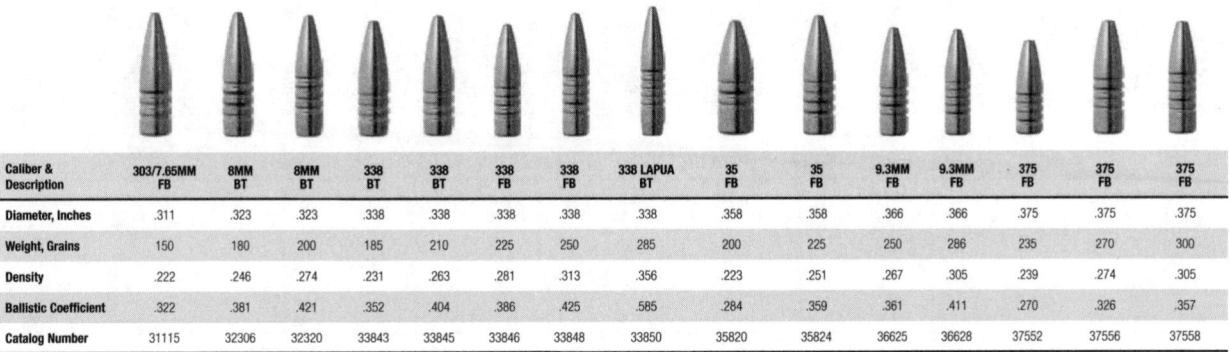

Caliber & Description	303/7.65MM FB	8MM BT	8MM BT	338 BT	338 BT	338 FB	338 FB	338 LAPUA BT	35 FB	35 FB	9.3MM FB	9.3MM FB	375 FB	375 FB	375 FB
Diameter, Inches	.311	.323	.323	.338	.338	.338	.338	.338	.358	.358	.366	.366	.375	.375	.375
Weight, Grains	150	180	200	185	210	225	250	285	200	225	250	286	235	270	300
Density	.222	.246	.274	.231	.263	.281	.313	.356	.223	.251	.267	.305	.239	.274	.305
Ballistic Coefficient	.322	.381	.421	.352	.404	.386	.425	.585	.284	.359	.361	.411	.270	.326	.357
Catalog Number	31115	32306	32320	33843	33845	33846	33848	33850	35820	35824	36625	36628	37552	37556	37558

Caliber & Description	375 FB	405 WIN FB	416 FB	416 FB	416 FB	404 JEFFREY FB	458 FB	458 FB	458 FB	458 FB	45/70 FN	45/70 FN	470 NITRO FB
Diameter, Inches	.375	.411	.416	.416	.416	.422	.458	.458	.458	.458	.458	.458	.474
Weight, Grains	350	300	300	350	400	400	300	350	450	500	250	300	500
Density	.356	.254	.248	.289	.330	.321	.204	.238	.306	.341	.170	.204	.318
Ballistic Coefficient	.425	.281	.298	.345	.392	.378	.234	.278	.369	.412	.136	.163	.363
Catalog Number	37560	41130	41683	41686	41689	42340	45814	45816	45819	45821	45841	45843	47452

Caliber & Description	505 GIBBS FB	500 NITRO FB	50 BMG BT	577 NITRO FB
Diameter, Inches	.505	.509	.510	.583
Weight, Grains	525	570	647	750
Density	.294	.314	.355	.315
Ballistic Coefficient	.320	.369	.572	.402
Catalog Number	50553	50958	51062	58472

From: $19.68–$64.91

VARMIN-A-TOR

Caliber & Description	20 FB	22 FB	22 FB	6mm FB	6mm FB
Diameter, Inches	.204	.224	.224	.243	.243
Weight, Grains	32	40	50	58	72
Density	.110	.114	.142	.140	.174
Ballistic Coefficient	.159	.153	.192	.173	.208
Catalog Number	20432	22429	22442	24329	24339

From: $20.96–$23.52

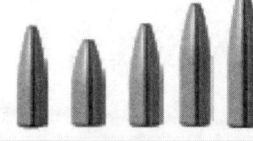

VARMINT GRENADE

Caliber & Description	"20 FB"	22 HORNET FB	22 FB	223 FB	6MM FB
Diameter, Inches	.204	.224	.224	.224	.243
Weight, Grains	26	30	36	50	62
Density	.089	.085	.102	.142	.150
Ballistic Coefficient	.131	.101	.149	.183	.199
Catalog Number	20426	22430	22436	22486	24372

Box 100: $18.91–$25.59

Handgun Bullets

M/LE TAC-XP PISTOL BULLETS

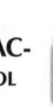

Caliber & Description	380 ACP	9MM	9MM	.357 SIG	38 SPL.	357 MAG.	10MM/40 S&W	10MM/40 S&W	10MM/40 S&W	44 SPL.	45 ACP/45 GAP	45 ACP
Diameter, Inches	.355	.355	.355	.355	.355	.357	.400	.400	.400	.429	.451	.451
Weight, Grains	80	95	115	125	110	125	125.	140	155	200	160	185
Density	.091	.108	.130	.142	.123	.140	.112	.125	.138	.155	.112	.130
Ballistic Coefficient	.107	.120	.167	.159	.156	.160	-	.128	.189	.138	.133	.167
Catalog Number	35500	35502	35501	35503	35703	35713	40003	40005	40006	42912	45106	45108

Box 40: $26.60–$36.17

Barnes Bullets

XPB Pistol Bullets

Caliber & Description	357 Mag.	41 Mag.	44 Mag.	44 Mag.	45 Colt	45 Colt	454 Casull	460 S&W	460 S&W	480 Ruger	500 S&W XPB	500 S&W XPB	500 S&W XPB
Diameter, Inches	.357	.410	.429	.429	.451	.451	.451	.451	.451	.475	.500	.500	.500
Weight, Grains	140	180	200	225	200	225	250	200	275	275	275	325	375
Density	.157	.153	.155	.175	.140	.158	.176	.140	.193	.174	.157	.186	.214
Ballistic Coefficient	.150	.126	.138	.166	•	.146	.141	.160	.215	.155	.141	.228	.261
Catalog Number	35714	41018	42920	42922	45116	45120	45123	45115	45105	48010	50025	50026	50028

Box 20: $16.49–$26.60

Berger Bullets

Famous for their superior performance in benchrest matches, Berger bullets also include hunting designs. From .17 to .30, all Bergers feature fourteen jackets with a wall concentricity tolerance of .0003. Lead cores are 99.9 percent pure and swaged in dies to within .0001 of a round. Berger's line includes several profiles: Match, Low Drag, Very Low Drag, Length Tolerant, and Maximum-Expansion, besides standard flat-base and boattail.

HUNTING

Caliber & Description	6mm VLD	6mm VLD	6mm	6mm VLD	6mm VLD	25 VLD"	6.5mm VLD	6.5mm VLD	270 VLD	270 Classic	270 VLD	270 VLD	7mm VLD	7mm VLD	7mm Classic	7mm VLD	30 VLD	30 VLD	30 Classic	30 VLD	30 VLD	30 Classic	30 VLD	30 VLD	338 Elite	338 Elite
Diameter, Inches	.243	.243	.243	.243	.243	.257	.264	.264	.277	.277	.277	.277	.284	.284	.284	.284	.308	.308	.308	.308	.308	.308	.308	.308	.338	.338
Weight, Grains	87	95	95	105	115	115	130	140	130	130	140	150	140	168	168	180	155	168	168	175	185	185	190	210	250	300
Density	.210	.230	-	.254	.278	.249	.266	.287	.241	-	.260	.279	.248	.298	-	.319	.233	.253	-	.264	.279	-	.286	.316	-	-
Ballistic Coefficient	.412	.480	.427	.532	.545	.466	.552	.612	.452	.497	.487	.531	.510	.617	.604	.659	.439	.473	.496	.498	.549	.547	.570	.631	.682	.818
Catalog Number	24524	24527	24570	24528	24530	25513	26503	26504	27501	27570	27502	27503	28503	28501	28570	28502	30508	30510	30570	30512	30513	30571	30514	30515	33554	33556

From: $38.18–$88.40

TARGET

Caliber & Description	22 FBHP	22 FBHP	22 VLD	22 BTHP	22 VLD	22 VLD	22 VLD	22 LRBTHP	22 VLD	6mm FBHP	6mm BR	6mm BTHP	6mm FBHP	6mm FBHP	6mm BTHP	6mm VLD
Diameter, Inches	.224	.224	.224	.224	.224	.224	.224	.224	.224	.243	.243	.243	.243	.243	.243	.243
Weight, Grains	52	55	70	73	75	80	80.5	82	90	62	-	65	65	68	90	95
Density	.148	.157	.199	.208	.214	.228	.229	.233	.256	.150	-	.157	.157	.165	.218	.230
Ballistic Coefficient	.242	.262	.371	.343	.423	.445	.436	.444	.551	.253	.277	.270	.265	.280	.411	.480
Catalog Number	22408	22410	22418	22420	22421	22422	22427	22424	22423	24404	24407	24408	24409	24411	24425	24427

Berger Bullets

Caliber & Description	6mm BTHP	6mm VLD	6mm Hybrid	6mm BTHP	6mm VLD	6.5mm BTHP	6.5mm VLD	6.5mm VLD	6.5mm LRBTHP	6.5mm Hybrid	7mm VLD	7mm VLD	7mm Hybrid
Diameter, Inches	.243	.243	.243	.243	.243	.264	.264	.264	.264	.264	.284	.284	.284
Weight, Grains	105	105	105	108	115	120	130	140	140	140	168	180	180
Density	.254	.254	.254	.261	.278	.245	.266	.287	.287	.287	.298	.319	.319
Ballistic Coefficient	.493	.495	.547	.551	.545	.453	.552	.612	.592	.618	.617	.659	.674
Catalog Number	24428	24429	24433	24431	24430	26402	26403	26401	26409	26414	28401	28405	28407

Caliber & Description	30 FBHP	30 FBHP	30 VLD	30 Hybrid	30 LRBTHP	30 VLD	30 Hybrid	30 LRBTHP	30 VLD	30 Juggernaut	30 VLD	30 Hybrid
Diameter, Inches	.308	.308	.308	.308	.308	.308	.308	.308	.308	.308	.308	.308
Weight, Grains	115	150	155	155	155.5	168	168	175	175	185	185	185
Density	.183	.226	.233	.233	.234	.253	.253	.264	.264	.279	.279	.279
Ballistic Coefficient	.296	.398	.439	.483	.464	.473	.519	.515	.498	.560	.549	.569
Catalog Number	30421	30407	30408	30426	30416	30410	30425	30420	30412	30418	30413	30424

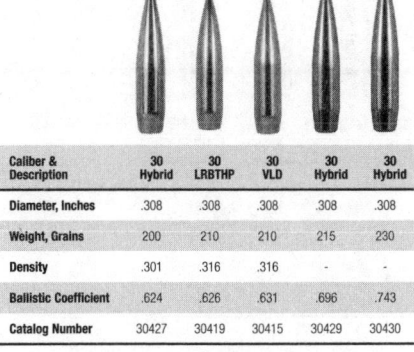

Caliber & Description	30 Hybrid	30 LRBTHP	30 VLD	30 Hybrid	30 Hybrid
Diameter, Inches	.308	.308	.308	.308	.308
Weight, Grains	200	210	210	215	230
Density	.301	.316	.316	-	-
Ballistic Coefficient	.624	.626	.631	.696	.743
Catalog Number	30427	30419	30415	30429	30430

From: $28.52–$67.54

VARMINT

Caliber & Description	17 FBHP	20 FBHP	20 BTHP	20 LRBTHP	22 FBHP	22 FBHP	22 FBHP	22 FBHP	22 FBHP	6mm LDHP	6mm FBHP	6mm LDHP
Diameter, Inches	.172	.204	.204	.204	.224	.224	.224	.224	.224	.243	.243	.243
Weight, Grains	25	35	40	55	40	52	55	60	64	69	80	88
Density	.121	.120	.137	.188	.114	.148	.157	.171	.182	.167	.194	.213
Ballistic Coefficient	.150	.176	.225	.381	.155	.197	.210	.278	.294	.291	.306	.391
Catalog Number	17308	20303	20304	20306	22303	22309	22311	22312	22316	24313	24321	24323

From: $28.35–$56.52

Hornady Bullets

Hornady's product line includes over 300 bullets, ranging from .17 caliber all the way up to the .50 caliber AMAX bullet for the .50 BMG. Hornady is always working to originate the next technological innovation. From prairie dogs to dangerous game, they have the perfect bullet to meet every hunting and shooting need.

Rifle Bullets

FMJ Bullets

Caliber & Description	22 FMJ-BT	30 FMJ	30 FMJ-BT	303 FMJ-BT	375 FMJ
Diameter, Inches	.224	.308	.308	.3105	.375
Weight, Grains	55	110	150	174	300
Density	.157	.166	.226	.255	.305
Ballistic Coefficient	.243	.178	.398	.470	.275
Catalog Number	2267	3017	3037	3131	37277

MSRP $18.98–$57.24

InterBond

Caliber & Description	6mm	25	6.5mm	270	270	7mm	7mm	30	30	30	338	416 RN
Diameter, Inches	.243	.257	.264	.277	.277	.284	.284	.308	.308	.308	.338	.416
Weight, Grains	85	110	129	130	150	139	154	150	165	180	225	400
Density	.206	.238	.264	.242	.279	.246	.525	.226	.248	.271	.281	.330
Ballistic Coefficient	.395	.390	.485	.460	.525	.486	.273	.415	.447	.480	.515	.311
Catalog Number	24539	25419	26209	27309	27409	28209	28309	30309	30459	30709	33209	41659

MSRP $60.87–$88.75

InterLock

Caliber & Description	22 SP"	6mm SP	6mm BT SP	25 SP"	25 BTSP	25 RN	25 HP	6.5mm SP	6.5mm SP	6.5mm RN	6.5mm Carcano RN	270 SP	270 BTSP	270 SP	7mm BTSP	7mm SP	7mm SP	7mm BTSP	7mm RN	7mm SP"
Diameter, Inches	.227	.243	.243	.257	.257	.257	.257	.264	.264	.264	.268	.277	.277	.277	.284	.284	.284	.284	.284	.284
Weight, Grains	70	100	100	100	117	117	120	129	140	160	160	130	140	150	139	139	154	162	175	175
Density	.194	.242	.242	.216	.253	.253	.260	.264	.287	.328	.321	.242	.261	.279	.246	.246	.273	.287	.310	.310
Ballistic Coefficient	.296	.381	.405	.357	.391	.243	.394	.445	.465	.283	.275	.409	.486	.462	.453	.392	.433	.514	.285	.462
Catalog Number	2280	2450	2453	2540	2552	2550	2560	2620	2630	2640	2645	2730	2735	2740	2825	2820	2830	2845	2855	2850

AMMUNITION

Caliber & Description	30 BTSP	30 RN	30 SP	30 BTSP	30 SP	30 FP	30 BTSP	30 RN	30 SP	30 BTSP	30 RN	7.62 SP	303 SP	303 RN	32 FP	8mm SP
Diameter, Inches	.308	.308	.308	.308	.308	.308	.308	.308	.308	.308	.308	.310	.312	.312	.321	.323
Weight, Grains	150	150	150	165	165	170	180	180	180	190	220	123	150	174	170	150
Density	.226	.226	.226	.248	.248	.256	.271	.271	.271	.286	.331	.183	.220	.255	.236	.205
Ballistic Coefficient	.349	.186	.338	.435	.387	.189	.452	.241	.425	.491	.300	.252	.361	.262	.249	.290
Catalog Number	3033	3035	3031	3045	3040	3060	3072	3075	3070	3085	3090	3140	3120	3130	3210	3232

Caliber & Description	8mm RN	8mm SP	338 SP-RP	338 SP-RP	338 RN	338 SP-RP	348 FP	35 RN	35 SP-RP	35 RN	35 SP-RP	9.3 SP-RP	375 FP	375 SP-RP	375 SP-RP	375 BTSP	375 RN
Diameter, Inches	.323	.323	.338	.338	.338	.338	.348	.358	.358	.358	.358	.366	.375	.375	.375	.375	.375
Weight, Grains	170	195	200	225	250	250	200	200	200	250	250	286	220	225	270	300	300
Density	.233	.267	.250	.281	.313	.313	.236	.223	.223	.279	.279	.305	.223	.229	.229	.305	.305
Ballistic Coefficient	.217	.410	.361	.397	.291	.431	.246	.195	.282	.271	.375	.410	.217	.320	.380	.460	.250
Catalog Number	3235	3236	3310	3320	3330	3335	3410	3515	3510	3525	3520	3560	3705	3706	3711	3725	3720

Caliber & Description	405 FP	405 SP	416 RN	44 FP	45 HP	45 FP	45 RN	45 RN
Diameter, Inches	.411	.411	.416	.430	.458	.458	.458	.458
Weight, Grains	300	300	400	265	300	350	350	500
Density	.251	.251	.330	.205	.204	.238	.238	.341
Ballistic Coefficient	.215	.250	.311	.186	.197	.195	.189	.287
Catalog Number	41050	41051	4165	4300	4500	4503	4502	4504

MSRP $28.20–$66.65

MATCH A-MAX

Caliber & Description	6.5mm	22	22 MOLY	22	22	6mm	6mm MOLY	6.5mm	6.5mm	6.5mm	7mm	30	30 MOLY	30	30 MOLY	30	30	50
Diameter, Inches	.264	.224	.224	.224	.224	.243	.243	.264	.264	.264	.284	.308	.308	.308	.308	.308	.308	.510
Weight, Grains	100	52	75	75	80	105	105	120	123	140	162	155	155	168	168	178	208	750
Density	.246	.148	.214	.214	.228	.254	.254	.246	.252	.287	.287	.233	.233	.253	.253	.268	.313	.412
Ballistic Coefficient	.390	.247	.435	.435	.453	.500	.500	.465	.510	.585	.625	.435	.435	.475	.475	.495	.325	1.050
Catalog Number	26101	22492	22794	22792	22832	24562	24564	26172	26171	26332	28402	30312	30314	30502	30504	30712	30732	5165

MSRP $25.47–$61.80

AMMUNITION

Hornady Bullets

SST

Caliber & Description	6mm	25	6.5mm	6.5mm	6.5mm	270	270	270	270	7mm SST	7mm SST	7mm SST	30	30	30	30
Diameter, Inches	.243	.257	.264	.264	.264	.277	.277	.277	.277	.284	.284	.284	.308	.308	.308	.308
Weight, Grains	95	117	123	129	140	120	130	140	150	139	154	162	125	150	150	165
Density	.230	.253	.252	.264	.287	.223	.242	.261	.279	.246	.273	.287	.185	.226	N/A	.248
Ballistic Coefficient	.355	.390	.510	.485	.520	.400	.460	.495	.525	.486	.525	.550	.305	.415	N/A	.447
Catalog Number	24532	25522	26173	26202	26302	2716	27302	27352	27402	28202	28302	28452	3019	30302	30303	30452

Caliber & Description	30	7.62	338	338
Diameter, Inches	.308	.310	.338	.338
Weight, Grains	180	123	200	225
Density	.271	.183	.250	.281
Ballistic Coefficient	.480	.260	.455	.515
Catalog Number	30702	3142	33102	33202

LEGEND

Type of Bullet

- BT – Boat Tail
- CT – Combat Target
- FMJ – Full Metal Jacket
- FP – Flat Point
- HB – Hollow Base
- L – Lead
- RN – Round Nose
- SP – Spire Point
- SX – Super Explosive
- SWC – Semi-Wadcutter
- WC – Wadcutter

MSRP $39.20–$50.85

Traditional Varmint

Caliber & Description	17 HP	20 SP	22 JET	22 Hornet	22 Hornet	22 HP BEE	22 SP	22 SP SX	22 SP	22 SP	22 SP SX	22 HP	22 SP	6mm HP
Diameter, Inches	.172	.204	.222	.223	.224	.224	.224	.224	.224	.224	.224	.224	.224	.243
Weight, Grains	25	45	40	45	45	45	50	50	55	55	55	60	60	75
Density	.121	.155	.116	.129	.128	.128	.142	.142	.157	.157	.157	.171	.171	.181
Ballistic Coefficient	.187	.245	.104	.202	.202	.108	.214	.214	.235	.235	.235	.271	.264	.294
Catalog Number	1710	22008	2210	2220	2230	2229	2245	2240	2265	2266	2260	2275	2270	2420

Caliber & Description	6mm BTHP	6mm SP	25 FP	25 HP	25 SP	6.5mm SP	270 SP	270 HP	270 BTHP	7mm HP	30 Short Jacket	30 SP	30 RN	30 SP
Diameter, Inches	.243	.243	.257	.257	.257	.264	.277	.277	.277	.284	.308	.308	.308	.308
Weight, Grains	87	87	60	75	87	100	100	110	110	120	100	110	110	130
Density	.210	.210	.130	.162	.188	.205	.186	.205	.205	.213	.151	.166	.166	.196
Ballistic Coefficient	.376	.327	.101	.257	.322	.358	.307	.352	.360	.334	.152	.256	.150	.295
Catalog Number	2442	2440	2510	2520	2530	2610	2710	2720	27200	2815	3005	3010	3015	3020

MSRP $18.17–$37.31

Hornady Bullets

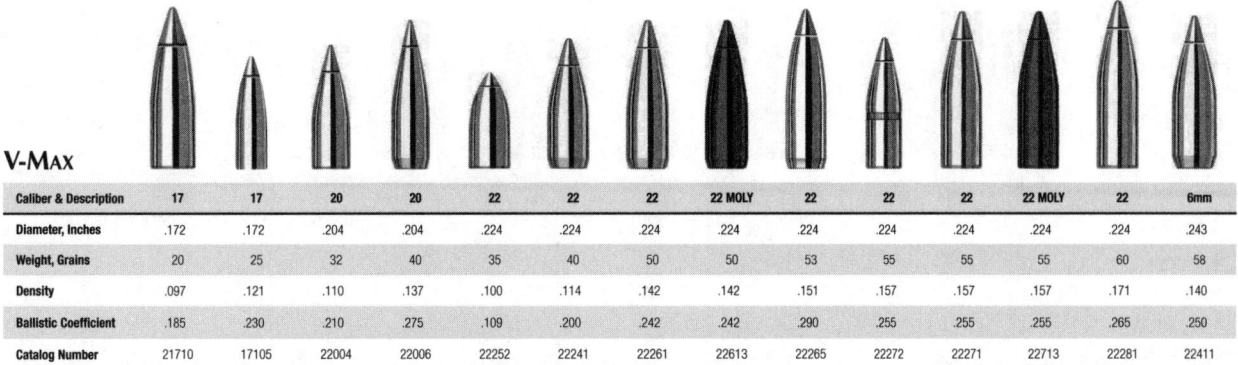

V-MAX

Caliber & Description	17	17	20	20	22	22	22	22 MOLY	22	22	22	22 MOLY	22	6mm
Diameter, Inches	.172	.172	.204	.204	.224	.224	.224	.224	.224	.224	.224	.224	.224	.243
Weight, Grains	20	25	32	40	35	40	50	50	53	55	55	55	60	58
Density	.097	.121	.110	.137	.100	.114	.142	.142	.151	.157	.157	.157	.171	.140
Ballistic Coefficient	.185	.230	.210	.275	.109	.200	.242	.242	.290	.255	.255	.255	.265	.250
Catalog Number	21710	17105	22004	22006	22252	22241	22261	22613	22265	22272	22271	22713	22281	22411

Caliber & Description	6mm	6mm	6mm	25	6.5mm	270	7mm	30
Diameter, Inches	.243	.243	.243	.257	.264	.277	.284	.308
Weight, Grains	65	75	87	75	95	110	120	110
Density	.157	.181	.210	.162	.195	.205	.213	.166
Ballistic Coefficient	.280	.330	.400	.290	.365	.370	.365	.290
Catalog Number	22415	22420	22440	22520	22601	22721	22810	23010

LEGEND

Type of Bullet

BT	–	Boat Tail
CT	–	Combat Target
FMJ	–	Full Metal Jacket
FP	–	Flat Point
HB	–	Hollow Base
L	–	Lead
RN	–	Round Nose
SP	–	Spire Point
SX	–	Super Explosive
SWC	–	Semi-Wadcutter
WC	–	Wadcutter

MSRP $22.32–$37.28

Handgun Bullets

FMJ BULLETS

Caliber & Description	9mm FMJ-RN	9mm FMJ-RN	10mm FMJ- FP	45 SWC	45 FMJ-RN	45 FMJ-FP	9mm FMJ	9mm FMJ-FP	9mm FMJ-RN	10mm FMJ-FP	"45 FMJ-CT"
Diameter, Inches	.355	.355	.400	.451	.451	.451	.355	.355	.355	.400	.451
Weight, Grains	115	124	180	185	230	230	100	124	147	200	200
Density	.130	.141	N/A	.130	.162	.162	.141	.141	.167	.179	.140
Ballistic Coefficient	.140	.145	N/A	.068	.184	.168	.158	.160	.212	.182	.115
Catalog Number	35557	355771	400471	45137	45177	451871	35527B	35567B	35597B	40077B	45157B

MSRP $22.52–$451.12

FRONTIER/ LEAD BULLETS

Caliber & Description	32 HBWC	32 SWC	38	38 HBWC	38 LRN	38 SWC	38 SWC HP	44 Cowboy	44 Cowboy
Diameter, Inches	.314	.314	.358	.358	.358	.358	.358	.427	.430
Weight, Grains	90	90	140	148	158	158	158	205	180
Density	.130	.130	.157	.165	.176	.176	.176	.161	.139
Ballistic Coefficient	.040	.096	.127	.047	.159	.135	.139	.123	.114
Catalog Number	10028	10008	10078	10208	10508	10408	10428	11208	11058

AMMUNITION

Hornady Bullets

FRONTIER/ LEAD BULLETS (CONT.)

Caliber & Description	44 SWC	44 SWC HP	"45 L-C/T"	45 SWC	45 LRN	45 FP Cowboy
Diameter, Inches	.430	.430	.452	.452	.452	.454
Weight, Grains	240	240	200	200	230	255
Density	.185	.185	.140	.140	.162	.177
Ballistic Coefficient	.182	.204	.081	.070	.207	.117
Catalog Number	11108	11118	12208	12108	12308	12458

MSRP $31.79–$50.24

HAP BULLETS

Caliber & Description	9mm	9mm	9mm	10mm	45	45	10mm
Diameter, Inches	.356	.356	.356	.400	.451	.451	.400
Weight, Grains	115	125	121	180	185	230	200
Density	.130	.141	.136	.161	.130	.162	.179
Ballistic Coefficient	.129	.158	.147	.164	.139	.188	.199
Catalog Number	355281	355721	35530B	400421	451051	451611	40061B

MSRP $77.65–$327.15

LEGEND
Type of Bullet

BT	–	Boat Tail
CT	–	Combat Target
FMJ	–	Full Metal Jacket
FP	–	Flat Point
HB	–	Hollow Base
L	–	Lead
RN	–	Round Nose
SP	–	Spire Point
SX	–	Super Explosive
SWC	–	Semi-Wadcutter
WC	–	Wadcutter

XTP BULLETS

Caliber & Description	30 RN	30 HP	32 HP	32 HP	32 HP	9mm HP	9mm HP	38 HP	9mm HP	38 FP	9mm HP	38 HP	38 HP	38 FP	38 HP	38 HP	9x18mm HP	10mm HP	10mm HP
Diameter, Inches	.308	.309	.312	.312	.312	.355	.355	.357	.355	.357	.355	.357	.357	.357	.357	.357	.365	.400	.400
Weight, Grains	86	90	60	85	100	90	115	110	124	125	147	125	140	158	158	180	95	155	180
Density	.130	.136	.088	.125	.147	.102	.130	.123	.141	.140	.167	.140	.157	.177	.177	.202	.102	.138	.161
Ballistic Coefficient	.105	.115	.090	.145	.170	.099	.129	.131	.165	.148	.212	.151	.169	.199	.206	.230	.127	.137	.164
Catalog Number	3100	31000	32010	32050	32070	35500	35540	35700	35571	35730	35580	35710	35740	35780	35750	35771	36500	40000	40040

Caliber & Description	10mm HP	41 HP	44 HP	44 HP	44 CL-SIL	44 HP	44 HP	45 HP	45 HP	45 HP	45	45 HP	45 HP	45	475 MAG	475	50	500 MAG	500 FP
Diameter, Inches	.400	.410	.430	.430	.430	.430	.300	.451	.451	.451	.452	.452	.452	.452	.475	.475	.500	.500	.500
Weight, Grains	200	210	180	200	240	240	300	185	200	230	240	250	300	300	325	400	300	350	500
Density	.179	.178	.139	.155	.185	.185	.232	.130	.140	.162	.168	.175	.210	.210	.206	.253	.171	.192	.275
Ballistic Coefficient	.199	.182	.138	.170	.174	.205	.245	.139	.151	.188	.160	.146	.180	.200	.150	.182	.120	.145	.185
Catalog Number	40060	41000	44050	44100	4425	44200	44280	45100	45140	45160	45220	45200	45230	45235	47500	47550	50101	50100	50105

MSRP $21.13–$57.97

AMMUNITION

Lapua

Rifle Bullets

Lapua precision bullets are made from the best raw materials and meet the toughest precision specifications. Each bullet is subject to visual inspection and tested with advanced measurement devices.

D46
The D46 bullet is manufactured to the strictest tolerances for concentricity, uniformity of shape, and weight.
From: $41.00–$45.99

D166
The Lapua's unique D166 construction has remained the same since the late 1930s: superb accurate FMJBT bullet for 7.62mm (.311) cartridges.
From: $51.99

FMJ
Ten rounds loaded with Lapua's .30 S374 8.0/123gr FMJ bullet from 100m can easily achieve groupings less than 30mm.
From: $27.99–$80.99

HOLLOW POINT
This HPCE bullet cuts a clean and easily distinguishable hole in your target. With ten rounds (G477 in .308 Win.) fired at 100m, this bullet typically achieves groupings of under 25mm—sometimes even less than 15mm.
From: $43.99–$89.99

LOCK BASE
A distinctive Full Metal Jacket Boat Tail bullet that has many applications from sport shooting to battlefield. Streamlined ballistic shape combined with patented base design
From: $49.99–$79.99

MEGA
This soft point bullet with a protective copper jacket bullet is at its best in the field and typically more than duplicates on impact. The mechanical bonding locks the lead alloy in place.
From: $50.99–$60.99

SCENAR
Scenar Hollow Point Boat Tail bullets have the IBS World Record in 600-yard Heavy Gun 5-shot group (.404") and hold the official world ISSF record of 600 out of 600 possible. Also available in Coated Silver Jacket version
From: $43.99–$89.99

SCENAR-L
The next generation Scenar, the Scenar-L is a refinement in all manufacturing steps that has resulted in closer weight tolerances, tighter jacket wall concentricity standards, and greater uniformity in every dimension, including the gilding metal cup, lead wire and jacket forming, ending up to core-jacket assembly, boat tail pressing, and tipping.
From: $50.99–$59.99

LAPUA D46

LAPUA D166

LAPUA FMJ S

LAPUA HP

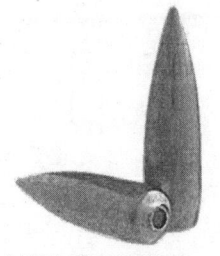
LAPUA LOCK BASE

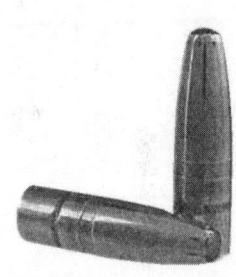
LAPUA MEGA

LAPUA SCENAR

LAPUA SCENAR-L

AMMUNITION

Nosler Bullets

Rifle Bullets

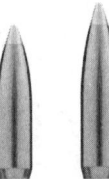

AccuBond

Caliber & Description	6mm S	25 SWT	6.5mm SWT	6.5mm	270 SWT	270 SWT	7mm SWT	7mm SWT	30 SWT	30 SWT	30 S	30 SWT	30 SWT
Diameter, inches	.243	.257	.264	.264	.277	.277	.277	.277	.284	.284	.308	.308	.308
Weight, Grains	90	110	130	140	100	110	130	140	140	160	125	150	165
Density	.218	.238	.266	.287	.186	.205	.242	.261	.248	.283	.188	.226	.248
Ballistic Coefficient	.376	.418	.488	.509	.323	.370	.435	.496	.485	.531	.366	.435	.475
Catalog Number	56357	53742	56902	57873	57845	54382	54987	54765	59992	54932	52165	56719	55602

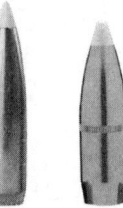

Caliber & Description	30 S	30 S	8mm S	338 S	338 S	338 S	338 S	338 S	35 Whelen S	35 Whelen S	9.3mm S	375 S	375 S
Diameter, inches	.308	.308	.323	.338	.338	.338	.338	.338	.358	.358	.366	.375	.375
Weight, Grains	180	200	200	180	200	225	250	300	200	225	250	260	300
Density	.271	.301	.274	.225	.250	.281	.313	.375	.223	.251	.267	.264	.305
Ballistic Coefficient	.507	.588	.450	.372	.414	.550	.575	.720	.365	.421	.494	.473	.485
Catalog Number	54825	54618	54374	57625	56382	54357	57287	54851	54425	50712	59756	54413	53662

MSRP $28.00–$57.00

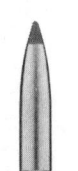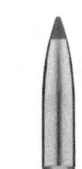

Ballistic Tip Hunting

Caliber & Description	6mm S	6mm S	25 S	25 S	6.5mm S	6.5mm S	6.5mm S	270 S	270 S	270 S	7mm S	7mm S
Diameter, inches	.243	.243	.257	.257	.264	.264	.264	.277	.277	.277	.284	.284
Weight, Grains	90	95	100	115	100	120	140	130	140	150	120	140
Density	.218	.230	.216	.249	.205	.246	.287	.242	.261	.279	.213	.248
Ballistic Coefficient	.365	.379	.393	.453	.350	.458	.509	.433	.456	.496	.417	.485
Catalog Number	24090	24095	25100	25115	26100	26120	26140	27130	27140	27150	28120	28140

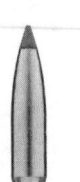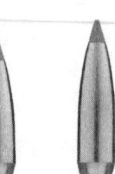

Caliber & Description	7mm S	30 S	30 S	30 S	30 S	30 S	8mm S
Diameter, inches	.284	.308	.308	.308	.308	.308	.323
Weight, Grains	150	125	150	165	168	180	180
Density	.266	.188	.226	.248	.253	.271	.247
Ballistic Coefficient	.493	.366	.435	.475	.490	.507	.394
Catalog Number	28150	30125	30150	30165	30168	30180	32180

MSRP $19.00–$26.00

LEGEND

Type of Bullet		Type of Tip	
BT	– Boat Tail	PT	– Purple Tip
HP	– Hollow Point	BT	– Blue Tip
J	– Jacketed	BrT	– Brown Tip
PP	– Protected Point	BuT	– Buckskin Tip
RN	– Round Nose	GT	– Green Tip
S	– Spitzer	GuT	– Gunmetal Tip
SS	– Semi Spitzer	MT	– Maroon Tip
W	– Whelen	OT	– Olive Tip
		RT	– Red Tip
		SLT	– Soft Lead Tip
		YT	– Yellow Tip

Nosler Bullets

BALLISTIC TIP VARMINT

Caliber & Description	204 S	204 S	22 S	22 S	22 S	22 S	6mm S	6mm S	6mm S	25 S
Diameter, inches	.204	.204	.224	.224	.224	.224	.243	.243	.243	.257
Weight, Grains	32	40	40	50	55	60	55	70	80	85
Density	.110	.137	.114	.142	.157	.171	.133	.169	.194	.184
Ballistic Coefficient	.206	.239	.221	.238	.27	.270	.276	.310	.329	.329
Catalog Number	35216	52111	39510	39522	39526	34992	24055	39532	24080	43004

MSRP $25.00–$33.00

CT BALLISTIC SILVERTIP HUNTING

Caliber & Description	6mm S	25 S	270 S	270 S	7mm S	7mm S	30 S	30 RN	30 S	30 S	8mm S	45-70 RN	338 S
Diameter, inches	.243	.257	.277	.277	.284	.284	.308	.308	.308	.308	.323	.458	.338
Weight, Grains	95	115	130	150	140	150	150	150	168	180	180	300	200
Density	.230	.249	.242	.279	.248	.266	.226	.226	.253	.271	.247	.204	.250
Ballistic Coefficient	.379	.453	.433	.496	.485	.493	.435	.232	.490	.507	.394	.191	.414
Catalog Number	51040	51050	51075	51100	51105	51110	51150	51165	51160	51170	51693	51834	51200

MSRP $23.00–$38.00

CUSTOM COMPETITION

Caliber & Description	22 HPBT	22 HPBT	22 HPBT	22 HPBT	6mm HPBT	6mm HPBT	6.5mm HPBT	6.5mm HPBT	6.8mm HPBT	7mm HPBT	30 HPBT	30 HPBT	30 HPBT	30 HPBT	30 HPBT	8mm HPBT	45 JHP
Diameter, Inches	.224	.224	.224	.224	.243	.243	.264	.264	.277	.284	.308	.308	.308	.308	.308	.323	.451
Weight, Grains	52	69	77	80	105	107	123	140	115	168	140	155	168	175	190	200	185
Density	.148	.196	.219	.228	.254	.259	.252	.287	.214	.298	.211	.233	.253	.264	.286	.274	.130
Ballistic Coefficient	.220	.305	.340	.415	.517	.525	.510	.529	.375	.520	.396	.450	.462	.505	.530	.520	.142
Catalog Number	53294	17101	22421	25116	53614	49742	53415	26725	45357	53418	53152	53155	53164	53952	53412	49524	44847

MSRP $24.00–$57.00

E-TIP

Caliber & Description	6mm S	25 S	6.8mm S	270 S	7mm S	7mm S	30 S	30 S	30 S	8mm S	338 S
Diameter, Inches	.243	.257	.277	.277	.284	.284	.308	.308	.308	.323	.338
Weight, Grains	90	100	85	130	140	150	150	168	180	180	200
Density	.218	.216	.158	.242	.248	.266	.226	.253	.271	.246	.250
Ballistic Coefficient	.403	.409	.273	.459	.489	.498	.469	.503	.523	.427	.425
Catalog Number	59165	59456	59543	59298	59955	59426	59378	59415	59180	59265	59186

MSRP $29.00–$45.00

Nosler Bullets

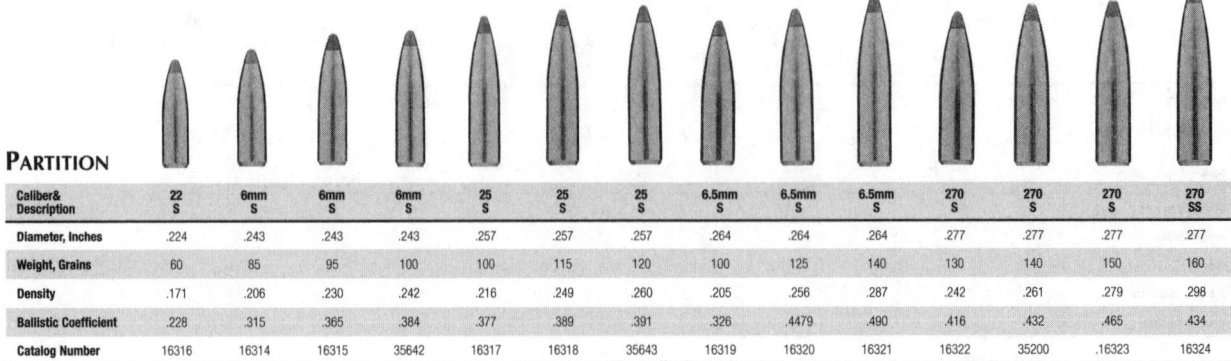

PARTITION

Caliber& Description	22 S	6mm S	6mm S	6mm S	25 S	25 S	25 S	6.5mm S	6.5mm S	6.5mm S	270 S	270 S	270 S	270 SS
Diameter, Inches	.224	.243	.243	.243	.257	.257	.257	.264	.264	.264	.277	.277	.277	.277
Weight, Grains	60	85	95	100	100	115	120	100	125	140	130	140	150	160
Density	.171	.206	.230	.242	.216	.249	.260	.205	.256	.287	.242	.261	.279	.298
Ballistic Coefficient	.228	.315	.365	.384	.377	.389	.391	.326	.4479	.490	.416	.432	.465	.434
Catalog Number	16316	16314	16315	35642	16317	16318	35643	16319	16320	16321	16322	35200	.16323	16324

Caliber & Description	7mm S	7mm S	7mm S	7mm S	30 S	30 S	30 RN	30 PP	30 S	30 S	30 SS	8mm S	338 S	338 S
Diameter, Inches	.284	.284	.284	.284	.308	.308	.308	.308	.308	.308	.308	.323	.338	.338
Weight, Grains	140	150	160	175	150	165	170	180	180	200	220	200	210	225
Density	.248	.266	.283	.310	.226	.248	.256	.271	.271	.301	.331	.274	.263	.281
Ballistic Coefficient	.434	.456	.475	.519	.387	.410	.252	.361	.474	.481	.351	.426	.400	.454
Catalog Number	16325	16326	16327	35645	16329	16330	16333	25396	16331	35626	16332	35277	16337	16336

Caliber & Description	338 S	35 S	35 S	9.3mm S	375 S	375 S	416 S	458 PP
Diameter, Inches	.338	.358	.358	.366	.375	.375	.416	.458
Weight, Grains	250	225	250	286	260	300	400	500
Density	.313	.251	.279	.307	.264	.305	.330	.389
Ballistic Coefficient	.473	.430	.446	.482	.314	.398	.390	.341
Catalog Number	35644	44800	44801	44750	44850	44845	45200	44745

MSRP $29.00–$80.60

LEGEND

Type of Bullet		Type of Tip	
BT	– Boat Tail	PT	– Purple Tip
HP	– Hollow Point	BT	– Blue Tip
J	– Jacketed	BrT	– Brown Tip
PP	– Protected Point	BuT	– Buckskin Tip
RN	– Round Nose	GT	– Green Tip
S	– Spitzer	GuT	– Gunmetal Tip
SS	– Semi Spitzer	MT	– Maroon Tip
W	– Whelen	OT	– Olive Tip
		RT	– Red Tip
		SLT	– Soft Lead Tip
		YT	– Yellow Tip

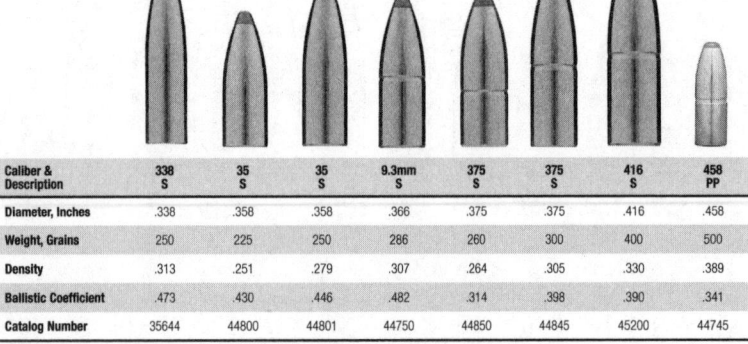

SOLID

Caliber & Description	9.3mm Solid	375 Solid	375 Solid	416 Solid	458 Solid	470 NE Solid
Diameter, Inches	.366	.375	.375	.416	.458	.474
Weight, Grains	286	260	300	400	500	500
Density	.305	.264	.305	.330	.341	.318
Ballistic Coefficient	.350	.254	.300	.289	.246	.237
Catalog Number	29825	29755	28451	23654	27452	28455

LEGEND

Type of Bullet			
		J	– Jacketed
BT	– Boattail	PP	– Protected Point
FMJ	– Full Metal Jacket	RN	– Round Nose
		S	– Spitzer

MSRP $70.00–$89.00

AMMUNITION

Nosler Bullets

VARMAGEDDON

Caliber & Description	17 FBHP	17 FB Tipped	20 FBHP	20 FB Tipped	22 FB Tipped	22 FBHP	22 FB Tipped	22 FBHP	22 FB Tipped	22 FBHP	6mm FBHP	6mm FB Tipped	6mm FB Tipped	30 FB Tipped
Diameter, Inches	.172	.172	.204	.204	.224	.224	.224	.224	.224	.224	.243	.243	.243	.308
Weight, Grains	20	20	32	32	35	40	40	55	55	62	55	55	70	110
Density	.097	.097	.110	.110	.100	.114	.114	.157	.157	.176	.133	.133	.169	.166
Ballistic Coefficient	.119	.183	.131	.204	.120	.158	.211	.210	.218	.251	.192	.252	.334	.293
Catalog Number	17205	17210	17215	17220	36763	17225	17230	17235	17240	35631	17245	17250	26123	34057

From: $13.99–$22.99

Handgun Bullets

SPORTING HANDGUN- PISTOL

Caliber & Description	9mm JHP	9mm JHP	10mm JHP	10mm JHP	10mm JHP	10mm JHP	45 JHP	45 FMJ
Diameter, Inches	.355	.355	.400	.400	.400	.400	.451	.451
Weight, Grains	115	124	135	150	180	200	230	230
Density	.109	.141	.093	.106	.161	.179	.1625	.162
Ballistic Coefficient	.130	.118	.121	.134	.147	.163	.175	.183
Catalog Number	44848	43123	44852	44860	44885	44952	44922	44964

MSRP $45.00–$62.00

SPORTING HANDGUN

Caliber & Description	38 JHP	41 JHP	44 JHP	44 JHP	44 JHP	44 JHP	45 Colt JHP
Diameter, Inches	.357	.410	.429	.429	.429	.429	.451
Weight, Grains	158	210	200	240	240	300	250
Density	.182	.170	.151	.173	.177	.206	.177
Ballistic Coefficient	.177	.178	155	.186	.186	.233	.176
Catalog Number	44841	43012	44846	44842	44868	42069	43013

MSRP $32.00–$62.00

Sierra Bullets

Rifle Bullets

BLITZKING

Caliber & Description	20	20	224	224	224	6mm	6mm	257	257
Diameter, Inches	.204	.204	.224	.224	.224	.243	.243	.257	.257
Weight, Grains	32	39	40	50	55	55	70	70	90
Density	.110	.134	.114	.142	.157	.133	.169	.151	.195
Ballistic Coefficient	.221	.287	.196	.248	.185	.225	.299	.260	.388
Catalog Number	1032	1039	1440	1450	1455	1502	1507	1605	1616

From: $26.45–$32.09

Sierra Bullets

GameKing

Caliber & Description	22 FMJBT	22 SBT	22 HPBT	22 SBT	6mm HPBT	6mm FMJBT	6mm SBT	25 HPBT	25 SBT	25 SBT	25 HPBT	6.5mm HPBT
Diameter, Inches	.224	.224	.224	.224	.243	.243	.243	.257	.257	.257	.257	.264
Weight, Grains	55	55	55	65	85	90	100	90	100	117	120	130
Density	.157	.257	.157	.185	.206	.218	.242	.195	.216	.253	.260	.266
Ballistic Coefficient	.272	.250	.185	.303	.282	.387	.430	.250	.355	.410	.350	.355
Catalog Number	1355	1365	1390	1395	1530	1535	1560	1615	1625	1630	1650	1728

Caliber & Description	6.5mm SBT	270 SBT	270 HPBT	270 SBT	270 SBT	7mm HPBT	7mm SBT	7mm SBT	7mm SBT	7mm HPBT	7mm SBT	30 FMJBT
Diameter, Inches	.264	.277	.277	.277	.277	.284	.274	.284	.284	.284	.284	.308
Weight, Grains	140	130	140	140	150	140	140	150	160	160	175	150
Density	.287	.242	.261	.261	.279	.248	.248	.266	.283	.283	.310	.226
Ballistic Coefficient	.495	.436	.337	.457	.483	.375	.416	.436	.455	.384	.533	.408
Catalog Number	1730	1820	1835	1845	1840	1912	1905	1913	1920	1925	1940	2115

Caliber & Description	30 SBT	30 HPBT	30 SBT	30 SBT	30 SBT	8mm SBT	338 SBT	338 SBT	35 SBT	375 SBT	375 SBT
Diameter, Inches	.308	.308	.308	.308	.308	.323	.338	.338	.358	.375	.375
Weight, Grains	150	165	165	180	200	220	215	250	225	250	300
Density	.226	.248	.248	.271	.301	.301	.269	.313	.251	.254	.305
Ballistic Coefficient	.380	.363	.404	.501	.560	.521	.485	.565	.370	.353	.475
Catalog Number	2125	2140	2145	2160	2165	2420	2610	2600	2850	2950	3000

From: $19.40–$41.93

MatchKing

Caliber & Description	22 HPBT	22 HP	22 HPBT	22 HPBT	22 HPBT	22 HPBT	22 HPBT	6mm HPBT	6mm HPBT	6mm HPBT	25 HPBT	6.5mm HPBT	6.5mm HPBT	6.5mm HPBT	6.5mm HPBT
Diameter, Inches	.224	.224	.224	.224	.224	.224	.224	.243	.243	.243	.257	.264	.264	.264	.264
Weight, Grains	52	53	69	77	77	80	90	70	107	95	100	107	120	123	140
Density	.148	.151	.196	.219	.219	.228	.256	.169	.259	.230	.216	.219	.246	.252	.287
Ballistic Coefficient	.225	.224	.301	.372	.372	.420	.504	.259	.527	.480	.394	.430	.421	.510	.535
Catalog Number	1410	1400	1380	9377T	9378T	9390T	9290T	1505	1570	1537	1628	1715	1725	1727	1740

Sierra Bullets

MatchKing

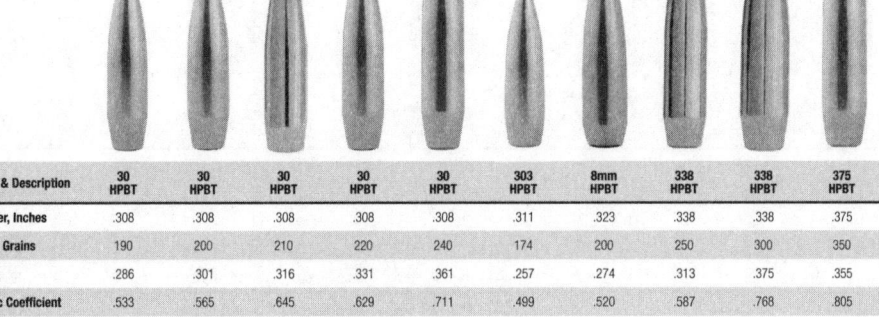

Caliber & Description	6.5mm HPBT	270 HPBT	270 HPBT	7mm HPBT	7mm HPBT	7mm HPBT	7mm HPBT	7mm HPBT	30 HP	30 HPBT	30 HPBT	30 HPBT	30 HPBT	30 HPBT	30 HPBT
Diameter, Inches	.264	.277	.277	.284	.284	.284	.284	.284	.308	.308	.308	.308	.308	.308	.308
Weight, Grains	142	115	135	130	150	168	175	180	125	135	150	155	168	175	180
Density	.291	.214	.251	.230	.266	.298	.310	.319	.188	.203	.226	.233	.253	.264	.271
Ballistic Coefficient	.595	.318	.488	.395	.429	.488	.608	.660	.349	.390	.417	.450	.462	.505	.475
Catalog Number	1742	1815	1833	1903	1915	1930	1975	1980	2121	2123	2190	2155	2200	2275	2220

Caliber & Description	30 HPBT	30 HPBT	30 HPBT	30 HPBT	30 HPBT	303 HPBT	8mm HPBT	338 HPBT	338 HPBT	375 HPBT
Diameter, Inches	.308	.308	.308	.308	.308	.311	.323	.338	.338	.375
Weight, Grains	190	200	210	220	240	174	200	250	300	350
Density	.286	.301	.316	.331	.361	.257	.274	.313	.375	.355
Ballistic Coefficient	.533	.565	.645	.629	.711	.499	.520	.587	.768	.805
Catalog Number	2210	2230	9240T	2240	9245T	2315	2415	2650	9300T	9350T

From: $17.36–$54.85

Pro-Hunter

Caliber & Description	6mm S	25 S	25 S	6.5mm S	270 S	270 S	7mm S	7mm S	30 HP/FN	30 FN	30 FN
Diameter, Inches	.243	.257	.257	.264	.277	.277	.284	.284	.308	.308	.308
Weight, Grains	100	100	117	120	110	130	120	140	125	150	170
Density	.242	.216	.253	.246	.205	.242	.213	.248	.188	.226	.256
Ballistic Coefficient	.373	.330	.388	.356	.318	.370	.328	.377	.119	.185	.205
Catalog Number	1540	1620	1640	1720	1810	1830	1900	1910	2020	2000	2010

Caliber & Description	30 RN	30 FMJ	30 S	30 S	30 RN	30 S	30 RN	30 RN
Diameter, Inches	.308	.308	.308	.308	.308	.308	.308	.308
Weight, Grains	110	110	125	150	150	180	180	220
Density	.166	.166	.188	.226	.226	.271	.271	.331
Ballistic Coefficient	.144	.144	.279	.336	.200	.407	.240	.310
Catalog Number	2100	2105	2120	2130	2135	2150	2170	2180

AMMUNITION

Sierra Bullets

Pro-Hunter (cont.)

Caliber & Description	303 S	303 S	303 S	8mm S	8mm S	338 S	35 RN	375 FN	45-70 HP/FN
Diameter, Inches	.311	.311	.311	.323	.323	.338	.358	.375	.458
Weight, Grains	125	150	180	150	175	225	200	200	300
Density	.185	.222	.266	.205	.240	.281	.223	.203	.204
Ballistic Coefficient	.274	.344	.411	.336	.381	.462	.148	.195	.120
Catalog Number	2305	2300	2310	2400	2410	2620	2800	2900	8900

Varminter

Caliber & Description	22 Hornet	22 Hornet	22 Hornet	22 Hornet	22 HP
Diameter, Inches	.223	.223	.224	.224	.224
Weight, Grains	40	45	40	45	40
Density	.115	.129	.114	.128	.114
Ballistic Coefficient	.117	.132	.116	.131	.155
Catalog Number	1100	1110	1200	1210	1385

From: $19.17–$34.83

Caliber & Description	22 S	22 S	22 S	22 Blitz	22 Blitz	22 SMP	22 S	22 HP	22 SMP	6mm HP	6mm HP	6mm SBT Blitz	6mm S	25 HP	25 S	6.5mm HP	6.5mm HP	270 HP	7mm HP	30 HP
Diameter, Inches	.224	.224	.224	.224	.224	.224	.224	.224	.224	.243	.243	.243	.243	.257	.257	.264	.264	.277	.284	.308
Weight, Grains	45	50	50	50	55	55	55	60	63	60	75	80	85	75	87	85	100	90	100	110
Density	.128	.142	.142	.142	.157	.157	.157	.171	.179	.145	.181	.194	.206	.162	.188	.174	.205	.168	.177	.166
Ballistic Coefficient	.210	.192	.222	.222	.237	.204	.237	.246	.231	.182	.217	.319	.315	.189	.293	.225	.259	.195	.209	.177
Catalog Number	1310	1320	1330	1340	1345	1350	1360	1375	1370	1500	1510	1515	1520	1600	1610	1700	1710	1800	1895	2110

From: $18.85–$30.59

Handgun Bullets

Sports Master

Caliber & Description	30 RN	32 JHC	9mm JHP	9mm JHP	9mm JHP	38 JHP Blitz	38 JHP	38 JSP	38 JHP	38 JHC	38 JSP	10mm JHP	10mm JHP
Diameter, Inches	.308	.312	.355	.355	.355	.357	.357	.357	.357	.357	.357	.400	.400
Weight, Grains	85	90	90	115	125	110	125	125	140	158	158	135	150
Density	.128	.132	.102	.130	.142	.123	.140	.140	.157	.177	.177	.121	.134
Ballistic Coefficient	.102	.125	.095	.107	.124	.120	.133	.133	.0776	.100	.100	.105	.120
Catalog Number	8005	8030	8100	8110	8125	8300	8320	8310	8325	8360	8340	8425	8430

Caliber & Description	10mm JHP	10mm JHP	41 JHC	41 JHC	44 JHC	44 JHC	44 JHC	44 JSP	45 JHP	45 JHP	45 JHC	45 JSP	50 JHP	50 JSP
Diameter, Inches	.400	.400	.410	.410	.4295	.4295	.4295	.4295	.4515	.4515	.4515	.4515	.500	.500
Weight, Grains	165	180	170	210	180	210	240	300	185	230	240	300	350	400
Density	.147	.161	.144	.178	.139	.163	.186	.232	.130	.161	.168	.210	.200	.229
Ballistic Coefficient	.130	.140	.123	.165	.130	.160	.185	.230	.100	.145	.150	.192	.155	.185
Catalog Number	8445	8460	8500	8520	8600	8620	8610	8630	8800	8805	8820	8830	5350	5400

From: $17.58–$34.49

Speer Bullets

Rifle Bullets

DeepCurl

This new line offers big game hunters of all types a consistent, tough, and accurate bullet, utilizing Speer's ability to bond bullets at the chemical level. Designed with a flat base for uniform bullet heel, DeepCurl is stable, accurate, and offers good weight retention.

Also available in handgun loads. ***Available in***: 6mm (80 Gr., 90 Gr.); 25 (120 Gr.); 6.5mm (140 Gr.); .270 (150 Gr.); 7mm (160 Gr., 175 Gr.); 30 (110 Gr., 150 Gr., 165 Gr., 170 Gr., 180 Gr.); .338 (225 Gr.)
From:. . . . . **$19.79–$32.99**

BOAT TAIL BULLETS

Caliber & Description	22 Match* HP	6mm SSP	6mm SSP	25 SHP	25 SSP	270 SSP	270 SSP	7mm SSP
Diameter, Inches	.224	.243	.243	.257	.257	.277	.277	.284
Weight, Grains	52	85	100	100	120	130	150	130
Density	.148	.206	.242	.216	.260	.242	.279	.230
Ballistic Coefficient	.253	.380	.446	.393	.480	.412	.489	.424
Catalog Number	1036	1213	1220	1408	1410	1458	1604	1624

Match bullets are not recommended for use on game animals.

Caliber & Description	7mm SSP	7mm Match* HP	7mm SSP	30 SSP	30 SSP	30 Match* HP	30 SSP	338 SSP	375 SSP
Diameter, Inches	.284	.284	.284	.308	.308	.308	.308	.338	.375
Weight, Grains	145	145	160	150	165	168	180	225	270
Density	.257	.257	.284	.226	.248	.253	.271	.281	.274
Ballistic Coefficient	.472	.468	.519	.417	.520	.534	.545	.497	.478
Catalog Number	1628	1631	1634	2022	2034	2040	2052	2406	2472

Match bullets are not recommended for use on game animals.

From: $19.29–$33.99

GRAND SLAM

Caliber & Description	6mm SP	25 HCSP	270 HCSP	270 HCSP	7mm HCSP	7mm HCSP	7mm HCSP	30 HCSP	30 HCSP	30 HCSP	338 HCSP	375 HCSP
Diameter, Inches	.243	.257	.277	.277	.284	.284	.284	.308	.308	.308	.338	.375
Weight, Grains	100	120	130	150	145	160	175	150	165	180	250	285
Density	.242	.260	.242	.279	.257	.283	.310	.226	.248	.271	.313	.290
Ballistic Coefficient	.327	.356	.332	.378	.353	.389	.436	.295	.354	.374	.436	.354
Catalog Number	1222	1415	1465	1608	1632	1638	1643	2026	2038	2063	2408	2473

From: $27.99–$59.99

LEGEND	
BT	– Boat Tail
FB	– Fusion Bonded
FMJ	– Full Metal Jacket
FN	– Flat Nose
GD	– Gold Dot®
HC	– Hot-Cor®
HP	– Hollow Point
L	– Lead
MHP™	– Molybdenum Disulfide Impregnated
S	– Spitzer
SS	– Semi-Spitzer
SB™	– For Short-Barrel Firearms
SP	– Soft Point
TMJ®	– Encased-Core Full Jacket
RN	– Round Nose
SWC	– Semi-Wadcutter
UC	– Uni-Cor®
WC	– Wadcutter

Speer Bullets

Hot-Cor Bullets*

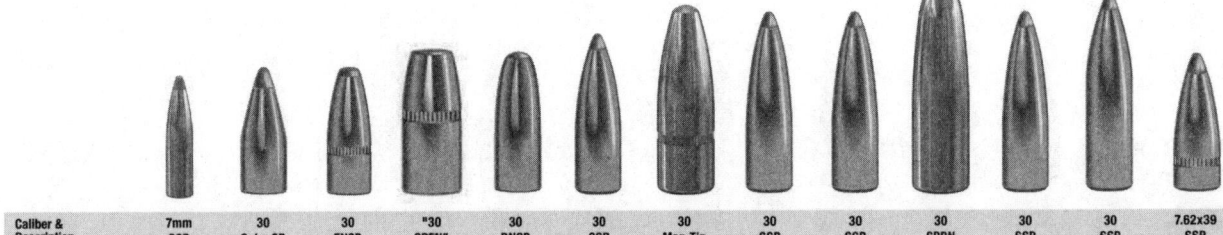

Caliber & Description	6mm SSP	25 SPFN	25 SSP	25 SSP	25 SSP	6.5mm SSP	6.5mm SSP	270 SSP	270 SSP	7mm SSP	7mm SPFN	7mm SSP
Diameter, Inches	.243	.257	.257	.257	.257	.264	.264	.277	.277	.284	.284	.284
Weight, Grains	90	75	87	100	120	120	140	130	150	130	130	145
Density	.218	.162	.188	.216	.260	.246	.287	.242	.279	.230	.230	.257
Ballistic Coefficient	.365	.135	.300	.334	.405	.392	.498	.383	.455	.394	.257	.416
Catalog Number	1217	1237	1241	1405	1411	1435	1441	1459	1605	1623	1625	1629

* Not recommended for lever-action rifles.

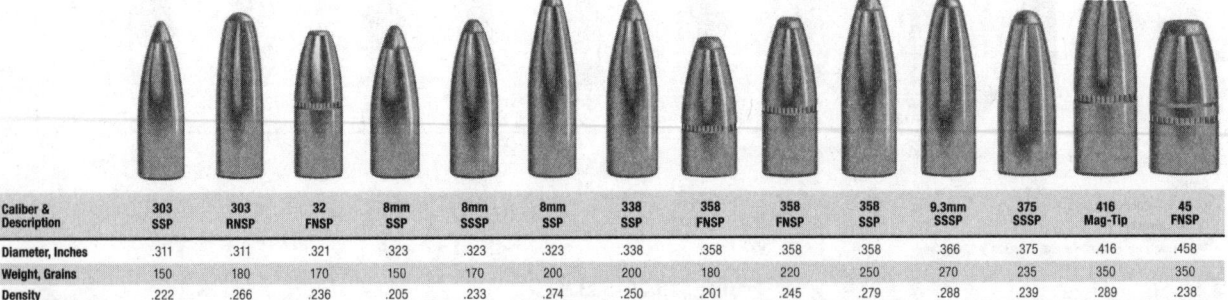

Caliber & Description	7mm SSP	30 Spire SP	30 FNSP	"30 SPFN"	30 RNSP	30 SSP	30 Mag-Tip	30 SSP	30 SSP	30 SPRN	30 SSP	30 SSP	7.62x39 SSP
Diameter, Inches	.284	.308	.308	.308	.308	.308	.308	.308	.308	.308	.308	.308	.310
Weight, Grains	160	110	130	150	150	150	150	165	170	180	180	200	123
Density	.283	.166	.196	.226	.226	.226	.226	.248	.256	.271	.271	.301	.183
Ballistic Coefficient	.504	.245	.213	.255	.235	.377	.301	.444	.298	.304	.441	.478	.283
Catalog Number	1635	1855	2007	2011	2017	2023	2025	2035	2041	2047	2053	2211	2213

* Not recommended for lever-action rifles.

Caliber & Description	303 SSP	303 RNSP	32 FNSP	8mm SSP	8mm SSSP	8mm SSP	338 SSP	358 FNSP	358 FNSP	358 SSP	9.3mm SSSP	375 SSSP	416 Mag-Tip	45 FNSP
Diameter, Inches	.311	.311	.321	.323	.323	.323	.338	.358	.358	.358	.366	.375	.416	.458
Weight, Grains	150	180	170	150	170	200	200	180	220	250	270	235	350	350
Density	.222	.266	.236	.205	.233	.274	.250	.201	.245	.279	.288	.239	.289	.238
Ballistic Coefficient	.351	.299	.283	.343	.311	.440	.426	.236	.286	.422	.361	.301	.332	.218
Catalog Number	2217	2223	2259	2277	2283	2285	2405	2435	2439	2453	2459	2471	2477	2478

From: $17.49–$36.49

Jacketed HP Bullets

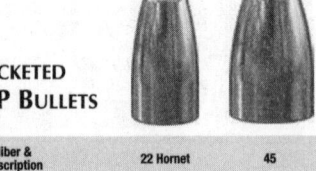

Caliber & Description	22 Hornet	45
Diameter, Inches	.224	.458
Weight, Grains	33	300
Density	.094	.204
Ballistic Coefficient	.080	.206
Catalog Number	1014	2482

From: $16.79–$29.49

Special Purpose Bullets*

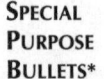   

Caliber & Description	30 SPRN	30 HP	45 SPFN
Diameter, Inches	.308	.308	.458
Weight, Grains	100	110	400
Density	.151	.166	.272
Ballistic Coefficient	.144	.128	.259
Catalog Number	1805	1835	2479

From: $17.79–$30.99

Speer Bullets

TNT BULLETS

Caliber & Description	204 HP	22 HP	22 HP	6mm HP	25 HP	6.5mm HP	270 HP	7mm HP	30 HP
Diameter, Inches	.204	.224	.224	.243	.247	.264	.277	.284	.308
Weight, Grains	39	50	55	70	87	90	90	110	125
Density	.134	.142	.157	.169	.188	.184	.168	.195	.188
Ballistic Coefficient	.202	.228	.233	.279	.337	.281	.303	.384	.341
Catalog Number	1015	1030	1032	1206	1246	1445	1446	1616	1986

From: $15.79–$26.99

Handgun Bullets

GOLD DOT BULLETS

Caliber & Description	25 HP	32 Auto HP	327 Fed. Mag. HP	327 Fed. Mag. HP	380 Auto HP	9mm HP	9mm HP	9mm HP	357 SIG HP	38 Spl. HPSB	38 HPSB	357 Mag. HP	40/10mm HP
Diameter, Inches	.251	.312	.312	.312	.355	.355	.355	.355	.355	.357	.357	.357	.400
Weight, Grains	35	60	100	115	90	115	124	147	125	110	135	125	155
Density	.079	.088	.147	.168	.102	.130	.141	.167	.142	.123	.151	.177	.138
Ballistic Coefficient	.091	.118	.137	.180	.101	.125	.134	.164	.141	.117	.141	.140	.123
Catalog Number	3985	3986	3990	3988	3992	3994	3998	4002	4360	4009	4014	4012	4400

Caliber & Description	40/10mm HP	40/10mm HP	40/10mm HPSB	44 Spl. HP	44 Mag. HP	45 Auto HP	45 Auto HP	45 Auto HP	45 HPSB
Diameter, Inches	.400	.400	.400	.429	.429	.451	.451	.451	.451
Weight, Grains	165	180	180	.200	210	185	200	230	230
Density	.147	.161	.161	.155	.163	.130	.140	.162	.162
Ballistic Coefficient	.138	.143	.148	.145	.154	.109	.138	.143	.148
Catalog Number	4397	4406	4401	4427	4428	4470	4478	4483	4482

From: $17.79–$29.99

LEGEND
BT	– Boat Tail
FB	– Fusion Bonded
FMJ	– Full Metal Jacket
FN	– Flat Nose
GD	– Gold Dot®
HC	– Hot-Cor®
HP	– Hollow Point
L	– Lead
MHP™	– Molybdenum Disulfide Impregnated
S	– Spitzer
SS	– Semi-Spitzer
SB™	– For Short-Barrel Firearms
SP	– Soft Point
TMJ®	– Encased-Core Full Jacket
RN	– Round Nose
SWC	– Semi-Wadcutter
UC	– Uni-Cor®
WC	– Wadcutter

Speer Bullets

Jacketed Bullets

Caliber & Description	9mm Luger FN JSP	38 Spl./357 Mag. JHP	38 Spl./357 Mag. JSP	38 Spl./357 Mag. JHP	38 Spl./357 Mag. JHP	38 Spl./357 Mag. JHP	38 Spl./357 Mag. JSP	38 Spl./357 Mag. JSP
Diameter, Inches	.355	.357	.357	.357	.357	.357	.357	.357
Weight, Grains	124	110	125	125	140	158	158	158
Density	.141	.123	.140	.140	.157	.177	.177	.177
Ballistic Coefficient	.115	.113	.129	.129	.145	.163	.164	.163
Catalog Number	3997	4007	4011	4013	4203	4211	4217	4732

Caliber & Description	44 Mag. JSP	44 Mag. JSP	45 Colt/460 S&W JHP	45 Colt/460 S&W JSP	50 Action Express JHP
Diameter, Inches	.429	.429	.451	.451	.186
Weight, Grains	240	300	260	300	325
Density	.186	.233	.183	.211	.186
Ballistic Coefficient	.169	.213	.183	.199	.169
Catalog Number	4454	4463	4481	4485	4495

LEGEND

FN	– Flat Nose		S	– Spitzer
HB	– Hollow Base		SP	– Soft Point
HC	– Hot-Cor®		SS	– Semi-Spitzer
HP	– Hollow Point		SWC	– Semi-Wadcutter
J	– Jacketed		WC	– Wadcutter
RN	– Round Nose			

From: $14.99–$27.49

Lead Handgun Bullets

Caliber & Description	32 S&W HBWC	9mm Luger RN	38 HBWC	38 SWC	38 SWC HP	38 RN	44 SWC	45 Auto SWC	45 Auto RN	45 Colt SWC
Diameter, Inches	.314	.356	.358	.358	.358	.358	.430	.452	.452	.452
Weight, grains	98	125	148	158	158	158	240	200	230	250
Density	.142	.141	.165	.176	.176	.176	.185	.140	.161	.175
Ballistic Coefficient	.044	.155	.050	.123	.121	.170	.151	.078	.160	.117
Bulk Part No.	4600	4602	4618	4624	4628	4648	4661	4678	4691	4684
Bulk Count	1000	500	500	500	500	500	500	500	500	500

From: $38.99–$70.99

Swift Bullets

Rifle Bullets

The Scirocco II rifle bullet starts with a tough, pointed polymer tip that reduces air resistance, prevents tip deformation, and blends into the radius of its secant ogive nose section. The Scirocco II has a bonded core construction with a pure lead core encased in a tapered, progressively thickening jacket of pure copper. The Swift A-Frame bullet with its midsection wall of copper is less aerodynamic than the Scirocco, but it produces a broad mushroom while carrying almost all its weight through muscle and bone.

A-Frame

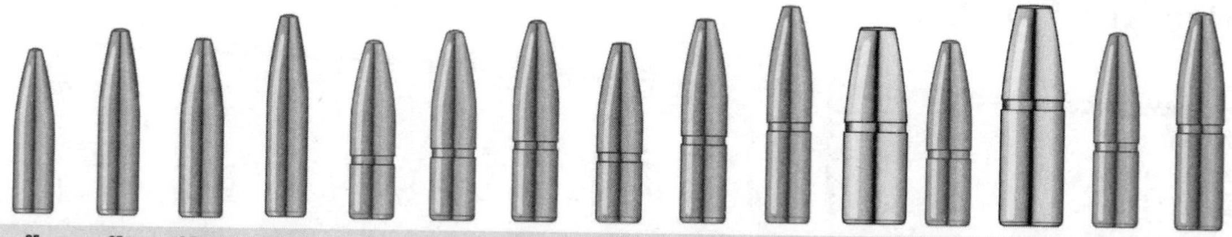

Caliber & Description	25 SS	25 SS	6.5mm SS	6.5mm SS	270 SS	270 SS	270 SS	7mm SS	7mm SS	7mm SS	30-30 FN	30 SS	30-30 FN	30 SS	30 SS
Diameter, Inches	.257	.257	.264	.264	.277	.277	.277	.284	.284	.284	.308	.308	.308	.308	.308
Weight, Grains	100	120	120	140	130	140	150	140	160	175	150	165	170	180	200
Density	.216	.260	.246	.287	.242	.261	.279	.248	.283	.310	.226	.248	.256	.271	.301
Ballistic Coefficient	.318	.382	.344	.401	.323	.414	.444	.335	.450	.493	.220	.367	.266	.400	.444

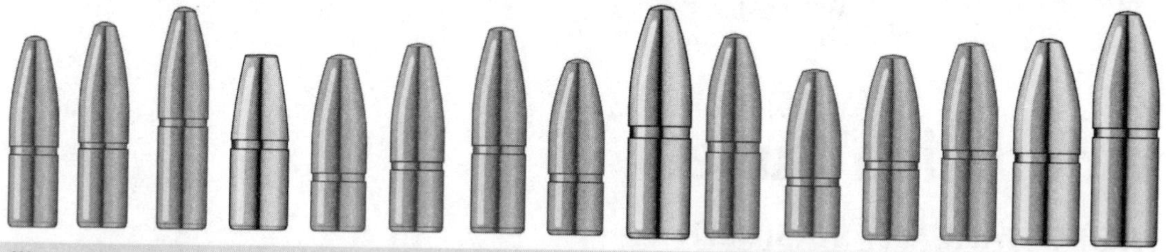

Caliber & Description	338 SS	338 SS	338 SS	348 FN	35 SS	35 SS	35 SS	9.3mm SS	9.3mm SS	9.3mm SS	375 SS	375 SS	375 SS	400 SS	400 SS
Diameter, Inches	.338	.338	.338	.348	.358	.358	.358	.366	.366	.366	.375	.375	.375	.410	.410
Weight, Grains	225	250	275	200	225	250	280	250	286	300	250	270	300	350	400
Density	.281	.313	.344	.236	.251	.279	.312	.267	.305	.320	.254	.274	.305	.297	.339
Ballistic Coefficient	.384	.427	.469	.245	.312	.347	.388	.285	.385	.342	.271	.349	.325	.321	.367

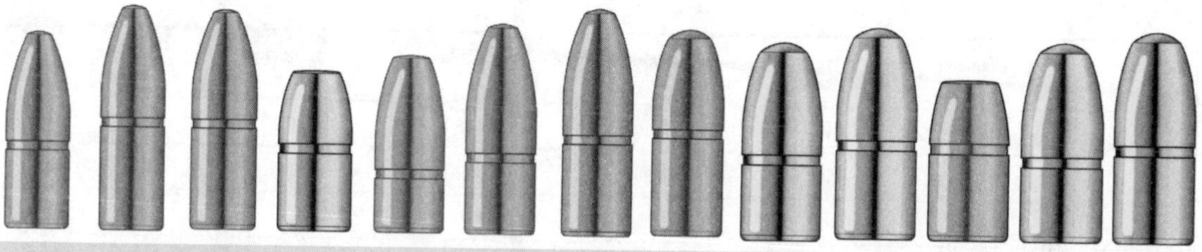

Caliber & Description	416 SS	416 SS	404 SS	45-70 FN	458 FN	458 SS	458 SS	470 RN	505 RN	505 RN	50 FN	500 RN	500 RN
Diameter, Inches	.416	.416	.423	.457	.458	.458	.458	.475	.505	.505	.509	.509	.509
Weight, Grains	350	400	400	350	400	450	500	500	535	570	450	535	570
Density	.289	.330	.319	.238	.272	.307	.341	.329	.300	.319	.247	.294	.313
Ballistic Coefficient	.321	.367	.375	.172	.258	.325	.361	.364	.285	.306	.180	.285	.306

MSRP $55.00–$114.50

Scirocco

Caliber & Description	224 BTS	224 BTS	6mm BTS	25 BTS	6.5mm BTS	270 BTS	7mm BTS	30 BTS	30 BTS	30 BTS	338 BTS
Diameter, Inches	.224	.224	.243	.257	.264	.277	.284	.308	.308	.308	.338
Weight, Grains	62	75	90	100	130	130	150	150	165	180	210
Density	.177	.214	.218	.216	.266	.242	.266	.226	.248	.271	.263
Ballistic Coefficient	.307	.419	.419	.429	.571	.450	.515	.430	.470	.520	.507

MSRP $52.25–$69.00

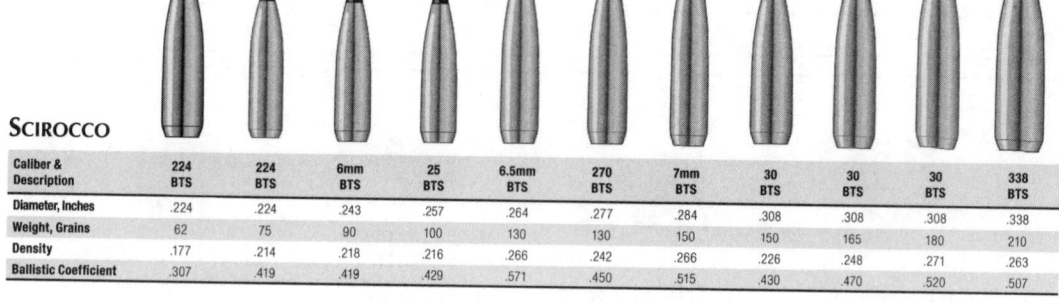

LEGEND
BT – Boattail
FN – Flat Nose
HP – Hollow Point
RN – Round Nose
S – Spitzer
SS – Semi-Spitzer

AMMUNITION

Swift Bullets

Handgun Bullets

A-FRAME HUNTING REVOLVER BULLETS										
Caliber & Description	357 HP	357 HP	41 HP	44 HP	44 HP	44 HP	45 HP	45 HP	45 HP	50 HP
Diameter, Inches	.357	.357	.410	.430	.430	.430	.452	.452	.452	.499
Weight, Grains	158	180	210	240	280	300	265	300	325	325
Density	.177	.202	.178	.185	.216	.232	.185	.210	.227	.186
Ballistic Coefficient	.183	.189	.159	.119	.139	.147	.129	.153	.171	.135

MSRP $54.00

Woodleigh Bullets

HYDROSTATICALLY STABILIZED

Hydrostatic stabilization is a method of producing pierced hollow bars to very precise concentricity to produce a bullet that resists deflection and achieves deep straight-line penetration. It's non-toxic and environmentally sensitive. It can be used in most nitro double and magazine rifles.

From: $35.49–$79.99

Caliber	Diameter	"Weight, Grains"	Catalog Number	Caliber	Diameter	"Weight, Grains"	Catalog Number
7mm	.308	140	H7mm	416	.416	400	H416
308	.308	150	H308A	404 Jeffery	.422	400	H404
308	.308	180	H308	450	.458	325	H450BPE
303	.312	215	H303	45/70	.458	400	H45/70
8mm	.323	170	H8mm	458	.458	450	H458A
338	.338	185	H338A	458	.458	480	H458
338	.338	225	H338	465	.468	480	H465
358	.358	225	H358	470	.474	500	H470
9.3	.366	"232 286"	"H9.3A H9.3"	500	.510	570	H500
375 Win.	.375	235	H375A	50 Alaskan	.510	400	H50 Alaskan
375	.375	300	H375	505	.505	525	H505
450/400 3"	.410	400	H450/400	577	.585	750	H577

98% & 95% RETAINED WEIGHT 300 WIN MAG 180GR PP

458 X 500GN SN RECOVERED FROM BUFFALO

270 WIN 150GN PP 86% RETAINED WEIGHT

94% RETAINED WEIGHT 300 WIN MAG 180GR PP

500/465 RECOVERED FROM BUFFALO

AMMUNITION

Woodleigh Bullets

TRADITIONAL BULLETS

Fashioned from gilding-metal-clad steel 2mm thick, jackets on FMJ bullets are heavy at the nose for extra impact resistance. The jacket then tapers toward the base to assist rifling engraving. Woodleigh Weldcore Soft Nose bullets are made from 90/100 gilding metal (90 percent copper; 10 percent zinc) 1.6 mm thick.
From: $30.49–$91.99

Caliber Diameter	Type	"Weight, Grains"	SD	BC	Catalog Number
6.5mm .264	PP SN	140	.287	.444	80
	PP SN	160	.328	.509	80A
	RN SN	160	.328	.285	80B
270 Win .277	PP SN	130	.242	.409	72
	PP SN	150	.279	.463	73
	PP SN	180	.334	.513	73A
7mm .284	PP SN	140	.248	.436	74
	PP SN	160	.283	.486	75
	PP SN	175	.310	.510	76
275 H&H .287	PP SN	160	.277	.474	77
	PP SN	175	.304	.509	78
308 .308	"PP SN	130	.189	.302	65I
	PP SN	150	.226	.310	65F
	PP SN	165	.248	.320	65A
	PP SN	180	.271	.376	65B
	RN SN	220	.331	.367	65C
	FMJ	220	.331	.359	65
30-30 .308	FN SN	150	.226	.246	65H
30/06 .308	PP SN	240	.361	.401	65G
300 Win. Mag. .308	PP SN	180	.271	.435	65D
	PP SN	200	.301	.450	65E
303 British .312	PP SN	174	.255	.362	68A
	RN SN	215	.316	.359	68
303/ 7.62mmx-39mm .312	PP SN	130	.312	.347	68B
8mm .323	RN SN	196	.268	.315	64B
	RN SN	220	.301	.355	64C
	RN SN	250	.343	.403	64D
325 Win. (8mm) .323	PP SN	200	.274	.406	64F
	PP SN	220	.301	.448	64G
8x57 .318	RN SN	200	.283	.331	64E
318 WR .330	RN SN	250	.328	.420	63
	FMJ	250	.328	.364	64
333 Jeffery .333	RN SN	250	.322	.335	60
	RN SN	300	.386	.418	61
	FMJ	300	.386	.418	62
338 Fed .338	PP SN	180	.226	.361	56C
	PP SN	200	.251	.401	56D
33 Win. .338	FN SN	200	.246	.234	56E
338 Mag .338	PP SN	225	.281	.425	56A
	RN SN	250	.313	.332	56
	PP SN	250	.313	.431	56B
	FMJ	250	.313	.326	57
	RN SN	300	.375	.416	58
	FMJ	300	.375	.414	59
348 Win. .348	FN SN	250	.295	.281	348

Caliber Diameter	Type	"Weight, Grains"	SD	BC	Catalog Number
358 .358	RN SN	225	.251	.263	51
	PP SN	225	.251	.372	51A
	FMJ	225	.251	.263	52
	RN SN	250	.279	.300	53
	PP SN	250	.279	.400	53A
	PP SN	275	.307	.450	53B
	RN SN	310	.346	.458	54
	FMJ	310	.346	.458	55
9.3 .366	RN SN	250	.267	.281	47A
	PP SN	250	.267	.381	47C
	RN SN	286	.305	.321	47
	PP SN	286	.305	.396	47B
	FMJ	286	.305	.305	48
	RN SN	320	.341	.359	49
	PP SN	320	.341	.457	49A
	FMJ	320	.341	.341	50
375 Mag. .375	PP SN	235	.239	.310	42A
	RN SN	270	.274	.250	42
	PP SN	270	.274	.370	43A
	RN SN	300	.305	.277	44HD
	RN SN	300	.305	.277	44
	PP SN	300	.305	.380	45A
	FMJ	300	.305	.275	46
	RN SN	350	.356	.321	46B
	RN SN	350	.356	.323	46BHD
	PP SN	350	.356	.400	46C
	FMJ	350	.356	.307	46D
400 Purdey .405	RN SN	230	.200	.181	81
450/400 Nitro .408	RN SN	400	.344	.307	40A
450/400 Nitro .411"	RN SN	400	.338	.307	40
450/400 Ruger .410	RN SN	400	.338	.307	40B
450/400 Ruger .408"	FMJ	400	.344	.300	41A
.410 Ruger	FMJ	400	.338	.300	41
405 Win. .412	RN SN	300	.252	.194	71
416 Rigby .416	PP SN	340	.281	.330	39
	RN SN	410	.338	.307	37A
	FMJ	410	.338	.300	38
	RN SN	450	.371	.338	37B
	FMJ	450	.371	.330	38B"
416 Rem. .416	RN SN	400	.330	.305	37C
	FMJ	400	.330	.300	38C
	RN SN	450	.371	.338	37N
	FMJ	450	.371	.330	38N
404 Jeffery .422	RN SN	350	.281	.293	35
	RN SN	400	.321	.335	33A
	FMJ	400	.321	.330	34
	RN SN	450	.361	.360	33B
	FMJ	450	.361	.355	34B
10.75x68mm .423	RN SN	347	.277	.290	36
	FMJ	347	.277	.288	36A
444 Marlin .430	FN SN	280	.216	.186	444

AMMUNITION

Woodleigh Bullets

Caliber Diameter	Type	"Weight, Grains"	SD	BC	Catalog Number
425 WR .435	RN SN	410	.310	.222	31
	FMJ	410	.310	.221	32
11.2 Schuler .440	RN SN	401	.296	.325	67
458 Mag. .458	PP SN	400	.272	.340	30
	RN SN	480	.327	.328	24A
	FMJ	480	.327	.325	25A
	RN SN	500	.341	.310	26
	PP SN	500	.341	.378	26A
	FMJ	500	.341	.310	28
	RN SN	550	.375	.340	27
	FMJ	550	.375	.326	29
450 BPE .458	RN SN	350	.238	.250	30A
45/70 .458	FN SN	405	.276	.204	30B
	FN SN	300	.205	.196	30C
450 Nitro .458	RN SN	480	.327	.328	24
	FMJ	480	.327	.325	25
465 Nitro .468	RN SN	480	.313	.334	22
	FMJ	480	.313	.330	23
470 Nitro .474	RN SN	500	.318	.374	20
	FMJ	500	.318	.370	21
476 WR .476	RN SN	520	.328	.385	18
	FMJ	520	.328	.380	19
475 No. 2 .483	RN SN	480	.294	.309	15
	FMJ	480	.294	.300	16
475 No. 2 Jeffery .488	RN SN	500	.300	.315	13
	FMJ	500	.300	.300	14

Caliber Diameter	Type	"Weight, Grains"	SD	BC	Catalog Number
500 S&W MAG .500	FN SN	400	.229	.182	83
505 Gibbs .505	RN SN	525	.294	.345	11
	FMJ	525	.294	.340	12
	PP SN	600	.336	.360	11A
	FMJ	600	.336	.360	12A
500 Jeffery .510	RN SN	535	.294	.350	9
	PP SN	535	.294	.310	9A
	FMJ	535	.294	.340	10
	PP SN	600	.330	.350	10B
	FMJ	600	.330	.355	10A
500 BP .510	RN SN	440	.242	.255	8
50 Alaskan & 50/110 Win. .510	FN SN	500	.275	.219	82
500 Nitro .510	RN SN	450	.247	.257	06A
	RN SN	570	.313	.368	6
	FMJ	570	.313	.350	7
577 BP Express .585	RN SN	650	.271	.292	5
577 Nitro .585	RN SN	650	.271	.292	3A
	RN SN	750	.313	.346	3
577 Nitro .584	FMJ	650	.272	.292	4A
	FMJ	750	.314	.351	4
600 Nitro .620	RN SN	900	.334	.371	1
	FMJ	900	.334	.334	2
700 Nitro .700	RN SN	1000	.292	.340	A
	FMJ	1000	.292	.340	B

AMMUNITION

HANDLOADING

POWDERS

RELOADING TOOLS

POWDERS

Accurate Powder

Rifle

1680
Extremely fast burning, double-base, spherical rifle powder well suited for large-capacity, high-performance handgun cartridges as well as low capacity rifle cartridges.
1lb: $19.25
8lbs:. $138.00

2015
Fast-burning, single-base, extruded rifle powder that performs very well in small to medium varmint calibers.
1lb: $21.05
8lbs:. $157.00

2200
High-performance, small caliber propellant; double-base, spherical propellant.
1lb: $19.25
8lbs:. $138.00

2230
Fast-burning, double-base, spherical rifle propellant. Excellent flow characteristics and grain size are ideal for progressive loading.
1lb: $19.25
8lbs:. $138.00

2460
Fast-burning, double-base, spherical rifle powder; slower derivative of the AA2230 powder; suitable for small and medium sized calibers.
1lb: $19.25
8lbs:. $138.00

2495
Single-base, extruded rifle powder that was developed for the .308 Win. and can be used over a wide range of rifle calibers.
1lb: $21.05
8lbs:. $157.00

2520
Medium-burning, double-base, spherical rifle propellant designed around the .308 Win.
1lb: $19.25
8lbs:. $138.00

2700
Medium-burning, double-base, spherical rifle powder that is suited for the .30-06 Spfd.
1lb: $19.25
8lbs:. $138.00

4064
Intermediate-burning, single-base, short cut extruded rifle powder designed around the .30-06 Spfd.
1lb: $21.05
8lbs:. $157.00

4350
Short-cut, single-base, extruded rifle powder in the extremely popular 4350 burn range.
1lb: $21.05
8lbs:. $157.00

5744
Low, bulky density and superior ignition characteristics; many rifle calibers and large-capacity black-powder cartridges
1lb: $24.85
8lbs:. $185.00

MAGPRO
Slow-burning, double-base, spherical rifle powder developed specifically for the short magnums of both Winchester and Remington.
1lb: $19.25
8lbs:. $138.00

Handgun

4100
Slow-burning with exceptional metering characteristics. Excellent choice for high-performance, full-power loads in magnum handgun cartridges.
1lb: $19.99
4lbs:. $74.99
8lbs:. $139.99

NO. 2
Extremely fast-burning, double-base, spherical powder. Low recoil and low flash; well suited for use in short barrel, concealed carry applications.
1lb: $16.80
5lbs:. $75.00

NO. 5
Wide performance range from target and Cowboy Action applications to full-power defense loads. Strikes a balance between ballistics and cost efficiency.
1lb: $18.10
8lbs:. $130.50

NO. 7
Intermediate-burning, double-base, spherical powder suitable for a wide range of handgun calibers, especially high performance semi-auto handguns.
1lb: $18.10
8lbs:. $130.50

NO. 9
Ideal for high power loads in traditional magnums such as the .357 Mag., .41 Rem. Mag., and .44 Rem. Mag.
1lb: $18.10
8lbs:. $130.50

Accurate Powder

Shotshell

NITRO 100

Fast-burning, flattened spherical, double-base shotshell powder that is a clean burning, cost-effective choice for all 12-gauge target applications.

12oz: $14.95
4lbs: $70.99
8lbs: $116.25

SOLO 1000

Ultra clean burning powder that is well suited for target handgun loads in .45 ACP and Cowboy Action cartridges.

12oz: $15.10
4lbs: $69.99
8lbs: $118.75

Alliant Powder
ALLIANT SMOKELESS POWDERS

20/28 SMOKELESS SHOTSHELL POWDER

Powder designed to deliver competition-grade performance to 20 and 28 Ga. clay target shooters. Extremely clean burning with proven lot-to-lot consistency.

1lb: $16.25
4lbs: $60.15
8lbs: $112.50

410

Cleanest .410 bore powder on the market.

1lb: $16.25
4lbs: $60.15
8lbs: $112.50

2400

Legendary for its performance in .44 Mag. and other magnum pistol loads. Originally developed for the .22 Hornet, it's also the shooter's choice for .410 bore.

1lb: $16.25
4lbs: $60.15
8lbs:$112.50

AMERICAN SELECT

This ultra-clean burning premium powder makes a versatile target load and superior 1 oz. load for improved clay target scores. Great for Cowboy Action handgun loading, too.

1lb: $15.65
4lbs: $65.99
8lbs: $106.80

AR-COMP

Developed specifically for AR-style rifles and ideally suited for heavy .223 and .308 match bullets, AR-Comp delivers high-performance ignition each and every time.

1lb: $19.40
8lbs: $144.50

BLACK MZ

Designed for shooters of all disciplines, Black MZ is an ideal choice for hunters as well as Cowboy Action shooters, reenactment shooters and the recent rise in .45-70, .45-90, and, .45-100 shooters.

1lb: $19.60

Alliant Powder

HANDLOADING

BLUE DOT
The powder of choice for magnum lead shotshell loads. 10, 12, 16, 20, and 28 Ga. Consistent and accurate. Doubles as magnum handgun powder.
1lb: $15.55
5lbs: $68.45

BULL'S-EYE
America's best known pistol powder. Unsurpassed for .45 ACP target loads.
1lb: $15.20
4lbs: $56.00
8lbs: $104.80

E3
The first of a new generation of high performance powders.
1lb: $15.65
4lb: $58.70
8lbs: $106.80

GREEN DOT
It delivers precise burn rates for uniformly tight patterns and you'll appreciat the lower felt recoil. Versatile for target and field.
1lb: $15.65
4lbs: $58.70
8lbs: $106.80

HERCO
Since 1920, a proven powder for heavy shotshell loads, including 10, 12, 16, 20, and 28 Ga. target loads. The ultimate in 12 Ga., 1¼ oz. upland game loads.
1lb: $15.65
4lbs: $58.70
8lbs: $106.80

POWER PISTOL
Designed for high performance in semi-automatic pistols (9mm, .40 S&W, and .357 SIG).
1lb: $15.20
4lbs: $55.90

RED DOT
America's #1 choice for clay target loads, now 50 percent cleaner. Since 1932, more 100 straights than any other powder.
1lb: $15.65
4lbs: $58.70
8lbs: $106.80

RELOADER 7
Designed for small caliber varmint loads, it meters consistently and meets the needs of the most demanding bench rest shooter. Great in .45-70 and .450 Marlin.
1lb: $19.15
5lbs: $89.40

RELOADER 10X
Best choice for light bullet applications in .222 Rem., .223 Rem., .22-250 Rem., and key benchrest calibers, as well as .308 Win. loads.
1lb: $19.15
5lbs: $89.40

Alliant Powder

RELOADER 15
An all-around medium speed rifle powder. It provides excellent .223 and .308 performance. Selected as the powder for U.S. Military's M118 Special Ball Long Range Sniper Round.
1lb: $19.15
5lbs: $89.40

RELOADER 19
Provides superb accuracy in most medium and heavy rifle loads and is the powder of choice for .30-06 and .338 calibers.
1lb: $19.15
5lbs: $89.40

RELOADER 22
This top performing powder for big-game loads provides excellent metering and is the powder of choice for .270, 7mm Mag., and .300 Win. Mag.
1lb: $19.15
5lbs: $89.40

RELOADER 25
This powder for big game hunting features improved slower burning and delivers the high-energy, heavy magnum loads needed.
1lb: $19.15
5lbs: $89.40

STEEL
Designed for waterfowl shotshells. Gives steel shot high velocity within safe pressure limits for 10 and 12 Ga. loads.
1lb: $15.70
4lbs: $58.00

UNIQUE
Shotgun/handgun powder for 12, 16, 20, and 28 Ga. loads. Use with most hulls, primers, and wads.
1lb: $15.65
4lbs: $58.70
8lbs: $106.80

Hodgdon

Smokeless Powders

CLAYS
Tailored for use in 12 Ga., 7/8 oz., 1 oz., and 1 1/8 oz. loads. Performs well in many handgun applications, including .38 Spl., .40 S&W, and .45 ACP.

14oz: $15.25
4lbs: $65.20
8lbs: $121.70

CLAYS, INTERNATIONAL
Ideal for 12 and 20 Ga. autoloaders who want reduced recoil.

14oz: $15.25
4lbs: $65.20
8lbs: $121.70

CLAYS, UNIVERSAL
Loads nearly all the straight-wall pistol cartridges as well as 12 Ga. 1 1/4 oz. thru 28 Ga. 3/4 oz. target loads.

1lb: $18.25
4lbs: $68.50
8lbs: $128.35

COPPER FOULING ERASER (CFE) 223
Versatile spherical rifle propellant incorporates in its formula Copper Fouling Eraser, an ingredient used in military propellant that deters copper fouling. It contributes to longer periods of top accuracy with less barrel clean-

---

ing time. Top velocities in .204 Ruger, .223 Rem./5.56mm NATO, .22-250 Rem., .308 Win./7.62mm NATO

1lb: $18.65
8lbs: $136.35

EXTREME BENCHMARK
A fine choice for small rifle cases like the .223 Rem. and PPC competition rounds. Appropriate also for the .30-30 and 7x57.

1lb: $21.35
8lbs: $152.00

EXTREME H50 BMG
Designed for the .50 BMG cartridge. Highly insensitive to extreme temperature changes.

1lb: $21.35
8lbs: $152.00

EXTREME H322
This powder fills the gap between H4198 and BL-C9(2). Performs best in small to medium capacity cases.

1lb: $21.35
8lbs: $152.00

EXTREME H1000 EXTRUDED POWDER
Fills the gap between H4831 and H87. Works especially well in overbore capacity cartridges (1,000-yd. shooters take note).

1lb: $21.35
8lbs: $152.00

EXTREME H4198
H4198 was developed especially for small and medium capacity cartridges.

1lb: $21.35
8lbs: $152.00

EXTREME H4350
Gives superb accuracy at optimum velocity for many large capacity metallic rifle cartridges.

1lb: $25.49
8lbs: $173.99

EXTREME H4831
Outstanding performance with medium and heavy bullets in the 6mm, .25-06, .270, and Magnum calibers. Also available with shortened grains (H4831SC) for easy metering.

1lb: $21.35
8lbs: $152.00

EXTREME H4895
4895 gives desirable performance in almost all cases from .222 Rem. to .458 Win. Reduced loads to as low as 3/5 maximum still give target accuracy.

1lb: $21.35
8lbs: $152.00

EXTREME RETUMBO
Designed for such cartridges as the .300 Rem. Ultra Mag., .30-378 Weatherby, the 7mm STW, and other cases with large capacities and small bores. Expect up to 40-100 fps more velocity than other magnum powders.

1lb: $21.35
8lbs: $152.00

EXTREME VARGET
Features small extruded grain powder for uniform metering, plus higher velocities/normal pressures in such calibers as .223, .22-250, .306, .30-06, and .375 H&H.

1lb: $21.35
8lbs: $152.00

H110
A spherical powder made especially for the .30 M1 carbine. H110 also does very well in .357, .44 Spl., .44 Mag., or .410 shotshell. Recommended for consistent ignition.

1lb: $18.10
8lbs: $133.30

HP-38
A fast pistol powder for most pistol loading. Especially recommended for mid-range .38 Spl.

1lb: $16.30
8lbs: $117.00

HS-6
HS-6 for magnum field loads is unsurpassed. Delivers uniform charges and is dense to allow sufficient wad column for best patterns.

1lb: $18.70
8lbs: $136.35

LONGSHOT
Spherical powder for heavy shotgun loads.

1lb: $18.05
4lbs: $69.35
8lbs: $133.30

PYRODEX PELLETS

Both rifle and pistol pellets eliminate powder measures, speeds shooting for black powder enthusiasts.

From: . . . . **$10.79–$26.49**

SPHERICAL BL-C(2)

Best performance is in the .222, .308, other cases smaller than .30-06.

1lb: **$18.65**
8lbs:. **$136.35**

SPHERICAL H335

H335 is popular for its performance in medium capacity cases, especially in .222 and .308 Win.

1lb: **$18.65**
8lbs:. **$136.35**

SPHERICAL H380

H380 is a superb performer in the .220 Swift, .243, .257 Roberts, and other fine varmint cartridges.

1lb: **$18.65**
8lbs:. **$136.35**

SPHERICAL H414

In many popular medium to medium large calibers, pressure velocity relationship is better.

1lb: **$18.65**
8lbs:. **$136.35**

SPHERICAL LEVEREVOLUTION

Same spherical propellant used in Hornady's high-performance factory ammunition. This fabulous propellant meters flawlessly and makes lever-action cartridges like the .30-30 Win. yield velocities in excess of 100 fps over any published handloads.

1lb: **$19.20**
8lbs:. **$138.50**

SPHERICAL SUPERFORMANCE

Superformance delivers striking velocities in Hornady cartridges like the .22-250 Rem., .243 Win. and .300 Win. Short Mag.

1lb: **$19.20**
8lbs:. **$138.50**

TITEGROUP

Excellent for most straight-walled pistol cartridges, including .38 Spl., .44 Spl., .45 ACP. Low charge weights, clean burning, position insensitive, and flawless ignition.

1lb: **$18.99**
4lbs:. **$68.99**
8lbs:. **$130.99**

TITEWAD

This 12 Ga. flattened spherical shotgun powder is ideal for 7/8 oz., 1 oz. and 1 1/8 oz. loads, with minimum recoil and mild muzzle report. The fastest fuel in Hodgdon's line.

1lb: **$16.29**
4lbs:. **$63.99**
8lbs:. **$116.99**

TRIPLE SEVEN PELLETS

Sulfur-free Triple Seven powder in 50-grain pellets. Formulated for use with 209 shotshell primers, Triple Seven leaves no rotten-egg smell, and the residue is easy to clean from the bore with only water. The pellets are sized for .50-caliber muzzleloaders and can be used singly (for target shooting or small game) as well as two at a time.

From: . . . . **$10.79–$29.49**

IMR

IMR 3031

A propellant with many uses, IMR 3031 is a favorite of .308 match shooters using 168 gr. match bullets. It is equally effective in small-capacity varmint cartridges from .223 Rem. to .22-250 Rem. and a great .30–30 Win. powder.

1lb: $20.60
8lbs: $147.80

IMR 4007 SSC

Powder that is made to be versatile. Perfect for a wide range of calibers (.17 to .416) and cut super short for smooth, even metering and more consistency.

1lb: $20.60
8lbs: $147.80

IMR 4198

This fast burning rifle powder gives outstanding performance in cartridges like the .222 Rem., .221 Fireball, .45-70 and .450 Marlin.

1lb: $20.60
8lbs: $147.80

IMR 4227

The choice for true magnum velocities and performance. In rifles, this powder delivers excellent velocity and accuracy in such cartridges as the .22 Hornet and .221 Fireball.

1lb: $20.60
8lbs: $147.80

IMR 4320

Short granulation, easy metering, and perfect for the .223 Remington, .22-250 Remington, .250 Savage, and other medium burn rate cartridges. It has long been a top choice for the vintage .300 Savage cartridge.

1lb: $20.60
8lbs: $147.80

IMR 4350

The No. 1 choice for the new short magnums, both Remington and Winchester versions. For magnums with light to medium bullet weights, IMR 4350 is the best choice.

1lb: $20.60
8lbs: $147.80

IMR 4895

Originally a military powder featured in the .30-06, IMR 4895 is extremely versatile. From .17 Rem. to the .243 Win. to the .375 H&H Mag., accuracy and performance are excellent. In addition, it is a longtime favorite of match shooters.

1lb: $20.60
8lbs: $147.80

IMR 7828

The big magnum powder. This slow burner gives real magnum performance to the large overbored magnums, such as the .300 Rem. Ultra Mag., the .30-378 Wby. Mag., and 7mm Rem. Ultra Mag.

1lb: $20.60
8lbs: $147.80

IMR 8208 XBR

Accurate metering, super short grained extruded rifle powder was designed expressly for match, varmint, and AR sniper cartridges. Ideally suited for cartridges like the .223 Rem./5.56mm, .308 Win./7.62mm NATO, and the 6mm PPC.

1lb: $20.60
8lbs: $147.80

Handguns & Shotgun Powders

HI-SKOR 700-X

This extruded flake type powder is ideally suited for shotshells in 12 and 16 Ga. where clay target and light field loads are the norm. It doubles as an excellent pistol target powder for such cartridges as the .38 Spl., .45 ACP, and many more.

1lb: $14.35
4lbs: $60.85
8lbs: $115.25

HI-SKOR 800-X

This large-grained flake powder is at its best when used in heavy field loads from 10 Ga. to 28 Ga. In handgun cartridges, 800-X performs superbly in cartridges such as the 10mm Auto, .357 Mag., and .44 Rem. Mag.

1lb: $16.50
4lbs: $62.15
8lbs: $116.35

PB

Named for the porous base structure of its grains by which the burning rate is controlled, PB is an extremely clean burning, single-base powder. It gives very low pressure in 12 and 20 Ga.

shotshell target loads and performs well in a wide variety of handgun loads.

14oz: **$19.30**
8lbs: **$160.00**

SR 4756

This fine-grained, easy-metering propellant has long been a favorite of upland and waterfowl handloaders. SR4756 performs extremely well in big handgun cartridges.

1lb: **$20.05**
8lbs: **$138.20**

SR 4759

This bulky handgun powder works great in the magnums, but really shines as a reduced load propellant for rifle cartridges. Its large grain size gives good loading density for reduced loads, enhancing velocity uniformity.

1lb: **$20.05**
8lbs: **$138.20**

SR 7625

SR7625 covers the wide range of shotshells from 10 Ga. to 28 Ga. in both target and field loadings. This versatile powder is equally useful in a large array of handgun cartridges for target, self-defense, and hunting loads.

1lb: **$22.25**
8lbs: **$162.30**

Ramshot

Ramshot (Western Powders, Inc.) powders are all double-base propellants, meaning they contain nitrocellulose and nitroglycerine. While some spherical or ball powders are known for leaving plenty of residue in barrels, these fuels burn very clean. They meter easily, as do all ball powders. Plastic canisters are designed for spill-proof use and include basic loading data on the labels.

BIG GAME

A versatile propellant for cartridges as diverse as the .30-06 and the .338 Win. and for light-bullet loads in small-bore magnums.

1lb: **$18.50**
8lbs: **$132.80**

COMPETITION

For the clay target shooter. A fast-burning powder comparable to 700-X or Red Dot, it performs well in a variety of 12 Ga. target loads, offering low recoil, consistent pressures, and clean combustion.

1lb: **$15.30**
4lbs: **$66.50**
8lbs: **$116.40**

Ramshot

ENFORCER
A match for high-performance hand-gun hulls like the .40 S&W. It is designed for full-power loading and high velocities. A fast burning rifle powder, it excels in small-caliber, medium-capacity cartridges.
1lb: $18.10
4lbs:......................$65.60

HUNTER
A double-base, clean-burning, high-performance propellant that is perfect for elk country cartridges such as the .270 Win., .300 WSM. and .338 Win. Mag.
1lb: $18.50
8lbs:...................$132.80

MAGNUM
The slowest powder of the Western line does its best work in cartridges with lots of case volume and small to medium bullet diameter. It is the pow-der of choice in 7mm and .30 mag-nums.
1lb: $18.50
8lbs:...................$132.80

SILHOUETTE
Ideal for the 9mm handgun cartridge, from light to heavy loads. It also works well in the .40 S&W and combat loads for the .45 Auto.
1lb: $18.10
4lbs:......................$65.60

TAC
Formulated for tactical rifle cartridges, specifically the .223 and .308. It has produced exceptional accuracy with a variety of bullets and charge weights.
1lb: $18.50
8lbs:...................$132.80

TRUE BLUE
Designed for small-to medium-size handgun cartridges. Similar to Win. 231 and Hodgdon HP-38, it has enough bulk to nearly fill most cases, thereby better positioning the powder for ignition.
1lb: $18.10
4lbs:......................$65.60

X-TERMINATOR
A clean-burning powder designed for the .222 Rem., .223 Rem., and .22 Benchrest calibers.
1lb: $18.50
8lbs:...................$132.80

ZIP
A fast-burning target powder for car-tridges like the .38 Spl. and .45 ACP, gives competitors uniform velocities.
1lb: $18.10
4lbs:......................$65.60

VihtaVuori

N100 SERIES RELOADING POWDERS
The N100 series powders are single-base powders used mainly in rifle cali-bers. There are ten N100 series pow-ders with different burning rates and suitability from the .17 Rem. up to the .458 Win. Mag. and two special pow-ders for .50 BMG
1lb: $29.15
8lbs:...................$189.00

N300 SERIES RELOADING POWDERS
The N300 series powders are single-base porous powders for handguns. There are altogether nine handgun powders with different kinds of shoot-ing properties and suitable applica-tions.
1lb: $29.95
4lbs:......................$100.50

N500 SERIES RELOADING POWDERS

The N500 series powders are impregnated extruded rifle powders with Nitroglycerol added as an extra energy component. If higher loading densities and more energy are needed, N500 series powders are competent alternatives for the N100 series powders.

N500 series High Energy powders are available in five different burning rates.

1lb: **$33.50**

TIN STAR PREMIUM POWDER

Intended for Cowboy Action Shooters. The primary benefit of Tin Star is its exceptionally high loading volume.

This porous powder fills the case much better than most conventional smokeless propellants, providing the loading density needed for those classic black powder cartridges.

From: **$29.95**

Reloading Tools

Dillon Precision Reloaders

RL 550B 4 STATION PROGRESSIVE LOADER

Able to load rifle as well as pistol cartridges; uses standard 7/8 by 14 thread per inch dies, as long as they deprime in the size die; manually indexed shellplate; manually fed cases and bullets; capable of loading 400 to 600 rounds per hour. It has 4 stations and includes a caliber conversion kit, powder measure with large and small powder bars, one tool head, one prime system and small priming parts, and one loaded cartridge catch bin.

MSRP **$439.95**

SL 900 SHOT SHELL RELOADER

This shot shell reloader reloads 12, 20, and 28 Ga. loaders. It has automatic indexing, auto powder and priming systems. Features easily adjustable, case-activated powder and shot sys-

tems that eliminate troublesome bushing changes along with spilled powder and shot. Adjustable shot dispenser uses the same design principle, with an extra large hopper that holds 25 pounds of shot. The frame is a heavy duty O-frame design, precision CNC machined to exacting tolerances. The tool head assembly slides out of the frame, keeping all your critical die and measurement adjustments intact and comes with factory adjusted dies.

MSRP **$919.95**

SQUARE DEAL B AUTO-INDEXING RELOADER

Designed to produce up to 400 or 500 handgun rounds per hour; comes with a factory-adjusted carbide die set; change from one caliber to another in minutes with a Square Deal B caliber conversion kit; automatic indexing; auto powder/priming systems; avail-

able in 14 handgun calibers; loading dies standard

MSRP **$379.95**

XL 650 5 STATION PROGRESSIVE LOADER

The XL 650 loads virtually every popular pistol and rifle cartridge utilizing standard dies. The optional powder charge check die on the third station sounds an alarm if the powder charge in a round is out of limits either high or low. An exclusive primer system uses a rotary indexing plate that positively controls each primer and keeps a steel shield between the primers and the operator. Features: automatic indexing; five-station interchangeable tool-head; auto powde/priming systems; uses standard 7/8-in. x 14-in. dies;rotary indexing plate for primers.

MSRP **$566.95**

Forster Reloading

3-IN-1 CASE MOUTH CUTTER

This carbide case trimmer accessory performs three functions simultaneously: It trims the case to length, chamfers the inside of the case to an angle of 14 degrees, and the outside of the mouth at 30 degrees. Blades never need sharpening if used on brass only. Currently available for three bullet diameters: .224, .243, .308.

MSRP **$86.00**

.50 BMG CASE TRIMMER

The .50 BMG Case Trimmer is designed specifically for the reloading needs of .50 BMG shooters. It does not require a collet, but it comes complete with a #510 pilot and rim holder.

MSRP **$132.00**

FORSTER RELOADING 3-IN-1 CASE MOUTH CUTTER

Forster Reloading

BENCH REST POWDER MEASURE

The superior design of our Bench Rest Powder Measure throws uniform charges. The charge arm/operating handle meters the powder and dispenses a flow of powder that is free from extremes in variation while minimizing powder shearing. The powder hopper's built-in baffle feeds powder into the charge arm very uniformly. Our Bench Rest measure can throw consistent charges from 2½ grains of Bulls-Eye to 95 grains of 432. Convenient and simple to use.
MSRP $155.00

BENCHREST SEATER DIES

Bench Rest Rifle Dies are glass-hard and polished mirror-smooth with special attention given to headspace, tapers, and diameters. Sizing die has an elevated expander button to ensure better alignment of case and neck.
Original Bench Rest
Seater Die: $67.00
Ultra Micrometer
 Seater Die: $102.00
Custom: . . . . $92–$127

CLASSIC CASE TRIMMER

Case Trimmer Classic (collet and pilot not included). Suitable for more than three hundred different big bore calibers from popular big-game rifles to classic black powder calibers. The Classic trims case lengths from 1⅞ in. long through 4⅛ in. long; shorter cases can be trimmed by mounting on a standard length base.
MSRP $122.00

CO-AX CASE AND CARTRIDGE INSPECTOR

Forster's exclusive Co-Ax Case and Cartridge Inspector provides you with the ability to ensure uniformity by measuring three critical dimensions: neck wall thickness, case neck concentricity, and bullet runout. The Inspector is unique because it checks both the bullet and case alignment in relation to the centerline (axis) of the entire cartridge or case.
MSRP $122.00

CO-AX PRIMER SEATER

Unlike other seaters, ours is designed so the operator can eliminate all slop when working with a specific cartridge. That translates into perfect seating, reliable ignition, and reduced misfires. The E-Z-Just jaws close to securely grip most modern rifle and pistol cases with a rim thickness of .045 in. to .072 in. Other features include a built-in primer flipper tray. Large and small primer tubes have an open slot and primers stack sideways for added safety.
MSRP $104.00

FORSTER BENCHREST SEATER DIE

FORSTER CO-AX CASE AND CARTRIDGE INSPECTOR

FORSTER CO-AX PRIMER SEATER

CO-AX RELOADING PRESS
Designed to make reloading easier and more accurate, this press offers the following features: snap-in and snap-out die change, positive spent primer catcher, automatic self-acting shell holder, floating guide rod, top priming device seats primers to factory specification, uses any standard 7/8 in x 14 in dies; short-throw handle.

MSRP **$440.00**

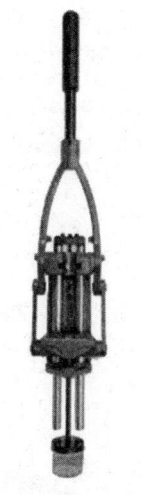

FORSTER CO-AX RELOADING PRESS

UNIVERSAL SIGHT MOUNTING FIXTURE
To drill and tap holes for the mounting of scope mounts, receiver sights, and shotgun beads. The fixture will accommodate any single-barrel long gun including bolt actions, lever actions, and pump actions as long as the barrel can be laid into the "V" blocks of the fixture. Tubular mag guns can be drilled. The two "V" blocks are made from hardened steel accurately ground on the "V" as well as the shaft. The blocks are adjustable for height. Universal Site Mounting Fixture includes 6-48 bushings.

MSRP **$488.00**

Frankford Arsenal

FRANKFORD ARSENAL DIGITAL RELOADING SCALE

FRANKFORD ARSENAL EZ SONIC CLEANER

FRANKFORD ARSENAL MAGNUM SONIC CLEANER

DS-750 DIGITAL RELOADING SCALE
A light, accurate, portable scale, the unit is suitable for use on the reloading bench, yet is at home on the shooting range or in the field. It weighs objects up to 750 grains. Accurate within ± .1 grains, it can be set to read in grains, grams, ounces, ct, or dwt. It comes with a protective sleeve and is small enough to fit in your shirt pocket. A calibration weight and batteries are also included.

MSRP **$59.99**

EZ SONIC CLEANER
Features: High frequency ultrasonic agitation quickly and quietly cleans the exterior and interior of brass without a mess, even breaking down the stubborn carbon build up found in primer pockets. Tank size of 5.8" x 4.8" x 1.9" gives it a capacity of .75L; capable of cleaning approximately 125 pieces of .223 brass per batch; 30 watt unit at 42KHz

MSRP **$76.99**

MAGNUM SONIC CLEANER
Features: Tank size of 7.7" x 6.5" x 2.6" gives it a capacity of 2L; capable of cleaning approximately 350 pieces of .223 brass per batch; provides added cleaning power with a heating function; offers a digital display and time controls; 100 watt unit at 42KHz

MSRP **$161.99**

Hornady

HANDLOADING

366 AUTO PROGRESSIVE RELOADER

The 366 Auto features full-length resizing with each stroke, automatic primer feed, swing-out wad guide, three-state crimping featuring Taper-Loc for factory-tapered crimp, automatic advance to the next station, and automatic ejection. The turntable holds 8 shells for 8 operations with each stroke. Automatic charge bar loads shot and powder, dies and crimp starters for 6 point, 8 point, and paper crimps.

12, 20, 28 Ga.: **$716.83**
.410: **$844.93**

HORNADY 366 AUTO PROGRESSIVE RELOADER

HANDHELD PRIMING TOOL

This portable tool primes new or cleaned cases—no need to use your press. Very useful for priming large quantities of cases before processing through a loader. The pliers-style design gives you more leverage, less fatigue, and a better feel than thumb-operated styles. Holds both small and large primers right side up for proper feeding. Uses standard Hornady shell holders, and a converter is available for RCBS shells.

MSRP **$48.60**

HORNADY HANDHELD PRIMING TOOL

LOCK-N-LOAD AP RELOADING PRESS

Dies and powder measure are inserted into Lock-N-Load die bushings. The bushings remain with the die and powder measure and can be removed in seconds. Other features include: deluxe powder measure, automatic indexing, off-set handle, power-pac linkage, case ejector, five die bushings, shellplate, primer catcher, Positive Priming System, powder drop, Deluxe Powder Measure, and automatic primer feed.

MSRP **$520.16**

HORNADY LOCK-N-LOAD AP RELOADING PRESS

LOCK-N-LOAD BENCH SCALE

Made from the same high-quality, precision load cell found on the Lock-N-Load Auto Charge. With a capacity of 1500 grains, you can weigh powder, bullets, cases, cartridges, and more. The large LCD display is easy to read and weighs precisely to one-tenth (.1) of a grain. Included are two calibration weights, AC adaptor, 220V adaptor, and metal powder pan.

MSRP **$122.72**

HORNADY LOCK-N-LOAD BENCH SCALE

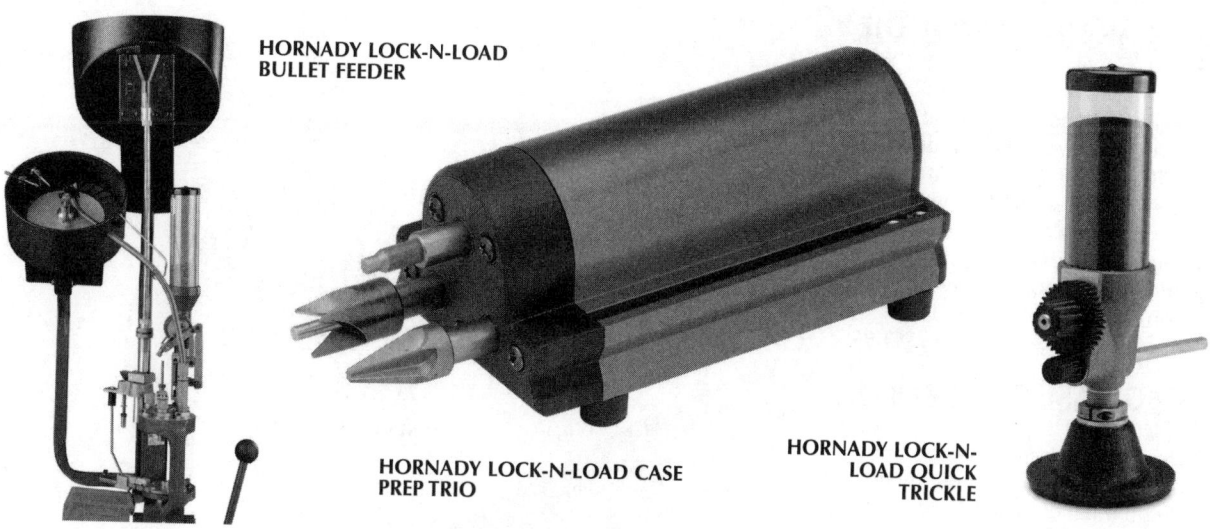

HORNADY LOCK-N-LOAD
BULLET FEEDER

HORNADY LOCK-N-LOAD CASE
PREP TRIO

HORNADY LOCK-N-
LOAD QUICK
TRICKLE

LOCK-N-LOAD BULLET FEEDER

The Lock-N-Load Bullet Feeder can be used with any press with $7/8$ in.–14 in. die threads. The bullet feeder die is case activated, which means the bullet will only feed upon contact with a case. The collets are made of solid steel. The setup and caliber change-overs are quick and easy and there are no special tools required for adjustments. The easy-feed bullet hopper holds up to 200 pistol bullets and features an adjustable center plate and bullet feed-wipers to ensure smooth feeding.

MSRP. $363.52

LOCK-N-LOAD CASE PREP TRIO

Features: Durable brushed aluminum housing and high torque, low speed motor. 3-tool capacity and onboard storage for optional accessories like our primer pocket cleaners, primer pocket reamers, case neck brushes, and any other 8-32 thread tools. With three active stations, you can chamfer, deburr, and clean primer pockets without having to change tools. Both inside diameter and outside diameter chamfer and deburr tools. Unit is compatible with 110V or 220V power.

MSRP. $129.38

LOCK-N-LOAD CLASSIC LOADER

Lock-N-Load is available on Hornady's single stage and progressive reloader models. This bushing system locks the die into the press like a rifle bolt. Instead of threading dies in and out of the press, you simply lock and unlock them with a slight twist. Dies are held firmly in a die bushing that stays with the die and retains the die setting. Features: Easygrip handle and O-style high-strength

MSRP. $146.50
Lock-N-Load Classic Kit: . . .$383.06

MATCH GRADE RIFLE DIES

The neck-size die features interchangeable, self-centering neck-size bushings (available in .002 in. increments) that eliminate the chance of oversizing your case necks and overworking the brass. Some calibers are available in two styles: full-length sizing and shoulder bump neck-size. Both styles feature interchangeable neck-sizing bushings.

MSRP. . . . . $53.20–$100.00

LOCK-N-LOAD QUICK TRICKLE

Features: This versatile powder trickler features hand-operated high and low speeds with up to a three-to-one gear ratio. Combined with double-sided, sealed ball bearings that prevent stray

powder from impeding operation, the Quick Trickle is the smoothest operating powder dispensing tool for your reloading bench.

MSRP. $115.84

LOCK-N-LOAD SONIC CLEANER 2L

Features: Features an 80 watt ceramic heater. Large 2L stainless steel tank holds up to three hundred .223 cases or one hundred fifty .308 cases. Microjet action of the Cleaner 2L removes carbon residue and other debris from cartridge cases, small gun parts, and other small metal equipment and it cleans internal and external surfaces of cartridge cases and primer pockets. 5 to 30 minute timer. 110V or 220V.

MSRP. $142.84

HORNADY LOCK-N-LOAD SONIC
CLEANER 2L

Lyman Reloading Tools

3-DIE CARBIDE PISTOL DIE SETS

Lyman originated the Tungsten Carbide (T-C) sizing die and the addition of extra seating screws for pistol die sets and the two-step neck expanding die. Multi-Deluxe Die sets offer these features: a one-piece hardened steel decapping rod, extra seating screws for all popular bullet-nose shapes, and all-steel construction.

MSRP....................$63.95

50 BMG CASE PREP MULTI-TOOL

Features: Lyman has engineered full-sized .50 caliber tools and put them together in a handy double ended storage handle—always ready and all in one place. The unique knurled handle unthreads in the middle to store all the parts. Both ends of the handle are threaded to allow a tool head to be mounted on each end. In addition to the double ended storage handle, the set includes: .50 cal. Outside Deburring Tool, .50 cal. VLD Inside Deburring Tool, .50 BMG Primer Pocket Reamer, Cleaner, and Uniformer

MSRP....................$59.99

55 CLASSIC BLACK POWDER MEASURE

Lyman's 55 Classic Powder Measure is ideal for the Cowboy Action Competition or black powder cartridge shooters. The one-pound-capacity aluminum reservoir and brass powder meter eliminate static. The internal powder baffle assures highly accurate and consistent charges. The 24 in. powder compacting drop tube allows the maximum charge in each cartridge. Drop tube works on calibers .38 through .50 and mounts easily to the bottom of the measure.

Model with tubes: $174.95
Powder Drop Tubes only: ...$37.50

1200 CLASSIC TUMBLER

This case tumbler features an improved base and drive system, plus a stronger suspension system and built-in exciters for better tumbling action and faster cleaning.

1200 Classic: .....$109.95–$117.50
Auto-Flo: ....$113.95–$124.00

LYMAN 3-DIE CARBIDE PISTOL DIE SET

LYMAN 50 BMG CASE PREP MULTI-TOOL

LYMAN 1200 CLASSIC TUMBLER

LYMAN 55 CLASSIC BLACK POWDER MEASURE

1200 DPS 3 (DIGITAL POWDER SYSTEM)

Imagine precisely weighing every charge you load nearly as fast as using a measure. With Lyman's new DPS 3, it can be a reality. This is the fastest powder system ever. In addition, the auto-repeat setting throws a precise charge automatically each time the pan is put in place. The DPS 3 is weighing your next charge while you're seating the bullet on your last charge. Now change powders faster and easier. Automatically throws the next charge each time the pan is put in place.
MSRP . . . . $374.95–$385

2500 PRO MAGNUM TUMBLER

The Lyman 2500 Pro Magnum tumbler handles up to 900 .38 Spl. cartridges at once.
MSRP . . . . $99.95–$117.50
Auto-Flo: . . . . $147.95–$148.00

ACCU-TRIMMER

Lyman's Accu-Trimmer can be used for all rifle and pistol cases from .22 to .458 Win. Mag. Standard shell holders are used to position the case, and the trimmer incorporates standard Lyman cutter heads and pilots. Mounting options include bolting to a bench, C-clamp, or vise.
MSRP $66.95

CASE PREP MULTI-TOOL

The unique new case prep accessory provides the reloader with all the essential Case Prep accessories in one compact, double-ended storage handle. Both ends of the handle are threaded to allow two tool heads to be mounted simultaneously. Plus the hollow, knurled handle unthreads in the center to store all parts and function equally well as two separate handles. The compact aluminum storage handle contains: an outside deburring tool, a VLD inside deburring tool, both large and small primer pocket cleaners, and reamers.
MSRP $27.95

LYMAN 1200 DPS 3 (DIGITAL POWDER SYSTEM)

LYMAN 2500 PRO MAGNUM TUMBLER

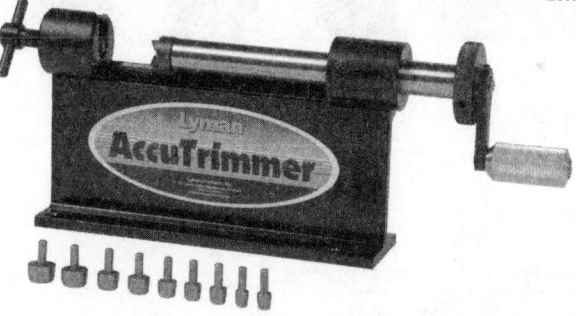

LYMAN ACCU-TRIMMER

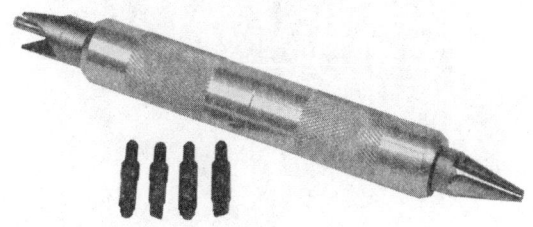

LYMAN CASE PREP MULTI-TOOL

Lyman Reloading Tools

CASE PREP XPRESS

Lyman introduces one of the most complete electric case prep systems yet developed. It features all the most popular case prep accessories driven by a high torque gear motor. The Case Prep Xpress allows the reloader to have five different case prep tools mounted vertically and powered, ready to instantly perform the desired operation. Every commonly-used case prep tool is included with the substantial five-position power base. In addition, a side-mounted, inside neck lube station is also part of the base with four neck brushes and Mica lube. For easy cleanup of fouling and brass shavings, a convenient removable dump pan is built in.

115 V Model: **$157.50**
230 V Model: **$162.50**

CLASSIC DIE SETS

Lyman Products offers new reloading dies sets for .40-60 Win., .45-65 Win., and .45-75 Win. cartridges. These cartridges have become popular with the introduction of the new '76 Win. lever action reproductions. Most importantly, these new dies have been carefully engineered to modern standards to provide precise reloads with either black or smokeless powder.

MSRP **$66.50**

CRUSHER II PRO KIT

Includes Crusher II press, loading block, case lube kit, primer tray, Model 500 Pro scale, powder funnel, and Lyman Reloading Handbook.

MSRP **$269.95**

CRUSHER II RELOADING PRESS

Our new Crusher II is the ideal press for reloading both rifle and pistol cartridges. The Crusher starts with a 1 in. diameter ram, compound linkage and a 4½ in. press opening, which makes even the largest magnum cartridges easy to load. Its classic "O" frame design takes all standard 7/8 in. x 14 in. dies. The Crusher II is equipped with hardened and ground linkage pins and retaining rings for a smooth and tight operation. The new base design has 14 square inches of "machined flat" surface area with three mounting bolt holes (vs. two slots for Rock ChuckerT) for perfect rigid mounting.

MSRP **$179.95**

LYMAN CLASSIC DIE SETS

LYMAN CASE PREP XPRESS

LYMAN CRUSHER II RELOADING PRESS

Lyman Reloading Tools

DEBURRING TOOL

Bevels and removes burrs from both inside and outside of case mouth. Precision machined and hardened, fits all cases from .17 to .45 caliber.
MSRP $19.95

DELUXE CARBIDE EXPANDER & DECAP DIE ROD COMPLETE

Features: The Lyman Deluxe Carbide expander and decapping rod assembly features a super hard and slick carbide expander button with an adjustable positioning sleeve. The carbide button will offer easier extraction through case necks, which will help prevent case stretching and lessen case trimming. The carbide button also floats free on the rod to allow for self-centering in the case neck. It will also allow the user to adjust when the button pulls through the case neck so the press linkage can be positioned for better leverage. Includes adapter for use with RCBS dies.
MSRP $29.95

E-ZEE CASE GAUGE

This improved version measures the case length of over 70 popular rifle and pistol cases. Many new cartridges are included like the Winchester Short Mags, .204 Ruger, .500 S&W, and others. Precisely made, this rugged metal gauge makes sorting cases quick, easy, and accurate.
MSRP $21.50

MAGNUM INERTIA BULLET PULLER

Safely strips loaded rounds in seconds without damage to bullet or case. Features newly-engineered head design that allows use on full range of calibers from tiny 5.7x28FN to the largest Magnums. New "full-size" ergonomic molded handle with rubber insert for comfort and sure grip. Traps components with just a few raps on the bench.
MSRP $22.98

MASTER CASTING KIT

Designed especially to meet the needs of blackpowder shooters, this kit features Lyman's combination round ball and maxi ball mould blocks. It also contains a combination double cavity mould, mould handle, mini-mag furnace, lead dipper, bullet lube, a user's manual, and a cast bullet guide. Kits are available in .45, .50, and .54 caliber.
MSRP . . . . $254.95–$265.00

MASTER RELOADING KIT

The complete reloading kit compares in price to other starter kits but is the first one that includes a state-of-the-art digital scale like the Lyman 1000 Grain. The new reloader can choose the turret T-Mag or single stage Crusher press kit and get all the high-end Lyman tools and accessories needed to start turning out top quality reloads. The only additional items needed are the dies and shellholder. Lyman's Trimmer Plus Case Conditioning Kit makes a perfect addition once the reloader is ready to further improve the performance of his reloads. The Lyman Master Reloading Kit includes a $7/8$ in. x 14 in. Adapter, 1000 grain electronic scale, #55 powder measure, a universal priming arm, a powder funnel, and an auto primer feed system.
T-Mag Master Kit: $489.95
Crusher Master Kit: $429.95

LYMAN DEBURRING TOOL

LYMAN DELUXE CARBIDE EXPANDER & DECAP DIE ROD COMPLETE

LYMAN E-ZEE CASE GAUGE

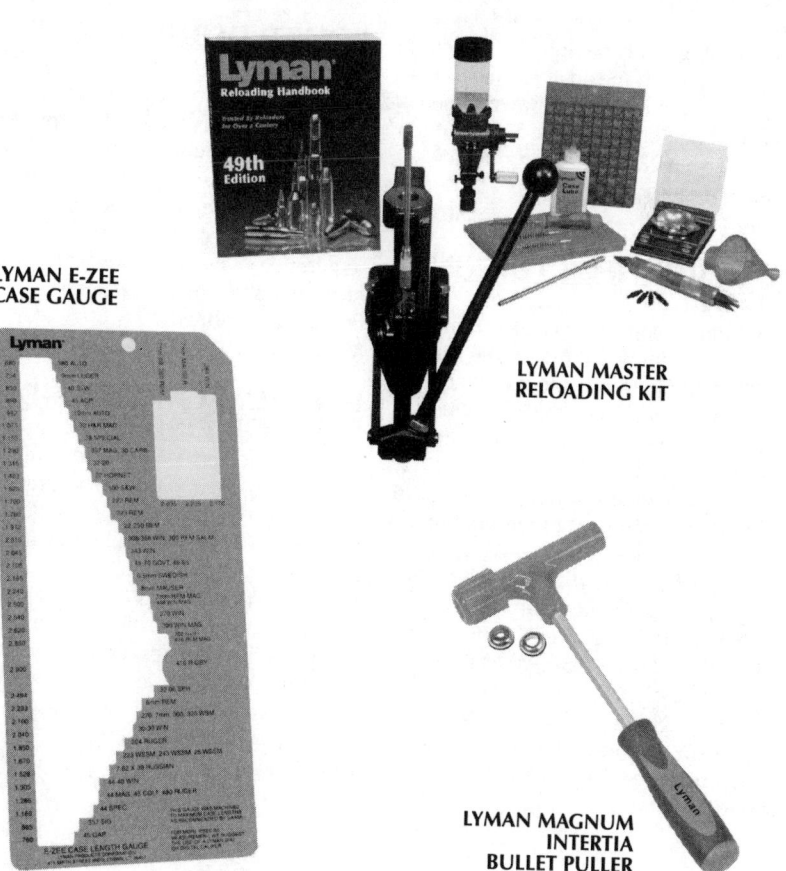

LYMAN MASTER RELOADING KIT

LYMAN MAGNUM INERTIA BULLET PULLER

Lyman Reloading Tools

LYMAN MICRO-TOUCH 1500
ELECTRONIC RELOADING SCALE

LYMAN OUTSIDE NECK TURNING TOOL

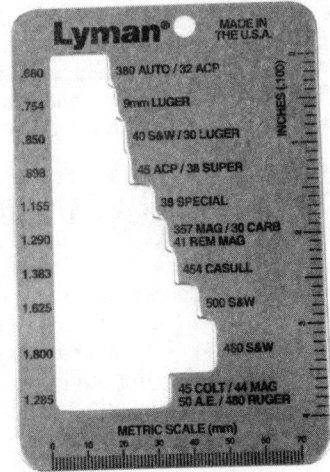

LYMAN PISTOL E-ZEE CASE GAUGE

MICRO-TOUCH 1500 ELECTRONIC RELOADING SCALE

Features: Lyman's newest electronic scale, the Micro-Touch 1500 has all the features of much larger models combined with state-of-the-art touch screen controls. Just 3.25" wide by 5.375" long and 1.25" tall with the dust cover in place, this scale has a full 1500 grain capacity. It is powered by an included AC adapter, but can also function on battery power when at the range or camp. The Micro-Touch 1500 also includes its own powder pan and calibration weight.
From: $69.95

OUTSIDE NECK TURNING TOOL

For both Lyman's Universal Trimmer and AccuTrimmer. Provides the user with a simple-to-operate tool that guarantees neck wall thickness and outside neck diameter. Essential for case reforming. Improves accuracy. Adjustable cutter (for length of cut and rate of feed) removes minimum brass to attain uniformity. Cutter blade can be adjusted to any diameter from .195 in. to .405 in. Comes with two extra cutting blades. Mandrels from .22 to .375. Includes six mandrel Multi-Pack (for .22, .243, .25, .270, 7mm, and .30 calibers). (Not adaptable to Power Trimmer.) Replacement parts and additional mandrels also available.
MSRP $42.50

PISTOL E-ZEE CASE GAUGE

Features: Here's Lyman's popular E-Zee Case Gauge in a smaller, more convenient size yet covering virtually any pistol case. The precise metal "no-go" gauge makes judging case length fast, easy, and accurate.
MSRP $14.95

POWER DEBURRING TOOL KIT

Features a high-torque, rechargeable power driver plus a complete set of accessories, including inside and outside deburr tools, large and small reamers, and cleaners, and case neck brushes. No threading or chucking required. Set also includes battery recharger and standard flat and Phillips driver bits.
MSRP $66.50

PREMIUM CARBIDE 4-DIE SETS FOR PISTOLS

Lyman 4-Die Sets feature a separate taper crimp die and powder charge/expanding die. The powder charge/expand die has a special hollow two-step neck expanding plug which allows powder to flow through the die from a powder measure directly into the case. The powder charge/expanding die has a standard 7/8 in. x 14 in. thread and will accept Lyman's 55 Powder Measure, or most other powder measures.
MSRP $84.95

PRO 1000 & 500 RELOADING SCALES

Features include improved platform system; hi-tech base design of high impact styrene; extra-large, smooth leveling wheel; dual agate bearings; larger damper for fast zeroing; built-in counter weight compartment; easy-tread beam.
Pro 1000 Scale: $87.50
Pro 500 Scale: $72.50

LYMAN POWER DEBURRING TOOL KIT

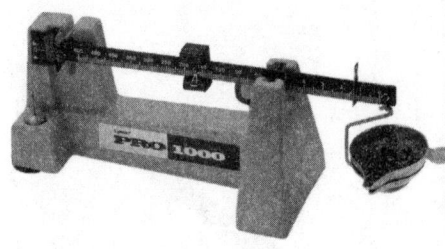

LYMAN PRO 1000 RELOADING SCALE

Lyman Reloading Tools

REVOLUTION ROTATING GUN VISE

This versatile gun vise is engineered with a full range of adjustments; it tilts, clamps, and has inserts to securely hold any firearm. The padded contact points protect the firearm during cleaning, maintenance, or gunsmithing, even bore sighting.
MSRP **$95.95**

RIFLE DIE SETS

Lyman precision rifle dies feature fine adjustment threads on the bullet seating stem to allow for precision adjustments of bullet seating depth. Lyman dies fit all popular presses using industry standard 7/8 in. x 14 in. threads, including RCBS, Lee, Hornady, Dillon, Redding and others. Each sizing die for bottle-necked rifle cartridges is carefully vented. Each sizing die is polished and heat treated for toughness.
MSRP **$22.50**

LYMAN REVOLUTION ROTATING GUN VISE

RIFLE 2-DIE SETS

Set consists of a full-length resizing die with decapping stem and neck expanding button and a bullet-seating die for loading jacketed bullets in bottlenecked rifle cases. For those who load cast bullets, use a neck-expanding die, available separately.
MSRP **$43.75**

RIFLE 3-DIE SETS

Straight wall rifle cases require these three-die sets consisting of a full-length resizing die with decapping stem, a two-step neck expanding (M) die, and a bullet-seating die. These sets are ideal for loading cast bullets due to the inclusion of the neck-expanding die.
MSRP **$56.95**

LYMAN RIFLE 3-DIE SET

TURBO SONIC 700

Features: Ultrasonic cleaning that allows the reloader to clean cases inside and out in less than 10 minutes. Used with Lyman's specially formulated cleaning solutions, these machines deliver superior cleaning of cases, steel and stainless steel gun frames and parts, tools, and even jewelry. The ultrasonic cavitation lifts and dissolves carbon, dirt, and residue. Cleans up to 100 9mm cases; uses advanced oscillation circuitry; two color LED display with five timed cleaning cycles; simple, push button digital controls; stainless tank with plastic parts basket; includes watch stand and CD holder
115V: **$79.95**
230V: **$82.50**

T-MAG II RELOADING PRESS

The T-Mag II has a hi-tech iron frame with state-of-the-art silver hammertone powder coat finish for guaranteed durability. Lyman's improved Turret Retention System allows smooth indexing while maintaining rock solid turret support. The T-Mag II's six station turret head lets the reloader mount up to six different reloading dies at one time. Like more expensive progressive presses the turret head detaches to easily change calibers while retaining precise setup. The turret handle doubles as a turret-removing wrench. Obtain extra turret heads and have all your favorite calibers set up to reload. The T-Mag II features a "flat machined" base that mounts easily to a wood or metal bench. Compound leverage assures a powerful and smooth operation. The handle mounts for either right or left hand use. The T-Mag II uses standard 7/8 in. x 14 in. dies and can be used for reloading rifle or pistol cases. It comes with universal priming arm, primer catcher, and turret handle.
MSRP **$260.00**

LYMAN T-MAG II RELOADING PRESS

Lyman Reloading Tools

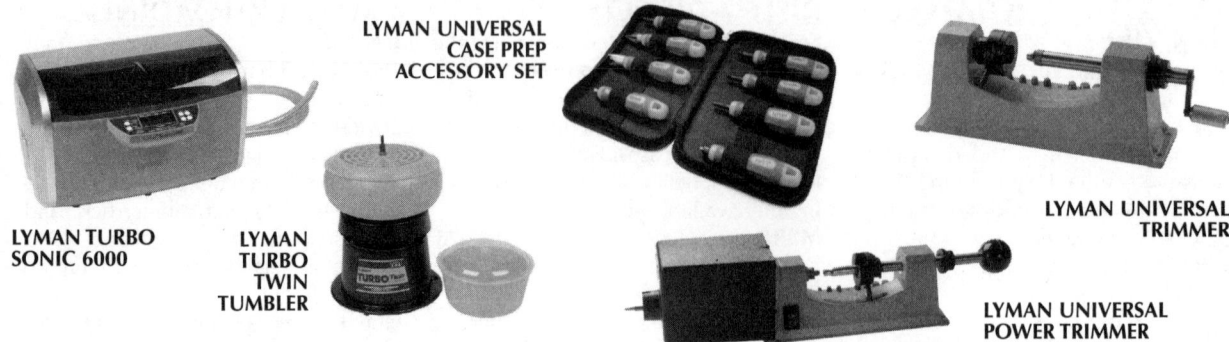

LYMAN UNIVERSAL CASE PREP ACCESSORY SET

LYMAN TURBO SONIC 6000

LYMAN TURBO TWIN TUMBLER

LYMAN UNIVERSAL TRIMMER

LYMAN UNIVERSAL POWER TRIMMER

TURBO SONIC 6000

Features: 6.3 quart tank (12.8"x8"x3.9") fits the biggest handguns or multiple pistol frames. Cleans up to 1300 9mm cases or four handgun frames. Powered by two industrial grade ultrasonic transducers. Tank has a built-in drain and hose for easy solution changes; comes with a large plastic parts basket with convenient handles; heated tank for optimum cleaning performance; two color LED display with five timed cleaning cycles.

115V: **$349.95**
230V: **$360**

TURBO TWIN TUMBLER

The Twin features Lyman 1200 Pro Tumbler with an extra 600 bowl system. Reloaders may use each bowl interchangeably for small or large capacity loads. 1200 Pro Bowl System has a built-in sifter lid for easy sifting of cases and media at the end of the polishing cycle. The Twin Tumbler features the Lyman Hi-Profile base design with built-in exciters and anti-rotation pads for faster, more consistent tumbling action.

115V: **$91.95**
230V: **$95.00**

UNIVERSAL CASE PREP ACCESSORY SET

This accessory features all the items necessary for quality case preparation in one deluxe set. Includes both large and small primer pocket reamers, primer pocket cleaners, outside deburring tool, inside (VLD) chamfer tool, and large and small primer pocket uniformer tools. All individual items have their own molded handle with rubber insert for sure grip. Includes custom zippered case for storage or easy transport to the range.

MSRP **$69.95**

UNIVERSAL POWER TRIMMER

The Universal Power Trimmer has all the accuracy and fast cartridge case lock/unlock of the original trimmer. Plus, the powerful 175 RPM motor adds real ease, speed, and powered primer pocket cleaning to the process. Trimming is rapid and uniform with precise, fully-adjustable settings for overall trim length. The replaceable cutter head accepts all Lyman pilots. Includes 9 pilot multi-pack and carbide cutter. Power Trimmer is available for 110 or 220 volt systems.

MSRP **$349.95**
230 Volt Model: **$355.00**

UNIVERSAL TRIMMER

This trimmer with patented chuckhead accepts all metallic rifle or pistol cases, regardless of rim thickness. To change calibers, simply change the case head pilot. Other features include coarse and fine cutter adjustments, an oil-impregnated bronze bearing, and a rugged cast base to assure precision alignment. Optional carbide cutter available.

MSRP **$105.00**
**Universal Trimmer
Power Pack Combo:** **$124.95**
**Universal Trimmer
Power Adapter:** **$28.00**

MEC Reloaders

600 JR. MARK 5

This single-stage reloader features a cam-action crimp die to ensure that each shell returns to its original condition. MEC's 600 Jr. Mark 5 can load six to eight boxes per hour and can be updated with the 285 CA primer feed. Press is adjustable for 3 in. shells.

MSRP . . . . **$192.96–$208.45**

MEC 600 JR. MARK 5

650N

This reloader works on six shells at once. A reloaded shell is completed with every stroke. The MEC 650 does not resize except as a separate operation. Automatic primer feed is standard. Simply fill it with a full box of primers and it will do the rest. Reloader has three crimping stations: the first one starts the crimp, the second closes the crimp and the third places a taper on the shell. Available in 12, 16, 20 and 28 Ga. and .410 bore. No die sets available.

MSRP . . . . $350.70–$379.98

MEC 650N

8567N GRABBER

This reloader features twelve different operations at all six stations, producing finished shells with each stroke of the handle. It includes a fully automatic primer feed and Auto-Cycle charging, plus MEC's exclusive three-stage crimp. The "Power Ring" resizer ensures consistent, accurately-sized shells without interrupting the reloading sequence. Simply put in the wads and shell casings, then remove the loaded shells with each pull of the handle. Available in 12, 16, 20, 28 Ga., and .410 bore.

MSRP . . . . $483.11–$524.80

9000 SERIES

Automatic indexing and finished shell ejection for quicker and easier reloading. The factory set speed provides uniform movement through every reloading stage. The reloader requires only a minimal adjustment from low to high brass domestic shells, any one of which can be removed for inspection from any station. Can be set up for automatic or manual indexing. Available in 12, 16, 20, 28 Ga., and .410 bore. No die sets are available.

9000GN: . . . . $591.58–$642.60
9001HN without
P&H: . . . . $663.45–$705.63
9000HN: . . . .$1231.50–$1246.50

SIZEMASTER

Sizemaster's "Power Ring" collet resizer returns each base to factory specifications. This resizing station handles brass or steel heads, both high and low base. An eight-fingered collet squeezes the base back to original dimensions, then opens up to release the shell easily. The E-Z Prime auto primer feed is standard equipment (not offered in .410 bore). Press is adjustable for 3 in. shells and is available in 10, 12, 16, 20, 28 Ga. and .410 bore.

MSRP . . . . $278.88–$299.50

STEELMASTER

Equipped to load steel shotshells as well as lead ones. Every base is resized to factory specs by a precision "power ring" collet. Handles brass or steel heads in high or low base. The E-Z prime auto primer feed dispenses primers automatically and is standard equipment. Separate presses are available for 12 Ga. 2¾ in., 3 in., 3½ in. and 10 Ga.

MSRP . . . . $319.02–$334.50

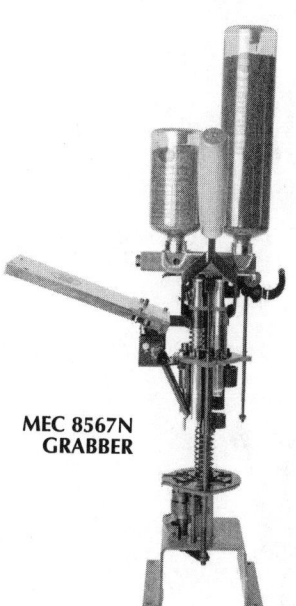

MEC 8567N
GRABBER

MEC 9000 SERIES

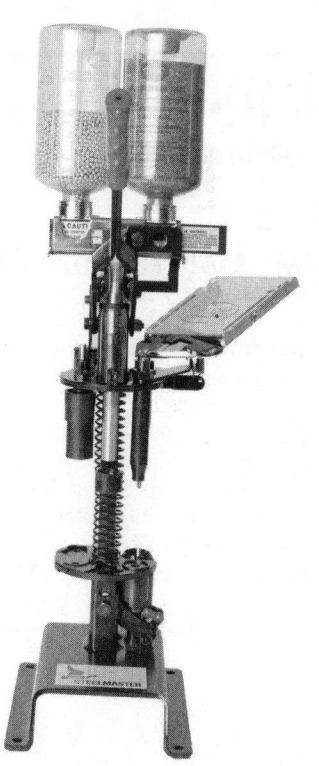

MEC STEELMASTER

MTM Case-Gard

DS-750 MINI DIGITAL RELOADING SCALE

Scale features a powder pan, custom designed to facilitate bullet, powder, and arrow weighing. It has up to a 750-grain capacity. It measures in grains, grams, carats, and ounces. The high-impact, plastic sensory cover doubles as a large powder pan.
MSRP **$42.49**

MTM CASE-GARD DS-750 MINI DIGITAL RELOADING SCALE

Nosler

CUSTOM BRASS

With uncompromising attention to detail, each round of NoslerCustom cartridge brass is made to precise dimensional standards and tolerances using top-grade materials to maximize accuracy, consistency, and enhance case life. Flash holes are deburred, necks are deburred and chamfered.
MSRP . . . .**$34.00–$77.00**

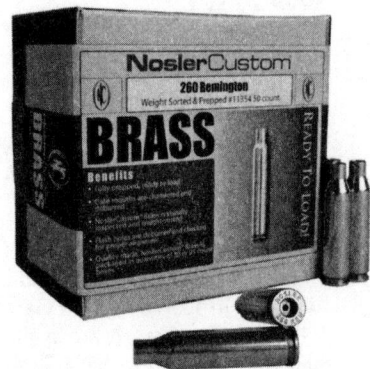

NOSLER CUSTOM BRASS

RCBS
Reloading Presses

AMMOMASTER-2 SINGLE STAGE PRESS

The AmmoMaster offers handloaders the freedom to configure a press to particular needs and preferences. It covers the complete spectrum of reloading, from single-stage through fully-automatic progressive reloading, from .25 Auto to .50 caliber. The AmmoMaster Auto has all the features of a five-station press.
MSRP **$362.95**

AMMOMASTER .50 BMG PACK

The Pack includes the press, dies, and accessory items needed, all in one box. The press is the Ammo Master Single Stage rigged for 1½ in. dies. It has a 1½ in. solid steel ram and plenty of height for the big .50. The kit also has a set of RCBS .50 BMG , 1½ in. reloading dies, including both full-length sizer and seater. Other items are a shell holder, ram priming unit, and a trim die.
MSRP **$787.95**

RCBS AMMOMASTER-2 SINGLE STAGE PRESS

RCBS AMMOMASTER .50 BMG PACK

GRAND SHOTSHELL PRESS

The combination of the powder system, shot system, and case holders allows the user to reload shells without fear of spillage. The powder system is case-actuated: no hull, no powder. Cases are easily removed with universal 12 and 20 Ga. case holders allowing cases to be sized down to the rim. Only one primer feeds at a time. Steel size ring provides complete resizing of high and low base hulls. Holds 25 lbs. of shot and 1½ lbs. of powder.

MSRP $1,025.95
Grand Conversion Kit: $489.95

MINI-GRAND SHOTSHELL PRESS

The Mini-Grand shotgun press, a seven-station single-stage press, loads 12 and 20 Ga. hulls, from 2¾ in. to 3½ in. in length. It utilizes RCBS, Hornady, and Ponsness Warren powder and shot bushings, with a half-pound capacity powder hopper and 12½ lb. capacity shot hopper. The machine will load both lead and steel shot.

From: $128.99

PARTNER PRESS

Easy-to-use, durable press in a compact package. Features compound linkage, durable steel links, priming arm. Reloads most standard calibers.
Partner Press: $96.95
Partner Standard Reloading Kit: . . . $243.95

PIGGYBACK 3 CONVERSION KIT

The Piggyback 3 conversion unit moves from single-stage reloading to five-station, manual-indexing, progressive reloading in one step. The Piggyback 3 will work with the RCBS Rock Chucker, Reloader Special-3, and Reloader Special-5.
MSRP $523.95

PRO 2000 PROGRESSIVE PRESS

Constructed of cast iron, the Pro-2000 features five reloading stations. The case-actuated powder measure assures repeatability of dispensing powder. A Micrometer Adjustment Screw allows precise return to previously recorded charges. All dies are standard ⅞ in. x 14 in., including the Expander Die. The press incorporates the APS Priming System. Allows full-length sizing in calibers from .32 Auto to .460 Wby Mag.
MSRP $693.95

RELOADER SPECIAL-5 PRESS

The Reloader Special press features a ball handle and primer arm so that cases can be primed and resized at the same time. Other features include a compound leverage system; solid aluminum "O" frame offset; corrosion resistant baked-powder finish; ⅞ in. x 14 in. thread for all standard reloading dies and accessories; optional Piggyback 2 conversion unit.
MSRP $165.95

RCBS MINI-GRAND SHOTSHELL PRESS

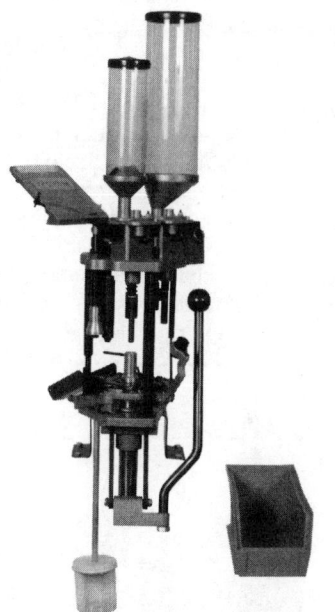

RCBS GRAND SHOTSHELL PRESS

RCBS PARTNER PRESS

RCBS PIGGYBACK 3 CONVERSION KIT

RCBS RELOADER SPECIAL-5 PRESS

RCBS

ROCK CHUCKER SUPREME MASTER RELOADING KIT

Kit includes all the tools and accessories needed to start handloading: Rock Chucker Press; RCBS 505 Reloading Scale; Speer Manual #13; Uniflow Powder Measure; deburring tool; case loading block; Primer Tray-2; hand priming tool; powder funnel; case lube pad; case neck brushes; fold-up hex key set; Trim Pro Manual Case Trimmer Kit.

MSRP **$472.95**

ROCK CHUCKER SUPREME PRESS

With its easy operation, outstanding strength and versatility, a Rock Chucker Supreme press serves beginner and pro alike. Heavy-duty cast iron for easy case resizing; larger window opening to accommodate longer cartridges; 1 in. ram held in place by 12½ sq. in. of ram bearing surface; ambidextrous handle; compound leverage system; ⅞ in. x 14 in. thread for all standard reloading dies and accessories

MSRP **$202.95**

TURRET PRESS

With pre-set dies in the six-station turret head, the Turret Press can increase production from 50 to 200 rounds per hour. The frame, links, and toggle block are constructed of cast iron and the handle offers compound leverage for full-length sizing of any caliber from .25 ACP to .460 Wby. Mag. Six stations allow for custom setup. The quick-change turret head makes caliber changes fast and easy. This press accepts all standard ⅞ in. x 14 in. dies and shell holders.

MSRP **$293.95**
Turret Press Deluxe
Reloading Kit: **$576.95**

Scales and Measures

505 RELOADING SCALE

This 511-grain capacity scale has a three-poise system with widely-spaced, deep-beam notches. Two smaller poises on right side adjust from .1 to 10 grains, larger one on left side adjusts in full 10-grain steps. The scale uses magnetic dampening to eliminate beam oscillation. The 5-0-5 also has a sturdy diecast base with large leveling legs. Self-aligning agate bearings support the hardened steel beam pivots for a guaranteed sensitivity to .1 grains.

MSRP **$119.95**

1010 RELOADING SCALE

Normal capacity is 510 grains, which can be increased without loss of sensitivity by attaching the included extra weight up to 1010 grains. Features include micrometer poise for quick, precise weighing, special approach-to weight indicator, easy-to-read graduation, magnetic dampener, agate bearings, anti-tip pan, and a dustproof lid snaps on to cover scale for storage. Sensitivity is guaranteed to .1 grains.

MSRP **$201.95**

CHARGEMASTER 1500 SCALE

High-performance reloading scale with 1500-grain capacity. Scale reads in grains or grams; calibration weights included. Available in 110 or 220 volt—AC adaptor included. Can be upgraded to an automatic dispensing system with the RCBS ChargeMaster.

MSRP **$254.95**

CHARGEMASTER COMBO

Performs as a scale or as a complete powder dispensing system. Scale can be removed and used separately. Dispenses from 2 to 300 grains. Reads and dispenses in grains or grams. Stores up to 30 charges in memory for quick recall of favorite loads. 110-volt or 220-volt adaptor included.

MSRP **$484.95**

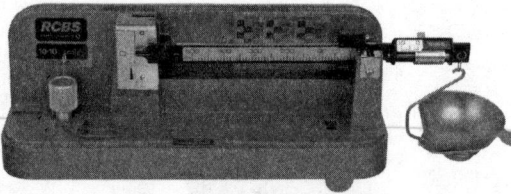

RCBS 1010 RELOADING SCALE

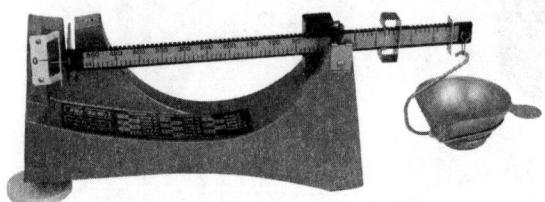

RCBS 505 RELOADING SCALE

RCBS CHARGEMASTER COMBO

RCBS

RANGEMASTER 750 SCALE

Compact, lightweight, and portable with 750-grain capacity. Scale reads in grams or grains; calibration weights included. Accurate to ± .1 of a grain; fast calibration; Powered by AC or 9-volt battery—AC adaptor included. 110- or 220-volt model available.

MSRP **$161.95**

RC-130 MECHANICAL SCALE

The RC130 features a 130-grain capacity and maintenance-free movement, plus a magnetic dampening system for fast readings. A three-poise design incorporates easy adjustments with a beam that is graduated in increments of 10 grains and 1 grain. A micrometer poise measures in .1-grain increments with accuracy to ±.1 grain.

MSRP **$56.95**

RCBS RANGEMASTER 750 SCALE

Reloading Tools

APS PRIMER STRIP LOADER

For those who keep a supply of CCI primers in conventional packaging, the APS primer strip loader allows quick filling of empty strips. Each push of the handle seats 25 primers.

From: **$31.99**

AR SERIES DIES

The RCBS AR Series is a must for the progressive reloader. It features a Small Base sizing die and a new Taper Crimp seating die. This combination makes reloading easier for AR-style or semi-auto shooters. The Small Base sizer guarantees that the cartridge will rechamber. The Taper Crimp Seater is more forgiving when various case lengths are loaded at the same time. Case neck crimp bulges and buckled shoulders are virtually eliminated when Taper crimping is used with cannelured bullets.

From: . . . . **$34.99–$69.99**

BULLET FEED DIE-PISTOL

RCBS's Pistol Bullet Feed Die allows the progressive pistol loader to leave the feed die set up on the removable die plate for quick caliber change-overs. The popular RCBS Bullet Feeder shortens reloading sessions while increasing load rates by approximately 50 percent. Rather than reinstalling on die plates and adjusting Bullet Fingers and Guides, simply install another Bullet Feed Die to save even more time during caliber changeovers. Includes one set of Bullet Fingers and retaining clip.

MSRP **$30.95**

RCBS APS PRIMER STRIP LOADER

RCBS AR SERIES DIE

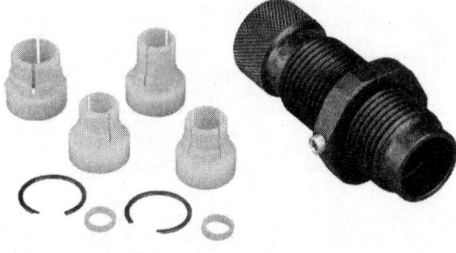

RCBS BULLET FEED DIE-PISTOL

RCBS

BULLET FEEDER

Designed to fit most progressive presses with $7/8$ in. x 14 in. Platform holes, this automatic unit features a rotating collator that orients the bullets to drop into the feed mechanism/ eat die. Choose .22 or .3. The hopper holds 250 .22 caliber bullets over .30s. Powdered by 110-240 VAC, the unit comes with plug adapters for foreign outlets.

Rifle: **$632.95**
Pistol: **$541.95**

CARBIDE REPLACEMENT TOOLS

Replacement carbide tipped cutters for your Case Trimmer, 3-Way Cutter and Trim Mate Chamfer, or Debur tool. These carbide tipped tools cut clean and stay sharp for a lifetime of use.
MSRP. **$44.95**

ELECTRONIC DIGITAL MICROMETER

Instant reading; large, easy-to-read numbers for error reduction with instant inch/millimeter conversion; zero adjust at any position; thimble lock for measuring like objects; replaceable silver oxide cell—1.55 Volt; auto off after five minutes for longer battery life; adjustment wrench included; fitted wooden storage cases.
MSRP. **$161.95**

HAND PRIMING TOOL

A patented safety mechanism separates the seating operation from the primer supply, virtually eliminating the possibility of tray detonation. Fits in your hand for portable primer seating. Primer tray installation requires no contact with the primers. Uses the same RCBS shell holders as RCBS presses. Made of cast metal.
MSRP. **$51.95**

POWDER TRICKLER-2

Today's trend is to use electronic scales to measure powder charges. Many of these scales have scale pans that are positioned out of reach of existing powder tricklers. The Powder Trickler-2 solves this problem by adding a height adjustable, non-skid base and powder tube extension.
MSRP. **$23.95**

POW'R PULL BULLET PULLER KIT

The RCBS Pow'r Pull bullet puller features a three-jaw chuck that grips the case rim—just rap it on any solid surface like a hammer, and powder and bullet drop into the main chamber for reuse. A soft cushion protects bullets from damage. Works with most centerfire cartridges from .22 to .45 (not for use with rimfire cartridges).
From:. **$19.99**

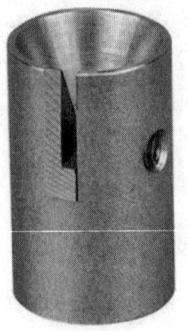

RCBS CARBIDE CHAMFER REPLACEMENT TOOL

RCBS ELECTRONIC DIGITAL MICROMETER

RCBS POWDER TRICKLER-2

RCBS CARBIDE CUTTER HEAD REPLACEMENT TOOL

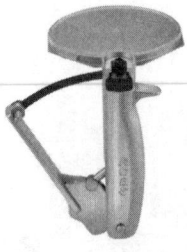

RCBS HAND PRIMING TOOL

RCBS CARBIDE CUTTER REPLACEMENT TOOL

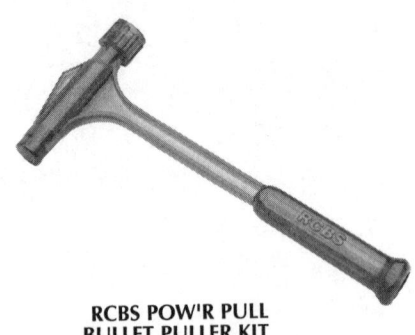

RCBS POW'R PULL BULLET PULLER KIT

RCBS

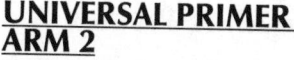

PRECISION BIPOD

Quick-adjust telescoping legs of 6061 T6 alloy secure your rifle for accurate shooting on uneven ground. Range of movement: 7 to 10 inches, with 25 degrees of cant. Skid-resistant polyurethane feet grip slick surfaces. Tool-free mounting adapts this bipod to any Picatinny rail. Paddle locks make for quick, easy deployment. Hard-coating anodizing ensures tough use.

MSRP **$219.95**

PRIMER POCKET SWAGER - BENCH TOOL

Features: Simplifies removal of staked primer pockets and requires 35 percent less force than other tools; rugged construction and foam padded handle; comes with hardened steel swaging heads and rods for small and large pockets; accommodates cases .22-caliber and larger

MSRP **$105.95**

SHELL HOLDER RACK

Twelve positions that hold two shell holders on each post; room to store six Trim Pro Shell Holders as well; clear cover keeps out the dust and dirt; mounted on the wall or used on the bench; wall mount spacing allows it to be hung off of standard 1-in. pegboard hooks; support legs angle the bottom out for wall mounting or the top up for bench use; Shell Holder Racks can be snapped together if more shell holder storage is needed; sticker labels are included

MSRP **$15.95**

TRIM PRO CASE TRIMMER

Cases are trimmed quickly and easily. The lever-type handle is more accurate to use than draw collet systems. A flat plate shell holder keeps cases locked in place and aligned. A micrometer fine adjustment bushing offers trimming accuracy to within .001 in. Made of diecast metal with hardened cutting blades.

120V: **$369.95**
240V: **$397.95**
Manual Kit: **$133.95**

TUBE PISTOL BULLET FEEDER

Features: Caliber specific; tube fed; allows use of jacketed, plated, cast or swaged lead bullets; compatible with any $7/8''$ x 14" threaded press; increase load rate up to 50 percent

MSRP **$35.95**

UNIVERSAL PRIMER ARM 2

Designed for fast and accurate primer seating. Primer plugs and sleeves included for large and small rifle and pistol primers. Universal primer for Rock Chucker Press.

MSRP **$16.95**

RCBS TUBE PISTOL BULLET FEEDER

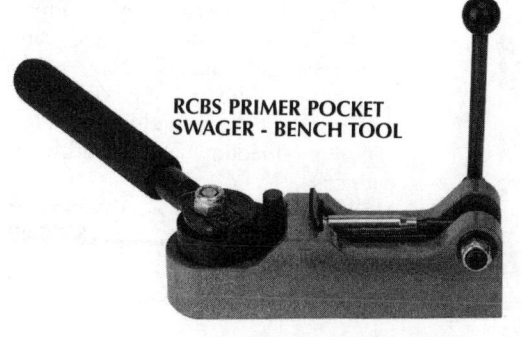

RCBS PRIMER POCKET SWAGER - BENCH TOOL

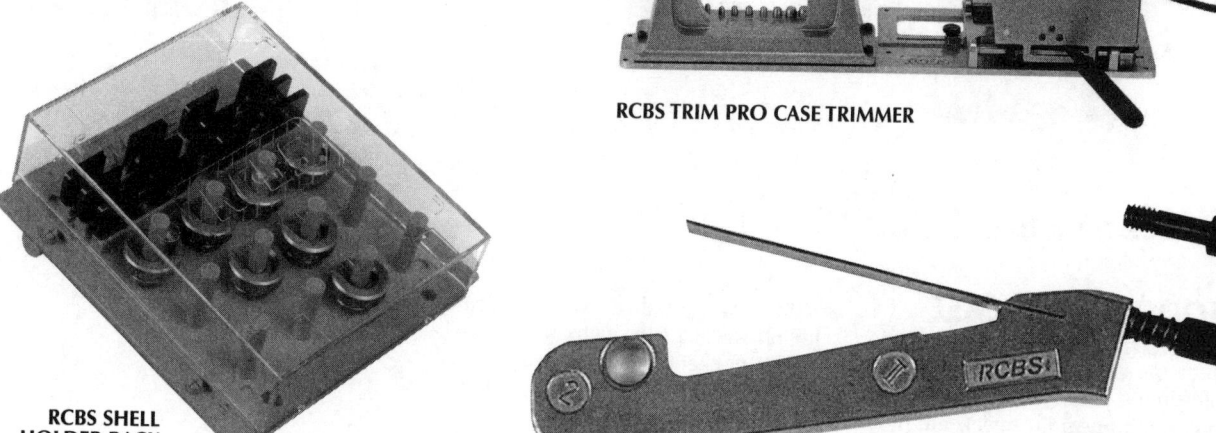

RCBS TRIM PRO CASE TRIMMER

RCBS SHELL HOLDER RACK

RCBS UNIVERSAL PRIMER ARM 2

Redding Reloading Tools

HANDLOADING

Handloading Presses

BIG BOSS RELOADING PRESS

A larger version of the Boss reloading press built on a heavier frame with a longer ram stroke for reloading magnum cartridges. It features a 1 in. diameter ram with over 3.8 in. of stroke; smart primer arm; offset ball handle; heavy-duty cast iron frame; heavy-duty compound linkage; steel adapter bushing accepts all standard 7/8 in. x 14 in. threaded dies.

Big Boss II:. $297.00
Big Boss: $266.00
Big Boss II Ram Only $52.50
Big Boss II Kit: $360.00
Big Boss Kit:. $329.00

BOSS RELOADING PRESS

This "O" type reloading press features a rigid cast iron frame whose 36-degree offset provides the best visibility and access of comparable presses. Its "Smart" primer arm moves in and out of position automatically with ram travel. The priming arm is positioned at the bottom of ram travel for lowest leverage and best feel. Model 721 accepts all standard 7/8 in. x 14 in. threaded dies and universal shell holders.

MSRP. $211.00
Boss Reloading Kit: $274.00

T-7 TURRET PRESS

The Redding T-7 Turret Press has a 7-station turret head that is easily turned to set the next die in place. With the addition of additional turret heads (sold separately) a reloader can switch between calibers without readjusting depth. The cast iron construction and stout compound linkage allow for reloading magnum cartridges with ease.

MSRP. $462.00
Turret Kit: $525.00

ULTRAMAG RELOADING PRESS

Highly recommended for the reloader needing a large frame press. The leverage system on this press (unlike most others) is connected to the top of the press frame which gives it literally tons of pressure without the usual concerns of press frame deflection or misalignment.

MSRP. $480.00
Kit:. $543.00

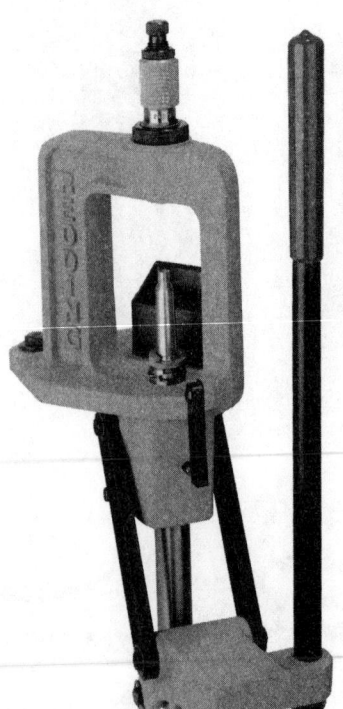

REDDING BIG BOSS RELOADING PRESS

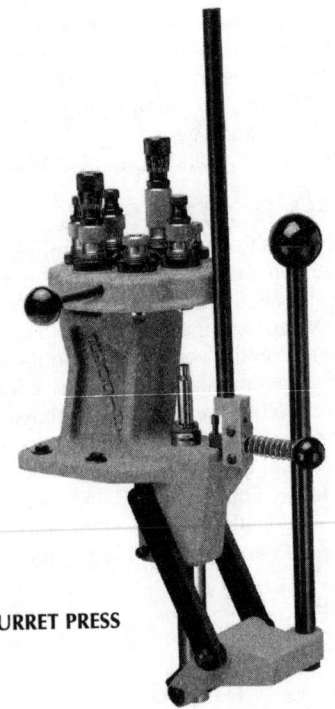

REDDING T-7 TURRET PRESS

Case Trimmers

MODEL 1400-XT CASE TRIMMING LATHE

The frame is cast iron with storage holes in the base for extra pilots. Coarse and fine adjustments are provided for case length. Also features: six pilots (.22, 6mm, .25, .270, 7mm, and .30); universal collet; two neck cleaning brushes (.22 through .30 cal.); two primer pocket cleaners; tin coated replaceable cutter; accessory power screwdriver adaptor.

Case Trimming Lathe: $149.00
Pilots: $6.75

Redding Reloading Tools

Dies & Bushings

BODY DIES

Designed to resize the case body and bump the shoulder position for proper chambering without disturbing the case neck. They are intended for use only to resize cases that have become increasingly difficult to chamber after repeated firing and neck sizing. Small Base Body Dies are available in .223 Rem., 6mm P.P.C, 6mm B. R. Rem., 6mm/284 Win., .260 Rem., 6.5mm/284 Win., .284 Win., .308 Win., and .30-06.

Category I:............$43.00
Category II:............$53.00
Category III:...........$65.00

COMPETITION BULLET SEATER DIE FOR HANDGUN & STRAIGHT-WALL RIFLE CARTRIDGES

The precision seating stem moves well down into the die chamber to accomplish early bullet contact. The seating stem's spring loading provides positive

alignment bias between the tapered nose and the bullet ogive. The Competition Bullet Seating Die features dial-in micrometer adjustment calibrated in .001-in. increments.

MSRP.................$123.00

FORM & TRIM DIES

Redding trim dies file trim cases without unnecessary resizing because they are made to chamber dimensions. For case forming and necking brass down from another caliber, Redding trim dies can be the perfect intermediate step before full-length resizing.

Series A: $43.00
Series B: $58.00
Series C: $72.50
Series D: $80.00

G-RX PUSH THRU BASE SIZING DIE

The G-Rx Carbide Push Thru Base Sizing Die is designed to restore fired cases from .40 S&W autoloading pis-

tols that exhibit a bulge near the base without the need for case lube. By passing the case completely through the new G-Rx Carbide Die, the bulge is removed and the case may be returned to service.

MSRP.................$56.00

NATIONAL MATCH DIE SET

Redding now offers a specialized die set for the military match shooter. Available in 6.8 SPC, .223 Rem., .308 Win., .30-06 Spfd., and .300 Blackout, the set includes a Full-Length Sizing Die a Competition Bullet Seating Die and a Taper Crimp Die.

MSRP.................$228.00

REDDING G-RX PUSH THRU BASE SIZING DIE

REDDING BODY DIE

REDDING COMPETITION BULLET SEATER DIE

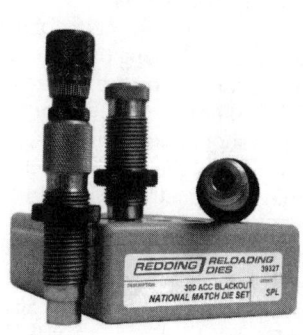

REDDING NATIONAL MATCH DIE SET

Redding Reloading Tools

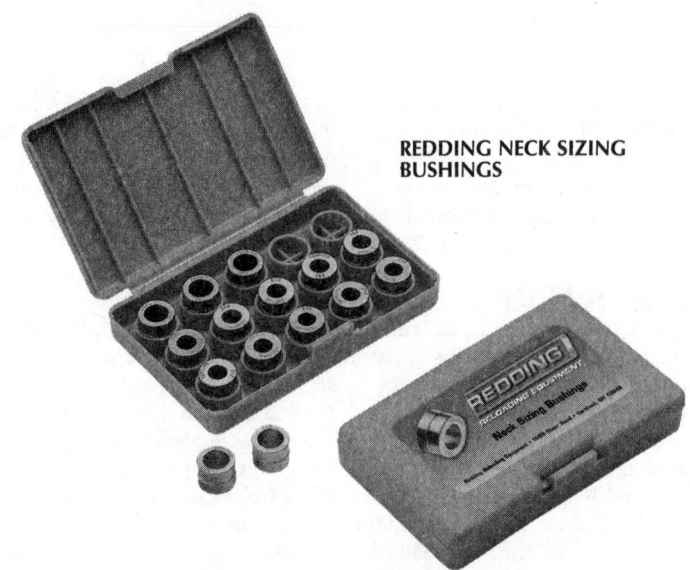

REDDING NECK SIZING BUSHINGS

NECK SIZING BUSHINGS

Redding Neck Sizing Bushings are available in two styles. Both share the same external dimensions (½ in. O.D. x ³/₈ in. long) and freely interchange in all Redding Bushing style Neck Sizing Dies. They are available in .001 in. size increments throughout the range of .185 in. through .365 in., covering all calibers from .17 to .338.

Heat Treated Steel: $21.00
Titanium Nitride Treatment: .$36.00
Storage Box: $3.72

NECK SIZING DIES

These dies size only the necks of bottleneck cases to prolong brass life and improve accuracy. These dies size only the neck and not the shoulder or body, fired cases should not be interchanged between rifles of the same caliber. Available individually or in Deluxe Die Sets.

Series A: $48.00
Series B: $64.50
Series C: $82.00
Series D: $92.50

PROFILE CRIMP DIES

For cartridges without head-space on the case mouth. These dies were designed for those who want the best possible crimp. Profile crimp dies provide a tighter, more uniform roll type crimp, and require the bullet to be seated to the correct depth in a previous operation.

Series A: $38.00
Series B: $38.00
Series C: $58.00
Series D: $64.50

TAPER & CRIMP DIES

Designed for cartridges with headspace on the case mouth where conventional roll crimping is undesirable. Available in the following rifle calibers: .223 Rem., 7.62MM x 39, .30-30, .308 Win, .30-06, .300 Win. Mag.

Series A: $38.00
Series B: $38.00
Series C: $58.00
Series D: $64.50

TRIM DIES

Redding trim dies allow trimming cases without excessive resizing. Trim dies require extended shell holders.

Series A: $43.00
Series B: $43.00
Series C: $72.50
Series D: $80.00

TYPE S-BUSHING STYLE DIES

The new Type S-Bushing Style Neck Sizing Die provides reloaders with a simple means to precisely control case neck size and tension. The Type-S features: interchangeable sizing bushings available in .001 in. increments; adjustable decapping rod with standard size button; self-centering resizing bushing; decapping pin retainer. All dies are supplied without bushings.

Category I: $84.00
Category II: $102.00
Category III: $126.00

REDDING PROFILE CRIMP DIE

Redding Reloading Tools

Handloading Accessories

CARBIDE SIZE BUTTON KITS

Make inside neck sizing smoother and easier without lubrication. Now die sets can be upgraded with a carbide size button kit. Available for bottleneck cartridges .22 through .338 cal. The carbide size button is free-floating on the decap rod, allowing it to self-center in the case neck. Kits contain: carbide size button, retainer, and spare decapping pin.
MSRP $43.00

COMPETITION MODEL 10X-PISTOL AND SMALL RIFLE POWDER MEASURE

This powder measure uses all of the special features of the Competition Model BR-30 combined with a drum and metering unit designed to provide the most uniform metering of small charge weights.
MSRP $294.00

COMPETITION MODEL BR-30 POWDER MEASURE

Combines all of the features of Competition Model BR-30, with a drum and metering unit designed to provide uniform metering of small charge weights. The diameter of the metering cavity is reduced and the metering plunger is given a hemispherical shape. Charge range: 1 to 25 grains.
MSRP $294.00

DROP TUBE ADAPTER

Features: The adapter is a simple friction fit and works with all Redding powder measures and the Redding powder funnel. Not simply a reducer, this adapter is manufactured with an integral chamber, engineered and tested to provide smooth powder flow and reduced bridging as the powder flows through the smaller orifice for the .17- and .20-caliber case necks.
From: $8.39

IMPERIAL BIO-GREEN CASE LUBE

Features: Redding now introduces a new plant, based sizing lube, which is highly effective, completely bio degradable, and totally renewable. Imperial Bio Green Case Lubricant sets a new standard for pad applied resizing lubricants. It will not stain your brass and offers easy water cleanup making it perfect for use with ultrasonic case cleaners.
From: $6.99

INSTANT INDICATOR HEADSPACE & BULLET COMPARATOR

The Instant Indicator checks the headspace from the case shoulder to the base. Bullet seating depths can be compared and bullets can be sorted by checking the base of bullets to give dimension. Case length can be measured. Available for 33 cartridges from .222 Rem to .338 Win. Mag., including WSSM cartridges.
With Dial Indicator: $184.50
Without Dial Indicator: $144.00
1-in. Dial Indicator: $46.00

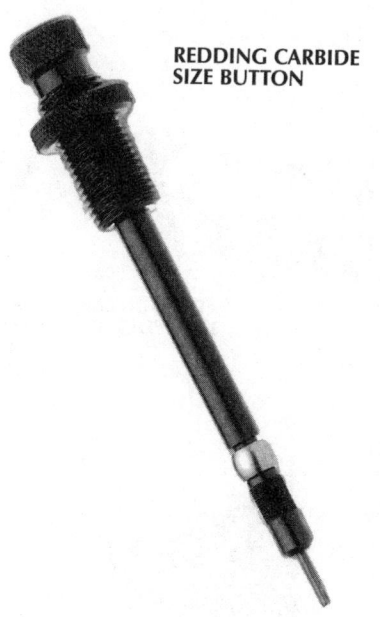

REDDING CARBIDE SIZE BUTTON

REDDING DROP TUBE ADAPTER

REDDING IMPERIAL BIO-GREEN CASE LUBE

Redding Reloading Tools

MATCH-GRADE MODEL 3BR POWDER MEASURE

Interchangeable universal-or pistol-metering chambers. Measures charges up to 100 grains. Unit is fitted with lock ring for fast dump with large clear plastic reservoir. See-through drop tube accepts all calibers from .22 to .6. Precision-fitted rotating drum is critically honed to prevent powder escape. Knife-edged powder chamber shears coarse-grained powders with ease, ensuring accurate charges.

Powder measure: **$249.00**
Measure with
both chambers: **$306.00**

MODEL 3 POWDER MEASURE

The Model 3 has a micrometer metering chamber in front. The frame is precision-machined cast iron with hand honed fit between the frame and hard surfaced drum to easily cut and meter powders. The Model 3 features a large capacity clear powder reservoir; see-through drop tube; body with standard 7/8 in. x 14 in. thread to fit mounting bracket and optional bench stand; cast mounting bracket included.

MSRP **$197.00**

VERSA PAK RELOADING KIT

Offers all of the products a serious handloader needs (without the press and dies), at a substantial savings over the cost of the individual items. The Versa Pak includes all the items listed in the Pro Pak (less press and dies) plus a Model 3 Master Powder Measure, a 1400 XT Case Trimmer, Imperial Dry Neck Lube in Application Media, a starter size of Imperial Sizing Die Wax and our DVD, "Advanced Handloading, Beyond the Basics."

MSRP **$600.00**

REDDING MATCH-GRADE MODEL 3BR POWDER MEASURE

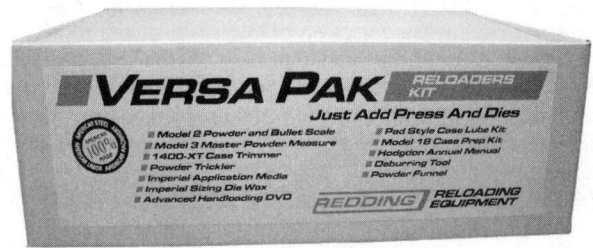

REDDING VERSA PAK RELOADING KIT

Powder Scales

MODEL NO. 2 POWDER AND BULLET SCALE

Model No. 2 features 505-grain capacity and .1-grain accuracy, a dampened beam, and hardened knife edges, and milled stainless bearing seats for smooth, consistent operation and a high level of durability.

MSRP **$132.00**

EZ FEED SHELLHOLDERS

Redding shell holders are of a universal "snap-in" design recommended for use with all Redding dies and presses, as well as all other popular brands. They are precision-machined to very close tolerances and heat-treated to fit cases and eliminate potential resizing problems. The outside knurling makes them easier to handle and change.

MSRP **$12.00**

REDDING MODEL NO. 2 POWDER AND BULLET SCALE

Shellholders

EXTENDED SHELLHOLDERS

Extended shell holders are required when trimming short cases under 1½ in. O.A.L. They are machined to the same tolerances as standard shell holders, except they're longer.

MSRP **$21.00**

REDDING EXTENDED SHELLHOLDER

REDDING EZ FEED SHELLHOLDER

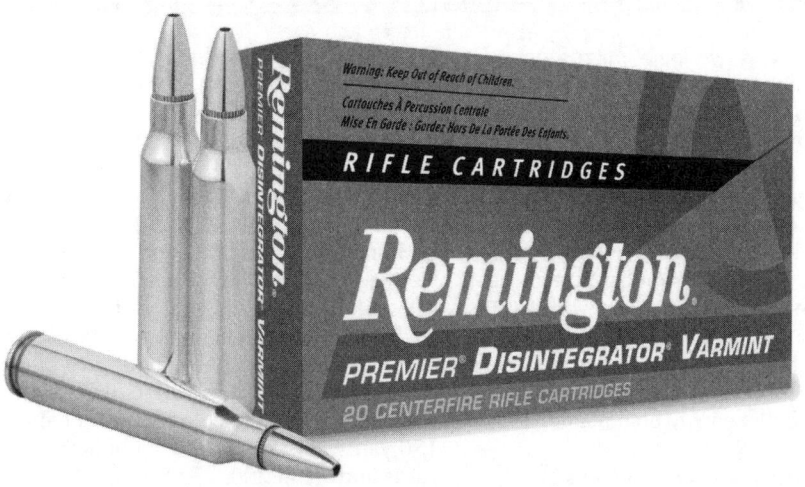

Centerfire Rifle Ballistics

Comprehensive Ballistics Tables for Currently Manufactured Sporting Rifle Cartridges

No more collecting catalogs and peering at microscopic print to find out what ammunition is offered for a cartridge, and how it performs relative to other factory loads! *Shooter's Bible* has assembled the data for you, in easy-to-read tables, by cartridge.

Data is taken from manufacturers' charts; your chronograph readings may vary. Listings are not intended as recommendations. For example, the data for the .44 Magnum at 400 yards shows its effective range is much shorter. The lack of data for a 285-grain .375 H&H bullet beyond 300 yards does not mean the bullet has no authority farther out. Besides ammunition, the rifle, sights, conditions and shooter ability all must be considered when contemplating a long shot. Accuracy and bullet energy both matter when big game is in the offing.

Barrel length affects velocity, and at various rates

depending on the load. As a rule, figure 50 fps per inch of barrel, plus or minus, if your barrel is longer or shorter than 22 inches.

Bullets are given by make, weight (in grains) and type. Most type abbreviations are self-explanatory: BT=Boat-Tail, FMJ=Full Metal Jacket, HP=Hollow Point, SP=Soft Point—except in Hornady listings, where SP is the firm's Spire Point. TNT and TXP are trademarked designations of Speer and Norma. XLC identifies a coated Barnes X bullet. HE indicates a Federal High Energy load, similar to the Hornady LM (Light Magnum) and HM (Heavy Magnum) cartridges.

Arc (trajectory) is based on a zero range published by the manufacturer, from 100 to 300 yards. If a zero does not fall in a yardage column, it lies halfway between—at 150 yards, for example, if the bullet's strike is "+" at 100 yards and "-" at 200.

.17 HORNET TO .22 HORNET

CARTRIDGE BULLET	RANGE, YARDS:	0	100	200	300	400
.17 HORNET						
Hornady 15.5 NXT SPF		0	100	200	300	400
	velocity, fps	3860	2924	2159	1531	1108
	energy, ft-lb	513	294	160	81	42
	arc, inches:	-1.5	+1.4	0	-9.1	-33.7
Hornady 20 V-MAX		0	100	200	300	400
	velocity, fps	3650	3077	2574	2122	1721
	energy, ft-lb	592	420	294	200	132
	arc, inches:	-1.5	+1.1	0	-6.4	-20.7
.17 REMINGTON						
Rem. 20 AccuTip BT	velocity, fps	4250	3594	3028	2529	2081
	energy, ft-lb	802	574	407	284	192
	arc, inches:		+1.3	+1.3	-2.5	-11.8
Rem. 20 Fireball	velocity, fps	4000	3380	2840	2360	1930
	energy, ft-lb	710	507	358	247	165
	arc, inches		+1.6	+1.5	-2.8	-13.5
Rem. 25 HP Power-Lokt	velocity, fps	4040	3284	2644	2086	1606
	energy, ft-lb	906	599	388	242	143
	arc, inches		+1.8	0	-3.3	-16.6
.204 RUGER						
Federal 32 Nosler Ballistic Tip	velocity, fps	4030	3465	2968	2523	2119
	arc, inches		+0.7	0	-4.7	-14.9
Hornady 32 V-Max	velocity, fps	4225	3632	3114	2652	2234
	energy, ft-lb	1268	937	689	500	355
	arc, inches:		+0.6	0	-4.2	-13.4
Hornady 40 V-Max	velocity, fps	3900	3451	3046	2677	2335
	energy, ft-lb:	1351	1058	824	636	485
	arc, inches:		+0.7	0	-4.5	-13.9
Rem. 32 AccuTip	velocity, fps	4225	3632	3114	2652	2234
	Energy, ft-lb:	1268	937	689	500	355
	Arc, inches:		+0.6	0	-4.1	-13.1

CARTRIDGE BULLET	RANGE, YARDS:	0	100	200	300	400
Rem. 40 AccuTip	velocity, fps	3900	3451	3046	2677	2336
	energy, ft-lb	1351	1058	824	636	485
	arc, inches:		+0.7	0	-4.3	-13.2
Win. 32 Ballistic Silver Tip	velocity, fps	4050	3482	2984	2537	2132
	energy, ft-lb	1165	862	632	457	323
	arc, inches		+0.7	0	-4.6	-14.7
Win. 34 HP	velocity, fps	4025	3339	2751	2232	1775
	energy, ft-lb	1223	842	571	376	238
	arc, inches:		+0.8	0	-5.5	-18.1
.218 BEE						
Win. 46 Hollow Point	velocity, fps	2760	2102	1550	1155	961
	energy, ft-lb:	778	451	245	136	94
	arc, inches:		0	-7.2	-29.4	
.22 HORNET						
Hornady 35 V-Max	velocity, fps:	3100	2278	1601	1135	929
	energy, ft-lb:	747	403	199	100	67
	arc, inches:		+2.8	0	-16.9	-60.4
Rem. 35 AccuTip	velocity, fps:	3100	2271	1591	1127	924
	energy, ft-lb:	747	401	197	99	66
	arc, inches:		+1.5	-3.5	-22.3	-68.4
Rem. 45 Pointed Soft Point	velocity, fps:	2690	2042	1502	1128	948
	energy, ft-lb:	723	417	225	127	90
	arc, inches:		0	-7.1	-30.0	
Rem. 45 Hollow Point	velocity, fps:	2690	2042	1502	1128	948
	energy, ft-lb:	723	417	225	127	90
	arc, inches:		0	-7.1	-30.0	
Win. 34 Jacketed HP	velocity, fps:	3050	2132	1415	1017	852
	energy, ft-lb:	700	343	151	78	55.
	arc, inches:		0	-6.6	-29.9	
Win. 45 Soft Point	velocity, fps:	2690	2042	1502	1128	948.
	energy, ft-lb:	723	417	225	127	90
	arc, inches:		0	-7.7	-31.3	

CARTRIDGE BULLET	RANGE, YARDS:	0	100	200	300	400
Win. 46 Hollow Point	velocity, fps:	2690	2042	1502	1128	948.
	energy, ft-lb:	739	426	230	130	92
	arc, inches:		0	-7.7	-31.3	

.221 REMINGTON FIREBALL

CARTRIDGE BULLET	RANGE, YARDS:	0	100	200	300	400
Rem. 50 AccuTip BT	velocity, fps:	2995	2605	2247	1918	1622
	energy, ft-lb:	996	753	560	408	292
	arc, inches:		+1.8	0	-8.8	-27.1

.222 REMINGTON

CARTRIDGE BULLET	RANGE, YARDS:	0	100	200	300	400
Federal 50 Hi-Shok	velocity, fps:	3140	2600	2120	1700	1350
	energy, ft-lb:	1095	750	500	320	200
	arc, inches:		+1.9	0	-9.7	-31.6
Federal 55 FMJ boat-tail	velocity, fps:	3020	2740	2480	2230	1990
	energy, ft-lb:	1115	915	750	610	484.
	arc, inches:		+1.6	0	-7.3	-21.5
Hornady 40 V-Max	velocity, fps:	3600	3117	2673	2269	1911
	energy, ft-lb:	1151	863	634	457	324
	arc, inches:		+1.1	0	-6.1	-18.9
Hornady 50 V-Max	velocity, fps:	3140	2729	2352	2008	1710.
	energy, ft-lb:	1094	827	614	448	325
	arc, inches:		+1.7	0	-7.9	-24.4
Norma 50 Soft Point	velocity, fps:	3199	2667	2193	1771	
	energy, ft-lb:	1136	790	534	348	
	arc, inches:		+1.7	0	-9.1	
Norma 50 FMJ	velocity, fps:	2789	2326	1910	1547	
	energy, ft-lb:	864	601	405	266	
	arc, inches:		+2.5	0	-12.2	
Norma 62 Soft Point	velocity, fps:	2887	2457	2067	1716	
	energy, ft-lb:	1148	831	588	405	
	arc, inches:		+2.1	0	-10.4	
PMC 50 Pointed Soft Point	velocity, fps:	3044	2727	2354	2012	1651
	energy, ft-lb:	1131	908	677	494	333
	arc, inches:		+1.6	0	-7.9	-24.5
PMC 55 Pointed Soft Point	velocity, fps:	2950	2594	2266	1966	1693
	energy, ft-lb:	1063	822	627	472	350
	arc, inches:		+1.9	0	-8.7	-26.3
Rem. 50 Pointed Soft Point	velocity, fps:	3140	2602	2123	1700	1350.
	energy, ft-lb:	1094	752	500	321	202
	arc, inches:		+1.9	0	-9.7	-31.7
Rem. 50 HP Power-Lokt	velocity, fps:	3140	2635	2182	1777	1432.
	energy, ft-lb:	1094	771	529	351	228
	arc, inches:		+1.8	0	-9.2	-29.6
Rem. 50 AccuTip BT	velocity, fps:	3140	2744	2380	2045	1740
	energy, ft-lb:	1094	836	629	464	336.
	arc, inches:		+1.6	0	-7.8	-23.9
Win. 40 Ballistic Silvertip	velocity, fps:	3370	2915	2503	2127	1786
	energy, ft-lb:	1009	755	556	402	283
	arc, inches:		+1.3	0	-6.9	-21.5
Win. 50 Pointed Soft Point	velocity, fps:	3140	2602	2123	1700	1350
	energy, ft-lb:	1094	752	500	321	202
	arc, inches:		+2.2	0	-10.0	-32.3

.222 REMINGTON MAGNUM

CARTRIDGE BULLET	RANGE, YARDS:	0	100	200	300	400
Nosler 40 BT	velocity, fps:	3600	3140	2726	2347	2000
	energy, ft-lb:	1150	876	660	489	355
	arc, inches:	-1.5	+1.0	0	-5.7	-17.8
Nosler 50 BT	velocity, fps:	3340	2917	2533	2179	1855
	energy, ft-lb:	1238	945	712	527	382
	arc, inches:	-1.5	+1.3	0	-6.8	-20.9

.223 REMINGTON

CARTRIDGE BULLET	RANGE, YARDS:	0	100	200	300	400
Black Hills 40 Nosler B. Tip	velocity, fps:	3600				
	energy, ft-lb:	1150				
	arc, inches:					
Black Hills 50 V-Max	velocity, fps:	3300				
	energy, ft-lb:	1209				
	arc, inches:					
Black Hills 52 Match HP	velocity, fps:	3300				
	energy, ft-lb:	1237				
	arc, inches:					
Black Hills 55 Softpoint	velocity, fps:	3250				
	energy, ft-lb:	1270				
	arc, inches:					
Black Hills 60 SP or V-Max	velocity, fps:	3150				
	energy, ft-lb:	1322				
	arc, inches:					
Black Hills 60 Partition	velocity, fps:	3150				
	energy, ft-lb:	1322				
	arc, inches:					
Black Hills 68 Heavy Match	velocity, fps:	2850				
	energy, ft-lb:	1227				
	arc, inches:					
Black Hills 69 Sierra MK	velocity, fps:	2850				
	energy, ft-lb:	1245				
	arc, inches:					
Black Hills 73 Berger BTHP	velocity, fps:	2750				
	energy, ft-lb:	1226				
	arc, inches:					
Black Hills 75 Heavy Match	velocity, fps:	2750				
	energy, ft-lb:	1259				
	arc, inches:					
Black Hills 77 Sierra MKing	velocity, fps:	2750				
	energy, ft-lb:	1293				
	arc, inches:					
Federal 50 Jacketed HP	velocity, fps:	3400	2910	2460	2060	1700
	energy, ft-lb:	1285	940	675	470	320
	arc, inches:		+1.3	0	-7.1	-22.7
Federal 50 Speer TNT HP	velocity, fps:	3300	2860	2450	2080	1750
	energy, ft-lb:	1210	905	670	480	340
	arc, inches:		+1.4	0	-7.3	-22.6
Federal 52 Sierra MatchKing BTHP	velocity, fps:	3300	2860	2460	2090	1760
	energy, ft-lb:	1255	945	700	505	360
	arc, inches:		+1.4	0	-7.2	-22.4
Federal 55 Hi-Shok	velocity, fps:	3240	2750	2300	1910	1550
	energy, ft-lb:	1280	920	650	445	295
	arc, inches:		+1.6	0	-8.2	-26.1
Federal 55 FMJ boat-tail	velocity, fps:	3240	2950	2670	2410	2170
	energy, ft-lb:	1280	1060	875	710	575
	arc, inches:		+1.3	0	-6.1	-18.3
Federal 55 Sierra GameKing BTHP	velocity, fps:	3240	2770	2340	1950	1610
	energy, ft-lb:	1280	935	670	465	315
	arc, inches:		+1.5	0	-8.0	-25.3
Federal 55 Trophy Bonded	velocity, fps:	3100	2630	2210	1830	1500.
	energy, ft-lb:	1175	845	595	410	275
	arc, inches:		+1.8	0	-8.9	-28.7
Federal 55 Nosler Bal. Tip	velocity, fps:	3240	2870	2530	2220	1920
	energy, ft-lb:	1280	1005	780	600	450
	arc, inches:		+1.4	0	-6.8	-20.8
Federal 55 Sierra BlitzKing	velocity, fps:	3240	2870	2520	2200	1910
	energy, ft-lb:	1280	1005	775	590	445
	arc, inches:		+-1.4	0	-6.9	-20.9

Centerfire Rifle Ballistics

.223 REMINGTON TO 5.6X52 R

CARTRIDGE BULLET	RANGE, YARDS:	0	100	200	300	400
Federal 62 FMJ	velocity, fps:	3020	2650	2310	2000	1710
	energy, ft-lb:	1225	970	735	550	405
	arc, inches:		+1.7	0	-8.4	-25.5
Federal 64 Hi-Shok SP	velocity, fps:	3090	2690	2325	1990	1680
	energy, ft-lb:	1360	1030	770	560	400
	arc, inches:		+1.7	0	-8.2	-25.2
Federal 69 Sierra MatchKing BTHP	velocity, fps:	3000	2720	2460	2210	1980
	energy, ft-lb:	1380	1135	925	750	600
	arc, inches:		+1.6	0	-7.4	-21.9
Hornady 40 V-Max	velocity, fps:	3800	3305	2845	2424	2044
	energy, ft-lb:	1282	970	719	522	371
	arc, inches:		+0.8	0	-5.3	-16.6
Hornady 53 Hollow Point	velocity, fps:	3330	2882	2477	2106	1710
	energy, ft-lb:	1305	978	722	522	369
	arc, inches:		+1.7	0	-7.4	-22.7
Hornady 55 V-Max	velocity, fps:	3240	2859	2507	2181	1891.
	energy, ft-lb:	1282	998	767	581	437
	arc, inches:		+1.4	0	-7.1	-21.4
Hornady 55 TAP-FPD	velocity, fps:	3240	2854	2500	2172	1871
	energy, ft-lb:	1282	995	763	576	427
	arc, inches:		+1.4	0	-7.0	-21.4
Hornady 55 Urban Tactical	velocity, fps:	2970	2626	2307	2011	1739
	energy, ft-lb:	1077	842	650	494	369
	arc, inches:		+1.5	0	-8.1	-24.9
Hornady 60 Soft Point	velocity, fps:	3150	2782	2442	2127	1837.
	energy, ft-lb:	1322	1031	795	603	450
	arc, inches:		+1.6	0	-7.5	-22.5
Hornady 60 TAP-FPD	velocity, fps:	3115	2754	2420	2110	1824
	energy, ft-lb:	1293	1010	780	593	443
	arc, inches:		+1.6	0	-7.5	-22.9
Hornady 60 Urban Tactical	velocity, fps:	2950	2619	2312	2025	1762
	energy, ft-lb:	1160	914	712	546	413
	arc, inches:		+1.6	0	-8.1	-24.7
Hornady 75 BTHP Match	velocity, fps:	2790	2554	2330	2119	1926
	energy, ft-lb:	1296	1086	904	747	617
	arc, inches:		+2.4	0	-8.8	-25.1
Hornacy 75 TAP-FPD	velocity, fps:	2790	2582	2383	2193	2012
	energy, ft-lb:	1296	1110	946	801	674
	arc, inches:		+1.9	0	-8.0	-23.2
Hornady 75 BTHP Tactical	velocity, fps:	2630	2409	2199	2000	1814
	energy, ft-lb:	1152	966	805	666	548
	arc, inches:		+2.0	0	-9.2	-25.9
PMC 40 non-toxic	velocity, fps:	3500	2606	1871	1315	
	energy, ft-lb:	1088	603	311	154	
	arc, inches:		+2.6	0	-12.8	
PMC 50 Sierra BlitzKing	velocity, fps:	3300	2874	2484	2130	1809
	energy, ft-lb:	1209	917	685	504	363
	arc, inches:		+1.4	0	-7.1	-21.8
PMC 52 Sierra HPBT Match	velocity, fps:	3200	2808	2447	2117	1817
	energy, ft-lb:	1182	910	691	517	381
	arc, inches:		+1.5	0	-7.3	-22.5.
PMC 53 Barnes XLC	velocity, fps:	3200	2815	2461	2136	1840
	energy, ft-lb:	1205	933	713	537	398.
	arc, inches:		+1.5	0	-7.2	-22.2
PMC 55 HP boat-tail	velocity, fps:	3240	2717	2250	1832	1473
	energy, ft-lb:	1282	901	618	410	265
	arc, inches:		+1.6	0	-8.6	-27.7
PMC 55 FMJ boat-tail	velocity, fps:	3195	2882	2525	2169	1843
	energy, ft-lb:	1246	1014	779	574	415
	arc, inches:		+1.4	0	-6.8	-21.1
PMC 55 Pointed Soft Point	velocity, fps:	3112	2767	2421	2100	1806
	energy, ft-lb:	1182	935	715	539	398
	arc, inches:		+1.5	0	-7.5	-22.9

CARTRIDGE BULLET	RANGE, YARDS:	0	100	200	300	400
PMC 64 Pointed Soft Point	velocity, fps:	2775	2511	2261	2026	1806.
	energy, ft-lb:	1094	896	726	583	464
	arc, inches:		+2.0	0	-8.8	-26.1
PMC 69 Sierra BTHP Match	velocity, fps:	2900	2591	2304	2038	1791
	energy, ft-lb:	1288	1029	813	636	492
	arc, inches:		+1.9	0	-8.4	-25.3
Rem. 50 AccuTip BT	velocity, fps:	3300	2889	2514	2168	1851
	energy, ft-lb:	1209	927	701	522	380
	arc, inches:		+1.4	0	-6.9	-21.2
Rem. 55 Pointed Soft Point	velocity, fps:	3240	2747	2304	1905	1554
	energy, ft-lb:	1282	921	648	443	295
	arc, inches:		+1.6	0	-8.2	-26.2
Rem. 55 HP Power-Lokt	velocity, fps:	3240	2773	2352	1969	1627
	energy, ft-lb:	1282	939	675	473	323
	arc, inches:		+1.5	0	-7.9	-24.8
Rem. 55 AccuTip BT	velocity, fps:	3240	2854	2500	2172	1871
	energy, ft-lb:	1282	995	763	576	427
	arc, inches:		+1.5	0	-7.1	-21.7
Rem. 55 Metal Case	velocity, fps:	3240	2759	2326	1933	1587
	energy, ft-lb:	1282	929	660	456	307
	arc, inches:		+1.6	0	-8.1	-25.5
Rem. 62 HP Match	velocity, fps:	3025	2572	2162	1792	1471
	energy, ft-lb:	1260	911	643	442	298
	arc, inches:		+1.9	0	-9.4	-29.9
Rem. 69 BTHP Match	velocity, fps:	3000	2720	2457	2209	1975
	energy, ft-lb:	1379	1133	925	747	598
	arc, inches:		+1.6	0	-7.4	-21.9
Win. 40 Ballistic Silvertip	velocity, fps:	3700	3166	2693	2265	1879.
	energy, ft-lb:	1216	891	644	456	314
	arc, inches:		+1.0	0	-5.8	-18.4
Win. 45 JHP	velocity, fps:	3600				
	energy, ft-lb:	1295				
	arc, inches:					
Win. 50 Ballistic Silvertip	velocity, fps:	3410	2982	2593	2235	1907.
	energy, ft-lb:	1291	987	746	555	404
	arc, inches:		+1.2	0	-6.4	-19.8
Win. 53 Hollow Point	velocity, fps:	3330	2882	2477	2106	1770
	energy, ft-lb:	1305	978	722	522	369
	arc, inches:		+1.7	0	-7.4	-22.7
Win. 55 Pointed Soft Point	velocity, fps:	3240	2747	2304	1905	1554.
	energy, ft-lb:	1282	921	648	443	295
	arc, inches:		+1.9	0	-8.5	-26.7
Win. 55 Super Clean NT	velocity, fps:	3150	2520	1970	1505	1165
	energy, ft-lb:	1212	776	474	277	166
	arc, inches:		+2.8	0	-11.9	-38.9
Win. 55 FMJ	velocity, fps:	3240	2854			
	energy, ft-lb:	1282	995			
	arc, inches:					
Win. 55 Ballistic Silvertip	velocity, fps:	3240	2871	2531	2215	1923
	energy, ft-lb:	1282	1006	782	599	451
	arc, inches:		+1.4	0	-6.8	-20.8
Win. 64 Power-Point	velocity, fps:	3020	2656	2320	2009	1724
	energy, ft-lb:	1296	1003	765	574	423
	arc, inches:		+1.7	0	-8.2	-25.1
Win. 64 Power-Point Plus	velocity, fps:	3090	2684	2312	1971	1664
	energy, ft-lb:	1357	1024	760	552	393
	arc, inches:		+1.7	0	-8.2	-25.4

5.6 x 52 R

CARTRIDGE BULLET	RANGE, YARDS:	0	100	200	300	400
Norma 71 Soft Point	velocity, fps:	2789	2446	2128	1835	
	energy, ft-lb:	1227	944	714	531	
	arc, inches:		+2.1	0	-9.9	

.22 PPC

CARTRIDGE BULLET	RANGE, YARDS:	0	100	200	300	400
A-Square 52 Berger	velocity, fps:	3300	2952	2629	2329	2049
	energy, ft-lb:	1257	1006	798	626	485
	arc, inches:		+1.3	0	-6.3	-19.1

.225 WINCHESTER

CARTRIDGE BULLET	RANGE, YARDS:	0	100	200	300	400
Win. 55 Pointed Soft Point	velocity, fps:	3570	3066	2616	2208	1838.
	energy, ft-lb:	1556	1148	836	595	412
	arc, inches:		+2.4	+2.0	-3.5	-16.3

.224 WEATHERBY MAGNUM

CARTRIDGE BULLET	RANGE, YARDS:	0	100	200	300	400
Wby. 55 Pointed Expanding	velocity, fps:	3650	3192	2780	2403	2056
	energy, ft-lb:	1627	1244	944	705	516
	arc, inches:		+2.8	+3.7	0	-9.8

.22-250 REMINGTON

CARTRIDGE BULLET	RANGE, YARDS:	0	100	200	300	400
Black Hills 50 Nos. Bal. Tip	velocity, fps:	3700				
	energy, ft-lb:	1520				
	arc, inches:					
Black Hills 60 Nos. Partition	velocity, fps:	3550				
	energy, ft-lb:	1679				
	arc, inches:					
Federal 40 Nos. Bal. Tip	velocity, fps:	4150	3610	3130	2700	2300
	energy, ft-lb:	1530	1155	870	645	470
	arc, inches:		+0.6	0	-4.2	-13.2
Federal 40 Sierra Varminter	velocity, fps:	4000	3320	2720	2200	1740
	energy, ft-lb:	1420	980	660	430	265
	arc, inches:		+0.8	0	-5.6	-18.4
Federal 55 Hi-Shok	velocity, fps:	3680	3140	2660	2220	1830
	energy, ft-lb:	1655	1200	860	605	410
	arc, inches:		+1.0	0	-6.0	-19.1
Federal 55 Sierra BlitzKing	velocity, fps:	3680	3270	2890	2540	2220
	energy, ft-lb:	1655	1300	1020	790	605
	arc, inches:		+0.9	0	-5.1	-15.6
Federal 55 Sierra GameKing BTHP	velocity, fps:	3680	3280	2920	2590	2280
	energy, ft-lb:	1655	1315	1040	815	630
	arc, inches:		+0.9	0	-5.0	-15.1
Federal 55 Trophy Bonded	velocity, fps:	3600	3080	2610	2190	1810.
	energy, ft-lb:	1585	1155	835	590	400.
	arc, inches:		+1.1	0	-6.2	-19.8
Hornady 40 V-Max	velocity, fps:	4150	3631	3147	2699	2293
	energy, ft-lb:	1529	1171	879	647	467
	arc, inches:		+0.5	0	-4.2	-13.3
Hornady 50 V-Max	velocity, fps:	3800	3349	2925	2535	2178
	energy, ft-lb:	1603	1245	950	713	527
	arc, inches:		+0.8	0	-5.0	-15.6
Hornady 53 Hollow Point	velocity, fps:	3680	3185	2743	2341	1974.
	energy, ft-lb:	1594	1194	886	645	459
	arc, inches:		+1.0	0	-5.7	-17.8
Hornady 55 V-Max	velocity, fps:	3680	3265	2876	2517	2183
	energy, ft-lb:	1654	1302	1010	772	582
	arc, inches:		+0.9	0	-5.3	-16.1
Hornady 60 Soft Point	velocity, fps:	3600	3195	2826	2485	2169
	energy, ft-lb:	1727	1360	1064	823	627
	arc, inches:		+1.0	0	-5.4	-16.3
Norma 53 Soft Point	velocity, fps:	3707	3234	2809	1716	
	energy, ft-lb:	1618	1231	928	690	
	arc, inches:		+0.9	0	-5.3	
PMC 50 Sierra BlitzKing	velocity, fps:	3725	3264	2641	2455	2103
	energy, ft-lb:	1540	1183	896	669	491
	arc, inches:		+0.9	0	-5.2	-16.2
PMC 50 Barnes XLC	velocity, fps:	3725	3280	2871	2495	2152
	energy, ft-lb:	1540	1195	915	691	514.
	arc, inches:		+0.9	0	-5.1	-15.9
PMC 55 HP boat-tail	velocity, fps:	3680	3104	2596	2141	1737
	energy, ft-lb:	1654	1176	823	560	368
	arc, inches:		+1.1	0	-6.3	-20.2
PMC 55 Pointed Soft Point	velocity, fps:	3586	3203	2852	2505	2178
	energy, ft-lb:	1570	1253	993	766	579
	arc, inches:		+1.0	0	-5.2	-16.0
Rem. 50 AccuTip BT (also in EtronX)	velocity, fps:	3725	3272	2864	2491	2147
	energy, ft-lb:	1540	1188	910	689	512
	arc, inches:		+1.7	+1.6	-2.8	-12.8
Rem. 55 Pointed Soft Point	velocity, fps:	3680	3137	2656	2222	1832
	energy, ft-lb:	1654	1201	861	603	410
	arc, inches:		+1.9	+1.8	-3.3	-15.5
Rem. 55 HP Power-Lokt	velocity, fps:	3680	3209	2785	2400	2046.
	energy, ft-lb:	1654	1257	947	703	511
	arc, inches:		+1.8	+1.7	-3.0	-13.7
Rem. 60 Nosler Partition (also in EtronX)	velocity, fps:	3500	3045	2634	2258	1914
	energy, ft-lb:	1632	1235	924	679	488
	arc, inches:		+2.1	+1.9	-3.4	-15.5
Win. 40 Ballistic Silvertip	velocity, fps:	4150	3591	3099	2658	2257
	energy, ft-lb:	1530	1146	853	628	453
	arc, inches:		+0.6	0	-4.2	-13.4
Win. 50 Ballistic Silvertip	velocity, fps:	3810	3341	2919	2536	2182
	energy, ft-lb:	1611	1239	946	714	529.
	arc, inches:		+0.8	0	-4.9	-15.2
Win. 55 Pointed Soft Point	velocity, fps:	3680	3137	2656	2222	1832
	energy, ft-lb:	1654	1201	861	603	410
	arc, inches:		+2.3	+1.9	-3.4	-15.9
Win. 55 Ballistic Silvertip	velocity, fps:	3680	3272	2900	2558	2240
	energy, ft-lb:	1654	1307	1027	799	613
	arc, inches:		+0.9	0	-5.0	-15.4
Win. 64 Power-Point	velocity, fps:	3500	3086	2708	2360	2038
	energy, ft-lb:	1741	1353	1042	791	590
	arc, inches:		+1.1	0	-5.9	-18.0

.220 SWIFT

CARTRIDGE BULLET	RANGE, YARDS:	0	100	200	300	400
Federal 52 Sierra MatchKing BTHP	velocity, fps:	3830	3370	2960	2600	2230
	energy, ft-lb:	1690	1310	1010	770	575
	arc, inches:		+0.8	0	-4.8	-14.9
Federal 55 Sierra BlitzKing	velocity, fps:	3800	3370	2990	2630	2310.
	energy, ft-lb:	1765	1390	1090	850	650
	arc, inches:		+0.8	0	-4.7	-14.4
Federal 55 Trophy Bonded	velocity, fps:	3700	3170	2690	2270	1880
	energy, ft-lb:	1670	1225	885	625	430
	arc, inches:		+1.0	0	-5.8	-18.5
Hornady 40 V-Max	velocity, fps:	4200	3678	3190	2739	2329
	energy, ft-lb:	1566	1201	904	666	482
	arc, inches:		+0.5	0	-4.0	-12.9
Hornady 50 V-Max	velocity, fps:	3850	3396	2970	2576	2215.
	energy, ft-lb:	1645	1280	979	736	545
	arc, inches:		+0.7	0	-4.8	-15.1
Hornady 50 SP	velocity, fps:	3850	3327	2862	2442	2060.
	energy, ft-lb:	1645	1228	909	662	471
	arc, inches:		+0.8	0	-5.1	-16.1
Hornady 55 V-Max	velocity, fps:	3680	3265	2876	2517	2183
	energy, ft-lb:	1654	1302	1010	772	582
	arc, inches:		+0.9	0	-5.3	-16.1
Hornady 60 Hollow Point	velocity, fps:	3600	3199	2824	2475	2156
	energy, ft-lb:	1727	1364	1063	816	619
	arc, inches:		+1.0	0	-5.4	-16.3
Norma 50 Soft Point	velocity, fps:	4019	3380	2826	2335	
	energy, ft-lb:	1794	1268	887	605	
	arc, inches:		+0.7	0	-5.1	

Centerfire Rifle Ballistics

.220 SWIFT TO .243 WINCHESTER

CARTRIDGE BULLET	RANGE, YARDS:	0	100	200	300	400
Rem. 50 Pointed Soft Point	velocity, fps:	3780	3158	2617	2135	1710
	energy, ft-lb:	1586	1107	760	506	325
	arc, inches:		+0.3	-1.4	-8.2	
Rem. 50 V-Max boat-tail (also in EtronX)	velocity, fps:	3780	3321	2908	2532	2185
	energy, ft-lb:	1586	1224	939	711	530
	arc, inches:		+0.8	0	-5.0	-15.4
Win. 40 Ballistic Silvertip	velocity, fps:	4050	3518	3048	2624	2238.
	energy, ft-lb:	1457	1099	825	611	445
	arc, inches:		+0.7	0	-4.4	-13.9
Win. 50 Pointed Soft Point	velocity, fps:	3870	3310	2816	2373	1972
	energy, ft-lb:	1663	1226	881	625	432
	arc, inches:		+0.8	0	-5.2	-16.7

.223 WSSM

CARTRIDGE BULLET	RANGE, YARDS:	0	100	200	300	400
Win. 55 Ballistic Silvertip	velocity, fps:	3850	3438	3064	2721	2402
	energy, ft-lb:	1810	1444	1147	904	704
	arc, inches:		+0.7	0	-4.4	-13.6
Win. 55 Pointed Softpoint	velocity, fps:	3850	3367	2934	2541	2181
	energy, ft-lb:	1810	1384	1051	789	581
	arc, inches:		+0.8	0	-4.9	-15.1
Win. 64 Power-Point	velocity, fps:	3600	3144	2732	2356	2011
	energy, ft-lb:	1841	1404	1061	789	574
	arc, inches:		+1.0	0	-5.7	-17.7

6MM PPC

CARTRIDGE BULLET	RANGE, YARDS:	0	100	200	300	400
A-Square 68 Berger	velocity, fps:	3100	2751	2428	2128	1850
	energy, ft-lb:	1451	1143	890	684	516
	arc, inches:		+1.5	0	-7.5	-22.6

6x70 R

CARTRIDGE BULLET	RANGE, YARDS:	0	100	200	300	400
Norma 95 Nosler Bal. Tip	velocity, fps:	2461	2231	2013	1809	
	energy, ft-lb:	1211	995	810	654	
	arc, inches:		+2.7	0	-11.3	

.243 WINCHESTER

CARTRIDGE BULLET	RANGE, YARDS:	0	100	200	300	400
Black Hills 55 Nosler B. Tip	velocity, fps:	3800				
	energy, ft-lb:	1763				
	arc, inches:					
Black Hills 95 Nosler B. Tip	velocity, fps:	2950				
	energy, ft-lb:	1836				
Federal 70 Nosler Bal. Tip	velocity, fps:	3400	3070	2760	2470	2200
	energy, ft-lb:	1795	1465	1185	950	755.
	arc, inches:		+1.1	0	-5.7	-17.1
Federal 70 Speer TNT HP	velocity, fps:	3400	3040	2700	2390	2100
	energy, ft-lb:	1795	1435	1135	890	685
	arc, inches:		+1.1	0	-5.9	-18.0
Federal 80 Sierra Pro-Hunter	velocity, fps:	3350	2960	2590	2260	1950
	energy, ft-lb:	1995	1550	1195	905	675
	arc, inches:		+1.3	0	-6.4	-19.7
Federal 85 Sierra GameKing BTHP	velocity, fps:	3320	3070	2830	2600	2380
	energy, ft-lb:	2080	1770	1510	1280	1070
	arc, inches:		+1.1	0	-5.5	-16.1
Federal 90 Trophy Bonded	velocity, fps:	3100	2850	2610	2380	2160.
	energy, ft-lb:	1920	1620	1360	1130	935
	arc, inches:		+1.4	0	-6.1	-19.2
Federal 100 Hi-Shok	velocity, fps:	2960	2700	2450	2220	1990
	energy, ft-lb:	1945	1615	1330	1090	880
	arc, inches:		+1.6	0	-7.5	-22.0
Federal 100 Sierra GameKing BTSP	velocity, fps:	2960	2760	2570	2380	2210
	energy, ft-lb:	1950	1690	1460	1260	1080
	arc, inches:		+1.5	0	-6.8	-19.8
Federal 100 Nosler Partition	velocity, fps:	2960	2730	2510	2300	2100
	energy, ft-lb:	1945	1650	1395	1170	975.

CARTRIDGE BULLET	RANGE, YARDS:	0	100	200	300	400
	arc, inches:		+1.6	0	-7.1	-20.9
Hornady 58 V-Max	velocity, fps:	3750	3319	2913	2539	2195
	energy, ft-lb:	1811	1418	1093	830	620
	arc, inches:		+1.2	0	-5.5	-16.4
Hornady 75 Hollow Point	velocity, fps:	3400	2970	2578	2219	1890
	energy, ft-lb:	1926	1469	1107	820	595
	arc, inches:		+1.2	0	-6.5	-20.3
Hornady 100 BTSP	velocity, fps:	2960	2728	2508	2299	2099
	energy, ft-lb:	1945	1653	1397	1174	979
	arc, inches:		+1.6	0	-7.2	-21.0
Hornady 100 BTSP LM	velocity, fps:	3100	2839	2592	2358	2138
	energy, ft-lb:	2133	1790	1491	1235	1014
	arc, inches:		+1.5	0	-6.8	-19.8
Norma 80 FMJ	velocity, fps:	3117	2750	2412	2098	
	energy, ft-lb:	1726	1344	1034	782	
	arc, inches:		+1.5	0	-7.5	
Norma 100 FMJ	velocity, fps:	3018	2747	2493	2252	
	energy, ft-lb:	2023	1677	1380	1126	
	arc, inches:		+1.5	0	-7.1	
Norma 100 Soft Point	velocity, fps:	3018	2748	2493	2252	
	energy, ft-lb:	2023	1677	1380	1126	
	arc, inches:		+1.5	0	-7.1	
Norma 100 Oryx	velocity, fps:	3018	2653	2316	2004	
	energy, ft-lb:	2023	1563	1191	892	
	arc, inches:		+1.7	0	-8.3	
PMC 80 Pointed Soft Point	velocity, fps:	2940	2684	2444	2215	1999
	energy, ft-lb:	1535	1280	1060	871	709
	arc, inches:		+1.7	0	-7.5	-22.1
PMC 85 Barnes XLC	velocity, fps:	3250	3022	2805	2598	2401
	energy, ft-lb:	1993	1724	1485	1274	1088
	arc, inches:		+1.6	0	-5.6	16.3
PMC 85 HP boat-tail	velocity, fps:	3275	2922	2596	2292	2009
	energy, ft-lb:	2024	1611	1272	991	761
	arc, inches:		+1.3	0	-6.5	-19.7
PMC 100 Pointed Soft Point	velocity, fps:	2743	2507	2283	2070	1869
	energy, ft-lb:	1670	1395	1157	951	776
	arc, inches:		+2.0	0	-8.7	-25.5
PMC 100 SP boat-tail	velocity, fps:	2960	2742	2534	2335	2144
	energy, ft-lb:	1945	1669	1425	1210	1021
	arc, inches:		+1.6	0	-7.0	-20.5
Rem. 75 AccuTip BT	velocity, fps:	3375	3065	2775	2504	2248
	energy, ft-lb:	1897	1564	1282	1044	842
	arc, inches:		+2.0	+1.8	-3.0	-13.3
Rem. 80 Pointed Soft Point	velocity, fps:	3350	2955	2593	2259	1951
	energy, ft-lb:	1993	1551	1194	906	676
	arc, inches:		+2.2	+2.0	-3.5	-15.8
Rem. 80 HP Power-Lokt	velocity, fps:	3350	2955	2593	2259	1951
	energy, ft-lb:	1993	1551	1194	906	676
	arc, inches:		+2.2	+2.0	-3.5	-15.8
Rem. 90 Nosler Bal. Tip (also in EtronX) or Scirocco	velocity, fps:	3120	2871	2635	2411	2199
	energy, ft-lb:	1946	1647	1388	1162	966
	arc, inches:		+1.4	0	-6.4	-18.8
Rem. 95 AccuTip	velocity, fps:	3120	2847	2590	2347	2118
	energy, ft-lb:	2053	1710	1415	1162	946
	arc, inches:		+1.5	0	-6.6	-19.5
Rem. 100 PSP Core-Lokt (also in EtronX)	velocity, fps:	2960	2697	2449	2215	1993
	energy, ft-lb:	1945	1615	1332	1089	882
	arc, inches:		+1.6	0	-7.5	-22.1
Rem. 100 PSP boat-tail	velocity, fps:	2960	2720	2492	2275	2069
	energy, ft-lb:	1945	1642	1378	1149	950
	arc, inches:		+2.8	+2.3	-3.8	-16.6
Speer 100 Grand Slam	velocity, fps:	2950	2684	2434	2197	
	energy, ft-lb:	1932	1600	1315	1072	

BALLISTICS

.243 WINCHESTER (continued)

CARTRIDGE BULLET	RANGE, YARDS:	0	100	200	300	400
Win. 55 Ballistic Silvertip	arc, inches:		+1.7	0	-7.6	-22.4
	velocity, fps:	4025	3597	3209	2853	2525
	energy, ft-lb:	1978	1579	1257	994	779
Win. 80 Pointed Soft Point	arc, inches:		+0.6	0	-4.0	-12.2
	velocity, fps:	3350	2955	2593	2259	1951.
	energy, ft-lb:	1993	1551	1194	906	676
Win. 95 Ballistic Silvertip	arc, inches:		+2.6	+2.1	-3.6	-16.2
	velocity, fps:	3100	2854	2626	2410	2203
	energy, ft-lb:	2021	1719	1455	1225	1024
Win. 95 Supreme Elite XP3	arc, inches:		+1.4	0	-6.4	-18.9
	velocity, fps:	3100	2864	2641	2428	2225
	energy, ft-lb:	2027	1730	1471	1243	1044
Win. 100 Power-Point	a rc, inches:		+1.4	0	-6.4	-18.7
	velocity, fps:	2960	2697	2449	2215	1993
	energy, ft-lb:	1945	1615	1332	1089	882
Win. 100 Power-Point Plus	arc, inches:		+1.9	0	-7.8	-22.6.
	velocity, fps:	3090	2818	2562	2321	2092
	energy, ft-lb:	2121	1764	1458	1196	972
	arc, inches:		+1.4	0	-6.7	-20.0

6MM REMINGTON

CARTRIDGE BULLET	RANGE, YARDS:	0	100	200	300	400
Federal 80 Sierra Pro-Hunter	velocity, fps:	3470	3060	2690	2350	2040
	energy, ft-lb:	2140	1665	1290	980	735
	arc, inches:		+1.1	0	-5.9	-18.2
Federal 100 Hi-Shok	velocity, fps:	3100	2830	2570	2330	2100
	energy, ft-lb:	2135	1775	1470	1205	985
	arc, inches:		+1.4	0	-6.7	-19.8
Federal 100 Nos. Partition	velocity, fps:	3100	2860	2640	2420	2220
	energy, ft-lb:	2135	1820	1545	1300	1090
	arc, inches:		+1.4	0	-6.3	-18.7
Hornady 100 SP boat-tail	velocity, fps:	3100	2861	2634	2419	2231
	energy, ft-lb:	2134	1818	1541	1300	1088
	arc, inches:		+1.3	0	-6.5	-18.9
Hornady 100 SPBT LM	velocity, fps:	3250	2997	2756	2528	2311
	energy, ft-lb:	2345	1995	1687	1418	1186
	arc, inches:		+1.6	0	-6.3	-18.2
Rem. 75 V-Max boat-tail	velocity, fps:	3400	3088	2797	2524	2267
	energy, ft-lb:	1925	1587	1303	1061	856
	arc, inches:		+1.9	+1.7	-3.0	-13.1
Rem. 100 PSP Core-Lokt	velocity, fps:	3100	2829	2573	2332	2104.
	energy, ft-lb:	2133	1777	1470	1207	983
	arc, inches:		+1.4	0	-6.7	-19.8
Rem. 100 PSP boat-tail	velocity, fps:	3100	2852	2617	2394	2183
	energy, ft-lb:	2134	1806	1521	1273	1058
	arc, inches:		+1.4	0	-6.5	-19.1
Win. 100 Power-Point	velocity, fps:	3100	2829	2573	2332	2104
	energy, ft-lb:	2133	1777	1470	1207	983
	arc, inches:		+1.7	0	-7.0	-20.4

.243 WSSM

CARTRIDGE BULLET	RANGE, YARDS:	0	100	200	300	400
Win. 55 Ballistic Silvertip	velocity, fps:	4060	3628	3237	2880	2550
	energy, ft-lb:	2013	1607	1280	1013	794
	arc, inches:		+0.6	0	-3.9	-12.0
Win. 95 Ballistic Silvertip	velocity, fps:	3250	3000	2763	2538	2325
	energy, ft-lb:	2258	1898	1610	1359	1140
	arc, inches:		+1.2	0	5.7	16.9
Win. 95 Supreme Elite XP3	velocity, fps	3150	2912	2686	2471	2266
	energy, ft-lb	2093	1788	1521	1287	1083
	arc, inches		+1.3	0	-6.1	-18.0
Win. 100 Power Point	velocity, fps:	3110	2838	2583	2341	2112
	energy, ft-lb:	2147	1789	1481	1217	991
	arc, inches:		+1.4	0	-6.6	-19.7

.240 WEATHERBY MAGNUM

CARTRIDGE BULLET	RANGE, YARDS:	0	100	200	300	400
Wby. 87 Pointed Expanding	velocity, fps:	3523	3199	2898	2617	2352
	energy, ft-lb:	2397	1977	1622	1323	1069
	arc, inches:		+2.7	+3.4	0	-8.4
Wby. 90 Barnes-X	velocity, fps:	3500	3222	2962	2717	2484
	energy, ft-lb:	2448	2075	1753	1475	1233
	arc, inches:		+2.6	+3.3	0	-8.0
Wby. 95 Nosler Bal. Tip	velocity, fps:	3420	3146	2888	2645	2414
	energy, ft-lb:	2467	2087	1759	1475	1229
	arc, inches:		+2.7	+3.5	0	-8.4
Wby. 100 Pointed Expanding	velocity, fps:	3406	3134	2878	2637	2408
	energy, ft-lb:	2576	2180	1839	1544	1287
	arc, inches:		+2.8	+3.5	0	-8.4
Wby. 100 Partition	velocity, fps:	3406	3136	2882	2642	2415
	energy, ft-lb:	2576	2183	1844	1550	1294
	arc, inches:		+2.8	+3.5	0	-8.4

.25-20 WINCHESTER

CARTRIDGE BULLET	RANGE, YARDS:	0	100	200	300	400
Rem. 86 Soft Point	velocity, fps:	1460	1194	1030	931	858
	energy, ft-lb:	407	272	203	165	141
	arc, inches:		0	-22.9	-78.9	-173.0
Win. 86 Soft Point	velocity, fps:	1460	1194	1030	931	858.
	energy, ft-lb:	407	272	203	165	141
	arc, inches:		0	-23.5	-79.6	-175.9

.25-35 WINCHESTER

CARTRIDGE BULLET	RANGE, YARDS:	0	100	200	300	400
Win. 117 Soft Point	velocity, fps:	2230	1866	1545	1282	1097
	energy, ft-lb:	1292	904	620	427	313
	arc, inches:		+2.1	-5.1	-27.0	-70.1

.250 SAVAGE

CARTRIDGE BULLET	RANGE, YARDS:	0	100	200	300	400
Rem. 100 Pointed SP	velocity, fps:	2820	2504	2210	1936	1684.
	energy, ft-lb:	1765	1392	1084	832	630
	arc, inches:		+2.0	0	-9.2	-27.7
Win. 100 Silvertip	velocity, fps:	2820	2467	2140	1839	1569
	energy, ft-lb:	1765	1351	1017	751	547
	arc, inches:		+2.4	0	-10.1	-30.5

.257 ROBERTS

CARTRIDGE BULLET	RANGE, YARDS:	0	100	200	300	400
Federal 120 Nosler Partition	velocity, fps:	2780	2560	2360	2160	1970
	energy, ft-lb:	2060	1750	1480	1240	1030
	arc, inches:		+1.9	0	-8.2	-24.0
Hornady 117 SP boat-tail	velocity, fps:	2780	2550	2331	2122	1925
	energy, ft-lb:	2007	1689	1411	1170	963
	arc, inches:		+1.9	0	-8.3	-24.4
Hornady 117 SP boat-tail LM	velocity, fps:	2940	2694	2460	2240	2031
	energy, ft-lb:	2245	1885	1572	1303	1071
	arc, inches:		+1.7	0	-7.6	-21.8
Rem. 117 SP Core-Lokt	velocity, fps:	2650	2291	1961	1663	1404
	energy, ft-lb:	1824	1363	999	718	512
	arc, inches:		+2.6	0	-11.7	-36.1
Win. 117 Power-Point	velocity, fps:	2780	2411	2071	1761	1488
	energy, ft-lb:	2009	1511	1115	806	576.
	arc, inches:		+2.6	0	-10.8	-33.0

.25-06 REMINGTON

CARTRIDGE BULLET	RANGE, YARDS:	0	100	200	300	400
Black Hills 100 Nos. Bal. Tip	velocity, fps:	3200				
	energy, ft-lb:	2273				
	arc, inches:					
Black Hills 100 Barnes XLC	velocity, fps:	3200				
	energy, ft-lb:	2273				
	arc, inches:					
Black Hills 115 Barnes X	velocity, fps:	2975				

Centerfire Rifle Ballistics

.25-06 REMINGTON TO 6.5X55 SWEDISH

CARTRIDGE BULLET	RANGE, YARDS:	0	100	200	300	400
	energy, ft-lb:	2259				
	arc, inches:					
Federal 90 Sierra Varminter	velocity, fps:	3440	3040	2680	2340	2030
	energy, ft-lb:	2365	1850	1435	1100	825
	arc, inches:		+1.1	0	-6.0	-18.3
Federal 100 Barnes XLC	velocity, fps:	3210	2970	2750	2540	2330
	energy, ft-lb:	2290	1965	1680	1430	1205
	arc, inches:		+1.2	0	-5.8	-17.0
Federal 100 Nosler Bal. Tip	velocity, fps:	3210	2960	2720	2490	2280
	energy, ft-lb:	2290	1940	1640	1380	1150.
	arc, inches:		+1.2	0	-6.0	-17.5
Federal 115 Nosler Partition	velocity, fps:	2990	2750	2520	2300	2100
	energy, ft-lb:	2285	1930	1620	1350	1120
	arc, inches:		+1.6	0	-7.0	-20.8
Federal 115 Trophy Bonded	velocity, fps:	2990	2740	2500	2270	2050
	energy, ft-lb:	2285	1910	1590	1310	1075
	arc, inches:		+1.6	0	-7.2	-21.1
Federal 117 Sierra Pro Hunt.	velocity, fps:	2990	2730	2480	2250	2030
	energy, ft-lb:	2320	1985	1645	1350	1100
	arc, inches:		+1.6	0	-7.2	-21.4
Federal 117 Sierra GameKing BTSP	velocity, fps:	2990	2770	2570	2370	2190
	energy, ft-lb:	2320	2000	1715	1465	1240
	arc, inches:		+1.5	0	-6.8	-19.9
Hornady 117 SP boat-tail	velocity, fps:	2990	2749	2520	2302	2096
	energy, ft-lb:	2322	1962	1649	1377	1141
	arc, inches:		+1.6	0	-7.0	-20.7
Hornady 117 SP boat-tail LM	velocity, fps:	3110	2855	2613	2384	2168
	energy, ft-lb:	2512	2117	1774	1476	1220
	arc, inches:		+1.8	0	-7.1	-20.3
PMC 100 SPBT	velocity, fps:	3200	2925	2650	2395	2145
	energy, ft-lb:	2273	1895	1561	1268	1019
	arc, inches:		+1.3	0	-6.3	-18.6
PMC 117 PSP	velocity, fps:	2950	2706	2472	2253	2047
	energy, ft-lb:	2261	1900	1588	1319	1088
	arc, inches:		+1.6	0	-7.3	-21.5
Rem. 100 PSP Core-Lokt	velocity, fps:	3230	2893	2580	2287	2014
	energy, ft-lb:	2316	1858	1478	1161	901
	arc, inches:		+1.3	0	-6.6	-19.8
Rem. 115 Core-Lokt Ultra	velocity, fps:	3000	2751	2516	2293	2081
	energy, ft-lb:	2298	1933	1616	1342	1106
	arc, inches:		+1.6	0	-7.1	-20.7
Rem. 120 PSP Core-Lokt	velocity, fps:	2990	2730	2484	2252	2032
	energy, ft-lb:	2382	1985	1644	1351	1100
	arc, inches:		+1.6	0	-7.2	-21.4
Speer 120 Grand Slam	velocity, fps:	3130	2835	2558	2298	
	energy, ft-lb:	2610	2141	1743	1407	
	arc, inches:		+1.4	0	-6.8	-20.1
Win. 85 Ballistic Silvertip	velocity, fps	3470	3156	2863	2589	2331
	energy, ft-lb:	2273	1880	1548	1266	1026
	arc, inches:		+1.0	0	-5.2	-15.7
Win. 90 Pos. Exp. Point	velocity, fps:	3440	3043	2680	2344	2034
	energy, ft-lb:	2364	1850	1435	1098	827
	arc, inches:		+2.4	+2.0	-3.4	-15.0
Win. 110 AccuBond CT	velocity, fps:	3100	2870	2651	2442	2243
	energy, ft-lb:	2347	2011	1716	1456	1228
	arc, inches:		+1.4	0	-6.3	-18.5
Win. 115 Ballistic Silvertip	velocity, fps:	3060	2825	2603	2390	2188
	energy, ft-lb:	2391	2038	1729	1459	1223
	arc, inches:		+1.4	0	-6.6	-19.2
Win. 120 Pos. Pt. Exp.	velocity, fps:	2990	2717	2459	2216	1987
	energy, ft-lb:	2382	1967	1612	1309	1053
	arc, inches:		+1.6	0	-7.4	-21.8

.25 WINCHESTER SUPER SHORT MAGNUM

CARTRIDGE BULLET	RANGE, YARDS:	0	100	200	300	400
Win. 85 Ballistic Silvertip	velocity, fps:	3470	3156	2863	2589	2331
	energy, ft-lb:	2273	1880	1548	1266	1026
	arc, inches:		+1.0	0	-5.2	-15.7
Win. 110 AccuBond CT	velocity, fps:	3100	2870	2651	2442	2243.
	energy, ft-lb:	2347	2011	1716	1456	1228
	arc, inches:		+1.4	0	-6.3	-18.5
Win. 115 Ballistic Silvertip	velocity, fps:	3060	2844	2639	2442	2254
	energy, ft-lb:	2392	2066	1778	1523	1298
	arc, inches:		+1.4	0	-6.4	-18.6
Win. 120 Pos. Pt. Exp.	velocity, fps:	2990	2717	2459	2216	1987
	energy, ft-lb:	2383	1967	1612	1309	1053
	arc, inches:		+1.6	0	-7.4	-21.8

.257 WEATHERBY MAGNUM

CARTRIDGE BULLET	RANGE, YARDS:	0	100	200	300	400
Federal 115 Nosler Partition	velocity, fps:	3150	2900	2660	2440	2220.
	energy, ft-lb:	2535	2145	1810	1515	1260
	arc, inches:		+1.3	0	-6.2	-18.4
Federal 115 Trophy Bonded	velocity, fps:	3150	2890	2640	2400	2180
	energy, ft-lb:	2535	2125	1775	1470	1210
	arc, inches:		+1.4	0	-6.3	-18.8
Wby. 87 Pointed Expanding	velocity, fps:	3825	3472	3147	2845	2563
	energy, ft-lb:	2826	2328	1913	1563	1269
	arc, inches:		+2.1	+2.8	0	-7.1
Wby. 100 Pointed Expanding	velocity, fps:	3602	3298	3016	2750	2500
	energy, ft-lb:	2881	2416	2019	1680	1388
	arc, inches:		+2.4	+3.1	0	-7.7
Wby. 115 Nosler Bal. Tip	velocity, fps:	3400	3170	2952	2745	2547
	energy, ft-lb:	2952	2566	2226	1924	1656.
	arc, inches:		+3.0	+3.5	0	-7.9
Wby. 115 Barnes X	velocity, fps:	3400	3158	2929	2711	2504
	energy, ft-lb:	2952	2546	2190	1877	1601
	arc, inches:		+2.7	+3.4	0	-8.1
Wby. 117 RN Expanding	velocity, fps:	3402	2984	2595	2240	1921
	energy, ft-lb:	3007	2320	1742	1302	956
	arc, inches:		+3.4	+4.31	0	-11.1
Wby. 120 Nosler Partition	velocity, fps:	3305	3046	2801	2570	2350
	energy, ft-lb:	2910	2472	2091	1760	1471
	arc, inches:		+3.0	+3.7	0	-8.9

6.53 (.257) SCRAMJET

CARTRIDGE BULLET	RANGE, YARDS:	0	100	200	300	400
Lazzeroni 85 Nosler Bal. Tip	velocity, fps:	3960	3652	3365	3096	2844
	energy, ft-lb:	2961	2517	2137	1810	1526
	arc, inches:		+1.7	+2.4	0	-6.0
Lazzeroni 100 Nosler Part.	velocity, fps:	3740	3465	3208	2965	2735
	energy, ft-lb:	3106	2667	2285	1953	1661.
	arc, inches:		+2.1	+2.7	0	-6.7

6.5x50 JAPANESE

CARTRIDGE BULLET	RANGE, YARDS:	0	100	200	300	400
Norma 156 Alaska	velocity, fps:	2067	1832	1615	1423	
	energy, ft-lb:	1480	1162	904	701	
	arc, inches:		+4.4	0	-17.8	

6.5x52 CARCANO

CARTRIDGE BULLET	RANGE, YARDS:	0	100	200	300	400
Norma 156 Alaska	velocity, fps:	2428	2169	1926	1702	
	energy, ft-lb:	2043	1630	1286	1004	
	arc, inches:		+2.9	0	-12.3	

6.5x55 SWEDISH

CARTRIDGE BULLET	RANGE, YARDS:	0	100	200	300	400
Federal 140 Hi-Shok	velocity, fps:	2600	2400	2220	2040	1860
	energy, ft-lb:	2100	1795	1525	1285	1080

CARTRIDGE BULLET	RANGE, YARDS:	0	100	200	300	400
	arc, inches:		+2.3	0	-9.4	-27.2
Federal 140 Trophy Bonded	velocity, fps:	2550	2350	2160	1980	1810
	energy, ft-lb:	2020	1720	1450	1220	1015
	arc, inches:		+2.4	0	-9.8	-28.4
Federal 140 Sierra MatchKg. BTHP	velocity, fps:	2630	2460	2300	2140	2000
	energy, ft-lb:	2140	1880	1640	1430	1235
	arc, inches:	+16.4	+28.8	+33.9	+31.8	
Hornady 129 SP LM	velocity, fps:	2770	2561	2361	2171	1994
	energy, ft-lb:	2197	1878	1597	1350	1138
	arc, inches:		+2.0	0	-8.2	-23.2
Hornady 140 SP Interlock	velocity, fps	2525	2341	2165	1996	1836
	energy, ft-lb:	1982	1704	1457	1239	1048
	arc, inches:		+2.4	0	-9.9	-28.5
Hornady140 SP LM	velocity, fps:	2740	2541	2351	2169	1999
	energy, ft-lb:	2333	2006	1717	1463	1242
	arc, inches:		+2.4	0	-8.7	-24.0
Norma 120 Nosler Bal. Tip	velocity, fps:	2822	2609	2407	2213	
	energy, ft-lb:	2123	1815	1544	1305	
	arc, inches:		+1.8	0	-7.8	
Norma 139 Vulkan	velocity, fps:	2854	2569	2302	2051	
	energy, ft-lb:	2515	2038	1636	1298	
	arc, inches:		+1.8	0	-8.4	
Norma 140 Nosler Partition	velocity, fps:	2789	2592	2403	2223	
	energy, ft-lb:	2419	2089	1796	1536	
	arc, inches:		+1.8	0	-7.8	
Norma 156 TXP Swift A-Fr.	velocity, fps:	2526	2276	2040	1818	
	energy, ft-lb:	2196	1782	1432	1138	
	arc, inches:		+2.6	0	-10.9	
Norma 156 Alaska	velocity, fps:	2559	2245	1953	1687	
	energy, ft-lb:	2269	1746	1322	986	
	arc, inches:		+2.7	0	-11.9	
Norma 156 Vulkan	velocity, fps:	2644	2395	2159	1937	
	energy, ft-lb:	2422	1987	1616	1301	
	arc, inches:		+2.2	0	-9.7	
Norma 156 Oryx	velocity, fps:	2559	2308	2070	1848	
	energy, ft-lb:	2269	1845	1485	1183	
	arc, inches:		+2.5	0	-10.6	
PMC 139 Pointed Soft Point	velocity, fps:	2850	2560	2290	2030	1790
	energy, ft-lb:	2515	2025	1615	1270	985
	arc, inches:		+2.2	0	-8.9	-26.3
PMC 140 HP boat-tail	velocity, fps:	2560	2398	2243	2093	1949
	energy, ft-lb:	2037	1788	1563	1361	1181
	arc, inches:		+2.3	0	-9.2	-26.4
PMC 140 SP boat-tail	velocity, fps:	2560	2386	2218	2057	1903
	energy, ft-lb:	2037	1769	1529	1315	1126
	arc, inches:		+2.3	0	-9.4	-27.1
PMC 144 FMJ	velocity, fps:	2650	2370	2110	1870	1650
	energy, ft-lb:	2425	1950	1550	1215	945
	arc, inches:		+2.7	0	-10.5	-30.9
Rem. 140 PSP Core-Lokt	velocity, fps:	2550	2353	2164	1984	1814
	energy, ft-lb:	2021	1720	1456	1224	1023
	arc, inches:		+2.4	0	-9.8	-27.0
Speer 140 Grand Slam	velocity, fps:	2550	2318	2099	1892	
	energy, ft-lb:	2021	1670	1369	1112	
	arc, inches:		+2.5	0	-10.4	-30.6
Win. 140 Soft Point	velocity, fps:	2550	2359	2176	2002	1836
	energy, ft-lb:	2022	1731	1473	1246	1048.
	arc, inches:		+2.4	0	-9.7	-28.1

6.5 GRENDEL

CARTRIDGE BULLET	RANGE, YARDS:	0	100	200	300	400
Hornady 123 A-MAX	velocity, fps:	2590	2420	2256	2099	1948
	energy, ft-lb:	1832	1599	1390	1203	1037
	arc, inches:	-2.4	+1.8	0	-8.6	-25.1
Hornady 123 SST	velocity, fps:	2620	2449	2284	2126	1974
	energy, ft-lb:	1875	1638	1425	1234	1064
	arc, inches:	-2.4	+1.7	0	-8.4	-24.5

6.5 CREEDMOOR

CARTRIDGE BULLET	RANGE, YARDS:	0	100	200	300	400
Hornady 120 GMX	velocity, fps:	3050	2850	2659	2476	2300
	energy, ft-lb:	2479	2164	1884	1634	1410
	arc, inches:	-1.5	+1.4	0	-6.3	-18.3
Hornady 129 SST	velocity, fps:	2950	2756	2571	2394	2223
	energy, ft-lb:	2493	2176	1894	1641	1415
	arc, inches:	-1.5	+1.5	0	-6.8	-19.7
Hornady 140 A-MAX	velocity, fps:	2710	2557	2410	2267	2129
	energy, ft-lb:	2283	2033	1805	1598	1410
	arc, inches:	-1.5	+1.9	0	-7.9	-22.6
Nosler 140 BT	velocity, fps:	2550	2380	2217	2060	1910
	energy, ft-lb:	2021	1761	1527	1319	1134
	arc, inches:	-1.5	+2.3	0	-9.4	-27.0

.260 REMINGTON

CARTRIDGE BULLET	RANGE, YARDS:	0	100	200	300	400
Federal 140 Sierra GameKing BTSP	velocity, fps:	2750	2570	2390	2220	2060
	energy, ft-lb:	2350	2045	1775	1535	1315
	arc, inches:		+1.9	0	-8.0	-23.1
Federal 140 Trophy Bonded	velocity, fps:	2750	2540	2340	2150	1970
	energy, ft-lb:	2350	2010	1705	1440	1210
	arc, inches:		+1.9	0	-8.4	-24.1
Rem. 120 Nosler Bal. Tip	velocity, fps:	2890	2688	2494	2309	2131
	energy, ft-lb:	2226	1924	1657	1420	1210
	arc, inches:		+1.7	0	-7.3	-21.1
Rem. 120 AccuTip	velocity, fps:	2890	2697	2512	2334	2163
	energy, ft-lb:	2392	2083	1807	1560	1340
	arc, inches:		+1.6	0	-7.2	-20.7
Rem. 125 Nosler Partition	velocity, fps:	2875	2669	2473	2285	2105.
	energy, ft-lb:	2294	1977	1697	1449	1230
	arc, inches:	+1.71	0	-7.4	-21.4	
Rem. 140 PSP Core-Lokt (and C-L Ultra)	velocity, fps:	2750	2544	2347	2158	1979
	energy, ft-lb:	2351	2011	1712	1448	1217
	arc, inches:		+1.9	0	-8.3	-24.0
Speer 140 Grand Slam	velocity, fps:	2750	2518	2297	2087	
	energy, ft-lb:	2351	1970	1640	1354	
	arc, inches:		+2.3	0	-8.9	-25.8

6.5/284

CARTRIDGE BULLET	RANGE, YARDS:	0	100	200	300	400
Norma 120 Nosler Bal. Tip	velocity, fps:	3117	2890	2674	2469	
	energy, ft-lb:	2589	2226	1906	1624	
	arc, inches:		+1.3	0	-6.2	
Norma 140 Nosler Part.	velocity, fps:	2953	2750	2557	2371	
	energy, ft-lb:	2712	2352	2032	1748	
	arc, inches:		+1.5	0	-6.8	

6.5/284 NORMA

CARTRIDGE BULLET	RANGE, YARDS:	0	100	200	300	400
Nosler 120 Ballistic Tip	velocity, fps:	3000	2792	2594	2404	2223
	energy, ft-lb:	2398	2077	1793	1540	1316
	arc, inches:	-1.5	+1.4	0	-6.6	-17.1
Nosler 125 PT	velocity, fps:	3000	2788	2585	2392	2207
	energy, ft-lb:	2497	2157	1855	1588	1352
	arc, inches:	-1.5	+1.5	0	-6.7	-19.5
Nosler 130 AccuBond	velocity, fps:	2900	2709	2526	2351	2182
	energy, ft-lb:	2427	2118	1842	1595	1374
	arc, inches:	-1.5	+1.5	0	-6.9	-18.4

6.5 REMINGTON MAGNUM

CARTRIDGE BULLET	RANGE, YARDS:	0	100	200	300	400
Nosler 125 PT	velocity, fps:	3025	2811	2608	2414	2228
	energy, ft-lb:	2539	2194	1888	1617	1377
	arc, inches:	-1.5	+1.5	0	-6.6	-19.1

Centerfire Rifle Ballistics

6.5 REMINGTON MAGNUM TO .270 WINCHESTER

CARTRIDGE BULLET	RANGE, YARDS:	0	100	200	300	400
Rem. 120 Core-Lokt PSP	velocity, fps:	3210	2905	2621	2353	2102
	energy, ft-lb:	2745	2248	1830	1475	1177
	arc, inches:		+2.7	+2.1	-3.5	-15.5

.264 WINCHESTER MAGNUM

CARTRIDGE BULLET	RANGE, YARDS:	0	100	200	300	400
Nosler 100 Ballistic Tip	velocity, fps:	3400	3105	2829	2569	2324
	energy, ft-lb:	2567	2141	1777	1465	1199
	arc, inches:	-1.5	+1.0	0	-5.5	-16.1
Nosler 130 AccuBond	velocity, fps:	3100	2900	2709	2527	2351
	energy, ft-lb:	2774	2428	2119	1843	1595
	arc, inches:	-1.5	+1.2	0	-6.0	-17.5
Rem. 140 PSP Core-Lokt	velocity, fps:	3030	2782	2548	2326	2114
	energy, ft-lb:	2854	2406	2018	1682	1389
	arc, inches:		+1.5	0	-6.9	-20.2
Win. 140 Power-Point	velocity, fps:	3030	2782	2548	2326	2114.
	energy, ft-lb:	2854	2406	2018	1682	1389
	arc, inches:		+1.8	0	-7.2	-20.8

6.8MM REMINGTON SPC

CARTRIDGE BULLET	RANGE, YARDS:	0	100	200	300	400
Hornady 110 BTHP	velocity, fps:	2570	2332	2107	1895	1697
	energy, ft-lb:	1613	1328	1084	877	703
	arc, inches:	-2.4	+2.0	0	-9.9	-29.5
Hornady 120 SST	velocity, fps:	2460	2250	2051	1863	1687
	energy, ft-lb:	1612	1349	1121	925	758
	arc, inches:	-2.4	+2.3	0	-10.5	-31.1
Rem. 115 Open Tip Match (and HPBT Match)	velocity, fps:	2800	2535	2285	2049	1828
	energy, ft-lb:	2002	1641	1333	1072	853
	arc, inches:		+2.0	0	-8.8	-26.2
Rem. 115 Metal Case	velocity, fps:	2800	2523	2262	2017	1789
	energy, ft-lb:	2002	1625	1307	1039	817
	arc, inches:		+2.0	0	-8.8	-26.2
Rem. 115 Sierra HPBT (2005; all vel. @ 2775)	velocity, fps:	2775	2511	2263	2028	1809
	energy, ft-lb:	1966	1610	1307	1050	835
	arc, inches:		+2.0	0	-8.8	-26.2.
Rem. 115 CL Ultra	velocity, fps:	2775	2472	2190	1926	1683
	energy, ft-lb:	1966	1561	1224	947	723
	arc, inches:		+2.1	0	-9.4	-28.2

.270 WINCHESTER

CARTRIDGE BULLET	RANGE, YARDS:	0	100	200	300	400
Black Hills 130 Nos. Bal. T.	velocity, fps:	2950				
	energy, ft-lb:	2512				
	arc, inches:					
Black Hills 130 Barnes XLC	velocity, ft-lb:	2950				
	energy, ft-lb:	2512				
	arc, inches:					
Federal 130 Hi-Shok	velocity, fps:	3060	2800	2560	2330	2110
	energy, ft-lb:	2700	2265	1890	1565	1285
	arc, inches:		+1.5	0	-6.8	-20.0
Federal 130 Sierra Pro-Hunt.	velocity, fps:	3060	2830	2600	2390	2190
	energy, ft-lb:	2705	2305	1960	1655	1390
	arc, inches:		+1.4	0	-6.4	-19.0
Federal 130 Sierra GameKing	velocity, fps:	3060	2830	2620	2410	2220.
	energy, ft-lb:	2700	2320	1980	1680	1420
	arc, inches:		+1.4	0	-6.5	-19.0
Federal 130 Nosler Bal. Tip	velocity, fps:	3060	2840	2630	2430	2230
	energy, ft-lb:	2700	2325	1990	1700	1440
	arc, inches:		+1.4	0	-6.5	-18.8
Federal 130 Nos. Partition And Solid Base	velocity, fps:	3060	2830	2610	2400	2200
	energy, ft-lb:	2705	2310	1965	1665	1400
	arc, inches:		+1.4	0	-6.5	-19.1.
Federal 130 Barnes XLC And Triple Shock	velocity, fps:	3060	2840	2620	2420	2220
	energy, ft-lb:	2705	2320	1985	1690	1425
	arc, inches:		+1.4	0	-6.4	-18.9

CARTRIDGE BULLET	RANGE, YARDS:	0	100	200	300	400
Federal 130 Trophy Bonded	velocity, fps:	3060	2810	2570	2340	2130
	energy, ft-lb:	2705	2275	1905	1585	1310
	arc, inches:		+1.5	0	-6.7	-19.8
Federal 140 Trophy Bonded	velocity, fps:	2940	2700	2480	2260	2060
	energy, ft-lb:	2685	2270	1905	1590	1315
	arc, inches:		+1.6	0	-7.3	-21.5
Federal 140 Tr. Bonded HE	velocity, fps:	3100	2860	2620	2400	2200.
	energy, ft-lb:	2990	2535	2140	1795	1500
	arc, inches:		+1.4	0	-6.4	-18.9
Federal 140 Nos. AccuBond	velocity, fps:	2950	2760	2580	2400	2230.
	energy, ft-lb:	2705	2365	2060	1790	1545
	arc, inches:		+1.5	0	-6.7	-19.6
Federal 150 Hi-Shok RN	velocity, fps:	2850	2500	2180	1890	1620
	energy, ft-lb:	2705	2085	1585	1185	870
	arc, inches:		+2.0	0	-9.4	-28.6
Federal 150 Sierra GameKing	velocity, fps:	2850	2660	2480	2300	2130
	energy, ft-lb:	2705	2355	2040	1760	1510
	arc, inches:		+1.7	0	-7.4	-21.4
Federal 150 Sierra GameKing HE	velocity, fps:	3000	2800	2620	2430	2260
	energy, ft-lb:	2995	2615	2275	1975	1700
	arc, inches:		+1.5	0	-6.5	-18.9
Federal 150 Nosler Partition	velocity, fps:	2850	2590	2340	2100	1880.
	energy, ft-lb:	2705	2225	1815	1470	1175
	arc, inches:		+1.9	0	-8.3	-24.4
Hornady 130 SST (or Interbond)	velocity, fps:	3060	2845	2639	2442	2254
	energy, ft-lb:	2700	2335	2009	1721	1467
	arc, inches:		+1.4	0	-6.6	-19.1
Hornady 130 SST LM (or Interbond)	velocity, fps:	3215	2998	2790	2590	2400
	energy, ft-lb:	2983	2594	2246	1936	1662
	arc, inches:		+1.2	0	-5.8	-17.0
Hornady 140 SP boat-tail	velocity, fps:	2940	2747	2562	2385	2214
	energy, ft-lb:	2688	2346	2041	1769	1524
	arc, inches:		+1.6	0	-7.0	-20.2
Hornady 140 SP boat-tail LM	velocity, fps:	3100	2894	2697	2508	2327.
	energy, ft-lb:	2987	2604	2261	1955	1684
	arc, inches:		+1.4	0	6.3	-18.3
Hornady 150 SP	velocity, fps:	2800	2684	2478	2284	2100
	energy, ft-lb:	2802	2400	2046	1737	1469
	arc, inches:		+1.7	0	-7.4	-21.6
Norma 130 SP	velocity, fps:	3140	2862	2601	2354	
	energy, ft-lb:	2847	2365	1953	1600	
	arc, inches:		+1.3	0	-6.5	
Norma 130 FMJ	velocity, fps:	2887	2634	2395	2169	
	energy, ft-lb:					
	arc, inches:		+1.8	0	-7.8	
Norma 150 SP	velocity, fps:	2799	2555	2323	2104	
	energy, ft-lb:	2610	2175	1798	1475	
	arc, inches:		+1.9	0	-8.3	
Norma 150 Oryx	velocity, fps:	2854	2608	2376	2155	
	energy, ft-lb:	2714	2267	1880	1547	
	arc, inches:		+1.8	0	-8.0	
PMC 130 Barnes X	velocity, fps:	2910	2717	2533	2356	2186
	energy, ft-lb:	2444	2131	1852	1602	1379
	arc, inches:		+1.6	0	-7.1	-20.4
PMC 130 SP boat-tail	velocity, fps:	3050	2830	2620	2421	2229
	energy, ft-lb:	2685	2312	1982	1691	1435
	arc, inches:		+1.5	0	-6.5	-19.0
PMC 130 Pointed Soft Point	velocity, fps:	2950	2691	2447	2217	2001
	energy, ft-lb:	2512	2090	1728	1419	1156
	arc, inches:		+1.6	0	-7.5	-22.1
PMC 150 Barnes X	velocity, fps:	2700	2541	2387	2238	2095
	energy, ft-lb:	2428	2150	1897	1668	1461
	arc, inches:		+2.0	0	-8.1	-23.1

BALLISTICS

Centerfire Rifle Ballistics

.270 WINCHESTER TO .270 WINCHESTER SHORT MAGNUM

CARTRIDGE BULLET	RANGE, YARDS:	0	100	200	300	400
PMC 150 SP boat-tail	velocity, fps:	2850	2660	2477	2302	2134
	energy, ft-lb:	2705	2355	2043	1765	1516.
	arc, inches:		+1.7	0	-7.4	-21.4
PMC 150 Pointed Soft Point	velocity, fps:	2750	2530	2321	2123	1936
	energy, ft-lb:	2519	2131	1794	1501	1248
	arc, inches:		+2.0	0	-8.4	-24.6
Rem. 100 Pointed Soft Point	velocity, fps:	3320	2924	2561	2225	1916
	energy, ft-lb:	2448	1898	1456	1099	815
	arc, inches:		+2.3	+2.0	-3.6	-16.2
Rem. 115 PSP Core-Lokt mr	velocity, fps:	2710	2412	2133	1873	1636
	energy, ft-lb:	1875	1485	1161	896	683
	arc, inches:		+1.0	-2.7	-14.2	-35.6
Rem. 130 PSP Core-Lokt	velocity, fps:	3060	2776	2510	2259	2022
	energy, ft-lb:	2702	2225	1818	1472	1180
	arc, inches:		+1.5	0	-7.0	-20.9
Rem. 130 Bronze Point	velocity, fps:	3060	2802	2559	2329	2110
	energy, ft-lb:	2702	2267	1890	1565	1285
	arc, inches:		+1.5	0	-6.8	-20.0
Rem. 130 Swift Scirocco	velocity, fps:	3060	2838	2677	2425	2232
	energy, ft-lb:	2702	2325	1991	1697	1438
	arc, inches:		+1.4	0	-6.5	-18.8
Rem. 130 AccuTip BT	velocity, fps:	3060	2845	2639	2442	2254
	energy, ft-lb:	2702	2336	2009	1721	1467
	arc, inches:		+1.4	0	-6.4	-18.6
Rem. 140 Swift A-Frame	velocity, fps:	2925	2652	2394	2152	1923
	energy, ft-lb:	2659	2186	1782	1439	1150
	arc, inches:		+1.7	0	-7.8	-23.2
Rem. 140 PSP boat-tail	velocity, fps:	2960	2749	2548	2355	2171
	energy, ft-lb:	2723	2349	2018	1724	1465
	arc, inches:		+1.6	0	-6.9	-20.1
Rem. 140 Nosler Bal. Tip	velocity, fps:	2960	2754	2557	2366	2187
	energy, ft-lb:	2724	2358	2032	1743	1487
	arc, inches:		+1.6	0	-6.9	-20.0
Rem. 140 PSP C-L Ultra	velocity, fps:	2925	2667	2424	2193	1975
	energy, ft-lb:	2659	2211	1826	1495	1212
	arc, inches:		+1.7	0	-7.6	-22.5
Rem. 150 SP Core-Lokt	velocity, fps:	2850	2504	2183	1886	1618
	energy, ft-lb:	2705	2087	1587	1185	872
	arc, inches:		+2.0	0	-9.4	-28.6
Rem. 150 Nosler Partition	velocity, fps:	2850	2652	2463	2282	2108
	energy, ft-lb:	2705	2343	2021	1734	1480
	arc, inches:		+1.7	0	-7.5	-21.6
Speer 130 Grand Slam	velocity, fps:	3050	2774	2514	2269	
	energy, ft-lb:	2685	2221	1824	1485	
	arc, inches:		+1.5	0	-7.0	-20.9
Speer 150 Grand Slam	velocity, fps:	2830	2594	2369	2156	
	energy, ft-lb:	2667	2240	1869	1548	
	arc, inches:		+1.8	0	-8.1	-23.6
Win. 130 Power-Point	velocity, fps:	3060	2802	2559	2329	2110
	energy, ft-lb:	2702	2267	1890	1565	1285.
	arc, inches:		+1.8	0	-7.1	-20.6
Win. 130 Power-Point Plus	velocity, fps:	3150	2881	2628	2388	2161
	energy, ft-lb:	2865	2396	1993	1646	1348
	arc, inches:		+1.3	0	-6.4	-18.9
Win. 130 Silvertip	velocity, fps:	3060	2776	2510	2259	2022.
	energy, ft-lb:	2702	2225	1818	1472	1180
	arc, inches:		+1.8	0	-7.4	-21.6
Win. 130 Ballistic Silvertip	velocity, fps:	3050	2828	2618	2416	2224
	energy, ft-lb:	2685	2309	1978	1685	1428
	arc, inches:		+1.4	0	-6.5	-18.9
Win. 140 AccuBond	velocity, fps:	2950	2751	2560	2378	2203
	energy, ft-lb:	2705	2352	2038	1757	1508
	arc, inches:		+1.6	0	-6.9	-19.9
Win. 140 Fail Safe	velocity, fps:	2920	2671	2435	2211	1999
	energy, ft-lb:	2651	2218	1843	1519	1242
	arc, inches:		+1.7	0	-7.6	-22.3
Win. 150 Power-Point	velocity, fps:	2850	2585	2336	2100	1879
	energy, ft-lb:	2705	2226	1817	1468	1175
	arc, inches:		+2.2	0	-8.6	-25.0
Win. 150 Power-Point Plus	velocity, fps:	2950	2679	2425	2184	1957
	energy, ft-lb:	2900	2391	1959	1589	1276
	arc, inches:		+1.7	0	-7.6	-22.6
Win. 150 Partition Gold	velocity, fps:	2930	2693	2468	2254	2051
	energy, ft-lb:	2860	2416	2030	1693	1402
	arc, inches:		+1.7	0	-7.4	-21.6
Win. 150 Supreme Elite XP3	velocity, fps:	2950	2763	2583	2411	2245
	energy, ft-lb:	2898	2542	2223	1936	1679
	arc, inches:		+1.5	0	-6.9	-15.5

.270 WINCHESTER SHORT MAGNUM

CARTRIDGE BULLET	RANGE, YARDS:	0	100	200	300	400
Black Hills 140 AccuBond	velocity, fps:	3100				
	energy, ft-lb:	2987				
	arc, inches:					
Federal 130 Nos. Bal. Tip	velocity, fps:	3300	3070	2840	2630	2430
	energy, ft-lb:	3145	2710	2335	2000	1705
	arc, inches:		+1.1	0	-5.4	-15.8
Federal 130 Nos. Partition And Nos. Solid Base And Barnes TS	velocity, fps:	3280	3040	2810	2590	2380
	energy, ft-lb:	3105	2665	2275	1935	1635
	arc, inches:		+1.1	0	-5.6	-16.3
Federal 140 Nos. AccuBond	velocity, fps	3200	3000	2810	2630	2450
	energy, ft-lb:	3185	2795	2455	2145	1865
	arc, inches:		+1.2	0	-5.6	-16.2
Federal 140 Trophy Bonded	velocity, fps:	3130	2870	2640	2410	2200
	energy, ft-lb:	3035	2570	2160	1810	1500
	arc, inches:		+1.4	0	-6.3	18.7
Federal 150 Nos. Partition	velocity, fps:	3160	2950	2750	2550	2370
	energy, ft-lb:	3325	2895	2515	2175	1870
	arc, inches:		+1.3	0	-5.9	-17.0
Norma 130 FMJ	velocity, fps:	3150	2882	2630	2391	
	energy, ft-lb:					
	arc, inches:		+1.5	0	-6.4	
Norma 130 Ballistic ST	velocity, fps:	3281	3047	2825	2614	
	energy, ft-lb:	3108	2681	2305	1973	
	arc, inches:		+1.2	0	-5.5	
Norma 140 Barnes X TS	velocity, fps:	3150	2952	2762	2580	
	energy, ft-lb:	3085	2709	2372	2070	
	arc, inches:		+1.3	0	-5.8	
Norma 150 Nosler Bal. Tip	velocity, fps:	3280	3046	2824	2613	
	energy, ft-lb:	3106	2679	2303	1972	
	arc, inches:		+1.1	0	-5.4	
Norma 150 Oryx	velocity, fps:	3117	2856	2611	2378	
	energy, ft-lb:	3237	2718	2271	1884	
	arc, inches:		+1.4	0	-6.5	
Win. 130 Bal. Silvertip	velocity, fps:	3275	3041	2820	2609	2408
	energy, ft-lb:	3096	2669	2295	1964	1673
	arc, inches:		+1.1	0	-5.5	-16.1
Win. 140 AccuBond	velocity, fps:	3200	2989	2789	2597	2413
	energy, ft-lb:	3184	2779	2418	2097	1810
	arc, inches:		+1.2	0	-5.7	-16.5
Win. 140 Fail Safe	velocity, fps:	3125	2865	2619	2386	2165
	energy, ft-lb:	3035	2550	2132	1769	1457
	arc, inches:		+1.4	0	-6.5	-19.0
Win. 150 Ballistic Silvertip	velocity, fps:	3120	2923	2734	2554	2380.
	energy, ft-lb:	3242	2845	2490	2172	1886.
	arc, inches:		+1.3	0	-5.9	-17.2

Centerfire Rifle Ballistics

.270 WINCHESTER SHORT MAGNUM TO 7MM-08 REMINGTON

CARTRIDGE BULLET	RANGE, YARDS:	0	100	200	300	400
Win. 150 Power Point	velocity, fps:	3150	2867	2601	2350	2113
	energy, ft-lb:	3304	2737	2252	1839	1487
	arc, inches:		+1.4	0	-6.5	-19.4
Win. 150 Supreme Elite XP3	velocity, fps:	3120	2926	2740	2561	2389
	energy, ft-lb:	3242	2850	2499	2184	1901
	arc, inches:		+1.3	0	-5.9	-17.1

.270 WEATHERBY MAGNUM

CARTRIDGE BULLET	RANGE, YARDS:	0	100	200	300	400
Federal 130 Nosler Partition	velocity, fps:	3200	2960	2740	2520	2320
	energy, ft-lb:	2955	2530	2160	1835	1550
	arc, inches:		+1.2	0	-5.9	-17.3
Federal 130 Sierra GameKing BTSP	velocity, fps:	3200	2980	2780	2580	2400
	energy, ft-lb:	2955	2570	2230	1925	1655
	arc, inches:		+1.2	0	-5.7	-16.6
Federal 140 Trophy Bonded	velocity, fps:	3100	2840	2600	2370	2150.
	energy, ft-lb:	2990	2510	2100	1745	1440
	arc, inches:		+1.4	0	-6.6	-19.3
Wby. 100 Pointed Expanding	velocity, fps:	3760	3396	3061	2751	2462
	energy, ft-lb:	3139	2560	2081	1681	1346
	arc, inches:		+2.3	+3.0	0	-7.6
Wby. 130 Pointed Expanding	velocity, fps:	3375	3123	2885	2659	2444
	energy, ft-lb:	3288	2815	2402	2041	1724
	arc, inches:		+2.8	+3.5	0	-8.4
Wby. 130 Nosler Partition	velocity, fps:	3375	3127	2892	2670	2458.
	energy, ft-lb:	3288	2822	2415	2058	1744
	arc, inches:		+2.8	+3.5	0	-8.3
Wby. 140 Nosler Bal. Tip	velocity, fps:	3300	3077	2865	2663	2470.
	energy, ft-lb:	3385	2943	2551	2204	1896
	arc, inches:		+2.9	+3.6	0	-8.4
Wby. 140 Barnes X	velocity, fps:	3250	3032	2825	2628	2438
	energy, ft-lb:	3283	2858	2481	2146	1848
	arc, inches:		+3.0	+3.7	0	-8.7
Wby. 150 Pointed Expanding	velocity, fps:	3245	3028	2821	2623	2434
	energy, ft-lb:	3507	3053	2650	2292	1973
	arc, inches:		+3.0	+3.7	0	-8.7
Wby. 150 Nosler Partition	velocity, fps:	3245	3029	2823	2627	2439.
	energy, ft-lb:	3507	3055	2655	2298	1981
	arc, inches:		+3.0	+3.7	0	-8.

7-30 WATERS

CARTRIDGE BULLET	RANGE, YARDS:	0	100	200	300	400
Federal 120 Sierra GameKing BTSP	velocity, fps:	2700	2300	1930	1600	1330.
	energy, ft-lb:	1940	1405	990	685	470
	arc, inches:		+2.6	0	-12.0	-37.6

7MM MAUSER (7X57)

CARTRIDGE BULLET	RANGE, YARDS:	0	100	200	300	400
Federal 140 Sierra Pro-Hunt.	velocity, fps:	2660	2450	2260	2070	1890.
	energy, ft-lb:	2200	1865	1585	1330	1110
	arc, inches:		+2.1	0	-9.0	-26.1
Federal 140 Nosler Partition	velocity, fps:	2660	2450	2260	2070	1890.
	energy, ft-lb:	2200	1865	1585	1330	1110
	arc, inches:		+2.1	0	-9.0	-26.1
Federal 175 Hi-Shok RN	velocity, fps:	2440	2140	1860	1600	1380
	energy, ft-lb:	2315	1775	1340	1000	740
	arc, inches:		+3.1	0	-13.3	-40.1
Hornady 139 SP boat-tail	velocity, fps:	2700	2504	2316	2137	1965
	energy, ft-lb:	2251	1936	1656	1410	1192
	arc, inches:		+2.0	0	-8.5	-24.9
Hornady 139 SP Interlock	velocity, fps:	2680	2455	2241	2038	1846
	energy, ft-lb:	2216	1860	1550	1282	1052
	arc, inches:		+2.1	0	-9.1	-26.6
Hornady 139 SP boat-tail LM	velocity, fps:	2830	2620	2450	2250	2070
	energy, ft-lb:	2475	2135	1835	1565	1330
	arc, inches:		+1.8	0	-7.6	-22.1
Hornady 139 SP LM	velocity, fps:	2950	2736	2532	2337	2152.
	energy, ft-lb:	2686	2310	1978	1686	1429
	arc, inches:		+2.0	0	-7.6	-21.5
Norma 150 Soft Point	velocity, fps:	2690	2479	2278	2087	
	energy, ft-lb:	2411	2048	1729	1450	
	arc, inches:		+2.0	0	-8.8	
PMC 140 Pointed Soft Point	velocity, fps:	2660	2450	2260	2070	1890
	energy, ft-lb:	2200	1865	1585	1330	1110.
	arc, inches:		+2.4	0	-9.6	-27.3
PMC 175 Soft Point	velocity, fps:	2440	2140	1860	1600	1380
	energy, ft-lb:	2315	1775	1340	1000	740
	arc, inches:		+1.5	-3.6	-18.6	-46.8
Rem. 140 PSP Core-Lokt	velocity, fps:	2660	2435	2221	2018	1827
	energy, ft-lb:	2199	1843	1533	1266	1037
	arc, inches:		+2.2	0	-9.2	-27.4
Win. 145 Power-Point	velocity, fps:	2660	2413	2180	1959	1754
	energy, ft-lb:	2279	1875	1530	1236	990
	arc, inches:		+1.1	-2.8	-14.1	-34.4

7x57 R

CARTRIDGE BULLET	RANGE, YARDS:	0	100	200	300	400
Norma 150 FMJ	velocity, fps:	2690	2489	2296	2112	
	energy, ft-lb:	2411	2063	1756	1486	
	arc, inches:		+2.0	0	-8.6	
Norma 154 Soft Point	velocity, fps:	2625	2417	2219	2030	
	energy, ft-lb:	2357	1999	1684	1410	
	arc, inches:		+2.2	0	-9.3	
Norma 156 Oryx	velocity, fps:	2608	2346	2099	1867	
	energy, ft-lb:	2357	1906	1526	1208	
	arc, inches:		+2.4	0	-10.3	

7MM-08 REMINGTON

CARTRIDGE BULLET	RANGE, YARDS:	0	100	200	300	400
Black Hills 140 AccuBond	velocity, fps:	2700				
	energy, ft-lb:					
	arc, inches:					
Federal 140 Nosler Partition	velocity, fps:	2800	2590	2390	2200	2020
	energy, ft-lb:	2435	2085	1775	1500	1265
	arc, inches:		+1.8	0	-8.0	-23.1
Federal 140 Nosler Bal. Tip And AccuBond	velocity, fps:	2800	2610	2430	2260	2100
	energy, ft-lb:	2440	2135	1840	1590	1360.
	arc, inches:		+1.8	0	-7.7	-22.3
Federal 140 Tr. Bonded HE	velocity, fps:	2950	2660	2390	2140	1900
	energy, ft-lb:	2705	2205	1780	1420	1120
	arc, inches:		+1.7	0	-7.9	-23.2
Federal 150 Sierra Pro-Hunt.	velocity, fps:	2650	2440	2230	2040	1860
	energy, ft-lb:	2340	1980	1660	1390	1150
	arc, inches:		+2.2	0	-9.2	-26.7
Hornady 139 SP boat-tail LM	velocity, fps:	3000	2790	2590	2399	2216
	energy, ft-lb:	2777	2403	2071	1776	1515
	arc, inches:		+1.5	0	-6.7	-19.4
Norma 140 Ballistic ST	velocity, fps:	2822	2633	2452	2278	
	energy, ft-lb:	2476	2156	1870	1614	
	arc, inches:		+1.8	0	-7.6	
PMC 139 PSP	velocity, fps:	2850	2610	2384	2170	1969
	energy, ft-lb:	2507	2103	1754	1454	1197
	arc, inches:		+1.8	0	-7.9	-23.3
Rem. 120 Hollow Point	velocity, fps:	3000	2725	2467	2223	1992
	energy, ft-lb:	2398	1979	1621	1316	1058
	arc, inches:		+1.6	0	-7.3	-21.7
Rem. 140 PSP Core-Lokt	velocity, fps:	2860	2625	2402	2189	1988
	energy, ft-lb:	2542	2142	1793	1490	1228
	arc, inches:		+1.8	0	-7.8	-22.9
Rem. 140 PSP boat-tail	velocity, fps:	2860	2656	2460	2273	2094
	energy, ft-lb:	2542	2192	1881	1606	1363
	arc, inches:		+1.7	0	-7.5	-21.7

BALLISTICS

BALLISTICS

CARTRIDGE BULLET	RANGE, YARDS:	0	100	200	300	400
Rem. 140 AccuTip BT	velocity, fps:	2860	2670	2488	2313	2145
	energy, ft-lb:	2543	2217	1925	1663	1431
	arc, inches:		+1.7	0	-7.3	-21.2
Rem. 140 Nosler Partition	velocity, fps:	2860	2648	2446	2253	2068
	energy, ft-lb:	2542	2180	1860	1577	1330
	arc, inches:		+1.7	0	-7.6	-22.0
Speer 145 Grand Slam	velocity, fps:	2845	2567	2305	2059	
	energy, ft-lb:	2606	2121	1711	1365	
	arc, inches:		+1.9	0	-8.4	-25.5
Win. 140 Power-Point	velocity, fps:	2800	2523	2268	2027	1802.
	energy, ft-lb:	2429	1980	1599	1277	1010
	arc, inches:		+2.0	0	-8.8	-26.0
Win. 140 Power-Point Plus	velocity, fps:	2875	2597	2336	2090	1859
	energy, ft-lb:	2570	1997	1697	1358	1075
	arc, inches:		+2.0	0	-8.8	26.0
Win. 140 Fail Safe	velocity, fps:	2760	2506	2271	2048	1839
	energy, ft-lb:	2360	1953	1603	1304	1051
	arc, inches:		+2.0	0	-8.8	-25.9
Win. 140 Ballistic Silvertip	velocity, fps:	2770	2572	2382	2200	2026
	energy, ft-lb:	2386	2056	1764	1504	1276
	arc, inches:		+1.9	0	-8.0	-23.8

7x64 BRENNEKE

CARTRIDGE BULLET	RANGE, YARDS:	0	100	200	300	400
Federal 160 Nosler Partition	velocity, fps:	2650	2480	2310	2150	2000
	energy, ft-lb:	2495	2180	1895	1640	1415
	arc, inches:		+2.1	0	-8.7	-24.9
Norma 140 AccuBond	velocity, fps:	2953	2759	2572	2394	
	energy, ft-lb:	2712	2366	2058	1782	
	arc, inches:		+1.5	0	-6.8	
Norma 154 Soft Point	velocity, fps:	2821	2605	2399	2203	
	energy, ft-lb:	2722	2321	1969	1660	
	arc, inches:		+1.8	0	-7.8	
Norma 156 Oryx	velocity, fps:	2789	2516	2259	2017	
	energy, ft-lb:	2695	2193	1768	1410	
	arc, inches:		+2.0	0	-8.8	
Norma 170 Vulkan	velocity, fps:	2756	2501	2259	2031	
	energy, ft-lb:	2868	2361	1927	1558	
	arc, inches:		+2.0	0	-8.8	
Norma 170 Oryx	velocity, fps:	2756	2481	2222	1979	
	energy, ft-lb:	2868	2324	1864	1478	
	arc, inches:		+2.1	0	-9.2	
Norma 170 Plastic Point	velocity, fps:	2756	2519	2294	2081	
	energy, ft-lb:	2868	2396	1987	1635	
	arc, inches:		+2.0	0	-8.6	
PMC 170 Pointed Soft Point	velocity, fps:	2625	2401	2189	1989	1801
	energy, ft lb:	2601	2175	1808	1493	1224
	arc, inches:		+2.3	0	-9.6	-27.9
Rem. 175 PSP Core-Lokt	velocity, fps:	2650	2445	2248	2061	1883
	energy, ft-lb:	2728	2322	1964	1650	1378
	arc, inches:		+2.2	0	-9.1	-26.4
Speer 160 Grand Slam	velocity, fps:	2600	2376	2164	1962	
	energy, ft-lb:	2401	2006	1663	1368	
	arc, inches:		+2.3	0	-9.8	-28.6
Speer 175 Grand Slam	velocity, fps:	2650	2461	2280	2106	
	energy, ft-lb:	2728	2353	2019	1723	
	arc, inches:		+2.4	0	-9.2	-26.2

7x65 R

CARTRIDGE BULLET	RANGE, YARDS:	0	100	200	300	400
Norma 150 FMJ	velocity, fps:	2756	2552	2357	2170	
	energy, ft-lb:	2530	2169	1850	1569	
	arc, inches:		+1.9	0	-8.2	
Norma 156 Oryx	velocity, fps:	2723	2454	2200	1962	
	energy, ft-lb:	2569	2086	1678	1334	
	arc, inches:		+2.1	0	-9.3	

CARTRIDGE BULLET	RANGE, YARDS:	0	100	200	300	400
Norma 170 Plastic Point	velocity, fps:	2625	2390	2167	1956	
	energy, ft-lb:	2602	2157	1773	1445	
	arc, inches:		+2.3	0	-9.7	
Norma 170 Vulkan	velocity, fps:	2657	2392	2143	1909	
	energy, ft-lb:	2666	2161	1734	1377	
	arc, inches:		+2.3	0	-9.9	
Norma 170 Oryx	velocity, fps:	2657	2378	2115	1871	
	energy, ft-lb:	2666	2135	1690	1321	
	arc, inches:		+2.3	0	-10.1	

.284 WINCHESTER

CARTRIDGE BULLET	RANGE, YARDS:	0	100	200	300	400
Win. 150 Power-Point	velocity, fps:	2860	2595	2344	2108	1886
	energy, ft-lb:	2724	2243	1830	1480	1185
	arc, inches:		+2.1	0	-8.5	-24.8

.280 REMINGTON

CARTRIDGE BULLET	RANGE, YARDS:	0	100	200	300	400
Federal 140 Sierra Pro-Hunt.	velocity, fps:	2990	2740	2500	2270	2060
	energy, ft-lb:	2770	2325	1940	1605	1320
	arc, inches:		+1.6	0	-7.0	-20.8
Federal 140 Trophy Bonded	velocity, fps:	2990	2630	2310	2040	1730
	energy, ft-lb:	2770	2155	1655	1250	925
	arc, inches:		+1.6	0	-8.4	-25.4
Federal 140 Tr. Bonded HE	velocity, fps:	3150	2850	2570	2300	2050
	energy, ft-lb:	3085	2520	2050	1650	1310
	arc, inches:		+1.4	0	-6.7	-20.0
Federal 140 Nos. AccuBond And Bal. Tip And Solid Base	velocity, fps:	3000	2800	2620	2440	2260
	energy, ft-lb:	2800	2445	2130	1845	1590
	arc, inches:		+1.5	0	-6.5	-18.9
Federal 150 Hi-Shok	velocity, fps:	2890	2670	2460	2260	2060
	energy, ft-lb:	2780	2370	2015	1695	1420
	arc, inches:		+1.7	0	-7.5	-21.8
Federal 150 Nosler Partition	velocity, fps:	2890	2690	2490	2310	2130
	energy, ft-lb:	2780	2405	2070	1770	1510.
	arc, inches:		+1.7	0	-7.2	-21.1
Federal 150 Nos. AccuBond	velocity, fps	2800	2630	2460	2300	2150
	energy, ft-lb:	2785	2455	2155	1885	1645
	arc, inches:		+1.8	0	-7.5	-21.5
Federal 160 Trophy Bonded	velocity, fps:	2800	2570	2350	2140	1940
	energy, ft-lb:	2785	2345	1960	1625	1340
	arc, inches:		+1.9	0	-8.3	-24.0
Hornady 139 SPBT LMmoly	velocity, fps:	3110	2888	2675	2473	2280.
	energy, ft-lb:	2985	2573	2209	1887	1604
	arc, inches:		+1.4	0	-6.5	-18.6
Norma 156 Oryx	velocity, fps:	2789	2516	2259	2017	
	energy, ft-lb:	2695	2193	1768	1410	
	arc, inches:		+2.0	0	-8.8	
Norma 170 Plastic Point	velocity, fps:	2707	2468	2241	2026	
	energy, ft-lb:	2767	2299	1896	1550	
	arc, inches:		+2.1	0	-9.1	
Norma 170 Vulkan	velocity, fps:	2592	2346	2113	1894	
	energy, ft-lb:	2537	2078	1686	1354	
	arc, inches:		+2.4	0	-10.2	
Norma 170 Oryx	velocity, fps:	2690	2416	2159	1918	
	energy, ft-lb:	2732	2204	1760	1389	
	arc, inches:		+2.2	0	-9.7	
Rem. 140 PSP Core-Lokt	velocity, fps:	3000	2758	2528	2309	2102
	energy, ft-lb:	2797	2363	1986	1657	1373
	arc, inches:		+1.5	0	-7.0	-20.5
Rem. 140 PSP boat-tail	velocity, fps:	2860	2656	2460	2273	2094
	energy, ft-lb:	2542	2192	1881	1606	1363
	arc, inches:		+1.7	0	-7.5	-21.7
Rem. 140 Nosler Bal. Tip	velocity, fps:	3000	2804	2616	2436	2263
	energy, ft-lb:	2799	2445	2128	1848	1593
	arc, inches:		+1.5	0	-6.8	-19.0

Centerfire Rifle Ballistics

.280 REMINGTON TO 7MM REMINGTON MAGNUM

CARTRIDGE BULLET	RANGE, YARDS:	0	100	200	300	400
Rem. 140 AccuTip	velocity, fps:	3000	2804	2617	2437	2265
	energy, ft-lb:	2797	2444	2129	1846	1594
	arc, inches:		+1.5	0	-6.8	-19.0
Rem. 150 PSP Core-Lokt	velocity, fps:	2890	2624	2373	2135	1912
	energy, ft-lb:	2781	2293	1875	1518	1217
	arc, inches:		+1.8	0	-8.0	-23.6
Rem. 165 SP Core-Lokt	velocity, fps:	2820	2510	2220	1950	1701
	energy, ft-lb:	2913	2308	1805	1393	1060.
	arc, inches:		+2.0	0	-9.1	-27.4
Speer 145 Grand Slam	velocity, fps:	2900	2619	2354	2105	
	energy, ft-lb:	2707	2207	1784	1426	
	arc, inches:		+2.1	0	-8.4	-24.7
Speer 160 Grand Slam	velocity, fps:	2890	2652	2425	2210	
	energy, ft-lb:	2967	2497	2089	1735	
	arc, inches:		+1.7	0	-7.7	-22.4
Win. 140 Fail Safe	velocity, fps:	3050	2756	2480	2221	1977
	energy, ft-lb:	2893	2362	1913	1533	1216
	arc, inches:		+1.5	0	-7.2	-21.5
Win. 140 Ballistic Silvertip	velocity, fps:	3040	2842	2653	2471	2297
	energy, ft-lb:	2872	2511	2187	1898	1640
	arc, inches:		+1.4	0	-6.3	-18.4

.280 ACKLEY IMPROVED

CARTRIDGE BULLET	RANGE, YARDS:	0	100	200	300	400
Nosler 140 AccuBond	velocity, fps:	3150	2947	2753	2567	2389
	energy, ft-lb:	3084	2700	2355	2048	1774
	arc, inches:	-1.5	+1.1	0	-5.0	-16.8
Nosler 150 ABLR	velocity, fps:	2930	2775	2626	2482	2342
	energy, ft-lb:	2858	2565	2297	2052	1827
	arc, inches:	-1.5	+1.5	0	-6.6	-18.7
Nosler 160 Partition	velocity, fps:	2950	2752	2562	2380	2206
	energy, ft-lb:	3091	2690	2332	2013	1729
	arc, inches:	-1.5	+1.5	0	-6.7	-19.4

7MM REMINGTON MAGNUM

CARTRIDGE BULLET	RANGE, YARDS:	0	100	200	300	400
A-Square 175 Monolithic Solid	velocity, fps:	2860	2557	2273	2008	1771
	energy, ft-lb:	3178	2540	2008	1567	1219
	arc, inches:		+1.92	0	-8.7	-25.9
Black Hills 140 Nos. Bal. Tip	velocity, fps:	3150				
	energy, ft-lb:	3084				
	arc, inches:					
Black Hills 140 Barnes XLC	velocity, fps:	3150				
	energy, ft-lb:	3084				
	arc, inches:					
Black Hills 140 Nos. Partition	velocity, fps:	3150				
	energy, ft-lb:	3084				
	arc, inches:					
Federal 140 Nosler Bal. Tip And AccuBond	velocity, fps:	3110	2910	2720	2530	2360.
	energy, ft-lb:	3005	2630	2295	1995	1725
	arc, inches:		+1.3	0	-6.0	-17.4
Federal 140 Nosler Partition	velocity, fps:	3150	2930	2710	2510	2320
	energy, ft-lb:	3085	2660	2290	1960	1670
	arc, inches:		+1.3	0	-6.0	-17.5
Federal 140 Trophy Bonded	velocity, fps:	3150	2910	2680	2460	2250.
	energy, ft-lb:	3085	2630	2230	1880	1575
	arc, inches:		+1.3	0	-6.1	-18.1
Federal 150 Hi-Shok	velocity, fps:	3110	2830	2570	2320	2090
	energy, ft-lb:	3220	2670	2200	1790	1450
	arc, inches:		+1.4	0	-6.7	-19.9
Federal 150 Sierra GameKing BTSP	velocity, fps:	3110	2920	2750	2580	2410
	energy, ft-lb:	3220	2850	2510	2210	1930
	arc, inches:		+1.3	0	-5.9	-17.0
Federal 150 Nosler Bal. Tip	velocity, fps:	3110	2910	2720	2540	2370
	energy, ft-lb:	3220	2825	2470	2150	1865
	arc, inches:		+1.3	0	-6.0	-17.4

CARTRIDGE BULLET	RANGE, YARDS:	0	100	200	300	400
Federal 150 Nos. Solid Base	velocity, fps:	3100	2890	2690	2500	2310
	energy, ft-lb:	3200	2780	2405	2075	1775
	arc, inches:		+1.3	0	-6.2	-17.8
Federal 160 Barnes XLC	velocity, fps:	2940	2760	2580	2410	2240
	energy, ft-lb:	3070	2695	2360	2060	1785
	arc, inches:		+1.5	0	-6.8	-19.6
Federal 160 Sierra Pro-Hunt.	velocity, fps:	2940	2730	2520	2320	2140
	energy, ft-lb:	3070	2640	2260	1920	1620
	arc, inches:		+1.6	0	-7.1	-20.6
Federal 160 Nosler Partition	velocity, fps:	2950	2770	2590	2420	2250.
	energy, ft-lb:	3090	2715	2375	2075	1800
	arc, inches:		+1.5	0	-6.7	-19.4
Federal 160 Nos. AccuBond	velocity, fps:	2950	2770	2600	2440	2280.
	energy, ft-lb:	3090	2730	2405	2110	1845
	arc, inches:		+1.5	0	-6.6	-19.1
Federal 160 Trophy Bonded	velocity, fps:	2940	2660	2390	2140	1900
	energy, ft-lb:	3070	2505	2025	1620	1280.
	arc, inches:		+1.7	0	-7.9	-23.3
Federal 165 Sierra GameKing BTSP	velocity, fps:	2950	2800	2650	2510	2370.
	energy, ft-lb:	3190	2865	2570	2300	2050
	arc, inches:		+1.5	0	-6.4	-18.4
Federal 175 Hi-Shok	velocity, fps:	2860	2650	2440	2240	2060
	energy, ft-lb:	3180	2720	2310	1960	1640
	arc, inches:		+1.7	0	-7.6	-22.1
Federal 175 Trophy Bonded	velocity, fps:	2860	2600	2350	2120	1900
	energy, ft-lb:	3180	2625	2150	1745	1400
	arc, inches:		+1.8	0	-8.2	-24.0
Hornady 139 SPBT	velocity, fps:	3150	2933	2727	2530	2341
	energy, ft-lb:	3063	2656	2296	1976	1692
	arc, inches:		+1.2	0	-6.1	-17.7
Hornady 139 SST (or Interbond)	velocity, fps:	3150	2948	2754	2569	2391
	energy, ft-lb:	3062	2681	2341	2037	1764
	arc, inches:		+1.1	0	-5.7	-16.7
Hornady 139 SST LM (or Interbond)	velocity, fps:	3250	3044	2847	2657	2475
	energy, ft-lb:	3259	2860	2501	2178	1890
	arc, inches:		+1.1	0	-5.5	-16.2
Hornady 139 SPBT HMmoly	velocity, fps:	3250	3041	2822	2613	2413
	energy, ft-lb:	3300	2854	2458	2106	1797.
	arc, inches:		+1.1	0	-5.7	-16.6
Hornady 154 Soft Point	velocity, fps:	3035	2814	2604	2404	2212
	energy, ft-lb:	3151	2708	2319	1977	1674
	arc, inches:		+1.3	0	-6.7	-19.3
Hornady 154 SST (or Interbond)	velocity, fps:	3035	2850	2672	2501	2337
	energy, ft-lb:	3149	2777	2441	2139	1867
	arc, inches:		+1.4	0	-6.5	-18.7
Hornady 162 SP boat-tail	velocity, fps:	2940	2757	2582	2413	2251
	energy, ft-lb:	3110	2735	2399	2095	1823
	arc, inches:		+1.6	0	-6.7	-19.7
Hornady 175 SP	velocity, fps:	2860	2650	2440	2240	2060.
	energy, ft-lb:	3180	2720	2310	1960	1640
	arc, inches:		+2.0	0	-7.9	-22.7
Norma 140 Nosler Bal. Tip	velocity, fps:	3150	2936	2732	2537	
	energy, ft-lb:	3085	2680	2320	2001	
	arc, inches:		+1.2	0	-5.9	
Norma 140 Barnes X TS	velocity, fps:	3117	2912	2716	2529	
	energy, ft-lb:	3021	2637	2294	1988	
	arch, inches:		+1.3	0	-6.0	
Norma 150 Scirocco	velocity, fps:	3117	2934	2758	2589	
	energy, ft-lb:	3237	2869	2535	2234	
	arc, inches:		+1.2	0	-5.8	
Norma 156 Oryx	velocity, fps:	2953	2670	2404	2153	
	energy, ft-lb:	3021	2470	2002	1607	
	arc, inches:		+1.7	0	-7.7	

7MM REMINGTON MAGNUM TO 7MM WINCHESTER SHORT MAGNUM

CARTRIDGE BULLET	RANGE, YARDS:	0	100	200	300	400
Norma 170 Vulkan	velocity, fps:	3018	2747	2493	2252	
	energy, ft-lb:	3439	2850	2346	1914	
	arc, inches:		+1.5	0	-2.8	
Norma 170 Oryx	velocity, fps:	2887	2601	2333	2080	
	energy, ft-lb:	3147	2555	2055	1634	
	arc, inches:		+1.8	0	-8.2	
Norma 170 Plastic Point	velocity, fps:	3018	2762	2519	2290	
	energy, ft-lb:	3439	2880	2394	1980	
	arc, inches:		+1.5	0	-7.0	
PMC 140 Barnes X	velocity, fps:	3000	2808	2624	2448	2279
	energy, ft-lb:	2797	2451	2141	1863	1614
	arc, inches:		+1.5	0	-6.6	18.9
PMC 140 Pointed Soft Point	velocity, fps:	3099	2878	2668	2469	2279
	energy, ft-lb:	2984	2574	2212	1895	1614
	arc, inches:		+1.4	0	-6.2	-18.1
PMC 140 SP boat-tail	velocity, fps:	3125	2891	2669	2457	2255
	energy, ft-lb:	3035	2597	2213	1877	1580
	arc, inches:		+1.4	0	-6.3	-18.4
PMC 160 Barnes X	velocity, fps:	2800	2639	2484	2334	2189
	energy, ft-lb:	2785	2474	2192	1935	1703
	arc, inches:		+1.8	0	-7.4	-21.2
PMC 160 Pointed Soft Point	velocity, fps:	2914	2748	2586	2428	2276
	energy, ft-lb:	3016	2682	2375	2095	1840
	arc, inches:		+1.6	0	-6.7	-19.4
PMC 160 SP boat-tail	velocity, fps:	2900	2696	2501	2314	2135
	energy, ft-lb:	2987	2582	2222	1903	1620
	arc, inches:		+1.7	0	-7.2	-21.0
PMC 175 Pointed Soft Point	velocity, fps:	2860	2645	2442	2244	2957
	energy, ft-lb:	3178	2718	2313	1956	1644
	arc, inches:		+2.0	0	-7.9	-22.7
Rem. 140 PSP Core-Lokt mr	velocity, fps:	2710	2482	2265	2059	1865
	energy, ft-lb:	2283	1915	1595	1318	1081
	arc, inches:		+1.0	-2.5	-12.8	-31.3
Rem. 140 PSP Core-Lokt	velocity, fps:	3175	2923	2684	2458	2243
	energy, ft-lb:	3133	2655	2240	1878	1564
	arc, inches:		+2.2	+1.9	-3.2	-14.2
Rem. 140 PSP boat-tail	velocity, fps:	3175	2956	2747	2547	2356
	energy, ft-lb:	3133	2715	2345	2017	1726
	arc, inches:		+2.2	+1.6	-3.1	-13.4
Rem. 150 AccuTip	velocity, fps:	3110	2926	2749	2579	2415
	energy, ft-lb:	3221	2850	2516	2215	1943
	arc, inches:		+1.3	0	-5.9	-17.0
Rem. 150 PSP Core-Lokt	velocity, fps:	3110	2830	2568	2320	2085
	energy, ft-lb:	3221	2667	2196	1792	1448
	arc, inches:		+1.3	0	-6.6	-20.2
Rem. 150 Nosler Bal. Tip	velocity, fps:	3110	2912	2723	2542	2367
	energy, ft-lb:	3222	2825	2470	2152	1867
	arc, inches:		+1.2	0	-5.9	-17.3
Rem. 150 Swift Scirocco	velocity, fps:	3110	2927	2751	2582	2419
	energy, ft-lb:	3221	2852	2520	2220	1948
	arc, inches:		+1.3	0	-5.9	-17.0
Rem. 160 Swift A-Frame	velocity, fps:	2900	2659	2430	2212	2006
	energy, ft-lb:	2987	2511	2097	1739	1430
	arc, inches:		+1.7	0	-7.6	-22.4
Rem. 160 Nosler Partition	velocity, fps:	2950	2752	2563	2381	2207
	energy, ft-lb:	3091	2690	2333	2014	1730
	arc, inches:		+0.6	-1.9	-9.6	-23.6
Rem. 175 PSP Core-Lokt	velocity, fps:	2860	2645	2440	2244	2057
	energy, ft-lb:	3178	2718	2313	1956	1644
	arc, inches:		+1.7	0	-7.6	-22.1
Speer 145 Grand Slam	velocity, fps:	3140	2843	2565	2304	
	energy, ft-lb:	3174	2602	2118	1708	
	arc, inches:		+1.4	0	-6.7	
Speer 175 Grand Slam	velocity, fps:	2850	2653	2463	2282	
	energy, ft-lb:	3156	2734	2358	2023	
	arc, inches:		+1.7	0	-7.5	-21.7
Win. 140 Fail Safe	velocity, fps:	3150	2861	2589	2333	2092
	energy, ft-lb:	3085	2544	2085	1693	1361
	arc, inches:		+1.4	0	-6.6	-19.5
Win. 140 Ballistic Silvertip	velocity, fps:	3100	2889	2687	2494	2310
	energy, ft-lb:	2988	2595	2245	1934	1659.
	arc, inches:		+1.3	0	-6.2	-17.9
Win. 140 AccuBond CT	velocity, fps:	3180	2965	2760	2565	2377
	energy, ft-lb:	3143	2733	2368	2044	1756
	arc, inches:		+1.2	0	-5.8	-16.9
Win. 150 Power-Point	velocity, fps:	3090	2812	2551	2304	2071
	energy, ft-lb:	3181	2634	2167	1768	1429
	arc, inches:		+1.5	0	-6.8	-20.2
Win. 150 Power-Point Plus	velocity, fps:	3130	2849	2586	2337	2102
	energy, ft-lb:	3264	2705	2227	1819	1472
	arc, inches:		+1.4	0	-6.6	-19.6
Win. 150 Ballistic Silvertip	velocity, fps:	3100	2903	2714	2533	2359
	energy, ft-lb:	3200	2806	2453	2136	1853
	arc, inches:		+1.3	0	-6.0	-17.5
Win. 160 AccuBond	velocity, fps:	2950	2766	2590	2420	2257
	energy, ft-lb:	3091	2718	2382	2080	1809
	arc, inches:		+1.5	0	-6.7	-19.4
Win. 160 Partition Gold	velocity, fps:	2950	2743	2546	2357	2176
	energy, ft-lb:	3093	2674	2303	1974	1682
	arc, inches:		+1.6	0	-6.9	-20.1
Win. 160 Fail Safe	velocity, fps:	2920	2678	2449	2331	2025
	energy, ft-lb:	3030	2549	2131	1769	1457
	arc, inches:		+1.7	0	-7.5	-22.0
Win. 175 Power-Point	velocity, fps:	2860	2645	2440	2244	2057
	energy, ft-lb:	3178	2718	2313	1956	1644
	arc, inches:		+2.0	0	-7.9	-22.7

7MM REMINGTON SHORT ULTRA MAGNUM

CARTRIDGE BULLET	RANGE, YARDS:	0	100	200	300	400
Rem. 140 PSP C-L Ultra	velocity, fps:	3175	2934	2707	2490	2283
	energy, ft-lb:	3133	2676	2277	1927	1620.
	arc, inches:		+1.3	0	-6.0	-17.7
Rem. 150 PSP Core-Lokt	velocity, fps:	3110	2828	2563	2313	2077
	energy, ft-lb:	3221	2663	2188	1782	1437
	arc, inches:		+2.5	+2.1	-3.6	-15.8
Rem. 160 Partition	velocity, fps:	2960	2762	2572	2390	2215
	energy, ft-lb:	3112	2709	2350	2029	1744
	arc, inches:		+2.6	+2.2	-3.6	-15.4
Rem. 160 PSP C-L Ultra	velocity, fps:	2960	2733	2518	2313	2117
	energy, ft-lb:	3112	2654	2252	1900	1592
	arc, inches:		+2.7	+2.2	-3.7	-16.2

7MM WINCHESTER SHORT MAGNUM

CARTRIDGE BULLET	RANGE, YARDS:	0	100	200	300	400
Federal 140 Nos. AccuBond	velocity, fps:	3250	3040	2840	2660	2470
	energy, ft-lb:	3285	2875	2515	2190	1900
	arc, inches:		+1.1	0	-5.5	-15.8
Federal 140 Nos. Bal. Tip	velocity, fps:	3310	3100	2900	2700	2520
	energy, ft-lb:	3405	2985	2610	2270	1975
	arc, inches:		+1.1	0	-5.2	15.2
Federal 150 Nos. Solid Base	velocity, fps:	3230	3010	2800	2600	2410
	energy, ft-lb:	3475	3015	2615	2255	1935
	arc, inches:		+1.3	0	-5.6	-16.3
Federal 160 Nos. AccuBond	velocity, fps:	3120	2940	2760	2590	2430
	energy, ft-lb:	3460	3065	2710	2390	2095
	arc, inches:		+1.3	0	-5.9	-16.8
Federal 160 Nos. Partition	velocity, fps:	3160	2950	2750	2560	2380.
	energy, ft-lb:	3545	3095	2690	2335	2015.
	arc, inches:		+1.2	0	-5.9	-16.9

BALLISTICS

Centerfire Rifle Ballistics

7MM WINCHESTER SHORT MAGNUM TO 7MM REMINGTON ULTRA MAGNUM

CARTRIDGE BULLET	RANGE, YARDS:	0	100	200	300	400
Federal 160 Barnes TS	velocity, fps:	2990	2780	2590	2400	2220
	energy, ft-lb:	3175	2755	2380	2045	1750
	arc, inches:		+1.5	0	-6.6	-19.4
Federal 160 Trophy Bonded	velocity, fps:	3120	2880	2650	2440	2230
	energy, ft-lb:	3460	2945	2500	2105	1765
	arc, inches:		+1.4	0	-6.3	-18.5
Win. 140 Bal. Silvertip	velocity, fps:	3225	3008	2801	2603	2414
	energy, ft-lb:	3233	2812	2438	2106	1812
	arc, inches:		+1.2	0	-5.6	-16.4
Win. 140 AccuBond CT	velocity, fps:	3225	3008	2801	2604	2415
	energy, ft-lb:	3233	2812	2439	2107	1812
	arc, inches:		+1.2	0	-5.6	-16.4
Win. 150 Power Point	velocity, fps:	3200	2915	2648	2396	2157
	energy, ft-lb:	3410	2830	2335	1911	1550
	arc, inches:		+1.3	0	-6.3	-18.6
Win. 160 AccuBond	velocity, fps:	3050	2862	2682	2509	2342
	energy, ft-lb:	3306	2911	2556	2237	1950
	arc, inches:		1.4	0	-6.2	-17.9
Win. 160 Fail Safe	velocity, fps:	2990	2744	2512	2291	2081
	energy, ft-lb:	3176	2675	2241	1864	1538
	arc, inches:		+1.6	0	-7.1	-20.8

7MM WEATHERBY MAGNUM

CARTRIDGE BULLET	RANGE, YARDS:	0	100	200	300	400
Federal 160 Nosler Partition	velocity, fps:	3050	2850	2650	2470	2290
	energy, ft-lb:	3305	2880	2505	2165	1865
	arc, inches:		+1.4	0	-6.3	-18.4
Federal 160 Sierra GameKing BTSP	velocity, fps:	3050	2880	2710	2560	2400
	energy, ft-lb:	3305	2945	2615	2320	2050
	arc, inches:		+1.4	0	-6.1	-17.4
Federal 160 Trophy Bonded	velocity, fps:	3050	2730	2420	2140	1880.
	energy, ft-lb:	3305	2640	2085	1630	1255
	arc, inches:		+1.6	0	-7.6	-22.7
Hornady 154 Soft Point	velocity, fps:	3200	2971	2753	2546	2348.
	energy, ft-lb:	3501	3017	2592	2216	1885
	arc, inches:		+1.2	0	-5.8	-17.0
Hornady 154 SST (or Interbond)	velocity, fps:	3200	3009	2825	2648	2478
	energy, ft-lb:	3501	3096	2729	2398	2100
	arc, inches:		+1.2	0	-5.7	-16.5
Hornady 175 Soft Point	velocity, fps:	2910	2709	2516	2331	2154
	energy, ft-lb:	3290	2850	2459	2111	1803
	arc, inches:		+1.6	0	-7.1	-20.6
Wby. 139 Pointed Expanding	velocity, fps:	3340	3079	2834	2601	2380.
	energy, ft-lb:	3443	2926	2478	2088	1748
	arc, inches:		+2.9	+3.6	0	-8.7
Wby. 140 Nosler Partition	velocity, fps:	3303	3069	2847	2636	2434
	energy, ft-lb:	3391	2927	2519	2159	1841
	arc, inches:		+2.9	+3.6	0	-8.5
Wby. 150 Nosler Bal. Tip	velocity, fps:	3300	3093	2896	2708	2527
	energy, ft-lb:	3627	3187	2793	2442	2127
	arc, inches:		+2.8	+3.5	0	-8.2
Wby. 150 Barnes X	veloctiy, fps:	3100	2901	2710	2527	2352
	energy, ft-lb:	3200	2802	2446	2127	1842
	arc, inches:		+3.3	+4.0	0	-9.4
Wby. 154 Pointed Expanding	velocity, fps:	3260	3028	2807	2597	2397
	energy, ft-lb:	3634	3134	2694	2307	1964
	arc, inches:		+3.0	+3.7	0	-8.8
Wby. 160 Nosler Partition	velocity, fps:	3200	2991	2791	2600	2417
	energy, ft-lb:	3638	3177	2767	2401	2075.
	arc, inches:		+3.1	+3.8	0	-8.9
Wby. 175 Pointed Expanding	velocity, fps:	3070	2861	2662	2471	2288
	energy, ft-lb:	3662	3181	2753	2373	2034
	arc, inches:		+3.5	+4.2	0	-9.9

7MM DAKOTA

CARTRIDGE BULLET	RANGE, YARDS:	0	100	200	300	400
Dakota 140 Barnes X	velocity, fps:	3500	3253	3019	2798	2587
	energy, ft-lb:	3807	3288	2833	2433	2081
	arc, inches:		+2.0	+2.1	-1.5	-9.6
Dakota 160 Barnes X	velocity, fps:	3200	3001	2811	2630	2455
	energy, ft-lb:	3637	3200	2808	2456	2140
	arc, inches:		+2.1	+1.9	-2.8	-12.5

7MM STW

CARTRIDGE BULLET	RANGE, YARDS:	0	100	200	300	400
A-Square 140 Nos. Bal. Tip	velocity, fps:	3450	3254	3067	2888	2715
	energy, ft-lb:	3700	3291	2924	2592	2292
	arc, inches:		+2.2	+3.0	0	-7.3
A-Square 160 Nosler Part.	velocity, fps:	3250	3071	2900	2735	2576.
	energy, ft-lb:	3752	3351	2987	2657	2357
	arc, inches:		+2.8	+3.5	0	-8.2
A-Square 160 SP boat-tail	velocity, fps:	3250	3087	2930	2778	2631
	energy, ft-lb:	3752	3385	3049	2741	2460
	arc, inches:		+2.8	+3.4	0	-8.0
Federal 140 Trophy Bonded	velocity, fps:	3330	3080	2850	2630	2420
	energy, ft-lb:	3435	2950	2520	2145	1815
	arc, inches:		+1.1	0	-5.4	-15.8
Federal 150 Trophy Bonded	velocity, fps:	3250	3010	2770	2560	2350.
	energy, ft-lb:	3520	3010	2565	2175	1830
	arc, inches:		+1.2	0	-5.7	-16.7
Federal 160 Sierra GameKing BTSP	velocity, fps:	3200	3020	2850	2670	2530.
	energy, ft-lb:	3640	3245	2890	2570	2275
	arc, inches:		+1.1	0	-5.5	-15.7
Nosler 175 ABLR	velocity, fps:	2900	2760	2625	2493	2366
	energy, ft-lb:	3267	2960	2677	2416	2175
	arc, inches:	-1.5	+1.5	0	-6.6	-18.8
Rem. 140 PSP Core-Lokt	velocity, fps:	3325	3064	2818	2585	2364
	energy, ft-lb:	3436	2918	2468	2077	1737
	arc, inches:		+2.0	+1.7	-2.9	-12.8
Rem. 140 Swift A-Frame	velocity, fps:	3325	3020	2735	2467	2215
	energy, ft-lb:	3436	2834	2324	1892	1525
	arc, inches:		+2.1	+1.8	-3.1	-13.8
Speer 145 Grand Slam	velocity, fps:	3300	2992	2075	2435	
	energy, ft-lb:	3506	2882	2355	1909	
	arc, inches:		+1.2	0	-6.0	-17.8
Win. 140 Ballistic Silvertip	velocity, fps:	3320	3100	2890	2690	2499
	energy, ft-lb:	3427	2982	2597	2250	1941
	arc, inches:		+1.1	0	-5.2	-15.2
Win. 150 Power-Point	velocity, fps:	3250	2957	2683	2424	2181
	energy, ft-lb:	3519	2913	2398	1958	1584
	arc, inches:		+1.2	0	-6.1	-18.1
Win. 160 Fail Safe	velocity, fps:	3150	2894	2652	2422	2204
	energy, ft-lb:	3526	2976	2499	2085	1727
	arc, inches:		+1.3	0	-6.3	-18.5

7MM REMINGTON ULTRA MAGNUM

CARTRIDGE BULLET	RANGE, YARDS:	0	100	200	300	400
Nosler 175 ABLR	velocity, fps:	3040	2896	2756	2621	2490
	energy, ft-lb:	3590	3258	2952	2669	2409
	arc, inches:	-1.5	+1.3	0	-5.9	-16.9
Rem. 140 PSP Core-Lokt	velocity, fps:	3425	3158	2907	2669	2444
	energy, ft-lb:	3646	3099	2626	2214	1856
	arc, inches:		+1.8	+1.6	-2.7	-11.9
Rem. 140 Nosler Partition	velocity, fps:	3425	3184	2956	2740	2534
	energy, ft-lb:	3646	3151	2715	2333	1995
	arc, inches:		+1.7	+1.6	-2.6	-11.4
Rem. 160 Nosler Partition	velocity, fps:	3200	2991	2791	2600	2417
	energy, ft-lb:	3637	3177	2767	2401	2075
	arc, inches:		+2.1	+1.8	-3.0	-12.9

CARTRIDGE BULLET	RANGE, YARDS:	0	100	200	300	400

7.21 (.284) FIREHAWK

CARTRIDGE BULLET		0	100	200	300	400
Lazzeroni 140 Nosler Part.	velocity, fps	3580	3349	3130	2923	2724
	energy, ft-lb	3985	3488	3048	2656	2308
	arc, inches		+2.2	+2.9	0	-7.0
Lazzeroni 160 Swift A-Fr.	velocity, fps	3385	3167	2961	2763	2574
	energy, ft-lb	4072	3565	3115	2713	2354
	arc, inches		+2.6	+3.3	0	-7.8

7.5x55 SWISS

		0	100	200	300	400
Norma 180 Soft Point	velocity, fps	2651	2432	2223	2025	
	energy, ft-lb	2810	2364	1976	1639	
	arc, inches		+2.2	0	-9.3	
Norma 180 Oryx	velocity, fps	2493	2222	1968	1734	
	energy, ft-lb	2485	1974	1549	1201	
	arc, inches		+2.7	0	-11.8	

7.62x39 RUSSIAN

		0	100	200	300	400
Federal 123 Hi-Shok	velocity, fps	2300	2030	1780	1550	1350
	energy, ft-lb	1445	1125	860	655	500.
	arc, inches		0	-7.0	-25.1	
Federal 124 FMJ	velocity, fps	2300	2030	1780	1560	1360
	energy, ft-lb	1455	1135	875	670	510
	arc, inches		+3.5	0	-14.6	-43.5
PMC 123 FMJ	velocity, fps	2350	2072	1817	1583	1368
	energy, ft-lb	1495	1162	894	678	507
	arc, inches		0	-5.0	-26.4	-67.8
PMC 125 Pointed Soft Point	velocity, fps	2320	2046	1794	1563	1350
	energy, ft-lb	1493	1161	893	678	505.
	arc, inches		0	-5.2	-27.5	-70.6
Rem. 125 Pointed Soft Point	velocity, fps	2365	2062	1783	1533	1320
	energy, ft-lb	1552	1180	882	652	483
	arc, inches		0	-6.7	-24.5	
Win. 123 Soft Point	velocity, fps	2365	2033	1731	1465	1248
	energy, ft-lb	1527	1129	818	586	425
	arc, inches		+3.8	0	-15.4	-46.3

.30 CARBINE

		0	100	200	300	400
Federal 110 Hi-Shok RN	velocity, fps	1990	1570	1240	1040	920
	energy, ft-lb	965	600	375	260	210
	arc, inches		0	-12.8	-46.9	
Federal 110 FMJ	velocity, fps	1990	1570	1240	1040	920
	energy, ft-lb	965	600	375	260	210
	arc, inches		0	-12.8	-46.9	
Magtech 110 FMC	velocity, fps	1990	1654			
	energy, ft-lb	965	668			
	arc, inches		0			
PMC 110 FMJ	(and RNSP)velocity, fps:1927		1548	1248		
	energy, ft-lb	906	585	380		
	arc, inches		0	-14.2		
Rem. 110 Soft Point	velocity, fps	1990	1567	1236	1035	923
	energy, ft-lb	967	600	373	262	208
	arc, inches		0	-12.9	-48.6	
Win. 110 Hollow Soft Point	velocity, fps	1990	1567	1236	1035	923
	energy, ft-lb	967	600	373	262	208
	arc, inches		0	-13.5	-49.9	

.30 T/C HORNADAY

		0	100	200	300	400
Hornady 150	velocity, fps	3000	2772	2555	2348	
	energy, ft-lb	2997	2558	2176	1836	
	arc, inches	-1.5	+1.5	0	-6.9	
Hornady 165	velocity, fps	2850	2644	2447	2258	
	energy, ft-lb	2975	2560	2193	1868	
	arc, inches	-1.5	+1.7	0	-7.6	

.30-30 WINCHESTER

CARTRIDGE BULLET		0	100	200	300	400
Federal 125 Hi-Shok HP	velocity, fps	2570	2090	1660	1320	1080
	energy, ft-lb	1830	1210	770	480	320
	arc, inches		+3.3	0	-16.0	-50.9
Federal 150 Hi-Shok FN	velocity, fps	2390	2020	1680	1400	1180
	energy, ft-lb	1900	1355	945	650	460
	arc, inches		+3.6	0	-15.9	-49.1
Federal 170 Hi-Shok RN	velocity, fps	2200	1900	1620	1380	1190
	energy, ft-lb	1830	1355	990	720	535
	arc, inches		+4.1	0	-17.4	-52.4
Federal 170 Sierra Pro-Hunt.	velocity, fps	2200	1820	1500	1240	1060
	energy, ft-lb	1830	1255	845	575	425
	arc, inches		+4.5	0	-20.0	-63.5
Federal 170 Nosler Partition	velocity, fps	2200	1900	1620	1380	1190
	energy, ft-lb	1830	1355	990	720	535
	arc, inches		+4.1	0	-17.4	-52.4
Hornady 150 Round Nose	velocity, fps	2390	1973	1605	1303	1095
	energy, ft-lb	1902	1296	858	565	399
	arc, inches		0	-8.2	-30.0	
Hornady 160 Evolution	velocity, fps	2400	2150	1916	1699	
	energy, ft-lb	2046	1643	1304	1025	
	arc, inches		+3.0	0.2	-12.1	
Hornady 170 Flat Point	velocity, fps	2200	1895	1619	1381	1191
	energy, ft-lb	1827	1355	989	720	535
	arc, inches		0	-8.9	-31.1	
Norma 150 Soft Point	velocity, fps	2329	2008	1716	1459	
	energy, ft-lb	1807	1344	981	709	
	arc, inches		+3.6	0	-15.5	
PMC 150 Starfire HP	velocity, fps	2100	1769	1478		
	energy, ft-lb	1469	1042	728		
	arc, inches		0	-10.8		
PMC 150 Flat Nose	velocity, fps	2300	1943	1627		
	energy, ft-lb	1762	1257	881		
	arc, inches		0	-7.8		
PMC 170 Flat Nose	velocity, fps	2150	1840	1566		
	energy, ft-lb	1745	1277	926		
	arc, inches		0	-8.9		
Rem. 55 PSP (sabot) "Accelerator"	velocity, fps	3400	2693	2085	1570	1187
	energy, ft-lb	1412	886	521	301	172
	arc, inches		+1.7	0	-9.9	-34.3
Rem. 150 SP Core-Lokt	velocity, fps	2390	1973	1605	1303	1095
	energy, ft-lb	1902	1296	858	565	399
	arc, inches		0	-7.6	-28.8	
Rem. 170 SP Core-Lokt	velocity, fps	2200	1895	1619	1381	1191
	energy, ft-lb	1827	1355	989	720	535
	arc, inches		0	-8.3	-29.9	
Rem. 170 HP Core-Lokt	velocity, fps	2200	1895	1619	1381	1191.
	energy, ft-lb	1827	1355	989	720	535
	arc, inches		0	-8.3	-29.9	
Speer 150 Flat Nose	velocity, fps	2370	2067	1788	1538	
	energy, ft-lb	1870	1423	1065	788	
	arc, inches		+3.3	0	-14.4	-43.7
Win. 150 Hollow Point	velocity, fps	2390	2018	1684	1398	1177
	energy, ft-lb	1902	1356	944	651	461
	arc, inches		0	-7.7	-27.9	
Win. 150 Power-Point	velocity, fps	2390	2018	1684	1398	1177
	energy, ft-lb	1902	1356	944	651	461
	arc, inches		0	-7.7	-27.9	
Win. 150 Silvertip	velocity,fps	2390	2018	1684	1398	1177
	energy, ft-lb	1902	1356	944	651	461
	arc, inches		0	-7.7	-27.9	

BALLISTICS

Centerfire Rifle Ballistics

.30-30 WINCHESTER TO .308 WINCHESTER

CARTRIDGE BULLET	RANGE, YARDS:	0	100	200	300	400
Win. 150 Power-Point Plus	velocity, fps:	2480	2095	1747	1446	1209
	energy, ft-lb:	2049	1462	1017	697	487
	arc, inches:		0	-6.5	-24.5	
Win. 170 Power-Point	velocity, fps:	2200	1895	1619	1381	1191
	energy, ft-lb:	1827	1355	989	720	535.
	arc, inches:		0	-8.9	-31.1	
Win. 170 Silvertip	velocity, fps:	2200	1895	1619	1381	1191
	energy, ft-lb:	1827	1355	989	720	535
	arc, inches:		0	-8.9	-31.1	

.300 SAVAGE

CARTRIDGE BULLET	RANGE, YARDS:	0	100	200	300	400
Federal 150 Hi-Shok	velocity, fps:	2630	2350	2100	1850	1630
	energy, ft-lb:	2305	1845	1460	1145	885
	arc, inches:		+2.4	0	-10.4	-30.9
Federal 180 Hi-Shok	velocity, fps:	2350	2140	1940	1750	1570
	energy, ft-lb:	2205	1825	1495	1215	985
	arc, inches:		+3.1	0	-12.4	-36.1
Rem. 150 PSP Core-Lokt	velocity, fps:	2630	2354	2095	1853	1631
	energy, ft-lb:	2303	1845	1462	1143	806.
	arc, inches:		+2.4	0	-10.4	-30.9
Rem. 180 SP Core-Lokt	velocity, fps:	2350	2025	1728	1467	1252
	energy, ft-lb:	2207	1639	1193	860	626
	arc, inches:		0	-7.1	-25.9	
Win. 150 Power-Point	velocity, fps:	2630	2311	2015	1743	1500
	energy, ft-lb:	2303	1779	1352	1012	749
	arc, inches:		+2.8	0	-11.5	-34.4

.307 WINCHESTER

CARTRIDGE BULLET	RANGE, YARDS:	0	100	200	300	400
Win. 180 Power-Point	velocity, fps:	2510	2179	1874	1599	1362
	energy, ft-lb:	2519	1898	1404	1022	742
	arc, inches:		+1.5	-3.6	-18.6	-47.1

.30-40 KRAG

CARTRIDGE BULLET	RANGE, YARDS:	0	100	200	300	400
Rem. 180 PSP Core-Lokt	velocity, fps:	2430	2213	2007	1813	1632.
	energy, ft-lb:	2360	1957	1610	1314	1064
	arc, inches, s:		0	-5.6	-18.6	
Win. 180 Power-Point	velocity, fps:	2430	2099	1795	1525	1298
	energy, ft-lb:	2360	1761	1288	929	673
	arc, inches, s:		0	-7.1	-25.0	

7.62x54R RUSSIAN

CARTRIDGE BULLET	RANGE, YARDS:	0	100	200	300	400
Norma 150 Soft Point	velocity, fps:	2953	2622	2314	2028	
	energy, ft-lb:	2905	2291	1784	1370	.
	arc, inches:		+1.8	0	-8.3	
Norma 180 Alaska	velocity, fps:	2575	2362	2159	1967	
	energy, ft-lb:	2651	2231	1864	1546	
	arc, inches:		+2.9	0	-12.9	
Winchester 180 FMJ	velocity, fps:	2580	2401	2230	2066	1909
	energy, ft-lb:	2658	2304	1987	1706	1457
	arc, inches:	-1.5	+2.6	0	-9.6	-27.3
Winchester 180 SP	velocity, fps:	2625	2302	2003	1729	1485
	energy, ft-lb:	2751	2117	1603	1195	882
	arc, inches:	-1.5	+2.9	0	-11.6	-34.9

.308 MARLIN EXPRESS

CARTRIDGE BULLET	RANGE, YARDS:	0	100	200	300	400
Hornady 160	velocity, fps	2660	2438	2226	2026	1836
	energy, ft-lb	2513	2111	1761	1457	1197
	arc, inches	-1.5	+3.0	+1.7	-6.7	-23.5
Hornady 140 MonoFlex	velocity, fps	2800	2532	2279	2040	1818
	energy, ft-lb	2437	1992	1614	1294	1027
	arc, inches	-1.5	+2.0	0	-8.7	-25.8

.308 WINCHESTER

CARTRIDGE BULLET	RANGE, YARDS:	0	100	200	300	400
Black Hills 150 Nosler B. Tip	velocity, fps:	2800				
	energy, ft-lb:	2611				
	arc, inches:					
Black Hills 165 Nosler B. Tip (and SP)	velocity, fps:	2650				
	energy, ft-lb:	2573				
	arc, inches:					
Black Hills 168 Barnes X (and Match)	velocity, fps:	2650				
	energy, ft-lb:	2620				
	arc, inches:					
Black Hills 175 Match	velocity, fps:	2600				
	energy, ft-lb:	2657				
	arc, inches:					
Black Hills 180 AccuBond	velocity, fps:	2600				
	energy, ft-lb:	2701				
	arc, inches:					
Federal 150 Hi-Shok	velocity, fps:	2820	2530	2260	2010	1770
	energy, ft-lb:	2650	2140	1705	1345	1050
	arc, inches:		+2.0	0	-8.8	-26.3
Federal 150 Nosler Bal. Tip.	velocity, fps:	2820	2610	2410	2220	2040
	energy, ft-lb:	2650	2270	1935	1640	1380
	arc, inches:		+1.8	0	-7.8	-22.7
Federal 150 FMJ boat-tail	velocity, fps:	2820	2620	2430	2250	2070
	energy, ft-lb:	2650	2285	1965	1680	1430
	arc, inches:		+1.8	0	-7.7	-22.4
Federal 150 Barnes XLC	velocity, fps:	2820	2610	2400	2210	2030
	energy, ft-lb:	2650	2265	1925	1630	1370
	arc, inches:		+1.8	0	-7.8	-22.9
Federal 155 Sierra MatchKg. BTHP	velocity, fps:	2950	2740	2540	2350	2170
	energy, ft-lb:	2995	2585	2225	1905	1620
	arc, inches:		+1.9	0	-8.9	-22.6
Federal 165 Sierra GameKing BTSP	velocity, fps:	2700	2520	2330	2160	1990
	energy, ft-lb:	2670	2310	1990	1700	1450
	arc, inches:		+2.0	0	-8.4	-24.3
Federal 165 Trophy Bonded	velocity, fps:	2700	2440	2200	1970	1760
	energy, ft-lb:	2670	2185	1775	1425	1135
	arc, inches:		+2.2	0	-9.4	-27.7
Federal 165 Tr. Bonded HE	velocity, fps:	2870	2600	2350	2120	1890
	energy, ft-lb:	3020	2485	2030	1640	1310
	arc, inches:		+1.8	0	-8.2	-24.0
Federal 168 Sierra MatchKg. BTHP	velocity, fps:	2600	2410	2230	2060	1890
	energy, ft-lb:	2520	2170	1855	1580	1340.
	arc, inches:		+2.1	0	+8.9	+25.9
Federal 180 Hi-Shok	velocity, fps:	2620	2390	2180	1970	1780
	energy, ft-lb:	2745	2290	1895	1555	1270
	arc, inches:		+2.3	0	-9.7	-28.3
Federal 180 Sierra Pro-Hunt.	velocity, fps:	2620	2410	2200	2010	1820
	energy, ft-lb:	2745	2315	1940	1610	1330
	arc, inches:		+2.3	0	-9.3	-27.1
Federal 180 Nosler Partition	velocity, fps:	2620	2430	2240	2060	1890
	energy, ft-lb:	2745	2355	2005	1700	1430.
	arc, inches:		+2.2	0	-9.2	-26.5
Federal 180 Nosler Part. HE	velocity, fps:	2740	2550	2370	2200	2030
	energy, ft-lb:	3000	2600	2245	1925	1645
	arc, inches:		+1.9	0	-8.2	-23.5
Hornady 110 TAP-FPD	velocity, fps:	3165	2830	2519	2228	1957
	energy, ft-lb:	2446	1956	1649	1212	935
	arc, inches:		+1.4	0	-6.9	-20.9
Hornady 110 Urban Tactical	velocity, fps:	3170	2825	2504	2206	1937
	energy, ft-lb:	2454	1950	1532	1189	916
	arc, inches:		+1.5	0	-7.2	-21.2

BALLISTICS

CARTRIDGE BULLET	RANGE, YARDS:	0	100	200	300	400
Hornady 150 SP boat-tail	velocity, fps:	2820	2560	2315	2084	1866
	energy, ft-lb:	2648	2183	1785	1447	1160
	arc, inches:		+2.0	0	-8.5	-25.2
Hornady 150 SST	velocity, fps:	2820	2593	2378	2174	1984
(or Interbond)	energy, ft-lb:	2648	2240	1884	1574	1311
	arc, inches:		+1.9	0	-8.1	-22.9
Hornady 150 SST LM	velocity, fps:	3000	2765	2541	2328	2127
(or Interbond)	energy, ft-lb:	2997	2545	2150	1805	1506.
	arc, inches:		+1.5	0	-7.1	-20.6
Hornady 150 SP LM	velocity, fps:	2980	2703	2442	2195	1964
	energy, ft-lb:	2959	2433	1986	1606	1285
	arc, inches:		+1.6	0	-7.5	-22.2
Hornady 155 A-Max	velocity, fps:	2815	2610	2415	2229	2051
	energy, ft-lb:	2727	2345	2007	1709	1448
	arc, inches:		+1.9	0	-7.9	-22.6
Hornady 155 TAP-FPD	velocity, fps:	2785	2577	2379	2189	2008
	energy, ft-lb:	2669	2285	1947	1649	1387
	arc, inches:		+1.9	0	-8.0	-23.3
Hornady 165 SP boat-tail	velocity, fps:	2700	2496	2301	2115	1937
	energy, ft-lb:	2670	2283	1940	1639	1375
	arc, inches:		+2.0	0	-8.7	-25.2
Hornady 165 SPBT LM	velocity, fps:	2870	2658	2456	2283	2078
	energy, ft-lb:	3019	2589	2211	1877	1583
	arc, inches:		+1.7	0	-7.5	-21.8
Hornady 165 SST LM	velocity, fps:	2880	2672	2474	2284	2103
(or Interbond)	energy, ft-lb:	3038	2616	2242	1911	1620
	arc, inches:		+1.6	0	-7.3	-21.2
Hornady 168 BTHP Match	velocity, fps:	2700	2524	2354	2191	2035.
	energy, ft-lb:	2720	2377	2068	1791	1545
	arc, inches:		+2.0	0	-8.4	-23.9
Hornady 168 BTHP Match	velocity, fps:	2640	2630	2429	2238	2056
LM	energy, ft-lb:	3008	2579	2201	1868	1577
	arc, inches:		+1.8	0	-7.8	-22.4
Hornady 168 A-Max Match	velocity fps:	2620	2446	2280	2120	1972
	energy, ft-lb:	2560	2232	1939	1677	1450
	arc, inches:		+2.6	0	-9.2	-25.6
Hornady 168 A-Max	velocity, fps:	2700	2491	2292	2102	1921
	energy, ft-lb:	2719	2315	1959	1648	1377
	arc, inches:		+2.4	0	-9.0	-25.9
Hornady 168 TAP-FPD	velocity, fps:	2700	2513	2333	2161	1996
	energy, ft-lb:	2719	2355	2030	1742	1486
	arc, inches:		+2.0	0	-8.4	-24.3
Hornady 178 A-Max	velocity, fps:	2965	2778	2598	2425	2259
	energy, ft-lb:	3474	3049	2666	2323	2017
	arc, inches:		+1.6	0	-6.9	-19.8
Hornady 180 A-Max Match	velocity, fps:	2550	2397	2249	2106	1974
	energy, ft-lb:	2598	2295	2021	1773	1557
	arc, inches:		+2.7	0	-9.5	-26.2
Norma 150 Nosler Bal. Tip	velocity, fps:	2822	2588	2365	2154	
	energy, ft-lb:	2653	2231	1864	1545	
	arc, inches:		+1.6	0	-7.1	
Norma 150 Soft Point	velocity, fps:	2861	2537	2235	1954	
	energy, ft-lb:	2727	2144	1664	1272	
	arc, inches:		+2.0	0	-9.0	
Norma 165 TXP Swift A-Fr.	velocity, fps:	2700	2459	2231	2015	
	energy, ft-lb:	2672	2216	1824	1488	
	arc, inches:		+2.1	0	-9.1	
Norma 180 Plastic Point	velocity, fps:	2612	2365	2131	1911	
	energy, ft-lb:	2728	2235	1815	1460	
	arc, inches:		+2.4	0	-10.1	
Norma 180 Nosler Partition	velocity, fps:	2612	2414	2225	2044	
	energy, ft-lb:	2728	2330	1979	1670	
	arc, inches:		+2.2	0	-9.3	

CARTRIDGE BULLET	RANGE, YARDS:	0	100	200	300	400
Norma 180 Alaska	velocity, fps:	2612	2269	1953	1667	
	energy, ft-lb:	2728	2059	1526	1111	
	arc, inches:		+2.7	0	-11.9	
Norma 180 Vulkan	velocity, fps:	2612	2325	2056	1806	
	energy, ft-lb:	2728	2161	1690	1304	
	arc, inches:		+2.5	0	-10.8	
Norma 180 Oryx	velocity, fps:	2612	2305	2019	1755	
	energy, ft-lb:	2728	2124	1629	1232	
	arc, inches:		+2.5	0	-11.1	
Norma 200 Vulkan	velocity, fps:	2461	2215	1983	1767	
	energy, ft-lb:	2690	2179	1747	1387	
	arc, inches:		+2.8	0	-11.7	
PMC 147 FMJ boat-tail	velocity, fps:	2751	2473	2257	2052	1859
	energy, ft-lb:	2428	2037	1697	1403	1150
	arc, inches:		+2.3	0	-9.3	-27.3
PMC 150 Barnes X	velocity, fps:	2700	2504	2316	2135	1964
	energy, ft-lb:	2428	2087	1786	1518	1284
	arc, inches:		+2.0	0	-8.6	-24.7
PMC 150 Pointed Soft Point	velocity, fps:	2750	2478	2224	1987	1766
	energy, ft-lb:	2519	2045	1647	1315	1039
	arc, inches:		+2.1	0	-9.2	-27.1
PMC 150 SP boat-tail	velocity, fps:	2820	2581	2354	2139	1935
	energy, ft-lb:	2648	2218	1846	1523	1247.
	arc, inches:		+1.9	0	-8.2	-24.0
PMC 168 Barnes X	velocity, fps:	2600	2425	2256	2095	1940
	energy, ft-lb:	2476	2154	1865	1608	1379
	arc, inches:		+2.2	0	-9.0	-26.0
PMC 168 HP boat-tail	velocity, fps:	2650	2460	2278	2103	1936
	energy, ft-lb:	2619	2257	1935	1649	1399
	arc, inches:		+2.1	0	-8.8	-25.6
PMC 168 Pointed Soft Point	velocity, fps:	2559	2354	2160	1976	1803
	energy, ft-lb:	2443	2067	1740	1457	1212
	arc, inches:		+2.4	0	-9.9	-28.7
PMC 168 Pointed Soft Point	velocity, fps:	2600	2404	2216	2037	1866
	energy, ft-lb:	2476	2064	1709	1403	1142
	arc, inches:		+2.3	0	-9.8	-28.7
PMC 180 Pointed Soft Point	velocity, fps:	2550	2335	2132	1940	1760
	energy, ft-lb:	2599	2179	1816	1504	1238.
	arc, inches:		+2.5	0	-10.1	-29.5
PMC 180 SP boat-tail	velocity, fps:	2620	2446	2278	2117	1962
	energy, ft-lb:	2743	2391	2074	1790	1538
	arc, inches:		+2.2	0	-8.9	-25.4
Rem. 125 PSP C-L MR	velocity, fps:	2660	2348	2057	1788	1546
	energy, ft-lb:	1964	1529	1174	887	663
	arc, inches:		+1.1	-2.7	-14.3	-35.8
Rem. 150 PSP Core-Lokt	velocity, fps:	2820	2533	2263	2009	1774
	energy, ft-lb:	2648	2137	1705	1344	1048
	arc, inches:		+2.0	0	-8.8	-26.2
Rem. 150 PSP C-L Ultra	velocity, fps:	2620	2404	2198	2002	1818
	energy, ft-lb:	2743	2309	1930	1601	1320
	arc, inches:		+2.3	0	-9.5	-26.4
Rem. 150 Swift Scirocco	velocity, fps:	2820	2611	2410	2219	2037
	energy, ft-lb:	2648	2269	1935	1640	1381
	arc, inches:		+1.8	0	-7.8	-22.7
Rem. 165 AccuTip	velocity, fps:	2700	2501	2311	2129	1958.
	energy, ft-lb:	2670	2292	1957	1861	1401.
	arc, inches:		+2.0	0	-8.6	-24.8
Rem. 165 PSP boat-tail	velocity, fps:	2700	2497	2303	2117	1941.
	energy, ft-lb:	2670	2284	1942	1642	1379
	arc, inches:		+2.0	0	-8.6	-25.0
Rem. 165 Nosler Bal. Tip	velocity, fps:	2700	2613	2333	2161	1996
	energy, ft-lb:	2672	2314	1995	1711	1460
	arc, inches:		+2.0	0	-8.4	-24.3

BALLISTICS

Centerfire Rifle Ballistics

.308 WINCHESTER TO .30-06 SPRINGFIELD

CARTRIDGE BULLET	RANGE, YARDS:	0	100	200	300	400
Rem. 165 Swift Scirocco	velocity, fps:	2700	2513	2233	2161	1996
	energy, fps:	2670	2313	1994	1711	1459
	arc, inches:		+2.0	0	-8.4	-24.3
Rem. 168 HPBT Match	velocity, fps:	2680	2493	2314	2143	1979
	energy, ft-lb:	2678	2318	1998	1713	1460
	arc, inches:		+2.1	0	-8.6	-24.7
Rem. 180 SP Core-Lokt	velocity, fps:	2620	2274	1955	1666	1414
	energy, ft-lb:	2743	2066	1527	1109	799
	arc, inches:		+2.6	0	-11.8	-36.3
Rem. 180 PSP Core-Lokt	velocity, fps:	2620	2393	2178	1974	1782
	energy, ft-lb:	2743	2288	1896	1557	1269
	arc, inches:		+2.3	0	-9.7	-28.3
Rem. 180 Nosler Partition	velocity, fps:	2620	2436	2259	2089	1927.
	energy, ft-lb:	2743	2371	2039	1774	1485
	arc, inches:		+2.2	0	-9.0	-26.0
Speer 150 Grand Slam	velocity, fps:	2900	2599	2317	2053	
	energy, ft-lb:	2800	2249	1788	1404	
	arc, inches:		+2.1	0	-8.6	-24.8
Speer 165 Grand Slam	velocity, fps:	2700	2475	2261	2057	
	energy, ft-lb:	2670	2243	1872	1550	
	arc, inches:		+2.1	0	-8.9	-25.9
Speer 180 Grand Slam	velocity, fps:	2620	2420	2229	2046	
	energy, ft-lb:	2743	2340	1985	1674	
	arc, inches:		+2.2	0	-9.2	-26.6
Win. 150 Power-Point	velocity, fps:	2820	2488	2179	1893	1633
	energy, ft-lb:	2648	2061	1581	1193	888
	arc, inches:		+2.4	0	-9.8	-29.3
Win. 150 Power-Point Plus	velocity, fps:	2900	2558	2241	1946	1678
	energy, ft-lb:	2802	2180	1672	1262	938
	arc, inches:		+1.9	0	-8.9	-27.0
Win. 150 Partition Gold	velocity, fps:	2900	2645	2405	2177	1962
	energy, ft-lb:	2802	2332	1927	1579	1282.
	arc, inches:		+1.7	0	-7.8	-22.9
Win. 150 Ballistic Silvertip	velocity, fps:	2810	2601	2401	2211	2028
	energy, ft-lb:	2629	2253	1920	1627	1370.
	arc, inches:		+1.8	0	-7.8	-22.8
Win. 150 Fail Safe	velocity, fps:	2820	2533	2263	2010	1775
	energy, ft-lb:	2649	2137	1706	1346	1049
	arc, inches:		+2.0	0	-8.8	-26.2
Win. 150 Supreme Elite XP3	velocity, fps:	2825	2616	2417	2226	2044
	energy, ft-lb:	2658	2279	1945	1650	1392
	arc, inches:		+1.8	0	-7.8	-22.6
Win. 168 Ballistic Silvertip	velocity, fps:	2670	2484	2306	2134	1971
	energy, ft-lb:	2659	2301	1983	1699	1449
	arc, inches:		+2.1	0	-8.6	-24.8
Win. 168 HP boat-tail Match	velocity, fps:	2680	2485	2297	2118	1948
	energy, ft-lb:	2680	2303	1970	1674	1415
	arc, inches:		+2.1	0	-8.7	-25.1
Win. 180 Power-Point	velocity, fps:	2620	2274	1955	1666	1414
	energy, ft-lb:	2743	2066	1527	1109	799
	arc, inches:		+2.9	0	-12.1	-36.9
Win. 180 Silvertip	velocity, fps:	2620	2393	2178	1974	1782
	energy, ft-lb:	2743	2288	1896	1557	1269
	arc, inches:		+2.6	0	-9.9	-28.9

.30-06 SPRINGFIELD

CARTRIDGE BULLET	RANGE, YARDS:	0	100	200	300	400
A-Square 180 M & D-T	velocity, fps:	2700	2365	2054	1769	1524
	energy, ft-lb:	2913	2235	1687	1251	928
	arc, inches:		+2.4	0	-10.6	-32.4
A-Square 220 Monolythic Solid	velocity, fps:	2380	2108	1854	1623	1424
	energy, ft-lb:	2767	2171	1679	1287	990
	arc, inches:		+3.1	0	-13.6	-39.9

CARTRIDGE BULLET	RANGE, YARDS:	0	100	200	300	400
Black Hills 150 Nosler B. Tip	velocity, fps:	2900				
	energy, ft-lb:	2770				
	arc, inches:					
Black Hills 165 Nosler B. Tip	velocity, fps:	2750				
	energy, ft-lb:	2770				
	arc, inches:					
Black Hills 168 Hor. Match	velocity, fps:	2700				
	energy, ft-lb:	2718				
	arc, inches:					
Black Hills 180 Barnes X	velocity, fps:	2650				
	energy, ft-lb:	2806				
	arc, inches:					
Black Hills 180 AccuBond	velocity, ft-lb:	2700				
	energy, ft-lb:					
	arc, inches:					
Federal 125 Sierra Pro-Hunt.	velocity, fps:	3140	2780	2450	2140	1850
	energy, ft-lb:	2735	2145	1660	1270	955
	arc, inches:		+1.5	0	-7.3	-22.3
Federal 150 Hi-Shok	velocity, fps:	2910	2620	2340	2080	1840
	energy, ft-lb:	2820	2280	1825	1445	1130
	arc, inches:		+1.8	0	-8.2	-24.4
Federal 150 Sierra Pro-Hunt.	velocity, fps:	2910	2640	2380	2130	1900
	energy, ft-lb:	2820	2315	1880	1515	1205
	arc, inches:		+1.7	0	-7.9	-23.3
Federal 150 Sierra GameKing BTSP	velocity, fps:	2910	2690	2480	2270	2070
	energy, ft-lb:	2820	2420	2040	1710	1430
	arc, inches:		+1.7	0	-7.4	-21.5
Federal 150 Nosler Bal. Tip	velocity, fps:	2910	2700	2490	2300	2110
	energy, ft-lb:	2820	2420	2070	1760	1485
	arc, inches:		+1.6	0	-7.3	-21.1
Federal 150 FMJ boat-tail	velocity, fps:	2910	2710	2510	2320	2150
	energy, ft-lb:	2820	2440	2100	1800	1535
	arc, inches:		+1.6	0	-7.1	-20.8
Federal 165 Sierra Pro-Hunt.	velocity, fps:	2800	2560	2340	2130	1920
	energy, ft-lb:	2875	2410	2005	1655	1360
	arc, inches:		+1.9	0	-8.3	-24.3
Federal 165 Sierra GameKing BTSP	velocity, fps:	2800	2610	2420	2240	2070.
	energy, ft-lb:	2870	2490	2150	1840	1580
	arc, inches:		+1.8	0	-7.8	-22.4
Federal 165 Sierra GameKing HE	velocity, fps:	3140	2900	2670	2450	2240.
	energy, ft-lb:	3610	3075	2610	2200	1845
	arc, inches:		+1.5	0	-6.9	-20.4
Federal 165 Nosler Bal. Tip	velocity, fps:	2800	2610	2430	2250	2080
	energy, ft-lb:	2870	2495	2155	1855	1585
	arc, inches:		+1.8	0	-7.7	-22.3
Federal 165 Trophy Bonded	velocity, fps:	2800	2540	2290	2050	1830.
	energy, ft-lb:	2870	2360	1915	1545	1230
	arc, inches:		+2.0	0	-8.7	-25.4
Federal 165 Tr. Bonded HE	velocity, fps:	3140	2860	2590	2340	2100
	energy, ft-lb:	3610	2990	2460	2010	1625.
	arc, inches:		+1.6	0	-7.4	-21.9
Federal 168 Sierra MatchKg. BTHP	velocity, fps:	2700	2510	2320	2150	1980
	energy, ft-lb:	2720	2350	2010	1720	1460
	arc, inches:		+16.2	+28.4	+34.1	+32.3
Federal 180 Hi-Shok	velocity, fps:	2700	2470	2250	2040	1850
	energy, ft-lb:	2915	2435	2025	1665	1360
	arc, inches:		+2.1	0	-9.0	-26.4
Federal 180 Sierra Pro-Hunt. RN	velocity, fps:	2700	2350	2020	1730	1470
	energy, ft-lb:	2915	2200	1630	1190	860
	arc, inches:		+2.4	0	-11.0	-33.6
Federal 180 Nosler Partition	velocity, fps:	2700	2500	2320	2140	1970
	energy, ft-lb:	2915	2510	2150	1830	1550
	arc, inches:		+2.0	0	-8.6	-24.6

CARTRIDGE BULLET	RANGE, YARDS:	0	100	200	300	400
Federal 180 Nosler Part. HE	velocity, fps:	2880	2690	2500	2320	2150
	energy, ft-lb:	3315	2880	2495	2150	1845
	arc, inches:		+1.7	0	-7.2	-21.0
Federal 180 Sierra GameKing BTSP	velocity, fps:	2700	2540	2380	2220	2080
	energy, ft-lb:	2915	2570	2260	1975	1720
	arc, inches:		+1.9	0	-8.1	-23.1
Federal 180 Barnes XLC	velocity, fps:	2700	2530	2360	2200	2040.
	energy, ft-lb:	2915	2550	2220	1930	1670
	arc, inches:		+2.0	0	-8.3	-23.8
Federal 180 Trophy Bonded	velocity, fps:	2700	2460	2220	2000	1800
	energy, ft-lb:	2915	2410	1975	1605	1290
	arc, inches:		+2.2	0	-9.2	-27.0
Federal 180 Tr. Bonded HE	velocity, fps:	2880	2630	2380	2160	1940
	energy, ft-lb:	3315	2755	2270	1855	1505
	arc, inches:		+1.8	0	-8.0	-23.3
Federal 220 Sierra Pro-Hunt. RN	velocity, fps:	2410	2130	1870	1630	1420
	energy, ft-lb:	2835	2215	1705	1300	985
	arc, inches:		+3.1	0	-13.1	-39.3
Hornady 150 SP	velocity, fps:	2910	2617	2342	2083	1843
	energy, ft-lb:	2820	2281	1827	1445	1131
	arc, inches:		+2.1	0	-8.5	-25.0
Hornady 150 SP LM	velocity, fps:	3100	2815	2548	2295	2058
	energy, ft-lb:	3200	2639	2161	1755	1410
	arc, inches:		+1.4	0	-6.8	-20.3
Hornady 150 SP boat-tail	velocity, fps:	2910	2683	2467	2262	2066.
	energy, ft-lb:	2820	2397	2027	1706	1421
	arc, inches:		+2.0	0	-7.7	-22.2
Hornady 150 SST (or Interbond)	velocity, fps:	2910	2802	2599	2405	2219
	energy, ft-lb:	3330	2876	2474	2118	1803
	arc, inches:		+1.5	0	-6.6	-19.3
Hornady 150 SST LM	velocity, fps:	3100	2860	2631	2414	2208
	energy, ft-lb:	3200	2724	2306	1941	1624
	arc, inches:		+1.4	0	-6.6	-19.2
Hornady 165 SP boat-tail	velocity, fps:	2800	2591	2392	2202	2020
	energy, ft-lb:	2873	2460	2097	1777	1495
	arc, inches:		+1.8	0	-8.0	-23.3
Hornady 165 SPBT LM	velocity, fps:	3015	2790	2575	2370	2176
	energy, ft-lb:	3330	2850	2428	2058	1734
	arc, inches:		+1.6	0	-7.0	-20.1
Hornady 165 SST (or Interbond)	velocity, fps:	2800	2598	2405	2221	2046
	energy, ft-lb:	2872	2473	2119	1808	1534
	arc, inches:		+1.9	0	-8.0	-22.8
Hornady 165 SST LM	velocity, fps:	3015	2802	2599	2405	2219
	energy, ft-lb:	3330	2878	2474	2118	1803.
	arc, inches:		+1.5	0	-6.5	-19.3
Hornady 168 HPBT Match	velocity, fps:	2790	2620	2447	2280	2120.
	energy, ft-lb:	2925	2561	2234	1940	1677.
	arc, inches:		+1.7	0	-7.7	-22.2
Hornady 180 SP	velocity, fps:	2700	2469	2258	2042	1846
	energy, ft-lb:	2913	2436	2023	1666	1362
	arc, inches:		+2.4	0	-9.3	-27.0
Hornady 180 SPBT LM	velocity, fps:	2880	2676	2480	2293	2114
	energy, ft-lb:	3316	2862	2459	2102	1786
	arc, inches:		+1.7	0	-7.3	-21.3
Norma 150 Nosler Bal. Tip	velocity, fps:	2936	2713	2502	2300	
	energy, ft-lb:	2872	2453	2085	1762	
	arc, inches:		+1.6	0	-7.1	
Norma 150 Soft Point	velocity, fps:	2972	2640	2331	2043	
	energy, ft-lb:	2943	2321	1810	1390	
	arc, inches:		+1.8	0	-8.2	
Norma 180 Alaska	velocity, fps:	2700	2351	2028	1734	
	energy, ft-lb:	2914	2209	1645	1202	
	arc, inches:		+2.4	0	-11.0	
Norma 180 Nosler Partition	velocity, fps:	2700	2494	2297	2108	
	energy, ft-lb:	2914	2486	2108	1777	
	arc, inches:		+2.1	0	-8.7	
Norma 180 Plastic Point	velocity, fps:	2700	2455	2222	2003	
	energy, ft-lb:	2914	2409	1974	1603	
	arc, inches:		+2.1	0	-9.2	
Norma 180 Vulkan	velocity, fps:	2700	2416	2150	1901	
	energy, ft-lb:	2914	2334	1848	1445	
	arc, inches:		+2.2	0	-9.8	
Norma 180 Oryx	velocity, fps:	2700	2387	2095	1825	
	energy, ft-lb:	2914	2278	1755	1332	
	arc, inches:		+2.3	0	-10.2	
Norma 180 TXP Swift A-Fr.	velocity, fps:	2700	2479	2268	2067	
	energy, ft-lb:	2914	2456	2056	1708	
	arc, inches:		+2.0	0	-8.8	
Norma 180 AccuBond	velocity, fps:	2674	2499	2331	2169	
	energy, ft-lb:	2859	2497	2172	1881	
	arc, inches:		+2.0	0	-8.5	
Norma 200 Vulkan	velocity, fps:	2641	2385	2143	1916	
	energy, ft-lb:	3098	2527	2040	1631	
	arc, inches:		+2.3	0	-9.9	
Norma 200 Oryx	velocity, fps:	2625	2362	2115	1883	
	energy, ft-lb:	3061	2479	1987	1575	
	arc, inches:		+2.3	0	-10.1	
PMC 150 X-Bullet	velocity, fps:	2750	2552	2361	2179	2005
	energy, ft-lb:	2518	2168	1857	1582	1339
	arc, inches:		+2.0	0	-8.2	-23.7
PMC 150 Pointed Soft Point	velocity, fps:	2773	2542	2322	2113	1916
	energy, ft-lb:	2560	2152	1796	1487	1222.
	arc, inches:		+1.9	0	-8.4	-24.6
PMC 150 SP boat-tail	velocity, fps:	2900	2657	2427	2208	2000
	energy, ft-lb:	2801	2351	1961	1623	1332
	arc, inches:		+1.7	0	-7.7	-22.5
PMC 150 FMJ	velocity, fps:	2773	2542	2322	2113	1916
	energy, ft-lb:	2560	2152	1796	1487	1222
	arc, inches:		+1.9	0	-8.4	-24.6
PMC 168 Barnes X	velocity, fps:	2750	2569	2395	2228	2067
	energy, ft-lb:	2770	2418	2101	1818	1565
	arc, inches:		+1.9	0	-8.0	-23.0
PMC 180 Barnes X	velocity, fps:	2650	2487	2331	2179	2034
	energy, ft-lb:	2806	2472	2171	1898	1652
	arc, inches:		+2.1	0	-8.5	-24.3
PMC 180 Pointed Soft Point	velocity, fps:	2650	2430	2221	2024	1839
	energy, ft-lb:	2807	2359	1972	1638	1351
	arc, inches:		+2.2	0	-9.3	-27.0
PMC 180 SP boat-tail	velocity, fps:	2700	2523	2352	2188	2030
	energy, ft-lb:	2913	2543	2210	1913	1646
	arc, inches:		+2.0	0	-8.3	-23.9
PMC 180 HPBT Match	velocity, fps:	2800	2622	2456	2302	2158
	energy, ft-lb:	3133	2747	2411	2118	1861
	arc, inches:		+1.8	0	-7.6	-21.7
Rem. 55 PSP (sabot) "Accelerator"	velocity, fps:	4080	3484	2964	2499	2080
	energy, ft-lb:	2033	1482	1073	763	528.
	arc, inches:		+1.4	+1.4	-2.6	-12.2
Rem. 125 PSP C-L MR	velocity, fps:	2660	2335	2034	1757	1509
	energy, ft-lb:	1964	1513	1148	856	632
	arc, inches:		+1.1	-3.0	-15.5	-37.4
Rem. 125 Pointed Soft Point	velocity, fps:	3140	2780	2447	2138	1853
	energy, ft-lb:	2736	2145	1662	1269	953.
	arc, inches:		+1.5	0	-7.4	-22.4
Rem. 150 AccuTip	velocity, fps:	2910	2686	2473	2270	2077
	energy, ft-lb:	2820	2403	2037	1716	1436
	arc, inches:		+1.8	0	-7.4	-21.5

BALLISTICS

Centerfire Rifle Ballistics

.30-06 SPRINGFIELD TO .300 BLACKOUT

CARTRIDGE BULLET	RANGE, YARDS:	0	100	200	300	400
Rem. 150 PSP Core-Lokt	velocity, fps:	2910	2617	2342	2083	1843
	energy, ft-lb:	2820	2281	1827	1445	1131
	arc, inches:		+1.8	0	-8.2	-24.4
Rem. 150 Bronze Point	velocity, fps:	2910	2656	2416	2189	1974
	energy, ft-lb:	2820	2349	1944	1596	1298
	arc, inches:		+1.7	0	-7.7	-22.7
Rem. 150 Nosler Bal. Tip	velocity, fps:	2910	2696	2492	2298	2112.
	energy, ft-lb:	2821	2422	2070	1769	1485
	arc, inches:		+1.6	0	-7.3	-21.1
Rem. 150 Swift Scirocco	velocity, fps:	2910	2696	2492	2298	2111
	energy, ft-lb:	2820	2421	2069	1758	1485
	arc, inches:		+1.6	0	-7.3	-21.1
Rem. 165 AccuTip	velocity, fps:	2800	2597	2403	2217	2039
	energy, ft-lb:	2872	2470	2115	1800	1523
	arc, inches:		+1.8	0	-7.9	-22.8
Rem. 165 PSP Core-Lokt	velocity, fps:	2800	2534	2283	2047	1825.
	energy, ft-lb:	2872	2352	1909	1534	1220
	arc, inches:		+2.0	0	-8.7	-25.9
Rem. 165 PSP boat-tail	velocity, fps:	2800	2592	2394	2204	2023
	energy, ft-lb:	2872	2462	2100	1780	1500
	arc, inches:		+1.8	0	-7.9	-23.0
Rem. 165 Nosler Bal. Tip	velocity, fps:	2800	2609	2426	2249	2080.
	energy, ft-lb:	2873	2494	2155	1854	1588
	arc, inches:		+1.8	0	-7.7	-22.3
Rem. 168 PSP C-L Ultra	velocity, fps:	2800	2546	2306	2079	1866
	energy, ft-lb:	2924	2418	1984	1613	1299
	arc, inches:		+1.9	0	-8.5	-25.1
Rem. 180 SP Core-Lokt	velocity, fps:	2700	2348	2023	1727	1466
	energy, ft-lb:	2913	2203	1635	1192	859
	arc, inches:		+2.4	0	-11.0	-33.8
Rem. 180 PSP Core-Lokt	velocity, fps:	2700	2469	2250	2042	1846
	energy, ft-lb:	2913	2436	2023	1666	1362
	arc, inches:		+2.1	0	-9.0	-26.3
Rem. 180 PSP C-L Ultra	velocity, fps:	2700	2480	2270	2070	1882
	energy, ft-lb:	2913	2457	2059	1713	1415
	arc, inches:		+2.1	0	-8.9	-25.8
Rem. 180 Bronze Point	velocity, fps:	2700	2485	2280	2084	1899.
	energy, ft-lb:	2913	2468	2077	1736	1441
	arc, inches:		+2.1	0	-8.8	-25.5
Rem. 180 Swift A-Frame	velocity, fps:	2700	2465	2243	2032	1833
	energy, ft-lb:	2913	2429	2010	1650	1343
	arc, inches:		+2.1	0	-9.1	-26.6
Rem. 180 Nosler Partition	velocity, fps:	2700	2512	2332	2160	1995
	energy, ft-lb:	2913	2522	2174	1864	1590
	arc, inches:		+2.0	0	-8.4	-24.3
Rem. 220 SP Core-Lokt	velocity, fps:	2410	2130	1870	1632	1422
	energy, ft-lb:	2837	2216	1708	1301	988
	arc, inches, s:		0	-6.2	-22.4	
Speer 150 Grand Slam	velocity, fps:	2975	2669	2383	2114	
	energy, ft-lb:	2947	2372	1891	1489	
	arc, inches:		+2.0	0	-8.1	-24.1
Speer 165 Grand Slam	velocity, fps:	2790	2560	2342	2134	
	energy, ft-lb:	2851	2401	2009	1669	
	arc, inches:		+1.9	0	-8.3	-24.1
Speer 180 Grand Slam	velocity, fps:	2690	2487	2293	2108	
	energy, ft-lb:	2892	2472	2101	1775	
	arc, inches:		+2.1	0	-8.8	-25.1
Win. 125 Pointed Soft Point	velocity, fps:	3140	2780	2447	2138	1853
	energy, ft-lb:	2736	2145	1662	1269	953
	arc, inches:		+1.8	0	-7.7	-23.0
Win. 150 Power-Point	velocity, fps:	2920	2580	2265	1972	1704
	energy, ft-lb:	2839	2217	1708	1295	967
	arc, inches:		+2.2	0	-9.0	-27.0
Win. 150 Power-Point Plus	velocity, fps:	3050	2685	2352	2043	1760
	energy, ft-lb:	3089	2402	1843	1391	1032
	arc, inches:		+1.7	0	-8.0	-24.3
Win. 150 Silvertip	velocity, fps:	2910	2617	2342	2083	1843
	energy, ft-lb:	2820	2281	1827	1445	1131
	arc, inches:		+2.1	0	-8.5	-25.0
Win. 150 Partition Gold	velocity, fps:	2960	2705	2464	2235	2019
	energy, ft-lb:	2919	2437	2022	1664	1358.
	arc, inches:		+1.6	0	-7.4	-21.7
Win. 150 Ballistic Silvertip	velocity, fps:	2900	2687	2483	2289	2103
	energy, ft-lb:	2801	2404	2054	1745	1473
	arc, inches:		+1.7	0	-7.3	-21.2
Win. 150 Fail Safe	velocity, fps:	2920	2625	2349	2089	1848
	energy, ft-lb:	2841	2296	1838	1455	1137
	arc, inches:		+1.8	0	-8.1	-24.3
Win. 165 Pointed Soft Point	velocity, fps:	2800	2573	2357	2151	1956
	energy, ft-lb:	2873	2426	2036	1696	1402
	arc, inches:		+2.2	0	-8.4	-24.4
Win. 165 Fail Safe	velocity, fps:	2800	2540	2295	2063	1846
	energy, ft-lb:	2873	2365	1930	1560	1249
	arc, inches:		+2.0	0	-8.6	-25.3
Win. 168 Ballistic Silvertip	velocity, fps:	2790	2599	2416	2240	2072
	energy, ft-lb:	2903	2520	2177	1872	1601
	arc, inches:		+1.8	0	-7.8	-22.5
Win. 180 Ballistic Silvertip	velocity, fps:	2750	2572	2402	2237	2080
	energy, ft-lb:	3022	2644	2305	2001	1728
	arc, inches:		+1.9	0	-7.9	-22.8
Win. 180 Power-Point	velocity, fps:	2700	2348	2023	1727	1466
	energy, ft-lb:	2913	2203	1635	1192	859
	arc, inches:		+2.7	0	-11.3	-34.4
Win. 180 Power-Point Plus	velocity, fps:	2770	2563	2366	2177	1997
	energy, ft-lb:	3068	2627	2237	1894	1594
	arc, inches:		+1.9	0	-8.1	-23.6
Win. 180 Silvertip	velocity, fps:	2700	2469	2250	2042	1846
	energy, ft-lb:	2913	2436	2023	1666	1362
	arc, inches:		+2.4	0	-9.3	-27.0
Win. 180 AccuBond	velocity, fps:	2750	2573	2403	2239	2082
	energy, ft-lb:	3022	2646	2308	2004	1732
	arc, inches:		+1.9	0	-7.9	-22.8
Win. 180 Partition Gold	velocity, fps:	2790	2581	2382	2192	2010
	energy, ft-lb:	3112	2664	2269	1920	1615
	arc, inches:		+1.9	0	-8.0	-23.2
Win. 180 Fail Safe	velocity, fps:	2700	2486	2283	2089	1904
	energy, ft-lb:	2914	2472	2083	1744	1450
	arc, inches:		+2.1	0	-8.7	-25.5
Win. 150 Supreme Elite XP3	velocity, fps:	2925	2712	2508	2313	2127
	energy, ft-lb:	2849	2448	2095	1782	1507
	arc, inches:		+1.6	0	-7.2	-20.8
Win. 180 Supreme Elite XP3	velocity, fps:	2750	2579	2414	2256	2103
	energy, ft-lb:	3022	2658	2330	2034	1768
	arc, inches:		+1.9	0	-7.8	-22.5

.300 BLACKOUT (.300 WHISPER)

CARTRIDGE BULLET	RANGE, YARDS:	0	100	200	300	400
Barnes 110 Tac/TX	velocity, fps:	2350	1810	1369		
	energy, ft-lb:	1349	800	458		
	arc, inches:	-1.5	-6.7	-55.5		
Hornady 110 V-MAX	velocity, fps:	2375	2094	1834	1597	
	energy, ft-lb:	1378	1071	821	623	
	arc, inches:	-1.5	+3.2	0	-13.7	
Hornady 208 A-MAX	velocity, fps:	1020	987	959		
	energy, ft-lb:	480	450	424		
	arc, inches:	-1.5	0	-34.1		

BALLISTICS

CARTRIDGE BULLET	RANGE, YARDS:	0	100	200	300	400
.300 H&H MAGNUM						
Handload, 165 Sierra HP	velocity, fps:	3000	2784	2579	2382	2195
	energy, ft-lb:	3297	2840	2436	2079	1764
	arc, inches:	-1.5	+1.5	0	-6.7	-19.5
Federal 180 Barnes TSX	velocity, fps:	2880	2680	2480	2290	2120
	energy, ft-lb:	3315	2860	2460	2105	1790
	arc, inches:	-1.5	+1.7	0	-7.3	-21.3
Hornady 180 InterBond	velocity, fps:	2870	2678	2493	2316	2146
	energy, ft-lb:	3292	2865	2484	2144	1841
	arc, inches:	-1.5	+1.7	0	-7.3	-21.0
Federal 180 Nosler Partition	velocity, fps:	2880	2620	2380	2150	1930
	energy, ft-lb:	3315	2750	2260	1840	1480
	arc, inches:		+1.8	0	-8.0	-23.4
Win. 180 Fail Safe	velocity, fps:	2880	2628	2390	2165	1952
	energy, ft-lb:	3316	2762	2284	1873	1523
	arc, inches:		+1.8	0	-7.9	-23.2
Handload, 190 Hornady	velocity, fps:	2800	2615	2437	2266	2102
	energy, ft-lb:	3307	2884	2505	2166	1864
	arc, inches:	-1.5	+1.8	0	-7.7	-22.1
.308 NORMA MAGNUM						
Norma 180 TXP Swift A-Fr.	velocity, fps:	2953	2704	2469	2245	
	energy, ft-lb:	3486	2924	2437	2016	
	arc, inches:		+1.6	0	-7.3	
Norma 180 Oryx	velocity, fps:	2953	2630	2330	2049	
	energy, ft-lb:	3486	2766	2170	1679	
	arc, inches:		+1.8	0	-8.2	
Norma 200 Vulkan	velocity, fps:	2903	2624	2361	2114	
	energy, ft-lb:	3744	3058	2476	1985	
	arc, inches:	0	+1.8	0	-8.0	
Nosler 180 AB	velocity, fps:	2975	2787	2608	2435	2269
	energy, ft-lb:	3536	3105	2718	2371	2058
	arc, inches:	-1.5	+1.5	0	-6.6	-19.1
.300 WINCHESTER MAGNUM						
A-Square 180 Dead Tough	velocity, fps:	3120	2756	2420	2108	1820
	energy, ft-lb:	3890	3035	2340	1776	1324
	arc, inches:		+1.6	0	-7.6	-22.9
Black Hills 180 Nos. Bal. Tip	velocity, fps:	3100				
	energy, ft-lb:	3498				
	arc, inches:					
Black Hills 180 Barnes X	velocity, fps:	2950				
	energy, ft-lb:	3498				
	arc, inches:					
Black Hills 180 AccuBond	velocity, fps:	3000				
	energy, ft-lb:	3597				
	arc, inches:					
Black Hills 190 Match	velocity, fps:	2950				
	energy, ft-lb:	3672				
	arc, inches:					
Federal 150 Sierra Pro Hunt.	velocity, fps:	3280	3030	2800	2570	2360.
	energy, ft-lb:	3570	3055	2600	2205	1860
	arc, inches:		+1.1	0	-5.6	-16.4
Federal 150 Trophy Bonded	velocity, fps:	3280	2980	2700	2430	2190
	energy, ft-lb:	3570	2450	2420	1970	1590
	arc, inches:		+1.2	0	-6.0	-17.9
Federal 180 Sierra Pro Hunt.	velocity, fps:	2960	2750	2540	2340	2160
	energy, ft-lb:	3500	3010	2580	2195	1860
	arc, inches:		+1.6	0	-7.0	-20.3
Federal 180 Barnes XLC	velocity, fps:	2960	2780	2600	2430	2260
	energy, ft-lb:	3500	3080	2700	2355	2050
	arc, inches:		+1.5	0	-6.6	-19.2

CARTRIDGE BULLET	RANGE, YARDS:	0	100	200	300	400
Federal 180 Trophy Bonded	velocity, fps:	2960	2700	2460	2220	2000
	energy, ft-lb:	3500	2915	2410	1975	1605
	arc, inches:		+1.6	0	-7.4	-21.9
Federal 180 Tr. Bonded HE	velocity, fps:	3100	2830	2580	2340	2110
	energy, ft-lb:	3840	3205	2660	2190	1790
	arc, inches:		+1.4	0	-6.6	-19.7
Federal 180 Nosler Partition	velocity, fps:	2960	2700	2450	2210	1990
	energy, ft-lb:	3500	2905	2395	1955	1585
	arc, inches:		+1.6	0	-7.5	-22.1
Federal 190 Sierra MatchKg. BTHP	velocity, fps:	2900	2730	2560	2400	2240
	energy, ft-lb:	3550	3135	2760	2420	2115
	arc, inches:		+12.9	+22.5	+26.9	+25.1
Federal 200 Sierra GameKing BTSP	velocity, fps:	2830	2680	2530	2380	2240
	energy, ft-lb:	3560	3180	2830	2520	2230
	arc, inches:		+1.7	0	-7.1	-20.4
Federal 200 Nosler Part. HE	velocity, fps:	2930	2740	2550	2370	2200
	energy, ft-lb:	3810	3325	2885	2495	2145
	arc, inches:		+1.6	0	-6.9	-20.1
Federal 200 Trophy Bonded	velocity, fps:	2800	2570	2350	2150	1950
	energy, ft-lb:	3480	2935	2460	2050	1690
	arc, inches:		+1.9	0	-8.2	-23.9
Hornady 150 SP boat-tail	velocity, fps:	3275	2988	2718	2464	2224
	energy, ft-lb:	3573	2974	2461	2023	1648
	arc, inches:		+1.2	0	-6.0	-17.8
Hornady 150 SST (and Interbond)	velocity, fps:	3275	3027	2791	2565	2352
	energy, ft-lb:	3572	3052	2593	2192	1842
	arc, inches:		+1.2	0	-5.8	-17.0
Hornady 165 SP boat-tail	velocity, fps:	3100	2877	2665	2462	2269.
	energy, ft-lb:	3522	3033	2603	2221	1887
	arc, inches:		+1.3	0	-6.5	-18.5
Hornady 165 SST	velocity, fps:	3100	2885	2680	2483	2296
	energy, ft-lb:	3520	3049	2630	2259	1930
	arc, inches:		+1.4	0	-6.4	-18.6
Hornady 180 SP boat-tail	velocity, fps:	2960	2745	2540	2344	2157
	energy, ft-lb:	3501	3011	2578	2196	1859
	arc, inches:		+1.9	0	-7.3	-20.9
Hornady 180 SST	velocity, fps:	2960	2764	2575	2395	2222
	energy, ft-lb:	3501	3052	2650	2292	1974
	arc, inches:		+1.6	0	-7.0	-20.1.
Hornady 180 SPBT HM	velocity, fps:	3100	2879	2668	2467	2275
	energy, ft-lb:	3840	3313	2845	2431	2068
	arc, inches:		+1.4	0	-6.4	-18.7
Hornady 190 SP boat-tail	velocity, fps:	2900	2711	2529	2355	2187
	energy, ft-lb:	3549	3101	2699	2340	2018
	arc, inches:		+1.6	0	-7.1	-20.4
Norma 150 Nosler Bal. Tip	velocity, fps:	3250	3014	2791	2578	
	energy, ft-lb:	3519	3027	2595	2215	
	arc, inches:		+1.1	0	-5.6	
Norma 150 Barnes TS	velocity, fps:	3215	2982	2761	2550	
	energy, ft-lb:	3444	2962	2539	2167	
	arc, inches:		+1.2	0	-5.8	
Norma 165 Scirocco	velocity, fps:	3117	2921	2734	2554	
	energy, ft-lb:	3561	3127	2738	2390	
	arc, inches:		+1.2	0	-5.9	
Norma 180 Soft Point	velocity, fps:	3018	2780	2555	2341	
	energy, ft-lb:	3641	3091	2610	2190	
	arc, inches:		+1.5	0	-7.0	
Norma 180 Plastic Point	velocity, fps:	3018	2755	2506	2271	
	energy, ft-lb:	3641	3034	2512	2062	
	arc, inches:		+1.6	0	-7.1	
Norma 180 TXP Swift A-Fr.	velocity, fps:	2920	2688	2467	2256	
	energy, ft-lb:	3409	2888	2432	2035	
	arc, inches:		+1.7	0	-7.4	

BALLISTICS

Centerfire Rifle Ballistics

.300 WINCHESTER MAGNUM TO .300 REMINGTON SHORT ULTRA MAGNUM

CARTRIDGE BULLET	RANGE, YARDS:	0	100	200	300	400
Norma 180 AccuBond	velocity, fps:	2953	2767	2588	2417	
	energy, ft-lb:	3486	3061	2678	2335	
	arc, inches:		+1.5	0	-6.7	
Norma 180 Oryx	velocity, fps:	2920	2600	2301	2023	
	energy, ft-lb:	3409	2702	2117	1636	
	arc, inches:		+1.8	0	-8.4	
Norma 200 Vulkan	velocity, fps:	2887	2609	2347	2100	
	energy, ft-lb:	3702	3023	2447	1960	
	arc, inches:		+1.8	0	-8.2	
Norma 200 Oryx	velocity, fps:	2789	2510	2248	2002	
	energy, ft-lb:	3455	2799	2245	1780	
	arc, inches:		+2.0	0	-8.9	
PMC 150 Barnes X	velocity, fps:	3135	2918	2712	2515	2327
	energy, ft-lb:	3273	2836	2449	2107	1803
	arc, inches:		+1.3	0	-6.1	-17.7
PMC 150 Pointed Soft Point	velocity, fps:	3150	2902	2665	2438	2222
	energy, ft-lb:	3304	2804	2364	1979	1644.
	arc, inches:		+1.3	0	-6.2	-18.3
PMC 150 SP boat-tail	velocity, fps:	3250	2987	2739	2504	2281
	energy, ft-lb:	3517	2970	2498	2088	1733
	arc, inches:		+1.2	0	-6.0	-17.4
PMC 180 Barnes X	velocity, fps:	2910	2738	2572	2412	2258
	energy, ft-lb:	3384	2995	2644	2325	2037
	arc, inches:		+1.6	0	-6.9	-19.8
PMC 180 Pointed Soft Point	velocity, fps:	2853	2643	2446	2258	2077
	energy, ft-lb:	3252	2792	2391	2037	1724
	arc, inches:		+1.7	0	-7.5	-21.9
PMC 180 SP boat-tail	velocity, fps:	2900	2714	2536	2365	2200
	energy, ft-lb:	3361	2944	2571	2235	1935
	arc, inches:		+1.6	0	-7.1	-20.3
PMC 180 HPBT Match	velocity, fps:	2950	2755	2568	2390	2219
	energy, ft-lb:	3478	3033	2636	2283	1968
	arc, inches:		+1.5	0	-6.8	-19.7
Rem. 150 PSP Core-Lokt	velocity, fps:	3290	2951	2636	2342	2068
	energy, ft-lb:	3605	2900	2314	1827	1859
	arc, inches:		+1.6	0	-7.0	-20.2
Rem. 150 PSP C-L MR	velocity, fps:	2650	2373	2113	1870	1646
	energy, ft-lb:	2339	1875	1486	1164	902
	arc, inches:		+1.0	-2.7	-14.3	-35.8
Rem. 150 PSP C-L Ultra	velocity, fps:	3290	2967	2666	2384	2120
	energy, ft-lb:	3065	2931	2366	1893	1496
	arc, inches:		+1.2	0	-6.1	-18.4
Rem. 180 AccuTip	velocity, fps:	2960	2764	2577	2397	2224
	energy, ft-lb:	3501	3053	2653	2295	1976
	arc, inches:		+1.5	0	-6.8	-19.6
Rem. 180 PSP Core-Lokt	velocity, fps:	2960	2745	2540	2344	2157
	energy, ft-lb:	3501	3011	2578	2196	1424
	arc, inches:		+2.2	+1.9	-3.4	-15.0
Rem. 180 PSP C-L Ultra	velocity, fps:	2960	2727	2505	2294	2093
	energy, ft-lb:	3501	2971	2508	2103	1751
	arc, inches:		+2.7	+2.2	-3.8	-16.4
Rem. 180 Nosler Partition	velocity, fps:	2960	2725	2503	2291	2089
	energy, ft-lb:	3501	2968	2503	2087	1744
	arc, inches:		+1.6	0	-7.2	-20.9
Rem. 180 Nosler Bal. Tip	velocity, fps:	2960	2774	2595	2424	2259.
	energy, ft-lb:	3501	3075	2692	2348	2039
	arc, inches:		+1.5	0	-6.7	-19.3
Rem. 180 Swift Scirocco	velocity, fps:	2960	2774	2595	2424	2259
	energy, ft-lb:	3501	3075	2692	2348	2039
	arc, inches:		+1.5	0	-6.7	-19.3
Rem. 190 PSP boat-tail	velocity, fps:	2885	2691	2506	2327	2156
	energy, ft-lb:	3511	3055	2648	2285	1961
	arc, inches:		+1.6	0	-7.2	-20.8

CARTRIDGE BULLET	RANGE, YARDS:	0	100	200	300	400
Rem. 190 HPBT Match	velocity, fps:	2900	2725	2557	2395	2239
	energy, ft-lb:	3547	3133	2758	2420	2115
	arc, inches:		+1.6	0	-6.9	-19.9
Rem. 200 Swift A-Frame	velocity, fps:	2825	2595	2376	2167	1970
	energy, ft-lb:	3544	2989	2506	2086	1722
	arc, inches:		+1.8	0	-8.0	-23.5
Speer 180 Grand Slam	velocity, fps:	2950	2735	2530	2334	
	energy, ft-lb:	3478	2989	2558	2176	
	arc, inches:		+1.6	0	-7.0	-20.5
Speer 200 Grand Slam	velocity, fps:	2800	2597	2404	2218	
	energy, ft-lb:	3481	2996	2565	2185	
	arc, inches:		+1.8	0	-7.9	-22.9
Win. 150 Power-Point	velocity, fps:	3290	2951	2636	2342	2068.
	energy, ft-lb:	3605	2900	2314	1827	1424
	arc, inches:		+2.6	+2.1	-3.5	-15.4
Win. 150 Fail Safe	velocity, fps:	3260	2943	2647	2370	2110
	energy, ft-lb:	3539	2884	2334	1871	1483
	arc, inches:		+1.3	0	-6.2	-18.7
Win. 165 Fail Safe	velocity, fps:	3120	2807	2515	2242	1985
	energy, ft-lb:	3567	2888	2319	1842	1445
	arc, inches:		+1.5	0	-7.0	-20.0
Win. 180 Power-Point	velocity, fps:	2960	2745	2540	2344	2157
	energy, ft-lb:	3501	3011	2578	2196	1859
	arc, inches:		+1.9	0	-7.3	-20.9
Win. 180 Power-Point Plus	velocity, fps:	3070	2846	2633	2430	2236
	energy, ft-lb:	3768	3239	2772	2361	1999
	arc, inches:		+1.4	0	-6.4	-18.7
Win. 180 Ballistic Silvertip	velocity, fps:	2950	2764	2586	2415	2250
	energy, ft-lb:	3478	3054	2673	2331	2023
	arc, inches:		+1.5	0	-6.7	-19.4
Win. 180 AccuBond	velocity, fps:	2950	2765	2588	2417	2253
	energy, ft-lb:	3478	3055	2676	2334	2028
	arc, inches:		+1.5	0	-6.7	-19.4
Win. 180 Fail Safe	velocity, fps:	2960	2732	2514	2307	2110
	energy, ft-lb:	3503	2983	2528	2129	1780
	arc, inches:		+1.6	0	-7.1	-20.7
Win. 180 Partition Gold	velocity, fps:	3070	2859	2657	2464	2280
	energy, ft-lb:	3768	3267	2823	2428	2078
	arc, inches:		+1.4	0	-6.3	-18.3
Win. 150 Supreme Elite XP3	velocity, fps:	3260	3030	2811	2603	2404
	energy, ft-lb:	3539	3057	2632	2256	1925
	arc, inches:		+1.1	0	-5.6	-16.2
Win. 180 Supreme Elite XP3	velocity, fps:	3000	2819	2646	2479	2318
	energy, ft-lb:	3597	3176	2797	2455	2147
	arc, inches:		+1.4	0	-6.4	-18.5

.300 REMINGTON SHORT ULTRA MAGNUM

CARTRIDGE BULLET	RANGE, YARDS:	0	100	200	300	400
Rem. 150 PSP C-L Ultra	velocity, fps:	3200	2901	2672	2359	2112
	energy, ft-lb:	3410	2803	2290	1854	1485
	arc, inches:		+1.3	0	-6.4	-19.l
Rem. 165 PSP Core-Lokt	velocity, fps:	3075	2792	2527	2276	2040
	energy, ft-lb:	3464	2856	2339	1828	1525
	arc, inches:		+1.5	0	-7.0	-20.7
Rem. 180 Partition	velocity, fps:	2960	2761	2571	2389	2214
	energy, ft-lb:	3501	3047	2642	2280	1959
	arc, inches:		+1.5	0	-6.8	-19.7
Rem. 180 PSP C-L Ultra	velocity, fps:	2960	2727	2506	2295	2094
	energy, ft-lb:	3501	2972	2509	2105	1753
	arc, inches:		+1.6	0	-7.1	-20.9
Rem. 190 HPBT Match	velocity, fps:	2900	2725	2557	2395	2239
	energy, ft-lb:	3547	3133	2758	2420	2115
	arc, inches:		+1.6	0	-6.9	-19.9

BALLISTICS

CARTRIDGE BULLET	RANGE, YARDS:	0	100	200	300	400

.300 WINCHESTER SHORT MAGNUM

CARTRIDGE BULLET		0	100	200	300	400
Black Hills 175 Sierra MKing	velocity, fps:	2950				
	energy, ft-lb:	3381				
	arc, inches:					
Black Hills 180 AccuBond	velocity, fps:	2950				
	energy, ft-lb:	3478				
	arc, inches:					
Federal 150 Nosler Bal. Tip	velocity, fps:	3200	2970	2755	2545	2345
	energy, ft-lb:	3410	2940	2520	2155	1830.
	arc, inches:		+1.2	0	-5.8	-17.0
Federal 165 Nos. Partition	velocity, fps:	3130	2890	2670	2450	2250
	energy, ft-lb:	3590	3065	2605	2205	1855.
	arc, inches:		+1.3	0	-6.2	-18.2
Federal 165 Nos. Solid Base	velocity, fps:	3130	2900	2690	2490	2290
	energy, ft-lb:	3590	3090	2650	2265	1920
	arc, inches:		+1.3	0	-6.1	-17.8
Federal 180 Barnes TS And Nos. Solid Base	velocity, fps:	2980	2780	2580	2400	2220
	energy, ft-lbs:	3550	3085	2670	2300	1970
	arc, inches:		+1.5	0	-6.7	-19.5
Federal 180 Grand Slam	velocity, fps:	2970	2740	2530	2320	2130
	energy, ft-lb:	3525	3010	2555	2155	1810
	arc, inches:		+1.5	0	-7.0	-20.5
Federal 180 Trophy Bonded	velocity, fps:	2970	2730	2500	2280	2080
	energy, ft-lb:	3525	2975	2500	2085	1725
	arc, inches:		+1.5	0	-7.2	-21.0
Federal 180 Nosler Partition	velocity, fps:	2975	2750	2535	2290	2126
	energy, ft-lb:	3540	3025	2570	2175	1825
	arc, inches:		+1.5	0	-7.0	-20.3
Federal 180 Nos. AccuBond	velocity, fps:	2960	2780	2610	2440	2280
	energy, ft-lb:	3500	3090	2715	2380	2075
	arc, inches:		+1.5	0	-6.6	-19.0
Federal 180 Hi-Shok SP	velocity, fps:	2970	2520	2115	1750	1430
	energy, ft-lb:	3525	2540	1785	1220	820
	arc, inches:		+2.2	0	-9.9	-31.4
Norma 150 FMJ	velocity, fps:	2953	2731	2519	2318	
	energy, ft-lb:					
	arc, inches:		+1.6	0	-7.1	
Norma 150 Barnes X TS	velocity, fps:	3215	2982	2761	2550	
	energy, ft-lb:	3444	2962	2539	2167	
	arc, inches:		+1.2	0	-5.7	
Norma 180 Nosler Bal. Tip	velocity, fps:	3215	2985	2767	2560	
	energy, ft-lb:	3437	2963	2547	2179	
	arc, inches:		+1.2	0	-5.7	
Norma 180 Oryx	velocity, fps:	2936	2542	2180	1849	
	energy, ft-lb:	3446	2583	1900	1368	
	arc, inches:		+1.9	0	-8.9	
Win. 150 Power-Point	velocity, fps:	3270	2903	2565	2250	1958
	energy, ft-lb:	3561	2807	2190	1686	1277
	arc, inches:		+1.3	0	-6.6	-20.2
Win. 150 Ballistic Silvertip	velocity, fps:	3300	3061	2834	2619	2414
	energy, ft-lb:	3628	3121	2676	2285	1941
	arc, inches:		+1.1	0	-5.4	-15.9
Win. 165 Fail Safe	velocity, fps:	3125	2846	2584	2336	2102
	energy, ft-lb:	3577	2967	2446	1999	1619
	arc, inches:		+1.4	0	-6.6	-19.6
Win. 180 Ballistic Silvertip	velocity, fps:	3010	2822	2641	2468	2301.
	energy, ft-lb:	3621	3182	2788	2434	2116
	arc, inches:		+1.4	0	-6.4	-18.6
Win. 180 AccuBond	velocity, fps:	3010	2822	2643	2470	2304
	energy, ft-lb:	3622	3185	2792	2439	2121
	arc, inches:		+1.4	0	-6.4	-18.5
Win. 180 Fail Safe	velocity, fps:	2970	2741	2524	2317	2120
	energy, ft-lb:	3526	3005	2547	2147	1797
	arc, inches:		+1.6	0	-7.0	-20.5
Win. 180 Power Point	velocity, fps:	2970	2755	2549	2353	2166
	energy, ft-lb:	3526	3034	2598	2214	1875
	arc, inches:		+1.5	0	-6.9	-20.1
Win. 150 Supreme Elite XP3	velocity, fps:	3300	3068	2847	2637	2437
	energy, ft-lb:	3626	3134	2699	2316	1978
	arc, inches:		+1.1	0	-5.4	-15.8
Win. 180 Supreme Elite XP3	velocity, fps:	3010	2829	2655	2488	2326
	energy, ft-lb:	3621	3198	2817	2473	2162
	arc, inches:		+1.4	0	-6.4	-18.3

.300 RUGER COMPACT MAGNUM

CARTRIDGE BULLET		0	100	200	300	400
Hornady 150 SST	velocity, fps:	3310	3065	2833	2613	2404
	energy, ft-lb:	3648	3128	2673	2274	1924
	arc, inches:	-1.5	+1.1	0	-5.4	-16.0
Hornady 165 GMX	velocity, fps:	3130	2911	2703	2504	2314
	energy, ft-lb:	3589	3105	2677	2297	1963
	arc, inches:	-1.5	+1.3	0	-6.1	-17.7
Hornady 180 SST	velocity, fps:	3040	2840	2649	2466	2290
	energy, ft-lb:	3693	3223	2804	2430	2096
	arc, inches:	-1.5	+1.4	0	-6.4	-18.5

.300 WEATHERBY MAGNUM

CARTRIDGE BULLET		0	100	200	300	400
A-Square 180 Dead Tough	velocity, fps:	3180	2811	2471	2155	1863.
	energy, ft-lb:	4041	3158	2440	1856	1387
	arc, inches:		+1.5	0	-7.2	-21.8
A-Square 220 Monolithic Solid	velocity, fps:	2700	2407	2133	1877	1653
	energy, ft-lb:	3561	2830	2223	1721	1334
	arc, inches:		+2.3	0	-9.8	-29.7
Federal 180 Sierra GameKing BTSP	velocity, fps:	3190	3010	2830	2660	2490
	energy, ft-lb:	4065	3610	3195	2820	2480
	arc, inches:		+1.2	0	-5.6	-16.0
Federal 180 Trophy Bonded	velocity, fps:	3190	2950	2720	2500	2290
	energy, ft-lb:	4065	3475	2955	2500	2105
	arc, inches:		+1.3	0	-5.9	-17.5
Federal 180 Tr. Bonded HE	velocity, fps:	3330	3080	2850	2750	2410
	energy, ft-lb:	4430	3795	3235	2750	2320
	arc, inches:		+1.1	0	-5.4	-15.8
Federal 180 Nosler Partition	velocity, fps:	3190	2980	2780	2590	2400
	energy, ft-lb:	4055	3540	3080	2670	2305
	arc, inches:		+1.2	0	-5.7	-16.7
Federal 180 Nosler Part. HE	velocity, fps:	3330	3110	2810	2710	2520
	energy, ft-lb:	4430	3875	3375	2935	2540
	arc, inches:		+1.0	0	-5.2	-15.1
Federal 200 Trophy Bonded	velocity, fps:	2900	2670	2440	2230	2030
	energy, ft-lb:	3735	3150	2645	2200	1820
	arc, inches:		+1.7	0	-7.6	-22.2
Hornady 150 SST (or Interbond)	velocity, fps:	3375	3123	2882	2652	2434
	energy, ft-lb:	3793	3248	2766	2343	1973
	arc, inches:		+1.0	0	-5.4	-15.8
Hornady 180 SP	velocity, fps:	3120	2891	2673	2466	2268.
	energy, ft-lb:	3890	3340	2856	2430	2055
	arc, inches:		+1.3	0	-6.2	-18.1
Hornady 180 SST	velocity, fps:	3120	2911	2711	2519	2335
	energy, ft-lb:	3890	3386	2936	2535	2180
	arc, inches:		+1.3	0	-6.2	-18.1
Rem. 180 PSP Core-Lokt	velocity, fps:	3120	2866	2627	2400	2184
	energy, ft-lb:	3890	3284	2758	2301	1905
	arc, inches:		+2.4	+2.0	-3.4	-14.9

BALLISTICS

Centerfire Rifle Ballistics

.300 WEATHERBY MAGNUM TO .303 BRITISH

CARTRIDGE BULLET	RANGE, YARDS:	0	100	200	300	400
Rem. 190 PSP boat-tail	velocity, fps:	3030	2830	2638	2455	2279
	energy, ft-lb:	3873	3378	2936	2542	2190.
	arc, inches:		+1.4	0	-6.4	-18.6
Rem. 200 Swift A-Frame	velocity, fps:	2925	2690	2467	2254	2052
	energy, ft-lb:	3799	3213	2701	2256	1870
	arc, inches:		+2.8	+2.3	-3.9	-17.0
Speer 180 Grand Slam	velocity, fps:	3185	2948	2722	2508	
	energy, ft-lb:	4054	3472	2962	2514	
	arc, inches:		+1.3	0	-5.9	-17.4
Wby. 150 Pointed Expanding	velocity, fps:	3540	3225	2932	2657	2399
	energy, ft-lb:	4173	3462	2862	2351	1916
	arc, inches:		+2.6	+3.3	0	-8.2
Wby. 150 Nosler Partition	velocity, fps:	3540	3263	3004	2759	2528
	energy, ft-lb:	4173	3547	3005	2536	2128
	arc, inches:		+2.5	+3.2	0	-7.7
Wby. 165 Pointed Expanding	velocity, fps:	3390	3123	2872	2634	2409
	energy, ft-lb:	4210	3573	3021	2542	2126
	arc, inches:		+2.8	+3.5	0	-8.5
Wby. 165 Nosler Bal. Tip	velocity, fps:	3350	3133	2927	2730	2542
	energy, ft-lb:	4111	3596	3138	2730	2367
	arc, inches:		+2.7	+3.4	0	-8.1
Wby. 180 Pointed Expanding	velocity, fps:	3240	3004	2781	2569	2366
	energy, ft-lb:	4195	3607	3091	2637	2237
	arc, inches:		+3.1	+3.8	0	-9.0
Wby. 180 Barnes X	velocity, fps:	3190	2995	2809	2631	2459
	energy, ft-lb:	4067	3586	3154	2766	2417
	arc, inches:		+3.1	+3.8	0	-8.7
Wby. 180 Bal. Tip	velocity, fps:	3250	3051	2806	2676	2503
	energy, ft-lb:	4223	3721	3271	2867	2504
	arc, inches:		+2.8	+3.6	0	-8.4
Wby. 180 Nosler Partition	velocity, fps:	3240	3028	2826	2634	2449
	energy, ft-lb:	4195	3665	3193	2772	2396
	arc, inches:		+3.0	+3.7	0	-8.6
Wby. 200 Nosler Partition	velocity, fps:	3060	2860	2668	2485	2308
	energy, ft-lb:	4158	3631	3161	2741	2366
	arc, inches:		+3.5	+4.2	0	-9.8
Wby. 220 RN Expanding	velocity, fps:	2845	2543	2260	1996	1751.
	energy, ft-lb:	3954	3158	2495	1946	1497
	arc, inches:		+4.9	+5.9	0	-14.6

.300 DAKOTA

CARTRIDGE BULLET	RANGE, YARDS:	0	100	200	300	400
Dakota 165 Barnes X	velocity, fps:	3200	2979	2769	2569	2377
	energy, ft-lb:	3751	3251	2809	2417	2070
	arc, inches:		+2.1	+1.8	-3.0	-13.2
Dakota 200 Barnes X	velocity, fps:	3000	2824	2656	2493	2336
	energy, ft-lb:	3996	3542	3131	2760	2423
	arc, inches:		+2.2	+1.5	-4.0	-15.2

.300 PEGASUS

CARTRIDGE BULLET	RANGE, YARDS:	0	100	200	300	400
A-Square 180 SP boat-tail	velocity, fps:	3500	3319	3145	2978	2817
	energy, ft-lb:	4896	4401	3953	3544	3172
	arc, inches:		+2.3	+2.9	0	-6.8
A-Square 180 Nosler Part.	velocity, fps:	3500	3295	3100	2913	2734
	energy, ft-lb:	4896	4339	3840	3392	2988
	arc, inches:		+2.3	+3.0	0	-7.1
A-Square 180 Dead Tough	velocity, fps:	3500	3103	2740	2405	2095
	energy, ft-lb:	4896	3848	3001	2312	1753
	arc, inches:		+1.1	0	-5.7	-17.5

.300 REMINGTON ULTRA MAGNUM

CARTRIDGE BULLET	RANGE, YARDS:	0	100	200	300	400
Federal 180 Trophy Bonded	velocity, fps:	3250	3000	2770	2550	2340
	energy, ft-lb:	4220	3605	3065	2590	2180
	arc, inches:		+1.2	0	-5.7	-16.8

CARTRIDGE BULLET	RANGE, YARDS:	0	100	200	300	400
Rem. 150 Swift Scirocco	velocity, fps:	3450	3208	2980	2762	2556
	energy, ft-lb:	3964	3427	2956	2541	2175
	arc, inches:		+1.7	+1.5	-2.6	-11.2
Rem. 180 Nosler Partition	velocity, fps:	3250	3037	2834	2640	2454
	energy, ft-lb:	4221	3686	3201	2786	2407
	arc, inches:		+2.4	+1.8	-3.0	-12.7
Rem. 180 Swift Scirocco	velocity, fps:	3250	3048	2856	2672	2495
	energy, ft-lb:	4221	3714	3260	2853	2487
	arc, inches:		+2.0	+1.7	-2.8	-12.3
Rem. 180 PSP Core-Lokt	velocity, fps:	3250	2988	2742	2508	2287
	energy, ft-lb:	3517	2974	2503	2095	1741
	arc, inches:		+2.1	+1.8	-3.1	-13.6
Rem. 200 Nosler Partition	velocity, fps:	3025	2826	2636	2454	2279
	energy, ft-lb:	4063	3547	3086	2673	2308
	arc, inches:		+2.4	+2.0	-3.4	-14.6

.30-378 WEATHERBY MAGNUM

CARTRIDGE BULLET	RANGE, YARDS:	0	100	200	300	400
Nosler 210 ABLR	velocity, fps:	3040	2907	2778	2653	2531
	energy, ft-lb:	4308	3940	3599	3282	2987
	arc, inches:	-1.5	+1.3	0	-5.8	-16.6
Wby. 165 Nosler Bal. Tip	velocity, fps:	3500	3275	3062	2859	2665
	energy, ft-lb:	4488	3930	3435	2995	2603
	arc, inches:		+2.4	+3.0	0	-7.4
Wby. 180 Nosler Bal. Tip	velocity, fps:	3420	3213	3015	2826	2645
	energy, ft-lb:	4676	4126	3634	3193	2797
	arc, inches:		+2.5	+3.1	0	-7.5
Wby. 180 Barnes X	velocity, fps:	3450	3243	3046	2858	2678.
	energy, ft-lb:	4757	4204	3709	3264	2865
	arc, inches:		+2.4	+3.1	0	-7.4
Wby. 200 Nosler Partition	velocity, fps:	3160	2955	2759	2572	2392.
	energy, ft-lb:	4434	3877	3381	2938	2541
	arc, inches:		+3.2	+3.9	0	-9.1

7.82 (.308) WARBIRD

CARTRIDGE BULLET	RANGE, YARDS:	0	100	200	300	400
Lazzeroni 150 Nosler Part.	velocity, fps:	3680	3432	3197	2975	2764
	energy, ft-lb:	4512	3923	3406	2949	2546.
	arc, inches:		+2.1	+2.7	0	-6.6
Lazzeroni 180 Nosler Part.	velocity, fps:	3425	3220	3026	2839	2661
	energy, ft-lb:	4689	4147	3661	3224	2831
	arc, inches:		+2.5	+3.2	0	-7.5
Lazzeroni 200 Swift A-Fr.	velocity, fps:	3290	3105	2928	2758	2594.
	energy, ft-lb:	4808	4283	3808	3378	2988
	arc, inches:		+2.7	+3.4	0	-7.9

7.65x53 ARGENTINE

CARTRIDGE BULLET	RANGE, YARDS:	0	100	200	300	400
Norma 174 Soft Point	velocity, fps:	2493	2173	1878	1611	
	energy, ft-lb:	2402	1825	1363	1003	
	arc, inches:		+2.0	0	-9.5	
Norma 180 Soft Point	velocity, fps:	2592	2386	2189	2002	
	energy, ft-lb:	2686	2276	1916	1602	
	arc, inches:		+2.3	0	-9.6	

.303 BRITISH

CARTRIDGE BULLET	RANGE, YARDS:	0	100	200	300	400
Federal 150 Hi-Shok	velocity, fps:	2690	2440	2210	1980	1780
	energy, ft-lb:	2400	1980	1620	1310	1055
	arc, inches:		+2.2	0	-9.4	-27.6
Federal 180 Sierra Pro-Hunt.	velocity, fps:	2460	2230	2020	1820	1630
	energy, ft-lb:	2420	1995	1625	1315	1060
	arc, inches:		+2.8	0	-11.3	-33.2
Federal 180 Tr. Bonded HE	velocity, fps:	2590	2350	2120	1900	1700
	energy, ft-lb:	2680	2205	1795	1445	1160
	arc, inches:		+2.4	0	-10.0	-30.0
Hornady 150 Soft Point	velocity, fps:	2685	2441	2210	1992	1787
	energy, ft-lb:	2401	1984	1627	1321	1064
	arc, inches:		+2.2	0	-9.3	-27.4

BALLISTICS

BALLISTICS

CARTRIDGE BULLET	RANGE, YARDS:	0	100	200	300	400
Hornady 150 SP LM	velocity, fps:	2830	2570	2325	2094	1884.
	energy, ft-lb:	2667	2199	1800	1461	1185
	arc, inches:		+2.0	0	-8.4	-24.6
Norma 150 Soft Point	velocity, fps:	2723	2438	2170	1920	
	energy, ft-lb:	2470	1980	1569	1228	
	arc, inches:		+2.2	0	-9.6	
PMC 174 FMJ (and HPBT)	velocity, fps:	2400	2216	2042	1876	1720
	energy, ft-lb:	2225	1898	1611	1360	1143
	arc, inches:		+2.8	0	-11.2	-32.2
PMC 180 SP boat-tail	velocity, fps:	2450	2276	2110	1951	1799
	energy, ft-lb:	2399	2071	1779	1521	1294
	arc, inches:		+2.6	0	-10.4	-30.1
Rem. 180 SP Core-Lokt	velocity, fps:	2460	2124	1817	1542	1311
	energy, ft-lb:	2418	1803	1319	950	687
	arc, inches, s:		0	-5.8	-23.3	
Win. 180 Power-Point	velocity, fps:	2460	2233	2018	1816	1629
	energy, ft-lb:	2418	1993	1627	1318	1060
	arc, inches, s:		0	-6.1	-20.8	

7.7x58 Japanese Arisaka

CARTRIDGE BULLET	RANGE, YARDS:	0	100	200	300	400
Norma 174 Soft Point	velocity, fps:	2493	2173	1878	1611	
	energy, ft-lb:	2402	1825	1363	1003	
	arc, inches:		+2.0	0	-9.5	
Norma 180 Soft Point	velocity, fps:	2493	2291	2099	1916	
	energy, ft-lb:	2485	2099	1761	1468	
	arc, inches:		+2.6	0	-10.5	

.32-20 Winchester

CARTRIDGE BULLET	RANGE, YARDS:	0	100	200	300	400
Rem. 100 Lead	velocity, fps:	1210	1021	913	834	769
	energy, ft-lb:	325	231	185	154	131
	arc, inches:		0	-31.6	-104.7	
Win. 100 Lead	velocity, fps:	1210	1021	913	834	769
	energy, ft-lb:	325	231	185	154	131
	arc, inches:		0	-32.3	-106.3	

.32 Winchester Special

CARTRIDGE BULLET	RANGE, YARDS:	0	100	200	300	400
Federal 170 Hi-Shok	velocity, fps:	2250	1920	1630	1370	1180
	energy, ft-lb:	1910	1395	1000	710	520
	arc, inches:		0	-8.0	-29.2	
Hornady 165 FTX	velocity, fps:	2410	2145	1897	1669	
	energy, ft-lb:	2128	1685	1318	1020	
	arc, inches:	-1.5	+3.0	0	-12.8	
Rem. 170 SP Core-Lokt	velocity, fps:	2250	1921	1626	1372	1175
	energy, ft-lb:	1911	1393	998	710	521
	arc, inches:		0	-8.0	-29.3	
Win. 170 Power-Point	velocity, fps:	2250	1870	1537	1267	1082
	energy, ft-lb:	1911	1320	892	606	442
	arc, inches:		0	-9.2	-33.2	

8mm Mauser (8x57)

CARTRIDGE BULLET	RANGE, YARDS:	0	100	200	300	400
Federal 170 Hi-Shok	velocity, fps:	2360	1970	1620	1330	1120
	energy, ft-lb:	2100	1465	995	670	475
	arc, inches:		0	-7.6	-28.5	
Hornady 195 SP	velocity, fps:	2550	2343	2146	1959	1782
	energy, ft-lb:	2815	2377	1994	1861	1375
	arc, inches:		+2.3	0	-9.9	-28.8.
Hornady 195 SP (2005)	velocity, fps:	2475	2269	2074	1888	1714
	energy, ft-lb:	2652	2230	1861	1543	1271
	arc, inches:		+2.6	0	-10.7	-31.3
Norma 123 FMJ	velocity, fps:	2559	2121	1729	1398	
	energy, ft-lb:	1789	1228	817	534	
	arc, inches:		+3.2	0	-15.0	
Norma 196 Oryx	velocity, fps:	2395	2146	1912	1695	
	energy, ft-lb:	2497	2004	1591	1251	
	arc, inches:		+3	0	-12.6	

CARTRIDGE BULLET	RANGE, YARDS:	0	100	200	300	400
Norma 196 Vulkan	velocity, fps:	2395	2156	1930	1720	
	energy, ft-lb:	2497	2023	1622	1289	
	arc, inches:		3.0	0	-12.3	
Norma 196 Alaska	velocity, fps:	2395	2112	1850	1611	
	energy, ft-lb:	2714	2190	1754	1399	
	arc, inches:		0	-6.3	-22.9	
Norma 196 Soft Point (JS)	velocity, fps:	2526	2244	1981	1737	
	energy, ft-lb:	2778	2192	1708	1314	
	arc, inches:		+2.7	0	-11.6	
Norma 196 Alaska (JS)	velocity, fps:	2526	2248	1988	1747	
	energy, ft-lb:	2778	2200	1720	1328	
	arc, inches:		+2.7	0	-11.5	
Norma 196 Vulkan (JS)	velocity, fps:	2526	2276	2041	1821	
	energy, ft-lb:	2778	2256	1813	1443	
	arc, inches:		+2.6	0	-11.0	
Norma 196 Oryx (JS)	velocity, fps:	2526	2269	2027	1802	
	energy, ft-lb:	2778	2241	1789	1413	
	arc, inches:		+2.6	0	-11.1	
PMC 170 Pointed Soft Point	velocity, fps:	2360	1969	1622	1333	1123
	energy, ft-lb:	2102	1463	993	671	476
	arc, inches:		+1.8	-4.5	-24.3	-63.8
Rem. 170 SP Core-Lokt	velocity, fps:	2360	1969	1622	1333	1123
	energy, ft-lb:	2102	1463	993	671	476
	arc, inches:		+1.8	-4.5	-24.3	-63.8.
Win. 170 Power-Point	velocity, fps:	2360	1969	1622	1333	1123
	energy, ft-lb:	2102	1463	993	671	476
	arc, inches:		+1.8	-4.5	-24.3	-63.8

.325 WSM

CARTRIDGE BULLET	RANGE, YARDS:	0	100	200	300	400
Win. 180 Ballistic ST	velocity, fps:	3060	2841	2632	2432	2242
	energy, ft-lb:	3743	3226	2769	2365	2009
	arc, inches:		+1.4	0	-6.4	-18.7
Win. 200 AccuBond CT	velocity, fps:	2950	2753	2565	2384	2210
	energy, ft-lb:	3866	3367	2922	2524	2170
	arc, inches:		+1.5	0	-6.8	-19.8
Win. 220 Power-Point	velocity, fps:	2840	2605	2382	2169	1968
	energy, ft-lb:	3941	3316	2772	2300	1893
	arc, inches:		+1.8	0	-8.0	-23.3

8mm Remington Magnum

CARTRIDGE BULLET	RANGE, YARDS:	0	100	200	300	400
A-Square 220 Monolythic Solid	velocity, fps:	2800	2501	2221	1959	1718
	energy, ft-lb:	3829	3055	2409	1875	1442
	arc, inches:		+2.1	0	-9.1	-27.6
Nosler 180 BT	velocity, fps:	3200	2923	2662	2416	2183
	energy, ft-lb:	4092	3414	2832	2333	1905
	arc, inches:	-1.5	+1.3	0	-6.2	-18.4
Rem. 200 Swift A-Frame	velocity, fps:	2900	2623	2361	2115	1885
	energy, ft-lb:	3734	3054	2476	1987	1577
	arc, inches:		+1.8	0	-8.0	-23.9

.338 Federal

CARTRIDGE BULLET	RANGE, YARDS:	0	100	200	300	400
Federal 180 AccuBond	velocity, fps:	2830	2590	2350	2130	1930
	energy, ft-lb:	3200	2670	2215	1820	1480
	arc, inches:	-1.5	+1.8	0	-8.2	-23.9
Federal 185 Barnes TSX	velocity, fps:	2750	2500	2260	2030	1820
	energy, ft-lb:	3105	2560	2090	1695	1355
	arc, inches:	-1.5	+2.0	0	-8.9	-26.2
Federal 200 Tr. Bonded T	velocity, fps:	2630	2430	2240	2060	1890
	energy, ft-lb:	3070	2625	2230	1885	1580
	arc, inches:	-1.5	+2.2	0	-9.2	-26.3
Federal 210 Partition	velocity, fps:	2630	2410	2200	2010	1820
	energy, ft-lb:	3225	2710	2265	1880	1545
	arc, inches:	-1.5	+2.3	0	-9.4	-27.3

Centerfire Rifle Ballistics

.338 MARLIN EXPRESS TO .340 WEATHERBY MAGNUM

CARTRIDGE BULLET	RANGE, YARDS:	0	100	200	300	400
.338 MARLIN EXPRESS						
Hornady 200 FTX	velocity, fps:	2565	2365	2174	1992	`1820
	energy, ft-lb:	2922	2484	2099	1762	1471
	arc, inches:	-1.5	+3.0	+1.2	-7.9	-25.9
.338-06						
A-Square 200 Nos. Bal. Tip	velocity, fps:	2750	2553	2364	2184	2011
	energy, ft-lb:	3358	2894	2482	2118	1796
	arc, inches:		+1.9	0	-8.2	-23.6
A-Square 250 SP boat-tail	velocity, fps:	2500	2374	2252	2134	2019
	energy, ft-lb:	3496	3129	2816	2528	2263
	arc, inches:		+2.4	0	-9.3	-26.0
A-Square 250 Dead Tough	velocity, fps:	2500	2222	1963	1724	1507
	energy, ft-lb:	3496	2742	2139	1649	1261
	arc, inches:		+2.8	0	-11.9	-35.5
Nosler 180 AB	velocity, fps:	2950	2698	2460	2234	2020
	energy, ft-lb:	3477	2909	2418	1994	1631
	arc, inches:	-1.5	+1.6	0	-7.4	-21.8
Nosler 225 AB	velocity, fps:	2600	2441	2287	2139	1997
	energy, ft-lb:	3376	2976	2614	2286	1992
	arc, inches:	-1.5	+2.2	0	-8.8	-25.3
Wby. 210 Nosler Part.	velocity, fps:	2750	2526	2312	2109	1916
	energy, ft-lb:	3527	2975	2403	2074	1712
	arc, inches:		+4.8	+5.7	0	-13.5
.338 RUGER COMPACT MAGNUM						
Hornady 185 GMX	velocity, fps:	2980	2755	2542	2338	2143
	energy, ft-lb:	3647	3118	2653	2242	1887
	arc, inches:	-1.5	+1.5	0	-6.9	-20.3
Hornady 200 SST	velocity, fps:	2950	2744	2547	2358	2177
	energy, ft-lb:	3846	3342	2879	2468	2104
	arc, inches:	-1.5	+1.6	0	-6.9	-20.1
Hornady 225 SST	velocity, fps:	2750	2575	2407	2245	2089
	energy, ft-lb:	3778	3313	2894	2518	2180
	arc, inches:	-1.5	+1.9	0	-7.9	-22.7
.338 WINCHESTER MAGNUM						
A-Square 250 SP boat-tail	velocity, fps:	2700	2568	2439	2314	2193
	energy, ft-lb:	4046	3659	3302	2972	2669
	arc, inches:		+4.4	+5.2	0	-11.7
A-Square 250 Triad	velocity, fps:	2700	2407	2133	1877	1653
	energy, ft-lb:	4046	3216	2526	1956	1516
	arc, inches:		+2.3	0	-9.8	-29.8
Federal 210 Nosler Partition	velocity, fps:	2830	2600	2390	2180	1980
	energy, ft-lb:	3735	3160	2655	2215	1835
	arc, inches:		+1.8	0	-8.0	-23.3
Federal 225 Sierra Pro-Hunt.	velocity, fps:	2780	2570	2360	2170	1980
	energy, ft-lb:	3860	3290	2780	2340	1960
	arc, inches:		+1.9	0	-8.2	-23.7
Federal 225 Trophy Bonded	velocity, fps:	2800	2560	2330	2110	1900
	energy, ft-lb:	3915	3265	2700	2220	1800
	arc, inches:		+1.9	0	-8.4	-24.5
Federal 225 Tr. Bonded HE	velocity, fps:	2940	2690	2450	2230	2010
	energy, ft-lb:	4320	3610	3000	2475	2025
	arc, inches:		+1.7	0	-7.5	-22.0
Federal 225 Barnes XLC	velocity, fps:	2800	2610	2430	2260	2090
	energy, ft-lb:	3915	3405	2950	2545	2190
	arc, inches:		+1.8	0	-7.7	-22.2
Federal 250 Nosler Partition	velocity, fps:	2660	2470	2300	2120	1960
	energy, ft-lb:	3925	3395	2925	2505	2130.
	arc, inches:		+2.1	0	-8.8	-25.1
Federal 250 Nosler Part HE	velocity, fps:	2800	2610	2420	2250	2080
	energy, ft-lb:	4350	3775	3260	2805	2395
	arc, inches:		+1.8	0	-7.8	-22.5

CARTRIDGE BULLET	RANGE, YARDS:	0	100	200	300	400
Hornady 225 Soft Point HM	velocity, fps:	2920	2678	2449	2232	2027
	energy, ft-lb:	4259	3583	2996	2489	2053
	arc, inches:		+1.8	0	-7.6	-22.0
Norma 225 TXP Swift A-Fr.	velocity, fps:	2740	2507	2286	2075	
	energy, ft-lb:	3752	3141	2611	2153	
	arc, inches:		+2.0	0	-8.7	
Norma 230 Oryx	velocity, fps:	2756	2514	2284	2066	
	energy, ft-lb:	3880	3228	2665	2181	
	arc, inches:		+2.0	0	-8.7	
Norma 250 Nosler Partition	velocity, fps:	2657	2470	2290	2118	
	energy, ft-lb:	3920	3387	2912	2490	
	arc, inches:		+2.1	0	-8.7	
PMC 225 Barnes X	velocity, fps:	2780	2619	2464	2313	2168
	energy, ft-lb:	3860	3426	3032	2673	2348.
	arc, inches:		+1.8	0	-7.6	-21.6
Rem. 200 Nosler Bal. Tip	velocity, fps:	2950	2724	2509	2303	2108
	energy, ft-lb:	3866	3295	2795	2357	1973
	arc, inches:		+1.6	0	-7.1	-20.8
Rem. 210 Nosler Partition	velocity, fps:	2830	2602	2385	2179	1983
	energy, ft-lb:	3734	3157	2653	2214	1834
	arc, inches:		+1.8	0	-7.9	-23.2
Rem. 225 PSP Core-Lokt	velocity, fps:	2780	2572	2374	2184	2003
	energy, ft-lb:	3860	3305	2815	2383	2004
	arc, inches:		+1.9	0	-8.1	-23.4
Rem. 225 PSP C-L Ultra	velocity, fps:	2780	2582	2392	2210	2036
	energy, ft-lb:	3860	3329	2858	2440	2071
	arc, inches:		+1.9	0	-7.9	-23.0
Rem. 225 Swift A-Frame	velocity, fps:	2785	2517	2266	2029	1808
	energy, ft-lb:	3871	3165	2565	2057	1633
	arc, inches:		+2.0	0	-8.8	-25.2
Rem. 250 PSP Core-Lokt	velocity, fps:	2660	2456	2261	2075	1898
	energy, ft-lb:	3927	3348	2837	2389	1999
	arc, inches:		+2.1	0	-8.9	-26.0
Speer 250 Grand Slam	velocity, fps:	2645	2442	2247	2062	
	energy, ft-lb:	3883	3309	2803	2360	
	arc, inches:		+2.2	0	-9.1	-26.2
Win. 200 Power-Point	velocity, fps:	2960	2658	2375	2110	1862
	energy, ft-lb:	3890	3137	2505	1977	1539
	arc, inches:		+2.0	0	-8.2	-24.3
Win. 200 Ballistic Silvertip	velocity, fps:	2950	2724	2509	2303	2108
	energy, ft-lb:	3864	3294	2794	2355	1972
	arc, inches:		+1.6	0	-7.1	-20.8
Win. 225 AccuBond	velocity, fps:	2800	2634	2474	2319	2170
	energy, ft-lb:	3918	3467	3058	2688	2353
	arc, inches:		+1.8	0	-7.4	-21.3
Win. 230 Fail Safe	velocity, fps:	2780	2573	2375	2186	2005
	energy, ft-lb:	3948	3382	2881	2441	2054
	arc, inches:		+1.9	0	-8.1	-23.4
Win. 250 Partition Gold	velocity, fps:	2650	2467	2291	2122	1960
	energy, ft-lb:	3899	3378	2914	2520	2134
	arc, inches:		+2.1	0	-8.7	-25.2
.340 WEATHERBY MAGNUM						
A-Square 250 SP boat-tail	velocity, fps:	2820	2684	2552	2424	2299
	energy, ft-lb:	4414	3999	3615	3261	2935
	arc, inches:		+4.0	+4.6	0	-10.6
A-Square 250 Triad	velocity, fps:	2820	2520	2238	1976	1741
	energy, ft-lb:	4414	3524	2781	2166	1683
	arc, inches:		+2.0	0	-9.0	-26.8
Federal 225 Trophy Bonded	velocity, fps:	3100	2840	2600	2370	2150
	energy, ft-lb:	4800	4035	3375	2800	2310
	arc, inches:		+1.4	0	-6.5	-19.4

CARTRIDGE BULLET	RANGE, YARDS:	0	100	200	300	400
Wby. 200 Pointed Expanding	velocity, fps:	3221	2946	2688	2444	2213
	energy, ft-lb:	4607	3854	3208	2652	2174
	arc, inches:		+3.3	+4.0	0	-9.9
Wby. 200 Nosler Bal. Tip	velocity, fps:	3221	2980	2753	2536	2329
	energy, ft-lb:	4607	3944	3364	2856	2409
	arc, inches:		+3.1	+3.9	0	-9.2
Wby. 210 Nosler Partition	velocity, fps:	3211	2963	2728	2505	2293
	energy, ft-lb:	4807	4093	3470	2927	2452
	arc, inches:		+3.2	+3.9	0	-9.5
Wby. 225 Pointed Expanding	velocity, fps:	3066	2824	2595	2377	2170
	energy, ft-lb:	4696	3984	3364	2822	2352
	arc, inches:		+3.6	+4.4	0	-10.7
Wby. 225 Barnes X	velocity, fps:	3001	2804	2615	2434	2260
	energy, ft-lb:	4499	3927	3416	2959	2551
	arc, inches:		+3.6	+4.3	0	-10.3
Wby. 250 Pointed Expanding	velocity, fps:	2963	2745	2537	2338	2149
	energy, ft-lb:	4873	4182	3572	3035	2563
	arc, inches:		+3.9	+4.6	0	-11.1
Wby. 250 Nosler Partition	velocity, fps:	2941	2743	2553	2371	2197
	energy, ft-lb:	4801	4176	3618	3120	2678
	arc, inches:		+3.9	+4.6	0	-10.9

.330 DAKOTA

CARTRIDGE BULLET	RANGE, YARDS:	0	100	200	300	400
Dakota 200 Barnes X	velocity, fps:	3200	2971	2754	2548	2350
	energy, ft-lb:	4547	3920	3369	2882	2452
	arc, inches:		+2.1	+1.8	-3.1	-13.4
Dakota 250 Barnes X	velocity, fps:	2900	2719	2545	2378	2217
	energy, ft-lb:	4668	4103	3595	3138	2727
	arc, inches:		+2.3	+1.3	-5.0	-17.5

.338 REMINGTON ULTRA MAGNUM

CARTRIDGE BULLET	RANGE, YARDS:	0	100	200	300	400
Federal 210 Nosler Partition	velocity, fps:	3025	2800	2585	2385	2190
	energy, ft-lb:	4270	3655	3120	2645	2230
	arc, inches:		+1.5	0	-6.7	-19.5
Federal 250 Trophy Bonded	velocity, fps:	2860	2630	2420	2210	2020
	energy, ft-lb:	4540	3850	3245	2715	2260
	arc, inches:		+0.8	0	-7.7	-22.6
Rem. 250 Swift A-Frame	velocity, fps:	2860	2645	2440	2244	2057
	energy, ft-lb:	4540	3882	3303	2794	2347
	arc, inches:		+1.7	0	-7.6	-22.1
Rem. 250 PSP Core-Lokt	velocity, fps:	2860	2647	2443	2249	2064
	energy, ft-lb:	4540	3888	3314	2807	2363
	arc, inches:		+1.7	0	-7.6	-22.0

.338 LAPUA

CARTRIDGE BULLET	RANGE, YARDS:	0	100	200	300	400
Black Hills 250 Sierra MKing	velocity, fps:	2950				
	energy, ft-lb:	4831				
	arc, inches:					
Black Hills 300 Sierra MKing	velocity, fps:	2800				
	energy, ft-lb:	5223				
	arc, inches:					
Hornady 285 BTHP	velocity, fps:	2745	2616	2491	2369	2251
	energy, ft-lb:	4768	4331	3926	3552	3206
	arc, inches:	-1.5	+1.8	0	-7.4	-21.0

CARTRIDGE BULLET	RANGE, YARDS:	0	100	200	300	600
Lapua 250 Scenar	velocity, fps:	2970	2823	2680	2539	2141
	energy, ft-lb:	4896	4424	3985	3579	2545
	arc, inches:	-1.5	+3.0	+4.0	0	-47.0
Lapua 300 Scenar	velocity, fps:	2723	2600	2482	2367	2042
	energy, ft-lb:	4938	4504	4102	3731	2778
	arc, inches:	-1.5	+4.0	+5.0	0	-54.0

CARTRIDGE BULLET	RANGE, YARDS:	0	100	200	300	400
Nosler 225 AB	velocity, fps:	3000	2826	2659	2498	2342
	energy, ft-lb:	4495	3990	3532	3117	2741
	arc, inches:	-1.5	+1.4	0	-6.3	-18.3

.338-378 WEATHERBY MAGNUM

CARTRIDGE BULLET	RANGE, YARDS:	0	100	200	300	400
Wby. 200 Nosler Bal. Tip	velocity, fps:	3350	3102	2868	2646	2434
	energy, ft-lb:	4983	4273	3652	3109	2631
	arc, inches:	0	+2.8	+3.5	0	-8.4
Wby. 225 Barnes X	velocity, fps:	3180	2974	2778	2591	2410.
	energy, ft-lb:	5052	4420	3856	3353	2902
	arc, inches:	0	+3.1	+3.8	0	-8.9
Wby. 250 Nosler Partition	velocity, fps:	3060	2856	2662	2475	2297
	energy, ft-lb:	5197	4528	3933	3401	2927
	arc, inches:	0	+3.5	+4.2	0	-9.8

8.59 (.338) TITAN

CARTRIDGE BULLET	RANGE, YARDS:	0	100	200	300	400
Lazzeroni 200 Nos. Bal. Tip	velocity, fps:	3430	3211	3002	2803	2613
	energy, ft-lb:	5226	4579	4004	3491	3033
	arc, inches:		+2.5	+3.2	0	-7.6
Lazzeroni 225 Nos. Partition	velocity, fps:	3235	3031	2836	2650	2471
	energy, ft-lb:	5229	4591	4021	3510	3052
	arc, inches:		+3.0	+3.6	0	-8.6
Lazzeroni 250 Swift A-Fr.	velocity, fps:	3100	2908	2725	2549	2379
	energy, ft-lb:	5336	4697	4123	3607	3143
	arc, inches:		+3.3	+4.0	0	-9.3

.338 A-SQUARE

CARTRIDGE BULLET	RANGE, YARDS:	0	100	200	300	400
A-Square 200 Nos. Bal. Tip	velocity, fps:	3500	3266	3045	2835	2634
	energy, ft-lb:	5440	4737	4117	3568	3081
	arc, inches:		+2.4	+3.1	0	-7.5
A-Square 250 SP boat-tail	velocity, fps:	3120	2974	2834	2697	2565.
	energy, ft-lb:	5403	4911	4457	4038	3652
	arc, inches:		+3.1	+3.7	0	-8.5
A-Square 250 Triad	velocity, fps:	3120	2799	2500	2220	1958
	energy, ft-lb:	5403	4348	3469	2736	2128
	arc, inches:		+1.5	0	-7.1	-20.4

.338 EXCALIBER

CARTRIDGE BULLET	RANGE, YARDS:	0	100	200	300	400
A-Square 200 Nos. Bal. Tip	velocity, fps:	3600	3361	3134	2920	2715
	energy, ft-lb:	5755	5015	4363	3785	3274
	arc, inches:		+2.2	+2.9	0	-6.7
A-Square 250 SP boat-tail	velocity, fps:	3250	3101	2958	2684	2553
	energy, ft-lb:	5863	5339	4855	4410	3998
	arc, inches:		+2.7	+3.4	0	-7.8
A-Square 250 Triad	velocity, fps:	3250	2922	2618	2333	2066
	energy, ft-lb:	5863	4740	3804	3021	2370
	arc, inches:		+1.3	0	-6.4	-19.2

.348 WINCHESTER

CARTRIDGE BULLET	RANGE, YARDS:	0	100	200	300	400
Win. 200 Silvertip	velocity, fps:	2520	2215	1931	1672	1443.
	energy, ft-lb:	2820	2178	1656	1241	925
	arc, inches:		0	-6.2	-21.9	

.357 MAGNUM

CARTRIDGE BULLET	RANGE, YARDS:	0	100	200	300	400
Federal 180 Hi-Shok HP Hollow Point	velocity, fps:	1550	1160	980	860	770
	energy, ft-lb:	960	535	385	295	235
	arc, inches:		0	-22.8	-77.9	-173.8
Win. 158 Jacketed SP	velocity, fps:	1830	1427	1138	980	883
	energy, ft-lb:	1175	715	454	337	274
	arc, inches:		0	-16.2	-57.0	-128.3

.35 REMINGTON

CARTRIDGE BULLET	RANGE, YARDS:	0	100	200	300	400
Federal 200 Hi-Shok	velocity, fps:	2080	1700	1380	1140	1000
	energy, ft-lb:	1920	1280	840	575	445
	arc, inches:		0	-10.7	-39.3	

BALLISTICS

Centerfire Rifle Ballistics

.35 REMINGTON TO 9.3X74 R

CARTRIDGE BULLET	RANGE, YARDS:	0	100	200	300	400
Hornady 200 Evolution	velocity, fps:	2225	1963	1721	1503	
	energy, ft-lb:	2198	1711	1315	1003	
	arc, inches:		+3.0	-1.3	-17.5	
Rem. 150 PSP Core-Lokt	velocity, fps:	2300	1874	1506	1218	1039
	energy, ft-lb:	1762	1169	755	494	359
	arc, inches:		0	-8.6	-32.6	
Rem. 200 SP Core-Lokt	velocity, fps:	2080	1698	1376	1140	1001
	energy, ft-lb:	1921	1280	841	577	445
	arc, inches:		0	-10.7	-40.1	
Win. 200 Power-Point	velocity, fps:	2020	1646	1335	1114	985
	energy, ft-lb:	1812	1203	791	551	431
	arc, inches:		0	-12.1	-43.9	

.356 WINCHESTER

CARTRIDGE BULLET	RANGE, YARDS:	0	100	200	300	400
Win. 200 Power-Point	velocity, fps:	2460	2114	1797	1517	1284
	energy, ft-lb:	2688	1985	1434	1022	732
	arc, inches:		+1.6	-3.8	-20.1	-51.2

.358 WINCHESTER

CARTRIDGE BULLET	RANGE, YARDS:	0	100	200	300	400
Hornady 200 SP	velocity, fps:	2475	2180	1906	1655	1434
	energy, ft-lb:	2720	2110	1612	1217	913
	arc, inches:	-1.5	+2.9	0	-12.6	-37.9
Win. 200 Silvertip	velocity, fps:	2490	2171	1876	1610	1379
	energy, ft-lb:	2753	2093	1563	1151	844
	arc, inches:		+1.5	-3.6	-18.6	-47.2

.35 WHELEN

CARTRIDGE BULLET	RANGE, YARDS:	0	100	200	300	400
Federal 225 Trophy Bonded	velocity, fps:	2600	2400	2200	2020	1840
	energy, ft-lb:	3375	2865	2520	2030	1690.
	arc, inches:		+2.3	0	-9.4	-27.3
Hornady 200 SP	velocity, fps:	2910	2585	2283	2001	1742
	energy, ft-lb:	3760	2968	2314	1778	1347
	arc, inches:	-1.5	+1.9	0	-8.6	-25.9
Rem. 200 Pointed Soft Point	velocity, fps:	2675	2378	2100	1842	1606
	energy, ft-lb:	3177	2510	1958	1506	1145
	arc, inches:		+2.3	0	-10.3	-30.8
Rem. 250 Pointed Soft Point	velocity, fps:	2400	2197	2005	1823	1652
	energy, ft-lb:	3197	2680	2230	1844	1515
	arc, inches:		+1.3	-3.2	-16.6	-40.0

.350 REMINGTON MAGNUM

CARTRIDGE BULLET	RANGE, YARDS:	0	100	200	300	400
Nosler 225 PT	velocity, fps:	2550	2349	2158	1976	1804
	energy, ft-lb:	3248	2758	2327	1951	1626
	arc, inches:	-1.5	+2.4	0	-9.9	-28.7

.358 NORMA MAGNUM

CARTRIDGE BULLET	RANGE, YARDS:	0	100	200	300	400
A-Square 275 Triad	velocity, fps:	2700	2394	2108	1842	1653
	energy, ft-lb:	4451	3498	2713	2072	1668
	arc, inches:		+2.3	0	-10.1	-29.8
Norma 250 TXP Swift A-Fr.	velocity, fps:	2723	2467	2225	1996	
	energy, ft-lb:	4117	3379	2748	2213	
	arc, inches:		+2.1	0	-9.1	
Norma 250 Woodleigh	velocity, fps:	2799	2442	2112	1810	
	energy, ft-lb:	4350	3312	2478	1819	
	arc, inches:		+2.2	0	-10.0	
Norma 250 Oryx	velocity, fps:	2756	2493	2245	2011	
	energy, ft-lb:	4217	3451	2798	2245	
	arc, inches:		+2.1	0	-9.0	

.358 STA

CARTRIDGE BULLET	RANGE, YARDS:	0	100	200	300	400
A-Square 275 Triad	velocity, fps:	2850	2562	2292	2039	1764
	energy, ft-lb:	4959	4009	3208	2539	1899.
	arc, inches:		+1.9	0	-8.6	-26.1

9.3x57

CARTRIDGE BULLET	RANGE, YARDS:	0	100	200	300	400
Norma 232 Vulkan	velocity, fps:	2329	2031	1757	1512	
	energy, ft-lb:	2795	2126	1591	1178	
	arc, inches:		+3.5	0	-14.9	
Norma 232 Oryx	velocity, fps:	2362	2058	1778	1528	
	energy, ft-lb:	2875	2182	1630	1203	
	arc, inches:		+3.4	0	-14.5	
Norma 285 Oryx	velocity, fps:	2067	1859	1666	1490	
	energy, ft-lb:	2704	2188	1756	1404	
	arc, inches:		+4.3	0	-16.8	
Norma 286 Alaska	velocity, fps:	2067	1857	1662	1484	
	energy, ft-lb:	2714	2190	1754	1399	
	arc, inches:		+4.3	0	-17.0	

9.3x62

CARTRIDGE BULLET	RANGE, YARDS:	0	100	200	300	400
Federal 286 TSX	velocity, fps:	2360	2160	1970	1790	
	energy, ft-lb:	3535	2965	2465	2035	
	arc, inches:	-1.5	+3.0	0	-12.0	
Federal 286 Woodleigh Hydro	velocity, fps:	2360	2050	1760	1510	
	energy, ft-lb:	3535	2665	1975	1445	
	arc, inches::	-1.5	+3.4	0	-14.7	
Hornady 286 SP-HP	velocity, fps:	2350	2155	1961	1778	
	energy, ft-lb:	3537	2949	2442	2008	
	arc, inches:	-1.5	+3.0	0	-12.1	
Norma 232 Oryx	velocity, fps:	2625	2294	1988	1708	
	energy, ft-lb:	3535	2700	2028	1497	
	arc, inches:	-1.5	+2.5	0	-11.4	
Norma 250 A-Frame	velocity, fps:	2625	2322	2039	1778	
	energy, ft-lb:	3826	2993	2309	1755	
	arc, inches:	-1.5	+2.5	0	-10.9	
Norma 286 Plastic Point	velocity, fps:	2362	2141	1931	1736	
	energy, ft-lb:	3544	2911	2370	1914	
	arc, inches:	-1.5	+3.1	0	-12.4	
Nosler 250 AccuBond	velocity, fps:	2550	2376	2208	2048	1894
	energy, ft-lb:	3609	3133	2707	2328	1992
	arc, inches:	-1.5	+2.3	0	-9.5	-27.2
Nosler 286 Partition	velocity, fps:	2350	2179	2015	1859	1711
	energy, ft-lb:	3506	3014	2578	2194	1859
	arc, inches:	-1.5	+2.9	0	-11.5	-33.1

9.3x64

CARTRIDGE BULLET	RANGE, YARDS:	0	100	200	300	400
A-Square 286 Triad	velocity, fps:	2700	2391	2103	1835	1602
	energy, ft-lb:	4629	3630	2808	2139	1631
	arc, inches:		+2.3	0	-10.1	-30.8

.370 SAKO

CARTRIDGE BULLET	RANGE, YARDS:	0	100	200	300	400
Federal 286 TSX	velocity, fps:	2550	2370	2190	2020	1860
	energy, ft-lb:	4130	3555	3045	2595	2195
	arc, inches:	-1.5	+2.4	0	-9.6	-27.5

9.3x74 R

CARTRIDGE BULLET	RANGE, YARDS:	0	100	200	300	400
A-Square 286 Triad	velocity, fps:	2360	2089	1844	1623	
	energy, ft-lb:	3538	2771	2157	1670	
	arc, inches:		+3.6	0	-14.0	
Hornady 286	velocity, fps	2360	2136	1924	1727	1545
	energy, ft-lb	3536	2896	2351	1893	1516
	arc, inches	-1.5	0	-6.1	-21.7	-49.0
Norma 232 Vulkan	velocity, fps:	2625	2327	2049	1792	
	energy, ft-lb:	3551	2791	2164	1655	
	arc, inches:		+2.5	0	-10.8	
Norma 232 Oryx	velocity, fps:	2526	2191	1883	1605	
	energy, ft-lb:	3274	2463	1819	1322	
	arc, inches:		+2.9	0	-12.8	

BALLISTICS

CARTRIDGE BULLET	RANGE, YARDS:	0	100	200	300	400
Norma 285 Oryx	velocity, fps:	2362	2114	1881	1667	
	energy, ft-lb:	3532	2829	2241	1758	
	arc, inches:		+3.1	0	-13.0	
Norma 286 Alaska	velocity, fps:	2362	2135	1920	1720	
	energy, ft-lb:	3544	2894	2342	1879	
	arc, inches:		+3.1	0	-12.5	
Norma 286 Plastic Point	velocity, fps:	2362	2135	1920	1720	
	energy, ft-lb:	3544	2894	2342	1879	
	arc, inches:		+3.1	0	-12.5	

.375 WINCHESTER

CARTRIDGE BULLET	RANGE, YARDS:	0	100	200	300	400
Win. 200 Power-Point	velocity, fps:	2200	1841	1526	1268	1089
	energy, ft-lb:	2150	1506	1034	714	
	arc, inches:			0	-9.5	-33.8

.375 FLANGED

CARTRIDGE BULLET	RANGE, YARDS:	0	100	200	300	400
Nosler 300 PT	velocity, fps:	2400	2191	1993	1806	1632
	energy, ft-lb:	3836	3198	2646	2173	1775
	arc, inches:	-1.5	+2.9	0	-11.7	-34.0

.375 H&H MAGNUM

CARTRIDGE BULLET	RANGE, YARDS:	0	100	200	300	400
A-Square 300 SP boat-tail	velocity, fps:	2550	2415	2284	2157	2034
	energy, ft-lb:	4331	3884	3474	3098	2755
	arc, inches:		+5.2	+6.0	0	-13.3
A-Square 300 Triad	velocity, fps:	2550	2251	1973	1717	1496
	energy, ft-lb:	4331	3375	2592	1964	1491
	arc, inches:		+2.7	0	-11.7	-35.1
Federal 250 Trophy Bonded	velocity, fps:	2670	2360	2080	1820	1580
	energy, ft-lb:	3955	3100	2400	1830	1380
	arc, inches:		+2.4	0	-10.4	-31.7
Federal 270 Hi-Shok	velocity, fps:	2690	2420	2170	1920	1700
	energy, ft-lb:	4340	3510	2810	2220	1740
	arc, inches:		+2.4	0	-10.9	-33.3
Federal 300 Hi-Shok	velocity, fps:	2530	2270	2020	1790	1580
	energy, ft-lb:	4265	3425	2720	2135	1665
	arc, inches:		+2.6	0	-11.2	-33.3
Federal 300 Nosler Partition	velocity, fps:	2530	2320	2120	1930	1750
	energy, ft-lb:	4265	3585	2995	2475	2040
	arc, inches:		+2.5	0	-10.3	-29.9
Federal 300 Trophy Bonded	velocity, fps:	2530	2280	2040	1810	1610
	energy, ft-lb:	4265	3450	2765	2190	1725
	arc, inches:		+2.6	0	-10.9	-32.8
Federal 300 Tr. Bonded HE	velocity, fps:	2700	2440	2190	1960	1740
	energy, ft-lb:	4855	3960	3195	2550	2020
	arc, inches:		+2.2	0	-9.4	-28.0
Federal 300 Trophy Bonded Sledgehammer Solid	velocity, fps:	2530	2160	1820	1520	1280.
	energy, ft-lb:	4265	3105	2210	1550	1090
	arc, inches, s:		0	-6.0	-22.7	-54.6
Hornady 270 SP HM	velocity, fps:	2870	2620	2385	2162	1957
	energy, ft-lb:	4937	4116	3408	2802	2296
	arc, inches:		+2.2	0	-8.4	-23.9
Hornady 300 FMJ RN HM	velocity, fps:	2705	2376	2072	1804	1560
	energy, ft-lb:	4873	3760	2861	2167	1621
	arc, inches:		+2.7	0	-10.8	-32.1
Norma 300 Soft Point	velocity, fps:	2549	2211	1900	1619	
	energy, ft-lb:	4329	3258	2406	1747	
	arc, inches:		+2.8	0	-12.6	
Norma 300 TXP Swift A-Fr.	velocity, fps:	2559	2296	2049	1818	
	energy, ft-lb:	4363	3513	2798	2203	
	arc, inches:		+2.6	0	-10.9	
Norma 300 Oryx	velocity, fps:	2559	2292	2041	1807	
	energy, ft-lb:	4363	3500	2775	2176	
	arc, inches:		+2.6	0	-11.0	

CARTRIDGE BULLET	RANGE, YARDS:	0	100	200	300	400
Norma 300 Barnes Solid	velocity, fps:	2493	2061	1677	1356	
	energy, ft-lb:	4141	2829	1873	1234	
	arc, inches:		+3.4	0	-16.0	
PMC 270 PSP	velocity, fps:					
	energy, ft-lb:					
	arc, inches:					
PMC 270 Barnes X	velocity, fps:	2690	2528	2372	2221	2076
	energy, ft-lb:	4337	3831	3371	2957	2582
	arc, inches:		+2.0	0	-8.2	-23.4
PMC 300 Barnes X	velocity, fps:	2530	2389	2252	2120	1993
	energy, ft-lb:	4263	3801	3378	2994	2644
	arc, inches:		+2.3	0	-9.2	-26.1
Rem. 270 Soft Point	velocity, fps:	2690	2420	2166	1928	1707
	energy, ft-lb:	4337	3510	2812	2228	1747
	arc, inches:		+2.2	0	-9.7	-28.7
Rem. 300 Swift A-Frame	velocity, fps:	2530	2245	1979	1733	1512
	energy, ft-lb:	4262	3357	2608	2001	1523
	arc, inches:		+2.0	0	-11.7	-35.0
Speer 285 Grand Slam	velocity, fps:	2610	2365	2134	1916	
	energy, ft-lb:	4310	3540	2883	2323	
	arc, inches:		+2.4	0	-9.9	
Speer 300 African GS Tungsten Solid	velocity, fps:	2609	2277	1970	1690	
	energy, ft-lb:	4534	3453	2585	1903	
	arc, inches:		+2.6	0	-11.7	-35.6
Win. 270 Fail Safe	velocity, fps:	2670	2447	2234	2033	1842
	energy, ft-lb:	4275	3590	2994	2478	2035
	arc, inches:		+2.2	0	-9.1	-28.7
Win. 300 Fail Safe	velocity, fps:	2530	2336	2151	1974	1806
	energy, ft-lb:	4265	3636	3082	2596	2173
	arc, inches:		+2.4	0	-10.0	-26.9

.375 DAKOTA

CARTRIDGE BULLET	RANGE, YARDS:	0	100	200	300	400
Dakota 270 Barnes X	velocity, fps:	2800	2617	2441	2272	2109
	energy, ft-lb:	4699	4104	3571	3093	2666
	arc, inches:		+2.3	+1.0	-6.1	-19.9
Dakota 300 Barnes X	velocity, fps:	2600	2316	2051	1804	1579
	energy, ft-lb:	4502	3573	2800	2167	1661
	arc, inches:		+2.4	-0.1	-11.0	-32.7

.375 RUGER

CARTRIDGE BULLET	RANGE, YARDS:	0	100	200	300	400
Hornady 270 SP	velocity, fps:	2840	2600	2372	2156	1951
	energy, ft-lb:	4835	4052	3373	2786	2283
	arc, inches:	-1.5	+1.8	0	-8.0	-23.6
Hornady 300 Solid	velocity, fps	2660	2344	2050	1780	1536
	energy, ft-lb	4713	3660	2800	2110	1572
	arc, inches	-1.5	+2.4	0	-10.8	-32.6
Nosler 260 AB	velocity, fps:	2900	2703	2514	2333	2160
	energy, ft-lb:	4854	4217	3649	3143	2693
	arc, inches:	-1.5	+1.6	0	-7.1	-20.7

.375 WEATHERBY MAGNUM

CARTRIDGE BULLET	RANGE, YARDS:	0	100	200	300	400
A-Square 300 SP boat-tail	velocity, fps:	2700	2560	2425	2293	2166
	energy, ft-lb:	4856	4366	3916	3503	3125
	arc, inches:		+4.5	+5.2	0	-11.9
A-Square 300 Triad	velocity, fps:	2700	2391	2103	1835	1602
	energy, ft-lb:	4856	3808	2946	2243	1710
	arc, inches:		+2.3	0	-10.1	-30.8
Wby. 300 Nosler Part.	velocity, fps:	2800	2572	2366	2140	1963
	energy, ft-lb:	5224	4408	3696	3076	2541
	arc, inches:		+1.9	0	-8.2	-23.9

BALLISTICS

Centerfire Rifle Ballistics

.375 JRS TO .416 REMINGTON MAGNUM

CARTRIDGE BULLET	RANGE, YARDS:	0	100	200	300	400
.375 JRS						
A-Square 300 SP boat-tail	velocity, fps:	2700	2560	2425	2293	2166.
	energy, ft-lb:	4856	4366	3916	3503	3125
	arc, inches:		+4.5	+5.2	0	-11.9
A-Square 300 Triad	velocity, fps:	2700	2391	2103	1835	1602
	energy, ft-lb:	4856	3808	2946	2243	1710
	arc, inches:		+2.3	0	-10.1	-30.8
.375 REMINGTON ULTRA MAGNUM						
Nosler 260 AB	velocity, fps:	2950	2750	2560	2377	2202
	energy, ft-lb:	5023	4367	3783	3262	2799
	arc, inches:	-1.5	+1.6	0	-6.9	-19.9
Nosler 300 PT	velocity, fps:	2750	2524	2309	2105	1912
	energy, ft-lb:	5036	4244	3553	2953	2435
	arc, inches:	-1.5	+2.0	0	-8.5	-24.9
Rem. 270 Soft Point	velocity, fps:	2900	2558	2241	1947	1678
	energy, fps:	5041	3922	3010	2272	1689
	arc, inches:		+1.9	0	-9.2	-27.8
Rem. 300 Swift A-Frame	velocity, fps:	2760	2505	2263	2035	1822
	energy, ft-lb:	5073	4178	3412	2759	2210
	arc, inches:		+2.0	0	-8.8	-26.1
.375 A-SQUARE						
A-Square 300 SP boat-tail	velocity, fps:	2920	2773	2631	2494	2360
	energy, ft-lb:	5679	5123	4611	4142	3710
	arc, inches:		+3.7	+4.4	0	-9.8
A-Square 300 Triad	velocity, fps:	2920	2596	2294	2012	1762
	energy, ft-lb:	5679	4488	3505	2698	2068
	arc, inches:		+1.8	0	-8.5	-25.5
.376 STEYR						
Hornady 225 SP	velocity, fps:	2600	2331	2078	1842	1625
	energy, ft-lb:	3377	2714	2157	1694	1319
	arc, inches:		+2.5	0	-10.6	-31.4
Hornady 270 SP	velocity, fps:	2600	2372	2156	1951	1759
	energy, ft-lb:	4052	3373	2787	2283	1855
	arc, inches:		+2.3	0	-9.9	-28.9
.378 WEATHERBY MAGNUM						
A-Square 300 SP boat-tail	velocity, fps:	2900	2754	2612	2475	2342
	energy, ft-lb:	5602	5051	4546	4081	3655
	arc, inches:		+3.8	+4.4	0	-10.0
A-Square 300 Triad	velocity, fps:	2900	2577	2276	1997	1747
	energy, ft-lb:	5602	4424	3452	2656	2034
	arc, inches:		+1.9	0	-8.7	-25.9
Wby. 270 Pointed Expanding	velocity, fps:	3180	2921	2677	2445	2225
	energy, ft-lb:	6062	5115	4295	3583	2968
	arc, inches:		+1.3	0	-6.1	-18.1
Wby. 270 Barnes X	velocity, fps:	3150	2954	2767	2587	2415
	energy, ft-lb:	5948	5232	4589	4013	3495
	arc, inches:		+1.2	0	-5.8	-16.7
Wby. 300 RN Expanding	velocity, fps:	2925	2558	2220	1908	1627.
	energy, ft-lb:	5699	4360	3283	2424	1764
	arc, inches:		+1.9	0	-9.0	-27.8
Wby. 300 FMJ	velocity, fps:	2925	2591	2280	1991	1725
	energy, ft-lb:	5699	4470	3461	2640	1983
	arc, inches:		+1.8	0	-8.6	-26.1
.38-40 WINCHESTER						
Win. 180 Soft Point	velocity, fps:	1160	999	901	827	
	energy, ft-lb:	538	399	324	273	
	arc, inches:		0	-23.4	-75.2	

CARTRIDGE BULLET	RANGE, YARDS:	0	100	200	300	400
.38-55 WINCHESTER						
Black Hills 255 FN Lead	velocity, fps:	1250				
	energy, ft-lb:	925				
	arc, inches:					
Win. 255 Soft Point	velocity, fps:	1320	1190	1091	1018	
	energy, ft-lb:	987	802	674	587	
	arc, inches:		0	-33.9	-110.6	
.41 MAGNUM						
Win. 240 Platinum Tip	velocity, fps:	1830	1488	1220	1048	
	energy, ft-lb:	1784	1180	792	585	
	arc inches:		0	-15.0	-53.4	
.450/.400 NITRO EXPRESS						
A-Square 400 Triad	velocity, fps:	2150	1910	1690	1490	
	energy, ft-lb:	4105	3241	2537	1972	
	arc, inches:		+4.4	0	-16.5	
Hornady 400 DGS, DGX	velocity, fps:	2050	1820	1609	1420	
	energy, ft-lb:	3732	2940	2298	1791	
	arc, inches:	-0.9	0	-9.7	-32.8	
.404 JEFFERY						
A-Square 400 Triad	velocity, fps:	2150	1901	1674	1468	1299
	energy, ft-lb:	4105	3211	2489	1915	1499
	arc, inches:		+4.1	0	-16.4	-49.1
Hornady 400 DGS, DGX	velocity, fps:	2300	2046	1809	1592	
	energy, ft-lb:	4698	3717	2906	2251	
	arc, inches:	-1.5	0	-6.9	-24.4	
Norma 450 Woodleigh SP	velocity, fps:	2150	2048	1949	1853	1760
	energy, ft-lb:	4620	4191	3795	3430	3096
	arc, inches:	-1.5	+.2	0	-2.5	-7.6
.405 WINCHESTER						
Hornady 300 Flatpoint	velocity, fps:	2200	1851	1545	1296	
	energy, ft-lb:	3224	2282	1589	1119	
	arc, inches:		0	-8.7	-31.9	
Hornady 300 SP Interlock	velocity, fps:	2200	1890	1610	1370	
	energy, ft-lb:	3224	2379	1727	1250	
	arc, inches:		0	-8.3	-30.2	
.416 TAYLOR						
A-Square 400 Triad	velocity, fps:	2350	2093	1853	1634	1443
	energy, ft-lb:	4905	3892	3049	2371	1849
	arc, inches:		+3.2	0	-13.6	-39.8
.416 HOFFMAN						
A-Square 400 Triad	velocity, fps:	2380	2122	1879	1658	1464
	energy, ft-lb:	5031	3998	3136	2440	1903
	arc, inches:		+3.1	0	-13.1	-38.7
.416 REMINGTON MAGNUM						
A-Square 400 Triad	velocity, fps:	2380	2122	1879	1658	1464
	energy, ft-lb:	5031	3998	3136	2440	1903
	arc, inches:		+3.1	0	-13.2	-38.7
Federal 400 Trophy Bonded Sledgehammer Solid	velocity, fps:	2400	2150	1920	1700	1500
	energy, ft-lb:	5115	4110	3260	2565	2005
	arc, inches:		0	-6.0	-21.6	-49.2
Federal 400 Trophy Bonded	velocity, fps:	2400	2180	1970	1770	1590
	energy, ft-lb:	5115	4215	3440	2785	2245
	arc, inches:		0	-5.8	-20.6	-46.9
Rem. 400 Swift A-Frame	velocity, fps:	2400	2175	1962	1763	1579
	energy, ft-lb:	5115	4201	3419	2760	2214
	arc, inches:		0	-5.9	-20.8	

.416 RIGBY

CARTRIDGE BULLET	RANGE, YARDS:	0	100	200	300	400
A-Square 400 Triad	velocity, fps:	2400	2140	1897	1673	1478
	energy, ft-lb:	5115	4069	3194	2487	1940
	arc, inches:		+3.0	0	-12.9	-38.0
Federal 400 Trophy Bonded	velocity, fps:	2370	2150	1940	1750	1570
	energy, ft-lb:	4990	4110	3350	2715	2190
	arc, inches:		0	-6.0	-21.3	-48.1
Federal 400 Trophy Bonded	velocity, fps:	2370	2120	1890	1660	1460
Sledgehammer Solid	energy, ft-lb:	4990	3975	3130	2440	1895
	arc, inches:		0	-6.3	-22.5	-51.5
Federal 410 Woodleigh	velocity, fps:	2370	2110	1870	1640	1440
Weldcore	energy, ft-lb:	5115	4050	3165	2455	1895
	arc, inches:		0	-7.4	-24.8	-55.0
Federal 410 Solid	velocity, fps:	2370	2110	2870	1640	1440
	energy, ft-lb:	5115	4050	3165	2455	1895
	arc, inches:		0	-7.4	-24.8	-55.0
Hornady 400 DGX, DGS	velocity, fps:	2415	2156	1915	1691	
	energy, ft-lb:	5180	4130	3256	2540	
	arc, inches:	-1.5	0	-6.0	-21.6	
Norma 400 TXP Swift A-Fr.	velocity, fps:	2350	2127	1917	1721	
	energy, ft-lb:	4906	4021	3266	2632	
	arc, inches:		+3.1	0	-12.5	
Norma 400 Barnes Solid	velocity, fps:	2297	1930	1604	1330	
	energy, ft-lb:	4687	3310	2284	1571	
	arc, inches:		+3.9	0	-17.7	

.416 RUGER

CARTRIDGE BULLET	RANGE, YARDS:	0	100	200	300	400
Hornady 400 DGS, DGX	velocity, fps:	2400	2151	1917	1700	
	energy, ft-lb:	5116	4109	3264	2568	
	arc, inches:	-1.5	0	-6.0	-21.6	

.500/416 NITRO EXPRESS

CARTRIDGE BULLET	RANGE, YARDS:	0	50	100	150	200
Norma 450 Woodleigh SP	velocity, fps:	2100	1991	1886	1785	1688
	energy, ft-lb:	4408	3963	3556	3185	2849
	arc, inches:	-1.5	+.3	0	-2.7	-8.2

.416 DAKOTA

CARTRIDGE BULLET	RANGE, YARDS:	0	100	200	300	400
Dakota 400 Barnes X	velocity, fps:	2450	2294	2143	1998	1859
	energy, ft-lb:	5330	4671	4077	3544	3068
	arc, inches:		+2.5	-0.2	-10.5	-29.4

.416 WEATHERBY

CARTRIDGE BULLET	RANGE, YARDS:	0	100	200	300	400
A-Square 400 Triad	velocity, fps:	2600	2328	2073	1834	1624
	energy, ft-lb:	6004	4813	3816	2986	2343
	arc, inches:		+2.5	0	-10.5	-31.6
Wby. 350 Barnes X	velocity, fps:	2850	2673	2503	2340	2182
	energy, ft-lb:	6312	5553	4870	4253	3700
	arc, inches:		+1.7	0	-7.2	-20.9
Wby. 400 Swift A-Fr.	velocity, fps:	2650	2426	2213	2011	1820
	energy, ft-lb:	6237	5227	4350	3592	2941
	arc, inches:		+2.2	0	-9.3	-27.1
Wby. 400 RN Expanding	velocity, fps:	2700	2417	2152	1903	1676
	energy, ft-lb:	6474	5189	4113	3216	2493
	arc, inches:		+2.3	0	-9.7	-29.3
Wby. 400 Monolithic Solid	velocity, fps:	2700	2411	2140	1887	1656
	energy, ft-lb:	6474	5162	4068	3161	2435
	arc, inches:		+2.3	0	-9.8	-29.7

10.57 (.416) METEOR

CARTRIDGE BULLET	RANGE, YARDS:	0	100	200	300	400
Lazzeroni 400 Swift A-Fr.	velocity, fps:	2730	2532	2342	2161	1987
	energy, ft-lb:	6621	5695	4874	4147	3508
	arc, inches:		+1.9	0	-8.3	-24.0

.425 EXPRESS

CARTRIDGE BULLET	RANGE, YARDS:	0	100	200	300	400
A-Square 400 Triad	velocity, fps:	2400	2136	1888	1662	1465
	energy, ft-lb:	5115	4052	3167	2454	1906
	arc, inches:		+3.0	0	-13.1	-38.3

.44-40 WINCHESTER

CARTRIDGE BULLET	RANGE, YARDS:	0	100	200	300	400
Rem. 200 Soft Point	velocity, fps:	1190	1006	900	822	756
	energy, ft-lb:	629	449	360	300	254
	arc, inches:		0	-33.1	-108.7	-235.2
Win. 200 Soft Point	velocity, fps:	1190	1006	900	822	756
	energy, ft-lb:	629	449	360	300	254
	arc, inches:		0	-33.3	-109.5	-237.4

.44 REMINGTON MAGNUM

CARTRIDGE BULLET	RANGE, YARDS:	0	100	200	300	400
Federal 240 Hi-Shok HP	velocity, fps:	1760	1380	1090	950	860
	energy, ft-lb:	1650	1015	640	485	395
	arc, inches:		0	-17.4	-60.7	-136.0
Rem. 210 Semi-Jacketed HP	velocity, fps:	1920	1477	1155	982	880
	energy, ft-lb:	1719	1017	622	450	361
	arc, inches:		0	-14.7	-55.5	-131.3
Rem. 240 Soft Point	velocity, fps:	1760	1380	1114	970	878
	energy, ft-lb:	1650	1015	661	501	411
	arc, inches:		0	-17.0	-61.4	-143.0
Rem. 240 Semi-Jacketed	velocity, fps:	1760	1380	1114	970	878
Hollow Point	energy, ft-lb:	1650	1015	661	501	411
	arc, inches:		0	-17.0	-61.4	-143.0
Rem. 275 JHP Core-Lokt	velocity, fps:	1580	1293	1093	976	896
	energy, ft-lb:	1524	1020	730	582	490
	arc, inches:		0	-19.4	-67.5	-210.8
Win. 210 Silvertip HP	velocity, fps:	1580	1198	993	879	795
	energy, ft-lb:	1164	670	460	361	295
	arc, inches:		0	-22.4	-76.1	-168.0
Win. 240 Hollow Soft Point	velocity, fps:	1760	1362	1094	953	861
	energy, ft-lb:	1650	988	638	484	395
	arc, inches:		0	-18.1	-65.1	-150.3
Win. 250 Platinum Tip	velocity, fps:	1830	1475	1201	1032	931
	energy, ft-lb:	1859	1208	801	591	481
	arc, inches:		0	-15.3	-54.7	-126.6.

.444 MARLIN

CARTRIDGE BULLET	RANGE, YARDS:	0	100	200	300	400
Rem. 240 Soft Point	velocity, fps:	2350	1815	1377	1087	941
	energy, ft-lb:	2942	1755	1010	630	472
	arc, inches:		+2.2	-5.4	-31.4	-86.7
Hornady 265 Evolution	velocity, fps:	2325	1971	1652	1380	
	energy, ft-lb:	3180	2285	1606	1120	
	arc, inches:		+3.0	-1.4	-18.6	
Hornady 265 FP LM	velocity, fps:	2335	1913	1551	1266	
	energy, ft-lb:	3208	2153	1415	943	
	arc, inches:		+ 2.0	-4.9	-26.5	

.45-70 GOVERNMENT

CARTRIDGE BULLET	RANGE, YARDS:	0	100	200	300	400
Black Hills 405 FPL	velocity, fps:	1250				
	energy, ft-lb:					
	arc, inches:					
Federal 300 Sierra Pro-Hunt.	velocity, fps:	1880	1650	1430	1240	1110
HP FN	energy, ft-lb:	2355	1815	1355	1015	810
	arc, inches:		0	-11.5	-39.7	-89.1
PMC 350 FNSP	velocity, fps:					
	energy, ft-lb:					
	arc, inches:					
Rem. 300 Jacketed HP	velocity, fps:	1810	1497	1244	1073	969
	energy, ft-lb:	2182	1492	1031	767	625
	arc, inches:		0	-13.8	-50.1	-115.7

BALLISTICS

Centerfire Rifle Ballistics

.45-70 GOVERNMENT TO .460 WEATHERBY MAGNUM

CARTRIDGE BULLET	RANGE, YARDS:	0	100	200	300	400
Rem. 405 Soft Point	velocity, fps	1330	1168	1055	977	918
	energy, ft-lb:	1590	1227	1001	858	758
	arc, inches:		0	-24.0	-78.6	-169.4
Win. 300 Jacketed HP	velocity, fps	1880	1650	1425	1235	1105
	energy, ft-lb:	2355	1815	1355	1015	810
	arc, inches:		0	-12.8	-44.3	-95.5
Win. 300 Partition Gold	velocity, fps	1880	1558	1292	1103	988
	energy, ft-lb:	2355	1616	1112	811	651
	arc, inches:		0	-12.9	-46.0	-104.9.

.450 BUSHMASTER

CARTRIDGE BULLET	RANGE, YARDS:	0	100	200	300	400
Hornady 250 SST-ML	velocity, fps	2200	1840	1524	1268	
	energy, ft-lb	2686	1879	1289	893	
	arc, inches	-2.0	+2.5	-3.5	-24.5	

.450 MARLIN

CARTRIDGE BULLET	RANGE, YARDS:	0	100	200	300	400
Hornady 325 FTX	velocity, fps:	2225	1887	1585	1331	
	energy, ft-lb:	3572	2569	1813	1278	
	arc, inches:	-1.5	+3.0	-2.2	-21.3	
Hornady 350 FP	velocity, fps:	2100	1720	1397	1156	
	energy, ft-lb:	3427	2298	1516	1039	
	arc, inches:		0	-10.4	-38.9	

.450 NITRO EXPRESS (3¼")

CARTRIDGE BULLET	RANGE, YARDS:	0	100	200	300	400
A-Square 465 Triad	velocity, fps:	2190	1970	1765	1577	
	energy, ft-lb:	4952	4009	3216	2567	
	arc, inches:		+4.3	0	-15.4	
Hornady 480 DGS, DGX	velocity, fps:	2150	1881	1635	1418	
	energy, ft-lb:	4927	3769	2850	2144	
	arc, inches:	-1.5	0	-8.4	-29.9	

.450 #2

CARTRIDGE BULLET	RANGE, YARDS:	0	100	200	300	400
A-Square 465 Triad	velocity, fps:	2190	1970	1765	1577	
	energy, ft-lb:	4952	4009	3216	2567	
	arc, inches:		+4.3	0	-15.4	

.458 WINCHESTER MAGNUM

CARTRIDGE BULLET	RANGE, YARDS:	0	100	200	300	400
A-Square 465 Triad	velocity, fps:	2220	1999	1791	1601	1433
	energy, ft-lb:	5088	4127	3312	2646	2121
	arc, inches:		+3.6	0	-14.7	-42.5
Federal 350 Soft Point	velocity, fps:	2470	1990	1570	1250	1060
	energy, ft-lb:	4740	3065	1915	1205	870
	arc, inches:		0	-7.5	-29.1	-71.1
Federal 400 Trophy Bonded	velocity, fps:	2380	2170	1960	1770	1590
	energy, ft-lb:	5030	4165	3415	2785	2255
	arc, inches:		0	-5.9	-20.9	-47.1
Federal 500 Solid	velocity, fps:	2090	1870	1670	1480	1320
	energy, ft-lb:	4850	3880	3085	2440	1945
	arc, inches:		0	-8.5	-29.5	-66.2
Federal 500 Trophy Bonded	velocity, fps:	2090	1870	1660	1480	1310
	energy, ft-lb:	4850	3870	3065	2420	1915
	arc, inches:		0	-8.5	-29.7	-66.8
Federal 500 Trophy Bonded Sledgehammer Solid	velocity, fps:	2090	1860	1650	1460	1300
	energy, ft-lb:	4850	3845	3025	2365	1865
	arc, inches:		0	-8.6	-30.0	-67.8
Federal 510 Soft Point	velocity, fps:	2090	1820	1570	1360	1190
	energy, ft-lb:	4945	3730	2790	2080	1605
	arc, inches:		0	-9.1	-32.3	-73.9
Hornady 500 FMJ-RN HM	velocity, fps:	2260	1984	1735	1512	
	energy, ft-lb:	5670	4368	3341	2538	
	arc, inches:		0	-7.4	-26.4	
Norma 500 TXP Swift A-Fr.	velocity, fps:	2116	1903	1705	1524	
	energy, ft-lb:	4972	4023	3228	2578	
	arc, inches:		+4.1	0	-16.1	

CARTRIDGE BULLET	RANGE, YARDS:	0	100	200	300	400
Norma 500 Barnes Solid	velocity, fps	2067	1750	1472	1245	
	energy, ft-lb:	4745	3401	2405	1721	
	arc, inches:		+4.9	0	-21.2	
Rem. 450 Swift A-Frame PSP	velocity, fps:	2150	1901	1671	1465	1289
	energy, ft-lb:	4618	3609	2789	2144	1659
	arc, inches:		0	-8.2	-28.9	
Speer 500 African GS Tungsten Solid	velocity, fps:	2120	1845	1596	1379	
	energy, ft-lb:	4989	3780	2828	2111	
	arc, inches:		0	-8.8	-31.3	
Speer African Grand Slam	velocity, fps:	2120	1853	1609	1396	
	energy, ft-lb:	4989	3810	2875	2163	
	arc, inches:		0	-8.7	-30.8	
Win. 510 Soft Point	velocity, fps:	2040	1770	1527	1319	1157
	energy, ft-lb:	4712	3547	2640	1970	1516
	arc, inches:		0	-10.3	-35.6	

.458 LOTT

CARTRIDGE BULLET	RANGE, YARDS:	0	100	200	300	400
A-Square 465 Triad	velocity, fps:	2380	2150	1932	1730	1551
	energy, ft-lb:	5848	4773	3855	3091	2485
	arc, inches:		+3.0	0	-12.5	-36.4
Federal 500 TSX	velocity, fps:	2280	2090	1900	1730	1560
	energy, ft-lb:	5770	4825	4000	3305	2715
	arc, inches:		-6.4	-22.7	-50.7	
Hornady 500 RNSP or solid	velocity, fps:	2300	2022	1776	1551	
	energy, ft-lb:	5872	4537	3502	2671	
	arc, inches:		+3.4	0	-14.3	
Hornady 500 InterBond	velocity, fps:	2300	2028	1777	1549	
	energy, ft-lb:	5872	4535	3453	2604	
	arc, inches:		0	-7.0	-25.1	

CARTRIDGE BULLET	RANGE, YARDS:	0	50	100	150	200
Norma 500 Woodleigh SP	velocity, fps:	2100	1982	1868	1758	1654
	energy, ft-lb:	4897	4361	3874	3434	3039
	arc, inches:	-1.5	+.3	0	-2.8	-8.4

.450 ACKLEY

CARTRIDGE BULLET	RANGE, YARDS:	0	100	200	300	400
A-Square 465 Triad	velocity, fps:	2400	2169	1950	1747	1567
	energy, ft-lb:	5947	4857	3927	3150	2534
	arc, inches:		+2.9	0	-12.2	-35.8

.450 RIGBY

CARTRIDGE BULLET	RANGE, YARDS:	0	50	100	150	200
Norma 550 Woodleigh SP	velocity, fps:	2100	1992	1887	1787	1690
	energy, ft-lb:	5387	4847	4352	3900	3491
	arc, inches:	-1.5	+.3	0	-2.7	-8.2

.460 SHORT A-SQUARE

CARTRIDGE BULLET	RANGE, YARDS:	0	100	200	300	400
A-Square 500 Triad	velocity, fps:	2420	2198	1987	1789	1613
	energy, ft-lb:	6501	5362	4385	3553	2890
	arc, inches:		+2.9	0	-11.6	-34.2

.450 DAKOTA

CARTRIDGE BULLET	RANGE, YARDS:	0	100	200	300	400
Dakota 500 Barnes Solid	velocity, fps:	2450	2235	2030	1838	1658
	energy, ft-lb:	6663	5544	4576	3748	3051
	arc, inches:		+2.5	-0.6	-12.0	-33.8

.460 WEATHERBY MAGNUM

CARTRIDGE BULLET	RANGE, YARDS:	0	100	200	300	400
A-Square 500 Triad	velocity, fps:	2580	2349	2131	1923	1737
	energy, ft-lb:	7389	6126	5040	4107	3351
	arc, inches:		+2.4	0	-10.0	-29.4
Wby. 450 Barnes X	velocity, fps:	2700	2518	2343	2175	2013
	energy, ft-lb:	7284	6333	5482	4725	4050
	arc, inches:		+2.0	0	-8.4	-24.1

BALLISTICS

.460 WEATHERBY MAGNUM TO .700 NITRO EXPRESS

CARTRIDGE BULLET	RANGE, YARDS:	0	100	200	300	400
Wby. 500 RN Expanding	velocity, fps:	2600	2301	2022	1764	1533.
	energy, ft-lb:	7504	5877	4539	3456	2608
	arc, inches:		+2.6	0	-11.1	-33.5
Wby. 500 FMJ	velocity, fps:	2600	2309	2037	1784	1557
	energy, ft-lb:	7504	5917	4605	3534	2690
	arc, inches:		+2.5	0	-10.9	-33.0

.500/.465

CARTRIDGE BULLET	RANGE, YARDS:	0	100	200	300	400
A-Square 480 Triad	velocity, fps:	2150	1928	1722	1533	
	energy, ft-lb:	4926	3960	3160	2505	
	arc, inches:		+4.3	0	-16.0	

.470 NITRO EXPRESS

CARTRIDGE BULLET	RANGE, YARDS:	0	100	200	300	400
A-Square 500 Triad	velocity, fps:	2150	1912	1693	1494	
	energy, ft-lb:	5132	4058	3182	2478	
	arc, inches:		+4.4	0	-16.5	
Federal 500 Trophy Bond	velocity, fps:	2150	1890	1660	1450	
(and Sledgehammer solid)	energy, ft-lb:	5130	3975	3045	2320	
	arc, inches:	-1.5	0	-9.4	-29.3	
Hornady 500 DGX, DGS	velocity, fps:	2150	1885	1643	1429	
	energy, ft-lb:	5132	3946	2998	2267	
	arc, inches:	-1.5	0	-8.9	-30.9	

CARTRIDGE BULLET	RANGE, YARDS:	0	50	100	150	200
Norma 500 Woodleigh	velocity, fps:	2100	2002	1906	1814	1725
(soft and solid)	energy, ft-lb:	4897	4449	4035	3654	3304
	arc, inches:	-1.5	+.3	0	-2.7	-8.0

.470 CAPSTICK

CARTRIDGE BULLET	RANGE, YARDS:	0	100	200	300	400
A-Square 500 Triad	velocity, fps:	2400	2172	1958	1761	1553
	energy, ft-lb:	6394	5236	4255	3445	2678
	arc, inches:		+2.9	0	-11.9	-36.1

.475 #2

CARTRIDGE BULLET	RANGE, YARDS:	0	100	200	300	400
A-Square 480 Triad	velocity, fps:	2200	1964	1744	1544	
	energy, ft-lb:	5158	4109	3240	2539	
	arc, inches:		+4.1	0	-15.6	

.475 #2 JEFFERY

A-Square 500 Triad	velocity, fps:	2200	1966	1748	1550	
	energy, ft-lb:	5373	4291	3392	2666	
	arc, inches:		+4.1	0	-15.6	

.495 A-SQUARE

A-Square 570 Triad	velocity, fps:	2350	2117	1896	1693	1513
	energy, ft-lb:	6989	5671	4552	3629	2899
	arc, inches:		+3.1	0	-13.0	-37.8

.500 NITRO EXPRESS (3")

A-Square 570 Triad	velocity, fps:	2150	1928	1722	1533	
	energy, ft-lb:	5850	4703	3752	2975	
	arc, inches:		+4.3	0	-16.1	
Federal 570 TSX	velocity, fps:	2100	1890	1700	1520	1370
	energy, ft-lb:	5580	4530	3655	2935	2355
	arc, inches:	0	-8.4	-28.7	-64.2	

CARTRIDGE BULLET	RANGE, YARDS:	0	100	200	300	400
Hornady 570 DGX, DGS	velocity, fps:	2150	1881	1635	1419	
	energy, ft-lb:	5850	4477	3384	2547	
	arc, inches:	-.9	0	-9.0	-31.1	

CARTRIDGE BULLET	RANGE, YARDS:	0	50	100	150	200
Norma 570 Woodleigh SP	velocity, fps:	2100	2000	1903	1809	1719
	energy, ft-lb:	5583	5064	4585	4145	3742
	arc, inches:	-1.5	+.3	0	-2.7	-8.0

50 BMG						
Hornady 750 A-MAX	velocity, fps:	2815	2727	2641	2557	2474
	energy, ft-lb:	13196	12386	11619	10889	10196
	arc, inches:	-1.8	+1.4	0	-6.4	-18.2

.500 JEFFERY

CARTRIDGE BULLET	RANGE, YARDS:	0	50	100	150	200
Norma 570 Woodleigh SP	velocity, fps:	2200	2097	1997	1901	1807
	energy, ft-lb:	6127	5568	5050	4573	4134
	arc, inches:	-1.5	+.2	0	-2.4	-7.1

.500 A-SQUARE

CARTRIDGE BULLET	RANGE, YARDS:	0	100	200	300	400
A-Square 600 Triad	velocity, fps:	2470	2235	2013	1804	1620
	energy, ft-lb:	8127	6654	5397	4336	3495
	arc, inches:		+2.7	0	-11.3	-33.5

.505 GIBBS

A-Square 525 Triad	velocity, fps:	2300	2063	1840	1637	
	energy, ft-lb:	6166	4962	3948	3122	
	arc, inches:		+3.6	0	-14.2	

CARTRIDGE BULLET	RANGE, YARDS:	0	50	100	150	200
Norma 600 Woodleigh SP	velocity, fps:	2100	1998	1899	1803	1711
	energy, ft-lb:	5877	5319	4805	4334	3904
	arc, inches:	-1.5	+.3	0	-2.7	-8.1

.577 NITRO EXPRESS

CARTRIDGE BULLET	RANGE, YARDS:	0	100	200	300	400
A-Square 750 Triad	velocity, fps:	2050	1811	1595	1401	
	energy, ft-lb:	6998	5463	4234	3267	
	arc, inches:		+4.9	0	-18.5	

.577 TYRANNOSAUR

A-Square 750 Triad	velocity, fps:	2460	2197	1950	1723	1516
	energy, ft-lb:	10077	8039	6335	4941	3825
	arc, inches:		+2.8	0	-12.1	-36.0

.600 NITRO EXPRESS

A-Square 900 Triad	velocity, fps:	1950	1680	1452	1336	
	energy, ft-lb:	7596	5634	4212	3564	
	arc, inches:		+5.6	0	-20.7	

.700 NITRO EXPRESS

A-Square 1000 Monolithic	velocity, fps:	1900	1669	1461	1288	
Solid	energy, ft-lb:	8015	6188	4740	3685	
	arc, inches:		+5.8	0	-22.2	

BALLISTICS

Long Range Rifle

6.6 CREEDMOOR TO .338 LAPUA

ballistics

CARTRIDGE BULLET	RANGE, YARDS:	0	400	600	800	1000
6.6 CREEDMOOR						
Nosler 140 HPBT	velocity, fps:	2550	2229	1932	1662	1426
	energy, ft-lb:	2021	1544	1160	859	632
	arc, inches:	-1.5	0	-26.7	-90.9	-205.9
.264 WINCHESTER MAGNUM						
Nosler 130 AccuBond	velocity, fps:	3100	2709	2350	2019	1718
	energy, ft-lb:	2773	2118	1594	1176	852
	arc, inches:	-1.5	0	-17.6	-60.6	-137.9
6.5/284 NORMA						
Nosler 129 AccuBond	velocity, fps:	2965	2633	2324	2036	1771
Long Range	energy, ft-lb:	2517	1985	1547	1188	899
	arc, inches:	-1.5	0	-18.7	-63.2	-141.6
.270 WSM						
Nosler 150 AccuBond	velocity, fps:	2960	2661	2381	2118	1873
Long Range	energy, ft-lb:	2917	2358	1888	1495	1169
	arc, inches:	-1.5	0	-18.2	-61.1	-135.1
7MM REMINGTON MAGNUM						
Nosler 168 AccuBond	velocity, fps:	2880	2598	2333	2084	1851
Long Range	energy, ft-lb:	3093	2518	2030	1620	1278
	arc, inches:	-1.5	0	-19.2	-64.0	-141.0
7MM STW						
Nosler 175 AccuBond	velocity, fps:	2900	2625	2366	2122	1893
Long Range	energy, ft-lb:	3267	2677	2175	1750	1393
	arc, inches:	-1.5	0	-18.8	-62.4	-137.1
7MM REMINGTON ULTRA MAG						
Nosler 175 AccuBond	velocity, fps:	3040	2756	2490	2239	2002
Long Range	energy, ft-lb:	3590	2952	2409	1948	1558
	arc, inches:	-1.5	0	-16.9	-56.2	-123.5
.308 WINCHESTER						
Barnes 175 OTM						
velocity, fps:		2650	2318	2011	1730	1480	1272
energy, ft-lb:		2730	2089	1571	1163	852	629
arc, inches:		-1.5	0	-24.6	-83.8	-189.9	-360.0
.300 WSM						
Nosler 190 AccuBond	velocity, fps:	2875	2588	2319	2066	1830
Long Range	energy, ft-lb:	3486	2826	2269	1801	1413
	arc, inches:	-1.5	0	-19.3	-64.7	-142.7

CARTRIDGE BULLET	RANGE, YARDS:	0	400	600	800	1000
.300 WINCHESTER MAGNUM						
Barnes 220 OTM						
velocity, fps:		2700	2420	2158	1912	1685	1481
energy, ft-lb:		3562	2862	2275	1786	1387	1072
arc, inches:		-1.5	0	-22.4	-74.7	-165.4	-305.3
Nosler 190 AccuBond	velocity, fps:	2870	2583	2314	2062	1826
Long Range	energy, ft-lb:	3474	2816	2260	1794	1407
	arc, inches:	-1.5	0	-19.4	-64.9	-143.3
.300 WEATHERBY MAGNUM						
Nosler 210 AccuBond	velocity, fps:	2825	2575	2339	2115	1905
Long Range	energy, ft-lb:	3720	3092	2551	2087	1691
	arc, inches:	-1.5	0	-19.5	-64.6	-140.8
.300 REMINGTON ULTRA MAG						
Nosler 210 AccuBond	velocity, fps:	2920	2665	2424	2196	1980
Long Range	energy, ft-lb:	3975	3311	2740	2248	1828
	arc, inches:	-1.5	0	-18.1	-60.0	-130.8
.30-378 WEATHERBY MAGNUM						
Nosler 210 AccuBond	velocity, fps:	3040	2778	2531	2297	2076
Long Range	energy, ft-lb:	4308	3599	2987	2461	2009
	arc, inches:	-1.5	0	-16.6	-54.9	-119.7
.338 REMINGTON ULTRA MAG						
Nosler 300 AccuBond	velocity, fps:	2600	2359	2131	1916	1716
	energy, ft-lb:	4502	3707	3026	2447	1963
	arc, inches:	-1.5	0	-23.6	-77.9	-170.2
.338 LAPUA						
Barnes 300 OTM						
velocity, fps:		2600	2375	2161	1958	1767	1591
energy, ft-lb:		4504	3757	3110	2554	2081	1687
arc, inches:		-1.5	0	-23.2	-76.4	-165.9	-300.1
Nosler 300 AccuBond	velocity, fps:	2650	2406	2176	1959	1755
	energy, ft-lb:	4677	3857	3154	2555	2053
	arc, inches:	-1.5	0	-22.6	-74.7	-163.1

582 • Shooter's Bible 105th Edition

www.skyhorsepublishing.com

Centerfire Handgun Ballistics

Data shown here is taken from manufacturers' charts; your chronograph readings may vary. Barrel lengths for pistol data vary, and depend in part on which pistols are typically chambered in a given cartridge. Velocity variations due to barrel length depend on the baseline bullet speed and the load. Velocity for the .30 Carbine, normally a rifle cartridge, was determined in a pistol barrel.

Listings are current as of February the year *Shooter's Bible* appears (not the cover year). Listings are not intended as recommendations. For example, the data for the .25 Auto gives velocity and energy readings to 100 yards. Few handgunners would call the little .25 a 100-yard cartridge.

Abbreviations: Bullets are designated by loading company, weight (in grains) and type, with these abbreviations for shape and construction: BJHP=brass-jacketed hollowpoint; FN=Flat Nose; FMC=Full Metal Case; FMJ=Full Metal Jacket; HP=Hollowpoint; L=Lead; LF=Lead-Free; +P=a more powerful load than traditionally manufactured for that round; RN=Round Nose; SFHP=Starfire (PMC) Hollowpoint; SP=Softpoint; SWC=Semi Wadcutter; TMJ=Total Metal Jacket; WC=Wadcutter; CEPP, SXT and XTP are trademarked designations of Lapua, Winchester and Hornady, respectively.

.25 AUTO TO .32 S&W LONG

CARTRIDGE BULLET	RANGE, YARDS:	0	25	50	75	100
.25 Auto						
Federal 50 FMJ	velocity, fps:	760	750	730	720	700
	energy, ft-lb:	65	60	60	55	55
Hornady 35 JHP/XTP	velocity, fps:	900		813		742
	energy, ft-lb:	63		51		43
Magtech 50 FMC	velocity, fps:	760		707		659
	energy, ft-lb:	64		56		48
PMC 50 FMJ	velocity, fps:	754	730	707	685	663
	energy, ft-lb:	62				
Rem. 50 Metal Case	velocity, fps:	760		707		659
	energy, ft-lb:	64		56		48
Speer 35 Gold Dot	velocity, fps:	900		816		747
	energy, ft-lb:	63		52		43
Speer 50 TMJ (and Blazer)	velocity, fps:	760		717		677
	energy, ft-lb:	64		57		51
Win. 45 Expanding Point	velocity, fps:	815		729		655
	energy, ft-lb	66		53		42
Win. 50 FMJ	velocity, fps:	760		707		
	energy, ft-lb	64		56		
.30 Luger						
Win. 93 FMJ	velocity, fps:	1220		1110		1040
	energy, ft-lb	305		255		225
7.62x25 Tokarev						
PMC 93 FMJ	velocity and energy figures not available					
.30 Carbine						
Win. 110 Hollow SP	velocity, fps:	1790		1601		1430
	energy, ft-lb	783		626		500
.32 Auto						
Federal 65 Hydra-Shok JHP	velocity, fps:	950	920	890	860	830
	energy, ft-lb:	130	120	115	105	100
Federal 71 FMJ	velocity, fps:	910	880	860	830	810
	energy, ft-lb:	130	120	115	110	105
Hornady 60 JHP/XTP	velocity, fps:	1000		917		849
	energy, ft-lb:	133		112		96
Hornady 71 FMJ-RN	velocity, fps:	900		845		797
	energy, ft-lb:	128		112		100
Magtech 71 FMC	velocity, fps:	905		855		810
	energy, ft-lb:	129		115		103
Magtech 71 JHP	velocity, fps:	905		855		810
	energy, ft-lb:	129		115		103

CARTRIDGE BULLET	RANGE, YARDS:	0	25	50	75	100
PMC 60 JHP	velocity, fps:	980	849	820	791	763
	energy, ft-lb:	117				
PMC 70 SFHP	velocity, fps:	velocity and energy figures not available				
PMC 71 FMJ	velocity, fps:	870	841	814	791	763
	energy, ft-lb:	119				
Rem. 71 Metal Case	velocity, fps:	905		855		810
	energy, ft-lb:	129		115		97
Speer 60 Gold Dot	velocity, fps:	960		868		796
	energy, ft-lb:	123		100		84
Speer 71 TMJ (and Blazer)	velocity, fps:	900		855		810
	energy, ft-lb:	129		115		97
Win. 60 Silvertip HP	velocity, fps:	970		895		835
	energy, ft-lb:	125		107		93
Win. 71 FMJ	velocity, fps:	905		855		
	energy, ft-lb	129		115		
.32 S&W						
Rem. 88 LRN	velocity, fps:	680		645		610
	energy, ft-lb:	90		81		73
Win. 85 LRN	velocity, fps:	680		645		610
	energy, ft-lb	90		81		73
.32 S&W Long						
Federal 98 LWC	velocity, fps:	780	700	630	560	500
	energy, ft-lb:	130	105	85	70	55
Federal 98 LRN	velocity, fps:	710	690	670	650	640
	energy, ft-lb:	115	105	100	95	90
Lapua 83 LWC	velocity, fps:	240		189*		149*
	energy, ft-lb:	154		95*		59*
Lapua 98 LWC	velocity, fps:	240		202*		171*
	energy, ft-lb:	183		130*		93*
Magtech 98 LRN	velocity, fps:	705		670		635
	energy, ft-lb:	108		98		88
Magtech 98 LWC	velocity, fps:	682		579		491
	energy, ft-lb:	102		73		52
Norma 98 LWC	velocity, fps:	787	759	732		683
	energy, ft-lb:	136	126	118		102
PMC 98 LRN	velocity, fps:	789	770	751	733	716
	energy, ft-lb:	135				
PMC 100 LWC	velocity, fps:	683	652	623	595	569
	energy, ft-lb:	102				
Rem. 98 LRN	velocity, fps:	705		670		635
	energy, ft-lb:	115		98		88

Centerfire Handgun Ballistics

.32 S&W LONG TO 9MM LUGER

CARTRIDGE BULLET	RANGE, YARDS:	0	25	50	75	100
Win. 98 LRN	velocity, fps:	705		670		635
	energy, ft-lb:	115		98		88

.32 SHORT COLT

CARTRIDGE BULLET	RANGE, YARDS:	0	25	50	75	100
Win. 80 LRN	velocity, fps:	745		665		590
	energy, ft-lb	100		79		62

.32-20

CARTRIDGE BULLET	RANGE, YARDS:	0	25	50	75	100
Black Hills 115 FPL	velocity, fps:	800				
	energy, ft-lb:					

.32 H&R MAG

CARTRIDGE BULLET	RANGE, YARDS:	0	25	50	75	100
Black Hills 85 JHP	velocity, fps	1100				
	energy, ft-lb	228				
Black Hills 90 FPL	velocity, fps	750				
	energy, ft-lb					
Black Hills 115 FPL	velocity, fps	800				
	energy, ft-lb					
Federal 85 Hi-Shok JHP	velocity, fps:	1100	1050	1020	970	930
	energy, ft-lb:	230	210	195	175	165
Federal 95 LSWC	velocity, fps:	1030	1000	940	930	900
	energy, ft-lb:	225	210	195	185	170
Hornady 80 FTX		0		50 yds.		100.
	velocity, fps:	1150		1039		963
	energy, ft-lb:	235		192		165

.38 SPECIAL LITE, 4"BBL

CARTRIDGE BULLET	RANGE, YARDS:	0	25	50	75	100
Hornady 90 FTX	velocity, fps:	1200		1037		938
	energy, ft-lb:	288		215		176

9MM MAKAROV

CARTRIDGE BULLET	RANGE, YARDS:	0	25	50	75	100
Federal 90 Hi-Shok JHP	velocity, fps:	990	950	910	880	850
	energy, ft-lb:	195	180	165	155	145
Federal 90 FMJ	velocity, fps:	990	960	920	900	870
	energy, ft-lb:	205	190	180	170	160
Hornady 95 JHP/XTP	velocity, fps:	1000		930		874
	energy, ft-lb:	211		182		161
PMC 100 FMJ-TC	velocity, fps:	velocity and energy figures not available				
Speer 95 TMJ Blazer	velocity, fps:	1000		928		872
	energy, ft-lb:	211		182		161

9x21 IMI

CARTRIDGE BULLET	RANGE, YARDS:	0	25	50	75	100
PMC 123 FMJ	velocity, fps:	1150	1093	1046	1007	973
	energy, ft-lb:	364				

9MM LUGER

CARTRIDGE BULLET	RANGE, YARDS:	0	25	50	75	100
Black Hills 115 JHP	velocity, fps:	1150				
	energy, ft-lb:	336				
Black Hills 115 FMJ	velocity, fps:	1150				
	energy, ft-lb:	336				
Black Hills 115 JHP +P	velocity, fps:	1300				
	energy, ft-lb:	431				
Black Hills 115 EXP JHP	velocity, fps:	1250				
	energy, ft-lb:	400				
Black Hills 124 JHP +P	velocity, fps:	1250				
	energy, ft-lb:	430				
Black Hills 124 JHP	velocity, fps:	1150				
	energy, ft-lb:	363				
Black Hills 124 FMJ	velocity, fps:	1150				
	energy, ft-lb:	363				
Black Hills 147 JHP subsonic	velocity, fps:	975				
	energy, ft-lb:	309				
Black Hills 147 FMJ subsonic	velocity, fps:	975				
	energy, ft-lb:	309				
Federal 105 EFMJ	velocity, fps:	1225	1160	1105	1060	1025
	energy, ft-lb:	350	315	285	265	245

CARTRIDGE BULLET	RANGE, YARDS:	0	25	50	75	100
Federal 115 Hi-Shok JHP	velocity, fps:	1160	1100	1060	1020	990
	energy, ft-lb:	345	310	285	270	250
Federal 115 FMJ	velocity, fps:	1160	1100	1060	1020	990
	energy, ft-lb:	345	310	285	270	250
Federal 124 FMJ	velocity, fps:	1120	1070	1030	990	960
	energy, ft-lb:	345	315	290	270	255
Federal 124 Hydra-Shok JHP	velocity, fps:	1120	1070	1030	990	960
	energy, ft-lb:	345	315	290	270	255
Federal 124 TMJ TMF Primer	velocity, fps:	1120	1070	1030	990	960
	energy, ft-lb:	345	315	290	270	255
Federal 124 Truncated FMJ Match	velocity, fps:	1120	1070	1030	990	960
	energy, ft-lb:	345	315	290	270	255
Federal 124 Nyclad HP	velocity, fps:	1120	1070	1030	990	960
	energy, ft-lb:	345	315	290	270	255
Federal 124 FMJ +P	velocity, fps:	1120	1070	1030	990	960
	energy, ft-lb:	345	315	290	270	255
Federal 135 Hydra-Shok JHP	velocity, fps:	1050	1030	1010	980	970
	energy, ft-lb:	330	315	300	290	280
Federal 147 Hydra-Shok JHP	velocity, fps:	1000	960	920	890	860
	energy, ft-lb:	325	300	275	260	240
Federal 147 Hi-Shok JHP	velocity, fps:	980	950	930	900	880
	energy, ft-lb:	310	295	285	265	255
Federal 147 FMJ FN	velocity, fps:	960	930	910	890	870
	energy, ft-lb:	295	280	270	260	250
Federal 147 TMJ TMF Primer	velocity, fps:	960	940	910	890	870
	energy, ft-lb:	300	285	270	260	245
Hornady 115 JHP/XTP	velocity, fps:	1155		1047		971
	energy, ft-lb:	341		280		241
Hornady 124 JHP/XTP	velocity, fps:	1110		1030		971
	energy, ft-lb:	339		292		259
Hornady 124 TAP-FPD	velocity, fps:	1100		1028		967
	energy, ft-lb:	339		291		257
Hornady 147 JHP/XTP	velocity, fps:	975		935		899
	energy, ft-lb:	310		285		264
Hornady 147 TAP-FPD	velocity, fps:	975		935		899
	energy, ft-lb:	310		285		264
Lapua 116 FMJ	velocity, fps:	365		319*		290*
	energy, ft-lb:	500		381*		315*
Lapua 120 FMJ CEPP Super	velocity, fps:	360		316*		288*
	energy, ft-lb:	505		390*		324*
Lapua 120 FMJ CEPP Extra	velocity, fps:	360		316*		288*
	energy, ft-lb:	505		390*		324*
Lapua 123 HP Megashock	velocity, fps:	355		311*		284*
	energy, ft-lb:	504		388*		322*
Lapua 123 FMJ	velocity, fps:	320		292*		272*
	energy, ft-lb:	410		342*		295*
Lapua 123 FMJ Combat	velocity, fps:	355		315*		289*
	energy, ft-lb:	504		397*		333*
Magtech 115 JHP +P	velocity, fps:	1246		1137		1056
	energy, ft-lb:	397		330		285
Magtech 115 FMC	velocity, fps:	1135		1027		961
	energy, ft-lb:	330		270		235
Magtech 115 JHP	velocity, fps:	1155		1047		971
	energy, ft-lb:	340		280		240
Magtech 124 FMC	velocity, fps:	1109		1030		971
	energy, ft-lb:	339		292		259
Norma 84 Lead Free Frangible (Geco brand)	velocity, fps:	1411				
	energy, ft-lb:	371				
Norma 124 FMJ (Geco brand)	velocity, fps:	1120				
	energy, fps:	341				
Norma 123 FMJ	velocity, fps:	1099	1032	980		899
	energy, ft-lb:	331	292	263		221
Norma 123 FMJ	velocity, fps:	1280	1170	1086		972
	energy, ft-lb:	449	375	323		259

BALLISTICS

Centerfire Handgun Ballistics

9MM LUGER TO .380 AUTO

CARTRIDGE BULLET	RANGE, YARDS:	0	25	50	75	100
PMC 75 Non-Toxic Frangible	velocity, fps:	1350	1240	1154	1088	1035
	energy, ft-lb:	303				
PMC 95 SFHP	velocity, fps:	1250	1239	1228	1217	1207
	energy, ft-lb:	330				
PMC 115 FMJ	velocity, fps:	1157	1100	1053	1013	979
	energy, ft-lb:	344				
PMC 115 JHP	velocity, fps:	1167	1098	1044	999	961
	energy, ft-lb:	350				
PMC 124 SFHP	velocity, fps:	1090	1043	1003	969	939
	energy, ft-lb:	327				
PMC 124 FMJ	velocity, fps:	1110	1059	1017	980	949
	energy, ft-lb:	339				
PMC 124 LRN	velocity, fps:	1050	1006	969	937	908
	energy, ft-lb:	304				
PMC 147 FMJ	velocity, fps:	980	965	941	919	900
	enerby, ft-lb:	310				
PMC 147 SFHP	velocity, fps:	velocity and energy figures not available				
Rem. 101 Lead Free Frangible	velocity, fps:	1220		1092		1004
	energy, ft-lb:	334		267		226
Rem. 115 FN Enclosed Base	velocity, fps:	1135		1041		973
	energy, ft-lb:	329		277		242
Rem. 115 Metal Case	velocity, fps:	1135		1041		973
	energy, ft-lb:	329		277		242
Rem. 115 JHP	velocity, fps:	1155		1047		971
	energy, ft-lb:	341		280		241
Rem. 115 JHP +P	velocity, fps:	1250		1113		1019
	energy, ft-lb:	399		316		265
Rem. 124 JHP	velocity, fps:	1120		1028		960
	energy, ft-lb:	346		291		254
Rem. 124 FNEB	velocity, fps:	1100		1030		971
	energy, ft-lb:	339		292		252
Rem. 124 BJHP	velocity, fps:	1125		1031		963
	energy, ft-lb:	349		293		255
Rem. 124 BJHP +P	velocity, fps:	1180		1089		1021
	energy, ft-lb:	384		327		287
Rem. 124 Metal Case	velocity, fps:	1110		1030		971
	energy, ft-lb:	339		292		259
Rem. 147 JHP subsonic	velocity, fps:	990		941		900
	energy, ft-lb:	320		289		264
Rem. 147 BJHP	velocity, fps:	990		941		900
	energy, ft-lb:	320		289		264
Speer 90 Frangible	velocity, fps:	1350		1132		1001
	energy, ft-lb:	364		256		200
Speer 115 JHP Blazer	velocity, fps:	1145		1024		943
	energy, ft-lb:	335		268		227
Speer 115 FMJ Blazer	velocity, fps:	1145		1047		971
	energy, ft-lb:	341		280		241
Speer 115 FMJ	velocity, fps:	1200		1060		970
	energy, ft-lb:	368		287		240
Speer 115 Gold Dot HP	velocity, fps:	1200		1047		971
	energy, ft-lb:	341		280		241
Speer 124 FMJ Blazer	velocity, fps:	1090		989		917
	energy, ft-lb:	327		269		231
Speer 124 FMJ	velocity, fps:	1090		987		913
	energy, ft-lb:	327		268		230
Speer 124 TMJ-CF (and Blazer)	velocity, fps:	1090		989		917
	energy, ft-lb:	327		269		231
Speer 124 Gold Dot HP	velocity, fps:	1150		1030		948
	energy, ft-lb:	367		292		247
Speer 124 Gold Dot HP+P	velocity, ft-lb:	1220		1085		996
	energy, ft-lb:	410		324		273
Speer 147 TMJ Blazer	velocity, fps:	950		912		879
	energy, ft-lb:	295		272		252

CARTRIDGE BULLET	RANGE, YARDS:	0	25	50	75	100
Speer 147 TMJ	velocity, fps:	985		943		906
	energy, ft-lb:	317		290		268
Speer 147 TMJ-CF (and Blazer)	velocity, fps:	985		960		924
	energy, ft-lb:	326		300		279
Speer 147 Gold Dot	velocity, fps:	985		960		924
	energy, ft-lb:	326		300		279
Win. 105 Jacketed FP	velocity, fps:	1200		1074		989
	energy, ft-lb:	336		269		228
Win. 115 Silvertip HP	velocity, fps:	1225		1095		1007
	energy, ft-lb:	383		306		259
Win. 115 Jacketed HP	velocity, fps:	1225		1095		
	energy, ft-lb:	383		306		
Win. 115 FMJ	velocity, fps:	1190		1071		
	energy, ft-lb:	362		293		
Win. 115 EB WinClean	velocity, fps:	1190		1088		
	energy, ft-lb:	362		302		
Win. 124 FMJ	velocity, fps:	1140		1050		
	energy, ft-lb:	358		303		
Win. 124 EB WinClean	velocity, fps:	1130		1049		
	energy, ft-lb:	352		303		
Win. 147 FMJ FN	velocity, fps:	990		945		
	energy, ft-lb:	320		292		
Win. 147 SXT	velocity, fps:	990		947		909
	energy, ft-lb:	320		293		270
Win. 147 Silvertip HP	velocity, fps:	1010		962		921
	energy, ft-lb:	333		302		277
Win. 147 JHP	velocity, fps:	990		945		
	energy, ft-lb:	320		291		
Win. 147 EB WinClean	velocity, fps:	990		945		
	energy, ft-lb:	320		291		

9 x 23 WINCHESTER

CARTRIDGE BULLET	RANGE, YARDS:	0	25	50	75	100
Win. 124 Jacketed FP	velocity, fps:	1460		1308		
	energy, ft-lb:	587		471		
Win. 125 Silvertip HP	velocity, fps:	1450		1249		1103
	energy, ft-lb:	583		433		338

.38 S&W

CARTRIDGE BULLET	RANGE, YARDS:	0	25	50	75	100
Rem. 146 LRN	velocity, fps:	685		650		620
	energy, ft-lb:	150		135		125
Win. 145 LRN	velocity, fps:	685		650		620
	energy, ft-lb:	150		135		125

.38 SHORT COLT

CARTRIDGE BULLET	RANGE, YARDS:	0	25	50	75	100
Rem. 125 LRN	velocity, fps:	730		685		645
	energy, ft-lb:	150		130		115

.38 LONG COLT

CARTRIDGE BULLET	RANGE, YARDS:	0	25	50	75	100
Black Hills 158 RNL	velocity, fps:	650				
	energy, ft-lb:					

.380 AUTO

CARTRIDGE BULLET	RANGE, YARDS:	0	25	50	75	100
Black Hills 90 JHP	velocity, fps:	1000				
	energy, ft-lb:	200				
Black Hills 95 FMJ	velocity, fps:	950				
	energy, ft-lb:	190				
Federal 90 Hi-Shok JHP	velocity, fps:	1000	940	890	840	800
	energy, ft-lb:	200	175	160	140	130
Federal 90 Hydra-Shok JHP	velocity, fps:	1000	940	890	840	800
	energy, ft-lb:	200	175	160	140	130
Federal 95 FMJ	velocity, fps:	960	910	870	830	790
	energy, ft-lb:	190	175	160	145	130
Hornady 90 JHP/XTP	velocity, fps:	1000		902		823
	energy, ft-lb:	200		163		135

Centerfire Handgun Ballistics

.380 AUTO TO .38 SPECIAL

CARTRIDGE BULLET	RANGE, YARDS:	0	25	50	75	100
Magtech 85 JHP + P	velocity, fps:	1082		999		936
	energy, ft-lb:	221		188		166
Magtech 95 FMC	velocity, fps:	951		861		781
	energy, ft-lb:	190		156		128
Magtech 95 JHP	velocity, fps:	951		861		781
	energy, ft-lb:	190		156		128
PMC 77 NT/FR	velocity, fps:	1200	1095	1012	932	874
	energy, ft-lb:	223				
PMC 90 FMJ	velocity, fps:	910	872	838	807	778
	energy, ft-lb:	165				
PMC 90 JHP	velocity, fps:	917	878	844	812	782
	energy, ft-lb:	168				
PMC 95 SFHP	velocity, fps:	925	884	847	813	783
	energy, ft-lb:	180				
Rem. 88 JHP	velocity, fps:	990		920		868
	energy, ft-lb:	191		165		146
Rem. 95 FNEB	velocity, fps:	955		865		785
	energy, ft-lb:	190		160		130
Rem. 95 Metal Case	velocity, fps:	955		865		785
	energy, ft-lb:	190		160		130
Rem. 102 BJHP	velocity, fps:	940		901		866
	energy, ft-lb:	200		184		170
Speer 88 JHP Blazer	velocity, fps:	950		920		870
	energy, ft-lb:	195		164		148
Speer 90 Gold Dot	velocity, fps:	990		907		842
	energy, ft-lb:	196		164		142
Speer 95 TMJ Blazer	velocity, fps:	945		865		785
	energy, ft-lb:	190		160		130
Speer 95 TMJ	velocity, fps:	950		877		817
	energy, ft-lb:	180		154		133
Win. 85 Silvertip HP	velocity, fps:	1000		921		860
	energy, ft-lb:	189		160		140
Win. 95 SXT	velocity, fps:	955		889		835
	energy, ft-lb:	192		167		147
Win. 95 FMJ	velocity, fps:	955		865		
	energy, ft-lb:	190		160		
Win. 95 EB WinClean	velocity, fps:	955		881		
	energy, ft-lb:	192		164		

.38 SPECIAL

CARTRIDGE BULLET	RANGE, YARDS:	0	25	50	75	100
Black Hills 125 JHP +P	velocity, fps:	1050				
	energy, ft-lb:	306				
Black Hills 148 HBWC	velocity, fps:	700				
	energy, ft-lb:					
Black Hills 158 SWC	velocity, fps:	850				
	energy, ft-lb:					
Black Hills 158 CNL	velocity, fps:	800				
	energy, ft-lb:					
Federal 110 Hydra-Shok JHP	velocity, fps:	1000	970	930	910	880
	energy, ft-lb:	245	225	215	200	190
Federal 110 Hi-Shok JHP +P	velocity, fps:	1000	960	930	900	870
	energy, ft-lb:	240	225	210	195	185
Federal 125 Nyclad HP	velocity, fps:	830	780	730	690	650
	energy, ft-lb:	190	170	150	130	115
Federal 125 Hi-Shok JSP +P	velocity, fps:	950	920	900	880	860
	energy, ft-lb:	250	235	225	215	205
Federal 125 Hi-Shok JHP +P	velocity, fps:	950	920	900	880	860
	energy, ft-lb:	250	235	225	215	205
Federal 125 Nyclad HP +P	velocity, fps:	950	920	900	880	860
	energy, ft-lb:	250	235	225	215	205
Federal 129 Hydra-Shok JHP+P	velocity, fps:	950	930	910	890	870
	energy, ft-lb:	255	245	235	225	215
Federal 130 FMJ	velocity, fps:	950	920	890	870	840
	energy, ft-lb:	260	245	230	215	205

CARTRIDGE BULLET	RANGE, YARDS:	0	25	50	75	100
Federal 148 LWC Match	velocity, fps:	710	670	630	600	560
	energy, ft-lb:	165	150	130	115	105
Federal 158 LRN	velocity, fps:	760	740	720	710	690
	energy, ft-lb:	200	190	185	175	170
Federal 158 LSWC	velocity, fps:	760	740	720	710	690
	energy, ft-lb:	200	190	185	175	170
Federal 158 Nyclad RN	velocity, fps:	760	740	720	710	690
	energy, ft-lb:	200	190	185	175	170
Federal 158 SWC HP +P	velocity, fps:	890	870	860	840	820
	energy, ft-lb:	280	265	260	245	235
Federal 158 LSWC +P	velocity, fps:	890	870	860	840	820
	energy, ft-lb:	270	265	260	245	235
Federal 158 Nyclad SWC-HP+P	velocity, fps:	890	870	860	840	820
	energy, ft-lb:	270	265	260	245	235
Hornady 125 JHP/XTP	velocity, fps:	900		856		817
	energy, ft-lb:	225		203		185
Hornady 140 JHP/XTP	velocity, fps:	825		790		757
	energy, ft-lb:	212		194		178
Hornady 140 Cowboy	velocity, fps:	800		767		735
	energy, ft-lb:	199		183		168
Hornady 148 HBWC	velocity, fps:	800		697		610
	energy, ft-lb:	210		160		122
Hornady 158 JHP/XPT	velocity, fps:	800		765		731
	energy, ft-lb:	225		205		188
Lapua 123 HP Megashock	velocity, fps:	355		311*		284*
	energy, ft-lb:	504		388*		322*
Lapua 148 LWC	velocity, fps:	230		203*		181*
	energy, ft-lb:	254		199*		157*
Lapua 150 SJFN	velocity, fps:	325		301*		283*
	energy, ft-lb:	512		439*		388*
Lapua 158 FMJLF	velocity, fps:	255		243*		232*
	energy, ft-lb:	332		301*		275*
Lapua 158 LRN	velocity, fps:	255		243*		232*
	energy, ft-lb:	332		301*		275*
Magtech 125 JHP +P	velocity, fps:	1017		971		931
	energy, ft-lb:	287		262		241
Magtech 148 LWC	velocity, fps:	710		634		566
	energy, ft-lb:	166		132		105
Magtech 158 LRN	velocity, fps:	755		728		693
	energy, ft-lb:	200		183		168
Magtech 158 LFN	velocity, fps:	800		776		753
	energy, ft-lb:	225		211		199
Magtech 158 SJHP	velocity, fps:	807		779		753
	energy, ft-lb:	230		213		199
Magtech 158 LSWC	velocity, fps:	755		721		689
	energy, ft-lb:	200		182		167
Magtech 158 FMC-Flat	velocity, fps:	807		779		753
	energy, ft-lb:	230		213		199
PMC 85 Non-Toxic Frangible	velocity, fps:	1275	1181	1109	1052	1006
	energy, ft-lb:	307				
PMC 110 SFHP +P	velocity, fps:	velocity and energy figures not available				
PMC 125 SFHP +P	velocity, fps:	950	918	889	863	838
	energy, ft-lb:	251				
PMC 125 JHP +P	velocity, fps:	974	938	906	878	851
	energy, ft-lb:	266				
PMC 132 FMJ	velocity, fps:	841	820	799	780	761
	energy, ft-lb:	206				
PMC 148 LWC	velocity, fps:	728	694	662	631	602
	energy, ft-lb:	175				
PMC 158 LRN	velocity, fps:	820	801	783	765	749
	energy, ft-lb:	235				
PMC 158 JSP	velocity, fps:	835	816	797	779	762
	energy, ft-lb:	245				

BALLISTICS

CARTRIDGE BULLET	RANGE, YARDS:	0	25	50	75	100
PMC 158 LFP	velocity, fps:	800		761		725
	energy, ft-lb:	225		203		185
Rem. 101 Lead Free Frangible	velocity, fps:	950		896		850
	energy, ft-lb:	202		180		162
Rem. 110 SJHP	velocity, fps:	950		890		840
	energy, ft-lb:	220		194		172
Rem. 110 SJHP +P	velocity, fps:	995		926		871
	energy, ft-lb:	242		210		185
Rem. 125 SJHP +P	velocity, ft-lb:	945		898		858
	energy, ft-lb:	248		224		204
Rem. 125 BJHP	velocity, fps:	975		929		885
	energy, ft-lb:	264		238		218
Rem. 125 FNEB	velocity, fps:	850		822		796
	energy, ft-lb:	201		188		176
Rem. 125 FNEB +P	velocity, fps:	975		935		899
	energy, ft-lb:	264		242		224
Rem. 130 Metal Case	velocity, fps:	950		913		879
	energy, ft-lb:	261		240		223
Rem. 148 LWC Match	velocity, fps:	710		634		566
	energy, ft-lb:	166		132		105
Rem. 158 LRN	velocity, fps:	755		723		692
	energy, ft-lb:	200		183		168
Rem. 158 SWC +P	velocity, fps:	890		855		823
	energy, ft-lb:	278		257		238
Rem. 158 SWC	velocity, fps:	755		723		692
	energy, ft-lb:	200		183		168
Rem. 158 LHP +P	velocity, fps:	890		855		823
	energy, ft-lb:	278		257		238
Speer 125 JHP +P Blazer	velocity, fps:	945		898		858
	energy, ft-lb:	248		224		204
Speer 125 Gold Dot +P	velocity, fps:	945		898		858
	energy, ft-lb:	248		224		204
Speer 158 TMJ +P (and Blazer)	velocity, fps:	900		852		818
	energy, ft-lb:	278		255		235
Speer 158 LRN Blazer	velocity, fps:	755		723		692
	energy, ft-lb:	200		183		168
Speer 158 Trail Blazer LFN	velocity, fps:	800		761		725
	energy, ft-lb:	225		203		184
Speer 158 TMJ-CF +P (and Blazer)	velocity, fps:	900		852		818
	energy, ft-lb:	278		255		235
Win. 110 Silvertip HP	velocity, fps:	945		894		850
	energy, ft-lb:	218		195		176
Win. 110 Jacketed FP	velocity, fps:	975		906		849
	energy, ft-lb:	232		201		176
Win. 125 Jacketed HP	velocity, fps:	945		898		
	energy, ft-lb:	248		224		
Win. 125 Jacketed HP +P	velocity, fps:	945		898		858
	energy, ft-lb:	248		224		204
Win. 125 Jacketed FP	velocity, fps:	850		804		
	energy, ft-lb:	201		179		
Win. 125 Silvertip HP + P	velocity, fps:	945		898		858
	energy, ft-lb:	248		224		204
Win. 125 JFP WinClean	velocity, fps:	775		742		
	energy, ft-lb:	167		153		
Win. 130 FMJ	velocity, fps:	800		765		
	energy, ft-lb:	185		169		
Win. 130 SXT +P	velocity, fps:	925		887		852
	energy, ft-lb:	247		227		210
Win. 148 LWC Super Match	velocity, fps:	710		634		566
	energy, ft-lb:	166		132		105
Win. 150 Lead	velocity, fps:	845		812		
	energy, ft-lb:	238		219		
Win. 158 Lead	velocity, fps:	800		761		725
	energy, ft-lb:	225		203		185

CARTRIDGE BULLET	RANGE, YARDS:	0	25	50	75	100
Win. 158 LRN	velocity, fps:	755		723		693
	energy, ft-lb:	200		183		168
Win. 158 LSWC	velocity, fps:	755		721		689
	energy, ft-lb:	200		182		167
Win. 158 LSWC HP +P	velocity, fps:	890		855		823
	energy, ft-lb:	278		257		238

.38-40

CARTRIDGE BULLET	RANGE, YARDS:	0	25	50	75	100
Black Hills 180 FPL	velocity, fps:	800				
	energy, ft-lb:					

.38 SUPER

CARTRIDGE BULLET	RANGE, YARDS:	0	25	50	75	100
Federal 130 FMJ +P	velocity, fps:	1200	1140	1100	1050	1020
	energy, ft-lb:	415	380	350	320	300
PMC 115 JHP	velocity, fps:	1116	1052	1001	959	923
	energy, ft-lb:	318				
PMC 130 FMJ	velocity, fps:	1092	1038	994	957	924
	energy, ft-lb:	348				
Rem. 130 Metal Case	velocity, fps:	1215		1099		1017
	energy, ft-lb:	426		348		298
Win. 125 Silvertip HP +P	velocity, fps:	1240		1130		1050
	energy, ft-lb:	427		354		306
Win. 130 FMJ +P	velocity, fps:	1215		1099		
	energy, ft-lb:	426		348		

.357 SIG

CARTRIDGE BULLET	RANGE, YARDS:	0	25	50	75	100
Federal 125 FMJ	velocity, fps:	1350	1270	1190	1130	1080
	energy, ft-lb:	510	445	395	355	325
Federal 125 JHP	velocity, fps:	1350	1270	1190	1130	1080
	energy, ft-lb:	510	445	395	355	325
Federal 150 JHP	velocity, fps:	1130	1080	1030	1000	970
	energy, ft-lb:	420	385	355	330	310
Hornady 124 JHP/XTP	velocity, fps:	1350		1208		1108
	energy, ft-lb:	502		405		338
Hornady 147 JHP/XTP	velocity, fps:	1225		1138		1072
	energy, ft-lb:	490		422		375
PMC 85 Non-Toxic Frangible	velocity, fps:	1480	1356	1245	1158	1092
	energy, ft-lb:	413				
PMC 124 SFHP	velocity, fps:	1350	1263	1190	1132	1083
	energy, ft-lb:	502				
PMC 124 FMJ/FP	velocity, fps:	1350	1242	1158	1093	1040
	energy, ft-lb:	512				
Rem. 104 Lead Free Frangible	velocity, fps:	1400		1223		1094
	energy, ft-lb:	453		345		276
Rem. 125 Metal Case	velocity, fps:	1350		1146		1018
	energy, ft-lb:	506		422		359
Rem. 125 JHP	velocity, fps:	1350		1157		1032
	energy, ft-lb:	506		372		296
Speer 125 TMJ (and Blazer)	velocity, fps:	1350		1177		1057
	energy, ft-lb:	502		381		307
Speer 125 TMJ-CF	velocity, fps:	1350		1177		1057
	energy, ft-lb:	502		381		307
Speer 125 Gold Dot	velocity, fps:	1375		1203		1079
	energy, ft-lb:	525		402		323
Win. 105 JFP	velocity, fps:	1370		1179		1050
	energy, ft-lb	438		324		257
Win. 125 FMJ FN	velocity, fps:	1350		1185		
	energy, ft-lb	506		390		

.357 MAGNUM

CARTRIDGE BULLET	RANGE, YARDS:	0	25	50	75	100
Black Hills 125 JHP	velocity, fps:	1500				
	energy, ft-lb:	625				
Black Hills 158 CNL	velocity, fps:	800				
	energy, ft-lb:					
Black Hills 158 SWC	velocity, fps:	1050				
	energy, ft-lb:					

BALLISTICS

Centerfire Handgun Ballistics

.357 MAGNUM TO .40 S&W

CARTRIDGE BULLET	RANGE, YARDS:	0	25	50	75	100
Black Hills 158 JHP	velocity, fps:	1250				
	energy, ft-lb:					
Federal 110 Hi-Shok JHP	velocity, fps:	1300	1180	1090	1040	990
	energy, ft-lb:	410	340	290	260	235
Federal 125 Hi-Shok JHP	velocity, fps:	1450	1350	1240	1160	1100
	energy, ft-lb:	580	495	430	370	335
Federal 130 Hydra-Shok JHP	velocity, fps:	1300	1210	1130	1070	1020
	energy, ft-lb:	490	420	370	330	300
Federal 158 Hi-Shok JSP	velocity, fps:	1240	1160	1100	1060	1020
	energy, ft-lb:	535	475	430	395	365
Federal 158 JSP	velocity, fps:	1240	1160	1100	1060	1020
	energy, ft-lb:	535	475	430	395	365
Federal 158 LSWC	velocity, fps:	1240	1160	1100	1060	1020
	energy, ft-lb:	535	475	430	395	365
Federal 158 Hi-Shok JHP	velocity, fps:	1240	1160	1100	1060	1020
	energy, ft-lb:	535	475	430	395	365
Federal 158 Hydra-Shok JHP	velocity, fps:	1240	1160	1100	1060	1020
	energy, ft-lb:	535	475	430	395	365
Federal 180 Hi-Shok JHP	velocity, fps:	1090	1030	980	930	890
	energy, ft-lb:	475	425	385	350	320
Federal 180 Castcore	velocity, fps:	1250	1200	1160	1120	1080
	energy, ft-lb:	625	575	535	495	465
Hornady 125 JHP/XTP	velocity, fps:	1500		1314		1166
	energy, ft-lb:	624		479		377
Hornady 125 JFP/XTP	velocity, fps:	1500		1311		1161
	energy, ft-lb:	624		477		374
Hornady 140 Cowboy	velocity, fps:	800		767		735
	energy, ft-lb:	199		183		168
Hornady 140 JHP/XTP	velocity, fps:	1400		1249		1130
	energy, ft-lb:	609		485		397
Hornady 158 JHP/XTP	velocity, fps:	1250		1150		1073
	energy, ft-lb:	548		464		404
Hornady 158 JFP/XTP	velocity, fps:	1250		1147		1068
	energy, ft-lb:	548		461		400
Lapua 150 FMJ CEPP Super	velocity, fps:	370		527*		303*
	energy, ft-lb:	664		527*		445*
Lapua 150 SJFN	velocity, fps:	385		342*		313*
	energy, ft-lb:	719		569*		476*
Lapua 158 SJHP	velocity, fps:	470		408*		359*
	energy, ft-lb:	1127		850*		657*
Magtech 158 SJSP	velocity, fps:	1235		1104		1015
	energy, ft-lb:	535		428		361
Magtech 158 SJHP	velocity, fps:	1235		1104		1015
	energy, ft-lb:	535		428		361
PMC 85 Non-Toxic Frangible	velocity, fps:	1325	1219	1139	1076	1025
	energy, ft-lb:	331				
PMC 125 JHP	velocity, fps:	1194	1117	1057	1008	967
	energy, ft-lb:	399				
PMC 150 JHP	velocity, fps:	1234	1156	1093	1042	1000
	energy, ft-lb:	512				
PMC 150 SFHP	velocity, fps:	1205	1129	1069	1020	980
	energy, ft-lb:	484				
PMC 158 JSP	velocity, fps:	1194	1122	1063	1016	977
	energy, ft-lb:	504				
PMC 158 LFP	velocity, fps:	800		761		725
	energy, ft-lb:	225		203		185
Rem. 110 SJHP	velocity, fps:	1295		1094		975
	energy, ft-lb:	410		292		232
Rem. 125 SJHP	velocity, fps:	1450		1240		1090
	energy, ft-lb:	583		427		330
Rem. 125 BJHP	velocity, fps:	1220		1095		1009
	energy, ft-lb:	413		333		283
Rem. 125 FNEB	velocity, fps:	1450		1240		1090
	energy, ft-lb:	583		427		330

CARTRIDGE BULLET	RANGE, YARDS:	0	25	50	75	100
Rem. 158 SJHP	velocity, fps:	1235		1104		1015
	energy, ft-lb:	535		428		361
Rem. 158 SP	velocity, fps:	1235		1104		1015
	energy, ft-lb:	535		428		361
Rem. 158 SWC	velocity, fps:	1235		1104		1015
	energy, ft-lb:	535		428		361
Rem. 165 JHP Core-Lokt	velocity, fps:	1290		1189		1108
	energy, ft-lb:	610		518		450
Rem. 180 SJHP	velocity, fps:	1145		1053		985
	energy, ft-lb:	542		443		388
Speer 125 Gold Dot	velocity, fps:	1450		1240		1090
	energy, ft-lb:	583		427		330
Speer 158 JHP Blazer	velocity, fps:	1150		1104		1015
	energy, ft-lb:	535		428		361
Speer 158 Gold Dot	velocity, fps:	1235		1104		1015
	energy, ft-lb:	535		428		361
Speer 170 Gold Dot SP	velocity, fps:	1180		1089		1019
	energy, ft-lb:	525		447		392
Win. 110 JFP	velocity, fps:	1275		1105		998
	energy, ft-lb:	397		298		243
Win. 110 JHP	velocity, fps:	1295		1095		
	energy, ft-lb:	410		292		
Win. 125 JFP WinClean	velocity, fps:	1370		1183		
	energy, ft-lb:	521		389		
Win. 145 Silvertip HP	velocity, fps:	1290		1155		1060
	energy, ft-lb:	535		428		361
Win. 158 JHP	velocity, fps:	1235		1104		1015
	energy, ft-lb:	535		428		361
Win. 158 JSP	velocity, fps:	1235		1104		1015
	energy, ft-lb:	535		428		361
Win. 180 Partition Gold	velocity, fps:	1180		1088		1020
	energy, ft-lb:	557		473		416

.40 S&W

CARTRIDGE BULLET	RANGE, YARDS:	0	25	50	75	100
Black Hills 155 JHP	velocity, fps:	1150				
	energy, ft-lb:	450				
Black Hills 165 EXP JHP	velocity, fps:	1150 (2005: 1100)				
	energy, ft-lb:	483				
Black Hills 180 JHP	velocity, fps:	1000				
	energy, ft-lb:	400				
Black Hills 180 JHP	velocity, fps:	1000				
	energy, ft-lb:	400				
Federal 135 Hydra-Shok JHP	velocity, fps:	1190	1050	970	900	850
	energy, ft-lb:	420	330	280	245	215
Federal 155 FMJ Ball	velocity, fps:	1140	1080	1030	990	960
	energy, ft-lb:	445	400	365	335	315
Federal 155 Hi-Shok JHP	velocity, fps:	1140	1080	1030	990	950
	energy, ft-lb:	445	400	365	335	315
Federal 155 Hydra-Shok JHP	velocity, fps:	1140	1080	1030	990	950
	energy, ft-lb:	445	400	365	335	315
Federal 165 EFMJ	velocity, fps:	1190	1060	970	905	850
	energy, ft-lb:	520	410	345	300	265
Federal 165 FMJ	velocity, fps:	1050	1020	990	960	935
	energy, ft-lb:	405	380	355	335	320
Federal 165 FMJ Ball	velocity, fps:	980	950	920	900	880
	energy, ft-lb:	350	330	310	295	280
Federal 165 Hydra-Shok JHP	velocity, fps:	980	950	930	910	890
	energy, ft-lb:	350	330	315	300	290
Federal 180 High Antim. Lead	velocity, fps:	990	960	930	910	890
	energy, ft-lb:	390	365	345	330	315
Federal 180 TMJ TMF Primer	velocity, fps:	990	960	940	910	890
	energy, ft-lb:	390	370	350	330	315
Federal 180 FMJ Ball	velocity, fps:	990	960	940	910	890
	energy, ft-lb:	390	370	350	330	315

CARTRIDGE BULLET	RANGE, YARDS:	0	25	50	75	100
Federal 180 Hi-Shok JHP	velocity, fps:	990	960	930	910	890
	energy, ft-lb:	390	365	345	330	315
Federal 180 Hydra-Shok JHP	velocity, fps:	990	960	930	910	890
	energy, ft-lb:	390	365	345	330	315
Hornady 155 JHP/XTP	velocity, fps:	1180		1061		980
	energy, ft-lb:	479		387		331
Hornady 155 TAP-FPD	velocity, fps:	1180		1061		980
	energy, ft-lb:	470		387		331
Hornady 180 JHP/XTP	velocity, fps:	950		903		862
	energy, ft-lb:	361		326		297
Hornady 180 TAP-FPD	velocity, fps:	950		903		862
	energy, ft-lb:	361		326		297
Magtech 155 JHP	velocity, fps:	1025		1118		1052
	energy, ft-lb:	500		430		381
Magtech 180 JHP	velocity, fps:	990		933		886
	energy, ft-lb:	390		348		314
Magtech 180 FMC	velocity, fps:	990		933		886
	energy, ft-lb:	390		348		314
PMC 115 Non-Toxic Frangible	velocity, fps:	1350	1240	1154	1088	1035
	energy, ft-lb:	465				
PMC 155 SFHP	velocity, fps:	1160	1092	1039	994	957
	energy, ft-lb:	463				
PMC 165 JHP	velocity, fps:	1040	1002	970	941	915
	energy, ft-lb:	396				
PMC 165 FMJ	velocity, fps:	1010	977	948	922	899
	energy, ft-lb:	374				
PMC 180 FMJ/FP	velocity, fps:	985	957	931	908	885
	energy, ft-lb:	388				
PMC 180 SFHP	velocity, fps:	985	958	933	910	889
	energy, ft-lb:	388				
Rem. 141 Lead Free Frangible	velocity, fps:	1135		1056		996
	energy, ft-lb:	403		349		311
Rem. 155 JHP	velocity, fps:	1205		1095		1017
	energy, ft-lb:	499		413		356
Rem. 165 BJHP	velocity, fps:	1150		1040		964
	energy, ft-lb:	485		396		340
Rem. 180 JHP	velocity, fps:	1015		960		914
	energy, ft-lb:	412		368		334
Rem. 180 FN Enclosed Base	velocity, fps:	985		936		893
	energy, ft-lb:	388		350		319
Rem. 180 Metal Case	velocity, fps:	985		936		893
	energy, ft-lb:	388		350		319
Rem. 180 BJHP	velocity, fps:	1015		960		914
	energy, ft-lb:	412		368		334
Speer 105 Frangible	velocity, fps:	1380		1128		985
	energy, ft-lb:	444		297		226
Speer 155 TMJ Blazer	velocity, fps:	1175		1047		963
	energy, ft-lb:	475		377		319
Speer 155 TMJ	velocity, fps:	1200		1065		976
	energy, ft-lb:	496		390		328
Speer 155 Gold Dot	velocity, fps:	1200		1063		974
	energy, ft-lb:	496		389		326
Speer 165 TMJ Blazer	velocity, fps:	1100		1006		938
	energy, ft-lb:	443		371		321
Speer 165 TMJ	velocity, fps:	1150		1040		964
	energy, ft-lb:	484		396		340
Speer 165 Gold Dot	velocity, fps:	1150		1043		966
	energy, ft-lb:	485		399		342
Speer 180 HP Blazer	velocity, fps:	985		951		909
	energy, ft-lb:	400		361		330
Speer 180 FMJ Blazer	velocity, fps:	1000		937		886
	energy, ft-lb:	400		351		313
Speer 180 FMJ	velocity, fps:	1000		951		909
	energy, ft-lb:	400		361		330

CARTRIDGE BULLET	RANGE, YARDS:	0	25	50	75	100
Speer 180 TMJ-CF (and Blazer)	velocity, fps:	1000		951		909
	energy, ft-lb:	400		361		330
Speer 180 Gold Dot	velocity, fps:	1025		957		902
	energy, ft-lb:	420		366		325
Win. 140 JFP	velocity, fps:	1155		1039		960
	energy, ft-lb:	415		336		286
Win. 155 Silvertip HP	velocity, fps:	1205		1096		1018
	energy, ft-lb	500		414		357
Win. 165 SXT	velocity, fps:	1130		1041		977
	energy, ft-lb:	468		397		349
Win. 165 FMJ FN	velocity, fps:	1060		1001		
	energy, ft-lb:	412		367		
Win. 165 EB WinClean	velocity, fps:	1130		1054		
	energy, ft-lb:	468		407		
Win. 180 JHP	velocity, fps:	1010		954		
	energy, ft-lb:	408		364		
Win. 180 FMJ	velocity, fps:	990		936		
	energy, ft-lb:	390		350		
Win. 180 SXT	velocity, fps:	1010		954		909
	energy, ft-lb:	408		364		330
Win. 180 EB WinClean	velocity, fps:	990		943		
	energy, ft-lb:	392		356		

10 MM AUTO

CARTRIDGE BULLET	RANGE, YARDS:	0	25	50	75	100
Federal 155 Hi-Shok JHP	velocity, fps:	1330	1230	1140	1080	1030
	energy, ft-lb:	605	515	450	400	360
Federal 180 Hi-Shok JHP	velocity, fps:	1030	1000	970	950	920
	energy, ft-lb:	425	400	375	355	340
Federal 180 Hydra-Shok JHP	velocity, fps:	1030	1000	970	950	920
	energy, ft-lb:	425	400	375	355	340
Federal 180 High Antim. Lead	velocity, fps:	1030	1000	970	950	920
	energy, ft-lb:	425	400	375	355	340
Federal 180 FMJ	velocity, fps:	1060	1025	990	965	940
	energy, ft-lb:	400	370	350	330	310
Hornady 155 JHP/XTP	velocity, fps:	1265		1119		1020
	energy, ft-lb:	551		431		358
Hornady 180 JHP/XTP	velocity, fps:	1180		1077		1004
	energy, ft-lb:	556		464		403
Hornady 200 JHP/XTP	velocity, fps:	1050		994		948
	energy, ft-lb:	490		439		399
PMC 115 Non-Toxic Frangible	velocity, fps:	1350	1240	1154	1088	1035
	energy, ft-lb:	465				
PMC 170 JHP	velocity, fps:	1200	1117	1052	1000	958
	energy, ft-lb:	543				
PMC 180 SFHP	velocity, fps:	950	926	903	882	862
	energy, ft-lb:	361				
PMC 200 TC-FMJ	velocity, fps:	1050	1008	972	941	912
	energy, ft-lb:	490				
Rem. 180 Metal Case	velocity, fps:	1150		1063		998
	energy, ft-lb:	529		452		398
Speer 200 TMJ Blazer	velocity, fps:	1050		966		952
	energy, ft-lb:	490		440		402
Win. 175 Silvertip HP	velocity, fps:	1290		1141		1037
	energy, ft-lb:	649		506		418

.41 REMINGTON MAGNUM

CARTRIDGE BULLET	RANGE, YARDS:	0	25	50	75	100
Federal 210 Hi-Shok JHP	velocity, fps:	1300	1210	1130	1070	1030
	energy, ft-lb:	790	680	595	540	495
PMC 210 TCSP	velocity, fps:	1290	1201	1128	1069	1021
	energy, ft-lb:	774				
PMC 210 JHP	velocity, fps:	1289	1200	1127	1068	1020
	energy, ft-lb:	774				
Rem. 210 SP	velocity, fps:	1300		1162		1062
	energy, ft-lb:	788		630		526

Centerfire Handgun Ballistics

.41 REMINGTON MAGNUM TO .45 AUTOMATIC (ACP)

CARTRIDGE BULLET	RANGE, YARDS:	0	25	50	75	100
Win. 175 Silvertip HP	velocity, fps:	1250		1120		1029
	energy, ft-lb:	607		488		412
Win. 240 Platinum Tip	velocity, ft-lb:	1250		1151		1075
	energy, ft-lb:	833		706		616

.44 COLT

CARTRIDGE BULLET	RANGE, YARDS:	0	25	50	75	100
Black Hills 230 FPL	velocity, fps:	730				
	energy, ft-lb:					

.44 RUSSIAN

CARTRIDGE BULLET	RANGE, YARDS:	0	25	50	75	100
Black Hills 210 FPL	velocity, fps:	650				
	energy, ft-lb:					

.44 SPECIAL

CARTRIDGE BULLET	RANGE, YARDS:	0	25	50	75	100
Black Hills 210 FPL	velocity, fps:	700				
	energy, ft-lb:					
Federal 200 SWC HP	velocity, fps:	900	860	830	800	770
	energy, ft-lb:	360	330	305	285	260
Federal 250 CastCore	velocity, fps:	1250	1200	1150	1110	1080
	energy, ft-lb:	865	795	735	685	645
Hornady 180 JHP/XTP	velocity, fps:	1000		935		882
	energy, ft-lb:	400		350		311
Magtech 240 LFN	velocity, fps:	750		722		696
	energy, ft-lb:	300		278		258
PMC 180 JHP	velocity, fps:	980	938	902	869	839
	energy, ft-lb:	383				
PMC 240 SWC-CP	velocity, fps:	764	744	724	706	687
	energy, ft-lb:	311				
PMC 240 LFP	velocity, fps:	750		719		690
	energy, ft-lb:	300		275		253
Rem. 246 LRN	velocity, fps:	755		725		695
	energy, ft-lb:	310		285		265
Speer 200 HP Blazer	velocity, fps:	875		825		780
	energy, ft-lb:	340		302		270
Speer 200 Trail Blazer LFN	velocity, fps:	750		714		680
	energy, ft-lb:	250		226		205
Speer 200 Gold Dot	velocity, fps:	875		825		780
	energy, ft-lb:	340		302		270
Win. 200 Silvertip HP	velocity, fps:	900		860		822
	energy, ft-lb:	360		328		300
Win. 240 Lead	velocity, fps:	750		719		690
	energy, ft-lb	300		275		253
Win. 246 LRN	velocity, fps:	755		725		695
	energy, ft-lb:	310		285		265

.44 REMINGTON MAGNUM

CARTRIDGE BULLET	RANGE, YARDS:	0	25	50	75	100
Black Hills 240 JHP	velocity, fps:	1260				
	energy, ft-lb:	848				
Black Hills 300 JHP	velocity, fps:	1150				
	energy, ft-lb:	879				
Federal 180 Hi-Shok JHP	velocity, fps:	1610	1480	1370	1270	1180
	energy, ft-lb:	1035	875	750	640	555
Federal 240 Hi-Shok JHP	velocity, fps:	1180	1130	1080	1050	1010
	energy, ft-lb:	740	675	625	580	550
Federal 240 Hydra-Shok JHP	velocity, fps:	1180	1130	1080	1050	1010
	energy, ft-lb:	740	675	625	580	550
Federal 240 JHP	velocity, fps:	1180	1130	1080	1050	1010
	energy, ft-lb:	740	675	625	580	550
Federal 300 CastCore	velocity, fps:	1250	1200	1160	1120	1080
	energy, ft-lb:	1040	960	885	825	775
Hornady 180 JHP/XTP	velocity, fps:	1550		1340		1173
	energy, ft-lb:	960		717		550
Hornady 200 JHP/XTP	velocity, fps:	1500		1284		1128
	energy, ft-lb:	999		732		565
Hornady 240 JHP/XTP	velocity, fps:	1350		1188		1078
	energy, ft-lb:	971		753		619
Hornady 300 JHP/XTP	velocity, fps:	1150		1084		1031
	energy, ft-lb:	881		782		708
Magtech 240 SJSP	velocity, fps:	1180		1081		1010
	energy, ft-lb:	741		632		623
PMC 180 JHP	velocity, fps:	1392	1263	1157	1076	1015
	energy, ft-lb:	772				
PMC 240 JHP	velocity, fps:	1301	1218	1147	1088	1041
	energy, ft-lb:	900				
PMC 240 TC-SP	velocity, fps:	1300	1216	1144	1086	1038
	energy, ft-lb:	900				
PMC 240 SFHP	velocity, fps:	1300	1212	1138	1079	1030
	energy, ft-lb:	900				
PMC 240 LSWC-GCK	velocity, fps:	1225	1143	1077	1025	982
	energy, ft-lb:	806				
Rem. 180 JSP	velocity, fps:	1610		1365		1175
	energy, ft-lb:	1036		745		551
Rem. 210 Gold Dot HP	velocity, fps:	1450		1276		1140
	energy, ft-lb:	980		759		606
Rem. 240 SP	velocity, fps:	1180		1081		1010
	energy, ft-lb:	721		623		543
Rem. 240 SJHP	velocity, fps:	1180		1081		1010
	energy, ft-lb:	721		623		543
Rem. 275 JHP Core-Lokt	velocity, fps:	1235		1142		1070
	energy, ft-lb:	931		797		699
Speer 240 JHP Blazer	velocity, fps:	1200		1092		1015
	energy, ft-lb:	767		636		549
Speer 240 Gold Dot HP	velocity, fps:	1400		1255		1139
	energy, ft-lb:	1044		839		691
Speer 270 Gold Dot SP	velocity, fps:	1250		1142		1060
	energy, ft-lb:	937		781		674
Win. 210 Silvertip HP	velocity, fps:	1250		1106		1010
	energy, ft-lb:	729		570		475
Win. 240 Hollow SP	velocity, fps:	1180		1081		1010
	energy, ft-lb:	741		623		543
Win. 240 JSP	velocity, fps:	1180		1081		
	energy, ft-lb:	741		623		
Win. 250 Partition Gold	velocity, fps:	1230		1132		1057
	energy, ft-lb:	840		711		620
Win. 250 Platinum Tip	velocity, fps:	1250		1148		1070
	energy, ft-lb:	867		732		635

.44-40

CARTRIDGE BULLET	RANGE, YARDS:	0	25	50	75	100
Black Hills 200 RNFP	velocity, fps:	800				
	energy, ft-lb:					
Hornady 205 Cowboy	velocity, fps:	725		697		670
	energy, ft-lb:	239		221		204
Magtech 225 LFN	velocity, fps:	725		703		681
	energy, ft-lb:	281		247		232
PMC 225 LFP	velocity, fps:	725		723		695
	energy, ft-lb:	281		261		242
Win. 225 Lead	velocity, fps:	750		723		695
	energy, ft-lb:	281		261		242

.45 AUTOMATIC (ACP)

CARTRIDGE BULLET	RANGE, YARDS:	0	25	50	75	100
Black Hills 185 JHP	velocity, fps:	1000				
	energy, ft-lb:	411				
Black Hills 200 Match SWC	velocity, fps:	875				
	energy, ft-lb:	340				
Black Hills 230 FMJ	velocity, fps:	850				
	energy, ft-lb:	368				

BALLISTICS

.45 AUTOMATIC (ACP) TO .45 GAP

CARTRIDGE BULLET	RANGE, YARDS:	0	25	50	75	100
Black Hills 230 JHP	velocity, fps:	850				
	energy, ft-lb:	368				
Black Hills 230 JHP +P	velocity, fps:	950				
	energy, ft-lb:	460				
Federal 165 Hydra-Shok JHP	velocity, fps:	1060	1020	980	950	920
	energy, ft-lb:	410	375	350	330	310
Federal 165 EFMJ	velocity, fps:	1090	1045	1005	975	942
	energy, ft-lb:	435	400	370	345	325
Federal 185 Hi-Shok JHP	velocity, fps:	950	920	900	880	860
	energy, ft-lb:	370	350	335	315	300
Federal 185 FMJ-SWC Match	velocity, fps:	780	730	700	660	620
	energy, ft-lb:	245	220	200	175	160
Federal 200 Exp. FMJ	velocity, fps:	1030	1000	970	940	920
	energy, ft-lb:	470	440	415	395	375
Federal 230 FMJ	velocity, fps:	850	830	810	790	770
	energy, ft-lb:	370	350	335	320	305
Federal 230 FMJ Match	velocity, fps:	855	835	815	795	775
	energy, ft-lb:	375	355	340	325	305
Federal 230 Hi-Shok JHP	velocity, fps:	850	830	810	790	770
	energy, ft-lb:	370	350	335	320	300
Federal 230 Hydra-Shok JHP	velocity, fps:	850	830	810	790	770
	energy, ft-lb:	370	350	335	320	305
Federal 230 FMJ	velocity, fps:	850	830	810	790	770
	energy, ft-lb:	370	350	335	320	305
Federal 230 TMJ TMF Primer	velocity, fps:	850	830	810	790	770
	energy, ft-lb:	370	350	335	315	305
Hornady 185 JHP/XTP	velocity, fps:	950		880		819
	energy, ft-lb:	371		318		276
Hornady 200 JHP/XTP	velocity, fps:	900		855		815
	energy, ft-lb:	358		325		295
Hornady 200 HP/XTP +P	velocity, fps:	1055		982		925
	energy, ft-lb:	494		428		380
Hornady 200 TAP-FPD	velocity, fps:	1055		982		926
	energy, ft-lbs:	494		428		380
Hornady 230 FMJ/RN	velocity, fps:	850		809		771
	energy, ft-lb:	369		334		304
Hornady 230 FMJ/FP	velocity, fps:	850		809		771
	energy, ft-lb:	369		334		304
Hornady 230 HP/XTP +P	velocity, fps:	950		904		865
	energy, ft-lb:	462		418		382
Hornady 230 TAP-FPD	velocity, fps:	950		908		872
	energy, ft-lb:	461		421		388
Magtech 185 JHP +P	velocity, fps:	1148		1066		1055
	energy, ft-lb:	540		467		415
Magtech 200 LSWC	velocity, fps:	950		910		874
	energy, ft-lb:	401		368		339
Magtech 230 FMC	veloctiy, fps:	837		800		767
	energy, ft-lb:	356		326		300
Magtech 230 FMC-SWC	velocity, fps:	780		720		660
	energy, ft-lb:	310		265		222
PMC 145 Non-Toxic Frangible	velocity, fps:	1100	1045	999	961	928
	energy, ft-lb:	390				
PMC 185 JHP	velocity, fps:	903	870	839	811	785
	energy, ft-lb:	339				
PMC 200 FMJ-SWC	velocity, fps:	850	818	788	761	734
	energy, ft-lb:	321				
PMC 230 SFHP	velocity, fps:	850	830	811	792	775
	energy, ft-lb:	369				
PMC 230 FMJ	velocity, fps:	830	809	789	769	749
	energy, ft-lb:	352				
Rem. 175 Lead Free Frangible	velocity, fps:	1020		923		851
	energy, ft-lb:	404		331		281

CARTRIDGE BULLET	RANGE, YARDS:	0	25	50	75	100
Rem. 185 JHP	velocity, fps:	1000		939		889
	energy, ft-lb:	411		362		324
Rem. 185 BJHP	velocity, fps:	1015		951		899
	energy, ft-lb:	423		372		332
Rem. 185 BJHP +P	velocity, fps:	1140		1042		971
	energy, ft-lb:	534		446		388
Rem. 185 MC	velocity, fps:	1015		955		907
	energy, ft-lb:	423		375		338
Rem. 230 FN Enclosed Base	velocity, fps:	835		800		767
	energy, ft-lb:	356		326		300
Rem. 230 Metal Case	velocity, fps:	835		800		767
	energy, ft-lb:	356		326		300
Rem. 230 JHP	velocity, fps:	835		800		767
	energy, ft-lb:	356		326		300
Rem. 230 BJHP	velocity, fps:	875		833		795
	energy, ft-lb:	391		355		323
Speer 140 Frangible	velocity, fps:	1200		1029		928
	energy, ft-lb:	448		329		268
Speer 185 Gold Dot	velocity, fps:	1050		956		886
	energy, ft-lb:	453		375		322
Speer 185 TMJ/FN	velocity, fps:	1000		909		839
	energy, ft-lb:	411		339		289
Speer 200 JHP Blazer	velocity, fps:	975		917		860
	energy, ft-lb:	421		372		328
Speer 200 Gold Dot +P	velocity, fps:	1080		994		930
	energy, ft-lb:	518		439		384
Speer 200 TMJ/FN	velocity, fps:	975		897		834
	energy, ft-lb:	422		357		309
Speer 230 FMJ (and Blazer)	velocity, fps:	845		804		775
	energy, ft-lb:	363		329		304
Speer 230 TMJ-CF (and Blazer)	velocity, fps:	845		804		775
	energy, ft-lb:	363		329		304
Speer 230 Gold Dot	velocity, fps:	890		845		805
	energy, ft-lb:	405		365		331
Win. 170 JFP	velocity, fps:	1050		982		928
	energy, ft-lb:	416		364		325
Win. 185 Silvertip HP	velocity, fps:	1000		938		888
	energy, ft-lb:	411		362		324
Win. 185 FMJ FN	velocity, fps:	910		861		
	energy, ft-lb:	340		304		
Win. 185 EB WinClean	velocity, fps:	910		835		
	energy, ft-lb:	340		286		
Win. 230 JHP	velocity, fps:	880		842		
	energy, ft-lb:	396		363		
Win. 230 FMJ	velocity, fps:	835		800		
	energy, ft-lb:	356		326		
Win. 230 SXT	velocity, fps:	880		846		816
	energy, ft-lb:	396		366		340
Win. 230 JHP subsonic	velocity, fps:	880		842		808
	energy, ft-lb:	396		363		334
Win. 230 EB WinClean	velocity, fps:	835		802		
	energy, ft-lb:	356		329		

.45 GAP

CARTRIDGE BULLET	RANGE, YARDS:	0	25	50	75	100
Federal 185 Hydra-Shok JHP And Federal TMJ	velocity, fps:	1090	1020	970	920	890
	energy, ft-lb:	490	430	385	350	320
Federal 230 Hydra-Shok And Federal FMJ	velocity, fps:	880	870	850	840	820
	energy, ft-lb:	395	380	3760	355	345
Win. 185 STHP	velocity, fps:	1000		938		887
	energy, ft-lb:	411		361		323
Win. 230 JHP	velocity, fps:	880		842		
	energy, ft-lb:	396		363		

BALLISTICS

Centerfire Handgun Ballistics

.45 GAP TO .500 SMITH & WESSON

CARTRIDGE BULLET	RANGE, YARDS:	0	25	50	75	100
Win. 230 EB WinClean	velocity, fps:	875		840		
	energy, ft-lb:	391		360		
Win. 230 FMJ	velocity, fps:	850		814		
	energy, ft-lb:	369		338		

.45 WINCHESTER MAGNUM

CARTRIDGE BULLET	RANGE, YARDS:	0	25	50	75	100
Win. 260 Partition Gold	velocity, fps:	1200		1105		1033
	energy, ft-lb:	832		705		616
Win. 260 JHP	velocity, fps:	1200		1099		1026
	energy, ft-lb:	831		698		607

.45 SCHOFIELD

CARTRIDGE BULLET	RANGE, YARDS:	0	25	50	75	100
Black Hills 180 FNL	velocity, fps:	730				
	energy, ft-lb:					
Black Hills 230 RNFP	velocity, fps:	730				
	energy, ft-lb:					

.45 COLT

CARTRIDGE BULLET	RANGE, YARDS:	0	25	50	75	100
Black Hills 250 RNFP	velocity, fps:	725				
	energy, ft-lb:					
Federal 225 SWC HP	velocity, fps:	900	880	860	840	820
	energy, ft-lb:	405	385	370	355	340
Hornady 255 Cowboy	velocity, fps:	725		692		660
	energy, ft-lb:	298		271		247
Magtech 250 LFN	velocity, fps:	750		726		702
	energy, ft-lb:	312		293		274
PMC 250 LFP	velocity, fps:	800		767		736
	energy, ft-lb:	355		331		309
PMC 300 +P+	velocity, fps:	1250	1192	1144	1102	1066
	energy, ft-lb:	1041				
Rem. 225 SWC	velocity, fps:	960		890		832
	energy, ft-lb:	460		395		346
Rem. 250 RLN	velocity, fps:	860		820		780
	energy, ft-lb:	410		375		340
Speer 200 FMJ Blazer	velocity, fps:	1000		938		889
	energy, ft-lb:	444		391		351
Speer 230 Trail Blazer LFN	velocity, fps:	750		716		684
	energy, ft-lb:	287		262		239
Speer 250 Gold Dot	velocity, fps:	900		860		823
	energy, ft-lb:	450		410		376
Win. 225 Silvertip HP	velocity, fps:	920		877		839
	energy, ft-lb:	423		384		352
Win. 255 LRN	velocity, fps:	860		820		780
	energy, ft-lb:	420		380		345
Win. 250 Lead	velocity, fps:	750		720		692
	energy, ft-lb:	312		288		266

.454 CASULL

CARTRIDGE BULLET	RANGE, YARDS:	0	25	50	75	100
Federal 300 Trophy Bonded	velocity, fps:	1630	1540	1450	1380	1300
	energy, ft-lb:	1760	1570	1405	1260	1130
Federal 360 CastCore	velocity, fps:	1500	1435	1370	1310	1255
	energy, ft-lb:	1800	1640	1500	1310	1260
Hornady 240 XTP-MAG	velocity, fps:	1900		1679		1483
	energy, ft-lb:	1923		1502		1172
Hornady 300 XTP-MAG	velocity, fps:	1650		1478		1328
	energy, ft-lb:	1813		1455		1175
Magtech 260 SJSP	velocity, fps:	1800		1577		1383
	energy, ft-lb:	1871		1437		1104
Rem. 300 Core-Lokt Ultra	velocity, fps:	1625		1472		1335
	energy, ft-lb:	1759		1442		1187

CARTRIDGE BULLET	RANGE, YARDS:	0	25	50	75	100
Speer 300 Gold Dot HP	velocity, fps:	1625		1477		1343
	energy, ft-lb:	1758		1452		1201
Win. 250 JHP	velocity, fps:	1300		1151		1047
	energy, ft-lb:	938		735		608
Win. 260 Partition Gold	velocity, fps:	1800		1605		1427
	energy, ft-lb:	1871		1485		1176
Win. 260 Platinum Tip	velocity, fps:	1800		1596		1414
	eneryg, ft-lb:	1870		1470		1154
Win. 300 JFP	velocity, fps:	1625		1451		1308
	energy, ft-lb:	1759		1413		1141

.460 SMITH & WESSON

CARTRIDGE BULLET	RANGE, YARDS:	0	25	50	75	100
Federal 275 Expander	velocity, fps:	1800		1640		1500
	energy, ft-lb:	1980		1650		1370
Federal 300 A-Frame	velocity, fps:	1750		1510		1300
	energy, ft-lb:	2040		1510		1125
Hornady 200 SST	velocity, fps:	2250		2003		1772
	energy, ft-lb:	2248		1395		1081
Win. 260 Supreme Part. Gold	velocity, fps	2000		1788		1592
	energy, ft-lb	2309		1845		2012

.475 LINEBAUGH

CARTRIDGE BULLET	RANGE, YARDS:	0	25	50	75	100
Hornady 400 XTP-MAG	velocity, fps:	1300		1179		1093
	energy, ft-lb:	1501		1235		1060

.480 RUGER

CARTRIDGE BULLET	RANGE, YARDS:	0	25	50	75	100
Federal 275 Expander	velocity, fps:	1350		1190		1080
	energy, ft-lb:	1115		870		710
Hornady 325 XTP-MAG	velocity, fps:	1350		1191		1076
	energy, ft-lb:	1315		1023		835
Hornady 400 XTP-MAG	velocity, fps:	1100		1027		971
	energy, ft-lb:	1075		937		838
Speer 275 Gold Dot HP	velocity, fps:	1450		1284		1152
	energy, ft-lb:	1284		1007		810
Speer 325 SP	velocity, fps:	1350		1224		1124
	energy, ft-lb:	1315		1082		912

.50 ACTION EXPRESS

CARTRIDGE BULLET	RANGE, YARDS:	0	25	50	75	100
Hornady 300 XTP/HP	velocity, fps:	1475		1251		1092
	energy, ft-lb:	1449		1043		795
Speer 300 Gold Dot HP	velocity, fps:	1550		1361		1207
	energy, ft-lb:	1600		1234		970
Speer 325 UCHP	velocity, fps:	1400		1232		1106
	energy, ft-lb:	1414		1095		883

.500 SMITH & WESSON

CARTRIDGE BULLET	RANGE, YARDS:	0	25	50	75	100
Federal 275 Expander	velocity, fps:	1660		1440		1250
	energy, ft-lb:	1680		1255		950
Federal 325 A-Frame	velocity, fps:	1800		1560		1350
	energy, ft-lb:	2340		1755		1315
Hornady 350 XTP Mag	velocity, fps:	1900		1656		1439
	energy, ft-lb:	2805		2131		1610
Hornady 500 FP-XTP	velocity, fps:	1425		1281		1164
	energy, ft-lb:	2254		1823		1505
Win. 350 Super-X	velocity, fps	1400		1231		1106
	energy, ft-lb	1523		1178		951
Win. 400 Platinum Tip	velocity, fps:	1800		1647		1505
	energy, ft-lb:	2877		2409		2012

Directory of Manufacturers & Suppliers

Accu-Tek Firearms
Ontario, CA
www.accu-tekfirearms.com

Accurate Powder
Miles City, MT
www.accuratepowder.com

Advanced Armament
Lawrenceville, GA
www.advanced-armament.com

Aimpoint
Chantilly, VA
www.aimpoint.com

Airforce Airguns
Fort Worth, TX
www.airforceairguns.com

Alliant Powder
Radford, VA
www.alliantpowder.com

Alpen Optics
Rancho Cucamonga, CA
www.alpenoptics.com

American Derringer
Waco, TX
www.amderringer.com

American Tactical Imports
Rochester, NY
www.americantactical.us

ArmaLite, Inc.
Geneso, IL
www.armalite.com

Arsenal Firearms
Gardone val Trompia, Italy
www.arsenalfirearms.com

Arsenal Inc.
Las Vegas, NV
www.arsenalinc.com

Auto-Ordnance
Worcester, MA
www.auto-ordnance.com

AYA
Eibar, Spain
www.aya-fineguns.com

Barnes Bullets
Mona, UT
www.barnesbullets.com

Barrett
Murfreesboro, TN
www.barrett.net

Beeman Precision Airguns
Santa Fe Springs, CA
www.beeman.com

Benelli USA
Pocomoke, MD
www.benelliusa.com

Beretta
Brescia, Italy
www.berettausa.com

Berger Bullets
Fullerton, CA
www.bergerbullets.com

Bernardelli
Brescia, Italy
www.bernardelli.com

Bersa
Wanamassa, NJ
www.bersa.com

Black Hills
Rapid City, SD
www.black-hills.com

Blaser
San Antonio , TX
www.blaser-usa.com

Bond Arms
Granbury, TX
www.bondarms.com

Brenneke USA
Clinton, IA
www.brennekeusa.com

Browning
Morgan, UT
www.browning.com

Brunton
Riverton, WY
www.bruntonhunting.com

BSA Optics
Ft. Lauderdale, FL
www.bsaoptics.com

Burris
Greeley , CO
www.burrisoptics.com

Bushmaster
Madison, NC
www.bushmaster.com

Bushnell Outdoor Products
Overland Park, KS
www.bushnell.com

Cabela's, Inc.
Sidney, NE
www.cabelas.com

Cabot Gun Company
Cabot, PA
www.cabotgun.com

Caesar Guerini USA, Inc.
Cambridge, MD
www.gueriniusa.com

Carl Zeiss Sports Optics
North Chesterfield, VA
www.sportsoptics.zeiss.com

CCI Ammunition
Lewiston, ID
www.cci-ammunition.com

Century International Arms, Inc.
Delray Beach, FL
www.centuryarms.com

Ceska Zbrojovka Arms (CZ)
Kansas City, KS
www.cz-usa.com

Charter Arms
Shelton, CT
www.charterfirearms.com

Chiappa Firearms
Dayton, OH
www.chiappafirearms.com

Chipmunk Rifles
Milton, PA
www.chipmunkrifles.com

Cimarron Firearms Co.
Fredericksburg, TX
www.cimarron-firearms.com

Citadel by Legacy Sports
see Legacy Sports

Colt Competition Rifle
Breckenridge, TX
www.coltcompetitionrifle.com

Colt's Manufacturing Company
Hartford, CT
www.coltsmfg.com

Connecticut Shotguns Mfg. Co.
New Britain, CT
www.connecticutshotgun.com

Connecticut Valley Arms (CVA)
Duluth, GA
www.cva.com

Coonan Inc.
Blaine, MN
www.coonaninc.com

Cooper Firearms
Stevensville, MT
www.cooperfirearms.com

CorBon / Glaser
Sturgis, SD
www.corbon.com

Crosman
Bloomfield, NY
www.crosman.com

Daisy
Rogers, AR
www.daisy.com

Dakota Arms
Sturgis, SD
www.dakotaarms.com

Dan Wesson Firearms Co.
Norwich, NY
www.cz-usa.com/products/by-brand/
dan-wesson

Del-Ton, Inc.
Elizabethtown, NC
www.del-ton.com

Dillon Precision Reloaders
Scottsdale, AZ
www.dillonprecision.com

Dixie Gun Works
Union City, TN
www.dixiegunworks.com

DoubleTap Defense LLC
St. Louis, MO
www.doubletapdefense.com

DPMS Firearms
St. Cloud, MN
www.dpmsinc.com

Eagle Imports
Wanamassa, NJ
www.eagleimportsinc.com

E.R. Shaw, Inc.
Bridgeville, PA
www.ershawbarrels.com

Ed Brown Products, Inc.
Perry, MO
www.edbrown.com

EMF Company, Inc.
Santa Ana, CA
www.emf-company.com

Enterprise Arms
Irwindale, CA
www.entreprise.com

ENVIRON-Metal, Inc.
Sweet Home, OR
www.hevishot.com

EOTech
Ann Arbor, MI
www.eotech-inc.com

Escort by Legacy Sports
Reno, NV
www.legacysports.com

European American Armory
Rockledge, FL
www.eaacorp.com

Excel Arms
Ontario, CA
www.excelarms.com

Fabarm
Brescia, Italy
www.fabarm.com

Fausti USA
Fredericksburg, VA
www.faustiusa.com

Federal Premium Ammunition
Anoka, MN
www.federalpremium.com

Fiocchi
Ozark, MO
www.fiocchiusa.com

Flodman
Jarsta, Sweden
www.flodman.com

FNH USA
McLean, VA
www.fnhusa.com

Forster Products
Lanark, IL
www.forsterproducts.com

Franchi USA
Pocomoke, MD
www.franchiusa.com

Frankford Arsenal
Columbia, MO
www.frankfordarsenal.com

Freedom Arms
Freedom, WY
www.freedomarms.com

Gamo USA
Ft. Lauderdale, FL
www.gamousa.com

Glock, Inc.
Smyrna, GA
www.glock.com

Hammerli
Ulm, Germany
www.haemmerli.info

Harrington & Richardson
Madison, NC
www.hr1871.com

Harvester Muzzleloading
Henderson, KY
www.harvestermuzzleloading.com

Heckler & Koch
Columbus, GA
www.hk-usa.com

Henry Repeating Arms
Bayonne, NJ
www.henryrepeating.com

Heritage Mfg., Inc.
Miami, FL
www.heritagemfg.com

High Standard
Houston, TX
www.highstandard.com

Hi-Point
Dayton, OH
www.hi-pointfirearms.com

Hodgdon Powder Company
Shawnee Mission, KS
www.hodgdon.com

Hornady Mfg., Co.
Grand Island, NE
www.hornady.com

Howa by Legacy Sports
Reno, NV
wwww.legacysports.com

H-S Precision
Rapid City, SD
www.hsprecision.com

IMR Powder Company
Shawnee, KS
www.imrpowder.com

ISSC by Legacy Sports
Reno, NV
www.legacysports.com

Ithaca Gun Company
Upper Sandusky, OH
www.ithacagun.com

IWI US, Inc.
Harrisburg, PA
www.iwi.us

J. P. Sauer & Sohn Rifles
San Antonio, TX
www.jpsauer.us/firearms

J.G. Anschutz
Ulm, Germany
www.jga.anschuetz-sport.com

Jarrett Rifles
Jackson, SC
www.jarrettrifles.com

K-Var Corp.
Las Vegas, NV
www.k-var.com

Kahr Arms
Worcester, MA
www.kahr.com

Kel-Tec CNC Industries, Inc.
Cocoa, FL
www.keltecweapons.com

Kimber Mfg. Inc.
Elmsford, NY
www.kimberamerica.com

Knight Rifles
Athens, TN
www.knightrifles.com

Directory of Manufacturers & Suppliers

Krieghoff International, Inc.
Ottsville, PA
www.krieghoff.com

Kriss USA
Virginia Beach, VA
www.kriss-usa.com

Kruger Optical
Sisters, OR
www.krugeroptical.com

Kynoch Ammunition
Englewood, CO
www.kynochusa.com

L.A.R. Mfg., Inc (Grizzly Firearms)
West Jordan, UT
www.largrizzly.com

LWRC International, LLC
Cambridge, MD
www.lwrci.com

Lapua Bullets
Lapua, Finland
www.lapua.com

Lazzeroni Arms, Inc.
Tuscon, AZ
www.lazzeroni.com

Leatherwood/Hi-Lux Optics
Torrance, CA
www.hi-luxoptics.com
www.leatherwoodoptics.com

Legacy Sports International
Reno, NV
www.legacysports.com

Leica
Allendale, NJ
www.us.leica-camera.com/sport_optics

Les Baer Custom
LeClaire, IA
www.lesbaer.com

Leupold and Stevens
Beaverton, OR
www.leupold.com

Ljutic LLC
Yakima, Washington
www.Ljuticgun.com

LUCID
Riverton, WY
www.mylucidgear.com

Lyman Products
Middletown , CT
www.lymanproducts.com

M.O.A. Corporation
Sundance, WY
www.moaguns.com

Magnum Research
Pillager, MN
www.magnumresearch.com

Magtech Ammunition Company, Inc.
Lino Lakes, MN
www.magtechammunition.com

Marlin
Madison, NC
www.marlinfirearms.com

Marocchi Arms
Sarezzo, Italy
www.marocchiarms.com

MasterPiece Arms
Carrollton, GA
www.masterpiecearms.com

Mauser
Isny, Germany
www.mauser.com

McMillian
Phoenix, AZ
www.mcmfamily.com

MEC Reloading
Mayville, Wisconsin
www.mecreloaders.com

Merkel
Trussville, AL
www.merkel-usa.com

MG Arms
Spring, TX
www.mgarmsinc.com

Millet Sights
Overland Park, KS
www.millettsights.com

Minox
Germany
www.minox.com

Montana Rifle Company
Kalispell, MT
www.montanarifleco.com

Mossberg
North Haven, CT
www.mossberg.com

MTM Molded Products Co.
Dayton, Ohio
www.mtmcase-gard.com

New Ultra Light Arms
Granville, WV
www.newultralight.com

Nightforce Optics, Inc.
Orofino, ID
www.nightforceoptics.com

Nighthawk Custom
Berryville, AR
www.nighthawkcustom.com

Nikon Sport Optics
Melville, NY
www.nikonsportoptics.com

Norma
Amotfors, Sweden
www.norma-usa.com

North American Arms
Provo, UT
www.naaminis.com

Nosler
Bend, OR
www.nosler.com

Olympic Arms
Olympia, WA
www.olyarms.com

P.M.C. Ammunition
Conroe, TX
www.pmcammo.com

PARA USA, LLC
Pineville, NC
www.para-usa.com

Pedersoli & C.
Brescia, Italy
www.davide-pedersoli.com

Pentax Ricoh Imaging Americas Corp.
Denver, CO
www.pentaximaging.com/sports-optics

Perazzi
Azusa, CA
www.perazzi.it

Powerbelt Bullets
Nampa, ID
www.powerbeltbullets.com

Puma by Legacy Sports
Reno, NV
www.legacysports.com

Purdey
London, England
www.purdey.com

Ramshot Powders
Miles City, MT
www.ramshot.com/powders

RCBS
Oroville, CA
www.rcbs.com

Redding Reloading Equipment
Cortland, NY
www.redding-reloading.com

Redfield
Beaverton, OR
www.redfield.com

Remington Arms
Madison, NC
www.remington.com

Rifles, Inc.
Pleasanton, TX
www.riflesinc.com

Rock River Arms
Colona, IL
www.rockriverarms.com

Rossi
Miami, FL
www.rossiusa.com

Ruger
Newport, NH
www.ruger.com

RWS
Furth, Germany
www.rws-munition.de/en

Sako
Riihimaki, Finland
www.sako.fi

Savage Arms
Westfield, MA
www.Savagearms.com

Schmidt & Bender
Claremont, NH
www.schmidtundbender.de/en

Shiloh
Big Timber, MT
www.shilohrifle.com

Sierra Bullets
Sedalia, MO
www.sierrabullets.com

Sig Sauer
Exeter, NH
www.sigsauer.com

Simmons Optics
Overland Park, KS
www.simmonsoptics.com

Smith & Wesson
Springfield, MA
www.smith-wesson.com

Speer Bullets
Lewiston, ID
www.speer-bullets.com

Springfield Armory
Geneso, IL
www.springfield-armory.com

Stag Arms
New Britain, CT
www.stagarms.com

Steiner Division
Greeley, CO
www.steiner-binoculars.com

Steyr Arms
Trussville, AL
www.steyrarms.com

STI International, Inc.
Georgetown, TX
www.stiguns.com

Stoeger Industries
Pocomoke, MD
www.stoegerindustries.com

Swarovski Optik
Cranston, RI
www.swarovskioptik.com

Swift Bullets
Quinter, KS
www.swiftbullets.com

Szecsei & Fuchs
Windsor, Ontario, Canada
www.fuchs-fine-guns.com or
www.szceseidoubleboltrepeater.ca

Tactical Rifles
Zephyrhills, FL
www.tacticalrifles.net

Taurus
Miami, FL
www.taurususa.com

Taylor's & Co.
Winchester , VA
www.taylorsfirearms.com

Thompson/Center
Springfield, MA
www.tcarms.com

Traditions Firearms
Old Saybrook, CT
www.traditionsfirearms.com

Tikka T3
Riihimaki, Finland
www.tikka.fi

Trijicon
Wixom, Michigan
www.trijicon.com

Tristar Sporting Arms
North Kansas City, MO
www.tristarsportingarms.com

Turnbull Mfg. Co.
Bloomfield, NY
www.turnbullmfg.com

Uberti
Pocomoke, MD
www.uberti.com

U.S. Firearms
Hartford, CT
www.usfirearms.com

UTAS USA
Des Plaines, IL
www.utas-usa.com

VihtaVuori
Bensenville, IL
www.vihtavuori-lapua.com

Volquartsen Custom
Carroll, IA
www.volquartsen.com

Walther Arms, Inc.
Fort Smith, AR
www.waltherarms.com

Weatherby
Paso Robles, CA
www.weatherby.com

Weaver Optics
Anoka, MN
www.weaveroptics.com

Western Powders, Inc.
Miles City, MT
www.accuratepowder.com

Wild West Guns
Anchorage, AK
www.wildwestguns.com

Wilson Combat
Berryville, AR
www.wilsoncombat.com

Winchester Repeating Arms & Ammunition
East Alton, IL
www.winchester.com

Woodleigh Bullets
Murrabit, Australia
www.woodleighbullets.com.au

MANUFACTURERS

Gunfinder Index

GUNFINDER INDEX

Gunfinder Index

GUNFINDER INDEX

Gunfinder Index